BUSINESS FINANCIAL MANAGEMENT

THIRD EDITION

BUSINESS FINANCIAL MANAGEMENT

THIRD EDITION

Philip L. Cooley

Trinity University

THE DRYDEN PRESS

Harcourt Brace College Publishers

Fort Worth   Philadelphia   San Diego   New York   Orlando   Austin   San Antonio
Toronto   Montreal   London   Sydney   Tokyo

Publisher	Elizabeth Widdicombe
Acquisitions Editor	Rick Hammonds
Developmental Editor	Stacey Fry
Project Management and Text Design	Elm Street Publishing Services, Inc.
Compositor	GTS Graphics
Text Type	10/12 Sabon
Cover Image	COMSTOCK, INC.

Chapter opening vignette photos in Chapters 1, 2, 5, 7, 9, 12, 13, 20, 21, and 22 © 1994, COMSTOCK, INC. The chapter opening vignette photo in Chapter 14 courtesy of T. Rosenthal/SUPERSTOCK Inc.

Address for Editorial Correspondence
The Dryden Press, 301 Commerce Street, Suite 3700, Fort Worth, TX 76102

Address for Orders
The Dryden Press, 6277 Sea Harbor Drive, Orlando, FL 32887
1-800-782-4479, or 1-800-433-0001 (in Florida)

ISBN: 0-03-097039-3

LIBRARY OF CONGRESS CATALOG NUMBER: 93-5795

Printed in the United States of America

3 4 5 6 7 8 9 0 1 2   069   9 8 7 6 5 4 3 2 1

THE DRYDEN PRESS

Harcourt Brace College Publishers

To Anne, Erika, Andria, Ruth, C. J., Fran, Wayne, and Ron

The Dryden Press Series in Finance

Amling and Droms
Investment Fundamentals

Berry and Young
Managing Investments:
A Case Approach

Bertisch
Personal Finance

Boyet
Security Analysis for Investment
Decisions: Text and Software

Brigham
Fundamentals of Financial
Management
Sixth Edition

Brigham and Gapenski
Cases in Financial Management:
Directed, Non-Directed, and by
Request

Brigham and Gapenski
Cases in Financial Management:
Module A

Brigham and Gapenski
Cases in Financial Management:
Module B

Brigham and Gapenski
Cases in Financial Management:
Module C

Brigham and Gapenski
Financial Management: Theory and
Practice
Seventh Edition

Brigham and Gapenski
Intermediate Financial Management
Fourth Edition

Brigham, Aberwald, and Gapenski
Finance with Lotus 1-2-3
Second Edition

Chance
An Introduction to Options and
Futures
Second Edition

Clauretie and Webb
The Theory and Practice of Real
Estate Finance

Cooley
Advances in Business Financial
Management: A Collection of
Readings

Cooley
Business Financial Management
Third Edition

Curran
Principles of Corporate Finance

Dickerson, Campsey, and Brigham
Introduction to Financial
Management
Fourth Edition

Evans
International Finance: A Markets
Approach

Fama and Miller
The Theory of Finance

Gardner and Mills
Managing Financial Institutions:
An Asset/Liability Approach
Third Edition

Gitman and Joehnk
Personal Financial Planning
Sixth Edition

Greenbaum and Thakor
Contemporary Financial
Intermediation

Harrington and Eades
Case Studies in Financial Decision
Making
Third Edition

Hayes and Meerschwam
Financial Institutions:
Contemporary Cases in the
Financial Services Industry

Johnson
Issues and Readings in Managerial
Finance
Third Edition

Kidwell, Peterson, and Blackwell
Financial Institutions, Markets, and
Money
Fifth Edition

Koch
Bank Management
Second Edition

Kohn
Money, Banking, and Financial
Markets
Second Edition

Lee and Finnerty
Corporate Finance: Theory,
Method, and Application

Maisel
Real Estate Finance
Second Edition

Martin, Cox, and MacMinn
The Theory of Finance:
Evidence and Applications

Mayo
Finance: An Introduction
Fourth Edition

Mayo
Investments: An Introduction
Fourth Edition

Pettijohn
PROFIT+

Reilly
Investment Analysis and Portfolio
Management
Fourth Edition

Reilly
Investments
Third Edition

Sears and Trennepohl
Investment Management

Seitz
Capital Budgeting and Long-Term
Financing Decisions

Siegel and Siegel
Futures Markets

Smith and Spudeck
Interest Rates: Principles and
Applications

Stickney
Financial Statement Analysis:
A Strategic Perspective
Second Edition

Turnbull
Option Valuation

Weston and Brigham
Essentials of Managerial Finance
Tenth Edition

Weston and Copeland
Managerial Finance
Ninth Edition

Wood and Wood
Financial Markets

The Harcourt Brace College Outline Series

Baker
Financial Management

PREFACE

Business Financial Management, Third Edition, is designed for students taking their first course in finance. Typical business students, both finance majors and nonmajors, have the ability to master the broad range of topics in this book. The writing style and organization of topics are aimed at beginning students.

The power and the fun of financial decision making come to life with real-world examples. Every chapter contains examples of corporate managers grappling with financial problems. Through these examples, students gain an appreciation of the relationship between theory and practice. Moreover, they gain confidence in their own abilities and become motivated to learn the principles of finance.

Maximizing shareholder wealth is the organizing principle of the book. Students learn to distinguish between good and bad decisions by seeing the resulting impact on a company's stock price. Thus the cornerstone of each chapter is valuation, which lies at the heart of the wealth-maximization objective. The book relates corporate financing and investing decisions to the financial objective.

ORGANIZATIONAL LOGIC OF THE BOOK

Part I, *Business Financial Management and Its Environment,* describes the financial environment in which companies operate. Heavy emphasis is placed on the objective of maximizing shareholder wealth, on financial securities, and on financial markets. To appreciate the guiding objective that pervades financial decision making, students need a solid understanding of securities and markets.

Part II, *Valuation and the Cost of Capital,* begins with the time value of money and discounted cash flow, providing the foundation for measuring and understanding value. The remaining three chapters of Part II build on the knowledge of discounted cash-flow analysis, securities, and markets. As students learn how to estimate the value of securities, they learn about the cost of securities that companies issue. They see and understand the intimate relationship between valuation and the cost of capital. The treatment of valuation and the cost of capital together makes each topic easier to grasp.

With the foregoing as background, students are prepared to use cost of capital in Part III, *Capital Budgeting.* The analysis of a company's capital investments follows the study of the financial environment and cost of capital for these reasons: To understand the investment selection process, students must know the objective of financial decision making as set out in Chapter 1; they must understand the nature of securities and markets, covered in Chapters 2 and 3; and they must know the meaning of cost of capital, covered in Part II. Part III of the book describes the estimation of cash flows for proposed capital investments, the methods of evaluation, and the analysis of risk.

Part IV, *Managing Working Capital,* maintains the focus on asset management. Analyzing a company's working capital—current assets and current liabilities—is only a small step from analyzing investments in long-term projects. Students already understand opportunity costs and therefore why excessive cash balances, accounts receivable, and inventory are undesirable. Studying working-capital management at this point gives them the opportunity to learn, in context, about selected financial ratios. For example, the inventory turnover ratio is meaningful when learned along with the principles of inventory management; it is less meaningful when presented before those principles. By studying ratios that help a financial manager to monitor a company's working capital, students recognize more easily the relevance of ratios.

Learning several financial ratios in context prepares students for a study of the big picture in Part V, *Analyzing and Planning Financial Performance.* Part V shows how to interpret financial statements and how to plan a company's future financial performance. Students learn not only the definition and calculation of financial ratios but also a procedure for unlocking the story contained in financial statements. Placing these topics earlier in the book (as some textbooks do) would require the analysis of a forest with the trees not yet introduced.

Part VI, *Institutional Features of Long-Term Financing,* details the nature and characteristics of long-term financial sources. In the preceding five parts, students learn sufficient information about bonds, preferred stock, common stock, and retained earnings to promote their understanding of valuation, cost of capital, and capital structure. Part VI adds to their understanding of stocks and bonds and introduces such features as convertibility, warrants, and options in general. Financing through retained earnings versus paying dividends concludes the discussion.

Part VII, *Special Topics,* closes the book with an in-depth treatment of selected topics discussed earlier in the book—leasing, mergers and acquisitions, bankruptcy, and international financial management. It presents additional ideas useful in the first finance course, if time permits.

ALTERNATIVE SEQUENCES OF THE PARTS

The sequence of the parts in the book presents a logical flow of ideas for students in their first finance course. For students with prior experience in finance, however, instructors may wish to reorder the parts to accommodate course objectives. To illustrate, when using the text to support a casebook, instructors may wish to cover the analysis and planning of financial performance (Part V) immediately after Part I. In addition, some instructors may find it necessary because of time constraints to cover only the first five parts, which by themselves provide a sound overview of business financial management. Other potential orderings of the parts include the following: (1) Cover the institutional features of long-term financing (Part VI) after valuation and the cost of capital (Part II); (2) cover the analysis and planning of financial performance (Part V) before working-capital management (Part IV). After covering Part I and Chapter 4 (present-value analysis), instructors will find great latitude in how they structure the remaining parts of the book.

MAJOR CHANGES IN THE THIRD EDITION

Staying abreast of the changing world of finance requires frequent updating and revision of a textbook. As the dynamic landscape of financial theory and practice changes, so too must a textbook in order to remain current. This edition reflects several changes in the discipline of finance, many of which were suggested for inclusion by users and reviewers of prior editions.

Several changes are spread throughout many parts of the book. Representative of these changes are the following: (1) a vignette on corporate practice at the beginning of each chapter; (2) a demonstration problem—incorporates key ideas of a chapter—at the end of Chapters 2 through 22; (3) video case problems—short case problems accompanied by a related video; (4) more than 200 new or modified questions and problems, many of which are based on real-world companies; (5) several new box highlights on interesting ideas from the business world; and (6) updates of all topical material.

In addition, this new edition:

- Uses Luby's Cafeterias Inc. to introduce the nature of financial statements and features a new section on ethics in business (Chapter 1).

- Revises the section on discount yield and investment yield of U.S. Treasury bills; presents the historical record of stock returns and interest rates; and includes a box highlight on the Federal Reserve System's influence on interest rates (Chapter 2).

- Expands the discussion of stock quotations to include the derivation of dividend payout ratio; presents the new format of over-the-counter stock quotations for small-cap issues; includes a box highlight on international financial markets; and adds a video case problem, NexStarr Broadcasting Inc., on financial markets (Chapter 3).

- Includes a box highlight on the difference between average rate of return and compound rate of return (Chapter 4).

- Features a new section describing the Ibbotson–Sinquefield data on historical rates of return: common stock, U.S. Treasury bills, and inflation (Chapter 5).

- Includes an appendix on financial problem solving with eight different calculators (Chapter 6).

- Presents a new video case problem, Riverfork Electric, on cost of capital (Chapter 7).

- Includes a box highlight on strategic planning in capital budgeting (Chapter 8).

- Simplifies the calculation of crossover rates in net present value profiles and features a new video case problem, West Coast Textiles Inc., on capital budgeting (Chapter 9).

- Uses AT&T to illustrate the statement of cash flows (Chapter 11).

- Revises the discussion of using interest rate futures to hedge temporarily excess cash and includes a new video case problem, Dos Amigos Petro Stores, on lockbox systems (Chapter 12).

- Includes a box highlight on inventory management (Chapter 13).
- Records historical prime rates, Treasury bill rates, and commercial paper rates and features a new video case problem, Northwest Lumber Inc., on short-term financing (Chapter 14).
- Includes a box highlight on industry average financial ratios, a new tabular summary of financial ratio definitions, and an updated case on comparing financial statements—The Coca-Cola Company versus PepsiCo (Chapter 15).
- Features a new video case problem, Rolled Oats Company, on financial planning (Chapter 16).
- Presents the new format of listed options quotations and revises the discussion of puts and calls (Chapter 17).
- Revises the discussion of cumulative voting to elect members of the board of directors (Chapter 18).
- Includes a box highlight on global mergers and acquisitions and notes the frequent violation of the absolute priority rule in bankruptcy proceedings (Chapter 21).
- Provides updated quotations of foreign-exchange rates (Chapter 22).

SPECIAL FEATURES

Business Financial Management, Third Edition, incorporates several special features to enhance the process of learning and teaching.

- **Opening vignettes.** To capture student interest, each chapter begins with a brief real-world story that relates to the chapter topic.
- **Running glossary.** New terms are defined not only in the text but also in the margin. The running glossary helps students to learn the language of finance and to review the key terms of chapters.
- **Examples.** Each chapter includes numerous in-text examples that show step by step how to solve problems. Examples immediately follow discussions on financial models and procedures so that students can quickly see how to apply them and gain hands-on experience.
- **Box highlights.** Some 30 boxes of special-interest material add richness and real-world seasoning to the book. The boxes direct attention to two types of material:
    - *Focus on Practice* presents real-world illustrations of financial practices and shows the relevance of financial concepts and theories.
    - *International Dimensions* examines the global concepts of business financial management. In addition to Chapter 22 on international financial management, these concepts are integrated within several chapters to add the international flavor of finance.
- **Summaries.** Each chapter concludes with summary statements that provide a crisp, succinct refresher of the chapter topics.
- **End-of-chapter material.** The following end-of-chapter material reinforces understanding of the information and techniques presented:
    - *Key Terms* provide a review of all running glossary terms from the chapter.

- *Questions* stress comprehension and do not require calculations.
- *Strategy Problems* help students learn problem-solving techniques. Marginal comments accompany each problem's step-by-step solution to provide a guide, or strategy, for solving the problem. Students may then apply the strategy to other problems.
- *Demonstration Problems* incorporate the key ideas of each chapter in a single problem. Selected transparencies provide a step-by-step illustration of how to solve these problems so that instructors may use them to structure lectures or as comprehensive assignments.
- *Problem Sets* provide an extensive variety of problems requiring calculations; answers to odd-numbered problems are in Appendix A at the end of the text.
- *Computer Problems* are included in chapters that lend themselves to computer work. Selected problems have been modeled on *Lotus*® *1-2-3*® and may be solved using the *Problem Diskette* that accompanies the book. No prior knowledge of *Lotus* is necessary to use the diskette.
- *Video Case Problems* are included at the end of Chapters 3, 7, 9, 12, 14, and 16. Instructors may show related videos prior to classroom discussion of the cases. Alternatively, video case problems can be used as regular case problems, similar to the use of those at the end of Chapters 4, 5, 10, 13, 15, 19, and 21. Although relatively short in length, each case provides an opportunity for in-depth analysis of a financial problem.
- *Selected References* provide a guide to published sources containing either special applications or advanced material.

- **Small-Business Perspective.** At the beginning of each of the seven parts of the book, readers look in on two entrepreneurs operating a small business. These seven vignettes illustrate the financial challenges of starting and running a small company.
- **Readiness Test.** The readiness test at the end of Chapter 1 is fun yet challenging. It requires students to recall ideas from previous courses and experiences and tests their ability to reason in financial terms.
- **Annual-Report Analysis.** The case problem in Chapter 15 includes excerpts from the 1991 Annual Report of The Coca-Cola Company. In addition to illustrating the nature of annual reports, these excerpts, along with data on PepsiCo, provide the opportunity for analysis of real-world financial statements.

ANCILLARY MATERIALS

Business Financial Management, Third Edition, is accompanied by a complete set of supplemental materials that are designed to aid learning and teaching:

- **Study Guide.** The *Study Guide,* by Jean Louis Heck and Nancy Nagele Heck, both of Villanova University, helps students to master the text material and gives them practice in solving problems. It includes an overview and outline of each chapter, a glossary of key terms, multiple-choice questions, and answers to the questions, problems, and solutions to the problems. The *Study Guide* may be ordered separately.

- **Readings Book.** *Advances in Business Financial Management: A Collection of Readings* (Hinsdale, IL: The Dryden Press, 1990), by Philip L. Cooley, consists of 48 finance articles from 26 different sources. The articles cover a wide range of finance topics, and each article lies within the intellectual grasp of students in their first finance course. The readings book may be ordered separately.

- **Instructor's Manual.** The *Instructor's Manual* contains an outline of each chapter, notes and teaching tips, learning objectives, answers to all text questions, and step-by-step solutions to all text problems. It also includes a diskette containing the solutions to the student Problem Diskette (see below).

- **Transparencies.** Available to instructors upon adoption of the book are more than 200 transparencies of figures, tables, and step-by-step solutions to problems.

- **Test Bank.** The *Test Bank,* by Jean Louis Heck and Nancy Nagele Heck, both of Villanova University, includes more than 1,100 questions and problems in objective format. It is available in both printed form and on diskette for IBM (and compatibles) and in a WordPerfect format. The *Test Bank* allows the instructor to edit questions and add new ones.

- **Problem Diskette.** A diskette containing Lotus 1-2-3 templates for solving designated end-of-chapter problems accompanies the text. The diskette provides an easy way for students to gain hands-on experience in using a spreadsheet to solve financial problems.

- **Videos.** Six short segments, ten to twenty minutes each, present the background for the video cases at the end of Chapters 3, 7, 9, 12, 14, and 16. Topics covered include financial markets (with a focus on the New York Stock Exchange); cost of capital (featuring a utility company—Minnesota Power—working to attract investors at an annual meeting of the New York Securities Analysts Association); capital budgeting (which discusses planning, evaluating, and selecting projects for company investments); cash management (which highlights the use of lockboxes in planning and controlling cash flows); short-term financing (which describes alternative sources of financing); and financial planning (which discusses the finance function in corporate planning and break-even analysis).

ACKNOWLEDGMENTS

Someone once said, "If I can see far, it is because I stand on the shoulders of giants." I feel the same way. A textbook builds on the shoulders of many previous authors, either directly or indirectly. The virtues of this book are due in large measure to these authors.

Reviewers played a key role in developing this book into a teachable instrument. The finished product is a monument to the reviewers of this and prior editions:

A. Frederic Banda	Donald Brown
Charles Barngrover	Severin Carlson
Thomas Berry	P. R. Chandy
Scott Besley	John Clinebell
Rahul Bishnoi	Maclyn Clouse
LeRoy Brooks	Maurice Corrigan

Charles Cox
Faramarz Damanpour
Zane Dennick-Ream
Gregg Dimkoff
Albert DiUlio
Eugene Dunham
James Feller
John Fletcher
George Flowers
Timothy Gallagher
R H Gilmer
Maurice Goudzwaard
Harry Grammatikos
Irene Hammerbacher
John Hammermeister
Hal Heaton
Charles Higgins
K. P. Hill
Robert Hollinger
Art Holt
Kenneth Huggins
Jerry Hunt
Hugh Hunter
Steven Isberg
James Jackson
Raymond Johnson
Robert Johnston
Fred Kaen
Dilip Kare
Richard Kaufman
Tom Klaasen

Duncan Kretovich
Gary Kundy
Richard LaNear
Martin Laurence
Wayne Lee
John Lindvall
Leo Mahoney
Gerald Martin
W. Joe Mason
Francis McGrath
James Millar
Lalatendu Misra
Donald Nast
Vivian Nazar
Edgar Norton
Ralph Pope
Gabriel Ramirez
Debra Reed
Linda Richardson
Antonio Rodriguez
John Settle
Neil Sicherman
Brent Stewart
Robert Sweeney
Paul Vanderheiden
Joseph Vinso
John Wachowicz
Herbert Weinraub
Kenneth Westby
C. Don Wiggins
Howard Williams

In addition to the reviewers, I am grateful for the work and specialized contributions of several people. For their research and writing contributions to Part VII, *Special Topics,* I thank Michael Gombola of Drexel University, James Wansley of the University of Tennessee, and David Ricks of the American Graduate School of International Management. For her research and writing contributions to the small-business perspectives, I thank Peggy Lambing of the University of Missouri at St. Louis. For their contributions in designing the computer exercises, I thank Topan Bhattacharya of Cameron University and Robert Hartwig of Worcester State College. For his research and writing contributions to the International Dimensions boxes, I thank Martin Laurence of William Paterson College. For his research and writing contributions to the case problems, I thank Carl Hubbard of Trinity University. Finally, the accuracy of the text and *Instructor's Manual* largely reflects the careful work of Stanley Jacobs of Central Washington University, who checked examples, questions, and problems.

My student assistants deserve special thanks for proofreading, running to the library, and taking care of odd jobs: Tracy Andrews, Mike Ashton, John Bojescul, Andria Cooley, Erika Cooley, Jay Hartzell, Bill Matthews, Wendy Nelson, Elissa Pritchard, and Paulina Salazar. I remember with gratitude the assistance of my patient and cheerful secretaries: Vilma Amell, Yvonne Cortright, Aurora Molina, and Kathaleen Zuehl.

The staff at The Dryden Press has the well-earned reputation of being "First in Finance." This slogan reflects the work of competent, confident, and caring people. My special thanks go to Diana Farrell, Stacey Fry, Rick Hammonds, and Sarah Jones at Dryden, and to Barb Bahnsen, John Beasley, Susan Jansen, and Stephanie Riley at Elm Street Publishing Services.

A CONCLUDING NOTE

Writing this book was a labor of love—most of the time. I hope you will be able to discern my effort to organize a paragraph just right, to construct a sentence with clarity, and to choose a word that hits the mark. When tempted to write for professorial colleagues, I tried to resist. Always foremost in my mind was the target readers—students taking their first course in finance. The reaction of students to this book is the final measure of its success.

Philip L. Cooley
San Antonio, Texas
November 1993

About the Author

Philip L. Cooley (Ph.D., Ohio State University; MBA, University of Hawaii; BME, General Motors Institute) is the Prassel Distinguished Professor of Business at Trinity University, San Antonio, Texas. Originally from Michigan, he taught at the University of South Carolina for 12 years and formerly served on the faculties of the U.S. Armed Forces Institute and the Far-East Division of the University of Maryland. He is past president of the Eastern Finance Association and the Southern Finance Association. He has also served as vice president of the Financial Management Association.

Professor Cooley's writings on capital budgeting, capital structure, working-capital management, financial analysis, and mergers have appeared in the *Journal of Financial Research, American Journal of Small Business, Journal of Finance, Journal of Financial and Quantitative Analysis, Journal of Business, Financial Review, Journal of Risk and Insurance, Financial Management, Real Estate Appraiser and Analyst, Journal of Business Research,* and other publications. He is author of the monograph *How to Value Oil Jobberships for Purchase or Sale* and editor of *Advances in Business Financial Management: A Collection of Readings.* Dr. Cooley is chairman of the board of directors of the Consumer Credit Counseling Service and associate editor of *Financial Management, Financial Review, Journal of Small Business Finance,* and *Journal of Managerial Issues.*

CONTENTS IN BRIEF

CONTENTS

BUSINESS FINANCIAL MANAGEMENT

THIRD EDITION

BUSINESS FINANCIAL MANAGEMENT AND ITS ENVIRONMENT

Part I

SMALL-BUSINESS PERSPECTIVE

Financial Management of Small Companies

For many years business financial management courses have focused on the operations of large corporations. In recent years many newly established small companies such as Apple Computer, Discovery Toys, and Federal Express have grown to become major corporations. The growth of well-known companies has led to a greater awareness of small companies and the role they play in the U.S. economy.

The Small Business Administration, an agency of the U.S. government, defines small businesses as those that have independent ownership, are not dominant in their field, and meet specific size guidelines. These size guidelines may include the number of employees, the sales volume, or the net worth of the company. "Small business" should not be equated solely with "mom and pop" operations. Although the local auto repair shop with sales of $250,000 is included under the "small business" umbrella, a wholesale company grossing $15,000,000 or a general contractor grossing $17,000,000 may also be included.

It is important to highlight small companies for several reasons. First, the importance of small companies may be overlooked, even though they contribute substantially to the U.S. economy. New jobs created by small companies have been estimated at 50 percent to 80 percent of the national total of all new jobs. In addition, over 70 percent of all employees in the wholesale and contract construction industries are employed by small companies. In terms of jobs, therefore, small companies play a vital role. Also, small companies are innovative. Many products, including cellophane, the jet engine, and microcomputers, were invented in small companies.

Another reason for highlighting small companies is that the owner of a small company needs to understand financial management. A small company does not have a finance department to analyze decisions. It may have an accountant who prepares the financial statements and offers advice, but the final decisions usually are made by the company owner. These decisions will directly affect the owner's personal wealth.

Finally, the financial problems small companies face are often somewhat different from those of large corporations, and the possible solutions are more limited. Small companies often start out without enough capital and frequently experience severe cash shortages even when prof-itable. The financing options available to large corporations are not always available to small companies. Competent cash management is therefore necessary for survival.

At the beginning of each part of the text, we follow the experiences of Kathy Griffin and Jim Sutherland, two entre-preneurs who establish "In Shape," a retail outlet for exercise equipment. The problems they face are typical of those facing all owners of small companies, as are the decisions they make. This ongoing story about In Shape illustrates financial management in a small company and suggests the many challenges faced by the owners of small companies.

Chapter 1

FINANCE AND BUSINESS

New-Age Executives

The former heavyweight champion Joe Louis said: "I don't like money actually, but it quiets my nerves." Although money cannot buy happiness, you should note that the word *wealth* is from *wela*—Anglo-Saxon for "happiness and well-being."

Creation of wealth takes imagination and vision, personal qualities often in short supply. Consider the hapless William Orton, president of Western Union in 1876. He decided against investing $100,000 to acquire the patent rights to Alexander Graham Bell's invention of the telephone. Mr. Orton agreed with the critics: "The telephone will never replace the telegraph." Because of the decision *not* to invest, Western Union missed the opportunity to create enormous wealth for its owners, the stockholders.

According to Management Practice Inc. (MPI), a New York consulting firm:

The qualities sought by directors when appointing the CEO [Chief Executive Officer] are increasingly determined by the need to build stockholder value. This quest puts pressure on the board to select the candidate most likely to ensure that profits are as robust as possible, the

price/earnings ratio above the industry average, the dividend rate stable or growing, and the stock and bond risk factors as low as possible.

But where do boards of directors find CEOs? MPI's 1991 report shows that most CEOs of large U.S. corporations—20.5 percent—come from the field of finance, followed by 19.1 percent from technical fields and 18.5 percent from operations. MPI's studies over several years show that CEOs who have strong financial education and experience are "best suited" for the challenges at the top.

Effective CEOs are intelligent, determined, forward-looking, honest, and straightforward, so say 204 corporate vice presidents surveyed by Pittsburgh-based Management Science & Development. The VPs also say that the most important leadership qualities of CEOs are persuasiveness, analytical competence, decisiveness, conceptual skills, oral communication, listening skills, creativity, diplomacy, and the ability to plan. As you might suspect, careful study of this book cannot assure that you will rise to the top of a large corporation. Careful study of the following chapters, however, can provide you with a firm foundation for your financial education.

Source: "Business Talk," *Financial Executive,* March/April 1992, 4–7.

The goal of this chapter is to introduce some essential concepts of business financial management and to explain the objective of financial decision making. The chapter begins by addressing the question: Why study finance? You will see the benefits gained from learning the theories and practices of finance. Examined next are the forms of business organization, a company's finance department, and the tasks of the financial manager. The most crucial idea in the chapter is the objective of business financial management: *maximization of shareholder wealth*. This objective is used for assessing the merit of financial decisions made by company managers.

WHY STUDY FINANCE?

What do you, a future business manager, need to know about business financial management? The answer depends partly on the career you contemplate, but all successful business managers need to understand how to interpret the financial condition and performance of the organization for which they work. Whether you work for a hospital, museum, university, United Way, Exxon, General Motors, Disney, or yourself, you need to understand the financial health of your employer; and you need to understand your contribution to your employer's financial success.

Completing your organizational tasks successfully depends on a sound knowledge of financial concepts, principles, and procedures. Business financial management takes you beyond just the facts, however, to a focus on financial decision making and the consequent cash flows. Your study of finance will empower you and enhance your ability to solve business problems creatively and analytically. Understanding decision making in business is what makes finance fun!

If you aspire to be a financial specialist—a banker, stockbroker, or financial manager of a corporation—then you will need a varied and technical knowledge of financial theories, securities, and markets, along with a strong background in accounting, taxes, economics, and quantitative methods. Once you master the field of finance, you can earn professional certification—as a chartered financial analyst (CFA), a certified management accountant (CMA), or a certified financial planner (CFP). An appendix at the end of this chapter describes the CFA, CMA, and CFP.

As you begin your formal study of finance, you will find that it is broken into three subdivisions: financial markets and institutions, investments, and business financial management. *Financial markets and institutions* concentrates on the ways in which money is loaned and borrowed and the organizations that create and deal in money. This area of finance explains the U.S. financial system—the roles of commercial banks, the Federal Reserve System, and other financial institutions. You also learn about the challenges of managing financial institutions. Studying financial markets and institutions helps you to understand how the value and behavior of money affect all financial decisions. Chapter 2 presents an overview that will help you to understand the U.S. financial system.

Investments is the study of how individuals and institutions allocate money to securities such as stocks and bonds. Investors hold stocks and bonds for the purpose of earning an income (dividends from stock and interest from bonds) or reselling at a higher price. The study of investments deals mainly with three questions: selection (what to buy), timing (when to buy), and portfolio (what combination to buy). A consideration of these questions must await your study in advanced courses in finance.

This book deals with investments, too, but they are the investments that companies make. To produce and distribute products, companies must invest in **assets**. Land, buildings, equipment, and inventory are examples of a company's assets—items of value that the company owns. In large part, *business financial management* concentrates on how people manage a company's assets; it also concentrates on how the company finances them. Generally, companies finance assets using a combination of debt and equity:

- **Debt** arises from a promise to pay, often evidenced by a promissory note or a bond—a long-term IOU.
- **Equity** comes from two sources: (1) sale of stock to investors and (2) retention of company earnings (profits).

A company's total assets equal its debt plus equity, and business financial management addresses the proper handling of each.

Courses in business financial management and investments have moved closer together in recent years because of a shift in the focus of financial objectives. In the past, business financial management focused on increasing company accounting profit. Now it focuses on increasing the company's stock price. This means that business financial management and investment courses are looking at stock price from different perspectives: Investment courses teach you how to select stocks that offer the greatest potential to increase in price (price appreciation); business financial management courses teach you how to make decisions that increase the company's stock price.

FORMS OF BUSINESS ORGANIZATION

Companies exist in three major forms: sole proprietorship, partnership, and corporation.[1] Each form is distinct insofar as its legal and tax statuses are concerned, even though the financial management of all three has much in common.

A **sole proprietorship** is a company owned by one person. Although size is not necessarily a distinguishing characteristic, a proprietorship is usually a small company that the owner manages. A **partnership** is a company owned by two or more persons who have entered into an agreement. Legal experts advise drawing up a formal partnership agreement, although legal documentation is not required.[2] A **corporation,** on the other hand, is a company formed by an agreement between the state and the persons forming the company, and the state requires legal documentation of the agreement. In contrast to a proprietorship and a partnership, a corporation legally exists apart from its owners, the holders of its **common stock**. In 1819 Chief Justice John Marshall defined a corporation

assets
Items of value owned by a company; total assets equal debt plus shareholder equity.

debt
Money a company owes; debt equals total assets less shareholder equity.

equity
Owners' investment in a company; equity equals total assets less debt.

sole proprietorship
Company owned by one person.

partnership
Company owned by two or more persons who have entered into an agreement.

corporation
Company formed by a legal agreement between the state and the persons establishing the company.

common stock
Security representing ownership in a corporation.

[1] *Company* is a generic term identifying a group of people associated for some purpose. In this book we generally use the term *company* in place of *corporation, proprietorship,* or *partnership*. Corporation is too limiting because many of the concepts and procedures are also applicable to proprietorships and partnerships. Whether *company* refers to a corporation only or to all three business organization forms will be clear from the context of the discussion.

[2] Each partner is liable for the partnership's debts unless stated otherwise in the partnership agreement. In a *limited partnership,* designated partners have limited liability, and the general partner(s) assumes the residual liability. Limited partners invest cash and share in profits, but they have no voice in running the partnership.

as "an artificial being, invisible, intangible, and existing only in the contemplation of law." Because of its separate legal identity, the corporate form prevails among large U.S. business organizations. Even though proprietorships and partnerships outnumber corporations, the corporation has the dominant impact on the U.S. economy. Because of this dominance, we pay special attention to corporations in this book.

Being an entity legally distinct from its owners and managers gives a corporation three financial advantages over a proprietorship and a partnership: (1) Owners (shareholders) of corporations have limited financial liability. For example, if you invest $5,000 in a corporation, then the most you can lose is $5,000. The same investment in a proprietorship or partnership could also be lost, but in addition you could be held personally accountable for the organization's debts and liabilities from lawsuits. (2) Corporate ownership can be divided into many small pieces—shares of common stock. Transferring ownership by selling stock is easier than transferring ownership of proprietorships and partnerships. (3) Corporations have perpetual lives and continue to exist after the deaths of managers and owners. In contrast, the death of a proprietor or partner causes the organization to cease to exist, although any remaining partners may form a new partnership. This feature permits the corporation to obtain financing—debt and equity—with a **maturity** greater than the managers' or owners' life expectancies.

maturity
Date when repayment is due.

In combination, limited financial liability, transferability of ownership, and perpetual life enhance the value of large organizations. Because they attract investors, these features enable corporations to raise large amounts of money to finance growth. Many organizations start small as proprietorships or partnerships, but if they grow successfully, their owners usually convert the organizations to the corporate form to ease the financing of growth. Apple Computer, for example, began as a partnership and converted to a corporation as its success grew.

A potential disadvantage of corporate organizations lies in their taxation. Unlike proprietorships and partnerships, corporations pay income taxes. Proprietors and partners pay income taxes, but their organizations do not; taxable income flows through the organizations to the proprietors or partners, who pay the taxes. Owners of a corporation, however, pay taxes twice:

- They pay as the corporation itself pays taxes on taxable income (sales revenues less all tax-deductible expenses).

cash dividend
Distribution of cash from a corporation to its shareholders.

- The shareholder-owners pay taxes on **cash dividends** they receive from the corporation.

This double taxation discourages small organizations from incorporating when the owners want to take large cash flows from the organization. On the other hand, if the owners of a small organization are content to leave cash in the organization, then incorporation may be advantageous. Despite double taxation, most large organizations incorporate because of limited liability, transferability of ownership, and the perpetual life of the corporation—all of which make raising money easier.

FINANCIAL ORGANIZATION WITHIN A COMPANY

Managers of a company need financial information so that they can measure current performance of the company, forecast future performance and resource needs, and plan for the future. People outside the company—potential investors,

FIGURE 1.1

Organization of a Company's Finance Department

Organization charts and titles given to managers vary from company to company, and this chart illustrates but one possibility. A company consists of three basic units: production, finance, and marketing. Detailed here is the organizational hierarchy within the finance department.

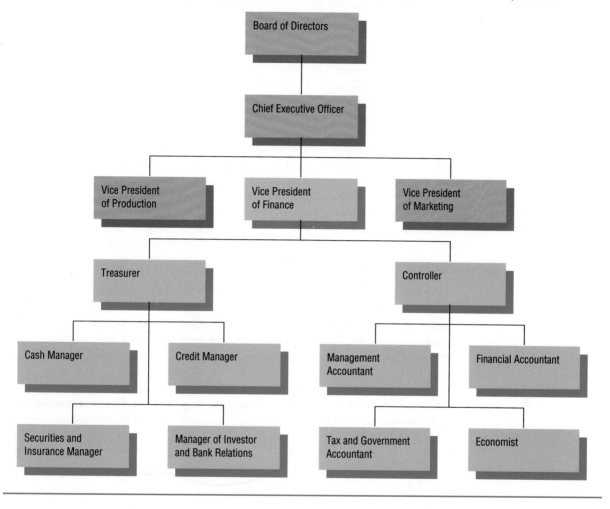

creditors, suppliers of raw materials, etc.—are equally interested in the financial well-being of the company. Personnel in the company's finance department have the responsibility of providing this information.

Figure 1.1 outlines the organizational structure of the finance department in a medium-sized manufacturing company. Heading the department is the vice president of finance, who reports to the chief executive officer (CEO).[3] The CEO is responsible to the board of directors, whose members the shareholders elect. As representatives of the shareholders, directors have ultimate authority for company policies and may hire and fire the CEO. In practice, removal of the CEO may be hindered by the number of inside directors—board members who also serve as operating officers of the company. Inside directors might include the

---

[3]In some companies the vice president of finance is given the title of chief financial officer (CFO); the vice president of production, chief operating officer (COO); the vice president of marketing, chief marketing officer (CMO).

CEO and the vice presidents. Outside directors might include bankers, consultants, attorneys, and community leaders.

Descending the organizational hierarchy through the vice president of finance, you see a finance department split into two sections, one headed by the treasurer and one by the controller. The treasurer's section has the following responsibilities: (1) manage the company's cash balances, (2) determine who receives credit from the company, (3) maintain contacts with the company's banks, and (4) manage the process of issuing new securities. These functions, among others, require people in the treasurer's section to represent the company to external constituents.

The controller's section includes the accounting function and might include computer services for the company's management information system. People in the controller's section manage the company's budgeting process, which provides for the planning and control of financial activity. To illustrate, the controller is responsible for planning and evaluating company investments in new plant and equipment (capital budgeting). People in the controller's section prepare budgets and reports for top management, file necessary tax forms, and interpret economic events relevant to the company.

TASKS OF A FINANCIAL MANAGER

The finance department illustrated in Figure 1.1 shows several financial specialists, each a financial manager of a particular activity. Many companies have even more specialists than the figure shows: manager of accounts payable, insurance and risk manager, inventory manager, manager of capital project analysis, and so on. In contrast, a small company may have only one person designated as the financial manager, a person who performs all of the financial functions. In this book we use the term *financial manager* to represent the various finance specialists in different companies. Defined in this way, the financial manager has three principal tasks:

1. Analyze and plan the company's performance.
2. Acquire the **funds** the company needs.
3. Allocate funds to acquire the most profitable assets.

funds
Cash raised from debt and equity sources.

These tasks are the *three A's* of the financial manager.

Analyze and Plan

Analyzing and planning occupy much of the financial manager's time. Company progress depends on management's knowing where the company now is and where in the future it wants the company to be. The financial manager gives operating management and investors an assessment of the company's current financial position and the financial consequences of alternative courses of action.

income statement
Financial statement detailing a company's earnings for a *period* of time.

Assessing the financial strengths and weaknesses of the company requires the financial manager to work with people from accounting, marketing, and production. Company accountants develop the **income statement** showing sales revenues less expenses for a period of time; they also put together the **balance sheet** listing company assets and the corresponding liabilities (debts) and shareholder equity. Based on these financial statements and projected versions of these statements, the financial manager assesses company financial strengths and weaknesses, both currently and in the future. To a large degree, the plans of the

balance sheet
Company's statement of financial position at a *point* in time; a listing of assets and claims against them—debt and equity.

FIGURE 1.2

Outline of a Company's Income Statement

The income statement shows a company's earnings (profit) for a period of time (year, quarter, month). Sales less all expenses equals earnings after taxes.

Item	Explanation
Net sales	Revenue from selling goods and services
− Cost of goods sold	Cost of goods sold to produce the sales
Gross profit	Gross income or gross earnings
− Operating expenses	Selling and administrative expenses
Earnings before interest and taxes	EBIT or net operating income
− Interest expense	Interest paid on short- and long-term debt
Earnings before taxes	Income, or profit, before payment of taxes
− Taxes	Federal, state, and local income taxes
Earnings after taxes	Income, or profit, after payment of taxes

production department and the sales forecasts of the marketing department determine the company's expected future *(pro forma)* financial performance and position.[4]

Figure 1.2 shows a skeletal outline of a company's income statement, based on the following equation:

$$\frac{\text{Net}}{\text{sales}} - \frac{\text{Cost of}}{\text{sales}} - \frac{\text{Operating}}{\text{expenses}} - \frac{\text{Interest}}{\text{expense}} - \text{Taxes} = \text{Earnings}$$

Net sales are gross sales less any discounts offered to customers or returns of goods previously sold. Earnings equal net sales for the accounting period less all expenses incurred to generate sales. The term *earnings* means the same as *profit* and *income*.

The format of the income statement may vary somewhat from company to company, and from the outline shown in Figure 1.2. For example, consider the 1991 income statement of Luby's Cafeterias Inc. shown in Table 1.1. This statement does not show a subtotal for gross profit, although you could calculate it as sales minus cost of sales. Note also that *Income from Operations* is the same as earnings before interest and taxes. As many companies do, Luby's shows its net income per share (or earnings per share) at the bottom of the statement. Net income per share ($1.18 for Luby's) equals net income ($32,346,000) divided by the average number of shares of common stock outstanding during the year (27,411,864 shares).

Acquire Funds

Financial managers acquire and manage the funds that a company needs to finance assets. To obtain these funds, the company can either issue shares of common stock (equity), borrow money (debt), or use some combination of the two.

---

[4] Chapters 15 and 16 discuss the way a financial manager analyzes and plans a company's financial performance and position. Some readers might prefer to study these two chapters immediately after Chapter 1. Chapters 15 and 16 are written to accommodate that alteration in chapter sequencing.

TABLE 1.1

Luby's Cafeterias Inc.
Statements of Income
Years Ended August 31, 1991 and 1990

	1991	1990
	(Thousands of dollars except per share data)	
Sales	$328,236	$311,325
Costs and Expenses		
Cost of sales	173,885	164,911
Operating, general, and administrative	107,094	99,474
	280,979	264,385
Income from Operations	47,257	46,940
Net Interest and Other Income	1,591	1,572
Income before Income Taxes	48,848	48,512
Provision for Income Taxes		
Current	18,211	15,173
Deferred	(1,709)	1,239
	16,502	16,412
Net Income	$ 32,346	$ 32,100
Net Income per Share	$ 1.18	$ 1.17

Source: Luby's Cafeterias Inc. 1991 Annual Report.

financial structure
Mix of all liabilities and equity.

capital structure
Mix of long-term debt and equity.

optimal capital structure
Best combination of long-term debt and equity.

financing decision
Process of choosing among alternative sources of financing.

The company that borrows must repay its debt at maturity. Debt may be short term with a maturity of one year or less, in which case it is a current liability of the company; or it may be long term with a maturity greater than one year, in which case it is a long-term liability. Common stock has no maturity and is always a long-term source of funds.

Figure 1.3 shows the way accountants organize assets, current liabilities, long-term debt, and equity on a company's balance sheet. Total liabilities plus equity equal total assets (required for balancing a balance sheet). The mix of liabilities and equity shows how the company finances its assets. The company's **financial structure** is the entire right side of a balance sheet—the mix of all liabilities (current and long term) and equity. More limited in scope, **capital structure** refers only to the mix of long-term debt and equity—the long-term portions of the financial structure.

Acquiring funds to support company assets requires financial managers to address two complex questions: (1) What are the appropriate proportions of long-term debt and shareholder equity in the capital structure? The best combination of long-term debt and equity is the **optimal capital structure.** (2) What proportion of total liabilities should be short term and long term? The process of choosing among alternative sources of financing is the **financing decision.** Part

FIGURE 1.3

Schematic of a Company's Balance Sheet

The balance sheet can be considered a photograph of a company's financial position at a point in time. Each time the company enters into a financial transaction, the photograph changes. The balance sheet conforms to the following accounting equation:

Total assets = Total liabilities + Shareholder equity

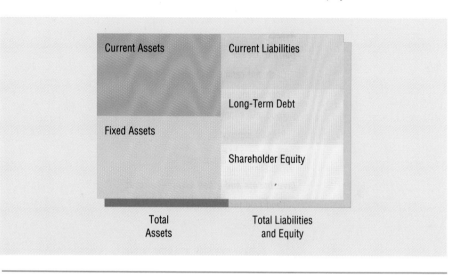

Current Assets	Current Liabilities
Fixed Assets	Long-Term Debt
	Shareholder Equity
Total Assets	Total Liabilities and Equity

II of the book covers the optimal capital structure; Part IV covers the decision on debt maturities.

Like the format of the income statement, the format of the balance sheet varies somewhat from company to company. A common format, illustrated by the balance sheet of Luby's Cafeterias Inc., is shown in Table 1.2. The table shows a top-to-bottom format wherein liabilities and shareholder equity are listed below assets. Luby's *fiscal* (from the Latin word *fiscus* meaning treasury) year ends August 31, so the figures in Table 1.2 reveal the company's investments in assets, its various liabilities, and shareholder equity as of August 31, not the calendar year-end December 31. On August 31, 1991, Luby's had $260,704,000 in assets, $57,922,000 in liabilities, and $202,782,000 in shareholder equity. Later chapters, especially Chapter 15, explain the details of a balance sheet and show you how to interpret the financial story embedded in the numbers.

Allocate Funds

investment decision
Process of allocating funds for investment in competing assets.

As equally critical as the financing decision to the success of a company is the **investment decision,** the process of allocating funds for investment in competing assets. Figure 1.3 shows that a company holds two types of assets, current and fixed:

- *Current assets* are cash and other assets normally converted into cash within a 12-month period. Current assets include: (1) marketable securities—low-risk securities for investment of temporarily idle cash, (2) accounts receivable—money customers owe to the company, and (3) inventory—company products available for sale.

- *Fixed assets* are noncurrent, or long-term, assets. Fixed assets include: (1) equipment, (2) buildings, and (3) land.

TABLE 1.2	·	**Luby's Cafeterias Inc.** **Balance Sheets** **August 31, 1991 and 1990**

	1991	1990
	(Thousands of dollars)	
Assets		
Current Assets		
Cash and cash equivalents	$ 14,200	$ 12,327
Accrued interest and other receivables	190	157
Food and supply inventories	4,267	3,732
Prepaid expenses	2,568	2,231
Total current assets	21,225	18,447
Investments and Other Assets—at cost		
Land held for future use	$ 10,682	$ 11,213
Other assets	1,989	1,732
Total investments and other assets	12,671	12,945
Property, Plant, and Equipment—at cost		
Less accumulated depreciation and amortization	226,808	203,952
	$260,704	$235,344
Liabilities and Shareholders' Equity		
Current Liabilities		
Current portion of long-term debt	$ 480	$ 455
Accounts payable—trade	8,157	8,925
Dividends payable	3,425	3,148
Accrued expenses and other liabilities	24,695	18,652
Income taxes payable	3,643	1,366
Total current liabilities	40,400	32,546
Long-Term Debt, net of current portion	1,851	2,328
Deferred Income Taxes and Other Credits	15,671	17,502
Shareholders' Equity		
Common stock, $.32 par value; authorized 50,000,000 shares, issued and outstanding 27,397,517 shares in 1991 and 27,374,206 shares in 1990	8,767	8,760
Paid-in capital	26,896	26,559
Retained earnings	167,119	147,649
Total shareholders' equity	202,782	182,968
	$260,704	$235,344

Source: Luby's Cafeterias Inc. 1991 Annual Report.

The investment decision must not overemphasize one sort of asset and slight another. For instance, it would be unwise to use so much cash to invest in a building that the company could not pay its bills when due. The financial manager plays a key role in the allocation of funds to competing assets. To illustrate, the financial manager evaluates a proposed investment in a fixed asset by examining its expected return and *risk*—the possibility that the actual return will differ from its expected level. The goal is to select fixed assets that will generate large returns with minimal risk. To understand the financial manager's concern with expected return and risk, consider this analogy: What grade do you expect to earn from the investment of time and money in your finance course? How confident are you about your expected grade? Is there some chance that your actual grade might be lower than what you expect? Your degree of uncertainty is the risk you face. If you are absolutely sure that you will earn an *A* (or a *B*, for that matter), then you face a risk-free grade.

THE OBJECTIVE OF BUSINESS FINANCIAL MANAGEMENT

The objective of business financial management in a corporation is to maximize shareholder wealth, which translates into maximization of stock price. By making decisions that maximize stock price, managers have done all that they can to maximize the wealth of the company's shareholders.[5] Corporate managers are hired hands (agents) of the corporation's shareholders (principals). As **agents,** managers should represent the principals by maximizing their wealth. Managers can best maximize shareholder wealth by maximizing stock price.

agent
Anyone who acts for another (the principal) with the other's consent.

Because proprietorships and partnerships have no common stock, we specify their financial objective differently from that of a corporation. A proprietor should make decisions to maximize the market value of his or her personal investment (proprietor net worth) in the business. Guided by this objective, the proprietor receives the maximum possible price when the business is sold. Similarly, partners should attempt to maximize the market value of their partnership's capital, which assures them the maximum possible price from the eventual sale of the business.

Maximizing stock price, or market value of the owners' investment, is a worthy objective on grounds other than the rights and desires of owners: (1) This objective motivates managers to be sure that customers are satisfied with the company's products and services. Satisfied customers mean increased sales and profits and an increase in stock price. (2) A fair day's wage to employees for a fair day's work naturally flows from the objective, thereby keeping morale and productivity up and work stoppages down. (3) Maximizing stock price motivates managers to create new products, which not only increase sales and profits but also create new jobs and enhance the general standard of living. (4) Concurrent

---

[5] Alternatives to this statement of objectives are as follows: (1) Maximize shareholders' utility, a general measure of satisfaction. Utility maximization is an excellent objective, but problems associated with defining and measuring utility pose overwhelming difficulties for financial managers. (2) Maximize total market value of common equity (price per share of common stock times the number of shares outstanding). This statement is acceptable for a broad range of circumstances, although total market value of equity can be increased simply by issuing more shares of stock, at any price. (3) Maximize total value of the company (market value of all the company's securities). This statement is also acceptable in many circumstances, although it ignores how value is distributed among the company's security holders. Focusing on maximization of stock price avoids the preceding problems, although it requires that we take as given some details of dividend policy—e.g., cash dividends and stock splits.

with satisfying customers and employees, managers must also seek efficient ways of producing the company's products. Low-cost production methods lead to high stock prices. (5) Finally, the company has a social responsibility to fulfill. It must consider the needs and concerns of the community in which it operates. Failure to consider issues such as pollution control and health standards not only violates business ethics but could lower stock price as well. Thus we see that maximizing stock price is consistent with several other objectives.

By adopting the objective of maximizing stock price, managers take on the challenge of successfully meeting the needs of company **stakeholders** and settling their conflicts. Customers want top-of-the-line products for low prices; employees want higher wages; suppliers want to sell their goods at higher prices; creditors want to charge higher interest rates; community leaders want more jobs for citizens and contributions to worthy causes; and, finally, shareholders want higher stock prices. Maximizing stock price for shareholders is constrained by the wants of these other stakeholders. Managers must seek ways of balancing these desires in order to maximize stock price.

Focusing on stakeholders and their stakes clarifies the essential nature of corporations. One school of thought views the corporation as *a nexus (a connected group) of contracts among stakeholders*. Figure 1.4 depicts the corporation as a focal point around which the stakeholders reside. Each stakeholder has a specific stake in the corporation: Employees earn wages, creditors receive interest, governments receive taxes, shareholders receive dividends, and so on. The alignment of these stakes at the bottom of Figure 1.4 reflects their ordering within the corporation's income statement. Customer purchases generate the sales revenue from which the financial stakes come. Viewing the corporation as a nexus of contracts reveals the corporation as a remarkable social invention for marshaling resources for production. It also reminds us that a corporation is a legal concept, "invisible, intangible, and existing only in the contemplation of law." As such, we recognize the ambiguity in statements that personify corporations. For example, corporations do not maximize shareholder wealth, corporate managers do.[6]

stakeholders

Groups who gain (or lose) as a company prospers (or fails)—customers, suppliers, employees, creditors, shareholders, and others.

AN OVERVIEW OF THE DETERMINANTS OF STOCK PRICE

Using the maximization of shareholder wealth as the objective of business financial management requires us to know what causes stock price to change. Interaction of three basic forces determines stock price: (1) the size of cash flows shareholders *expect* to receive from owning the stock, (2) the risk of the cash flows that is *perceived* by shareholders, and (3) shareholders' *expectations* of when they will receive the cash flows.

Size of Expected Cash Flows

After purchasing common stock, shareholders may receive two types of cash flows: (1) cash dividends declared by the board of directors and paid by the company, and (2) cash from eventually selling their stock to other investors. Selling stock for a price greater than that paid results in a capital gain; selling stock for

---

[6] For an elaboration on the concept of the corporation as a nexus of contracts, see Michael C. Jensen and William H. Meckling, "Theory of the Firm: Managerial Behavior, Agency Costs and Ownership Structure," *Journal of Financial Economics*, 3(1976), 305–360.

FIGURE 1.4

View of the Corporation as a Nexus of Contracts

The corporation may be viewed as a legal entity that brings together different groups of people. These groups, the stakeholders, have stakes in the success of the corporation. In this view, stakeholders act through or on behalf of the corporation, which is incapable of action because it exists only as a legal device.

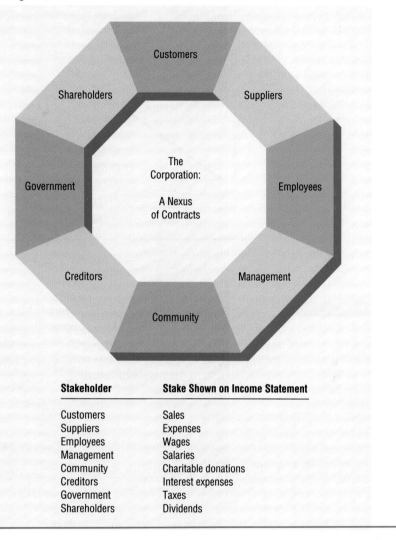

Stakeholder	Stake Shown on Income Statement
Customers	Sales
Suppliers	Expenses
Employees	Wages
Management	Salaries
Community	Charitable donations
Creditors	Interest expenses
Government	Taxes
Shareholders	Dividends

rate of return
Dollar return expressed as a percentage of investment.

less produces a capital loss. Assuming that a shareholder owns the stock for, say, one year, we calculate the **rate of return** as follows:

$$\text{Rate of return} = \frac{\text{Selling price} - \text{Buying price}}{\text{Buying price}} + \frac{\text{Cash dividends}}{\text{Buying price}}$$

$$= \frac{(\text{Selling price} - \text{Buying price}) + \text{Cash dividends}}{\text{Buying price}}$$

In other words, the shareholder's rate of return for the year equals the capital gain, or capital loss, plus cash dividends, all divided by the dollars invested (measured by the original buying price).

FIGURE 1.5

Effect of Expected Cash Flows on Stock Price

The size of expected cash flows and the stock price are positively related. The risk of these cash flows, however, is inversely related to stock price.

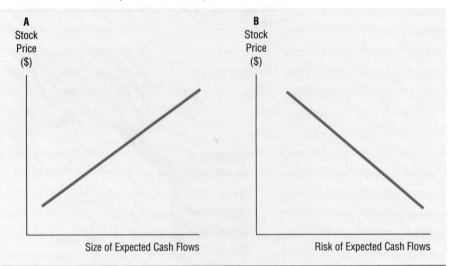

EXAMPLE

Suppose that you buy a share of General Motors common stock for $50 and sell it one year later for $60. Also suppose that General Motors pays you a $2 dividend just before you sell the share. You calculate your rate of return as follows:

$$\text{Rate of return} = \frac{(\$60 - \$50) + \$2}{\$50}$$

$$= \frac{\$12}{\$50}$$

$$= 0.24, \text{ or } 24\% \text{ for the year}$$

If you sell the share for only $40, then your rate of return is −16 percent, [($40 − $50) + $2]/$50.

In the above example, we calculate an actual (historical, or *ex post*) rate of return based on historical cash flows. Today's price of General Motors (GM) stock, however, depends on expected (future, or *ex ante*) cash flows—dividends and prices that GM shareholders (and potential investors) expect from GM stock. Higher *expected* cash flows lead to increases in *today's* stock price, as illustrated in Figure 1.5A. As expected cash flows rise and fall, the stock price rises and falls in the same direction.

By making company decisions—financing and investment decisions—that increase shareholders' expected cash flows, managers increase stock price. The art of successful management lies in knowing how to increase shareholders' expected cash flows without increasing their risk. To maximize stock price, managers must balance risk and expected return in company decisions.

Risk of Expected Cash Flows

risk
Perceived uncertainty in future cash flows or in expected rate of return.

Risk, the second major influence on a company's stock price, is the uncertainty shareholders perceive surrounding future cash flows: cash dividends and the future selling price of the stock. From the equation for rate of return, we can also say that risk is the uncertainty surrounding shareholders' expected rate of return. What shareholders expect, of course, may not actually occur. Actual cash dividends and the future selling price of the stock may differ dramatically from their expected values. Shareholders may be disappointed by smaller cash flows than expected. The greater the potential for disappointment, the greater the risk.

risk averse
Desiring to avoid risk.

Most investors are **risk averse;** that is, they do not like risk. This risk aversion establishes the negative, or inverse, relationship between stock price and risk: An increase in risk, holding other influences constant, causes a decline in stock price. Figure 1.5B shows us that as risk of cash flows rises and falls, the stock price falls and rises. By minimizing risk perceived by shareholders and maximizing their expected cash flows, managers increase stock price. Unfortunately, as we shall see later, larger expected cash flows and greater risk often go hand in hand.[7]

Timing of Expected Cash Flows

The third major influence on stock price is the timing of cash flows to shareholders. Shareholders prefer to receive cash earlier rather than later because cash in hand is worth more than cash in the future.

What causes this "bird-in-the-hand" reasoning? Three reasons that shareholders might offer for valuing near-term cash flows more highly than distant-future cash flows are: (1) "Who knows what tomorrow will bring? The future is cloudy and fraught with uncertainty." (2) "The prices of goods and services will continue to rise. A dollar will buy less in the future than it does today." (3) "I can invest a dollar received now to earn a return." These responses are valid reasons for valuing cash in hand more highly than cash in the future. The third response requires some explanation, however, because it prevails even in the absence of risk and **inflation.**

inflation
Decline in the purchasing power of money measured by an increase in the average price level.

Imagine a land where everybody knows the timing and amount of future cash flows with certainty and where no inflation exists. Living in such a land, shareholders know for certain the cash flow they will receive from their investment in a company's common stock. And they have no fear of the purchasing power of the dollar eroding. Even under these conditions, timing of cash flows is important to the shareholders because of the opportunity to invest. The return on their money is a reward for abstinence and patience, and the ability to earn a return makes investors prefer an immediate cash flow to a deferred cash flow.[8]

DO MANAGERS MAXIMIZE STOCK PRICE?

Do managers really try to maximize stock price through the size, risk, and timing of expected cash flows to shareholders? Perhaps they do in some companies, perhaps not in other companies. This financial objective is only one of several cor-

---

[7]See Chapters 5 and 10 for detailed discussions of risk.

[8]Chapter 4 discusses the time value of money.

porate objectives, and as such it may not necessarily dominate in every decision. When managers subordinate this financial objective to other objectives, however, they should assess the effect on the value of the company's common stock. Corporate managers who ignore the goal of stock price maximization may be forgetting that shareholders not only are beneficiaries of a corporation's financial success, but they are also referees who determine management's financial power. Failure to please common shareholders means that managers may find themselves looking for employment elsewhere.

A low stock price makes a company a tempting target for a takeover—another company or group of investors purchase enough stock to gain control. Each share of common stock usually carries with it one vote for electing members to the board of directors. After purchasing a controlling interest in the outstanding shares, the new owners may fire the managers. The best protection for managers is a high and rising stock price, making the company too expensive for takeover artists.

Despite the threat of takeover, some managers might be more preoccupied with their personal interests than with shareholder interests. These managers focus on *perquisites*—fringe benefits such as expensively appointed offices, numerous assistants, and jet airplanes. Such an attitude from professional managers, who might not even own shares in the company, creates an **agency problem:** The agents (managers) do not work hard nor do they make the same decisions that would be made if the principals (owners) were in charge.[9]

The agency problem creates **agency costs**—costs of monitoring management decisions and costs incurred through lower stock prices than would be the case with highly motivated managers. Examples of costs incurred to lessen the agency problem are: (1) expenditures for auditing financial statements, (2) committee decisions on major expenditures, (3) bonding costs to protect against malfeasance, (4) limitations on managerial decisions that inadvertently cause missed financial opportunities, and (5) executive compensation policies.

One way to motivate managers to make decisions consistent with the interests of shareholders is to tie their compensation to stock price performance. For example, the directors of many companies give **executive stock options** to top managers, which enable the managers to buy company stock in the future at a fixed price per share. The managers therefore have an incentive to try to increase stock price, because to do so will increase the value of their options.

Now return to the opening question: Do managers try to maximize stock price? The answer is: Some do and some don't. Normatively speaking, managers *should* try to maximize stock price.

ETHICS IN BUSINESS

In addition to agency questions on the relationship between corporate managers and shareholders, important ethical issues pervade the relationship between corporate managers and stakeholders in general. These issues deal with fair and just treatment of customers, employees, suppliers, the community at large, and others. Ethical behavior demands more of managers than just adhering to the letter of the law. Ethics impose a moral duty and an obligation to do what is right.

---

agency problem
Potential conflict of interest between agents (managers) and principals (shareholders).

agency costs
Costs arising from the separation of ownership and control of corporations; e.g., monitoring costs and lower stock price resulting from decisions by managers (agents).

executive stock options
Incentive compensation to executives, enabling them to buy their company's stock in the future at a fixed price.

---

[9]For the seminal work on agency problems, see the article by Jensen and Meckling cited in Note 6.

INTERNATIONAL DIMENSIONS

What Makes International *Financial Management Different?*

In today's global economy many companies, large and small, conduct business across national boundaries. Some companies are importers or exporters of goods for ultimate resale in markets other than the country of origin. Others engage in production outside the home (or parent) country, in a host country. They may sell products in either the home country, host country, a third country, or some combination of these markets.

Companies viewed as "purely domestic" also need to recognize international financial variables. Product pricing, raw-material and labor costs, interest rates, and availability of funds in countries other than the home country have an impact on domestic companies as the world economy rapidly integrates. For example, financial managers who ignore interest rates abroad may make their companies uncompetitive by obtaining higher-cost funds locally (domestically) rather than lower-cost funds internationally.

While financial management concepts and goals are universal, *international* financial management adds unique and vital characteristics. To illustrate, managing current assets and current liabilities for *all* companies entails cash, marketable securities, accounts receivable, and inventory in relation to accounts payable and other short-term liabilities. Similarly, shareholder wealth maximization is the goal of international as well as domestic companies. In multinational companies, however, managers contend with these responsibilities in an environment where assets, liabilities, revenues, expenses, and profits are recorded in different currencies whose values may change over time. For U.S. domestic companies, the value of a U.S. dollar is the same whether business transactions take place in California, Texas, New York State, or across a number of state boundaries.

The international financial manager has to monitor supply and demand factors determining currency prices—called *exchange rates*. The price of German deutsche marks or French francs expressed in U.S. dollars (or other currencies) can differ from minute to minute in the global marketplace. This attribute of the international financial environment—*floating exchange rates*—adds to the international financial manager's task. Decisions on hedging (insuring or protecting) become necessary for cash accounts, expected cash inflows from the collection of accounts receivable, and expected cash outflows for the payment of accounts payable and other liabilities.

Further complicating the job of the international financial manager—indeed *all* financial managers—is the need to be aware of sources and costs of capital worldwide. Over time, financial markets have evolved from a high degree of *segmentation* toward *integration*. Financial markets formerly separated by legal, political, and technological barriers now tend toward accessibility to borrowers and lenders irrespective of national origin. Previously, many financial managers telephoned a local banker to ask for a loan when the company needed funds. Now, competent financial managers literally "shop" the world to ensure finding the best deal for the company.

Additionally, companies that invest overseas incur distinct risks. Besides the usual business risks, investments across national boundaries bear political risk, ranging from limitations on funds repatriation (transfer) to expropriation (seizure) of assets. The international financial manager therefore needs to understand and analyze a foreign country's political, cultural, economic, and social systems in order to make decisions effectively. These systems determine the country's laws, accounting rules, and tax regulations, which in turn affect the international company's investment decisions and performance measurement.

According to one study, business executives believe that ethical standards within companies must originate at the top. Emphasis on ethical action by top executives serves as a role model for other employees. When Chrysler Corporation sold cars with disconnected odometers as new, chairman Lee Iacocca offered compensation to the buyers of the cars and promised to stop the practice. His openness about the incident probably lessened its impact on Chrysler's customers and stock price. Similarly, when Sears auto centers overcharged customers, CEO Edward Brennan offered $15 million in compensation to past customers.

Although rules, policies, and procedures cannot cover all contingencies, many large companies have adopted a code of ethics for employees to follow. These codes usually contain a general statement emphasizing management's commitment to ethical behavior and a list of specific "do and don't" statements. Ethical top management and a code of ethics may not deter the employee committed to unethical acts, but they can sensitize employees on the importance of ethical conduct.

Former U.S. Secretary of the Treasury and successful businessman William Simon states: "History teaches us that no free society or free economy can long survive without an ethical base. It is only through a shared moral foundation—a set of binding rules for fair conduct—that free associations, be they social, diplomatic, or commercial, can flourish and endure." Despite these compelling arguments, ethical lapses occur with regularity in business. For example, the names Charles Keating, Michael Milken, Ivan Boesky, Dennis Levine, and Jim Bakker have become notorious because of violations of trust and moral conduct. Still, it seems doubtful that ethical lapses occur proportionately more frequently in business than in other professions—politics, law, medicine, academia, to name a few. Moreover, it seems reasonable to conclude that ethical behavior of corporate managers is a necessary ingredient in the maximization of stock price.

BUSINESS FINANCIAL MANAGEMENT AND STOCK PRICE

All financial decisions have the potential for altering a company's stock price. Because of this potential and the financial objective of maximizing shareholder wealth through maximization of stock price, we analyze decisions in terms of their consequences in the stock market. This logic, in turn, requires that we understand the forces acting upon a company's stock.

Figure 1.6 summarizes the relationship between financial decisions and the company's stock price. Investment and financing decisions by corporate managers generate the corporate cash flow from which cash payments are made to shareholders. The total cash flow of the corporation holds implications for the size of cash flows expected by shareholders, risk of the expected cash flows, and their timing. Maximizing stock price calls for decisions that tend to:

1. Increase size of expected cash flows.
2. Decrease perceived risk of expected cash flows.
3. Produce cash flows as soon as possible.

Reductions in the size of expected cash flows, increases in risk, and postponement of cash flows lead to a lower stock price.

Business financial management examines the way financial decisions within a company affect cash flows to shareholders, and thereby the company's stock price. In this book we explore company decisions on investments and their financing. *Investment decisions* include issues in cash management, credit policy, inventory control, and the selection of fixed assets. *Financing decisions* include issues in managing credit extended to the company, bank borrowing, issuing stocks and bonds, and retaining earnings for internal financing. Before addressing

FIGURE 1.6

The Effect of Financial Decisions on Stock Price

Financial decisions affect the cash flows received by shareholders. Large expected cash flows, low risk, and early cash flows contribute to a high stock price.

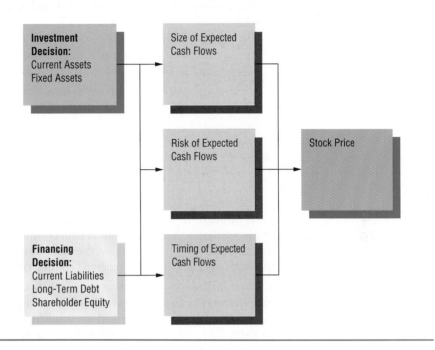

these issues, we examine, in Chapters 2 and 3, the U.S. financial system and the markets for stocks and bonds.

SUMMARY

• The study of finance consists of three parts: (1) financial markets and institutions, (2) investments, and (3) business financial management. In large part, the study of financial markets and institutions focuses on depository institutions and the securities markets, and the study of investments focuses on "Wall Street finance"—the study of how individuals and institutions invest in stocks, bonds, and other securities. Business financial management, the topic of this book, concentrates on cash flows to and from a company resulting from investment and financing decisions. Understanding business financial management will help you to make better business decisions.

• The three basic forms of business organization are sole proprietorship, partnership, and corporation. Although proprietorships and partnerships outnumber corporations, they tend to be small. Large businesses tend to be corporations because of three financial advantages of this organizational form: (1) limited financial liability of owners, the shareholders; (2) ease of transferring ownership by selling common stock; and (3) the unlimited lives of corporations. Shareholders own the corporation and usually have one vote for each share of stock; shareholders elect the members of the board of directors.

- The finance department within a company often consists of two sections, one headed by the treasurer and one headed by the controller. Heading the finance department is the vice president of finance, the chief financial officer (CFO).

- You can remember the financial manager's principal tasks by knowing the three A's:

   Analyze and plan the company's performance.
   Acquire funds from debt and equity in the optimal proportions.
   Allocate funds among competing assets, assessing risk and expected return.

- A company's *income statement* is based on the following equation:

$$\frac{\text{Net}}{\text{sales}} - \frac{\text{Cost of}}{\text{sales}} - \frac{\text{Operating}}{\text{expenses}} - \frac{\text{Interest}}{\text{expense}} - \text{Taxes} = \text{Earnings}$$

A company's *balance sheet* is based on the following equation:

$$\text{Total assets} = \text{Total liabilities} + \text{Shareholder equity}$$

- The objective of business financial management is to maximize shareholder wealth through the maximization of stock price. Stock price depends on: (1) the size of cash flows that shareholders expect, (2) the perceived risk of the expected cash flows, and (3) the timing of the cash flows. Shareholders prefer large cash flows with low risk that are received sooner rather than later.

- Thinking of the corporation as a nexus of contracts helps us to avoid the personification of the corporation, which is simply a legal concept. Each stakeholder has a contract, expressed or implied, with the corporation. Corporate managers and shareholders—two of the stakeholders—may have divergent interests, which creates an agency problem. Agency costs are the resources and effort spent to lessen the agency problem. Ethical treatment of all stakeholders by corporate managers is a necessary condition for shareholder wealth maximization.

- Financial decisions on investments and financing affect company cash flows. The company's cash flows, in turn, determine its potential for paying cash dividends to shareholders. Large cash flows generated by the company lead shareholders to expect large cash flows from dividends, and this expectation leads to stock price increases. Managers maximize stock price by making decisions that balance expected cash flows against their risk.

Key Terms

assets	funds	stakeholders
debt	income statement	rate of return
equity	balance sheet	risk
sole proprietorship	financial structure	risk averse
partnership	capital structure	inflation
corporation	optimal capital structure	agency problem
common stock	financing decision	agency costs
maturity	investment decision	executive stock options
cash dividend	agent	

Questions

1.1. What are the three divisions of finance? Which one does this book emphasize?

1.2. Investment courses and business financial management courses have moved closer together because both concentrate on stock price, but from different perspectives. Explain the role of stock price in investment courses and business financial management courses.

1.3. Why does the corporate form of business organization dominate among large U.S. companies?

1.4. Describe the three principal tasks of financial managers.

1.5. Branch-Moses Company's (BMC) financial statements are given below. Describe the purpose of the balance sheet and the income statement. (No calculations are required.)

Balance Sheet, December 31, 199X

Current assets	$250,000	Total debt	$200,000
Fixed assets	150,000	Total equity	200,000
Total assets	$400,000	Total claims	$400,000

Income Statement for Year Ending December 31, 199X

Net sales	$800,000
Expenses	750,000
Earnings	$ 50,000

1.6. What would likely happen to the price of the company's common stock after each of the following announcements? Explain.
   a. IBM makes a large investment to develop small computers that use the software of large computers. Delays in design and production prevent delivery.
   b. Occidental Petroleum must pay $724,000,000 to Coastal Corporation as a result of a federal court ruling in Wyoming.
   c. Union Carbide settles its financial liability for a major industrial accident in India. The cost of the settlement is less than expected.

1.7. Explain how stock price varies with changes in (a) size of expected cash flows, and (b) risk.

1.8. Some items affecting a common stock's price are within the control of a financial manager and some are beyond it. Comment on management's ability to control each of the following items: (a) foreign competition, (b) speculation in the stock market, and (c) labor costs.

1.9. "Risk is beyond the control of management, so we shouldn't be concerned with it." Explain why you agree or disagree with this statement.

1.10. "The financial objective of business is to maximize stock price and thereby increase shareholder wealth." Comment on this objective and discuss whether other parties with a stake in the corporation are necessarily being ignored in the pursuit of this objective. Who are these stakeholders?

1.11. Two corporations are similar in every respect. However, the Kooper International shareholders perceive greater risk associated with the company's future dividends than do the shareholders of Cochran Corporation with its dividends. Which corporation's common stock has a greater market value? Support your choice with a brief discussion.

1.12. Jerry Lee purchased 100 shares of Motor Car Company common stock for $26 per share. He sold it for $52 a share and received a dividend of $6 per share immediately before selling the shares. If Mr. Lee held the stock for one year, what was his rate of return? What is the difference between a capital gain and a rate of return?

1.13. Assume that you purchase 300 shares of Nalco Chemical Company common stock for $34.50 per share. Having held the stock for one year, you sell it for $38 per share. Prior to sale, you also receive a cash dividend of $1 per share.
   a. Calculate your rate of return.
   b. Calculate your rate of return assuming that you sell the stock for $30 per share.

1.14. Charles Plott of the California Institute of Technology, Mark Isaac of the University of Arizona, and James Walker of Indiana University devised a game to explore the free-rider problem—attempts to gain advantage at the expense of one's neighbors. Up to five people can play the game, which makes use of the following table of payoffs:

Number of Players Choosing Alternative A	Payoff for Choosing: A	B
0	—	$ 0
1	$10	20
2	20	40
3	30	60
4	40	80
5	50	—

Each player chooses either A or B to determine his or her individual payoff, but the level of payoff also depends on the number of players choosing A. For example, if all 5 players choose A, then each player would receive $50. If all 5 players choose B, then each player would receive zero. Similarly, if 4 players choose A and one player chooses B, then the player choosing B gets $80 and the others get $40 each.

a. To play the game, each player writes either A or B on a slip of paper. Collect and analyze the papers to determine the payoffs. Repeat the game 2 or 3 times with each player making independent choices—no deal making or colluding.

b. Now play the game and allow players to make deals with each other.

Did you notice any ethical lapses during the game?

Readiness Test

In spirit, the readiness test below is like a puzzle—fun yet challenging to the intellect. As you take the test, enjoy its subtle, odd, and ironic flavor. The test requires you to recall ideas from previous courses and experiences, and it may force you to search for ideas in later chapters of this book. In either case the test should be a healthy exercise and fun. It calls for a large dose of common sense—as does decision making in a company. Feel free to use the index at the end of the book if you need to.

1.1. Phyllis Brent can take a job paying $35,000 per year when she graduates from college, or she can go to graduate school for two years and pay $18,000 per year. Measured in dollars, what is her opportunity cost of going to graduate school for the next two years?

1.2. Oscar Martinez, a clothing wholesaler, sold a quantity of goods for $18,775. He deducts 5 percent for cash and then finds that he has made 10 percent on his investment. What did he pay for the goods?

1.3. Which one of the following groups typically is hurt the most by unexpected inflation?
a. Bondholders
b. Borrowers
c. Farmers
Explain your choice.

1.4. The interest on an $80 investment from March 1st to June 1st is $2. What is the rate per year compounded quarterly?

1.5. The rate of interest a company pays on its borrowed money increases from 10.5 percent annually to 11.9 percent annually. By what percentage did the rate of interest increase? By how many percentage points did the rate of interest increase?

1.6. Company X earns $1,000,000 profit after taxes and Company Y earns $100,000. Is Company X necessarily more profitable than Company Y? Explain your answer, and be sure to comment on the difference between *profit* and *profitability*.

1.7. A company reports $180,000 in after-tax profit. If it paid income taxes at a 40 percent rate, what was its profit before taxes?

1.8. In percentage terms, the price of Glaxmonn Drug stock drops 1.4 times as fast as the overall stock market. A measure of the overall stock market drops from 2,500 to 1,700. To what price does Glaxmonn stock move from $48 per share?

1.9. A company sells items for $7 each. Its fixed overhead costs are $150 and variable costs are $4 per unit. What profit does it make selling (a) 100 items, (b) 120 items? By what percentage does its profit increase as sales increase from 100 to 120 units?

1.10. A company's annual sales amount to four times its total assets. Its profit on sales is 3.6 percent. What is its rate of profit on its total assets?

1.11. A company has $3 debt for every $9 equity. How much debt does it have for each $1 of assets?

1.12. Adam Lane plans to organize a company that will sell water. He plans to sell 10 gallons of water for twice the price of a half-carat diamond. After all, he reasons, water is far more necessary for life than are diamonds. His friend Marshall Jevons thinks the price is too high. Do you agree with Mr. Jevons or with Mr. Lane? Why?

1.13. LuAnn Watson buys a super-large malted milk for $3. "Wow, that really hits the spot," exclaims Ms. Watson. If the malted milk is so good and she has the money, then why doesn't Ms. Watson order another one for $3? Use the economic concept of utility in your answer.

1.14. Carnes Studios has liabilities and equity in the ratio of 3 to 1. The size of the liabilities is fixed. By what percentage does equity increase when assets increase 25 percent?

1.15. In 1989 Sears, Roebuck announced that because of deteriorating profits, it would dramatically *lower* prices in its stores. How might lower prices increase the company's profits?

1.16. Bolten Belt Company (BBC) has 750 shares of common stock outstanding. It earned $4 per share in 19X1. If BBC buys back 20 percent of the outstanding shares and total earnings increase 10 percent in 19X2, what are its earnings per share in 19X2?

1.17. Wheeler Corporation's earnings before interest and taxes are 5 times its interest expense. If its earnings after taxes are $3,600 and its tax rate is 40 percent, how much interest did it pay?

1.18. LBJ Company sells trinkets for $2.50 each. Labor and material for each trinket produced cost $1.25. The company's fixed costs are $1,000. How many trinkets must LBJ Company produce and sell to break even (EBIT = 0)?

1.19. Rudy Soza invested $1,000 and earned 8 percent during the first year. His goal is to earn 10 percent per year for 2 years. Assuming that Mr. Soza reinvests his first-year earnings, what percentage must he earn during the second year to achieve his goal?

1.20. Suppose that *Teen Age*, a teenage magazine, proposed a doubling of the minimum wage that businesses must pay teens. If placed into law, what effect would the doubling most likely have on teen wages and on employment in a market economy?

Selected References

Coffman, Richard B. "Is Profit Maximization vs. Value Maximization Also Economics vs. Finance?" *Journal of Financial Education,* Fall 1983: 37–40.

Cooley, Philip L. "On the Nature of Risk: A Comment." *Journal of Financial Research,* Spring 1979: 81–85.

Cooley, Philip L., and Charles E. Edwards. "Financial Objectives of Small Firms." *American Journal of Small Business,* July–September 1983: 27–31.

Findlay, M. Chapman, III, and G. A. Whitmore. "Beyond Shareholder Wealth Maximization." *Financial Management,* Winter 1974: 25–35.

Gombola, Michael J., and George P. Tsetsekos. "The Information Content of Plant Closing Announcements: Evidence from Financial Profiles and the Stock Price Reaction." *Financial Management,* Summer 1992: 31–40.

Meckling, William H., and Michael C. Jensen. "Reflections on the Corporation as a Social Invention." *Midland Corporate Finance Journal,* Fall 1983: 6–15.

Parker, Jeffrey M., and Menachem Rosenberg. "Equity-Oriented Compensation Plans for Executives." *Financial Executive,* June 1981: 22–26.

Rappaport, Alfred. "Selecting Strategies That Create Shareholder Value." *Harvard Business Review,* May–June 1981: 139–149.

Seitz, Neil. "Shareholder Goals, Firm Goals and Firm Financing Decisions." *Financial Management,* Autumn 1982: 20–26.

Treynor, Jack L. "The Financial Objective in the Widely Held Corporation." *Financial Analysts Journal,* March–April 1981: 68–71.

Wenner, David L., and Richard W. LeBer. "Managing for Shareholder Value—From Top to Bottom." *Harvard Business Review,* November–December 1989: 52–54ff.

Appendix 1A PROFESSIONAL CERTIFICATION IN FINANCE

Three widely recognized and respected certification programs in finance permit finance professionals to become chartered financial analysts (CFA), certified management accountants (CMA), and certified financial planners (CFP). These programs give finance professionals designations that rival the CPA in accounting.

The following discussion briefly describes each certification program. If interested, you may write for more information and an application to sit for one or more of the examinations.

CHARTERED FINANCIAL ANALYST

The Financial Analysts Federation established the Institute of Chartered Financial Analysts in 1959. The ICFA gave its first examination in 1963. The term *financial analyst* refers to someone who is professionally engaged in investment management and securities research.

A college degree and three character references are required for admission to the program. The examination, which is given at about 100 locations each year, consists of three levels, with a candidate sitting for a subsequent level only after successfully passing the previous level. Each level requires a progressively greater depth of understanding of material and covers a broader range of subjects within each topic. The topics are:

1. Economics, including analysis and forecasting, historical and structural perspectives, and economic policy.

2. Financial accounting, including principles and construction of accounting statements, areas of judgment, and current accounting principles and practices.

3. Techniques of analysis, including fixed-income securities, bonds and credit evaluation, credit markets, mathematical properties of bonds, bond management, policy and implementation, and bond performance.

4. Techniques of analysis, including equity securities, sources of information and financial instruments, and industry and company appraisal and evaluation.

5. Objectives of analysis, including portfolio analysis, investor objectives and constraints, and portfolio strategy and construction.

6. Conduct of analysis, including ethical and professional standards, securities laws, and regulations.

For more information and to receive announcement forms about the examination, write or call:

> Association for Investment Management & Research
> #5 Boars Head Lane
> Charlottesville, Virginia 22903
> (804) 977–6600

CERTIFIED MANAGEMENT ACCOUNTANT

The CMA is a professional designation for management accountants and financial managers. The National Association of Accountants administered the first CMA examination in 1972.

The CMA program requires candidates to pass a series of uniform examinations and to meet specific educational and professional standards to qualify for and maintain the CMA. The Institute of Certified Management Accountants administers the program, conducts the examinations, and grants certificates to those who qualify. Anyone with a college degree and two years of relevant experience may sit for the examination, which consists of the following parts:

1. Economics and business finance.
2. Organization and behavior, including ethical considerations.
3. Public reporting standards, auditing, and taxes.
4. Periodic reporting for internal and external purposes.
5. Decision analysis, including modeling and information systems.

Each part takes $3\frac{1}{2}$ hours, scheduled consecutively over a $2\frac{1}{2}$-day period. You may take all five parts at one sitting.

For more information about the CMA and to receive information about examinations, write or call:

> Institute of Certified Management Accountants
> 10 Paragon Drive
> Montvale, New Jersey 07645–1759
> (201) 573–6300

CERTIFIED FINANCIAL PLANNER

The International Board of Standards and Practices for Certified Financial Planners established the CFP designation to standardize the requirements for candidates to be considered competent in financial planning. To become a CFP, a candidate must enroll in a college or university that has a financial planning program registered with the International Board, pass a series of examinations, complete specified experience requirements, and agree to uphold the International Board's code of ethics.

The CFP examination is composed of six parts, which reflect the broad range of financial services with which financial planners must deal. CFPs help individuals by offering them financial advice—in contrast to CFAs and CMAs, who usually advise companies about investment and financing decisions.

CFP candidates take one or two parts of the examination at one sitting after they have completed the appropriate course work. The examination's six parts are as follows:

1. Introduction to financial planning.
2. Risk management.
3. Investments.
4. Tax planning and management.
5. Retirement planning and employee benefits.
6. Estate planning.

For more information about the CFP and to receive information about examinations, write or call:

> International Board of Standards and Practices for
>   Certified Financial Planners Inc.
> 5445 DTC Parkway, Suite P-1
> Englewood, Colorado 80111
> (303) 850–0333

Chapter 2

BUSINESS AND THE FINANCIAL SYSTEM

The S&L Mess

Unveiled in the 1970s, the popular savings vehicle known as the IRA (Individual Retirement Account) is just one part of a large financial system comprising numerous savings and lending methods. Participating in this system are companies, individuals, governments, commercial banks, savings and loan associations (S&Ls), insurance companies, pension funds, mutual funds, and other groups.

Unfortunately for the U.S. taxpayer, the S&L part of the financial system has performed poorly in recent years. Hundreds of S&Ls have failed and have been liquidated or merged with other companies during the 1980s and 1990s. To protect depositors from losing their savings, the federal government will ultimately use more than $200 billion of taxpayers' money to restructure the S&L industry.

Management incompetence and corruption account for some of the S&L failures, but many of them got into trouble doing what they are supposed to do: take in short-term deposits from savers and lend on long-

term mortgages to home buyers. The nature of the process violates a cardinal principle of finance: Match the maturity of sources of funds with the maturity of uses of funds. Violation of this rule did not seem to matter until interest rates rose to modern-day highs in the early 1980s. To compete with the high rates offered by money market mutual funds, S&Ls had to raise the rates that they paid on deposits. The rates they earned on money loaned for home mortgages, however, were fixed at the low levels prevailing during most of the 1970s. As a consequence of paying more and earning less, S&L profits plummeted and turned into deficits. Eventually many S&Ls had more dollars of liabilities than dollars of assets—they were insolvent!

Perhaps President Franklin Roosevelt was right when he commented in 1933 on the government guaranteeing deposits in financial institutions: ". . . the minute the government starts to do that . . . the government runs into a probable loss."

Source: Lindley H. Clark, Jr., "Perils of Insuring Bank Deposits," *The Wall Street Journal,* May 8, 1989, A1; "American Thrifts: Pyramidists," *Economist,* July 2, 1988, 66–67.

This chapter examines the financial system comprising financial markets and financial institutions. Once you understand the financial system, you will see the choices companies have for raising funds for their investments. This chapter prepares you for the detailed discussion of the stock and bond markets in Chapter 3. You need to understand the financial system, particularly the markets for a company's securities, to understand the financial objective of maximizing shareholder wealth. In later chapters, as you learn financial techniques for maximizing shareholder wealth, you will understand the impact of managerial decisions in the marketplace.

THE FINANCIAL SYSTEM

security
Documentary evidence of claims on future cash flows—stocks, bonds, and other promises to pay.

The financial system shifts funds from savers to users. Users of funds exchange securities for the funds they receive from savers. Securities give savers a claim on the users' future cash flows. A **security** in itself is evidence of the claim, and it specifies the rights of the security holder. Figure 2.1 illustrates the exchange of funds and securities between savers and users. In the role of users, companies, individuals, and governments may obtain funds from other companies, individuals, and governments in the role of savers. Briefly, the types of securities issued by users of funds include the following:

- Companies issue common stock, bonds, and other securities. In return for their funds, savers who buy common stock receive fractional ownership in the company; this ownership confers the rights to receive dividends (when declared by the board of directors) and to vote in major company decisions. Purchasers of bonds have the right to receive interest (a legal obligation of the company) and a return of the bond's face value at maturity. A bond is evidence of the company's debt, which makes bondholders creditors of the company.

- Individuals sign (issue) promissory notes for the funds they borrow. A promissory note is an IOU specifying the amount borrowed, the interest rate, the maturity, and other conditions of the loan.

- Local, state, and federal governments issue bonds to savers in exchange for the savers' surplus funds. Like corporate bonds, government bonds entitle savers to interest payments at specified times in the future. When the bonds mature on their repayment dates, the issuer-debtor returns to savers their initial investment in the bonds.

direct placement
Issuing securities directly to savers in return for funds, bypassing all intermediaries.

The process of obtaining funds in the way illustrated in Figure 2.1 is **direct placement.** To be successful with direct placement, the user must have information on which savers are willing to purchase the user's securities. Moreover, the user often needs to raise dollar amounts far larger than are available from any one saver. In these cases users must identify numerous savers. Because of the difficulties inherent in direct placement, users frequently do not appeal directly to savers for funds. Instead, they seek help from other participants in the financial system.

financial market
Mechanism for facilitating the issuance of securities; also known as the securities market.

financial institution
Commercial bank or other organization that collects funds from savers and makes loans to users.

Two mechanisms for easing the flow of funds between savers and users are financial markets and financial institutions. **Financial markets** provide the system for issuing stocks, bonds, and other securities. **Financial institutions** include commercial banks and other organizations that collect funds from savers and make loans to users. The existence of financial markets and institutions greatly reduces

FIGURE 2.1

Flow of Funds between Savers and Users

Savers transfer funds to users. Savers are companies, individuals, and governments with funds they presently do not need to cover expenses. Users have insufficient funds to meet their needs for projects and expenditures. In return for funds, users issue securities, claims on future cash flows.

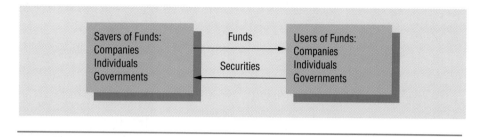

the number of individuals with whom a user of funds must transact business. For example, a company borrowing $1,000,000 from a commercial bank must negotiate with only one person, the bank's corporate loan officer, because the bank has performed the function of collecting funds from thousands of depositors (savers). The bank loans the depositors' funds to the user.

Figure 2.2 expands Figure 2.1 by showing the relationship of financial markets and institutions to savers and users. The direct flow of funds and securities between savers and users is the same as that shown in Figure 2.1. However, by inserting financial markets and institutions into the system, we see the alternative routes to direct placement for the flow of funds and securities:

1. Users issue securities and savers buy them in financial markets (also known as securities markets). Financial markets contain organizations that assist in the exchange of securities for funds.

2. Users borrow funds from financial institutions that collect funds from savers.

3. Acting as users, financial institutions may issue securities for funds in the financial markets. Acting as savers, financial institutions may purchase securities for funds in the financial markets.

After users have issued securities for funds, many of the securities can be resold at a later time by the savers who initially bought them. Say that you buy 100 shares of common stock issued by Exxon Corporation, hold the shares for a year, and then decide to sell them. As the bottom of Figure 2.2 shows, you may sell previously issued securities in the financial markets. Thus financial markets provide a means for savers to purchase securities being issued by users of funds and securities being sold by other savers who now want cash instead of securities.

FUNCTIONS OF FINANCIAL MARKETS

investment banking firm
Organization that specializes in the distribution of corporate securities to investor-savers.

Financial markets encompass the New York Stock Exchange, **investment banking firms,** and other places and organizations. You meet some of these organizations and places as you examine the three major functions of financial markets: (1) to transfer funds from savers to users, (2) to provide liquidity for investors, and (3) to provide signals and targets for financial managers.

FIGURE 2.2

Flow of Funds through the Financial System

The financial markets and institutions in the financial system provide an efficient means of bringing together savers and users of funds. Users issue securities in the financial markets in exchange for funds; savers provide the funds in exchange for the securities. Financial institutions collect funds from savers, giving them claims on future cash flows (securities); these institutions, in turn, provide the funds to users. Institutions provide funds to financial markets by purchasing securities. Buyers and sellers of previously issued securities operate in the secondary market.

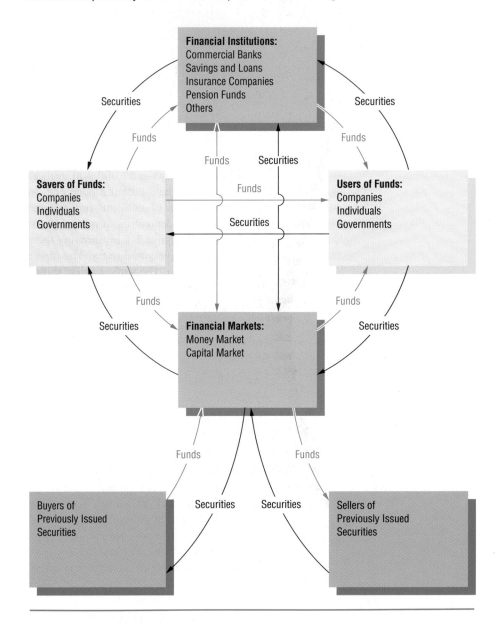

Transfer Funds from Savers to Users

Financial markets enable users of funds to gather and mobilize large dollar sums from thousands of savers. The following examples illustrate how financial markets facilitate transactions between users and savers:

1. A company needing funds for long-term purposes issues common stock (or bonds) through an investment banking firm such as Goldman Sachs, Salomon Brothers, or Morgan Stanley. Investment bankers advise company managers wanting to sell new securities, bear some of the risk of successfully selling the securities, and do the actual selling.[1]

2. A company needing funds for only a few months sells short-term debt securities through dealers who specialize in such securities.[2] These dealers provide services similar to those provided by investment bankers, who specialize in long-term securities.

Investment bankers and securities dealers have more experience and are better equipped to sell securities than are most company managers. Experience in selling securities over time for numerous companies creates operational efficiency and sound judgment in the sale of new securities. By issuing securities through these specialists, companies take advantage of this efficiency and sound judgment.

Provide Liquidity for Investors

liquidity
Ease with which securities can be converted into cash with little or no loss in current value.

Liquidity is the ease with which investors can convert their securities into cash with little or no loss in current value. Cash is the standard of liquidity because it can be used to buy goods and services. Financial markets provide liquidity by providing the means for buyers and sellers to exchange cash for securities and securities for cash.[3]

Suppose that you bought 100 shares of common stock when a company first issued it and now you wish to sell the shares. You can sell your shares by using the services of a **stockbroker**—Merrill Lynch, PaineWebber, Dean Witter, A. G. Edwards, to name a few. Operating in the retail, or resale, portion of financial markets, stockbrokers help you buy and sell previously issued securities.

stockbroker
Company (or individual) that executes customer orders to buy or sell securities.

A resale market for securities greatly enhances their liquidity. Investors are more willing to buy securities when first issued by companies if the investors are confident in their ability to sell the securities later. Thus financial markets not only help companies to raise funds initially, but they also provide liquidity for outstanding securities. Because investors like liquidity, they demand lower rates of return on securities actively trading in financial markets than on securities without a ready market. Lower required rates of return mean that (1) companies pay less interest on bonds, and (2) investors willingly pay higher prices per share of common stock.

---

[1] Chapter 3 presents a more detailed examination of investment banking.

[2] Companies issue short-term IOUs known as commercial paper. Chapter 14 discusses the process and cost of issuing commercial paper.

[3] Here the term *cash* is used as part of the more encompassing term *funds*. Broadly defined, *funds* are any means of payment, including cash. Funds might also include cash deposits at a financial institution such as a commercial bank or credit union.

Provide Signals and Targets for Financial Managers

Like the markets for other goods and services, financial markets are governed by the forces of supply and demand. The collective actions of buyers and sellers determine the prices of securities, which reflect the expectations of buyers and sellers. Changes in security prices sometimes provide financial managers with readable signals about the economic future. For example, if investors expect an economic recession, they will obtain funds to help them through the recession by selling securities. In addition, they will sell securities before the onset of the recession in order to avoid losses. As momentum gathers for selling securities, the prices of securities decline. In this way the financial markets signal an impending recession.

Financial markets also help managers to determine whether they are achieving the goal of maximizing price per share of common stock. When investors expect larger future cash dividends and perceive lower risk, they begin to buy more shares, thus bidding up the stock price. When they expect smaller future cash dividends and perceive higher risk, they begin to sell shares, thus driving down the stock price.

A financial manager can monitor the company's stock price movements and thereby obtain information about how shareholders view the company's investment and financing decisions. Sustained price movements in the same direction for many months are especially informative. If the company's stock price rises relative to other stock prices, then management is making decisions that investors like. If the company's stock price falls relative to other stock prices, then management is making decisions that investors dislike. Once management adopts the goal of maximizing stock price, shareholders become the final judges of company success. Thus the financial markets furnish a target—the stock price—for measuring the success of the company's decisions.

TYPES OF FINANCIAL MARKETS

Financial markets consist of many separate markets; there is no single market for all securities. Markets differ by the customers they serve, the types of securities traded within them, and their geographic locations—some have no central location at all. The commonly used classifications of financial markets overlap each other and are not mutually exclusive. Still, the classifications provide a useful and systematic view of financial markets. The classifications are: (1) primary and secondary markets, (2) debt and equity markets, and (3) money and capital markets.

Primary and Secondary Markets

primary market
Financial market where securities are first issued.

The **primary market** is the financial market where securities are first issued, and it is sometimes called the *new-issues market*. Figure 2.2 illustrates transactions in the primary market by the arrows extending from the Users of Funds box. When companies issue securities in the primary market, they usually solicit the assistance of an investment banker to distribute the new securities to investors.

secondary market
Financial resale market where investors buy and sell previously issued securities.

In contrast to the primary market, the **secondary market** is a resale market where investors buy and sell previously issued securities (see the bottom of Figure 2.2). All securities are first issued in the primary market, but subsequent trades occur in the secondary market. Most likely, you are more familiar with the secondary market, which includes the New York Stock Exchange, than with the primary market. The secondary market includes the activities of brokers and dealers. Brokers arrange for the purchase and sale of previously issued securities. For example, stockbrokers execute customer orders to trade without buying or selling the stock themselves. Brokers earn profits by charging commissions to customers for executing trades. **Dealers,** by contrast, buy and sell securities for their own accounts. Dealers take title to the securities and earn profits on the difference between the buying and selling prices.

dealer
Company (or individual) that buys and sells securities for its own account.

The primary and secondary markets serve different functions. The primary market eases the transfer of funds from savers to users. The secondary market provides liquidity for outstanding securities. In addition, the secondary market sends signals to financial managers and furnishes a target—the stock price—for assessing the success of investment and financing decisions.

Debt and Equity Markets

Whenever a company, individual, or government issues or sells a debt security such as a bond, the transaction takes place in the **debt market.** Whenever a company or individual issues or sells a common stock, the transaction takes place in the **equity market.** Notice that if these were initial sales, then they would be primary-market transactions in either the debt or equity market; otherwise, they would be secondary-market transactions.

debt market
Financial market where debt securities such as bonds are traded.

equity market
Financial market where common stock is traded.

The debt and equity financial markets are further classified as organized exchanges or over-the-counter markets. An **organized exchange** consists of coordinated, centrally located trading facilities with specific rules for members of the exchange. Brokerage firms are members of an exchange, which entitles them to buy and sell securities on behalf of clients. The New York Stock Exchange is an example of an organized, secondary, equity market in which investors and speculators trade the stocks of corporations. There is no organized exchange for the primary market. Unlike an organized exchange, the **over-the-counter (OTC) market** is not located at a specific geographic location. Instead, the OTC market is a decentralized network of brokers and dealers connected electronically by telephones and computers. An example of the over-the-counter market is the one for U.S. government securities, which are traded among brokers, dealers, and individuals over telephones and cables without the need for a centrally located facility.

organized exchange
Coordinated, centrally located trading facility whose members buy and sell securities.

over-the-counter (OTC) market
Decentralized, electronically connected network of brokers and dealers.

Money and Capital Markets

The **money market** is any place where securities with a maturity of one year or less are traded. The **capital market** is any place where securities with a maturity greater than one year are traded. Money and capital markets may be primary (new issue) or secondary (existing issue), organized (traded in a central location) or over the counter (no central location). The following discussion of financial markets uses the distinction between money and capital markets to introduce you to the securities that trade in them.

money market
Financial market where securities with a maturity of one year or less are traded.

capital market
Financial market where securities with a maturity greater than one year are traded.

THE MONEY MARKET

Companies use the money market in either of two ways: (1) They issue short-term debt securities to raise funds to finance temporary increases in assets (say, increases in inventory), or (2) they invest temporarily excess cash in money market securities. Companies such as General Motors Acceptance Corporation, Citicorp, Sears, and General Electric issue money market securities. The U.S.

TABLE 2.1   **Characteristics of Money Market Securities**

Security	Issuer	Secondary Market	Maturities When Issued	Denomination
Treasury bill	U.S. government obligation	Excellent	13 weeks 26 weeks 52 weeks	$10,000 (sold in multiples of $5,000 above the minimum)
U.S. agency security	Obligation of U.S. agency established by congressional act	Fair to good	30 days to 1 year	$1,000 to $100,000
Commercial paper	Promissory note of issuing company (industrial and financial)	Weak	30–270 days	$25,000 to $5,000,000; $100,000 basic trading unit
Negotiable certificate of deposit (CD)	Obligation of bank accepting the deposit	Good	Usually 1 to 6 months but occasionally up to several years	$100,000 and up
Banker's acceptance	Credit instrument guaranteed by a bank	Fair	30–180 days; 90 days is most common primary-market maturity	Issued in odd denominations
Federal funds	Loanable excess reserves at a bank	None	Usually overnight but occasionally up to a year	Negotiated among participants

government issues money market securities weekly to help finance the national debt. Although individual money market securities differ from one another, they share several characteristics in common. All money market securities:

- Are debt securities.
- Have short-term maturities.
- Have low **default risk.**
- Usually offer relatively low expected rates of return compared with capital market securities.

Table 2.1 lists six money market securities and outlines some of their attributes. The following sections elaborate on the facts the table presents by detailing the nature of each security.

U.S. Treasury Bills and Agency Securities

The market for U.S. Treasury securities (also known as "Treasuries") is the largest part of the money market.[4] Short-term securities issued by the U.S. government are known as **Treasury bills,** also known as T-bills. The U.S. Treasury sells T-bills

default risk
Uncertainty surrounding a debtor's ability to pay interest and principal.

U.S. Treasury bill
Short-term debt obligation of the United States.

---

[4]Paul Meek describes the operation of the U.S. government securities market in *U.S. Monetary Policy and Financial Markets* (New York: Federal Reserve Bank of New York, 1982).

each week with maturities of 13 and 26 weeks; 52-week T-bills are sold each month. T-bills are denominated and issued in $10,000 units and larger.

Because the U.S. government, with its taxing authority, is the issuer of T-bills, they have virtually no default risk. In addition, they have excellent liquidity because of an active secondary market. Low default risk and excellent liquidity lead investors to demand relatively low returns from their investments in T-bills.

Closely linked to U.S. Treasury bills are the short-term debt obligations issued by agencies of the U.S. government. The U.S. Congress has created numerous agencies to assist financially the development of housing, farming, foreign trade, and other activities. These agencies include the Federal Home Loan Mortgage Corporation, Federal Land Bank, Federal Farm Credit, and Inter-American Development Bank. Federal agency obligations are guaranteed by the issuing agency and are only indirectly supported by the U.S. government. But no one expects Congress to let agency obligations default; consequently, these securities enjoy almost as high an investment standing and offer almost as low a yield as U.S. Treasury securities of the same maturities.

Discount Yield and Investment Yield.   U.S. Treasury bills do not pay dollar interest like a savings account at a bank. Instead investors buy T-bills and cash them in later for an amount greater than the purchase price. T-bills trade at a discount from *face value,* which is the cash flow an investor receives when the bill matures. To illustrate, suppose you pay $9,800 for a 6-month T-bill with a face value of $10,000. In 6 months, you will receive $10,000, $200 more than the $9,800 you paid.

By convention, when dealers offer to buy or sell T-bills, they quote them on a discount basis and use a 360-day year instead of a 365-day year. For example, a dealer might offer to sell a $10,000, 360-day T-bill for a 5 percent **discount yield.** In this case, you would pay $9,500 for the T-bill, which is a 5 percent discount from its face value of $10,000. The annual discount yield is calculated as follows:

discount yield

Discount percentage from face value based on a 360-day year; used for quoting yields on T-bills.

$$\frac{\text{Annual}}{\text{discount yield}} = \frac{\text{Face value} - \text{Purchase price}}{\text{Face value}} \times \frac{360}{\text{Days to maturity}}$$

$$= \frac{\$10,000 - \$9,500}{\$10,000} \times \frac{360}{360}$$

$$= 0.05 \times 1.0$$

$$= 0.05, \text{ or } 5\% \text{ per year}$$

The first term on the right side of the equation is the discount yield for the period remaining until maturity (360 days in this case). Multiplying the first term by the number of interest periods in a 360-day year (360/Days to maturity, or 1.0 in this case) annualizes the discount yield.

Figure 2.3 presents a sample of T-bill quotations from *The Wall Street Journal.* The first column gives the maturity date of each bill being quoted. For convenience, the second column shows *Days to Maturity* of each. *Days to Maturity* of a T-bill is based on the settlement date (the effective date when ownership of the bills is determined), which is 4 days prior to the maturity date. The next two columns contain the dealer's bid and asked discount yields: *bid* is the price the dealer will pay for the T-bill in terms of yield (from which purchase price can be calculated); *asked* is the yield at which the dealer will sell it. *Chg.* is change (in hundredths) in the asked discount yield from the preceding trading day.

FIGURE 2.3

Treasury Bill Quotations from *The Wall Street Journal*

Representative over-the-counter quotations are based on transactions of $1,000,000 or more, for the day preceding the publication date. *Days to Maturity* are based on the settlement date, which is 4 days prior to the *Maturity* date. *Bid* (offer to buy) and *Asked* (offer to sell) quotations are discount yields offered by dealers. *Chg.* is change (in hundredths) in the asked quotation from the preceding trading day. The annual investment yield in the last column is expected rate of return based on the asked price, which can be calculated from the asked discount yield. Latest 13-week and 26-week bills are boldfaced.

TREASURY BILLS

Maturity	Days to Mat.	Bid	Asked	Chg.	Ask Yld.
Sep 24 '92	3	2.65	2.55	+0.03	2.59
Oct 01 '92	10	2.59	2.49	....	2.53
Oct 08 '92	17	2.73	2.63	+0.03	2.67
Oct 15 '92	24	2.73	2.63	+0.04	2.67
Oct 22 '92	31	2.81	2.77	+0.01	2.82
Oct 29 '92	38	2.79	2.75	+0.01	2.80
Nov 05 '92	45	2.82	2.78	+0.01	2.83
Nov 12 '92	52	2.82	2.78	−0.01	2.83
Nov 19 '92	59	2.84	2.82	−0.01	2.88
Nov 27 '92	67	2.85	2.83	....	2.88
Dec 03 '92	73	2.88	2.86	−0.01	2.92
Dec 10 '92	80	2.88	2.86	−0.01	2.92
Dec 17 '92	**87**	**2.88**	**2.86**	**−0.02**	**2.93**
Dec 24 '92	94	2.88	2.86	−0.01	2.92
Dec 31 '92	101	2.84	2.82	−0.02	2.88
Jan 07 '93	108	2.88	2.86	−0.02	2.92
Jan 14 '93	115	2.89	2.87	−0.03	2.94
Jan 21 '93	122	2.91	2.89	....	2.96
Jan 28 '93	129	2.91	2.89	−0.01	2.96
Feb 04 '93	136	2.92	2.90	....	2.97
Feb 11 '93	143	2.92	2.90	−0.01	2.98
Feb 18 '93	150	2.93	2.91	....	2.99
Feb 25 '93	157	2.93	2.91	....	2.99
Mar 04 '93	164	2.93	2.91	....	2.99
Mar 11 '93	171	2.91	2.89	−0.01	2.97
Mar 18 '93	**178**	**2.92**	**2.90**	**−0.01**	**2.98**
Apr 08 '93	199	2.93	2.91	....	2.99
May 06 '93	227	2.95	2.93	−0.01	3.02
Jun 03 '93	255	2.95	2.93	−0.01	3.02
Jul 01 '93	283	3.00	2.98	+0.01	3.08
Jul 29 '93	311	3.02	3.00	....	3.10
Aug 26 '93	339	3.03	3.01	....	3.12

Source: The Wall Street Journal, September 18, 1992, C14.

EXAMPLE

The T-bill in Figure 2.3 that matures March 18, 1993, has 178 days to maturity. The discount yield bid by the dealer is 2.92 percent; the asked yield is 2.90 percent. Calculate the bid and asked prices corresponding to these yields (using a $10,000 face value):

Bid Price

$$0.0292 = \frac{\$10,000 - \text{Purchase price}}{\$10,000} \times \frac{360}{178}$$

$$\frac{0.0292 \times 178 \times \$10,000}{360} = \$10,000 - \text{Purchase price}$$

$$\text{Purchase price} = \$10,000 - \$144.38 = \$9,855.62$$

Asked Price

$$0.0290 = \frac{\$10,000 - \text{Purchase price}}{\$10,000} \times \frac{360}{178}$$

$$\frac{0.0290 \times 178 \times \$10,000}{360} = \$10,000 - \text{Purchase price}$$

$$\text{Purchase price} = \$10,000 - \$143.39 = \$9,856.61$$

In the preceding example, the bid price per $10,000 face value corresponding to 2.92 percent is $9,855.62; the asked price corresponding to 2.90 percent is $9,856.61. The bid yield is higher than the asked yield, but the bid price is lower than the asked price. The difference between the bid and asked price ($0.99) is the dealer's gross profit. For a $10,000,000 transaction (a typical transaction size for the quotations in Figure 2.3), the dealer's gross profit would be $990.

The last column in Figure 2.3 contains the annual investment yield based on the asked price. This yield is the investor's expected rate of return and is calculated as follows:

$$\frac{\text{Annual}}{\text{investment yield}} = \frac{\text{Face value} - \text{Purchase price}}{\text{Purchase price}} \times \frac{365}{\text{Days to maturity}}$$

The first term on the right side of the equation is the yield (rate of return) for the period remaining until maturity. Multiplying the first term by the number of interest periods in a year (365/Days to maturity) annualizes the yield.[5] Note closely the difference between *annual discount yield* and *annual investment yield*.

EXAMPLE

The T-bill in Figure 2.3 that matures March 18, 1993 (178 days to maturity), has an annual investment yield (last column) of 2.98 percent. From the preceding example, you know that the purchase price is $9,856.61 per $10,000 face value, based on the asked discount yield. Show how to calculate the annual investment yield of 2.98 percent:

$$\frac{\text{Annual}}{\text{investment yield}} = \frac{\$10,000 - \$9,856.61}{\$9,856.61} \times \frac{365}{178}$$

$$= 0.01455 \times 2.05056$$

$$= 0.298, \text{ or } 2.98\%$$

The annual investment yield, or expected rate of return, is 2.98 percent.

To summarize, dealers quote T-bills using the discount yield. Investors in T-bills, however, are primarily interested in the investment yield, their expected rate of return based on the price they pay and a 365-day year.

Commercial Paper

commercial paper
Short-term promissory notes issued by corporations.

Companies issue short-term promissory notes, known as **commercial paper,** as an alternative to borrowing from banks. Major issuers of commercial paper include finance companies and banks—General Motors Acceptance Corporation, Ford Motor Credit Company, Citicorp, for example—and nonfinancial companies such as public utility companies. These companies either place their commercial paper directly with large purchasers (other companies and financial institutions) or sell their paper through dealers.

Companies generally issue commercial paper with maturities of 30 to 270 days. Like U.S. Treasury bills, commercial paper trades at a discount from face

---

[5] Although this equation is used by the financial press for reporting investment yields, it actually provides only an approximation of the true annual yield. (Chapter 14 presents a procedure for calculating true yield.) The financial press uses this equation for T-bills with maturities of 6 months or less. For longer maturities, a more complex equation is used.

value: Investors pay less than face value at time of issuance and expect to receive face value at maturity. Investors perceive a higher risk in commercial paper than in T-bills, which the U.S. government guarantees.[6] Thus commercial paper must offer a larger investment yield than T-bills to attract investors.

EXAMPLE

The financial manager of Finman Enterprises plans to buy $100,000 (the basic trading unit) of commercial paper issued by Household Finance Company. The paper matures in 90 days and can be purchased for $98,500, a $1,500 discount from face value ($100,000). Finman's financial manager expects to earn $1,500 over the 90-day period on the $98,500 investment, producing the following annual investment yield:

$$\begin{aligned} \text{Annual investment yield} &= \frac{\text{Face value} - \text{Purchase price}}{\text{Purchase price}} \times \frac{365}{\text{Days to maturity}} \\ &= \frac{\$100,000 - \$98,500}{\$98,500} \times \frac{365}{90} \\ &= 0.0152 \times 4.056 \\ &= 0.062, \text{ or } 6.2\% \text{ per year} \end{aligned}$$

As Table 2.1 indicates, companies issue commercial paper in large denominations, $100,000 and even $1,000,000 units being commonplace. Buyers of commercial paper, therefore, tend to be other large organizations rather than individuals. Buyers generally hold commercial paper to maturity, but in some cases they can sell the paper back to the issuer or dealer. For most issues of commercial paper, the buyer must be sure that the maturity meets organizational needs, because the weak secondary market often makes reselling commercial paper difficult.

Other Money Market Securities

negotiable certificate of deposit

Claim on funds deposited at a commercial bank, issued for a specified number of days at a specified interest rate.

Other types of money market securities include negotiable certificates of deposit, bankers' acceptances, and federal funds. A **negotiable certificate of deposit** (CD) is a claim on funds deposited at a commercial bank, for a specified number of days at a specified interest rate. In exchange for a deposit of funds, the bank issues a CD, agreeing to pay the amount deposited plus interest to the CD owner on the maturity date. Commercial banks issue CDs in negotiable form in denominations of $100,000 or larger. Unlike the $1,000 CDs offered by banks, savings and loan associations, and credit unions, negotiable CDs are traded in the secondary market among securities dealers (hence the word *negotiable*). They are bought and sold in the secondary market on a yield basis, meaning that the buyer pays face value plus the interest accrued to date. Negotiable CDs are no riskier than the issuing bank; if the probability of the bank failing is small, then the default risk of the CD is small. Yields on negotiable CDs are normally comparable to the yields on commercial paper with equivalent maturities.

---

[6] Although companies rarely default on commercial paper, it does happen. In 1970 Penn Central Railroad issued $195 million of commercial paper. Penn Central declared bankruptcy later that year and defaulted on almost $100 million of its commercial paper.

banker's acceptance
Credit instrument issued by an importer's bank that guarantees payment of an exporter's invoice.

A **banker's acceptance** is a form of credit that begins as a company's promise to pay suppliers for goods, usually imported goods like automobiles, personal computers, and commodities. This promise to pay becomes an acceptance when the importer's bank agrees to make payment upon delivery of the goods. Essentially, bankers' acceptances are claims against future deposits at commercial banks. An acceptance trades in the secondary market at a discount from face value, and investors holding acceptances until maturity earn the dollar discount. Yields on acceptances are comparable with yields on negotiable CDs and commercial paper.

federal funds
Excess reserves at commercial banks that can be loaned to other banks having reserve deficiencies.

Finally, Table 2.1 shows federal funds trading in the money market. **Federal funds** are excess reserves at commercial banks that can be loaned to other banks having reserve deficiencies. Banks loan federal funds, normally in denominations of $1,000,000 or larger, overnight or for several days; other banks borrow (buy) federal funds and pay interest on the amount borrowed. Financial managers watch the federal funds rate for clues to changes in **monetary policy.**

monetary policy
Action by the Federal Reserve System to control the money supply and interest rates.

THE CAPITAL MARKET

Companies use the capital market to issue long-term securities such as bonds and common stock. The U.S. government and its agencies and state and local governments issue only bonds in the capital market. Table 2.2 lists characteristics of the long-term securities issued by these organizations. The second column of the table comments on (1) the degree of liquidity provided by the secondary market and (2) the quality of the securities themselves. For debt securities, high quality means low default risk, and low quality means high default risk. Quality of preferred stock and common stock refers to the degree of uncertainty surrounding their dividends and price per share.

There is greater diversity among capital market securities than among money market securities. Money market securities are all debt; capital market securities consist of both debt and equity. Money market securities have maturities ranging up to one year; capital market securities have maturities ranging from one year (plus one day) to infinity. Money market securities are generally low risk; the risk of capital market securities varies from low to extremely high. Because of their higher risk and longer maturity, the required rate of return on securities trading in the capital market normally exceeds that on securities trading in the money market.

U.S. Treasury and Agency Securities

The U.S. Treasury offers two classes of long-term securities: notes with maturities of ten years or less and bonds with maturities longer than ten years. Some bonds are callable any time within five years of maturity. **Callability** means that the issuer can redeem the bonds (call them in) before maturity at a stated cash price. Minimum denominations of U.S. Treasury and agency securities vary from $1,000 to $100,000. After their initial issuance, government securities trade primarily in the over-the-counter market.

callability
Right of a bond issuer to redeem bonds before maturity at a stated cash price.

The U.S. Treasury pays semiannual interest on notes and bonds to the *registered owner,* which means that the U.S. Treasury keeps a list of owners and mails interest payments to the names and addresses on the list. U.S. agencies also pay semiannual interest on their obligations, but in some cases they do not keep a list of the security owners. Instead, they pay interest to the *bearer,* whoever

TABLE 2.2

Characteristics of Capital Market Securities

Issuer/Security	Secondary Market and Quality	Maturities When Issued	Denominations
U.S. Treasury and Agency Securities			
U.S. Treasury notes and bonds	Excellent to good; highest quality	1–30 years	$1,000 minimum
U.S. Agency:			
Federal Home Loan Mortgage Corporation	Average; extremely high quality	1–30 years	$100,000 minimum
Government National Mortgage Association	Average; extremely high quality	1–25 years	$25,000 minimum
Tennessee Valley Authority	Average; very high quality	3–50 years	$1,000 minimum
Corporate Securities			
Bonds	Good to below average; quality varies	1–30 years	$1,000 typically
Preferred stock	Average to below average; quality varies	Usually no maturity	Any size
Common stock	Average to above average; quality varies greatly	No maturity	Any size
State and Local Government Bonds	Average to below average; very high to low quality	1–30 years	$5,000 minimum

currently holds the bond. The bearer clips a coupon (small attachment to the bond) from the bond and mails it to the agency, notifying the agency to send an interest payment. Most agency (and other) securities are now being registered, in response to pressure from the Internal Revenue Service (IRS). The IRS wants access to the names of bondholders so it can verify that they (1) pay taxes on interest income and (2) pay estate taxes.

Corporate Securities

coupon rate
Promised rate of interest on a bond.

perpetuity
Security that investors expect will pay a level dollar amount forever.

Corporate securities trading in the capital market include bonds, preferred stock, and common stock. Corporate bonds normally pay interest semiannually to bondholders, and most trade in denominations of $1,000. Thus a corporate bond with a promised rate, or **coupon rate,** of 10 percent pays $100 per year (0.10 × $1,000), with actual payments of $50 every six months. Preferred stock pays a specified dividend and has no maturity period. Essentially, preferred stocks are **perpetuities,** although many preferreds are callable by the issuing corporation. Preferred stockholders must receive their promised dividends before common shareholders can receive any dividends (hence the term *preferred*). Also, by law a corporation must pay interest before it can pay dividends on either preferred or common stock. Common shareholders are the last to be paid.

Because of the difference in rights granted to investors, corporate securities differ in risk:

- From the *investor's* point of view, bonds offer the least risk and common stock the most. Because they are legal claims on corporate income and assets, bonds have less risk than either preferred or common stock. Interest on bonds is a legal obligation and must be paid. Because it has the lowest claim on corporate income, common stock has more risk than either bonds or preferred stock. In terms of risk to investors, preferred stock falls between bonds and common stock: Companies pay preferred-stock dividends *after* paying interest on bonds but *before* paying any dividends on common stock.

- From the *company's* point of view, bonds present the most risk because they legally require semiannual cash payments (interest) and future repayment (principal). Common stock presents the issuing company with the least risk because common stock does not carry with it any obligation for the company to pay dividends—they are optional. Preferred stock has less risk than bonds because a preferred-stock dividend may go unpaid without forcing the company into bankruptcy; preferred stock has more risk than common stock because the corporation must pay the dividend on its preferred stock before its board of directors may declare a common-stock dividend.

After being issued in the primary market, corporate securities trade in the secondary market, either over the counter or on organized exchanges. Securities of small companies generally trade over the counter, although securities of many large companies trade there as well. Common and preferred stock of large companies generally trade on the New York Stock Exchange (NYSE) or the other exchange in New York City, the American Stock Exchange (AMEX). Investors call the NYSE the Big Board because about 80 percent of the volume of shares traded on exchanges trades there; the AMEX is a distant second with less than 10 percent of the shares. Regional exchanges account for the remaining trades: Chicago Stock Exchange, Pacific Stock Exchange, Philadelphia Stock Exchange, Cincinnati Stock Exchange, Boston Stock Exchange, and others. Many corporate managers view the listing of their company's common stock on an exchange, especially on the NYSE, as bringing prestige and visibility to the company—and perhaps an increase in price of the company's common stock.

State and Local Government Bonds

State and local governments issue bonds in the capital market to finance their capital-spending programs—construction of water treatment plants, municipal office buildings, generation of electricity, road improvements, and so on. Investors call these bond issues *municipals* because they are issued by municipalities, subdivisions of states; they also call them *tax-exempts* because the interest investors receive is exempt from federal taxation. Most states exempt state income tax as well on the interest earned from their bonds. For example, a citizen of South Carolina does not pay state income tax on the interest earned from South Carolina municipal bonds; the same citizen, however, pays state income tax on interest earned from municipal bonds issued by other states.

Table 2.2 notes that state and local governments issue bonds with minimum denominations of $5,000. Also noted there is the average to below-average secondary market for municipals. Secondary markets for municipal issues are often weak (or "thin") because individuals, banks, and other investors tend to buy and hold the bonds until they mature. Secondary markets for many corporate bonds are also thin for the same reason. The risk incurred in the purchase of municipals varies greatly and depends on the financial strength of the issuing state or municipality.

REVIEW OF FINANCIAL MARKETS

In foreign economies where financial markets are not well developed, companies have difficulty expanding to produce goods for customers. Even in the U.S. economy, with its well-developed financial markets, successful proprietorships and partnerships often grow slowly; both types of companies are effectively excluded from issuing securities in financial markets to raise funds for expansion. The existence of financial markets efficiently mobilizes capital within an economy for productive uses by corporations and governments.

U.S. financial markets can be classified into two parts: (I) the money market and (II) the capital market. These parts can be subdivided further according to the following outline:

I. Money market
   A. Primary market
   B. Secondary market

II. Capital market
   A. Primary market
   B. Secondary market
      1. Over-the-counter market
      2. Organized exchanges

Both the money and capital markets consist of primary (new issue) and secondary (resale) markets. Further, the secondary capital market consists of the over-the-counter and organized-exchange markets. The securities issued and traded in these markets expose investors to varying degrees of risk. High-risk securities must be accompanied by high expected cash flows, or investors will shun the high-risk securities in favor of those with low risk.

Experience bears out the proposition that the actual rate of return an investor receives increases, on average, with the risk of the security. For example, Figure 2.4 shows that the average (mean) return on common stock was 10.3 percent per year for the 64-year period between 1926 and 1989. In contrast, U.S. Treasury bills produced 3.6 percent per year for the same period of time. As the right side of Figure 2.4 shows, the annual rate of return on T-bills varied little over the 64-year period. The rate of return on common stock, however, ranged from large negative to large positive percentages. Annual returns on stocks of small companies varied even more than the returns on the stocks of all companies. Variability of returns on long-term corporate and government bonds fell between that of common stock and T-bills. Figure 2.4 demonstrates that higher actual rates of return go hand in hand with greater risk (measured by variability of actual rates of return).[7]

---

[7]The mean return in Figure 2.4 is the geometric mean, or compound annual rate of return for the 64-year period. To illustrate, you interpret the 10.3 percent as the average annual rate you would have earned over the 64-year period by investing in a broadly diversified portfolio of common stocks. (Chapter 4 explains the calculation of compound rates.) In comparison, the 64-year arithmetic mean (add up the 64 annual rates of return and divide by 64) for common stocks is 12.4 percent. You interpret the 12.4 percent as the rate of return in a typical year during the 64-year period; alternatively, the 12.4 percent is the average of the distribution of 64 annual rates of return. Standard deviation (explained in Chapter 5) of the 64 annual rates is 20.9 percent.

FIGURE 2.4

Annual Rates of Return on Securities for the Period 1926–1989

Historically, the average rate of return on securities with high risk has exceeded that on securities with low risk. Common stock returned, on average, 10.3 percent annually, while T-bills averaged 3.6 percent.

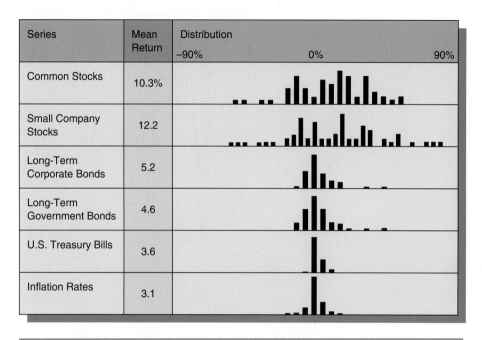

Source: R. Ibbotson and R. Sinquefield, *Stocks, Bonds, Bills, and Inflation: Historical Returns* (Chicago: Dow Jones-Irwin, 1989); updated in *SBBI 1990 Yearbook* (Chicago: Ibbotson Associates).

INTEREST RATES IN THE MONEY AND CAPITAL MARKETS

The rate of return on a debt security is commonly known as an interest rate—the charge a borrower pays to use the lender's funds. The interest rate on a security depends in part on *risk, liquidity,* and *maturity* of the security. Higher risk leads investors to require a higher rate of return as compensation. Investors prefer highly liquid securities because they can easily convert them into cash. To encourage investors to buy illiquid securities, borrowers pay high interest rates. Investor attitudes toward the maturity of debt securities are more complex and are the focus here. We begin by looking at interest rate *levels* and proceed to the *difference* between short- and long-term interest rate levels in the money and capital markets.

Interest Rate Levels

Interest rates on the debt securities traded in financial markets tend to move up and down together. So when news reports indicate that interest rates have risen or declined, they usually mean interest rates in general, not the interest rate on a specific security. Figure 2.5 shows short- and long-term interest rates for the past several years, from which we can make the following observations: (1) Interest rates generally declined during the period; (2) long-term rates typically were higher than short-term rates; and (3) short-term rates were more volatile than long-term rates.

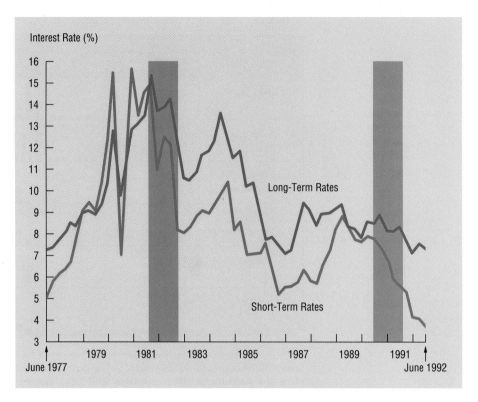

FIGURE 2.5

Short- and Long-Term Interest Rates

Interest rates generally declined during the 1980s and early 1990s. Short-term rates tended to be lower and more volatile than long-term rates.

Note: Three-month Treasury bills and 10-year Treasury bonds represent the short- and long-term rates, respectively. The shaded areas denote recessions (downturns in business activity).
Source: Federal Reserve Bulletin.

Economists who study financial markets have proposed a number of reasons for the behavior of interest rates. Two of the explanations are:

open-market operations
Federal Reserve purchase and sale of U.S. Treasury securities to control the money supply.

- Federal Reserve actions (or monetary policy): Federal Reserve (Fed) **open-market operations** control the money supply and take place in the money market. When the Fed buys U.S. T-bills, it bids up the price and bids down the yield; when it sells T-bills, it drives down the price and drives up the yield. The Fed's efforts through monetary policy to keep the economy growing and the inflation rate low cause changes in interest rate levels, especially short-term ones.

- Government deficits (or fiscal policy): When the federal government spends more money than it takes in from tax revenues, it creates a deficit. To finance the deficit, the U.S. Treasury issues T-bills, notes, and bonds. Issuance of more government securities drives down their prices and increases their yields. In addition, a deficit may lead to an increase in expected inflation, which also contributes to an increase in the general level of interest rates.

Most financial economists agree that the government's monetary and fiscal policies strongly influence interest rates. Additional theories also exist on why

FIGURE 2.6

Yield Curves Based on U.S. Treasury Securities

Yield curves show the term structure of interest rates for U.S. treasury securities. Interest rates generally declined from November 10, 1987, to September 18, 1992 (especially short-term rates).

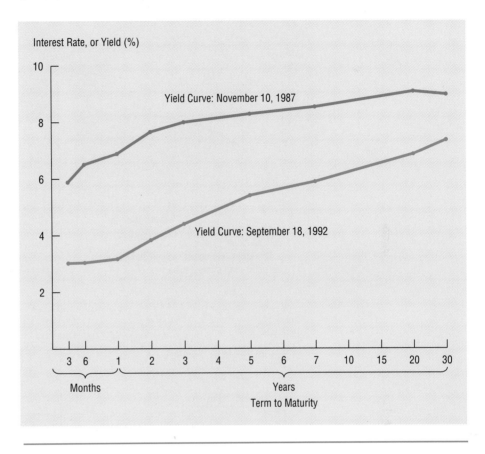

short- and long-term interest rate levels differ, as the following discussion explains.

Term Structure of Interest Rates

term structure of interest rates
Relationship between yields and maturities of debt securities.

yield curve
Graph of yields on debt securities of differing maturities.

The relationship, at a point in time, among interest rates on debt securities that differ only in maturity is known as the **term structure of interest rates.** A **yield curve** provides a graphic portrayal of the term structure of interest rates. Understanding yield curves helps financial managers determine whether to issue short- or long-term debt securities. Yield curves also help investors decide between the purchase of short- and long-term securities.

Figure 2.6 shows yield curves for November 10, 1987, and for September 18, 1992. Each yield curve depicts interest rates (yields) on U.S. Treasury securities arrayed by term to maturity. Using interest rates on U.S. Treasury securities to draw yield curves holds default risk and other variables constant. The yield curves in Figure 2.6 are upward-sloping, and they show that interest rates declined from 1987 to 1992, especially short-term rates. Issuing debt securities in 1992 would have cost much less than issuing them in 1987.

FIGURE 2.7

Four Typical Yield-Curve Shapes

Yield curves take on many different shapes. The four yield-curve shapes illustrated here show the major features observed historically.

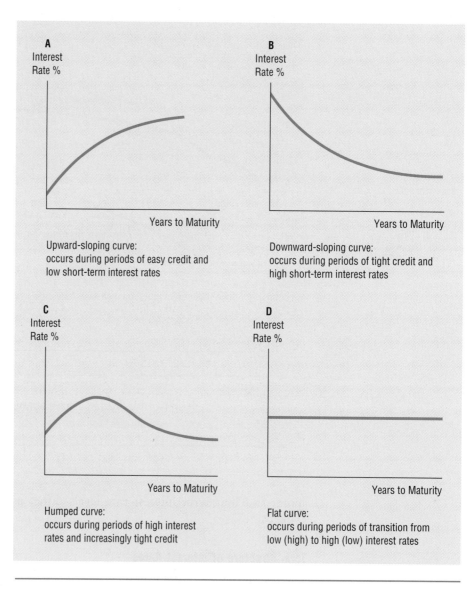

A
Interest Rate %

Years to Maturity

Upward-sloping curve:
occurs during periods of easy credit and low short-term interest rates

B
Interest Rate %

Years to Maturity

Downward-sloping curve:
occurs during periods of tight credit and high short-term interest rates

C
Interest Rate %

Years to Maturity

Humped curve:
occurs during periods of high interest rates and increasingly tight credit

D
Interest Rate %

Years to Maturity

Flat curve:
occurs during periods of transition from low (high) to high (low) interest rates

Although upward-sloping yield curves have occurred frequently in past years, yield curves often take on other shapes as well. Figure 2.7 illustrates four typical yield-curve shapes: upward-sloping, downward-sloping, humped, and flat. A brief description of the economic period that usually accompanies the yield-curve shape is shown in each panel of Figure 2.7. For example, an upward-sloping yield curve usually occurs during periods of easy credit and low short-term interest rates. Opposite conditions usually prevail when the downward-sloping yield curve appears.

Economists have developed three primary theories to explain the shape of the yield curve: (1) liquidity preference theory, (2) market segmentation theory, and (3) expectations theory.

Liquidity Preference Theory. The *liquidity preference theory* argues that long-term rates are higher than short-term rates because of the preferences of lenders and borrowers:

- Lenders (investors in debt securities) prefer to invest in short-term securities because they are liquid—readily convertible into cash with little chance of loss of principal. Investors thus accept lower interest rates on short-term bonds than on long-term bonds.

- Borrowers (issuers of debt securities) prefer to raise funds with long-term securities. Long-term financing avoids frequent refinancings, which are costly and risky (rates may go up). Thus borrowers willingly pay higher rates on long-term bonds than on short-term bonds.

Combining the preferences of lenders and borrowers leads to the prediction that long-term rates will exceed short-term rates. This prediction is consistent with the upward-sloping yield curve in Figure 2.7 but not with the other yield-curve shapes illustrated.

Market Segmentation Theory. According to the *market segmentation theory,* the market for debt securities is segmented by maturity. The interest rate on securities in a specific maturity range is determined by the supply of and demand for securities within that range. For example, commercial banks invest in liquid, short-term debt securities as reserves to cover unexpected deposit withdrawals. In contrast, life insurance companies invest in long-term debt securities to cover long-term yield commitments made on life insurance policies. The market segmentation theory asserts that debt maturities are not substitutable because of the preferred habitats of borrowers and lenders. At any given time corporate borrowers may need short-term loans to finance temporary increases in inventory; at other times they may need long-term loans to finance plant and equipment. If strong demand exists for long-term funds when they are in short supply, then long-term rates will be high and the yield curve will be upward-sloping. On the other hand, if strong demand exists for short-term funds when they are in short supply, then short-term rates will be high and the yield curve will be downward-sloping. According to the market segmentation theory, the shape of each yield curve in Figure 2.7 depends on supply and demand conditions for the different maturities.

Expectations Theory. The *expectations theory* asserts that investors purchase short- and long-term debt securities to maximize expected rate of return over a planned investment horizon. Acting in this way, investors, through their buying and selling activity, cause long-term rates to depend on expected short-term rates (future rates).

EXAMPLE

Suppose a newspaper reports the following rates on U.S. Treasury securities: 1-year rate, 6 percent; 2-year rate, 8 percent per year. According to the expectations theory, if you had a 2-year investment horizon, you would not buy the 1-year security unless you expected to earn 10 percent on a 1-year security during the second year. Earning 6 percent during the first year and 10 percent during the second year gives you an average of 8 percent per year, the same rate that is available on the 2-year security.

The expectations theory can be used to estimate future short-term interest rates. Such forecasts are useful in the timing of corporate borrowing to minimize interest costs. Financial managers observe both short- and long-term interest rates in newspaper quotations, but they cannot observe future short-term rates; these rates must be estimated.

To illustrate further the relationship between short- and long-term interest rates, suppose that you know what the 1-year interest rate will be during each of the next 4 years: 6 percent, 8 percent, 10 percent, and 12 percent. According to the expectations theory, the present 4-year interest rate will be the average of these 4 one-year rates, or 9 percent. Investors would be indifferent between earning the 4-year series of 1-year rates or 9 percent per year for 4 years. Their indifference causes investors collectively to price the securities so that the average of the 4 future 1-year rates equals the 4-year rate. Note that the present 1-year rate of 6 percent and 4-year rate of 9 percent join to form an upward-sloping yield curve like the one in Figure 2.7A. Moreover, the upward slope correctly implies that future short-term rates will rise. A downward-sloping yield curve implies that future short-term rates will fall, and a flat yield curve implies that future short-term rates will not change from the present short-term rate.

The expectations theory helps to explain why short-term rates are more volatile than long-term rates. A long-term rate is an average of expected short-term rates, and an average is inherently more stable than the elements in it. Suppose the present 1-year rate rises from 6 to 8 percent, a 2 percentage point (or 33.3 percent) increase. For simplicity, hold the expected 1-year rates constant from the preceding illustration and calculate the new average, or the new 4-year rate: 9.5 percent $(8 + 8 + 10 + 12)/4$.[8] A 33.3 percent increase in the present 1-year rate leads to only a 5.6 percent increase (from 9 percent to 9.5 percent) in the 4-year rate. In general, short-term interest rates are more volatile than long-term rates, as Figure 2.5 illustrates.

In summary, when investors expect higher future interest rates, liquidity preferences and expectations operate together to cause a pronounced upward-sloping yield curve. When investors expect lower future interest rates, the slope of the yield curve depends on the comparative strengths of liquidity preferences and expectations. Changes in supply and demand conditions at various maturities of debt securities (reflecting market segmentation) are the wild card in determining yield-curve shapes in each circumstance.

---

[8] For simplicity, we ignore compounding in the explanation of expectations theory. Instead of using a simple arithmetic average, we gain precision by using a geometric average, which for the latter example is:

$$\text{Geometric average} = [(1 + i_1)(1 + i_2) \cdots (1 + i_n)]^{1/n} - 1$$
$$= [(1 + 0.08)(1 + 0.08)(1 + 0.10)(1 + 0.12)]^{1/4} - 1$$
$$= 1.0949 - 1$$
$$= 0.0949, \text{ or } 9.49\%$$

The arithmetic average serves well as an approximation of the geometric average if the short-term rates $(i_1, i_2, \cdots)$ do not vary widely over time.

FINANCIAL INSTITUTIONS

Like financial markets, financial institutions such as banks and insurance companies match users of funds with savers of funds. As we saw in Figure 2.2, financial institutions provide an alternative to financial markets for companies needing to raise funds to finance assets. Using financial markets, a company issues securities, usually with the help of an investment banker, to investors in return for their funds. Using a financial institution, a company issues securities such as promissory notes (IOUs) to the institution in return for its funds. The financial institution acquires funds to lend from companies, individuals, and governments that have available savings; in return, the institution grants to these savers claims (securities) on future funds evidenced by savings passbooks and certificates of deposit. Financial institutions such as banks and credit unions are **financial intermediaries.** They do more than shift funds and securities between buyers and sellers, which is the function of brokers and investment bankers. Intermediaries go a step further and create new securities such as CDs.

In addition to commercial banks, three other financial institutions (often called *thrift institutions*) accept **checkable deposits:** savings and loan associations, savings banks, and credit unions. All four institutions take funds deposited by companies, individuals, and governments and lend funds to other companies, individuals, and governments. These intermediaries are called **depository institutions.**

Historically, financial institutions were classified as either banks or nonbanks; however, that is no longer the case. The distinction disappeared as a result of the Depository Institutions Deregulation and Monetary Control Act of 1980. This act (usually called the Monetary Control Act) permits federally chartered savings and loan associations, savings banks, and credit unions to offer checkable deposits. Before 1980 the law permitted only commercial banks to offer checkable deposits; savings and loan associations, savings banks, and credit unions could offer only savings deposits. States have enacted similar regulations permitting state-chartered institutions to do the same. With the expansion of checking-account services, financial institutions are now classified as either *depository* or *nondepository* to designate whether or not they offer checkable deposits. The Monetary Control Act of 1980 largely blurred the distinctions among depository institutions, making them more homogeneous in nature.

Nondepository financial institutions include insurance companies and pension funds, among others. Both insurance companies and pension funds collect substantial amounts of cash prior to having to pay promised cash payouts. Insurance companies collect cash payments (insurance premiums) from customers and promise to pay them should a specified peril occur, such as death or an accident. Pension funds collect cash from employees and employers and promise to pay an income to the employees upon their retirement. Insurance companies and pension funds make this cash available to users by buying large amounts of government and corporate bonds as well as corporate stock. In addition, they make direct loans to businesses.

Nondepository financial institutions also include *mutual funds,* called *open-end investment companies* because they raise money by continually issuing new shares in the fund itself. A mutual fund issues shares in return for funds from individuals and institutions, then invests these funds on behalf of the shareholders. Shareholders may buy shares from or sell shares to the mutual fund anytime they wish. Individual mutual funds have specific investment objectives: (1) money market fund—to invest in money market securities in order to generate income

financial intermediary
Financial institution that creates new securities as it serves as agent between savers and users of funds.

checkable deposits
Accounts on which depositors may write checks.

depository institution
Financial institution that accepts deposits and loans funds.

The Fed Sets Only One Interest Rate

The Federal Reserve Act of 1913 established the Federal Reserve System, often called the Federal Reserve or simply the Fed. Commercial banks use the Fed, the central bank of the United States, as you use your personal bank to deposit and withdraw money.

Although the Fed strongly influences interest rates in general, it actually sets only one rate—the discount rate. When a depository institution is short on the reserves it needs to meet regulatory requirements, it may borrow reserves from its regional Federal Reserve Bank at the discount rate. The discount rate is an administered rate, set at a certain level and held there by administrative decision. Changes in the discount rate are initiated by the boards of directors of the individual Reserve Banks, but the Federal Reserve's Board of Governors in Washington must approve all changes. This coordination generally results in roughly simultaneous changes at all twelve Reserve Banks.

The Federal Reserve's monetary policy can be defined as the Fed's use of its influence on reserves in the banking system to influence money and credit and, through them, the economy. The discount rate and the federal funds rate figure importantly in the conduct of monetary policy, and many observers regard these two rates as the principal indicators of the direction of policy. Declines in these rates are taken as signs that the Federal Reserve wants to encourage money and credit growth, or ease money and credit conditions, while increases in these rates are interpreted as Fed efforts to restrain money and credit growth, or tighten money and credit conditions.

Federal funds are reserves lent overnight by depository institutions with excess reserves to depository institutions with insufficient reserves. The federal funds rate is a market rate of interest determined by the supply and demand for reserves. The Fed directly affects the funds rate by buying and selling government securities in the open market to influence the supply of reserves, and federal funds in the banking system. When the Federal Reserve wants to ease money and credit conditions through open-market operations, it supplies additional reserves to the banking system by purchasing additional short-term government securities.

The ability of the Federal Reserve to influence the level of interest rates diminishes greatly at longer maturities. The reason is that longer-term interest rates, such as mortgage rates and corporate bond yields, are largely determined by the expected rate of inflation. In order to appreciate the influence of inflation expectations on longer-term rates, suppose that the long-term expected inflation rate were 5 percent. Lenders would be unwilling to lend at 5 percent because the interest income would be completely offset by the inflation loss. Lenders want to cover the expected inflation loss and earn some real rate of return, considered usually to be 3 to 4 percent. Borrowers, for their part, are willing to pay the inflation premium because they expect to repay their debts with cheaper dollars. Therefore, one can reasonably expect long-term interest rates to be about 3 to 4 percentage points above the expected inflation rate. It follows that the primary way to reduce long-term rates is to lower the expected rate of inflation, a difficult task even for the Fed.

Source: Adapted from Craig Carlock, "How the Federal Reserve Influences Interest Rates," *Cross Sections* (Federal Reserve Bank of Richmond, Fall 1991): 12–14.

but maintain liquidity and low risk; (2) balanced equity fund—to invest in common and preferred stocks in order to generate dividend income and capital gains; (3) growth fund—to invest in common stock in order to achieve long-term growth of capital. Listed according to increasing risk and expected return, these funds illustrate only three possible investment objectives among many.

Another type of investment company is a *closed-end investment company,* which raises funds by initially selling shares in itself and then investing in securities on behalf of the shareholders. In contrast to mutual funds, closed-end companies do not sell (or buy) shares in themselves based on daily demand. Instead, they raise a specified amount of money by selling shares, and the shares thus issued then trade in the secondary market just like the shares of any other company. Closed-end and open-end investment companies offer two major attractions to investors: (1) full-time professional management of funds and (2) reduction of risk through investment in a diversified **portfolio.**

portfolio
Collection of securities.

Other financial institutions include the following: (1) sales finance companies (such as General Motors Acceptance Corporation), which buy installment debt contracts from sellers of durable goods such as automobiles and appliances; (2) consumer finance companies, which make small personal loans to individuals; (3) commercial finance companies, which make large loans to individuals and businesses, typically those with low credit standings disqualifying them from getting loans from commercial banks; and (4) mortgage companies, which buy agency-backed (Federal Housing Administration and Veterans Administration) **mortgages** and make mortgage loans to real estate developers and builders, and then sell the loans to investors.

mortgage
Long-term IOU collateralized with (backed by) real estate.

The character of financial institutions, both depository and nondepository, has changed greatly during the 1980s and early 1990s, due in large part to government deregulation. Historical differences among financial institutions have decreased and homogeneity has increased. Each type of financial institution seems headed toward becoming a department store of financial services—a one-stop center where customers can satisfy all of their financial needs for checking accounts, savings accounts, stock market investments, life insurance, mortgage financing, and credit-card accounts. Some observers believe the trend toward unification of financial services will continue to intensify, increase competition, and drive down the cost of financial services to individuals and companies.

SUMMARY

- The U.S. financial system transfers funds from savers to users. In return for funds from savers, users issue securities, or claims on future cash flows.

- Financial markets (securities markets) are places and/or facilities that (1) help companies and governments issue securities for funds and (2) assist in the subsequent reselling of securities once they are issued. Financial markets have three basic functions: to transfer funds from savers to users, to provide liquidity for investors, and to serve as a system of signals and targets (stock prices) for financial managers.

- Securities with a maturity of one year or less trade in the money market. U.S. Treasury bills, securities issued by U.S. government agencies, and commercial paper dominate the money market. Besides having short-term maturities, these securities are low-risk debt obligations of the issuers. Treasury bills and commercial paper trade on a discount basis; the difference between face value and purchase price represents dollar interest earned by the investor.

- Dealers quote U.S. Treasury bill yields in the financial press on a discount basis—percentage discount from face value based on a 360-day year. The annual discount yield is calculated as follows:

$$\text{Annual discount yield} = \frac{\text{Face value} - \text{Purchase price}}{\text{Face value}} \times \frac{360}{\text{Days to maturity}}$$

Given the quoted annual discount yield, you can solve this equation for the purchase price of the T-bill. The annual investment yield (expected rate of return on the purchase price) on T-bills and other discount securities is calculated as follows:

$$\frac{\text{Annual}}{\text{investment yield}} = \frac{\text{Face value} - \text{Purchase price}}{\text{Purchase price}} \times \frac{365}{\text{Days to maturity}}$$

Note carefully the difference between the equations for annual *discount* yield and annual *investment* yield.

• Securities with a maturity greater than one year trade in the capital market. U.S. Treasury securities, U.S. agency bonds, corporate issues of bonds, preferred stock, common stock, and state and local government bonds trade in the capital market.

• Both the money and capital markets consist of primary and secondary markets. The primary market is anyplace where securities are first issued, and it is sometimes referred to as the new-issues market. The secondary market is anyplace where securities trade after having been issued; this market consists of security trades over the counter and on organized exchanges—the New York Stock Exchange, the American Stock Exchange, and the regional exchanges.

• Money market securities expose investors to less risk than do capital market securities. To encourage investors to buy them, capital market securities usually must offer rates of return that exceed those on money market securities. Evidence suggests a positive relationship between actual rates of return and risk. For investor behavior, this evidence suggests that the *greater* the risk investors perceive a security to have, the *higher* will be the rate of return they require.

• Government monetary and fiscal policies have a substantial effect on short- and long-term interest rate levels. Three major theories explain the difference between short- and long-term interest rate levels as depicted by the yield curve: (1) liquidity preference theory, (2) market segmentation theory, and (3) expectations theory.

• Financial institutions take the savings of individuals, companies, and governments and lend them directly to borrowers or invest them in the money and capital markets. Acting as intermediaries between savers and users, financial institutions issue their own securities (for example, certificates of deposit) to savers in return for funds. Lending these funds to borrowers, financial institutions receive securities such as promissory notes.

• Depository institutions offer checkable and savings deposits to individuals and businesses. The four types of depository institutions in the United States are commercial banks, savings and loan associations, savings banks, and credit unions. Nondepository institutions include insurance companies, pension funds, investment companies, finance companies, and mortgage companies.

• Financial institutions are undergoing change in an increasingly competitive environment. To combat financial failure, many financial institutions are merging and offering new services. More and more institutions are becoming department stores of financial services.

Key Terms

security	financial institution	stockbroker
direct placement	investment banking firm	primary market
financial market	liquidity	secondary market

dealer	discount yield	open-market operations
debt market	commercial paper	term structure of interest rates
equity market	negotiable certificate of deposit	yield curve
organized exchange	banker's acceptance	financial intermediary
over-the-counter (OTC) market	federal funds	checkable deposits
money market	monetary policy	depository institution
capital market	callability	portfolio
default risk	coupon rate	mortgage
U.S. Treasury bill	perpetuity	

Questions

2.1. Explain the crucial role of the financial system in providing funds for business investments. Use Figure 2.2 in preparing your answer.

2.2. Explain how the financial markets (a) transfer funds, (b) provide liquidity, and (c) serve as a system of signals and targets for financial managers.

2.3. Your uncle explains the primary and secondary markets this way: "The primary market is to new cars as the secondary market is to used cars." Elaborate on your uncle's analogy.

2.4. Contrast each of the following types of securities:
   a. Money market versus capital market.
   b. Debt versus equity.
   c. Low-risk versus high-risk.

2.5. The money market is the market for short-term debt securities. List two reasons for its importance to a financial manager.

2.6. Examine Table 2.1 and explain which security (or securities) fits (or fit) each of the following descriptions:
   a. Minimum denomination is $10,000.
   b. Obligation of a commercial bank.
   c. Obligation of an industrial corporation.
   d. No secondary market.

2.7. What is the difference between *annual investment yield* and *annual discount yield?*

2.8. Table 2.2 lists capital market securities. Refer to this table and explain which security (or securities) fits (or fit) each of the following descriptions:
   a. Exempt from federal taxation.
   b. Excellent secondary market.
   c. Trades in $1,000 denominations.
   d. No maturity.

2.9. Describe the cash flows a company's common shareholders and bondholders expect to receive. How do these two cash flows differ in terms of risk?

2.10. Describe the cash flows a company's common shareholders and preferred stockholders expect to receive. How do these two cash flows differ with respect to risk?

2.11. "From the investor's viewpoint, a company's common stock is riskier than its bonds, but from the company's viewpoint, the bonds are riskier than the stock." Is this statement true? Explain your answer.

2.12. Why do investors expect and require higher rates of return on securities with higher risk levels?

2.13. Define *term structure of interest rates* and *yield curve.*

2.14. The following three theories have been developed for what purpose: (1) liquidity preference theory, (2) market segmentation theory, and (3) expectations theory? Briefly describe each theory.

2.15. What role do financial institutions play in the United States? What is the trend in the services they offer? Explain why this trend is occurring. What are the benefits to individuals and companies?

2.16. Explain the difference between depository and nondepository financial institutions. List four examples of each type of institution.

2.17. Obtain a copy of *The Wall Street Journal* and examine its table of contents to find the Credit Markets Report. Read the article and summarize present conditions in the bond market.

Strategy Problem

Ramos Gonzaga, chief financial officer for Allied American Company, is considering investing nearly $5 million of the company's cash in a Treasury bill. He consults *The Wall Street Journal* and records the bid and asked discount yields for a 150-day T-bill: bid, 2.93; asked, 2.91. He also notes that 1-year and 2-year Treasury securities are yielding 3 percent and 4 percent, respectively.

a. Calculate the purchase price of the 150-day T-bill based on the asked discount yield of 2.91 percent.

b. Assuming that Mr. Gonzaga buys the 150-day T-bill at the asked price, what is the company's annual investment yield?

c. Based on expectations theory, what is the 1-year rate one year from now implied by the 1-year and 2-year Treasury securities?

Strategy

Use the equation for annual discount yield.

Solution

a. Purchase price of the T-bill in millions of dollars:

$$0.0291 = \frac{\$5 - \text{Purchase price}}{\$5} \times \frac{360}{150}$$

$$0.0291 = (\$5 - \text{Purchase price})\,0.48$$

$$\text{Purchase price} = \$5 - \frac{0.0291}{0.48}$$

$$= \$4.939375, \text{ or } \$4,939,375$$

b. Annual investment yield:

Use the equation for annual investment yield and the purchase price from Part a.

$$\text{Annual investment yield} = \frac{\$5 - \$4.939375}{\$4.939375} \times \frac{365}{150}$$

$$= 0.0299, \text{ or } 2.99\%$$

c. Envision the future 1-year rate on a time line:

	0	1	2
End of year			
1-year rates		3%	?%
2-year rate		4% per year	

According to the expectations theory, the average of the 1-year rates will equal the 2-year rate:

Use the arithmetic average to approximate the more complicated geometric average in Note 8.

$$\frac{3\% + ?\%}{2} = 4\%$$

$$?\% = 5\%, \text{ which is the 1-year future rate}$$

Presumably, you would be indifferent between (1) earning 3 percent the first year and 5 percent the second and (2) earning 4 percent per year for 2 years.

◆ ## Demonstration Problem

Suppose your finance instructor asks you to demonstrate your knowledge of the U.S. financial system. The demonstration will take place during your next finance class and will take the form of you teaching your classmates. Your instructor tells you to feel free to select the topics for discussion but be sure to include example calculations of *annual discount yield* and *annual investment yield*. After studying Chapter 2 of this book, you decide on the following topics and exercises, for which you must now develop explanations and answers:

a. Imagine that you are the financial manager of a large company and have the responsibility for acquiring the funds to build a new factory. In what ways might you use the U.S. financial system to help you carry out your responsibility?

b. Explain how the financial markets (securities markets) provide liquidity for investors.

c. U.S. financial markets can be classified as follows: (1) money market versus capital market, (2) primary market versus secondary market, and (3) over-the-counter market versus organized exchanges. Define each of these contrasting markets. Identify the securities that trade in the money market and in the capital market.

d. The U.S. Treasury bill in Figure 2.3 that matures December 17, 1992, has 87 days to maturity. The discount yield bid by the dealer is 2.88 percent; the asked yield is 2.86 percent. Calculate the bid and asked prices per $1,000,000 of face value corresponding to these yields.

e. If you were to buy the T-bill described in Part *d*, what would be your annual investment yield (expected rate of return)? Support your answer with the calculation of the annual investment yield.

f. Each edition of *The Wall Street Journal* usually contains a drawing of a yield curve based on U.S. Treasury securities. Obtain a recent copy of the *Journal* and trace the yield curve. Compare that yield curve to the ones shown in Figure 2.6. Based on these yield curves, describe what has happened to interest rates over the past few years.

g. Economists have developed three primary theories to explain the shape of the yield curve: (1) liquidity preference theory, (2) market segmentation theory, and (3) expectations theory. Briefly describe each theory. Does each theory seem consistent with recent yield curves?

h. A few years ago, 1-year and 2-year U.S. Treasury securities were yielding 9 percent per year and 10 percent per year, respectively. Draw a yield curve based on these two rates. Based on expectations theory and the yield curve, explain whether future short-term rates are likely to be higher or lower than present short-term rates. Use the expectations theory to calculate the expected 1-year rate following the first year.

i. Explain how the Federal Reserve System influences the level of interest rates.

Problems

Annual investment yield

2.1. A T-bill with a $10,000 face value trades in the money market for $9,900. A buyer of the T-bill will earn the $100 discount in 90 days. Calculate the annual investment yield on the T-bill.

Annual rate of return on money market securities

2.2. Commercial paper, Treasury bills, and bankers' acceptances trade on a discount basis. Explain what the term *discounted from face value* means and calculate the expected annual rate of return (annual investment yield) in each of the following examples. Use a 365-day year in your calculations.

a. A $10,000 U.S. Treasury bill matures in 180 days. An investor pays $9,750 for the bill.

b. A $100,000 banker's acceptance matures in 180 days. An investor pays $97,000 for it.

c. A corporation issues $100,000 of commercial paper to mature in 180 days. An investor pays $96,500 for it.

Quotes on money market rates

2.3. *The Wall Street Journal* is a source of information about financial markets. Use it to complete the following assignment. Refer to the *Journal*'s table of contents to locate Money Rates. Find the rates and report the yields on federal funds (the day's high), commercial paper (for directly placed, 150–270 days), certificates of deposit (for 3 months), bankers' acceptances (for 3 months), and U.S. Treasury bills (for 13 weeks). Which has the lowest annual rate?

Expected and actual returns

2.4. Mary Uribe purchased a 180-day Treasury bill for $9,750. She planned to hold the bill to maturity, at which time she would receive $10,000. After 70 days of owning the bill, Mary changed her mind and sold it for $9,870 in the secondary market.

a. What annual rate of return did Ms. Uribe *expect to earn* when she purchased the T-bill?

b. What annual rate of return did Ms. Uribe *actually earn* upon selling the T-bill?

c. What annual rate of return does the investor who purchased the T-bill from Ms. Uribe expect to earn?

d. Why did Ms. Uribe earn a higher annual rate than she originally expected?

Investing temporarily excess cash

2.5. Ailine Cross is considering what to do with her company's $300,000 in cash, which it will not need for 60 days. At the end of 60 days the company will make its quarterly dividend payment. Table 2.1 lists the various short-term securities that she is considering. The present prices for $10,000 face values on 60-day securities are:

U.S. Treasury bills	$9,930
U.S. agency paper	9,915
Prime commercial paper	9,890
Bankers' acceptances	9,900

a. Calculate the expected annual rate of return on each of these securities.

b. Which security should Ms. Cross buy? Support your answer with a discussion of each security's characteristics.

Discount yield

2.6. Maynard Wayne is taking his first course in business financial management, and he is trying to understand discount yields. "Let's see," he says, "the face value of the security is $100,000." Thinking aloud, he continues, "I can buy the security for $90,000 and it matures in 360 days. How do I calculate the annual discount yield?" Help Mr. Wayne by calculating the yield for him. Explain the meaning of the yield.

T-bill price based on the discount yield

2.7. Jeffrey Lynn, corporate treasurer of KLN Pest Control, is confused by the T-bill quotations in *The Wall Street Journal*. He is looking for T-bill prices but instead finds two discount yields: bid 2.82 and asked 2.78.

a. Help Mr. Lynn by calculating the T-bill prices that correspond to the bid and asked discount yields. Assume a $1,000,000 face value for the T-bill and 46 days to maturity.

b. Calculate the annual investment yield based on the asked price.

Yield curves and inflation

2.8. U.S. interest rates were high in the early 1980s and low in the early 1990s. Illustrative of the two periods are the following yields on U.S. Treasury securities:

Maturity	Early 1980s	Early 1990s
3-month	14%	3%
6-month	13	3
3-year	12	4
10-year	11	6

a. Draw the yield curve for the *early 1980s* and for the *early 1990s* on the same graph.

b. The inflation rate was high in the early 1980s and low in the early 1990s. Why do interest rates tend to be positively related with the inflation rate?

Estimating a future short-term rate

2.9. Suppose that 1-year bonds yield 5 percent per year and 2-year bonds yield 6 percent per year. Using the expectations theory, find the expected 1-year rate one year from now.

Expectations theory and yield curve

2.10. Robin Larkin is attempting to understand the relationship between short-term and long-term interest rates. Her company's president has asked her to make a report on this relationship to the executive committee. She has heard of two theories about interest rates—the expectations theory and the liquidity preference theory. Her assistant has collected the following data pertaining to expected short-term rates in each of the next four years:

Beginning of Year	Expected Rate
1	9%
2	7
3	7
4	5

Assume that these expected rates are reflected in bond market prices.

a. According to the expectations theory, what is the 4-year bond rate that would be quoted in *The Wall Street Journal*?

b. Draw a yield curve based on your calculation and the given information.

Annual discount and investment yields, expectations theory, yield curve

2.11. J. Peters and Company, a dealer in U.S. government securities, receives a phone call from the chief financial officer of Fong Enterprises. She wants to buy $20 million of face value 96-day maturity T-bills. Because of the large size of the purchase, she offers to buy them at an annual discount yield of 8.3 percent instead of the asked yield of 8.28 percent. (She offers a high-yield bid to get a low price.)

a. How many dollars of gross profit implied by the bid-asked yields will J. Peters and Company forgo if it sells the T-bills to Fong Enterprises at the price offered?

b. What is the annual investment yield for Fong Enterprises based on the price offered?

c. In determining whether or not to sell the T-bills to Fong Enterprises for the price offered, J. Peters and Company will consider the trend in interest rates. If interest rates are rising, then selling the securities at the price offered may be justified. The company's financial economist has circulated the following forecast of 1-year interest rates:

Beginning of Year	Expected Rate
1	5%
2	8
3	12
4	7

Calculate the interest rates on 2-, 3-, and 4-year securities based on the expectations theory of interest rates. Present your results in a yield curve.

Selected References

"Deregulation of the Financial Sector." Excerpts from papers delivered to the Conference on Bank Structure and Competition, Federal Reserve Bank of Chicago. *Economic Perspective,* Fall 1982: 26–36.

Jauch, Heinz. "Four Keys to Savings and Loan Profitability." *Financial Analysts Journal,* May–June 1981: 31–44.

Jones, Charles P., and Jack W. Wilson. "Stocks, Bonds, Paper, and Inflation: 1870–1985." *Journal of Portfolio Management,* Fall 1987: 20–24.

Marks, Kenneth R., and Warren A. Law. "Hedging against Inflation with Floating Notes." *Harvard Business Review,* March–April 1980: 106–112.

Marlin, Matthew R. "The Role of Sectoral Demand in Influencing Tax-Exempt Bond Yields: A Reexamination." *Financial Review,* February 1992: 35–57.

Melton, William C., and Jean M. Mahr. "Bankers' Acceptances." Federal Reserve Bank of New York *Quarterly Review,* Summer 1981: 39–55.

Pyle, David H. "On the Theory of Financial Intermediation." *Journal of Finance,* June 1971: 737–747.

Segall, Patricia. "Commercial Paper: New Tunes on an Old Instrument." *Journal of Commercial Bank Lending,* April 1987: 16–23.

Shawkey, Hany, Ronald Forbes, and Alan Frankle. "Liquidity Services and Capital Market Equilibrium: The Case for Money Market Mutual Funds." *Journal of Financial Research,* Summer 1983: 141–152.

Van Horne, James C. *Financial Market Rates and Flows,* 4th ed. Englewood Cliffs, NJ: Prentice-Hall, 1990.

Chapter 3

MARKETS FOR STOCKS AND BONDS

Hotcakes and Cappuccino

The International House of Pancakes (IHOP) restaurant chain initially offered common stock to the public for $10 per share. Trading in the secondary market a couple of months later, the stock was going for $15 per share. Ironically, IHOP executives were surprised by investors hungry for their stock. IHOP's IPO (Initial Public Offering) was priced too low. Had the company issued the stock at, say, $15 per share, it would have raised more cash. Or, it could have issued one-third fewer shares and still have ended up with the same amount of cash.

Setting a proper price for an IPO is difficult to do, and, by definition, there is no secondary market price to provide guidance. Set the price too low, and you suffer IHOP's fate. Set the price too high, and investors

will not buy your stock.

The Starbucks Corporation, a specialty coffee retailer, apparently set its price just right. Starbucks announced that it would issue 2,100,000 shares of common stock, priced at $14 to $16—more than 60 times the preceding year's earnings per share, $0.24. Despite what seemed to be a high price relative to earnings, the stock offering was successful, thanks in large part to Starbucks' investment bankers: Alex. Brown & Sons Inc. and Wertheim Schroder & Company.

Investment bankers play a key role in IPOs and in the issuance of securities in general. They advise company managers on the type of security to issue, when to make the offering, security pricing, and relevant government regulations. In some cases, groups of investment bankers act as underwriters; they actually buy the securities from the company and then offer them at a higher price to investors.

Source: Gene G. Marcial, "IHOP Has Plenty of Sizzle," *Business Week,* October 14, 1991, 110; Lawrence M. Fisher, "A Coffee Trend Is Going Public," *The New York Times,* May 28, 1992, D10.

Before a company can issue securities, it must fulfill a number of government requirements. The first part of the chapter describes these requirements and explains how investment bankers help companies to issue securities in the primary market. The remaining parts of the chapter address the secondary market. Here you will learn how to read stock and bond quotations published in *The Wall Street Journal* and other financial publications. Quotations of stock prices provide the scorecard on the value of financial decisions.

THE PRIMARY MARKET

Companies needing to raise funds in the primary market through offerings of stocks and bonds must comply with government regulations. These regulations, requiring a description of the securities being offered and public disclosure of the company's financial condition, stem largely from the 1929 stock market crash, a precipitous decline in stock prices. Prior to the crash, from 1927 to 1929, many companies issued massive volumes of securities lacking sound financial backing. These securities, combined with institutional and personal speculation, resulted in the loss of many personal fortunes and heralded the Great Depression of the 1930s. Congressional investigations after the crash revealed that much abuse and fraud had occurred in the primary market. To prevent abuse in the future, Congress enacted legislation governing the way companies issue securities.

Regulation of the Primary Market

Laws regulating the issuance of new securities exist at both the federal and state levels. Federal law is the dominant force in regulating the primary market, and federal compliance usually means state compliance as well. State law becomes effective for many securities that are exempt from federal law. The following sections briefly describe these laws and their implications for issuing securities.

Securities Act of 1933.   Congress passed the **Securities Act of 1933** in an attempt to prevent fraud and misrepresentation in the issuance of securities. The act does this by requiring disclosure to security buyers of all relevant information pertaining to an issue. A company issuing securities must prepare two documents disclosing facts about the securities and the company itself. First, the company must file a **registration statement (Form S-1)** with the **Securities and Exchange Commission (SEC)**, the federal agency that regulates the U.S. financial markets.[1] Second, the company (or its agent) must deliver a **prospectus,** an abridged version of the registration statement, to investors before they purchase the securities.

The registration statement contains detailed information about the security issuer—its management, directors, divisions, finances, accounting history, operations, earnings—that may have a bearing on the value of the security to investors. The SEC is not concerned with the issuing company's profit potential, or even the legality of its operations. The SEC requires only that relevant information on securities be fully disclosed and made available to prospective buyers.

After a company files its registration statement with the Securities and Exchange Commission, it must wait at least 20 days before offering the issue to

---

Securities Act of 1933
Federal act requiring a company to register its new issues of securities with the Securities and Exchange Commission.

registration statement (Form S-1)
Detailed financial and operating information filed with the SEC about a company.

Securities and Exchange Commission (SEC)
Federal agency that regulates U.S. financial markets.

prospectus
Abridged version of the registration statement, giving investors information relevant to the purchase of securities.

---

[1] Before passing the Securities Exchange Act of 1934, which established the Securities and Exchange Commission, Congress made the Federal Trade Commission responsible for registering new issues.

the investing public. During this waiting period the company may amend the statement and publicly announce the issue, but it may not sell the issue until it has SEC approval and has a prospectus ready to present to prospective buyers. During the waiting period and before the issue's final approval, however, the company may give a preliminary prospectus, called a **red herring,** to prospective buyers. The red herring increases public awareness of the issue and exposes it to increased public scrutiny.

red herring
Preliminary prospectus given to potential buyers of securities prior to SEC approval of the issue.

Figure 3.1 shows the cover page of a red herring for the initial public offering of common stock of Taco Cabana. The cover page of a red herring must bear in red ink the statement that the issue is being registered with the Securities and Exchange Commission (see the left margin of Figure 3.1). Because it is preliminary, the prospectus cover excludes the issue price of the stock and other details that the issuer will provide in the final prospectus. Toward the center of Figure 3.1 is the required disclaimer stating that the SEC has not approved or disapproved the security, nor has it evaluated the accuracy or adequacy of the prospectus.

To avoid later charges that they did not fully disclose all relevant information, companies usually include an enormous number of facts in the registration statement. In addition, the statement tends to take on a negative tone, which avoids charges that the company hyped its securities to investors. An analogy makes the point. During World War II, if General Dwight Eisenhower's D-Day order for the 1944 allied invasion of Europe had been registered on an S-1 form with the Securities and Exchange Commission, then it probably would have read something like this:

> *The officers planning the invasion, including myself, have never before planned anything on so grand a scale. The invasion uses the greatest armada in the history of the world, and the number of troops transported has never before been seen in one location.*
>
> *The Commander in Chief (President Franklin D. Roosevelt) has no experience in commanding troops in combat. Airborne and other attack methods have never before been attempted by our army. German gun emplacements on the French coast are 18-inch concrete, complemented with land mines, barbed wire, machine guns, howitzers, and field-hardened combatants. The weather is modestly favorable, but there is a great deal of uncertainty surrounding the forecast.*
>
> *There is no assurance that any allied soldiers will cross the channel safely and, if they do, that they can secure the beach. In short, the likelihood of failure is great and that of success small.*

Despite the generally negative tone of a registration statement, the record of information it provides is a major contribution of the Securities Act of 1933. The act enables security buyers wronged by falsehoods and omissions of material facts to sue the issuing company and its investment bankers. The court's interpretation of whom else the wronged purchaser may sue has expanded to include the auditors, printers, attorneys, and anyone else involved in the issue.

Regulation by the Securities and Exchange Commission focuses on large issues of long-term securities issued across state lines. Several types of new issues are exempt from the registration requirement: (1) intrastate issues in which the issuer and purchasers are residents of the same state; (2) debt securities with maturities of less than 270 days (commercial paper); (3) small issues sold to no more than 35 purchasers; (4) issues of companies (**public utilities** and railroads) regulated by other federal commissions; (5) issues of charitable and other non-profit organizations; and (6) all U.S. government, federal agency, and state or local government obligations.

public utility
Shareholder-owned corporation providing a service important to the public welfare—for example, electric, gas, and telephone service.

FIGURE 3.1   **Cover Page of the Preliminary Prospectus for Common Stock of Taco Cabana**

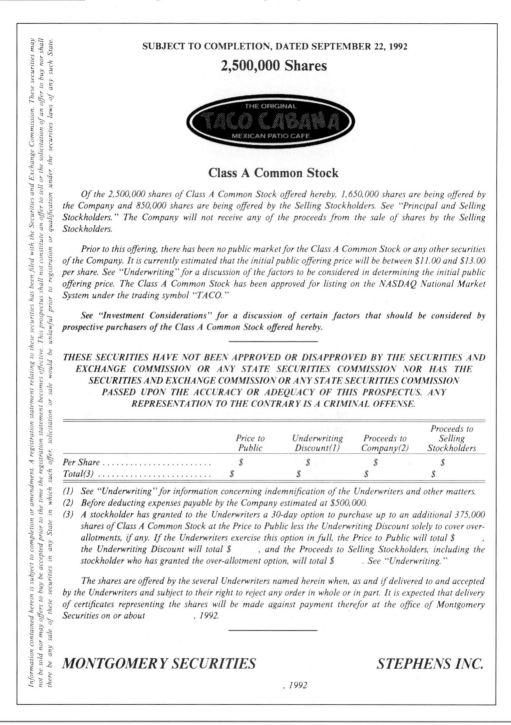

SUBJECT TO COMPLETION, DATED SEPTEMBER 22, 1992

2,500,000 Shares

Class A Common Stock

Of the 2,500,000 shares of Class A Common Stock offered hereby, 1,650,000 shares are being offered by the Company and 850,000 shares are being offered by the Selling Stockholders. See "Principal and Selling Stockholders." The Company will not receive any of the proceeds from the sale of shares by the Selling Stockholders.

Prior to this offering, there has been no public market for the Class A Common Stock or any other securities of the Company. It is currently estimated that the initial public offering price will be between $11.00 and $13.00 per share. See "Underwriting" for a discussion of the factors to be considered in determining the initial public offering price. The Class A Common Stock has been approved for listing on the NASDAQ National Market System under the trading symbol "TACO."

See "Investment Considerations" for a discussion of certain factors that should be considered by prospective purchasers of the Class A Common Stock offered hereby.

THESE SECURITIES HAVE NOT BEEN APPROVED OR DISAPPROVED BY THE SECURITIES AND EXCHANGE COMMISSION OR ANY STATE SECURITIES COMMISSION NOR HAS THE SECURITIES AND EXCHANGE COMMISSION OR ANY STATE SECURITIES COMMISSION PASSED UPON THE ACCURACY OR ADEQUACY OF THIS PROSPECTUS. ANY REPRESENTATION TO THE CONTRARY IS A CRIMINAL OFFENSE.

	Price to Public	Underwriting Discount(1)	Proceeds to Company(2)	Proceeds to Selling Stockholders
Per Share	$	$	$	$
Total(3)	$	$	$	$

(1) *See "Underwriting" for information concerning indemnification of the Underwriters and other matters.*

(2) *Before deducting expenses payable by the Company estimated at $500,000.*

(3) *A stockholder has granted to the Underwriters a 30-day option to purchase up to an additional 375,000 shares of Class A Common Stock at the Price to Public less the Underwriting Discount solely to cover over-allotments, if any. If the Underwriters exercise this option in full, the Price to Public will total $, the Underwriting Discount will total $, and the Proceeds to Selling Stockholders, including the stockholder who has granted the over-allotment option, will total $. See "Underwriting."*

The shares are offered by the several Underwriters named herein when, as and if delivered to and accepted by the Underwriters and subject to their right to reject any order in whole or in part. It is expected that delivery of certificates representing the shares will be made against payment therefor at the office of Montgomery Securities on or about   , 1992.

MONTGOMERY SECURITIES   *STEPHENS INC.*

, 1992

Information contained herein is subject to completion or amendment. A registration statement relating to these securities has been filed with the Securities and Exchange Commission. These securities may not be sold nor may offers to buy be accepted prior to the time the registration statement becomes effective. This prospectus shall not constitute an offer to sell or the solicitation of an offer to buy nor shall there be any sale of these securities in any State in which such offer, solicitation or sale would be unlawful prior to registration or qualification under the securities laws of any such State.

Source: Courtesy of Montgomery Securities.

In 1982 the Securities and Exchange Commission reduced the number of required registrations even further by issuing Rule 415. This rule allows an issuing company to register all of the securities it expects to offer over a two-year period and then to take all or part of them "off of the shelf" by filing a short-form statement. The subsequent issues are known as **shelf offerings.** Shelf offerings have proven popular among financial managers for two reasons: (1) They reduce paperwork and costs, and (2) managers can be poised to issue securities when financial market conditions appear favorable—low interest rates and high security prices.

shelf offering
Offering of new securities during a 24-month period whose registration is covered by a single Form S-1.

Blue Sky Laws. The Securities Act of 1933 requires full disclosure of relevant financial and operating information on interstate security issues. Each state has laws regulating securities issued and sold within its borders. These state regulations are **blue sky laws,** so called because a Kansas state legislator in 1911 (the year when Kansas enacted the first such law) commented that the law should prevent unscrupulous stock sellers from promising the blue sky to unsuspecting residents. The phrase caught the public's fancy, and we now call all state security laws regulating new issues blue sky laws. Any new issue must comply with these regulations before an issuer can offer the security within the borders of the state.

blue sky laws
State laws regulating securities issued and sold within state borders.

Blue sky laws seek to protect a state's residents from investing in unworthy securities. The state's securities commissioner determines what *unworthy* means. Typically, anything in the state registration statement or accompanying documents that appears to be unfair, unjust, inequitable, or oppressive to investors is sufficient to prohibit sale of the issue in a state.

How Companies Issue Securities

Companies have two basic alternatives for issuing new stocks and bonds in the primary market. They can issue the securities directly to investors or use an investment banking firm to do the selling. To issue stocks and bonds directly requires company managers to locate and persuade investors to purchase the securities, often a difficult task. Alternatively, companies can transfer the selling task to investment bankers, who sell securities for a living.[2]

Investment Banking Functions. Although an investment banking firm sounds like a commercial bank, it is totally different. Investment banking firms, unlike commercial banks, do not take deposits from savers and do not make loans to companies, individuals, and governments. The role of investment bankers is simply to assist issuers of securities in the primary market. To carry out this role, investment bankers perform four functions:

1. **Origination.** In originating a security issue, the investment banker advises company managers on the type of security to issue in order to maintain the company's optimal capital structure. The investment banker also gives advice on timing the issue to take best advantage of low interest rates and high security prices. Operationally, the investment banker helps the company to prepare the registration statement for the SEC and the prospectus for investors.

2. **Underwriting.** When investment bankers underwrite a security issue,

origination
Planning a new issue of securities through negotiations between the investment banker and the issuing corporation.

underwriting
Guaranteeing proceeds from a new issue of securities by buying the entire issue for resale.

---

[2]Technically, an investment banker is an individual who works for an investment banking firm. Common practice uses the term *investment banker* to refer to either the individual or the firm.

they guarantee the proceeds to the company by buying outright the entire issue for resale to investors. Underwriting transfers the risk of an unsuccessful security sale from the issuing company to the investment banker.

3. **Syndication.** When the dollar size of a security issue is too large for one investment banker to handle alone, the originating investment banker invites other investment bankers to help with the issue. By banding together in a syndicate, investment bankers spread the underwriting risk of reselling the securities at a loss. The syndicate continues to exist either until the securities have been sold at the offering price or until it becomes evident that sales at this price are impossible. In the latter case, the syndicate breaks up, each member taking its unsold securities and selling them at the best obtainable price.

4. **Distribution.** After purchasing a company's securities, syndicate members set about selling them to the investing public. Actual distribution of the securities may take place through either of two channels: (1) Syndicate members sell directly to investors, or (2) they sell to dealers who, in turn, sell to investors. Selling securities through a large number of dealers requires syndicate members to give up part of their profit, but it also assures them of a quick sale, thus lessening the probability of holding unsold securities.

Methods for Issuing Securities. Although investment bankers stand ready to perform their four functions, an issuing company may not require all of them to be performed. A company itself may perform one or more of the functions. Which functions a company requests from an investment banker depends on the method it selects for selling its securities.

Figure 3.2 illustrates the methods that companies use to issue securities. With private placements, the company bypasses investment bankers and issues its securities directly to investors. Companies often use private placement to issue bonds and preferred stock to an institutional investor such as a life insurance company or a pension fund. Even in these cases, however, the company may employ an investment banker to help find an institution willing to buy the security issue. By placing securities privately with an institution, the company avoids having to register the issue with the Securities and Exchange Commission. In addition, **flotation costs** (or *placement costs*) are less because of lower marketing costs. Offsetting these advantages, interest and dividend costs are normally higher for private placements than for public offerings because of the relatively low liquidity of private placements.

In public offerings of securities, companies rely on one or more of the services provided by investment bankers, who have an advantage in marketing securities to far-flung investors. Figure 3.2 shows two basic methods for issuing securities through investment bankers: a negotiated sale and a competitive bid. More common of the two, a **negotiated sale** is one in which company managers meet with the investment banker to negotiate the services to be rendered and the fee to be paid. The parties may agree to have the investment banker perform all four functions: originate the issue, underwrite it, syndicate other investment bankers, and distribute the securities to investors. Alternatively, the parties may forge a **best-efforts agreement,** in which the investment banker does not underwrite the issue but simply acts as a broker. Under this agreement, typically used for speculative securities, the investment banker promises only best efforts to sell

syndication
Temporary banding together of investment bankers to share the risk of issuing new securities.

distribution
Marketing a new issue of securities to investors.

flotation costs
All costs associated with issuing new securities.

negotiated sale
Agreement between the investment banker and securities-issuing corporation on services and fee.

best-efforts agreement
Agreement between the investment banker and securities-issuing corporation that the banker will serve only as a broker for a new issue.

FIGURE 3.2

Methods for Issuing Securities in the Primary Market

Companies raise funds by issuing securities privately to large investors or by using investment bankers to sell the securities to the investing public. Company managers may negotiate with an investment banker on the security sale or have several investment bankers bid competitively for the securities. Companies use negotiated sales—underwritings, best efforts, or standby underwritings—more frequently than competitive bids.

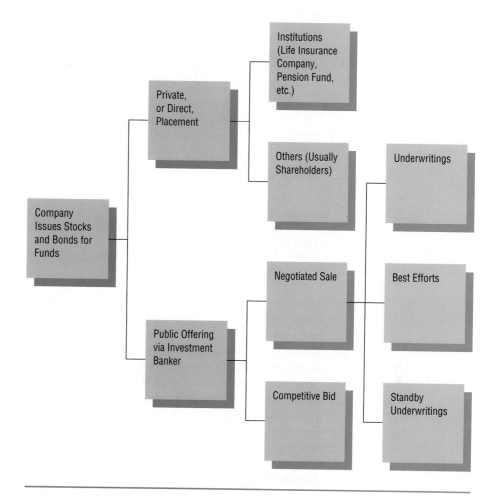

standby underwriting
Agreement between the investment banker and securities-issuing corporation that the banker will buy all unsold shares of a new issue for resale.

competitive-bid procedure
Process in which the issuer sells its securities to the highest-bidding investment banker.

the securities; all unsold securities are returned to the issuing company. When a company plans a private placement of new common stock to its shareholders, it may hire an investment banker for backup help in case some shares remain unsold.[3] Under this agreement, called a **standby underwriting,** the investment banker agrees to buy all unsold shares for a specified price and to offer them to the public.

In contrast to a negotiated sale, the **competitive-bid procedure** is one in which the issuing company sells its securities to the investment banker (or syndicate) bidding the highest price. The bidder underwrites, syndicates, and dis-

[3]Issuing new common stock to shareholders is a rights offering. Companies using this procedure provide an incentive to their shareholders by pricing the new stock below the prevailing market price. Chapter 18 presents details of rights offerings.

TABLE 3.1

The Top Ten Investment Bankers

Firm	1991			1990		
	Market Share	Number of Issues	Rank	Market Share	Number of Issues	Rank
Merrill Lynch	18.0%	567	1	16.8%	372	1
Goldman Sachs	14.8	454	2	12.6	200	2
Morgan Stanley	10.3	281	3	7.3	191	6
Alex. Brown	9.6	66	4	9.4	33	4
Lehman Brothers	7.3	498	5	6.4	116	7
First Boston	7.3	312	6	8.1	167	5
Salomon Brothers	6.2	199	7	9.9	142	3
Dean Witter Reynolds	2.5	41	8	3.9	21	9
PaineWebber	2.4	75	9	4.7	38	8
Kidder Peabody	2.3	199	10	2.0	82	11

Note: Rankings are based on fees earned from underwriting new security issues.
Source: The Wall Street Journal, January 2, 1992, R32. Reprinted by permission of *The Wall Street Journal,* Dow Jones & Company, Inc. All Rights Reserved Worldwide.

tributes the securities, but it does not advise the company on security features, timing of the issue, or registration. If necessary, the company can buy this advice from an investment banker not bidding on the issue. Regulatory agencies or law require some issuers to use the competitive-bid procedure. For example, the Interstate Commerce Commission requires railroad companies to use competitive bidding; some public utility commissions require electric and gas companies to use it; and some states require it for municipal bond issues. Most nonregulated companies shun competitive bids in favor of negotiated sales, presumably because company managers value the personal relationship and advice investment bankers provide.

Negotiated Sales in Detail.   The first step in issuing securities via negotiation is to select an investment banker. Almost every large company has an ongoing relationship with an investment banker. In many cases, an officer of the investment banking firm serves on the board of directors of the issuing company. For companies making an **initial public offering (IPO)**, however, or those dissatisfied with their current relationship, an investment banker must be selected.

initial public offering (IPO)
Issuing a type of security (e.g., common stock) for the first time.

Table 3.1 lists the names of 10 prominent investment bankers, each a nationally known company. Selecting an investment banker from this list or one of numerous other firms is an important first step in a negotiated sale for two reasons: (1) The client company must trust the integrity of its investment banker. Reputable investment bankers help to establish a fair price for their client's securities. (2) The client company must trust its investment banker's competence. Capable investment bankers have their fingers on the pulse of the primary market, know security regulations, and understand the issuer's operations and finances.

After the issuing company and its investment banker have agreed on (1) the securities to be issued, (2) the timing of their sale, and (3) the fee for services,

FIGURE 3.3

The Network for Issuing Corporate Securities in the Primary Market

The managing, or lead, investment banker performs all four functions: origination, underwriting, syndication, and distribution. Other investment bankers in the syndicate perform two functions: underwriting and distribution. Members of the selling group perform one function: distribution.

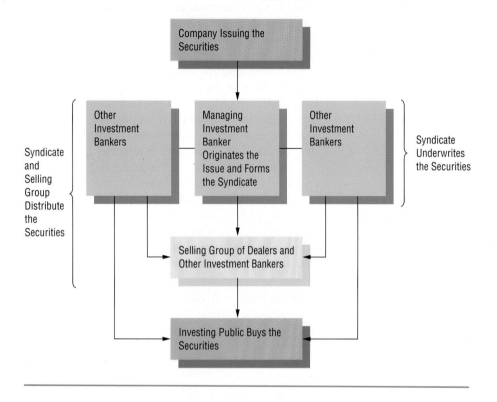

the investment banker organizes the underwriting syndicate. Many corporate security issues are too large to be acquired by one investment banking firm. Should the investment banking firm have the financial capability to buy the issue without the need for a syndicate, strong reasons still argue for sharing the tasks and the fees. Using a syndicate of investment bankers reduces the risk of loss to individual investment bankers, and it assures the rapid sale and distribution of the securities.

Figure 3.3 illustrates the flow of securities from the issuer to the investing public. The managing investment banker originates the issue and invites other investment bankers to join the syndicate. Each member of the syndicate underwrites a portion of the issue by agreeing to purchase a specified number of securities. Syndicate members sell the securities at both the retail and wholesale levels. They retail securities to the investing public and wholesale them to members of the selling group—dealers and investment bankers not included in the syndicate. Members of the selling group buy relatively small numbers of the securities and resell them to investors.

Compensation to members of the network for issuing securities depends on the functions they perform. Members performing the selling function, for example, may receive 50 percent of the spread between the market value of the securities and the proceeds to the issuing company. Underwriting may command 30 percent of the spread, and the managing investment banker may take 20 percent.

Receiving approval of the registration statement from the Securities and Exchange Commission energizes the network for issuing the securities. Members of the syndicate and selling group send the approved prospectuses to potential investors and make phone calls and personal visits in attempts to place the securities. At the same time, an advertisement appears in the financial press (*The Wall Street Journal,* among others) announcing the new issue of securities; because of its appearance, the advertisement is known as a **tombstone** (see Figure 3.4). Besides announcing the new issue of securities, the tombstone provides institutional advertising for investment bankers, who take very seriously the location of their names in the ad. The tombstone lists first the co-managers of the security issue, followed generally by the other firms according to their prestige within the investment banking industry. Prestige is a determinant of how much of a security issue the firm gets to underwrite. Prestigious investment banking firms are frequently asked to participate in underwriting syndicates.

tombstone
Advertisement announcing a new issue of securities.

After the syndicate and selling group sell all of the securities, the syndicate dissolves, for it has accomplished its goal. In some cases the managing investment banker actively buys and sells the securities in the secondary market to provide the issue with liquidity. Making a market in this way is helpful for small-company stocks that trade over the counter and lack an active secondary market. When investors know that the managing investment banker will make a market in the stock, they are more inclined to purchase stock in an initial public offering.

Flotation Costs.   A company incurs flotation costs (or placement costs) when issuing new securities. Total flotation costs for securities issued through investment bankers consist of two parts:

$$\frac{\text{Total flotation}}{\text{costs}} = \frac{\text{Underwriting}}{\text{spread}} + \frac{\text{Issuing expenses}}{\text{of company}}$$

underwriting spread
Difference between the market value of the security and the proceeds to the company.

The **underwriting spread** is the difference between the market value of the security and the proceeds the issuing company receives:

$$\frac{\text{Underwriting}}{\text{spread}} = \frac{\text{Market value}}{\text{of security}} - \frac{\text{Proceeds to}}{\text{company}}$$

Proceeds to the company are paid by investment bankers.

EXAMPLE

Midwest Airlines issued $35,000,000 of common stock in 1993, but its proceeds were $33,650,000. The underwriting spread of $1,350,000 ($35,000,000 − $33,650,000) compensated investment bankers for services rendered. In other words, the investment bankers received $35,000,000 from the public offering and paid Midwest Airlines $33,650,000. Stated as a percentage, the underwriting spread equaled 3.9 percent:

$$\frac{\text{Underwriting spread}}{\text{as a percentage}} = \frac{\text{Market value} - \text{Proceeds}}{\text{Market value}}$$

$$= \frac{\$35,000,000 - \$33,650,000}{\$35,000,000}$$

$$= 0.039, \text{ or } 3.9\%$$

Midwest Airlines issued 1,000,000 shares of stock, so on a per-share basis the underwriting spread equaled $1.35 ($1,350,000/1,000,000 shares).

FIGURE 3.4   **A Tombstone Announcing the Issuance of Common Stock**

*This advertisement is neither an offer to sell nor a solicitation of an offer to buy any of these securities.
The offering is made only by the Prospectus.*

August 10, 1992

2,000,000 Shares

SOMATOGEN

Common Stock

Price $19 Per Share

*Copies of the Prospectus may be obtained from such of the Underwriters as may legally offer these securities
in compliance with the securities laws of the respective states.*

ALEX. BROWN & SONS   MONTGOMERY SECURITIES
INCORPORATED

DILLON, READ & CO. INC.   A.G. EDWARDS & SONS, INC.   HAMBRECHT & QUIST
                                                                        INCORPORATED

KIDDER, PEABODY & CO.   LEHMAN BROTHERS   MERRILL LYNCH & CO.
    INCORPORATED

OPPENHEIMER & CO., INC.   PAINEWEBBER INCORPORATED   SBCI SWISS BANK CORPORATION
                                                                 INVESTMENT BANKING

ADVEST, INC.   WILLIAM BLAIR & COMPANY   COWEN & COMPANY   DAIN BOSWORTH
                                                                             INCORPORATED

FURMAN SELZ   KEMPER SECURITIES, INC.   McDONALD & COMPANY
INCORPORATED   SECURITIES, INC.

PIPER JAFFRAY INC.   RAYMOND JAMES & ASSOCIATES, INC.   THE ROBINSON-HUMPHREY COMPANY, INC.

SUTRO & CO. INCORPORATED   WESSELS, ARNOLD & HENDERSON

BREAN MURRAY, FOSTER SECURITIES INC.   DOMINICK & DOMINICK   HANIFEN, IMHOFF INC.
                                              INCORPORATED

LAIDLAW EQUITIES, INC.   PENNSYLVANIA MERCHANT GROUP LTD   RAFFENSPERGER, HUGHES & CO.
                                                                    INCORPORATED

VAN KASPER & COMPANY   VECTOR SECURITIES INTERNATIONAL, INC.

Source: The Wall Street Journal, August 10, 1992, C17.

Of the two parts of flotation costs, the underwriting spread is larger by far. Underwriting spreads typically account for 65 to 90 percent of total flotation costs. The remaining costs are out-of-pocket expenses the issuing company incurs: (1) legal fees, (2) printing and engraving expenses, (3) accounting expenses, and (4) numerous smaller expenses. Printing the security certificates and prospectuses accounts for a large portion of the company's out-of-pocket expenses.

By type of security issued, underwriting spreads as a percentage of market value are highest for common stock and lowest for bonds, with preferred stock in the middle. Common stock is the most expensive for two reasons: (1) Being the highest risk security, common stock presents investment bankers with the most underwriting risk; hence investment bankers demand a larger underwriting fee on common stock than on either preferred stock or bonds. (2) Common stock is typically sold in small lots to individual investors, whereas large portions of preferred stock and bonds are sold to large institutional investors; hence investment bankers charge a larger fee for the time-consuming process of distributing common stock than they charge for distributing preferred stock and bonds.

Underwriting spreads also vary by the dollar size (market value) of a security issue. Companies incur larger underwriting fees for larger issues than for smaller ones. Underwriting spreads expressed as a percentage of dollar size, however, vary inversely with size of the security issue. For example, a company issuing $1,000,000 of common stock may pay 20 percent ($200,000) in fees, but a company issuing $50,000,000 of common stock may pay 3 percent ($1,500,000). Similar relationships hold for bonds (and preferreds), but the costs are smaller. Issuing $1,000,000 of bonds may cost 15 percent, or $150,000, but issuing $50,000,000 of bonds may cost only 1 percent, or $500,000.

Flotation costs as a percentage of market value decline with issue size partly because some of the issue expenses stay about the same regardless of issue size, legal and accounting expenses being good examples. Also, large issues are normally made by well-known, established companies, which lessens the risk of underwriting and, therefore, the underwriting spread. For any company, issuing securities is an expensive proposition. Thus a financial manager needs to analyze and anticipate the company's long-term financing requirements in order to reduce the frequency of issuing securities.

THE SECONDARY MARKET

Once they are issued by companies, securities trade in the secondary market either over the counter or on organized exchanges. The following sections describe the process of buying and selling common stock in the secondary market and the way the press reports stock and bond prices. To monitor the impact of corporate decision making on stock price, a financial manager must understand the way the market works. To develop this understanding, we begin with government regulations and proceed to common-stock trading.

Regulation of the Secondary Market

In addition to the abuses and fraud surrounding new security issues prior to the 1929 stock market crash, investors trading securities in the secondary market suffered losses from various stock manipulation schemes. Congress put in place the Securities Act of 1933, but that act regulates only the disclosure of information in the primary market. So in the following year Congress passed the **Securities Exchange Act of 1934,** which requires disclosure of information in the secondary market. The 1934 act established the Securities and Exchange Commission (SEC) to enforce regulations in both the primary and the secondary markets.

Securities Exchange Act of 1934
Federal law governing activities in the secondary market.

To provide investors with information that might help them make informed investment decisions, the 1934 act requires companies with securities listed on organized exchanges (and some with stock trading in the over-the-counter market) to file periodic reports. Each year companies must file Form 10-K with the SEC. The 10-K, available to the public upon request, consists of detailed, audited financial statements and substantial information on company operations during the operating year. Companies must also file an unaudited quarterly financial report, Form 10-Q. Companies send variations of these SEC filings, both 10-K and 10-Q, to their common shareholders.

In addition to company filings, the 1934 act requires corporate insiders to file with the Securities and Exchange Commission monthly reports of their holdings and transactions in the common stock of the company for which the SEC considers them insiders. Corporate insiders include company directors, upper-level managers, and major shareholders. The 1934 act prohibits anyone from using confidential information to make profits from trading in the company's stock. Insiders are legally bound to wait until the information has been announced publicly.

The 1934 act also requires organized exchanges to register with the Securities and Exchange Commission. Thus the SEC collects information from the places where securities trade, the companies whose securities trade there, and investors with nonpublic (inside) information. In general, the SEC seeks to prevent manipulation of security prices and the defrauding of investors. It prevents such abuses by monitoring and regulating the activities of organized exchanges and the over-the-counter market.

The Stock Market

The organized stock exchanges—the New York, American, Chicago, Pacific Coast, and others—and the over-the-counter (OTC) market provide stock-trading facilities. Bonds trade mostly over the counter, although the New York and American Exchanges have floor areas for bond trading. The term **stock market** refers collectively to any place involving stock trading in the secondary market, whether on an exchange or over the counter.

stock market
Financial market for trading stock; any place that stock trades in the secondary market.

Organized Exchanges.   If a company's stock is not listed on an exchange, then by definition it trades in the over-the-counter market. To list a stock on an exchange, a company must pay a fee and meet several listing requirements dealing with size of earnings, number of shares outstanding, market value of shares, and number of shareholders. In general, companies on the NYSE are larger than those on the AMEX; in turn, AMEX companies tend to be larger than OTC companies and those listed on regional exchanges. Whenever a company violates a listing requirement, the exchange will consider delisting it—removing the stock from the exchange listing. Most managers prefer to have their stock listed on an exchange, preferably the NYSE, because it gives the company free daily publicity in newspaper listings of stock prices. Also, a NYSE company has an aura of prestige in the business community. The NYSE has existed since 1792, and it is well known around the world.

Organized exchanges rely on *auction trading,* in which stock shares sell to the highest bidder. The key person here is a *broker.* When brokers receive buy and sell orders from investors in St. Paul, Des Moines, Seattle, or other cities, they send the orders electronically to the trading floor of the exchange. There a representative of the brokerage firm takes the order to a designated trading post where the stock trades. The representative may trade with another broker or with a specialist. A **specialist** is an exchange member who makes a market in a specific stock by standing ready to buy or sell when no one else will. A specialist also maintains a record of those wanting to trade at other than the prevailing price.

specialist
Stock exchange member who makes a market in a specific stock.

EXAMPLE

Suppose that Xerox common stock trades at $72\frac{1}{2}$, or $72.50 per share. Brokers for investors who want to buy at prices under $72\frac{1}{2}$ leave the buy orders with the specialist; brokers for investors who want to sell at prices above $72\frac{1}{2}$ leave the sell orders with the specialist. If possible, the specialist plays the role of a broker and matches the buy and sell orders. If necessary, the specialist plays the role of a dealer and personally buys from investors wanting to sell and sells to investors wanting to buy. The specialist's job is to maintain an orderly market, with gradually increasing and decreasing stock prices and no abrupt price changes from one transaction to the next.

---

round lot
Block of 100 shares of a stock.

odd lot
Fewer than 100 shares of a stock.

Investors often buy and sell stock in **round lots,** blocks of 100 shares. They may also buy and sell **odd lots,** one to 99 shares of stock. Odd-lot commissions paid to brokers are slightly higher than round-lot commissions, which typically range from 1 to 4 percent of the stock price. Investors pay brokerage commissions coming and going—that is, when they buy and when they sell.

The Wall Street Journal and other newspapers publish daily price quotations for stocks listed on various stock exchanges. Figure 3.5 presents a sample of price quotations taken from the Friday, October 2, 1992, issue of *The Wall Street Journal.* Friday's *Journal* contains the quotations for Thursday, the preceding trading day. Look at the quotation for the first listed stock. Here is the way to interpret the information:

52 Weeks		
Hi	**Lo**	Over the past 52 weeks, the price per share reached a high of $15.875 and a low of $10.625. Most stocks are quoted in eighths of a dollar; $\frac{1}{8}$ is $0.125.
$15\frac{7}{8}$	$10\frac{5}{8}$	

Stock	
AAR	AAR is the abbreviated name of the company Adams and Russell Inc., a manufacturer of electronic equipment. (Letters preceding some quotations refer to explanatory footnotes.)

Sym	
AIR	AIR is the company's symbol on the NYSE "ticker" tape, which shows price per share and number of shares for each transaction.

Div	
.48	The indicated annual dividend per share is $0.48, which equals the most recent quarterly dividend ($0.12) times 4.

FIGURE 3.5

Stock Price Quotations from *The Wall Street Journal:* New York Stock Exchange Composite Transactions

The term *composite transactions* means that these stock quotations include trades on the New York, Chicago, Pacific, Philadelphia, Boston, and Cincinnati stock exchanges; also included are trades reported by the National Association of Securities Dealers. Most trades are on the New York Stock Exchange.

Quotations as of 5 p.m. Eastern Time
Thursday, October 1, 1992

52 Weeks Hi	Lo	Stock	Sym	Div	Yld %	PE	Vol 100s	Hi	Lo	Close	Net Chg
		-A-A-A-									
15⅞	10⅝	AAR	AIR	.48	4.1	19	424	11⅞	11⅝	11⅝	– ⅛
11⅝	10⅛	ACM Gvt Fd	ACG	.96	8.4	...	1044	11⅜	11¼	11⅜	...
10⅜	9	ACM OppFd	AOF	.80	8.2	...	164	9⅞	9¾	9¾	...
11⅞	10	ACM SecFd	GSF	.96	8.4	...	1448	11⅜	11¼	11⅜	...
9¾	8¼	ACM SpctmFd	SI	.79	8.5	...	984	9½	9¼	9¼	– ¼
10⅝	8¼	ACM MgdIncFd	AMF	1.08	10.2	...	697	10⅝	10½	10⅝	...
12⅞	9⅞	ACM MgdMultFd	MMF	1.08	10.5	...	233	10¼	10⅛	10¼	...
2½	**1**	**ADT wt**			...	...	**67**	1¼	1⅛	1¼	+ ⅛
9½	5	ADT	ADT		...	...	1196	7	6⅞	7	– ⅛
34	23¼	AFLAC	AFL	.44	1.4	15	941	31¾	31¼	31½	...
26	17⅝	AL Labs A	BMD	.18	.8	92	819	23⅞	23½	23⅞	+ ⅛
2⅛	**½**	**AM Int**	**AM**		...	...	**56**	⅝	9/16	9/16	– 1/16
10¾	**1⅝**	**AM Int pf**			...	...	**15**	2⅛	2	2	– ⅛
11⅞	10⅞	AMEV Sec	AMV	1.02	8.8	...	112	11¾	11½	11⅝	...
80¼	54½	AMR	AMR		...	...	3768	57¼	56½	56⅝	– ½
28	25	ANR pf		2.67	9.5	...	3	28	28	28	...
47¼	34½	ARCO Chm	RCM	2.50	5.6	24	39	44⅞	44⅝	44¾	+ ⅛
2⅜	**1**	**ARX**	**ARX**		...	**15**	**64**	1½	1⅜	1⅜	– ⅛
53½	33⅞	ASA	ASA	2.00	5.8	...	423	34¾	34½	34½	– ⅛
6½	¼	ATT Cap yen wt			...	...	20	1	1	1	...
s 34¾	26⅛	AbbotLab	ABT	.60a	2.1	20	11133	28¾	28¼	28⅜	+ ⅛
n 9⅞	5⅛	Abex	ABE		...	...	153	5⅜	5⅛	5⅛	– ¼
14	11⅜	Abitibi g	ABY	.50	...	...	9	11⅜	11⅜	11⅜	– ⅛
6¼	**3⅞**	**AcmeElec**	**ACE**		...	**32**	**29**	4⅜	4⅛	4⅛	– ¼
37⅜	14⅜	Acuson	ACN		...	10	687	15⅞	15⅝	15⅝	– ⅛
20¼	17½	AdamsExp	ADX	1.63e	8.4	...	250	19¾	19⅜	19⅜	– ⅛
21½	7⅜	AdvMicro	AMD		...	4	8918	11⅛	10⅝	10⅞	– ⅜
49⅛	29½	AdvMicro pf		3.00	8.1	...	47	37½	37	37	– ½

Source: The Wall Street Journal, October 2, 1992, C3.

Yld
%
4.1

The dividend yield equals 4.1 percent, which is the annualized dividend per share divided by the closing price per share: \$0.48/\$11.625 = 0.041, or 4.1%. Dividend yield is one part of an investor's total rate of return; the other part is capital-gain yield.

P-E
Ratio
19

P-E ratio (here 19) is the price-earnings ratio, or closing price ($11\frac{5}{8}$) divided by the latest annual earnings per share (EPS). EPS is not given, but it can be derived: 19 = \$11.625/EPS; or EPS = \$11.625/19 = \$0.61. P-E ratios indicate how many dollars investors are willing to pay for one dollar of a company's earnings.

Vol
100s
424

The number of 100-share units (round lots) sold during the day is 424. This day a total of 42,400 shares were traded.

Hi	**Lo**	**Close**
$11\frac{7}{8}$	$11\frac{5}{8}$	$11\frac{5}{8}$

High price per share for the day, low price for the day, and closing or last price recorded for the day.

Net
Chg
$-\frac{1}{8}$

Net change in closing price from the trading day before today's close is $-\frac{1}{8}$, or −\$0.125 per share. The closing quote the previous day must have been $11\frac{3}{4}$ ($11\frac{5}{8} + \frac{1}{8}$).

dividend payout ratio
Percentage of a company's earnings paid out as dividends on common stock; dividends per share divided by earnings per share.

dividend yield
Percentage return on stock price based solely on dividends; dividends per share divided by price per share of stock.

price-earnings (P-E) ratio
Price investors pay for $1 of a company's earnings per share; earnings multiple; price per share divided by earnings per share.

From the information provided by a stock quotation, you can indirectly calculate a company's **dividend payout ratio,** the percentage of earnings paid out as dividends:

$$\frac{\text{Dividend}}{\text{payout ratio}} = \frac{\text{Dividends per share}}{\text{Earnings per share}}$$

The calculation uses the **dividend yield** and the **price-earnings (P-E) ratio,** each defined as follows:

$$\frac{\text{Dividend}}{\text{yield}} = \frac{\text{Dividends per share}}{\text{Price per share}}$$

$$\frac{\text{Price-earnings}}{\text{ratio}} = \frac{\text{Price per share}}{\text{Earnings per share}}$$

Multiplying the dividend yield by the P-E ratio produces the dividend payout ratio:

$$\frac{\text{Dividend}}{\text{payout ratio}} = \text{Dividend yield} \times \text{P-E ratio}$$

$$= \frac{\text{Dividends per share}}{\text{Price per share}} \times \frac{\text{Price per share}}{\text{Earnings per share}}$$

$$= \frac{\text{Dividends per share}}{\text{Earnings per share}}$$

Low payout ratios provide investors assurance that the company will be able to continue paying the dividend indicated in the stock quotation. High payout ratios create concern about the company's ability to continue paying the indicated dividend.

EXAMPLE

Calculate the dividend payout ratio for AAR based on the stock quotation in Figure 3.5:

$$\frac{\text{Dividend}}{\text{payout ratio}} = \text{Dividend yield} \times \text{P-E ratio}$$

$$= 4.1\% \times 19$$

$$= 77.9\%$$

AAR's dividend payout ratio, based on the indicated dividend, is 77.9 percent. Investors usually consider payout ratios above the 40 to 60 percent range to be high, so they probably have some concern about AAR's ability to continue paying the indicated dividend.

Most newspapers use the format in Figure 3.5 to report stock quotations for trades on organized exchanges. Over-the-counter (OTC) quotations are formatted in two different ways, as explained below.

Over-the-Counter Market.   The OTC market is a nationwide network of thousands of securities dealers and brokerage firms. Collectively, these dealers and brokerage firms make a market (stand ready to buy and sell shares) in about

FIGURE 3.6

OTC Stock Price Quotations: NASDAQ Small-Cap Issues

NASDAQ is an acronym for National Association of Securities Dealers Automated Quotations. *Small Cap* is a shortened form of *small capitalization,* where capitalization refers to the total market value of a company's common stock: price per share times the number of shares outstanding. The stock quotations below are for small companies with regional-investor interest.

Quotes at 4 p.m. Eastern Time Thursday, October 1, 1992						Issue	Div	Vol 100s	Last	Chg
Issue	Div	Vol 100s	Last	Chg		CBT Cp s.36i		3	27	+ 1/2
						CCAIR		62	4 1/8	+ 1/8
						CCR s		20	13/16	...
A&A Fd g		66	2 9/16	+ 1/16		CEC In s		4	3 1/2	...
AAON		59	5/16	− 1/32		CNS		33	1 5/8	− 1/8
ACTV		34	15/16	− 3/16		CPI un		330	5	...
ACTV wt		225	11/16	+ 1/16		CPT Hld		4	2 3/4	...
ADM Tr		296	1/4			CTEC B		38	14 3/4	− 1 3/8
AFN		530	1 1/4	+ 1/8		CblCar		456	31/32	− 5/32
AFP		8	13/16	− 1/32		CblC wt		75	3/32	...
AGBag		340	2 7/8	+ 1/8		Cadiz s		4	1 3/4	− 1/4
AGBag wt		10	9/32	− 1/32		CalJam		6	4 5/8	+ 1/8
APA		13	3 9/16	...		Calnetcs		30	1 3/4	+ 1/2
ASA Int		52	1 7/8	...		CamNt g		417	11 3/4	− 3/8
ATC Env		105	2 1/2	− 3/16		Camelot		30	1 3/4	...
ATC		135	2 1/4	− 1/8		CamPlat		57	1 3/4	− 3/32
Abatlx		118	1 1/16	+ 1/16		Camlz		5	2 1/4	− 3/8
Accuhlt		193	5 3/8	...		CdnPiper		192	3/32	...
ActnPr		30	1 13/16	− 1/16		Canav		261	17/32	− 3/32
Adelph h		1	16	− 1/4		CandBk		5	7 1/4	− 1/4
Admar		917	2 7/16	+ 1/16		CndyTor		98	4 7/8	...
AdvEnv		317	1 1/2	+ 1/8		Cantbry		30	1 1/2	...
AdvEn wt		213	11/32	+ 1/32		CapMult		332	8 1/4	+ 1/2
AdvF wtA		8	7/8	− 3/8		CapMl wt		369	3 1/2	+ 1/4
AdvFin		112	5	+ 1/4		Caprck		10	7/32	− 1/32
AdvMed		79	3 1/4	− 3/8		Capucln		133	7/16	− 1/32
AdNMR		806	2 1/2	+ 1/8		CarMrt		109	3 1/4	− 1/8
A NMR wt		2	2 3/4	+ 1/2		CarMt wt		20	1	...
AdvLfe		177	19/32	− 3/32		vjCreEn		150	2 1/4	− 1/16
Aerody		58	5	+ 1/8		Caretnd		388	2 5/16	+ 1/16
Aero wtA		5	1	...		CarolB		15	4 7/8	+ 1/8
Agristr		5	5/8	− 1/16		CascSBk		21	8 5/8	− 3/8
AirSen h		440	5/8	...		CasinAm		367	12 1/4	+ 1/4
ArCur wt		47	1 1/16	+ 1/16		CasnA wt		538	6 1/2	+ 1/2
Airlnt		626	13/32	− 1/32		Cavco s		10	8 1/2	...
Airln wtA		10	5/32	...		vjCedrG		106	1/4	− 1/16
Airln wtB		10	5/32	...		Cedarl	.52	80	3 5/8	− 3/8

Source: The Wall Street Journal, October 2, 1992, C8.

50,000 separate stock issues. Dealers stand ready to buy at one price (the bid) and to sell at another—and slightly higher—price (the asked). The difference between the bid and asked prices is the *spread,* a dealer's expected gross profit on a transaction. Investors buy stock in the OTC market at the asked price from a dealer, who maintains an inventory of shares for sale; investors sell their stock at the bid price to a dealer. Dealers maintain markets by trying to keep bid and asked prices, and the spread between them, at levels where the amounts of stock they buy and sell are roughly equal over time. If dealers start buying more stock than they sell, they respond by dropping both the bid and asked prices. This action discourages investors from selling so much stock and encourages them to buy more stock. Dealers raise bid and asked prices if they start selling out of inventory.[4]

An investor is usually one party in an OTC stock transaction, the other party being a dealer. The investor asks a broker to buy or sell an OTC stock, and the broker contacts the dealer with the best price—lowest price if the investor is buying and highest price if the investor is selling. The broker charges a commission to execute the buy or sell order, and the dealer earns the spread between the asked price and the bid price. Total transaction costs for the investor, therefore, equal the dealer's spread plus the broker's commission.

---

[4]Technically, most over-the-counter quotations are bids to buy, and offers to sell, 100 shares between dealers at the stated prices. Larger or smaller transactions with the public are subject to further negotiation.

The Wall Street Journal and other newspapers publish price quotations for over-the-counter stocks in two ways: (1) For companies followed by investors nationally, newspapers format stock quotations the same way as shown in Figure 3.5 for organized-exchange quotations. The listing is titled *NASDAQ National Market Issues,* where NASDAQ stands for National Association of Securities Dealers Automated Quotations. The National Association of Securities Dealers (NASD) licenses dealers and supervises trading procedures. (2) For less well-known companies, those of perhaps regional interest only, newspapers format stock quotations as shown in Figure 3.6. The first column gives the name of the company, and the second column gives its annual dividend, if any, based on the most recent quarterly payment. The third column gives the day's trading volume in hundreds of shares. The fourth column gives the price per share of the last trade of the day, and the final column gives the change in last price per share from the preceding trading day.

Corporate Bond Quotations.   In addition to stock price quotations, some newspapers also publish corporate bond quotations. Many bonds never trade in the secondary market because the initial buyers hold them until maturity. Also, institutional investors such as life insurance companies and pension funds often trade bonds among themselves without the transactions being recorded in published bond quotations. By printing daily quotations of the bonds that trade publicly, the financial press makes it easy for financial managers and investors to track bond prices and yields.

Although most bonds trade in the over-the-counter market, the New York Stock Exchange lists more bonds than it does stocks. Figure 3.7 presents a sample of quotations for New York Exchange Bonds as reported in *The Wall Street Journal*. The first column identifies the issuer, coupon rate, and year of maturity. For example, AMR (parent company of American Airlines) has a bond issue with a 9 percent coupon rate that matures in the year 2016. Similar to most corporate bonds, each of these AMR bonds has a face value (par value) of $1,000. Both the coupon rate and face value are fixed and remain unchanged over the life of the bond. Annual dollar interest per bond, paid to the bondholder, is:

$$\text{Annual dollar interest} = \text{Coupon rate} \times \text{Face value}$$
$$= 0.09 \times \$1,000$$
$$= \$90$$

Like most corporate bonds, AMR's bond pays interest semiannually, so the bondholder actually would receive $45 each 6-month period until the bond matures in 2016. At maturity, the bond repays the face value, $1,000, to the bondholder.

current yield
Rate of return on a bond based on dollar interest but ignoring changes in bond prices.

The second column of the bond quotations in Figure 3.7 reports the **current yield,** annual dollar interest divided by closing price:

$$\text{Current yield} = \frac{\text{Coupon rate} \times \text{Face value}}{\text{Closing price}}$$

Applying this equation to "AMR's 9s" produces the following:

$$\text{Current yield} = \frac{0.09 \times \$1,000}{\$1,008.75}$$
$$= 0.089, \text{ or } 8.9\%$$

FIGURE 3.7

Corporate Bond Quotations: New York Exchange Bonds

Corporate bond quotations include the following information: company name, coupon rate, year of maturity, current yield, number of bonds traded (volume), closing price, and change in closing price from that of the preceding trading day. Bond prices are quoted as a percentage of face value (par value).

CORPORATION BONDS Volume, $49,990,000					Bonds	Cur Yld	Vol	Close	Net Chg
Bonds	Cur Yld	Vol	Close	Net Chg	DetEd 8.15s00	7.9	10	102⅞	...
AForP 5s30	8.6	28	58⅛ +	⅝	DetEd 7⅜s01	7.3	10	100⅝ +	⅛
AMR 9s16	8.9	539	100⅞ +	⅝	DIsney zr05	...	357	47⅛	
AMR zr06	...	18	43	− ¼	duPnt 8.45s04	8.2	37	103¼ +	¼
AMR 8.10s98	7.9	81	103	− ½	duPnt dc6s01	6.3	539	95⅞ +	⅞
Advst 9s08	cv	115	88 +	1	DuqL 8¾s00	8.4	2	104 +	½
AlrbF 6¾s01	cv	80	89¾ −	¼	E Kod 8⅝s16	8.3	198	104¼ +	½
AlaBn 4.20s99†	4.3	15	98½ −	1	E Kod zr11	...	43	29⅜	
AlaP 7⅞s02	7.8	75	101⅜ −	⅝	Eatn dc7s11	8.0	1	87⅝ +	⅜
AlaP 8¼s03	7.9	1	104¼ +	⅞	EmbSult 10½s94	10.2	45	102⅞ +	⅛
AlskAr 6⅞s14	cv	109	82½ −	1	EmbSult 10⅞s02	10.3	52	106 +	1
AlskAr zr06	...	129	35⅝ +	⅛	EBP 6¾s06	cv	127	68½ +	1½
AlldC zr96	...	29	84½ +	1	Exxon 6s97	6.0	93	100⅜ −	⅛
AlldC zr2000	...	48	57½ +	2	Exxon 6½s98	6.4	46	101	...
AlldC zr95	...	10	86⅜ +	½	FairCp 12s01	12.7	5	94⅛ +	1⅞
AlldC zr03	...	15	45 +	1½	FairCp 13⅛s06	14.6	156	90⅛ −	1½
AlegCp 6½s14	cv	19	87⅝	...	FdMog 8⅜s93	8.3	400	101¼ −	⅛
AldSig 9⅞s97	9.5	291	103⅞ +	⅜	FedN zr14s	...	10	16½ −	⅝
AMAX 14½s94	12.5	2	116	...	FedDS 10s00	10.0	155	100½ +	¼
ACyan 8⅜s06	8.2	10	102	− ¼	Fldcst 6s12	cv	47	70¾	
AmStor 01	cv	86	111	...	FUnRE 8⅜s94	8.4	50	100	...
ATT 5⅛s97	5.5	247	100 +	¼	FrdC 8⅜s01	8.3	40	100¾ −	⅝
ATT 4⅜s99	4.8	3	91¼ +	1¼	FrpMCG zr11	...	50	32½ −	¾
ATT 6s00	6.1	113	98⅜ +	⅜	Frpt dc6.55s01	cv	5	92½ +	¼
ATT 5⅛s01	5.7	165	90½ +	¾	FreptM zr06	...	118	29⅞	
					Fuqua 9½s98	9.9	103	95¾ +	½

Source: The Wall Street Journal, October 2, 1992, C14.

Corporate bond quotations express the bond price as a percentage of face value (par value), *not in dollars*. Therefore, the AMR closing price is $100\frac{7}{8}$ percent of $1,000, *not* $100\frac{7}{8}$. The decimal equivalent of $100\frac{7}{8}$ percent is 1.00875, which when multiplied by the $1,000 face value yields $1,008.75, the closing price in dollars. An investor who pays this price for AMR's bond would earn a return of 8.9 percent for the year, ignoring any capital gain or loss due to change in bond price. For example, if market interest rates rise, the bond price would decline, producing a capital loss. Chapter 6 shows how to calculate yields that include changes in bond price.

Figure 3.7 omits the current yield for two types of bonds: (1) For convertible bonds, CV appears in the current-yield column. Holders of convertible bonds may convert them into a specified number of shares of the company's common stock. (2) For zero-coupon bonds, ellipsis dots (. . .) appear in the current-yield column. Zero-coupon bonds do not pay interest; instead, investors buy them at a discount from face value, which investors receive when the bond matures.[5]

The third column of the corporate bond quotations shows volume, the number of bonds traded for the day. Volume of bonds traded is often quite low because of the buy-and-hold strategy of many bondholders and because of off-exchange trading in bonds by institutional investors. The final column shows the change in closing price from that of the preceding trading day. For example, "AMR's 9s" closed up $\frac{5}{8}$. Note that $+\frac{5}{8}$ indicates a price increase of $6.25 (0.00625 × $1,000), *not* $0.625.

---

[5] Chapter 17 describes convertible bonds and zero-coupon bonds in detail.

margin buying

Borrowing a percentage of the purchase price to buy stock.

Margin Buying and Short Selling.   Security price quotations are crucial in the decision making of investors. For example, if they believe that a stock price is low compared with the price justified by the basic determinants—amount and timing of expected cash flows and required rate of return—then they would buy the stock; otherwise they would sell the stock, if already owned. In addition to these ordinary transactions, investors may also buy stock on margin or sell it short.

Margin buying means borrowing a percentage of the purchase price when buying stock. Literally, margin is the equity money an investor provides for the transaction, and the amount that the investor borrows is the debit balance or broker's loan. The Securities Exchange Act of 1934 empowers the Federal Reserve Board to set initial margin requirements on purchases of both stocks and bonds. *Initial margin* is the minimum amount of equity money an investor must provide at the time of purchasing a security.

EXAMPLE

If the initial margin requirement is 50 percent, then you would have to put up $5,000 in cash to buy $10,000 worth of stock. If you expect that the value of the stock will rise to $12,000 and that you will receive no dividend, then (ignoring transaction costs) you would expect to earn 40 percent:

$$\frac{\text{Expected}}{\text{rate of return}} = \frac{\text{Selling price} - \text{Purchase price}}{\text{Cash investment}} + \frac{\text{Dividends}}{\text{Cash investment}}$$

$$= \frac{\$12,000 - \$10,000}{\$10,000 - \$5,000} + 0$$

$$= 0.40, \text{ or } 40\%$$

If you had not margined the stock, then your expected rate of return falls to 20 percent because your cash investment rises to the full purchase price:

$$\text{Expected rate of return} = \frac{\$12,000 - \$10,000}{\$10,000} + 0$$

$$= 0.20, \text{ or } 20\%$$

Note that buying on margin magnifies not only potential gains but also potential losses. Compare your losses with a margin versus a cash purchase if the stock value drops from $10,000 to $8,000. (*Answer:* −40 percent versus −20 percent.)

When you borrow money from a broker to buy stock, you must pay interest on the loan. Sometimes interest charges on margin accounts rise to very high levels, cooling off speculation in the market. Besides the initial margin requirements imposed by the Federal Reserve Board, brokers also require you to preserve a maintenance margin in your account. *Maintenance margin* is the difference between the value of the stock in your account and the amount you owe the broker. Typically, maintenance margin requirements are at least 25 percent of the value of stock held in a margin account.[6]

short sale

Security sale made with borrowed securities.

A **short sale** is any security sale completed with borrowed securities. Investors sell a stock short when they firmly believe that its price will decline. When

---

[6]The minimum to which the stock price can fall without a request from the broker for more maintenance margin (a *margin* or *house call*) is calculated as follows:

$$\frac{(V - D)}{V} = 0.25$$

short-selling, an investor tries to sell a stock at a high price, then buy it back later at a low price to cover the short sale. Here is what happens in a successful short sale: (1) The short-seller borrows stock from a broker and sells the stock through the same broker. (2) Later, when the stock price drops, the investor buys shares of the stock to replace those previously borrowed. (3) The investor pockets the difference between the selling price in Step 1 and the buying price in Step 2. Brokerage companies have standard operating procedures set up to allow investors to sell short.

EXAMPLE

American Hermetics (AH) common stock trades at $70 a share and you sell short 100 shares through your broker because you strongly believe the price will decline. Two months later the price per share has dropped to $55, and you call your broker to cover (close out) the short position:

Sold short 100 shares of AH at $70 a share	$7,000
Less 100 shares of AH bought at $55 a share	− 5,500
Gain (ignoring transaction costs)	$1,500

What happens if American Hermetics stock rises to $85 a share when you close out your short position? [*Answer:* You lose $1,500: 100 shares × ($85 − $70).] What is the most you can lose? (*Answer:* Depends on how high the stock price rises.)

Generally, an investor can hold open a short sale for an indefinite period of time, although the investor must close it out eventually. During this period of time the investor pays the broker any dividends paid on the borrowed shares.[7] In addition, the investor must have a specified amount of collateral (determined by margin rates) on hand at the brokerage company.

Measuring Stock Price Behavior

The collective transactions of all stock investors—buying, selling, buying on margin, and short-selling—cause stock prices to change daily. Corporate financial managers pay attention to these changes for two reasons. First, the overall direction of stock prices helps managers to forecast business conditions because the stock market is a leading indicator of general business activity. Second, the

---

where V = current value of the stock

D = debit balance, the dollar amount owed the broker

In the example a broker issues a margin call for more cash when the market value of the stock drops to $6,667:

$$\frac{V - \$5,000}{V} = 0.25$$

$$V = \$6,667$$

[7] Actually, the short-seller pays the dividend through the broker to the investor who loaned the stock. Stocks that are loaned for short sales are held in *street name* (broker's name), although they are owned by one of the broker's customers. The investor who bought the shorted stock receives the dividend from the paying company. The buyer's name replaces the lender's name on the company's registry of shareholders.

behavior of stock prices in general is associated in varying degrees with the price of each stock trading in the market. As the overall market for stocks rises and falls, there is a tendency for an individual stock price to rise and fall. Consequently, financial managers need to be aware of market movements to assess their influence on the company's stock price.

The major factor affecting the general level of common-stock prices is investor expectations of economic growth and stability. If investors become confident that a business expansion will be sustained and company profits will rise, then stock prices will generally increase (a **bull market**). In contrast, if investors lose confidence and expect an economic recession or depression that will cause company profits to decline, then stock prices will generally decrease (a **bear market**). Because companies tend to do well when the economy as a whole grows and to do poorly when it stagnates or declines, the stock prices of different companies tend to rise and fall in unison.

Financial managers and investors look at movements in the averages and indexes of stock prices to see whether the stock market is bullish or bearish. Managers and investors typically use the terms *average* and *index* interchangeably, but technically they are different measures. An *average*, for example, might be the arithmetic average price of a group of stocks at a point in time; an *index* measures the current price of a group of stocks in relation to a base value at an earlier point in time. Of the several publicly available averages and indexes, we examine two that are widely followed: (1) the Dow Jones Industrial Average and (2) Standard & Poor's 500 Index.

bull market
Period of rising stock prices.

bear market
Period of falling stock prices.

Dow Jones Industrial Average (DJIA)
Stock price average of a group of 30 industrial companies.

Dow Jones Industrial Average.   The **Dow Jones Industrial Average (DJIA)** consists of 30 industrial common stocks of companies such as General Motors, Sears, Exxon, IBM, and McDonald's. Prepared by Dow Jones & Company Inc., publishers of *Barron's* and *The Wall Street Journal*, the DJIA dates back to 1884. Its longevity largely explains its present popularity as a stock market indicator.

Financial managers and investors use *changes* in the DJIA to assess what is happening to stock prices in general. Generally, if they know what is happening to the DJIA, then they know what is happening to the stock market. The actual level of the DJIA is not what is important; changes are the important information.

EXAMPLE

On Thursday, January 8, 1987, the DJIA broke the 2000 level for the first time in its history by closing at 2002.25. What can you conclude? Probably very little, unless you knew where it started. For example, if the Average started at 1943 on Thursday's opening and moved to 2002.25 on the close, you might be impressed; a 3 percent movement in one day is unusual. Alternatively, a movement from 1993.95 (the actual opening) to 2002.25 is not impressive.

Some historical values for the DJIA will give you a feel for its interpretation. The Average reached 386 in 1929 just before the great market crash; in 1932 it stood at 41, an extraordinary decline of 90 percent. Not until 1954, 25 years later, did the Average again reach the 386 level of 1929. It reached 1500 for the first time in 1985 and 2000 for the first time in 1987. Later in 1987 it broke 2700 (intramonth), but astonishingly, it crashed to 1738, on October 19, 1987.

The loss was made up by 1989, and the Average rose above 3000 in 1991 and 3600 in 1993. Figure 3.8 shows the Average's recent history.

Although investors refer to the Dow Jones Industrial Average as an average, it is not really an arithmetic average price of stocks. The average price of the 30 stocks in the DJIA is nowhere near $2,000, $1,000, or even $200. At the beginning of 1992 the average price per share of the 30 stocks approximated $49.

The disparity between average stock price and the Dow Jones Industrial Average occurs because, among other reasons, Dow Jones & Company occasionally changes the stocks in the index.[8] We can illustrate the effects of these changes with the following simplified example. First, construct an average for, say, three stocks, X, Y, and Z:

Stock	Price per Share
X	$10
Y	20
Z	30
	Total $60

Arithmetic average: $60/3 = $20

At this point in time, the average stands at $20. Suppose Company Z is replaced with Company N (for New), whose price is only $15 per share. We might make this change because Company Z is no longer an important corporation and Company N is a fast-growing manufacturer of compact disks. With no adjustment to recognize the switch in companies, the arithmetic average drops from $20 to $15 [($10 + $20 + $15)/3]. Such a decline would give a false signal to investors and financial managers. The average drops from $20 to $15 simply because Stock N replaces Stock Z, not because of a general decline in stock prices.

Dow Jones & Company wants its Average to reflect changes in stock prices, not switches in companies. Following its system, we want the preceding arithmetic average to stay at $20 because stock prices have not changed. To force the average back to $20 from $15, we must change the divisor from 3 to a smaller number that will keep the average at $20:

$$\text{Adjusted average} = \text{Sum of stock prices/New divisor}$$

$$20 = \$45/\text{New divisor}$$

$$\text{New divisor} = 2.25$$

The dollar sign is omitted from this 20 because it is not an average of three stock prices; it is an average adjusted for the substitution of Stock N for Stock Z. As a result of such adjustments, the changes in the DJIA are stated in *points* rather than dollars.

Although simpler than the Dow Jones Industrial Average, the average in the above example illustrates the process that Dow Jones & Company follows to adjust for changes in the composition of the 30 stocks. Without adjustments to the divisor, the DJIA would jump up or down each time the composition of the Average is changed. So when Dow Jones & Company computes the DJIA, it does not divide 30 stock prices by the number 30. It divides the 30 stock prices by a divisor that was 8.92 in 1950, 1.443 in 1979, 1.09 in 1985, and 0.4627 in 1992.

---

[8] Stock splits and stock dividends (not *cash* dividends) also create a disparity between average stock price and the DJIA. Chapter 19 explains the nature of stock splits and stock dividends.

FIGURE 3.8   **Dow Jones Industrial Average: Month-End Values for 1950–1992**

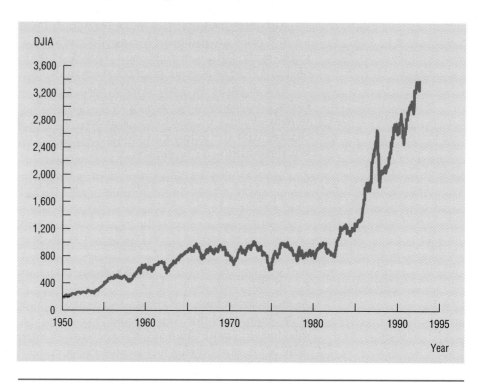

Source: The Wall Street Journal, various issues.

You can find today's divisor in *The Wall Street Journal* below the charts located in the stock quotation section.

Some investors criticize the DJIA because it consists of only 30 stocks. Moreover, all 30 stocks in the DJIA are blue-chip stocks, stocks of highly regarded and well-established companies. Critics charge that the DJIA is not representative of the broad market. In its defense, we should note that although the DJIA contains less than 2 percent of all stocks listed on the New York Stock Exchange, those stocks account for roughly one-fourth of the total market value of all NYSE-listed stocks. Investors wanting a market indicator consisting of more than 30 stocks can use Standard & Poor's 500 Index.

Standard & Poor's 500 Index (S&P 500)

Stock price index of 500 industrial, utility, transportation, and financial corporations.

Standard & Poor's 500 Index.   Standard & Poor's 500 Index (S&P 500) consists of 500 common stocks: 400 industrial companies, 40 public utilities, 20 transportation companies, and 40 financial firms. The Index is therefore more representative of the broad market than is the Dow Jones Industrial Average. Movements in the Index generally reflect movements in the price of a typical common stock.

Unlike the DJIA, which is a modified arithmetic average of prices, the S&P 500 Index compares the total market value of 500 stocks with their base value during the years 1941–1943:

$$\text{S\&P 500 Index} = \frac{\text{Total market value of 500 stocks}}{\text{Average total market value, 1941–1943}} \times 10$$

Standard & Poor's 500 Index: Month-End Values for 1950–1992

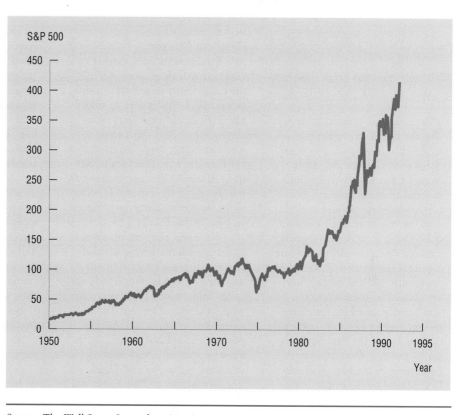

Source: *The Wall Street Journal*, various issues.

For the period 1941–1943 the value in the numerator equals that in the denominator, producing a ratio of 1. Not wanting to start the Index with such a small number, Standard & Poor's Corporation multiplied the Index by 10, and this number begins the average Index value for 1941–1943.

Figure 3.9 shows a recent history of the S&P 500. Starting at 20 in 1950, it climbed to 118 in the early 1970s. It broke 300 for the first time in 1987 and reached 417 in 1992. A comparison of Figures 3.8 and 3.9 shows the similarity between the peaks and valleys. Both Standard & Poor's 500 Index and the Dow Jones Industrial Average show the economic downturn caused by the OPEC oil embargo in 1973. Both indicators also reflect the bull market of the 1980s. The Index and the Average, although quite different in composition, react similarly to market expectations of economic growth and stability.[9]

Chapter 5 uses Standard & Poor's 500 Index in a procedure to estimate the risk in owning individual common stocks. Comparing individual stock prices with the Index permits us to classify the risk of stocks relative to the risk of the market as measured by the Index.

[9] *The Wall Street Journal* reports values for several other stock indexes. For example, it reports on the New York Stock Exchange Composite Index, which includes all common stocks on the NYSE; and on the Wilshire 5000, which contains more than 6,000 common stocks, including many from the over-the-counter market.

I N T E R N A T I O N A L   D I M E N S I O N S

International Financial Markets

Supply and demand determine the cost and availability of funds in international financial markets just as they do in domestic financial markets. International financial markets, however, include money and capital markets that have attributes not shared with their domestic counterparts. For example, the international money market is not simply the totality of local money markets available in each country. It also contains markets for currencies on deposit in banks outside the country of the currency's origin. A primary illustration is the *Eurocurrency* market, in which U.S. dollars on deposit in banks located in Europe or other non-U.S. locations *(Eurodollars)* are loaned out to borrowers. *Euroyen* deposits—Japanese currency deposited in the United States or some other country—are another example, as are *Euromark* depos-

its—German currency deposited outside of Germany.

The Eurocurrency market's rapid growth since inception in the early 1950s to trillions of dollars in the 1990s is easy to understand. Financial managers often can invest surplus short-term funds at higher rates in this market than are available locally. Similarly, financial managers often can borrow short term in the Eurocurrency market at lower rates than are obtainable locally.

The bond segment of international capital markets is divided into two categories: *Eurobonds* and *foreign bonds*. Eurobonds are issues sold outside the country in whose currency they are denominated. For example, a U.S. company might sell bonds denominated in U.S. dollars to investors in Europe and Japan. The advantages of Eurobonds are the lax governmental and disclosure requirements for issuers and the comparatively lenient tax rules for investors.

Foreign bonds are issues sold in one country, denominated in the currency of that country, by

an issuer from another country. A typical case is the "Samurai" bond: A U.S. (or other non-Japanese) company sells bonds in Japan, denominated in yen, to Japanese investors. Foreign bonds sold in the United States are "Yankee" bonds, and those sold in the United Kingdom are "Bulldog" bonds.

International equity markets afford companies the opportunity to broaden ownership of their shares and possibly lower the cost of equity funds. For this reason and despite operational peculiarities of foreign stock exchanges, the number of companies listing their shares in both domestic and overseas markets has been increasing. Dual listings are leading to further integration of the world's capital markets.

Because of the globalization of business, financial managers need to be familiar with foreign currencies, some of which have odd names. The following table lists several countries and their corresponding currencies:

Country	Currency	Country	Currency
Argentina	Peso	Greece	Drachma
Australia	Dollar	Hungary	Forint
Austria	Schilling	India	Rupee
Bahrain	Dinar	Indonesia	Rupiah
Belgium	Franc	Ireland	Punt
Brazil	Cruzeiro	Israel	Shekel
Britain	Pound	Italy	Lira
Canada	Dollar	Japan	Yen
China	Renminbi	Malaysia	Ringgit
Denmark	Krone	Mexico	Peso
Ecuador	Sucre	Netherlands	Guilder
Finland	Markka	Saudi Arabia	Riyal
France	Franc	Thailand	Baht
Germany	Mark	Venezuela	Bolivar

SUMMARY

- The Securities Act of 1933 and the blue sky laws regulate the primary (or new-issues) market. The Act of 1933 requires nonexempt companies to file a registration statement (Form S-1) and to deliver a prospectus to a purchaser before completing a security sale. Exempt offerings include intrastate issues. The Act of 1933 prohibits fraud in the preparation and distribution of information to investors. States impose blue sky laws that regulate new issues within state borders.

- Investment banking firms are the primary force in the public new-issues market. The major functions performed by investment banking firms are origination, underwriting, syndication, and distribution. Origination consists of the planning of features and the timing of a new security issue. Underwriting is the outright purchase for resale of a security issue by a group of investment banking firms. Syndication is the temporary combining of investment banking firms to acquire and distribute a new issue. A tombstone ad published in the financial press portrays the underwriting syndicate. Distribution is the marketing of a new issue to investors.

- A company incurs two kinds of flotation (or placement) costs when issuing securities through investment bankers:

$$\frac{\text{Total flotation}}{\text{costs}} = \frac{\text{Underwriting}}{\text{spread}} + \frac{\text{Issuing expenses}}{\text{of company}}$$

The underwriting spread, earned by the investment bankers, is the difference between the market value of the securities and the proceeds received by the issuing company. Issuing expenses of the company are out-of-pocket expenses such as attorney fees, accounting expenses, and costs for printing security certificates and prospectuses.

- Private placement is the issuance of a security in a nonpublic offering, usually to avoid registration and other flotation costs, including investment banking fees. Private placements frequently involve placing bonds with large institutional investors.

- The Securities Exchange Act of 1934 regulates the secondary market. This act established the Securities and Exchange Commission (SEC) and gave it regulatory responsibility for both the primary and secondary markets. Companies listed on organized exchanges must file annual (10-K) and quarterly (10-Q) reports with the SEC. Organized exchanges themselves must register with the SEC. The 1934 act prohibits the use of inside information for making profit in the stock market.

- The stock market consists of both organized exchanges and the over-the-counter (OTC) market. The OTC market is a network of dealers who make markets in about 50,000 different common stocks. A major characteristic of an organized exchange is the auction process conducted by a specialist. Specialists make markets for specific stocks assigned to them. *The Wall Street Journal* and other newspapers publish price quotations of stocks and bonds listed on organized exchanges and those that trade in the OTC market.

- Organized exchanges and the over-the-counter market permit investors to buy on margin and to sell short. To buy on margin means to borrow a percentage of a stock's purchase price. To sell short means to sell a stock that you do not own but can borrow with the help of a broker. A short-seller hopes that the stock price will decline so that the stock may subsequently be purchased cheaply to replace the borrowed shares.

• An index or market average measures the general level of stock prices. Two widely used measures are the Dow Jones Industrial Average (DJIA) and Standard & Poor's 500 Index (S&P 500). Persistent increases in these measures denote a bull market; persistent decreases denote a bear market.

Key Terms

Securities Act of 1933	flotation costs	odd lot
registration statement (Form S-1)	negotiated sale	dividend payout ratio
Securities and Exchange Commission (SEC)	best-efforts agreement	dividend yield
prospectus	standby underwriting	price-earnings ratio
red herring	competitive-bid procedure	current yield
public utility	initial public offering (IPO)	margin buying
shelf offering	tombstone	short sale
blue sky laws	underwriting spread	bull market
origination	Securities Exchange Act of 1934	bear market
underwriting	stock market	Dow Jones Industrial Average (DJIA)
syndication	specialist	Standard & Poor's 500 Index (S&P 500)
distribution	round lot	

Questions

3.1. Clearly distinguish between the Securities Act of 1933 and the Securities Exchange Act of 1934. Make sure that you identify which one regulates the use of inside information.

3.2. The Securities Act of 1933 exempts U.S. agency issues from the requirements for registration with the Securities and Exchange Commission. What reasoning can you suggest for this exemption?

3.3. *(CMA examination, modified)*[10]   The Securities and Exchange Commission's fraud rule prohibits stock trading on the basis of inside information by:
  a. Officers.
  b. Officers and directors.
  c. All officers, directors, and stockholders.
  d. Officers, directors, and holders of 10 percent of the corporation's stock.
  e. Anyone who bases trading activities on nonpublic information.

  Explain your choice and define the term *inside information*.

3.4. Blue sky laws are similar in some respects to the Securities Act of 1933 and dissimilar in others. List and discuss the similarities and dissimilarities.

3.5. Consult Figure 3.2 and provide responses to the following:
  a. Contrast a negotiated sale and a competitive bid.
  b. Describe the three types of negotiated sales listed in Figure 3.2.

3.6. Although investment bankers stand ready to perform four basic functions, a company issuing securities may not require all of them to be performed. The company itself may perform one or more of the functions.
  a. Describe the four basic functions performed by investment bankers.
  b. Which function does an investment banker exclude in a *best-efforts agreement*? Explain.

3.7. Describe the two types of flotation costs incurred by a company that issues securities. Which one is likely to be larger?

[10]The CMA examination is a five-part examination that a candidate must pass in order to become a certified management accountant (CMA). See Appendix 1A for more information about the CMA certification program.

3.8. Listing a security on an exchange provides advantages to a corporation. Indicate whether each statement below is true or false and explain the italicized words.
   a. Listing is likely to lower the investor's *required rate of return*.
   b. A good *secondary market* is likely to facilitate the sale of new issues.
   c. Issuing new common stock through a *specialist* is likely to result in lower transaction costs to the firm.
   d. *Delisting* is likely to decrease a stock's *liquidity*.

3.9. Stocks trade in both the over-the-counter market and on organized exchanges. (a) Explain the major differences between these two markets, and (b) comment specifically on the contrast between the roles of dealers and specialists.

3.10. Define the following terms: *dividend payout ratio, dividend yield,* and *price-earnings ratio.* Show the relationship among these terms in an equation.

3.11. Corporate bond quotations show a bond's *coupon rate* and *current yield.* Define the two terms and show the relationship between them in an equation.

3.12. Margin trading and short-selling are two ways to participate in securities trading that are usually considered to be speculative. Define each of these terms and comment on which type of trade you would like to have during (a) a bull market, (b) a bear market.

3.13. *(CFA examination, modified)*[11] The SEC requires publicly traded corporations to make 10-Q forms available to shareholders. Explain what a 10-Q form is and discuss why the SEC places this requirement on corporations.

3.14. *(CFA examination, modified)* From your knowledge of a company, you estimate that 19X7 earnings per share will be about $1.50. Based on your estimate, you believe you should sell the company's stock short. The next day you visit the company's president, who tells you in confidence that her earnings estimate is $6.60 because the company received a large contract to supply material to General Dynamics. If you now buy the stock, do you risk legal action? Explain your answer.

3.15. Compare and contrast the Dow Jones Industrial Average with Standard & Poor's 500 Index. Why do we call one an average and one an index?

3.16. The Dow Jones Industrial Average (DJIA) plunged a record 39.10 points to 1526.61 on January 8, 1986. In percentage terms, this slide in the DJIA came nowhere near that of the Great Crash in 1929. The 39.10 points, however, did exceed the previous record decline of 38.33 points on October 28, 1929. Moreover, the 39.10-point decline occurred on a day when volume on the NYSE reached 180,000,000 shares, the fifth largest total on record.
   a. What is the relevance and importance of the large volume of shares traded on the day of the record decline in the DJIA?
   b. What do you suppose happened to the S&P 500 on January 8, 1986? How confident are you of your answer? Explain.
   c. One day recently the DJIA increased by two points. What do you suppose happened to the S&P 500 on that day? How confident are you of your answer? Explain.

Strategy Problem

Suppose that you see in the newspaper the following stock quotation for SuperCo Corporation Inc.:

$40\frac{1}{8}$ $15\frac{3}{8}$ SprCo SPC .85 3.9 10 421 $21\frac{3}{4}$ $21\frac{1}{8}$ $21\frac{3}{4}$ $+\frac{5}{8}$

a. Calculate the company's earnings per share.
b. What would be your percentage gain if you bought SuperCo at its low price for the past 12 months and sold it at its high price? Include the annual dividend in your calculation.
c. Suppose that you sell short a round lot of SuperCo common stock at its closing price and cover the sale 3 weeks later at $15\frac{1}{4}$. To sell stock short, your broker requires you to invest 55 percent of the short-sale price. If transaction costs total $100 when you cover your short sale, then what is your percentage gain? (The company did not pay a dividend.)
d. Suppose that you buy a round lot on margin at the closing price. The margin requirement is 55 percent, and your broker charges $78.30 interest on the debit balance. SuperCo pays the dividend indicated in the stock quotation above. Calculate your rate of return on the investment assuming you sell the stock one year later for $26\frac{7}{8}$ and brokerage commissions are $72 on each transaction (buying and selling).

[11] The CFA examination is a three-level examination that a candidate must pass in order to become a chartered financial analyst (CFA). See Appendix 1A for more information about the CFA certification program.

Strategy	**Solution**

a. The stock quotation gives the closing price ($21\frac{3}{4}$) and the earnings multiple (10):

The P-E ratio is 10 and P is $21.75.

$$\frac{P}{E} = 10$$

$$\frac{\$21.75}{E} = 10$$

Solve for E, the earnings per share.

$$E = \$2.175 \text{ per share}$$

b. The percentage gain on the stock is the capital gain yield plus the dividend yield:

Combine the capital gain and dividend.

Divide by the cash investment, or buying price.

$$\frac{\text{Percentage}}{\text{gain}} = \frac{(\text{Selling price} - \text{Buying price}) + \text{Cash dividend}}{\text{Buying price}}$$

$$= \frac{(\$40.125 - \$15.375) + \$0.85}{\$15.375}$$

$$= 1.665, \text{ or } 166.5\%$$

c. The percentage gain is the dollar gain adjusted for transaction costs, all expressed as a percentage of the cash investment:

Start by calculating net gain.

Selling price (100 shares × $21.75)	$2,175
Less purchase price (100 shares × $15.25)	1,525
Gain	$ 650
Less transaction costs	100
Net gain	$ 550

Divide net gain by the cash investment.

$$\text{Percentage gain} = \frac{\$550}{0.55 \times \$2,175}$$

$$= 0.46, \text{ or } 46\%$$

d. The rate of return is the net proceeds less the cash investment, all expressed as a percentage of the cash investment:

Begin by calculating the cash investment.

Cash investment

Total cost of 100 shares (100 shares × $21.75)	$2,175.00
Multiply by margin rate	× 0.55

Do not overlook the commission.

Cash invested in stock	$1,196.25
Add commission	72.00
Cash investment	$1,268.25

Calculate net proceeds. Add total dividend to selling price of 100 shares.

Net proceeds

Selling price of 100 shares (100 × $26.875)	$2,687.50
Add dividend (100 × $0.85)	85.00
Cash received from stock	$2,772.50

Do not forget interest expense and the selling commission.

Less costs		
Interest charges	$78.30	
Commission	72.00	150.30
Proceeds		$2,622.20
Less loan repayment (0.45 × $2,175)		978.75
Net proceeds		$1,643.45

Calculate rate of return.

$$\text{Rate of return} = \frac{\$1,643.45 - \$1,268.25}{\$1,268.25}$$

$$= 0.296, \text{ or } 29.6\% \text{ per year}$$

◆ **Demonstration Problem**

Michael Olmsted is the sole owner of a large dairy manufacturing and wholesaling company. Mr. Olmsted wants to expand his business, but he does not have sufficient personal funds for the expansion. To finance it, he is considering the issuance of common stock and bonds to the investing public. His major competitor is Borden Inc., whose common stock and bonds were recently quoted as follows:

Common Stock
$34\frac{7}{8}$ $26\frac{1}{4}$ BordenInc. BN 1.20 4.5 14 3025 27 $26\frac{5}{8}$ $26\frac{7}{8}$ $+\frac{1}{4}$

Corporate Bond
Bordn $10\frac{1}{4}$95 10.0 17 $102\frac{1}{4}$ $-\frac{1}{4}$

Because of his unfamiliarity with the primary and secondary capital markets, Mr. Olmsted has yet to contact an investment banker about his expansion plans. Instead, he has hired you to explain to him various aspects of capital markets. In response to a preliminary discussion with Mr. Olmsted, you decide to cover several topics during the next meeting with him. The meeting is scheduled for tomorrow, and you must now develop responses for each topic.

a. Contrast the Securities Act of 1933 with the Securities Exchange Act of 1934.
b. Describe the basic functions of investment bankers in helping companies issue securities in the primary market.
c. Assume that Mr. Olmsted issues 1,000,000 shares of common stock at $50 per share. The underwriting spread is $1.50 per share, and Mr. Olmsted's out-of-pocket costs are $500,000 for legal fees, accounting services, and printing and engraving. Calculate (1) total flotation costs, (2) flotation costs as a percentage of gross proceeds ($50,000,000), and (3) flotation costs per share of stock issued.
d. Identify each part of the common-stock quotation for Borden Inc.
e. Based on the common-stock quotation, calculate the following for Borden Inc.: (1) closing price on the preceding trading day, (2) dividend yield, (3) earnings per share, and (4) dividend payout ratio.
f. Identify each part of the bond quotation for Borden Inc.
g. Based on the bond quotation, calculate the following for Borden Inc.: (1) closing price in dollars, (2) net change in closing price in dollars, and (3) current yield.
h. Contrast the calculation of the Dow Jones Industrial Average with the calculation of Standard & Poor's 500 Index.

Problems

Flotation costs: dollars, percentage, per share

3.1. Textron Inc. issued 500,000 shares of common stock through investment bankers. The stock sold to the public for $35 a share, but Textron received $33.25 a share. Textron's out-of-pocket costs equaled $225,000.
a. Calculate Textron's total flotation costs in dollars.
b. Calculate Textron's total flotation costs as a percentage of gross proceeds (selling price).
c. Calculate Textron's total flotation costs per share of stock issued.

Proceeds and underwriting spreads

3.2. Fellner, Fall, Fallon, and Little is an investment banking firm managing a $350,000,000 (at market or resale value) bond issue.
a. The gross spread on this issue is 70 basis points (100 basis points = 1 percent). How much cash does the issuing corporation receive on the issue?
b. The spread is allocated in the following manner: manager, 20 percent; underwriters, 30 percent; and distributors, 50 percent. Determine how much Fellner, Fall, Fallon, and Little earns on a $10,000,000 sale that it:
(1) Makes to investors.

(2) Makes to dealers in the selling group.

(3) Merely manages.

Spreads and losses on OTC stock

3.3. Suppose you buy 10,000 shares of Oronco Company common stock. The stock trades over the counter and the dealer's bid and asked prices are $1.50 and $1.75, respectively. The commission cost for buying (or selling) 10,000 shares is $250.

a. How much money do you pay in total for the 10,000 shares?

b. Suppose that you must sell the shares two days later because of a financial emergency. How much money do you receive, assuming the bid-asked prices remain unchanged?

c. Calculate the percentage loss on your two-day investment.

Spreads and gains on OTC stock

3.4. Bob Jennings bought 500 shares of Cadiz common stock and sold them one year later. The dealer's bid-asked prices were as follows:

	Bid Price	Asked Price
Beginning of year	$9\frac{7}{8}$	10
End of year	$14\frac{1}{4}$	$15\frac{3}{8}$

Cadiz common stock does not pay dividends. Mr. Jennings paid a $100 commission when he bought the stock and $150 when he sold. Calculate Mr. Jennings' rate of return on the investment.

Interpreting NYSE quotations

3.5. The following is a stock quotation for Winn Dixie, a supermarket chain listed on the NYSE:

$$50\tfrac{5}{8} \quad 37\tfrac{1}{2} \quad \text{Winn Dixie} \quad \text{WIN} \quad 1.92 \quad 3.9 \quad 14 \quad 101 \quad 49\tfrac{3}{4} \quad 49\tfrac{1}{4} \quad 49\tfrac{1}{4} \quad -\tfrac{3}{8}$$

a. Identify each part of the stock quotation.

b. What was the closing price on the preceding trading day?

c. Show with an equation the way to calculate Winn Dixie's dividend yield.

Interpreting NYSE quotations

3.6. The following is a stock quotation for Exxon Company, a major oil company listed on the NYSE:

$$47\tfrac{3}{4} \quad 40\tfrac{3}{8} \quad \text{Exxon} \quad \text{XON} \quad 2.20 \quad 5.0 \quad 11 \quad 19785 \quad 44\tfrac{1}{8} \quad 43\tfrac{5}{8} \quad 43\tfrac{3}{4} \quad -\tfrac{1}{2}$$

a. Identify each part of the stock quotation.

b. Calculate Exxon's dividend yield.

c. Calculate Exxon's earnings per share.

d. Calculate Exxon's dividend payout ratio.

Interpreting NYSE quotations

3.7. The following stock quotations for Coca-Cola and Pepsi Cola were taken from *The Wall Street Journal,* Friday's issue:

$$60\tfrac{1}{8} \quad 36\tfrac{1}{4} \quad \text{Coca Cola} \quad \text{KO} \quad 1.36 \quad 2.4 \quad 19 \quad 7442 \quad 58\tfrac{1}{8} \quad 57\tfrac{1}{4} \quad 57\tfrac{1}{2} \quad -\tfrac{1}{2}$$
$$55\tfrac{1}{4} \quad 33\tfrac{1}{2} \quad \text{PepsiCo} \quad \text{PEP} \quad 1.00 \quad 1.9 \quad 17 \quad 7311 \quad 54\tfrac{1}{8} \quad 53\tfrac{1}{4} \quad 53\tfrac{1}{2} \quad -\tfrac{3}{4}$$

a. These data are for stock trades on what day?

b. Which company provides the larger dividend yield? Show how both yields are calculated.

c. Calculate the earnings per share for each company.

d. Calculate the dividend payout ratio for each company.

Interpreting a bond quotation

3.8. The following is a quotation of one of Rapid American Corporation's bonds:

$$\text{RapA} \quad 7\text{s}94 \quad 11.3 \quad 5 \quad 62 \quad +2$$

a. Identify each part of the bond quotation. (Some bond quotations, such as this one, have the letter *s* following the coupon rate. The *s* pluralizes the coupon rate so investors may refer to the bond as Rapid American's 7s.)

b. Calculate the current yield on the bond.

c. What was the price of the bond on the preceding trading day? (Face value is $1,000.)

Bond quotation, dollar interest, and volume

3.9. *The Wall Street Journal* quoted Eastman Kodak's bond as follows:

$$\text{Ekod} \quad 8\tfrac{5}{8}16 \quad 8.3 \quad 198 \quad 104 \quad +\tfrac{1}{2}$$

    a. How much money would it cost you to buy 10 of these bonds?

    b. How much dollar interest would you receive each year if you bought 10 of these bonds?

    c. Calculate the current yield on the bond.

    d. Why do most corporate bond quotations show relatively small volumes—numbers of bonds traded for the day?

Variation in bond quotations

3.10. Figure 3.7 in this chapter shows two bond quotations for Alaska Airlines. Consult that figure to answer the following questions:

    a. What type of bond does the first quotation describe?

    b. What type of bond does the second quotation describe?

    c. Why is the price of the bond in the second quotation so low?

Bond quotation and capital gains

3.11. The following is a quotation for one of several different bonds issued by American Telephone and Telegraph (AT&T):

$$\text{ATT} \quad 5\tfrac{1}{8}01 \quad 5.7 \quad 165 \quad 90\tfrac{1}{2} \quad +\tfrac{3}{4}$$

    a. Calculate the current yield on the bond.

    b. In what year does the bond mature?

    c. In addition to the interest payment, how much money will AT&T pay the holder of one bond at maturity?

    d. If you buy one AT&T bond at $90\tfrac{1}{2}$ and hold it until maturity, how many dollars of capital gain will you earn?

Rate of return on a short sale

3.12. Carol Ruff had a bearish outlook on Southwest Oil Company (SOC). She thought it likely that the members of the OPEC oil cartel would break ranks and increase their production of oil. If that happened, the price per 42-gallon barrel of oil would decline, causing the value of SOC's oil production to decline as well. Ms. Ruff believed that SOC's profits and stock price were going to fall. Acting on her beliefs, she sold short 1,000 shares of SOC stock at $26 per share. Ms. Ruff's broker, John Whitehorne, said she needed cash on hand at the brokerage firm equal to 50 percent of the short-sale value. Moreover, Mr. Whitehorne charged her $350 in commissions for the short sale. Regrettably for Ms. Ruff, the price per barrel of oil skyrocketed, carrying SOC's stock price with it. Becoming nervous over her losses, Ms. Ruff finally closed out the short sale by purchasing 1,000 shares of SOC stock at $35 per share. Mr. Whitehorne charged her $390 to make the purchase. Assuming that SOC did not pay a dividend while Ms. Ruff held open her short position, what was her percentage loss?

Rate of return on margined stock

3.13. R. L. Roddy bought 100 shares of Apex Development common stock at $148\tfrac{7}{8}$ a share. He purchased the stock on margin when the margin requirement was 55 percent, and he paid his broker $172 in commissions. By year-end Mr. Roddy decided to sell his stock after he read it was selling for $170\tfrac{1}{8}$ a share. His broker charged him $186 in commissions and $669.94 interest on the debit balance. If Apex Development paid a $4.40 dividend per share at the end of the year, what was Mr. Roddy's rate of return?

Calculating the DJIA

3.14. Assume that the Dow Jones Industrial Average (DJIA) consists of only four stocks. Call them A, B, C, and D. Prices per share of the stocks are: A = $10, B = $20, C = $30, and D = $40. Using the procedure employed by Dow Jones & Company, compute the following:

    a. DJIA.

    b. The simple average if Stock H replaces Stock D. Stock H's price is $8 per share.

    c. Compute the new divisor necessary to keep the DJIA at its amount in Part *a* above.

(VHS)

VIDEO CASE PROBLEM

NexStarr Broadcasting Inc.

By 1981 Kevin Wyatt had saved and borrowed enough money to follow his dream of owning a television broadcasting station. The small station catered to the young and the young at heart with a mix of western-swing and rock video programming. The format was a great success, with more and better programming each year. Audience ratings were on the rise, as was the station's profitability.

After three years of operating the station, Wyatt realized that he had "hit a wall." His vision of broadcasting extended well beyond what could be accomplished with one station. Thus during the next eight years, Wyatt acquired and operated six more stations, but he still remained unsatisfied. He envisioned a broadcasting company that would reach all of the major U.S. markets—perhaps Canada and Mexico as well. His vision even carried him to Europe and the Far East, especially Japan.

With the help of the investment banking firm Kidder, Peabody & Co., Wyatt merged his company with NexStarr, a medium-sized cable company. The merger agreement called for Wyatt to be the chief executive officer of NexStarr, the surviving company. Former CEO Richard Carter became chairman of the board, and Liddy Farrel continued as chief financial officer. Having successfully completed the merger, Wyatt turned his attention toward global expansion.

Carter and Farrel agree in principle with the concept of expansion, but they are concerned about how to raise the $200,000,000 needed to finance the plan: (1) Should NexStarr issue common stock, bonds, or some combination of the two? (2) Currently, NexStarr has 8,000,000 shares of stock outstanding. Carter owns 35 percent of the shares, Wyatt owns 15 percent, and Farrel owns 5 percent. The remaining shares trade in the over-the-counter market. Would a stock issue cause a loss of control? (3) NexStarr's present capital structure includes $160,000,000 of debt in the form of bonds and $140,000,000 of shareholder equity. Would a bond issue cause undue financial risk for the company? (4) How much money would an investment banker charge to underwrite an issuance of common stock? An issuance of bonds?

Wyatt realizes that these concerns will have to be addressed at the meeting of the board of directors next month. He expects approval of the expansion, but he is unsure of the board's position on financing for the expansion. In fact, he is unsure of his own position on the matter and asks Farrel for more information to clarify the issues.

The second agenda item for the upcoming board meeting concerns whether or not management should apply to list NexStarr's common stock on the New York Stock Exchange (NYSE). The stock currently trades over-the-counter among NASDAQ's National Market Issues. Joseph Hardiman, CEO of the National Association of Securities Dealers (NASD) and its subsidiary NASDAQ, describes the market in a *Schwab Report* newsletter:

> The traditional stock exchange is built around trading floors, where buyers and sellers of stock physically interact with each other. NASDAQ, on the other hand, is built around computerized, or, as we say, "screen-based" trading. . . . We have a large central computer complex in Trumbull, Connecticut, and a second back-up facility in Rockville, Maryland. The two centers are connected by more than 100,000 miles of leased telephone lines. Participants access the system through workstations that provide a broad array of information and automated trading systems . . . . The day will come when there's a global stock market . . . driven by computers, linked by superfast telecommunications technology . . . and open to individual investors 24 hours a day.

Wyatt believes that NexStarr's stock should be removed from the NASDAQ system of trading. He plans to ask the board members for authority to seek listing of the stock on the NYSE. In his opinion, a listing on the Big Board will bring more visibility to the stock, improve its liquidity, and perhaps even increase its market value. Farrel is not persuaded by Wyatt's arguments for listing. In her opinion, NASDAQ is the stock market of the future, and she sees little advantage in the proposed change. Despite her reservations, Farrel agrees that the proposal should be considered by the board. At Wyatt's request she prepares the following background memorandum to be mailed to the board members before their meeting:

Board Memorandum

> The New York Stock Exchange celebrated its bicentennial on May 17, 1992. Started in 1792 as the New York Stock & Exchange Board, the NYSE is not the oldest nor the largest exchange in the world. The Philadelphia Stock Exchange came before it in the United States, and the Tokyo Stock Exchange, by several measures, is now larger. But the NYSE is still viewed as the most significant and best regulated exchange in the international marketplace.
>
> Under New York state law, the NYSE is a nonprofit corporation owned exclusively by members of the exchange. In 1990, there were 1,444 members, 1,366 of whom own seats on the exchange from which they conduct trades in securities. Others may pay an annual fee to have access to the trading floor, but approval must be granted by two-thirds of the NYSE board of directors. Seats may be bought and sold, given or leased, with the approval of the exchange. But the number of seats has not changed since 1953, and the value of a seat varies with public interest in the stock market. The price of a seat hit a high of $1,150,000 in 1987 and dropped to about $350,000 in the early 1990s.

More than 1,800 company stocks, valued at several trillion dollars, are listed on the NYSE; more than 150,000,000 shares are traded during a typical day. To be listed on the NYSE, companies must pay a fee and meet several criteria dealing with size of earnings, number of shares outstanding, market value of shares, and number of shareholders. The exchange monitors all stock trades in an attempt to prevent unfair trading practices harmful to shareholders.

Until recently, the NYSE's combination of traders and computers seemed to be the best of all worlds. But now the NYSE faces growing competition from off-exchange, all-electronic trading systems. As a consequence, NYSE's percentage of trading volume has declined recently. Some analysts even speculate that the trading floor of the NYSE will eventually give way to computers. The continued preeminence of the NYSE will depend on its answer to this challenge.

A week before the board meeting, Farrel reports to Wyatt on the estimated flotation costs of issuing new common stock and bonds. If NexStarr issues $100,000,000 each of common stock and bonds in a negotiated-sales arrangement, then total costs will be approximately $5,000,000. Underwriting spreads will be $3,400,000 and $1,100,000, respectively, for stock and bonds. Out-of-pocket costs will be $300,000 for stock and $200,000 for bonds.

Pleased with her report, Wyatt instructs Farrel to present her findings and respond to questions at the upcoming board meeting. In her preparation, she obtains the following quotations on NexStarr's common stock and bonds:

52 Weeks Hi	Lo	Stock	Sym	Div	Yld %	PE	Vol 100s	Hi	Lo	Close	Net Chg
38	$27\frac{1}{2}$	NexStarr	NEXS	.51	1.7	18	103	$30\frac{1}{4}$	30	30	$+\frac{1}{4}$

Bonds	Cur Yld	Vol	Close	Net Chg
NexStarr 9s06	9.2	71	$97\frac{1}{2}$	$+\frac{1}{4}$

She also develops a series of questions and issues for her assistant to analyze. Farrel will use these analyses in her presentation, so they must be accurate. Put yourself in the assistant's position and respond to Farrel's request.

a. Carter and Farrel are concerned that a stock issuance will cause a loss of control. Assume that NexStarr issues $100,000,000 of common stock at $30 per share to the investing public. Calculate the percentage ownership of outstanding stock for Carter, Wyatt, and Farrel. Are the three of them combined still likely to have control of the company?

b. Carter and Farrel also are concerned that a bond issuance will cause undue financial risk. In what way would a bond issuance cause financial risk? Assume that NexStarr issues $100,000,000 each of common stock and bonds. Calculate NexStarr's percentage of debt and percentage of equity in its capital structure: (1) before issuing new securities and (2) after issuing new securities. Has NexStarr's financial risk increased?

c. Describe the role of an investment banker in the flotation of corporate securities. What is the difference between a *negotiated sale* and a *competitive bid*?

d. Assume that NexStarr issues $100,000,000 of common stock at $30 per share. After paying all flotation costs, how much money does NexStarr receive in total? Per share issued? Total flotation costs are what percentage of $100,000,000? Describe the two parts of total flotation costs: (1) underwriting spread and (2) issuing expenses of company (out-of-pocket costs).

e. Assume that NexStarr issues $100,000,000 of bonds at $1,000 per bond. After paying all flotation costs, how much money does NexStarr receive in total? Per bond issued? Total flotation costs are what percentage of $100,000,000? Why is the flotation-cost percentage for bonds less than that for common stocks?

f. If you were the CEO of NexStarr, would you prefer to have the company's common stock listed on the New York Stock Exchange (NYSE) or among NASDAQ's National Market Issues? Explain.

g. Describing the difference between stock trades on the NYSE and in the NASDAQ market, one observer stated: "The NYSE is an *auction* market, and NASDAQ is a *dealer* market." Explain the meaning of this statement.

h. If you were bullish on NexStarr's stock, you might buy shares on margin. But if you were bearish on the stock, you might sell shares short. Explain the terms *margin buying* and *short-selling*.

i. Assume that NexStarr: (1) issues $100,000,000 of common stock at $30 per share, (2) issues $100,000,000 of bonds at $1,000 per bond, each with a coupon rate of $9\frac{1}{4}$ percent, (3) continues to pay the dividend per share indicated in its stock quotation, and (4) has 140,000 bonds outstanding, each with a face value (par value) of $1,000, prior to issuing additional bonds. Based on these assumptions, calculate NexStarr's total dividend payment and total interest payment for one year.

References: Allan H. Pessin, *An Illustrated Encyclopedia of the Securities Industry,* New York, NY: NYIF Corp., 1988; William Power, "Bicentennial Battle: Big Board, at Age 200, Scrambles to Protect Grip on Stock Market," *The Wall Street Journal,* May 13, 1992, A1 and A8; "Technology, the Markets and You," *Schwab Report,* Summer 1992, 1 and 4.

Selected References

Dubofsky, David A., and John C. Groth. "Exchange Listing and Stock Liquidity." *Journal of Financial Research,* Winter 1984: 291–302. .

Eckardt, Walter L., Jr., and Bruce B. Bagamery. "Short Selling: The Mutual Fund Alternative." *Journal of Financial Research,* Fall 1983: 231–238.

Fabozzi, Frank J. "Does Listing on the Amex Increase the Value of Equity?" *Financial Management,* Spring 1981: 43–50.

Hakansson, Nils H., Avroham Beja, and Jinendra Kale. "On the Feasibility of Automated Market Making by a Programmed Specialist." *Journal of Finance,* March 1985: 1–20.

Hasbrouck, Joel. "Security Markets, Information and Liquidity." *Financial Practice and Education,* Fall/Winter 1991: 7–16.

Marr, M. Wayne, and G. Rodney Thompson. "The Influence of Offering Yield on Underwriting Spread." *Journal of Financial Research,* Winter 1984: 323–328.

Santoni, G. J. "The Great Bull Markets 1924–29 and 1982–87: Speculative Bubbles or Economic Fundamentals?" Federal Reserve Bank of St. Louis, *Review,* November 1987: 16–29.

Szewczyk, Samuel H., George P. Tsetsekos, and Raj Varma. "Institutional Ownership and the Liquidity of Common Stock Offerings." *Financial Review,* May 1992: 211–225.

Van Horne, James C. "Of Financial Innovations and Excesses." *Journal of Finance,* July 1985: 632–633.

Wansley, James W., and Terrence M. Clauretie. "The Impact of CreditWatch Placement on Equity Returns and Bond Prices." *Journal of Financial Research,* Spring 1985: 31–42.

VALUATION AND THE COST OF CAPITAL

SMALL-BUSINESS PERSPECTIVE

Financing a New Business

Kathy Griffin and Jim Sutherland, both in their mid-twenties, had been friends since college. Their mutual interest in athletics and fitness and their love of competition served as the basis for many weekend activities. They enjoyed entering marathons, including biking and jogging, and also enjoyed helping other people train for these events. Because of their success in various competitions and their willingness to help others, they developed an excellent reputation among sports enthusiasts.

Kathy and Jim worked in fitness-related businesses: Kathy taught aerobics and Jim managed a health club. Although both enjoyed their work, their competitive natures constantly made them think of ways to improve the services available to health enthusiasts. Kathy and Jim believed that the general public was not knowledgeable about health equipment and therefore often exercised on inferior machines.

They knew that existing training programs for marathon participants did not meet their standards.

After several months of discussion and planning, Kathy and Jim decided to open a retail outlet, to be called In Shape Inc., that would sell fitness equipment— exercise bicycles, treadmills, rowing machines, weight machines, and the like. Kathy and Jim also planned to offer individualized training programs for those who purchased equipment. The outlet would also sell equipment to hotels, resorts, and other institutions that wanted to establish exercise rooms for their customers.

Kathy and Jim selected a location in a Chicago suburb where many young professional people resided. There was only one other fitness equipment outlet within ten miles, and its equipment was a lower quality than that which Kathy and Jim planned to sell at In Shape. They gathered information to estimate their start-up costs and their projected income statement. The figures are given below.

Kathy and Jim each had $25,000 that they could invest in the business. They planned to borrow additional funds from a local bank that was offering a relatively low (10 percent) rate

of interest. They were undecided, however, about how much to invest and how much to borrow. Kathy thought that the entire $50,000 of their personal funds should be invested to keep loan payments as low as possible. Jim believed that only $30,000 should be invested, leaving $81,400 to be borrowed and the remaining $20,000 of their personal funds to be set aside in case unforeseen problems arose.

All companies, regardless of size, must determine their appropriate levels of debt and equity. This part of the text details the concepts of a company's debt and equity and illustrates methods for estimating the costs of each.

Start-Up Costs

Inventory	$ 80,000
Building renovations	3,000
Lease deposit	3,400
Grand-opening advertising	1,000
Cash balances	20,000
Accounting and legal fees	1,000
Cash register, file cabinets, office furniture	3,000
Total	$111,400

Projected Income Statement

Sales	$400,000
Cost of goods sold	292,000
Gross profit	$108,000
Operating expenses	$88,000
Earnings before interest and taxes	$20,000

Chapter 4

TIME VALUE OF MONEY AND DISCOUNTED CASH FLOW

The Magic of Compounding

*L*ife magazine published this letter in August 1959:

Sir:

The Indian who sold Manhattan for $24 was a sharp salesman. If he had put the $24 away at 6 percent compounded semiannually, it would now be $9.5 billion, and he could buy most of the now-improved land back.

> S. Branch Walker
> Stamford, Connecticut

If the original $24 had continued to earn 6 percent compounded semiannually, it would have grown to $79.8 billion by fall 1995. Such is the "magic of compounding."

Most financial decisions involve a trade-off between present and future cash flows. By investing the $24 for future cash returns, the Indian exchanges present purchasing power (consumption opportunities) for purchasing power (consumption) in the future. In August 1959, the Indian would have had to forgo spending $9.5 billion to reach $79.8 billion by fall 1995. The rate of exchange between present and future cash flows depends on the time value of money—for the Indian, 6 percent compounded semiannually.

Suppose that you are 20 years old and would like to be a multimillionaire when you reach 65. Further suppose that you can earn an average of 10.3 percent per year, as suggested in Chapter 2, by investing in a broadly diversified portfolio of common stocks—say, a mutual fund. How much money would you need to invest each year to have $2,000,000 when you are 65 years old? The amount is surprisingly small—$2,531 per year—because of, once again, the "magic of compounding." Unfortunately, most people lack the discipline to save annually for long periods. Also, "Watch out for the inflation monster!" A $15,000 automobile will cost $87,618 by the time you are 65 if the inflation rate averages only 4 percent per year.

Each of the preceding illustrations involves the time value of money, which, according to many professors in the field, is the most important idea in finance. Its importance derives from the objective of creating value, or the maximization of shareholder wealth. To understand how financial decisions create value, you must learn about valuation—the process of estimating value.

Photo Source: Brad Holland.

In this chapter you learn how to evaluate financial decisions involving differing cash flows. The first part of the chapter presents an analysis of how an investor or financial manager values cash flows received or paid at different points in time. The chapter concludes with some sample problems to help you refine your skills in analyzing financial decisions.

TIME VALUE

Money has time value, meaning that a dollar received today is worth more than a dollar received tomorrow. Time value arises from the time preferences of individuals for consumption. For example, dollar interest received on an investment rewards you for patience in not using your money for consumption. The origin of interest and dividends is the investments by companies in factories and other productive assets. Such basic investments provide the future cash flows that reward individuals for investing—that is, postponing consumption.

In a productive economy, individuals have several investment opportunities, which create *opportunity cost*. To illustrate, suppose you are considering either spending $100 for clothes or investing in a certificate of deposit yielding 8 percent per year. In this case, you incur an 8 percent opportunity cost if you buy the clothes.

Productive investments by companies give rise to opportunity cost, which coupled with time preferences of individuals give rise to the time value of money. As a result, individuals demand compensation for exchanging money today for money in the future. Only if the future amount exceeds the present amount will an exchange occur. In the presence of expected inflation, individuals demand even greater compensation to offset the erosion of money's purchasing power. Regardless of expected inflation, however, money still has time value.

The time value of money establishes a relationship between cash flows received at different times. Calculating the present value (today's value) of a future cash flow requires **discounting,** and the process is called *discounted-cash-flow (DCF) analysis,* or *present-value analysis.* Calculating the future value of a cash investment requires **compounding,** and the process is called *future-value analysis.* The following sections discuss the procedures for calculating present value and future value.

discounting
Calculating the present value of a future cash flow.

compounding
Calculating the future value of a present cash flow.

FUTURE VALUE

To illustrate the calculation of future value, consider a 2-year loan of $100 at 10 percent annual interest. Based on **simple interest,** the calculation of future value requires the use of the following equation:

$$\text{Interest} = \text{Principal} \times \text{Rate} \times \text{Time}$$

The principal is the amount of the loan ($100), rate is the interest rate charged (10 percent), and time is the period of the loan (2 years):

$$\text{Interest} = \$100 \times 0.10 \times 2$$
$$= \$20$$

At the end of 2 years, the lender receives the $100 principal plus $20 of interest, for a total of $120, the future value. This type of interest is *simple interest*

simple interest
Interest paid or earned on the principal of a loan but *not* on interest accumulated during prior periods.

because the lender earns interest only on the principal and not on the interest earned during Year 1.

compound interest
Interest paid or earned on the principal of a loan *and* on interest accumulated during prior periods.

Loans at simple interest are rarely made because lenders want to be compensated for forgoing the opportunity to invest the interest they have earned. Unlike simple interest, **compound interest** is the amount that the lender earns on the original principal plus the accumulated interest. Compound interest reflects the opportunity cost of both principal and interest.

EXAMPLE

Using compound interest, calculate the future value of a 2-year loan of $100 at 10 percent annual interest. By the end of one year, interest equals $10:

$$\text{Interest} = \$100 \times 0.10 \times 1$$
$$= \$10$$

Adding $10 to the principal ($100) yields $110 at the end of one year. With compounding, the lender earns interest during Year 2 on both the principal and the interest from Year 1:

$$\text{Interest} = \$110 \times 0.10 \times 1$$
$$= \$11$$

At the end of 2 years, the lender receives $121 ($110 + $11). Comparing this future value ($121) with that using simple interest ($120) reveals the benefit to lenders (and cost to borrowers) of compounding.

Calculating future values with compound interest as done in this example is time-consuming, especially for loans or investments of more than a few years. To simplify the calculations involving compound interest, we use the following equation:

$$FV = PV(1 + i)^n$$

where FV = future value at the end of *n* periods (e.g., years)

PV = present value, or the beginning dollar amount

i = compound interest rate per period (e.g., per year)

n = number of periods (years in many problems) separating the future and present values

The $(1 + i)^n$ part of the equation compounds the rate of interest. Applying the equation to the preceding example yields the following:

$$FV = \$100(1 + 0.10)^2$$
$$= \$100(1.21)$$
$$= \$121$$

Intuitive understanding of the equation for future value follows from the nature of compounding. For example, investing *PV* dollars at interest rate *i* will earn (PV × i) by year-end. Adding this dollar interest, (PV × i), to the original investment *PV* yields the year-end total: PV + (PV × i), which simplifies to PV(1 + i). Note the similarity between the 1-year future-value (FV) equation and the general equation:

One-year equation: $FV = PV(1 + i)^1$

General equation: $FV = PV(1 + i)^n$

Leaving the one-year future value, $PV(1 + i)$, invested during Year 2 yields dollar interest of $PV(1 + i)$ times i. Adding this dollar interest to the value of the investment at the *beginning* of Year 2 yields the value at the *end* of Year 2:

$$FV = \frac{\text{Beginning}}{\text{investment}} + \frac{\text{Interest}}{\text{earned}}$$

$$= PV(1 + i)\ +\ PV(1 + i)i$$

Factoring simplifies the equation to:

$$FV = PV(1 + i)(1 + i)$$

One more simplification produces:

$$FV = PV(1 + i)^2$$

Note the similarity between the 2-year future-value equation and the general equation. Future values for other time periods are developed in the same manner: $n = 3$, $FV = PV(1 + i)^3$; $n = 4$, $FV = PV(1 + i)^4$; and so on.

Figure 4.1 shows how future value (FV) grows over time (n) at various interest rates (i). Larger values for n and i produce larger future values. At 5 percent, for example, a \$100 investment doubles in value after approximately 14 years; at 15 percent, the investment doubles in value after 5 years. With no interest, the \$100 investment does not grow but remains at \$100.

So far we have used a mathematical equation to calculate future value. Two alternative ways to calculate future value are to use an interest factor equation or a financial calculator. Consider each of these three methods, in turn, applied to the earlier example: $PV = \$100$, $n = 2$ years, and $i = 10$ percent per year.

1. *Mathematical equation.* In equation form, $FV = \$100(1 + 0.10)^2$. Multiply 1.1 times 1.1, and multiply the result times \$100 to get $FV = \$121$. Or use a regular, handheld calculator: Enter 1.1, press the y^x key, enter 2, and press the equals (=) key to get 1.21. Multiply \$100 times 1.21 to get $FV = \$121$. The y^x key is especially useful when n is a large number. (Key sequences may vary for different calculators. See the reference guide for your calculator.)

2. *Interest factor equation.* The interest factor equation for calculating future value is:

$$FV = PV(FVIF_{i,n})$$

future-value interest factor

Future value of \$1 earning *i* percent per period for *n* periods; $FVIF_{i,n} = (1 + i)^n$.

where $FVIF_{i,n}$ is the **future-value interest factor** equivalent to $(1 + i)^n$. Table 4.1 (excerpted from a larger table in Appendix B.1) contains values of FVIF for various values of *i* and *n*. In other words, the values of $(1 + i)^n$ for selected values of *i* and *n* are precalculated and tabulated in Appendix B.1.

To apply the interest factor equation to the preceding example, you first select the correct value for $FVIF_{10\%,2}$ from Table 4.1: Enter the table in Row 2 and proceed to the 10 percent column to find $FVIF_{10\%,2} = 1.21$. The number 1.21 is the future value of \$1 when $i = 10\%$ and $n = 2$; so for \$100, multiply \$100 times 1.21: $FV = \$100(1.21)$, or $FV = \$121$, the same answer calculated using the mathematical equation. Because of rounding error, answers using the interest factor equa-

| FIGURE 4.1 | **Relationship between Future Value, Time, and Compound Interest Rate** |

$FV = PV(1 + i)^n$: The future value (FV) of an investment such as \$100 (PV) grows larger over time (n) at positive interest rates (i). Larger interest rates contribute to larger future values.

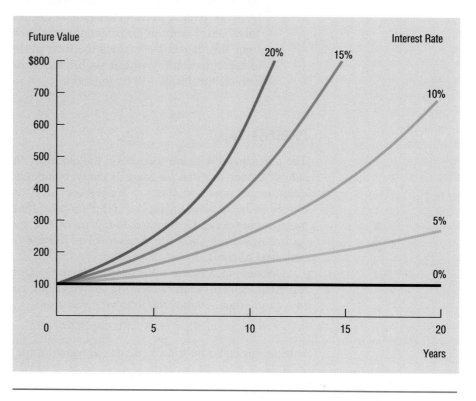

tion sometimes vary a little from those calculated using the mathematical equation.

3. *Financial calculator.* Financial calculators have the following four financial keys (among others):

| n | i | PV | FV |

Entering in any order the values for any three of the four keys enables you to find the value represented by the fourth key. For the example,

| TABLE 4.1 | **Future Value of \$1: $FVIF_{i,n} = (1 + i)^n$, $FV = PV(FVIF_{i,n})$** |

Period (n)	1%	2%	3%	4%	5%	6%	7%	8%	9%	10%
1	1.0100	1.0200	1.0300	1.0400	1.0500	1.0600	1.0700	1.0800	1.0900	1.1000
2	1.0201	1.0404	1.0609	1.0816	1.1025	1.1236	1.1449	1.1664	1.1881	1.2100
3	1.0303	1.0612	1.0927	1.1249	1.1576	1.1910	1.2250	1.2597	1.2950	1.3310
4	1.0406	1.0824	1.1255	1.1699	1.2155	1.2625	1.3108	1.3605	1.4116	1.4641
5	1.0510	1.1041	1.1593	1.2167	1.2763	1.3382	1.4026	1.4693	1.5386	1.6105

enter 100 for *PV*, 10 for *i*, and 2 for *n*; then press the *FV* key to get the answer, $121. Some calculators require you to press a key for compute *(CPT)* before pressing the *FV* key. Also, some calculators attach a minus sign to *FV*, reminding you that paying the loan requires a cash outflow. (A major danger in using a financial calculator is that you treat it as a "black box" without understanding the underlying logic. You can overcome this danger by learning the logic of the mathematical and interest factor equations. Without such understanding, your ability to solve financial problems will be limited.)

PRESENT VALUE

The preceding discussion focuses on the question: What is the future value of a sum of money invested (or loaned) today, compounded at rate *i*? Reversing the question, we now ask: What is the present value, or today's value, of a sum of money to be received in the future? Phrased differently, the question is: How much money must be invested today to have a specific dollar amount in the future? Answering these questions involves present-value analysis, or discounted-cash-flow analysis.

Discounting a future value to the present time is the reverse of compounding a present value to a future time. As shown earlier, compounding a present value to a future time requires the following equation:

$$FV = PV(1 + i)^n$$

Solving this equation for *PV* yields the equation for calculating present value:

present-value interest factor

Present value of $1 due in *n* periods discounted at *i* percent per period; $PVIF_{i,n} = 1/(1 + i)^n$.

$$PV = \frac{FV}{(1 + i)^n} \quad \text{or} \quad PV = FV\left[\frac{1}{(1 + i)^n}\right]$$

The **present-value interest factor** ($PVIF_{i,n}$), $1/(1 + i)^n$, is the reciprocal of the future-value interest factor ($FVIF_{i,n}$), $(1 + i)^n$. This reciprocal relationship is the reason that we say discounting is the opposite of compounding.[1]

EXAMPLE

Suppose you can earn 10 percent per year on a 2-year certificate of deposit. How much money must you invest today to have $100 at the end of 2 years?

$$PV = \frac{FV}{(1 + i)^n}$$

$$PV = \frac{\$100}{(1 + 0.10)^2}$$

$$= \$82.64$$

$82.64 grows to $90.90 ($82.64 × 1.10) by the end of the first year and to $100 ($90.90 × 1.10) by the end of the second year.

---

[1] Mathematically, $(1 + i)^{-n}$ is equivalent to $1/(1 + i)^n$. Thus the equation for calculating present value is sometimes shown as $PV = FV(1 + i)^{-n}$.

FIGURE 4.2

Relationship between Present Value, Time, and Discount Rate

$PV = FV/(1 + i)^n$: The present value (PV) of a future value (FV) such as $100 declines with increases in time (n) and the discount rate (i).

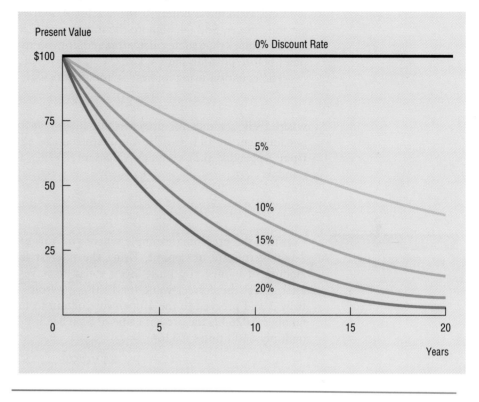

In this example three numbers are given for the calculation of present value: (1) future value, FV = $100, (2) number of years to the future value, n = 2, and (3) interest rate, i = 10 percent. The interest rate in present-value problems is also known as the **discount rate** because it penalizes (discounts, or reduces in size) future cash flows. *Required rate of return* is another name for the interest rate in present-value problems.

Figure 4.2 illustrates the effect of the discount rate (i) and time (n) on the present value of $100. For a given discount rate (say, 10 percent), present value declines as the time before receiving the $100 increases. In addition, for a given number of years (say, 5 years) before receiving the $100, present value declines as the discount rate (required rate of return) increases. At a discount rate of 5 percent, the present value of $100 received in 5 years is $78.35; at 20 percent, the present value is only $40.19. Similarly, at a discount rate of 5 percent, the present value of $100 received in 20 years is $37.69; at 20 percent, the present value is only $2.61.

Like the calculation of future value, present value can be calculated using: (1) a mathematical equation, (2) an interest factor equation, or (3) a financial calculator. The preceding example illustrates the use of a mathematical equation. Employing a financial calculator to find present value requires the use, once again, of the following keys:

discount rate

Percentage used in discounting future cash flows; rate of return that measures the time value of money.

At a 10 percent discount rate, the present value of $100 to be received in 2 years is found as follows: Enter 10 for *i*, 2 for *n*, and 100 for *FV*; then press *PV* to get the answer, $82.64. (Ignore the minus sign if it appears on your calculator, and remember that some calculators require you to press the *CPT* key [for compute] before pressing the *PV* key.)

The equation using interest factors to calculate present value is:

$$PV = FV(PVIF_{i,n})$$

where $PVIF_{i,n}$ stands for present-value interest factor based on *i* and *n*. $PVIF_{i,n}$ is equivalent to $1/(1 + i)^n$ in the mathematical equation. Table 4.2 (excerpted from Appendix B.2) contains values of $PVIF_{i,n}$ for various combinations of *i* and *n*.

EXAMPLE

Consider the preceding example where you can earn 10 percent per year on a 2-year certificate of deposit. Using the interest factor equation, calculate the amount of money you must invest today to have $100 at the end of 2 years. First, select the correct value for $PVIF_{10\%,2}$ from Table 4.2: Enter the table in Row 2 and proceed to the 10 percent column to find $PVIF_{10\%,2} = 0.8264$. The number 0.8264 is the present value of $1 when i = 10% and n = 2; so for $100, multiply $100 times 0.8264:

$$PV = FV(PVIF_{10\%,2})$$
$$= \$100(0.8264)$$
$$= \$82.64$$

The answer, $82.64, is the same as that calculated in the previous example.

A comparison of the entries in Table 4.1 (future value of $1) and Table 4.2 (present value of $1) reveals that they are reciprocals. To illustrate, for n = 2 and i = 10%, the entry is 1.21 in Table 4.1 and 0.8264 in Table 4.2: 1/1.21 = 0.8264, and 1/0.8264 = 1.21. This reciprocal relationship is also shown by:

$$FVIF_{i,n} = \frac{1}{PVIF_{i,n}} \quad \text{and} \quad (1 + i)^n = \frac{1}{1/(1 + i)^n}$$

Although Tables 4.1 and 4.2 provide essentially the same information, it is convenient to have both tables when solving future-value and present-value problems.

So far in this chapter, we have analyzed two types of problems:

Solve for	Given	Example Problem
FV	PV, i, n	Future value of an investment
PV	FV, i, n	Present value of a promised sum of money

TABLE 4.2

Present Value of $1: $PVIF_{i,n} = 1/(1 + i)^n$, $PV = FV(PVIF_{i,n})$

Period (n)	1%	2%	3%	4%	5%	6%	7%	8%	9%	10%
1	.9901	.9804	.9709	.9615	.9524	.9434	.9346	.9259	.9174	.9091
2	.9803	.9612	.9426	.9246	.9070	.8900	.8734	.8573	.8417	.8264
3	.9706	.9423	.9151	.8890	.8638	.8396	.8163	.7938	.7722	.7513
4	.9610	.9238	.8885	.8548	.8227	.7921	.7629	.7350	.7084	.6830
5	.9515	.9057	.8626	.8219	.7835	.7473	.7130	.6806	.6499	.6209

The following two types of problems can also be solved using the information already presented:

Solve for	Given	Example Problem
i	PV, FV, n	Interest rate on a single-payment loan
n	PV, FV, i	Years to achieve an investment goal

EXAMPLE

Your Uncle Bertrom offers to loan you $48,743 provided that you pay him $75,000 five years later. What rate of interest is Uncle Bertrom charging you? Using the interest factor equation, you can calculate the rate of interest as follows:

$$PV = FV(PVIF_{i,n})$$

$$\$48,743 = \$75,000(PVIF_{i,5})$$

$$PVIF_{i,5} = \frac{\$48,743}{\$75,000}$$

$$PVIF_{i,5} = 0.6499$$

Table 4.2 (and Appendix B.2) shows that an *n* of 5 and a *PVIF* of 0.6499 are associated with an *i* of 9 percent. Hence Uncle Bertrom is charging you 9 percent per year on the loan. A financial calculator yields the same answer: Enter 75000 for *FV*, 48743 for *PV*, and 5 for *n*; then press *i* (or *CPT* and then *i*) to get the answer—9 percent.

EXAMPLE

You deposit $1,000 at a bank offering 9 percent interest compounded annually. How long will it take to double your money? To show the equivalence between procedures, answer the question using future-value (FVIF) and present-value interest factors (PVIF):

FVIF (See Appendix B.1)
$$FV = PV(FVIF_{i,n})$$
$$\$2,000 = \$1,000(FVIF_{9\%,n})$$

PVIF (See Appendix B.2)
$$PV = FV(PVIF_{i,n})$$
$$\$1,000 = \$2,000(PVIF_{9\%,n})$$

$$FVIF_{9\%,n} = \frac{\$2,000}{\$1,000}$$

$$PVIF_{9\%,n} = \frac{\$1,000}{\$2,000}$$

$$FVIF_{9\%,n} = 2.0000$$

$$PVIF_{9\%,n} = 0.5000$$

Appendix B.1 shows that an *i* of 9 percent and a *FVIF* of 2.0000 are associated with an *n* between 8 and 9.

Appendix B.2 shows that an *i* of 9 percent and a *PVIF* of 0.5000 are associated with an *n* between 8 and 9.

Based on Appendixes B.1 and B.2, the best estimate is 8 years for you to double your money. A financial calculator shows the precise answer to be 8.04 years.

PRESENT AND FUTURE VALUE OF AN UNEVEN SERIES OF CASH FLOWS

The preceding examples deal with cash flows occurring at only two points in time—the present and sometime in the future. In many cases, cash flows occur periodically and vary in amount over time. For example, the cash flows a company earns from investing in equipment are likely to vary over time, and common stock often pays a variable stream of dividends.

The present value of an uneven series of cash flows is calculated by summing the present values of the individual cash flows. To illustrate, consider the following series of cash flows resulting from a company's investment in a piece of equipment:

End of Year	Cash Flow
0	−$10,000
1	+3,000
2	+5,000
3	+7,000

The company invests $10,000, denoted as −$10,000 to indicate a cash outflow, and earns a 3-year series of cash inflows (denoted by +). The present value of all 4 cash flows (positive and negative) equals the sum of the individual present values. Using a discount rate of 10 percent per year (the required rate of return on the equipment), you calculate present value as follows:

$$PV = \frac{-\$10,000}{(1 + 0.10)^0} + \frac{\$3,000}{(1 + 0.10)^1} + \frac{\$5,000}{(1 + 0.10)^2} + \frac{\$7,000}{(1 + 0.10)^3}$$

$$= -\$10,000 + \$2,727.27 + \$4,132.23 + \$5,259.20$$

$$= \$2,118.70$$

The present value of the cash inflows exceeds the cash investment by $2,118.70 (a good investment, as Chapter 9 explains). Figure 4.3 illustrates the discounting process applied to these cash flows. Discounting each individual cash flow and summing the results yields the present value $2,118.70.

EXAMPLE

Using present-value interest factors (PVIF$_{i,n}$) and i = 10 percent, calculate the present value of the 4 cash flows shown on the time line in Figure 4.3:

FIGURE 4.3

Time Line of an Uneven Series of Cash Flows: Present Value, i = 10%

Calculate the present value of an uneven series of cash flows by discounting each cash flow separately, then totaling the separate present values.

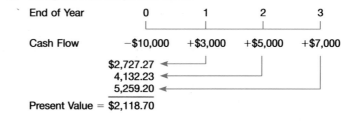

$$PV = -\$10{,}000(PVIF_{10\%,0}) + \$3{,}000(PVIF_{10\%,1}) + \$5{,}000(PVIF_{10\%,2})$$
$$+ \$7{,}000(PVIF_{10\%,3})$$
$$= -\$10{,}000(1.0000) + \$3{,}000(0.9091) + \$5{,}000(0.8264)$$
$$+ \$7{,}000(0.7513)$$
$$= \$2{,}118.40$$

Note the following observations: (1) The present-value interest factors are from Appendix B.2. (2) $(PVIF_{10\%,0}) = 1.0$; PVIF is always 1.0 for cash flows occurring at time zero. (3) The answer here ($2,118.40) differs from the answer in Figure 4.3 ($2,118.70) because of rounding error in the present-value interest factors; a small rounding error is tolerable in many cases.

The general equation for calculating the present value of an uneven series of cash flows is:

$$PV = C_0 + \frac{C_1}{(1 + i)^1} + \frac{C_2}{(1 + i)^2} + \cdots + \frac{C_n}{(1 + i)^n}$$

where $C_0, C_1, C_2, \cdots, C_n$ represent cash flows occurring at different times. Using the Greek capital letter Σ (sigma) to indicate summation, we can show the general equation in a more compact form:

$$PV = \sum_{t=0}^{n} \frac{C_t}{(1 + i)^t}$$

which states that the present value of cash flows C_t equals the summation of C_t divided by $(1 + i)^t$, where t equals zero to n. t is an index for time, and $t = 0$ indicates the present time; $t = 1$ is one period from now, and $t = n$ is n periods from now. This shorthand notation is commonly used in finance because of its convenience.

The need to calculate the present value of an uneven series of cash flows occurs frequently in financial problems. Although occurring less frequently, the need to calculate the *future value* of an uneven series of cash flows arises in the analysis of corporate investments (e.g., in Chapter 9). Using an example from personal finance, suppose that you put $1,000 in a bank account today and plan to make the following future deposits: $2,000 1 year from today, $3,000 2 years

| FIGURE 4.4 | **Time Line of an Uneven Series of Cash Flows: Future Value, i = 8%** |

Calculate the future value of an uneven series of cash flows by compounding each cash flow separately, then totaling the separate future values.

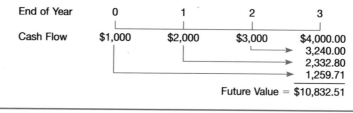

from today, and $4,000 3 years from today. If the bank pays 8 percent annual compound interest, how much money will you have in the bank after 3 years?

To answer this question, calculate the future value of each deposit, then total the individual future values. As Figure 4.4 shows, each cash deposit earns interest for a different number of years; $1,000, 3 years; $2,000, 2 years; $3,000, 1 year; $4,000, zero years:

$$FV = \$1,000(1 + 0.08)^3 + \$2,000(1 + 0.08)^2 + \$3,000(1 + 0.08)^1 + \$4,000$$
$$= \$1,259.71 + \$2,332.80 + \$3,240.00 + \$4,000.00$$
$$= \$10,832.51$$

Making the four bank deposits as planned yields $10,832.51 by the end of Year 3.

The general equation for calculating the future value of an uneven series of cash flows is:

$$FV = \sum_{t=0}^{n} C_t(1 + i)^{n-t}$$

which states that the future value of cash flows C_t equals the summation (Σ) of C_t times $(1 + i)^{n-t}$, where t equals zero to n. The unusual-looking exponent $(n - t)$ is the number of periods for which each cash flow earns interest at rate i. Consider, for example, the first cash deposit ($c_0 = \$1,000$) in the preceding illustration: n = 3 years, the point in time of the future value; t = 0, the point in time of the $1,000 cash deposit; $(n - t) = 3 - 0$, or 3, the number of years that the deposit earns interest.

FUTURE VALUE OF AN ANNUITY

annuity
Even series of cash flows, constant in amount, that occur at fixed intervals such as years or months.

The calculation of the future value of an *uneven* series of cash flows is tedious because each cash flow must be analyzed individually. In contrast, the calculation of the future value of an even series of cash flows is relatively easy, as this section now shows. Fortunately, many problems in finance involve an *even* series of cash flows, called an annuity.

ordinary annuity
Annuity in which the payments (cash flows) occur at the end of each period.

An **annuity** is an even series of cash flows, constant in amount, that occur at regular fixed periods of time (e.g., years or months). Figure 4.5 illustrates two types of annuities that are commonplace in finance. An **ordinary annuity**, also known as a *deferred annuity*, has payments (cash flows) occurring at the end of

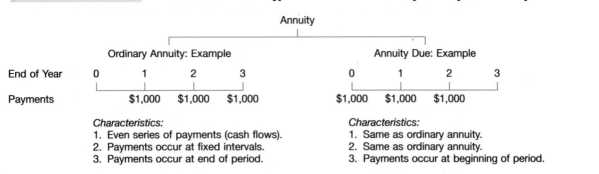

FIGURE 4.5   **Illustration of Two Types of Annuities: Ordinary Annuity and Annuity Due**

each period.[2] Payments on a home mortgage take the form of an ordinary annuity. An **annuity due** has payments occurring at the beginning of each period. Payments of apartment rent and insurance premiums often take the form of an annuity due. By convention and because ordinary annuities are so common in finance, we use the term *annuity* as shorthand for *ordinary annuity* unless otherwise specified.

annuity due

Annuity in which the payments occur at the beginning of each period.

Ordinary Annuity

If the payments of the ordinary annuity illustrated in Figure 4.5 were invested at 8 percent annual compound interest, then one way to calculate their future value is:

(1) End of Year	(2) Payment	(3) Years to Earn Interest	(4) $FVIF_{8\%,n}$	(2) × (4) = (5) Product
1	$1,000	2	1.1664	$1,166.40
2	1,000	1	1.0800	1,080.00
3	1,000	0	1.0000	1,000.00
			3.2464	$3,246.40

The first $1,000 earns interest for 2 years, the second $1,000 earns interest for 1 year, and the third $1,000 earns no interest. Multiplying each $1,000 payment by its future-value interest factor ($FVIF_{8\%,n}$ in Appendix B.1 and Table 4.1) and summing the products gives the future value of the annuity, $3,246.40. Figure 4.6 illustrates the $1,000 payments compounding to the end of Year 3 to produce the future value of $3,246.40.

An easier way to calculate the future value of an annuity is to use the interest factors in Table 4.3 (excerpted from Appendix B.3). These interest factors are the future value of a series of $1 payments earning interest rate *i* for a number of periods *n*. For example, the interest factor in the row for 3 years and the column for 8 percent annually is 3.2464; a $1 annuity compounding at 8 percent per

---

[2]The cash flows (C_t) of an annuity equal one another: $C_1 = C_2 = \cdots = C_n$. Because of this equality, one symbol can be used to represent all of the cash flows. This book uses PMT for payments because most financial calculators use this symbol.

FIGURE 4.6

Future Value of a 3-Year, $1,000 Annuity Compounded at 8 Percent Annually

The future value of an annuity is the sum of the future values of the individual payments.

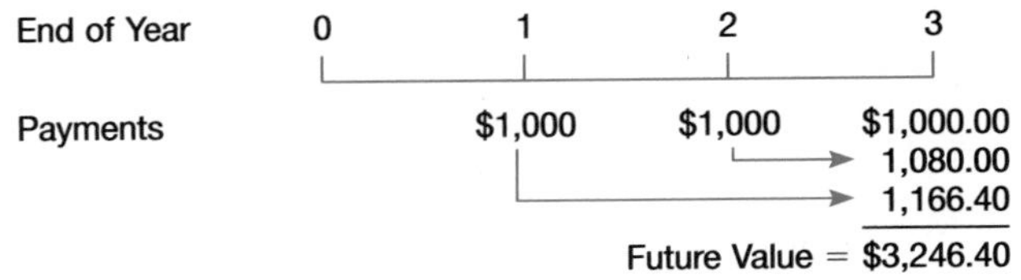

End of Year	0	1	2	3
Payments		$1,000	$1,000	$1,000.00
				1,080.00
				1,166.40

Future Value = $3,246.40

year will total $3.2464 at the end of 3 years. Note that 3.2464 is the sum of the FVIFs (1.1664 + 1.0800 + 1.0000) in the preceding calculation of future value of the ordinary annuity. In general, the interest factor for any period n in Table 4.3 (Appendix B.3) equals 1.0 plus the sum of the interest factors in Table 4.1 (Appendix B.1) up to and including Period $n - 1$.

Using interest factors, the equation for calculating the future value of an ordinary annuity is:

$$FVA = PMT(FVIFA_{i,n})$$

where FVA = future value of an ordinary annuity

PMT = payments, or amount of cash flows

FVIFA = future-value interest factor of an annuity (Appendix B.3)

i = compound interest rate per period

n = number of periods

Applying the equation to the 3-year, $1,000 annuity earning 8 percent annually yields:

$$FVA = \$1,000(FVIFA_{8\%,3})$$
$$= \$1,000(3.2464)$$
$$= \$3,246.40$$

This calculation is less tedious than analyzing each payment separately. Generally, the equation for FVA should be used for calculating the future value of an ordinary annuity.

The *sinking-fund problem* involves the question: How much money must be invested each period to achieve a specific financial goal? For example, suppose you are 20 years old and want to have $1 million by the time you are 60. If you can earn 10 percent annual compound interest, how much money must you invest at the end of each of the next 40 years?

$$FVA = PMT(FVIFA_{10\%,40})$$
$$\$1,000,000 = PMT(442.59)$$
$$PMT = \$2,259.43$$

The payment is small relative to the $1 million because of the long savings period—40 years!

TABLE 4.3

Future Value of an Annuity of $1:

$$FVIFA_{i,n} = \frac{(1 + i)^n - 1}{i}; \quad FVA = PMT(FVIFA_{i,n})$$

Period (n)	1%	2%	3%	4%	5%	6%	7%	8%	9%	10%
1	1.0000	1.0000	1.0000	1.0000	1.0000	1.0000	1.0000	1.0000	1.0000	1.0000
2	2.0100	2.0200	2.0300	2.0400	2.0500	2.0600	2.0700	2.0800	2.0900	2.1000
3	3.0301	3.0604	3.0909	3.1216	3.1525	3.1836	3.2149	3.2464	3.2781	3.3100
4	4.0604	4.1216	4.1836	4.2465	4.3101	4.3746	4.4399	4.5061	4.5731	4.6410
5	5.1010	5.2040	5.3091	5.4163	5.5256	5.6371	5.7507	5.8666	5.9847	6.1051

The interest factors ($FVIFA_{i,n}$) in Table 4.3 and Appendix B.3 are determined solely by the values of i and n. To understand how these interest factors are calculated, consider the following derivation of the future value of an ordinary annuity (FVA):

$$FVA = PMT(1 + i)^{n-1} + PMT(1 + i)^{n-2} + \cdots + PMT(1 + i)^0$$
$$= PMT[(1 + i)^{n-1} + (1 + i)^{n-2} + \cdots + (1 + i)^0]$$
$$= PMT \sum_{t=1}^{n} (1 + i)^{n-t}$$

Mathematicians identify equations like this one as the sum of a geometric series. The sum simplifies to the following equation (as shown in Appendix 4A):

$$FVA = PMT \left[\frac{(1 + i)^n - 1}{i} \right]$$

The bracketed term, denoted $FVIFA_{i,n}$, is used to calculate the interest factors in Appendix B.3. The bracketed term can also be used to calculate FVA for fractional and other values of i and n not contained in Appendix B.3.

EXAMPLE

Calculate the future value of a 5-year, $2,000 ordinary annuity that earns 8.5 percent annually:

$$FVA = \$2,000 \left[\frac{(1 + 0.085)^5 - 1}{0.085} \right]$$
$$= \$2,000(5.925373)$$
$$= \$11,850.75$$

Financial calculators with the following keys easily handle fractional (and other) values for i and n:

To find *FVA* for the preceding example, enter 5 for *n*, 8.5 for *i*, and 2000 for *PMT*; then press *FV* (or *CPT* and then *FV*) to get the answer—$11,850.75. (Ignore the minus sign if present.)

Annuity Due

If the payments of the *annuity due* illustrated in Figure 4.5 are invested at 8 percent annual compound interest, then one way to calculate their future value is:

(1)	(2)	(3) Years to	(4)	(2) × (4) = (5)
End of Year	**Payment**	**Earn Interest**	**FVIF$_{8\%,n}$**	**Product**
0	$1,000	3	1.2597	$1,259.70
1	1,000	2	1.1664	1,166.40
2	1,000	1	1.0800	1,080.00
3	—	—	—	—
				Future value = $3,506.10

Compared to the payments of the ordinary annuity shown in Figure 4.5, each payment of the *annuity due* earns interest for one more year. For example, the first $1,000 of the annuity due earns interest for 3 years, not 2 years. As a result, the future value of the annuity due, $3,506.10, exceeds that of the ordinary annuity ($3,246.40).

An easier way to calculate the future value of an annuity due, FVA(Due), is:

$$\text{FVA(Due)} = \text{PMT}(\text{FVIFA}_{i,n})(1 + i)$$

PMT(FVIFA$_{i,n}$) is the future value of an *ordinary* annuity; multiplying it by $(1 + i)$ compounds each payment for one extra period. Applied to the preceding illustration, the equation is:

$$\text{FVA(Due)} = \$1,000(\text{FVIFA}_{8\%,3})(1 + 0.08)$$
$$= \$1,000(3.2464)(1.08)$$
$$= \$3,506.11$$

For an annuity due, multiplying the interest factors in Appendix B.3 by $(1 + i)$ accounts for the extra period of compounding.[3]

On a financial calculator, the keystrokes for finding FVA(Due) are similar to those for finding the future value of an ordinary annuity. There is one important exception, however: Using a switch or a key typically marked *due* or *begin,* you must indicate that the payments occur at the beginning of each period. Because financial calculators tend to differ on the required keystrokes for an annuity due, you should consult the reference guide accompanying your calculator.

PRESENT VALUE OF AN ANNUITY

Financial problems often involve the present value of an annuity. Prominent examples are the calculations for payments on car loans, home mortgages, and

---

[3] The $0.01 difference ($3,506.11 − $3,506.10) between the answers is rounding error in the first calculation.

FIGURE 4.7

Present Value of a 3-Year, $1,000 Annuity Discounted at 8 Percent Annually

The present value of an annuity is the sum of the present values of the individual payments.

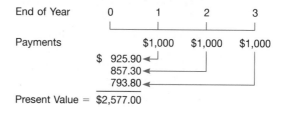

Note: Minor rounding error arises from using the interest factors in Appendix B.2. A financial calculator shows that the present value is $2,577.10.

multiyear business loans. The ideas presented below are essential for calculating such payments.

Ordinary Annuity

The present value of an ordinary annuity equals the sum of the present values of the individual payments. Consider, for example, the present value of the 3-year, $1,000 ordinary annuity shown in Figure 4.7. Discounting the payments one at a time at 8 percent per year requires the following calculations:

(1) End of Year	(2) Payment	(3) Years to Discount	(4) $PVIF_{8\%,n}$	(2) × (4) = (5) Product
1	$1,000	1	0.9259	$ 925.90
2	1,000	2	0.8573	857.30
3	1,000	3	0.7938	793.80
			2.5770	$2,577.00

Calculating the present value this way requires three multiplications and one summation, and it requires the use of interest factors in Appendix B.2. Figure 4.7 graphically illustrates the calculations and shows that the $1,000 payments have a present value of $2,577.00.

To reduce the number of calculations, we use the interest factors in Table 4.4 (excerpted from Appendix B.4). These interest factors are the present value of a series of $1 payments discounted at rate *i* for a number of periods *n*. For exam-

TABLE 4.4

Present Value of an Annuity of $1:

$$PVIFA_{i,n} = \frac{1 - [1/(1 + i)^n]}{i}; \ PVA = PMT(PVIFA_{i,n})$$

Period (n)	1%	2%	3%	4%	5%	6%	7%	8%	9%	10%
1	0.9901	0.9804	0.9709	0.9615	0.9524	0.9434	0.9346	0.9259	0.9174	0.9091
2	1.9704	1.9416	1.9135	1.8861	1.8594	1.8334	1.8080	1.7833	1.7591	1.7355
3	2.9410	2.8839	2.8286	2.7751	2.7232	2.6730	2.6243	2.5771	2.5313	2.4869
4	3.9020	3.8077	3.7171	3.6299	3.5460	3.4651	3.3872	3.3121	3.2397	3.1699
5	4.8534	4.7135	4.5797	4.4518	4.3295	4.2124	4.1002	3.9927	3.8897	3.7908

ple, the interest factor in the row for 3 years and the column for 8 percent annually is 2.5771; discounting a 3-year, $1 annuity at 8 percent per year yields a present value of $2.5771. Note that 2.5771 is the sum (with rounding error) of the PVIFs (0.9259 + 0.8573 + 0.7938) in the preceding calculation of the present value of the ordinary annuity. In general, the interest factor for any period n in Table 4.4 (Appendix B.4) equals the sum of the interest factors in Table 4.2 (Appendix B.2) up to and including period n.[4]

Using interest factors, the equation for calculating the present value of an ordinary annuity is:

$$PVA = PMT(PVIFA_{i,n})$$

where PVA = present value of an ordinary annuity

PMT = payments, or amount of cash flows

PVIFA = present-value interest factor of an annuity (Appendix B.4)

i = discount rate, or compound interest rate per period

n = number of periods

Applying the equation to the 3-year, $1,000 annuity discounted at 8 percent annually yields:

$$PVA = \$1,000(PVIFA_{8\%,3})$$
$$= \$1,000(2.5771)$$
$$= \$2,577.10$$

This method of calculating the present value of an ordinary annuity requires fewer steps than the summation of present values of individual payments. When the number of annuity payments is large, the time-saving advantage of this method becomes especially important.

EXAMPLE

amortize
Provide for the gradual repayment of a loan.

Borrowers and lenders use the equation for PVA to calculate the payments necessary to **amortize** (pay off) a loan. Suppose, for example, that you borrow $4,000 at 8 percent annual compound interest and plan to repay the loan by making 3 end-of-year payments. The loan amount, $4,000, is the present value of the payments, calculated as follows:

$$PVA = PMT(PVIFA_{8\%,3})$$
$$\$4,000 = PMT(2.5771)$$
$$PMT = \frac{\$4,000}{2.5771}$$
$$= \$1,552.13$$

---

[4]The interest factors in Appendix B.4 (PVIFA$_{i,n}$) are related to the interest factors in Appendixes B.1 (FVIF$_{i,n}$) and B.3 (FVIFA$_{i,n}$) as follows:

$$(FVIF_{i,n})(PVIFA_{i,n}) = FVIFA_{i,n}$$

$$(1 + i)^n \left[\frac{1 - [1/(1 + i)^n]}{i} \right] = \frac{(1 + i)^n - 1}{i}$$

For example, consider i = 8% and n = 3:

$$(1.2597)(2.5771) = 3.2464$$
$$3.2464 = 3.2464$$

TABLE 4.5

Loan Amortization Schedule for a 3-Year, $4,000 Loan at 8 Percent Interest

(1) Year	(2) Beginning Balance	(3) Payment	0.08 × (2) = (4) Interest	(3) − (4) = (5) Repayment of Principal	(2) − (5) = (6) Ending Balance
1	$4,000.00	$1,552.13	$320.00	$1,232.13	$2,767.87[a]
2	2,767.87	1,552.13	221.43	1,330.70	1,437.17
3	1,437.17	1,552.13	114.97	1,437.16	0[b]

[a]Interest for the first year is $320 (0.08 × $4,000), and repayment of principal is $1,232.13 ($1,552.13 − $320). Therefore the ending balance of the loan is $2,767.87 ($4,000 − $1,232.13); $2,767.87 is the beginning balance for Year 2.

[b]The ending balance is zero when a loan matures. Although shown to be zero, the ending balance here is $0.01 due to rounding error.

loan amortization schedule

Table showing the timing of payments necessary to amortize a loan, and the breakdown of each payment into interest and repayment of principal.

Each payment consists of interest and repayment of principal. Table 4.5 is a **loan amortization schedule,** which details the amounts of interest and principal in each payment. The interest portion (Column 4) declines each year even though the interest rate remains constant because the loan principal (Column 2) declines each year. The portion of each payment repaying principal (Column 5) increases each year as the portion paying interest declines.

Like other interest factors, those $(PVIFA_{i,n})$ in Table 4.4 and Appendix B.4 are determined solely by values of i and n, as the following derivation of present value of an annuity (PVA) shows:

$$PVA = \frac{PMT}{(1+i)} + \frac{PMT}{(1+i)^2} + \cdots + \frac{PMT}{(1+i)^n}$$

$$= PMT \left[\frac{1}{(1+i)} + \frac{1}{(1+i)^2} + \cdots + \frac{1}{(1+i)^n} \right]$$

$$= PMT \sum_{t=1}^{n} \frac{1}{(1+i)^t}$$

This sum of a geometric series simplifies (as shown in Appendix 4B) to the following:

$$PVA = PMT \left[\frac{1 - [1/(1+i)^n]}{i} \right]$$

The bracketed term, denoted $PVIFA_{i,n}$, is used to calculate the interest factors in Appendix B.4. Interest factors for values of i and n not contained in Appendix B.4 can also be calculated using the bracketed term.

Once again, financial calculators easily handle all values of i and n. For example, to find the payments for a $4,000 loan, n = 3 years and i = 8 percent, use the following keystrokes: Enter 3 for *n*, 8 for *i*, and 4000 for *PV*; then press *PMT* (or *CPT* and then *PMT*) to get the answer, $1,552.13.

Annuity Due

The present value of an *annuity due* is larger than the present value of the comparable ordinary annuity because payments occur at the beginning of each period, not the end. To illustrate, consider the annuity due shown in Figure 4.5 discounted at 8 percent:

(1) End of Year	(2) Payment	(3) Years to Discount	(4) PVIF$_{8\%,n}$	(2) × (4) = (5) Product
0	$1,000	0	1.0000	$1,000.00
1	1,000	1	0.9259	925.90
2	1,000	2	0.8573	857.30
3	—	—	—	—
			Present value =	$2,783.20

The present value here is $2,783.20; if the payments occurred at the end of each period, however, the present value would be only $2,577.00 (as shown in the preceding section). Timing of the payments causes the difference in present value.

Using interest factors to calculate the present value of an annuity due, PVA(Due), requires the following equation:

$$\text{PVA(Due)} = \text{PMT}(\text{PVIFA}_{i,n})(1 + i)$$

PMT(PVIFA$_{i,n}$) is the present value of an ordinary annuity; multiplying it by $(1 + i)$ accounts for the payments occurring one period earlier. Applied to the preceding illustration, the equation is:

$$\text{PVA(Due)} = \$1,000(\text{PVIFA}_{8\%,3})(1 + 0.08)$$

$$= \$1,000(2.5771)(1.08)$$

$$= \$2,783.27$$

The interest factors in Appendix B.4 multiplied by $(1 + i)$ account for the beginning-of-period payments of an annuity due.[5]

Perpetuities

Unlike the annuities discussed so far, a *perpetuity* is an annuity with an infinite life—a perpetual annuity. In other words, the payments of a perpetuity go on forever. Examples of perpetuities include the dividend payments of some preferred stock and the interest payments of some bonds issued by sovereign countries.

The present value of a perpetuity (PVP) can be shown as follows:

$$\text{PVP} = \frac{\text{PMT}}{(1 + i)} + \frac{\text{PMT}}{(1 + i)^2} + \cdots + \frac{\text{PMT}}{(1 + i)^n}$$

where n approaches infinity. Based on the mathematical equation for present value of an ordinary annuity, the present value of a perpetuity can also be shown as:

$$\text{PVP} = \text{PMT} \left[\frac{1 - [1/(1 + i)^n]}{i} \right]$$

---

[5] The $0.07 difference ($2,783.27 − $2,783.20) between the answers is rounding error.

where *n* approaches infinity. But when *n* approaches infinity, the second term within the brackets approaches zero, leaving:

$$PVP = PMT \left[\frac{1 - 0}{i} \right]$$

Simplifying the equation yields:

$$PVP = \frac{PMT}{i}$$

In words, the present value of a perpetuity equals the payment divided by the discount rate. This conclusion is supported by the interest factors ($PVIFA_{i,n}$) in Appendix B.4. As *n* becomes increasingly large (becoming increasingly similar to a perpetuity) for a given discount rate, the value of the interest factor approaches $1/i$. For example, when n = 60 and i = 10 percent, the interest factor equals 9.9672, or approximately $1/0.10$. At a discount rate of 10 percent, the value of a $1 perpetuity is $10 ($1/0.10).

EXAMPLE

Calculate the present value of a perpetuity paying $100 annually. The required rate of return (discount rate) on the perpetuity is 10 percent per year. *Solution:*

$$PVP = \frac{\$100}{0.10}$$

$$= \$1,000$$

What is the present value of the perpetuity for a required rate of return equaling 20 percent per year?

$$PVP = \frac{\$100}{0.20}$$

$$= \$500$$

Notice that doubling the required rate of return halves the value of the perpetuity. In general, rising required rates of return cause the values of perpetuities (and other securities) to drop.

Like the equation for present value of an ordinary annuity, the equation for PVP requires that payments occur at the *end* of each period. If the payments occur at the beginning of each period, the equation must be modified by adding PMT to PMT/i. This addition of PMT accounts for the occurrence of a payment at time zero, the present time.

EXAMPLE

Assume that the payments in the first part of the preceding example are received at the beginning of each period and that the other facts remain unchanged. What is the present value of the payments? Adding $100 to $100/0.10 yields the answer: $1,100. The only difference between this answer and the preceding answer is the $100 payment occurring at time zero.

Because a perpetuity produces payments forever, the future value of a perpetuity is a meaningless concept. To be meaningful, the future value of an annuity (FVA) requires a stopping point, but a perpetuity extends to infinity. Inserting infinity for *n* in the mathematical equation for FVA yields infinity for all sizes of payments. In contrast, present value of a perpetuity yields finite answers that have meaning, as we shall see again in later chapters.

FREQUENCY OF COMPOUNDING AND THE EFFECTIVE ANNUAL RATE

Compound interest means that interest is paid or earned on principal plus accumulated interest. **Frequency of compounding** indicates how often the interest is accumulated. For example, a credit card may charge annual interest that compounds monthly, or a savings account may pay interest at an annual rate compounded quarterly (every 3 months). In such cases interest is paid or earned more frequently than once per year, and the equations for future and present value must be modified accordingly. Additionally, the greater frequency of compounding leads to a rate of return called the **effective annual rate.**

frequency of compounding
Frequency with which interest is accumulated; e.g., an annual rate of 8 percent compounded quarterly accumulates interest every 3 months.

effective annual rate
A rate per year compounded annually; e.g., 8 percent per year compounded annually.

Frequency of Compounding

As an illustration of the impact of frequency of compounding, consider the future value of a bank account that pays 8 percent per year compounded semiannually. The account pays 4 percent (8 percent/2) each 6 months, and there are two 6-month periods in one year. Placing $1,000 in the account yields $40 (0.04 × $1,000) interest during the first 6 months; during the second 6 months the account earns $41.60 (0.04 × $1,040). Interest earned on the accumulated interest is $1.60 (0.04 × $40). By the end of the year the account is worth $1,081.60: the $1,000 principal plus $40 interest during the first 6 months plus $41.60 interest during the second 6 months.

In the preceding illustration, we divide 8 percent by 2 and multiply 1 year by 2, where 2 is the frequency of compounding (twice per year). In general, letting *m* represent frequency of compounding, we write the equation for future value as follows:

$$FV = PV \left(1 + \frac{i}{m} \right)^{mn}$$

Applying the equation to the preceding illustration yields:

$$FV = \$1,000 \left(1 + \frac{0.08}{2} \right)^{2(1)}$$
$$= \$1,000(1.04)^2$$
$$= \$1,081.60$$

If the 8 percent annual rate is compounded quarterly, the future value becomes:

$$FV = \$1,000 \left(1 + \frac{0.08}{4} \right)^{4(1)}$$
$$= \$1,000(1.02)^4$$
$$= \$1,082.43$$

TABLE 4.6

Effect of Frequency of Compounding on the Future Value of $1,000: i = 8% per Year and n = 1 Year

Principal	Frequency of Compounding	Future Value: End of Year 1
$1,000	Annually	$1,080.00
1,000	Semiannually	1,081.60
1,000	Quarterly	1,082.43
1,000	Monthly	1,083.00
1,000	Daily	1,083.28
1,000	Continuously	1,083.29

Note: Continuous, or instantaneous, compounding is the upper limit of the frequency of compounding. As Appendix 4C shows, $FV = PV(e)^{in}$ for continuous compounding, where $e = 2.71828$ is the base number for natural logarithms: $FV = \$1,000(e)^{0.08(1)} = \$1,083.29$.

Table 4.6 shows the future value for several other frequencies of compounding. Compounding annually, for example, the $1,000 investment grows to $1,080 at the end of 1 year; compounding monthly, it grows to $1,083. The $3 difference arises because of the more frequent compounding. In general, Table 4.6 shows that the $1,000 principal grows to larger future values with more frequent compounding, which explains why depositors prefer more frequent compounding. (Continuous compounding is the upper limit of the frequency of compounding, as Appendix 4C explains.)

EXAMPLE

Using interest factors, calculate the future value of $1,000 invested for 2 years at 10 percent per year compounded semiannually. *Solution:* $i/m = 10\%/2 = 5\%$ per 6-month period; $mn = 2 \times 2$ years = four 6-month periods in 2 years:

$$FV = \$1,000(FVIF_{5\%,4})$$
$$= \$1,000(1.2155)$$
$$= \$1,215.50$$

Frequency of compounding also affects present value. To accommodate different frequencies of compounding, we modify the equation for present value as follows:

$$PV = \frac{FV}{[1 + (i/m)]^{mn}}$$

For example, apply the equation to $1,000 received 1 year in the future, discounted at 8 percent compounded semiannually:

$$PV = \frac{\$1,000}{[1 + 0.08/2]^{2(1)}}$$
$$= \$924.56$$

TABLE 4.7

Effect of Frequency of Compounding on the Present Value of $1,000: i = 8% per Year and n = 1 Year

Principal	Frequency of Compounding	Present Value
$1,000	Annually	$925.93
1,000	Semiannually	924.56
1,000	Quarterly	923.85
1,000	Monthly	923.36
1,000	Daily	923.124
1,000	Continuously	923.116

Note: For continuous compounding, $PV = FV/(e)^{in}$: $PV = \$1,000/(e)^{0.08(1)} = \$923.116$.

Table 4.7 shows the present value for several other frequencies of compounding. In general, more frequent compounding leads to smaller present values. Borrowers prefer *less* frequent compounding because they receive larger loans (PV represents dollar size of a loan) for a given future payment.

EXAMPLE

Using interest factors, calculate the present value of $1,000 paid 2 years in the future, discounted at 10 percent per year compounded semiannually. *Solution:* i/m = 10%/2 = 5% per 6-month period; mn = 2 × 2 years = four 6-month periods in 2 years:

$$PV = \$1,000(PVIF_{5\%,4})$$

$$= \$1,000(0.8227)$$

$$= \$822.70$$

Given the discount rate of 10 percent compounded semiannually, repaying a 2-year loan of $822.70 requires one $1,000 payment. Consider the size of loan that you can repay with 4 semiannual payments of $1,000 each:

$$PVA = PMT(PVIFA_{5\%,4})$$

$$= \$1,000(3.5460)$$

$$= \$3,546.00$$

Given the discount rate of 10 percent compounded semiannually, you fully amortize (pay off) the $3,546 loan by making 4 semiannual payments of $1,000.[6]

---

[6] Note that the payments occur at the end of each 6-month period. The calculations become cumbersome and tedious if payments occur at times other than on discounting (or compounding) dates. We assume in this book that annuity payments occur at the same time as discounting and compounding dates—e.g., *semiannual* payments compounding *semiannually*, *quarterly* payments compounding *quarterly*, and so on. Appendixes B.3 and B.4 are based on this assumption. For a discussion of payments that occur at times other than compounding dates, see *Business Analyst Guidebook* (Texas Instruments Inc., 1982): 9-45 through 9-52.

FOCUS ON PRACTICE

Confused about Rate of Return?

Some ideas are more complex than they, at first, may appear. Take rate of return, for instance.

If you invest $100 and get back $125, then your rate of return is 25 percent, right? Well, not exactly. The dollar return "to" you is $125, consisting of a $100 return "of" your investment and a $25 return "on" your investment. You, therefore, have a 25 percent *gain*. Superimpose the 25 percent gain on *time*—say, one year—and you have a rate of return: 25 percent per year.

Now consider an investment for more than one year. Suppose that you invest $100, then suffer a 50 percent loss during the first year and a 50 percent gain during the second year, leaving you $75. Your average rate of return is

zero: $(-50\% + 50\%)/2 = 0$. But you have lost 25 percent of your investment during the two years! Your compound annual return is −13.4 percent:

$$FV = PV(1 + i)^n$$
$$\$75 = \$100(1 + i)^2$$
$$i = -13.4\% \text{ per year}$$
compounded annually.

Mutual funds, brokers, insurance companies, and money managers use both *average* return and *compound* return to report investment performance. Both calculations are perfectly legitimate, but they require different interpretations. "The average return is going to give you some information about what is most likely to happen, but used together with the

compound return, you also get the idea of the risk involved," says David Ferrier, a Merrill Lynch vice president. The larger the swings in return from one period to the next, the lower the compound return becomes in comparison to the average return.

As the accompanying table demonstrates, increasingly higher volatility leads to a compound return that is increasingly smaller than the average return. In each illustration, the sum of the three annual returns is 27 percent, for an average of 9 percent. The compound return, however, varies from 9 percent to 6.96 percent, depending on the sequence of gains and losses.

Investment Return Averages Can Mask Wide Swings

Here are six sets of investment returns totaling 27% over three years. While the average return in each case is 9% a year, compound annual returns vary. Looking at average and compound returns together gives an indication of year-to-year performance swings.

	Investment Performance					
First year	9%	5%	0%	0%	−1%	−5%
Second year	9	10	7	0	−1	−8
Third year	9	12	20	27	29	40
Average return	9.00	9.00	9.00	9.00	9.00	9.00
Compound return	9.00	8.96	8.69	8.29	8.13	6.96

Source: Reprinted by permission of *The Wall Street Journal,* © 1990 Dow Jones & Company, Inc. All Rights Reserved Worldwide.

nominal annual rate
A stated rate per year that compounds more frequently than once per year; e.g., 8 percent per year compounded daily.

Effective Annual Rate

The word *nominal* means "in name only." Examples of a **nominal annual rate** are those in the preceding section: 8 percent per year compounded semiannually; 8 percent per year compounded quarterly; and so on. These are nominal rates because they are not adjusted for frequency of compounding. Valid comparisons of investments and the making of financial decisions require the transformation of nominal rates into effective annual rates, or true rates of return. By convention, the *effective annual rate* is the rate per year compounded annually.

Table 4.6 shows that annual compounding produces a future value of $1,080 from a $1,000 investment earning 8 percent for 1 year. In this case, the nominal and effective annual rates are the same—8 percent compounded annually. With semiannual compounding, however, the $1,000 investment grows to $1,081.60 at the end of 1 year, and the effective rate exceeds the nominal rate of 8 percent. One way to calculate the effective annual rate is to use the future-value equation and solve for i:

$$FV = PV(1 + i)^n$$

$$\$1,081.60 = \$1,000(1 + i)^1$$

$$i = (\$1,081.60/\$1,000) - 1$$

$$= 0.0816, \text{ or } 8.16\% \text{ per year compounded annually}$$

Investors are indifferent between earning an effective annual rate of 8.16 percent and the nominal annual rate of 8 percent compounded semiannually because the rates yield the same future value, $1,081.60.

A more direct way of calculating the effective annual rate from the nominal annual rate i is to use this equation:[7]

$$\text{Effective annual rate} = \left(1 + \frac{i}{m}\right)^m - 1$$

where m is the frequency of compounding each year. Applied to the preceding example, the equation is:

$$\text{Effective annual rate} = \left(1 + \frac{0.08}{2}\right)^2 - 1$$

$$= (1.04)^2 - 1$$

$$= 0.0816, \text{ or } 8.16\% \text{ per year compounded annually}$$

For 8 percent per year, compounded daily, the equation is:

$$\text{Effective annual rate} = \left(1 + \frac{0.08}{365}\right)^{365} - 1$$

$$= 1.0833 - 1$$

$$= 0.0833, \text{ or } 8.33\% \text{ per year compounded annually}$$

---

[7] For annual compounding, $FV = PV(1 + i)^n$. For higher frequencies of compounding:

$$FV = PV\left(1 + \frac{i}{m}\right)^{mn}$$

To derive the equation for effective annual rate, set the preceding equations equal to each other:

$$PV(1 + i)^n = PV\left(1 + \frac{i}{m}\right)^{mn}$$

Dividing each side by PV and taking the *n*th root of each side yields:

$$1 + i = \left(1 + \frac{i}{m}\right)^m$$

Subtracting 1 from each side leaves i on the left side denoted as the effective annual rate:

$$\text{Effective annual rate} = \left(1 + \frac{i}{m}\right)^m - 1$$

Consistent with its larger future value in Table 4.6, daily compounding yields a higher effective annual rate than does semiannual compounding.

EXAMPLE

Some credit cards require the user to pay $1\frac{1}{2}$ percent per month (nominal annual rate of 18 percent) on the unpaid balance. What effective annual rate does the user pay on the unpaid balance? *Solution:*

$$\text{Effective annual rate} = \left(1 + \frac{0.18}{12}\right)^{12} - 1$$
$$= (1.015)^{12} - 1$$
$$= 0.196, \text{ or } 19.6\% \text{ per year compounded annually}$$

To perform this calculation using a regular, handheld calculator, enter 1.015 and press y^x; then enter 12 and press the equals (=) sign to get 1.196; 1.196 − 1 = 0.196, or 19.6 percent. (No wonder financial advisers say that you should pay credit-card balances within the grace period to avoid interest charges!)

STRATEGY IN PROBLEM SOLVING

Solving time-value-of-money problems requires careful interpretation of the given information. Illustrating each problem on a time line helps in the interpretation. To do so, draw a horizontal line and scale it to show different points of time—one like any of those shown earlier in the chapter. Next, at the appropriate points in time, plot the cash flows from the problem. Graphic analysis ensures that you understand the problem, and it should suggest the correct solution.

Figure 4.8 diagrams the steps to follow in solving problems involving the time value of money—both discounting and compounding. After studying the problem and drawing a time line, ask yourself: "Is this a problem involving level cash flows that occur at equal intervals of time?" If the answer is no, then you may use *either* the future-value equation or the present-value equation; or you may use the appropriate interest factor from either Appendix B.1 or B.2. However, if the answer is yes, then you are dealing with an annuity. When analyzing an annuity, ask yourself if you are dealing with an annuity that accumulates to some future value. If you are, then you must use Appendix B.3. Similarly, if the problem asks for the present value of an annuity or gives you the present value, then you must use Appendix B.4.

Vince Lombardi, ex–football coach of the Green Bay Packers and the Washington Redskins, said, "Practice doesn't make perfect. Perfect practice makes perfect!" With his maxim in mind, we turn our attention to some examples and "perfect" practice problems. The time spent working through the following problems will pay you large dividends in studying the remainder of this book.

EXAMPLE

(Growth rate) Reprographics Inc. earned $4.21 per share of common stock during 19X2 and $7.42 per share during 19X7. What is the compound annual growth rate of the company's earnings per share?

FIGURE 4.8

Flowchart of Logic for Solving Problems Involving the Time Value of Money

Solving a problem involving the time value of money begins with a time line and progresses through several logical questions. Answering the questions will help to solve the problem successfully.

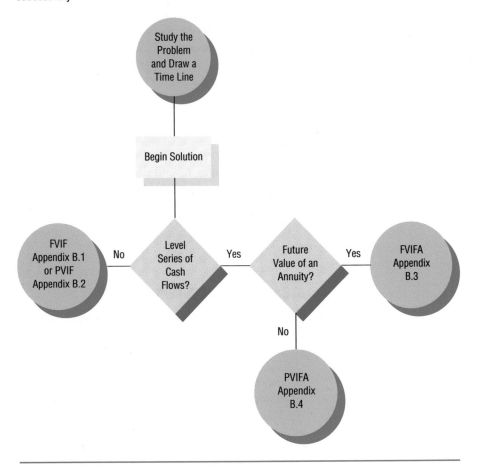

$$FV = PV(FVIF_{i,5})$$

$$\$7.42 = \$4.21\,(FVIF_{i,5})$$

$$FVIF_{i,5} = \frac{\$7.42}{\$4.21}$$

$$= 1.7625$$

Appendix B.1 shows that an *n* of 5 and an *FVIF* of 1.7625 are associated with an *i* of 12 percent. Hence the earnings per share grew at a compound annual rate of 12 percent.

EXAMPLE

(Rule of 72) The "Rule of 72" is a fun way of finding (approximate) answers for questions involving doubling and halving. The rule calls for dividing 72 by *i* (stated as a nondecimal) to find *n*, and for dividing 72 by *n* to find *i* (stated as a nondecimal). For example, if you earn 9 percent per year, then you will double

your money in approximately 8 years (72/9). And if you double your money in 6 years, you are earning approximately 12 percent per year (72/6). Other applications of the rule are as follows:

1. In how many years will you triple your money if you earn 9 percent per year? *Solution:* 72/9 = 8 years to double, plus 4 more years to triple, for a total of 12 years to triple your money. (Remember that the rule provides only approximate answers; a financial calculator shows the answer to be 12.75 years.)

2. If the gross national product (GNP) quadruples in 24 years, what is its annual rate of growth? *Solution:* It quadruples in 24 years and doubles in 12 years; so 72/12 = 6 percent per year.

3. The half-life of a dollar is the time during which inflation erodes the dollar's purchasing power by one-half. What is the half-life of a dollar when the inflation rate is 6 percent per year? *Solution:* 72/6 = 12 years. If you currently earn $30,000 per year, your earnings will be worth only $15,000 in today's purchasing power at the end of 12 years.

EXAMPLE

(Required rate for a financial goal) You plan to buy a house after working for 5 years. The down payment will be $25,000, and your budget permits you to set aside $4,095 annually. If you invest $4,095 in an account at the end of each of the next 5 years, what compound annual rate must the account pay for you to make the down payment? The solution, in steps, is as follows:

1. Your annual savings of $4,095 takes the form of an annuity.
2. The future value of the annuity is $25,000, your financial goal.
3. Because you know the future value of the annuity ($25,000), you use Appendix B.3 to find the compound annual rate:

$$FVA = PMT (FVIFA_{i,n})$$
$$\$25,000 = \$4,095 (FVIFA_{i,5})$$
$$FVIFA_{i,5} = \frac{\$25,000}{\$4,095}$$
$$= 6.1050$$

Now check Appendix B.3 and note that the interest rate associated with n = 5 and FVIFA = 6.1050 is 10 percent. You will accumulate enough money for the down payment if the account pays 10 percent per year.

EXAMPLE

(Present value of deferred payments) Evelyn Leonard is analyzing a strange opportunity that will pay her $3,000 per year for 6 years. The strange part is that she will receive the first $3,000 payment at the end of 15 years. Ms. Leonard wonders what the present value of the payments would be using a discount rate of 9 percent per year.

This problem involves the present value of an annuity with deferred payments. Solving the problem requires two steps. First, calculate the present value of the 6-year, $3,000 annuity:

FIGURE 4.9

Present Value of a 6-Year, $3,000 Annuity Discounted at 9 Percent Annually with the First Payment in 15 Years

The present value of an annuity with the first payment occurring in 15 years requires two steps: (1) Calculate the value of the annuity at the beginning of Year 15 (end of Year 14). (2) Calculate the present value of the answer in the preceding step.

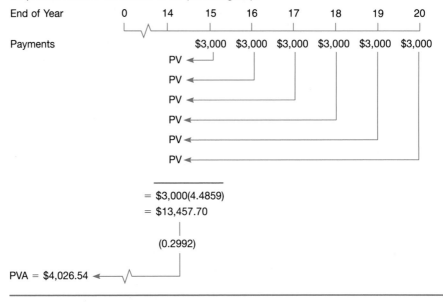

$$PVA = PMT(PVIFA_{9\%,6})$$

$$= \$3,000\,(4.4859)$$

$$= \$13,457.70$$

The $13,457.70 is the value of the annuity at Year-end 14. Figure 4.9 shows that the annuity has been discounted to the beginning of Year 15, which is the *end* of Year 14. The second step is to discount the $13,457.70 back to time zero (today) at 9 percent. Combining Steps 1 and 2 into one equation yields:

$$PVA = PMT(PVIFA_{9\%,6})\ (PVIF_{9\%,14})$$

$$= \$3,000(4.4859)\ (0.2992)$$

$$= \$4,026.54$$

Make sure that you understand why we discount the $13,457.70 using n = 14 rather than n = 15, and note the usefulness of drawing a time line for interpreting this problem.

An alternative way to solve this problem is to: (1) Calculate PVA assuming that Ms. Leonard receives a $3,000 payment each year for 20 years, then (2) subtract the present value of the first 14 payments:

$$PVA = PMT(PVIFA_{9\%,20}) - PMT(PVIFA_{9\%,14})$$

$$= \$3,000(9.1285) - \$3,000(7.7862)$$

$$= \$27,385.50 - \$23,358.60$$

$$= \$4,026.90$$

Within rounding error, $4,026.90 is the same answer as that provided by the first procedure.

SUMMARY

- Money has time value because of the time preferences of individuals and their opportunities for investment. To induce someone to loan money and forgo an alternative use of money, a borrower must promise to pay a return that is greater than the lender's opportunity cost.

- *Compounding* converts a present cash flow to a future value (FV), and *discounting* converts a future cash flow to a present value (PV). Future and present values can be calculated using mathematical equations, interest factors (in Appendix B), or a financial calculator. Table 4.8 summarizes the mathematical and interest factor equations for compounding and discounting: i represents the interest rate, or discount rate; n represents the number of periods.

- An *ordinary annuity* is a series of level payments (PMT) received or paid at the end of equally spaced time intervals. An *annuity due* is the same as an ordinary annuity except that the payments occur at the beginning of each time period. Multiplying the future value of an ordinary annuity (FVA) by $(1 + i)$ yields the future value of an annuity due, FVA(Due). Also, multiplying the present value of an ordinary annuity (PVA) by $(1 + i)$ yields the present value of an annuity due, PVA(Due).

- The equations in Table 4.8 for compounding and discounting a single cash flow provide the basis for solving the following types of problems:

Solve for	Given	Example Problem
FV	PV, i, n	Future value of an investment
PV	FV, i, n	Present value of a promised sum of money
i	PV, FV, n	Growth rate, or interest rate
n	PV, FV, i	Years required for growth

- The equations in Table 4.8 for compounding and discounting annuities provide the basis for solving the following types of problems:

Solve for	Given	Example Problem
PVA	PMT, i, n	Present value of an annuity
PMT	PVA, i, n	Payments to amortize a loan
i	PVA, PMT, n	Rate of interest on a loan
n	PVA, PMT, i	Years to amortize a loan
FVA	PMT, i, n	Future value of an annuity
PMT	FVA, i, n	Sinking-fund payment
i	FVA, PMT, n	Required rate for accumulation
n	FVA, PMT, i	Years to accumulate a sum of money

- The present (future) value of an uneven series of cash flows equals the sum of the present values (future values) of the individual cash flows. Although a laborious chore, each cash flow must be analyzed individually. Appendixes B.3

TABLE 4.8		**Compounding and Discounting with Mathematical Equations and Interest Factors**	
	Mathematical Equation	**Interest Factor Equation**	**Appendix for Interest Factor**
Compounding			
Single cash flow	$FV = PV(1 + i)^n$	$FV = PV(FVIF_{i,n})$	B.1
Ordinary annuity	$FVA = PMT\left[\dfrac{(1 + i)^n - 1}{i}\right]$	$FVA = PMT(FVIFA_{i,n})$	B.3
Discounting			
Single cash flow	$PV = \dfrac{FV}{(1 + i)^n}$	$PV = FV(PVIF_{i,n})$	B.2
Ordinary annuity	$PVA = PMT\left[\dfrac{1 - [1/(1 + i)^n]}{i}\right]$	$PVA = PMT(PVIFA_{i,n})$	B.4

and B.4 cannot be used to calculate the future and present value of an uneven series of cash flows. (Sophisticated financial calculators easily handle uneven cash flows.)

• A *perpetuity* is an annuity with an infinite life—a perpetual annuity. The present value of a perpetuity (PVP) equals the payment (PMT) divided by the discount rate (i). If the payments occur at the beginning of each period, the present value is: PMT + PMT/i.

• *Frequency of compounding (m)* is the number of times interest is accumulated. To accommodate a frequency of compounding that is more than once per year, we modify the equations for future value (FV) and present value (PV) as follows:

$$FV = PV\left(1 + \frac{i}{m}\right)^{mn} \quad \text{and} \quad PV = \frac{FV}{[1 + (i/m)]^{mn}}$$

• A *nominal annual rate* is a stated rate that does not reflect frequency of compounding. Adjusting the nominal rate (i), as follows, produces the *effective annual rate*:

$$\text{Effective annual rate} = \left(1 + \frac{i}{m}\right)^m - 1$$

For example, a nominal annual rate of 8 percent compounded semiannually is equivalent to an effective annual rate of 8.16 percent (per year, compounded annually). The effective annual rate is always higher than the nominal annual rate when the frequency of compounding is more than once per year.

• The ideas this chapter presents are used throughout the remainder of the book. For example, present-value analysis (discounted-cash-flow analysis) is used to estimate the value of stocks and bonds; it is also used to analyze corporate decisions on investing in fixed assets. In addition, effective annual rates are used to compare the costs of borrowing from a bank with the cost of issuing commercial paper.

Key Terms

discounting	present-value interest factor	amortize
compounding	discount rate	loan amortization schedule
simple interest	annuity	frequency of compounding
compound interest	ordinary annuity	effective annual rate
future-value interest factor	annuity due	nominal annual rate

Questions

4.1. Congratulations! You are the winner of a $5 million lottery, payable $125,000 per year for 40 years. In what sense is your prize worth less than $5 million?

4.2. The Internal Revenue Service (IRS) requires corporations to pay income taxes quarterly during the year in which the income is earned. This rule took effect in 1967. In 1949 the IRS allowed corporations to pay income taxes quarterly during the year following that in which income was earned. Explain why the IRS moved income tax payments closer to current payment.

4.3. What is the mathematical relationship between the interest factors in Appendixes B.1 and B.2?

4.4. What is the mathematical relationship between the interest factors in Appendixes B.3 and B.4?

4.5. An individual makes two $1,000 investments at the same time. Each investment has a $2,000 future value at the end of 5 years. Do these investments have the same effective annual return? Do these investments have the same nominal annual return if one compounds annually and the other quarterly? Explain.

4.6. Which interest rate would you prefer to *receive* on a $1,000 deposit: 12 percent annually, compounded quarterly, or 12 percent annually, compounded annually? Which interest rate would you prefer to *pay* on a $1,000 loan: 12 percent annually, compounded quarterly, or 12 percent annually, compounded annually? Explain your choices.

Strategy Problem

Myrie Wright plans to invest in a suburban mall offering her a cash flow of $3,500 at the end of each of the next 5 years with the payment at the end of Year 3 omitted. On an investment like this one, Ms. Wright requires a 15 percent annual rate of return.

To finance the investment, Ms. Wright will borrow money from Easton Savings Association. Easton Savings will charge her 12 percent per year compounded monthly.
a. Calculate the present value of the investment.
b. Suppose that Ms. Wright borrows an amount equal to the present value of the investment. Show the initial three entries on a monthly amortization schedule if the maturity of the loan is 5 years.
c. What is the effective (true) rate of interest on the loan?

Strategy	Solution

Sketch a time line.

+$3,500   +$3,500   0   +$3,500   +$3,500

Use equations for present value of an annuity and a single cash flow.

$$PVA = \$3,500(PVIFA_{15\%,2}) + \$3,500(PVIFA_{15\%,2})(PVIF_{15\%,3})$$

$$= \$3,500(1.6257) + \$3,500(1.6257)(0.6575)$$

$$= \$5,689.95 + \$3,741.14$$

$$= \$9,431.09$$

Use the equation for present value of an annuity. The beginning balance is PVA = $9,431.09.

$$PVA = PMT(PVIFA_{i/12,n \times 12})$$

$$\$9,431.09 = PMT(PVIFA_{1\%,60})$$

$$\$9,431.09 = PMT(44.955)$$

$$PMT = \frac{\$9,431.09}{44.955}$$

$$= \$209.79$$

	(1)	(2) Beginning	(3)	0.01 × (2) = (4)	(3) − (4) = (5) Repayment of	(2) − (5) = (6)
Separate payments into interest and repayment of principal.	Month	Balance	Payment	Interest	Principal	Ending Balance
	1	$9,431.09	$209.79	$94.31	$115.48	$9,315.61
	2	9,315.61	209.79	93.16	116.63	9,198.98
	3	9,198.98	209.79	91.99	117.80	9,081.18

Use the equation for effective annual rate and note that the effective rate is higher than the nominal rate.

c.

$$\text{Effective annual rate} = \left(1 + \frac{i}{m}\right)^m - 1$$

$$= \left(1 + \frac{0.12}{12}\right)^{12} - 1$$

$$= 0.1268, \text{ or } 12.68\% \text{ per year compounded annually}$$

Demonstration Problem

Andria Lee, a recent college graduate, now works as a staff consultant for Engler and Yong (E&Y), a business consulting firm. Ms. Lee completed two months of intensive training at E&Y and shortly thereafter was assigned to a project team. As the team just completed a successful engagement with a client, Ms. Lee thinks to herself: "Finally, I have some time to get my own financial house in order."

Ms. Lee has three financial concerns. First, she wants to begin a disciplined savings plan and is considering 5-year certificates of deposit at two local banks: Frost Bank pays 8 percent per year compounded annually on its 5-year CDs, and Bankers Trust pays 8 percent per year compounded quarterly. Second, Ms. Lee has been offered a credit card with a $3,000 spending limit and an annual percentage rate (APR) of 20.87 percent. The application form provides the following illustration:

Money You Receive	Monthly Payment	Number of Payments	Total of Payments	Finance Charge
$3,000	$112.82	36	$4,061.52	$1,061.52

Third, she wants to buy a condominium unit, which she expects will cost $100,000 and require a $20,000 down payment. Local rates on 30-year mortgages are 9 percent per year. Your task, as a close personal friend of Ms. Lee's, is to help her by analyzing the following questions and problems. (Looking at the task ahead, you soon realize that a financial calculator will be helpful in solving some of the problems.)

a. Ms. Lee has $7,000 to invest in a 5-year CD. Both Frost Bank and Bankers Trust have CDs that allow reinvestment of interest at the rate offered when the CD is purchased. In which bank should Ms. Lee deposit her $7,000? Support your answer by calculating the value of the CD in each bank at the end of 5 years.

b. Calculate the present value of each future value that you calculated in Part *a*. For the Frost Bank CD, use a discount rate of 8 percent per year compounded annually; for the Bankers Trust CD, use a discount rate of 8 percent per year compounded quarterly. In view of your analyses in Parts *a* and *b*, describe the relationship between the calculation of future value and the calculation of present value.

c. Calculate the effective annual rate on the CD offered by each bank. Do these rates support your decision in Part *a*? Explain.

d. Suppose that instead of investing in a CD, Ms. Lee decides to invest $7,000 in seven perpetual bonds issued by the United Kingdom. Each bond has a face value of $1,000 and a coupon rate of 8 percent, meaning that it pays $80 interest each year. Five years later, after interest rates have declined, the market price of the bond has increased, and it is yielding 7 percent. Ms. Lee then decides to sell her seven bonds. What is her total capital gain on the bonds?

e. Repeat the calculations for Part *d* but assume that interest rates have risen and the bond is yielding 9 percent. Compare the risk of the perpetual bonds with the risk of the CDs. Which investment is riskier? Explain.

f. The application form for the credit card shows that Ms. Lee can borrow $3,000 and pay 36 payments of $112.82 each. Use this information to calculate the effective annual rate.

g. The application form for the credit card states that the APR is 20.87 percent. Use this information to calculate the effective annual rate. Speculate on why the credit card company prominently displays the APR but not the effective annual rate.

h. If Ms. Lee purchases the condominium unit, how much money will she need to pay each month on her mortgage loan?

i. Calculate the effective annual rate of the mortgage loan.

j. Show the first three monthly entries of the monthly amortization schedule for the mortgage loan.

Problems

Future value

4.1. Your friend has $1,000 to invest in an account that pays 10 percent annually. How much money will be in the account at the end of 6 years?
  a. Solve this problem using the mathematical equation.
  b. Solve this problem using the interest factor equation.

Future value

4.2. Philpot Realty invests $50,000 in rental property and expects the price to appreciate 5 percent annually for 6 years. Calculate the expected price of the property at the end of 3 years and at the end of 6 years.

Present value

4.3. If you require a 15 percent annual return on an investment, what are the following cash flows worth to you today?
  a. $20,000 expected 10 years from today.
  b. $15,000 expected 5 years from today.
  c. $8,000 today.

Present value

4.4. Calculate the present value of $100,000 to be received 8 years from now. Use a discount rate of 6 percent compounded annually.

Growth rate

4.5. E. F. A. Carnes was 4 feet tall on her tenth birthday. By her eighteenth birthday, she had grown to 6 feet tall. What was Ms. Carnes's compound annual rate of growth?

Years required for growth

4.6. How many years will it take for the gross national product to increase from $6 trillion to $9 trillion if it increases by 3 percent compounded annually?

Compound rate of return

4.7. What compound annual rate of return is required for an investment amount to increase by 50 percent in 3 years?

Uneven series of cash flows

4.8. Calculate the present value of the cash flows shown below using a discount rate of (a) 10 percent, (b) zero percent, and (c) infinite percent:

End of Year	Cash Flow
1	$100,000
2	200,000
3	300,000

Uneven series of cash flows

4.9. What is the value of the following cash flows at the end of 3 years, assuming that you invest them at an annual rate of 7 percent?

End of Year	Cash Flow
1	$10,500
2	6,459
3	4,250

Present value of annuities   **4.10.** Assuming a 9 percent annual opportunity cost, which amount is worth more today: $6,000 at the end of each of the next 10 years or $3,000 at the end of each of the next 20 years?

Future value of an annuity   **4.11.** Jay Triffits plans to invest $5,000 at the end of each year for 30 years. He expects to earn 9 percent annual interest on the investment. How much money will Jay have at the end of 30 years?

Comparing present values   **4.12.** Using a 12 percent discount rate compounding annually, indicate and defend your preferences for the following financial alternatives:
a. $20,000 immediately or a 6-year annuity that pays $3,000 at the end of each of the next 3 years and $10,000 at the end of each of the following 3 years.
b. $20,000 six years from now or a 6-year annuity that pays $3,000 at the end of each of the next 3 years and $10,000 at the end of each of the following 3 years.

Required rate on an annuity   **4.13.** Modani Metals establishes a $50,000 account to repair a deteriorating scrap compactor. The company's president tells you that $8,000 must be withdrawn at the end of each year during the scrap compactor's 10-year life to replace worn parts. No cash will remain in the account at the end of the 10 years. What compound annual interest rate must be earned on the account to permit Modani Metals to withdraw $8,000 at the end of each of the next 10 years?

Long-term future value   **4.14.** The Indian who sold Manhattan for $24 worth of then high-tech items such as axes and metal kettles learned quickly about negotiation and the time value of money. Indians later sold Brooklyn for $4,800 and retained hunting rights. If the Indians had invested the $4,800 at 6 percent per year compounded annually, how much money would they have accumulated in 25 years? In 60 years?

Value of a perpetuity   **4.15.** What should you be willing to pay in order to receive $2,000 annually forever, if you require 10 percent per year on the investment?

Expected rate of return   **4.16.** Ezra Leonard purchased 200 shares of preferred stock for $50 a share. Each share pays a $4 dividend annually. Calculate Mr. Leonard's annual income from the investment and his expected rate of return.

Capital loss on a perpetuity   **4.17.** Kim Walker paid $1,000 for a perpetual bond issued by the Canadian government. The coupon rate on the bond is 5 percent, meaning that it pays $50 interest each year. Two years later, after interest rates have risen, the price of the bond has declined, and it is yielding 10 percent per year. Ms. Walker then decides to sell her bond. What is her capital loss (price decline) on the bond?

Rate of return on preferred stock   **4.18.** Ferrous Metals Inc. (FM) issued 100,000 shares of preferred stock for $25 a share. FM pays a $2.50 dividend annually on each share. Barney Palmer bought 10,000 shares of FM's preferred stock but sold them one year later. At year-end the required rate of return on the preferreds was 8 percent per year.
a. What was the trading price per share at the end of the year?
b. What was Mr. Palmer's rate of return?

Price of a perpetuity   **4.19.** The country of Orlanga has a bond outstanding that pays investors $50 at the end of each year. The bond is a perpetuity, meaning that it has no maturity date. The investors' required rate of return is presently 10 percent per year. The bond must therefore be priced to yield investors 10 percent per year.
a. Calculate the price of the bond.
b. If the required rate of return rises to 12 percent, what happens to the price? Show your calculations.

c. Explain the relationship between required rate of return and price that your calculations illustrate.

d. How much money per bond do the investors lose if the bond is purchased yielding 10 percent and sold yielding 12 percent?

Future value and frequency of compounding	4.20.	You deposit $50,000 in an account earning 12 percent per year for 6 years. How much money will be in the account at the end of 6 years if the 12 percent rate is compounded annually? Compounded semiannually? Compounded quarterly? Compounded monthly?
Present value and frequency of compounding	4.21.	Joe Rader will receive $10,000 in 5 years from a trust account. Calculate the present value of the $10,000, assuming a 10 percent discount rate compounded annually. Compounded semiannually. Compounded quarterly. Compounded monthly.
Future value of an annuity and semiannual compounding	4.22.	The retirement plan for the Toro Corporation calls for a semiannual contribution by the company of $2,000 per employee. If the cash earns 8 percent per year compounded semiannually, how much would an employee accumulate after 15 years?
Number of semiannual compounding periods	4.23.	How many semiannual compounding periods are required for $1,000 to grow to $2,653 at an annual growth rate of 10 percent per year compounded semiannually?
Effective annual rate	4.24.	Grand National Financial Services offers two types of savings accounts, one paying 8 percent per year compounded annually and the other paying 8 percent per year compounded quarterly. a. In which account would you prefer to invest your money? Show the effective annual interest rate for each account. b. Support your answer in Part *a* by showing the future value of $500 left on deposit for 6 years compounding annually and quarterly.
Effective annual rate	4.25.	Suppose that the balance on your credit card averages $1,000 through the year. Further suppose that the finance charge on the balance is 1.25 percent per month, an annual percentage rate (APR) of 15 (1.25 percent $\times$ 12 months). a. Calculate the effective annual rate on the credit-card balance. b. How many dollars of interest do you pay per year to the credit-card company?
Amortization payment	4.26.	Joanne Knoll has been working in a high-paying job for 15 years, and she is ready to "move up" in the housing market. She plans to sell her present house for $150,000, which will net her $110,000 after transaction costs and repayment of the existing mortgage. She will use the $110,000 for a down payment on a new and larger house costing $500,000. The rate on 30-year jumbo mortgages (over $202,000) is 12 percent per year. a. Calculate Ms. Knoll's monthly mortgage payment. b. How much money will Ms. Knoll pay the lender over the life of the loan? c. How much dollar interest will Ms. Knoll pay the lender over the life of the loan? d. Do you think the lender is being fair to Ms. Knoll? Explain.
Amortization payment	4.27.	Betty Freed borrowed $50,000 for 10 years and agreed to pay 10 percent annually on the loan. a. How much is each annual payment? b. How much total interest will Ms. Freed pay over the life of the loan? Does this total suggest that the lender is ripping off Ms. Freed by charging her excessive interest? Explain.
Deferred payments on debt	4.28.	A vendor allows a company to purchase a piece of machinery with payments deferred until the end of the third year. From the end of Year 3 through the end of Year 10, the company must pay $3,000 per year. At a 10 percent discount rate, what is the present value (at time zero) of the annuity payments? Sketch a time line to illustrate the cash flows.

Debt payments

4.29. Anchor Industries borrows $720,000 from State Bank and Trust. The bank loans the money for 12 years and charges 14 percent annual interest.
a. How much is each annual payment?
b. Assume that the bank will make the loan only on condition that Anchor Industries' initial 6 payments are $175,000 each. How much will each subsequent payment be?
c. How much is each semiannual payment under the original conditions but with interest compounded semiannually?

Debt payments

4.30. Datalife Corporation borrows $200,000 from a wealthy individual. Terms of the loan are 16 percent per year for 8 years, and the loan must be repaid in equal end-of-year payments.
a. How much is each annual payment? What is the total amount of cash Datalife pays over the life of the loan? How much interest does the company pay?
b. Suppose that the individual insists that the final 3 payments be $34,000 each. How much is each of the initial 5 payments?

Amortization schedule

4.31. Mallory Gambola plans to borrow $100,000 from John Wamsley Enterprises, which agrees that Mr. Gambola should repay the loan in 4 equal end-of-year payments. The company loans Mr. Gambola the money at 12 percent interest compounded annually.
a. What is the amount of each annual payment?
b. Complete the following loan amortization schedule, rounding amounts to the nearest dollar:

(1) Year	(2) Beginning Balance	(3) Annual Payment	0.12 × (2) = (4) Dollar Interest (12%)	(3) − (4) = (5) Principal Repayment	(2) − (5) = (6) Ending Balance
1	$100,000	————	$12,000	$20,924	$79,076
2	79,076	————	9,489	23,435	————
3	————	————	————	————	————
4	————	————	————	————	————

c. How much interest will Mr. Gambola pay John Wamsley Enterprises over the life of the loan? In your opinion, is he getting a good deal? Defend your opinion.

Monthly payments on a loan

4.32. Edward Frank would like to purchase a Mercedes 450 SL that sells for $50,000. He plans to take out a 5-year loan at a 12 percent annual rate (1 percent per month). The most that Mr. Frank can afford for monthly payments is $1,000, but he can sell his current car to raise additional cash for a down payment. What is the minimum amount that Mr. Frank can accept for his current car and still be able to purchase the Mercedes?

Investing for a financial goal

4.33. Your child will begin college 10 years from today. You expect college costs to be $10,000 per year at that time. To assure that enough money will be available to cover this expense, you decide to make one deposit today and to leave it untouched until your child starts college. The account will pay 8 percent compounded annually. At the beginning of the first year of college you will withdraw $10,000, and you will do the same at the beginning of each of the other 3 years, leaving a zero balance in the account after the fourth withdrawal. How much money do you need to deposit today in order to accomplish this goal?

Investing for a financial goal

4.34. Suppose you have set a specific goal for the balance in your savings account 12 years from today. You have been making year-end deposits of $2,000 per year for the past 8 years, and this annual deposit (if continued for 12 more years) would have been sufficient to reach your goal under the 10 percent average annual interest rate (annual compounding) that you have been receiving. However, you believe that the average annual interest rate on your deposits will be only 9 percent per year compounded annually over the remaining 12 years of the investment period. If your goal remains unchanged, you must adjust your annual deposit to reflect this new interest rate. Assuming that your next deposit will be made one year from today, what must be the amount of each of the remaining 12 deposits in order to reach your original goal?

Choosing between financing plans

4.35. Kris Owen plans to purchase a new $15,000 drill for his machine shop. The drill manufacturer has offered Mr. Owen two alternative 4-year financing plans: (1) Pay 10 percent annual interest and receive a $2,000 cash rebate, or (2) pay 5 percent annual interest but receive no cash rebate. If Mr. Owen's opportunity cost is 8 percent per year, which financing plan should he choose? Support your answer with calculations.

Nominal and effective interest rates

4.36. Compute the effective annual rate of return for each of the following nominal rates:
a. 9% per year compounded annually.
b. 9% per year compounded semiannually.
c. 9% per year compounded quarterly.
d. 9% per year compounded monthly.
e. 9% per year compounded daily (use 365 days in a year).
What principle does this exercise demonstrate?

Extra credit: continuous compounding

4.37. Continuous compounding is the upper limit on the frequency of compounding. A continuously (or instantaneously) compounded rate (i) is related to an annually compounded rate in the following way (see Appendix 4C):

$$i = \ln (1 + \text{Effective annual rate})$$

where *ln* is the natural logarithm. An annually compounded rate is related to a continuously compounded rate by:

$$\text{Effective annual rate} = (e)^i - 1$$

where *e* is the base of the natural logarithm.
a. Compute the effective annual rate of 9 percent per year compounded continuously.
b. Compare your answer in Part *a* with your answers to Problem 4.36. Are there any important differences?
c. An effective rate of 10 percent per year is equivalent to what continuously compounded rate per year?

Annuity due

4.38. Appendix B.4 helps you compute the present value of an ordinary annuity, which requires that receipts and payments occur at the end of each period. If receipts and payments occur at the beginning of each period, then you are dealing with an *annuity due*, and you can use Appendix B.4 only after multiplying the interest factors by $(1 + i)$. Suppose that a company pays $10,000 per year, payable at the beginning of each year, to lease a piece of equipment. What is the present value of the lease payments if the company leases the equipment for 10 years and the discount rate is 9 percent?

Rule of 72

4.39. Use the Rule of 72 in the following problems:
a. Your mother purchased land 12 years ago for $50,000, and it has now doubled in price. What is the approximate annual rate of growth of the land's price?
b. A promoter tells you that investments in rare coins double their value in 24 years. What annual rate of return is the promoter implying?
c. If you invest $10,000 at 8 percent per year, in approximately how many years will your money double? In how many years will you quadruple your money?
d. How many years will it take for you to double your money at 100 percent per year? Use the Rule of 72, then use common sense. Note the difference between your answers.

Present value and changing interest rates

4.40. A real estate firm must receive $100,000 from the sale of a house in order to preserve its $16,000 profit. The present market interest rate on 20-year mortgages is 15 percent per year.

a. Calculate the annual debt-service payments on a $100,000 mortgage at 15 percent per year for 20 years.

b. To sell the house, the firm decides to offer a low-interest loan of 12 percent per year for 20 years. Suppose that the realtor sells the house for $100,000 and receives a 20-year, 12 percent mortgage. Then, after deciding it does not want to carry the note for 20 years, the firm sells the mortgage in the secondary market to Freddie Mac to yield Freddie Mac 15 percent. What is the dollar loss the realtor incurs? Show all calculations.

c. To preserve its $16,000 profit, the real estate firm decides to sell the house for more than $100,000 with a 20-year, 12 percent mortgage. The price must be high enough so that when the realtor discounts the note to Freddie Mac, the discounted price will be $100,000 with 20 payments yielding 15 percent. Calculate the selling price of the house. (*Hint:* Use the 20 annual payments you found in Part *a* and the interest factor for 20 years and 12 percent.)

d. Using the proper annuity equation, verify that if the realtor discounts the mortgage by selling it for $100,000, then Freddie Mac will in fact receive a 15 percent return per year. (*Hint:* To find *i*, use the debt-service payments from Part *c*, $100,000, and 20 years.)

e. What does this example demonstrate about the relationship between the interest rate and the price of the house?

Computer Problems

Time value of money: template TIMVAL

4.41. On her twenty-first birthday, Alexis Timmerman received a letter from the trustees of her late Uncle Samuel's estate. Her uncle had left her a sizable sum of money that she could draw upon in any of the following ways:

(1) $100,000 per year for 10 years, starting a year from now.
(2) $650,000 in a lump sum immediately.
(3) $1,500,000 in a lump sum, 10 years from now.
(4) An increasing stream of money, starting with $80,000 after one year and increasing by $5,000 each year for a total period of 10 years.
(5) A decreasing stream starting with $140,000 next year and declining by $10,000 per year for a total of 10 years.

a. Assuming a discount rate of 10 percent, which option should Alexis choose?

b. What would her decision be if the discount rate were 8 percent? 9 percent?

Loan amortization: template AMORT

4.42. After two months of looking, you have finally found the condominium you want. It costs $60,000 with a down payment of $30,000 and an interest rate of 12 percent per year on the amount borrowed. The loan is for a period of 40 years.

a. What is the annual payment you have to make?

b. Recalculate Part *a* for interest rates of 8 percent, 9 percent, 10 percent, 11 percent, and 13 percent.

c. Recalculate Part *a* for loan maturities of 15, 20, 25, 30, and 35 years.

d. Recalculate Part *a* assuming the down payment is zero, $10,000, $20,000, $40,000, and $50,000.

Annuity: template ANNUITY

4.43. Larry Johnstone is celebrating his daughter's sixth birthday. Exactly 12 years from now she will be entering college. Mr. Johnstone wants to start saving for her college education, which will cost $10,000 per year for four years, payable at the beginning of each year. Assuming a constant interest rate of 8 percent annually over the entire period, calculate the annual payments he needs to make from her seventh birthday until her eighteenth birthday in order to provide for her education. What would the payments be if the annual interest rate were 6 percent, 10 percent, and 12 percent?

Case Problem

Melkin Housing USA

Melkin Housing USA is trying to sell homes during a period of high interest rates. The interest rate for a 20-year loan is 18 percent per year, a rate that discourages many potential buyers from buying homes. Melkin Housing decides to offer "low interest" financing, but management wants to make sure that the company will make a sufficient amount of money to maintain its profitability.

At present, the company finances a $60,000 house at 18 percent interest for 20 years with annual debt-service payments due at the end of each year.

Larry Melkin, the company's marketing director, decides that low-interest financing can boost sales dramatically. He suggests that offering home loans at 12 percent interest will be eye-popping.

Elizabeth Melkin, the company's financial manager and Larry's sister, is called in to help Larry determine the financial impact of changing the interest rate. A discussion follows in which Larry and Elizabeth consider several alternatives.

Elizabeth points out that lowering the interest rate from 18 percent to 12 percent will cause Melkin Housing USA to lose money. "We aren't a charity," she says. After talking with Larry for a while, she comes up with a proposal that will give the company a profit "up front"—that is, on the selling price.

"We can price the houses to reflect a 12 percent interest rate, but use the annual loan repayments based on a $60,000 selling price for 20 years at 18 percent," she points out. "That will make our selling price somewhere around $83,000."

Larry thinks for a moment, then asks, "How will that solve our problem?"

"Look, we sell the houses at this higher price and then offer the loan for 20 years at 12 percent annual interest. Presto!" she continues, "The buyer gets a low-interest loan, and we get our profit."

"Wait a minute," says Larry. "I've noticed that many borrowers have trouble making payments that are too high. Buyers may not be able to qualify for a loan. We don't want that to happen."

"How about this?" Elizabeth counters. "We sell the house for $83,724 and require a $23,724 down payment, with the remaining amount financed at 12 percent for 20 years." She adds, "That will still preserve our profit, yet give the buyer a break on interest rates."

After considering these proposals, Larry comes up with one more problem. "The market for housing is soft now, and I don't see selling our $60,000 houses for much more than that. Can't we do something else?"

After a moment's reflection, Elizabeth suggests that perhaps houses can be sold for $60,000, but changing the length of time over which repayment occurs may permit a lower annual interest rate. "We can keep the annual payments at $11,209 but price the house at $60,000 and make the loan at 12 percent annual interest." With a grin she leans back in her chair. "That should make all parties happy."

a. How much is each equal annual debt-service payment for a $60,000 house at the 18 percent annual interest rate for 20 years?
b. If the company markets houses at a 12 percent interest rate, how much is each equal annual payment for a $60,000 loan for 20 years?
c. For how much must Melkin Housing USA sell a house under the conditions that Elizabeth initially suggests: interest rate 12 percent, 20 years, loan payments $11,209 annually?

d. Elizabeth suggests selling the house for $83,724 with a $23,724 down payment. What is the annual debt-service payment on the amount financed at 12 percent annual interest for 20 years?

e. The final suggestion is for payments to be $11,209 annually and interest to be 12 percent per year on a loan for $60,000. What will be the maturity (time period) of this loan?

f. Do you believe that below-market interest rates offered to increase sales of houses (or cars) are likely to be reflected in their selling prices? Explain your answer.

Selected References

Cissell, Robert, Helen Cissell, and David C. Flashpohler. *Mathematics of Finance*, 5th ed. Boston: Houghton-Mifflin, 1978.

Clayton, Gary E., and Christopher B. Spivey. *The Time Value of Money*. New York: Dryden Press, 1978.

Greynolds, Elbert B., Jr., Julius S. Aronofsky, and Robert J. Frame. *Financial Analysis Using Calculators: Time Value of Money*. New York: McGraw-Hill, 1979.

Horvath, Philip A. "A Pedagogical Note on Intra-Period Compounding and Discounting." *Financial Review,* February 1985: 116–118.

Shao, Stephen P. *Mathematics for Management and Finance*, 3rd ed. Cincinnati: South-Western Publishing, 1974.

Appendix 4A FUTURE VALUE OF AN ORDINARY ANNUITY

The future value of an ordinary annuity (FVA) having payments PMT can be shown as follows:

$$\text{FVA} = \text{PMT}(1 + i)^{n-1} + \text{PMT}(1 + i)^{n-2} + \cdots + \text{PMT}(1 + i)^0 \quad (4A.1)$$

where *i* is the compound interest rate per period and *n* is the number of periods. Equation 4A.1 is a geometric series that can be simplified by first multiplying it by the repetitive term $(1 + i)$:

$$(1 + i)\text{FVA} = \text{PMT}(1 + i)^n + \text{PMT}(1 + i)^{n-1} + \cdots + \text{PMT}(1 + i) \quad (4A.2)$$

Subtracting Equation 4A.1 from Equation 4A.2 yields:

$$(1 + i)\text{FVA} - \text{FVA} = \text{PMT}(1 + i)^n - \text{PMT}(1 + i)^0$$

Factoring both sides of the equation gives:

$$\text{FVA}(1 + i - 1) = \text{PMT}[(1 + i)^n - 1]$$

which simplifies to:

$$\text{FVA} = \text{PMT}\left[\frac{(1 + i)^n - 1}{i}\right]$$

The bracketed term, denoted $\text{FVIFA}_{i,n}$, is used to calculate the interest factors in Appendix B.3.

Appendix 4B PRESENT VALUE OF AN ORDINARY ANNUITY

The present value of an ordinary annuity (PVA) having payments PMT can be shown as follows:

$$\text{PVA} = \frac{\text{PMT}}{(1 + i)} + \frac{\text{PMT}}{(1 + i)^2} + \cdots + \frac{\text{PMT}}{(1 + i)^n} \quad (4B.1)$$

where i is the discount rate and n is the number of periods. Equation 4B.1 is a geometric series that can be simplified by first multiplying it by the repetitive term $(1 + i)$:

$$(1 + i)PVA = PMT + \frac{PMT}{(1 + i)} + \cdots + \frac{PMT}{(1 + i)^{n-1}} \qquad (4B.2)$$

Subtracting Equation 4B.1 from Equation 4B.2 yields:

$$(1 + i)PVA - PVA = PMT - \frac{PMT}{(1 + i)^n}$$

Factoring both sides of the equation gives:

$$PVA(1 + i - 1) = PMT \left[1 - \frac{1}{(1 + i)^n} \right]$$

which simplifies to:

$$PVA = PMT \left[\frac{1 - [1/(1 + i)^n]}{i} \right]$$

The bracketed term, denoted $PVIFA_{i,n}$, is used to calculate the interest factors in Appendix B.4.

Appendix 4C CONTINUOUS COMPOUNDING AND DISCOUNTING

Time-value-of-money problems ordinarily involve compounding and discounting for discrete intervals of time: years, quarters, months, and so on. However, many problems in the scientific literature of finance involve continuous compounding and discounting. Also, some financial institutions pay continuously compounded rates on savings accounts. This appendix explains the reasoning underlying continuous compounding and discounting.

Continuous Compounding

Consider a commercial bank that pays 8 percent per year continuously compounded, on a savings account. How much would a $1,000 account at this bank be worth in 1 year? Answering this question requires the use of the future-value equation for continuous compounding.

Before answering this question, recall the equation for calculating future value (FV) for discrete compounding:

$$FV = PV \left(1 + \frac{i}{m} \right)^{mn} \qquad (4C.1)$$

If, instead of continuous compounding, the bank used daily compounding ($m = 365$), the future value of the $1,000 account would be:

$$FV = \$1,000 \left(1 + \frac{0.08}{365} \right)^{365(1)}$$

$$= \$1,000(1.0002192)^{365}$$

$$= \$1,000(1.08328)$$

$$= \$1,083.28$$

By letting m = 8,760 (365 days × 24 hours per day), we can even use Equation 4C.1 for hourly compounding; but we cannot use it for continuous compounding by letting *m* equal infinity.

To derive the future-value equation for continuous compounding, let a = m/i and restate Equation 4C.1 as follows:

$$FV = PV \left(1 + \frac{1}{a}\right)^{ain} \tag{4C.2}$$

Note that 1/a = i/m and ain = mn, so that Equation 4C.2 is equivalent to Equation 4C.1. Rearrange Equation 4C.2 as follows:

$$FV = PV \left[\left(1 + \frac{1}{a}\right)^a\right]^{in} \tag{4C.3}$$

As *a* approaches infinity, $(1 + 1/a)^a$ becomes the base number for natural logarithms, denoted as *e* and equal to 2.71828. As the frequency of compounding, *m*, increases without limit (becoming continuous), *a* approaches infinity. The result is the future-value equation for continuous compounding:

$$FV = PV(e)^{in} \tag{4C.4}$$

where *i* is the annual rate compounded continuously and *n* is the number of years. Now we can answer the question: How much would \$1,000 be worth in 1 year if it earned 8 percent per year compounded continuously?

$$FV = \$1,000(e)^{0.08(1)}$$
$$= \$1,000(1.08329)$$
$$= \$1,083.29 \quad \text{(shown in Table 4.6)}$$

Using a calculator to find *FV*, enter .08 and press e^x. (On some calculators, e^x is a second-level function, which requires you to press another key—e.g., *2nd*—before pressing e^x.) Multiply by \$1,000 to get \$1,083.29.

Continuous Discounting

Continuous discounting is present-value analysis based on a discount rate that is compounded continuously. In this case, we use a transformed version of Equation 4C.4 to calculate present value (PV):

$$PV = \frac{FV}{(e)^{in}} \tag{4C.5}$$

Equation 4C.5 can also be written in the following equivalent form:

Thus the present value of \$1,000 received 1 year in the future, discounted at an 8 percent annual rate compounded continuously, is calculated as follows:

$$PV = \frac{\$1,000}{(e)^{0.08(1)}} = \$1,000(e)^{-0.08(1)}$$

$$= \frac{\$1,000}{1.08329} = \$1,000(0.92312)$$

$$= \$923.12 \quad \text{(shown in Table 4.7)}$$

Effective Annual Rate

By convention, the *effective annual rate* is defined as an annual rate compounded annually. A continuously compounded rate, therefore, is not an effective rate; rather, it is a *nominal* rate. Effective annual rates are higher than their corresponding continuously compounded rates.

A continuously compounded rate (i) is related to the effective annual rate as follows:

$$i = \ln(1 + \text{Effective annual rate})$$

where *ln* is the natural logarithm (base e = 2.71828). To illustrate, for an effective annual rate of 8 percent, the equivalent rate compounded continuously is:

$$i = \ln(1 + 0.08)$$

$$= 0.0770, \text{ or } 7.70\% \text{ per year compounded continuously}$$

Using a calculator to find *i*, enter 1.08 and press *ln x*. (If *ln x* is a second-level function on your calculator, you must press another key before *ln x*.)

Perhaps more common than calculating continuous rates from effective rates is the reverse: calculating effective rates from continuous rates. Effective rates provide a common basis for comparing alternative nominal rates. The effective annual rate is related to a continuously compounded rate (i) as follows:

$$\text{Effective annual rate} = (e)^i - 1$$

For example, calculate the effective annual rate for 8 percent per year compounded continuously:

$$\text{Effective annual rate} = (e)^{0.08} - 1$$

$$= 1.0833 - 1$$

$$= 0.0833, \text{ or } 8.33\% \text{ per year compounded annually}$$

As always, the effective annual rate (8.33 percent) exceeds the continuously compounded rate (8 percent). The following listing further illustrates the relationship between continuously compounded rates and effective rates:

Continuously Compounded Rate	Effective Annual Rate
8%	8.33%
12	12.74
16	17.35
20	22.14
30	34.99

RISK AND RATE OF RETURN

Janus Complains about AIG

Janus Fund is a longtime successful mutual fund made up of common stocks. Investors buy shares of the fund and Janus managers invest their money, seeking long-term growth without undue risk. During the 10-year period ending June 30, 1992, Janus Fund earned 19.2 percent per year.

In a recent newsletter to their shareholders, Janus managers express displeasure with one of their common-stock investments. The target of their ire is American International Group (AIG), a leading, global company in the insurance business. Ironically, AIG is a great company whose management team is recognized as one of the best in the industry. So admired is AIG that its stock trades on the New York Stock Exchange at a high price relative to its earnings. Why, then, are the Janus managers displeased with AIG?

The managers are annoyed because AIG bought an aircraft leasing business, International Lease Finance, and about 15 percent of AIG's income will now come from the leasing business. The Janus managers say: "We don't like the prospects for aircraft leasing. If we did, we would have been owners of International Lease stock; it's not as if AIG discovered a heretofore unknown company." Sim-

ilarly, Janus Fund owns shares of Chambers Development (waste management) and U.S. Surgical Corporation (surgical instruments), but the Janus managers would not want the latter company to purchase the former.

According to the Janus managers: "Many corporate managers feel that they need to diversify their businesses to enhance shareholder value. Often, they buy businesses which are of lower quality than their primary business. What they don't understand is that if a shareholder wants to diversify his or her portfolio into another business, they can accomplish that very easily by buying shares." In other words, corporate managers should concentrate on their primary business and not play portfolio manager.

The objective of business financial management is to maximize shareholder wealth through maximization of stock price. Stock price depends on (1) the size of expected cash flows to shareholders, (2) the risk of the cash flows, and (3) the timing of the cash flows. To make decisions that maximize shareholder wealth, therefore, a financial manager must understand the viewpoint of the investor.

Source: "Winners and Losers," *Janus Report,* 3–4.

This chapter adopts the investor's viewpoint to explain (1) the definition of risk, (2) the measurement of risk, and (3) the relationship between risk and rate of return. In general, risk is the uncertainty surrounding the expected rate of return on an investment, and quantitative measures of risk reflect the degree of uncertainty. The *capital asset pricing model (CAPM),* a major theory of asset pricing, relates risk to the rate of return required by investors. Because investors are risk averse (they dislike it), they require higher rates of return on higher-risk investments. Understanding the CAPM will further your knowledge of stock pricing: What market forces are set into motion when investors believe a stock is overpriced or underpriced? What happens to stock prices when interest rates rise or when investors expect an increase in the inflation rate? The CAPM gives you a framework for answering these questions.

EXPECTED RATE OF RETURN

Suppose you are considering an investment in Ottawa Oatmeal Corporation's common stock. The stock presently trades at $50 per share. After careful analysis of the company's performance, you forecast that its stock price will increase to $55 per share by year-end. If it pays its usual $2 year-end dividend, then your expected rate of return for the year is 14 percent:

$$\text{Expected rate of return} = \frac{\text{Expected}}{\text{dividend yield}} + \frac{\text{Expected capital}}{\text{gain yield}}$$

$$= \frac{\$2}{\$50} + \frac{(\$55 - \$50)}{\$50}$$

$$= 0.04 + 0.10$$

$$= 0.14, \text{ or } 14\%$$

You may recognize that this 14 percent is the rate relating the expected cash flow one year hence ($55 + $2) to the present $50 invested today. Using the future-value equation from Chapter 4, you find the same expected 14 percent rate of return calculated above:

$$FV = PV(1 + i)^n$$

$$\$55 + \$2 = \$50(1 + i)^1$$

$$1.14 = (1 + i)^1$$

$$i = 1.14 - 1$$

$$= 0.14, \text{ or } 14\%$$

Perhaps your investment in Ottawa Oatmeal will in fact earn a 14 percent return. It is more likely, however, that you will be either pleasantly surprised or sorely disappointed, because the actual return will be either greater or less than your expected 14 percent. This means that your investment is subject to risk. Recall that risk involves the possibility that the actual return will differ from the expected return. Your investment in the common stock of Ottawa Oatmeal is therefore risky, just like any other investment in common stock.

If you are a prudent investor, rather than keeping your investment funds only in Ottawa Oatmeal's common stock, you will consider **diversification** into other stocks, say, Paris Perfume common stock. A portfolio of just two common stocks demonstrates the benefits of diversifying. Suppose that when the price of Paris

diversification

Investing in more than one security to reduce risk.

FIGURE 5.1

An Illustration of Portfolio Return

Ottawa Oatmeal stock performs well during recessions but poorly during boom years. Paris Perfume stock performs well during boom years but poorly during recessions. Individually and separately each stock is risky, but combined in a portfolio they produce constant returns under varying economic conditions.

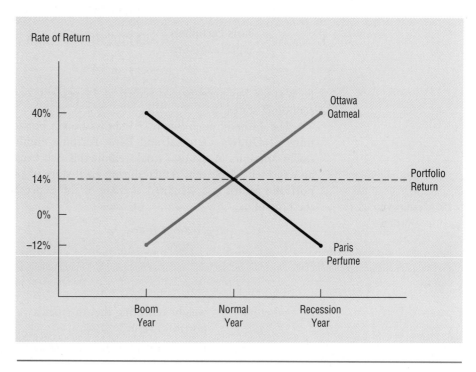

Perfume's common stock rises, the price of Ottawa Oatmeal's declines, and vice versa. This phenomenon causes the rates of return on these two common stocks to move opposite to each other. Figure 5.1 illustrates the tendency: When one stock's rate of return is high, the other stock's is low.

To illustrate the calculation of expected rate of return based on probabilities, suppose that each economic state described in Figure 5.1 is equally probable: Boom Year, $\frac{1}{3}$; Normal Year, $\frac{1}{3}$; and Recession Year, $\frac{1}{3}$. Paris Perfume's return moves with the business cycle, high during an economic boom and low during a recession. Ottawa Oatmeal's return moves counter to the business cycle, low during an economic boom and high during a recession. Each stock performs midlevel during a normal year. The following equation combines the probabilities with the possible returns to calculate $\bar{K}$, the expected rate of return based on probabilities:

$$\bar{K} = P_1K_1 + P_2K_2 + \cdots + P_nK_n$$

$$= \sum_{j=1}^{n} P_jK_j$$

where $\bar{K}$ ("K-bar") = expected rate of return; probability-weighted average of possible returns

P_j = probability of *j*th possible rate of return K_j

n = number of possible rates of return

Applied to Ottawa Oatmeal and Paris Perfume, the equation yields the following:

$$\begin{array}{l}\text{Ottawa Oatmeal's} \\ \text{expected return}\end{array} = P_1K_1 + P_2K_2 + P_3K_3$$

$$= 0.333(-0.12) + 0.333(0.14) + 0.333(0.40)$$

$$= 0.14, \text{ or } 14\%$$

$$\begin{array}{l}\text{Paris Perfume's} \\ \text{expected return}\end{array} = 0.333(0.40) + 0.333(0.14) + 0.333(-0.12)$$

$$= 0.14, \text{ or } 14\%$$

Each stock has an expected return of 14 percent, considering all three possible economic states.[1]

The dashed line in Figure 5.1 shows how a portfolio made up of equal portions of Ottawa Oatmeal and Paris Perfume eliminates risk. Investing equal dollar amounts in the two stocks eliminates risk because the portfolio produces an expected 14 percent return during each state of the business cycle. **Expected portfolio return** is a weighted average of the expected returns on the stocks in the portfolio:

expected portfolio return
Weighted average of the expected returns on the stocks in a portfolio.

$$\begin{array}{l}\text{Expected portfolio} \\ \text{return}\end{array} = W_1\bar{K}_1 + W_2\bar{K}_2 + \cdots + W_n\bar{K}_n$$

$$= \sum_{i=1}^{n} W_i \bar{K}_i$$

where W_i = weight reflecting the *i*th stock's value as a percentage of portfolio value

$\bar{K}_i$ = Expected return from investing in the *i*th stock (i = 1, 2, ..., n)

Equal investments in Ottawa Oatmeal and Paris Perfume mean that W for each is one-half (0.50). Using these values for W and the expected return ($\bar{K}$ = 14 percent) on each stock, we calculate the expected portfolio return as follows:

$$\begin{array}{l}\text{Expected portfolio} \\ \text{return}\end{array} = W_1\bar{K}_1 + W_2\bar{K}_2$$

$$= 0.50(0.14) + 0.50(0.14)$$

$$= 0.14, \text{ or } 14\%$$

Because the portfolio of these two stocks eliminates risk, the portfolio yields 14 percent regardless of the economic state. If an economic boom occurs, Ottawa Oatmeal yields -12 percent and Paris Perfume yields 40 percent for a portfolio return of 14 percent:

$$\begin{array}{l}\text{Portfolio return} \\ \text{during boom year}\end{array} = 0.50(-0.12) + 0.50(0.40)$$

$$= 0.14, \text{ or } 14\%$$

During a recession the 40 percent on Ottawa Oatmeal increases the portfolio return, offsetting the poorly performing Paris Perfume stock's -12 percent. Again, the portfolio return is 14 percent:

[1] The terms *expected return* and *expected rate of return* are used interchangeably.

$$\text{Portfolio return} \atop \text{during recession year} = 0.50(0.40) + 0.50(-0.12)$$

$$= 0.14, \text{ or } 14\%$$

In a normal year each stock yields 14 percent, as does the portfolio:

$$\text{Portfolio return} \atop \text{during normal year} = 0.50(0.14) + 0.50(0.14)$$

$$= 0.14, \text{ or } 14.0\%$$

Ottawa Oatmeal and Paris Perfume demonstrate the sage advice of the maxim: "Never put all of your eggs in one basket." Despite being risky when held individually, combined the stocks form a portfolio without risk. Reduction in risk through forming portfolios is the benefit that diversification produces.

RISK AND STANDARD DEVIATION

probability distribution
Listing of possible returns and their associated probabilities of occurrence.

standard deviation, σ
Measure of dispersion around the expected return of a distribution of possible returns; a measure of total risk.

Another way to illustrate the benefit of diversification is by calculating standard deviation, a measure of *total risk*. Standard deviation measures the variability of possible returns in a **probability distribution,** with larger standard deviations indicating greater variability and smaller ones indicating lesser variability. Using the Greek letter σ (sigma), we calculate **standard deviation** as follows:

$$\sigma = [P_1(K_1 - \bar{K})^2 + P_2(K_2 - \bar{K})^2 + \cdots + P_n(K_n - \bar{K})^2]^{1/2}$$

$$= \sqrt{\sum_{j=1}^{n} P_j(K_j - \bar{K})^2}$$

where σ = sigma, the standard deviation
  P_j = probability of the *j*th possible rate of return K_j
  $\bar{K}$ = expected rate of return
  n = number of possible rates of return

Table 5.1 shows the calculation of standard deviation for Ottawa Oatmeal, Paris Perfume, and the portfolio comprising 50 percent of each company. The following steps are used to calculate each standard deviation:

1. Calculate the deviation of each possible return from the expected return: $(K_j - \bar{K})$.
2. Square each deviation: $(K_j - \bar{K})^2$.
3. Multiply each squared deviation by the probability of its occurrence: $P_j(K_j - \bar{K})^2$.

variance, σ²
The square of standard deviation.

4. Sum the products from Step 3 to obtain the **variance** of returns:

$$\sigma^2 = \sum_{j=1}^{n} P_j(K_j - \bar{K})^2$$

5. Take the square root of the variance to obtain the standard deviation:

$$\sigma = \sqrt{\sigma^2} = \sqrt{\sum_{j=1}^{n} P_j(K_j - \bar{K})^2}$$

Based on the preceding five steps, Table 5.1 shows that the standard deviation of possible returns for Ottawa Oatmeal and Paris Perfume, taken individ-

TABLE 5.1

Calculating Standard Deviation: Ottawa Oatmeal, Paris Perfume, and a Portfolio Containing Both Stocks

Stock/Portfolio	(1) Deviation $(K_j - \bar{K})$	$(1)^2 = (2)$ Deviation Squared	(3) Probability	$(2) \times (3) = 4$ Product
Ottawa Oatmeal	$(-12 - 14) = -26$	676	0.333	225.11
	$(14 - 14) = \quad 0$	0	0.333	0
	$(40 - 14) = \quad 26$	676	0.333	225.11
			Variance $= \sigma^2 =$	450.22
			Standard deviation $= \sigma = $ 21.22%	
Paris Perfume	$(40 - 14) = \quad 26$	676	0.333	225.11
	$(14 - 14) = \quad 0$	0	0.333	0
	$(-12 - 14) = -26$	676	0.333	225.11
			Variance $= \sigma^2 =$	450.22
			Standard deviation $= \sigma = $ 21.22%	
Portfolio[a]	$(14 - 14) = \quad 0$	0	0.333	0
	$(14 - 14) = \quad 0$	0	0.333	0
	$(14 - 14) = \quad 0$	0	0.333	0
			Variance $= \sigma^2 = 0$	
			Standard deviation $= \sigma = $ 0%	

[a] Half of the portfolio is Ottawa Oatmeal and half is Paris Perfume.

ually, is 21.22 percent. Combining the two stocks in a portfolio (50 percent of the portfolio in each stock), however, yields a standard deviation of zero. In other words, if you invest all of your money in Ottawa Oatmeal (or Paris Perfume), your expected return is 14 percent accompanied by a standard deviation of 21.22 percent, which means that you face substantial risk. In contrast, if you invest half of your money in each stock, your expected return is still 14 percent, but the standard deviation is zero, which means that you face no risk. The simple act of diversification lessens your exposure to risk—in this illustration diversification eliminates risk.[2]

Standard deviation in the preceding example is based on a distribution of *known* possible returns and probabilities. Identifying such a distribution in practice is a difficult task. To overcome this difficulty, analysts often use a sample of past returns as a proxy for the distribution of future returns. Standard deviation of the sample returns then becomes an estimate of the standard deviation of possible future returns. The estimated standard deviation (σ) based on a sample of past returns is calculated as follows:

$$\text{Estimated } \sigma = \sqrt{\frac{\sum_{t=1}^{n} (K_t - K_{avg})^2}{n - 1}}$$

[2] For bell-shaped distributions (normal or Gaussian) of possible rates of return, σ has a special interpretation. The probability is 68.3 percent that the actual rate of return will be within 1.0σ of the expected rate of return: Prob($-1\sigma < K_j < +1\sigma$) = 68.3 percent. The probability is 95.5 percent that the actual rate of return will be within 2.0σ of the expected rate of return, and 99.7 percent that it will be within 3.0σ. The latter case encompasses virtually all possible rates of return. Diversification causes total risk (σ) of a portfolio to become smaller. When σ becomes smaller, investors become more certain about the future rate of return that they expect to earn on the portfolio.

K_t represents the past rate of return in Period t, and K_{avg} is the average rate of return during the past n periods.

Calculate the estimated standard deviation based on the following annual rates of return on a common stock: 19X4, 25%; 19X5, −15%; 19X6, 20%.

$$K_{avg} = \frac{25 - 15 + 20}{3} = 10\%$$

$$\text{Estimated } \sigma = \sqrt{\frac{(25 - 10)^2 + (-15 - 10)^2 + (20 - 10)^2}{3 - 1}}$$

$$= \sqrt{\frac{950}{2}} = 21.8\%$$

Based on only three (n = 3) past returns, the average return (K_{avg}) is 10 percent, and the estimated standard deviation is 21.8 percent. For brevity, the example contains only three returns; to obtain a good estimate of σ in practice, you should use a much larger number of returns.

The magnitudes in the preceding example for K_{avg} (10%) and estimated σ (21.8 percent) are not unusual for individual common stocks. Note also that estimated σ is often a satisfactory measure of future variability, but K_{avg} is rarely a satisfactory measure of expected future return. In general, rates of return on individual stocks vary too much (in the example, 25, −15, and 20 percent) for the past average to be a good indicator of expected future return.

RISK AND CORRELATION

correlation
Degree to which a series of returns changes systematically with another series.

Real-life common stocks rarely behave like Ottawa Oatmeal and Paris Perfume. Totally eliminating risk by joining Ottawa Oatmeal with Paris Perfume is possible only because each one's return always moves opposite to the other's. If the returns varied in some other way, then risk could not have been totally eliminated. The way in which returns move together is known as correlation. **Correlation** is a statistical measure of the degree to which one series of returns changes systematically with another series of returns.

Figure 5.2 suggests the significance of perfect negative correlation between two stocks, O and P. *Perfect negative correlation* means that when one series of numbers increases or decreases, the other series *always* does exactly the opposite. Notice in Figure 5.2 that when the rate of return on Stock O is up, the rate of return on Stock P is down, and vice versa. This perfect negative correlation describes the relationship between Ottawa Oatmeal and Paris Perfume in Figure 5.1. Opposite to Stocks O and P, Stocks X and Y in Figure 5.2 display perfect positive correlation. *Perfect positive correlation* means that when one series of numbers increases or decreases, the other series *always* does exactly the same. In fact, Stocks X and Y are perfect substitutes for one another. Midway between these two extremes is *zero correlation*, in which the two series do not move together in a systematic way—when one increases, the other may decrease,

FIGURE 5.2

Illustrations of Perfect Negative and Perfect Positive Correlation between Rates of Return

When returns always move exactly opposite to each other, like those in the left panel, the returns have perfect negative correlation. When returns always move exactly in the same way, like those in the right panel, the returns have perfect positive correlation.

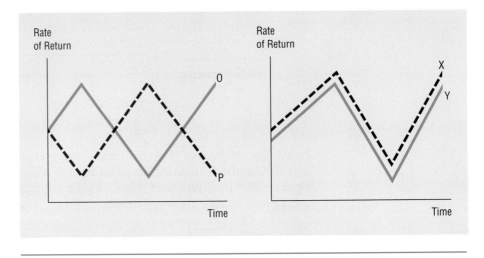

increase, or remain unchanged. Whenever two series of returns have zero correlation, information about one series provides no information about the other.

A portfolio of two stocks can be constructed to eliminate risk totally when their returns have perfect negative correlation. When returns have perfect positive correlation, diversification does not reduce risk. In the preceding example we looked at an idealized world in which Stocks O and P were perfectly negatively correlated. In reality, the correlation between rates of return on most pairs of common stocks is positive but not perfectly so. That is, their actual rates of return (and prices) *tend* to change in the same direction but not always. Usually, one will increase and the other one will too. But sometimes the other one will decrease. This lack of perfect positive correlation enables diversification to reduce risk. In real-life portfolios the extreme winners balance against the extreme losers and the moderate winners support the moderate losers.[3]

DIVERSIFIABLE AND NONDIVERSIFIABLE RISK

Combining different stocks into a portfolio reduces total risk as measured by standard deviation. The standard deviation becomes smaller as it reflects the reduced variability in portfolio returns and greater certainty about the expected

---

[3] A correlation coefficient (denoted by Corr) lies within the following range: $-1 \leq \text{Corr} \leq +1$. Technically, the correlation coefficient for two rates of return (K_x and K_y) is:

$$\text{Corr} = \text{Cov}(K_x, K_y)/\sigma_x \sigma_y$$

$\text{Cov}(K_x, K_y)$ stands for covariance between rates of return K_x and K_y; it is a statistical measure of the way K_x and K_y covary together and is defined mathematically as follows:

$$\text{Cov}(K_x, K_y) = E[(K_x - \bar{K}_x)(K_y - \bar{K}_y)]$$

where E is the expectations operator (tells you to take the expected value of what follows). σ_x and σ_y are the standard deviations of K_x and K_y, respectively.

return. To illustrate the decline in total risk with increased diversification, we first decompose total risk into two parts:

$$\text{Total risk} = \text{Diversifiable risk} + \text{Nondiversifiable risk}$$

Diversifiable risk is also known as *unsystematic* risk or *company-specific* risk. Nondiversifiable risk is also known as *systematic* risk or *market* risk.

Diversifiable risk approaches zero in portfolios of several stocks because it arises from company-specific factors whose effects on individual stock returns offset each other. The following unexpected events are diversifiable because investors can offset adverse effects by diversifying their investments among stocks of several different companies:

diversifiable risk
Portion of stock risk that is unique to the company.

- A company's labor force unexpectedly goes on strike.
- A company unexpectedly hires a new management team.
- A company's top management dies in a plane crash.
- A one-million-gallon oil tank bursts and floods a company's production area.

The above list stresses unexpected changes, because stock prices already reflect the changes that investors expect. Expected events do not cause returns and stock prices to change because investors have already acted on their expectations by buying or selling certain stocks. Unexpected changes, however, cause returns and stock prices to change in ways investors cannot anticipate.

Portfolios need not be large to reduce diversifiable risk significantly. On average, according to Figure 5.3, only 20 randomly selected stocks with equal dollar investments would rid the investor of most of the diversifiable risk. Because diversifiable risk constitutes about 50 percent of the total risk of a typical common stock, getting rid of it through diversification is clearly beneficial.

Although a well-diversified portfolio virtually eliminates diversifiable risk, it nevertheless contains **nondiversifiable risk,** and its actual return may still differ from what the investor expects. Consider, for example, the performance of Standard & Poor's 500 Index, which we examined in Chapter 3. It is a well-diversified portfolio containing 500 stocks and therefore has very little diversifiable risk. Despite being a portfolio of 500 stocks, the S&P 500 varies considerably over time and is difficult for investors to predict.

Several economic influences contribute to nondiversifiable risk, causing swings in returns on diversified portfolios. Notice in the following examples of nondiversifiable events that each factor affects all stocks taken collectively, even though each individual stock may respond differently:

nondiversifiable risk
Portion of stock risk that arises from general economic conditions affecting all stocks simultaneously.

- Unexpected changes in interest rates—interest rate risk.
- Unexpected changes in inflation—inflation risk.
- Unexpected changes in cash flows such as those resulting from tax rate changes, foreign competition, and the business cycle.

As with diversifiable events, the list above stresses unexpected events that cause returns and stock prices to change in ways investors cannot anticipate.

Nondiversifiable risk is a relevant concept of risk because simply diversifying a portfolio cannot eliminate it. Based on this logic, nondiversifiable risk is the only type of risk needed to determine required rates of return on stocks. Figure 5.3 shows that nondiversifiable risk is the irreducible component of total risk:

$$\text{Nondiversifiable risk} = \text{Total risk} - \text{Diversifiable risk}$$

Reducing Total Risk by Diversifying

Increasing the number of different stocks in a portfolio enables an investor to reduce diversifiable risk. Total risk (variability of returns) of the portfolio therefore declines as well. Studies of historical annual rates of return show that the standard deviation (σ) of a typical common stock is about 30 percent; σ of a portfolio of all stocks is only about 15 percent.

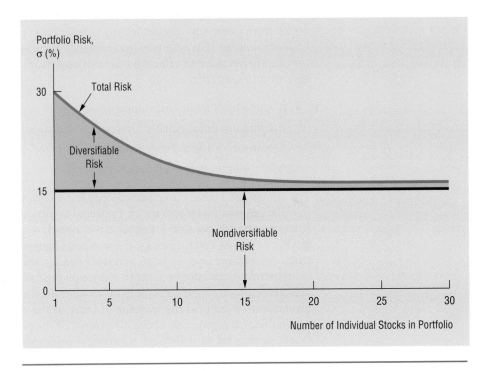

For well-diversified portfolios, nondiversifiable risk approximately equals total risk because diversifiable risk approaches zero.

MEASURING NONDIVERSIFIABLE RISK

According to the capital asset pricing model (described in the next section), the marketplace rewards investors with a percentage premium for incurring nondiversifiable risk only; it does not reward investors for risk that can be easily eliminated by diversification. To estimate the rate of return required on a common stock, therefore, we must have a method for measuring nondiversifiable risk.

Figure 5.4 illustrates how historical *(ex post)* rates of return are used to measure nondiversifiable risk. The slope of the line in Figure 5.4 provides an estimate of how a particular stock's historical rates of return relate to returns on a market index. A slope of 0.95 means that the stock's rate of return is slightly less volatile than the market's. When the market earns a positive 10 percent return for a particular period, this stock tends to produce a positive 9.5 percent return (0.95 × 10). A 10 percent decline in the market index (say, Standard & Poor's 500 Index) tends to be associated with a −9.5 percent return on the stock. The slope of the line in Figure 5.4 is the *beta coefficient*, or simply *beta* (β). **Beta** is

beta, β
Measure of nondiversifiable risk.

FIGURE 5.4

Graph of Historical Rates of Return for Estimating a Stock's Beta

To estimate beta, many analysts use the most recent 60 monthly rates of return on the common stock and the market index (e.g., Standard & Poor's 500 Index). Rate of return for one month equals the change in price plus any dividends paid, all divided by the beginning price. Each dot represents an actual rate of return on the stock and the market index for a particular month. A statistical technique (regression analysis) fits the line whose slope we call beta. Some analysts use weekly periods instead of monthly periods, and they sometimes make statistical adjustments to beta to make it a better predictor.

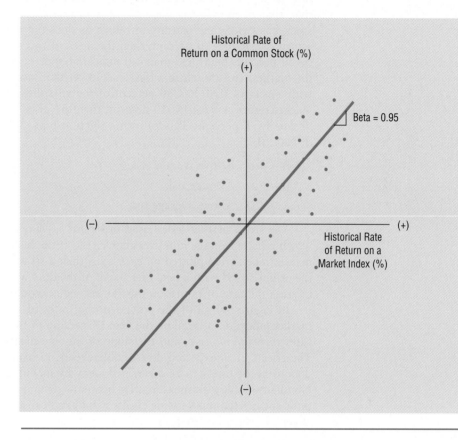

the measure of nondiversifiable risk.[4] By looking at the historical relationship, a financial manager hopes to gain some idea of how a stock's rate of return will react to market movements in the future.

---

[4]Technically, beta is a regression coefficient defined as follows:

$$\beta = \frac{\text{Cov}(K_j, K_m)}{\text{Var}(K_m)}$$

$\text{Cov}(K_j, K_m)$ is the covariance between the stock return (K_j) and the market portfolio (K_m). $\text{Var}(K_m)$ is the variance of the market portfolio return. Alternatively, beta can be defined in terms of the correlation (Corr) between K_j and K_m:

$$\beta = \left(\frac{\sigma_j}{\sigma_m}\right) \text{Corr}$$

where σ_j is the standard deviation of K_j and σ_m is the standard deviation of K_m. The average correlation coefficient between stock returns (K_j) and market returns (K_m) is about 0.5. Since the average stock beta is 1.0, the average ratio of σ_j to σ_m is approximately 2.0; that is, uncertainty of return on a typical stock is about twice that of the market portfolio.

A beta of 1.0 indicates that a common stock has average nondiversifiable risk. Stated differently, a beta of 1.0 tells us that the stock has nondiversifiable risk equal to that of the *market portfolio* of all stocks (as represented by the market index used to estimate beta). Percentage changes in the price of the stock tend to be the same as those of the market index. Volatility of the stock price and therefore its rate of return tend to be equivalent to that of the market index.

Betas different from 1.0 mean that nondiversifiable risk differs from that of the market portfolio. Betas greater than 1.0 indicate nondiversifiable risk greater than that of the market generally. For example, a beta of 2.0 indicates that a stock has twice the volatility in return as does the market index. If the market return is *negative* 10 percent, then the price of this stock would tend to *decline* by 20 percent. Betas less than 1.0 indicate nondiversifiable risk less than that of the market, and therefore a risk level lower than average. For example, a stock with a beta of 0.80 has 80 percent of the volatility of the market index. If the market return is *negative* 10 percent, then the price of this stock would tend to *decline* by 8 percent. The following relationships summarize the interpretation of beta (β):

$\beta < 1.0$ Below-average risk

$\beta = 1.0$ Average risk

$\beta > 1.0$ Above-average risk

The stock market index used in Figure 5.4 has a beta of 1.0 by definition, which reflects average nondiversifiable risk. If the historical rate of return on the market index were plotted on *each* axis, then a straight line would radiate from the origin at 45° with a beta of 1.0. All of the dots would fall directly on the line because the rate of return on the market index would be plotted against itself.

In Figure 5.4 all of the dots, denoting rates of return on the stock and the market index, do not fall on the line. Dispersion of the dots around the line measures *diversifiable* risk, and the slope of the line measures nondiversifiable risk. The effects of unexpected diversifiable events, measured by the distances of the dots from the line, can be diversified away by including the stock in a portfolio. Nondiversifiable risk measured by beta still remains, however, after diversification; unexpected marketwide events would still cause returns and stock prices to change in ways investors cannot anticipate.

Most betas of common stocks fall within the range of 0.70 to 1.60, although betas occasionally reach as low as 0.40 and as high as 2.50. Table 5.2 presents the betas for 25 different common stocks calculated by the *Value Line Investment Survey*. The betas included in Table 5.2 range from 0.45 to 1.90. In addition to *Value Line*, Merrill Lynch, Wells Fargo National Bank, and other firms regularly publish estimates of betas for hundreds of companies.

The simple numerical average of the betas in Table 5.2 is 1.15. This average is the beta of the portfolio of all 25 stocks assuming an equal dollar investment in each stock. For example, if you invested a total of $25,000 with $1,000 in each stock, then your portfolio's beta would be 1.15.

portfolio beta (β_p)

Weighted average of the stock betas in a portfolio.

In general, a **portfolio beta (β_p)** is the weighted average of the stock betas in the portfolio, with the weights assigned according to the amount invested in each stock as a percentage of the total invested:

$$\beta_p = W_1\beta_1 + W_2\beta_2 + \cdots + W_n\beta_n$$

$$= \sum_{i=1}^{n} W_i \beta_i$$

TABLE 5.2

Betas for Selected Common Stocks

Company	Beta	Company	Beta
1. Battle Mountain Gold Co.	0.45	14. General Cinema	1.10
2. Wisconsin Energy	0.60	15. Walt Disney	1.20
3. Franklin Electric	0.70	16. Pep Boys	1.25
4. Exxon Corp.	0.75	17. Blockbuster Entertainment	1.30
5. Cadbury Schweppes	0.80	18. Raychem Corp.	1.35
6. BIC Corp.	0.85	19. American Express	1.40
7. Playboy Enterprises	0.85	20. Circuit City Stores	1.50
8. Clorox Co.	0.90	21. Liz Claiborne	1.60
9. Hormel	0.95	22. Harley Davidson	1.67
10. Anheuser-Busch	0.95	23. Spiegel Inc. "A"	1.75
11. Colgate Palmolive	1.00	24. Tyson Foods	1.85
12. Boeing	1.05	25. Micropolis Corp.	1.90
13. Campbell Soup	1.05		

Source: Value Line Investment Survey (New York: Arnold Bernhard, 1992).

where W_i = weight reflecting the ith stock's value as a percentage of portfolio value

β_i = beta of the ith stock (i = 1, 2, . . . , n)

The beta of a stock measures its contribution to the riskiness of a portfolio. Adding high-beta stocks to the portfolio increases its risk, and adding low-beta stocks lowers its risk. Investors can adjust their exposure to portfolio risk by buying and selling stocks with differing betas.

Many analysts estimate and use betas for common stock but not for other securities. Theoretically, all securities have betas, but estimation problems have precluded their widespread use for securities other than common stock. Betas for long-term corporate bonds probably range from 0.10 to 0.40.

EXAMPLE

Cortland Hansen decides to invest 65 percent of his money in Harley Davidson stock, 10 percent in Clorox Co. stock, and 25 percent in Walt Disney stock. Cortland's research indicates that Harley Davidson is riskiest with a 1.67 beta, Clorox Co. is least risky with a 0.9 beta, and Walt Disney falls between with a 1.2 beta. The portfolio beta is 1.48, calculated as follows:

$$\beta_p = 0.65(1.67) + 0.10(0.90) + 0.25(1.20)$$

$$= 1.48$$

In tabular form, the solution appears as follows:

(1) Stock	(2) Proportion of Portfolio	(3) Stock Beta β_i	(2) × (3) = (4) Product
Harley Davidson	0.65	1.67	1.09
Clorox Co.	0.10	0.90	0.09
Walt Disney	0.25	1.20	0.30
	1.00	Portfolio beta (β_p) =	1.48

•

Valuing Stocks *the* Value Line *Way*

The *Value Line Investment Survey* is one source of beta values. Published by Arnold Bernhard & Company, *Value Line* develops financial information (including betas) for about 1,700 publicly held corporations. A typical report on a company is shown in Figure 5.5. Notice that in addition to such information as monthly stock prices, growth rates in dividends, and other information about the company, *Value Line* presents the stock's beta in the upper left corner of the report. The beta is calculated with the New York Stock Exchange Index as the measure of the market.

Arnold Bernhard started *Value Line* in the depths of the 1930s depression, seeking to develop a rational, unemotional, and objective system for evaluating stocks. He later expanded into mutual fund management "to prove my theories about stock selection."

Value Line tries to identify industry groups and individual stocks that will outperform the rest of the market and those that will do worse. Among the items it considers are long-term price and earnings trends, price momentum (the stock's 10-week average price relative to its 52-week average

price compared with the market), and the surprise factor—the degree to which analysts' earnings forecasts differ from what the company actually reported.

Value Line does not rank the performance of its own investment advice. But based on the service's own criteria, it would probably carry no better than a No. 3 ranking for timeliness because of lag times in publication. The information in the upper left corner of Figure 5.5 tells us that a timeliness ranking of 3 is average.

Source: Based on reports in *Business Week*, Jan. 24, 1983, 72, and May 27, 1985, 134; and *Value Line*'s 1989 brochure.

capital asset pricing model (CAPM)
Model that relates required rate of return to the risk-free rate plus a risk premium.

risk-free rate of return
Rate of return known with certainty; estimated with yields on U.S. Treasury securities.

risk premium
Additional percentage points required by investors for investment in risky securities; in the CAPM, the excess return over the risk-free rate.

THE CAPITAL ASSET PRICING MODEL

For stocks held in a well-diversified portfolio, the risk of each stock is appropriately represented by beta, which measures the risk contributed by each stock to the portfolio. The **capital asset pricing model (CAPM)** incorporates beta as the relevant measure of risk and relates it to required rate of return. According to the CAPM, risk-averse investors require higher rates of return (pay smaller prices, other things being constant) on stocks with larger betas. To induce investors to forgo the **risk-free rate of return** (R_f, proxied by the return on U.S. Treasury securities), stocks must provide the expectation of a return in excess of R_f. The general idea is as follows:

$$\text{Required rate of return} = R_f + \text{Risk premium}$$

The risk-free return accounts for the time value of money, and the **risk premium** is the additional percentage points necessary to compensate investors for risk (beta).

The primary focus of the capital asset pricing model is on the risk premium added to the risk-free return to derive the required return. Prior to development of the model in 1964, risk premiums were based largely on judgment and intuition. Complementing judgment and intuition with more scientific procedures constitutes the major contribution of the model to the practice of finance.

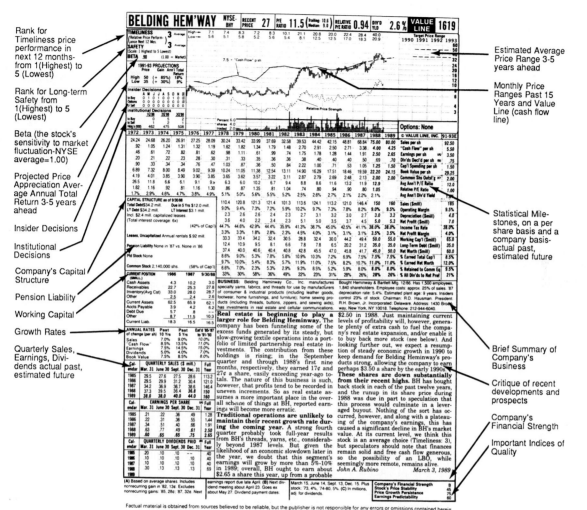

FIGURE 5.5

A Typical *Value Line* Report

Rank for Timeliness price performance in next 12 months—from 1(Highest) to 5 (Lowest)

Rank for Long-term Safety from 1(Highest) to 5 (Lowest)

Beta (the stock's sensitivity to market fluctuation-NYSE average=1.00)

Projected Price Appreciation Average Annual Total Return 3-5 years ahead

Insider Decisions

Institutional Decisions

Company's Capital Structure

Pension Liability

Working Capital

Growth Rates

Quarterly Sales, Earnings, Dividends actual past, estimated future

Estimated Average Price Range 3-5 years ahead

Monthly Price Ranges Past 15 Years and Value Line (cash flow line)

Statistical Milestones, on a per share basis and a company basis-actual past, estimated future

Brief Summary of Company's Business

Critique of recent developments and prospects

Company's Financial Strength

Important Indices of Quality

Source: Value Line Inc., 1989.

market price of risk
Required rate of return on the market portfolio (or average-risk stock) less the risk-free rate; in the CAPM, the slope of the security market line.

market portfolio
Portfolio of all risky securities; Standard & Poor's 500 Index is often used as a proxy for the market portfolio.

According to the CAPM, the risk premium consists of two parts multiplied together:

$$\text{Risk premium} = \frac{\text{Market price}}{\text{of risk}} \times \frac{\text{Nondiversifiable}}{\text{risk}}$$

Nondiversifiable risk is measured with beta, β, as discussed in the preceding section. The **market price of risk** is the reward per unit of risk measured in market terms. It is measured with the required rate of return on the average-risk common stock minus the risk-free rate of return (R_f). The required rate of return on the average-risk common stock is equivalent to the required rate of return on the collection of all common stocks (K_m). The collection of all common stocks trading in the secondary market is called the **market portfolio.**

Putting together these ideas yields the following measure of the percentage points for the risk premium in the required rate of return:

$$\text{Risk premium} = \frac{\text{Market price}}{\text{of risk}} \times \frac{\text{Nondiversifiable}}{\text{risk}}$$

$$= (K_m - R_f)\beta$$

Adding this risk premium to the risk-free rate of return yields the *capital asset pricing model:*

$$K_c = R_f + (K_m - R_f)\beta$$

where K_c is the required rate of return on a common stock. Each company's common stock has its own particular value for nondiversifiable risk (β): Higher values indicate higher risk levels and correspondingly higher required rates of return (K_c). Values for the risk-free return (R_f) and the required return on the market portfolio (K_m) are the *same* for *all* companies.

EXAMPLE

Claymore Company's common stock has a beta of 1.5, and Pacific Power's common stock has a beta of 0.7. The risk-free return (R_f) is 8 percent, and the required return on the market portfolio (K_m) is 14 percent. Calculate the required rate of return on each common stock:

$$\text{Claymore Company:} \quad K_c = 0.08 + (0.14 - 0.08)1.5$$
$$= 0.08 + 0.09$$
$$= 0.170, \text{ or } 17.0\%$$

$$\text{Pacific Power:} \quad K_c = 0.08 + (0.14 - 0.08)0.7$$
$$= 0.08 + 0.042$$
$$= 0.122, \text{ or } 12.2\%$$

The larger beta of Claymore Company causes its required rate of return to be larger than Pacific Power's.

Figure 5.6 presents a graphic portrayal of the capital asset pricing model, with required rate of return (K_c) on the vertical axis and beta on the horizontal axis. The security market line (SML) shows the relationship between nondiversifiable risk and the rate of return investors require on common stock. The trade-off between risk and return determines the line's slope—to obtain a greater return, an investor must be willing to incur greater nondiversifiable risk. Added risk leads to a quantifiable increase in the required rate of return. The graph makes it easier to visualize and understand the capital asset pricing model.

Intercept and Slope of the Security Market Line

The capital asset pricing model suggests that when beta is zero, the required rate of return equals the risk-free return R_f:

$$K_c = R_f + (K_m - R_f)\beta$$
$$= R_f + (K_m - R_f)0$$
$$= R_f$$

FIGURE 5.6

Graphic Portrayal of the Capital Asset Pricing Model

The security market line is a straight line connecting the risk-free rate accompanying a zero beta and the point representing the required rate of return on the market portfolio, K_m, and its beta of 1.0. The slope of the SML is the market price of risk, $K_m - R_f$.

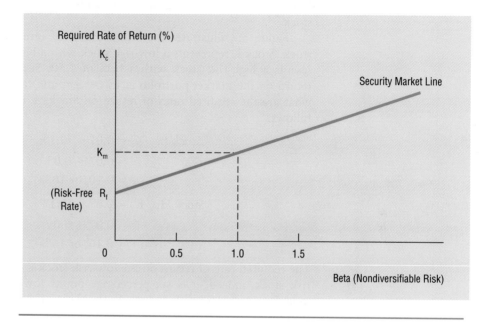

Figure 5.6 shows $K_c = R_f$ when beta equals zero. One more point on the security market line is known, the point denoting the return on the market portfolio and its beta of 1.0. If beta of a stock equals 1.0, then it has the same nondiversifiable risk as the market portfolio or average stock, and the required rate of return is K_m, the return required on the market portfolio:

$$K_c = R_f + (K_m - R_f)\beta$$
$$= R_f + (K_m - R_f)1.0$$
$$= R_f + K_m - R_f$$
$$= K_m$$

We can use these two points (K_m and a beta of 1.0, and R_f and a beta of 0) to construct the equation of the security market line in Figure 5.6:

$$\text{Intercept} = R_f$$

$$\text{Slope} = \frac{\text{Rise}}{\text{Run}} = \frac{K_m - R_f}{1.0 - 0}$$
$$= K_m - R_f$$

The slope represents the market price of risk: ($K_m - R_f$) is the return in excess of the risk-free rate necessary to induce investors to buy an average stock with the same risk as the market portfolio (for example, Standard & Poor's 500 Index).

Basic geometry tells us that K_c equals the intercept (R_f) plus the slope times β. The result is the capital asset pricing model with which this section began:

$$K_c = R_f + (K_m - R_f)\beta$$

Note that beta is the slope of the line in Figure 5.4, but it is the value along the horizontal axis in Figure 5.6. Estimating betas requires historical returns on the stock and on the market portfolio (see Figure 5.4). Once estimated, beta is used in the capital asset pricing model to estimate the required rate of return on the stock.

Figure 5.7 illustrates the required rate of return on a low- and high-risk stock. Stock L represents a low-risk stock with a beta of 0.50, and Stock H represents a high-risk stock with a beta of 1.50. Supposing the required rate of return on the market portfolio is 13 percent and the risk-free rate is 7 percent, what are the required rates of return on Stocks L and H? The solutions are as follows:

$$\text{Stock L:} \quad K_c = 0.07 + (0.13 - 0.07)0.50$$
$$= 0.07 + 0.03$$
$$= 0.10, \text{ or } 10\%$$

$$\text{Stock H:} \quad K_c = 0.07 + (0.13 - 0.07)1.50$$
$$= 0.07 + 0.09$$
$$= 0.16, \text{ or } 16\%$$

The required rate of return on the low-risk stock is lower than that on the high-risk stock; indeed, it is six percentage points lower. The capital asset pricing model quantifies for different stocks the trade-off between risk and required rate of return.

Underpriced and Overpriced Stocks

The points in Figure 5.7 representing Stocks L and H lie squarely on the security market line. Investors in Stocks L and H are fully compensated for their risk exposure because their *expected* rates of return equal their *required* rates of return. Stocks L and H are in equilibrium.

To illustrate equilibrium, consider Stock L on which an investor both expects and requires a 10 percent rate of return. Suppose that Stock L is a no-growth common stock offering a $1 dividend; the $1 dividend will be paid annually forever. We calculate its **intrinsic value** with the perpetuity model, which incorporates the investor's required rate of return:

intrinsic value

Value of an asset based on the present value of its expected future cash flows.

$$\text{Intrinsic value} = \frac{\text{Expected cash flow}}{\text{Required rate of return}}$$
$$= \frac{\$1}{0.10}$$
$$= \$10$$

If the market price per share of Stock L equals the $10 intrinsic value, then the investor will *expect* the following rate of return:

$$\text{Expected rate of return} = \frac{\text{Expected cash flow}}{\text{Stock price}}$$
$$= \frac{\$1}{\$10}$$
$$= 0.10, \text{ or } 10\%$$

FIGURE 5.7

Required Rates of Return for Two Stocks

The required rate of return on the low-risk stock (L) equals 10 percent, but the required rate of return on the high-risk stock (H) equals 16 percent. The SML shows the trade-off between risk and required rate of return.

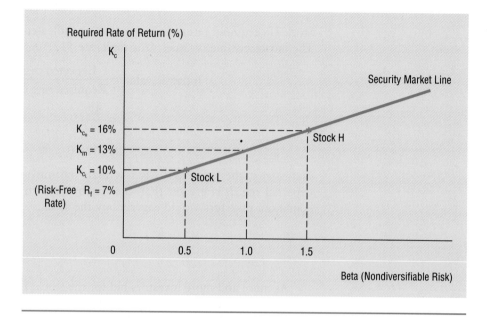

The investor expects a 10 percent rate of return when the market price of Stock L is $10 a share, and 10 percent is the investor's required rate of return. For this investor the $10 price of Stock L is neither too high nor too low. If all investors share this view, then the market price of Stock L is in equilibrium and will remain at $10 a share until new information about the company arrives in the stock market.

Consider what happens in the stock market when unexpected information becomes publicly available. Perhaps, for example, the company receives a new government contract or is prosecuted for price fixing by the Department of Justice. Investors act on the information by either buying or selling the stock, which drives its price to a new equilibrium level, the point where its expected and required rates of return are equal.

Imagine what would happen in the market to a stock with an expected rate of return represented by Point U in Figure 5.8. The expected rate of return is 20 percent at Point U, but the required rate of return on the stock is only 16 percent, as indicated by Point H on the security market line. At Point U the expected rate of return exceeds the required rate dictated by the 1.5 beta of the stock. When investors notice this condition, they will buy the stock.

EXAMPLE

Suppose that Stock U is trading at $10 per share. An investor in Stock U would expect a 20 percent return from buying the stock, measured by the ratio of its expected perpetual $2 dividend and $10 price:

$$\text{Expected rate of return} = \frac{\text{Expected cash flow}}{\text{Stock price}}$$

$$= \frac{\$2}{\$10}$$

$$= 0.20, \text{ or } 20\%$$

Stock U's required return is 16 percent, as indicated by the security market line. The intrinsic value of Stock U is therefore $12.50:

$$\text{Intrinsic value} = \frac{\text{Expected cash flow}}{\text{Required rate of return}}$$

$$= \frac{\$2}{0.16}$$

$$= \$12.50$$

Notice that the price ($10) is less than the intrinsic value ($12.50), and the expected return is greater than the required return (20% > 16%). Under this condition, investors would eagerly buy the stock.

As more and more investors bid for the stock, they bid up the price and bid down the expected return, thereby restoring equilibrium. At Point U in Figure 5.8, therefore, the stock is *underpriced* because its expected return exceeds its required return. Stock U's expected return would quickly move to the equilibrium point (H) on the security market line. *All stocks with expected returns greater than their required returns on the security market line are underpriced.*

By similar reasoning, a stock with an expected return plotting below the security market line is *overpriced*. Consider what happens to Stock O in Figure 5.8:

1. Expected rate of return on Stock O is 6 percent, which is less than the required 10 percent rate of return at Point L on the security market line.

2. Investors notice this unfavorable condition and sell Stock O, which lowers its price.

3. A lower price means a higher expected return. Remember the inverse, or negative, relationship between price and return. The expected return quickly rises to Point L on the security market line, where the stock price is in equilibrium—there is no tendency for the price to change.

All stocks with expected returns less than their required returns on the security market line are overpriced.

Now you can see why the following equation is called the capital asset *pricing* model:

$$K_c = R_f + (K_m - R_f)\beta$$

The model can be used to judge whether a stock price is too low or too high based on its expected return relative to its required return. Investors buy or sell the stock based on the difference between expected and required return, causing the stock price to move into equilibrium.

FIGURE 5.8

Two Stocks with Differing Expected and Required Rates of Return

When the expected rate of return differs from the required rate of return, intrinsic value differs from the stock price. The buying and selling behavior of investors will drive the market price to the intrinsic value, where the expected and required rates of return equal each other. Both Point U and Point O will be driven to the SML in equilibrium.

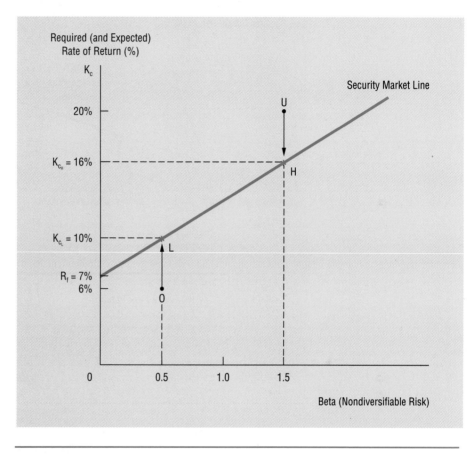

Required Rate of Return and Inflation

Inflation causes a decline in the purchasing power of money as measured by an increase in the average price level of goods and services. Investors expecting inflation require higher rates of return than they would in its absence.

To understand the way inflation affects the required rate of return, view the risk-free rate R_f as consisting of two components:

$$R_f = \frac{\text{Real rate}}{\text{of return}} + \frac{\text{Premium for}}{\text{expected inflation}}$$

In an inflation-free world, R_f is the real rate of return, which economists estimate has ranged from 2 to 5 percent per year, averaging about 3 percent per year. Changes in the expected inflation rate affect all required rates of return, not only R_f, because investors in securities at all risk levels try to maintain the purchasing power of their money. They do this by offering lower prices on securities when

FIGURE 5.9

Impact of Expected Inflation on Required Rates of Return

Increases in expected inflation cause increases in rates of return required by shareholders. For example, a two-percentage-point increase in expected inflation leads to a two-percentage-point increase in required rates of return.

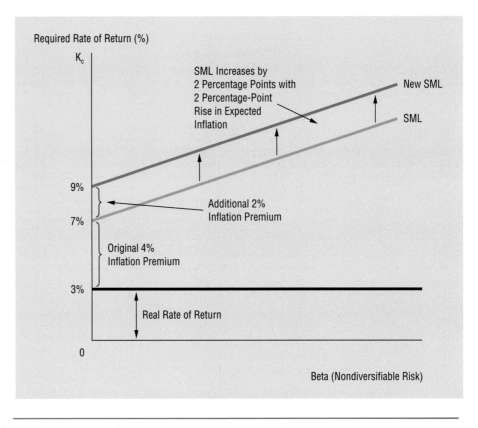

the expected inflation rate increases. Lower security prices are a consequence of higher required rates of return.

Figure 5.9 illustrates the impact of a change in the expected inflation rate on shareholders' required rates of return. Initially, the risk-free rate R_f equals 7 percent, the sum of a 3 percent real rate and a 4 percent inflation premium. Then, because of federal monetary policy, the expected inflation rate increases from 4 to 6 percent. The increased inflation rate causes R_f to increase from 7 to 9 percent. In addition, the entire security market line shifts upward for all risk levels. You can understand why this parallel shift occurs by recalling the fundamental capital asset pricing model:

$$\text{Required rate of return} = R_f + \text{Risk premium}$$

If R_f increases because of increases in the expected inflation rate, then *all* required rates of return must increase. The risk premium $(K_m - R_f)\beta$ remains constant because the expected inflation rate increases both K_m and R_f by equal amounts. Beta is unaffected by changes in *expected* inflation.

| TABLE 5.3 | | | | **Historical Rates of Return (%)** | | | |

Year	Common Stock	U.S. Treasury Bill	Inflation	Year	Common Stock	U.S. Treasury Bill	Inflation
1926	11.62	3.27	−1.49	1959	11.96	2.95	1.50
1927	37.49	3.12	−2.08	1960	0.47	2.66	1.48
1928	43.61	3.56	−0.97	1961	26.89	2.13	0.67
1929	−8.42	4.75	0.20	1962	−8.73	2.73	1.22
1930	−24.90	2.41	−6.03	1963	22.80	3.12	1.65
1931	−43.34	1.07	−9.52	1964	16.48	3.54	1.19
1932	−8.19	0.96	−10.30	1965	12.45	3.93	1.92
1933	53.99	0.30	0.51	1966	−10.06	4.76	3.35
1934	−1.44	0.16	2.03	1967	23.98	4.21	3.04
1935	47.67	0.17	2.99	1968	11.06	5.21	4.72
1936	33.92	0.18	1.21	1969	−8.50	6.58	6.11
1937	−35.03	0.31	3.10	1970	4.01	6.52	5.49
1938	31.12	−0.02	−2.78	1971	14.31	4.39	3.36
1939	−0.41	0.02	−0.48	1972	18.98	3.84	3.41
1940	−9.78	0.00	0.96	1973	−14.66	6.93	8.80
1941	−11.59	0.06	9.72	1974	−26.47	8.00	12.20
1942	20.34	0.27	9.29	1975	37.20	5.80	7.01
1943	25.90	0.35	3.16	1976	23.84	5.08	4.81
1944	19.75	0.33	2.11	1977	−7.18	5.12	6.77
1945	36.44	0.33	2.25	1978	6.56	7.18	9.03
1946	−8.07	0.35	18.16	1979	18.44	10.38	13.31
1947	5.71	0.50	9.01	1980	32.42	11.24	12.40
1948	5.50	0.81	2.71	1981	−4.91	14.71	8.94
1949	18.79	1.10	−1.80	1982	21.41	10.54	3.87
1950	31.71	1.20	5.79	1983	22.51	8.80	3.80
1951	24.02	1.49	5.87	1984	6.27	9.85	3.95
1952	18.37	1.66	0.88	1985	32.16	7.72	3.77
1953	−0.99	1.82	0.62	1986	18.47	6.16	1.13
1954	52.62	0.86	−0.50	1987	5.23	5.47	4.41
1955	31.56	1.57	0.37	1988	16.81	6.35	4.42
1956	6.56	2.46	2.86	1989	31.49	8.37	4.65
1957	−10.78	3.14	3.02	1990	−3.17	7.81	6.11
1958	43.36	1.54	1.76	1991	30.55	5.60	3.06

Source: R. Ibbotson and R. Sinquefield, *Stocks, Bonds, Bills and Inflation, 1992 Yearbook.*

Historical Rates of Return

The history of rates of return on securities has been documented by R. Ibbotson and R. Sinquefield. Their study includes annual rates of return on common stock and U.S. Treasury bills, among other securities. They calculate annual rates of return on Standard & Poor's 500 Index, comprising 500 different common stocks and annual rates of return on a portfolio of 3-month U.S. T-bills. Their study also includes annual inflation rates based on changes in the consumer price index.

Table 5.3 contains Ibbotson and Sinquefield's results for the 66-year period from 1926 to 1991. By studying the table, you can get a feel for: (1) K_m, the required rate of return on the market portfolio, as indicated by historical returns on Standard & Poor's 500 Index; and (2) $(K_m − R_f)$, the market price of risk, or the risk premium of the market portfolio relative to U.S. T-bills. The following observations are based on data in the table:

1. *Common stock:* arithmetic mean, 12.4 percent; standard deviation, 20.8 percent.
2. *U.S. T-bills:* arithmetic mean, 3.9 percent; standard deviation, 3.4 percent.
3. *Inflation:* arithmetic mean, 3.2 percent; standard deviation, 4.7 percent.

Based on common stock and T-bills, the average risk premium on the market portfolio $(K_m - R_f)$ is 8.5 percent, 12.4 percent minus 3.9 percent.

Additional observations on the 66-year history of common-stock returns are as follows: (1) maximum return, 53.99 percent in 1933; (2) minimum return, −43.34 percent in 1931; (3) 46 years of positive returns and 20 years of negative returns; (4) longest period of positive returns, 1982 to 1989; (5) longest period of negative returns, 1929 to 1932; (6) number of years with returns greater than the mean of 12.4 percent, 35 of 66 years.

DIFFICULTIES IN APPLYING THE CAPITAL ASSET PRICING MODEL

Although the capital asset pricing model helps you to understand risk-return relationships and pricing dynamics, using it to estimate required returns is a difficult task. Difficulties encountered in its application include: (1) Estimating a reliable beta for the future based on historical data; betas tend to change over time. (2) Deciding whether to use the yield on short- or long-term U.S. Treasury bonds as the proxy for the risk-free rate of return; when the yield curve is relatively flat, however, short-term yields approximately equal long-term yields, and the choice does not matter much. (3) Estimating the market price of risk, $(K_m - R_f)$; historical data are helpful here, but some error in the estimate will likely remain.[5]

An additional difficulty is theoretical: The model stresses a one-dimensional measure of risk (beta). Critics of the model suggest that relevant risk must consist of more than a stock's nondiversifiable risk, in part because not all investors can or will diversify their portfolios. Some investors put all of their eggs in one basket, then watch the basket carefully.

Arbitrage Pricing Model

arbitrage pricing model (APM)

Model that relates required rate of return to several risk factors.

The theoretical critics suggest that the arbitrage pricing model is superior to the capital asset pricing model because it introduces several influences (not just beta) on required return. *Arbitrage* means to buy and sell the same or similar capital assets at the same time to make a profit. The **arbitrage pricing model (APM)** is an equation relating required rate of return to several factors. According to the APM, more than one risk premium (RP) should be added to the risk-free rate R_f:

$$K_c = R_f + RP_1 + RP_2 + \cdots + RP_n$$

[5] The complete theory surrounding the CAPM rests on several assumptions: (1) Capital markets are perfect, meaning there are no transaction costs (broker fees, taxes, and so on). (2) Investors have homogeneous expectations, meaning that they all expect the same returns, standard deviations, and correlations among securities. (3) Investors try to maximize their personal wealth. Despite the strong assumptions, theoretical extensions of CAPM theory and empirical tests indicate that the basic model presented here is reasonably robust; that is, it has explanatory and predictive power.

Exactly what these risk premiums should be is difficult to say. Some researchers, however, suggest premiums for the following four influences: (1) unexpected changes in inflation, (2) unexpected changes in industrial production, (3) unexpected changes in the yield differential between low- and high-rated bonds, and (4) unexpected changes in the yield differential between long- and short-term bonds. Conceptually, the arbitrage pricing model is merely a commonsense adding up of the percentage points of return that investors need to equalize the attraction of a specific stock with that of stocks in general. When the relative attraction of stocks is equal, the market is in equilibrium. Arbitrage, or the trade-offs that investors make, gives the model its name: If a stock is underpriced according to the APM, then investors engage in arbitrage by simultaneously selling overpriced stocks and buying underpriced stocks.

Despite the theoretical debate and the difficulty in obtaining accurate betas, some investors use the capital asset pricing model because it systematically relates return with risk and shows how key variables interact. In any event, the model provides you with an understanding of investor behavior and market dynamics. In addition, it provides financial managers with a means of estimating a company's cost of retained earnings, as Chapter 6 explains.

Financial Management and Stock Betas

To this point we have looked at risk primarily from the viewpoint of investors. This viewpoint is valid and necessary for financial managers who attempt to maximize stock price. Financial managers need to understand the impact of investors' perceived risk on required rate of return and stock price.

According to the capital asset pricing model, understanding beta is the key to understanding why required rates of return differ across companies. The required rate of return on the market portfolio (K_m) and the risk-free rate (R_f) are the same for all companies, but betas differ depending on company characteristics. In general, any managerial decision that makes a company's stock returns more sensitive to broad changes in stock market prices causes an increase in the stock's beta. Any decision that makes the returns less sensitive decreases beta. A company's investment and financing decisions potentially affect beta and, therefore, the required rate of return.

An example of a financing decision that causes a stock's beta to change is an increase in the amount of debt the company uses. Larger debt levels lead to larger stock betas because stock performance becomes more sensitive to what happens in the market. During a bull market, stocks of companies with a great deal of debt tend to perform better than average; during a bear market they tend to perform worse than average. Do not conclude from this point that a company should use no debt! The objective of business financial management is to increase stock price, not to minimize beta. In Chapter 7 you will see that prudent use of debt increases stock price.

An example of an investment decision that causes a stock's beta to change is an increased commitment to automated production processes. Investments in equipment reduce **variable costs** such as labor, but increase **fixed costs** such as depreciation and maintenance. Fixed costs do not change with changes in output and must be paid regardless of the output level. During upswings in the business cycle when there is a bull market, stocks of companies with large fixed costs relative to variable costs tend to perform better than the stocks of companies with large variable costs; during a business cycle downswing and bear market, they tend to perform worse. As a result, stocks of companies with large fixed oper-

variable costs
Operating costs that change as output changes.

fixed costs
Operating costs that do not change as output changes.

Diversification International Style

Conducting business across national boundaries potentially creates two financial advantages for a multinational company: (1) additional cash flows from sales in foreign markets and (2) a reduction in the nondiversifiable risk of the company's common stock. If investments abroad lower a company's stock beta (measure of nondiversifiable risk), then according to the capital asset pricing model the required rate of return on the company's stock will decline. Moreover, the company's stock price will rise.

Empirical studies show that the GNPs (gross national products) or indexes of industrial production among nations are less than perfectly correlated. The growth in output of Country A may be high when the growth in output of Country B is low. The cash flows of a company that invests in countries with contracyclical economies tend to be more stable (less uncertain) than the cash flows generated from investment in only one country.

The lack of perfect correlation among national economies enables a multinational company to diversify away some of its domestic *nondiversifiable* (market) risk. In effect, the company converts its domestic risk to a lower international risk. Investing abroad enables the company to lessen risk while engaged in its customary business lines in which it has expertise. Furthermore, it may be

Total Risk: σ of Company Returns

able to earn a high return on assets while reducing the risk of the assets.

The figure illustrates the decline in total risk (σ, or standard deviation of company returns) as a company increases its number of investments. As shown, the total risk accompanying international investments is lower than that of domestic investments alone. Also, the relative independence of different national economies causes the beta (nondiversifiable risk) of a multinational company's assets and common stock to be lower than the betas of equivalent domestic companies.

Despite the lower beta, the benefit of *corporate* international diversification must be interpreted cautiously. After all, if shareholders desire, they can diversify for

themselves across many of the world's stock markets. Still, corporations have access to more countries than do shareholders, largely because of underdeveloped stock markets in many countries. Empirical studies indicate that multinational companies provide some beneficial international diversification for shareholders. Worldwide diversification by investors themselves, however, provides a greater reduction in the uncertainty of returns.

Although shareholders appear to have the advantage in diversifying to reduce uncertainty, corporations have the advantage in generating additional cash flows from foreign sales. Corporate international investments add value in large part because of increased cash flows, not because of reductions in uncertainty.

ating costs relative to variable costs tend to be sensitive to market volatility. In other words, they have large betas and high required rates of return.

Virtually all of management's decisions affect beta to some degree. Fast-growing companies tend to have larger betas than do their slow-growing counterparts. Companies with stable demand for their products tend to have smaller betas than do their counterparts with an unstable demand. In short, any company characteristic that increases or decreases the sensitivity of stock return to the general market affects the company's stock beta. Beta, in turn, affects the company's cost of capital, as Chapter 6 shows.

SUMMARY

- The expected rate of return on a common stock equals the sum of the expected dividend yield and the expected capital gain yield. Alternatively, the expected rate of return ($\bar{K}$) can be viewed as a probability-weighted average of possible returns (K_j):

$$\bar{K} = P_1K_1 + P_2K_2 + \cdots + P_nK_n$$

$$= \sum_{j=1}^{n} P_jK_j$$

where P_j is the probability of K_j, and *n* is the number of possible returns.

- The expected rate of return on a portfolio of stocks is a weighted average of the expected returns on the stocks in the portfolio:

$$\text{Expected portfolio return} = W_1\bar{K}_1 + W_2\bar{K}_2 + \cdots + W_n\bar{K}_n$$

$$= \sum_{i=1}^{n} W_i\bar{K}_i$$

where W_i is the weight reflecting the *i*th stock's value as a percentage of portfolio value, and $\bar{K}_i$ is the expected return from investing in the *i*th stock (i = 1, 2, . . . , n).

- Standard deviation is a statistical measure of variability. Applied to the possible returns (K_j) on common stock, standard deviation (σ) represents total risk (uncertainty surrounding the expected rate of return, $\bar{K}$):

$$\sigma = [P_1(K_1 - \bar{K})^2 + P_2(K_2 - \bar{K})^2 + \cdots + P_n(K_n - \bar{K})^2]^{\frac{1}{2}}$$

$$= \sqrt{\sum_{j=1}^{n} P_j(K_j - \bar{K})^2}$$

A large standard deviation indicates a wide dispersion around $\bar{K}$, and a small standard deviation indicates a "tight" dispersion around $\bar{K}$. Combining stocks into a portfolio reduces an investor's exposure to total risk (σ) because returns on different stocks are less than perfectly correlated with each other. In other words, winners tend to offset losers.

- Analysts often use a sample of historical rates of return on a common stock as a proxy for the probability distribution of future rates of return. They then use the standard deviation of the sample as an estimate of the future standard deviation:

$$\text{Estimated } \sigma = \sqrt{\frac{\sum_{t=1}^{n} (K_t - K_{avg})^2}{n-1}}$$

where K_t is the past rate of return for Period t, and K_{avg} is the average rate of return during the past n periods.

- Most investors are averse to risk; they dislike it. Because of risk aversion, investors normally diversify their investment portfolios. Well-diversified portfolios easily eliminate the diversifiable risk shown in the following equations:

Total risk = Diversifiable risk + Nondiversifiable risk

Nondiversifiable risk = Total risk − Diversifiable risk

The only risk that the market rewards is nondiversifiable risk, which is measured by beta. Nondiversifiable risk is the driving force affecting required rates of return because it cannot be eliminated by diversifying. The market does not reward diversifiable risk because an investor can easily eliminate it.

- To estimate beta, analysts plot a stock's historical rates of return against a market index's historical rates of return. They then fit a line in the scatter diagram. The slope of the line measures the stock's beta:

Beta < 1.0   Below-average risk

Beta = 1.0   Average risk

Beta > 1.0   Above-average risk

- The beta of a portfolio of stocks is a weighted average of the betas of the stocks in the portfolio:

$$\beta_p = W_1\beta_1 + W_2\beta_2 + \cdots + W_n\beta_n$$

$$= \sum_{i=1}^{n} W_i\beta_i$$

where W_i is the weight reflecting the ith stock's value as a percentage of portfolio value, and β_i is the beta of the ith stock ($i = 1, 2, \ldots, n$). Investors who want low exposure to nondiversifiable risk must include some low-beta securities in their portfolios.

- The graph of the capital asset pricing model (see Figure 5.6) is described by:

$$K_c = R_f + (K_m - R_f)\beta$$

The vertical axis represents the required rate of return (K_c) and the horizontal axis represents nondiversifiable risk (β). The risk-free rate of return (R_f) is the vertical intercept on the graph, and ($K_m - R_f$) is the slope of the security market line. K_c on the vertical axis depends on β on the horizontal axis. Common stocks in equilibrium lie on the security market line. In equilibrium, expected return equals required return and the price of a stock fully reflects its nondiversifiable risk. If expected return is greater than required return, then a stock is underpriced. If expected return is less than required return, then a stock is overpriced. Underpriced and overpriced stocks are in disequilibrium.

- Investors demand compensation for erosion of their purchasing power due to expected inflation. They require higher rates of return and offer lower prices for securities when they expect higher inflation rates. Required rates of return relate to the expected inflation rate as follows:

$$\text{Required rate} \atop \text{of return} = {\text{Real rate} \atop \text{of return}} + {\text{Premium for} \atop \text{expected inflation}} + {\text{Risk} \atop \text{premium}}$$

The real rate of return plus the premium for expected inflation equals the risk-free rate of return.

- The capital asset pricing model (CAPM) provides an excellent framework to help you understand changes in security prices. Applying it to estimate required rates of return, however, demands carefully justified estimates of R_f, $(K_m - R_f)$, and β.

Key Terms

diversification	nondiversifiable risk	market portfolio
expected portfolio return	beta, β	intrinsic value
probability distribution	portfolio beta	arbitrage pricing model (APM)
standard deviation, σ	capital asset pricing model (CAPM)	variable costs
variance, σ^2	risk-free rate of return	fixed costs
correlation	risk premium	
diversifiable risk	market price of risk	

Questions

5.1. Alcoa Corporation's stock beta as recently measured by *Value Line* is 1.1. Does Alcoa common stock have more or less nondiversifiable risk than the average stock in the market portfolio? Explain.

5.2. Figure 5.6 presents the relationship between risk and required rate of return. Using the symbols in Figure 5.6, write the equation for the security market line.

5.3. Explain why Point U in Figure 5.8 represents an underpriced common stock. Explain why Point O represents an overpriced common stock.

5.4. Keong Chew selects common stocks for investment in a rather strange way. He throws darts at the stock quotation section of *The Wall Street Journal*. If a dart hits a particular stock quote, he buys that stock. Using Figure 5.3 to guide your discussion, compare the total portfolio risks that you would expect under the following circumstances:
   a. Mr. Chew throws 5 darts.
   b. Mr. Chew throws 40 darts.
   c. Mr. Chew throws 50 darts.

   Explain the process of reducing total risk through diversification.

5.5. Sharon Copely wants to estimate the beta of AMR's common stock. List the steps she might take to achieve her goal.

5.6. This chapter presents three types of returns: expected return, actual return, and required return. Define each type.

5.7. Describe why beta is a useful measure of risk. What does beta mean?

5.8. U.S. Treasury securities have no default risk. Does this fact mean that when you buy a 20-year U.S. Treasury bond you incur no risk? Explain your answer.

5.9. The common stock of Woodway Lumber Company has a 1.8 beta. Fully interpret the meaning of Woodway's beta to its shareholders and its managers.

5.10. This chapter points out that nondiversifiable risk influences investors' required rates of return. What is the reason for this assertion? In your explanation, use the terms *total risk* and *diversifiable risk*.

5.11. What estimation problems do you face when you use the capital asset pricing model to estimate required rate of return?

5.12. If investors expect the inflation rate to decrease from 6 percent to 3 percent annually, what will happen to the security market line? Holding other influences constant, what will happen to stock prices? Explain.

Strategy Problem

Horace Ibsen has $40,000 invested in common stock, allocated as follows:

Company	Dollar Investment	Beta	Expected Return
American Capital	$12,000	0.55	9.65%
Dart & Kraft, Inc.	18,000	0.75	10.25
H. J. Heinz	10,000	0.75	10.25

Mr. Ibsen is considering investing $18,000 in Alcoa common stock. After reading several research reports in addition to *Value Line*, he expects Alcoa common stock to yield a 14.5 percent annual rate of return over the next several years. Current conditions in the capital markets are as follows: yield on U.S. government securities, 8 percent; expected return on the S&P 500, 11 percent.

a. Calculate the beta of and the required return on Mr. Ibsen's portfolio.
b. Why would he want to invest in Alcoa common stock? Support your answer by comparing the required rate of return on Alcoa with Mr. Ibsen's expected rate of return. *Value Line*'s estimate of Alcoa's beta is 1.1.
c. Calculate the portfolio beta, expected return, and required return assuming Mr. Ibsen liquidates his Dart & Kraft shares and replaces them with $18,000 of Alcoa shares. Ignore taxes and brokerage fees in your calculations.
d. Suppose that Mr. Ibsen and other investors revise their expectations of inflation. They expect inflation to be 2 percentage points more than they originally thought. What is the rate of return Mr. Ibsen requires on Alcoa common stock after the revision?

Strategy	Solution

a. The portfolio beta is the weighted average of the stock betas:

Calculate a weighted average based on each beta and proportion of the portfolio.

$$\beta_p = \frac{\$12,000}{\$40,000}(0.55) + \frac{\$18,000}{\$40,000}(0.75) + \frac{\$10,000}{\$40,000}(0.75)$$

$$= 0.69$$

The required return on the portfolio (K_p) is calculated using the capital asset pricing model (CAPM):

Use the portfolio beta in the CAPM.

$$K_p = 0.08 + (0.11 - 0.08)0.69$$

$$= 0.101, \text{ or } 10.1\%$$

b. Mr. Ibsen, like any investor, would want to invest in Alcoa common stock if its expected return is higher than its required return—that is, if the stock is underpriced. The required rate of return is calculated using the capital asset pricing model and Alcoa's beta of 1.1:

Use beta, R_f, and K_m in the CAPM.

$$K_c = 0.08 + (0.11 - 0.08)1.1$$

$$= 0.113, \text{ or } 11.3\%$$

The expected return (14.5 percent) is higher than the required return (11.3 percent), so Mr. Ibsen is correct in wanting to buy Alcoa common stock.

c. Portfolio beta after selling Dart & Kraft and buying Alcoa:

Substitute Alcoa for Dart & Kraft, then calculate a weighted average of betas.

$$\beta_p = \frac{\$12,000}{\$40,000}(0.55) + \frac{\$18,000}{\$40,000}(1.10) + \frac{\$10,000}{\$40,000}(0.75)$$

$$= 0.85$$

The expected return on the portfolio is a weighted average of the expected return on each stock:

Substitute Alcoa for Dart & Kraft, then calculate a weighted average of returns.

$$\text{Expected portfolio return} = \frac{\$12,000}{\$40,000}(0.0965) + \frac{\$18,000}{\$40,000}(0.145) + \frac{\$10,000}{\$40,000}(0.1025)$$

$$= 0.120, \text{ or } 12.0\%$$

The required return on the portfolio is calculated with the capital asset pricing model and the weighted average beta:

Use the CAPM to find required return.

$$K_p = 0.08 + (0.11 - 0.08)0.85$$

$$= 0.106, \text{ or } 10.6\%$$

d. An increase in the expected rate of inflation causes all rates of return to increase by the same percentage points—the risk-free rate and the required return on the market portfolio increase by 2 percentage points, making the required rate of return on Alcoa increase by 2 percentage points:

Use the CAPM; note the market price of risk does not change.

$$K_c = (0.08 + 0.02) + [(0.11 + 0.02) - (0.08 + 0.02)]1.1$$

$$= 0.133, \text{ or } 13.3\%$$

◆ **Demonstration Problem**

Carevest Company is an investment management firm that manages money for wealthy individuals and private and public pension funds. Carevest's 12 employees, including the portfolio manager, nine security analysts, and two office workers, manage a total of $750,000,000. One of the security analysts is Carlos Padea, who recently graduated from college and is now beginning Carevest's training program for security analysts. Because Carevest is a small firm, its training program consists solely of an informal mentoring process: New hires are assigned to work with a senior analyst, who advises and instructs the junior analysts. Mr. Padea's first assignment involves the analysis of the following distributions of stock returns:

***Ex Ante* Distribution of Returns on Common Stock**

State of Economy	Probability of Economic State	Goldstake Mining	Computer Technologies
Recession	0.3	25%	−10%
Normal	0.4	15	20
Boom	0.3	−5	30

***Ex Post* Distribution of Returns on Common Stock**

Year	Cola Soda	Clothier Designs
19X2	18%	10%
19X3	−20	18
19X4	14	33
19X5	32	−9

Assume that you are the senior analyst and mentor for Mr. Padea, and that your task is to explain to Mr. Padea the basic concepts of risk and rate of return by answering the following questions and analyzing the following problems.

a. What is an *ex ante* distribution of returns on common stock? *Ex post* distribution of returns on common stock? Explain the implicit assumption necessary for the relevance of an *ex post* distribution of returns on common stock.
b. Calculate the expected rate of return for Goldstake Mining and for Computer Technologies. Calculate the average rate of return for Cola Soda and for Clothier Designs. Why do we say *expected* rate of return for the first two companies and *average* rate of return for the second two? Is the *average* rate of return a very good predictor of the *expected* rate of return?

c. Calculate the standard deviation (σ) for Goldstake Mining and for Computer Technologies. Calculate the estimated σ for Cola Soda and for Clothier Designs. Why are the standard deviations for Cola Soda and Clothier Designs said to be *estimated*? Which one of the four stocks appears riskiest for an investor who for some reason invests in only one stock?

d. Both an investor who invests in only one stock and an investor who invests in a well-diversified portfolio of stocks should view standard deviation of portfolio returns as an appropriate measure of risk. For the well-diversified investor, however, the appropriate measure of risk of each stock is its *contribution* to the standard deviation of the portfolio returns. A stock's contribution to the risk of a well-diversified portfolio is measured by its beta (β), an index of nondiversifiable risk. Use the foregoing logic and the following equation to explain why β is a relevant measure of risk of a common stock:

$$\text{Total risk} = \text{Diversifiable risk} + \text{Nondiversifiable risk}$$

e. Calculate the expected rate of return on a portfolio consisting of $100,000 invested in Goldstake Mining and $100,000 invested in Computer Technologies. Calculate the standard deviation (σ) of the portfolio returns. Explain why σ of the portfolio is smaller than the σ of either Goldstake Mining or Computer Technologies.

f. Calculate the average rate of return on a portfolio consisting of $100,000 invested in Cola Soda and $100,000 invested in Clothier Designs. Calculate the estimated σ of the portfolio returns. Explain why the estimated σ of the portfolio is smaller than the estimated σ of either Cola Soda or Clothier Designs.

g. Suppose that the expected rate of return and the beta for each stock are as follows:

Company	Expected Rate of Return	Beta
Goldstake Mining	12%	0.60
Computer Technologies	10	1.25
Cola Soda	11	1.00
Clothier Designs	17	1.40

Expected rate of return reflects the expectations of Carevest's security analysts, based on their analyses of the four companies. The analysts estimate that the required rate of return on the market portfolio of all stocks is 12 percent, and the risk-free rate is 6 percent. Use the capital asset pricing model (CAPM) to calculate the required rate of return on each of the four stocks. Which of the four stocks do you recommend for investment?

h. Assume that you invest $100,000 in each of the stocks that you recommend in Part g. For your total investment, calculate beta, required rate of return, and expected rate of return.

i. Suppose that investors expect the inflation rate to increase by 2 percentage points. Does this fact alter your recommendations in Part g? Explain.

Problems

Expected return and
standard deviation

5.1. The probability distributions of possible returns for Stocks X and Y are as follows:

Economic State	Probability	X	Y
Recession economy	0.2	−15%	−5%
Normal economy	0.6	20	15
Boom economy	0.2	30	25

a. Calculate the expected rate of return on each stock.
b. Calculate the standard deviation for each stock.
c. Which stock do you consider riskier? Explain.
d. In which stock would you prefer to invest? Explain.

Expected return and standard deviation: portfolio

5.2. Possible rates of return for Stocks P and Q are described by the following probability distributions:

Economic State	Probability	Stock P	Stock Q
Recession economy	0.1	−20%	30%
Normal economy	0.4	10	20
Above-average economy	0.4	30	20
Boom economy	0.1	40	−10

a. Calculate the expected rate of return on each stock.
b. Calculate the standard deviation for each stock.
c. Assume that you invest $10,000 in each stock; now calculate the expected rate of return and the standard deviation for your portfolio.
d. Explain why the standard deviation for your portfolio is smaller than that for either Stock P or Stock Q.

Risk aversion

5.3. Suppose that a business tycoon visits your finance class and offers you the following probability distributions:

The Sure Thing		The Gamble	
Probability	Payoff to You	Probability	Payoff to You
1.0	$1,000,000	0.50	$0
		0.50	$2,000,000

The business tycoon says that it will cost you nothing to play this game. If you choose *The Sure Thing*, you will receive a $1,000,000 check immediately. If you choose *The Gamble*, the business tycoon will flip a coin: Tails—you get zero; Heads—you get a $2,000,000 check immediately.

a. Calculate the expected value of your payoff from *The Sure Thing* and from *The Gamble.*
b. Which probability distribution would you choose? Explain.
c. Does your choice in Part *b* reflect risk aversion or risk seeking? Explain.
d. If you were as wealthy as the business tycoon, would you likely alter your choice in Part *b*? Explain.
e. Assume that *The Gamble* offers you a 50–50 chance at zero and $10,000,000. Respond to Parts *a, b, c,* and *d* based on this revised gamble.

Historical rates of return

5.4. Stocks H and L have the following historical rates of return:

Year	Stock H	Stock L
19X1	31.2%	−10.3%
19X2	15.4	25.8
19X3	−29.5	13.2
19X4	10.1	9.7

a. Calculate the average rate of return on each stock for the period 19X1 to 19X4.
b. Using the 19X1-to-19X4 samples of historical rates of return, estimate the standard deviation for each stock.

c. Calculate the average rate of return on a portfolio consisting of 50 percent of Stock H and 50 percent of Stock L.

d. Using the 19X1-to-19X4 samples of historical rates of return, estimate the standard deviation for the portfolio described in Part *c*.

e. Explain why the estimated standard deviation for the 50–50 portfolio is smaller than that for either Stock H or Stock L.

Required rate of return

5.5. A company's financial manager wants to use the capital asset pricing model to estimate the required rate of return on her company's common stock. She estimates the beta of the stock to be 1.5. She uses the 7 percent yield on 4-year, U.S. Treasury bonds as a proxy for the risk-free rate. Finally, she estimates the required rate of return on the market portfolio to be 14 percent. What will be her estimated required rate of return on the company's stock?

Expected and required rate of return

5.6. Jeff Wyatt is considering an investment in Ravine Company common stock. He expects to earn 15 percent on the stock and estimates its beta to be 1.9. In addition, he has developed the following estimates: $R_f = 7$ percent and $K_m = 14$ percent. Would you recommend that Mr. Wyatt buy Ravine Company common stock? Support your recommendation with calculations.

Required rate of return and inflation

5.7. Phillips-Dodge has an estimated beta of 0.60. The annual yield on U.S. Treasury securities is 9 percent, and the required rate of return on a typical share of common stock (as measured by a market index) is 14 percent per year.

a. Calculate the rate of return investors require from their investment in Phillips-Dodge common stock.

b. If expected inflation declines by 2 percentage points, what is the new required rate of return for Phillips-Dodge?

Stock price, inflation, and required rate of return

5.8. ABC Corporation pays a $5 annual dividend on its common stock, and investors expect the dividend to remain unchanged for the foreseeable future; that is, they view the stock as a perpetuity. Yesterday's closing price of ABC Corporation's stock was $46.30 a share. After the stock exchange closed, the chairman of the Federal Reserve Board gave a speech in which he led investors to expect a 2-percentage-point increase in the inflation rate. The resulting impact on R_f and K_m is as follows:

	Yesterday	Today
R_f	6%	8%
K_m	12	14

ABC Corporation's stock beta remains unchanged at 0.8.

a. Draw the security market line (SML) based on yesterday's information. Label the vertical axis *Required Rate of Return* and the horizontal axis *Beta*.

b. Show the shift in the SML due to the change in expected inflation.

c. Calculate the required rate of return on ABC Corporation's common stock based on yesterday's information. Repeat the calculation based on today's information. Plot both points on your graph in Part *b*.

d. What is ABC Corporation's stock price based on today's information?

e. Describe the relationship between *stock price* and *change in expected inflation*, as illustrated above.

Portfolio beta

5.9. Malcolm Bolingbroke has $100,000 invested in common stock allocated as follows:

Company	Dollar Investment	Beta
Kaiser Donuts	$50,000	1.6
Argo Plants	20,000	0.8
Conner Rails	30,000	1.2

Calculate the beta of Mr. Bolingbroke's portfolio. Is his portfolio more or less risky than average, according to its beta? Explain.

Portfolio beta and diversifiable risk

5.10. Nancy Pritchard manages a portfolio of 10 different common stocks for her mother. The current market value of the portfolio is $500,000, and its beta is 0.90. Ms. Pritchard's mother plans to add $100,000 to the portfolio, and Ms. Pritchard is considering alternative investments for the additional funds: T-bills with a beta of zero, or stock of a high-tech company with a beta of 1.5.

a. Calculate the portfolio beta assuming that Ms. Pritchard invests the additional funds in T-bills. Is this portfolio more or less risky than average, according to its beta? Explain.

b. Calculate the portfolio beta assuming that Ms. Pritchard invests the additional funds in the stock of the high-tech company. Is this portfolio more or less risky than average, according to its beta? Explain.

c. In your opinion, is the portfolio in Part *b* likely to be well diversified? Provide a verbal assessment of the portfolio's *total* risk. Use the term *diversifiable risk* in your assessment.

Portfolio beta and expectations

5.11. K. K. Roy is considering investments in four securities with the following betas:

Security	Beta
Alpha	0.00
Gamma	0.55
Iota	1.00
Omega	1.35

a. If Mr. Roy invests equal amounts in each security, what will be the beta of his portfolio?

b. If Mr. Roy invests 40 percent of his money in Alpha and 20 percent in each of the remaining securities, what will be the beta of his portfolio?

c. If Mr. Roy wishes to speculate on a bull market, which portfolio composition should he select—the one in Part *a* or the one in Part *b*? Explain your answer.

Portfolio beta and the SML

5.12. Lucille McIntosh wants to invest in a portfolio of common stocks. She expects the returns on the five stocks that she has selected to be as follows:

	Expected Return	Beta
Browning Ferris	12.8%	1.20
Circle K	12.6	1.15
Coleco Industries	12.6	1.15
Federal Express	13.6	1.40
The Gap	13.0	1.25

According to her best estimates, the expected (and required) return on a well-diversified portfolio of common stocks is 12 percent annually, and the risk-free rate of return is 8 percent annually.

a. Draw the security market line. Label the vertical axis *Required Rate of Return* and the horizontal axis *Beta*. Is each stock price in equilibrium? Explain your answer.

b. Ms. McIntosh will invest equal dollar amounts in each stock. Calculate the portfolio beta and expected return, and locate the portfolio on the SML you drew in Part *a* above.

c. Why would Ms. McIntosh want to invest in a portfolio like this one made up of stocks with high betas?

Beta and required rates of return

5.13. Amalgam Corporation of North America is a company owning 100 percent of the equity of three subsidiaries:

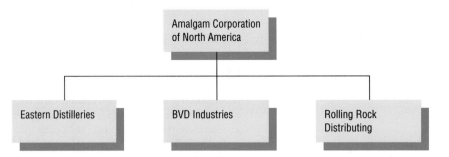

Amalgam's management refers to *Value Line* and finds betas for companies similar to each subsidiary. The estimated betas for each subsidiary are: (1) Eastern Distilleries, 0.90, (2) BVD Industries, 1.20, and (3) Rolling Rock Distributing, 1.80. In addition, management calculates Amalgam's investment in each of the three subsidiaries to be roughly equal. Amalgam borrows money only through its subsidiaries, and Amalgam's stock is listed on a regional stock exchange.

a. Estimate the stock beta for Amalgam, the parent company.

b. If the risk-free rate is 8 percent and the required rate of return on the market portfolio is 14 percent, what is the required rate of return on Amalgam stock?

c. Compute the required rate of return on each subsidiary and show that the weighted average of these returns equals the solution to Part *b*. Use $R_f = 8\%$ and $K_m = 14\%$.

Computer Problems

Portfolio selection: template PORTFOL

5.14. Kirk Jones has received a gift of $49,000 from an uncle. He wants to invest this amount in common stock. His broker has suggested that he invest $7,000 in each of the following companies:

Company	Expected Return	Beta
A	13%	0.80
B	15	0.90
C	14	1.00
D	17	1.10
E	18	1.20
F	17	1.30
G	18	1.40

The current risk-free rate of return is 7 percent per year, and the required rate of return on the market portfolio is 15 percent per year.

a. Calculate the required return for each stock using the capital asset pricing model.

b. Calculate the portfolio beta, expected return, and required return.

c. Plot the security market line and the position of each stock on the graph. If Mr. Jones invests wisely and puts equal amounts in each underpriced stock, which stocks would he buy and what would be the portfolio beta, expected return, and required return?

d. In light of the need to diversify and at the same time maximize returns, Mr. Jones decides to invest in a minimum of three stocks with the constraint that not more than 50 percent and not less than 20 percent of his total investment should be in any one stock. What should be the composition of his portfolio, and what will be the portfolio beta, expected return, and required return on the portfolio?

Expected return and standard deviation: template EXPRET

5.15. The probability distributions of returns for Stocks V and W are as follows:

Economic State	Probability	Stock V	Stock W
Deep recession	0.1	−10%	0%
Mild recession	0.2	0	5
Average economy	0.4	20	10
Strong economy	0.2	30	15
Boom economy	0.1	40	20

a. Calculate the expected return for Stock V and for Stock W.
b. Calculate the standard deviation for Stock V and for Stock W.
c. Calculate the expected return and standard deviation for portfolios composed of:
(1) 25% V and 75% W
(2) 50% V and 50% W
(3) 75% V and 25% W

The SML and stock selection: template SML

5.16. Paula Butler is studying a dozen stocks recommended by her brother, and she wishes to use the capital asset pricing model to determine which ones are acceptably priced. Her broker's recommendations with their expected rates of return and betas are listed below. The risk-free rate is 7.5 percent, and the expected return on the market portfolio is 15 percent.

Stock	Expected Return	Beta
ABC	12.00%	0.60
BCD	13.20	0.70
CDE	19.15	1.55
DEF	16.45	1.22
EFG	12.65	0.70
FGH	25.38	2.25
GHI	15.09	1.12
HIJ	16.77	1.37
IJK	14.00	0.86
JKL	16.95	1.26
KLM	12.90	0.95
LMN	18.60	1.48

a. Calculate the required rate of return for each stock.
b. Indicate for each stock whether or not it is acceptably priced (i.e., whether the expected return equals or exceeds the required return).
c. Repeat Parts *a* and *b* assuming that the risk-free rate rises by 0.5 percentage point and the required return on the market portfolio rises by 1.0 percentage point.

Portfolio beta and expected return: template PORTBETA

5.17. Mark Ellis wishes to invest $120,000 in common stocks. Although he is relatively young and will accept some risk in his pursuit of high rates of return, he wishes to eliminate as much unnecessary risk as possible. He has decided to begin his planning with an imaginary investment of equal amounts in each of 12 randomly selected stocks. Before making a real investment, he will try to modify the original portfolio to suit his objectives.

The selected stocks are arranged below in order of their beta and expected rate of return. All of the stocks lie on the security market line (SML).

Stock	Beta	Expected Return
A	0.80	12.80%
B	0.80	12.80
C	0.90	13.40
D	0.95	13.70
E	1.05	14.30
F	1.05	14.30
G	1.10	14.60
H	1.15	14.90
I	1.20	15.20
J	1.20	15.20
K	1.30	15.80
L	1.40	16.40

a. Compute the beta and the expected return of the original portfolio consisting of equal investments (1/12 or $10,000) in each stock.

b. Recompute Part *a* assuming the four stocks with the lowest betas are eliminated and the amounts invested in the four stocks with the highest betas are doubled.

c. Recompute Part *a* assuming the four stocks with the lowest betas are replaced with four new stocks having the same betas and rates of return as the four highest-beta stocks (change the betas and rates of return for Stocks A–D).

d. Recompute Part *a* assuming the four stocks with the highest betas are eliminated and the amounts invested in the four stocks with the lowest betas are doubled.

e. Which is the better strategy for increasing the portfolio's beta and expected return, Part *b* or Part *c*? Explain.

Case Problem

Henry Lewis, Attorney at Law

Henry Lewis is an attorney who has just settled a lucrative lawsuit to the advantage of his client. His share of the settlement is $100,000. After expenses associated with the lawsuit and after providing for other needs, Mr. Lewis has $50,000 to invest. At present he has a diversified portfolio of common stocks with a total market value of $250,000. The beta coefficient of the portfolio is 1.15, and the average dividend yield is 2.5 percent per year.

At age 35, Mr. Lewis believes he can afford to accept higher-than-average risk in his investment decisions. His life insurance is adequate, and he has a savings account balance equal to four months' living expenses. Mr. Lewis, his wife, who is a college professor, and their two children live comfortably. Because of the near-term tax consequences of receiving dividend and interest income, Mr. Lewis prefers to avoid high-yielding securities.

After receiving the settlement income, Mr. Lewis telephoned his broker, who is employed at a full-service brokerage firm, for advice on investing the $50,000. Anticipating windfall commissions, the broker gave Mr. Lewis the following list of candidate stocks.

Common Stock	Price per Share	Annual Dividend per Share	Beta	Standard Deviation
Cincinnati Gas & Electric	$28	$2.32	0.58	19%
Compaq	95	—	1.45	43
Exxon	45	2.40	0.73	39
Genentech	22	—	1.41	45
Jostens Inc.	24	0.64	1.09	35
Meredith Corp.	35	0.64	1.10	52
National Convenience Stores	8	0.36	1.02	40
Texaco	50	3.00	0.49	25

The broker also provided the following market information: The market index used to estimate betas is Standard & Poor's 500 Index, the beta of the index is 1.00, and the standard deviation of the annual returns on the index is 20 percent.

Mr. Lewis has approached you to assist him in evaluating the list of stocks provided by the broker.

a. Describe the steps that the brokerage firm might have taken to estimate the betas and standard deviations.
b. Which measurement of risk is more relevant to Mr. Lewis, beta or standard deviation? Explain your answer.
c. If Mr. Lewis invests half of the $50,000 in Compaq and half in Genentech, what is the beta of the $50,000 investment? What is the beta of the entire $300,000 portfolio?
d. Mr. Lewis's tax rate on investment income is 28 percent. Calculate the additional income tax he will owe during the first year if he invests $25,000 each in Jostens and National Convenience Stores. How much additional tax will he owe if he invests $25,000 each in Compaq and Genentech?
e. Mr. Lewis learns from his broker that the annual yield on U.S. Treasury bonds is 8 percent. In addition, analysts at the brokerage firm expect an annual return of 14 percent on average-risk stocks. Moreover, the analysts believe that the market is in equilibrium (expected rate of return equals required rate of return). Using the capital asset pricing model, calculate the expected rate of return on Texaco, Exxon, Meredith Corp., Compaq, and Genentech. Comparing the expected rate of return on Texaco with that on Compaq, which company is more likely to disappoint Mr. Lewis?
f. Which stocks in the above list would you suggest that Mr. Lewis consider in light of his objectives? Explain your answer.
g. *(Optional)* Using Standard & Poor's NYSE Reports, make a list of three additional stocks that are consistent with Mr. Lewis's investment objectives.

The author thanks Professor Carl M. Hubbard of Trinity University for contributing this case problem.

Selected References

Callahan, Carolyn M., and Rosanne M. Mohr. "The Determinants of Systematic Risk: A Synthesis." *Financial Review,* May 1989: 157–181.

Chan, Louis K. C., and Josef Lakonishok. "Robust Measurement of Beta Risk." *Journal of Financial and Quantitative Analysis,* June 1992: 265–282.

Duvall, Richard M., and John M. Cheney. "Bond Beta and Default Risk." *Journal of Financial Research,* Fall 1984: 243–254.

Grauer, Robert R. "Further Ambiguity When Performance Is Measured by the Security Market Line." *Financial Review,* November 1991: 569–585.

Harrington, Diana. "Whose Beta Is Best?" *Financial Analysts Journal,* July–August 1983: 67–73.

Lee, Chi-Wen Jevons. "Market Model Stationarity and Timing of Structural Change." *Financial Review,* November 1985: 329–342.

Markowitz, Harry M. *Portfolio Selection: Efficient Diversification of Investments.* New York: Wiley, 1959.

Mullins, David W. "Does the Capital Asset Pricing Model Work?" *Harvard Business Review,* January–February 1982: 105–114.

Roll, Richard, and Stephen A. Ross. "The Arbitrage Pricing Theory Approach to Strategic Portfolio Planning." *Financial Analysts Journal,* May–June 1984: 14–26.

Rosenberg, Barr. "The Capital Asset Pricing Model and the Market Model." *Journal of Portfolio Management,* Winter 1981: 5–16.

Sharpe, William F. "Capital Asset Prices: A Theory of Market Equilibrium under Conditions of Risk." *Journal of Finance,* September 1964: 425–442.

Wagner, W. H., and S. C. Lau. "The Effect of Diversification on Risk." *Financial Analysts Journal,* November–December 1971: 48–53.

Wiggins, James B. "Betas in Up and Down Markets." *Financial Review,* February 1992: 107–123.

Chapter 6

SECURITY VALUATION AND THE COST OF CAPITAL

A Winner and a Loser

At the end of October 1992, the total market value of IBM common stock—price per share times the number of shares outstanding—was $38.2 billion. IBM's market value ranked eighth among U.S. corporations. Unfortunately for IBM shareholders, the company's 1992 market value reflected a 20 percent decline from $47.9 billion a decade earlier, at which time IBM ranked second only to AT&T. Even more shocking, this decline occurred while the Dow Jones Industrial Average climbed 225 percent.

AT&T's stock market value moved in a dramatically different pattern from IBM's during the decade. Counting the seven regional phone companies (Baby Bells), whose shares were spun off to AT&T shareholders in 1984, AT&T's stock market value grew by 272 percent. The once-stodgy telephone monopoly soared, while the computer juggernaut plummeted.

Although the reasons for the divergent stock values are many,

consider these: (1) AT&T continued to dominate the long distance telephone market, and the Baby Bells continued to raise local phone rates, while prospering from the cellular phone business. (2) The proliferating manufacturers of desktop computers sold systems to customers who had formerly purchased only IBM mainframe computers. In the meantime, IBM failed to compete effectively in the desktop computer industry.

Each of the foregoing events affected investor perceptions of company prospects. As noted before, events that lead investors to expect higher sales, profits, and dividends bring about an increase in demand for a company's stock, causing its price to rise. Opposite conditions cause a company's stock price to decline. As assessed by the stock market from October 1982 to October 1992, the managers of AT&T and the Baby Bells made a series of good decisions. Moreover, the shareholders of these companies undoubtedly were pleased with the increase in their wealth. As IBM shareholders watched their company's stock price decline, along with their wealth, they undoubtedly were displeased—surely many were angry—with the decisions of IBM's managers.

Source: Randall Smith, "The Biggest Stocks Aren't Always a Safe Bet," *The Wall Street Journal,* November 19, 1992, C1.
Photo Source: John Madere for AT&T.

valuation
Process of estimating the value of an asset.

cost of capital
Percentage cost a company pays for funds to finance its investments.

This chapter discusses value and the way investors estimate the value of major corporate securities—bonds, preferred stock, and common stock. The importance of **valuation** (the process of estimating value) derives naturally from the objective of maximizing stock price. In addition, financial managers use valuation procedures to estimate what a company must pay for financing assets—the company's percentage **cost of capital.** What is the percentage cost of issuing bonds, preferred stock, and common stock? Answering this question reveals the close linkage between valuation and the cost of each source of capital to a company. Thus it is logical to combine into one chapter the valuation of securities and the cost of issuing them.

INTRINSIC VALUE AND MARKET VALUE

The *intrinsic value* of a security is the present value of its expected cash flows. To calculate intrinsic value, you need two estimates: (1) the expected cash flows from the security and (2) the required rate of return on the security. The required rate of return, or *discount rate*, together with the expected cash flows enable you to calculate the value of bonds, preferred stock, and common stock.

zero-coupon bond
Bond that does not pay coupon interest; issued at a discount from par value.

Consider the simple case of a **zero-coupon bond,** a bond that does not pay coupon interest. In 1981 J. C. Penney issued zero-coupon bonds scheduled to mature in 8 years. In exchange for not paying coupon interest, the company willingly sold the bonds well below par value. Each bond's *par value,* or face value, was $1,000, meaning that J. C. Penney would pay the bondholder $1,000 in 8 years. Interest rates were high in 1981, and investors in the bonds required a 14.76 percent annual rate of return. Based on the equation for present value (PV) in Chapter 4, the intrinsic value of the bond is calculated as follows:

$$PV = \frac{FV}{(1 + i)^n} = \frac{\$1,000}{(1 + 0.1476)^8} = \$332.41$$

market value
Price at which a security trades.

Based on a discount rate of 14.76 percent and a par value of $1,000, the intrinsic value of each bond is $332.41. Because a sufficient number of investors were satisfied to earn 14.76 percent per year on the bond, J. C. Penney was able to issue each bond for $332.41. In other words, the **market value** of the bond equaled its intrinsic value.

Each investor may come up with a different intrinsic value for a security because each may estimate different future cash flows and require a different rate of return. In a market where investors make different forecasts, there are as many intrinsic values as there are investors. The consensus judgment of investors gives rise to market value, the price at which a security trades. Marginally satisfied investors, through their buying and selling transactions, establish the market price of a security.

Professional investors compare market value with intrinsic value to decide whether they want to buy or sell a security. If intrinsic value exceeds market value, then an investor will (1) buy the security or (2) hold any securities already acquired. Conversely, if a security's market value exceeds its intrinsic value, then an investor will (1) not buy the security or (2) sell any securities already acquired. When the market consensus is that intrinsic value equals market value, the security is in *equilibrium*—a condition in which the price reflects all relevant information and there is no tendency for the price to change. Investor decisions made by comparing price (P) and intrinsic value (V) are summarized as follows:

Relationship	Decision
P < V	Buy (or do not sell)
P > V	Sell (or do not buy)
P = V	Equilibrium

EXAMPLE

Aston Enterprises common stock trades for $17 per share, and you estimate the present value of its future cash flows to be $24 per share. Under these conditions you would buy the common stock because its market value (price) is less than its intrinsic value. If several investors share your evaluation of the stock, an increase in demand will cause the price to rise toward equilibrium ($24). Alternatively, if the stock were trading for $28, investors would sell shares and cause the price to fall toward equilibrium.

EFFICIENT CAPITAL MARKETS

In an efficient capital market, expected cash flows, required rate of return, intrinsic value, and price relate to each other as follows:

$$\left.\begin{array}{l}\text{Expected cash flows} \\ \text{Required rate of return}\end{array}\right\} \longrightarrow \text{Intrinsic value} \longrightarrow \text{Price}$$

efficient capital market
Market in which security prices quickly reflect new information, causing price to equal intrinsic value.

Many finance theorists have studied the relationship between price and intrinsic value of stocks trading on organized exchanges such as the New York and American Stock Exchanges. Most of the evidence suggests that price equals intrinsic value in these markets, and when prices closely reflect intrinsic values, the market is efficient. An **efficient capital market** is one in which the prices of securities reflect all information available to investors. In an efficient market, when new information regarding the timing or amount of expected cash flows becomes available, security prices will change quickly.

The assertion that security prices reflect all known information is called the *efficient market hypothesis (EMH)*. Based on three types of information, finance theorists define three versions of the EMH:

1. *Weak-form efficiency* asserts that the current price of a security reflects all information contained in *past prices* and rates of return. If this is true, studying trends in stock prices will not help an investor to select underpriced stocks. Weak-form efficiency implies that *technical analysis,* or the charting of past security prices, is of no value, because stock prices already reflect this information.

2. *Semistrong-form efficiency* asserts that the current price of a security reflects *all publicly available* information. This set of information includes not only that generated in the market itself (stock prices), but also all other public information about the issuer of the security: for example, dividends, earnings, and data contained in balance sheets and income statements. Semistrong-form efficiency implies that *fundamental analysis,* or the study of economic and financial factors affecting the issuer of a security, will not help an investor to select underpriced stocks, because stock prices already reflect this information.

3. *Strong-form efficiency* asserts that the current price of a security reflects *all information*, public and private. This set of information includes the preceding two sets of information plus insider information. Strong-form efficiency implies that corporate officers and other insiders cannot use their privileged information effectively to earn an *abnormal return—* excessive return in relation to the riskiness of the stock.

Hundreds of researchers in finance have empirically tested the three forms of market efficiency. In general, their work supports the weak-form and semi-strong-form of efficiency, implying that "You can't consistently beat the stock market using publicly available information." Thousands of analysts scour the market daily and react quickly to the arrival of information. Good news and bad news lead to (almost) immediate changes in stock prices because of the buying and selling of securities by professionals. Your challenge in "beating the market" using public information is to outwit thousands of analysts. Of course, the challenge is less formidable for stocks of small companies followed by only a few analysts.

The third version of the EMH, strong-form efficiency, deals with the use of insider information to "beat the market." This version of the hypothesis does not hold true, because many investors with insider information have earned abnormal returns. Note, however, that some of these "insiders" are in prison. As Chapter 3 points out, the Securities Exchange Act of 1934 outlaws insider trading. To lessen insider trading, the Securities and Exchange Commission monitors stock trading by corporate officers and prosecutes any investor believed to have used inside information for personal gain.

EXAMPLE   Aston Enterprises' management calls a press conference to announce that it has won a lucrative government contract to produce nuclear submarines for the U.S. Navy. The concept of intrinsic value operating in an efficient market suggests that the company's stock price will increase quickly to a new equilibrium. Why? The increase in expected cash flows to the company encourages investors to expect bigger dividends, and the reduction in risk through a contractual arrangement with the government causes investors to reduce their required rate of return.

SECURITY VALUATION

The preceding ideas are used in the following sections on valuing corporate bonds, preferred stock, and common stock trading in efficient markets. In these sections we take the view of an investor and use required rate of return and expected cash flows to estimate a security's intrinsic value. Later in the chapter we take the view of a financial manager and use security price and expected cash flows to estimate the rates of return required by bondholders, preferred stockholders, and common shareholders. These estimates provide the basis for calculating a company's cost of capital.

Valuing Bonds

Unlike the zero-coupon bond introduced earlier, most corporate bonds pay interest. These bonds (long-term debt obligations) promise two types of cash flows to an investor: (1) fixed interest payments at regular intervals and (2) the repayment of principal when the bond matures. Bond principal is called the *par value*, or *face value*, and is usually $1,000 per bond.

The interest payments on a bond are based on its *coupon rate* and par value. Annual dollar interest equals the coupon rate times the par value, although most corporations pay bond interest in semiannual installments. For example, a corporate bond with a 14 percent coupon rate offers an investor $140 (0.14 × $1,000) interest annually in two $70 semiannual installments, payable until the bond matures.[1]

When investors calculate the intrinsic value of a bond, they use a present-value equation adjusted for semiannual compounding. The intrinsic value of a bond is calculated as follows:

$$VB = \sum_{t=1}^{2n} \frac{I/2}{[1 + (K_d/2)]^t} + \frac{Par}{[1 + (K_d/2)]^{2n}}$$

$$= (I/2)(PVIFA_{K_d/2,2n}) + Par(PVIF_{K_d/2,2n})$$

where VB = intrinsic value of a bond

    I = annual dollar interest payments; coupon rate times par value

    K_d = market interest rate compounded semiannually; investor's annual required rate of return

   Par = par value, or face value (usually $1,000)

    n = number of years remaining until the bond matures; 2n is the number of semiannual periods

(Recall that Appendix B.4 contains the interest factor PVIFA and that Appendix B.2 contains the interest factor PVIF. Also, see Appendix 6A for instructions on using a calculator to value a bond.)

EXAMPLE

Calculate the intrinsic value of a corporate bond that matures in 6 years, has a 14 percent coupon rate, and trades to yield a 12 percent required rate of return. The bond has a $1,000 par value. Because the corporation pays bond interest in semiannual installments, the calculation of bond value contains the following adjustments:

---

[1] The names and addresses of holders of registered bonds are recorded by the issuing corporation. Bearer bonds, which are not registered with the corporation, have interest coupons attached to the bond certificate. Each coupon is dated and carries the right to one semiannual interest payment. A new 30-year bond would have 60 coupons and pay semiannual interest by check to each bondholder. Commercial banks "clip coupons" and collect the interest for bearers for a small fee. Registered bonds, which have become more common than bearer bonds in recent years, do not have coupons, but pay semiannual interest by check to the registered bondholder. The issuing corporation must therefore maintain a record, or transfer book, showing the names of bondholders and the number of bonds each owns. The term *coupon rate* is used for registered bonds even though they do not have coupons.

FIGURE 6.1

Intrinsic Value of a 14 Percent Coupon, 6-Year Corporate Bond Trading to Yield 12 Percent Annually

The intrinsic value of a bond is the present value of the semiannual interest payments plus the present value of the par value. Each cash flow is discounted at the investor's required rate of return, adjusted for semiannual compounding.

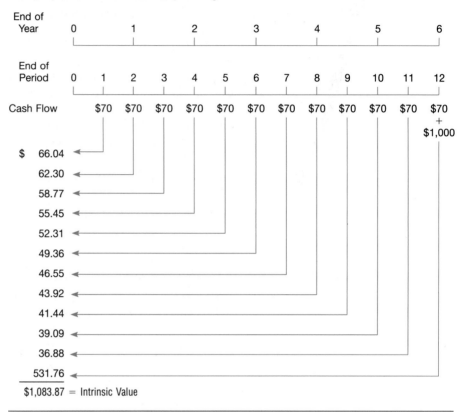

Adjustment to n: 2 × 6 years = 12 six-month periods
Adjustment to K_d: $K_d/2$ = 0.12/2 = 6% per six months
Adjustment to I: (0.14 × $1,000)/2 = $70 per six months

$$VB = \frac{\$140}{2}(PVIFA_{12\%/2,2\times6}) + \$1,000(PVIF_{12\%/2,2\times6})$$

$$= \$70(8.3838) + \$1,000(0.4970)$$

$$= \$586.87 + \$497.00$$

$$= \$1,083.87$$

Figure 6.1 illustrates that the intrinsic value of the bond in the above example is $1,083.87 when discounted at a 12 percent required rate of return. Stated differently, if investors pay $1,083.87 for this bond, then, by holding the bond to maturity, they receive a 12 percent annual rate of return compounded semiannually. Note two points: First, the equation for intrinsic value uses the same discount rate ($K_d/2$) and number of periods (2n) for *both* the interest payments and par value. Second, in an efficient market the intrinsic value and market price of the bond both equal $1,083.87.

Premiums and Discounts.   After a company issues bonds, they trade in the secondary market. In an efficient market a change in the present value of a bond will lead quickly to a change in its price. When a bond's price is greater than its par value, the bond trades **at a premium.** When a bond's price is less than its par value, it trades **at a discount.** Most bonds trade at a premium or a discount because of changes in interest rates over time.

at a premium
Trading at a price above par value; said of a premium bond.

at a discount
Trading at a price below par value; said of a discount bond.

EXAMPLE

The bond described in Figure 6.1 trades at a premium because its coupon rate (14 percent) exceeds the return (12 percent) required by investors. When the company issued the bond 2 years ago, investors required 14 percent, but market interest rates subsequently declined and investors now require only 12 percent. Calculate the value of the bond when the company issued it, using n = 8 and K_d = 14%:

$$VB = \frac{\$140}{2}(\text{PVIFA}_{14\%/2,2\times8}) + \$1,000(\text{PVIF}_{14\%/2,2\times8})$$

$$= \$70(9.4466) + \$1,000(0.3387)$$

$$= \$661.26 + \$338.70$$

$$= \$999.96, \text{ or } \$1,000 \text{ excluding rounding error}$$

When the required rate of return equals the coupon rate, the value of a bond equals its par value, $1,000. If market interest rates had risen instead of fallen and investors required 16 percent on the bond 2 years after its issuance, then what would the bond be worth? *Solution* (K_d = 16%, n = 6):

$$VB = \frac{\$140}{2}(\text{PVIFA}_{16\%/2,2\times6}) + \$1,000(\text{PVIF}_{16\%/2,2\times6})$$

$$= \$70(7.5361) + \$1,000(0.3971)$$

$$= \$527.53 + \$397.10$$

$$= \$924.63$$

The bond would be worth $924.63, and it would trade at a discount.

The preceding example illustrates the following principles:

If:	Then:
K_d < coupon rate	Bond trades at a premium.
K_d = coupon rate	Bond trades at par.
K_d > coupon rate	Bond trades at a discount.

Furthermore, as market interest rates (required rates of return, K_d) rise, the value (price) of a bond falls; and as market interest rates fall, the value (price) of a bond rises.

Interest Rate Risk.   The inverse (or opposite) relationship between bond prices and market interest rates creates **interest rate risk:** Investors' actual returns may differ from their expected returns as a result of unexpected changes in market interest rates. All securities (including default-free U.S. Treasury securities) are subject to varying amounts of interest rate risk. Other things being equal, the longer the maturity of a bond, the greater the interest rate risk will be, as the following example illustrates.

EXAMPLE

Suppose that investors can purchase an 8 percent U.S. Treasury bond with 1 year remaining until maturity. Alternatively, they can purchase an 8 percent U.S. Treasury bond with 10 years to maturity. Each bond pays interest semiannually. What happens to the price of each bond if market interest rates increase above 8 percent per year compounded semiannually?

In the above example, if investors require an 8 percent rate of return on a U.S. Treasury security with an 8 percent coupon rate, then the bond will be priced at par, $1,000 (see Table 6.1). If market interest rates rise to 10 percent after the investors purchase the bonds, then they lose money on each bond: *interest rates up, bond prices down.* This drop in price resulting from increased interest rates reflects interest rate risk. Table 6.1 shows that investors lose more on the 10-year bond ($124.61 per bond) than they do on the 1-year bond ($18.62 per bond). Stated differently, investors lose only 1.862 percent on the 1-year bond, but they lose 12.461 percent on the 10-year bond. On the other hand, if the market interest rate on the bonds drops to 6 percent, then the 10-year bond price appreciates more ($148.80 = $1,148.80 − $1,000) than does the 1-year bond price ($19.14 = $1,019.14 − $1,000). This differing impact of interest rate changes on bond price demonstrates that long-term bonds have more interest rate risk than do short-term bonds.[2]

The preceding analysis illustrates the following principles:

	Short-Term Bond	Long-Term Bond
Interest rates increase	Price falls	Price falls more
Interest rates decrease	Price rises	Price rises more
Bond price volatility	Less	More
Interest rate risk	Less	More

Figure 6.2 further illustrates the inverse relationship between bond prices and market interest rates. It also illustrates the greater price swing of a long-term bond in comparison to a short-term bond in response to changes in market interest rates (required rates of return).[3]

[2] Financial calculators easily handle the calculation of bond value. Consider, for example, the first calculation in Table 6.1: Enter 2 for *n*, 4 for *i*, 40 for *PMT*, and 1000 for *FV*; then press *PV* (or *CPT*, then *PV*) to get the answer, $1,000. See Appendix 6A.

[3] Many bond analysts quantify interest rate risk with *duration*, a measure expressed in units of time; it is the average deferred time of the cash flows. Duration (D) is the weighted-average number of years until the investor receives the cash flows from a bond:

$$D = \sum_{t=1}^{n} \frac{tC_t/(1 + K_d)^t}{VB}$$

TABLE 6.1

Changes in Short- and Long-Term Bond Prices for a Given Change in Interest Rates

One-Year Bond, 8% Coupon Rate

Trading at 8%: Bond price = $40(PVIFA$_{4\%,2}$) + $1,000(PVIF$_{4\%,2}$)
= $40(1.8861) + $1,000(0.9246)
= $75.44 + $924.60
= $1,000[a]

Trading at 10%: Bond price = $40(PVIFA$_{5\%,2}$) + $1,000(PVIF$_{5\%,2}$)
= $40(1.8594) + $1,000(0.9070)
= $74.38 + $907.00
= $981.38

Ten-Year Bond, 8% Coupon Rate

Trading at 8%: Bond price = $40(PVIFA$_{4\%,20}$) + $1,000(PVIF$_{4\%,20}$)
= $40(13.5903) + $1,000(0.4564)
= $543.61 + $456.40
= $1,000[a]

Trading at 10%: Bond price = $40(PVIFA$_{5\%,20}$) + $1,000(PVIF$_{5\%,20}$)
= $40(12.4622) + $1,000(0.3769)
= $498.49 + $376.90
= $875.39

[a]Rounded to $1,000.

Required rates of return on corporate bonds reflect not only interest rate risk but also the default risk of the issuing company. For example, two bonds with the same maturity and coupon rate may have different prices because they have different default risk—the uncertainty surrounding the borrower's ability to service the debt. Greater default risk leads investors to require a higher rate of return on a bond, which lowers its price.

Valuing Preferred Stock

Calculating the intrinsic value of a share of preferred stock requires the equation for a perpetuity (presented in Chapter 4). A *perpetuity* is a perpetual annuity, an annual dollar amount an investor receives through infinity. A preferred stock is a perpetuity because it pays a stated, level dividend indefinitely.

where C_t = cash flow at time t

t = time of cash flow

K_d = interest rate

n = years to maturity

VB = market value of the bond

As the duration of a bond increases, its interest rate risk increases as well. If a bond returns only one cash flow at maturity, then its duration is the same as its years to maturity. For a coupon bond with more than one cash flow, duration is less than years to maturity. A readable and informative source on this topic is G. J. Santoni, "Interest Rate Risk and the Stock Prices of Financial Institutions," Federal Reserve Bank of St. Louis, *Review,* August–September 1984, 12–20.

The expected annual dividend divided by the required rate of return yields the intrinsic value.[4] This method assumes that the investor acquires the stock at the beginning of the first period (that is, at time zero) and receives dividends at the *end* of each year including the first one. The equation is:

$$VP = \frac{D_p}{K_p}$$

where VP = intrinsic value of a share of preferred stock on the day following the most recent dividend

D_p = preferred share's annual end-of-year dividend

K_p = investor's annual required rate of return

EXAMPLE

A share of preferred stock offers a $5 annual dividend. If you require a return of 8 percent per year and buy the stock at the beginning of the year, then the stock's intrinsic value is:

$$VP = \frac{\$5}{0.08}$$

$$= \$62.50$$

If you buy the preferred stock in the above example at a time when you receive the first dividend *immediately* rather than at the end of a year, then intrinsic value will rise by the amount of the dividend. This is why: The present value of the immediate $5 is clearly $5, so you add this amount to the present value of the future dividends. The solution becomes $5 + $62.50 = $67.50. This adjustment suggests why stock prices (of both preferred and common) decline on the day following a dividend. Investors buying the stock on this day will not receive the dividend immediately, and so the intrinsic value declines. As the intrinsic value declines, investors bid less for the shares and the price falls toward its

---

[4] Although the result is quite simple, the derivation of the perpetuity equation is more complex. Algebraically, the value of a perpetuity (VP) is:

$$VP = \frac{D_p}{(1 + K_p)^1} + \frac{D_p}{(1 + K_p)^2} + \cdots + \frac{D_p}{(1 + K_p)^n} \tag{6.1}$$

where D_p is the cash dividend each year and K_p is the annual required rate of return. First, multiply Equation 6.1, a geometric series, by the repetitive factor $(1 + K_p)$:

$$VP(1 + K_p) = D_p + \frac{D_p}{(1 + K_p)^1} + \frac{D_p}{(1 + K_p)^2} + \cdots + \frac{D_p}{(1 + K_p)^{n-1}} \tag{6.2}$$

Next subtract Equation 6.1 from Equation 6.2:

$$VP(1 + K_p) - VP = D_p - \frac{D_p}{(1 + K_p)^n} \tag{6.3}$$

Because we are working with a perpetuity, let $n \to \infty$, which causes $D_p/(1 + K_p)^n \to 0$. Thus Equation 6.3 becomes:

$$VP(1 + K_p) - VP = D_p$$

which simplifies to $VP(1 + K_p - 1) = VP(K_p) = D_p$. Therefore the value of a preferred stock is $VP = D_p/K_p$. Although many preferred stocks pay dividends quarterly, analysts often ignore this detail, as we do, and assume that dividends are paid annually.

FIGURE 6.2

Relationship between Bond Values and Interest Rates

Bond values, or prices, are inversely related to interest rates. Also, changes in interest rates cause long-term bond prices to change more than short-term bond prices. Thus long-term bonds have more interest rate risk than do short-term bonds with similar coupons.

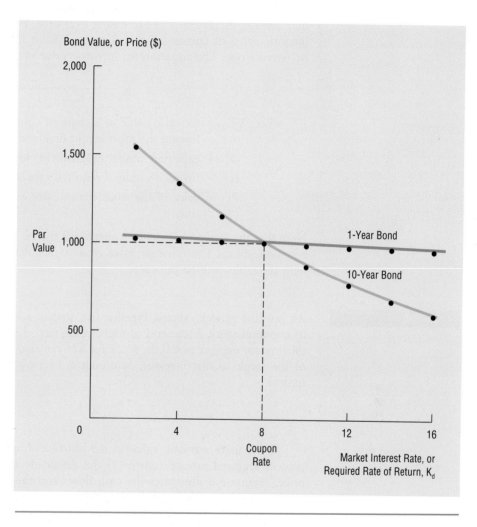

equilibrium level dictated by intrinsic value. In the above example the price of the stock would fall from $67.50 to $62.50 on the day following the dividend.

Some preferred stocks are *callable*, meaning that the issuers can redeem them by paying stockholders a prespecified **call price**. Callability gives corporate managers a measure of control over a preferred stock and enables them to plan its retirement. If interest rates and required rates of return fall after a company issues preferred stock, then management might wish to call it in and issue new preferred stock with a smaller dividend, thus reducing the company's cash outflow. Calculating the value of a preferred stock likely to be called is similar to that of a corporate bond: First you estimate when the call will likely occur; then you add the present value of dividends expected prior to the call to the present value of the call price.

call price

Price a company pays to investors for early redemption of bonds or preferred stock.

Valuing Common Stock

As with bonds and preferred stock, the intrinsic value of a share of common stock is the present value of its future cash flows. Its future cash flows are (1) expected cash dividends and (2) an expected sale price, or disposal value. Unlike most bonds and preferred stock, common stock offers an investor cash flows that may change, increasing and decreasing over time. For this reason estimating the intrinsic value of common stock is more difficult than doing so for a bond or preferred stock. The equation for intrinsic value of a common stock is:

$$VC = \sum_{t=1}^{n} \frac{D_t}{(1 + K_c)^t} + \frac{P_n}{(1 + K_c)^n}$$

where VC = intrinsic value of a share of common stock on the day following the most recent dividend

D_t = expected annual dollar dividend at time t

K_c = investor's annual required rate of return

P_n = price of the stock the investor expects upon selling it at time n

Note that the interest factors in Appendix B can be used as an alternative to the equation above. The intrinsic value of a stock calculated with the equation or with the tables will be the same.

EXAMPLE

An investor expects Mason Pipeline Inc. to pay a $2.80 dividend per share on its common stock at the end of each of the next 3 years. At the end of 3 years the investor expects to sell the stock for $26 per share. What is the intrinsic value of the stock to this investor, assuming a 16 percent annual required rate of return?

To calculate intrinsic value in the above example, you discount at the 16 percent required rate of return (1) the dividends and (2) the expected selling price.[5] Figure 6.3 illustrates the cash flows and the discounting process, which yields an intrinsic value of $22.95. Unlike the dividends in this example, expected future dividends from most stocks will not form an ordinary annuity. When dividends vary, you must discount *each* expected dividend—whatever its amount—with the required rate of return and add this amount to the present value of the expected sale price.

The price at which you can sell a stock depends on the dividends expected by the purchaser. So in the preceding example the expected sale price, $26, depends on the dividends expected after Year 3. Viewed this way, the only cash flows received from stock ownership by a series of shareholders over time—are dividends! Collectively, shareholders receive no cash flows other than dividends (assuming that the company is not taken over by another company). The value of common stock can therefore be viewed in terms of dividends only, ignoring

---

[5] Many companies pay quarterly common-stock dividends. Although many analysts ignore this detail and assume dividends to be paid at year-end, we can increase precision by recognizing the quarterly payments. For convenience and simplicity, we consider only annual dividends in the valuation models in this book.

any consideration of a future selling price. This viewpoint results in a most useful model for valuing common stock.

Constant-Growth Model. Because the estimation of individual annual dividends is tedious and difficult to do accurately, analysts often estimate the *growth rate* of dividends instead. By assuming that the growth rate is constant over time, they can use a simple model to calculate the intrinsic value of a stock. The model is the **constant-growth** (or **Gordon**) **model,** popularized by Professor Myron Gordon, who has written a great deal about security valuation. If dividends are expected to grow perpetually at a constant annual rate, then the intrinsic value of a share of common stock becomes the present value of the perpetually growing dividends found with the constant-growth model:[6]

constant-growth (Gordon) model
Model that equates intrinsic value with the present value of dividends growing at a constant rate into the indefinite future.

$$VC = \frac{D_1}{K_c - g}$$

where VC = intrinsic value of a share of common stock on the day following the most recent dividend

D_1 = cash dividend expected one year from now

K_c = investor's annual required rate of return

g = expected annual growth rate of the cash dividend

[6]Derivation of the constant-growth model is similar to that for the value of a preferred stock in Note 4. If you work through the derivation, you will better understand the basic ideas of the model. Express the value of common stock (VC) as the present value of all future dividends:

$$VC = \frac{D_1}{(1 + K_c)^1} + \frac{D_2}{(1 + K_c)^2} + \cdots + \frac{D_n}{(1 + K_c)^n} \tag{6.4}$$

If dividends are expected to grow at a constant rate g, you can express next year's dividend as $D_1 = D_0(1 + g)$, where D_0 is the dividend paid and received at time zero. The second-year dividend is $D_2 = D_1(1 + g)$, or:

$$D_2 = D_1(1 + g) = D_0(1 + g)(1 + g) = D_0(1 + g)^2$$

For the year n, $D_n = D_0(1 + g)^n$. Equation 6.4 now becomes:

$$VC = \frac{D_0(1 + g)^1}{(1 + K_c)^1} + \frac{D_0(1 + g)^2}{(1 + K_c)^2} + \cdots + \frac{D_0(1 + g)^n}{(1 + K_c)^n} \tag{6.5}$$

Equation 6.5 is a geometric series, which can be simplified by first multiplying it by $(1 + K_c)/(1 + g)$:

$$\left(\frac{1 + K_c}{1 + g}\right) VC = D_0 + \frac{D_0(1 + g)^1}{(1 + K_c)^1} + \frac{D_0(1 + g)^2}{(1 + K_c)^2} + \cdots + \frac{D_0(1 + g)^{n-1}}{(1 + K_c)^{n-1}} \tag{6.6}$$

Next subtract Equation 6.5 from Equation 6.6:

$$\left(\frac{1 + K_c}{1 + g}\right) VC - VC = D_0 - \frac{D(1 + g)^n}{(1 + K_c)^n} \tag{6.7}$$

Because we are working with a perpetuity, let n → ∞. Also assume $K_c > g$, causing the second term on the right side of Equation 6.7 to approach zero, leaving:

$$\left(\frac{1 + K_c}{1 + g}\right) VC - VC = D_0 \tag{6.8}$$

Multiplying each term by $(1 + g)$ produces:

$$(1 + K_c)VC - VC(1 + g) = D_0(1 + g)$$

Factoring out VC leaves:

$$VC(1 + K_c - 1 - g) = D_0(1 + g)$$

which simplifies to:

$$VC = \frac{D_0(1 + g)}{K_c - g}$$

Therefore, the value of a common stock with constant-growth dividends is $VC = D_1/(K_c - g)$.

FIGURE 6.3

Intrinsic Value of Common Stock: Mason Pipeline Inc. (Discounted at 16 Percent Annually)

The intrinsic value of a share of common stock paying a constant dividend is the present value of the annuity formed by the dividends plus the present value of the expected sale price, each discounted at the investor's required rate of return.

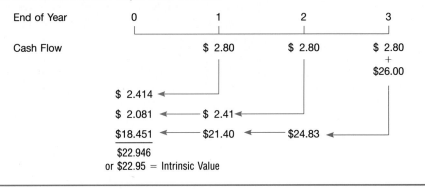

EXAMPLE

Tapesco recently paid a $3.00 dividend per share on its common stock. Investors expect the dividend to grow at a 12 percent annual rate for the indefinite future. How much is the stock worth to investors requiring a 16 percent return? The first step is to estimate the dividend one year from now. It is the $3.00 dividend increased by the 12 percent growth rate:

$$D_1 = D_0(1 + g)$$
$$= \$3.00(1 + 0.12) = \$3.36$$

Now use the constant-growth model to find the answer:

$$VC = \frac{\$3.36}{0.16 - 0.12} = \$84$$

zero-growth stock
Stock whose dividends investors expect will remain constant into the indefinite future; $g = 0$ in the constant-growth model.

The constant-growth model easily handles **zero-growth stocks**, which pay a constant dividend. Just let $g = 0$, and intrinsic value becomes:

$$VC = \frac{D_1}{K_c}$$

This equation is essentially the same as that used to value preferred stock, which pays a constant dividend and is therefore a zero-growth stock.

EXAMPLE

What is the intrinsic value of Tapesco's common stock (in the preceding example) if investors expect the company to pay a dividend of $3.00 per share, require a 16 percent annual rate of return, and expect zero growth in the dividend?

$$VC = \frac{\$3.00}{0.16}$$
$$= \$18.75$$

Stock value drops to \$18.75 from \$84 per share because expected dividend growth declines from 12 percent to zero. What happens to Tapesco's stock value if investors expect dividend growth to be -4 percent, a negative growth rate?

$$VC = \frac{\$3.00(1 - 0.04)}{0.16 - (-0.04)} = \frac{\$2.88}{0.20}$$

$$= \$14.40$$

In this case the expected dividend D_1 is \$2.88, not \$3.00; dividing \$2.88 by 0.20 yields the intrinsic value, \$14.40. Note that when g is 12 percent, VC is \$84; when g is zero, VC is \$18.75; and when g is -4 percent, VC is \$14.40.

The preceding examples and the constant-growth model illustrate the substantial impact that expected dividend growth has on stock value. The challenge to corporate managers is to find ways of increasing sustainable dividend growth through investment and financing decisions—for example, through product innovation, improved operating efficiency, and the use of low-cost debt. As the model indicates, a reduction in the required rate of return through a reduction in the risk perceived by investors also increases value. In summary, increases in D_1 and g and decreases in K_c lead to increases in stock value, the objective of business financial management.

Investors, analysts, and financial managers use the constant-growth model despite the limitations its simplifying assumptions impose. In practice, successful application of the model to estimate a stock's intrinsic value depends primarily on one's ability to estimate the expected growth rate in dividends (g). Small variations in estimates of growth can lead to large variations in estimates of value.

The growth rate is defined explicitly as the expected growth rate of dividends per share. In practical applications, g usually applies also to the expected growth rates of earnings and price per share of common stock. For the per-share growth rates of *dividends, earnings,* and *price* to be the same requires (1) a constant ratio between dividends and earnings per share and (2) a constant ratio between price and earnings per share. The constant-growth model also assumes that the required rate of return is greater than the growth rate (that is, $K_c > g$). If that were not the case, the model would yield meaningless solutions. A growth rate greater than the required rate of return, for example, results in a negative stock value, which implies that the expected cash flows have negative present value. Also, a growth rate equaling the required rate of return results in an undefined stock value. When $g \geq K_c$, an alternative model must be used to estimate intrinsic value.

Nonconstant-Growth Model. Many companies experience high growth rates in sales and earnings when they are newly established and as they market new products and services. Recent examples are companies engaged in genetic engineering, computer software, and overnight delivery services. Rapidly growing companies often pay no dividends in the early years, but instead reinvest all earnings in expansion projects. Investors willingly buy the stock of growth companies because they believe that dividends will one day be forthcoming, even if only in the distant future. As growth companies begin to mature, the dividends they pay tend to grow at high but unsustainable rates. Reaching maturity, the companies pay dividends that grow at more normal rates and in accordance with general

nonconstant-growth model
Model for valuing stocks whose dividends investors expect will grow at varying rates.

Buying Stocks with Low P-E Ratios

Intrinsic value is easier to conceptualize than to estimate because, in the real world of investments, growth rates can change in unexpected ways. Consequently, analysts have developed many different models for determining intrinsic values. Some analysts apply the constant-growth model and the present-value models we examine in this chapter. Others compare a stock's price with its annual earnings per share—in investors' jargon, the price–earnings, or P-E, ratio. If the price of a share of Widget Inc. is $10 and the company earned $1 per share in the last 12 months, its P-E ratio is 10.

Some analysts suggest that companies with low P-E ratios have intrinsic values higher than their prices, making them good investments. Others have a different view: Companies with low P-E ratios have high risk (and other

problems), making them poor investments.

Michael Berry, at the University of Virginia Business School, looked at 1,000 widely traded stocks, sorting them into five equal groups according to P-E rankings. His conclusion: The stocks with the lowest P-E ratios averaged a total return of 22.8 percent annually from mid-1975 to mid-1985, while those with the highest P-E ratios produced only 9.6 percent per year.

Investors wanting to follow the low P-E ratio selection method may want to supplement it with other information. For example, David Dreman, a professional money manager with the New York firm of Dreman & Embry, suggests that successful stock selection results from buying the stocks of companies showing successful financial performance for a period of time. He likes companies

that have a growth rate of at least 10 percent annually in their earnings after taxes.

A study by Robert Jones, of Goldman, Sachs & Co., shows that low P-E strategies tend to do poorly when economic growth is slower than usual. When a slowdown occurs, the prices of low P-E stocks tend to fall quickly, because the companies tend to be small, fragile, and risky.

The low P-E method has its limitations, so it does not make sense simply to buy the bottom of the heap. You would more than likely wind up with mostly troubled companies. Diversification and investing in the stocks of different companies with different P-E ratios are probably essential to success. Mr. Dreman suggests that an ideal low P-E portfolio would contain 15 to 20 stocks in about a dozen industries.

Source: Based on articles by Pamela Sherrid, *U.S. News & World Report,* Feb. 3, 1986, 60; and Barbara Donnelly, *The Wall Street Journal,* Apr. 25, 1989, C1.

economic growth. This life-cycle scenario describes dividends that grow at nonconstant rates over time; and for such cases a **nonconstant-growth model** can be used to estimate intrinsic value of common stock.

EXAMPLE   Intercomp is a high-tech and high-growth company founded several years ago. Intercomp has never paid dividends and does not plan to do so for another 2 years, at which time it is expected to pay $2 per share. Analysts also expect the dividend to grow 50 percent per year for 2 years, then decline to 8 percent per year indefinitely. How much is Intercomp stock worth to investors requiring a 15 percent annual return?

The above example characterizes a company that pays dividends at a nonconstant growth rate. Expressed in words, the nonconstant-growth model for calculating intrinsic value in such cases is as follows: (1) Calculate the present value

| FIGURE 6.4 | **Intrinsic Value of a Common Stock with a Nonconstant Growth Rate in Dividends** |

(1) Calculate the present value of the dividends during the high-growth period. (2) Use the constant-growth model to calculate stock value at the end of the high-growth period; discount this value to the present. (3) Add the present value from Step 1 to the present value from Step 2 to obtain the intrinsic value.

$$VC = \$2(0.7561_{15\%,2}) + \$3(0.6575_{15\%,3}) + \$4.50(0.5718_{15\%,4}) + \$69.43(0.5718_{15\%,4})$$

$$= \$1.51 + \$1.97 + \$2.57 + \$39.70$$

$$= \$45.75$$

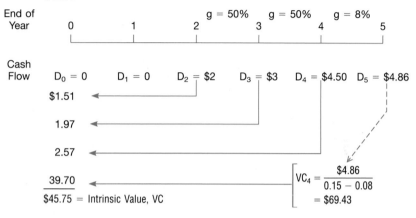

of the dividends during the high-growth period—in the example, the dividends occurring at Year-ends 2, 3, and 4. (2) Use the constant-growth model to calculate stock value at the end of the high-growth period—in the example, Year-end 4; discount this value to the present. (3) Add the present value from Step 1 to the present value from Step 2 to obtain the intrinsic value of the stock.

Figure 6.4 summarizes the calculation of intrinsic value for the preceding example: (1) The present values ($K_c = 15\%$) of D_2, D_3, and D_4 are $1.51, $1.97, and $2.57, respectively. (2) D_5 is the dividend used in the constant-growth model; D_5 equals $D_4(1 + g)$, or $4.86 = $4.50 × 1.08. VC_4 is the value at Year-end 4 of all future dividends beginning with Year-end 5. The present value of VC_4 ($K_c = 15\%$, n = 4) is $39.70. (3) Intrinsic value of the stock is the present value of D_2, D_3, D_4, and VC_4, or $45.75.

To summarize, the nonconstant-growth model is a step-by-step procedure for calculating intrinsic value of a stock paying dividends at varying growth rates. Although only one dividend scenario is discussed here, the general ideas of the model can be tailored to fit a wide range of dividend patterns.

component cost of capital
Estimated percentage cost of a component—bonds, preferred stock, new common stock, and retained earnings—in a company's capital structure.

COST OF CAPITAL

To raise funds, a company must compensate investors for their opportunity cost—the required rate of return used in valuing securities. In an efficient market the percentage cost of each source of capital is the investors' required rate of return adjusted where needed for flotation costs and tax effects. The logical flow of ideas for estimating the **component cost of capital** to a company is as follows:

FIGURE 6.5 **Corporate Securities Portrayed on the Security Market Line (SML)**

Arrayed in terms of increasing required rate of return and cost to a company are bonds, preferred stock, and common stock.

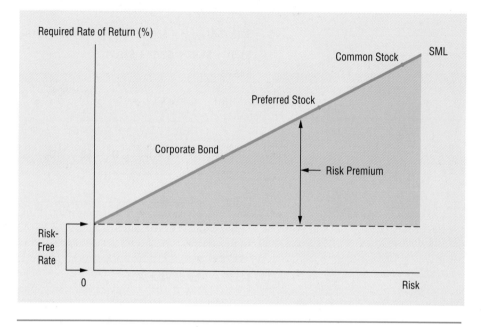

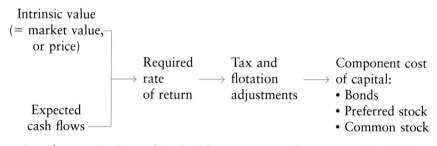

The price of a security is combined with an estimate of its expected cash flows in a present-value equation to solve for the required rate of return, which is the basis for a component cost of capital.

The cost-of-capital concept needs to be understood because it affects a company's market value. As a matter of fact, the cost of capital and the value of a company are inversely related: The higher the cost of capital, the lower the value of the company. The combined market values of a company's bonds, preferred stock, and common stock equal the company's total market value. Therefore, if the cost of the company's capital can be reduced, or the price of its securities increased, the company's market value will be increased.

Figure 6.5 presents the way three major sources of capital (bonds, preferred stock, and common stock) appear when each source's required rate of return is related with its risk to an investor. Common stock presents the greatest risk to investors because any company loss is first shouldered by common shareholders. The least risky security of a given company for an investor to hold is a bond.

The risk of owning a preferred stock falls between that of a bond and a common stock because a preferred stockholder has a claim on assets and earnings ranking ahead of that for a common shareholder but behind that for a bondholder.[7] In order of increasing cost, the sources of capital to a company are: (1) corporate bonds, (2) preferred stock, and (3) common stock. We analyze the cost of each of these components in the following sections.

Cost of Bonds

cost of bonds
Investors' required rate of return on the bonds, adjusted for flotation costs and the tax deductibility of interest payments.

The percentage **cost of bonds** issued by a company is *the rate of return required by investors in the bonds,* adjusted for flotation costs and tax effects. For example, a financial manager might discover, after a discussion with the company's investment banker, that the interest rate on a bond the company wants to issue must be 10 percent per year. This 10 percent is the company's before-tax cost of bond financing. If the financial manager borrows $500,000 at 10 percent interest on behalf of the company, the company must pay $50,000 (0.10 × $500,000) interest each year.

Taxes play an important role in the cost of bonds. Interest is a tax-deductible expense, making the annual after-tax cost of bond financing less than its before-tax cost. Therefore we start the analysis by discussing the impact of taxes on bond financing before calculating the cost of this component.

EXAMPLE

Dinah Apparel Company's earnings before paying its interest and income taxes are $400,000. If the company's marginal tax rate[8] is 34 percent and it pays $50,000 interest on a bond issue, then its earnings after taxes without the bond and with the bond are as follows:

	Without Bond	With Bond
Earnings before interest and taxes	$400,000	$400,000
Less interest expense	0	50,000
Earnings before taxes	$400,000	$350,000
Less income taxes (34%)	136,000	119,000
Earnings after taxes	$264,000	$231,000

Despite paying $50,000 interest on the bond, Dinah Apparel Company's earnings after taxes decline only $33,000 rather than $50,000. The $17,000 difference occurs because income taxes decline by $17,000. For each $1 Dinah Apparel pays in interest, its taxable earnings decline by $1 and its income taxes decline by $0.34.

---

[7] Considered here is the risk of a single company's securities. Company A's bond may, in fact, be riskier than Company B's common stock.

[8] A marginal tax rate refers to the percentage paid on the *last* unit of taxable income. The Tax Reform Act of 1986 forces corporations to pay taxes according to the following schedule: 15 percent on the first $50,000, 25 percent on the next $25,000, 39 percent on the next $235,000, and 34 percent on all taxable income over $335,000. Therefore, if a corporation has a taxable income of $400,000, its *marginal* tax rate is 34 percent. (In 1993, the U.S. Congress increased the top corporate tax rate to 35 percent.)

The relationship between after-tax and before-tax cost of interest in the preceding example can be expressed in the following way:

$$\frac{\text{After-tax}}{\text{dollar cost}} = \frac{\text{Before-tax}}{\text{dollar cost}} - \text{Tax savings}$$

Alternatively, the relationship is:

$$\frac{\text{After-tax}}{\text{dollar cost}} = \frac{\text{Before-tax}}{\text{dollar cost}} \times (1 - \text{Marginal tax rate})$$

$$\$33,000 = \$50,000 \times (1 - 0.34)$$

Because interest expense is tax deductible to the company, the bond investor's required rate of return must be adjusted to calculate the after-tax cost of funds raised from issuing a bond. In general, the after-tax percentage cost of a bond relates to the before-tax percentage in the following way:

$$\frac{\text{After-tax}}{\text{percentage cost}} = \frac{\text{Before-tax}}{\text{percentage cost}} \times (1 - \text{Marginal tax rate})$$

Letting K_i be the after-tax cost, T the company's marginal tax rate, and K_d the bondholder's required rate of return, we have the general relationship:

$$K_i = K_d(1 - T)$$

EXAMPLE

Consider the example above in which the company paid $50,000 interest on $500,000 of bonds. The before-tax cost (K_d) is 10 percent, and the after-tax cost (K_i) is 6.6 percent:

$$K_i = K_d(1 - T)$$
$$= 0.10(1 - 0.34)$$
$$= 0.066, \text{ or } 6.6\%$$

yield to maturity
Average annual rate of return investors expect to receive on a bond by holding it to maturity.

Yield to Maturity.   The required rate of return (K_d) on a bond has a special name, yield to maturity. **Yield to maturity** is the average annual rate of return an investor expects to receive from buying and holding a bond until the company repays the principal at maturity. Stated differently, the yield to maturity is the discount rate in a present-value equation equating a bond's price to the present value of its debt-service payments—future cash flows consisting of (1) interest payments and (2) repayment of principal (par value) at maturity.

Calculating the yield to maturity requires the use of an iterative procedure. *Iterative* means that we repeat calculations with different discount rates until we find the one equating the present value of the bond's future cash flows to the bond price. A bond trading at par value ($1,000) requires no searching. The bondholder's required rate of return and the before-tax percentage cost of the bond (K_d) is the coupon interest rate.

EXAMPLE

Colite Industries issues a bond at par ($1,000) with a coupon rate of 10 percent per year. Colite pays interest semiannually, and the bond will mature in 15 years (n). The yield to maturity (K_d) is 10 percent annually, as the following steps show you:

Adjustment to n: 15 years $\times$ 2 = 30 six-month periods

Adjustment to the
required rate of return: $K_d/2 = 0.10/2 = 5\%$ per 6-month period

Adjustment to interest
payments: $(0.10 \times \$1,000)/2 = \$50$ per 6-month period

$$\$1,000 = \$50(\text{PVIFA}_{5\%,30}) + \$1,000(\text{PVIF}_{5\%,30})$$
$$= \$50(15.3725) + \$1,000(0.2314)$$
$$= \$768.63 + \$231.40$$
$$\$1,000 = \$1,000 \text{ (rounded)}$$

The discount rate that forces the present value of interest and principal payments to equal bond price is 10 percent per year compounded semiannually. This rate is the yield to maturity and the investors' required rate of return.[9] If Colite's tax bracket is 25 percent, then the cost of this component of capital is:

$$K_i = 0.10(1 - 0.25)$$
$$= 0.075, \text{ or } 7.5\%$$

Remember from this example that when companies issue bonds at par value, the before-tax cost is the coupon rate of interest. Multiplying this rate by $1 - T$ produces the after-tax cost.

Although present-value procedures provide a more accurate calculation of yield to maturity, the following approximation aids understanding of bond prices and yields:

$$\frac{\text{Approximate yield}}{\text{to maturity}} = \frac{\text{Average annual dollar return}}{\text{Average annual investment}}$$
$$= \frac{\text{Annual interest + Prorated capital gain (loss)}}{\text{Average annual investment}}$$
$$= \frac{I + [(\text{Par} - \text{VB})/n]}{(\text{VB} + \text{Par})/2}$$

VB is the value of the bond, or the current market price. Notice that if a bond trades at a discount, then VB < Par and the second term in the numerator is positive—a capital gain prorated over the life (n) of the bond. If the bond trades at a premium, then VB > Par and the second term is negative—a capital loss prorated over the life of the bond. The average annual investment is approximated by the beginning plus ending bond values divided by 2. Knowing the equation for approximate yield to maturity helps you to understand the nature of

---

[9]Because of semiannual compounding, the effective annual rate on the bond is:

$$\text{Effective annual rate} = (1 + 0.05)^2 - 1$$
$$= 0.1025, \text{ or } 10.25\% \text{ per year compounded annually}$$

Although many analysts ignore the effect of compounding, precision is increased by recognizing it. For convenience and simplicity, however, we ignore the effect when calculating yield to maturity and the component cost of bonds.

bonds. It also helps you to narrow the search for the more accurate yield to maturity in present-value analysis.

EXAMPLE

Suppose you pay $1,100 for a 10-year bond with a 12 percent coupon rate and a $1,000 par value. What is the approximate yield to maturity on your bond?

$$\frac{\text{Approximate yield}}{\text{to maturity}} = \frac{\$120 + (\$1,000 - \$1,100)/10}{(\$1,100 + \$1,000)/2}$$

$$= \frac{\$120 - \$10}{\$1,050}$$

$$= 0.105, \text{ or } 10.5\%$$

Your annual dollar interest ($120) less the annual prorated capital loss ($10) yields 10.5 percent on your average investment, $1,050. (*Note:* We seek only an approximate yield to maturity and therefore use annual dollar interest, not semi-annual dollar interest. Despite the "roughness" of the procedure, the equation often produces fairly accurate answers: in this example, 10.5 percent versus 10.35 percent.)

Issue Price and Flotation Costs.   Two problems may prevent the use of the after-tax coupon rate as a company's cost of bonds. First, bonds often trade at prices other than par value. Issuers and their investment bankers tinker with the *issue price* after setting the coupon rate in order to attract investors with a yield to maturity competitive in the market—not too high, not too low. In recent years, some companies have issued **deep-discount bonds,** whose prices are well below par value. The issuer places a low coupon rate on the bond, then offers it at a very large discount from par value. Investors buying these bonds receive a large cash return at maturity, but they must accept small interest payments in the meantime.

deep-discount bond
Bond trading at a substantial discount from par value.

The second problem is *flotation costs,* costs associated with issuing a new security. Examples of flotation costs are investment banking fees, expenses for printing certificates and other documents, accounting costs, and legal fees. Cash proceeds to the company from a new offering will be less than the issue price as a result of flotation costs. Proceeds are used in the yield-to-maturity equation to calculate the cost of bonds (K_i).

EXAMPLE

Prescott Corporation plans a bond issue with a coupon rate of 10 percent per year and a maturity of 8 years. The bond will have a face value of $1,000 and pay interest semiannually. Because competitive market rates currently exceed the coupon rate, the bond will initially trade at a discount. Considering this factor and flotation costs, Prescott expects proceeds of $898.90 from each bond issued. What is Prescott's after-tax cost of debt (K_i) if the company's marginal income tax rate (federal and state) is 40 percent?

The first step in the solution to the example problem is to adjust all values to reflect semiannual payments and compounding:

Adjustment to *n*:   8 years $\times$ 2 = 16 six-month periods

Adjustment to the required rate of return: $K_d/2$

Adjustment to interest payments: $(0.10 \times \$1,000)/2 = \$50$
per 6-month period

Now find the discount rate that forces the present value of future cash flows from the bond to equal the \$898.90 proceeds to Prescott. Because these proceeds are less than the \$1,000 face value, you know that the before-tax cost of debt must be *greater* than the coupon rate of 10 percent per year.

Iteration 1.   Try 14 percent per year (7 percent semiannually):

$$\$898.90 = \$50(PVIFA_{7\%,16}) + \$1,000(PVIF_{7\%,16})$$

$$= \$50(9.4466) + \$1,000(0.3387)$$

$$= \$472.33 + \$338.70$$

$$\$898.90 \neq \$811.03$$

This iteration tells you that the before-tax cost of the bond is *not* 14 percent annually because the present value of the bond's future cash flows is less than Prescott's \$898.90 proceeds. Try a smaller discount rate to raise the present value.

Iteration 2.   Try 12 percent per year (6 percent semiannually):

$$\$898.90 = \$50(10.1059) + \$1,000(0.3936)$$

$$= \$505.30 + \$393.60$$

$$\$898.90 = \$898.90$$

Prescott's before-tax cost of new bond financing (K_d) is 12 percent per year compounded semiannually, because that is the discount rate forcing the present value of the bond's future cash flows to equal the bond proceeds.[10] Note that investors paid more than \$898.90 for the bond and therefore earn less than 12 percent interest. Prescott pays more than investors earn because of flotation costs. Prescott's after-tax cost of new bond financing, including the effects of flotation costs and issuing the bond at a discount, is calculated as follows:

$$K_i = K_d(1 - T)$$

$$= 0.12(1 - 0.40)$$

$$= 0.072, \text{ or } 7.2\%$$

Cost of Preferred Stock

cost of preferred stock
Investors' required rate of return on the preferred stock, adjusted for flotation costs.

In an efficient market, and ignoring flotation costs, the percentage **cost of preferred stock** is *the rate of return required by investors in the company's preferred stock*. The cost of preferred stock is estimated with the perpetuity valuation model because, as we have seen, a company promises a dividend on its preferred

---

[10] Financial calculators easily handle the calculation of yield to maturity and K_d. The keystrokes for the present example are as follows: Enter 16 for *n*, 50 for *PMT*, 898.9 for *PV*, and 1000 for *FV*; then press *i* (or *CPT* and then *i*) to get the answer, 6 percent per 6 months. Multiply by 2 to get 12 percent per year compounded semiannually. See Appendix 6A.

stock that remains level and has no maturity date. An investor in preferred stock therefore buys the perpetual dividend stream at market value.

Unlike interest expense on bonds, preferred-stock dividends are not tax deductible to the issuing company. The company subtracts preferred-stock dividends from after-tax earnings, as the following calculations for Dinah Apparel Company show. The company has $500,000 in bonds outstanding with a 10 percent coupon rate and 80,000 shares of preferred stock outstanding on which the company pays a $1 dividend per share:

Earnings before interest and taxes	$400,000
Less interest expense (0.10 × $500,000)	50,000
Earnings before taxes	$350,000
Less income taxes (34%)	119,000
Earnings after taxes	$231,000
Less preferred-stock dividends ($1 × 80,000)	80,000
Earnings available to common shareholders	$151,000

Because dividends on preferred stock are not tax deductible to the paying company, there is no tax adjustment in the calculation of the cost of this component of capital.

Preferred-stock financing is an external source of capital that requires a company to issue new shares to investors. Consequently, the investors' required rate of return must be adjusted for flotation costs to calculate the cost of preferred stock to the company: Subtract the per-share flotation costs from the price of a preferred stock to find the proceeds to the issuing company. The resulting equation for the cost of preferred stock is:

$$K_p = \frac{D_p}{P_{net}}$$

where D_p = dollar dividend per share of preferred stock paid at the end of Year 1 and annually thereafter

P_{net} = proceeds the issuing company receives per share of preferred stock; price per share minus flotation costs per share.

EXAMPLE

Stoneman Corporation is offering a new issue of preferred stock to raise funds for a plant expansion. The stock will pay a $2.50 annual dividend per share. If Stoneman issues the stock at $25 per share and flotation costs are $1 per share, then the cost of preferred stock to the corporation is 10.4 percent, calculated as follows:

$$K_p = \frac{D_p}{P_{net}}$$

$$= \frac{\$2.50}{\$25 - \$1}$$

$$= 0.104, \text{ or } 10.4\%$$

Cost of Common Equity

The percentage cost of common equity in an efficient market, and ignoring flotation costs, is *the rate of return required by investors in the company's common stock*. Because common equity has the greatest risk to investors, they require a higher rate of return on common stock than they do on either bonds or preferred stock.

Although the concept is straightforward, calculating the cost of common equity is complicated by a company's having two sources of common equity: (1) earnings retained from profitable operations and (2) issuance of new common stock. Dividends paid to common shareholders are subtracted from **earnings available to common shareholders**. The remaining earnings increase not only assets, but also retained earnings on the balance sheet. Companies normally retain some earnings each year to support future growth in sales.

The relationships between earnings and dividends are illustrated by the lower part of Dinah Apparel Company's income statement; the company pays a $0.25 dividend per share on its 40,000 shares of common stock outstanding:

Earnings after taxes	$231,000
Less preferred-stock dividends ($1 × 80,000)	80,000
Earnings available to common shareholders	$151,000
Less common-stock dividends ($0.25 × 40,000)	10,000
Earnings retained during the year	$141,000

In addition to increasing its equity investment by retaining earnings, a company can increase equity by issuing new shares of common stock. The two sources of equity financing—earnings and new issues of common stock—lead to a distinction used in calculating the cost of equity: The earnings retained during the year are **internal equity**—financing generated within the company from profit; and the issuance of new common stock is **external equity**.

Common equity
— Earnings retained during the year (internal equity)
— New common stock (external equity)

The following discussion shows how a company's financial manager estimates the cost of these two sources of common equity.

Cost of Retained Earnings. The percentage **cost of retained earnings** is, by definition, the *shareholders' required rate of return*. Shareholders incur an opportunity cost when the company retains earnings on their behalf. If management uses the earnings wisely, then shareholders are eager for the company to retain earnings. The earnings thus retained are *not* a free source of equity capital, however, because of the shareholders' opportunity cost.

One equation for calculating the percentage cost of retained earnings (internal equity) is the constant-growth valuation model examined earlier, but solved for K_c:

$$VC = \frac{D_1}{K_c - g}$$

Solve the equation for K_c (required rate of return) as follows:

1. Multiply each side of the equation by $(K_c - g)$:

$$(K_c - g)VC = D_1$$

---

earnings available to common shareholders
Amount of earnings after taxes and preferred-stock dividends have been paid by the company.

internal equity
Financing generated within a company from the retention of earnings.

external equity
Financing generated from the issuance of new common stock.

cost of retained earnings
Shareholders' required rate of return on the company's common stock.

2. Divide each side by *VC*:

$$K_c - g = \frac{D_1}{VC}$$

3. Solve for the shareholders' required rate of return and the company's cost of retained earnings (K_c):

$$K_c = \frac{D_1}{VC} + g$$

VC is intrinsic value, which equals market value in an efficient market. This equality permits us to use the market's view on the value of common stock: The price per share P_0 (at time zero, today) replaces *VC* in the model to yield the measure of a company's cost of retained earnings:

$$K_c = \frac{D_1}{P_0} + g$$

Estimates of the expected dividend for next year (D_1) are generally straightforward: Multiply the most recent yearly dividend per share by $1 + g$, or the most recent quarterly dividend per share by 4, then by $1 + g$ to get next year's expected dividend. To gauge the expected growth in dividends (g), analysts often examine historical growth rates for different periods. In some cases, subjective estimates by analysts of future growth rates may be more accurate than estimates from historical data. The *Value Line Investment Survey* provides a readily available source of expected growth rates based on its assessments of past growth rates and assessments of future market and economic conditions confronting specific companies.

The expected growth rate in dividends per share (g) is equivalent to expected capital gain yield under the following conditions: (1) a constant ratio of dividends to earnings per share (dividend payout ratio) and (2) a constant ratio of price to earnings per share (P-E ratio). Assuming these conditions enables analysts to *interpret K_c as the sum of expected dividend yield (D_1/P_0) and expected capital gain yield (g).* In equilibrium, expected rate of return (K_c) equals required rate of return.

EXAMPLE

Nefron Corporation's most recent annual dividend per share (D_0) is $3. Historical growth rates suggest an average 8 percent annual rate (g) over the indefinite future. Nefron's common stock trades at $50 per share ($P_0$). What is the company's cost of retained earnings?

$$K_c = \frac{D_1}{P_0} + g$$

$$= \frac{\$3(1.08)}{\$50} + 0.08$$

$$= 0.145, \text{ or } 14.5\%$$

An alternative method for estimating a company's cost of retained earnings is the capital asset pricing model (CAPM). As Chapter 5 explains, the CAPM is an equation that relates required rate of return (K_c) to the risk-free rate (R_f) plus a risk premium:

$$K_c = R_f + (K_m - R_f)\beta$$

The second term of the equation is the risk premium added to R_f: K_m is the required rate of return on the market portfolio (or equivalently, the average common stock), and β (beta) is a measure of nondiversifiable risk.

A company's cost of retained earnings is the opportunity cost of its shareholders. Earnings *not* paid in dividends to shareholders prevent them from investing funds they own in other securities of equivalent risk. This missed opportunity gives rise to the company's cost of retained earnings—the shareholders' required rate of return on the company's common stock. The CAPM is an alternative to the constant-growth model for calculating required rate of return.

EXAMPLE	Max Claiborne Company's common stock has a beta of 1.3. Using Standard & Poor's 500 Index as a measure of market prices, the company's managers project a 14 percent annual rate of return on the market portfolio of all common stocks. Based on U.S. Treasury securities, they judge the risk-free rate to be 8 percent per year. What is Max Claiborne's cost of retained earnings?

$$K_c = 0.08 + (0.14 - 0.08)1.3$$
$$= 0.08 + 0.078$$
$$= 0.158, \text{ or } 15.8\%$$

Cost of New Common Stock. In an efficient market and without flotation costs, the percentage **cost of new common stock** is the rate of return needed to urge investors to buy the company's *new issue* of common stock. Companies try to set the offering price of the stock so that the rate of return investors expect equals their required rate of return. Only then will intrinsic value equal the offering price. If the offering price is too high, no one will buy the stock. If the offering price is too low, the company fails to raise new equity capital at the lowest cost.

cost of new common stock
Investors' required rate of return on the company's common stock, adjusted for flotation costs.

The cost of new common stock is the investors' required rate of return adjusted for the flotation costs incurred from issuing the stock. We calculate the cost of new common stock (K_{nc}) with the constant-growth model:

$$K_{nc} = \frac{D_1}{P_{net}} + g$$

where P_{net} is the proceeds to the company per share of common stock issued. Stated differently, P_{net} is price per share minus flotation costs per share.

EXAMPLE	Consider again the Nefron Corporation. We estimated Nefron's cost of retained earnings to be 14.5 percent using the following values: $D_0 = \$3$, $P_0 = \$50$, and $g = 8$ percent. If Nefron issues new common stock and flotation costs are $4 per share, the cost is 15 percent, calculated as follows:

$$K_{nc} = \frac{\$3(1 + 0.08)}{\$50 - \$4} + 0.08$$
$$= 0.15, \text{ or } 15\%$$

Because of flotation costs, the cost of new common stock in the above example is one-half percentage point more than the cost of retained earnings. Why would a company issue new common stock when it costs more than retained earnings? A company issues new common stock when its need for equity financing exceeds the earnings available for retention. In other words, the company seeks external equity only when it runs out of internal equity.

EXAMPLE

Suppose that Nefron Corporation plans to invest $30 million of equity in land, buildings, and equipment. If management expects the company to generate $15 million in earnings available to common shareholders and to pay $5 million in dividends, then Nefron must issue $20 million worth of new shares:

Equity needed	$30,000,000
Less equity from earnings retention ($15,000,000 − $5,000,000)	10,000,000
New common stock needed	$20,000,000

A Warning and a Rule of Thumb.   Estimating the percentage cost of common equity for a company can be a difficult task. Accurate estimates require a financial manager to understand how investors value stocks and how intrinsic value influences prices in the market.

With the constant-growth model, $K_c = (D_1/P_0) + g$, the primary challenge is to develop an accurate estimate of the expected growth rate (g). With the capital asset pricing model, $K_c = R_f + (K_m - R_f)\beta$, the primary challenge is to develop an accurate estimate of beta (β). Yet a great deal of research shows that growth rates and betas estimated with historical data are nonstationary—they change over time. Thus, for example, historical betas as measures of future betas may contain appreciable error. A good portion of this error persists even when adjustments are made to reflect the tendency of high betas to fall and low betas to rise.

Ultimately, a financial manager must use good judgment to estimate the cost of common equity. As noted banker Walter Wriston states, "Good judgment comes from experience. Experience comes from bad judgment." Experience suggests a rule of thumb for estimating the cost of retained earnings: K_c often falls between three and six percentage points higher than the before-tax cost of a company's new bond issue (K_d). Check calculations with the above models using the following equation:

$$K_c = K_d + (0.03 \text{ to } 0.06)$$

In words, estimate the before-tax cost of new bonds and add to it a risk premium of three to six percentage points. The total is a rough-and-ready estimate of the company's cost of common equity. Some thumbs are thicker than others, so be careful in applying this rough-and-ready rule. Using it, however, may prevent a gross estimation error. An estimate above or below the suggested range would require careful substantiation.

•

Beating the Market

Most people interested in the stock market fall into one of three categories: (1) academic scholars who doubt that anybody really knows how to beat the market on a risk-adjusted basis; (2) professional investors who reject this view; and (3) amateur investors who believe they can beat the market but don't realize how controversial this assumption is. Although a great deal of research supports the academic view, there seem to be several anomalies (irregularities) that don't fit the view:

1. *Superior investors.* Some investors repeatedly make a greater return than would be expected based on the nondiversifiable risk of their portfolios. Who are these successful investors? Many are followers of the late Benjamin Graham, author of a classic study in stock selection titled *Security Analysis*. First published in 1934 and still in print, the book's core idea is that investors should look for companies that for some reason are undervalued and then hold the stock for as long as it takes the market to see the value.

2. *The discount on closed-end investment companies.* Many closed-end funds, which trade publicly, have sold for years at large discounts from their net asset values. After several of the heavily discounted closed-end funds went open-end (mutual funds) in the 1970s, the discounts disappeared. No one has satisfactorily explained why closed-end funds sold at a discount in the first place. "I've heard a hundred convoluted explanations of the discount," says Stephen Ross, professor of finance at Yale University, "and not one that makes any sense."

3. *The calendar effect.* Stock prices perform better during different calendar periods. For example, the January effect refers to a distinct, statistically significant pattern of above-average returns to investors that occurs during January, with the gains heavily concentrated during the first five trading days of the month. There is also a weekend effect: Returns on Monday tend to be negative even though other daily returns tend to be positive. Finally, there is a monthly effect: Stock returns are higher during the first half of the month than they are during the second half. As one researcher points out, the stock market's overall advance during the past 19 years is attributable to its performance during the first half of each month. The last half contributed nothing.

4. *The small-firm effect.* Stocks of small firms offer a return well in excess of what their nondiversifiable risk would predict. The small-firm effect suggests that investors should load up their portfolios with stocks of small firms in order to reap what they have not sown; that is, they will receive a return in excess of what is expected based on the capital asset pricing model.

Some of these anomalies will probably be explained as academicians make strides toward understanding risk and institutional features of markets. The hardest part will be to explain the presence of persistently superior investors. Be careful, however, about assuming that the existence of superior investors means that you, too, can outperform the market. Even though you recognize their presence, it could be a mistake to act as though you and your stockbroker are among them!

Source: Based on Daniel Seligman, "Can You Beat the Stock Market?" *Fortune*, Dec. 26, 1983, 81–91; and Robert A. Ariel, "Monthly Market Patterns," *American Association of Individual Investors Journal*, January 1987, 8–11.

Table 6.2 summarizes the equations for calculating the costs of debt, preferred stock, and common equity. Common equity consists of both retained earnings and new common stock. Chapter 7 uses these equations to calculate a company's weighted-average cost of capital.

| TABLE 6.2 | **Summary of Equations for Calculating Costs of Debt, Preferred Stock, and Common Equity** |

Cost of Debt	After-tax cost = Before-tax cost × (1 − Tax rate)
	$K_i = K_d(1 - T)$

Cost of Preferred Stock	$K_p = \dfrac{\text{Dividend per share}}{\text{Proceeds per share}}$
	$K_p = \dfrac{D_p}{P_{net}}$

Cost of Retained Earnings

1. $K_c = \dfrac{\text{Next year's dividend per share}}{\text{Stock price per share}} + \text{Expected growth rate in dividends}$

$$K_c = \dfrac{D_1}{P_0} + g$$

2. $K_c = \text{Risk-free rate} + \text{Risk premium}$

$$K_c = R_f + (K_m - R_f)\beta$$

3. *Rule of thumb:*

$$K_c = \dfrac{\text{Company's before-tax cost of debt}}{} + \dfrac{\text{3 to 6 percentage points}}{}$$

$$K_c = K_d + (0.03 \text{ to } 0.06)$$

Cost of New Common Stock

$$K_{nc} = \dfrac{\text{Next year's dividend per share}}{\text{Proceeds per share}} + \text{Expected growth rate in dividends}$$

$$K_{nc} = \dfrac{D_1}{P_{net}} + g$$

SUMMARY

- Valuation is the process of estimating value. To estimate the intrinsic value of a bond, preferred stock, or common stock, investors discount expected future cash flows. The discount rate, or required rate of return, should be commensurate with the risk of the security. Conceptually, the "flip side" of valuation is cost of capital, the percentage cost of issuing securities. The cost of issuing a security is the investors' required rate of return, adjusted where necessary for flotation costs and corporate income taxes.

- In efficient capital markets, security prices quickly reflect all information available to investors. The price of a security represents the consensus judgment of investors on the intrinsic value of the security. The assertion that markets are efficient is called the efficient market hypothesis (EMH). Finance theorists define three versions of the EMH: weak-form, semistrong-form, and strong-form efficiency. Empirical evidence supports the first two versions but not the third one.

- The intrinsic value of a bond (*VB*) is the present value of its future semi-annual interest payments (I/2) and par value (face value):

$$VB = (I/2)(PVIFA_{K_d/2,2n}) + Par\,(PVIF_{K_d/2,2n})$$

where K_d is the investors' required rate of return, or yield to maturity (assuming bond price equals VB), and n is the number of years to maturity. The semiannual interest payments (I/2) equal the coupon rate times par value, divided by 2. If $K_d <$ coupon rate, the bond trades at a premium and VB > par value; if $K_d >$ coupon rate, the bond trades at a discount and VB < par value.

• Bond prices are inversely related to market interest rates, or required rates of return—for example, when interest rates go up, bond prices go down. Changes in market interest rates cause long-term bond prices to fluctuate more than short-term bond prices. The uncertainty in bond prices due to changing interest rates is called interest rate risk.

• The intrinsic value of a preferred stock (VP) and a zero-growth common stock equals the expected dividend (D_p) divided by the required rate of return:

$$VP = \frac{D_p}{K_p}$$

This equation is the valuation model for perpetuities.

• Valuing common stock (VC) requires the expected dividends (D_t) and expected sale price (P_n) to be discounted to the present at the required rate of return (K_c):

$$VC = \sum_{t=1}^{n} \frac{D_t}{(1 + K_c)^t} + \frac{P_n}{(1 + K_c)^n}$$

The sale price at time n (P_n) can be viewed as a function of dividends expected to be paid after time n. Valuing a common stock solely in terms of dividends and assuming they grow at a constant annual rate g throughout the indefinite future, we can use the constant-growth model for *VC*:

$$VC = \frac{D_1}{K_c - g}$$

where D_1 is the expected year-end dividend per share.

• The cost of each source of capital to a company is the investors' required rate of return, adjusted where necessary for flotation costs and tax effects. Each component—bonds, preferred stock, new issues of common stock, and retained earnings—of a company's capital structure has a cost. These costs, called component costs of capital, are calculated using security prices and expected cash flows.

• A company's before-tax cost of bonds (K_d) is the discount rate that equates the present value of dollar interest payments and par value to the company's proceeds from issuing the bonds. The after-tax cost of bonds (K_i) is:

$$K_i = K_d(1 - T)$$

where T is the company's marginal tax rate.

• The cost of preferred stock (K_p) is the ratio of the year-end dividend per share (D_p) divided by the proceeds per share (P_{net}) to the issuing company:

$$K_p = \frac{D_p}{P_{net}}$$

• The cost of retained earnings (K_c) can be estimated using either of two equations. The constant-growth model adds expected dividend yield (D_1/P_0) to the expected capital gain yield measured by the expected annual growth rate (g) in dividends:

$$K_c = \frac{D_1}{P_0} + g$$

The capital asset pricing model adds a risk premium to the risk-free rate of return (R_f). The risk premium equals beta (β) multiplied by the market price of risk, the difference between the required rate of return on the market portfolio (K_m) and R_f:

$$K_c = R_f + (K_m - R_f)\beta$$

- Because of flotation costs, issuing new common stock is more costly to a company than retaining earnings. We use the constant-growth model to estimate the cost of new common stock but change P_0 to the proceeds per share (P_{net}) the issuing company receives:

$$K_c = \frac{D_1}{P_{net}} + g$$

Key Terms

valuation	call price	cost of preferred stock
cost of capital	constant-growth (Gordon) model	earnings available to common shareholders
zero-coupon bond	zero-growth stock	
market value	nonconstant-growth model	internal equity
efficient capital market	component cost of capital	external equity
at a premium	cost of bonds	cost of retained earnings
at a discount	yield to maturity	cost of new common stock
interest rate risk	deep-discount bond	

Questions

6.1. Intrinsic and market values are closely related. Describe how they relate to each other and explain what would happen to the market value of a $13.50 share of common stock if, upon reconsidering the stock, investors realize that the stock's intrinsic value is $12.

6.2. What is an efficient capital market? Describe the three versions of the efficient market hypothesis and the implications of each for investors.

6.3. Ruth Leonard smiles to herself as she finishes graphing CBS's stock price. The price is trending upward and is gathering momentum, she concludes. Hastily, she calls her broker to purchase 100 shares of CBS stock. Do you believe that Ms. Leonard's graphs are useful for selecting stocks? Explain.

6.4. Two individuals are considering whether or not each should buy a share of Burroughs Corporation common stock. One person estimates that the stock's intrinsic value is $46 per share and the other estimates $32 per share.

  a. Explain how each person may have estimated intrinsic value.

  b. Assuming that each person used the constant-growth model, explain what might cause the difference between the two intrinsic values.

  c. What action would each person take if the market value of Burroughs is $36 per share?

6.5. The intrinsic value of a security is the present value of its expected future cash flows. List the types of cash flows associated with owning (a) a bond, (b) a preferred stock, and (c) a common stock. Which security has the greatest risk for an investor? Explain your answer.

6.6. Define *interest rate risk* and explain the inverse relationship between interest rates and bond prices. Use the terms *required rate of return* and *coupon rate* in your explanation.

6.7. "Where should I invest the $100,000?" asks the assistant treasurer. "I don't care," responds the corporate treasurer. "Just make sure it's nearly risk-free. We can't take any chances with that money." Thinking to himself, the assistant treasurer decides to invest the $100,000 in 30-year U.S. Treasury bonds. "The United States won't default on the bonds," he chuckles silently. Assess the wisdom of the assistant treasurer's decision.

6.8. Which component cost of capital would be directly affected if Congress changes the corporate tax rates?
a. Preferred stock.
b. Retained earnings.
c. Common stock.
d. Corporate bonds.

Explain your choice.

6.9. Flotation costs play an important role in estimating the costs of bonds, preferred stock, and common stock. Explain what the term *flotation costs* means and describe their role in the calculations.

6.10. Figure 6.5 shows the relative required rates of return for three sources of financial capital. Explain why each source is located where it is and what the intercept (intersection of the SML with the vertical axis) of the diagonal line represents.

6.11. Which of the following conditions would decrease the cost of retained earnings, all other things being equal?
a. Investors become more risk averse.
b. Investors become more risk-seeking.

Explain your choice.

6.12. True or false: Corporate bonds have the highest component cost of any of the capital sources available to a corporation. Explain your choice.

6.13. A classmate in marketing sees your finance notes and comments on what must be an error. "How can that be?" he asks. "Retained earnings are a free source of financing for a company!" Explain how and why retained earnings not only have a cost but are an expensive source of capital to a company.

6.14. Which is the more expensive source of capital, retained earnings or new common stock? Explain your choice and show an equation for calculating the cost of each source of capital.

Strategy Problem

Your task is to analyze yields and rates associated with securities issued by Sample Corporation. The securities are described as follows: (1) Sample Corporation issued a bond 4 years ago. It originally had a 16-year maturity, $1,000 par value, and a 9 percent coupon rate. The bond offers interest semiannually and now trades at $946.28. (2) Sample Corporation's common stock now trades at $28 per share. Five years ago the stock price averaged $15.20. The company pays a quarterly dividend, and its most recent dividend was $0.46 per share. Your analysis indicates that stock price and dividend per share have been growing at the same rate.
a. Calculate the yield to maturity on the bond and the expected rate of return on the stock.
b. Determine the after-tax cost to Sample Corporation of issuing the following bond: Coupon rate = 9 percent;

years to maturity = 12; par value = $1,000. Sample Corporation pays interest on the bond semiannually, and the proceeds from issuing each bond are $922.40. Assume that the company is in the 34 percent marginal tax bracket.
c. Estimate Sample Corporation's cost of new common stock with flotation costs of $1.50 per share.
d. Sample Corporation's financial manager refers to *The Wall Street Journal* and determines that the annual yield on U.S. Treasury securities is 7 percent. The manager expects the rate of return on the S&P 500 Index to be 15 percent annually, and the estimated beta of Sample Corporation's common stock is 1.675. Estimate the required rate of return on the company's common stock.

Strategy	Solution

a. *Bond:* The yield to maturity is the discount rate relating future bond payments to the price of the bond:

Set the bond price equal to the present value of bond payments.

$$\$946.28 = \frac{\$90}{2}(\text{PVIFA}_{K_d/2,12\times2}) + \$1,000(\text{PVIF}_{K_d/2,12\times2})$$

Sketch a time line.

0	1/2	1	1 1/2	2	$\cdots$	11 1/2	12
$946.28	$45	$45	$45	$45	$\cdots$	$45	$ 45 $1,000

Use a calculator for yield to maturity, or calculate the yield using Appendix B.

Solve for $K_d/2$, then multiply by 2. A financial calculator with the following information yields the answer: Enter 24 for n; 45 for *PMT*; 946.28 for *PV*; and 1000 for *FV*; then press i (or *CPT* and then i) to get $K_d/2 = 4.88\%$. Solve for $K_d = 9.76\%$.

Stock: The expected rate of return on the stock equals the expected dividend yield plus the expected capital gain yield:

$$K_c = \frac{D_1}{P_0} + g$$

Calculate the historical growth rate using the future-value equation.

Growth rate (g):

$$FV = PV(1 + g)^n$$

$$\$28 = \$15.20(1 + g)^5$$

$$1.8421 = (1 + g)^5$$

$$1.13 = 1 + g$$

$$g = 0.13, \text{ or } 13\%$$

Note that 4 times the quarterly dividend is the annual dividend.

Dividend one year hence:

$$D_1 = D_0(1 + g)^1$$

$$= (4 \times \$0.46)(1 + 0.13)^1$$

$$= \$2.08$$

Use the constant-growth model.

Expected rate of return:

$$K_c = \frac{\$2.08}{\$28} + 0.13$$

$$= 0.204, \text{ or } 20.4\%$$

b. The component cost of bond financing before taxes is the discount rate relating the future payments to the proceeds:

Use proceeds to the company.

$$\$922.40 = \frac{\$90}{2}(PVIFA_{K_d/2,12\times2}) + \$1,000(PVIF_{K_d/2,12\times2})$$

Sketch a time line.

Use a calculator or Appendix B.

Adjust K_d for tax deductibility of interest.

A financial calculator with the following information yields the answer: Enter 24 for n; 45 for *PMT*; 922.4 for *PV*; and 1000 for *FV*; then press i (or *CPT* and then i) to get $K_d/2 = 5.07\%$. Solve for $K_d = 10.14\%$.

$$K_i = K_d(1 - T)$$

$$= 10.14(1 - 0.34) = 6.7\%$$

c. Estimate the cost of new common stock with the constant-growth model adjusted for flotation costs:

Proceeds per share equal price per share less flotation costs per share.

$$K_{nc} = \frac{D_1}{P_{net}} + g$$

$$= \frac{\$2.08}{\$28 - \$1.50} + 0.13$$

$$= 0.208, \text{ or } 20.8\%$$

*Use the CAPM to estimate
required rate of return.*

d. Estimate the required rate of return on common stock with the capital asset pricing model:

$$K_c = R_f + (K_m - R_f)\beta$$

$$= 0.07 + (0.15 - 0.07)1.675$$

$$= 0.07 + 0.134$$

$$= 0.204, \text{ or } 20.4\%$$

Demonstration Problem

JATX, a manufacturer of office furniture, has sales revenue of $150,000,000 during 19X5. Its cost of goods sold and operating expenses total $130,000,000, producing earnings before interest and taxes (EBIT) of $20,000,000. JATX has bonds, preferred stock, and common stock outstanding, each described as follows: (1) *Bonds:* number of bonds outstanding, 40,000; par value of each bond, $1,000; coupon rate, 8 percent per year payable semiannually; and years to maturity, 10. (2) *Preferred stock:* number of shares outstanding, 600,000; dividend per share, $5. (3) *Common stock:* number of shares outstanding, 3,000,000; dividend per share paid during 19X5, $1. JATX's income tax rate, federal and state combined, is 40 percent.

a. Calculate the earnings retained by JATX during 19X5.
b. How much money does JATX save in income taxes due to interest payments? Calculate the after-tax dollar cost of JATX's interest payments.
c. Assuming that the required rate of return on the bonds is 10 percent per year compounded semiannually, what is the value of one bond? Of all of the bonds? Why are the bonds worth less than par value?
d. In addition to the 10-year bonds described above, suppose that JATX has bonds outstanding with 2 years remaining to maturity, a par value of $1,000 per bond, and a coupon rate of 8 percent per year payable semiannually. Which bonds have more *interest rate risk,* the 2-year bonds or the 10-year bonds? Support your answer by comparing the values of the 2-year bonds and the 10-year bonds, using required annual rates of return of 8 percent and 10 percent, each compounded semiannually. (*Hint:* At 8 percent, each bond is worth par value, $1,000. Also, the answer to Part *c* provides the value of the 10-year bond at 10 percent.)
e. Suppose that JATX issues new bonds with the following characteristics: par value of each bond, $1,000; coupon rate, 10 percent per year payable semiannually; proceeds per bond received by JATX, $891.72; and years to maturity, 9. Calculate JATX's after-tax percentage cost for this bond. What possible reasons account for the proceeds being less than par value?
f. Calculate the value per share and the total value of JATX's preferred stock for each of the following required rates of return: (1) 8 percent, (2) 10 percent, and (3) 12 percent. What financial principle do your answers illustrate?
g. Suppose that JATX issues new preferred stock to investors for $40 per share. Investment banking fees, legal fees, accounting costs, and printing charges sum to $2.50 per share. What is the percentage cost of the preferred stock if JATX pays an annual $4.50 dividend per share? Explain why the cost of the preferred stock is independent of JATX's income tax rate.
h. Use the constant-growth model to value a share of JATX's common stock under the following conditions: The required rate of return (K_c) on the stock is 13 percent per year, and the expected growth rate (g) in dividends per share for the foreseeable future is 5 percent per year. Show what happens to the stock value if the expected inflation rate rises 2 percentage points, causing K_c to rise to 15 percent. Return to the original conditions and show what happens to the stock value if the growth rate (g) rises to 7 percent.

i. Assume that JATX's stock beta (β) is 1.2, the risk-free rate (R_f) is 7 percent, and the required rate of return on the market portfolio (K_m) is 14 percent. Use the capital asset pricing model (CAPM) to calculate the required rate of return (K_c) on JATX's stock. Now use this K_c and a 7-percent growth rate (g) in the constant-growth model to value a share of JATX's common stock. What is JATX's total equity value?

j. K_c in Part *i* is a measure of JATX's percentage cost of retained earnings (which are calculated in Part *a*). Explain why retained earnings are *not* a free source of equity capital for JATX. Describe two alternative procedures (other than the CAPM) for estimating the cost of retained earnings.

k. Suppose that JATX issues new common stock to investors for $12 per share and incurs flotation costs of $1 per share. JATX presently pays a $1 dividend per share, and historical growth rates indicate that dividends will grow 7 percent per year into the indefinite future. Calculate the percentage cost of new common stock. Why does the cost of new common stock exceed the cost of retained earnings?

l. A hypothesis is a declarative sentence. Write a declarative sentence for each of the three versions of the efficient market hypothesis.

Problems

Valuing a bond

6.1. How much money would investors pay for a bond with a 12-year maturity, a 6 percent coupon rate, and a $1,000 par value? Assume that competitive bond yields are 10 percent per year compounded semiannually and that the bond pays interest semiannually.

Bond value and required rate of return

6.2. American Telephone & Telegraph has a bond outstanding that matures in 10 years. The bond's coupon rate is 7 percent and its par value is $1,000. The company pays bond interest semiannually. Calculate the value of the bond to investors under each of the following scenarios, and state the financial principle that is demonstrated.
a. Investors require a 6 percent annual rate of return, compounded semiannually.
b. Investors require an 8 percent annual rate of return, compounded semiannually.
c. Investors require a 10 percent annual rate of return, compounded semiannually.

Bond value and interest rate risk

6.3. Alamo Ocean World has the following two bonds outstanding:

Terms	Bond A	Bond B
Years to maturity	2	10
Coupon rate	9%	9%
Par value	$1,000	$1,000

The company pays semiannual interest on the bonds. Calculate the value of Bond A and Bond B to investors under each of the following scenarios:
a. Investors require a 10 percent annual rate of return, compounded semiannually.
b. Investors require a 12 percent annual rate of return, compounded semiannually. Which bond has more interest rate risk—Bond A or Bond B? Explain.

Valuing a preferred stock on different days

6.4. Ringling and Barnum preferred stock has a $20 par value and pays an $0.80 dividend each year. Assume that the required rate of return is 8 percent per year.
a. What maximum price would investors pay for this stock if they buy it on the day following the most recent dividend and the company pays the dividend at the end of each year?
b. Assume the original conditions. What maximum price would investors pay if they bought the stock on the day preceding the next dividend payment?
c. What do your solutions to Parts *a* and *b* suggest happens to the price of a preferred stock on the *ex*-dividend day—the day when buyers of the stock do not receive the dividend?

Compound annual rate of return

6.5. You invest $1,000 in the common stock of the Weber Company. Ten years later you sell the shares for $2,500. Disregarding personal taxes, what is the compound annual rate of return on your investment if the company paid no dividends over the period?

Compound growth of stock price

6.6. Correcto Machinery's common stock was $27 per share in 19X1 and $73 per share 6 years later. Calculate the compound annual growth rate in the common-stock price.

Valuing common stock: constant-growth model

6.7. Howard Distribution is offering its common stock to the public on January 25. All indications suggest that the typical purchaser of the stock anticipates a 7 percent annual growth rate in dividends for the foreseeable future. The present dividend per share (all shares are presently owned by the Howard family) is $2.

a. What is the size of the dividend expected at the end of Year 1?

b. If Sylvia Potter requires a 10 percent annual rate of return, what will be the maximum price that she will pay for a share? (*Hint:* Use the constant-growth model.)

c. Explain what happens to the stock price under each of the following conditions. No calculations are called for and each condition is independent of the other.

(1) The expected dividend growth rate rises.

(2) The required rate of return rises.

(3) Investors expect to receive the first dividend immediately after purchase instead of one year from now.

Effect of growth rate on stock value

6.8. Taggart Machinery recently paid a $5 cash dividend on each share of its common stock. Investors require a 15 percent annual rate of return on the stock.

a. Use the constant-growth model to calculate the market value per share of stock under each of the following conditions: (1) g = 5.0 percent, (2) g = 0.0 percent, and (3) g = −5.0 percent (g is the expected annual growth rate of the cash dividend).

b. What financial principle do your answers for Part *a* illustrate?

Valuing common stock

6.9. Investors expect Centrum to pay a $3.60 dividend on its common stock at the end of each of the next 4 years. They expect the price in 4 years to be $46.80 and require a 20 percent rate of return on Centrum's common stock. Calculate the stock's intrinsic value based on its 4-year cash flow.

Valuing common stock: nonconstant-growth model

6.10. Investors expect Swift Company's dividends to grow 20 percent per year for the next 2 years, 15 percent during the third year, and 7 percent per year thereafter. Swift's most recent dividend was $2 per share. Calculate the intrinsic value of Swift's common stock. Use a discount rate of 10 percent.

Valuing common stock: nonconstant-growth model

6.11. MCR Inc. manufactures and distributes office equipment. Because of its high-quality products and excellent service, MCR has been profitable and is growing rapidly. During the 8 years since its founding, MCR has not paid dividends to its shareholders; earnings retention has helped fuel its growth. Most professional observers expect MCR to continue to retain 100 percent of its earnings during the next 5 years. They expect MCR to initiate a $1 dividend per share at the end of 5 years. According to this scenario, dividends will then grow 50 percent per year for 4 years and 7 percent per year thereafter. Investors require a 16 percent annual return on MCR stock.

a. What are the expected end-of-year dividends for Years 5, 6, 7, 8, 9, and 10?

b. Calculate the present value of the dividends expected during Years 5, 6, 7, 8, and 9.

c. Calculate the value at the end of Year 9 of all the future dividends; then calculate the present value of this Year 9 value.

d. What is MCR stock worth?

Required rate of return and stock price

6.12. Jesco Iron Works recently paid a $5 dividend per share to its common shareholders. The present risk-free rate of return is 7 percent, and the required rate of return on the market portfolio is 15 percent. Jesco's common-stock beta is 1.36. If investors expect Jesco's dividend per share to grow at a rate of 3 percent per year, what is the present price of the company's common stock? (*Hint:* Use the capital asset pricing model and the constant-growth model.)

Required rate of return in an acquisition

6.13. The management of Seaman's Grocery is considering whether or not to acquire Greenspoint Oil Distributors. The acquisition would have the following impact on Seaman's stock beta and expected growth rate in dividends per share:

	Before Acquisition	After Acquisition
Beta	0.90	1.40
Growth rate	3%	5%

Seaman's most recent dividend was $2.35 per share, R_f is 6 percent, and K_m is 14 percent. Should Seaman's management acquire Greenspoint?

Calculation of earnings and after-tax cost

6.14. Melicher Services (MS), a Colorado company, generated $5,500,000 in sales revenues during 19X6. The company's cost of goods sold and operating expenses totaled $2,300,000. MS paid $800,000 in interest on bonds, $500,000 in dividends on preferred stock, and $700,000 in dividends on common stock. MS's tax rate is 34 percent.
   a. Calculate the following items for MS: (1) earnings before interest and taxes (EBIT), (2) earnings before taxes (EBT), (3) earnings after taxes (EAT), (4) earnings available to common shareholders (EACS), and (5) earnings retained during 19X6.
   b. Holding other things constant, assume that MS does *not* pay any interest expenses. Based on this assumption, recalculate the items in Part *a*.
   c. What is the after-tax dollar cost of MS's $800,000 interest expense? Calculate the tax shield (tax savings) created by the $800,000 interest expense.
   d. Suppose that the total market value of MS's bonds is $10,000,000. What is the before-tax percentage cost of the bonds? The after-tax percentage cost?

Yield to maturity

6.15. Suppose you are considering the purchase of a 7-year bond with a 12 percent coupon rate. Par value of the bond is $1,000, and it pays interest semiannually. If you purchase the bond for $912.54 and hold it to maturity, what annual rate of return will you earn? Use the present-value procedure for your analysis.

Approximate yield to maturity

6.16. Wiley Petroleum has a $200,000 bond issue outstanding that will mature in 8 years. The coupon rate on the $1,000 par value of each bond is 7 percent and interest is paid semiannually. Each bond is trading at $941.73.
   a. Using the approximation equation, calculate the bond's yield to maturity.
   b. Using the present-value procedure, calculate the bond's yield to maturity.
   c. If Wiley Petroleum is in the 34 percent marginal tax bracket, what is the cost (K_i) of its new debt capital? (Assume that flotation costs are zero.)

Yield to maturity and cost of a bond

6.17. Random Computing Services issued a 20-year bond with a $1,000 par value and a 15 percent coupon rate. The bond has 6 years remaining to maturity, and it pays interest semiannually. Calculate the yield to maturity on the bond assuming it trades for $1,221.55. Determine the cost to Random Computing of a similar but new bond if flotation costs are zero and the company is in the 40 percent marginal tax bracket.

Cost of a bond

6.18. Alma Products issued $50 million worth of bonds that were scheduled to mature in 15 years. Each bond has a par value of $1,000 and a coupon rate of 9 percent, with interest payable semiannually. The bonds have 7 years remaining until maturity, and they currently trade for $869 each. To finance its expansion plans, the company needs to issue an additional $60 million worth of bonds. The company's treasurer believes the new bonds will have to offer a rate of return competitive with that on the outstanding bonds. Discussions with the company's investment banker suggest that flotation costs on newly issued bonds will be $8.42 per bond. Alma Products is in the 34 percent marginal tax bracket. What is the after-tax cost of the new bonds to be issued by Alma Products?

Cost of preferred stock

6.19. A company plans to issue preferred stock for $100 per share. The stock pays a $10 dividend each year. If the company incurs $6 per-share flotation costs, what is the cost of the preferred stock to the company under each of the following conditions?

a. The company's marginal tax rate is 34 percent.
b. The company's marginal tax rate is 15 percent.
(Be careful. This is a trick question.)

Cost of retained earnings: CAPM

6.20. Winsome Company's financial manager is calculating the company's cost of equity with the capital asset pricing model. Presently the yield on U.S. Treasury securities is 8 percent per year, and investors expect the return on Standard & Poor's 500 Index to be 15 percent per year for the foreseeable future. *Value Line Investment Survey* reports that Winsome's beta is 1.2. Calculate the cost of retained earnings based on the above information.

Cost of retained earnings and new common stock: constant-growth model

6.21. Lexicon Imports' common stock trades at $28 per share, and the company will pay a $4 dividend at the end of the year. Investors expect Lexicon's dividend per share and earnings per share to grow 3 percent per year. Any new shares the company issues will net $22 per share.

a. If the ratio of price per share to earnings per share remains constant, what is the likely growth rate in price per share of Lexicon stock?
b. Calculate the estimated cost of retained earnings to Lexicon using the constant-growth model.
c. Calculate the estimated cost of new common stock to the company using the constant-growth model.

Cost of bonds, preferred stock, retained earnings, and new common stock

6.22. Anderson Cosmetics is a company in the 40 percent marginal tax bracket (federal and state). The company needs to raise new long-term funds. Calculate Anderson's cost of new bonds, preferred stock, retained earnings, and new common stock if present market conditions are as follows:

• The company's new bonds will have an 8 percent coupon rate with a $1,000 par value and will net the company $908.68 per bond. The issue will mature in 20 years. Interest will be paid annually.

• Anderson's outstanding preferred stock now trades at $80 per share. Investors expect it to pay an $8 dividend at the end of the year. Flotation costs of a new issue of preferred stock will be $4 per share, and the stock will trade at $60 a share. (*Hint:* You must calculate the dividend on the new stock.)

• The company's common stock trades at $30 per share, and the company presently pays a $3 dividend per share. Historical growth rates indicate that dividends will grow 5 percent per year. Flotation costs of new common stock will be $4 per share.

Dividends and cost of retained earnings: constant-growth model

6.23. Plasticoat Inc. is considering raising equity via an issue of new common stock. Presently the shareholders' equity component of its balance sheet appears as follows:

Common Stock (1,000,000 shares authorized, 416,000 outstanding)	$ 416,000
Paid-in Capital in Excess of Par	3,220,000
Retained Earnings	2,700,000

The price of the common stock is now $30 per share. The company's common shareholders expect the dividend growth rate of 5 percent annually to persist through the indefinite future. The company's financial manager expects after-tax earnings to be $3.8 million, and the company will pay out 30 percent in dividends. The company plans to issue an additional 40,000 shares. A financial adviser suggests that flotation costs on a new issue of common stock will be $4 per share.

a. Is the retained-earnings figure of $2.7 million on the balance sheet relevant to the calculation of the cost of equity? Explain your answer.

b. How much of the company's new equity will be from earnings retention and how much will be from new common stock?

c. Calculate Plasticoat's expected end-of-year dividend per share based on the expected earnings and number of shares shown on the company's balance sheet.

d. Use the constant-growth model to calculate the costs of retained earnings and new common stock.

Valuation and changing rates of return: CAPM

6.24. Jay Heck collected the following data on M&M Mining and the general market:

- M&M's current dividend, D_0, is $2.
- M&M's stock beta, $\beta_{M\&M}$, is 1.2.
- M&M's dividend growth, g, is expected to continue through the indefinite future at 6 percent per year.
- Required rate of return on the market portfolio, K_m, is 14 percent per year.
- Risk-free rate of return, R_f, is 8 percent per year.

a. Estimate the price per share of M&M's common stock on the day following the most recent dividend.

b. If R_f and K_m each decline by two percentage points and beta stays at 1.2, what will be the new price per share of M&M stock?

c. Return to the original conditions, with the beta staying at 1.2. If R_f and K_m each increase by two percentage points, what will be the new price per share of M&M stock?

d. What financial principles do your answers to Parts *a*, *b*, and *c* illustrate?

Computer Problems 🖫

Bond valuation: template BNDPRICE

6.25. Ralston Inc. has an outstanding bond issue with the following characteristics: par value, $1,000; years to maturity, 10; and coupon rate, 12%. Interest is paid semi-annually. The required rate of return is 15 percent per year.

a. Calculate the price of the bond.

b. What would be the price if the coupon rate were 11 percent, 13 percent, and 16 percent?

c. Recalculate Part *b* for years to maturity of 5 years and 15 years.

d. Recalculate Part *a* for required rates of return of 10 percent, 14 percent, and 18 percent.

e. What conclusions can you draw regarding the movement of bond prices with changes in the coupon rate, years to maturity, and yield to maturity? Explain your answer.

f. If the company is able to issue 12 percent, 10-year bonds for $894.06, what is the cost of the bonds to the company? Assume that the company's marginal tax rate is 34 percent.

Bond yield: template BNDYTM

6.26. Your investment adviser places before you the following information about four different bonds listed on the NYSE:

	A	B	C	D
Par value	$1,000	$1,000	$1,000	$1,000
Years to maturity	10	15	10	15
Coupon rate	8%	8%	9%	9%
Market price	$701	$642	$783	$693

Each bond pays semiannual interest. Which bond would you buy? Explain your choice. Why do the bonds have different yields to maturity?

Stock valuation: template
STKCONSG

6.27. The dividends paid by Companies A, B, C, and D during the past six years are given below:

Year	Company A	Company B	Company C	Company D
19X2	$ 2.50	$ 3.00	$ 1.80	$ 5.00
19X3	2.75	3.20	2.00	5.00
19X4	3.10	3.40	2.25	5.00
19X5	3.40	3.60	2.50	5.00
19X6	3.70	3.80	2.75	5.00
19X7	4.00	4.10	3.00	5.00
Price of stock	**$80.00**	**$72.00**	**$71.25**	**$38.00**

Investors expect the average growth rates to remain unchanged. Assume that all investors have the same required rate of return of 15 percent per year for each company.

a. Which stock (or stocks) would investors buy? Explain your answer.

b. Use the data table to calculate the stock price of Company A for annual required rates of return of 11 percent, 12 percent, 13 percent, 14 percent, 15 percent, 16 percent, 17 percent, and 18 percent. (The diskette gives instructions for preparing the data table.)

Stock valuation: template
STKNCGR

6.28. Barry Martin is considering investing in the common stock of Globe Motors Inc. He expects the company to pay a dividend of $2.40 next year and $2.70, $3.40, $4.00, and $4.40 during the subsequent 4 years. The dividends are thereafter expected to grow at a constant rate of 8 percent annually. Mr. Martin's required rate of return is 15 percent per year.

a. Calculate the intrinsic value of Globe Motors' stock.

b. The dividend growth could be subject to changes. Calculate the intrinsic value assuming the growth rate after the initial 5 years is 4 percent, 6 percent, 10 percent, and 12 percent.

c. Suppose the price per share is $54.39. What growth rate do investors apparently expect after the initial 5 years?

Selected References

Brigham, Eugene F., and Louis C. Gapenski. "Flotation Cost Adjustments." *Financial Practice and Education,* Fall/Winter 1991: 29–34.

Cooley, Philip L. "A Review of the Use of Beta in Regulatory Proceedings." *Financial Management,* Winter 1981: 75–81.

Dawson, Steven M. "An Explanation of Large Share Price Changes." *Securities Industry Review,* April 1986: 9–17.

Gordon, M. J., and L. I. Gould. "Comparison of the DCF and HPR Measures of the Yield on Common Shares." *Financial Management,* Winter 1984: 40–47.

Hubbard, Carl M. "Flotation Costs in Capital Budgeting: A Note on the Tax Effect." *Financial Management,* Summer 1984: 38–40.

Joy, O. Maurice. "Hunting the Stock Market Snark." *Sloan Management Review,* Spring 1987: 17–24.

Linke, Charles M., and J. Kenton Zumwalt. "Estimation Biases in Discounted Cash Flow Analysis of Equity Capital Cost in Rate Regulation." *Financial Management,* Autumn 1984: 15–21.

Modani, Naval K., Philip L. Cooley, and Rodney L. Roenfeldt. "Stability of Market Risk Surrogates." *Journal of Financial Research,* Spring 1983: 33–40.

Siegel, Jeremy J. "The Application of the DCF Methodology for Determining the Cost of Equity." *Financial Management,* Spring 1985: 46–53.

Taggart, Robert A., Jr. "Consistent Valuation and Cost of Capital Expressions with Corporate and Personal Taxes." *Financial Management,* Autumn 1991: 8–20.

Timme, Stephen G., and Peter C. Eisemann. "On the Use of Consensus Forecasts of Growth in the Constant Growth Model: The Case of Electric Utilities." *Financial Management,* Winter 1989: 23–35.

Appendix 6A   FINANCIAL PROBLEM SOLVING WITH A CALCULATOR

Texas Instruments BA-35

The *BA-35* operates in "modes". Before solving a financial problem, users must enter financial mode by pressing [2nd] {FIN}. Housekeeping functions needed to perform basic operations such as setting display formats, clearing calculator memory and adjusting for annuities due are summarized below.

Housekeeping Functions

Set Display Format to Two Decimal Places	[2nd] {Decimal}
Set Financial Mode	[2nd] {FIN}
Clear Display	[ON/C]
Clear TVM Registers	[2nd] {FIN}
Adust for Payments at Beginning of Period	[DUE] *

* Press the [DUE] key just prior to the last keystroke needed to solve problem

Future Value of a Present Sum

Harry just deposited $1000 into a savings account paying 6 percent coumpounded annually. How much will he have in the account at the end of five years?

1000.00	[PV]
6.00	[%i]
5.00	[N]
[CPT] [FV]	1338.23

Harry will have accumulated $1,338.23 at the end of five years.

Present Value of an Annuity

Nancy has obtained an $11,000 bank loan to finance the purchase of a new car. The loan is for 48 months at an interest rate of 12 percent, compounded monthly. What is the amount of her monthly payment?

11000.00	[PV]
1.00	[%i]
48.00	[N]
[CPT] [PMT]	289.67

Nancy's monthly payment is $289.67.

Finding an Unknown Interest Rate

Exactly five years ago, Dave and Cindy purchased 100 shares of Gro-Tex Corporation at $45 per share. They now wish to sell their holdings at the current market price of $75 per share. What was their average annual rate of return over this period?

45.00	[PV]
5.00	[N]
75.00	[FV]
[CPT] [%i]	10.76

Dave and Cindy earned a 10.76 percent holding period rate of return.

Finding an Unknown Number of Periods

Stacy received her retirement pension in a lump sum, and has invested it in an account which guarantees her a 10 percent annual rate of return. She wishes to make annual withdrawals of $35,000 beginning at the end of this year. If her current account balance is

$250,000, how long will it be until she exhausts her account?

250000.00	[PV]
10.00	[%i]
35000.00	[PMT]
[CPT] [N]	13.14

Her account balance will be exhausted in 13.14 periods; her last withdrawal (which will be smaller than her earlier ones) will be made 14 years from today.

Simple Bond Pricing

What is the price of an 8 percent semiannual coupon bond maturing EXACTLY six years from now? It has a par value of $1000, and bonds of similar risk are yielding 10 percent.

40.00	[PMT]
12.00	[N]
5.00	[%i]
1000.00	[FV]
[CPT] [PV]	-911.37

The bond should sell for $354.53 + 556.84 = $911.37

Simple Bond Yields to Maturity

What is the yield to maturity on a 10 percent annual coupon bond currently selling for $1,038.31? It matures in exactly three years.

1038.31	[PV]
100.00	[PMT]
1000.00	[FV]
3.00	[N]
[CPT] [%i]	8.50

The bond is priced to yield 8.50 percent per year.

Loan Amortization

Prepare an amortization schedule for a one-year, $2,000 computrer loan at 12 percent annual interest, compounded monthly. Monthly payments are $177.70.

2000.00	[PV]
1.00	[%i]
177.70	[PMT]
1 [2nd] [INT]	20.00
[STO] [2nd] [RCL] [PMT] [-] [RCL] [=]	157.70
1 [2nd] [BAL]	1842.30
2 [2nd] [INT]	18.42
[STO] [2nd] [RCL] [PMT] [-] [RCL] [=]	159.28
2 [2nd] [BAL]	1683.02

Interest porfion of 1st payment = $20.00
Principal portion of 1st payment = $157.70
Loan balance after 1st payment = $1,842.30
Interest portion of 2nd payment = $18.42
Principal portion of 2nd payment = $159.28
Loan balance after 2nd payment = $1,683.02

Interest Rate Conversions

A furniture store offers loan terms of 18 percent, compounded monthly. What is the loan's effective annual rate?

12.00	[2nd] {APR> >}
18.00 [≡]	19.56

The effective annual rate is 19.56 percent.

Source: Appendix 6A is taken from Mark A. White, "Financial Problem-Solving with an Electronic Calculator," *Financial Practice and Education,* Fall/Winter 1991, 73–88. Permission granted.

Texas Instruments BA-II

The *BA-II* operates in "modes." Before solving a financial problem, users must enter financial mode by pressing [2nd] {MODE}. Housekeeping functions needed to perform basic operations such as setting display formats, clearing calculator memory and adjusting for annuities due are summarized below.

Housekeeping Functions

Set Display Format to Two Decimal Places	[FIX] 2
Set Financial Mode	[2nd] {MODE}
Clear Display	[ON/C]
Clear TVM Registers	[2nd] {CMR}
Adjust for payments at Beginning of Period	[DUE] *

*
Press the [DUE] key just prior to the last keystroke needed to solve the problem.

Future Value of a Present Sum

Harry has just deposited $1000 into a savings account paying 6 percent, compounded annually. How much will he have in the account at the end of five years?

1000.00	[PV]
6.00	[%i]
5.00	[N]
[2nd] [FV]	1338.23

Harry will have accumulated $1,338.23 at the end of five years.

Present Value of an Annuity

Nancy had obtained an $11,000 bank loan to finance the purchase of a new car. The loan is for 48 months at an interest rate of 12 percent, compounded monthly. What is the amount of her monthly payment?

11000.00	[PV]
1.00	[%i]
48.00	[N]
[2nd] [PMT]	289.67

Nancy's monthly payment is $289.67.

Copyright © 1991 by *Financial Management Association.*

Finding an Unknown Interest Rate

Exactly five years ago, Dave and Cindy purchased 100 shares of Gro-Tex Corporation at $45 per share. They now wish to sell their holdings at the current market price of $75 per share. What was their average annual rate of return over this period?

45.00	[PV]
5.00	[N]
75.00	[FV]
[2nd] [%i]	10.76

Dave and Cindy earned a 10.76 percent holding period rate of return.

Finding an Unknown Number of Periods

Stacy received her retirement pension in a lump sum, and has invested it in an account which guarantees her a 10 percent annual rate of return. She wishes to make annual withdrawals of $35,000 beginning at the end of this year. If her current account balance is $250,000, how long will it be until she exhausts her account?

250000.00	[PV]
10.00	[%i]
35000.00	[PMT]
[2nd] [N]	13.14

Her account balance will be exhausted in 13.14 periods; her last withdrawal (which will be smaller than her earlier ones) will be made 14 years from today.

Simple Bond Pricing

What is the price of an 8 percent semiannual coupon bond maturing EXACTLY six years from now? It has a par value of $1000, and bonds of similar risk are yielding 10 percent.

40.00	[PMT]
12.00	[N]
5.00	[%i]
[2nd] [PV]	354.53

1000.00	[FV]
12.00	[N]
5.00	[%i]
[2nd] [PV]	556.84

The bond should sell for $354.53 + $556.84 = $911.37.

Simple Bond Yields to Maturity

What is the yield to maturity on a 10 percent annual coupon bond currently selling for $1,038.31? It matures in exactly three years.

1038.31	[PV]
100.00	[PMT]
1000.00	[FV]
3.00	[N]
[2nd] [%i]	Error

Unfortunately, the BA-II cannot compute bond yields-to-maturity in a single step. The correct answer is 8.50 percent and must be obtained using a "trial and error" approach.

Texas Instruments - Financial Investment Analyst

Housekeeping functions needed to perform basic operations such as setting display formats, clearing calculator memory and adjusting for annuities due are summarized below.

Housekeeping Functions

Set Display Format to 2 Decimal Places	[2nd] {FORMAT} 2 [DEC]
Set Financial Mode	[TVM]
Clear Display	[CE/C]
Clear TVM Registers	[2nd] {CLR COL}
Adjust for Payments at Beginning of Period	[BGN], [END]
Set Compounding Frequency to 1x per Period	1 [P/Y]

Future Value of a Present Sum

Harry has just deposited $1000 into a saving account paying 6 percent, compounded annually. How much will he have in the account at the end of five years?

-1,000.00	[PV]
6.00	[I/Y]
5.00	[N]
[Compute] [FV]	1,338.23

Harry will have accumulated $1,338.23 at the end of five years.

Present Value of an Annuity

Nancy has obtained an $11,000 bank loan to finance the purchase of a new car. The loan is for 48 months at an interest rate of 12 percent, compounded monthly. What is the amount of her monthly payment?

11,000.00	[PV]
1.00	[I/Y]
48.00	[N]
[Compute] [PMT]	-289.67

Nancy's monthly payment is $289.67.

Finding an Unknown Interest Rate

Exactly five years ago, Dave and Cindy purchased 100 shares of Gro-Tex Corporation at $45 per share. They now wish to sell their holding at the current market price of $75 per share. What was their average annual rate of return over this period?

-45.00	[PV]
5.00	[N]
75.00	[FV]
[Compute] [I/YR]	10.76

Finding an Unknown Number of Periods

Stacy received her retirement pension in a lump sum, and has invested it in an account which guarantees her a 10 percent annual rate of return. She wishes to make annual withdrawals of $35,000 beginning at the end of this year. If her current account balance is $250,000, how long will it be until she exhausts her account?

-250,000.00	[PV]
10.00	[I/YR]
35,000.00	[PMT]
[Compute] [N]	13.14

Her account balance will be exhausted in 13.14 periods; her last withdrawal (which will be smaller than her earlier ones) will be made 14 years from today.

Simple Bond Pricing

What is the price of an 8 percent semiannual coupon bond maturing EXACTLY six years from now? It has a par value of $1000, and bonds of similar risk are yielding 10 percent.

40.00	[PMT]
12.00	[N]
5.00	[I/YR]
1,000.00	[FV]
[Compute] [PV]	-911.37

The bond should sell for $911.37.

Simple Bond Yields to Maturity

What is the yield to maturity on a 10 percent annual coupon bond currently selling for $1,038.31? It matures in exactly three years.

-1,038.31	[PV]
100.00	[PMT]
1,000.00	[FV]
3.00	[N]
[Compute] [I/YR]	8.50

The bond is priced to yield 8.50 percent per year.

Cash Flow Analysis

An investment project promises the following schedule of cash flows. The project's initial outlay is -$100,000 and the appropriate discount rate is 10%. Use the NPV and IRR criteria to determine acceptance or rejection of this project.

Year 1:	$15,000
Year 2:	$20,000
Year 3:	$20,000
Year 4:	$20,000
Year 5:	$20,000
Year 6:	$60,000

-100,000.00	[CF$_o$]
[↓]	
15,000.00	[CF$_n$]
20,000.00	[CF$_n$]

4	[FRQ]
[↓]	
60,000.00	[CF$_n$]
10.00	[I]
[CashF]	
[Compute] [NPV]	5,138.72
[Compute] [IRR]	11.42

The project should be accepted because its NPV of $5,138.72 is greater than zero and its IRR of 11.42% is greater than the discount rate of 10 percent.

Loan Amortization

Prepare an amortization schedule for a one-year, $2,000 computer loan at 12 percent annual interest, compounded monthly. Monthly payments are $177.70.

2,000.00	[PV]
1.00	[I/Y]
-177.70	[PMT]
[↓] [Compute]	1,842.30
	-157.70
	-20.00

2 [P1] 2 [P2]	1,683.02
[Compute]	-159.28
	-18.42

Interest portion of 1st payment = $20.00
Principal portion of 1st payment = $157.70
Loan balance after 1st payment = $1,842.30

Interest portion of 2nd payment = $18.42
Principal portion of 2nd payment = $159.28
Loan balance after 2nd payment = $1,683.02

Interest Rate Conversions

A furniture store offers loan terms of 18 percent, compounded monthly. What is the loan's effective annual rate?

12.00	[C/Y]
18.00	[APR]
[Compute] [AER]	19.56

The effective annual rate is 19.56 percent.

Sharp Electronics EL-731

The *EL-731* operates in "modes." Before solving a financial problem, users must enter financial mode by pressing [2ndF] {MODE}. Housekeeping functions needed to perform basic operations such as setting display formats, clearing calculator memory and adjusting for annuities due are summarized below.

Housekeeping Functions

Set Display Format to Two Decimal Places	[2ndF] {TAB} 2
Set Financial Mode	[2ndF] {MODE}
Clear Display	[C-CE]
Clear TVM Registers	[2ndF] {CA}
Adjust for Payments at Beginning of Period	[BGN]

Future Value of a Present Sum

Harry has just deposited $1000 into a savings account paying 6 percent, compounded annually. How much will he have in the acccount at the end of five years?

-1'000.00	[PV]
6.00	[i]
5.00	[n]
[COMP] [FV]	1'338.23

Harry will have accumulated $1,338.23 at the end of five years.

Present Value of an Annuity

Nancy has obtained an $11,000 bank loan to finance the purchase of a new car. The loan is for 48 months at an interest rate of 12 percent, compounded monthly. What is the amount of her monthly payment?

11'000	[PV]
1.00	[i]
48.00	[n]
[COMP] [PMT]	-289.67

Nancy's monthly payment is $289.67.

Finding an Unknown Interest Rate

Exactly five years ago, Dave and Cindy purchased 100 shares of Gro-Tex Corporation at $45 per share. They now wish to sell their holdings at the current market price of $75 per share. What was their average annual rate of return over this period?

-45.00	[PV]
5.00	[n]
75.00	[FV]
[COMP] [i]	10.76

Dave and Cindy earned a 10.76 percent holding rate of return.

Finding an Unknown Number of Periods

Stacy received her retirement pension in a lump sum, and has invested it in an account which guarantees her a 10 percent annual rate of return. She wishes to make annual withdrawals of $35,000 beginning at the end of this year. If her current account balance is $250,000, how long will it be until she exhausts her account?

-250'000.00	[PV]
10.00	[i]
35'000.00	[PMT]
[COMP] [n]	13.14

Her account balance will be exhausted in 13.14 periods; her last withdrawal (which will be smaller than her earlier ones) will be made 14 years from today.

Simple Bond Pricing

What is the price of an 8 percent semiannual coupon bond maturing EXACTLY six years from now? It has a par value of $1000, and bonds of similar risk are yielding 10 percent.

40.00	[PMT]
12.00	[n]
5.00	[i]
1'000.00	[FV]
[COMP] [PV]	-911.37

The bond should sell for $911.37.

Simple Bond Yields to Maturity

What is the yield to maturity on a 10 percent annual coupon bond currently selling for $1,038.31? It matures in exactly three years.

-1'038.31	[PV]
100.00	[PMT]
1'000.00	[FV]
3.00	[n]
[COMP] [i]	8.50

The bond is priced to yield 8.50 percent per year.

Loan Amortization

Prepare an amortization schedule for a one-year, $2,000 computer loan at 12 percent annual interest, compounded monthly. Monthly payments are $177.70.

2'000.00	[PV]
1.00	[i]
-177.70	[PMT]
1 [AMRT]	-157.70
[AMRT]	-20.00
[AMRT]	1'842.30
2 [AMRT]	-159.28
[AMRT]	-18.42
[AMRT]	1'683.02

Interest portion of 1st payment = $20.00
Principal portion of 1st payment = $157.70
Loan balance after 1st payment = $1,842.30

Interest portion of 2nd payment = $18.42
Principal portion of 2nd payment =$159.28
Loan balance after 2nd payment = $1,638.02

Interest Rate Conversions

A furniture store offers loan terms of 18 percent, compounded monthly. What is the loan's effective annual rate?

12.00	[2ndF] {>>EFF}
18.00 [≡]	19.56

The effective annual rate is 19.56 percent.

Sharp Electronics EL-733, EL-735

Users of the *EL-733* must first enter financial mode by pressing [2ndF] {MODE} before solving financial problems. Housekeeping functions needed to perform basic operations such as setting display formats, clearing calculator memory and adjusting for annuities due are summarized below.

Housekeeping Functions

Set Display Format to Two Decimal Places	[2ndF] {TAB} 2
Set Financial Mode	[2ndF] {MODE}
Clear Display	[C-CE]
Clear TVM Registers	[2ndF] {CA}
Adjust for Payments at Beginning of Period	[BGN]

Future Value of a Present Sum

Harry has just deposited $1000 into a savings account paying 6 percent, compounded annually. How much will he have in the account at the end of five years?

-1'000.00	[PV]
6.00	[ⅈ]
5.00	[n]
[COMP] [FV]	1'338.23

Harry will have accumulated $1,338.23 at the end of five years.

Present Value of an Annuity

Nancy has obtained an $11,000 bank loan to finance the purchase of a new car. The loan is for 48 months at an interest rate of 12 percent, compounded monthly. What is the amount of her monthly payment?

11'000	[PV]
1.00	[ⅈ]
48.00	[n]
[COMP] [PMT]	-289.67

Nancy's monthly payment is $289.67.

Finding an Unknown Interest Rate

Exactly five years ago, Dave and Cindy purchased 100 shares of Gro-Tex Corporation at $45 per share. They now wish to sell their holdings at the current market price of $75 per share. What was their average annual rate of return over this period?

-45.00	[PV]
5.00	[n]
75.00	[FV]
[COMP] [ⅈ]	10.76

Dave and Cindy earned a 10.76 percent holding rate of return.

Finding an Unknown Number of Periods

Stacy received her retirement pension in a lump sum, and has invested it in an account which guarantees her a 10 percent annual rate of return. She wishes to make annual withdrawals of $35,000 beginning at the end of this year. If her current account balance is $250,000, how long will it be until she exhausts her account?

-250'000	[PV]
10.00	[ⅈ]
35'000	[PMT]
[COMP] [n]	13.14

Her account balance will be exhausted in 13.14 periods; her last withdrawal (which will be smaller than her earlier ones) will be made 14 years from today.

Simple Bond Pricing

What is the price of an 8 percent semiannual coupon bond maturing EXACTLY six years from now? It has a par value of $1000, and bonds of similar risk are yielding 10 percent.

40.00	[PMT]
12.00	[n]
5.00	[ⅈ]
1'000.00	[FV]
[COMP] [PV]	-911.37

The bond should sell for $911.37.

Simple Bond Yields to Maturity

What is the yield to maturity on a 10 percent annual coupon bond currently selling for $1,038.31? It matures in exactly three years.

-1'038.31	[PV]
100.00	[PMT]
1'000.00	[FV]
3.00	[n]
[COMP] [ⅈ]	8.50

The bond is priced to yield 8.50 percent per year.

Cash Flow Analysis

An investment project promises the following schedule of cash flows. The project's initial outlay is -$100,000 and the appropriate discount rate is 10%. Use the NPV and the IRR criteria to determine acceptance or rejection of this project.

Year 1:	$15,000
Year 2:	$20,000
Year 3:	$20,000
Year 4:	$20,000
Year 5:	$20,000
Year 6:	$60,000

-100'000.00	[CFi]
15'000.00	[CFi]
4	[2ndF] {Ni}
20'000.00	[CFi]
60'000.00	[CFi]
10.00	[ⅈ]
[NPV]	5'138.72
[IRR]	11.42

The project should be accepted because its NPV of $5,138.72 is greater than zero and its IRR of 11.42 percent is greater than the discount rate of 10 percent.

Loan Amortization

Prepare an amortization schedule for a one-year, $2,000 computer loan at 12 percent annual interest, compounded monthly. Monthly payments are $177.70.

2'000.00	[PV]
1.00	[ⅈ]
-177.70	[PMT]
1 [AMRT]	-157.70
[AMRT]	-20.00
[AMRT]	1'842.30
2 [AMRT]	-159.28
[AMRT]	-18.42
[AMRT]	1'683.02

Interest portion of 1st payment = $20.00
Principal portion of 1st payment = $157.70
Loan balance after 1st payment = $1,842.30

Interest portion of 2nd payment = $18.42
Principal portion of 2nd payment = $159.28
Loan balance after 2nd payment = $1,638.02

Interest Rate Conversions

A furniture store offers loan terms of 18 percent, compounded monthly. What is the loan's effective annual rate?

12.00	[2ndF] {> > EFF}
18.00 [≡]	19.56

The effective annual rate is 19.56 percent.

Hewlett-Packard HP-10B

By default, the *HP-10B* assumes monthly compounding, or 12 times per period. Beginning students should change this setting to once per period by pressing 1 [_] {P/YR}. Additional housekeeping functions needed to perform basic operations such as setting display formats, clearing calculator memory and adjusting for annuities due are summarized below.

Housekeeping Functions

Set Display Format to Two Decimal Places	[_] [DSP] 2
Clear Display	[C]
Clear TVM Registers	[_] {CLEAR ALL}
Adjust for Payments at Beginning of Period	[_] {BEG/END}
Set Compounding Frequency to 1x per Period	1 [_] {P/YR}

Future Value of a Present Sum

Harry has just deposited $1000 into a savings account paying 6 percent, compounded annually. How much will he have in the acccount at the end of five years?

-1,000.00	[PV]	
6.00	[I/YR]	
5.00	[N]	
[FV]	1,338.23	

Harry will have accumulated $1,338.23 at the end of five years.

Present Value of an Annuity

Nancy has obtained an $11,000 bank loan to finance the purchase of a new car. The loan is for 48 months at an interest rate of 12 percent, compounded monthly. What is the amount of her monthly payment?

11,0000.00	[PV]	
1.00	[I/YR]	
48.00	[N]	
[PMT]	-289.67	

Nancy's monthly payment is $289.67.

Finding an Unknown Interest Rate

Exactly five years ago, Dave and Cindy purchased 100 shares of Gro-Tex Corporation at $45 per share. They now wish to sell their holdings at the current market price of $75 per share. What was their average annual rate of return over this period?

-45.00	[PV]	
5.00	[N]	
75.00	[FV]	
[I/YR]	10.76	

Dave and Cindy earned a 10.76 percent holding period rate of return.

Finding an Unknown Number of Periods

Stacy received her retirement pension in a lump sum, and has invested it in an account which guarantees her a 10 percent annual rate of return. She wishes to make annual withdrawals of $35,000 beginning at the end of this year. If her current account balance is $250,000, how long will it be until she exhausts her account?

-250,000.00	[PV]	
10.00	[I/YR]	
35,000.00	[PMT]	
[N]	13.14	

Her account balance will be exhausted in 13.14 periods; her last withdrawal (which will be smaller than her earlier ones) will be made 14 years from today.

Simple Bond Pricing

What is the price of an 8 percent semiannual coupon bond maturing EXACTLY six years from now? It has a par value of $1000, and bonds of similar risk are yielding 10 percent.

40.00	[PMT]	
12.00	[N]	
5.00	[I/YR]	
1,000.00	[FV]	
[PV]	-911.37	

The bond should sell for $911.37.

Simple Bond Yields to Maturity

What is the yield to maturity on a 10 percent annual coupon bond currently selling for $1,038.31? It matures in exactly three years.

-1,038.31	[PV]	
100.00	[PMT]	
1,000.00	[FV]	
3.00	[N]	
[I/YR]	8.50	

The bond is priced to yield 8.50 percent per year.

Cash Flow Analysis

An investment project promises the following schedule of cash flows. The project's initial outlay is -$100,000 and the appropriate discount rate is 10%. Use the NPV and the IRR criteria to determine acceptance or rejection of this project.

Year 1:	$15,000
Year 2:	$20,000
Year 3:	$20,000
Year 4:	$20,000
Year 5:	$20,000
Year 6:	$60,000

-100,000.00	[CFj]	
15,000.00	[CFj]	
20,000.00	[CFj]	
4.00	[_] [Nj]	
60,000.00	[CFj]	
10.00	[I/YR]	
[_] {NPV}	5,138.72	
[_] {IRR/YR}	11.42	

The project should be accepted because its NPV of $5,138.72 is greater than zero and its IRR of 11.42 percent is greater than the discount rate of 10 percent.

Loan Amortization

Prepare an amortization schedule for a one-year, $2,000 computer loan at 12 percent annual interest, compounded monthly. Monthly payments are $177.70.

2,000.00	[PV]	
1.00	[I/YR]	
-177.70	[PMT]	

1[INPUT][ ][AMORT]	[=]	-20.00
	[=]	-157.70
	[=]	1,842.30
2[INPUT][ ][AMORT]	[=]	-18.42
	[=]	-159.28
	[=]	1,683.02

Interest portion of 1st payment =	$20.00
Principal portion of 1st payment =	$157.70
Loan balance after 1st payment =	$1,842.30

Interest portion of 2nd payment =	$18.42
Principal portion of 2nd payment =	$159.28
Loan balance after 2nd payment =	1,638.02

Interest Rate Conversions

A furniture store offers loan terms of 18 percent, compounded monthly. What is the loan's effective annual rate?

12.00	[_] {P/YR}	
18.00	[_] {NOM%}	
[_] {EFF%}	19.56	

The effective annual rate is 19.56 percent.

Hewlett-Packard HP-12C

Some users may find the *HP-12C* difficult to operate because it evaluates arithmetic expressions using RPN logic.   The *HP-12C* Owner's Handbook provides instructions in the use ot this method of data entry. Housekeeping functions needed to perform basic operations such as setting display formats, clearing calculator memory and adjusting for annuites due are summarized below.

Housekeeping Functions

Set Display Format to [f] 2 Two Decimal Places	
Display Numbers in [f] [.] Scientific Notation	
Clear Display [CLX]	
Clear TVM Registers [f] CLEAR {FIN}	
Adjust for Payments at [g] {BEG}, [g] {END} Beginning of Period	

Future Value of a Present Sum

Harry has just deposited $1000 into a savings account paying 6 percent, compounded annually. How much will he have in the account at the end of five years?

-1,000.00	[PV]
6.00	[i]
5.00	[n]
[FV]	1,338.23

Harry will have accumulated $1,338.23 at the end of five years.

Present Value of an Annuity

Nancy has obtained an $11,000 bank loan to finance the purchase of a new car. The loan is for 48 months at an interest rate of 12 percent, compounded monthly.   What is the amount of her monthly payment?

11,0000.00	[PV]
1.00	[i]
48.00	[n]
[PMT]	-289.67

Nancy's monthly payment is $289.67.

Finding an Unknown Interest Rate

Exactly five years ago, Dave and Cindy purchased 100 shares of Gro-Tex Corporation at $45 per share. They now wish to sell their holdings at the current market price of $75 per share.   What was their average annual rate of return over this period?

-45.00	[PV]
5.00	[n]
75.00	[FV]
[i]	10.76

Dave and Cindy earned a 10.76 percent holding period rate of return.

Finding an Unknown Number of Periods

Stacy received her retirement pension in a lump sum, and has invested it in an account which guarantees her a 10 percent annual rate of return. She wishes to make annual withdrawals of $35,000 beginning at the end of this year. If her current account balance is $250,000, how long will it be until she exhausts her account?

-250,000.00	[PV]
10.00	[i]
35,000.00	[PMT]
[n]	14.00

Her account balance will be exhausted in 13.14 periods; her last withdrawal (which will be smaller than her earlier ones) will be made 14 years from today.

Simple Bond Pricing

What is the price of an 8 percent semiannual coupon bond maturing EXACTLY six years from now? It has a par value of $1000, and bonds of similar risk are yielding 10 percent.

40.00	[PMT]
12.00	[n]
5.00	[i]
1,000.00	[FV]
[PV]	-911.37

The bond should sell for $911.37.

Simple Bond Yields to Maturity

What is the yield to maturity on a 10 percent annual coupon bond currently selling for $1,038.31? It matures in exactly three years.

-1,038.31	[PV]
100.00	[PMT]
1,000.00	[FV]
3.00	[n]
[i]	8.50

The bond is priced to yield 8.50 percent per year.

Cash Flow Analysis

An investment project promises the following schedule of cash flows.   The project's initial outlay is -$100,000 and the appropriate discount rate is 10%. Use the NPV and the IRR criteria to determine acceptance or rejection of this project.

Year 1:	$15,000
Year 2:	$20,000
Year 3:	$20,000
Year 4:	$20,000
Year 5:	$20,000
Year 6:	$60,000

-100,000.00	[g] {CF$_0$}
15,000.00	[g] {CF$_j$}
20,000.00	[g] {CF$_j$}
4.00	[g] {Nj}
60,000.00	[g] {CF$_j$}
10.00	[i]
[f] {NPV}	5,138.72
[f] {IRR})	11.42

The project should be accepted because its NPV of $5,138.72 is greater than zero and its IRR of 11.42 percent is greater than the discount rate of 10 percent.

Loan Amortization

Prepare an amortization schedule for a one-year, $2,000 computer loan at 12 percent annual interest, compounded monthly. Monthly payments are $177.70.

2,000.00	[PV]
1.00	[i]
-177.70	[PMT]

1 [f] {AMORT}	-20.00
[x >< y]	-157.70
[RCL] [PV]	1,842.30

1 [f] {AMORT}	-18.42
[x >< y]	-159.28
[RCL] [PV]	1,683.02

Interest portion of 1st payment =	$20.00
Principal portion of 1st payment =	$157.70
Loan balance after 1st payment =	$1,842.30

Interest portion of 2nd payment =	$18.42
Principal portion of 2nd payment =	$159.28
Loan balance after 2nd payment =	$1,638.02

Miscellany

- To perform a calculator self-test, turn the calculator on while holding down the [x] key.
- To change between American and European display formats, turn the calculator on while holding down the [.] key.
- Press [STO] {EEX} to toggle the 'c' annunciator, which determines whether intra-period interest is calculated on a simple or compound basis.

Hewlett-Packard HP-17B II, HP-19B II

Housekeeping functions needed to perform basic operations such as setting display formats, clearing calculator memory and adjusting for annuities due are summarized below.

Housekeeping Functions

Set Display Format to Two Decimal Places	[DSP] [FIX] 2 [INPUT]
Clear Display	[___] {CLEAR}
Clear TVM Registers	[___] {CLEAR DATA}
Adjust for Payments at Beginning of Period	[BEG], [END] *
Set Compounding Frequency to 1x per Period	1 [P/YR] *

* Press [FIN] [TVM] [OTHER] to access the menus needed to change these options.

Future Value of a Present Sum

Harry has just deposited $1000 into a savings account paying 6 percent, compounded annually. How much will he have in the account at the end of five years?

-1,000.00	[PV]
6.00	[I%YR]
5.00	[n]
[FV]	1,338.23

Harry will have accumulated $1,338.23 at the end of five years.

Present Value of an Annuity

Nancy has obtained an $11,000 bank loan to finance the purchase of a new car. The loan is for 48 months at an interest rate of 12 percent, compounded monthly. What is the amount of her monthly payment?

11,0000.00	[PV]
1.00	[I%YR]
48.00	[N]
[PMT]	-289.67

Nancy's monthly payment is $289.67.

Finding an Unknown Interest Rate

Exactly five years ago, Dave and Cindy purchased 100 shares of Gro-Tex Corporation at $45 per share. They now wish to sell their holdings at the current market price of $75 per share. What was their average annual rate of return over this period?

-45.00	[PV]
5.00	[N]
75.00	[FV]
[I%YR]	10.76

Dave and Cindy earned a 10.76 percent holding rate of return.

Finding an Unknown Number of Periods

Stacy received her retirement pension in a lump sum, and has invested it in an account which guarantees her a 10 percent annual rate of return. She wishes to make annual withdrawals of $35,000 beginning at the end of this year. If her current account balance is $250,000, how long will it be until she exhausts her account?

-250,000.00	[PV]
10.00	[I%YR]
35,000.00	[PMT]
[N]	13.14

Her account balance will be exhausted in 13.14 periods; her last withdrawal (which will be smaller than her earlier ones) will be made 14 years from today.

Simple Bond Pricing

What is the price of an 8 percent semiannual coupon bond maturing EXACTLY six years from now? It has a par value of $1000, and bonds of similar risk are yielding 10 percent.

40.00	[PMT]
12.00	[N]
5.00	[I%YR]
1,000.00	[FV]
[PV]	-911.37

The bond should sell for $911.37.

Simple Bond Yields to Maturity

What is the yield to maturity on a 10 percent annual coupon bond currently selling for $1,038.31? It matures in exactly three years.

-1,038.31	[PV]
100.00	[PMT]
1,000.00	[FV]
3.00	[N]
[I%YR]	8.50

The bond is priced to yield 8.50 percent per year.

Cash Flow Analysis

An investment project promises the following schedule of cash flows. The project's initial outlay is -$100,000 and the appropriate discount rate is 10%. Use the NPV and the IRR criteria to determine acceptance or rejection of this project.

Year 1:	$15,000
Year 2:	$20,000
Year 3:	$20,000
Year 4:	$20,000
Year 5:	$20,000
Year 6:	$60,000

-100,000.00	[INPUT]
15,000.00	[INPUT]
1.00	[INPUT]
20,000.00	[INPUT]
4.00	[INPUT]
60,000.00	[INPUT]
1.00	[INPUT]
[CALC]	
10.00	[I%]
[NPV]	5,138.72
[IRR%]	11.42

The project should be accepted because its NPV of $5,138.72 is greater than zero and its IRR of 11.42 percent is greater than the discount rate of 10 percent.

Loan Amortization

Prepare an amortization schedule for a one-year, $2,000 computer loan at 12 percent annual interest, compounded monthly. Monthly payments are $177.70.

2,000.00	[PV]
1.00	[I%YR]
-177.70	[PMT]

[OTHER] [AMRT]		
1 [#P] [INT]	-20.00	
[PRIN]	-157.70	
[BAL]	1,842.30	
[NEXT] [INT]	-18.42	
[PRIN]	-159.28	
[BAL]	1,683.02	

Interest portion of 1st payment =	$20.00
Principal portion of 1st payment =	$157.70
Loan balance after 1st payment =	$1,842.30
Interest portion of 2nd payment =	$18.42
Principal portion of 2nd payment =	$159.28
Loan balance after 2nd payment =	$1,638.02

Interest Rate Conversions

A furniture store offers loan terms of 18 percent, compounded monthly. What is the loan's effective annual rate?

12.00	[P]
18.00	[NOM%]
[EFF%]	19.56

The effective annual rate is 19.56 percent.

Chapter 7

COST OF CAPITAL AND CAPITAL STRUCTURE

A Weakened Giant

Newspaper headlines during 1992 told a sad story about General Motors Corporation: "GM Aims to Break Even Next Year on North American Operations"; "S&P Issues Warning on GM Stock"; "Moody's Cuts Rating on GM Bonds"; "GM Issues Preferred Stock, Again." Apparently, breaking even was a lofty goal for a company skidding toward its third consecutive annual loss.

During the 18-month period ending November 1992, GM made eight trips to the capital markets. The number one auto manufacturer raised $7.9 billion, principally to cover losses from operations. Noted one analyst, "They're burning cash at a rapid rate." Amid the internal turmoil, GM issued preferred stock repeatedly, signaling that its difficulties probably would continue. The issuance of preferred stock, for which dividends are *not* tax deductible, instead of bonds, for which interest payments are tax deductible, was interpreted by some analysts as an indication that management expected future tax rates to be zero because of continued losses.

The tax-deductibility of

interest has no value to a company not paying income taxes. Moreover, preferred stock provides more flexibility to the company than do bonds. Preferred-stock dividends need not be paid until declared by the board of directors, but interest on bonds must be paid on time as scheduled. Like most companies in financial distress, GM needed flexibility much more than tax deductibility.

As bad news surfaced, GM's common-stock price declined. Pressure mounted from credit-rating companies as they placed the company's bonds under review for a possible down-grade. Standard & Poor's said GM preferred stock might sink to "junk" ratings if the company issued more preferred stock to cover losses. Subsequently, Moody's Investors Service lowered GM's senior bond rating from *A* to *Baa,* indicating a rise in risk level. In general, investors supplying capital to GM began to require higher rates of return on its securities. GM's cost of capital had risen.

Source: Douglas Lavin and Joseph B. White, "GM Will Issue Up to $1 Billion of Preferred," *The Wall Street Journal,* November 11, 1992, A3; Joseph B. White, "S&P Issues New Warning on GM Stock," *The Wall Street Journal,* November 12, 1992, A3.

The preceding chapter describes ways to estimate the costs of debt, preferred stock, and common equity. This chapter describes the weighted average of these costs—the average percentage cost of a company's capital. To maximize shareholder wealth, financial managers must use the mix of capital sources that minimizes the *average cost of capital*. Financial managers use the *marginal cost of capital* in the selection of investment projects. The chapter begins with the calculation of average cost of capital and the logic behind it. Discussed next is the impact of the debt-equity mix on average cost of capital, including the celebrated theories of capital structure. Following is a discussion of the relationship between average and marginal cost of capital and the role the latter plays in selecting capital projects for investment. Concluding the chapter is a practical method (EBIT-EPS analysis) for comparing the benefits of alternative financing plans.

AVERAGE COST OF CAPITAL

average cost of capital
Weighted average of the component costs of capital.

After a financial manager has calculated the *component costs of capital*—debt, preferred stock, and common equity—it is not difficult to find the average cost of these financing sources. The **average cost of capital** is a weighted average of the component costs: Multiply each component's percentage cost by its contribution to the total amount of capital, and then total the products. The calculation in equation form is:

$$K_a = W_i K_i + W_p K_p + W_c K_c$$

where K_a = average cost of capital

K_i = after-tax cost of debt

K_p = cost of preferred stock

K_c = cost of common equity

W = weight or proportion of total capital represented by each capital source (all must total 100 percent)

EXAMPLE

A company raises $1,000,000 in long-term capital. The individual amounts of each source are: $300,000 debt, $200,000 preferred stock, and $500,000 common equity. If the cost of each capital source is 8, 14, and 18 percent, respectively, the average cost of capital is:

$$K_a = \frac{\$300,000}{\$1,000,000}(0.08) + \frac{\$200,000}{\$1,000,000}(0.14) + \frac{\$500,000}{\$1,000,000}(0.18)$$

$$= 0.024 + 0.028 + 0.090$$

$$= 0.142, \text{ or } 14.2\%$$

Placing the cost of each component of financing in the equation for average cost of capital makes it easy to see the contribution each makes to the overall cost of financing and to compare the individual costs with the average. Examining the costs in the example above, you might wonder why a company would use a mix that includes 50 percent common equity with a component cost of 18 percent when debt financing with a component cost of 8 percent is available.

explicit cost
Percentage cost of a source of capital.

implicit cost
Change in the percentage cost of a source of capital resulting from the use of another source.

Each of the values used in the example (8 percent, 14 percent, and 18 percent) is an **explicit cost,** the percentage cost of a component without regard to its impact on the cost of another component. In addition to its explicit cost, debt has an implicit cost. The **implicit cost** of a capital component is the increase in the cost of another component as a result of using the first component. The major *implicit cost of debt is the increase in the cost of common equity resulting from the use of debt;* the cost of preferred stock may increase as well.

Here is the reason debt has an implicit cost: A company with no common equity would find it impossible to borrow money. No investor or financial institution would loan a company enough money to finance its investments 100 percent. If the 50 percent equity base in the example above were not in place, then the company would not be able to borrow at 8 percent interest. Using debt, which has a low explicit cost, thus depends on the presence of common equity, which has a high cost. The explicit cost of debt understates its true cost. The true cost of debt equals the explicit cost plus the implicit cost. Fortunately for us, we need not separately estimate the implicit cost of debt because the weighted-average cost of capital automatically takes into account any prevailing implicit costs. The high cost of common equity, the mid-level cost of preferred stock, and the low cost of debt are combined into one equation for calculating the average cost of capital.

FINANCIAL LEVERAGE AND COST OF CAPITAL

financial leverage
Use of a fixed-cost source of capital.

A company that uses debt financing is said to employ **financial leverage.** The term *leverage* has its origins in the physical sciences: ". . . the action or mechanical effect of a lever." Leverage in the business world is analogous to that in the physical sciences. Financial leverage results from using debt or other fixed-cost capital (preferred stock) to partially finance assets. Interest payments, like a fulcrum in the physical sciences, are fixed; the borrower must pay the interest whether or not the investment in assets proves profitable. If the return on assets exceeds borrowing costs, then leverage increases (levers up) the borrower's return on equity (earnings after taxes divided by equity). Unfortunately, if return on assets turns out to be less than borrowing costs, then the return on equity drops.

debt-equity ratio
Amount of debt per dollar of common equity.

financial risk
Possibility that actual earnings after taxes will differ from their expected value because a company uses debt financing.

Increases in a company's **debt-equity ratio** lead to increases in financial leverage and the potential for gains *and losses.* The increased uncertainty surrounding earnings after taxes is **financial risk.** Because the company must use a portion of its before-tax earnings for interest payments, its after-tax earnings become more volatile in the presence of debt. Changes in earnings volatility, or changes in financial risk, cause security holders to revise their opinion of a company, which in turn causes its cost of capital to change.

Cost of Debt

Consider first the viewpoint of bondholders when a company increases its financial leverage. Bondholders have a claim on earnings senior to, or prior to, that of common shareholders and must receive interest before the company pays dividends. Because of this senior claim, bondholders normally react indifferently as companies raise capital through reasonable amounts of debt. At some high debt level, however, they become concerned about a company's ability to service its debt. This concern leads them to demand a higher rate of return on any new bonds the company might issue. Thus the greater financial leverage measured by

FIGURE 7.1

Effect of Financial Leverage on the Costs of Debt and Common Equity

Panel A illustrates the way the cost of debt capital remains relatively constant as financial leverage increases up to some point, then increases because of the enlarged financial risk from the high debt level. Panel B illustrates the way the cost of common equity increases over the entire range of financial leverage, accelerating at higher levels. Cost of equity consists of the risk-free rate (R_f) plus premiums for business risk and financial risk.

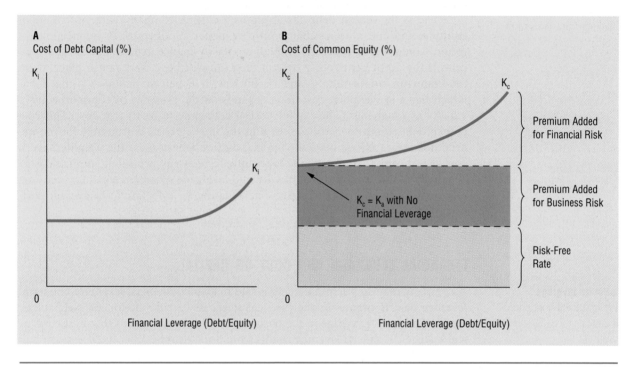

the higher debt-equity ratio increases the company's cost of debt capital. Figure 7.1A illustrates how the after-tax cost of debt (K_i) changes with changes in financial leverage. The after-tax cost of debt stays relatively constant as the debt-equity ratio increases, but at some unspecified point it begins to increase. The precise point at which the curve begins to rise is difficult to specify, but additional debt will eventually increase the after-tax cost of debt to a company because of the added financial risk.

Cost of Common Equity

The cost of common equity (K_c) also increases with increasing financial leverage. In fact, the financial risk that leverage creates falls most heavily on common shareholders, the junior, or lesser, claimants on a company's earnings and assets. Because of this, the cost of common equity rises more dramatically, in comparison with the cost of debt, at all levels of financial leverage. Figure 7.1B illustrates the relationship between the cost of common equity and financial leverage. At zero leverage the cost of common equity consists of the risk-free rate of return plus a percentage premium for **business risk**—the risk inherent in a company's operations without debt. A company's operations reflect management's investment decisions. Think of business risk as the risk of the company's assets without

business risk

Uncertainty surrounding future earnings before interest and taxes as a result of company operations.

considering the way they are financed. At the minimum, a company would have no business risk if all of its funds were invested in U.S. Treasury bills. As you can see from the lower dashed line in Figure 7.1B, such an investment policy would cause the cost of common equity K_c to equal the risk-free rate. From the perspective of shareholders, the company has become a mutual fund investing in T-bills on their behalf. As management invests in riskier projects, shareholders incur greater risk and therefore require a higher rate of return.

When the company increases financial leverage, the implicit cost of debt makes itself felt: Shareholders require a higher rate of return to compensate them for the increased financial risk they perceive in the company. As a result, the cost of common equity rises because of the added premium for financial risk.[1] Although not illustrated in Figure 7.1, the cost of preferred stock (K_p) also rises with increases in financial leverage. The cost of preferred stock is omitted here and in the following discussion of average cost of capital for two reasons: (1) Omitting preferred stock simplifies the analysis and discussion, and (2) preferred stock is not a widely used source of financing by industrial corporations.

Average Cost of Capital

Increases in financial leverage and the accompanying financial risk cause capital suppliers to require higher rates of return, thereby ultimately increasing the costs of debt and equity. However, the *average* cost of capital (K_a) *declines* as financial leverage initially increases. Figure 7.2A illustrates this principle. It shows average cost of capital passing through three phases as financial leverage increases:

- *Falling K_a:* For small increases in debt, the costs of debt and equity do not increase much because the increase in debt-service payments (interest and principal) is too small to strain the cash resources of the company. In this phase, average cost of capital (K_a) declines because the company uses cheap debt, with its tax-deductible interest, instead of costly equity.

- *Minimum K_a:* The minimum average cost of capital identifies the **optimal capital structure**, the best mix of debt and equity. Optimal capital structure minimizes the average cost of capital and maximizes the value of the com-

optimal capital structure
Debt-equity ratio that minimizes a company's cost of capital and maximizes its stock price.

---

[1]Nondiversifiable risk, measured by a stock's beta, increases as a company's debt-equity ratio increases. Recall that the capital asset pricing model shows higher betas leading to higher required rates of return and, therefore, to higher equity costs. Under the assumptions of the capital asset pricing model, we express a common stock's beta (β_c) as a function of the debt-equity ratio measured with market values:

$$\beta_c = \beta_u \left[1 + \frac{(1 - T)D}{S} \right]$$

$$= \beta_u + \beta_u \left[\frac{(1 - T)D}{S} \right]$$

where β_u = unlevered beta

T = company's marginal tax rate

D and S = market values of the levered company's debt and equity

If the company borrows no money, then the beta of its common stock would be β_u, which reflects the company's business (operating) risk. Note that as the debt-equity ratio increases, the stock beta increases as well.

FIGURE 7.2   **Effect of Financial Leverage on the Average Cost of Capital and Company Value**

The average cost of capital (K_a) and the value of a company change as financial leverage changes. Panel A shows that K_a initially falls, reaches a minimum, and then rises as financial leverage increases. Panel B shows that the value of the company initially rises, reaches a maximum, then falls as financial leverage increases. The company's maximum value in Panel B occurs at its minimum cost of capital in Panel A.

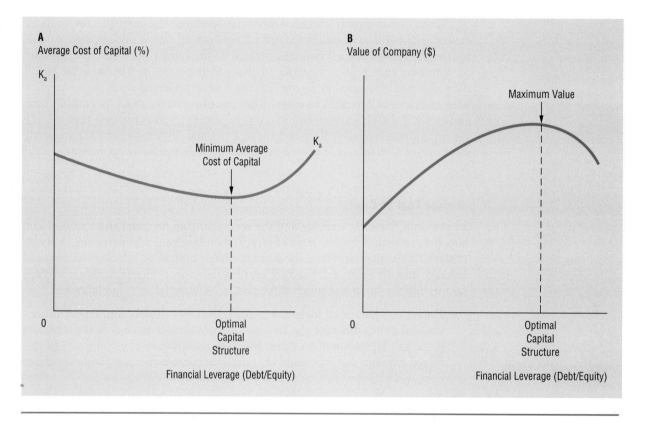

pany because it minimizes the discount rate used to find the present value of the company's future cash flows. Maximizing the value of the company also maximizes the value of common equity and price per share of common stock.

- *Rising K_a:* Beyond the optimal capital structure, financial risk rises rapidly. The possibility of bankruptcy emerges. Bond buyers pay less for the company's bonds, requiring the company to issue more bonds to raise needed funds at greater interest cost. Default risk increases and common shareholders become increasingly alarmed about the possibility of a default on company debt. Shareholders demand an increasingly higher rate of return, and this, along with the increase in debt-service payments (which reduces the cash flow available to pay dividends), leads to a decline in company value and the price of the common stock. In summary, beyond the optimal capital structure, higher rates of return required by capital suppliers more than offset the tax advantage of using debt.

EXAMPLE

To illustrate the behavior of average cost of capital (K_a) for various proportions of debt (W_i) and equity (W_c) and for the costs of debt (K_i) and equity (K_c), consider the following:

(1) W_i	×	(2) K_i	+	(3) W_c	×	(4) K_c	=	(5) K_a
0.0		—%		1.0		13.0%		13.0%
0.1		5.0		0.9		13.1		12.3
0.2		5.0		0.8		13.2		11.6
0.3		5.2		0.7		13.4		10.9
0.4		**5.5**		**0.6**		**14.0**		**10.6**
0.5		6.2		0.5		15.4		10.8
0.6		7.0		0.4		16.9		11.0

Costs of the individual capital sources in the example table above are consistent with what Figure 7.1 illustrates: Column 2 shows the cost of debt remaining constant over some reasonable range of financial leverage, then increasing. The cost of equity gradually increases with financial leverage (see Column 4), then increases rapidly. Notice that the average cost of capital in Column 5 equals the cost of equity in Column 4 for the special case when the company uses no debt financing. The weighted-average costs in Column 5 are consistent with Figure 7.2: There is an optimal, or least-cost, weighted average even though each component cost increases. When debt becomes 40 percent of total capital, K_a is at a minimum of 10.6 percent. At this point the debt-equity ratio is $0.40/0.60 = 0.667$, and the company is using $0.667 of debt for each $1 of equity. Beyond the debt-equity ratio of 0.667 the costs of debt and equity rise rapidly and cause the average cost of capital to increase and the value of the company to decrease.

THEORY OF CAPITAL STRUCTURE

The impact of a company's capital structure (or financial leverage) on its market value and average cost of capital has been the focus of theoretical study for many years. Hundreds of financial theorists have sought to answer the question: How much debt should a company use optimally to finance its assets? Depending on their assumptions, the theorists provide wide-ranging answers: (1) A company can use any amount of debt desired because capital structure is irrelevant; it has no effect on company value. (2) A company should use close to 100 percent debt because the interest paid on debt is tax deductible; the reduction in tax payments increases company value. Contrary to these answers, today's financial theorists generally agree that capital structure *does* matter and that much less than 100 percent debt is optimal. The following sketch highlights the evolution of theory toward these conclusions.

Modigliani and Miller

The debate on capital structure began more than three decades ago. In 1958 Franco Modigliani and Merton Miller (hereafter MM) argued that capital structure does not matter because company value depends solely on the earning power of the company's assets.[2] They concluded that the proportion of company earnings paid to holders of bonds versus that paid to the holders of stock did not matter. How you slice the pie (company earnings and company value) does not change the size of the pie. Using the perpetuity model, MM equated company value to the present value of net operating income (or earnings before interest and taxes):

$$\text{Value of a company} = \frac{\text{Net operating income}}{K_a}$$

where K_a is the weighted-average cost of capital. MM argued that neither net operating income nor K_a is affected by capital structure, thus causing the value of a company to be independent of capital structure. They noted: (1) Net operating income represents earnings before any interest payments, and so it is unaffected by the use of debt. (2) K_a is unaffected by the use of debt because as the debt-equity ratio increases, the increase in equity cost is exactly offset by the lower cost of debt. To reach their conclusion, and for simplicity, MM assumed the absence of corporate taxes, personal taxes, and bankruptcy costs. In other words, they assumed that securities trade in *perfect markets,* which also means that investors have access to the same information as corporate managers, transactions costs are zero, and investors can borrow at the same rate as corporations.

Making outlandish assumptions to develop a theory is fine as long as the assumptions do not affect the explanatory and predictive power of the theory. In 1963 MM realized that one of their assumptions—the absence of corporate taxes—was harmful to their theory. They corrected their model to show that the value of a company does indeed depend on its capital structure:

$$\begin{matrix} \text{Value of a} \\ \text{levered company} \end{matrix} = \begin{matrix} \text{Value as an} \\ \text{unlevered company} \end{matrix} + \begin{matrix} \text{Present value of tax} \\ \text{savings from interest} \end{matrix}$$

With corporate taxation, the value of a levered (partially debt-financed) company equals its unlevered (all equity-financed, no debt) value plus the present value of future tax savings created by tax-deductible interest.[3] MM's 1963 model suggests that companies should finance assets with almost 100 percent debt: Higher debt levels create higher present values of tax savings from interest and lead to higher

---

[2] The seminal articles on the theory of capital structure include the following: Franco Modigliani and Merton H. Miller, "The Cost of Capital, Corporation Finance and the Theory of Investment," *American Economic Review,* June 1958, 261–297; "Taxes and the Cost of Capital: A Correction," *American Economic Review,* June 1963, 433–443; Merton H. Miller, "Debt and Taxes," *Journal of Finance,* May 1977, 261–278. In conformance to these articles, the discussion here focuses on maximizing company value, which usually is equivalent to maximizing shareholder wealth and stock price. Exceptions to this equivalence can occur when managerial decisions cause transfers of wealth from bondholders to stockholders; that is, a managerial decision might maximize shareholder wealth but cause bond values and company value to decline. For example, after issuing bonds, a company might invest in riskier projects than expected by the bond investors. The increase in business risk causes a decline in bond values and shifts wealth from the bondholders to the stockholders. Investors in bonds usually demand protection from such Machiavellian strategies by restricting managerial discretion through protective covenants (described in Chapter 17).

[3] The tax savings, or tax shield, from interest payments equals the company's tax rate (T) times the dollar interest (I) it pays: T(I). If the interest rate is K_d, then $I = K_d(VB)$, where VB is the value of the bonds, or amount borrowed. The tax shield thus becomes $T(K_d)(VB)$. If the company maintains the debt level permanently, then the present value of the tax shield can be calculated using the perpetuity model: $T(K_d)(VB)/K_d$, where the discount rate K_d is commensurate with the risk of the tax shield $T(K_d)(VB)$. Simplifying the expression yields the present value of the tax shield: T(VB), the company's tax rate times the value of its bonds. For a company that pays no taxes, T = 0, and the present value of the tax shield is zero. A company's tax rate and therefore the present value of the tax shield may decline at high debt-equity ratios because of the substantial dollar interest the company pays. In this case, the value of the company declines at high debt levels.

company values. Because real-world companies do not come close to 100 percent debt levels, however, the model lacks intuitive appeal. Assuming that countless financial managers cannot all be wrong in their debt decisions, most financial theorists believe something is missing from the model.

In 1977 Merton Miller (the second M in MM) argued once again for the irrelevance of financial leverage to a company's value. Including personal taxes incurred by investors in addition to corporate taxes, he concluded:

$$\begin{array}{cc}\text{Value of a} & \text{Value as an} \\ \text{levered company} & = \ \text{unlevered company}\end{array}$$

Miller argued that a company should minimize both personal and corporate taxes, not just the latter; and under his assumptions he demonstrated that when a corporation pays a dollar each to a bondholder and to a stockholder, they end up with the same amount of money after corporate and personal taxes. Under this scenario, whether a corporation issues stocks or bonds to investors is irrelevant. To reach this conclusion, Miller assumed: (1) The investors' tax rate (at the margin) on income from common stock is zero, and (2) the investors' personal tax rate on bond income equals the corporate tax rate.

Shortly after 1977 several financial theorists attacked Miller's key assumptions and concluded:

$$\begin{array}{ccc}\text{Value of a} & \text{Value as an} & \text{Present value of} \\ \text{levered company} & = \ \text{unlevered company} & + \ \text{net tax effects}\end{array}$$

This result mirrors the 1963 conclusion and suggests again that corporate capital structures should contain extremely high levels of debt.[4] In contrast to the 1963 conclusion, however, the second term on the right-hand side of the equation includes the net effects of both personal and corporate taxes. Because the present value of net tax effects is smaller than the present value of corporate tax savings only, the theory implies less incentive for using debt than was suggested in the 1963 model.

Trade-Off Theory

trade-off theory
Applied to capital structure, description of the trade-off between the tax advantage of debt and bankruptcy costs; implies the existence of an optimal capital structure.

Many theorists since the late 1970s have become convinced that the threat of bankruptcy costs offsets the advantage of net tax effects at some point. As a company increases the debt in its capital structure, the likelihood becomes increasingly probable that bankruptcy costs will be drained from the company. According to the **trade-off theory,** the value of a levered company is:

$$\begin{array}{cccc}& \text{Value as an} & \text{Present value} & \text{Present value} \\ \text{Value of a} & \text{unlevered} & + \ \text{of net tax} & - \quad \text{of probable} \\ \text{levered company} & = \ \text{company} & \text{effects} & \text{bankruptcy costs}\end{array}$$

Bankruptcy costs include direct costs such as legal and accounting fees and the managerial time spent to administer the bankruptcy; also included are indirect costs such as lost sales, lost investment opportunities, and the inability to obtain credit except under onerous terms. According to this theory, financial managers face a trade-off between the tax advantage of debt and bankruptcy costs when making capital-structure decisions.

---

[4]For a contrary conclusion because of the effect of tax shields other than that created by interest expense see H. DeAngelo and R. Masulis, "Optimal Capital Structure Under Corporate and Personal Taxation," *Journal of Financial Economics*, March 1980: 5–29.

Figure 7.3 graphically summarizes the evolution of capital-structure theory since MM's rigorous analysis in 1958. Undoubtedly, more theoretical developments will unfold in the future. For now, the trade-off theory provides a plausible defense for the existence of an optimal capital structure. Note, however, that present theory is incapable of specifying exactly what debt-equity ratio supplies the optimal capital structure.

Pecking-Order Theory

pecking-order theory
Description of managerial preference for internal financing over external financing, because of flotation costs and asymmetric information.

An alternative to the preceding trade-off theory is called the **pecking-order theory**, which describes managerial preferences for types of financing.[5] According to this theory, financial managers prefer to finance assets with internal equity—retained earnings; if external financing is required, then they prefer to issue low-risk bonds first, proceeding to common stock last. One obvious reason for this pecking order is that internal financing, unlike external financing, involves no flotation costs. Furthermore, the flotation costs of bonds are less than the flotation costs of common stock. Managers who try to minimize flotation costs therefore tend to use retained earnings, bonds, and common stock, in that order.

Financial managers need to be concerned also about signals transmitted to the capital market. For example, the announcement of a stock issue sends a negative signal. Empirical studies show that when industrial companies announce a stock issue, their stock price falls, on average, 3 percent—which amounts to millions of dollars each for many companies. In contrast, the announcement of a low-risk bond issue has little or no effect on stock price. It is not surprising then, that financial managers put bonds ahead of stock in the pecking order.

asymmetric information
Imbalance of information on company prospects; corporate managers have better information than do investors.

One explanation for the drop in stock price on announcement of a stock issue involves **asymmetric information:** Corporate managers (insiders) have better information about their company's financial prospects than do investors (outsiders). Professional investors work hard to redress this imbalance of information but are likely to fall short. Knowing their disadvantage, they attempt to read signals based on corporate behavior. To illustrate, suppose a company's stock is overpriced, and the company's managers know it. Issuing stock in this circumstance helps the company's present shareholders but hurts the new ones. Just the opposite occurs when a company's stock is underpriced (when issuing stock hurts present shareholders and helps new ones). Based on this logic, investors greet the announcement of a stock issue as an admission by corporate managers that company prospects are less than favorable and that the stock is overpriced; investors then proceed to bid down the stock price. Exceptions to this scenario include: (1) public utility companies, whose capital structures follow the dictates of state and federal regulatory agencies, and (2) rapidly growing companies perceived by investors as needing external equity to support profitable investment opportunities.

The pecking-order theory implies that companies will use less debt than indicated by the trade-off theory illustrated in Figure 7.3. By doing so, they maintain borrowing capacity and can use debt to finance future investment opportunities that otherwise they might have had to forgo or finance with underpriced common stock. Another difference between the two theories concerns their implications for the behavior of profitable companies. According to the pecking-order theory, if a profitable company is able to finance its projects internally, then it

---

[5] Stewart Myers, "The Capital Structure Puzzle," *Journal of Finance*, July 1984: 575–592.

FIGURE 7.3

Effect of Financial Leverage on the Value of a Company

This figure highlights the evolution of capital-structure theory: (1) MM's 1958 model indicates that financial leverage has no effect on company value. (2) MM's 1963 model indicates that financial leverage increases company value because of the tax deductibility of interest payments. (3) Miller's 1977 model indicates that the corporate tax advantage of debt is exactly offset by its personal tax disadvantage, causing the debt-equity decision to be irrelevant. (4) Theorists later argue that investors' personal taxes only partially offset the corporate tax advantage of debt. (5) Later still, theorists argue that the present value of probable bankruptcy costs offsets the net tax advantage of debt at some point, which creates an optimal capital structure.

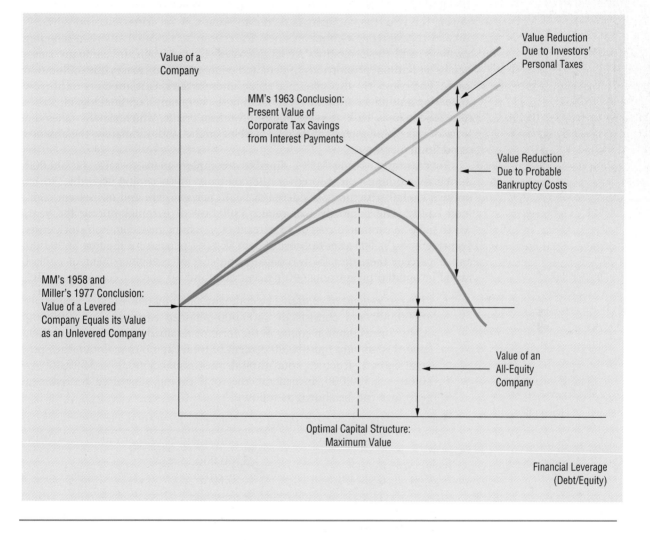

will not simply issue bonds to move toward the optimal capital structure that Figure 7.3 describes. On the other hand, an unprofitable company in the same industry may have a debt-equity ratio that exceeds the optimum because of its attempt to avoid issuing common stock.

As you may have gathered, much is known about the impact of capital structure on value and the cost of capital, but much remains unknown. Financial theory provides useful guidelines for financial practice, but the final decision on debt-equity levels rests on informed judgment.

MARGINAL COST OF CAPITAL

marginal cost of capital (MCC)

Cost of the final increment of capital raised in optimal proportions of debt and equity.

capital project

Capital expenditure, or capital investment; project usually involving depreciable assets that generate cash flows over several years.

The **marginal cost of capital** (MCC) is the percentage cost of the last dollar of capital raised by a company during a planning period. MCC is equal to or greater than the average cost of capital. If the last dollar raised during the planning period costs more than average, then MCC exceeds the average cost of capital; otherwise, the two costs are equal.

Consider a company that plans to raise capital during the coming year to finance **capital projects**—also called *capital investments* or *capital expenditures*. If the dollar size of the company's capital budget exhausts all earnings retained during the year, the company is forced to issue new securities. Because of flotation costs, issuing new common stock, for example, is more costly than retaining earnings, and the company's MCC increases. Even though the company raises capital in optimal proportions of debt and equity, MCC increases due to flotation costs. The company also may face rising interest rates as it attempts to borrow increasing amounts during the year. Despite the company's optimal capital structure, lenders may balk at some point and ration credit, which usually takes the form of increasing interest rates (the price of credit) and, ultimately, the absence of additional credit.

To illustrate a rising MCC, suppose a company plans to raise $2,300,000 during the coming year. Moreover, the company raises capital according to its optimal capital structure, considered to be 40 percent debt and 60 percent common equity. The company will retain $300,000 of earnings during the year, which have an estimated cost of 15 percent (K_c); issuing new common stock costs 16 percent (K_{nc}). The after-tax cost of debt (K_i) is 7 percent for the first $600,000 and 8 percent thereafter. Now, consider the cost of each increment of capital raised in optimal proportions, 40 percent debt and 60 percent common equity.

1. *First increment of capital.* The company's first increment of capital totals $500,000 and consists of $300,000 retained earnings and $200,000 debt. Since common equity in the form of retained earnings is $300,000, and this amount must be 60 percent of total capital to maintain the optimal capital structure, total capital must equal $500,000: $300,000 = 0.60 \times $500,000. In general, the total capital supported by retained earnings can be shown as follows:

$$\frac{\text{Total capital supported}}{\text{by retained earnings}} = \frac{\text{Retained earnings}}{\text{Optimal equity proportion}}$$

$$= \frac{\$300,000}{0.60}$$

$$= \$500,000$$

The company's cost for this increment of capital is the weighted average of the cost of debt ($K_i = 7\%$) and cost of retained earnings ($K_c = 15\%$):

$$K_a = W_i K_i + W_c K_c$$

$$= 0.40(0.07) + 0.60(0.15)$$

$$= 0.118, \text{ or } 11.8\%$$

Figure 7.4 shows the 11.8 percent cost of the first $500,000 increment of capital consisting of 60 percent equity ($W_c = 0.60$) and 40 percent debt ($W_i = 0.40$). The $300,000 retained earnings provide an equity

FIGURE 7.4

Illustration of a Marginal Cost of Capital Schedule

The marginal cost of capital schedule identifies the cost of capital for all dollar levels of financing. A company faces a rising MCC as it plans to raise increasing amounts of capital during the planning period. MCC first rises because equity cost increases due to flotation costs; then MCC rises because debt cost increases.

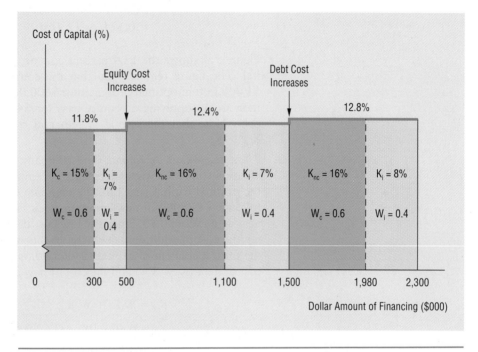

base for the $200,000 debt, and the total supplies the initial $500,000 increment of capital.

2. *Second increment of capital.* The company must raise additional capital because $500,000 falls short of its $2,300,000 goal. The second increment of capital totals $1,000,000 ($600,000 new common stock and $400,000 debt), bringing the total of the first two increments to $1,500,000. Here is the reasoning: (1) Only $600,000 of low-cost (7 percent) debt is available, and this amount must be 40 percent of total capital to maintain the optimal capital structure. (2) The $600,000 of low-cost debt is used up when total capital is $1,500,000: $600,000 = 0.40 × $1,500,000. (3) $1,500,000 less $500,000, the size of the first increment, equals $1,000,000, the size of the second increment. In general, the total capital supported by low-cost debt can be shown as follows:

$$\begin{aligned} \text{Total capital supported} \atop \text{by low-cost debt} &= \frac{\text{Amount of low-cost debt}}{\text{Optimal debt proportion}} \\ &= \frac{\$600,000}{0.40} \\ &= \$1,500,000 \end{aligned}$$

The company's cost for the $1,000,000 increment of capital is the weighted average of the cost of debt ($K_i = 7\%$) and the cost of new common stock ($K_{nc} = 16\%$):

$$K_a = W_iK_i + W_cK_{nc}$$
$$= 0.40(0.07) + 0.60(0.16)$$
$$= 0.124, \text{ or } 12.4\%$$

Figure 7.4 shows the 12.4 percent cost of the second increment of capital. The figure reminds you that the company raises the incremental $1,000,000 in optimal proportions: $600,000 ($W_c = 0.60$) of new common stock supplying an equity base for $400,000 ($W_i = 0.40$) of new debt. Note that the second incremental cost exceeds the first because $K_{nc} > K_c$.

3. *Third increment of capital.* The company needs to raise $800,000 in addition to the first two increments of capital ($1,500,000). To maintain the optimal capital structure the company must raise the $800,000 as follows: $480,000 of new common stock, $W_c = 0.60$; and $320,000 of new debt, $W_i = 0.40$. Since the low-cost debt (7 percent) has been used up, the cost of additional debt rises to 8 percent. The company's cost for the third increment of capital ($800,000) is the weighted average of the cost of debt ($K_i = 8\%$) and the cost of new common stock ($K_{nc} = 16\%$):

$$K_a = W_iK_i + W_cK_{nc}$$
$$= 0.40(0.08) + 0.60(0.16)$$
$$= 0.128, \text{ or } 12.8\%$$

Figure 7.4 shows the 12.8 percent cost of the third increment of capital. Note that the third incremental cost exceeds the second because of the rise in the cost of debt.

✶ Read from here to end

marginal cost of capital schedule

Line depicting the cost of capital for various increments of capital.

The stairstep line (Figure 7.4) depicting the cost of capital for various levels of financing is called the **marginal cost of capital schedule.** According to this schedule, the company's marginal cost of capital depends on the dollar amount of financing. In turn, the dollar amount of financing the company needs depends on the dollar cost of its planned capital projects. For example, if the company needs less than $500,000, MCC is 11.8 percent; between $500,000 and $1,500,000, MCC is 12.4 percent; and between $1,500,000 and $2,300,000, MCC is 12.8 percent.

capital budgeting

Evaluating and selecting capital investments for a planning period.

Financial managers use MCC in **capital budgeting**—the process of evaluating and selecting capital projects. For an average-risk project (risk characteristics similar to the company's) to be acceptable, its expected rate of return must exceed MCC. Otherwise, the project is unacceptable because investing in it would lower shareholder wealth. *If a company's cost of capital is independent of the amount of capital raised (MCC schedule in Figure 7.4 is a straight, horizontal line), then the average cost of capital may be used in the selection of average-risk projects.* The task of successfully selecting capital projects is essential for any company, and Part III of this book discusses what it entails.

ISSUES IN COST OF CAPITAL AND CAPITAL STRUCTURE

Like estimating value, estimating a company's average and marginal cost of capital is difficult to do well. Besides potential errors in estimation, problems may arise that make calculating cost of capital easier in theory than in practice. This section examines some of the gray areas placed by the realities of business practice on the theoretical model.

Market Weights vs. Book Weights

market weights
Proportions of long-term capital sources based on market values.

book weights
Proportions of long-term capital sources based on book values.

Either of two weights might be used to calculate average and marginal cost of capital: market or book. **Market weights** refer to the proportions of bonds, preferred stock, and common stock based on market values of a company's securities. **Book weights** refer to the proportions based on balance sheet (book) values. Market weights are superior to book weights because they reflect the way investors currently value the company's securities. Financial managers estimate the cost of *new* capital raised in the marketplace to invest in *new* capital projects; they do not estimate a historical cost of capital. Also, because they use market costs of individual capital sources, to be consistent they must use market values to weight the market costs. Because book values are accounting numbers based on historical cost, they often differ from market values, which reflect investors' evaluations of future cash flows discounted at required rates of return.

Long-Term vs. Short-Term View

The calculation of marginal cost of capital is based on the assumption that the company raises capital in a way that preserves the optimal capital structure. It may be impractical to do this because stock prices may be down when bond prices are up, or vice versa. Moreover, it takes time to register and issue stocks and bonds, and conditions may make one take longer than the other, causing the securities to be issued at different times. In the short term, then, companies may deviate from optimality. They frequently issue common stock one year and bonds the next, instead of issuing both in the same year. Alternating the issuance of securities causes the debt-equity ratio to wobble over time, presumably around the optimal ratio. If the debt-equity ratio becomes too large as a result of relying excessively on bond financing, then in the subsequent period the company will use equity financing and reduce its debt-equity ratio toward the target level. In this way short-term financial leverage continually moves away from and back toward its optimal level.

Short-Term vs. Long-Term Debt

As a rule, only long-term debt and equity are included in the calculation of average and marginal cost of capital. Only these sources are included because generally a company should use only long-term funds to finance long-term investment projects. As Chapter 11 explains, companies should not use short-term sources for this purpose. Some companies violate this financial rule, however, and use short-term debt as a permanent source of capital by refinancing (rolling over) each time the short-term debt becomes payable. If the amount of such short-term debt is significant, then the financial manager should consider including its cost in the calculation of cost of capital.

I N T E R N A T I O N A L   D I M E N S I O N S

Cost of Capital and the Multinational Company

Raising funds in more than one country potentially affects a company's cost of capital. For example, the supply of capital available to the company increases with the number of sources. Increased supply tends to lower the company's cost of capital.

In competitive, integrated capital markets, securities of comparable quality (expected return, risk, and maturity) carry identical prices. This *law of one price* results from *arbitrage*—the simultaneous purchase and sale of equivalent securities when more than trivial differences appear between their prices. Arbitrage causes uniformity in the cost of capital raised in integrated capital markets, but not in *segmented* capital markets.

Unlike the reasonably well-integrated capital markets of the United States and Canada, the capital markets of many pairs of countries are relatively segmented—for example, the United States and Spain. Technological, governmental, and/or informational barriers impede arbitrage across segmented markets and create the possibility of different prices for securities of like quality. Segmentation (not integration) creates opportunities for issuing securities in markets offering the highest price, thus lowering the company's cost of capital.

In addition to issuing debt and equity securities in foreign markets, multinational companies also invest in assets in foreign countries. These foreign investments carry risks not present in domestic investments. For example, foreign-exchange risk (uncertainty in the price of foreign currency) exacerbates the multinational company's riskiness. The value of cash flows generated abroad can fluctuate merely because of changes in exchange rates. In addition, political risk can hamper operations, limit repatriation of cash flows, and even culminate in seizure of assets. The increased risk due to uncertain exchange rates and political events increases a company's cost of capital.

Offsetting the disadvantage of added risks from investing abroad are special tax rules applicable to U.S. companies. One such rule allows U.S. multinational companies to defer taxes on foreign earnings until the repatriation date. The tax advantages and potential cash flows coupled with opportunities to lessen cost of capital provide strong incentives for U.S. companies to engage in international business.

Project-Specific Financing vs. Total Capital Budget

When financial managers evaluate investment projects, they normally assume that each project will be financed with debt-equity proportions equal to the company's optimal capital structure. This assumption is probably a good one for most company projects. For some projects, however, the financial manager may seek *project-specific financing*—debt and equity for specific projects. Some projects have higher debt capacities than others because they involve less business risk. **Debt capacity** is the optimal amount of debt a company should use to finance a project. Different capital projects (and lines of business) have different debt capacities and, as a result, have different optimal capital structures. Project-specific financing normally becomes an issue for large investment projects in lines of business differing from the usual.

debt capacity
Amount of debt with which a specific project optimally should be financed.

EBIT-EPS ANALYSIS

One widely used method for planning capital structures relies on an equation that expresses earnings per share (EPS) as a function of earnings before interest and taxes (EBIT) and capital structure:

$$EPS = f(EBIT \text{ and capital structure})$$

where f means "function of." This notation shows that a company's earnings per share depend on its earnings before interest and taxes and its chosen capital structure. High earnings before interest and taxes lead to high earnings per share; and capital structures that include debt can produce even higher earnings per share for a given level of earnings before interest and taxes.

EXAMPLE

The management of Coleman Company has completed its capital budget and discovers that $6,000,000 are needed to finance a proposed project. The company faces the following capital structure choices: (1) Coleman can net $30 a share from selling common stock, which would require issuing 200,000 shares. Coleman currently has 800,000 shares of common stock outstanding and no debt. (2) Coleman can borrow $6,000,000 through a bond issue at 10 percent per year. The financial manager wants to know the impact of each alternative financing source on earnings per share if earnings before interest and taxes reach $2,000,000 and $4,000,000.

Consider the way that each financing alternative in the above example affects earnings per share when earnings before interest and taxes are $2,000,000. Table 7.1 shows that Coleman earns $1.20 per share with common-stock financing. With bond financing Coleman earns only $1.05. At this earnings level, common stock appears to be the superior financing alternative. However, if Coleman is able to generate $4,000,000 in earnings before interest and taxes, then bond financing produces earnings per share of $2.55 in contrast to $2.40 from common-stock financing.

Under the common-stock plan, a doubling of earnings before interest and taxes from $2,000,000 to $4,000,000 causes earnings per share to double from $1.20 to $2.40. Under the bond plan, this same doubling causes earnings per share to *more than* double from $1.05 to $2.55, a 143 percent increase. If management could be relatively sure that earnings before interest and taxes would reach $4,000,000, then the bond issue appears the better financing choice.

What implication for risk do these financing alternatives contain? Debt increases a company's financial leverage and financial risk, and Table 7.1 shows that bond financing creates a greater range and uncertainty in earnings per share than does stock financing. *This greater range in earnings per share illustrates the financial risk that accompanies financial leverage.*[6]

Mathematically, the relationship between earnings per share (EPS) and earnings before interest and taxes (EBIT) is as follows:

$$EPS = \frac{(EBIT - I)(1 - T)}{N}$$

where I = dollar interest paid

   T = company's marginal tax rate

   N = number of common-stock shares outstanding

---

[6] Chapter 16 presents the way to measure a company's *degree* of financial leverage.

Earnings per Share of Coleman Company Common Stock: Two Financing Plans and Two EBIT Levels

	Financing Plans	
	Common Stock	**Corporate Bonds**
Assuming EBIT = $2,000,000		
Earnings before interest and taxes	$2,000,000	$2,000,000
Less interest expense	0	600,000
Earnings before taxes	$2,000,000	$1,400,000
Less income taxes (40%)	800,000	560,000
Earnings after taxes	$1,200,000	$ 840,000
Number of shares outstanding	1,000,000	800,000
Earnings per share	**$1.20**	**$1.05**
Assuming EBIT = $4,000,000		
Earnings before interest and taxes	$4,000,000	$4,000,000
Less interest expense	0	600,000
Earnings before taxes	$4,000,000	$3,400,000
Less income taxes (40%)	1,600,000	1,360,000
Earnings after taxes	$2,400,000	$2,040,000
Number of shares outstanding	1,000,000	800,000
Earnings per share	**$2.40**	**$2.55**

The expression (EBIT − I) represents earnings before taxes. Multiplying this expression by 1 − T yields earnings after taxes. Hence the equation shows that earnings per share of common stock equal a company's earnings after taxes divided by the number of common shares issued and outstanding.

To calculate the EBIT that causes earnings per share to be the same under *either* the new-stock *or* the bond-financing plan, begin with the equality:

$$\text{EPS}_{\text{stock financing}} = \text{EPS}_{\text{bond financing}}$$

With new-stock financing, the number of shares outstanding and the dollar interest paid (N_s and I_s) differ from those for bond financing (N_b and I_b). Equating earnings per share under the two financing plans yields the following:

indifference EBIT

EBIT that yields the same earnings per share whether management selects debt or common-stock financing.

$$\frac{(\text{EBIT}^* - I_s)(1 - T)}{N_s} = \frac{(\text{EBIT}^* - I_b)(1 - T)}{N_b}$$

EBIT* is the **indifference EBIT,** which causes equality between earnings per share under the two financing plans.

EXAMPLE

Coleman Company's earnings before interest and taxes that generate the same earnings per share under the two financing alternatives in Table 7.1 are $3,000,000:

TABLE 7.2

Indifference Earnings before Interest and Taxes for Coleman Company: Common-Stock vs. Bond Financing

	Financing Plans	
	Common Stock	**Corporate Bonds**
Earnings before interest and taxes[a]	$3,000,000	$3,000,000
Less interest expense	0	600,000
Earnings before taxes	$3,000,000	$2,400,000
Less income taxes (40%)	1,200,000	960,000
Earnings after taxes	$1,800,000	$1,440,000
Number of shares outstanding	1,000,000	800,000
Earnings per share	**$1.80**	**$1.80**

[a] $3,000,000 is the indifference EBIT because it produces the same earnings per share under either financing plan.

$$\frac{(EBIT^* - 0)(1 - 0.40)}{800,000 + 200,000} = \frac{(EBIT^* - \$600,000)(1 - 0.40)}{800,000}$$

$$EBIT^* = \$3,000,000$$

Table 7.2 verifies that under either financing plan the $3,000,000 earnings before interest and taxes yield the same earnings per share: $1.80.

Figure 7.5 is a graph of the EBIT-EPS analysis of the financing alternatives facing Coleman Company. The horizontal axis represents earnings before interest and taxes, and the vertical axis represents earnings per share. Below the indifference EBIT ($3,000,000), the common-stock line, indicating higher EPS, dominates the bond line. Above the indifference EBIT, a reversal occurs and the bond line dominates the common-stock line. If management expects EBIT to exceed $3,000,000, then bond financing *appears* to be a better choice; below $3,000,000, common-stock financing *appears* to be a better choice.

EBIT-EPS analysis emphasizes the impact of alternative financing plans on the company's earnings per share. Maximizing earnings per share, however, leads to maximizing stock price *only* if the change in the company's price-earnings (P-E) ratio does not cancel out the change in earnings per share. If the P-E ratio differs under the alternative financing plans because of risk, then the effect of the ratio should be included in the analysis.

EXAMPLE

Suppose the management of Coleman Company believes that the company can generate $4,000,000 in earnings before interest and taxes, well above the indifference EBIT of $3,000,000. Table 7.1 shows that earnings per share would equal $2.40 with common-stock financing and $2.55 with bond financing. Further sup-

FIGURE 7.5   **EBIT-EPS Graph Showing the Indifference EBIT**

When earnings before interest and taxes are below $3,000,000, the common-stock alternative dominates the bond alternative by producing larger earnings per share. For EBITs above $3,000,000 the reverse holds, and bond financing produces larger earnings per share.

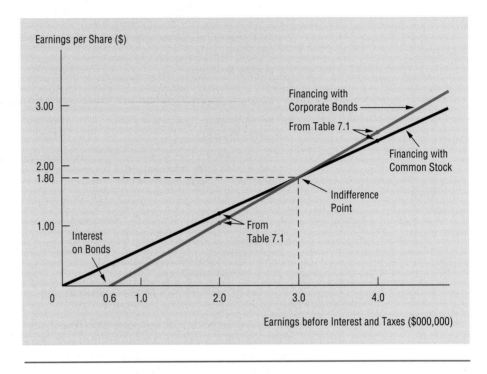

pose that the stock market places on Coleman's earnings per share a P-E ratio of 12 if it finances the project with an issue of common stock, but drops the P-E to 10 if it finances the project with bonds, because of the increased risk. The price per share of stock under the alternative plans would be:

Stock plan: $P_0 = (\text{P-E})\text{EPS} = 12 \times \$2.40 = \$28.80$

Bond plan: $P_0 = (\text{P-E})\text{EPS} = 10 \times \$2.55 = \$25.50$

Under these conditions Coleman Company should issue common stock instead of bonds to raise capital even though doing so results in lower earnings per share. Stock price is greater under the stock plan, and stock price matters more to shareholders than do earnings per share.

EBIT-EPS analysis provides insight into the way a company should finance a specific project. To use the analysis effectively, however, requires a financial manager to extend it to include expected changes in stock price. Because expectations usually contain errors, financial managers should consider these four criteria before selecting a financing alternative:

1. *Cost.* Assess the component cost of each source of long-term financing and be wary of relying exclusively on one source and the resulting

impact on the company's P-E ratio and stock price. New common stock costs the most, followed by retained earnings. Cost of preferred stock is next, with debt having the lowest explicit cost. Tax deductibility of interest, a powerful influence in reducing the explicit cost of debt, creates a strong attraction to debt financing.

2. *Risk.* From the company's viewpoint, the risk of securities stems from the legal obligations they create. Borrowing money creates the greatest risk because interest and principal payments represent legal, contractual obligations. If a company defaults on these obligations, creditors may take legal action that can cause bankruptcy. Preferred stock creates less risk than do bonds because dividends may be omitted without fear of legal action. With **cumulative preferred stock,** however, the company must eventually pay omitted dividends or it cannot pay dividends to common shareholders. Common stock represents ownership in the company and creates the least risk.

3. *Control.* Each share of common stock usually gives its owner the right to one vote in the election of company directors and in other company matters. Thus when a company issues new common stock, it gives away votes. Unless the present shareholders purchase some of the new stock, they may incur **dilution of control.** Preferred stockholders normally cannot vote on company matters except in special circumstances. For example, the preferred stockholders of General Motors Corporation can vote for one-fourth of the company's directors if the company remains in arrears six months or more in paying preferred dividends. Bondholders and other creditors have no vote in company affairs. Nevertheless, creditors may get control of the company if the company does not meet its legal obligations.

4. *Maneuverability.* Today's financing decisions may influence how a company finances itself in the future. **Financial maneuverability** is the ability of a company manager to maneuver, or move at will, between debt and equity financing. Maneuverability in sequential financing decisions comes about by making choices today that keep future financing options open. Loss of maneuverability results from heavy debt financing over a period of time, which greatly restricts a company's future borrowing power. Managers of highly levered companies may well discover that creditors have effectively shut off their access to the debt market. Even though the company's stock price appears severely depressed, management may have no other option but to issue common stock. In contrast, a company with a solid equity base has the option of borrowing, issuing preferred stock, or issuing common stock.

cumulative preferred stock
Preferred stock on which a company must pay dividends in arrears before it can pay a dividend on its common stock.

dilution of control
Loss of a shareholder's relative voting power as a result of the company's issuance of new shares.

financial maneuverability
Ability of a company to shift between debt and equity sources.

SUMMARY

- The average cost of capital is calculated as follows:

$$K_a = W_i K_i + W_p K_p + W_c K_c$$

where K_i, K_p, and K_c are the costs of debt, preferred stock, and common equity, respectively. Each cost is weighted by the proportion (W) of total capital measured in the market values of each capital source.

Theories That Have an Impact on Your Monthly Utility Bill

Financial experts use the theories and principles discussed in Part II of this book to help public utility commissions set your monthly utility bill. Utility companies charge prices for energy that will allow them to pay both operating expenses and capital costs. Because utility companies must make large investments in plant and equipment, they must raise substantial amounts of capital in the marketplace. Capital costs are thus a major portion of your utility bill. The following exchange between a utility commission attorney and an expert witness illustrates the analysis of cost of capital in practice.

Attorney: What is the basic objective of your testimony?
Witness: To determine an independent estimate of the cost of equity capital and an average cost of capital for South Carolina Electric and Gas Company (SCE&G).
Attorney: Please summarize the possible required rates of return

on SCE&G common stock as produced by application of the capital asset pricing model.
Witness: Using the model $K_c = R_f + (K_m - R_f)\beta$ and the best estimates of R_f, K_m, and β, the best estimate of required rate of return on SCE&G common stock is:

$$12.36\% = 6.71\% + (11.5\% - 6.71\%)1.18$$

Although 12.36 percent is the best CAPM estimate, scientific objectivity and rigor require recognition of potential errors in measurement of beta. Adding and subtracting one standard deviation from the best estimate of beta provide the upper and lower reasonable bounds on beta and the required rate of return:

$$13.00\% = 6.71\% + (11.5\% - 6.71\%)1.313$$

$$11.73\% = 6.71\% + (11.5\% - 6.71\%)1.047$$

Attorney: What is the formulation

for the cost of equity capital using the discounted cash flow [constant-growth] method?
Witness: The cost of equity capital (K_c) is given by:

$$K_c = \frac{D_1}{P_0} + g$$

D_1 is the expected dividend next period, P_0 is the current stock price, and g is the expected growth rate in dividends.
Attorney: What estimate of the cost of equity does the discounted cash flow [constant-growth] procedure provide?
Witness: The estimated range is from 11.16 to 12.36 percent, with a most likely estimate of 11.76 percent.

	K_c		D_1/P_0		g
Upper limit	12.36%	=	8.16%	+	4.2%
Most likely	11.76%	=	8.16%	+	3.6%
Lower limit	11.16%	=	8.16%	+	3.0%

Attorney: Is there a difference between the cost of internally

---

• The optimal capital structure (mix of capital sources) minimizes the average cost of capital and maximizes price per share of common stock. In practice, companies may deviate in the short run from the optimal capital structure and oscillate around optimality in the long run.

• As a company introduces debt into its capital structure, the average cost of capital declines because of the low explicit cost of debt. Explicit cost of debt is relatively low because creditors have senior claims and because of the tax deductibility of interest. As financial leverage from debt usage advances to a critical level, the accompanying default and financial risks offset the debt advantage. Lenders of funds and buyers of common stock require higher rates of return, causing the average cost of capital to rise.

• The theory of capital structure has a rich and varied history. Professors Modigliani and Miller (MM) in 1958 provided a rigorous foundation for the theory. Much of the subsequent development of the theory uses MM's original

and externally generated equity capital?

Witness: The cost of equity capital previously estimated using the discounted cash flow procedure is the cost of internally generated equity. External equity from a new stock issue will exceed the internal cost because of flotation cost. For the portion of funds raised externally, the discounted cash flow (DCF) model must be adjusted as follows:

$$K_{nc} = \frac{D_1}{P_0(1 - F)} + g$$

where F is the percentage flotation cost. This is the same as dividing the expected dividend one year hence by proceeds rather than by price. Mathematically, we obtain the same result if we divide the expected dividend yield D_1/P_0 by $(1 - F)$:

$$K_{nc} = \left(\frac{D_1/P_0}{1 - F}\right) + g$$

Attorney: Based on the CAPM and DCF methods, what is your best estimate of the cost of equity capital for SCE&G?

Witness: Considering the amounts of internal and external equity, the best estimates from these two procedures provide a most likely estimate between 12.00 and 12.60 percent.

Attorney: What is your estimate of the overall, or weighted-average, cost of capital?

Witness: The best estimate of the overall cost of capital is between 9.01 percent and 9.20 percent based on the weights and costs shown in the table.

The weighted-average cost of capital that public utility commissions accept as the best estimate becomes a part of the total costs that the commissions use to set rates. A higher average cost of capital means higher total costs and therefore the higher monthly rates that all of us must pay. No wonder, then, that expert witnesses and public utility commissions place so much emphasis on the theories and principles examined in Part II.

Type of Capital	Percentage Cost	Percentage of Total Capitalization	Weighted Percentage Cost
Debt	7.60%	55.70%	4.23%
Preferred stock	7.91	13.01	1.03
Common equity	12.00–12.60	31.29	3.75–3.94
		Weighted-average cost of capital: K_a =	9.01–9.20%

Source: Adapted from Robert Glenn Rhyne, South Carolina Electric and Gas Company, Docket No. 75-645-E.

work as a starting point. According to the trade-off theory, the value of a levered company is as follows:

$$\text{Value of a levered company} = \text{Value as an unlevered company} + \text{Present value of net tax effects} - \text{Present value of probable bankruptcy costs}$$

Increasing debt levels increase the present value of net tax effects, but at some point the present value of probable bankruptcy costs offsets the tax advantage of debt—hence the trade-off. The pecking-order theory asserts the following managerial preference ranking of financing sources: retained earnings, bonds, and common stock. Flotation costs favor retained earnings over external financing, as does investor interpretation of signals due to asymmetric information. According to the pecking-order theory, companies use less debt than implied by the trade-off theory in order to maintain financial maneuverability. Despite many years of study by financial theorists and despite their many findings, key aspects of capital structure remain a puzzle.

- When companies use up retained earnings, they issue common stock, which causes an increase in the cost of capital. At some point the cost of debt may increase, causing another increase in the cost of capital. The cost of the final increment of capital raised in optimal proportions of debt and equity is the marginal cost of capital. The financial manager uses marginal cost of capital to determine in which projects a company should invest.

- EBIT-EPS analysis assists management in selecting financing alternatives for projects. For given levels of earnings before interest and taxes (EBIT), the analysis shows which alternative produces the highest earnings per share (EPS). The indifference EBIT occurs where earnings per share are the same regardless of the financing alternative used. EBIT-EPS analysis implies that management should (1) issue new common stock if expected EBIT *falls below* the indifference point, and (2) use debt if expected EBIT *exceeds* the indifference point. In practice, management must also consider the impact of financing alternatives on the company's price-earnings (P-E) ratio. Using debt increases the company's financial risk and may lower the P-E ratio, causing a decline in stock price per share even though earnings per share rise.

- Alternative sources of financing carry with them different implications for company cost, risk, control, and maneuverability. Management should evaluate each of these criteria when considering alternative plans for financing projects.

Key Terms

average cost of capital	trade-off theory	book weights
explicit cost	pecking-order theory	debt capacity
implicit cost	asymmetric information	indifference EBIT
financial leverage	marginal cost of capital (MCC)	cumulative preferred stock
debt-equity ratio	capital project	dilution of control
financial risk	marginal cost of capital schedule	financial maneuverability
business risk	capital budgeting	
optimal capital structure	market weights	

Questions

7.1. How does the explicit cost of debt differ from its implicit cost?

7.2. "Look, our cost of debt is less than our cost of equity," exclaims the new employee. "We should never issue common stock—it's too expensive," he goes on. "I don't know, but maybe you're right," responds the listener. Do you agree with the new employee? Explain your answer.

7.3. A company's cost of capital can increase for these two reasons: (1) increasing the amount of financial leverage above the optimal level and (2) expanding more rapidly than internal equity can support. Referring to Figures 7.2 and 7.4, elaborate on each of these reasons.

7.4. Identify and explain the expected impact of each of the following on a company's average cost of capital:
   a. The risk-free rate increases.
   b. Business risk declines.
   c. Management increases the debt-equity ratio from zero to 0.10.
   d. Management increases the debt-equity ratio from 1.0 to 4.0.

7.5. What is meant by the term *optimal capital structure*? What real-world factors cause an optimal capital structure to exist?

7.6. What signals can management read to assess

whether or not a company operates near its optimal capital structure?

7.7. Modigliani and Miller's 1958 model implies that capital structure is irrelevant, but their 1963 model implies that it is *relevant*. What causes the change from irrelevance to relevance? Explain.

7.8. Describe the trade-off theory of capital structure. Include in your description the roles played by tax-deductible interest and bankruptcy costs.

7.9. Describe the pecking-order theory of capital structure. Include in your description the roles played by flotation costs and asymmetric information.

7.10. In what sense is the marginal cost of capital a weighted average?

7.11. The maximum-size capital budget a company can finance with retained earnings is $300,000, and the company's debt-equity ratio is 0.30.
   a. If the budget is $299,999, then how does management calculate the marginal cost of capital?
   b. If the budget is $300,001, then how does management calculate the marginal cost of capital?

7.12. The chapter discusses two weighting systems to calculate K_a: market and book weights. Explain how the financial manager uses each of these weighting systems, and point out which one is conceptually preferable and why.

7.13. The chapter discussion points out that a company's new capital consists of blocks composed of debt, preferred stock, and common equity. Experience shows, however, that many companies use various sources of capital at different times, using only retained earnings in one period, for example, and in a subsequent period using long-term debt and no equity. Explain how the concept and calculation of marginal cost of capital in this chapter are compatible with what is observed in the real world.

7.14. One method of evaluating alternative plans for financing is EBIT-EPS analysis.
   a. Explain how management uses EBIT-EPS analysis. What is meant by the *indifference EBIT*?

b. Discuss the primary reason that EBIT-EPS analysis may be misleading.

7.15. Joe Sleipko calculates his company's indifference EBIT and obtains the following:

Source	Number of Shares Outstanding	EBIT	EPS
Debt	400,000	$1,260,000	$4.60
Equity	600,000	1,260,000	4.60

He is somewhat confused by this information because he has never studied finance.
   a. Explain why the number of shares outstanding differs with each financing alternative.
   b. What does the relationship between the column labeled EBIT and that labeled EPS indicate?
   c. Mr. Sleipko checks with the corporate forecasters and is told that expected earnings before interest and taxes are $1,600,000. Which financial source should the company use? Explain your choice.
   d. Sketch a figure relating the indifference EBIT to earnings per share. Be sure to label each axis and both lines and to note the source of financing to be used according to the relationship between the expected and indifference EBITs.

7.16. Answer the following questions regarding a company issuing bonds, preferred stock, and common stock. Take the *company's* viewpoint.
   a. Which type of security creates the most risk? Least risk? Why?
   b. Which type of security gives up the most control? Next most? Why?
   c. Which type of security provides the most flexibility in future financing? Why?
   d. Which type of security costs the least (explicitly)? State two reasons why.

Strategy Problem

Susong Enterprises, a U.S. manufacturer of digital tape, is about to invest in several capital projects in order to remain competitive with Japanese imports. The company will obtain financing for the proposed projects from a combination of bonds, preferred stock, common stock, and retained earnings in proportions conforming to the company's current optimal capital structure. The company's financial manager has analyzed conditions in the capital market and has developed the following information:

Source of Funds	Par Value	Interest or Dividend Rate	Proceeds per Security
Bonds (15-year maturity)	$1,000	8%	$845.92
Preferred stock	100	9	76.10
Common stock	1		80.00

The market and book values of Susong's outstanding debt and equity are as follows:

	Book Value	**Market Value**
Bonds	$ 720,000	$ 686,000
Preferred stock	210,000	186,000
Common equity:		
Common stock		
(50,000 shares at		
$1 par value)	$ 50,000	
Paid-in capital	1,020,000	
Retained earnings	2,400,000	
Total common equity	3,470,000	4,200,000
Total	$4,400,000	$5,072,000

Susong's common stock presently trades at $84 per share. Stock price and dividends have been growing at an average annual rate of 12 percent and are expected to continue growing at this rate through the foreseeable future. The most recent annual dividend was $3.00 per share.

The financial manager expects the company to have $590,000 available from earnings retention. The company's marginal tax rate is 34 percent.

a. Calculate Susong's component costs of bonds, preferred stock, retained earnings, and new common stock.

b. What is the maximum capital expenditure that Susong can make based on the expected earnings retention and the company's present capital structure?

c. Calculate Susong's marginal cost of capital assuming it invests (1) $712,559 and (2) $712,561 in the proposed projects.

d. Susong's financial manager is considering investing $169,184 in a project using the proceeds from either an issue of bonds or new common stock. The company's annual interest expense is presently $64,800. Calculate the indifference EBIT of Susong Enterprises for the alternative financing plans.

Strategy

Sketch a time line.

Solve for K_d by finding the yield to maturity based on proceeds.

Adjust the yield to reflect the company's marginal tax rate.

Use the perpetuity equation and proceeds.

Use the constant-growth model.

Use the constant-growth model and proceeds.

Solution

a. Component costs of capital:

Cost of bonds:

End of 6-month period	0	1	2	3	...	29	30
Cash Flow	$845.92	$40	$40	$40	...	$40	$1,000 $ 40 $1,040

$$\$845.92 = \sum_{t=1}^{30} \frac{\$80/2}{(1 + K_d/2)^t} + \frac{\$1,000}{(1 + K_d/2)^{30}}$$

$$K_d = 0.05 \times 2 = 0.100, \text{ or } 10.0\%$$

$$K_i = K_d(1 - T) = 0.100(1 - 0.34) = 0.066, \text{ or } 6.6\%$$

Cost of preferred stock:

$$K_p = \frac{D_p}{P_{net}} = \frac{\$9.00}{\$76.10} = 0.118, \text{ or } 11.8\%$$

Cost of retained earnings:

$$K_c = \frac{D_1}{P_0} + g = \frac{\$3.00(1 + 0.12)}{\$84} + 0.12$$

$$= 0.040 + 0.12 = 0.16, \text{ or } 16.0\%$$

Cost of new common stock:

$$K_{nc} = \frac{D_1}{P_{net}} + g = \frac{\$3.00(1 + 0.12)}{\$80} + 0.12$$

$$= 0.042 + 0.12 = 0.162, \text{ or } 16.2\%$$

Find the proportion of equity using market values and solve for the budget size.

b. Maximum size of the capital budget determined by earnings retention:

$$\text{Equity as a percent of total capital} = \frac{\$4,200,000}{\$5,072,000} = 0.828, \text{ or } 82.8\%$$

$$\text{Equity (\%)} \times \text{Budget size} = \text{Retained earnings}$$
$$0.828 \times \text{Budget size} = \$590,000$$
$$\text{Budget size} = \$712,560$$

c. Marginal cost of capital:

(1) *Invest $712,559:*

Use market weights and costs.

$$K_a = \frac{\$686,000}{\$5,072,000}(0.066) + \frac{\$186,000}{\$5,072,000}(0.118) + \frac{\$4,200,000}{\$5,072,000}(0.160)$$
$$= 0.146, \text{ or } 14.6\%$$

(2) *Invest $712,561:*

Note the only difference: use of the cost of new common stock.

$$K_a = \frac{\$686,000}{\$5,072,000}(0.066) + \frac{\$186,000}{\$5,072,000}(0.118) + \frac{\$4,200,000}{\$5,072,000}(0.162)$$
$$= 0.147, \text{ or } 14.7\%$$

Begin by calculating the number of new shares and the interest on the new bonds.

d.

$$\frac{\text{Number of new shares}}{\text{with stock financing}} = \frac{\$169,184}{\$80} = 2,115$$

$$\frac{\text{Number of bonds issued}}{\text{with debt financing}} = \frac{\$169,184}{\$845.92} = 200$$

$$\frac{\text{Interest paid}}{\text{on new bonds}} = 200 \text{ bonds} \times \$80 = \$16,000 \text{ annually}$$

Solve the EPS equations for the indifference EBIT.

$$EPS_{stock} = EPS_{bonds}$$

$$\frac{(EBIT^* - \$64,800)(1 - 0.34)}{50,000 + 2,115} = \frac{(EBIT^* - \$80,800)(1 - 0.34)}{50,000}$$

$$EBIT^* = \$459,051$$

	Common Stock	Bonds
EBIT	$459,051	$459,051
Less interest	64,800	80,800
Earnings before taxes	$394,251	$378,251
Less taxes (34%)	134,045	128,605
Earnings after taxes	$260,206	$249,646
	EPS = $260,206/52,115	EPS = $249,646/50,000
	= $4.99	= $4.99

A good habit: Check your solution to make sure you get the same EPS with each alternative.

Susong's indifference EBIT including present operations and the proposed project is $459,051. If expected EBIT is greater than $459,051, then bond financing will produce a larger EPS than stock financing. If expected EBIT is less than $459,051, then stock financing will produce a larger EPS than bond financing.

◆ ## Demonstration Problem

American Medical Enterprises (AME) owns and operates a chain of 11 for-profit hospitals with a total of 1,550 beds. AME's capital structure based on book values and market values is as follows:

Sources of Capital	Book Value	Market Value
Bonds (9% coupon rate)	$ 61,000,000	$53,980,000
Common stock ($2 par value)	20,000,000	
Retained earnings	154,500,000	
Total common equity	$174,500,000	$215,920,000
Total claims	$235,500,000	$269,900,000

The yield to maturity on AME's bonds equals 10 percent, and AME is subject to a 40 percent income tax rate. The company's financial analysts expect AME to retain $10,000,000 of its earnings during the coming year. In addition, they estimate the cost of retained earnings (K_c) to be 15 percent and the cost of issuing new common stock (K_{nc}) to be 16 percent.

a. Calculate the book weights and market weights of AME's debt and equity capital. Explain why you should use market weights in the calculation of average cost of capital.

b. Based on market weights, what is AME's average cost of capital (K_a)? (*Hint:* Use K_c in your calculation.)

c. Based on market weights and the expected retention of $10,000,000, what is the maximum level of capital expenditures before the company must issue new common stock? Calculate the company's marginal cost of capital, assuming that it must issue new common stock.

d. Draw a graph of AME's marginal cost of capital schedule. Put *cost of capital* on the vertical axis and *dollar amount of financing* on the horizontal axis. (*Hint:* See Figure 7.4 for help.) For what purpose do financial managers use a company's marginal cost of capital?

e. AME has a relatively small amount of debt in its capital structure. Suppose that management plans to alter the capital structure by issuing bonds and using the proceeds to buy shares of AME's stock in the secondary market. Based on consultations with an investment banker, management expects the cost of debt (K_i) and the cost of equity (K_c) to rise with increasing debt levels as follows:

Market Weight of Debt	After-Tax Cost of Debt (K_i)	Cost of Equity (K_c)
0.00	—	14.0%
0.10	6.0%	14.2
0.20	6.0	15.0
0.30	6.5	15.5
0.40	7.0	16.0
0.50	8.0	17.4
0.60	9.5	19.5

Calculate the average cost of capital (K_a) for each debt level and determine the optimal capital structure. Should AME's shareholders be concerned about the company's current market weight of debt being only 20 percent? Explain.

f. Financial theorists have developed the trade-off theory and the pecking-order theory of capital structure. Describe each theory.

g. AME currently pays $5,490,000 annual interest, and it has 10,000,000 shares of common stock outstanding. AME management is considering investing $20,000,000 in a new hospital that can be financed in one of two ways: (1) issue 1,000,000 shares of new common stock, with proceeds per share of $20 to the company or (2) borrow $20,000,000 from a life insurance company, paying an annual interest rate of 10 percent. Calculate the indifference EBIT (earnings before interest and taxes) for the two financing plans. Check your answer by calculating the earnings per share under each plan at the indifference EBIT.

h. Management expects AME's EBIT to be $50,000,000 after investing in the new hospital described in Part *g*. Based on EBIT-EPS analysis and your analysis of optimal capital structure in Part *e*, which financing alternative would you select? What impact would your choice have on AME's financial risk? Financial maneuverability? Explain.

Problems

Average cost of capital

7.1. Orex Corporation has the following capital structure and component costs of capital:

Component of Capital	Market Value	Market Weight	After-Tax Cost
Long-term debt	$ 2,000,000	0.20	8%
Preferred stock	3,000,000	0.30	13
Common equity	5,000,000	0.50	17
Total	$10,000,000	1.00	

a. Calculate Orex Corporation's average cost of capital.
b. Define the terms *market weights* and *book weights* in the calculation of average cost of capital.
c. Why are market weights superior to book weights in the calculation of average cost of capital?

Average cost of capital

7.2. Elissa Maness is attempting to calculate the average cost of capital for her company, Arkansas Crafts. Based on consultations with an investment banker, she believes the company's optimal capital structure and component costs of capital are as follows:

Component of Capital	Market Value	Market Weight	After-Tax Cost
Bonds	$17,170,000	0.20	0.075
Preferred stock	21,462,500	0.25	0.100
Common equity	47,217,500	0.55	0.165
Total	$85,850,000	1.00	

a. Calculate the average cost of capital for Arkansas Crafts.
b. Define the term *optimal capital structure*, noting its impact on the company's average cost of capital and market value.

Optimal capital structure

7.3. Stonewood Enterprises has only debt and common equity in its capital structure. The company faces the following schedules for the cost of debt and common equity:

Debt Proportion of Capital Structure	After-Tax Cost of Debt	Cost of Equity
0.00	—	14.0%
0.10	6.0%	14.0
0.30	6.1	14.2
0.50	7.5	14.9
0.60	8.5	16.0
0.70	9.7	17.3
0.80	11.5	18.5

a. Calculate the debt-equity ratios for debt proportions 0.10, 0.50, and 0.80. (*Note:* The debt proportion plus the equity proportion equals 1.00.)

b. Determine Stonewood's optimal capital structure.

c. If Stonewood's management is excessively conservative and selects the debt proportion of 0.10, why should the stockholders care?

d. Sketch a figure for Stonewood similar to Figure 7.2A.

Marginal cost of capital and size of capital budget

7.4. Western Industries expects to have $300,000 in after-tax earnings by the end of this year. Von Mundy, the financial manager, estimates the cost of internal equity to be 18 percent and that of external equity to be 20 percent. The cost of preferred stock is 16 percent, and the after-tax cost of debt is 12 percent. Debt, preferred stock, and equity are used in equal proportions.

a. What is the maximum size of the capital budget before the company must sell new common stock? Assume that Western pays no dividend.

b. Calculate the cost of capital for Western assuming it plans to raise $900,000.

c. What happens to Western's cost of capital if the company raises more than $900,000? Explain your answer.

Costs of retained earnings and new common stock, marginal cost of capital, and size of the capital budget

7.5. James Thompson, vice president of finance at Walker Company, is preparing for the company's annual capital investments meeting. The purpose of the meeting is to determine which projects the company should invest in and the amounts of the financial commitments for the coming year. Mr. Thompson must present an investment analysis for each of the potential projects. In order to prepare a complete analysis of each project, Mr. Thompson must calculate the company's marginal cost of capital.

Walker's board of directors has indicated that the company's present capital structure should be maintained: 70 percent common equity and 30 percent long-term debt. The company's projected earnings accompanied by periodic common-stock sales will permit it to maintain the present 70 percent owners' equity structure.

After consulting with the company's investment banker, Mr. Thompson determines that bonds could be sold to yield 8 percent and new common stock could be sold to provide net proceeds of $50 per share to the company. The common stock currently trades at $52 in the market. The company currently pays a dividend of $4 per share, and the dividends are expected to grow at an annual rate of 7 percent. The company's effective income tax rate is 40 percent.

a. Calculate Walker's cost of retained earnings and cost of new common stock.

b. Calculate Walker's marginal cost of capital assuming that new common stock need not be issued.

c. If Mr. Thompson expects retained earnings to equal $700,000, how large can the capital budget be before Walker must issue new common stock?

d. Calculate Walker's marginal cost of capital for capital budget levels exceeding your answer to Part *c*.

Marginal cost of capital schedule

7.6. J. T. Zietlow Company plans to raise $20,000,000 during the next 12 months. The company plans to raise capital according to its optimal capital structure, considered to be 60 percent debt and 40 percent common equity. The company will retain $2,000,000 of its earnings during the year, which have an estimated cost of 16 percent (K_c); issuing new common stock costs 17 percent (K_{nc}). The after-tax cost of debt (K_i) is 8 percent for the first $6,000,000 and 9 percent thereafter.

a. Calculate the total capital supported by retained earnings; then calculate the total capital supported by low-cost debt (8 percent). (*Hint:* These levels of total capital are the break points in the company's marginal cost of capital schedule.)

b. Calculate the company's average cost of capital for the following combinations of capital components: (1) retained earnings and low-cost debt; (2) new common stock and low-cost debt; (3) new common stock and high-cost debt (9 percent).

c. Draw a graph depicting the company's marginal cost of capital schedule. (*Hint:* See Figure 7.4.)

Marginal cost of capital schedule

7.7. Lease Corporation (LC) manufactures fan blades and supplies them to automobile manufacturers. LC plans to expand internationally, which will require an investment of $50,000,000. Funds for the expansion project will consist of 45 percent debt and 55 percent common equity. LC will retain $5,500,000 of its earnings during the coming year. According to LC's investment banker, the company's component costs of capital are as follows:

• Cost of retained earnings, 14 percent.

• Cost of new common stock, 15 percent.

• After-tax cost of debt, 7 percent for the first $9,000,000; 8 percent on amounts above $9,000,000.

Draw a graph of Lease Corporation's marginal cost of capital schedule. (*Hint:* See Figure 7.4.)

Costs of retained earnings and bonds, marginal cost of capital, and size of capital budget

7.8. The FAX Corporation is preparing to evaluate the company's capital expenditure proposals for next year. To start the evaluation, management must estimate marginal cost of capital for the company. FAX Corporation's financial vice president provides the following information:

• The market price of common stock is $50 per share.

• The dividend expected at the end of the year is $4.

• Expected growth in dividends is a constant 10 percent annually.

• The current capital structure of 40 percent long-term debt and 60 percent common equity is considered optimal.

• New bonds can be issued at face value with a 13 percent before-tax cost to the company.

• Anticipated earnings to be retained in the coming year are $3 million.

• The company has a 40 percent marginal tax rate.

a. Calculate the after-tax cost of the new bond issue.
b. Calculate the cost of retained earnings.
c. Calculate the cost of new common stock. (Flotation costs are 10 percent of stock price.)
d. If FAX Corporation plans a $7 million capital budget, what percentage is its marginal cost of capital?

CMA examination, modified: costs of capital sources, marginal cost of capital, and size of capital budget

7.9. Timel Company is in the process of determining its capital budget for the next fiscal year. Timel's balance sheet reflects five sources of long-term financial capital. The current outstanding amounts from these five sources are shown below:

Source	Amount (000,000)	Percent
Mortgage bonds ($1,000 par, $7\frac{1}{2}$%, due 19X7)	$135	15.0%
Debenture bonds ($1,000 par, 8%, due 19X5)	225	25.0
Preferred stock ($100 par, 900,000 shares, $7\frac{1}{2}$%)	90	10.0
Common stock ($10 par, 15,000,000 shares)	150	16.7
Retained earnings	300	33.3
	$900	100.0%

Timel will raise the long-term capital necessary to support the selected capital investment projects in proportion to its historical distribution of capital sources. Thus 15 percent will be obtained from additional mortgage bonds on new plant, 25 percent from debenture (unsecured) bonds, 10 percent from preferred stock, and 50 percent from common-equity sources. Timel's policy is to reinvest a portion of each year's earnings in new projects, and it issues new common stock only after exhausting all financing from retained earnings.

The dividend payout ratio will be 40 percent of earnings available to common shareholders; management expects these earnings to be $6.00 per share. Preferred stockholders will receive $6,750,000 ($7.50 per share). Management will use the earnings retained as needed to support the capital investment program.

The capital-budgeting staff, in conjunction with Timel's investment adviser, has developed the following data regarding Timel's sources of long-term financing and their costs in the current market:

Source of Funds	Par Value	Interest or Dividend Rate	Proceeds per Security
Mortgage bonds	$1,000	10%	$1,000.00
Debenture bonds	1,000	$12\frac{1}{2}$	1,000.00
Preferred stock	100	$13\frac{1}{2}$	98.00
Common stock	10		56.00

The financial adviser believes that Timel's P-E ratio of 10 is consistent with a 10 percent growth rate in dividends expected by the market. Timel is subject to a 40 percent income tax rate.

a. Calculate the after-tax cost of each of the five sources of capital for Timel.

b. Calculate Timel's marginal cost of capital assuming no new common stock needs to be sold.

c. Calculate Timel's marginal cost of capital with a new common-stock issue.

d. Timel follows the practice that 50 percent of any long-term financing will be derived from common-equity sources. Determine the point of expansion (the size of the capital budget) at which Timel's source of common equity would switch from retained earnings to new common stock in the coming year. In other words, determine the maximum capital budget financed 50 percent from the $54,000,000 in retained earnings.

e. If the business risks are similar for all companies in the industry in which Timel participates, would each have approximately the same cost of capital? Explain your answer.

Capital structure and financial risk

7.10. Two manufacturers of tables and chairs, Avanter and Sovren, are similar in most respects. They have the same product mix, and both are headquartered in Indiana. Even their sales, total assets, and earnings are similar in size. They differ dramatically, however, in capital structure:

	Avanter	Sovren
Debt (before-tax cost, 10%)	$1,900,000	$ 100,000
Common equity	100,000	1,900,000
Total assets	2,000,000	2,000,000
Number of common shares outstanding	2,000	38,000
Tax rate	40%	40%

Assume that Avanter's and Sovren's earnings before interest and taxes are $190,000 during recession periods and $380,000 during expansion periods.

a. Calculate earnings per share for each company during recessions and expansions.

b. Which company has more financial risk? Explain.

Asymmetric information and financing

7.11. Imtrex Company's common stock trades at $15 per share, but Imtrex's managers have reason to believe that it is worth $20 per share. They plan to introduce a profitable new product called Imtrex Classic, which will add $1 million to Imtrex's equity value. Introduction of the new product will require a $2 million investment.

Imtrex has 200,000 shares of common stock currently outstanding, making its aggregate equity value equal to $3 million.

a. If Imtrex issues common stock to finance the new project, how many shares will it need to issue? (Assume zero flotation costs.)

b. According to management's beliefs, what is the true worth of the new issue of common stock?

c. If issuing common stock is Imtrex's only financing alternative, should it go forward with the investment plan? Explain.

d. If Imtrex spends $200,000 on investor relations, it can eliminate the problem of asymmetric information. Should Imtrex spend $200,000 on investor relations? Explain.

Indifference EBIT and EPS	7.12.	Marianna Rota, treasurer of Eckerd Imports, is considering whether or not her company should issue new common stock or bonds to invest in a $280,000 project. Her alternative financial sources are the following:

- Issue new common stock. Market price of the common stock is $15 per share, and flotation cost is $1 per share.

- Issue bonds. Interest on the 20-year bonds would be 10 percent, and no principal would be repaid before maturity.

Eckerd Imports pays 40 percent marginal tax, and the company has 150,000 shares of common stock authorized and 60,000 shares outstanding.

a. Calculate the indifference EBIT for the new common-stock and debt alternatives.

b. Verify your answer in Part *a* by calculating earnings per share for each alternative at the indifference EBIT. Graph EPS as a function of EBIT for each alternative; label each axis and note the indifference point for EBIT and EPS on your graph.

c. Explain how the financial manager makes the choice between the alternatives in Part *a* above. Do you recognize a potential problem in this method of choosing financial sources? Explain your answer.

Indifference EBIT and EPS	7.13.	Taiwan Imports is examining the financial implications of expanding its productive capacity with an $800,000 investment. The company's financial manager has determined that the company now has 80,000 shares outstanding, and to finance the project with new equity requires an additional 20,000 shares. Alternatively, to finance it with debt requires $800,000 of 12 percent bonds. The company is in the 40 percent marginal tax bracket.

a. Calculate the indifference EBIT.

b. Calculate earnings per share at the indifference EBIT.

c. If the financial manager expects EBIT to be $518,000, then Taiwan Imports should finance the expansion with debt. True or false? Why?

d. Explain why a slavish reliance on EBIT-EPS analysis may not lead to the correct decision regarding which source of capital to select.

CMA examination, modified: indifference EBIT, EPS, and preserving dividends per share	7.14.	The directors of Pogler Inc. will meet in the near future to select one of two plans to finance the company's entry into the market for small kitchen appliances. The final choice will be made between a common-stock issue and a bond issue.

The company normally earns $6,000,000 before interest and taxes. However, it has earned as little as $1,500,000 and as much as $7,000,000 before interest and taxes on its current resources. The company is subject to a 40 percent income tax rate. The assets of Pogler total $25,000,000 and are financed by $1,000,000 of current liabilities, $5,000,000 from a long-term loan, and $19,000,000 in shareholder equity. The long-term loan carries an 8 percent interest rate.

There are 2,000,000 shares of common stock outstanding. The company has paid a $0.75 dividend per share for the past 4 years and expects to continue this policy in the near future.

Management expects the new $10,000,000 investment to earn an additional $1,500,000 annually before interest and taxes. However, business conditions may cause these earnings to vary from $500,000 to $2,000,000. The company can raise funds by issuing 800,000 shares of common stock at $12.50 a share or by a $10,000,000 bond issue that would bear a 14 percent interest rate.

a. The directors of Pogler would like the following amounts calculated for each plan:
   (1) The earnings per share at the expected income level for the company after the expansion has taken place.
   (2) The minimum after-expansion company earnings before interest and taxes that will permit the $0.75 per-share dividend to be covered by current earnings.

b. Calculate the earnings before interest and taxes at which both plans will have the same earnings per share.

c. Explain how the directors of Pogler should weigh the information from Part *b* in their analysis of the two financial plans.

Computer Problems 💾

Weighted-average cost of capital: template WACC

7.15. The financial manager of Semrad Enterprises is estimating the cost of raising $1,000,000 to invest in a new mainframe computer and peripherals. The optimal capital structure for the company is:

Debt	40%
Preferred stock	10
Common stock	50

The company's tax rate is 40 percent and current earnings before taxes are $1,000,000. The dividend payout ratio is 50 percent. Given the following data, calculate the cost of each source of financing and the weighted-average cost of capital.

- The company can issue 8 percent 15-year bonds of $1,000 par value at $960. Flotation costs will be $20 per bond.

- It can issue 8 percent preferred stock at par value of $100 with 3 percent flotation cost.

- The company's current stock price is $50 per share. The dividend next year is expected to be $2 per share, and it is expected to grow at a constant rate of 6 percent per year. New stock can be issued at $50 per share and flotation costs will be $3.50 per share.

Marginal cost of capital: template MARGINAL

7.16. Lenihan Associates estimated the costs of its sources of external capital and compiled the following table:

Source of Capital	Range of New Financing	After-Tax Cost
Debt	$0 to $500,000	5%
	$500,001 to $1,000,000	6
	$1,000,001 to $2,000,000	7
Preferred stock	$0 to $200,000	10
	$200,001 to $750,000	11
Common stock	$0 to $1,000,000	15
	$1,000,001 to $2,000,000	17
	$2,000,001 to $4,000,000	19

The company's target capital structure is 30 percent debt, 10 percent preferred stock, and 60 percent common stock.

a. Calculate the cost of each increment of capital and the range of financing for which it is applicable.

b. What is the marginal cost of capital for capital budgets of $1,000,000, $2,000,000, $3,000,000, $4,000,000, $5,000,000, and $6,000,000?

Capital structure: template
CAPSTR

7.17. Joe Lyndon, the financial manager of Gallagher Inc., is planning Gallagher's capital structure. To do this, he collects information about expected sales during a recession, normal economy, and boom. Gallagher Inc. will have fixed operating costs of $5,000,000 and variable costs of 45 percent of sales. In a normal economy Mr. Lyndon expects sales of $15,000,000. In a recession they could fall to $10,000,000, and in a booming economy they could rise to $20,000,000. The probability of a normal economy is 50 percent, recession 25 percent, and boom 25 percent. Mr. Lyndon expects that Gallagher Inc., a new company for distributing tires, will require total assets of $15,000,000. Gallagher Inc. can issue common stock at $10 per share to finance these assets. Alternatively, the company can issue some combination of common stock and bonds to finance the assets. The company will have a 40 percent marginal tax rate.

For evaluating the proposed capital structure, Mr. Lyndon has collected the additional following information:

Debt Ratio (D/TA)	Pre-Tax Cost of Debt (K_d)	Cost of Equity (K_c)
0	—	11.50%
0.2	8.00%	12.00
0.4	10.00	13.00
0.6	13.00	16.00
0.8	17.00	20.00

a. Calculate the following for each debt ratio (total debt divided by total assets):
   (1) The weighted-average cost of capital.
   (2) Interest expense.
   (3) Number of shares outstanding.
   (4) Earnings per share during recession, a normal economy, and a boom economy.
   (5) The price per share of stock estimated with expected earnings per share divided by the cost of equity. (This assumes constant earnings and that all earnings are paid out as dividends.)

b. Which of the above capital structures would you recommend and why?

((VHS))

VIDEO CASE PROBLEM

Riverfork Electric

Riverfork Electric, a utility company in the Southeast, sells electric power to residential and commercial accounts. The company generates electricity by burning high-sulfur coal mined in Kentucky. Recent studies have shown that this type of coal produces significant amounts of sulfur dioxide, the main ingredient in acid rain. To lessen the problem of acid rain, new environmental regulations require that Riverfork's generating plant be adapted to reduce its emissions of sulfur dioxide. Emissions must be cut by 30 percent this year and by another 40 percent over the next three years. To comply with the legislation, management has the choice of switching to low-sulfur coal or installing filter-like scrubbers to screen emissions. Since Riverfork has a large investment in high-sulfur coal mines, management has decided to go with the costly scrubbers.

The estimated cost of installing the scrubbers is $44 million, which will be financed with either debt, equity, or a combination of both. Management believes that investors will require a higher rate of return in the coming year than in recent years, because of increased risk from environmental regulatory uncertainty and expectations of higher inflation. This higher required rate of return means a higher cost of capital. To cover these higher costs, management plans to petition the Public Utility Commission (PUC) for an increase in price per kilowatt-hour (kwh) charged to customers.

As a regulated monopoly, Riverfork cannot raise prices without approval from the PUC of the state in which it operates. The commission attempts to set energy prices just high enough for Riverfork to cover operating costs and capital costs. The guiding legal standard for just and reasonable energy prices is based on a Supreme Court case (Bluefield Water Works & Investment Co. *v.* Public Service Commission of the State of West Virginia, 1923, 693):

> *A public utility is entitled to such rates as will permit it to earn a return on the value of the property which it employs for the convenience of the public equal to that generally being made at the same time and in the same general part of the country on investments in other business undertakings which are attended by corresponding risks and uncertainties. . . .*

The guiding legal standard on capital costs also comes from a Supreme Court case (Federal Power Commission *v.* Hope Natural Gas Company, 1944, 603):

> *From the investor or company point of view it is important that there be enough revenue not only for operating expenses but also for capital costs of the business. These include service on the debt and dividends on the stock. . . . By that standard the return to the equity owner should be commensurate with returns on investments in other enterprises having corresponding risks.*

Based on the foregoing legal principles, the PUC will set Riverfork's price per kwh to cover all estimated costs: operating expenses, income taxes, interest on debt, dividends on preferred stock, and return on equity. The sum of these costs equals total required revenue, which divided by the forecast demand (number of kilowatt-hours) produces price charged per kwh. Each of the estimates that goes into calculating price per kwh will be hotly contested in the hearing room (similar to a courtroom) by PUC staff economists, Riverfork's analysts, and interveners on behalf of various customer groups. After listening to evidence from each interested party, the commissioners will pass judgment on the price Riverfork is allowed to charge customers.

Often the most controversial and debated estimates are those related to capital costs, especially the cost of equity capital. To calculate the revenue necessary to cover all capital costs, expert witnesses in utility rate cases estimate the company's percentage average cost of capital, and multiply this rate by the rate base (capital base allowed by the PUC) to obtain the revenue necessary to

cover capital costs. The average cost of capital (K_a) before taxes is calculated as follows:

$$K_a = W_d K_d + W_p K_p + W_c K_c$$

where K_d is before-tax cost of debt, K_p is cost of preferred stock, K_c is cost of common equity, and W_d, W_p, and W_c are weights, or proportions of total capital represented by the individual capital sources. Since K_d is used in the calculation instead of K_i—the after-tax cost of debt—the tax deductibility of interest must be taken into account in the calculation of income taxes. From past experience, Riverfork management expects the PUC to define "allowable rate base" as the market value of the company's bonds and stocks.

Riverfork management's request for rate relief hinges significantly on its ability to convince the PUC that the company's cost of capital justifies higher prices. In preparation for the PUC hearing, management begins to collect data for the estimates related to cost of capital, including the following information on Riverfork's capital structure:

| | In Thousands of Dollars | |
Sources of Capital	Book Value	Market Value
Bonds (9% coupon rate; $1,000 par)	$119,000	$119,000
Preferred stock (9.5%; 200,000 shares)	20,000	20,000
Common stock ($5 par value)	$54,200	
Capital in excess of par	8,700	
Retained earnings	96,600	
Total common equity	$159,500	$176,150
Total claims	$298,500	$315,150

The market value of Riverfork's recently issued bonds and preferred stock equals book value; the market value of common equity, however, exceeds book value by $16,650,000.

Riverfork's 10,840,000 shares of common stock trade in the secondary market for $16.25 per share. Dividends per share, earnings per share, and price per share each have grown at an annual rate of 5 percent over the past ten years, with the expected dividend for the coming year being $1.30 per share. The company's 200,000 shares of preferred stock pay an annual dividend of $9.50 per share, and its 119,000 bonds pay annual interest of $90.00 per bond.

Forecast demand for Riverfork's electric output during the coming year is 2.915 billion kilowatt-hours. To achieve this level of output, the company will incur operating expenses of $152,005,000. In addition, the company will pay income taxes totaling 40 percent of taxable income.

Management plans to hire a consultant to analyze Riverfork's request for rate relief. The consultant will present written and oral testimony to the PUC. As a candidate for the consulting job, your initial task is to respond to a series of questions and problems developed by management.

a. What is the difference between the *explicit* and *implicit* cost of debt?

b. In your opinion, does Riverfork's capital structure expose common shareholders to undue financial risk? Explain.

c. Calculate K_d, K_p, and K_c for Riverfork. You may ignore flotation costs in your calculations because they will be included in the company's operating expenses.

d. Use market weights to calculate K_a for Riverfork. (*Note:* Use 6-place accuracy in your calculation of the weights and K_a. This degree of accuracy is needed below to avoid large rounding errors.)

e. Begin at the bottom of the table below and work your way upward to calculate Riverfork's total required revenue:

Total required revenue —Operating expenses	$
Required EBIT —Interest expense	$
Required EBT —Income taxes	$
Required EAT —Preferred-stock dividends	$
Fair return to equity	$

Calculate price per kwh based on *Total required revenue* and the forecast demand.

Notes: (1) Fair return to equity equals K_c times the market value of common equity. (2) Required earnings before taxes (EBT) equal required earnings after taxes (EAT) divided by $(1 - T)$, where T is the tax rate. (3) EBIT stands for earnings before interest and taxes.

f. To check your work in Part *e*, calculate the sum of interest expense, preferred-stock dividends, and fair return to equity. Within rounding error, this sum should equal K_a times the rate base. Show the equivalence between the two calculations.

g. (1) Use the capital asset pricing model (CAPM) to calculate K_c, assuming that the required rate of return on the market portfolio (K_m) is 14 percent, the risk-free rate of return (R_f) is 7 percent, and the common-stock beta (β) is 0.70. (2) Use this value of K_c to recalculate total required revenue as described in Part *e*. (3) Compare the total required revenue and fair return to equity calculated here with that calculated in Part *e*. Of the two methods used to calculate K_c—the CAPM and the constant-growth model—which method would each of the following groups likely support: Riverfork management, interveners on behalf of various customer groups, and PUC staff economists?

h. During oral testimony in the hearing room, your method and estimated inputs used to calculate K_c will be severely attacked by attorneys representing opposing groups. What are the likely lines of attack on your use of the constant-growth model? The CAPM?

References: Alexander A. Robichek, "Regulation and Modern Finance Theory," *Journal of Finance,* June 1978, 693–705; James Cook, "Jim Roger's First 1,000 Days," *Forbes,* December 9, 1991, 78–80; Stewart C. Myers, "The Application of Finance Theory to Public Utility Rate Cases," *Bell Journal of Economics and Management Science,* Spring 1972, 58–97.

Selected References

Antia, Murad, J., and Richard L. Meyer. "The Growth Optimal Capital Structure: Manager Versus Shareholder Objectives." *Journal of Financial Research,* Fall 1984: 259–267.

Appleyard, A. R., and N. C. Strong. "Textbook Inconsistencies in Graphing Valuation Equations: A Note." *The Financial Review,* November 1985: 361–367.

Arzac, Enrique R. "On the Capital Structure of Leveraged Buyouts." *Financial Management,* Spring 1992: 16–26.

Conine, Thomas E., Jr., and Maurry Tamarkin. "Divisional Cost of Capital Estimation: Adjusting for Leverage." *Financial Management,* Spring 1985: 54–58.

Edwards, Charles E., and Philip L. Cooley. "Leverage Financing Choices for Real Estate Investments." *Real Estate Appraiser and Analyst,* Summer 1984: 73–78.

Gardner, John C., and Charles A. Trzcinka. "All-Equity Firms and the Balancing Theory of Capital Structure." *Journal of Financial Research,* Spring 1992: 77–90.

Gehr, Adam K., Jr. "Financial Structure and Financial Strategy." *Journal of Financial Research,* Spring 1984: 69–80.

Harris, John M., Jr., Rodney L. Roenfeldt, and Philip L. Cooley. "Evidence of Financial Leverage Clienteles." *Journal of Finance,* September 1983: 1125–1132.

Kolodny, Richard, and Dianne Rizzuto Suhler. "Changes in Capital Structure, New Equity Issues, and Scale Effects." *Journal of Financial Research,* Summer 1985: 127–135.

Pinegar, J. Michael, and Lisa Wilbricht. "What Managers Think of Capital Structure Theory: A Survey." *Financial Management,* Winter 1989: 82–91.

"Reflections on the MM Propositions: Thirty Years Later." *Financial Management,* Summer 1989: 12–38.

Taggart, Robert A., Jr. "Corporate Financing: Too Much Debt?" *Financial Analysts Journal,* May–June 1986: 35–42.

CAPITAL BUDGETING

SMALL-BUSINESS PERSPECTIVE

Investing in New Equipment

After several discussions with the bank's loan officer about the financing of their new retail outlet, Kathy Griffin and Jim Sutherland decided to invest $50,000 and to borrow $61,400 for 7 years. The projected net income would be sufficient to cover the loan payments, and the $20,000 in cash balances that they included in their projected start-up costs should cover any unforeseen problems.

In Shape Inc. opened for business in January 19X6. Jim and Kathy held a grand-opening reception the night before the store officially opened for business. They invited friends, relatives, and reporters from local newspapers who might give the store free publicity. The reception was well attended and provided excellent exposure.

After the store was open and operating smoothly, Kathy assumed responsibility for retail sales and Jim assumed responsibility for sales to hotels and resorts. Jim was also responsible for the delivery and setup of all fitness equipment. In Shape provided free delivery and setup of the larger pieces of equipment to both residential and institutional customers.

The store was successful in its first year, earning $11,000 before taxes. Kathy and Jim attributed the success to a good location, quality products, and excellent customer service (including free delivery). However, as the reputation of the business grew, the demand for delivery service also increased. Jim spent almost all of his time making deliveries, setting up equipment, and making sales calls.

The constant demand for deliveries began to take its toll on the truck that Jim drove. In order to reduce start-up costs, Kathy and Jim had decided to use a truck that Jim already owned. Consequently, after 18 months of constant use, the truck frequently developed mechanical problems. Delivery schedules were often interrupted, and customer service did not meet Kathy and Jim's standards. Also, repair bills were becoming excessive.

Toward the end of the second year, Kathy and Jim realized that the continuing success of the company would cause another problem. The company would pay several thousand dollars in taxes over the next few years. Their concern was based on projected income statements.

If past growth continued at the same rate during the future, the tax liability would be large. The growth of the company was already straining cash flows, and Kathy and Jim needed to keep as much cash in the company as possible. Any taxes would drain the company of working capital it desperately needed.

The solution to the increasing truck repair bills and possibly the tax problem seemed to be the purchase of a delivery van. Jim knew that a new van would cost approximately $20,000 but he was not sure if this purchase would substan-

tially reduce the company's taxes. Kathy reviewed the first year's income statement and the year-to-date figures for the second year. She found that the depreciation expense on the old truck was very low, but she was not familiar enough with the tax regulations to calculate the amount of depreciation on a new van. She was also concerned that the tax savings might be offset by the new loan payments, with the result that cash flows might not improve.

The three chapters in Part III present information that helps answer the questions raised by Kathy and Jim. Chapter 8 describes the relevant cash flows in capital investments and explains the impact of depreciation and taxes. Chapter 9 illustrates how the cash flows should be evaluated to make investment decisions. Concluding the discussion, Chapter 10 describes methods for incorporating risk into the decision-making process.

CAPITAL INVESTMENTS AND CASH FLOWS

Cash Flows from Oil?

As an example of the importance of capital investments, consider the experience of companies in the petroleum industry. After the Arab oil embargo in 1973, the oil business enjoyed the strongest boom in its history. The boom lasted until the end of 1981, when the posted price of OPEC (Organization of Petroleum Exporting Countries) crude oil peaked at $34 a barrel.

While oil prices were rising, oil companies made large investments aimed at finding more oil, and they financed many of these investments with bonds. Financial managers estimated future cash flows based on their expectations of increasing oil prices over the foreseeable future. Some companies implemented small capital investment programs, but most leaned toward large, ambitious projects because of the tantalizing profits and the seemingly permanent nature of the cash flows.

In early 1982 the economic bubble burst. Because of the worldwide glut of oil, OPEC cut

prices. A precipitous decline in oil company profits and cash flows followed. Capital investments that had been profitable based on an oil price of $34 a barrel were miserable failures at $17 a barrel. A large number of companies went bankrupt, and many continued to teeter on the brink, with cash flows barely above the level required to service debt.

The severely troubled oil companies shared a common experience. The projected cash flows from capital investment projects failed to live up to expectations. When cash flows declined below expected levels, company efforts to cut back on expenses and to sell assets to generate cash were inadequate, and lenders and investors were unwilling to advance additional funds to companies already on the verge of bankruptcy. The results for the oil industry were widespread declines in stock prices and increases in the number of bankruptcies.

Photo Source: © L. Lee/West Light.

Capital investments normally require large cash outlays and last for many years. Thus an error in the decision-making process can have serious consequences for a company. Financial managers have the challenging task of analyzing capital investments—from the standpoint of cash flows and impact on stock price—and recommending the action to be taken by the company. To understand this process, we begin with an overview describing the steps in capital investment decisions. We then turn our attention to the cash flows associated with a capital investment. Armed with the information from this chapter, you will be ready to consider the evaluation methods presented in Chapter 9.

INTRODUCTION TO CAPITAL BUDGETING

The process of planning capital investments and evaluating and selecting the best projects from a range of alternatives is called *capital budgeting*. Capital investments (alternatively called *capital expenditures* or *capital projects*) are easy to identify because they usually involve a depreciable asset. Examples are investments in plant and equipment, other companies (called acquisitions), property, and less tangible assets such as exploration ventures, research and development, and new-product development.

Although the process of planning and evaluating capital investments varies among companies, capital budgeting basically consists of the following steps:

1. *Generate ideas* for increasing shareholder wealth through new products, new production methods, replacement of worn-out facilities, and acquisition of other companies.

2. *Estimate the cash outflows and inflows* for each project proposal.

3. *Evaluate the risks* of each project proposal. Assess the uncertainty of both the required cash outlay and the estimated cash inflows.

4. *Select projects* that are expected to increase the company's stock price; use the cash flow estimates and risk assessments (Steps 2 and 3) for the selection process.

5. *Monitor the accepted projects* for variance from expected performance and conduct a postaudit upon project completion.

This chapter discusses the sources of ideas for capital investments (Step 1) and the measurement of estimated cash flows (Step 2). Chapters 9 and 10 address the remaining three steps.

Sources of Ideas for Capital Investments

Ideas for capital investments may come from planning committees, research and development groups, vendors, or individual employees. Some companies try to encourage capital-budgeting ideas by offering monetary incentives to employees who suggest them.

The cash expenditures for capital projects are usually sizable and, to a large extent, irrevocable. For example, if management accepts someone's idea to acquire a company or build a new factory to expand production and later decides the decision was wrong, then the company may not be able to recover much of the investment in the unwanted acquisition or partially constructed factory. Consider the case of General Dynamics' acquisition of Cessna Aircraft in 1985 for $663 million. The subsequent slump in the aviation industry was unanticipated

FIGURE 8.1

Proposal Form for Capital Investments: Willard Trucking Inc.

Division:	Date:	Project Cost	
		Fixed Assets (Purchased)	_____
		Fixed Assets (Leased)	_____
	Sponsor:	Net Working Capital	_____
		Total	

Proposal Description:

Appropriation Group:		Economic Life	Payback Period	Net Present Value
Growth Project	1			
Replacement Machinery	2	Internal Rate of Return	Commitment Date:	
Replacement Trucks	3			
Additional Trucks	4		Completion Date:	
Miscellaneous	5			

Priority: Justification:
A. Absolutely Essential
B. Necessary
C. Economically Desirable
D. General Improvement

Company Approvals:		Remarks:
Financial Manager	_____	
Plant Manager	_____	
Division Manager	_____	
Chair, Capital Budgeting Committee	_____	

when management approved the proposed capital investment. Fifteen months after the acquisition, General Dynamics abandoned much of the investment and wrote off $420 million, or $9.80 per share, in the fourth quarter of 1986.

Because of the large expenditures involved, most companies organize the capital-budgeting procedure so that decisions to accept or reject ideas are made with great care. The initial idea for a project must be documented with production and marketing data so that the financial manager can estimate cash flows and the potential impact of the project on the price of the company's common stock.

Approval of Ideas for Capital Investments

Many companies require the person recommending a capital investment to complete part of a form describing the proposed project. Figure 8.1 shows the form used by Willard Trucking Inc., a medium-sized truck rental company. Most proposal forms are designed to give the financial manager necessary information for analyzing project cash flows. The proposal form usually has additional pages of information and analysis to support the proposed project.

After the project sponsor has provided background information on the project, the financial manager begins the financial evaluation. Willard Trucking's financial manager begins by assigning one of the following priorities to the proposed project:

A. *Absolutely essential.* Legally required or necessary for health and safety. Example: Compliance with federal safety standards.

B. *Necessary.* Needed to sustain existing business; expenditure may be delayed temporarily but cannot long be avoided. Example: Replacement of worn-out trucks.

C. *Economically desirable.* Needed for cost savings, to produce new products, or to expand capacity. Examples: Purchase of more efficient equipment; rental of cars and construction equipment.

D. *General improvement.* Needed for morale, prestige, and convenience. Example: Paving the employee parking lot.

Having assigned priority to the project, the financial manager summarizes the economic evaluation (middle-right side of Figure 8.1); Chapters 9 and 10 explain these evaluation methods.

The financial manager then sends the completed form to the proper authority for review and final approval. Approval authority in Willard Trucking depends on the dollar outlay. For example, a plant manager approves any outlay up to $10,000, subject to a $50,000 annual total. A division manager approves outlays ranging between $10,000 and $60,000, subject to a $200,000 annual total. The capital-budgeting committee, consisting of the chief executive officer and the company vice presidents, approves all proposals exceeding $60,000. Like most companies, Willard Trucking requires larger projects to be approved by higher-ranking company officials.

Cash Flows and Capital Investments

Most methods used by financial managers to evaluate acceptability of proposed projects depend on estimates of cash flows. Ideally, these methods:

1. Include all incremental cash flows (after taxes) over the entire life of the proposed project.

2. Recognize the time value of money.

3. Incorporate the required rate of return on the project.

net investment cash outflow (NICO)

Capital expenditure to get a capital project in working order; typically includes expenditures for depreciable assets and net working capital.

Project analysis emphasizes cash flows because cash has an opportunity cost, which causes the preference in timing of cash flows. Conventional projects require a cash outlay at time zero and earn the company cash inflows at future points in time. Table 8.1 identifies the initial cash outlay as the **net investment cash outflow (NICO)**; the subsequent cash inflows consist of operating cash flows and the cash flow from terminating the project. Figure 8.2 illustrates the expected cash flows from a hypothetical three-year capital investment project. The initial investment leads to three years of cash inflows, including a disposal cash inflow at the end of the project's life. Not all projects produce cash flow patterns like the one in Figure 8.2. Chapter 9 discusses alternative patterns, but here we focus on the conventional pattern of an outlay followed by cash inflows.

TABLE 8.1

Expected Cash Flows of a Typical Capital Investment

Net Investment Cash Outflow (NICO)

Depreciable Assets:	Investment adjusted for delivery and installation costs and for investment tax credit (when allowed).
Net Working Capital:	Investment in additional current assets less current liabilities.

Cash Inflows

Operating Cash Flow:	After-tax increase in cash from operations, including the tax savings from depreciation.
Disposal (Liquidation) Cash Flow:	*Depreciable assets:* Selling price adjusted for taxes. *Net working capital:* Current assets less current liabilities.

FIGURE 8.2

Cash Flow Pattern of a Typical Capital Investment

A typical capital investment requires an initial cash outflow for depreciable assets and net working capital, followed by several years of operating cash inflows and a final disposal cash inflow when management terminates the project.

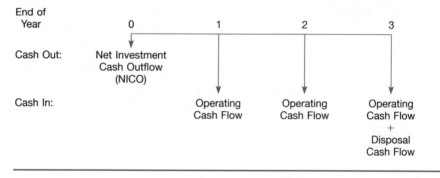

The cash flows relevant in capital budgeting are those directly attributable to the project. Cash flows of the company *with* the project less cash flows of the company *without* the project are the only relevant cash flows. These changes in cash flows are called **incremental cash flows**. It makes no difference whether the cash flows occur at one point in time or at several points, or whether they vary or are constant, so long as they are new, incremental cash flows. Nonincremental cash flows (for example, sunk costs) are irrelevant in capital budgeting.

incremental cash flows
Changes in a company's cash flows attributable to a capital investment.

sunk cost
Cash outlay that cannot be recouped and therefore is not attributable to a capital project.

Sunk Costs.   A **sunk cost** is a cash outlay that a company has made or has a legal commitment to make. Sunk costs are *not* incremental cash flows and therefore are irrelevant in capital budgeting. To illustrate, Louisianne Food Products (LFP) paid $85,000 to a consultant for a market survey to determine the need for an additional factory outlet. Based on the survey, the consultant concluded that a need did, in fact, exist. Later, in its analysis of the investment in the factory outlet, LFP correctly ignored the $85,000 fee paid to the consultant. Whether LFP chose to invest or not, the $85,000 was gone. LFP's $85,000 payment is an example of a sunk cost.

indirect cash flows
Incremental cash flows in parts of a company other than the capital project, but caused by the capital project.

Indirect Cash Flows.   Indirect cash flows are cash inflows and outflows that occur in other parts of a company's operations as a result of the company investing in a capital project. As with sunk costs, indirect cash flows can be difficult to recognize. Unlike sunk costs, however, they are incremental cash flows and therefore are relevant in capital budgeting. The following examples illustrate the nature of indirect cash flows.

EXAMPLE

Cybertaks paid $350,000 for a sheet-metal press 10 years ago. The press is still functional but is technologically inferior to the new model. Cybertaks management is planning to replace the old press with the new one. Total cost of the new press is $500,000, and the old press can be sold to net $100,000 after taxes. The decision to invest in the new press *causes* the sale of the old press and Cybertak's receipt of $100,000. Consequently, Cybertak's net investment cash outflow (NICO) for the new press is $400,000 ($500,000 − $100,000), not $500,000. In general, the after-tax value, or salvage value, of assets being replaced offsets the investment in the replacement assets.

EXAMPLE

A financial manager is evaluating a proposal to construct a building to house the production of a new line of cosmetics. If the workers used to construct the building are already on the payroll and presently productively employed, then the manager must include in the analysis the wages of *workers hired* to replace those used in construction. Because the workers taken from some productive use must be replaced, the analysis includes the cost of the *new* employees. Thus the wages of the new employees are the incremental cash outflows.

NET INVESTMENT CASH OUTFLOW

The first incremental cash flow that occurs in a capital investment is the net investment cash outflow (NICO). For *expansion* projects, NICO usually consists of cash outflows to acquire depreciable assets and additional net working capital. Expansion projects are investments in new assets for the purpose of increasing sales revenue. A company's strategic plan usually limits the types of expansion projects that need to be evaluated. More routine in nature, *replacement* projects are investments in new assets to replace existing ones. Although the calculation of cash flows for expansion and replacement projects follows the same principles, some differences exist in the cash flows, as described in the Appendix to this chapter. The focus here is expansion projects.

Investment in Depreciable Assets

depreciable asset
Property on which the U.S. tax code permits a company to charge depreciation against income.

A **depreciable asset** is property on which the Internal Revenue Service allows a company to charge depreciation against income. Depreciable assets have useful lives longer than one year and include such things as desks, computer hardware and software, machinery, and buildings. The expected cash expenditure for a project includes all cash outlays necessary to make the depreciable asset useful, that is, to bring it on line. These additional costs may consist of delivery charges, installation costs, and land costs.

investment tax credit (ITC)
Percentage of the cost of a depreciable asset that the U.S. tax code allows as a reduction in a company's tax bill; repealed in 1986.

Cash expended for depreciable assets is reduced by the **investment tax credit (ITC),** an investment incentive to businesses sometimes provided by the federal government. The ITC reduces the cash needed to invest in a project because it reduces, dollar for dollar, the company's tax bill. Among other changes in the tax laws, the U.S. Congress increases the ITC when it wants to boost the economy by encouraging capital investment, and it reduces the ITC when it wants to increase federal tax revenues. Although eliminated in 1986, the ITC may well appear again in the future. When permissible, the financial manager multiplies the ITC percentage times the cost of depreciable assets and reduces the company's tax bill by the resulting amount.

EXAMPLE

Friedhoffer Associates invests in a fleet of trucks costing $680,000. Shipping charges increase the cost to $700,000. A 6 percent investment tax credit is available, so Friedhoffer Associates may reduce its tax bill by $42,000 ($700,000 × 0.06). Friedhoffer Associates adjusts the cash outflow for investment in depreciable assets to $658,000 ($700,000 − $42,000).

The investment in depreciable assets is the first cash flow of the project, and it occurs at time zero, the beginning of the project's expected life. Graphically, this outflow appears as follows for a three-year project:

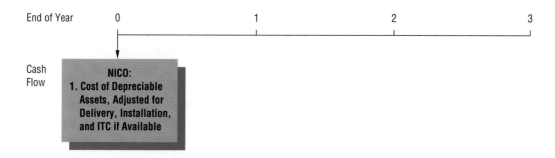

Investment in Net Working Capital

net working capital
Current assets minus current liabilities.

Undertaking a capital project often causes a company to increase its investment in **net working capital**—current assets minus current liabilities. For example, the project may require additional investment in inventory and accounts receivable. Offsetting the additional investment may be a rise in accounts payable to suppliers and accrued expenses (taxes payable and wages payable), all attributable to the project. In this case, the incremental increase in the company's net working capital is a cash outflow caused by undertaking the project.

For some projects, net working capital increases gradually over time as sales increase. Thus the investment in net working capital might increase in several steps, not just at time zero. These increases could be subtracted from the future cash inflows, or the discounted value of the increases could be included in the net investment cash outflow (NICO). To simplify the discussion, we assume that the increased net working capital caused by a project occurs at time zero, depicted as follows:

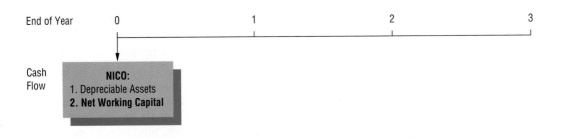

The net investment cash outflow consists of expenditures for depreciable assets and the increase in net working capital.

OPERATING CASH FLOWS FROM CAPITAL INVESTMENTS

A company receives cash inflows over time from operating a project as well as cash inflows at the end of the project's life from selling remaining assets and recapturing net working capital. The true picture of the benefit of accepting a project requires the inclusion of all these cash inflows in the capital-budgeting analysis. Many capital projects contribute to a company's operating cash flows by increasing sales revenues more than expenses or by reducing expenses with no effect on sales. As a general rule, the larger the operating cash flows a typical project generates, the larger will be the increase in the company's stock price. Before looking at the calculation of operating cash flows, you must understand the effects of income taxes and depreciation expense. Each has a profound effect on an operating cash flow: Income taxes reduce it and depreciation expense increases it.

Corporate Income Taxes and Operating Cash Flow

marginal tax rate
Tax rate applied to the last, or marginal, dollar of taxable income.

average tax rate
Tax rate applied to the average dollar of taxable income; total taxes paid divided by taxable income.

A corporation pays federal income taxes, state income taxes, and capital gains taxes separate from those paid by the corporation's shareholders.[1] Income is taxed at the federal tax rates presented in Table 8.2. State tax rates vary from state to state. To illustrate the federal tax rates, suppose a company has $60,000 taxable income. The company pays $7,500 ($0.15 \times \$50,000$) on the first $50,000 and $2,500 ($0.25 \times \$10,000$) on the next $10,000. The company's **marginal tax rate**—the rate on the last dollar of income—is 25 percent. Its **average tax rate**, however, is 16.7 ($10,000/$60,000) percent—total taxes paid divided by the amount of taxable income.

The rate the financial manager applies to the taxable income of a proposed project is the company's marginal tax rate. The marginal rate affects a company's incremental cash flows and therefore the cash flows of the project.[2]

[1] Proprietorships and partnerships do not pay income taxes as organizational entities. All taxable income passes through these organizations to the owners. The proprietors and partners, not the organizations, pay the income taxes, as discussed in Chapter 1. The tax code permits corporations with 35 or fewer common shareholders to avoid paying any income tax as a corporation. A corporation may become an S corporation, in which common shareholders report a proportional share of corporate income (whether or not distributed as dividends) as their own for tax purposes. Corporations are required to estimate their annual tax liability and to pay it in quarterly installments on the fifteenth of April, June, September, and December.

[2] A capital investment sometimes results in a loss, perhaps during the early years while a new product is being developed or its distribution is being established. In that event the company may apply the rule of *loss carryback, carryforward*. If the project loss exceeds the company's taxable income for the taxable year, then the *company's* loss may be carried back 3 years and forward 15 years to reduce

TABLE 8.2

Federal Tax Rates on Corporate Income

Taxable Income	Federal Tax Rate[a]
Up to $50,000	15%
$50,000 to $75,000	25
$75,000 to $100,000	34
$100,000 to $335,000	39
More than $335,000	34

[a]The Tax Reform Act of 1986 specifies these rates for taxable years beginning in 1987. For taxable income in the $100,000–$335,000 range, the act adds a 5 percent surtax to the 34 percent rate, thus creating a tax rate of 39 percent within this range. The effect of the surtax is to eliminate the tax break on income below $75,000. As a consequence, corporations with a taxable income of $335,000 or more effectively pay a flat tax of 34 percent: For example, 0.34($335,000) = $113,900; and 0.15($50,000) + 0.25($25,000) + 0.34($25,000) + 0.39($235,000) = $113,900. In this situation the corporation's marginal tax rate equals its average tax rate, 34 percent.

Depreciation Expense and Operating Cash Flow

Companies use up depreciable assets over time and deduct a depreciation expense from revenue. *Depreciation expense* often bears little resemblance to the actual decline in asset value, but instead represents a recovery allowance prescribed by law. For tax purposes, the U.S. Congress requires companies to calculate depreciation according to the **modified accelerated cost recovery system (MACRS)**, which replaces the accelerated cost recovery system (ACRS) in force through 1986. Companies have the option, however, of using straight-line depreciation in place of accelerated depreciation.

Depreciation methods used for financial reporting to investors may differ from those used for tax reporting to the Internal Revenue Service (IRS). In other words, companies *may keep two sets of books.* For example, a company may use straight-line depreciation for financial reporting because it results in higher reported earnings than does accelerated depreciation. At the same time, the company may use accelerated depreciation for tax reporting to the IRS because it results in less taxes payable than does straight-line depreciation. The focus here is depreciation methods used for tax reporting because they affect a company's marginal tax rate, the rate applicable to a proposed capital investment.

The U.S. tax code, which consists of acts passed by Congress and interpretations by the Internal Revenue Service and federal courts, lists asset class lives. **Class life** is the number of years over which an asset may be depreciated for tax purposes. Table 8.3 shows class lives specified in the Tax Reform Act of 1986. The class lives range from 3 years to 20 years, depending upon the asset. A financial manager evaluating a proposed capital investment matches the depreciable assets of the project with their allowed class lives in order to calculate the annual depreciation expense. The designated class lives may differ from the expected life of a proposed project. For example, a financial manager may evaluate a project with a 9-year expected life and use a 5-year class life for depreciation.

modified accelerated cost recovery system (MACRS)
Congressionally imposed depreciation procedures for tax purposes.

class life
Number of years over which an asset may be depreciated for tax purposes.

---

taxable income in those years. The reduction in taxable income empowers the company to obtain a tax refund from the Internal Revenue Service. The company uses its loss to reduce taxable income in the third preceding year, then the second preceding year, then the first preceding year. Subject to specific conditions too detailed for us to consider here, the company carries forward any remaining loss for up to 15 years into the future to be applied against taxable income. A company may elect to forgo the carryback provision and simply carry forward its operating loss for 15 years.

TABLE 8.3

Class Lives and Depreciation Rates for Assets Placed in Service after 1986

Class Life	Assets	Accelerated Depreciation Method
3-Year	Assets with estimated lives of 4 years or less except cars and light trucks, and including some horses.	200% declining balance
5-Year	Assets with estimated lives of more than 4 years and less than 10 years, including cars, light trucks, semiconductor manufacturing equipment, and R&D property.	200% declining balance
7-Year	Assets with estimated lives of more than 10 years and less than 16 years and assets without an IRS-designated life span.	200% declining balance
10-Year	Assets with estimated lives of more than 16 years and less than 20 years.	200% declining balance
15-Year	Assets with estimated lives of more than 20 years and less than 25 years, including municipal wastewater treatment plants and some telephone company equipment.	150% declining balance
20-Year	Assets with estimated lives of more than 25 years other than real property,[a] including municipal sewers.	150% declining balance

[a] Real property is real estate—land and buildings. Class-life designations and depreciation methods become more complex for real property than shown here for personal property.

Source: Tax Reform Act of 1986, Coopers & Lybrand, 1986, 99.

straight-line depreciation
Depreciation method requiring allocation of equal annual percentages of an asset's historical cost over the asset's class life.

historical cost
Acquisition cost of a depreciable asset consisting of its purchase price plus delivery charges and installation costs.

half-year convention
U.S. tax code requirement that a company take a half-year's depreciation in the year of acquisition and a half-year's depreciation in the year of retirement.

Straight-Line Depreciation.   **Straight-line depreciation** requires the allocation of equal annual percentages of an asset's historical cost over the asset's class life. **Historical cost** is the total of purchase price, delivery charges, and installation costs. The annual depreciation rate (or percentage) is 1 divided by the asset class life designated in Table 8.3:

$$\text{Annual straight-line depreciation rate} = \frac{1}{\text{Class life}}$$

To find the *dollar* depreciation for the proposed capital investment, the financial manager multiplies the historical cost by the annual straight-line rate.[3]

Before applying the rates, the financial manager must include an adjustment for the half-year convention the tax code requires. The **half-year convention** means that the company can take only a half-year of depreciation in the year of acquisition and a half-year of depreciation in the year of retirement. The year of retirement is the year *following* the class life. Regardless of the month in which the company buys a depreciable asset, the IRS considers the asset bought at the midpoint of the year. As a result, the company receives only one-half of the first year's depreciation expense.

---

[3] For tax purposes, the depreciation rate applies to historical cost, not historical cost less expected salvage value. For the purpose of financial reporting to investors, however, the depreciation rate is often applied to historical cost less expected salvage value. In comparison to the tax method, this latter method reduces depreciation expense and raises reported earnings. Generally accepted depreciation methods used by companies in their *Annual Report to Shareholders* include: (1) straight-line, (2) double-declining-balance, (3) sum-of-years'-digits, and (4) units-of-production.

EXAMPLE

Marwicke Enterprises' financial manager is evaluating a proposal to invest in a microcomputer system for its branch offices in the northeastern United States. The depreciable assets cost $91,000 and have a 5-year class life. Installation and delivery require an additional $9,000, for a total cost of $100,000. The annual depreciation rate is $\frac{1}{5}$, or 0.20. The annual depreciation expense is the depreciation rate times historical cost: $20,000 = 0.20 × $100,000. Because of the half-year convention, the company will report one-half of the annual depreciation expense in Year 1 and one-half in Year 6. Hence the annual depreciation expense associated with the proposed depreciable assets is as follows:

	Year	Depreciation Expense
Last half of Year	1	$ 10,000
All of Year	2	20,000
All of Year	3	20,000
All of Year	4	20,000
All of Year	5	20,000
First half of Year	6	10,000
		Total = $100,000

Accelerated Depreciation (MACRS).   Accelerated depreciation means that a company writes off more of a depreciable asset in the early years than it would with straight-line depreciation. As Table 8.3 shows, assets with class lives falling in the 3- through 10-year range are depreciated with the 200 percent declining-balance method; for assets with 15- and 20-year class lives, the 150 percent declining-balance method is used. To illustrate, the depreciation rate for the 200 percent declining-balance method is:

$$\text{Depreciation rate: 200\% declining-balance method} = 2 \times \text{Straight-line rate}$$

depreciable basis

Portion of asset value that can be depreciated for tax purposes.

The resulting rate is applied to the asset's **depreciable basis**—historical cost less accumulated depreciation, or equivalently, the remaining undepreciated value of the asset.

Two complications occur with the accelerated method of depreciation. First, each asset is depreciated with the half-year convention. As with straight line, this convention complicates the calculation of depreciation expense in the first and final year. The second complication involves depreciating the entire cost of the asset. Applying the declining-balance method to an annually declining book value means that the asset will never be entirely depreciated—you continue forever to take a percentage of a declining value. Adjusting for this complication requires a convention called the *straight-line switch,* which means that the accelerated depreciation method switches to straight line whenever the straight-line method results in a *larger* depreciation expense.

Table 8.4 presents the accelerated depreciation rates for assets with class lives of 3, 5, 7, and 10 years. The IRS publishes these rates for convenience, because of the complexity of their calculation. You too will find it convenient to use Table 8.4 when calculating accelerated depreciation expense. For instance, consider again the $100,000 microcomputer system being evaluated by Marwicke Enterprises' financial manager in the preceding example. According to the MACRS

TABLE 8.4

Accelerated Depreciation Rates on Personal Property

Year of Ownership	Class Life of Asset			
	3-Year[a]	5-Year	7-Year	10-Year
1	33.33%	20.00%	14.29%	10.00%
2	44.44	32.00	24.49	18.00
3	14.82	19.20	17.49	14.40
4	7.41	11.52	12.49	11.52
5		11.52	8.93	9.22
6		5.76	8.93	7.37
7			8.92	6.56
8			4.46	6.55
9				6.55
10				6.55
11				3.28
Totals	100%	100%	100%	100%

[a]These rates are based on the 200 percent declining-balance method. To illustrate the method, consider the 5-year class life: (1) Straight-line rate = $\frac{1}{5}$ = 0.20, or 20%. (2) 2 × Straight-line rate = 2 × 0.20 = 0.40, or 40%. (3) Because of the half-year convention, the rate for Year 1 is one-half of 40%, or 20%. (4) The depreciable basis for Year 2 is 80% (100% of historical cost less 20%); multiply 0.40 times 80% to get the Year 2 rate, 32%. (5) The depreciable basis for Year 3 is 48% (100% − 20% − 32%); multiply 0.40 times 48% to get the Year 3 rate, 19.2%. (6) The depreciable basis for Year 4 is 28.8% (100% − 20% − 32% − 19.2%); multiply 0.40 times 28.8% to get the Year 4 rate, 11.52%. (7) The depreciable basis for Year 5 is 17.28% (100% − 20% − 32% − 19.2% − 11.52%); now is the time for the straight-line switch because straight-line depreciation exceeds 0.40 × 17.28 = 6.91% for Year 5; prorating 17.28% over the remaining 1.5 years yields 5.76% per half-year (17.28% ÷ 3); therefore the Year 5 rate is 2 × 5.76% = 11.52%, and the Year 6 rate is 5.76%.

(modified accelerated cost recovery system) guidelines, the computer has a 5-year class life. To calculate annual depreciation expense, the financial manager simply multiplies the rates in the 5-year column of Table 8.4 times $100,000. Having the precalculated rates enables the financial manager to avoid the complicated steps described in the note to Table 8.4.

The annual depreciation expense for the $100,000 capital expenditure is profiled in Figure 8.3 for the straight-line and 200 percent declining-balance method. Accelerated depreciation results in larger write-offs during the first two years of the project's life, but smaller write-offs during the remaining years. Clearly, the method the financial manager uses will affect the company's annual depreciation expense. Which one, then, should the financial manager choose? The answer depends on the impact of depreciation expense on cash flow.

Depreciation Tax Shelters.   Depreciation increases a proposed project's operating cash flow "through the back door" by reducing the company's tax bill. Depreciation is a **tax shelter,** a noncash, tax-deductible expense that saves tax dollars for the company. Some financial managers call a tax shelter a *tax shield*.

tax shelter

A noncash, tax-deductible expense; also known as tax shield.

The tax savings that depreciation provides can be calculated by multiplying the company's marginal tax rate times the depreciation expense:

$$\text{Tax savings} = \text{Marginal tax rate} \times \text{Depreciation expense}$$

A proposed project with depreciation expense has greater operating cash flow than it would have without depreciation expense.

FIGURE 8.3

Profiles of Annual Depreciation Expense: Straight Line vs. Accelerated for the 5-Year Class Life

During the early years of a project's life, accelerated depreciation results in larger write-offs than does straight-line depreciation. Total depreciation expense taken over the project's life, however, is the same under either method and equals the project's depreciable basis ($100,000 in the illustration).

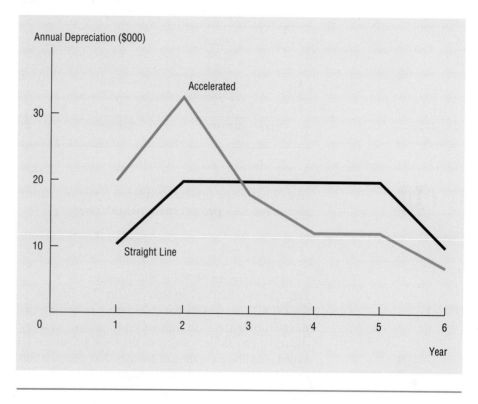

Consider once again Marwicke Enterprises' proposed capital investment of $100,000. Table 8.5 shows the tax savings for both straight-line and accelerated depreciation. The total tax savings over six years are the same with each method, but the timing of the tax savings differs. Accelerated depreciation leads to larger tax savings early in the life of the asset, and straight line leads to larger tax savings later in its life. The preferable method is the one that generates the higher present value of tax savings—accelerated in this case, for all positive discount rates less than infinity.

Calculating Operating Cash Flow

The tax savings from depreciation are part of a project's operating cash flow—the cash flow arising from the operation of the project. A *pro forma* (projected) operating statement provides the information necessary to identify the cash inflows and outflows generated by a project.

EXAMPLE

Prev Corporation's financial manager forecasts that a project will generate $20,000 of sales revenue and require a $6,000 labor expense during the year. The project's depreciation expense for tax purposes will be $8,000 during the

TABLE 8.5   **Tax Savings from Straight-Line and Accelerated Depreciation (Marginal Tax Rate = 34 Percent)**

	Straight Line		Accelerated (MACRS)	
(1) **Year**	**(2)** **Depreciation Expense**	**(0.34) × (2) = (3)** **Tax Savings**	**(4)** **Depreciation Expense**	**(0.34) × (4) = (5)** **Tax Savings**
1	$ 10,000	$ 3,400	$ 20,000	$ 6,800
2	20,000	6,800	32,000	10,880
3	20,000	6,800	19,200	6,528
4	20,000	6,800	11,520	3,917
5	20,000	6,800	11,520	3,917
6	10,000	3,400	5,760	1,958
Totals	$100,000	$34,000	$100,000	$34,000

year. What is the project's expected operating cash flow for the year if the company pays a 15 percent marginal tax rate?

The top part of Table 8.6 presents the *pro forma* operating statement for Prev Corporation's proposed project. The bottom part shows the operating cash flow (OCF) statement for calculating operating cash flow. The OCF statement includes only the cash inflows and outflows and excludes noncash items such as depreciation. Table 8.6 shows the OCF statement *without* and *with* depreciation expense to illustrate the tax savings that depreciation creates. Without the $8,000 depreciation expense, OCF equals $11,900; with the $8,000 depreciation expense, OCF equals $13,100. In other words, OCF with depreciation is $1,200 greater ($13,100 − $11,900) than without it because the proposed project's depreciation expense reduces the company's tax bill. This example demonstrates that the impact of depreciation on operating cash flow comes "through the back door" through tax savings. The tax savings equal the marginal tax rate times the depreciation expense: $1,200 = 0.15 × $8,000.

For the sake of emphasis, Table 8.6 shows Prev paying no interest expense associated with the project. Even if Prev had paid interest, however, the operating cash flow (OCF) from the project would remain unchanged. For example, if Prev had financed the project in part with debt requiring a $1,000 interest expense, the OCF would still be $13,100. OCF from a project is the cash flow generated by operating assets, irrespective of the way they are financed. The percentage cost of debt is included in the weighted-average cost of capital, used to discount OCF. Including interest expense in OCF *and* the percentage cost of debt in the discount rate would be double counting. Therefore OCF *excludes interest expense.*

For operating statements (such as the one in Table 8.6) that exclude interest expense, the following equation can be used to calculate operating cash flow (OCF):

$$OCF = EAT + Depreciation$$
$$= \$5,100 + \$8,000$$
$$= \$13,100$$

TABLE 8.6

Pro Forma Operating Statements of a Proposed Project Showing the Impact of Depreciation on Operating Cash Flow

Pro Forma Operating Statement

	Without Depreciation	With Depreciation
Sales revenue	$20,000	$20,000
Less labor expense (cash)	6,000	6,000
Less depreciation	0	8,000
Earnings before interest and taxes	$14,000	$ 6,000
Less interest expense	0	0
Earnings before taxes	$14,000	$ 6,000
Less income taxes (15%)	2,100	900
Earnings after taxes	$11,900	$ 5,100

Operating Cash Flow Statement

	Without Depreciation	With Depreciation
Cash inflow (sales revenue)	$20,000	$20,000
Less labor expense (cash)	6,000	6,000
Less income taxes	2,100	900
Operating cash flow	$11,900	$13,100

where EAT represents earnings after taxes (same as net income and net profit). This equation yields an OCF of $13,100 for the example, just as the OCF statement does in Table 8.6.[4]

An alternative method for calculating operating cash flow (OCF) relates OCF to earnings before interest and taxes (EBIT), the marginal tax rate (T), and depreciation:

$$OCF = EBIT(1 - T) + Depreciation$$
$$= \$6,000(1 - 0.15) + \$8,000$$
$$= \$13,100$$

[4]The restricted use of the equation can be shown by first expressing earnings after taxes (EAT) in terms of earnings before interest and taxes (EBIT), dollar interest (I), and the marginal tax rate (T):

$$EAT = (EBIT - I)(1 - T)$$
$$= EBIT - I - T(EBIT) + T(I)$$
$$= EBIT(1 - T) - I(1 - T)$$

Rearranging the equation produces:

$$EBIT(1 - T) = EAT + I(1 - T)$$

Substitute the right side of this equation for EBIT(1 − T) in the following equation:

$$OCF = EBIT(1 - T) + Depreciation$$
$$= EAT + I(1 - T) + Depreciation$$

Now you can see that OCF equals EAT plus depreciation if, and only if, I = 0 or is excluded from the operating statement.

This method also generates the same OCF as that from the statement in Table 8.6. The logic of the equation is: (1) EBIT = EBT (earnings before taxes) because of the exclusion of interest expense. (2) Therefore EBIT(1 − T) represents earnings after taxes (EAT). (3) Adding depreciation to EBIT(1 − T), or equivalently EAT, to get OCF recognizes that depreciation is a noncash expense. If other noncash expenses (e.g., deferred taxes and amortized expenses) had been included in the operating statement, then they too would be added back.[5]

Regardless of method, capital budgeting requires the calculation of annual operating cash flows during the estimated life of a proposed project. Operating cash flows, not earnings after taxes, are the dollar amounts used in evaluating proposed capital investments. Operating cash flows typically occur over several years, with the amount in each year differing because of varying sales revenues, production and distribution costs, materials costs, and depreciation expense. For a three-year project, the cash flows discussed so far look like this:

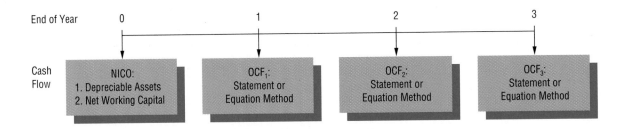

At this point, only one more cash flow needs to be estimated: the expected cash flow arising from terminating the project.

PROJECT-DISPOSAL CASH FLOW

Proposed capital projects have a life limited to a specified number of years. Depreciable assets do not last forever, and products that a company sells as a result of a capital investment will not command a market forever. Because capital projects have a finite life, capital-budgeting analysis includes the cash flow associated with terminating the project.

---

[5] An equivalent equation for operating cash flow (OCF) can be derived as follows:

$$OCF = EBIT(1 - T) + Depreciation$$
$$= EBIT(1 - T) + Depreciation - T(Depreciation) + T(Depreciation)$$
$$= EBIT(1 - T) + Depreciation(1 - T) + T(Depreciation)$$
$$= (EBIT + Depreciation)(1 - T) + T(Depreciation)$$

Applied to the data in Table 8.6, the equation becomes:

$$OCF = (\$6,000 + \$8,000)(1 - 0.15) + 0.15(\$8,000)$$
$$= \$11,900 + \$1,200$$
$$= \$13,100$$

The operating cash flow of $13,100 is the same as that obtained with the alternative methods.

Cash Flow from Disposal of Depreciable Assets

Selling depreciable assets at the end of a project's life may create a capital gain or a capital loss. Either case affects the company's tax bill. The cash flow from disposal of depreciable assets is the selling price adjusted for tax consequences.

A taxable gain occurs when a corporation sells a depreciable asset for more than its book value for tax purposes. Since the Tax Reform Act of 1986, the gain is taxed at the corporation's marginal *income* tax rate. Prior to this act, corporations used an alternative rate of 28 percent if their income tax rate was higher.[6] A capital loss occurs when a corporation sells a depreciable asset for less than its book value. The loss is tax deductible as an ordinary expense because it represents an understatement of past depreciation charges on the company's tax returns. Like depreciation, the loss produces a tax shelter—a noncash, tax-deductible expense.[7]

EXAMPLE

Strand Corporation sells for $70,000 a depreciable asset originally acquired about 2 years ago for $60,000. The company has used MACRS depreciation, resulting in a book value of $30,000. The company pays marginal income taxes at the 34 percent rate. What is the cash flow from disposal?

In the above example Strand Corporation disposes of an asset for more than its book value. Strand therefore has a taxable gain:

Selling price	$70,000
Less book value	30,000
Taxable gain	$40,000
Multiplied by tax rate	× 0.34
Total taxes	$13,600

Strand's cash flow from disposal of the asset is the difference between cash inflows and outflows:

Cash inflow (selling price)	$70,000
Less cash outflow (taxes)	13,600
Cash flow from disposal	$56,400

What would be the cash flow from disposal if Strand sold the asset for $26,000? Then the company would have a tax-deductible loss measured by the

[6] The U.S. tax code specifies that a gain in excess of book value but less than the historical acquisition cost is *depreciation recapture*. The gain larger than depreciation recapture (measured by selling price less historical cost) is 1231 Gain, named for a section of the tax code. The alternative tax rate of 28 percent applied to the 1231 Gain.

[7] Generally, corporations may deduct from taxable income only those losses on capital assets used for the production of income. Other capital losses may be deducted from capital gains but not from taxable income. If these capital losses exceed capital gains, the excess may be carried back three years, and any part still unused may be carried forward five years, in each case to the earliest year first. By offsetting the capital gains, such capital losses reduce a corporation's tax liability.

difference between the MACRS book value and the selling price. The loss produces a tax savings:

Book value	$30,000
Less selling price	26,000
Loss	$ 4,000
Multiplied by tax rate	× 0.34
Tax savings	$ 1,360

Strand's cash flow in this case equals $27,360:

Cash inflow (selling price)	$26,000
Add tax savings	1,360
Cash flow from disposal	$27,360

The following illustration portrays the cash flow from disposal of depreciable assets at the end of a three-year project:

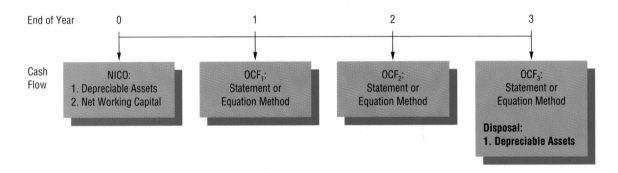

Cash Flow from Disposal of Net Working Capital

Recall that part of the investment in a capital project may consist of net working capital—cash, receivables, and inventory less current liabilities. At the end of a project's life, the company liquidates the project's current assets and pays the project's current liabilities. The difference between the current assets and the current liabilities is the cash flow from disposal of net working capital. As a practical matter, financial managers usually assume that the company will liquidate current assets at book values. This assumption means that the initial investment in net working capital is returned upon completion of the project. This return is the final cash flow from the project.[8]

EXAMPLE

Strand Corporation expects to invest $28,000 in inventory and receivables as part of its investment in a proposed capital project. The company will rely on trade creditors to finance $12,000 of the current assets. Strand's incremental investment in net working capital (current assets less current liabilities) is

---

[8] There are situations in which disposal of inventory results in a gain or a loss—the selling price may be greater or less than the book value. In addition, accounts receivable may be uncollectible, causing a tax-deductible write-off.

$16,000. The financial manager assumes for capital-budgeting purposes that the future cash flow from disposal of net working capital will be at book value:

Liquidated current assets	$28,000
Less amount paid to short-term creditors	12,000
Cash flow from disposal of net working capital	$16,000

The following illustration portrays the cash flow from disposal of net working capital at the end of a three-year project:

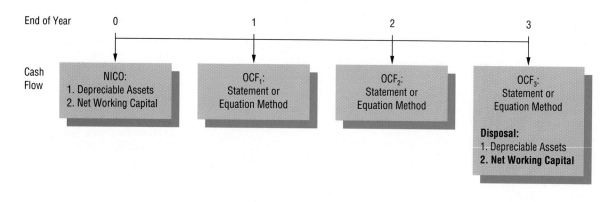

REVIEW OF THE CASH FLOWS

When financial managers evaluate a proposed capital investment, they must forecast the amount and timing of incremental, after-tax cash flows attributable to the project. Here is a summary of the cash flows involved in the evaluation of a typical project:

1. The first group of cash flows consists of those included in the net investment cash outflow, the cash required to initiate the project.
   a. Determine the cost of depreciable assets involved in the project and add to this cost any delivery charges and installation costs necessary to put the assets in working order. (Reduce this amount by the investment tax credit if allowed. The ITC reduces the income taxes the company will pay.)
   b. The second part of the proposed project's net investment cash outflow is the investment in net working capital. Take the required increase in the company's cash balance, accounts receivable, and inventory, and subtract the expected increase in current liabilities attributable to the project.[9] The resulting amount is the incremental

---

[9] Normally, the increase in current liabilities will consist of increases in accounts payable to suppliers and accrued expenses such as wages and taxes. Increases in notes payable to banks are normally excluded for one of the following reasons: (1) The borrowing is temporary and will not be refinanced. (2) If continually refinanced, the cost of the bank borrowing is included in the company's cost of capital; in this case the effect of the notes payable is taken care of in the discount rate, not in the net investment cash outflow.

Strategic Planning and Capital Budgeting

Strategic planning helps companies cope with competition and provides direction for capital budgeting. Viewed broadly, competition is characterized for a company in the following ways: (1) jockeying for position among current competitors, (2) threat of new entrants to the industry, (3) threat of substitute products, (4) bargaining power of customers, and (5) bargaining power of suppliers. Attempts to cope with these competitive forces narrow management's focus on potential capital expenditures. Project proposals that help a company to meet or beat the competition receive high priority.

Consider the competitive challenge of new entrants to an industry. New entrants bring new capacity, take market share, and generally cause turmoil. The key for existing competitors in generating successful capital projects is to erect and maintain barriers to entry against the potential newcomers. Successful projects usually involve building defenses against potential competitors or creating products and services where competition is weakest.

Companies may create, preserve, or enhance their competitive advantages by investing in projects that raise the following barriers to entry:

1. **Economies of scale.** Large capital requirements go hand-in-hand with economies of scale, which exist whenever costs rise less than proportionally with increases in scale of production, marketing, or financing. Scale economies force potential entrants to invest on a large scale or face cost disadvantages. These economies, especially in production, account for the small number of automobile manufacturers.

2. **Product differentiation.** Brand loyalty creates a barrier by forcing aspirants to spend heavily to gain recognition for their products. Coca-Cola Company and PepsiCo Inc. take advantage of large advertising expenditures and superior marketing skills to sell soft drinks worldwide. Approximately two out of every three soft drinks consumed in the United States are sold by these two companies.

3. **Cost disadvantages.** Entrenched companies may have cost advantages not available to potential entrants, independent of economies of scale. Low-cost producers take advantage of the learning curve, proprietary technology, or low-cost raw materials. For example, Wal-

Mart and Southwest Airlines are each low-cost competitors in their respective industries.

4. **Distribution channels.** Limited access to channels of distribution often deters newcomers to an industry. A new potato-chip manufacturer, for example, will have trouble displacing Frito-Lay from the supermarket shelf. Also, replicating Avon's network of 900,000 independent sales representatives seems nearly impossible.

5. **Government policy.** Government controls, regulations, and licensing requirements may limit or foreclose entry of new competitors. Quotas on Japanese cars have limited the ability of Toyota and Mitsubishi to expand sales in the United States. Also, rigorous regulations controlling waste disposal help protect Browning Ferris Industries and WMX Technologies.

In summary, a run-of-the-mill company in a highly competitive industry will have difficulty in generating good ideas for capital investments. The key to success in capital budgeting is *competitive advantage.*

Source: Based on Michael E. Porter, "How Competitive Forces Shape Strategy," *Harvard Business Review,* March–April 1979, 137–145; and Alan C. Shapiro, "Corporate Strategy and the Capital Budgeting Decision," *Midland Corporate Finance Journal,* Spring 1985, 22–36.

investment in net working capital associated with the proposed project.

2. The second group of cash flows consists of the operating cash flows. Estimate the expected operating cash flow for each year of the life of the proposed project. Begin by calculating a *pro forma* operating statement

for each year. Then calculate the operating cash flow with the statement method or with the equation method.

3. The third group of cash flows consists of the project-disposal cash flows.
   a. Estimate the after-tax cash flow from liquidating depreciable assets: selling price less taxes (if sold for a gain), or selling price plus tax savings (if sold at a loss).
   b. Estimate the cash flow from disposal of net working capital. This cash flow is usually assumed to be the same as the investment in net working capital considered in *1b* above.

This chapter presents the administrative features of investing in proposed capital projects and examines the way a financial manager calculates cash flows. Chapter 9 focuses on the way financial managers combine the timing and size of cash flows to determine whether or not the company should invest in a proposed project.

SUMMARY

• Capital budgeting is the process of evaluating and selecting capital investment projects. Ideas for capital investments may come from several different sources—planning committees, vendors, or employees, for example. Many companies formalize the process of capital budgeting because of the large cash outlays and long-term nature of the projects. Large investment projects must usually be approved by high-ranking company managers.

• The financial manager estimates all incremental, after-tax cash flows of a project and completes the capital-budgeting analysis based on the amount and timing of these cash flows. Cash flows normally vary from year to year because of changes in depreciation expense, sales revenue, cost of raw materials, and salaries.

• The net investment cash outflow of a typical project consists of two parts: (1) the cost of depreciable assets (including delivery charges and installation costs) reduced by the amount of the investment tax credit when allowed, and (2) the investment in net working capital—current assets minus current liabilities.

• Corporations pay a 34 percent tax rate, marginal and average, on taxable income over $335,000. Income taxes reduce operating cash flows. The loss carryback, carryforward rule applies to losses, meaning that a company may receive a refund as a result of a loss.

• Companies may use either MACRS or straight-line depreciation for calculating operating cash flow. Each method requires the depreciable asset to be assigned a class life specified by the tax code. The half-year convention requires the company to take only a half-year of depreciation in the year of acquisition and a half-year of depreciation in the year of retirement. The depreciation method employed in evaluating proposed projects should be the same as that used by the company on its tax return.

• MACRS results in larger tax savings than straight line early in the life of an asset. Straight line results in larger tax savings than MACRS late in the life of an asset. The financial manager should use the method producing the larger present value of tax savings—MACRS in most cases.

• Operating cash flows arise from the operation of a capital project. An operating cash flow statement can be used to calculate operating cash flow (OCF), or alternatively, the following equation can be used:

$$OCF = EBIT(1 - T) + Depreciation$$

where EBIT is earnings before interest and taxes, and T is the company's marginal income tax rate. If interest expense is excluded, as it should be, from the *pro forma* operating statement, then OCF can be calculated as follows:

$$OCF = Earnings\ after\ taxes + Depreciation$$

Each of these methods provides the same dollar estimate.

• The project-disposal cash flow is the project's final cash flow. One part of the disposal cash flow is the after-tax cash flow from selling (liquidating) depreciable assets. The company may realize either a gain or a loss from the disposal. A gain is taxable at the company's marginal income tax rate. A capital loss is tax deductible from a company's ordinary income. The second part of disposal cash flow is the return of net working capital.

Key Terms

net investment cash outflow (NICO)

incremental cash flows

sunk cost

indirect cash flows

depreciable asset

investment tax credit (ITC)

net working capital

marginal tax rate

average tax rate

modified accelerated cost recovery system (MACRS)

class life

straight-line depreciation

historical cost

half-year convention

depreciable basis

tax shelter

Questions

8.1. Define the following terms: *capital expenditure, capital budget,* and *capital budgeting.*

8.2. Describe the five basic steps in capital budgeting.

8.3. Richard J. Marshuetz, chief financial officer of American Can, states: "Once the proposal's value is calculated, the approval process begins." He goes on to say that the general manager of a business unit in American Can may approve projects amounting to $250,000; sector executives have authority up to $1 million; an investment committee approves projects involving $1 million to $3 million; and the board of directors must approve all projects larger than $3 million. Mr. Marshuetz says that "these levels may be raised as we gain experience." Explain the probable reasoning for American Can's authorization procedure.

8.4. A typical capital project involves a *net investment cash outflow,* followed by several years of *operating cash flows* and a final *disposal cash flow.* Describe each of these three types of cash flows.

8.5. What is meant by *incremental cash flows?* Are sunk costs incremental cash flows? Explain. When a company replaces an old machine with a new

one, is the salvage value of the old machine an incremental cash flow? Explain.

8.6. In their research at Santa Clara University, Professors Meir Statman and David Caldwell pose the following scenario: Suppose you are involved in a business venture in which you have already lost $2,000. Now you face a choice between a sure gain of $1,000 and an even chance to earn $2,000 or nothing. Which will you choose if you are risk averse? Explain your choice and the role of sunk cost in it.

8.7. The following outline shows a history of the investment tax credit (ITC):

Date	Congressional Action
January 1962	7% ITC instituted
October 1966	ITC suspended
March 1967	7% ITC reinstated
April 1969	ITC suspended
April 1971	7% ITC reinstated
January 1975	ITC increased to 10%
January 1986	ITC suspended

a. What is the purpose of the ITC?

b. Prior to January 1986, corporations could use the ITC to offset the cost of movable office partitions but not to offset the cost of permanent walls. What impact do you suppose this rule had on corporate office environments during the early 1980s?

8.8. The *pro forma* operating statement for a capital project, without depreciation expense and with depreciation expense, is provided below:

	Without Depreciation	With Depreciation
Sales revenue	$100,000	$100,000
Cash expenses	50,000	50,000
Depreciation	0	20,000
EBIT	$ 50,000	$ 30,000
Income taxes (15%)	7,500	4,500
Earnings after taxes	$ 42,500	$ 25,500

a. What is the project's operating cash flow without depreciation? With depreciation? Describe the alternative methods that you can use to answer these questions.

b. What accounts for the increase in the project's operating cash flow when depreciation is present? Use the term *tax shelter* or *tax shield* in your answer.

c. Assume that the owner of the project finances it partially with debt, thus creating interest expense of $10,000. What impact does the interest expense have on the project's operating cash flow? Explain.

8.9. The Tax Reform Act of 1986 allows companies to calculate depreciation on personal property in either of two ways for tax purposes: (1) modified accelerated cost recovery system (MACRS) or (2) straight line. Two companies, Alpha and Omega, have each purchased a $200,000 piece of equipment. Alpha's earnings are large and growing. Omega will operate at a deficit for 2 years, at which time it will begin to turn large profits.

Which depreciation method, MACRS or straight line, should each company adopt? Explain.

8.10. The modified accelerated cost recovery system (MACRS) permits companies to expense the outlay for a depreciable asset over a specified period of time.

a. Identify the class lives associated with MACRS.

b. Explain the meaning of 200 percent declining balance with half-year convention.

c. If a company uses MACRS for tax-reporting purposes and uses straight-line depreciation for financial-reporting purposes, then which method should the financial manager use to calculate a proposed project's cash flows?

8.11. Place a minus sign $(-)$ before each of the following if it represents an incremental cash outflow, a plus sign $(+)$ if it represents an incremental cash inflow, and a zero (0) if it is not incremental:

_____a. Purchase of a $78,000 depreciable asset.

_____b. The corporation charges a project $8,000 annually for accounting and computer time. The corporate staff has sufficient capacity to handle these services without hiring new personnel or buying new equipment.

_____c. The corporation charges a project $8,000 annually for accounting and computer time. The corporate staff incurs $8,000 annual additional salary expense for overtime to information system personnel.

_____d. Depreciation expense of $13,000 annually for financial reporting.

_____e. MACRS depreciation for tax reporting.

_____f. Income taxes of $7,200 associated with a project.

_____g. Interest expense of $976 on the bonds sold to finance a depreciable asset.

_____h. Gain of $4,200 from selling a depreciable asset at the end of the project's life.

_____i. Disposal of net working capital.

Strategy Problem

The financial manager of American Pencil Corporation is evaluating an investment in a new process that uses lasers to put lead in pencils. The project will have a 5-year life and require the purchase of new equipment for $226,000. The new equipment has a 3-year class life and will be depreciated on a straight-line basis using the half-year convention. Net working capital of $42,700 will be invested when the company implements the project. American Pencil's financial manager expects to sell the equipment for $34,000 and to recover the entire amount of net working capital upon termination of the project.

The company's marketing manager estimates that incremental sales will be $275,000 in the first year and will increase 10 percent each year during the life of the project. Incremental overhead and rental expenses associated with the project will be $85,000 annually. The company's cost accountant anticipates variable costs equaling 45 percent of sales. In addition, the project will be charged 5 percent of sales in order to account for information systems and accounting support; however, the company will not experience additional cash outflows for these items because there is sufficient capacity to service the demands of the project. American Pencil is in the 34 percent marginal tax bracket. Calculate all incremental cash flows associated with the project.

Strategy

Add the cost of equipment and net working capital.

Use straight-line depreciation; don't forget the half-year convention.

Construct pro forma *operating statements; ignore the 5 percent overhead charges.*

Use the operating statements to calculate operating cash flows.

Don't forget disposal cash flow!

Cash flow from disposal of depreciable assets.

Solution

Begin by calculating the net investment cash outflow:

$$\text{NICO} = \text{Depreciable equipment} + \text{Net working capital}$$

$$= \$226,000 + \$42,700 = \$268,700$$

Before calculating operating cash flow, determine the yearly depreciation expense for tax purposes:

$$\text{Depreciation expense} = \frac{\$226,000}{3 \text{ years}} = \$75,333 \text{ per year}$$

The half-year convention means that depreciation expense will be $75,333/2 = \$37,667$ in Year 1 and in Year 4.

Pro Forma Operating Statement

	Year 1	Year 2	Year 3	Year 4	Year 5
Sales	$275,000	$302,500	$332,750	$366,025	$402,628
Less costs:					
Variable	123,750	136,125	149,738	164,711	181,182
Fixed	85,000	85,000	85,000	85,000	85,000
Depreciation	37,667	75,333	75,333	37,667	0
Earnings before taxes	$ 28,583	$ 6,042	$ 22,679	$ 78,647	$136,446
Less taxes (34%)	9,718	2,054	7,711	26,740	46,392
Earnings after taxes	$ 18,865	$ 3,988	$ 14,968	$ 51,907	$ 90,054

Operating Cash Flow Statement

	Year 1	Year 2	Year 3	Year 4	Year 5
Cash inflows (sales)	$275,000	$302,500	$332,750	$366,025	$402,628
Less cash outflows:					
Variable costs	123,750	136,125	149,738	164,711	181,182
Fixed costs	85,000	85,000	85,000	85,000	85,000
Taxes	9,718	2,054	7,711	26,740	46,392
Operating cash flow	$ 56,532	$ 79,321	$ 90,301	$ 89,574	$ 90,054
Add disposal cash flow:					
Equipment[a]					22,440
Net working capital					42,700
Annual cash flow	$ 56,532	$ 79,321	$ 90,301	$ 89,574	$155,194

[a] Cash flow from disposal of the equipment is the sale price net of taxes:

Sale price	$34,000
Less book value	0
Gain	$34,000
Less taxes (34%)	11,560
Cash flow	$22,440

Show results on a time line.

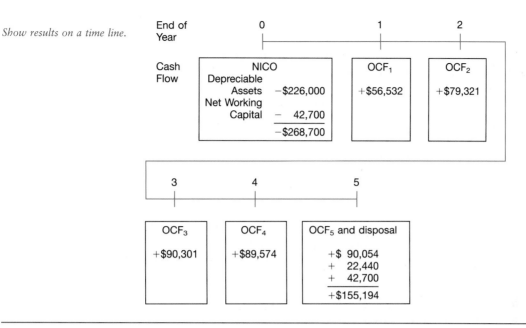

End of Year	0	1	2
Cash Flow	NICO	OCF₁	OCF₂

NICO
Depreciable
  Assets   −$226,000
Net Working
  Capital   −   42,700
              ─────────
              −$268,700

OCF$_1$ +$56,532

OCF$_2$ +$79,321

3	4	5

OCF$_3$ +$90,301

OCF$_4$ +$89,574

OCF$_5$ and disposal
  +$ 90,054
  +   22,440
  +   42,700
  ──────────
  +$155,194

◆ Demonstration Problem

The R. Porter Company (RPC) is considering an investment in equipment to expand sales of its steel products—angle iron, scrap metal, and sheet metal. The equipment will cost $500,000, and its delivery and installation will cost $130,000. Plans call for the equipment to be housed in a fully depreciated $300,000 building that RPC owns but has never used and for which RPC has no other use. If the company goes forward with the project, its inventory investment will rise $75,000, and its accounts payable will rise $45,000.

For tax purposes RPC will use the MACRS procedure to calculate annual depreciation charges for the project, which has a 3-year class life. The project will terminate at the end of 4 years, at which time the company will recoup its investment in net working capital and sell the equipment as salvage for $50,000.

The project will produce annual sales revenue of $490,000, but it will cause an annual decline of $80,000 in sales of other RPC products viewed as close substitutes for the steel products. Cash expenses associated with the project are $110,000 per year. RPC's marginal tax rate is 34 percent.

a. How do companies like RPC generate ideas for capital expenditures?
b. A capital-budgeting analyst for a Fortune 500 company said: "Generating ideas for capital projects is a *creative* exercise, but estimating their cash flows is *laborious.*" What does the analyst mean?
c. Define the term *sunk cost*. What is the sunk cost associated with RPC's project? Is this cost relevant to RPC's investment decision? Explain.
d. Calculate the net investment cash outflow for the project. Explain why the increase in net working capital is part of the cash outflow.
e. Calculate the project-disposal cash flow.
f. Use the following MACRS rates to calculate the project's annual depreciation charges: 0.3333, 0.4444, 0.1482, and 0.0741 for Years 1 through 4, respectively.
g. Use an operating cash flow (OCF) statement to calculate the OCF for each year of the project's life. Calculate the tax shield created by depreciation in Year 1.
h. Use the following equations to calculate the operating cash flow (OCF) for Year 1:

$$OCF = EBIT\,(1 - T) + D$$
$$OCF = (EBIT + D)(1 - T) + TD$$

where EBIT is earnings before interest and taxes, T is the marginal tax rate, and D is depreciation expense. (*Note:* You should get the same answer with the two equations.)

i. Summarize the annual incremental cash flows attributable to the project by filling in the following blanks:

End of Year	Incremental Cash Flow
0	$_____
1	_____
2	_____
3	_____
4	_____

j. Suppose that RPC partially financed the project with a bank loan and incurred annual interest payments of $60,000. What impact would these payments have on operating cash flow? No calculations are called for but explain your answer.

k. In view of the cash flows in Part *i*, do you believe that RPC should invest in the project? No calculations are called for but explain your answer.

Problems

Relevant tax rate

8.1. Suppose you own 100 percent of the common stock of a corporation that will have a taxable income of $50,000 during the coming year. The corporation's tax liability will be $7,500 (0.15 × $50,000). Now suppose you decide (on behalf of your corporation) to invest in a project that will increase the corporation's taxable income to $70,000. As a result, the corporation's tax liability will be $12,500 [0.15($50,000) + 0.25($20,000)].

a. What is the corporation's average tax rate if you decide to invest in the project?

b. What is the corporation's marginal tax rate if you decide to invest in the project?

c. Which tax rate, average or marginal, is relevant to your decision to invest in the project? Explain.

Taxes and depreciation tax shield

8.2. Hanzel Corporation's sales revenue for 19X3 is $2,300,000. Its depreciation expense is $50,000, and its earnings before taxes are $300,000.

a. What is the corporation's marginal tax rate?

b. Calculate the corporation's average tax rate.

c. Calculate the tax savings associated with the corporation's depreciation expense.

Marginal vs. average tax rate

8.3. Bulgar Company's taxable income is $1 million. Calculate the company's average tax rate and compare it to the company's marginal tax rate. Which is larger, the average or the marginal tax rate? For what range of taxable income would your answer remain unchanged?

Depreciation methods

8.4. For $160,000 Alar Corporation purchases a depreciable asset with a 3-year class life.

a. Use the straight-line method to calculate the annual depreciation expense for tax purposes.

b. Use MACRS (modified accelerated cost recovery system) to calculate the annual depreciation expense.

c. Alar Corporation uses units-of-production depreciation for financial reporting to investors. Which method—MACRS or units-of-production—is relevant for calculating the project's operating cash flows? Explain your choice.

Tax liabilities

8.5. Letter Corporation's income before taxes is $500,000 for 19X3. In addition, the corporation has a $110,000 capital gain. Assuming a 34 percent income tax rate, what is Letter's total tax liability for 19X3?

Benefit of MACRS vs. straight line

8.6. Leslie Meer must decide which depreciation method to use for her company's proposed $360,000 investment in hydraulic drilling equipment. The class life of the equipment is 5 years.
   a. Calculate the depreciation for each year for the following choices (include the half-year convention): (1) MACRS depreciation and (2) straight-line depreciation.
   b. If the company were in the 34 percent marginal tax bracket, what would be the tax savings each year with each of the two depreciation methods?
   c. Demonstrate why a financial manager would prefer MACRS over straight-line depreciation by calculating the present value of each year's tax savings discounted at 12 percent. Assume the tax savings occur at the end of each year. Interpret your results.

Operating cash flow

8.7. The *pro forma* annual operating statement for a capital investment is provided below:

Sales revenue	$2,500,000
Cash expenses	1,250,000
Depreciation	450,000
EBIT	$ 800,000

The tax rate relevant to the investment is 34 percent.
   a. Use an operating cash flow (OCF) statement to calculate the annual OCF for the project.
   b. Use an equation method to calculate the annual OCF for the project.

Operating cash flow

8.8. The financial manager of Kovos Company is estimating the annual operating cash flows for a proposed project to manufacture a new product. The accounting and marketing departments provide the following annual revenue and cost estimates:

Sales revenue	$200,000
Materials and labor	128,000
Supervision and maintenance	19,000
Depreciation	30,000
Earnings before taxes	$ 23,000

Kovos Company's marginal tax rate (federal and state) is 40 percent.
   a. Calculate the additional income taxes per year the company must pay if management accepts the proposed project.
   b. Use an operating cash flow (OCF) statement to calculate the OCF for each year of the project's life.
   c. Use an equation method to calculate the OCF for each year of the project's life.

Operating cash flow

8.9. Mechanico Corporation's financial manager is considering an investment in a new product with an expected 5-year life. The company will spend $160,000 on depreciable assets to produce and market the product and $26,000 to increase net working capital. The increase in annual sales from the product is an expected 20,000 units at $10 each, or $200,000 in each year of the product's 5-year life. Incremental salaries and rent of facilities associated with the project will be $60,000 annually, and the company's cost accountant anticipates variable costs per unit to be $3.20. Assume that depreciation expense is $32,000 annually for tax-reporting purposes. Mechanico pays an average tax rate of 34 percent and is in the 40 percent marginal tax bracket. The financial manager expects to finance the project with bonds having $16,000 annual interest. Calculate the annual operating cash flow associated with this project.

Operating cash flow

8.10. Aronson Company plans to invest in an information system that will save $30,000 annually in cash expenses. Annual depreciation charges (D) attributable to the system are $10,000. Therefore, the project will cause the company's annual earnings before interest and taxes (EBIT) to rise $20,000. The company's marginal tax rate is 34 percent. Use the following equations to calculate the annual operating cash flow (OCF) produced by the investment:

$$OCF = EBIT(1 - T) + D$$

$$OCF = (EBIT + D)(1 - T) + TD$$

You should get the same answer with the two equations.

Cash flow from disposal

8.11. Merrill Enterprises Inc. is disposing of depreciable assets it has had for 3 years. Merrill's purchasing agent acquired the assets for $160,000, and the MACRS accumulated depreciation presently equals $92,800. The marginal income tax rate for the company is 34 percent.
  a. Calculate Merrill's disposal cash flow from the following transactions:
     (1) Selling the assets for $180,000.
     (2) Selling the assets for $67,200.
     (3) Selling the assets for $40,000.
  b. Comment on the following statement (no calculations are needed): "Your company's treasurer is aware of the tax benefits from incurring a tax-deductible loss. Management's judgment indicates that your interests would be best served if the company incurs tax losses. For this reason, we accepted a $40,000 price rather than $67,200 for the asset discussed above."

Incremental cash flows

8.12. The financial manager of G. F. Booth Company is evaluating a proposed capital project with a delivered price of $125,000. Installation of the project will cost $15,000. As a result of the project, the company's inventory will rise $20,000 and its accounts payable will rise $10,000. The company has already spent $2,000 on search costs, trying to identify reputable vendors of the project.

   The financial manager expects the project to terminate at the end of 4 years, at which time the net working capital will be recovered, and the depreciable assets will be sold for $25,000. For tax purposes, the class life of the project is 3 years, and the financial manager will use the MACRS procedure to calculate depreciation expense.

   Booth's sales revenue will rise $200,000 per year as a result of the project. In addition, the proposed project will cause a $10,000 per year drop in cash expenses associated with an existing project. Direct cash expenses per year associated with the proposed project are $100,000. The company's marginal tax rate is 34 percent.
  a. Calculate Booth's net investment cash outflow for the proposed project.
  b. Calculate the project-disposal cash flow.
  c. Calculate the annual depreciation expense associated with the proposed project.
  d. Calculate the annual incremental cash inflows attributable to the proposed project.

Incremental cash flows

8.13. Freeman Company recently hired Jay Hartz to assist Marie Stoller, the chief financial officer. Arriving for his first day on the job, Mr. Hartz discovers that Ms. Stoller has been called out of town on important business. Ms. Stoller's secretary gives him the following message: "Please calculate the relevant incremental cash flows for the Ajax Project. My secretary will give you the necessary information." Looking up from the note, Mr. Hartz has thrust in his face another piece of paper with the following information on it:

   • Expected project life, 4 years.

- Class life of equipment, 3 years; price of equipment, $300,000; installation costs, $80,000.
- Additional net working capital, $50,000.
- Use MACRS to calculate depreciation expenses.
- Expected first-year sales revenue from project, $400,000; expected growth rate in sales revenue, 8 percent per year; expected cash expenses, 60 percent of sales revenue.
- Assume that the equipment can be sold for $50,000 at the end of 4 years; net working capital will also be recovered at that time.
- Freeman Company's marginal tax rate is 34 percent.

Mr. Hartz feels overwhelmed by his assignment. Although a recent college graduate, he did not study business financial management—too tough, he had thought at the time. Mr. Hartz decides to get help and calls you, his close personal friend. Please help him to complete the assignment by calculating the incremental cash flows for the Ajax Project.

Comprehensive problem   **8.14.**   The financial manager of Calcax Industries is considering a proposal for the company to develop a new system of bagging chemical fertilizers. The depreciable assets to cut and form the bags will cost $104,000, and delivery charges will increase the cost to $120,000. According to Calcax's tax consultant, the depreciable equipment will have a 5-year class life for MACRS. The financial manager expects the company to carry an inventory of $52,000 and to have accounts receivable of $58,000 associated with the proposed project. Calcax will use trade credit to finance $40,000 of the increase in current assets. The financial manager expects to dispose of the depreciable assets for $30,000 at the end of the 4-year life of the project and to recover the net working capital in the project.

The company uses straight-line depreciation with the required half-year convention for tax reporting and straight-line depreciation without the half-year convention for financial reporting. A 10 percent investment tax credit is available (its use does not affect the depreciation calculation).

The company's cost accountant informs the financial manager that the labor and material required to produce the bags will be $4.50 per bag, consisting of $3.00 in labor and material and $1.50 in additional variable overhead. The marketing manager expects to spend $4,000 annually for advertising the bags. Each bag will sell for $5.00, and the demand for the bags is expected to vary over the project's 4-year life. Personnel anticipates hiring an additional machine-tool operator for $26,000 annually. The following table summarizes the cost and sales information:

Price and Cost Information

Unit selling price		$5.00
Unit production costs:		
Labor and material	$3.00	
Variable overhead	$1.50	
		$4.50
Unit contribution margin		$0.50

Estimated Unit Sales

Year 1	Year 2	Year 3	Year 4
90,000	120,000	120,000	120,000

Incremental annual fixed costs

Salaries	$26,000
Advertising	$ 4,000

Calcax pays a 34 percent marginal tax rate. The company's tax consultant believes that this rate will prevail over the next 6 to 8 years. Calculate all incremental cash flows associated with this project and place them on a time line like that in Figure 8.2 to summarize your results.

Computer Problems 🖫

Depreciation: template
DEPRN

8.15. Chang Tools acquired a new jig boring machine for $42,000. Delivery and installation costs are $8,000. The class life of the machine is 5 years.
   a. Calculate the annual depreciation for each year using:
      (1) Straight-line depreciation with the half-year convention.
      (2) Modified accelerated cost recovery system.
   b. Recalculate Part *a* assuming the class life of the machine is 3 years.
   c. Calculate the company's annual tax savings from depreciation for marginal tax rates of 25 and 34 percent.
   d. For each of the above cases calculate the present value of tax savings assuming a discount rate of 14 percent, 18 percent, and 24 percent.
   e. How do the class life and the tax rate affect the present value of tax savings?

Tax on sale of assets:
template TAXASST

8.16. Hill Oil purchased a drilling rig for $100,000 in 19X2 and sold it 3 years later in 19X5 for $60,000. The class life of the rig is 5 years. The company's marginal income tax rate is 34 percent.
   a. Calculate the total taxes payable on the sales proceeds.
   b. What would be the taxes payable if the rig had been sold for $150,000, $100,000, and $20,000?
   c. Recalculate Part *a* and Part *b* assuming the rig had been used for one year.
   d. Recalculate Part *a*, Part *b*, and Part *c* assuming the class life of the rig had been 3 years.

Cash flow estimation:
template CASHFLOW

8.17. The financial manager of Apex Industries is evaluating a project to increase the production and sales of the company's lawn mowers. She has collected the following data:

Cost of depreciable assets	$182,000
Delivery and installation costs	18,000

An investment tax credit is unavailable. The assets have a class life of 5 years and will be used for 4 years, after which they will be disposed of at a price of $50,000. Inventories, accounts receivable, and accounts payable will increase by $100,000, $80,000, and $90,000, respectively. Projected sales both with and without the investment are estimated as follows:

Year	Without the Investment	With the Investment
1	$2,000,000	$2,500,000
2	2,100,000	2,650,000
3	2,150,000	2,750,000
4	2,250,000	2,900,000

Selling and administrative costs without the investment are projected at $500,000 in Year 1 and will increase by $25,000 per year. If the investment is made, the costs will be $600,000 in Year 1 and will increase by $25,000 annually. Variable costs are 60 percent of sales and will remain at that level. The company's marginal tax rate is 34 percent.

    a. What are the annual cash flows of the project?

    b. Recalculate Part *a* assuming the class life of the depreciable assets is 3 years.

    c. Recalculate Part *a* assuming the salvage value is $220,000, $150,000, and $80,000.

    d. Recalculate Part *a* assuming the marginal tax rate is 25 percent.

    e. What is the impact on cash flows of changes in the class life, salvage value, and tax rates?

Selected References

Angell, Robert J. "Depreciable Basis/ITC Decisions When the ITC Is Deferred." *Financial Management,* Summer 1985: 43–47.

Angell, Robert J. "The Effect of the Tax Reform Act on Capital Investment Decisions." *Financial Management,* Winter 1988: 82–86.

Drtina, Ralph E., and James A. Largay III. "Pitfalls in Calculating Cash Flow from Operations." *The Accounting Review,* April 1985: 314–326.

Kroll, Yoram. "On the Difference between Accrual Accounting Figures and Cash Flows: The Case of Working Capital." *Financial Management,* Spring 1985: 75–82.

Marshuetz, Richard J. "How American Can Allocates Capital." *Harvard Business Review,* January–February 1985: 82–91.

McCarty, Daniel E., and William R. McDaniel. "A Note on

Expensing Versus Depreciating under the Accelerated Cost Recovery System: Comment." *Financial Management,* Summer 1983: 37–39.

Ross, Marc. "Capital Budgeting Practices of Twelve Large Manufacturers." *Financial Management,* Winter 1986: 15–22.

Stancill, James McNeill. "Where Is There Cash in Cash Flow?" *Harvard Business Review,* March–April 1987: 38–49.

Statman, Meir, and David Caldwell. "Applying Behavioral Finance to Capital Budgeting." *Financial Management,* Winter 1987: 7–15.

Statman, Meir, and Tyzoon T. Tyebjee. "Optimistic Capital Budgeting Forecasts: An Experiment." *Financial Management,* Autumn 1985: 27–33.

Appendix 8A   CASH FLOWS OF REPLACEMENT PROJECTS

Chapter 8 emphasizes the cash flows of *expansion projects* where the intention is to increase a company's sales revenue. *Replacement projects,* in contrast, are not intended to increase sales revenue. Instead, their purpose usually is to increase efficiency through technology and thereby reduce costs. The principles of capital budgeting that apply to expansion projects also apply to replacement projects. However, identifying the relevant incremental cash flows of replacement projects tends to be more challenging. The analysis of the following example demonstrates how it is done.

EXAMPLE

Suppose a financial manager is considering replacing an old machine with a new one to reduce production costs. Although inefficient, the old machine is usable for another 4 years, at which time it would have a zero salvage value. Book value of the old machine is currently $100,000, but because of its inefficiency it can be sold for only $70,000. Scheduled depreciation expense for the old machine is $28,571 for each of the next 3 years and $14,287 for the fourth year. The new machine will cost $400,000, plus $80,000 for freight and installation. In addition, net working capital will increase $50,000 to accommodate the inventory requirement of the new machine. For tax purposes, the class life of the new machine is 3 years, and the financial manager will use the MACRS (modified accelerated cost recovery system) procedure to calculate its annual depreciation expense. The financial manager expects to sell the new machine for $80,000 and recover the $50,000 of net working capital at the end of 4 years. Replacing the old machine with the new one will not affect sales revenue, but it will reduce costs by $90,000 per year, which will cause *earnings before depreciation and taxes* to rise $90,000 per year. The company's marginal tax rate (state and federal) is 40 percent.

The incremental cash flows associated with the replacement project in the preceding example include: (1) the net investment cash outflow, (2) operating cash flows, and (3) the project-disposal cash flow. These cash flows are calculated as follows:

1. *Net investment cash outflow (NICO):*

Purchase price of new machine	$400,000
Freight and installation costs	80,000
Increase in net working capital	50,000
Sale price of old machine	(70,000)
Tax savings on loss: old machine	(12,000)
Net investment cash outflow	$448,000

   Note: (1) Purchase of the new machine causes the sale of the old machine, so NICO is reduced $70,000. (2) Tax savings caused by the loss on the sale of the old machine equal the tax rate times the loss: 0.40($30,000), or $12,000.

2. *Operating cash flows (OCF):*

Change in	Year 1	Year 2	Year 3	Year 4
Earnings before depreciation and taxes	$ 90,000	$ 90,000	$90,000	$90,000
Depreciation	131,413	184,741	42,565	21,281
Earnings before taxes	($ 41,413)	($ 94,741)	$47,435	$68,719
Taxes (40%)	(16,565)	(37,896)	18,974	27,488
Earnings after taxes	($ 24,848)	($ 56,845)	$28,461	$41,231
Add depreciation	131,413	184,741	42,565	21,281
Operating cash flows	$106,565	$127,896	$71,026	$62,512

   Note: (1) Each number in the preceding table represents a *change* caused by acceptance of the new machine. (2) The losses in the first two years reduce the company's taxable income from other sources; tax savings are 40 percent of each loss. (3) Depreciation on the new machine is calculated as follows (use the percentages in Table 8.4):

   Year 1: $159,984 = 0.3333 ($480,000)

   Year 2: $213,312 = 0.4444 ($480,000)

   Year 3: $71,136 = 0.1482 ($480,000)

   Year 4: $35,568 = 0.0741 ($480,000)

   Change in depreciation equals depreciation on the new machine less depreciation on the old machine:

   Year 1: $131,413 = $159,984 − $28,571

   Year 2: $184,741 = $213,312 − $28,571

$$\text{Year 3:} \quad \$42,565 = \$71,136 - \$28,571$$
$$\text{Year 4:} \quad \$21,281 = \$35,568 - \$14,287$$

Change in OCF equals change in earnings after taxes plus change in depreciation, because interest expense is (correctly) excluded from the calculations.

3. *Project-disposal cash flow:*

Sale price of new machine	$80,000
Taxes on sale price (40%)	(32,000)
Recovery of net working capital	50,000
Project-disposal cash flow	$98,000

The following time line summarizes the cash outflows and inflows associated with the replacement project:

End of Year	0	1	2	3	4
Cash Flow	−$448,000	+$106,565	+$127,896	+$71,026	+$62,512
					+ 98,000
					$160,512

Chapter 9 explains the methods for evaluating such cash flows to decide whether the project should be accepted or rejected.

Computer Problem

Cash flows for a replacement project: template REPLACE

8A.1. Thornton Abrasives is considering replacement of its present equipment for producing precision grinding wheels. The purchase price of the old equipment two years ago was $65,000. Although Thornton expects this equipment to last another seven years, the new equipment is more efficient. Thornton has a firm offer from another company to buy the old equipment for $75,000.

New equipment will cost $125,000 delivered and installed. For tax purposes, both the old and the new equipment are depreciated using MACRS percentages for a 5-year class life. Thornton estimates the salvage value of the new machine will be $25,000. No investment tax credit was taken on the old equipment, nor is it available on the new equipment.

The new equipment is expected to save $0.60 per unit manufactured over the next seven years. Because the new equipment greatly simplifies setups for custom orders, Thornton will be able to reduce inventories by $5,000. Accounts receivable, on the other hand, are expected to increase by $3,000, and this investment will be recovered at the end of the project's seven-year life. Production in the first year is expected to be 10,000 units, but it is expected to increase by 1,000 units per year throughout the seven-year life of the equipment.

Thornton's marginal tax rate is 40 percent on both ordinary income and capital gains.

a. Compute the net investment cash outflow, the operating cash flows, and the project-disposal cash flow resulting from replacement of the old equipment.
b. Recalculate Part *a* assuming production increases by only 500 units per year.
c. Recalculate Part *a* assuming production increases by 1,500 units per year.
d. Recalculate Part *a* assuming the savings realized are only $0.30 per unit.
e. Recalculate Part *a* assuming the savings realized are $0.90 per unit.
f. Recalculate Part *a* assuming Thornton's tax rate is 30 percent.

EVALUATING CAPITAL INVESTMENTS

Eastman Kodak's Property Puzzle

The executives at Eastman Kodak Company look at their holdings of land and buildings as financial assets. They run their real-estate operations as a business in order to create value for shareholders. Kodak's mission statement includes objectives relating to not only solving the company's real-estate problems but also to rate of return and cash flow.

Kodak's portfolio of real estate consists of approximately 400 locations—office, commercial, and industrial properties around the world. Managing the portfolio begins with strategies to create value from surplus properties, underutilized properties, and properties not functioning at their "highest and best use." H. Bruce Russell, vice president of corporate real estate, says: "Before we build new facilities or a new infrastructure, we look on the outside to acquire distressed

properties from developers. Or we may decide to look for an existing, underutilized asset or surplus asset and adapt it to our needs."

When new construction appears necessary, Kodak analysts first look at space requirements, the justification for construction, and how long the company plans to use the property. Next comes the capital-budgeting analysis, including a *pro forma* statement of the property's cash flows. Based on a present-value analysis of the after-tax cash flows, the analyst develops a recommendation for management. Incorporating these procedures into a strategic plan for each property in its portfolio, Kodak has created millions of dollars in shareholder value.

Source: H. Bruce Russell, "The Property Puzzle," *Financial Executive,* July/August 1992, 42–45.

This chapter begins with a brief analysis of the incremental cash flows from a capital project, following the procedures in Chapter 8. These cash flows are then used to illustrate the methods available to a financial manager for selecting projects from those proposed. To avoid complicating the analysis, we evaluate the project as though its risk were equivalent to that of the company's average or typical project. Chapter 10 presents procedures for analyzing projects with differing risk levels.

PROJECT CASH FLOWS: AN ILLUSTRATION

Suppose that the financial manager of Bally Manufacturing is evaluating a proposal to expand the fashion boutique in the company's hotel. The project sponsor, the manager of the boutique, has completed the necessary paperwork, and now the financial manager is developing estimates of the cash flows.

Depreciable equipment (such as new displays and fixtures) is expected to cost $104,000. Delivery charges and installation costs bring the total outlay to $120,000. The manager expects accounts receivable and inventory to increase by $96,000 as a result of the expansion. Current liabilities (primarily increases in accounts payable associated with buying inventory) should increase by $26,000. The increase in net working capital associated with the proposal is therefore $70,000 ($96,000 − $26,000). The company's tax adviser tells the financial manager that a 10 percent investment tax credit is available on the depreciable equipment.[1] Considering this credit, the financial manager calculates the following net investment cash outflow:

Investment in depreciable equipment	$120,000
Less investment tax credit (10%)	12,000
Net investment in depreciable equipment	$108,000
Add increase in net working capital	70,000
Net investment cash outflow	$178,000

Working with the marketing manager, cost accountant, and personnel manager, the financial manager develops the *pro forma* operating statements and operating cash flow statements for the project. Although the project has a 5-year class life for depreciation, it has a 6-year economic life. The top part of Table 9.1 shows the *pro forma* operating statements based on the estimated sales revenues, incremental operating costs, and the company's marginal tax rate of 34 percent. The bottom part of Table 9.1 shows the operating cash flow statements based on the cash items from the *pro forma* operating statements.[2]

The financial manager forecasts that the depreciable assets will be sold for $14,000 at the end of the economic life of the project. At that time the assets

---

[1] Although the Tax Reform Act of 1986 repealed the investment tax credit (perhaps temporarily), the ITC here makes the example more general.

[2] Chapter 8 presents two equation methods for calculating operating cash flow (OCF). Consider the calculation of OCF at the end of Year 1, for example:

$$OCF = EBIT (1 - T) + Depreciation$$
$$= \$41,000(1 - 0.34) + \$24,000$$
$$= \$27,060 + \$24,000$$
$$= \$51,060$$

TABLE 9.1	**Pro Forma Operating Statements and Operating Cash Flow Statements: Proposed Boutique Expansion**

Pro Forma Operating Statements

	Year 1	Year 2	Year 3	Year 4	Year 5	Year 6
Projected sales revenue	$450,000	$600,000	$600,000	$600,000	$350,000	$240,000
Less incremental costs						
Variable costs	315,000	420,000	420,000	420,000	245,000	154,000
Fixed costs	70,000	70,000	70,000	70,000	70,000	70,000
Depreciation[a]	24,000	38,400	23,040	13,824	13,824	6,912
Earnings before interest and taxes[b]	$ 41,000	$ 71,600	$ 86,960	$ 96,176	$ 21,176	$ 9,088
Less taxes (34%)	13,940	24,344	29,566	32,700	7,200	3,090
Earnings after taxes	$ 27,060	$ 47,256	$ 57,394	$ 63,476	$ 13,976	$ 5,998

Operating Cash Flow Statements

	Year 1	Year 2	Year 3	Year 4	Year 5	Year 6
Cash inflow (sales revenues)	$450,000	$600,000	$600,000	$600,000	$350,000	$240,000
Less cash outflows						
Variable costs	315,000	420,000	420,000	420,000	245,000	154,000
Fixed costs	70,000	70,000	70,000	70,000	70,000	70,000
Taxes	13,940	24,344	29,566	32,700	7,200	3,090
Operating cash flow	$ 51,060	$ 85,656	$ 80,434	$ 77,300	$ 27,800	$ 12,910

[a] Depreciation is based on MACRS and the 5-year class life in Table 8.4. Assume that ITC does not affect depreciation calculations.

[b] Operating cash flows include operating expenses but *exclude* financial expenses such as interest paid to creditors. In the *pro forma* operating statements, EBIT equals earnings before taxes, the taxable income a project produces.

will have a zero book value. The cash flow from disposal of depreciable assets will therefore be $9,240:

Sale price	$14,000
Less book value	0
Gain	$14,000
Less taxes (34%)	4,760
Cash inflow from disposal of depreciable assets	$ 9,240

The disposal of current assets and payment of the current liabilities associated with the project will lead to a cash inflow equal to the original net working capital, $70,000. Disposal cash flows total $79,240 ($9,240 + $70,000).

Figure 9.1 illustrates the cash flows from the proposed expansion of the boutique. The net investment cash outflow occurs at the beginning of the project, so Figure 9.1 shows it at the beginning of Year 1, or time zero. Operating cash flows occur at the end of each year for six years. The disposal cash flow from depre-

$$OCF = EAT + Depreciation$$
$$= \$27,060 + \$24,000$$
$$= \$51,060$$

The second method requires that interest expense be excluded from the *pro forma* operating statement (as in Table 9.1).

FIGURE 9.1

Time Line of Cash Flows: Proposed Boutique Expansion

The time line details all incremental cash flows of a proposed project: net investment cash outflow at time zero, followed by annual operating cash flows and a disposal cash flow when the company terminates the project.

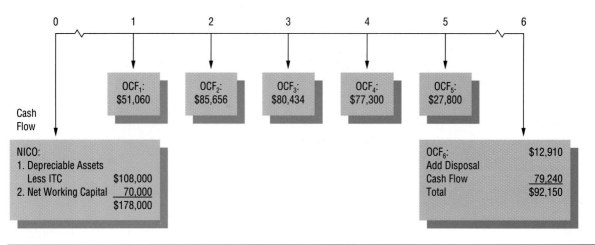

ciable assets and net working capital occurs at the end of the project's economic life.[3]

The financial manager now has estimates of the size and timing of cash flows for the proposed project. Several different methods can be used to evaluate the cash flows, but the ideal evaluation method should (1) include all cash flows occurring during the entire life of a project, (2) be consistent with the principle of time value of money, and (3) incorporate the required rate of return on the project. The *payback period* does not meet these criteria as well as do the discounted cash flow methods—*internal rate of return, net present value,* and *profitability index*. Using the project cash flows described above, we apply in sequence each of these evaluation methods.

PAYBACK PERIOD

payback period
Time required to recover a project's net investment cash outflow through incremental cash inflows.

The **payback period** is the time required to recover through incremental cash inflows a project's net investment cash outflow (NICO). In the example in Figure 9.1, it takes 2.51 years to recover the $178,000 investment:

[3] The time line in Figure 9.1 reflects conventional assumptions about the timing of cash flows. Although adequate for many projects, these assumptions can be relaxed when necessary. Examples of the need for different assumptions are: (1) NICO occurs over several years, as happens for large construction projects; (2) net working capital increases over the years as sales increase; (3) a large part of operating cash flow occurs early in the year, making questionable the year-end assumption; and (4) the disposal cash flows occur over several years, as happens in land reclamation after strip mining.

FIGURE 9.2

Payback Period: Proposed Boutique Expansion

The payback period, 2.51 years, is the number of years for the incremental cash inflows of the project to equal the $178,000 net investment cash outflow: 2.51 years = 2 + $41,284/$80,434, where $80,434 is OCF_3.

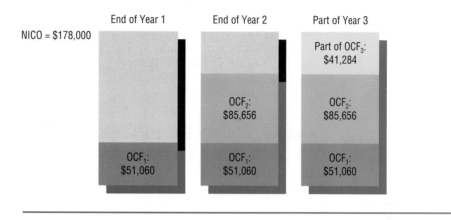

	Year 1	Year 2	Year 3
Cash flows	$51,060	$ 85,656	$ 80,434
Cumulative sum of cash flows	$51,060	$136,716	$217,150
Sum of years	1	2	$41,284/$80,434 = 0.51
			2 + 0.51 = 2.51 years

The calculation locates the point at which the inflows equal the net investment cash outflow. The company recaptures the entire $178,000 cash outflow sometime during the third year. The first two years of cash inflows total $136,716, and the third year must supply the remaining $41,284 ($178,000 − $136,716). If we assume that cash inflows occur uniformly during the year, the project will require $41,284/$80,434 = 0.51, or 51 percent of Year 3, to generate the needed cash inflow. Figure 9.2 illustrates the incremental cash inflows in each year and the way the project recovers the $178,000 net investment cash outflow in 2.51 years.

Financial managers use the payback period to evaluate a project by comparing it with some standard. For example, if the standard is two years, then this project is not acceptable. If the standard is three years, then the project is acceptable. In general, financial managers prefer short payback periods.

Payback period suffers from not meeting any of the criteria of an ideal evaluation method. You know from Chapter 4 that $178,000 paid out at time zero is not equivalent to $178,000 received over a three-year period. Also, the method does not include the cash flows beyond the payback period: Whether the cash flows end at 2.51 years or whether they increase or decline thereafter is not evaluated. Finally, there is no consideration of a required rate of return on the project: Whether the company requires a 15 percent return or a 30 percent return on the investment in this project is ignored.

In fact, payback period does not measure return on investment at all. Payback measures speed of capital recovery, a return *of* capital rather than a return *on* capital. It is a popular evaluation method because it reflects a project's liquidity and is easy to understand. Payback analysis appeals to financial managers whose companies are short of cash and are operating in the face of large uncertainties. For example, a company in the highly competitive business of manufacturing tennis rackets might use the payback method because of the uncertainties surrounding the product life of a racket. If a company must recover its cash quickly to avoid either going broke or suffering financial strain, then a short payback standard makes sense.[4]

DISCOUNTED CASH FLOW METHODS

discounted cash flow (DCF) methods

Capital-budgeting methods that discount cash flows to account for the time value of money: internal rate of return, net present value, and profitability index.

To apply the **discounted cash flow (DCF) methods** to the boutique example, we assume the following: The $178,000 net investment cash outflow occurs at the beginning of Year 1 (that is, at time zero); all other cash flows occur at the end of each year. These assumptions cause DCF methods to understate the value of projects for which cash flows occur throughout each year as the company makes sales and pays bills. In most cases, the understatement is small and need not trouble us. In those cases where the understatement is large, recognition should be given to the peculiarities in timing of the cash flows.

Internal Rate of Return

internal rate of return (IRR)

Return on invested capital; discount rate that causes equality between the present value of cash inflows and the net investment cash outflow.

The **internal rate of return (IRR)** on a project is the company's rate of return on its invested capital. Stated differently, *the IRR is the discount rate that equates the present value of a project's expected cash inflows with its net investment cash outflow.*

Solving for the internal rate of return requires an iterative, or repeating, process: Try several discount rates until you find the one that makes the present value of cash inflows equal to the net investment cash outflow. Financial calculators with an IRR key also use an iterative procedure. Mathematically, the following equation determines IRR:

$$\text{NICO} = \sum_{t=1}^{n} \frac{CF_t}{(1 + IRR)^t}$$

where NICO = net investment cash outflow at time zero

CF = annual cash inflow

IRR = solved-for IRR

t = time (years)

n = estimated life of the project in years

For the proposed boutique expansion in Figure 9.1, you might begin the search for the internal rate of return by first trying a discount rate of 25 percent.

---

[4] Payback period is an example of an undiscounted evaluation method in capital budgeting. Another is *accounting rate of return* (ARR), which equals earnings after taxes produced by the project divided by investment in the project. Earnings and investment often vary over time, so analysts sometimes use an average of each variable. ARR fails to meet the criteria for an ideal evaluation method, and financial managers use it much less frequently than payback period. Because of the theoretical weakness and infrequent use of ARR, this book omits further discussion of it.

Substitute 0.25 for IRR in the preceding equation and check to see if the present value of the cash inflows equals the $178,000 net investment cash outflow:

$$\$178,000 \overset{?}{=} \frac{\$51,060}{(1 + 0.25)^1} + \frac{\$85,656}{(1 + 0.25)^2} + \frac{\$80,434}{(1 + 0.25)^3}$$
$$+ \frac{\$77,300}{(1 + 0.25)^4} + \frac{\$27,800}{(1 + 0.25)^5} + \frac{\$92,150}{(1 + 0.25)^6}$$

(Instead of using the equation, you could use interest factors such as those in Appendix B.2.) Figure 9.3 shows the result of the first trial using 25 percent as the IRR. The present value of the future cash flows, $201,779, exceeds the $178,000 net investment cash outflow. The IRR is not 25 percent, and you must try another rate. Should it be larger or smaller than 25 percent? At 25 percent the present value of cash inflows is too high, and a look at the equation for IRR suggests that you should use a *larger* discount rate because that will *reduce* the present value.

Figure 9.4 shows the result for a 30 percent discount rate. The present value of the future cash flows is still above the net investment cash outflow, so the IRR does not equal 30 percent, but it is close to 30 percent. Because the present value of the cash inflows slightly exceeds the net investment cash outflow, you know that the IRR is slightly greater than 30 percent. At 31 percent the present value of the cash flows equals $176,356, which is less than the net investment cash outflow. The IRR, therefore, must lie between 30 and 31 percent. For most purposes this degree of accuracy is acceptable, and you would stop the calculations here. If necessary, the more precise answer, 30.6 percent, can be found by using a calculator with an IRR key.[5]

Interpreting IRR. The internal rate of return is the *return on invested capital,* where the amount of invested capital may stay the same, decrease, or increase over time.

Invested Capital Stays the Same. Consider a $1,000 investment that nets the company $100 annually for 2 years and returns the $1,000 at Year-end 2:

The amount of invested capital ($1,000) at the beginning of each year is the same in this case. The company earns $100, or 10 percent, on a $1,000 investment in Year 1 *and in Year 2*. The internal rate of return—return on invested capital— is 10 percent per year because that discount rate makes the present value of future cash inflows equal to the initial investment:

$$\$1,000 = \frac{\$100}{(1 + 0.10)^1} + \frac{\$1,100}{(1 + 0.10)^2}$$

---

[5] Financial calculators with an IRR key and personal computers with appropriate software remove the drudgery from the calculation of IRR. To illustrate, here are the keystrokes on a Hewlett-Packard 12C to find the IRR of the proposed boutique expansion: (1) Press *f*, then *REG* to clear the calculator. (2) Enter 178000, then press *CHS*, *g*, and *CFo*. (3) Enter 51060, then press *g* and *CFj*. (4) Repeat Step 3 for the remaining cash flows, entering the appropriate cash flow for each year. (5) Press *f*, then *IRR*, and wait for the answer, 30.6 percent. Of course, other calculators may require different keystrokes. The owner's handbook will explain them to you.

FIGURE 9.3

First Trial in Solving for an Internal Rate of Return (Trying 25 Percent)

The IRR calculation begins with a guess: Select a discount rate, use it to find the present value of all incremental cash inflows, then compare the present value with the net investment cash outflow. An inequality, such as the one here, means that you have not found the IRR.

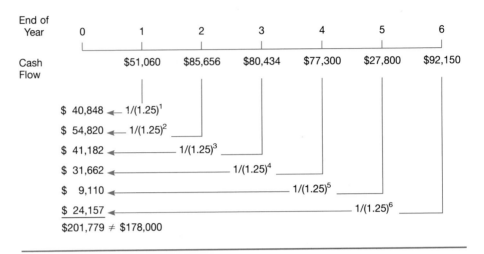

This pattern of cash flows is typical of corporate coupon bonds, in which case the 10 percent is better known as *yield to maturity* instead of IRR.

Invested Capital Decreases.   Most capital-budgeting projects are similar to the boutique expansion that Figure 9.1 illustrates: The invested capital declines over time. The internal rate of return is a return on the declining capital investment at the beginning of each year. Consider a $1,000 investment that produces cash flows of $576.20 at the end of Year 1 and $576.18 at the end of Year 2:

End of Year	0	1	2
Cash Flow	−$1,000	+$576.20	+$576.18

The IRR equals 10 percent per year:

$$\$1,000 = \frac{\$576.20}{(1 + 0.10)^1} + \frac{\$576.18}{(1 + 0.10)^2}$$

The actual investment in the project declines from the beginning of Year 1 to the beginning of Year 2, as Column 2 below shows:

(1) Year	(2) Beginning Balance	(2) × 10% = (3) Dollar Return at 10%	(2) + (3) = (4) Ending Balance	(5) Actual Cash Withdrawal	(4) − (5) = (6) Remaining Investment
1	$1,000.00	$100.00	$1,100.00	$576.20	$523.80
2	523.80	52.38	576.18	576.18	0

The project yields a 10 percent IRR, which means that by Year-end 1 the project owes the company $1,100 (1.10 × $1,000); but the project pays only $576.20, which means that $523.80 ($1,100 − $576.20) remains invested for the second

FIGURE 9.4

Second Trial in Solving for an Internal Rate of Return (Trying 30 Percent)

The discount rate here is larger than the 25 percent rate used in Figure 9.3. Using a larger discount rate reduces the present value of cash inflows. As shown here, a discount rate of 30 percent reduces the present value to $180,215, which is still too large. IRR must be slightly more than 30 percent.

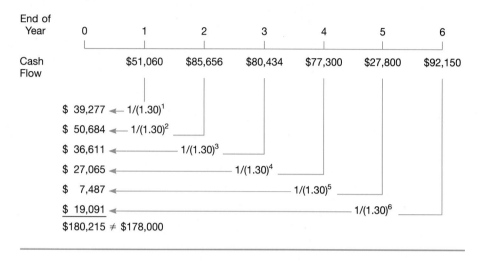

year. By Year-end 2 the $523.80 grows to $576.18 (1.10 × $523.80), which exactly equals the cash withdrawal from the project, leaving zero capital invested. In this example the IRR is 10 percent on $1,000 during Year 1 and 10 percent on $523.80 during Year 2.

Invested Capital Increases. To illustrate invested capital that increases over time, consider a $1,000 investment for 2 years that pays $1,210 at Year-end 2:

End of Year	0	1	2
Cash Flow	−$1,000	0	+$1,210

The project's internal rate of return equals 10 percent per year:

$$\$1,000 = \frac{\$1,210}{(1 + 0.10)^2}$$

By Year-end 1 the project owes the company $1,100 (1.10 × $1,000), but it pays nothing. Invested capital therefore grows from $1,000 at time zero to $1,100 at Year-end 1. During the second year the $1,100 grows to $1,210 (1.10 × $1,100), which equals the cash flow received by the company. In this example the internal rate of return is 10 percent on $1,000 during Year 1 and 10 percent on $1,100, during Year 2.

In each case above, the return on invested capital and the internal rate of return are 10 percent annually. The IRR in each case is the discount rate equating the present value of future cash flows to the net investment cash outflow.

Decision Rule. How should the financial manager interpret the internal rate of return for the proposed boutique expansion? The project offers an expected 30.6

hurdle rate

Minimum rate of return
required for accepting a
capital project; cutoff or
screening rate for capital
budgeting.

percent IRR. Investment in the project will yield the company 30.6 percent
annually on invested capital that declines over the 6-year period.

If a project's internal rate of return exceeds the project's **hurdle rate,** then the
financial manager should accept the project. If not, then the project should be
rejected. *For projects with risk characteristics similar to those of the typical project in which the company has invested, the appropriate hurdle rate is the company's marginal cost of capital (MCC).* The decision rule for IRR follows:

- IRR > MCC: Accept the project; stock price will rise.
- IRR < MCC: Reject the project; accepting the project will cause stock price
  to fall.

If IRR = MCC, then the financial manager would be indifferent toward the project because its acceptance or rejection would have no impact on stock price. As
a practical matter, the financial manager might wish to reexamine the cash flow
estimates to make sure they are reasonable when IRR = MCC.

The rationale for using MCC as the hurdle rate for a company's average-risk
projects is based on the continual evaluation of the company's securities in the
marketplace. MCC is a weighted average of the required rates of return on these
securities and, therefore, reflects risk perceived by investors. Moreover, the risk
of the securities derives from the risk of company assets, which means that MCC
is in proportion to the risk of company assets—that is, the company's average-
risk project. If the IRR of an average-risk project exceeds MCC, then the company earns more on the project than it pays for capital to finance the project.
Accepting such projects causes an increase in stock price and shareholder wealth.

Appraising IRR.   The internal rate of return satisfies all criteria for an ideal capital-budgeting method. It uses cash flows over the entire life of the project; it
adjusts cash flows for the time value of money; and the decision rule for IRR
incorporates the project's required rate of return (for example, through the use
of the marginal cost of capital). In addition, many financial managers feel comfortable with the concept of a rate of return on invested capital. Hence they find
IRR understandable and easy to explain.

Despite the generally good report on internal rate of return, it presents a
problem in some circumstances. For some patterns of cash flows, you may calculate two or more IRRs! When that occurs, the IRR method has malfunctioned,
and you dare not interpret the calculated rates as rates of return on invested
capital—the usual interpretation.

Conventional capital projects have a cash outflow at time zero, followed by
annual cash inflows. The cash flows might follow any of these patterns:

$$- + + + + + + + + +$$
$$- + + +$$
$$- + + + + + +$$

The boutique expansion in Figure 9.1 is a conventional project because the
$178,000 net investment cash outflow is followed by 6 years of cash inflows.
Notice that in conventional projects you observe only one change in the direction
of cash flows—a cash outflow (a negative) followed by a series of cash inflows
(positives). Conventional projects have only one internal rate of return, interpreted as the rate of return on invested capital.

Nonconventional capital projects have varying cash inflows and outflows throughout their lives. Some cash flow patterns might be:

$$- + -\qquad\text{(two sign changes)}$$
$$- + + + + + -\ \text{(two sign changes)}$$
$$- + + - + + +\ \ \text{(three sign changes)}$$

An example of two sign changes occurs in a project involving the strip mining of coal. Such a project requires an initial net investment cash outflow followed first by a series of operating cash inflows; then when the coal vein is exhausted, another cash outflow occurs because the federal government requires the company to restore the mined property to its original state. Thus the project has two changes in the direction of cash flows:

$$- + + + + + -$$

Nonconventional capital projects sometimes have more than one internal rate of return. The maximum possible number of IRRs is limited to the number of sign changes in the cash flows. Although multiple sign changes are necessary for multiple IRRs, they are not sufficient conditions. The magnitude of the cash flows also affects whether multiple IRRs exist.

The following cash flows have the necessary and sufficient conditions for two internal rates of return:

Year-End	Cash Flow
0	−$ 800
1	+$5,000
2	−$5,000

The two IRRs are 25 and 400 percent.[6] You should not interpret either percentage as a rate of return on invested capital. Also, comparing either of these IRRs to MCC to determine project acceptance may be hazardous to shareholder wealth.[7]

---

[6] The following calculations show that 25 percent and 400 percent are the internal rates of return:

$$\textit{For 25\%:}\ \$800 = \frac{\$5,000}{(1 + 0.25)^1} - \frac{\$5,000}{(1 + 0.25)^2}$$
$$= \$4,000 - \$3,200$$
$$= \$800$$

$$\textit{For 400\%:}\ \$800 = \frac{\$5,000}{(1 + 4)^1} - \frac{\$5,000}{(1 + 4)^2}$$
$$= \$1,000 - \$200$$
$$= \$800$$

[7] Textbooks specializing in capital budgeting provide more thorough treatments of the problem of multiple internal rates of return. You will find the most rigorous treatment in the article by Daniel Teichroew, Alexander A. Robichek, and Michael Montalbano, "An Analysis of Criteria for Investment and Financing Decisions under Certainty," *Management Science*, November 1965, 151–179.

Net Present Value

net present value (NPV)
Present value of cash
inflows less net investment
cash outflow.

Like internal rate of return, **net present value** (**NPV**) is a discounted cash flow procedure for evaluating capital projects. Unlike IRR, which is a percentage rate, NPV is a dollar amount. Mathematically, net present value is defined as follows:

$$NPV = \sum_{t=1}^{n} \frac{CF_t}{(1 + K)^t} - NICO$$

where CF = annual cash inflow

K = required rate of return on the project (equal to the company's MCC for average-risk projects)

NICO = net investment cash outflow at time zero

t = time (years)

n = estimated life of the project in years

The equation shows that NPV is the present value of a project's cash inflows less the net investment cash outflow:

$$NPV = \frac{\text{Present value}}{\text{of cash inflows}} - \frac{\text{Net investment}}{\text{cash outflow}}$$

To illustrate the calculation of net present value, consider again the proposal to expand the boutique. The net investment cash outflow equals $178,000, and the annual cash inflows vary as Figure 9.1 shows. Because the boutique expansion has the same risk as the company's average or typical project, the financial manager uses the company's marginal cost of capital to discount the incremental cash inflows. Based on an MCC of 20 percent, the present value of the future cash inflows is $227,891. Figure 9.5 shows the NPV to be $49,891, calculated as follows:[8]

$$NPV = \$227,891 - \$178,000$$
$$= \$49,891$$

Interpreting NPV. A project's NPV measures the dollar change in shareholder wealth due to the company's acceptance of the project. In the preceding example NPV equals $49,891, which means that accepting the project would add $49,891 to the wealth of Bally Manufacturing's current shareholders. For the increase in wealth to materialize, however, investors in the stock market must be aware of the project and must believe the accuracy of the NPV calculation. If so, then they will bid up the company's stock price, adding $49,891 to the overall value of the company's common equity, and thus to the wealth of current shareholders. If the company has 100,000 shares of stock outstanding, then the price per share will increase approximately $0.50 ($49,891/100,000). For a company with millions of shares outstanding, an NPV of $49,891 would not have a noticeable effect on stock price.

Net present value can also be interpreted as a measure of how good a bargain

---

[8]Financial calculators with an IRR key also have an NPV key. After entering the cash flows as described in Note 5, enter the discount rate, 20, and press *i*; then press *f* and *NPV* for the answer, $49,891.

FIGURE 9.5

Calculating Net Present Value of the Proposed Boutique Expansion (MCC = 20 Percent)

The company must pay $178,000 to get cash inflows with a present value of $227,891. Net present value equals $227,891 − $178,000 = $49,891.

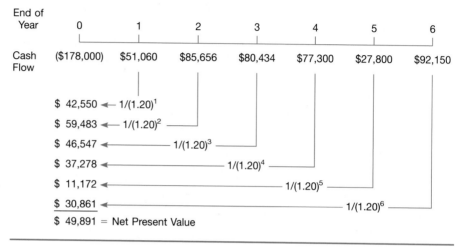

a project represents. Large NPVs represent great bargains, as implied by the following equation:

$$NPV = \frac{\text{Maximum price}}{\text{of the project}} - \frac{\text{Actual price}}{\text{of the project}}$$

$$= \$227,891 - \$178,000$$

$$= \$49,891$$

The maximum price Bally Manufacturing could afford to pay for the boutique expansion is $227,891, the present value of cash inflows. But since the company needs to pay only $178,000, it is getting a bargain: The proposed project is underpriced by $49,891 in comparison with its maximum price, $227,891. Cash inflows after paying all operating expenses and taxes are sufficient to: (1) repay the $178,000 investment, (2) pay 20 percent to the capital suppliers, and (3) provide a $49,891 bonus to the common shareholders.

To understand better the nature of net present value, consider its reaction as the discount rate varies. Figure 9.6 shows this reaction for the boutique expansion project by illustrating its **NPV profile**—a graph of NPV as a function of the discount rate. NPV declines as the discount rate rises.

The NPV profile for the boutique expansion project is constructed by calculating NPV using four discount rates and plotting the results. Consider first the discount rate of infinity. NPV approaches −$178,000 as the discount rate approaches infinity (∞):

NPV profile

Graph of NPV as a function of the discount rate.

$$NPV = \left(\frac{\$51,060}{(1 + \infty)^1} + \frac{\$85,656}{(1 + \infty)^2} + \frac{\$80,434}{(1 + \infty)^3} + \frac{\$77,300}{(1 + \infty)^4}\right.$$

$$\left. + \frac{\$27,800}{(1 + \infty)^5} + \frac{\$92,150}{(1 + \infty)^6}\right) - \$178,000$$

$$= -\$178,000$$

FIGURE 9.6   **NPV Profile of the Proposed Boutique Expansion**

Net present value declines as the discount rate rises. The discount rate causing NPV = 0 is the internal rate of return, 30.6 percent. When the discount rate is zero, NPV = $236,400; when the discount rate approaches infinity, NPV approaches −$178,000. The NPV profile is convex toward the origin.

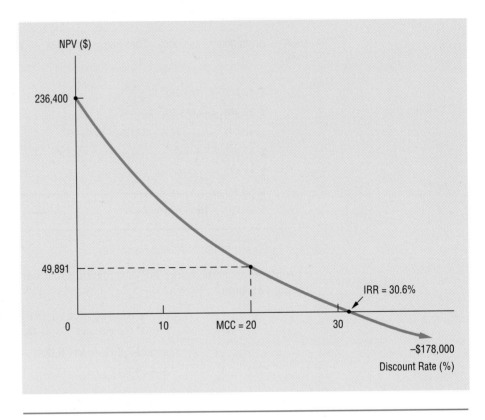

The first six terms approach zero as the discount rate approaches infinity, leaving only −$178,000, the net investment cash outflow. Next use the other extreme, a discount rate of zero. It produces an NPV of $236,400:

$$\text{NPV} = \left(\frac{\$51,060}{(1+0)^1} + \frac{\$85,656}{(1+0)^2} + \frac{\$80,434}{(1+0)^3} + \frac{\$77,300}{(1+0)^4} \right.$$
$$\left. + \frac{\$27,800}{(1+0)^5} + \frac{\$92,150}{(1+0)^6} \right) - \$178,000$$
$$= \$236,400$$

Because dividing by $(1+0)^t$ does not affect the cash inflows, you simply add the cash inflows and subtract the net investment cash outflow to determine NPV with a zero discount rate.

The third point of interest is the company's marginal cost of capital (required rate of return on the project), 20 percent in the example. Figure 9.5 shows that at 20 percent, NPV for the project equals $49,891, indicating an acceptable project. Figure 9.6 locates the point relating the 20 percent discount rate to the $49,891 NPV.

The last point of special interest on the NPV profile is where the profile intersects the horizontal axis. At this intersection point, NPV = 0. *Using the following logic, you will recognize the discount rate causing NPV = 0 to be the internal rate of return:*

$$\text{NPV} = \frac{\text{Present value}}{\text{of cash inflows}} - \frac{\text{Net investment}}{\text{cash outflow}}$$

$$0 = \frac{\text{Present value}}{\text{of cash inflows}} - \frac{\text{Net investment}}{\text{cash outflow}}$$

$$\frac{\text{Present value}}{\text{of cash inflows}} = \frac{\text{Net investment}}{\text{cash outflow}}$$

The discount rate (IRR) causing NPV = 0 also causes this last equality, which is the basic equation for calculating IRR. Figure 9.6 shows that (1) IRR is the discount rate when NPV = 0, and (2) any discount rate between zero and 30.6 percent produces a positive NPV.

Decision Rule. A financial manager should accept any project with a positive net present value and reject any project with a negative net present value. A major task of management is to create and to discover projects with positive NPVs, and successful management teams have a knack for generating project ideas with positive NPVs. The decision rule for NPV follows:

- NPV > 0: Accept the project; the project's internal rate of return exceeds its required rate of return; stock price will rise.

- NPV < 0: Reject the project; the project's internal rate of return is less than its required rate of return; project acceptance will cause stock price to fall.

If NPV = 0, then the financial manager would be indifferent toward the project: The project's internal rate of return equals its required rate of return, and project acceptance will have no impact on stock price or shareholder wealth.

Appraising NPV. Like the internal rate of return, net present value satisfies all criteria for an ideal evaluation method. It uses all incremental cash flows, recognizes the time value of money, and incorporates the project's required rate of return (for example, through the use of marginal cost of capital).

Net present value has two advantages over internal rate of return. First, NPV requires only one calculation. You use the required rate of return on the project and solve directly for NPV (no trial and error). Second, NPV provides a dollar measure of change in shareholder wealth. Because maximizing shareholder wealth is our objective, it is convenient to use a method that measures wealth changes directly. Unfortunately, some people find NPV difficult to understand, which may be its primary disadvantage.

profitability index (PI)
Present value of cash inflows per dollar of investment; benefit-cost ratio.

Profitability Index

The profitability index is a discounted cash flow method similar to net present value. Sometimes called a benefit–cost ratio, the **profitability index (PI)** measures the present value of cash inflows per dollar invested:

$$\text{Profitability index} = \frac{\text{Present value of cash inflows}}{\text{Net investment cash outflow}}$$

$$= \frac{\sum_{t=1}^{n} CF_t/(1+K)^t}{\text{NICO}}$$

where all variables are as defined in the equation for NPV.

The equations for net present value and the profitability index are closely related in that they use the same cash flows and discount rate. They merely present the same information differently. PI requires that the present value of cash inflows be *divided* by NICO, whereas NPV requires that NICO be *subtracted* from the present value of cash inflows. As a result, NPV yields a dollar amount and PI yields a number representing present value per dollar invested.

For the boutique expansion project (see Figure 9.5) and based on a 20 percent required rate of return, PI is calculated as follows:

$$\text{Profitability index} = \frac{\$227,891}{\$178,000}$$

$$= 1.28$$

The company receives $1.28 in present value for each $1 invested. Because the present value of cash inflows exceeds the net investment cash outflow, the financial manager should accept the project—the same decision indicated by internal rate of return and net present value.

The decision rule for the profitability index is as follows:

- PI > 1.0:   Accept the project; stock price will rise.
- PI < 1.0:   Reject the project; acceptance will cause stock price to fall.

If PI = 1.0, then the financial manager would be indifferent toward the project. When PI = 1.0, net present value equals zero, and the internal rate of return equals the required rate of return. Under these conditions project acceptance would have no impact on stock price or shareholder wealth—hence the indifference.

The profitability index satisfies all criteria for an ideal evaluation procedure. In addition, the profitability index has intuitive appeal—some managers prefer to work with benefit-cost ratios, or present value of cash inflows per dollar of investment. For accept-reject decisions, however, the profitability index yields the same decision as the other discounted cash flow methods, internal rate of return and net present value. Because of this redundancy, the method chosen depends on personal preference.

Table 9.2 summarizes the four evaluation methods. The payback period fails to consider cash flows over the life of a project, ignores the time value of money, and neglects the required rate of return. Each of the three discounted cash flow methods—IRR, NPV, and PI—satisfies the criteria for an ideal evaluation method. *Any project that is acceptable using one of the DCF methods will be acceptable using either of the other two DCF methods.*

RANKING AND SELECTING PROJECTS

The preceding section examines methods of evaluation without giving consideration to how one project might affect another. The analysis implicitly assumes that projects are independent of each other. The meaning of *independence* is that

TABLE 9.2

Summary of Evaluation Methods for Capital Budgeting

Evaluation Method	Comments
Payback Period	A popular procedure in practice that measures the time required to recapture through cash inflows a project's net investment cash outflow. Payback ignores time value of money and post-payback cash flows. It measures return *of* capital, not return *on* capital.
Discounted Cash Flow Methods	
Internal rate of return $$NICO = \sum_{t=1}^{n} \frac{CF_t}{(1 + IRR)^t}$$	IRR is the rate of return on invested capital. IRR forces equality between the net investment cash outflow and the present value of cash inflows. IRR satisfies the criteria for an ideal evaluation method. Accept projects with an IRR greater than the required rate of return. Nonconventional capital projects may have more than one IRR, none of which represents return on invested capital.
Net present value $$NPV = \sum_{t=1}^{n} \frac{CF_t}{(1 + K)^t} - NICO$$	NPV measures the dollar change in shareholder wealth if management accepts a proposed project. It equals the present value of incremental cash inflows minus the net investment cash outflow. If NPV > 0, then IRR exceeds the required rate of return. NPV meets the criteria for an ideal evaluation method, although some managers find it difficult to interpret.
Profitability index $$PI = \frac{\sum_{t=1}^{n} CF_t/(1 + K)^t}{NICO}$$	PI measures the present value of cash inflows per dollar of net investment cash outflow. If PI > 1.0, then IRR exceeds the project's required rate of return (K) and NPV > 0. PI meets the criteria for an ideal evaluation method but contains no information beyond that provided by NPV.

mutually exclusive projects
Dependency among projects wherein acceptance of one precludes acceptance of the other projects.

capital rationing
Capital available to a company is limited; requires a company to forgo some projects with positive NPVs.

the selection of one project does not affect the acceptance or the rejection of another project.

To illustrate the problem created when acceptance of one project depends on the acceptance or rejection of another project, consider the projects being evaluated by the financial manager of Quick Shop Company. The company's marginal cost of capital is 9 percent, and the manager's calculations produce the results shown in Table 9.3. With independent projects, the manager would accept Projects A through E because for each IRR > 9 percent, NPV > 0 and PI > 1.0. Quick Shop's capital budget would total $180,000, the sum of the net investment cash outflows for each acceptable project. For *accept-reject decisions,* IRR, NPV, and PI provide the same, consistent signals for Projects A through F: Accept A through E, but reject F.

Besides deciding whether to accept or reject a project, financial managers need to *rank-order* projects under either of the following conditions: (1) The projects are **mutually exclusive projects,** so that accepting one precludes accepting another. For example, Projects D and E in Table 9.3 may be substitutes for one another, such as two competing microcomputer networks—DEC vs. IBM. (2) A company faces **capital rationing,** which means that it has a limited supply of capital and cannot accept all projects with positive net present values.[9] Quick

---

[9]Sophisticated solutions to capital-budgeting problems under capital rationing using mathematical programming are provided in H. Martin Weingartner, *Mathematical Programming and the Analysis of Capital Budgeting Problems,* Englewood Cliffs, NJ: Prentice-Hall, 1963.

		Net Investment			
	Project	Cash Outflow	IRR	NPV	PI
	A	$10,000	22%	$ 1,795	1.2
	B	10,000	19	1,919	1.2
	C	30,000	16	26,000	1.9
	D	80,000	14	40,000	1.5
	E	50,000	12	30,000	1.6
MCC = 9% (Reject)	F	36,000	8	(4,600)	0.9

TABLE 9.3

Project Evaluation: Quick Shop Company

Shop may not have $180,000 to invest in Projects A through E. Perhaps creditors refuse to lend more money to the company, or management may be afraid of the added financial risk that accompanies borrowing. Also, powerful shareholders may not want the company to issue common stock to raise capital because they fear losing voting control.

Regardless of the reason, circumstances occasionally force financial managers to rank-order projects, accepting for investment the best ones—that is, those that will produce the largest increase in stock price and shareholder wealth. When ranking is called for, the financial manager may face a problem: *The discounted cash flow methods—IRR, NPV, and PI—sometimes conflict in the rankings they produce.*

Using NPV and PI to Rank Projects

To illustrate the potential conflict in rankings by net present value and profitability index, consider only the following two equally risky projects from Table 9.3:

	Project D (DEC)	Project E (IBM)
Present value of cash inflows	$120,000	$80,000
Less net investment cash outflow	80,000	50,000
Net present value	$ 40,000	$30,000
Profitability index	1.5	1.6

Project D is a DEC microcomputer system and Project E is the IBM equivalent. Each system is acceptable because NPV > 0 and PI > 1.0. However, the fact that they are two competing systems forces the financial manager of Quick Shop to select only one. Which one should it be? The DEC system has the larger net present value and the IBM system has the larger profitability index. The financial manager may be tempted to choose IBM, with the larger profitability index, because the cash outflow is less than that for DEC ($50,000 vs. $80,000). This choice, however, forces Quick Shop to incur an opportunity cost. The DEC system adds $40,000 to shareholder wealth, but the IBM system adds only $30,000. The $10,000 difference is the opportunity cost to the shareholders of selecting the IBM system.

If Quick Shop can raise the capital (assume no capital rationing), then it should invest in Project D, whose net present value exceeds that of Project E.

With no capital rationing, the $30,000 ($80,000 − $50,000) difference in net investment cash outflow is of no consequence. With capital rationing, by contrast, the financial manager must weigh the advantage of choosing Project E to save the $30,000 against the disadvantage of losing the $10,000 in NPV. The choice depends on the severity of the capital-rationing constraint.

Using NPV and IRR to Rank Projects

In general, net present value and internal rate of return provide the same signals on whether to accept or reject a project. For rank-ordering projects, however, the two procedures may produce conflicting results.

Consider, for example, only two projects from Table 9.3. Projects A and B are mutually exclusive because they are alternative ways to do the same thing—move products and supplies from the receiving dock to various areas in the warehouse. Project A is a conveyor system and Project B is a forklift truck. Investing in one project precludes investing in the other because Quick Shop needs only one way to move products from the dock.

To illustrate the dilemma that arises when using net present value and internal rate of return to rank mutually exclusive projects, try your hand at selecting the better project from equally risky and mutually exclusive investments in the conveyor system and the forklift truck:

	Project A: Conveyor System	Project B: Forklift Truck
Net investment cash outflow	$10,000	$10,000
Cash inflow, Year-end 1	$ 6,705	0
Cash inflow, Year-end 2	$ 6,705	$14,161
Required rate of return	9%	9%
Internal rate of return	22%	19%
Net present value at 9%	$ 1,795	$ 1,919

If the projects were independent of each other and no capital rationing existed, then you would accept both of them. The conflict in ranking would be meaningless. But if the projects are mutually exclusive, which one do you select? According to IRR, you select the conveyor system. Now look at NPV, which tells you to select the forklift truck. To answer the question and to resolve the conflict, we construct NPV profiles as shown in Figure 9.7.

Construction of the NPV profiles for the two projects requires the following series of calculations:

1. *Net present value at 0 percent:*

$$\text{Conveyor system:} \quad \text{NPV}_A = -\$10,000 + \frac{\$6,705}{(1+0)^1} + \frac{\$6,705}{(1+0)^2}$$

$$= \$3,410$$

$$\text{Forklift truck:} \quad \text{NPV}_B = -\$10,000 + \frac{\$14,161}{(1+0)^2}$$

$$= \$4,161$$

2. *Internal rate of return (rate at which NPV = 0):* Use a financial calculator, the equations, or the interest factors in Appendix B. The following calculations use interest factors:

FIGURE 9.7

NPV Profiles Showing Conflict in Rankings by NPV and IRR

NPV profiles for two mutually exclusive projects show the condition for conflict in ranking by NPV and IRR. For discount rates less than the crossover rate (11.2 percent), NPV ranks the forklift truck over the conveyor system, just the opposite of the IRR ranking. For discount rates greater than the crossover rate, NPV and IRR yield the same ranking.

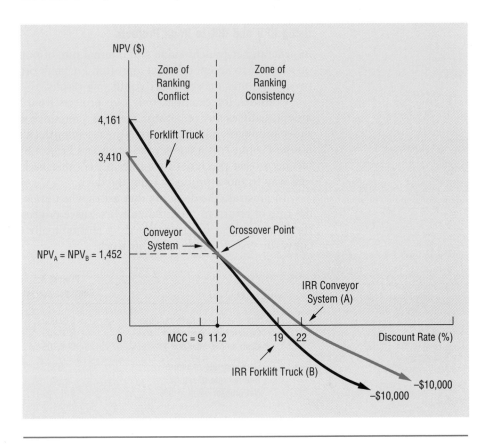

Conveyor system:

$$\text{NPV} = 0 = -\$10,000 + (\text{PVIFA}_{\text{IRR},2})\$6,705$$

$$\$10,000 = (\text{PVIFA}_{\text{IRR},2})\$6,705$$

$$\text{PVIFA}_{\text{IRR},2} = \frac{\$10,000}{\$6,705} = 1.4914$$

$$\text{IRR}_A = 22\% \quad \textit{(see Appendix B.4)}$$

Forklift truck:

$$\$10,000 = (\text{PVIF}_{\text{IRR},2})\$14,161$$

$$\text{PVIF}_{\text{IRR},2} = 0.7062$$

$$\text{IRR}_B = 19\% \quad \textit{(see Appendix B.2)}$$

3. *Net present value at* ∞ *percent:*

Conveyor system:

$$\text{NPV}_A = -\$10,000 + \frac{\$6,705}{(1 + \infty)^1} + \frac{\$6,705}{(1 + \infty)^2}$$

$$= -\$10,000$$

$$\text{Forklift truck:} \quad NPV_B = -\$10,000 + \frac{\$14,161}{(1 + \infty)^2}$$
$$= -\$10,000$$

4. *Crossover rate (rate equating NPVs):* The crossover rate occurs where $NPV_A = NPV_B$, or $NPV_B - NPV_A = 0$. To calculate the crossover rate, first subtract the cash flows of Project A from those of Project B: Year-end 0, \$0; Year-end 1, $-\$6,705$; Year-end 2, \$7,456. Then calculate the internal rate of return for the cash-flow differences:

$$\$6,705 = (PVIF_{IRR,1})\$7,456$$

$$PVIF_{IRR,1} = \frac{\$6,705}{\$7,456} = 0.8993$$

$$11\% < IRR < 12\% \quad \text{(see Appendix B.2)}$$

The IRR (crossover rate) lies between 11 percent and 12 percent. A financial calculator shows more precisely that the rate is 11.2 percent.

Where Conflicts Occur. Figure 9.7 depicts the results from the preceding four calculations. Critical to understanding the conflict in ranking between net present value and internal rate of return is the **crossover rate**, 11.2 percent:

- If the discount rate used to calculate the NPV is *greater than* the crossover rate, then NPV and IRR rank projects in the same order (A over B). There is no conflict in ranking in the **zone of ranking consistency.**
- If the discount rate used to calculate the net present value is *less than* the crossover rate, then NPV and IRR rank projects in conflicting order. Figure 9.7 shows the conflicts occurring in the **zone of ranking conflict.**

If the financial manager of Quick Shop had calculated net present value with a discount rate greater than 11.2 percent, then no ranking conflict would have occurred. The 9 percent rate used creates the conflict between NPV and IRR. The following discussion shows how to evaluate projects in the zone of ranking conflict.

Resolving Conflicts. Understanding the relationship between the crossover rate and the reinvestment rate helps us to resolve the conflict in ranking. The **reinvestment rate** is the rate of return the company can earn from investing a project's cash inflows. Here are the rules for resolving conflict in ranking:

- If the company can invest each project's cash inflows at a rate *greater than* the crossover rate, then choose the project with the greater internal rate of return.
- If the company can invest each project's cash inflows at a rate *less than* the crossover rate, then choose the project with the greater net present value.

As these rules state, the *crossover rate* determines the point at which the financial manager should use either IRR or NPV to rank conflicting projects, and it identifies the zone of ranking conflict.

Reinvestment Rate Greater than Crossover Rate. If Quick Shop can invest each project's cash inflows at a rate *greater than* 11.2 percent (the crossover rate), then

crossover rate
Discount rate that causes equality between the net present values of projects; point where the NPV profiles intersect.

zone of ranking consistency
Range of discount rates where net present value and internal rate of return rank projects identically.

zone of ranking conflict
Range of discount rates where net present value and internal rate of return rank projects differently.

reinvestment rate
Rate of return a company can earn from investing a project's cash inflows.

the conveyor system ranks ahead of the forklift truck, as the internal rate of return indicates. Suppose that the financial manager estimates a 12 percent annual reinvestment rate over the life of each project. At 12 percent the **terminal value** of each project is as follows:

Conveyor System	*Forklift Truck*
$TV_A = \$6,705(1 + 0.12) + \$6,705$	$TV_B = 0(1 + 0.12) + \$14,161$
$= \$7,509.60 + \$6,705$	$= 0 + \$14,161$
$= \$14,214.60$	$= \$14,161$

With a 12 percent reinvestment rate, the conveyor system's terminal value ($14,214.60) is greater than the forklift truck's ($14,161), and the present value of its terminal value exceeds the forklift truck's for all discount rates. Thus the financial manager ranks the conveyor system ahead of the forklift truck for all reinvestment rates exceeding the crossover rate of 11.2 percent. Ranking by the internal rate of return is correct in this case. Note that *selecting* the conveyor system instead of the forklift truck *implicitly assumes a reinvestment rate* greater than 11.2 percent.

Reinvestment Rate Less than Crossover Rate. If Quick Shop can invest each project's cash inflows at rates *less than* 11.2 percent, then the forklift truck ranks ahead of the conveyor system, as the net present value indicates. Suppose that the financial manager forecasts a 10 percent annual reinvestment rate. Then the terminal value of each project is:

Conveyor System	*Forklift Truck*
$TV_A = \$6,705(1 + 0.10) + \$6,705$	$TV_B = 0(1 + 0.10) + \$14,161$
$= \$7,375.50 + \$6,705$	$= 0 + \$14,161$
$= \$14,080.50$	$= \$14,161$

With a 10 percent reinvestment rate, the conveyor system's terminal value ($14,080.50) is less than the forklift truck's ($14,161). The financial manager ranks the forklift truck ahead of the conveyor system because of its higher terminal value and, therefore, its higher present values for all discount rates. In this case the ranking indicated by net present value (discount rate at 9 percent) is correct. Note that even if the financial manager makes no explicit assumption about the reinvestment rate, *selecting* the forklift truck instead of the conveyor system *implicitly assumes* that the reinvestment rate is less than 11.2 percent.

Reinvestment Rate Equal to Crossover Rate. If Quick Shop can reinvest each project's cash inflows at precisely 11.2 percent, then the terminal values for each project equal $14,161:

Conveyor System	*Forklift Truck*
$TV_A = \$6,705(1 + 0.112) + \$6,705$	$TV_B = 0(0.112) + \$14,161$
$= \$7,456 + \$6,705$	$= 0 + \$14,161$
$= \$14,161$	$= \$14,161$

In this case the projects rank equally, and the financial manager would be indifferent to the selection of either project.

FIGURE 9.8

Capital Rationing Leads to a High Reinvestment Rate

Under capital rationing a company has profitable projects that its budget constraint prevents it from accepting. If the projects will be available in the future, then the company has a high reinvestment rate.

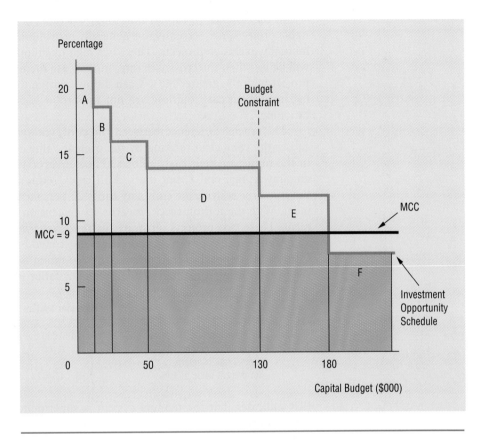

A Rule of Thumb. Resolving conflicts in ranking by NPV and IRR requires a financial manager to forecast what the future reinvestment rate will be, then compare it with the crossover rate. That is no easy task. Common sense, however, suggests the following rule of thumb for ranking projects: *Use internal rate of return under conditions of severe capital rationing and net present value in its absence.* This is why: A company experiencing severe capital rationing has profitable projects that its budget constraint prevents it from accepting. These profitable projects will likely be available in the future so that future cash inflows can be reinvested at a high return.

investment opportunity schedule

Line depicting descending rates of return on proposed capital projects.

To illustrate, Quick Shop faces the **investment opportunity schedule**—the line depicting descending rates of return on proposed capital projects—shown in Figure 9.8. The financial manager accepts Projects A through E in the absence of capital rationing because in each case IRR > MCC of 9 percent. The size of the capital budget is $180,000, determined by the intersection of the investment opportunity schedule and the MCC. However, with capital restricted to $130,000, the financial manager accepts Projects A through D and rejects Project E, with a relatively high rate of return. The capital budget is $50,000 ($180,000 − $130,000) less with capital rationing than without it.

In general, for companies facing severe capital rationing, the reinvestment rate is high and exceeds the crossover rate. In this case internal rate of return is superior to net present value for rank-ordering mutually exclusive projects because there is a high probability that the reinvestment rate will be greater than the crossover rate.

In the absence of capital rationing, where a company can invest in all profitable projects, net present value generally provides the superior rank-ordering of mutually exclusive projects. There is a high likelihood that the reinvestment rate will be less than the crossover rate. In this case the financial manager accepts the project with the greater NPV. Cash inflows during the early years and size of the net investment cash outflow are not important issues in the absence of capital rationing.

The crucial difference between the conveyor system and forklift truck that causes the conflict in ranking by net present value and internal rate of return is in the timing of their cash inflows. The conveyor system returns a large dollar amount at Year-end 1, but the forklift truck returns nothing at that time. With the conveyor system, the company earns 22 percent on a declining capital investment. With the forklift truck, it earns 19 percent on an increasing capital investment. These two projects illustrate the *time disparity* problem.

Another cause of ranking conflict is illustrated by the *size disparity* problem. Consider a proposal to computerize an accounting system, which is capital intensive, versus using a manual system, which is labor intensive:

	Computer System	**Manual System**
Net investment cash outflow	$100,000	$20,000
Cash inflow, Year-end 1	$115,000	$24,000
Internal rate of return	15%	20%
Net present value at 10%	$ 4,545	$ 1,818

IRR indicates that the manual system is superior to the computer system, but NPV indicates the reverse. In essence, the manual system offers the opportunity to earn a large-percentage return (20 percent) on a small investment ($20,000). The computer system offers the opportunity to earn a small-percentage return (15 percent) on a large investment ($100,000). Despite the smaller rate of return, the larger size of the computer system causes its NPV to be larger than that of the manual system. In the absence of capital rationing, the financial manager should choose the computer system, as indicated by NPV. If the financial manager chooses the manual system, then that choice implies that the company can invest the $80,000 difference in NICOs ($100,000 − $20,000) at a rate exceeding 13.75 percent. Here is why: The $80,000 difference generates an extra $91,000 ($115,000 − $24,000), for a rate of return of 13.75 percent [($91,000 − $80,000)/$80,000]. Only if the $80,000 can be invested elsewhere at a rate exceeding 13.75 percent should the financial manager choose the manual system over the computer system. The 13.75 percent is the crossover rate of the NPV profiles of the two projects.[10]

[10] Mathematical programming (see Note 9) provides the theoretically correct solution to the problem of project ranking. Unfortunately, estimating the necessary input for this procedure makes it difficult to implement in practice.

MONITORING PROJECTS AND THE POST-COMPLETION AUDIT

After the capital-budgeting committee approves the company's capital budget, projects are implemented and eventually completed or abandoned. The final step in capital budgeting is to monitor projects as they develop and evaluate the success or failure of completed or abandoned projects. The responsibility for monitoring often lies with the controller's office and is usually undertaken by the company's cost accountants and information systems specialists. The financial manager usually undertakes the **post-completion audit.**

post-completion audit

Performance appraisal of a capital project to assess its success.

The post-completion audit is often a weak link in the capital-budgeting process because financial managers are busy with today's problems and planning for tomorrow. Furthermore, they know they cannot change what has already been completed. Yet a post-completion audit is important for two reasons: (1) It assesses the actual success or failure of projects so that the company can reward the managers involved in successful projects. (2) It aids the financial manager in improving the capital-budgeting process by uncovering weaknesses in the system.

Figure 9.9 shows a post-completion audit form for a company. It compares expected and actual net operating profit after taxes and the return on investment (internal rate of return). It also compares the expected payback period with the actual one. The form requires the signatures of the line manager and the financial manager involved. Before signing, each manager probes for explanations of any differences between expected and actual results.

Thus far we have assumed that each project has risk equal to that of the company's average project. This assumption has allowed us to focus on the various evaluation methods and to use the same hurdle rate for each project—the company's marginal cost of capital (MCC). However, financial managers often examine proposed projects that differ from the average. Some projects have substantially more risk than the average project (for example, a proposal to open a manufacturing facility abroad), whereas others have substantially less risk (for example, a proposal to reconfigure the floor space in a retail area). Chapter 10 addresses the way a financial manager can introduce risk analysis into the decision process.

SUMMARY

Table 9.2 provides a summary of the evaluation methods that this chapter presents.

- Capital budgeting starts with the creative act of generating project ideas, followed by the crucial process of estimating expected cash flows. Next is the challenging step of evaluating risks, followed by the mechanical step of evaluating project acceptability. The final step is monitoring and auditing project results.

- An ideal method for evaluating and selecting projects should (1) recognize the time value of money, (2) consider cash flows over a project's entire life, and (3) incorporate a project's required rate of return—the company's marginal cost of capital for average-risk projects.

- Payback period measures the length of time required to recover through cash inflows a project's net investment cash outflow. It is a measure of liquidity, stressing a project's return *of* capital rather than a return *on* capital. This method fails to meet the criteria of an ideal evaluation method.

Global Capital Investments

Investing in capital projects around the globe is commonplace for U.S. (and non-U.S.) companies. For example, General Motors has manufacturing facilities in Japan and Mexico, and Ford has manufacturing facilities in England and Brazil. Citibank has a joint venture (partnership) with Dai-Ichi Kangyo Bank in Japanese retail banking.

The evaluation of foreign capital investments is conceptually the same as that for domestic capital investments. A project with a positive net present value (NPV) is acceptable, but one with a negative NPV is not. A major difference arises between foreign and domestic investments, however, in the size, timing, and risk of cash flows.

Cash flows in foreign currency generated by an overseas subsidiary (corporation owned by the parent corporation), by a branch office, or by an affiliate are sometimes not immediately available to the parent company. Government regulations in the host country may bar or limit repatria-

tion (transmittal to the parent in the home country) of the cash flows. Operating under such regulations means that the parent company must reinvest part of its cash flows in projects within the host country. It also means that the blocked cash flows cannot be paid in dividends to shareholders. In addition, during the time of blockage, the cash flows are exposed to *foreign-exchange risk,* the uncertainty in the value of the foreign currency.

Another impact on cash flows stems from foreign income taxes on earnings generated abroad. The maximum corporate income tax rates among countries vary greatly: United States, 34 percent; Canada, 44 percent; Japan, 42 percent; Sweden, 52 percent; Germany, 56 percent; and Italy, 36 percent, for example. U.S. companies, however, are not taxed twice on the same earnings. Payment of foreign income taxes entitles U.S. companies to *foreign tax credits* against U.S. income taxes. In general, U.S. tax laws are designed so that worldwide earnings are taxed no less than earnings generated within the United States. Earnings generated in countries with tax rates higher than the U.S. tax rates are taxed at the higher rates.

Higher tax rates cause a greater reduction in cash flows from capital investments.

Occasionally, governments discriminate against foreign companies by imposing extra taxes. In the extreme, a government can impose the ultimate tax: the confiscation of company assets. *Expropriation,* the seizure of assets, is uncommon, but such political risks should be included in the evaluation of overseas projects.

To account for restrictions on repatriating cash flows, foreign-exchange risk, foreign taxes, and political risks, financial managers typically evaluate overseas projects in two ways: (1) from the foreign subsidiary's viewpoint and (2) from the parent company's viewpoint. The subsidiary's viewpoint subjects a project to local conditions: inflation rates, discount rates, and business risks. Projects yielding a negative NPV to the subsidiary are rejected. Those surviving the subsidiary's analysis are next analyzed from the parent company's viewpoint to account for the size, timing, and risk of cash flows to the parent. Only with a positive NPV from the parent's viewpoint is a project finally accepted.

• The discount rate that causes equality between present value of cash inflows and net investment cash outflow is known as internal rate of return (IRR). An iterative search process is required to calculate IRR, which is best interpreted as the return on invested capital. When multiple IRRs occur for a nonconventional project, the IRRs should not be interpreted as returns on invested capital. If a conventional project's IRR exceeds the required rate of return, then the project should be accepted for investment.

• Net present value (NPV) equals the present value of cash inflows, discounted at the project's required rate of return, minus the net investment cash outflow. NPV measures the dollar change in shareholder wealth, or market value of com-

FIGURE 9.9

Post-Completion Audit Form

Capital Expenditures and
Extraordinary Expenses
(Dollar Amounts in Thousands)

Group/Location

Project No.

Project Name

Date Initial Proj.
Funds Expended

Date Prepared

Project Funds	Approved	Actual	Actual (O)/U Approved	Cash Flow Payback Years
Fixed Assets	$	$	$	Original
Expense				Revised
Other (Detail)				
Total	$	$	$	

Return on Incremental Investment		FY 19__	FY 19__	FY 19__	FY 19__	FY 19__	Annual Average of __ Years
Company Net Profit after Taxes	Original	$	$	$	$	$	$
	Revised	$	$	$	$	$	$
	Incr./(Decr.)	$	$	$	$	$	$
Return on Investment after Taxes	Original	%	%	%	%	%	%
	Revised	%	%	%	%	%	%
	Incr./(Decr.)	Pts	Pts	Pts	Pts	Pts	Pts

EXPLANATION OF CHANGES

Signatures

Senior Financial Executive
Submitting Operating Unit

Senior Executive
Submitting Operating Unit

Source: Arthur V. Corr, *The Capital Expenditure Decision* (New York: National Association of Accountants, 1983), 100.

mon equity, caused by investing in a project. NPV must exceed zero for a project to be acceptable.

• Profitability index (PI) equals the present value of cash inflows divided by the net investment cash outflow. PI shows the present value of cash inflows per dollar invested in the project. If PI is greater than 1.0, then the project is acceptable.

• For conventional projects, the three discounted cash flow methods—IRR, NPV, and PI—provide the same accept-reject signals. If one method indicates project acceptability, then the other two do also. Any project unacceptable with one method is unacceptable with either of the others.

• Although the three discounted cash flow methods provide consistent evaluations for accept-reject decisions, they may produce conflicting rank orderings of projects. Independent projects require only accept-reject decisions, whereas mutually exclusive projects or the presence of capital rationing requires ranking to select the better ones.

• NPV profiles illustrate why NPV and IRR rank-order projects differently. These profiles reveal the zone of ranking conflict and the zone of ranking consistency. The zone of ranking conflict exists where the discount rate is less than the crossover rate of the mutually exclusive projects. Within the zone of conflict, NPV ranks projects correctly if the reinvestment rate is less than the crossover rate; IRR ranks projects correctly if the reinvestment rate is greater than the crossover rate.

• The decision regarding which mutually exclusive project to select depends on the financial manager's assumption about the reinvestment rate for intermediate cash inflows. Under capital rationing the reinvestment rate is likely to be high; for companies that can invest each year in all acceptable projects, the reinvestment rate is likely to be lower. A rule to use when a ranking conflict exists between IRR and NPV is the following: *Under capital rationing, use internal rate of return to rank-order projects; in the absence of capital rationing, use net present value to rank-order projects.*

Key Terms

payback period	NPV profile	zone of ranking conflict
discounted cash flow (DCF) methods	profitability index (PI)	reinvestment rate
	mutually exclusive projects	terminal value
internal rate of return (IRR)	capital rationing	investment opportunity schedule
hurdle rate	crossover rate	post-completion audit
net present value (NPV)	zone of ranking consistency	

Questions

9.1. What are the shortcomings of payback period as an evaluation method in capital budgeting?

9.2. Describe the role of a project's required rate of return in the following methods for evaluating proposed capital projects: (1) internal rate of return, (2) net present value, and (3) profitability index.

9.3. Explain the decision rules for accepting and rejecting projects when using the following capital-budgeting methods: (1) internal rate of return, (2) net present value, and (3) profitability index.

9.4. The management of Magnum Optics is considering the following list of proposed capital investment projects for 19X8:

Project	Investment	IRR	NPV
A	$70,000	28%	$18,000
B	12,000	16	12,000
C	18,000	12	16,000
D	6,000	8	(2,000)
E	26,000	7	(6,000)

a. The present value of Project C's future cash flows is:
   (1) $12,000.   (3) $26,000.
   (2) $19,000.   (4) $34,000.

b. If the projects are not mutually exclusive and there is no capital rationing, then the size of the optimal capital budget is nearest:

(1) $32,000.   (3) $100,000.

(2) $70,000.   (4) $106,000.

c. Project A has an $18,000 NPV. Interpret what this amount tells the financial manager will happen to the company's stock price if the project is accepted.

d. Explain which project, B or C, management should select if the two are mutually exclusive and there is no capital rationing.

9.5. If time has no value, then the discount rate is zero. Assuming time has no value, what is the net present value of the following cash inflows (+) and outflows (−)?

Year-End	Cash Flow
0	−$10,000
1	+$30,000
2	+$10,000
3	−$20,000

9.6. What is the net present value of the following cash flows as the discount rate approaches infinity?

Year-End	Cash Flow
0	−$2,000
1	+$1,000,000
2	+$3,000

9.7. The following configuration of cash flows represents a nonconventional project:

Year-End	Cash Flow
0	−$ 1,600
1	+$10,000
2	−$10,000

This project has two internal rates of return, 25 and 400 percent. Show that these are IRRs for the cash flows by using the equation for IRR.

9.8. If the net present value of a project exceeds zero, then the internal rate of return exceeds K, the required rate of return on the project. Also, under these conditions the profitability index exceeds 1. Explain why these relationships hold true.

9.9. "It seems to me that net present value is somehow related to the profitability index," says Aurora, while studying with her friend Donna for their finance exam. "I think you're right, but how, that's the question," replies Donna. "I've got it," says Aurora. "Divide NPV by NICO and add 1." Is Aurora's conclusion correct? Explain.

9.10. Why is it necessary to rank-order mutually exclusive projects but unnecessary to rank-order independent projects? In your answer define *mutually exclusive* and *independent*.

9.11. What are the negative consequences of capital rationing? Why does capital rationing exist in some companies?

9.12. Anne Alexander and David Price work in the controller's office of the Metal Fab Company. They work as capital-budget analysts and are having the following discussion:

David: Since Metal Fab can borrow at 12 percent, I say we go ahead with it.

Anne: What's the project's expected rate of return?

David: 14 percent.

Anne: Sounds okay to me. As long as we make more than we pay—that's good business.

Where have Anne and David gone wrong? Explain the fallacy in their reasoning.

9.13. The net present value of a capital project varies with the discount rate as follows:

Discount Rate	NPV
0%	$145,600
12	50,000
20	0
∞	−200,000

Sketch the NPV profile of the project. Label each axis and note the location of the internal rate of return.

9.14. a. Explain the relationship between the crossover rate and K (required rate of return on the project) in determining when a ranking conflict occurs between NPV and IRR. Be sure to refer to the zone of ranking conflict in your answer.

b. How does a financial manager use the relationship between the reinvestment rate and the crossover rate to resolve a conflict in ranking by NPV and IRR?

9.15. Explain why internal rate of return is useful for rank-ordering mutually exclusive projects when capital rationing exists.

9.16. Explain why net present value is useful for rank-ordering mutually exclusive projects when capital rationing is absent.

Strategy Problem

I. Evaluation Methods

The financial manager of American Pencil Company must evaluate a project with a 5-year life requiring an investment in equipment of $226,000. The equipment will be depreciated using the MACRS procedure and a 3-year class life. Net working capital of $42,700 will be invested when the company implements the project. American Pencil's financial manager expects to sell the equipment for $34,000 and to recapture the entire amount of net working capital when the company terminates the project.

The accompanying schedule shows the *pro forma* operating statements and incremental cash flows associ-

ated with the project. American Pencil is in the 34 percent marginal income tax bracket, and its marginal cost of capital is 18 percent. Since the project is typical of the company's other projects, the financial manager will use the marginal cost of capital in the discounted cash flow analysis.

a. Calculate the project's payback period. Should the financial manager accept the project if the maximum acceptable payback period is 3 years?

b. Calculate and interpret the project's internal rate of return, net present value, and profitability index.

Pro Forma Operating Statements

	Year 1	Year 2	Year 3	Year 4	Year 5
Sales	$275,000	$302,500	$332,750	$366,025	$402,628
Less costs					
Variable	123,750	136,125	149,738	164,711	181,182
Fixed	85,000	85,000	85,000	85,000	85,000
Depreciation	75,334	100,446	33,480	16,740	0
Earnings before taxes	($ 9,084)	($ 19,071)	$ 64,532	$ 99,574	$136,446
Less taxes (34%)[a]	(3,089)	(6,484)	21,941	33,855	46,392
Earnings after taxes	($ 5,995)	($ 12,587)	$ 42,591	$ 65,719	$ 90,054

Operating Cash Flow Statements

	Year 1	Year 2	Year 3	Year 4	Year 5
Cash inflows					
Sales	$275,000	$302,500	$332,750	$366,025	$402,628
Tax savings[a]	3,089	6,484			
Less cash outflows					
Variable costs	123,750	136,125	149,738	164,711	181,182
Fixed costs	85,000	85,000	85,000	85,000	85,000
Taxes	0	0	21,941	33,855	46,392
Operating cash flow	$ 69,339	$ 87,859	$ 76,071	$ 82,459	$ 90,054
Add disposal cash flow:					
Equipment					22,440
Net working capital					42,700
Cash flow	$ 69,339	$ 87,859	$ 76,071	$ 82,459	$155,194

[a]The company has other profitable operations that permit it to reduce taxable income by the amount of loss from this project. The tax savings are 34 percent of the taxable loss.

Strategy	Solution

a. The payback period is the time required to recover through incremental cash inflows the project's net investment cash outflow ($268,700 = $226,000 + $42,700):

Arrange the cash flows on a time line and accumulate them.

	Year 1	Year 2	Year 3	Year 4
Cash flows	$69,339	$ 87,859	$ 76,071	$82,459
Cumulative cash flows	$69,339	$157,198	$233,269	$35,431/$82,459 = 0.43
Sum of years	1	2	3	3.43

Based on the 3-year maximum acceptable period, the financial manager will reject the proposed project using the payback method.

b. Begin the discounted cash flow analysis by drawing a time line depicting all incremental cash flows:

Draw a time line for the annual cash flows.

End of Year	0	1	2	3	4	5
	NICO	CF_1	CF_2	CF_3	CF_4	CF_5
Cash Flow	−$268,700	+$69,339	+$87,859	+76,071	+$82,459	+$155,194

The *internal rate of return* is the rate of return on the capital invested in the project. Solve the following equation for IRR:

$$NICO = \sum_{t=1}^{n} \frac{CF_t}{(1 + IRR)^t}$$

Use a financial calculator with an IRR key (or use Appendix B.2 and trial and error).

Using a financial calculator yields the IRR: 19.4 percent. The financial manager should accept the proposed project because the internal rate of return on the project is greater than the MCC (19.4% > 18%).

The *net present value* measures the change in shareholder wealth upon acceptance of the project. Solve the following equation for NPV:

$$NPV = \sum_{t=1}^{n} \frac{CF_t}{(1 + K)^t} - NICO$$

Use a financial calculator with an NPV key (or use Appendix B.2 and K = 18%).

Letting K = 18% and using a financial calculator yield the NPV: $9,827. The financial manager should accept this project because its NPV is greater than zero. In fact, accepting the project will increase shareholder wealth by $9,827.

The *profitability index* is the present value of cash inflows per dollar invested. Solve the following equation:

Divide the present value of cash inflows by NICO.

$$\text{Profitability index} = \frac{\sum_{t=1}^{n} \frac{CF_t}{(1 + K)^t}}{NICO}$$

A financial calculator yields the result: 1.037. The financial manager should accept the project because its PI > 1.0. The company receives $1.037 in present value for each $1 invested.

II. Conflict in Ranking

A financial manager must evaluate two proposed projects that are mutually exclusive. Project S (for *Small*) requires a net investment cash outflow of $33,333, and Project L (for *Large*) requires one of $66,539. The cash flows are as follows:

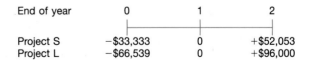

End of year	0	1	2
Project S	−$33,333	0	+$52,053
Project L	−$66,539	0	+$96,000

The hurdle rate of an investment in either project is 12 percent.

a. Do NPV and IRR conflict in their rank orderings of the two projects?

b. Which project should the financial manager accept if the reinvestment rate is 12 percent?

Strategy	Solution

Solution

a. To determine whether or not there is a conflict in the rank order, calculate the NPV and IRR for each project. Using a financial calculator yields the solutions:

Calculate NPV and IRR for each project.

	NPV	IRR
Project S	$8,163	25.0%
Project L	9,992	20.1

There is a conflict in ranking because Project S has the higher IRR, and Project L has the higher net present value.

b. To determine which project is preferable, calculate the crossover rate, then compare it with the reinvestment rate.

Crossover rate calculation:

Calculate the crossover rate by setting $NPV_S = NPV_L$.

$$NPV_S = NPV_L$$

$$\$52,053(PVIF_{i,2}) - \$33,333 = \$96,000(PVIF_{i,2}) - \$66,539$$

$$\$43,947(PVIF_{i,2}) = \$33,206$$

$$PVIF_{i,2} = 0.756$$

When the reinvestment rate is less than the crossover rate, use NPV for rank ordering.

Appendix B.2 shows that an n of 2 and an interest factor of 0.756 are associated with an i of 15 percent. Thus the crossover rate is 15 percent. Now compare the reinvestment rate with the crossover rate: 12% < 15%. When the reinvestment rate is less than the crossover rate, the financial manager should select the project with a higher net present value: Project L in this problem.

  If the company could invest the difference in the projects' NICO ($33,206 = $66,539 − $33,333) at a rate greater than 15 percent, then the financial manager should select Project S. But the reinvestment rate indicates that the difference can be invested at 12 percent, so the financial manager should select Project L. Note that 20.1 percent on $66,539 is more profitable than 25 percent on $33,333 plus 12 percent on $33,206 ($66,539 − $33,333).

◆ **Demonstration Problem**

Karen Johnson is interviewing for a job as a capital-budgeting analyst with a Fortune 500 company. She will spend 30 minutes each with a company representative from the department of human resources and from the department of capital budgeting. Based on prior interviews, she expects the capital-budgeting representative to check out her technical expertise. She decides to prepare for the interview by reviewing some principles of capital budgeting. In a textbook she finds an illustration of cash flows from two capital projects. Assume that you are in Ms. Johnson's position and respond to the series of questions and exercises associated with the cash flows.

	Incremental Cash Flows	
Year-End	Project C	Project D
0	−$350,000	−$350,000
1	+$163,558	0
2	+$163,558	0
3	+$163,558	+$532,306

a. What are *incremental cash flows*?
b. What is the payback period for Project C and for Project D? To answer this question, assume that the cash inflows occur uniformly throughout the year. Which project should be accepted, assuming a payback criterion of 2 years? What are the shortcomings of payback period as an evaluation method in capital budgeting?
c. Calculate the internal rate of return for Project C and for Project D. Should either project be accepted, assuming a required rate of return of 10 percent? Explain.
d. Fill in the blanks of the following table for Project C (round off to nearest dollar):

Year	Beginning Balance	Dollar Return at 19%	Ending Balance	Actual Cash Withdrawal	Remaining Investment
1	$350,000	$66,500	$416,500	$163,558	$252,942
2	252,942	____	____	____	____
3	____	____	____	____	____

Does the capital invested in Project C at the beginning of each year increase, decrease, or stay the same? Answer the same question for Project D without constructing a table to do so, but explain your reasoning.
e. Use a required rate of return of 10 percent to calculate net present value for Project C and for Project D. Should either project be accepted? Explain.
f. Calculate net present value for Project C and for Project D using the following discount rates: (1) zero and (2) infinity. What is the implication of these discount rates for the time value of money?
g. Use a required rate of return of 10 percent to calculate the profitability index for Project C and for Project D. Should either project be accepted? Explain.
h. (1) Why does a company use its marginal cost of capital to evaluate average-risk projects? (2) Why do some companies face capital rationing? (3) What is the difference between *independent* projects and *mutually exclusive* projects?
i. Assume that Project C and Project D are mutually exclusive. Draw NPV profiles for the projects. If you choose Project C instead of Project D, how high is the reinvestment rate implied by your choice?

Problems

Payback period, IRR, NPV, and PI

9.1. Dick Waldron, a capital-budgeting analyst for Tovar Foods, is analyzing a project proposed by the marketing department. According to his research to date, the project will cost $250,000 and produce cash inflows of $70,000 per year for 8 years. As a matter of policy on projects of this sort, Tovar Foods requires a maximum payback period of 4 years and a minimum annual rate of return of 20 percent.
a. Calculate payback period, internal rate of return, net present value, and the profitability index for the project.
b. Should Mr. Waldron recommend acceptance of the project? Explain.

Present value of reducing expenses

9.2. Ella Cochran is employed by Tustin Products and has come up with an idea for a labor-saving device. If the company's capital-budgeting committee accepts the device, its only impact will be to reduce wages—an operating expense—by $216,000 annually in each of the next 6 years. Tustin Products is in the 40 percent marginal tax bracket. Calculate the annual dollar impact on operating cash flows assuming the company implements Ms. Cochran's suggestion. Using the company's 12 percent cost of capital as the discount rate, calculate the present value of the labor-saving device.

Cash flows, payback period, and NPV

9.3. Sanka Venkswar is the controller for Collingswood Crosstiks, a company that publishes and distributes crossword puzzles. His immediate task is to analyze an investment project proposed by a planning committee. Mr. Venkswar's boss places before him the following data on the proposed project:

	Amount per year
Sales revenue	$2,920,000
Direct labor cost	520,000
Direct materials cost	840,000
Marketing cost	760,000
Depreciation	400,000
Earnings before taxes	$ 400,000

His boss also tells him the following: (1) The company's marginal tax bracket is 40 percent. (2) Depreciable assets for the project will cost $2 million and be worthless at the end of the project's 5-year life. (3) The project requires a $60,000 investment in net working capital, which will be recovered at the end of the project's life. (4) For this preliminary analysis, use $400,000 to approximate the annual depreciation associated with the project. (5) The required rate of return on the project is 14 percent per year.
a. Calculate the net investment cash outflow *and* disposal cash flow associated with the project.
b. Calculate the annual operating cash flow from the proposed project.
c. Calculate the payback period for the proposed project. Should Mr. Venkswar recommend acceptance of the project if the maximum acceptable payback period is 3 years?
d. Calculate the net present value of the project. Should Mr. Venkswar recommend acceptance of the project based on NPV?

Cash flows, payback period, and NPV

9.4. Donald Walz recently joined the Graphic Design Company as a capital-budgeting analyst. His first assignment involves the analysis of a $500,000 investment to expand sales. The investment will increase annual sales revenue by $1,300,000 and annual cash expenses by $900,000. For tax purposes, annual depreciation charges will be $100,000. Mr. Walz expects the project to last for 5 years, at which time the assets of the project will be sold for $50,000. Graphic Design Company's marginal tax bracket is 34 percent, and company policy requires a 15 percent annual return on investments.
a. Calculate the annual operating cash flow from the proposed project.
b. Calculate the payback period for the project. Should Mr. Walz recommend acceptance of the project if the maximum acceptable payback period is 4 years?
c. Calculate the net present value of the project. Should Mr. Walz recommend acceptance of the project based on NPV?

Interpretation of IRR

9.5. Projects A and B each require a $10,000 investment and produce the following cash inflows:

End of Year	Project A	Project B
1	$ 1,200	$6,073
2	11,200	6,073

a. What is the internal rate of return (IRR) of Project A? Try to answer the question without calculations.
b. Calculate the IRR of Project B.
c. Fill in the blanks of the following table for Project A:

Year	Beginning Balance	Dollar Return at 12%	Ending Balance	Actual Cash Withdrawal	Remaining Investment
1	$10,000	$1,200	$11,200	_____	_____
2	_____	_____	11,200	_____	0

Does the capital invested in Project A at the beginning of each year increase, decrease, or stay the same?

d. Develop a table for Project B like the one in Part *c*. Does the capital invested in Project B at the beginning of each year increase, decrease, or stay the same?

IRR and uneven cash flows

9.6. Suppose you can invest $770 today, entitling you to the following cash flows:

End of Year	Cash Flow
1	$500
2	125
3	252

a. Calculate the internal rate of return on your investment.

b. Calculate your dollar amount invested immediately after the $500 cash flow at Year-end 1, the $125 cash flow at Year-end 2, and the $252 cash flow at Year-end 3.

Interpretation of NPV

9.7. Victoria Williams is a capital-budgeting analyst for Dynamicron Company. She is analyzing a capital project with the following annual earnings:

	Per Year
Sales revenue	$5,650,000
Cash expenses	4,120,000
Depreciation	750,000
Earnings before taxes	$ 780,000

The net investment cash outflow for the 6-year project is $4,500,000, which occurs at the beginning of Year 1. Cash flows from terminating the project at the end of 6 years will be zero. Ms. Williams judges the project to have risk characteristics typical of Dynamicron Company's other projects. She estimates the company's marginal cost of capital to be 12 percent and its marginal tax bracket to be 40 percent.

a. Calculate the net present value (NPV) of the project.

b. What is the maximum dollar amount that Dynamicron Company could invest in the project and it still be acceptable?

c. Based on the NPV in Part *a*, what change in shareholder wealth do you expect to occur upon acceptance of the project? What assumptions are implicit in your answer?

d. Ms. Williams tells her boss: "Revenues from the project will cover cash operating expenses and taxes, repay the $4,500,000 investment, pay 12 percent on the $4,500,000 provided by capital suppliers, and still provide a bonus to our shareholders." Explain how this is possible.

Interpretation of NPV

9.8. Greg Demkoff, a new employee in the department of finance of Pace Products, just received his first assignment. His task is to calculate the net present value of a capital project with a net investment cash outflow of $500,000. The 10-year project is expected to produce incremental cash inflows of $120,000 per year. Relative to Pace Products' other investments, the project has average-risk characteristics.

Mr. Demkoff's immediate supervisor told him that the company's marginal cost of capital is 15 percent. He also told him to be prepared to explain the meaning of his calculations to the head of the department of finance.

a. Calculate the net present value of the project.

b. What answers should Mr. Demkoff give to the following questions raised by the department head:

(1) "Why do you use 15 percent to discount the cash inflows?"

(2) "Do you recommend that we invest in the project?"

(3) "What happens to your recommendation if the project costs $600,000, not $500,000? Also, what's the most we can pay for the project and still have it be an acceptable venture?"

(4) "What do you expect to happen to the wealth of our shareholders if we accept the project? And what are the hidden assumptions in your answer?"

Interpretation of NPV

9.9. Goodman Corporation has been presented with an investment opportunity that will yield the 10 years of incremental cash flows presented below. The net investment cash outflow is an immediate $125,000, and the financial manager estimates the marginal cost of capital to be 10 percent. What is the net present value of the investment? What does the net present value represent?

End of Year(s)	Cash Inflows
1	$90,000
2–9	25,000
10	30,000

Payback period and DCF methods

9.10. Alomito Steel is considering investing in two projects with the following cash flows:

Year-End	Project L	Project M
0	−$80,000	−$100,000
1	+$40,000	+$40,000
2	+$40,000	+$40,000
3	+$40,000	+$40,000

a. For each project compute the payback period and internal rate of return. Also compute their net present values and profitability indexes using a 12 percent annual discount rate.

b. Should the financial manager accept Projects L and M? Assume that 12 percent per year is the required rate of return on each project.

Ranking conflict, crossover rate vs. reinvestment rate, and NPV profiles

9.11. Two mutually exclusive projects have the following expected cash flows:

Year-End	Fast Payoff	Slow Payoff
0	−$220,000	−$220,000
1	+$100,000	0
2	+$100,000	0
3	+$100,000	+$334,593

a. Calculate the internal rate of return for each project. Based on IRR, which project do you prefer?

b. Calculate the net present value for each project, assuming a 10 percent marginal cost of capital. Based on NPV, which project do you prefer?

c. Sketch NPV profiles for the projects, noting the crossover rate of 11.1 percent. Under what condition would you choose *Fast Payoff*?

Ranking conflict, crossover rate vs. reinvestment rate, and NPV profiles

9.12. The following three projects are mutually exclusive and have the indicated internal rates of return:

Year-End	X	Y	Z
0	−$1,000	−$1,000	−$1,000
1	0	+$100	+$576.20
2	+$1,210	+$1,100	+$576.20
IRR	10%	10%	10%

a. The IRR is the return on invested capital. Invested capital at the beginning of each year in Project X is increasing. Explain what is happening to invested capital at the beginning of each year in Projects Y and Z.
b. Sketch NPV profiles for Projects X, Y, and Z. Place all three profiles on the same sketch.
c. Under what condition should a company choose Project X instead of either Project Y or Project Z?
d. Under what condition should a company choose Project Z instead of either Project X or Project Y?

Crossover rate and resolving ranking conflict

9.13. The Richmond Company faces severe capital rationing. At the same time Richmond must select between two mutually exclusive projects described as follows:

Project	Outlay, t = 0	Cash Inflow, t = 1	Internal Rate of Return
A	$100,000	$125,000	25%
B	200,000	240,000	20

Richmond's marginal cost of capital is 12 percent. At 12 percent Project A's net present value equals $11,607 and Project B's equals $14,286.
a. Calculate the crossover rate.
b. Which project should Richmond select? Base your choice on the IRR. What is your assumption about the difference in outlays for Projects A and B?

Meeting the required rate of return

9.14. FiestaWare Inc., a manufacturer of ceramic products, has the opportunity to produce a faddish product—a ceramic pet stone. The project will cost $100,000 after taxes and will last only one year. At the end of the year FiestaWare will receive $115,000 after taxes shown as follows:

	Cash Flow
Cash sales	$250,000
Wages	75,000
Materials	45,000
Taxes	10,000
Miscellaneous	5,000
Operating cash flow	$115,000

No other incremental, after-tax cash flows result from the pet stone project. FiestaWare requires a 15 percent annual rate of return on short-lived products. Should FiestaWare introduce the ceramic pet stone? Support your answer with calculations.

Cash flows, depreciation, payback, and NPV

9.15. A project sponsor presents a project to the capital-budgeting committee of Helstrom Fish Hatchery that will expand capacity at the company's Lake Como plant by 30 percent. The initial outlay is $500,000 for plant and equipment and $60,000 for net working capital. The required rate of return on the project is 20 percent.

Incremental sales revenues in each of the project's 5 years are $420,000, and cash operating costs are $200,000 annually. Management plans to liquidate the project at the end of the fifth year, liquidating current assets at their book values and paying current liabilities. Management will sell the plant and equipment for $22,000. The company is in the 40 percent marginal tax bracket.

a. Calculate the net investment cash outflow assuming that the company takes a 6 percent investment tax credit.

b. Calculate the operating cash flow for each year. For tax purposes the company uses straight-line depreciation with the half-year convention. The assets have a 3-year class life, and the ITC does not affect the depreciable amounts.

c. Calculate the payback period for the project and explain what action management should take if the maximum acceptable period is 2.5 years.

d. Calculate the net present value of the project. Should management accept the project? What will happen to the company's stock price if it does?

e. Calculate the internal rate of return on the project. Should management accept the project? Explain your answer.

Cash flows, payback period, and DCF methods

9.16. Peltan Concessions is considering installing a concession stand at an amusement park. *Pro forma* operating income before taxes will be as follows for the next 5 years:

			Year-End		
	1	**2**	**3**	**4**	**5**
Sales					
Units	90,000	100,000	110,000	110,000	70,000
Revenues	$450,000	$500,000	$550,000	$550,000	$350,000
Less costs					
Variable costs					
Labor	$170,000	$200,000	$230,000	$230,000	$110,000
Material	67,500	75,000	82,500	82,500	52,500
Overhead	67,500	75,000	82,500	82,500	52,500
Fixed costs	100,000	100,000	100,000	100,000	100,000
Depreciation	18,370	36,630	36,630	18,370	0
Operating income	$ 26,630	$ 13,370	$ 18,370	$ 36,630	$ 35,000

The total investment will be $110,000 in equipment and $8,000 in net working capital. Peltan's marginal cost of capital and the required rate of return on the project are 20 percent, and a 10 percent investment tax credit is available on the equipment. Assume that the depreciation expenses above are applicable to Peltan's tax return, and no cash flows occur from liquidating the depreciable assets. Liquidating current assets and paying off current liabilities will result in an $8,000 cash flow. Peltan is in the 40 percent marginal tax bracket.

a. Peltan's accountant points out that the concession stand will be charged overhead at a rate of 20 percent of variable costs each year for support services from the central administration. These budgeted costs are not included in the above calculations. Explain under which of the following conditions Peltan would correctly include these costs in measuring the operating cash flows from the concession stand:

(1) Central administration requires no new outlays because there is sufficient excess capacity (labor, equipment, storage space, and so on) to service the concession stand.

(2) The central administration must hire new employees. This cost is estimated to be equal to 20 percent of the project's variable costs.

b. What is the net investment cash outflow for the project?

   c. Calculate the operating cash flow for each year (ignoring the allocable overhead in Part *a* above).

   d. Calculate each of the following and then state whether or not the financial manager should accept the proposal:

     (1) Payback period ($2\frac{1}{2}$ years or less is acceptable).

     (2) Internal rate of return.

     (3) Net present value.

     (4) Profitability index.

CMA examination, modified: depreciation, operating cash flow, undiscounted and discounted cash flow methods

9.17. Hazman Company plans to replace an old piece of equipment that is obsolete and expected to be unreliable under the stress of daily operations. The equipment is fully depreciated, and no salvage value can be realized upon its disposal. New equipment will provide an additional $7,000 annual cash flow from operations before considering depreciation expense.

     The equipment will cost $18,000 and have an estimated useful life of 5 years. Hazman's management will take an 8 percent investment tax credit, which will not affect annual depreciation expense. Hazman uses the straight-line depreciation method on all equipment for financial reporting and tax purposes. For tax purposes the company employs the half-year convention and uses a 3-year class life. The company is subject to a 40 percent marginal tax rate and has a 32 percent average tax rate. Hazman's marginal cost of capital and the required rate of return on the project are 20 percent. There will be no disposal cash flows.

   a. How might the financial manager have estimated the required rate of return to be 20 percent?

   b. Calculate and interpret the meaning of the following measures for Hazman's proposed investment in new equipment:

     (1) Payback period (maximum acceptable: 3 years)

     (2) Net present value.

     (3) Profitability index.

     (4) Internal rate of return.

   c. Should Hazman's management invest in the new equipment? Explain your answer by referring to your calculations in Part *b*.

Computer Problems 🖫

Capital budgeting techniques: template CAPBUDTC

9.18. North American Automotive Inc. plans to set up a factory to manufacture spark plugs. The total investment will be $7 million in plant and equipment and $1 million in net working capital. The class life of the plant and equipment is 3 years. At the end of 5 years the plant and equipment will be sold and the site turned into a park and handed to the local civic authorities. The salvage value will cover the cost of landscaping the site. Sales revenues will be $10 million in Year 1 and will increase by 10 percent every year. The variable cost is 60 percent of the sales revenue, and the fixed cost (excluding depreciation) will be $1 million per year over the entire period. The company is in the 34 percent tax bracket. The required rate of return on the project is 20 percent per year.

   a. Calculate the following:

     (1) Payback period.

     (2) Internal rate of return.

     (3) Net present value.

     (4) Profitability index.

   b. Recalculate Part *a* assuming sales remain unchanged for the entire period.

   c. Recalculate Part *a* assuming sales increase 20 percent every year.

Project selection: template PROJSEL

9.19. Robinson Compressors is considering the replacement of its existing fractional horsepower assembly line with a more automated line. Two different technologies are being considered. Project A is a semiautomated process that would require an initial investment of $1,500,000 and would result in an incremental after-tax cash flow of $550,000 per year due to labor cost reduction. Project B is a highly automated process using robotics technology that would cost $2,500,000 and would result in a savings of $1,300,000 per year in labor costs. Each assembly line has an economic life of 6 years. The semiautomated line will have a disposal value of $450,000 and the highly automated line will have a disposal value of $800,000. The company is in the 34 percent marginal tax bracket. Neither project requires additional working capital. The salvage value of the existing line will exactly offset the cost of dismantling it. For projects A and B:

a. Calculate internal rate of return.
b. Calculate net present value assuming a discount rate of 10 percent, 15 percent, 20 percent, 25 percent, 30 percent, 35 percent, and 40 percent.
c. Which project should the company acquire if it has a marginal cost of capital of 18 percent and (1) unlimited funds? (2) capital rationing? Explain your answer.

((VHS))

VIDEO CASE PROBLEM

West Coast Textiles Inc.

Jan Smith is the capital-budgeting officer of West Coast Textiles Inc., an industrial textiles weaving company in California. Ms. Smith, who recently completed her MBA degree, is responsible for the analysis of capital project proposals for WCT. Her responsibilities include completing an analysis of each project proposal presented to the vice president of finance and preparing a report with her own recommendations.

Ms. Smith was recently invited to attend a meeting of the executive committee, comprising the president and vice presidents of the company. The topic discussed was a report by Tom Sales, vice president of marketing, who presented a proposal to bid for a new defense contract. A large defense contractor is soliciting bids for silk cloth to be used in the production of parachutes. WCT has produced high-quality silk materials for a number of years and could easily add parachute material to its existing product lines. Established supply contacts plus WCT's experience in silk manufacturing are clear advantages in bidding for the contract.

The amount of silk material required in the contract is 100,000 pounds per year for 5 years. According to Mr. Sales, the new contract could be won with a bid of $2.00 per pound of finished material. An internal study of the production costs of silk indicates that variable production costs—raw material and labor—would be 50 percent of revenue, or $1.00 per pound at current prices. Because of the additional bookkeeping and warehouse expenses, WCT's annual fixed costs would increase by $25,000 at current prices if it bids successfully for the contract.

At the present time WCT is operating at or near full capacity. Current sales and production are under long-term contract with various textile buyers. Thus none of the current weaving capacity can be diverted to the defense contract. New equipment must be purchased if production is to be increased.

A study of the current weaving technology has provided information on a new weaving machine that could produce the silk. The equipment costs $250,000 delivered and installed. As an incentive to WCT to purchase the new equipment, vendor technicians would train WCT operators at the vendor's factory prior to the installation of the machine, at no additional cost to WCT.

The new equipment has a 5-year class life and would be depreciated according to the MACRS (modified accelerated cost recovery system) procedure. At the end of 5 years WCT could sell the weaving machine to a smaller weaving company for $75,000.

At the meeting Ms. Smith expressed her concern about the effect of inflation on the future profitability of the parachute material. Raw material costs, labor costs, and fixed costs increase annually with the general inflation in production costs. Unless there is a clause in the contract allowing WCT to increase its price with inflation, WCT would experience reduced profits in each succeeding year of the contract. Mr. Sales replied that the contract provided for an annual increase in price equal to the rate of increase in the Producer Price Index (PPI). It was agreed that the price and cost estimates above would be appropriate for the first year of production and sales. In Years

2 through 5, however, prices and costs would increase at the expected rate of inflation of 5 percent per annum.

At the close of the meeting, Ms. Smith was assigned the responsibility of completing a capital-budgeting analysis of the defense contract proposal. Her report is due at the next weekly meeting of the executive committee.

In addition to the data provided by Mr. Sales, Ms. Smith estimates that an immediate investment in net working capital of $50,000 would be required if the project were accepted. The net working capital would be recovered at the end of 5 years. From recent analyses of capital projects, Ms. Smith notes that the company's marginal cost of capital is 12 percent. Since the risk of the new product line is equivalent to that of the company generally, no additional risk adjustment to the cost of capital is necessary. WCT's marginal income tax rate is 34 percent.

a. Calculate the net investment cash outflow of the proposed project.

b. Calculate the annual depreciation expense of the new equipment and its book value at the end of Year 5. (*Hint:* See Table 8.4.)

c. Calculate the expected operating cash flows over the 5-year life of the project. Adjust sales revenue and costs for expected inflation in Years 2 through 5.

d. Calculate the project-disposal cash flow at the end of Year 5.

e. Calculate payback period, net present value, and internal rate of return for the project. (*Hint:* For IRR, initially try 13 percent.)

f. Prepare Ms. Smith's report to the executive committee. Indicate whether or not the project should be accepted and defend your recommendation.

The author thanks Professor Carl M. Hubbard of Trinity University for contributing this case problem.

Selected References

Brick, Ivan E., and Daniel G. Weaver. "A Comparison of Capital Budgeting Techniques in Identifying Profitable Investments." *Financial Management,* Winter 1984: 29–39.

Brigham, Eugene F., and T. Craig Tapley. "Financial Leverage and Use of the Net Present Value Investment Criterion." *Financial Management,* Summer 1985: 48–52.

Chen, Son-Nan, and William T. Moore. "Project Abandonment under Certainty: A Bayesian Approach." *Financial Review,* November 1983: 306–313.

Cooley, Philip L., Rodney L. Roenfeldt, and It-Keong Chew. "Capital Budgeting Procedures under Inflation." *Financial Management,* Winter 1975: 12–17.

Dudley, Carlton L., Jr. "A Note on Reinvestment Assumptions in Choosing between Net Present Value and Internal Rate of Return." *Journal of Finance,* September 1972: 907–915.

Lewellen, Wilbur G., Howard P. Lanser, and John J. McConnell. "Payback Substitutes for Discounted Cash Flow." *Financial Management,* Summer 1973: 17–23.

Logue, Dennis E., and T. Craig Tapley. "Performance Monitoring and the Timing of Cash Flows." *Financial Management,* Autumn 1985: 34–39.

Mehta, Dileep R., Michael D. Curley, and Hung-Gay Fung. "Inflation, Cost of Capital, and Capital Budgeting Procedures." *Financial Management,* Winter 1984: 48–54.

Myers, Stewart C. "Finance Theory and Financial Strategy." *Interfaces,* January–February 1984: 126–137.

Scott, David F., Jr., and J. William Petty II. "Capital Budgeting Practices in Large American Firms: A Retrospective Analysis and Synthesis." *Financial Review,* March 1984: 111–123.

Shapiro, Alan C. "Corporate Strategy and the Capital Budgeting Decision." *Midland Corporate Finance Journal,* Spring 1985: 22–36.

Sweeney, Robert J. "Reinvestment Bias When Analyzing Mutually Exclusive Assets." *Journal of Applied Business Research,* Spring 1986: 71–78.

Weingartner, H. Martin. "Capital Rationing: *n* Authors in Search of a Plot." *Journal of Finance,* December 1977: 1403–1431.

Woods, John C., and Maury R. Randall. "The Net Present Value of Future Investment Opportunities: Its Impact on Shareholder Wealth and Implications for Capital Budgeting Theory." *Financial Management,* Spring 1989: 85–92.

Appendix 9A COMPARING PROJECTS HAVING DIFFERENT LIVES

It is not uncommon for investment proposals to have differing economic lives. When that occurs for mutually exclusive projects or under capital rationing, a financial manager normally must adjust the evaluation process to avoid an incorrect decision.

EXAMPLE   A financial manager is considering two proposed capital investments, Project 5 and Project 10. Project 5 is expected to have a 5-year life and Project 10 a 10-

year life. It may be inappropriate to compare the calculated net present values of these *mutually exclusive* projects, because only the initial 5 years are in fact comparable.

Figure 9A.1 illustrates the problem associated with the differing project lives in the above example. The period of comparability is only the initial 5 years. Project 5 expires at the end of 5 years and Project 10 continues to generate cash flows for an additional 5 years.

There are four ways to cope with the problem of differing lives when comparing mutually exclusive projects:

1. The financial manager can ignore the differing life spans and base the decision on the calculated net present values. This choice ignores the possibility of participating in a replacement opportunity (at the beginning of Year 6 in Figure 9A.1) with a positive NPV.

2. The financial manager can limit the analysis to the end of the shorter project by determining a disposal flow for the longer project at that point and counting this cash flow as part of the longer project's cash flows. In this way each becomes a 5-year project.

3. Alternatively, the financial manager can extend the analysis to the life of the longer project with a *replacement chain,* a series of cash flows for an assumed replacement investment at the end of the shorter project's life. The period covered by the replacement project is the difference between the lives of the original two projects. In this way each becomes a 10-year project.

4. Finally, the financial manager can choose to extend the analysis to infinity by calculating the present value of a perpetuity measured by an annuity equivalent to the net present value of each project. The perpetuity is discounted at each project's required rate of return. In this way each project becomes an infinite-life project. Some analysts call this procedure the *equivalent annual annuity method.*

To illustrate each of these four methods, assume that the annual operating cash flows from Project 5 are $610; and for Project 10 they are $380. Also assume that each project requires a $2,000 investment and that the required rate of return on each project is 10 percent:

1. Ignoring the different life spans leads to selection of Project 10 because of its greater net present value:

	Project 5	Project 10
Present value of operating cash flows:		
$610 × 3.7908 =	$2,312	$380 × 6.1446 = $2,335
Less investment	2,000	2,000
NPV	$ 312	$ 335

2. Cutting off the analysis at the end of Year 5 requires the estimation of a liquidation value for Project 10 at that time and including this estimate

FIGURE 9A.1

Period of Comparability for Mutually Exclusive Projects with Differing Lives

When mutually exclusive projects have differing lives, their cash flows can be compared only for the overlapping years. Adjustments before calculating net present values must be made for the nonoverlapping years.

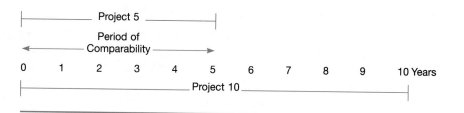

in Project 10's NPV. Assume that Project 10's liquidation value at the end of Year 5 is $1,000. The NPV of Project 10 is the present value of the first 5 years of operating cash flows plus the present value of the $1,000 liquidation value:

PV of operating cash flows: $380 × 3.7908	$1,441
Add PV of liquidation value: $1,000 × 0.6209	621
Present value	$2,062
Less investment	2,000
NPV	$ 62

With this analysis Project 5 becomes preferable to Project 10 ($312 > $62). Notice, however, that Project 10's appeal differs according to what we assume its liquidation value to be.

3. Project 5 may be treated as a replacement chain. Suppose management estimates that at the end of 5 years (that is, at the beginning of Year 6) it can find a new 5-year project generating $650 annual operating cash flows. The investment outlay is, say, $2,200:

a. Calculate NPV of the replacement project:

Present value of operating cash flows: $650 × 3.7908	$2,464
Less investment outlay	2,200
NPV (beginning of Year 6)	$ 264
Discounted to beginning of Year 1 (n = 5)	×0.6209
NPV of replacement project	$ 164

b. NPV of the entire investment is the sum of the original NPV plus the replacement NPV:

NPV of Project 5	$312
Add NPV of replacement project	164
Adjusted NPV	$476

Under these conditions the financial manager should select Project 5 rather than Project 10. The appeal of Project 5, however, depends upon assumptions regarding the replacement project.

4. Converting each project into a perpetuity involves finding an annuity equivalent to each project's NPV (use a financial calculator or Appendix B.4):

Project 5	Project 10
$PVA = PMT(PVIFA_{10\%,5})$	$PVA = PMT(PVIFA_{10\%,10})$
$\$312 = PMT(3.7908)$	$\$335 = PMT(6.1446)$
$PMT = \dfrac{\$312}{3.7908}$	$PMT = \dfrac{\$335}{6.1446}$
$= \$82.30$	$= \$54.52$

Estimate the present value of the perpetuity using the required rate of return:

Project 5	Project 10
$PV = \dfrac{\$82.30}{0.10}$	$PV = \dfrac{\$54.52}{0.10}$
$= \$823.00$	$= \$545.20$

Under these conditions the financial manager chooses Project 5 because the present value of its perpetuity is greater than that of Project 10.

The method that leads to maximizing shareholder wealth depends on which assumptions about the future best approximate reality. Note, however, that differing project lives is not a problem when the NPV method is used in the absence of capital rationing and mutually exclusive projects; all projects with positive net present values are chosen. The financial manager must consider the above adjustments for differing lives only when capital rationing or mutually exclusive projects exist.

Computer Problem

Projects with unequal lives: template UNEQLIF

9A.1. John Hu Enterprises is considering three projects (P, Q, and R) to improve materials handling in its jobbing plant. The company's cost of capital is 18 percent per year. The net investment cash outflow and annual cash inflows over the life of each project are as follows:

Year	Project P	Project Q	Project R
0	−$100,000	−$150,000	−$90,000
1	25,000	50,000	62,000
2	26,000	62,000	65,000
3	28,000	69,000	
4	27,000	75,000	
5	29,000		
6	30,000		
7	30,000		
8	32,000		

a. Calculate the net present value and internal rate of return of each project and rank the projects by NPV in descending order.

b. Use the replacement chain method to calculate the NPV and IRR of each project. Does the ranking by this method differ from the ranking by NPV in Part *a*?

c. Convert each project into a perpetuity and calculate the annuity equivalent of the net present values. Rank the projects based on these results.

d. Compare the rankings obtained by using the above three methods. Which method do you prefer? Explain your answer.

Chapter 10

CAPITAL BUDGETING AND RISK

Risk Is a Four-Letter Word

Think of the uncomfortable position in which financial managers find themselves when recommending the investment of millions of dollars in a project. The expenditure may be larger than any they have dealt with in their previous experience; the uncertainty surrounding project cash flows may be almost impossible to evaluate; and similar projects as a basis of comparison may not exist.

The financial managers at Ford probably had a few sleepless nights in 1987 while wrestling with a proposal to open branches of Ford's First Nationwide Bank in 150 K marts. Some retail chains had their own financial services operations, but Ford was the first corporation to move into stores of a nonaffiliated company. Consider also the risk faced by Federal Express when it purchased Tiger International in 1989 for

$900 million. While other overnight-delivery companies used commercial airlines, the managers at Federal Express decided to purchase their own airline for the delivery of letters and packages. In another industry, RJR Nabisco invested hundreds of millions of dollars in developing a smokeless cigarette. Unfortunately, the "breakthrough" cigarette tasted bad and was hard to light.

When General Motors develops and markets electric cars, when Sears goes into the brokerage business, when Lockheed designs and manufactures a new airplane, each company faces substantial risks. Determining which risks are worth taking is a function of careful analysis and managerial perspective. Here are the perceptions of *risk* as a business term from three different perspectives: (1) *Capital-budgeting analyst:* uncertainty surrounding expected net present value; (2) *Accountant:* errors and irregularities; (3) *Lee Trevino:* a $20 bet on 18 holes when you have only $2 in your pocket.

Photo Source: Courtesy of Bankers Trust Company.

In Chapter 9 we simplify capital budgeting by assuming equivalence between the risk of the proposed project and the risk of projects already accepted by the company. This assumption permits the discussion to focus on the methods for evaluating cash flows. It also permits the use of a company's marginal cost of capital (MCC) as the discount rate. In reality, financial managers frequently analyze proposed projects with risks that differ from the average. This chapter extends the discussion of capital budgeting to answer questions such as: How should a financial manager analyze a project when its risk differs substantially from that of a company's average project? Moreover, how can it be determined whether or not the project's risk is different? To answer these questions, the chapter opens with an examination of the origins of risk in capital projects. It then presents some methods for assessing the degree of risk inherent in a project. The chapter concludes with procedures for incorporating risk into the analysis of investment decisions. Throughout the chapter you should be aware of the limitations in the treatment of risk. Unfortunately, there are no unequivocal procedures for risk analysis in capital budgeting. Judgment and intuition are integral to capital-budgeting decisions—particularly in projecting the cash flows for a proposed capital project and in assessing risk.

RISK IN CAPITAL PROJECTS

Like the outcome of any investment, the actual return from a capital investment is likely to vary from the financial manager's expectation. An investment in a capital project is made for a long period of time, and cash flows normally become more difficult to forecast as they extend into the future. For example, cash flows three years from now are harder to forecast accurately than cash flows occurring three weeks from now. Forecast errors occur because the financial manager cannot see into the future with certainty. It is this inability to foresee the future with clarity that causes risk in capital budgeting.

The risk of a capital project results from unforeseen variation in the values of key inputs to the capital-budgeting analysis:

- The possibility that the net investment cash outflow will differ from what the financial manager expects.
- The possibility that operating cash flows will be more or less than expected.
- The possibility that disposal cash flows will vary from the financial manager's expectation.
- The possibility that the marginal cost of capital will differ from what the financial manager used in the evaluation.

A project is *risky* if its actual net present value (or internal rate of return and profitability index) might possibly differ from its expected value. For example, the financial manager of Quick Shop Company may invest in a conveyor system with an expected 22 percent IRR and a $1,795 NPV. The possibility that the actual IRR may be 7 percent or 25 percent and that the NPV may be −$380 or $7,480 means that the investment carries risk.

There are numerous specific reasons for NPV to vary from the amount expected when the financial manager analyzes the project. The net investment cash outflow may change unexpectedly because of changes in the cost of land, buildings, and equipment. The U.S. Congress may repeal the investment tax credit (as it did in 1986) on depreciable assets during the planning process, causing an increase in NICO. Required net working capital may also differ from what the financial manager expects. Taken together, these variations may lead to either *cost overruns* or *cost underruns.*

Incremental operating cash flows equal the operating cash inflows of the project minus the operating cash outflows. Incremental cash flows may differ from estimates because of unforeseen changes in product prices, product demand, cost of goods sold, selling and administrative expenses, and income taxes. For cost-saving projects, the cost saved might differ from the expected savings. Finally, the cash flow from terminating the project may differ from the expected amount as a result of changes in the tax rate applicable to capital gains (as in 1986) and unexpected changes in the disposal values of depreciable and current assets.

EXAMINING POSSIBLE NPV LEVELS

An expected value is the probability-weighted average of possible outcomes. Applying this idea to net present value yields the *expected net present value* $(\overline{NPV})$:

$$\overline{NPV} = P_1 NPV_1 + P_2 NPV_2 + \cdots + P_n NPV_n$$

$$= \sum_{j=1}^{n} P_j NPV_j$$

where $\overline{NPV}$ ("NPV bar") = expected NPV, a probability-weighted average of the possible NPVs

P_j = probability of the possible net present value NPV_j (probabilities must total 1.00)

n = number of possible NPVs

discrete probability distribution

Probability distribution comprising a limited number of outcomes and their associated probabilities.

The possible NPVs and their associated probabilities constitute a **discrete probability distribution:** Possible NPVs have specific probabilities of occurring, and there are gaps between the possible NPVs.

Consider the discrete probability distributions in Table 10.1. Each distribution describes the possible NPVs and associated probabilities for a capital project. Project A has a 50–50 chance of yielding net present values of −$50,000 and $100,000. Project A is risky because of the uncertainty about what its NPV will be. Project B has a 70 percent probability of yielding an NPV equaling −$50,000 and only a 30 percent probability of yielding an NPV of $100,000. B's higher probability of the negative outcome (−$50,000) causes its expected value (−$5,000) to be less than A's ($25,000). Common sense tells us that we would prefer A over B. Does our preference mean that A is less risky than B? Before you answer, consider Projects C and D.

Project C appears even worse than Project B. With C, we are reasonably sure (90 percent probability) that the net present value will be −$50,000. C's expected NPV is an unprofitable −$35,000. Again, common sense tells us we would prefer B over C. Furthermore, we would prefer A, B, and C over D. With D there is a 100 percent probability of the bad outcome and a zero percent probability of the good outcome. D's expected NPV is −$50,000.

Because we least prefer Project D, do we conclude that D is riskiest? The answer is no. The net present value of D is a certainty—certainty of a bad outcome—because the probability assigned to its −$50,000 outcome is 100 percent.

TABLE 10.1   **Expected Net Present Values for Four Capital Projects**

(1) Project	(2) Probability	(3) Net Present Value	(2) × (3) = (4) Product
A	0.50	−$ 50,000	−$25,000
	0.50	$100,000	$50,000
		Expected NPV$_A$ =	**$25,000**
B	0.70	−$ 50,000	−$35,000
	0.30	$100,000	$30,000
		Expected NPV$_B$ =	**−$ 5,000**
C	0.90	−$ 50,000	−$45,000
	0.10	$100,000	$10,000
		Expected NPV$_C$ =	**−$35,000**
D	1.00	−$ 50,000	−$50,000
	0.00	$100,000	0
		Expected NPV$_D$ =	**−$50,000**

In fact, C's expected NPV is relatively more certain than B's, which in turn is relatively more certain than A's. We prefer A because of its high expected net present value and *despite* the high degree of uncertainty.

The above discussion demonstrates that expected net present value is not a measure of risk but *is* a determinant of preference. As a matter of fact, the preference for a project is a function of (or depends on) two variables, expected net present value and risk:

$$\text{Preference} = f(\overline{\text{NPV}}, \text{risk})$$

Project A is preferable to Project D because the impact of expected NPV dominates the impact of risk.[1]

Standard Deviation of Net Present Value

Standard deviation (σ) quantifies risk by measuring the dispersion of a distribution of possible net present values, as described by the following equation:

$$\sigma = [P_1(NPV_1 - \overline{NPV})^2 + P_2(NPV_2 - \overline{NPV})^2 + \cdots$$
$$+ P_n(NPV_n - \overline{NPV})^2]^{1/2}$$
$$= \sqrt{\sum_{j=1}^{n} P_j(NPV_j - \overline{NPV})^2}$$

A large standard deviation reflects a wide dispersion of possible outcomes and the likelihood that the actual outcome will differ from the one expected. A small standard deviation reflects a tight dispersion. Essentially, standard deviation measures the uncertainty about what will happen in the future.

Figure 10.1 graphically depicts the probability distributions of net present

---

[1] We take some liberty in this illustration when we assert a preference ordering for Projects A through D. After all, preference is personal. Logic and past surveys of preference, however, are on our side. The illustration emphasizes the necessity of keeping separate the definitions and connotations of *perception, preference, risk, outcome, probability,* and *expected value.*

FIGURE 10.1

Discrete Probability Distributions of Net Present Values for Four Capital Projects

Each project has the same possible NPVs, but the differing probabilities cause the expected NPVs ($\overline{NPV}$) and standard deviations to differ. Project A has the largest standard deviation and $\overline{NPV}$, and Project D has the smallest standard deviation and $\overline{NPV}$.

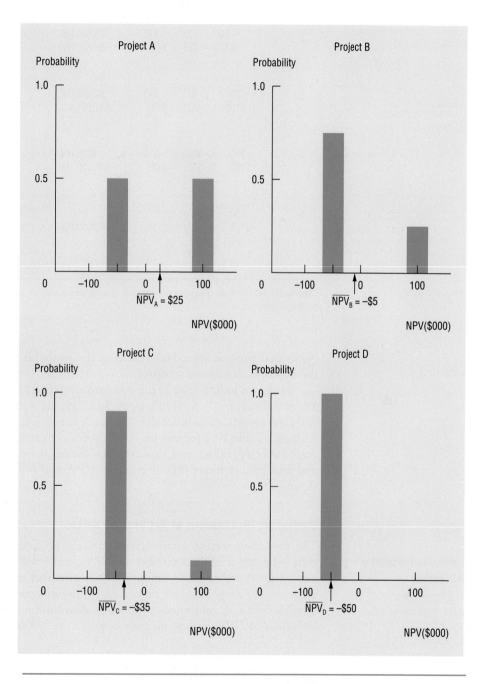

values that Table 10.1 presents. The possible NPVs on the horizontal axes are the same for each project, but the associated probabilities on the vertical axes differ. Because the distributions contain discrete NPV outcomes, there are gaps between the possible NPVs. Moreover, the expected NPV ($\overline{NPV}$) need not be one of the possible NPVs; $\overline{NPV}$ is a mathematical expectation based on possible

TABLE 10.2   **Standard Deviations for Projects A, B, C, and D (in Thousands)**

Project	(1) Deviation[a] $(NPV_j - \overline{NPV})$	$(1)^2 = (2)$ Deviation Squared	(3) Probability	$(2) \times (3) = (4)$ Product
A	$-\$50 - \$25 = -\$75$	$\$5,625,000$	0.50	$\$2,812,500$
	$\$100 - \$25 = \$75$	$\$5,625,000$	0.50	$2,812,500$
			1.00	$\sigma_A^2 = \$5,625,000$
				$\sigma_A = \$75$
B	$-\$50 - (-\$5) = -\$45$	$\$2,025,000$	0.70	$\$1,417,500$
	$\$100 - (-\$5) = \$105$	$\$11,025,000$	0.30	$3,307,500$
			1.00	$\sigma_B^2 = \$4,725,000$
				$\sigma_B = \$68.739$
C	$-\$50 - (-\$35) = -\$15$	$\$225,000$	0.90	$\$\ 202,500$
	$\$100 - (-\$35) = \$135$	$\$18,225,000$	0.10	$1,822,500$
			1.00	$\sigma_C^2 = \$2,025,000$
				$\sigma_C = \$45$
D	$-\$50 - (-\$50) = 0$	0	1.00	$\$0$
	$\$100 - (-\$50) = \$150$	$\$22,500,000$	0	0
			1.00	$\sigma_D^2 = \quad \$0$
				$\sigma_D = \quad \$0$

[a] See Table 10.1 for the possible net present values, expected net present values, and the associated probabilities.

NPVs and probabilities. Differences in the probabilities for each project cause the standard deviations to differ.

As shown in Table 10.2, the standard deviations for Projects A, B, C, and D are as follows: $\sigma_A = \$75,000$, $\sigma_B = \$68,739$, $\sigma_C = \$45,000$, and $\sigma_D = 0$. The standard deviations indicate that Project A is riskiest, followed by B, C, and D.[2] Although Table 10.2 focuses on NPV, equivalent calculations can be used to generate expected values and standard deviations of internal rate of return (IRR) and profitability index (PI). In place of NPV_j and $\overline{NPV}$, insert IRR_j and $\overline{IRR}$ or PI_j and $\overline{PI}$.

Continuous Distributions of Net Present Values

continuous probability distribution

Probability distribution that includes all dollar values of NPV.

The preceding section characterizes probability distributions of NPVs as discrete—having a limited number of NPVs, each with its own probability. For many capital projects, this limitation on the number of NPVs is not descriptively accurate. For these cases we may use a continuous probability distribution of all possible NPVs. A **continuous probability distribution** is one that includes all dollar values of NPV, leaving no gaps between the NPVs.

[2] As noted in Chapter 5, standard deviation is a measure of total risk. A portion of total risk can be diversified away, leaving only nondiversifiable risk, which beta measures. (Beta is discussed later in this chapter.) Another statistic occasionally used as a risk measure is the *coefficient of variation (CV)*, which equals standard deviation divided by expected value (mean). CV can be interpreted as risk per unit of expected value. Cast in this light, CV appears more like a criterion for making decisions than it does a risk measure. For Project A, $CV_A = \$75,000/\$25,000 = 3.0$. Because of the negative expected net present values for Projects B, C, and D, coefficient of variation does not seem very useful in these cases.

In contrast to the discrete distributions in Figure 10.1, the continuous distributions in Figure 10.2 are drawn with smooth lines. Figure 10.2 illustrates the distributions of cash flows and the net present value for a two-year project. As shown, the minimum value for NICO (net investment cash outflow) is zero, but the cash inflows, CF_1 and CF_2, may be negative as well as positive. The distributions peak at the expected cash flows, $\overline{NICO}$, $\overline{CF_1}$, and $\overline{CF_2}$.

The expected cash flows are the financial manager's best estimates made during the planning period (t_{-1} to t_0). Using these expected cash flows produces the expected net present value, $\overline{NPV}$. To recognize the uncertainty surrounding an expected cash flow, the financial manager assigns a probability distribution to it, using any one of several distributions described in statistics books. Because of the different possible values for NICO, CF_1, and CF_2, the actual NPV may be negative as well as positive. Figure 10.2 shows, however, that in this case the chances are that NPV will be greater than zero.[3]

The Normal Distribution.   If each cash flow turns out to be what the financial manager expects, then the net present value will turn out to be the expected value, $\overline{NPV}$. $\overline{NPV}$ can also result from other combinations of cash flows:

1. $\overline{NICO}$ occurs, but $CF_1 > \overline{CF_1}$ and $CF_2 < \overline{CF_2}$ in just the right proportions to yield $\overline{NPV}$.
2. $NICO < \overline{NICO}$, $CF_1 < \overline{CF_1}$, and $CF_2 < \overline{CF_2}$, again in just the right proportions to yield $\overline{NPV}$.

Because of these and several other combinations of cash flows that produce an NPV around $\overline{NPV}$, the distribution of possible NPVs for many projects can be assumed normal and continuous. This means that the distribution of possible NPVs follows a normal, bell-shaped curve, with no gaps between the NPVs (that is, they are not discrete.). In a **normal distribution** each possible NPV is a *normal random value*, which means that the actual NPV cannot be known in advance.[4]

Figure 10.2B shows a normal distribution of possible NPVs. When NPVs are normal random values, you can assign probabilities to *ranges* of possible outcomes but not to the outcomes themselves. For example, in a normal distribution an actual value will fall within ± 1 standard deviation of the expected value about 67 percent of the time and within ± 2 standard deviations about 95 percent of the time. Even a normal distribution of NPVs, however, may serve up disappointments or pleasant surprises. Here are two examples:

Disappointment: $NICO > \overline{NICO}$, $CF_1 < \overline{CF_1}$, $CF_2 < \overline{CF_2}$

normal distribution

Symmetrical, bell-shaped curve depicting a distribution of possible outcomes; distribution is fully described by the mean and standard deviation.

---

[3] Which discount rate should be used in developing a distribution of NPVs is an issue. Some analysts argue for the risk-free rate, which accounts for the value of time in discounting. The distribution of NPVs can then be used to formulate judgments about risk. Separating the time and risk dimensions helps the decision maker to avoid double-counting risk—once when calculating NPV and once when judging the distribution of NPVs. A high discount rate reflecting high risk penalizes a project's future cash inflows, and the project should not be penalized again when the decision maker judges risk based on the distribution of NPVs. On the other hand, some decision makers are more comfortable with an $\overline{NPV}$ calculated with a discount rate reflecting risk, along with a distribution of NPVs at that rate. They simply want to know the probability of NPV being less than zero, assuming a risk-adjusted discount rate. Which discount rate should be used depends on the decision maker's use of the NPV distribution. Although Figure 10.2 shows a risk-adjusted discount rate, K, you should be aware of the possibility of double-counting risk.

[4] The normal, or Gaussian, distribution is often assumed to be applicable in finance problems. The assumption seems a good approximation for net present values, and we make use of it in this chapter.

FIGURE 10.2

Uncertain Cash Flows for a Two-Year Project and Its Uncertain Net Present Value

A. During the planning period (t_{-1} to t_0), the financial manager estimates cash flows ($\overline{NICO}$, $\overline{CF}_1$, and $\overline{CF}_2$) for a two-year project. Because of the uncertainty of the estimates, each has a distribution of possible values.

B. The expected net present value ($\overline{NPV}$) of the investment equals the present value of the expected cash inflows less the expected net investment cash outflow. Because the cash flows are uncertain, so is the NPV, as depicted by its distribution.

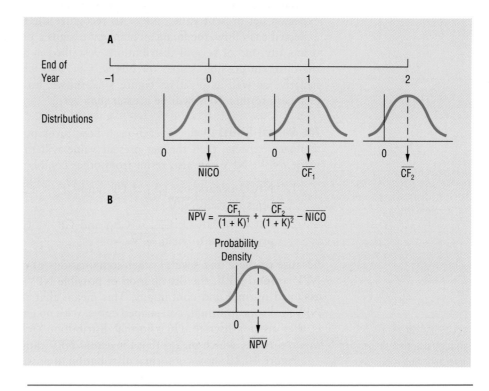

Pleasant surprise: NICO $< \overline{NICO}$, CF$_1$ $> \overline{CF}_1$, CF$_2$ $> \overline{CF}_2$

A normal distribution of net present values for a project contains a great deal of information, far more information than indicated solely by the expected value, $\overline{NPV}$.

Using the Normal Distribution.   Having both $\overline{NPV}$ and standard deviation and assuming normally distributed NPVs enables the financial manager to make probability statements about the range of NPVs that will likely occur.[5] For example, the manager can calculate the probability of an NPV being less than zero, which is the probability of an accepted project reducing stock price and shareholder wealth.

---

[5] We use the terms *mean* and *expected value* interchangeably, both of them referring to the probability-weighted average of possible outcomes. For a skewed distribution, however, we must be more careful. Skewness causes the mean to differ from the *median*—the midpoint of the distribution, with equal areas under the curve to the left and to the right of the median. For a normal distribution the mean equals the median. You will find a discussion of skewness in Alan H. Kvanli, C. Stephen Guynes, and Robert J. Pavur, *Introduction to Business Statistics: A Computer Integrated Approach*, St. Paul: West Publishing, 1986, 53–54.

FIGURE 10.3

Normal Probability Distribution of Net Present Values:
$\overline{NPV}$ = $10,000, σ = $5,000

The normal distribution of NPVs is completely described by expected NPV and standard deviation. $\overline{NPV}$ = $10,000 denotes the central location of the distribution, and σ = $5,000 denotes the dispersion around $\overline{NPV}$. Based on this information, the financial manager can find the probability of the actual NPV being less than zero.

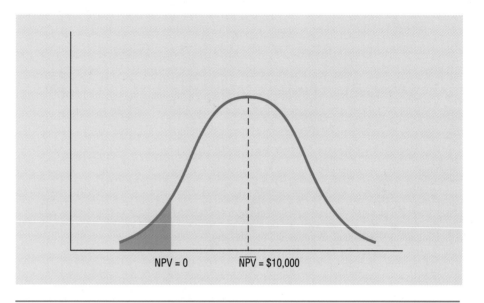

To find the probability of NPV < 0, we first calculate Z, the difference between the normal random variable NPV and $\overline{NPV}$ all divided by standard deviation:

$$Z = \frac{\text{Normal random variable NPV} - \overline{NPV}}{\text{Standard deviation } (\sigma)}$$

Z measures the distance of a specified NPV (say, NPV = 0) from $\overline{NPV}$ in terms of standard deviation.

EXAMPLE

Assume that the NPV distribution in Figure 10.2B has the following mean and standard deviation:

$$\overline{NPV} = \$10,000$$

$$\sigma = \$\ 5,000$$

What is the probability of NPV being less than zero? Pictorially, we seek the area in Figure 10.3 to the left of NPV = 0.

Stated differently, the question in the above example is: How many standard deviations is NPV = 0 from the expected net present value ($\overline{NPV}$)? Answering this question begins as follows:

TABLE 10.3   **Normal Probability Distribution**

Number of Standard Deviations (σ) from the Mean Z	Probability of Outcome Being Farther Away from the Mean[a]
0.00	0.5000
0.10	0.4602
0.20	0.4207
0.30	0.3821
0.40	0.3446
0.50	0.3085
0.60	0.2743
0.70	0.2420
0.80	0.2119
0.90	0.1841
1.00	0.1587
1.10	0.1357
1.20	0.1151
1.30	0.0968
1.40	0.0808
1.50	0.0668
1.60	0.0548
1.70	0.0446
1.80	0.0359
1.90	0.0287
2.00	0.0228
2.50	0.0062
3.00	0.0013
3.50	0.0002
4.00	0.00003

[a] Area in one tail of the normal distribution beyond the specified number of standard deviations.

$$Z = \frac{\text{NPV} - \overline{\text{NPV}}}{\sigma}$$

$$= \frac{0 - \$10,000}{\$5,000}$$

$$= -2.0$$

In other words, NPV = 0 is −2.0 standard deviations away from the expected net present value, $\overline{\text{NPV}}$. The negative sign indicates that NPV = 0 is to the *left* of $\overline{\text{NPV}}$. A positive Z would indicate that NPV is to the *right* of $\overline{\text{NPV}}$.

Find the area to the left of NPV = 0 by using the data in Table 10.3. The column labeled Z contains values for any standard normal random variable. The column denoting the probability of an outcome lists *areas* under the normal curve. *Probability is merely an area under the normal curve.* The column lists only one side of the normal curve because the other side is exactly the same— the curve is symmetrical about the expected value. For example, beyond a Z of 1.00 lies 0.1587, or 15.87 percent of the area of a normal curve. Because the curve is symmetrical, there is also 0.1587, or 15.87 percent of the area beyond a Z of −1.00. For the Z = −2.0 in the example, Table 10.3 shows a corresponding 0.0228, or 2.28 percent; 2.28 percent of the area under the normal curve lies in the far left tail beyond 2.0 standard deviations. In other words, there are only 2.28 chances in 100 that NPV will be less than zero. Faced with this probability, a financial manager would be confident in the acceptability of a capital investment.

EXAMPLE

In the preceding example, what is the probability of net present value being *greater than* zero? The area (probability) we seek extends from Z = −2.0 to plus infinity, depicted graphically as follows:

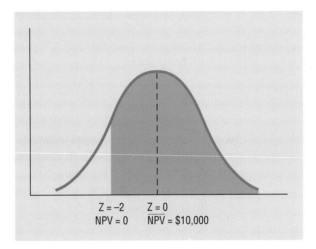

According to the equation for Z, NPV = 0 corresponds to Z = −2.0, and $\overline{\text{NPV}}$ = $10,000 corresponds to Z = 0. Table 10.3 shows that the area to the left of Z = −2.0 is 0.0228; the area to the right is therefore 0.9772 (1.00 − 0.0228). The probability of NPV being greater than zero is 97.72 percent.

Should a financial manager accept the project above with $\overline{\text{NPV}}$ = $10,000 and a standard deviation of $5,000? Based strictly on the discussion so far, $\overline{\text{NPV}}$ and standard deviation do not yield a specific answer to the question. In fact, a universal accept-reject decision rule does not exist. Despite this shortcoming, having the standard deviation in addition to $\overline{\text{NPV}}$ provides the basis for a well-informed decision. The financial manager knows there is a 97.72 percent probability that NPV will exceed zero. Although many of us would accept the project under these conditions, the ultimate choice rests on personal preference.

METHODS FOR ASSESSING RISK

Developing a distribution of net present values is not easy to do in practice because the range and probabilities of NPVs are subject to many influences. Unexpected changes in sales, wages, the cost of materials, the life of the proposed project, and tax rates are only a few of the influences a financial manager must consider. For major capital projects, however, financial managers might find it

TABLE 10.4

Scenario Analysis: Performance Summary

Scenario	Expected Year-End Cash Flows		
	0	1	2
Pessimistic case	−$125,000	$52,300	$52,300
Most likely case	−$100,000	$65,455	$65,455
Optimistic case	−$90,000	$76,100	$76,100

Expected Results	Scenario		
	Pessimistic Case	Most Likely Case	Optimistic Case
Net present value (12%)	−$36,610	$10,622	$38,613
Internal rate of return	−11.1%	20.0%	43.5%
Profitability index	0.71	1.11	1.43
Payback period	No payback	1.53 years	1.18 years

worthwhile to expend the effort and to incur the cost necessary to develop such a distribution. For other project evaluations they might wish simply to get a feel for the uncertainty surrounding $\overline{NPV}$.

Three methods for assessing the risk of a capital project are *scenario analysis, sensitivity analysis,* and *Monte Carlo simulation.* The following sections describe the use of each of these methods in capital-budgeting analysis.

Scenario Analysis

scenario analysis
Analysis of a capital project's acceptability under three sets of assumptions: pessimistic, most likely, and optimistic.

In **scenario analysis** a financial manager analyzes a project under three different sets of assumptions: pessimistic (or worst) case, most likely (or best-guess) case, and optimistic (or best) case. In addition to the analysis of project cash flows based on expected values, the manager uses scenarios in which things generally go wrong (a pessimistic scenario) or go right (an optimistic scenario). The pessimistic scenario provides some idea of the project's downside risk. On the bright side, the optimistic scenario indicates upside potential.

Table 10.4 presents a performance summary of a scenario analysis for a two-year project discounted with a 12 percent required rate of return. In the pessimistic case the project costs more and produces smaller cash inflows than it does in the most likely case. The opposite occurs in the optimistic case.

The bottom part of Table 10.4 shows that the project is expected to increase shareholder wealth: The most likely net present value ($10,622) exceeds zero, the internal rate of return (20 percent) exceeds the required rate of return (12 percent), the profitability index (1.11) exceeds 1.0, and the payback period is reasonably short at 1.53 years. Confronted with these performance measures, the financial manager might feel comfortable accepting the project.

The pessimistic scenario, however, waves a red flag. Pessimistically, unit sales will fall short of the target and competition will drive down price per unit sold. The drop in project sales revenue might be accompanied by increases in labor and materials cost. As a result, operating cash flow will be low. Under this scenario, accepting the project reduces shareholder wealth by $36,610, and the company does not even recapture its $125,000 investment. Of course, if sales revenues exceed the target and expenses are less than expected, then the optimistic conditions hold, and the project adds $38,613 to shareholder wealth.

Whether or not the financial manager should accept the project depends on intuition and judgment. Interpretation of the assumptions accompanying the pessimistic case and the other two cases helps guide the decision. Knowledge of the probabilities attached to the scenarios would help greatly. Often, financial managers assign a 5 percent to 10 percent probability to the optimistic and pessimistic scenarios and an 80 percent to 90 percent probability to the most likely scenario, with the probabilities totaling 1.00. How much confidence anyone can place in these probabilities is open to question.

Despite its shortcomings, scenario analysis provides more information than the analysis of only the most likely case. It forces the financial manager to consider the possibility of variables gone awry and to plan for contingencies.

Sensitivity Analysis

sensitivity analysis

Analysis of the effects that key input variables, changed one at a time, have on the acceptability of a capital project.

Sensitivity analysis shows the responsiveness of net present value to changes in other variables, taken one at a time. For example, sensitivity analysis shows the percentage change in NPV as the discount rate changes by some specified percentage. Some financial managers refer to sensitivity analysis as *what if* analysis. *What* happens to the NPV of the project *if*: The net investment cash outflow changes? Operating expenses increase? Sales revenues decline?

Whereas scenario analysis examines the impact on net present value of *simultaneous* changes in a number of variables, sensitivity analysis focuses *sequentially* on percentage changes in one variable at a time, holding the rest constant. Sensitivity analysis locates the variables having the greatest impact on NPV. An error in estimating some variables would have more impact on the project's NPV than a similar error with other variables. Sensitivity analysis shows where to focus attention and which variables would require the closest monitoring if management accepts the project.

Figure 10.4 illustrates the sensitivity of net present value to two variables that affect the most likely case in Table 10.4—net investment cash outflow and the discount rate. The most likely NICO is $100,000. A 10 percent swing in that number (between $110,000 and $90,000) causes NPV to swing between a low of $622 and a high of $20,622. A 10 percent change in the 12 percent discount rate (between 13.2 percent and 10.8 percent) causes NPV to swing between a low of $8,902 and a high of $12,392. The same percentage change (10 percent) is applied to each variable to make comparisons easy.

The slopes of the lines in Figure 10.4 show the degree of sensitivity of net present value to a specific variable. The steeper the line is, the greater the sensitivity will be. NPV is far more sensitive in this case to 10 percent changes in net investment cash outflow than it is to similar changes in the discount rate.

Sensitivity analysis is applicable to any DCF measure—internal rate of return and profitability index—to check its sensitivity to changes in inputs. Furthermore, a wide variety of different inputs can be evaluated: estimated project lives, cash inflows, operating costs, number of units sold, price per unit sold, and changes in tax laws.

The value of sensitivity analysis lies in its ability to isolate the importance of individual inputs. After scenario analysis stakes out the extreme outcomes, sensitivity analysis reveals the inputs primarily responsible for the extreme results. Personal computers and electronic spreadsheets like Lotus 1-2-3 and Multiplan

FIGURE 10.4

Sensitivity of Net Present Value to Changes in Net Investment Cash Outflow and Discount Rate

Sensitivity analysis measures the change in NPV associated with a specified percentage change in other variables. The steeper the slope of the line, the greater the sensitivity. This figure shows NPV to be more sensitive to changes in NICO than to changes in the discount rate.

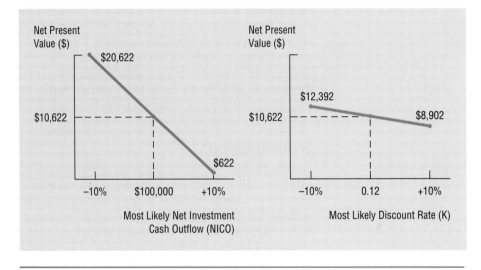

greatly simplify the process of sensitivity analysis. Financial managers easily obtain the answers to dozens of *what if* questions, and in the process they get a feel for a project's risk. This assessment enables intuition and informed judgment to enter the decision on whether or not to invest in a risky project.

Monte Carlo Simulation

Monte Carlo simulation
Method for producing a probability distribution of NPVs based on probability distributions of key input variables.

Named after the city in Monaco, **Monte Carlo simulation** develops a probability distribution of net present values. To simulate the performance of a capital project means to imitate what might actually happen.

Compared with Monte Carlo simulation, scenario analysis and sensitivity analysis are elementary. Monte Carlo simulation produces a probability distribution of net present values, but the other two procedures do not. The distribution gives Monte Carlo simulation the advantage of providing more information, but it comes at a cost. The financial manager must develop probability distributions of key input variables in order to generate the distribution of NPVs.

Accurate input distributions are difficult to develop, a disadvantage that normally restricts the application of Monte Carlo simulation to major projects only. Realistic applications of simulation require access to a computer with the large capacity needed to run the program.

The major steps in a Monte Carlo simulation are as follows:

1. Identify the inputs needed to estimate project cash flows.

2. Assign probability distributions to each key input variable, noting each one's minimum and maximum values, expected value, and standard deviation.

FIGURE 10.5

Monte Carlo Simulation of Net Present Value

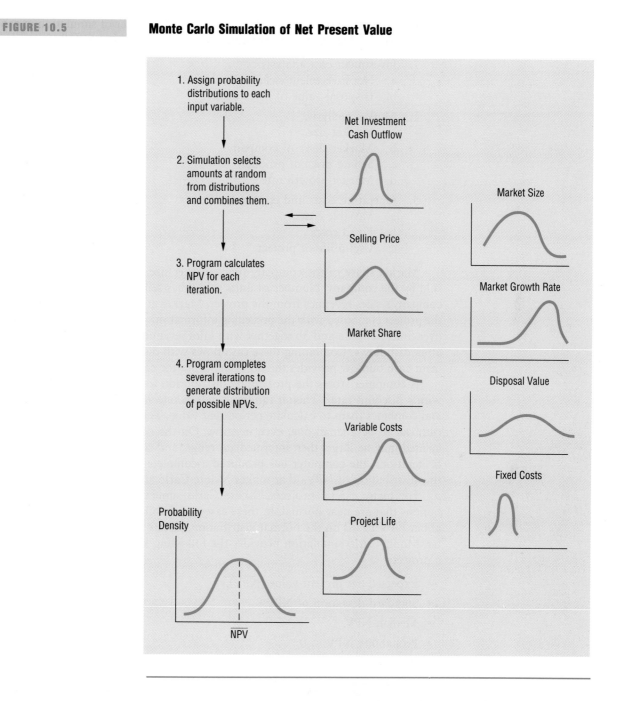

3. Select values randomly from the distributions for each input variable in Step 2. Combine the selected values to calculate net present value.

4. Repeat Step 3 a large number of times—say 1,000—to generate a distribution of NPVs for the project.

5. Interpret the distribution of NPVs.

Figure 10.5 depicts simulation of net present values. On the left side are shown the major steps in the simulation. On the right side are the key input variables originally suggested by David B. Hertz, the father of simulation in capital budgeting.[6] Hertz's nine input variables can be organized as follows:

1. Investment cost analysis.
   a. Net investment cash outflow.
   b. Disposal value of investment.
2. Market analysis.
   a. Market size.
   b. Market share of company.
   c. Selling price of product.
   d. Market growth rate.
3. Operating costs and economic life.
   a. Variable costs.
   b. Fixed costs.
   c. Useful life of project.

Market share of the company times market size yields the number of units sold by the company. Number of units sold times selling price per unit gives the company's sales revenues from the project. Market growth rate and useful life of the project combined with the preceding information yields project sales revenues over time. Items 3a and 3b together with sales revenue provide the project's operating cash flows. Combining these cash flows with disposal value and net investment cash outflow provides the necessary input for calculating net present value.

A computer stores the probability distribution for each input variable along with a discount rate.[7] Then it randomly selects one value from each distribution and combines them to calculate net present value. The NPV thus calculated may turn out to be a small one, even negative. On the next iteration, the NPV calculated may be large, then intermediate-range, and so on. After a large number of iterations, the computer has produced a complete distribution of NPVs. It is this distribution of NPVs that makes Monte Carlo simulation appealing.

For many capital projects, Monte Carlo simulation produces NPV distributions that are near normal. In these cases, probability statements can be made about NPV based on the normal distribution, just as we did earlier in this chapter. Monte Carlo simulation provides the following kinds of information about a project:

- Expected net present value ($\overline{\text{NPV}}$).
- Standard deviation of NPV.
- Median NPV.
- Probability NPV < 0.
- Probability NPV > X, where the financial manager specifies X.

Simulation, like scenario analysis and sensitivity analysis, does not provide a decision rule. It does, however, provide information on which to base decisions. The following section develops evaluation methods that yield decision rules.

---

[6] A classic discussion of Monte Carlo simulation is found in David B. Hertz, "Risk Analysis in Capital Investments," *Harvard Business Review*, January–February 1964, 95–106.

[7] Which discount rate should be used in a simulation is an issue, as discussed in Note 3.

EVALUATION METHODS INCORPORATING RISK

In practice, financial managers make capital-budgeting decisions by balancing a proposed project's expected return against its risk. The treatment of risk is often informal and subjective. Nevertheless, evaluation methods are available that do include risk. Here are two methods for incorporating risk directly into the evaluation process: risk-adjusted discount rate (RADR) and certainty equivalent adjustment (CEA).

Risk-Adjusted Discount Rate

risk-adjusted discount rate (RADR)
Rate of return adjusted for the uncertainty in future cash flows; technique for analyzing risky capital investments.

A **risk-adjusted discount rate (RADR)** is a rate of return adjusted for the uncertainty perceived in the timing and amount of future cash flows. Marginal cost of capital is an example of a risk-adjusted discount rate. MCC is used to evaluate projects having the same risk as a company's average capital project.

Using the Marginal Cost of Capital.   The rationale for using the marginal cost of capital to evaluate projects with typical or average risk is based on investors' continual evaluation of a company's securities for potential return and risk. The rates of return investors require on a company's bonds, preferred stock, and common stock reflect risk. A weighted average of these required rates of return reflects the risk of company assets as a whole. In other words, the risk of the company's assets is a major influence on the rate of return that its security holders require. Financial managers therefore evaluate projects having risk similar to that of the company at a required rate of return equal to the company's marginal cost of capital. If they accept an average-risk project earning less, then the company's stock price declines.

Just as Chapter 9 suggests, projects with risk typical of the company are evaluated using the discount rate K:

$$\text{NPV} = \frac{\overline{\text{CF}}_1}{(1 + K)^1} + \frac{\overline{\text{CF}}_2}{(1 + K)^2} + \cdots + \frac{\overline{\text{CF}}_n}{(1 + K)^n} - \overline{\text{NICO}}$$

$$= \sum_{t = 1}^{n} \frac{\overline{\text{CF}}_t}{(1 + K)^t} - \overline{\text{NICO}}$$

where $\overline{\text{CF}}_t$ = expected future cash inflows
K = company's marginal cost of capital
t = time (years)
n = estimated life of the project in years
$\overline{\text{NICO}}$ = expected net investment cash outflow at t_0

If the project's net present value exceeds zero, then the internal rate of return exceeds K, and the project should therefore be accepted.

Evaluating Projects with Differing Risk.   Projects with risk levels that differ from the risk of the company's typical project present a problem. The risk-adjusted discount rate (RADR) method tells us to select a discount rate consistent with project risk, but it does not specify how to make the selection. In general, the discount rate should be higher, say, K^* ($K^* > K$) for higher-risk projects. Net present value is calculated as follows with K^*:

TABLE 10.5

Risk Classes for Assigning Discount Rates

Discount Rate	Project Description
Risk Class 1:	
Company's marginal cost of capital (MCC)	Replacement of old equipment with new labor-saving equipment. Product expansions where markets are well-established and the manufacturing process is well-known.
Risk Class 2:	
Company's MCC plus risk premium of a few percentage points	Expansion of plant and equipment. Market penetration of familiar products, or introduction of new products closely allied with existing product mix. Uncertain environment creates more risk than is present in company's current business.
Risk Class 3:	
Company's MCC plus risk premium of several percentage points	Expansion in new lines of business. Introduction of new products. Manufacturing processes differ from those currently used by the company. Risk clearly exceeds the company's present level of business risk.

$$\text{NPV} = \frac{\overline{\text{CF}}_1}{(1 + K^*)^1} + \frac{\overline{\text{CF}}_2}{(1 + K^*)^2} + \cdots + \frac{\overline{\text{CF}}_n}{(1 + K^*)^n} - \overline{\text{NICO}}$$

$$= \sum_{t=1}^{n} \frac{\overline{\text{CF}}_t}{(1 + K^*)^t} - \overline{\text{NICO}}$$

As with the decision above for the average-risk project, if NPV > 0 despite the higher discount rate K^*, then the project should be accepted. Also, if IRR > K^*, then again the project should be accepted.[8]

To deal with the problem of selecting an appropriate discount rate (K^*), some managers establish risk classes for capital projects. For example, Table 10.5 lists three risk classes, each with its own prescribed discount rate. For typical replacement projects, the financial manager uses the company's marginal cost of capital (MCC). Expansion in related lines of business calls for a small risk premium—say, three to five percentage points—to be added to the MCC. Expansion in new business lines calls for a larger risk premium—say, five to ten percentage points. The subjectivity in the guidelines is clear. Still, the risk classification guidelines benefit financial managers who are facing the difficulties that risk analysis poses.

EXAMPLE

The financial manager of Leonard Oil Company is analyzing an expansion into electrical machines—motors, generators, relays, and the like. She estimates the net investment cash outflow at $10,000,000 and incremental, after-tax cash inflows at $2,100,000 annually for 10 years. Leonard's marginal cost of capital equals 12 percent, and company guidelines list a premium of 6 percentage points for expansions into unrelated businesses. Using the 12 percent marginal cost of

---

[8] Considered here is the common case where project risk exceeds company risk, so $K^* > K$. If project risk were less than company risk, then $K^* < K$. Of course, if NPV > 0 at K, then it will be even larger at $K^* < K$.

capital and the risk-adjusted 18 percent, the financial manager of Leonard Oil Company calculates two NPVs:

Considered as typical project (MCC):

$$NPV = \$2,100,000(PVIFA_{12\%,10}) - \$10,000,000$$
$$= \$2,100,000(5.6502) - \$10,000,000$$
$$= \$11,865,420 - \$10,000,000$$
$$= \$1,865,420$$

Considered substantially riskier (MCC + 6 percentage points):

$$NPV = \$2,100,000(PVIFA_{18\%,10}) - \$10,000,000$$
$$= \$2,100,000(4.4941) - \$10,000,000$$
$$= \$9,437,610 - \$10,000,000$$
$$= -\$562,390$$

These results show that Leonard would accept the project using the company's marginal cost of capital but reject it using the appropriate risk-adjusted discount rate for a substantially riskier project.

pure-play method
Technique for estimating the required rate of return on a proposed investment; use the estimated MCC of a publicly held company in the same line of business as the proposed project.

Rather than relying on subjectively designed risk classes and percentage premiums to determine the risk-adjusted discount rate, some financial managers prefer to use another technique, the **pure-play method**. This technique requires financial managers to find a company engaged purely (only) in the same business as the proposal. In other words, the project is considered, for purposes of analysis, a microbusiness, the mirror image of the pure-play alternative. If the pure-play company has publicly traded securities, then the financial manager estimates that company's marginal cost of capital. This market-determined, risk-adjusted discount rate is used as the project's discount rate. Because so many companies have diversified product lines and differing debt levels, pure-play companies may be difficult to find for some products and projects.

Certainty Equivalent Adjustment

certainty equivalent adjustment (CEA)
Adjustment to a risky cash flow making it equally desirable to a risk-free cash flow; technique for analyzing risky capital investments.

In 1966 Alexander Robichek and Stewart Myers developed an alternative to adjusting discount rates for risk.[9] They reasoned that if we can adjust discount rates for risk, then we should be able to adjust cash flows too. Their method is called the **certainty equivalent adjustment (CEA)**.

A *certainty equivalent* is a cash flow to be received for certain in the future, equal in desirability to a larger expected but uncertain cash flow. For example, if you were indifferent between receiving $700 for certain one year from now and an expected but uncertain $1,000 at that time, then the $700 is your certainty equivalent to the $1,000. In other words, you judge a risk-free $700 to be equally preferable to the risky $1,000. For exceptionally risky future cash inflows, you would drastically reduce the certainty equivalent. Perhaps you would be indifferent between only $200 for sure and an expected $1,000 that is

---

[9]See Alexander A. Robichek and Stewart C. Myers, "Conceptual Problems in the Use of Risk-Adjusted Discount Rates," *Journal of Finance*, December 1966, 727–730.

exceptionally risky. Note the inverse relationship between risk and certainty equivalent cash inflows: Higher risk leads to smaller certainty equivalents.

The relationship between a certain cash inflow and a risky cash inflow is as follows:

$$\text{Certain cash inflow} = \alpha_t \times \text{Risky cash inflow}$$

where α_t (Greek letter alpha) is the certainty equivalent factor for the risky cash inflow occurring at time t. The certainty equivalent factors for the examples above are calculated as follows:

Less risky cash inflow:

$$\$700 = \alpha_t \times \$1,000$$

$$\alpha_t = 0.70$$

Riskier cash inflow:

$$\$200 = \alpha_t \times \$1,000$$

$$\alpha_t = 0.20$$

Multiplying each risky cash inflow by its certainty equivalent factor yields the certainty equivalent cash inflows.

The preceding step completes the risk adjustment process. What remains is the calculation of the present values of the certainty equivalent cash inflows. Because the risky cash inflows have been reduced to their certainty equivalents, we use the risk-free rate R_f as the discount rate:

$$NPV = \frac{\alpha_1 \overline{CF_1}}{(1 + R_f)^1} + \frac{\alpha_2 \overline{CF_2}}{(1 + R_f)^2} + \cdots + \frac{\alpha_n \overline{CF_n}}{(1 + R_f)^n} - \alpha_0 \overline{NICO}$$

$$= \sum_{t=1}^{n} \frac{\alpha_t \overline{CF_t}}{(1 + R_f)^t} - \alpha_0 \overline{NICO}$$

If the cost of the net investment is certain, then the certainty equivalent factor for the net investment cash outflow ($\overline{NICO}$) is $\alpha_0 = 1.0$. In this case the actual net investment cash outflow is used in the calculation of net present value.

For risky cash *inflows*, certainty equivalent factors (α_t) range from 0 to 1.0. Factors within this range properly penalize cash inflows for being risky. For risky cash *outflows*, however, the certainty equivalent factors (α_0) exceed 1.0. Say that $\alpha_0 = 1.2$ for a risky cash outflow expected to be $10,000. The certainty equivalent outflow equals $12,000 ($1.2 \times \$10,000$). In other words, we would be indifferent between a certain $12,000 expenditure and an expected but uncertain $10,000, which may ultimately cost us more than $10,000. The extra $2,000 ($12,000 - \$10,000$) is analogous to an insurance premium.

EXAMPLE

Ballinger Winery has under consideration a project to diversify its wine business. The project has a 4-year life, costs $300,000, and the financial manager expects the project to produce annual cash flows as follows:

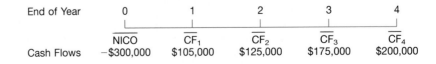

End of Year	0	1	2	3	4
	NICO	CF_1	CF_2	CF_3	CF_4
Cash Flows	−$300,000	$105,000	$125,000	$175,000	$200,000

Ballinger's financial manager believes the cash flows are increasingly uncertain over time. Furthermore, company policy requires that certainty equivalents be used in calculating net present value. Using a risk-free rate of 7 percent and the following certainty equivalent factors, the financial manager estimates NPV to be $51,947:

(1)	(2)	(3)	(2) × (3) = (4)	(5)	(4) × (5) = (6)
			Certainty Equivalent	PVIF	Present Value
Year-End	$\overline{CF}_t$	α_t	Cash Flow	at 7%	of Cash Flows
0	−$300,000	1.0	−$300,000	1.0000	−$300,000
1	105,000	0.9	94,500	0.9346	88,320
2	125,000	0.8	100,000	0.8734	87,340
3	175,000	0.7	122,500	0.8163	99,997
4	200,000	0.5	100,000	0.7629	76,290

Certainty equivalent NPV = $ 51,947

Should Ballinger's financial manager recommend acceptance of the proposed project? Yes, because its certainty equivalent NPV, $51,947, exceeds zero.

Notice in the above example two features of the certainty equivalent method for evaluating the project: (1) Certainty equivalent factors for cash inflows decline over time, reflecting increasing uncertainty in the cash inflows. (2) Certainty equivalent cash flows are discounted at the risk-free rate, R_f.

The major advantage of certainty equivalent adjustments is the period-by-period adjustment for risk. The financial manager can tailor each α_t for the risk level of the specific cash flow. Ironically, this degree of freedom is also a disadvantage: Financial managers (and others) find it difficult to estimate appropriate alphas. Thus certainty equivalents are not widely used in practice.[10]

CAPITAL BUDGETING AND THE CAPITAL ASSET PRICING MODEL

Chapter 5 describes how the capital asset pricing model (CAPM) is used to estimate the required rate of return on common stock. The model can also help structure your thinking about the required rate of return on a project and its risk level.

The CAPM can be used in capital budgeting for capital projects that trade in markets similar to those for common stocks as well as for projects with securities that trade. Consider, for example, the purchase of a subsidiary or an entire company whose securities actively trade in the securities markets. Most capital projects do not have traded securities, however, nor do product markets exist for the projects themselves. This absence of markets greatly limits the practical application of the CAPM in capital budgeting. Nevertheless, the absence of markets does not prevent us from exploiting the model for the insight it provides.

---

[10]Certainty equivalent adjustment (CEA) factors can be derived from risk-adjusted discount rates (RADR). Yet managers seem more comfortable with RADR than with CEA. Robichek and Myers, cited in Note 9, developed the CEA method to expose an implicit assumption in the RADR method. They showed that a constant RADR implies a risk increasing at a specific rate over time. A risk premium that gets compounded in present-value mathematics implies the increasing risk.

To see how the capital asset pricing model can help a financial manager quantify risk premiums, consider a company financed solely with common equity that plans to retain earnings for a project. Recall from Chapter 6 that the cost of the company's retained earnings is the rate of return that common shareholders require (K_c). According to the CAPM, the cost of retained earnings is:

$$K_c = R_f + (K_m - R_f)\beta$$

where R_f = risk-free rate of return

K_m = required rate of return on an average common stock, or the market portfolio of all common stocks

β = the stock's beta, a measure of nondiversifiable risk

EXAMPLE

Suppose that the equity-financed company in our discussion is a manufacturer of grinding wheels, Emery Products.[11] Above average in risk, Emery's common-stock beta is 1.2; K_m is 14 percent, and R_f is 8 percent. The cost of retained earnings to Emery is:

$$K_c = 0.08 + (0.14 - 0.08)1.2$$

$$= 0.08 + 0.072$$

$$= 0.152, \text{ or } 15.2\%$$

Because Emery's risk exceeds that of a typical stock ($\beta = 1.2 > 1.0$), shareholders demand an above-average (15.2% > 14%) rate of return.

For prospective projects with risk levels similar to its typical or average capital project, a company must earn at least its marginal cost of capital. To accept projects with equal risk but earning less than the MCC causes a decline in the common-stock price. In the example above, Emery management accepts typical projects offering at least a 15.2 percent internal rate of return. If Emery accepts a typical project ($\beta = 1.2$) and the cash flows from the project generate less than a 15.2 percent IRR, then the price of Emery's stock will fall.

EXAMPLE

The management of Emery Products is considering investing $3,000,000 in a project, bringing the market value of the company's assets to $13,000,000. The proposed project and the company's typical project have the following characteristics:

Project	Beta	Expected Return
Typical	1.2	15.2%
Proposed	1.2	10.0

If management accepts the project, then Emery's stock price falls.

[11] For simplicity, not necessity, we assume that Emery Products is entirely equity financed. If Emery were partially financed with debt, its marginal cost of capital would be a weighted average of both debt and equity costs. Chapter 7 discusses this calculation in detail.

In the above example Emery's stock price falls because shareholders dissatisfied with management's decision to invest in a project offering the same risk but lower expected return will sell their stock. When management accepts the proposed project, the beta and the return on the company's portfolio of total assets each become a weighted average of the betas and the returns on its present projects and the proposed project.[12] The proposed project requires a $3,000,000 net investment cash outflow, and Emery's present capital projects total $10,000,000. The expected rate of return and the beta for Emery after accepting the proposed project become:

$$\text{Expected rate of return} = \left(\frac{\$10}{\$13}\right)0.152 + \left(\frac{\$3}{\$13}\right)0.10$$

$$= 0.14, \text{ or } 14.0\%$$

$$\text{Beta} = \left(\frac{\$10}{\$13}\right)1.2 + \left(\frac{\$3}{\$13}\right)1.2$$

$$= 1.2$$

Now consider what happens to the company's stock price. Emery's shareholders require a 15.2 percent rate of return for betas of 1.2. When they realize that Emery's expected rate of return has declined to 14.0 percent without a reduction in risk, they sell their shares, placing downward pressure on the stock price. The price declines until the expected return on the market value of Emery's assets equals the required rate of return, 15.2 percent.

From this example you can see that investing in a project with an internal rate of return less than the marginal cost of capital reduces stock price and shareholder wealth. Emery's financial manager should reject the proposed project because its internal rate of return (10 percent) is less than the marginal cost of capital (15.2 percent).

The capital asset pricing model permits the calculation of *multiple hurdle rates* for a company, discount rates that differ according to the risks of proposed projects. The financial manager incorporates directly into the model a proposed project's nondiversifiable risk measured by beta.

EXAMPLE

The financial manager of Emery Products is considering a proposed capital investment in the mining of aluminum oxide, Al_2O_3, commonly known as corundum. If it mines this abrasive material, the company will gain a reliable and low-cost source of raw materials for its manufacture of grinding wheels. If it does not mine the corundum, the company must buy the material at a higher price from suppliers who often fail to make deliveries as scheduled. Based on estimates of beta for other mining companies (pure plays), Emery's management estimates that the beta of the proposed project is 1.7.

Using the capital asset pricing model, calculate the required rate of return (K) on Emery's proposed expansion into mining. K_m is 14 percent, R_f is 8 percent, and beta is 1.7:

$$K = 0.08 + (0.14 - 0.08)1.7$$

$$= 0.08 + 0.102$$

$$= 0.182, \text{ or } 18.2\%$$

---

[12]Chapter 5 points out that a portfolio beta is simply a value-weighted average of the betas of the stocks making up the portfolio. A company's collection of assets can be viewed as a portfolio of capital projects. Conceptually, the beta of a company's total assets measures its business risk and is the value-weighted average beta of its individual assets.

Because the project risk (1.7) exceeds that of Emery's present assets (1.2), the required rate of return (18.2 percent) on the project exceeds that for Emery's present assets (15.2 percent). The financial manager calculates a risk-adjusted net present value using an 18.2 percent discount rate.

◼

The security market line in Figure 10.6 depicts Emery's proposed mining project. Relative to Emery's typical capital project, the mining project has above-average risk and therefore a higher required rate of return. If the mining project were expected to yield a 15.2 percent internal rate of return (Emery's marginal cost of capital), then it would be rejected to avoid a decline in Emery's stock price.

Consider what happens to Emery's stock price if it accepts a proposed project with a 1.7 beta and 15.2 percent expected internal rate of return. The proposed project requires a $3,000,000 net investment cash outflow, and the company's assets before accepting the project total $10,000,000. The company's expected rate of return is unchanged after accepting the project, but its beta increases:

$$\text{Expected rate} \atop \text{of return} = \left(\frac{\$10}{\$13}\right)0.152 + \left(\frac{\$3}{\$13}\right)0.152$$

$$= 0.152, \text{ or } 15.2\%$$

$$\text{Beta} = \left(\frac{\$10}{\$13}\right)1.2 + \left(\frac{\$3}{\$13}\right)1.7$$

$$= 1.32$$

Adding the mining project to its portfolio of assets causes Emery's beta to increase from 1.2 to 1.32. The mining project, however, does not cause expected return to rise. Hence accepting the project causes a decline in Emery's stock price. Alternatively, if the mining project yielded 18.2 percent, then it would provide an increase in return consistent with the increased risk, and stock price would be unchanged:

$$\text{Expected rate of return} = \left(\frac{\$10}{\$13}\right)0.152 + \left(\frac{\$3}{\$13}\right)0.182$$

$$= 0.159, \text{ or } 15.9\%$$

This 15.9 percent corresponds to Emery's new marginal cost of capital (beta = 1.32), as the capital asset pricing model shows:

$$K = 0.08 + (0.14 - 0.08)1.32$$

$$= 0.08 + 0.079$$

$$= 0.159, \text{ or } 15.9\%$$

In this case Emery Products would move up the security market line in Figure 10.6 from its present location toward the location of the mining project.

To summarize the discussion, financial managers should accept all proposed projects with expected internal rates of return plotting above the security market line. They should reject those plotting below it. Finally, they should be indifferent to projects with IRRs plotting on the SML. Here, then, are the decision rules provided by the capital asset pricing model:

FIGURE 10.6

Risk-Adjusted Discount Rates Using the Capital Asset Pricing Model

To be acceptable, proposed capital investments with nondiversifiable risk equal to that of Emery Products' typical projects must offer at least a 15.2 percent return. All proposed investments plotting above the SML should be accepted; all those plotting below the SML should be rejected.

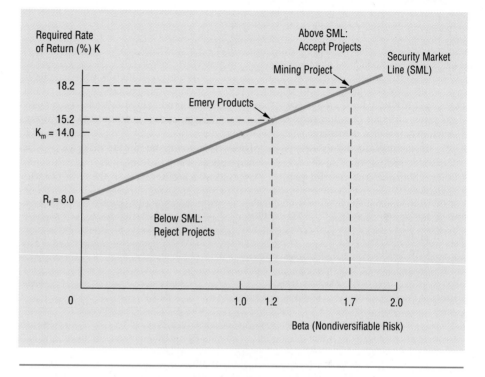

- Project's expected rate of return > Required rate of return: Accept the project; acceptance causes stock price to increase.
- Project's expected rate of return < Required rate of return: Reject the project; acceptance causes stock price to decrease.

The capital asset pricing model offers another evaluation method that a financial manager can use to determine how capital investments affect a company's stock price. One of its serious drawbacks in practice, however, is the difficulty of estimating project betas. Pure-play procedures, subjective estimates, and projects with active markets provide partial solutions. Like the other risk-adjusted capital-budgeting techniques, the CAPM does not offer an ironclad recommendation for project selection, but it does provide insight to help make decisions.

COPING WITH RISK IN CAPITAL BUDGETING

Financial managers making decisions on which projects a company will undertake need to assess both expected return and risk exposure. In the extreme, project selection without regard to risk may lead the company to bankruptcy. Short of that, new projects could lead to a decline in the price of the company's common stock.

Multiple Hurdle Rates, or Divisional Cost of Capital

Financial managers are moving in the direction of using multiple hurdle rates in capital budgeting rather than a single hurdle rate measured by the marginal cost of capital. Multiple hurdle rates refer to using different discount rates in each division of a company.

In the past, financial managers tended to use one hurdle rate throughout the company for two reasons:

- One rate is relatively easy to understand and apply throughout the company.

- Estimates of prospective cash flows from capital projects are approximations at best. Why attempt to refine the discount rate when a rough yardstick might serve as well in this imperfect environment?

These reasons for one hurdle rate had appeal. They did not, however, allow for differences in the cost of capital across different types of businesses. And differences in business risk were ignored totally.

Many managers assign hurdle rates to divisions. Developing a hurdle rate for each proposed project also makes sense, but the time involved can be prohibitive. The result is often a sliding hurdle rate that reflects the risk and required return for specific divisions, but not for individual projects.

Consider, for example, Interstate Business Services, a company with three operating divisions. Each division has a marginal cost of capital that reflects the division's cost of equity and debt, its marginal tax rate, and its optimal capital structure:

Machine Tools (20%)	Electronics (50%)	Metal Products (30%)
$K_c = 0.19$	$K_c = 0.22$	$K_c = 0.17$
$K_d = 0.07$	$K_d = 0.08$	$K_d = 0.07$
$T = 0.40$	$T = 0.40$	$T = 0.40$
$D/TA = 0.50$	$D/TA = 0.40$	$D/TA = 0.60$
$MCC = 0.042(0.50)$	$MCC = 0.048(0.40)$	$MCC = 0.042(0.60)$
$+ 0.19(0.50)$	$+ 0.22(0.60)$	$+ 0.17(0.40)$
$= 0.116$, or 11.6%	$= 0.151$, or 15.1%	$= 0.093$, or 9.3%

To find the cost of equity for each division, the financial manager uses the pure-play method described in this chapter. To determine the optimal capital structure for each division, the financial manager uses the average debt ratio measured with market values for the industry in which the division operates. By using divisional hurdle rates, Interstate Business Services recognizes divisional differences in business risk and financial risk. The overall marginal cost of capital for Interstate Business Services is the weighted average of each division's MCC:

$$MCC_{company} = 0.20(0.116)$$
$$+ 0.50(0.151)$$
$$+ 0.30(0.093)$$
$$= 0.127, \text{ or } 12.7\%$$

Source: Based on Allen H. Seed III, "Structuring Capital Spending Hurdle Rates," *Financial Executive,* February 1982, 22; Enrique R. Arza, "Do Your Business Units Create Shareholder Wealth?" *Harvard Business Review,* January–February 1986, 121–126; and Samuel C. Weaver, "Divisional Hurdle Rates and the Cost of Capital," *Financial Management,* Spring 1989, 18–25.

Some projects do not warrant elaborate risk analysis and the consequent expenditure of time and money. For example, government-mandated pollution control equipment simply must be purchased, which reduces the problem to one of getting the job done at the lowest cost. Some projects are undertaken for convenience and comfort—a well-appointed front office, paved parking lots for employees, an air-conditioning system. In these cases decisions tend to be based on intangible benefits and project cost.

Setting aside the trivial, the mandated, and the judgmental projects leaves numerous projects meriting close study. Financial managers analyze large-scale projects with the methods—preferably more than one—described in this chapter. The concept of risk, its measurement, and its impact on stock price are all too elusive for reliance solely on the validity of one method.

Ultimately, financial managers who understand company operations and have a firm grasp of the trends and vagaries within the industry make successful capital-budgeting decisions. For these managers, judgment can be formed with and tempered by the following kinds of information:

- *Scenario analysis:* Identification of the most likely outcome along with the pessimistic and optimistic cases.
- *Sensitivity analysis:* Knowledge of the key variable(s) affecting net present value.
- *Monte Carlo simulation:* Probability that the net present value will be less than zero.
- *RADR and CEA:* Net present value of the project after assessing penalties for risk.
- *Capital asset pricing model:* Quantification of the risk-adjusted discount rate; importance of nondiversifiable risk.

Taken together, these procedures provide a useful arsenal for the financial manager. But, as pointed out at the beginning of this chapter, they do not provide easy answers to the hard questions that risk poses.

SUMMARY

- Risk in capital budgeting results from the uncertainty in cash flows of a proposed capital investment. The actual rate of return on a project might differ from what the financial manager expects because of variance in cash flows.

- A probability distribution of net present values includes the possible NPVs and their associated probabilities of occurring. Expected net present value ($\overline{NPV}$) is a probability-weighted average of possible NPVs, and standard deviation (σ) is a measure of dispersion around $\overline{NPV}$:

$$\overline{NPV} = \sum_{j=1}^{n} P_j NPV_j$$

$$\sigma = \sqrt{\sum_{j=1}^{n} P_j (NPV_j - \overline{NPV})^2}$$

where P_j is the probability of NPV_j occurring. A large standard deviation reflects a wide dispersion of possible NPVs and great risk. Assuming that NPV is normally distributed (bell-shaped), the financial manager can use the normal distribution to assign a probability to a range of actual NPVs, say, the probability of $NPV < 0$.

- The following three methods help a financial manager to assess the risk present in a proposed capital project:

1. *Scenario analysis* provides three estimates of a project's net present value: the most likely case; a pessimistic, or worst, case; and an optimistic, or best, case.

2. *Sensitivity analysis* measures the impact of changes in inputs—estimated cash flows, discount rate, project life, and so on—taken one at a time on a project's net present value.

3. *Monte Carlo simulation* develops a probability distribution of net present values for a project. Based on this distribution, the financial manager can make probability statements about NPV—for example, the probability of NPV < 0.

• One way for financial managers to account for risk in capital budgeting is to use a risk-adjusted discount rate (RADR). This procedure requires the discount rate to be commensurate with project risk. For example, if a project has greater risk than the company's typical or average asset, then the discount rate exceeds the company's marginal cost of capital. Net present value with a risk-adjusted discount rate (K*) is calculated as follows:

$$NPV = \sum_{t=1}^{n} \frac{\overline{CF}_t}{(1 + K^*)^t} - \overline{NICO}$$

where $\overline{CF}_t$ = expected cash inflow at time t

$\overline{NICO}$ = expected net investment cash outflow

If NPV > 0, then the financial manager should accept the project.

• Certainty equivalent adjustments (CEA) provide an alternative to RADR. In this procedure the financial manager multiplies expected but uncertain cash flows $(\overline{CF}_t)$ by certainty equivalent factors (α_t). These factors range between zero and 1.0 for risky cash inflows; α_t is smaller for a more risky cash inflow. Net present value with certainty equivalents is calculated as follows:

$$NPV = \sum_{t=1}^{n} \frac{\alpha_t \overline{CF}_t}{(1 + R_f)^t} - \alpha_0 \overline{NICO}$$

where R_f is the risk-free rate of return. The discount rate equals the risk-free rate because the expected but uncertain cash inflows have already been adjusted for risk. If NPV > 0, then the financial manager should accept the project.

• According to the capital asset pricing model (CAPM), only the nondiversifiable portion of project risk should be used to adjust the discount rate. More specifically, the CAPM describes the required rate of return (K, or RADR) on a project as follows:

$$K = R_f + (K_m - R_f)\beta$$

where β (beta) measures the project's nondiversifiable risk. If the expected internal rate of return on a proposed project exceeds K, the required rate of return, then the financial manager should accept the project.

• Financial managers who understand not only the operations of their companies but also the trends in their industries cope best with risk in capital budgeting. The concepts and procedures described in this chapter help financial managers develop informed judgments on whether or not benefits from proposed projects adequately compensate for the risks.

Key Terms

discrete probability distribution

continuous probability distribution

normal distribution

scenario analysis

sensitivity analysis

Monte Carlo simulation

risk-adjusted discount rate (RADR)

pure-play method

certainty equivalent adjustment (CEA)

Questions

10.1. Explain what the term *risk* means in capital budgeting and why financial managers should consider it in decision making.

10.2. In what sense is standard deviation a measure of distance?

10.3. Suppose you invested $1,000 and later discovered that your possible cash benefits are best described by the following probability distribution:

Probability	Cash Benefit
0.95	0
0.05	$3,000

  a. Do you regret making the investment? Why or why not?

  b. Would you describe your possible cash benefits as being uncertain? Explain your answer.

10.4. Explain the major difference between *scenario analysis* and *sensitivity analysis*. Point out which one emphasizes extreme values and which one emphasizes percentage changes.

10.5. *True or false:* Monte Carlo simulation is a good procedure for assessing risk of small, routine projects. Explain your choice.

10.6. Monte Carlo simulation selects values from probability distributions of key variables to calculate a net present value. Explain how simulation develops a probability distribution of net present values.

10.7. Suppose that you are evaluating the sensitivity analysis of a proposed capital project. You receive the following sensitivity measures:

Variable	Change in Variable	Change in NPV
Investment outlay	10%	28%
Product (output) selling price	10	3
Market share	10	13
Variable cost per unit	10	5
Life of the project	10	24
Residual value	10	8

  a. What is the significance of this information and how might it be useful to you?

  b. Which variable(s) would you concentrate on measuring most accurately before accepting the project? Explain your choice(s).

10.8. One of your friends comments on risk-adjusted discount rates and their application in the following way: "Using risk-adjusted discount rates always causes net present value to be less than that calculated using the company's marginal cost of capital." Do you agree with this observation? Explain your answer.

10.9. Explain why a company's marginal cost of capital is the appropriate discount rate for evaluating the company's average-risk projects.

10.10. Compare and contrast the use of risk-adjusted discount rates and certainty equivalent adjustments in capital budgeting. Comment on the role of the discount rate in each method.

10.11. *True or false:* Certainty equivalent factors are inversely related to the riskiness of expected cash inflows. Explain your choice.

10.12. According to the capital asset pricing model, the required rate of return on a project is:

$$K = R_f + (K_m - R_f)\beta$$

  a. What is the name of the line this equation represents? Draw the graph and label each axis, noting the location of R_f and K_m.

  b. Note on the graph the location of the required rate of return for a proposed project with a beta of 2.0.

10.13. The graph on the following page shows two projects that a financial manager is analyzing. The company's beta is 1.1, Project A's is 0.7, and Project B's is 1.7. Should the company invest in Project A or in Project B? Explain your answer.

10.14. Wolfe Shoe Manufacturing merges with Eastern Shoe Wholesalers. The market value of Wolfe's common equity equals that of Eastern, and each has the same debt level. Despite these similarities, Wolfe's stock beta is 1.4 and Eastern's is 0.9.

a. What are the possible reasons for Wolfe's beta being larger than Eastern's?

b. What is the stock beta of the merged companies, now called Eastern-Wolfe Shoes?

c. Is Eastern-Wolfe's cost of equity capital higher or lower than Wolfe's? On the basis of your answer, can you say that the merger was a good idea? A bad idea? Explain your answer.

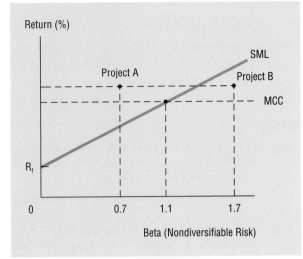

Strategy Problem

The capital-budgeting committee of the Pave Distributing Company has begun deliberation on several capital investment proposals for the next year. One of the projects, submitted by the company's facilities manager, requires a $30,000 net investment cash outflow and has the following cash inflows:

Scenario	Year 1	Year 2	Year 3
Optimistic	$18,000	$24,000	$10,000
Most likely	15,000	20,000	7,000
Pessimistic	12,000	19,000	6,000

The committee has turned to the company's financial manager, Don Dunn, and has asked him to evaluate the project using discounted cash flow procedures. Mr. Dunn favors risk-adjusted net present value, which allows for the risk that he perceives in the project. He has calculated a 17 percent marginal cost of capital for the company, and the risk-free rate of return is 7 percent.

a. Calculate the net present value of the proposed project under each scenario. Use the marginal cost of capital as the discount rate.

b. After reflecting on the three scenarios, Mr. Dunn believes that there is a 20 percent probability that the optimistic scenario will occur; a 60 percent probability that the most likely scenario will occur; and a 20 percent probability that the pessimistic scenario will occur. Based on this information and your solutions in Part *a*, what is the probability that the net present value will be negative? Assume that NPV is normally distributed and use Table 10.3.

c. As a part of the analysis, Mr. Dunn decides to use a risk-adjusted discount rate. Company guidelines indicate that a project with risk characteristics such as this one requires the addition of a two percentage point premium to Pave Distributing Company's marginal cost of capital. Calculate the NPV based on this information and the most likely scenario.

d. To complete the analysis, Mr. Dunn uses certainty equivalent adjustments. Based on the risk levels of the cash flows, he decides to use the following certainty equivalent factors: 1.00 for the net investment cash outflow, 0.95 for the cash flow one year hence, 0.90 for the cash flow in two years, and 0.88 for the cash flow in three years. Calculate the NPV of the project based on this information and the most likely scenario.

Strategy

Draw a time line of the cash flows.

Solution

a. Net present value of the project under each scenario using the marginal cost of capital 17 percent:

End of Year:	0	1	2	3
Cash Flows:				
Optimistic	−$30,000	$18,000	$24,000	$10,000
Most likely	−$30,000	$15,000	$20,000	$ 7,000
Pessimistic	−$30,000	$12,000	$19,000	$ 6,000

$$NPV = \frac{\text{Present value}}{\text{of cash inflows}} - NICO$$

Calculate NPV for each scenario.

$$NPV_{(\text{optimistic})} = \$39,161 - \$30,000$$
$$= \$9,161$$
$$NPV_{(\text{most likely})} = \$31,801 - \$30,000$$
$$= \$1,801$$
$$NPV_{(\text{pessimistic})} = \$27,882 - \$30,000$$
$$= -\$2,118$$

Calculate expected net present value, $\overline{NPV}$.

b. To calculate the standard deviation, begin by calculating the expected net present value, a probability-weighted average of possible net present values:

Scenario	(1) NPV	(2) Probability	(1) × (2) = (3) Product
Optimistic	$9,161	0.20	$1,832
Most likely	$1,801	0.60	$1,081
Pessimistic	−$2,118	0.20	−$ 424
		$\overline{NPV} =$	$2,489

Calculate standard deviation, σ.

Now, calculate the squared deviations from $\overline{NPV}$, multiply each by its probability of occurrence, sum the products, and take the square root of the total:

Scenario	(1) Deviation $(NPV_j - \overline{NPV})$	$(1)^2 = (2)$ Deviation Squared	(3) Probability	(2) × (3) = (4) Product
Optimistic	$9,161 − $2,489 = $6,672	$44,515,584	0.20	$ 8,903,117
Most likely	$1,801 − $2,489 = −$ 688	$ 473,344	0.60	$ 284,006
Pessimistic	−$2,118 − $2,489 = −$4,607	$21,224,449	0.20	$ 4,244,890
			$\sigma^2 =$	$13,432,013

$$\text{Standard deviation } (\sigma_{NPV}) = \sqrt{\$13,432,013} = \$3,665$$

Calculate the Z statistic:

$$Z = \frac{NPV - \overline{NPV}}{\sigma}$$
$$= \frac{0 - \$2,489}{\$3,665}$$
$$= -0.679$$

Use the Z statistic and Table 10.3 to estimate the probability of NPV < 0.

Refer to Table 10.3 to find the area under the normal curve beyond a Z of −0.679. The percentage of the normal distribution beyond this Z is between 24.20 and 27.43 percent. The probability of NPV being less than zero is about 25 percent. Without the assumption of NPV being normally distributed, the probability would be 20 percent—the probability associated with the pessimistic scenario.

c. The risk-adjusted discount rate is the company's marginal cost of capital (17 percent) adjusted to reflect the project's risk. The discount rate for this project is 19 percent (17% + 2%):

Calculate NPV using a discount rate of 19 percent.

$$NPV = \$30,882 - \$30,000 = \$882$$

d. Adjust each expected cash flow to find the certainty equivalent; then, discount the certainty equivalents at the risk-free rate:

End of Year:	0	1	2	3
Certainty Equivalent:	−$30,000	$14,250	$18,000	$6,160

Multiply cash flows by the certainty equivalent factors; discount the certainty equivalent cash flows at the risk-free rate, 7 percent.

(1)	(2)	(3)	(2) × (3) = (4)	(5)	(4) × (5) = (6)
Year-End	$\overline{CF}_t$	α_t	Certainty Equivalent Cash Flow	PVIF at 7%	Present Value of Cash Flows
0	−$30,000	1.00	−$30,000	1.0000	−$30,000
1	$15,000	0.95	$14,250	0.9346	$13,318
2	$20,000	0.90	$18,000	0.8734	$15,721
3	$ 7,000	0.88	$ 6,160	0.8163	$ 5,028

Certainty equivalent NPV = $ 4,067

Demonstration Problem

Elena Garza is a capital-budgeting analyst for Santa Barbara Shoes (SBS), a small manufacturer of athletic footwear. One of the proposed projects sponsored by the production department requires a $100,000 investment and has the following incremental cash inflows under three scenarios:

Scenario	Year 1	Year 2	Year 3
Best case	$58,000	$58,000	$58,000
Most likely	47,000	47,000	47,000
Worst case	40,000	40,000	40,000

Ms. Garza's supervisor tells her to assume the following probabilities for the three scenarios: best case, 10 percent; most likely, 80 percent; worst case, 10 percent. SBS's marginal cost of capital is 12 percent, the risk-free rate of return is 7 percent, and the required rate of return on an average common stock (or the market portfolio) is 14 percent.

a. What causes capital projects to be risky?
b. Use the marginal cost of capital to calculate net present value (NPV) of the project under each scenario.
c. Calculate the expected value and standard deviation of the three NPVs in Part *b*.
d. Based on the information provided by Ms. Garza's supervisor, what is the probability that NPV will be less than zero? Now assume that NPV is normally distributed and use Table 10.3 to calculate the probability that NPV will be less than zero. Why do these two probabilities differ?
e. Suppose that beta (index of nondiversifiable risk) of the project is 1.0. Use the capital asset pricing model to calculate the project's risk-adjusted discount rate; then use this rate to calculate the project's NPV under the most likely scenario. Why does this risk-adjusted discount rate differ from the company's marginal cost of capital?
f. Instead of calculating project betas, many financial managers assign projects to risk classes such as: (1) replacement projects, (2) expansion in old lines of business, and (3) expansion in new lines of business. Assess the relative risk of projects in these three categories. How does the risk-adjusted discount rate relate to the categories?
g. What is the purpose of *scenario analysis, sensitivity analysis,* and *Monte Carlo simulation?* What is the principal difference between scenario analysis and sensitivity analysis?
h. As part of the analysis, Ms. Garza decides to apply certainty equivalent factors to the most likely cash flows: 1.0 for the net investment cash outflow and 0.9, 0.8, and 0.7 for the cash inflows in Years 1, 2, and 3, respectively. Calculate NPV based on certainty equivalents.

i. In your opinion and based on the preceding analyses, should Ms. Garza recommend acceptance of the project? Explain.

Problems

Expected NPV

10.1. The Butters Company must choose between two mutually exclusive projects. The probability distributions of net present values for the projects are:

Project A		Project B	
Probability	**NPV**	**Probability**	**NPV**
0.05	$10,000	0.05	($10,000)
0.25	40,000	0.25	20,000
0.40	50,000	0.40	50,000
0.25	60,000	0.25	80,000
0.05	80,000	0.05	100,000

a. Based solely on expected net present value ($\overline{\text{NPV}}$), which project should Butters' financial manager select?
b. Which project appears more risky? Why? (No calculations are needed.)

Expected cash flow and standard deviation

10.2. A financial manager is evaluating a project with the following probability distribution of cash inflows to be received one year from now:

Probability	Cash Inflow
0.20	$46,000
0.60	47,000
0.20	60,000

a. Calculate the expected value of these cash inflows.
b. Calculate the standard deviation of these cash inflows.

Probabilities and a normal distribution

10.3. A statistician would refer to the probability distribution in Problem 10.2 as *discrete* because there are gaps between the possible cash inflows. In answering the following questions, use your answers to Problem 10.2 but assume that the probability distribution is continuous (not discrete). (*Hint:* Use Table 10.3.)
a. How large is the cash inflow 2 standard deviations below the expected value?
b. How large is the cash inflow 1 standard deviation above the expected value?
c. What is the probability that the actual cash inflow will fall below $44,086?
d. What is the probability that the actual cash inflow will be greater than $28,144?

Probability and a normal distribution

10.4. A project proposal has an expected net present value of $100,000 and a standard deviation of $100,000. Use Table 10.3 to determine the probability of receiving a negative NPV (NPV < 0).

Expected cash flows and RADR

10.5. The financial manager of Styco Inc. is analyzing a $20,000 investment with a 2-year life. The distributions of cash inflows are:

	Probability	Cash Inflow
Year 1	0.20	$22,000
	0.60	15,000
	0.20	13,000
Year 2	0.20	15,600
	0.60	15,200
	0.20	10,800

Styco uses a risk-adjusted discount rate of 15 percent per year to calculate the project's net present value.
a. Calculate the expected cash inflows $\overline{CF}_t$ for Years 1 and 2.
b. Calculate the risk-adjusted NPV of the project.
c. Should Styco invest in the project? Explain your answer by referring to shareholder wealth and stock price.

NPV and RADR   10.6. Subramanyam Enterprises (SE) is a manufacturer of toys, primarily low-cost pocket toys. SE's director of research and development has suggested an expansion into larger, higher-cost toys. The suggestion calls for SE to experiment during the first year with a super-hero-airplane transformer. SE's director of research and development estimates the cost of introducing the toy at $280,000. He expects the toy to produce year-end cash inflows of $100,000 for 4 years. SE's marginal cost of capital is 14 percent, and the risk-free rate is 8 percent. According to SE's policy guidelines, the minimum required rate of return on expansion products is 18 percent.
a. Calculate net present value of the proposed new toy using a discount rate of 8 percent, 14 percent, and 18 percent.
b. Which of the NPVs calculated in Part *a* is most appropriate? Explain.

NPV and RADR   10.7. Terrel Industries, a manufacturer of C-rations for the U.S. army, is considering extending its product lines to include bakery products for civilian institutions such as schools, hospitals, and public cafeterias. Company managers believe the product extension will require an investment of $1,000,000. According to company policy, required rates of return on capital projects are as follows: 12 percent on replacement projects; 15 percent on the introduction of new products closely allied with the existing product mix; 18 percent on expansion in lines of business with manufacturing processes different from those currently used by the company. The investment in manufacturing bakery products is expected to produce annual cash inflows of $275,000 for 6 years.
a. Calculate net present value of the project using a discount rate of 12 percent, 15 percent, and 18 percent.
b. Explain why the discount rates of 12 percent and 18 percent provide misleading information on the project.

Certainty equivalent NPV   10.8. Tanco Inc. has an opportunity to invest in a new product line costing $250,000. The company's capital-budgeting analyst estimates the cash inflows and their associated certainty equivalent factors as follows:

Year-End	Expected Cash Inflow	Certainty Equivalent Factor
1	$ 85,000	0.95
2	95,000	0.90
3	105,000	0.85
4	115,000	0.80

The company's marginal cost of capital (MCC) is 14 percent, and the risk-free rate of return is 7 percent.
a. Calculate net present value using MCC and the expected cash flows.
b. Calculate net present value using the certainty equivalent factors.
c. Describe the implicit assumption about project risk in Part *a*.
d. Should Tanco Inc. invest in the project? Explain.

Certainty equivalent NPV   10.9. Vinny Pazienda is a financial manager for Z-Mart Companies. Mr. Pazienda's assignment is to analyze a proposed project for investment by Z-Mart. After talking to product vendors, Z-Mart engineers, and accountants, he put together the following information on the project:

Expected net investment cash outflow ($\overline{\text{NICO}}$) = \$100,000
Expected cash inflows per year ($\overline{\text{CF}}_t$) = \$40,000
Expected project life ($\bar{n}$) = 5 years

Because of his uncertainty about the cash inflows, Mr. Pazienda decides to let α_0 = 1 and to apply the following certainty equivalent factors to the cash inflows:

Year	α_t
1	0.9
2	0.8
3	0.7
4	0.5
5	0.5

The risk-free rate of return is 7 percent.
a. What is the risk-adjusted net present value calculated by Mr. Pazienda?
b. What should be the recommendation to his boss?
c. If you were the boss, what questions might you raise about the assumptions and methods used in the analysis?

Depreciation, operating cash flows, and RADR

10.10. Shores Clothiers is considering an opportunity to invest in a catalog-merchandising program that calls for a \$28,000 outlay for fixed assets and an \$8,000 increase in net working capital. The project will last 4 years, and Shores Clothiers uses for tax purposes straight-line depreciation with the half-year convention and a 3-year class life. Per-unit expected costs and revenues associated with the project are:

Price	\$7.00
Labor costs	2.50
Materials and overhead	1.50

Depreciable assets will be disposed of at the end of the project's life with no cash realized. The company will recover net working capital in the project. The marketing department has made the following forecast:

Year	Expected Sales Volume (Units)
1	3,500
2	3,600
3	7,000
4	4,000

Shores Clothiers is in the 40 percent marginal tax bracket. Its marginal cost of capital is 13 percent, but for projects in this risk class Shores adds a risk premium of three percentage points. Assume that all cash flows except those associated with the net investment occur at the end of each year.

Should Shores Clothiers invest in the project? Support your decision using the risk-adjusted discount rate to calculate the project's net present value.

CAPM, operating cash flows, and NPV

10.11. Roderick Harold and Arkley Kelley are evaluating a \$300,000 4-year investment to produce a hexa-photo cybernetic oscillator. The project also requires \$15,000 of net working capital and will have the following characteristics for each of the next 4 years:

Total revenue (38,000 units)	$696,000
Variable costs per unit	
Materials	$7.12
Labor	$5.30
Administrative and selling	$2.60
Depreciation (annual) for tax purposes	$75,000

The net investment cash outflow for the project is $315,000, and the company's marginal tax rate is 40 percent. Messrs. Harold and Kelley agree to use a risk-free rate (R_f) of 8 percent, and they estimate the required rate of return on the market portfolio (K_m) to be 15 percent. Using the pure-play method, they estimate the project's beta at 1.0.

a. Calculate the required rate of return on the project.
b. Calculate each year's expected operating cash inflow.
c. Calculate the project's net present value. Should the project be accepted? (Assume that liquidation value of net working capital and equipment is zero.)

CAPM and project selection

10.12. Northwest Industries is a conservatively financed company. C. J. Leonard, the president, remembers the Great Depression of the 1930s and refuses to use debt financing. Northwest's beta is 1.3. Because Northwest has only equity financing, its beta measures the market risk of both its assets and its common stock.

    Ms. Leonard is not sure she should approve a proposed capital expenditure. The proposed project's beta is estimated at 1.6, and Ms. Leonard is concerned about raising the risk level of company assets. Northwest's financial manager assures her of the project's merit. After all, he notes, its expected rate of return is 16 percent, which approximately equals the profitability of Northwest Industries. Still, Ms. Leonard is troubled by the proposal, perhaps because of its size; the proposed project would increase Northwest's assets by 50 percent. Northwest's capital-budgeting analysts provide the following market benchmarks: R_f is 7 percent and K_m is 14 percent.

a. According to the capital asset pricing model, what are the required rates of return on the company and the project?
b. If Ms. Leonard approves the project, what will be the new required rate of return on the company?
c. If she approves the project, what will be the new expected rate of return on the company?
d. Should she approve the project? Explain your answer.

CAPM, marginal cost of capital, and project selection

10.13. Frankie Manley, financial manager of Venus Velvet Enterprises, is evaluating a prospective investment project with a beta of 1.1. Venus Velvet has an optimal capital structure described as follows:

Component	Proportion
Debt	0.40
Common equity	0.60

Venus Velvet's debt costs average 11 percent before taxes, and its stock beta is 1.1. Ms. Manley's analysis of the securities markets turns up the following two estimates: R_f is 7 percent and K_m is 14 percent. The company's marginal tax bracket is 40 percent.

a. Calculate Venus Velvet's marginal cost of capital.
b. Calculate the required rate of return on the prospective project.
c. Should Ms. Manley recommend that the capital-budgeting committee accept the project if she expects the project to have a 15 percent rate of return? Explain your answer.

NPV and payback period

10.14. The management of Fredonia Manganese and Calcite is considering investing in a project with the following characteristics:

> Expected life of project = 10 years
> Expected cash inflow per year = $26,000
> Expected net investment in project = $120,000

Management policy requires projects of this sort to produce 14 percent per year. Because of management's aversion to risk, each project must have a payback period of 4 years or less. Management's reasoning for the payback cutoff is as follows: Cash inflows beyond 4 years are so unpredictable that they are unsettling. Management therefore will treat expected values of cash inflows occurring beyond 4 years as zeros.

a. Calculate the net present value of the project using all 10 years of cash inflows. Should management accept the project based on NPV?

b. Calculate the payback period of the project. Should management accept the project based on payback period?

c. What do you think of management's payback policy? Present your reasoning.

Scenario analysis, NPV, IRR, PI, and payback period

10.15. Sally Fowler believes that, if everything goes exceptionally well, a proposed project she is evaluating will cost $1,000,000 and produce $350,000 per year for 10 years, all after taxes. Ms. Fowler also knows about Murphy's Law: "If anything can go wrong, it will." She begins to think about the downside possibilities of the project. She believes the following is the worst the project will do:

> Worst-case cost = $1,300,000
> Worst-case cash inflow = $255,000 per year
> Worst-case expected life = 7 years

Reflecting further on the project, she concludes that most likely the project will cost $1,100,000 and produce $300,000 per year for 8 years. The required rate of return on the project is 17 percent per year.

a. Calculate the following for the project under the three scenarios envisioned by Ms. Fowler: net present value, internal rate of return, profitability index, and payback period.

b. Based on your judgment, should Ms. Fowler recommend investing in the project?

c. If you could ask her questions about the project, what would be your line of inquiry?

Computer Problems 🖫

Scenario analysis: template SCENARIO

10.16. McCormicks is planning a second fast-food restaurant in Norman City. The company paid $20,000 to McCammon Associates for the market survey and site selection. The consultants estimated that the company's sales over the 6-year life of the project would be $1,700,000 in the first year with a 5 percent annual increase thereafter, assuming an average economy.

The expected investment in depreciable assets is $500,000. The assets have a class life of 5 years. The land and building would be rented at $5,000 per month. Other fixed cash costs would be $500,000 per year, and variable costs would be 40 percent of sales. Net working capital of 60 percent of monthly sales would be required. Investment in net working capital is required at the beginning of the year. Due to the presence of the second restaurant, the loss of sales at the existing restaurant would be 20 percent of sales of the second restaurant.

In a recession sales growth would be zero, whereas in an economic boom sales would increase 10 percent annually. The probability of a recession is 10 percent, the probability of an average economy is 60 percent, and the probability of a boom economy is 30 percent. In a boom economy the assets have a disposal value of $200,000, in an average economy they have a disposal value of $100,000, and in a recession salvage value is zero. McCormicks's marginal cost of capital is 15 percent, and its marginal tax rate is 34 percent.

a. Calculate the initial investment, and explain why you exclude the $20,000 to McCammon Associates.

b. Calculate the net present value in a recession, in an average economy, and in a boom economy. Also calculate the expected NPV.

c. Based on the scenario analysis in Part *b*, should McCormicks invest in the second restaurant?

d. McCormicks has a policy of adding two percentage points to the cost of capital for risky projects. Using this criterion, would the project be accepted?

Sensitivity analysis: template
SENSITIV

10.17. General Sales Inc. is evaluating an offer from Williard Batteries to take on its franchise for selling automotive batteries in Kansas City. Total market demand is expected to be 200,000 batteries next year, increasing at the rate of 2 percent each year thereafter. The average price of a battery is $50. The gross margin is expected to be 30 percent. General Sales expects to attain a market share of 5 percent of total market demand in the first year, 10 percent in the second year, and 15 percent from the third year on. The investment is expected to be $100,000 in inventory and $30,000 in accounts receivable. Accounts payable will be $60,000. Depreciable assets worth $20,000 with a class life of 5 years will be required. The assets have a 6-year economic life and no salvage value. Selling and administrative expenses will be $300,000 per year. The company is in the 34 percent tax bracket, and its marginal cost of capital is 20 percent.

a. Calculate the net present value of the project.

b. Recalculate Part *a* under the following independent conditions taken one at a time:

(1) Market share from the third year on is 10 percent, 12.5 percent, 17.5 percent, and 20 percent.

(2) Gross margin is 20 percent, 25 percent, 35 percent, and 40 percent.

(3) Selling and administrative expenses per year are $200,000, $250,000, $350,000, and $400,000.

(4) Initial investment is $60,000, $75,000, $105,000, and $120,000.

c. Which variable or variables should General Sales concentrate on estimating most accurately before accepting the franchise? Explain your choice(s).

Risk analysis in capital
budgeting: template
CAPBRISK

10.18. Schofield Industries is evaluating the feasibility of five projects. The probability distributions of net present values using a 15 percent discount rate for the projects are as follows:

	Net Present Value ($)				
Probability	**A**	**B**	**C**	**D**	**E**
0.05	10,000	80,000	(10,000)	80,000	(180,000)
0.15	50,000	100,000	60,000	85,000	(50,000)
0.30	100,000	120,000	115,000	90,000	130,000
0.30	110,000	150,000	150,000	95,000	140,000
0.15	160,000	170,000	200,000	100,000	250,000
0.05	200,000	190,000	280,000	105,000	370,000

a. Calculate the expected NPV for each project and rank the projects.

b. Calculate the standard deviation and coefficient of variation of the NPV of each project. Average-risk projects have a coefficient of variation of 0.5. Based on your judgment, assign each project to one of the following risk classes: low, average, moderately high, and high.

c. The expected internal rates of return on each project are as follows:

Project A	20%
Project B	22
Project C	25
Project D	18
Project E	27

Acceptable internal rates of return are:

Low-risk projects	15%
Average-risk projects	20
Moderately high-risk projects	25
High-risk projects	30

Which project(s) should Schofield accept? Explain your choice(s).

Case Problem

Menego Company

The Menego Company manufactures toys and trinkets with short economic lives. The research and development department has come up with an item that would make a good promotional gift for office equipment dealers. Aggressive and effective effort by Menego's sales personnel has resulted in almost firm commitments for the product for the next three years. Management expects that the product's value will be exhausted by that time.

Investment Information. In order to produce the quantity demanded, Menego will need to buy additional machinery and rent additional factory space. It appears that about 25,000 square feet will be needed; Menego now has 12,500 square feet of unused space it is leasing from AmeriLease Corporation. The present lease with 10 years to run costs $3 per square foot annually. Menego's management anticipates no other use of the space in the foreseeable future. Another 12,500 square feet in an adjoining building can be rented for 3 years at $4 per square foot annually. No incremental cash outflows for general overhead costs will be incurred, but the home office will charge the project for general overhead.

Management will purchase the equipment for $900,000 and must spend an additional $180,000 to deliver and set up the equipment. All of the expenditures will be made on January 1, 19X3, and they are depreciable for tax purposes. A 6 percent investment tax credit is available. The company uses straight-line depreciation and a $100,000 salvage value for financial reporting purposes. For tax purposes it uses a 3-year class life and straight-line depreciation with the half-year convention applied to the entire $1,080,000 outlay. The financial manager expects that the equipment can be sold for $120,000 in 3 years—the end of the project's estimated life.

In addition to the capital expenditures required for the project, management must also provide for net working capital. Additional net working capital will be $160,000 at the beginning of the project and will remain level throughout the project's life. The company will recover the net working capital at the end of the project's life.

The company's accountant has prepared the accompanying *pro forma* operating statements for the project based on generally accepted accounting principles. The statements include straight-line depreciation for financial reporting purposes.

The capital-budgeting committee assigned an analyst the task of estimating the project's beta. He had already estimated the beta of Menego's assets using a weighted average of its stock and bond betas. He believed that the proposed project's beta was greater than that of the average or typical asset that the company already owned. To estimate the proposed project's beta, he decided to use the pure-play procedure.

After identifying three companies engaged primarily in manufacturing promotional items, the analyst set about analyzing market data on their securities. Using various sources of information (including *Value Line*), he estimated stock and bond betas, which in turn he used to estimate the average beta of each company's assets. The resulting betas are:

Company	Beta
A	1.45
B	1.56
C	1.62

The company's investment guidelines call for a 46 percent ordinary tax rate (includes state and local taxes) in evaluating proposed projects.

Pro Forma Financial Statements

	19X3	19X4	19X5
Sales	$1,000,000	$1,600,000	$870,000
Less costs			
Variable material and labor	$ 400,000	$ 750,000	$350,000
Assigned general overhead (home office)	40,000	75,000	35,000
Rent ($37,500 + $50,000)	87,500	87,500	87,500
Depreciation	326,667	326,667	326,667
Total operating costs	$ 854,167	$1,239,167	$799,167
Earnings before taxes	145,833	360,833	70,833
Income taxes	67,083	165,983	32,583
Earnings after taxes	$ 78,750	$ 194,850	$ 38,250

Financing Information.   The financial manager of Menego meets with the company's accountants, financial consultants, and bankers to collect relevant financial information. She determines from this meeting that Menego's book-value capital structure is as follows:

Bonds (8 percent coupon, $1,000 par, mature in 20 years)		$20,000,000
Shareholder equity		
Common stock (400,000 shares)	$16,000,000	
Retained earnings	12,000,000	
Total shareholder equity		28,000,000
Total capital		$48,000,000

Additional items of information regarding the costs of individual capital sources and conditions in the financial markets are:

- Menego can issue mortgage bonds to yield investors 9 percent. Placement costs on the bonds will increase the cost to Menego to $9\frac{1}{4}$ percent. The company's outstanding bonds pay interest annually and trade at $909 to yield bondholders a 9 percent annual return.

- Menego's common stock has been trading around $100 per share. Menego pays out 50 percent of its earnings after taxes as dividends, and the company's directors intend to continue this policy through the foreseeable future. The stock's price-earnings multiple has remained fairly constant and probably won't change in the near future. Dividends and earnings per share have grown approximately 5 percent annually over the preceding 5 years.

- The most recent annual dividend was $12 per share.

- If the company issues new common stock, the company will net $94 per share after all costs.

- The company's common stock is trading at a 1.43 multiple of its book value.

- The annualized yield on U.S. Treasury securities is 8 percent, and the company's financial consultant expects the rate of return on broad market portfolios to average 14 percent annually over the next 4 years.

a. Calculate the cost of internal equity and the cost of new common stock for Menego.

b. Calculate Menego's marginal cost of capital with debt and new common stock, using market weights for each component. (Use the information above to calculate the market value of outstanding securities.)

c. Calculate the net investment cash outflow for the equipment and net working capital.

d. Prepare *pro forma* operating statements that include only incremental amounts. Be sure to use the appropriate depreciation and ignore the assigned general overhead and the lease payments for which the company is already committed.

e. Prepare a schedule showing the project's annual, incremental, after-tax cash flows. Explain why you do not include in your calculations the assigned general overhead and the cost of the presently unused but leased space.

f. If Menego requires a 2-year payback period for its investment, should it undertake the project? Show your supporting calculations.

g. The financial manager of Menego wants to evaluate the project using net present value. Assume that all operating revenues and expenses occur at the end of each year.

  (1) Calculate the risk-adjusted net present value of the project based on the company's marginal cost of capital. Round the MCC to its nearest whole percentage point for the calculation.

  (2) Calculate the risk-adjusted NPV of the project using a discount rate calculated with the capital asset pricing model. Round the discount rate to its nearest whole percentage point for the calculation.

  (3) Should the capital-budgeting committee accept the proposed project? Explain your answer based on what you believe will happen to the price of Menego's stock if the committee accepts the project.

h. Barry Menego has recently earned his BBA. In a finance course that he took, the professor suggested that sensitivity analysis is a useful capital-budgeting tool. Explain what sensitivity analysis is and how it might be helpful in evaluating this project.

Selected References

Ang, James S., and Wilbur G. Lewellen. "Risk Adjustment in Capital Investment Project Evaluations." *Financial Management,* Summer 1982: 5–14.

Bower, Richard S., and Jeffrey M. Jenks. "Divisional Screening Rates." *Financial Management,* Autumn 1975: 42–49.

Cooley, Philip L., and Rodney L. Roenfeldt. "Ranking Investments by Risk and Return." *Atlanta Economic Review,* July–August 1977: 13–18.

Denis, David J. "Corporate Investment Decisions and Corporate Control: Evidence from Going-Private Transactions." *Financial Management,* Autumn 1992: 80–94.

Gallagher, Timothy J. "A Pedagogical Note on Risk Aversion." *Journal of Financial Education,* Fall 1982: 40–46.

Gup, Benton, and Samuel E. Norwood III. "Divisional Cost of Capital: A Practical Approach." *Financial Management,* Spring 1982: 20–24.

Harrington, Diana R. "Stock Prices, Beta, and Strategic Planning." *Harvard Business Review,* May–June 1983: 157–164.

Harris, Robert S., Thomas J. O'Brien, and Doug Wakeman. "Divisional Cost-of-Capital Estimation for Multi-Industry Firms." *Financial Management,* Summer 1989: 74–84.

Henderson, Glenn V., Jr., and Stephen E. Skomp. "Geometric Exposition of CAPM-Based Capital Budgeting." *Journal of Financial Education,* Fall 1983: 1–16.

Weaver, Samuel C. "Capital Budgeting." *Financial Management,* Spring 1989: 10–17.

Weston, J. Fred. "Investment Decisions Using the Capital Asset Pricing Model." *Financial Management,* Spring 1973: 25–33.

MANAGING WORKING CAPITAL

Part IV

SMALL-BUSINESS PERSPECTIVE

Working-Capital Problems in a Small Company

Because Kathy Griffin and Jim Sutherland were unsure about purchasing a delivery van for their exercise equipment outlet, they decided to ask a friend, Susan Bethel, for financial advice. Susan, a finance major at a local university, was happy to help her friends determine the best course of action. After Susan had shown them the net present value of the project, Kathy and Jim decided to purchase the van.

In Shape Inc. continued to grow and prosper for the next several years. Kathy's sales to area residents increased rapidly, and Jim's sales calls to hotels and resorts added new commercial customers. Kathy projected that sales would reach $600,000 by the fifth year of operation.

Excellent customer service continued to be the hallmark of the company. Customer opinions and suggestions were often solicited and were frequently implemented. If Kathy and Jim were asked by customers to carry a new line of accessories such as sweatbands or jogging shorts, they would contact a supplier and order a small quantity of the product to see if it would sell. The increasing volume of equipment sales and the addition of accessories resulted in higher inventory levels. The original inventory of $80,000 had gradually increased to $200,000 over 5 years.

Equipment inventory was often ordered in large quantities for two reasons. First, the suppliers usually offered quantity discounts. For example, if 10 treadmills were purchased, they would cost $2,000 each, but if 5 treadmills were purchased, they would cost $2,300 each. Second, freight costs were high because of the weight of the equipment. Freight costs could be reduced by making one shipment of 10 treadmills instead of two shipments of 5 each.

Purchases by area residents were paid for by cash or credit card, but hotels and resorts were given 30 days credit on all purchases. (This was typical for the industry and not unique to In Shape.) A credit check was run on each new customer. Based on the information obtained in the credit check, Kathy would establish the credit limit and notify the customer of the amount. Although In Shape incurred some bad debts, the total amount was very low compared with its sales volume. Since In Shape offered no discounts for early payment, receivables were never paid earlier than 30 days after purchase.

The company's rapid growth resulted in a corresponding increase in accounts receivable. Combined with the inventory expansion, this led to a chronic shortage of cash. Although the company was profitable, Kathy often found it difficult to pay the bills on time. One of the most frustrating consequences of the cash shortage was not being able to take advantage of the standard 2 percent discount most of the company's suppliers offered for early payment. In Shape could pay all of its bills only if payables were stretched to roughly 45 days. Kathy was concerned about this situation for two reasons. First, she knew that the lost discounts were substantial, although she had never calculated how much more the equipment cost due to lost discounts. Second, she was concerned that In Shape's credit rating might suffer if the stretching of payables continued.

This part of the text describes working-capital management, methods to improve cash flow, managing accounts receivable and inventory, and sources of short-term funds. The focus is the management of current assets and current liabilities.

Chapter 11

OVERVIEW OF WORKING-CAPITAL MANAGEMENT

More Than Just Soup

The treasury department of Campbell Soup manages more than $5 billion of cash flow annually for the company and its subsidiaries, including Pepperidge Farm, Vlasic Foods, and Godiva Chocolatier. Because it is highly automated, the department has only seven staff members. Housed at Campbell's corporate headquarters in Camden, New Jersey, the department is responsible for short-term investing, short-term borrowing, cash-flow management, banking relations, and commercial paper. Accounts payable and payroll are decentralized and managed at the plant level.

Through efficient operations and constant planning sessions with bankers, the treasury department reduced annual banking fees for cash management services by $3 million in five years. A key component of the department's mission is "to develop systems and strategies that ensure the most effective utilization, control, and security of our cash resources."

James D. Moss, director of treasury operations, states:

"We're no longer concerned with just cash, float, and bank fees. Today's treasury management team must work with all organizations within the company that affect *working capital* or that have information the team can use to better manage that capital."

The changes in its goals are illustrative of how the treasury department has evolved. In the 1980s, its goals included: Do a lockbox study; do a disbursement study; consolidate banks; reduce banking fees. In the 1990s, its goals included: Partic-ipate in a company task force to reduce working capital; use an electronic data interchange to pay certain vendors; work with sales personnel to evaluate the effect on sales of offering additional discounts for receiving electronic payments. The changing goals at Campbell Soup's treasury department increasingly focus on working capital and not just cash.

Source: James D. Moss, "Campbell Soup Company Cutting-Edge Cash Management," *Financial Executive,* September/October 1992, 39–42.

Working-capital management is the management of all components of a company's current assets and current liabilities. These managerial activities consume a large part of a financial manager's time because of continual changes in the components: Accounts receivable and inventory expand and contract with sales, payables rise and fall with purchases, and managers use cash to pay taxes and other bills. Managers need to monitor each of these and other current accounts to avoid financial difficulties that could discredit the company.

This chapter describes the principles of working-capital management and presents the statement of cash flows, a statement showing the change in a company's cash balance due to operating, investing, and financing activities. The statement of cash flows accompanies the balance sheet and income statement in a company's annual report to shareholders. Perspectives provided in this chapter form the foundation for the next three chapters on cash management, receivables and inventory management, and the management of current liabilities.

LIQUIDITY

The *liquidity* of an asset is the ease with which it can be converted into cash at the prevailing market value without large transaction costs. Assets possess different degrees of liquidity, some being easily and quickly converted into cash and others not. Because of its use as a medium of exchange, cash is the most liquid of all assets. Real estate is relatively illiquid because its conversion into cash usually takes a long time and creates large transaction costs and because it may have to be sold below market value. In contrast, Treasury bills are highly liquid because they can be sold quickly at or near market value for a small fee.

Company Liquidity

A company that is liquid has the ability to meet its short-term, maturing obligations; that is, it can pay its bills. A large investment in liquid assets (cash, T-bills, and other money market securities) relative to the need for cash increases a company's liquidity. Not all companies, however, need the same level of liquid investments to maintain company liquidity. For example, typical of the fast-food industry, McDonald's and Wendy's have relatively small investments in liquid assets. The rapid cash flows from product sales lessen the need for these companies to hold large amounts of liquid assets.

Like other managerial decisions, the decision to increase or decrease a company's liquid assets requires the financial manager to weigh benefits against costs. Liquid assets increase the likelihood of the company's being able to take advantage of business opportunities, such as taking cash discounts offered by suppliers for prompt payment. In addition, they reduce the company's risk of becoming *illiquid*—being unable to repay its maturing debts. Running counter to these benefits are the costs of holding liquid assets. For example, holding cash causes the company to incur an opportunity cost—the missed opportunity to invest the cash elsewhere to earn a return. Holding inventory for sale creates an opportunity cost and out-of-pocket costs as well: storage fees, insurance, taxes, spoilage, pilferage, and obsolescence.

Liquidity and Expected Profitability

The costs and benefits of holding liquid assets result in a trade-off between a company's liquidity and its expected profitability. As Figure 11.1 illustrates, an increase in liquidity causes a decrease in expected profitability, whereas a

FIGURE 11.1

Trade-off between Liquidity and Expected Profitability

An increase in liquidity, measured on the horizontal axis, causes a decline in expected profitability. A decrease in liquidity causes an increase in expected profitability. (The precise shape of the curve depends on company circumstances. Also, extremely low liquidity may cause expected profitability to decline.)

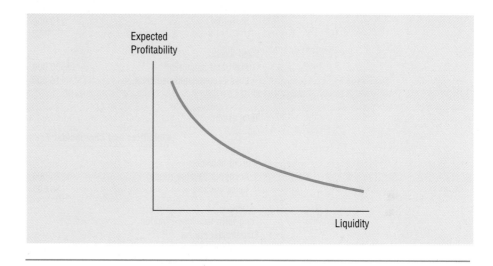

decrease in liquidity causes an increase in expected profitability. As a general rule, assets with high liquidity have a low expected return and those with low liquidity have a high expected return. For example, holding cash offers the company maximum liquidity but no return. Machinery employed in production or an expansion of retail floor space offer little liquidity, but they offer high expected profitability.

The trade-off between liquidity and expected profitability is sometimes called the "eat-well, sleep-well trade-off": A manager choosing a low liquidity level in an attempt to raise profitability has high expectations of eating well but may spend some sleepless nights worrying about impending cash shortages. Alternatively, another manager may choose a high degree of liquidity by maintaining large cash balances and investments in Treasury bills. In this case the manager sleeps well but may not enjoy the high salary and large bonuses that come from improved profitability.

A company's balance sheet (statement of financial position) can be interpreted as a trade-off between liquidity and expected profitability. Table 11.1 presents the balance sheet for Oakmont Marketing Company. Note that the assets are listed according to decreasing liquidity and increasing expected profitability. Liabilities and shareholder equity (claims against assets) also reflect a trade-off between liquidity and expected profitability. Moving down this portion of the statement, note that liquidity increases in two ways: (1) Long-term liabilities need not be repaid until some time in the distant future, whereas the company must pay current liabilities (or replace them with new current liabilities) within 12 months, and (2) shareholder equity has no default risk. Using long-term debt and equity increases liquidity by reducing near-term cash needs, whereas using short-term debt has the opposite effect.

In contrast to the increasing liquidity, expected profitability decreases moving downward on the claims portion of the balance sheet. The cost of long-term

TABLE 11.1

Oakmont Marketing Company: Balance Sheet, December 31, 19X1[a]

Assets

Current assets		
Cash	$280,000	
Accounts receivable	340,000	
Inventory	210,000	
		$ 830,000
Fixed assets		
Plant and equipment	$500,000	
Less accumulated depreciation	(110,000)	
		390,000
Total assets		$1,220,000

Liabilities and Shareholder Equity

Current liabilities		
Accounts payable (trade)	$220,000	
Taxes payable	80,000	
		$ 300,000
Long-term liabilities—bonds		432,000
Shareholder equity		
Common stock	$280,000	
Paid-in capital in excess of par	40,000	
Retained earnings	168,000	
		488,000
Total claims		$1,220,000

[a] The arrow by assets indicates decreasing liquidity and increasing expected profitability. The arrow by liabilities and shareholder equity indicates increasing liquidity and decreasing expected profitability.

borrowing usually exceeds that of short-term borrowing, as shown by the normally upward-sloping yield curve (see Chapter 2). Furthermore, companies normally do not pay interest on money owed suppliers (accounts payable), taxes payable, and certain other current liabilities. Using long-term sources of capital therefore increases liquidity but decreases expected profitability.

WORKING-CAPITAL POLICY

The trade-off between liquidity and expected profitability sets up a dilemma for the financial manager. The aggressive financial manager, seeking added profitability, attempts to operate with a minimum of *working capital,* defined as *current assets.* The conservative financial manager, willing to sacrifice some profitability, chooses to operate with a maximum of working capital to reduce the risk of being unable to meet the company's short-term obligations, such as its payroll and bank loan repayments.

working-capital policy
Company policy regarding the management of current assets and current liabilities.

conservative working-capital policy
Policy that emphasizes liquidity over profitability.

Working-capital policy consists of a set of rules describing the way a company deals with the dilemma arising from the trade-off between liquidity and expected profitability. Consider first a **conservative working-capital policy,** which emphasizes liquidity at the expense of profitability. In this case the company's investment in current assets will be large in comparison with its current liabilities.

current ratio
Investment in current assets per dollar of current liabilities; measure of a company's liquidity.

The **current ratio** measures the company's liquidity by indicating the investment in current assets per dollar of current liabilities:

$$\text{Current ratio} = \frac{\text{Current assets}}{\text{Current liabilities}}$$

A large current ratio means that the company has the potential to pay current liabilities by liquidating its current assets. In other words, a large current ratio reflects a conservative working-capital policy and a highly liquid company.[1]

EXAMPLE

Calculate and interpret the current ratio of Oakmont Marketing Company in Table 11.1:

$$\text{Current ratio} = \frac{\$830,000}{\$300,000}$$

$$= 2.77$$

Oakmont has $2.77 in current assets for each $1 of current liabilities. Based on balance sheet totals, Oakmont's financial manager could liquidate the company's current assets and comfortably pay the liabilities maturing within 12 months.

net working capital
Current assets minus current liabilities; dollar amount of current assets financed with long-term debt and equity.

A large current ratio implies that a company has a large **net working capital**—current assets minus current liabilities:

$$\text{Net working capital} = \text{Current assets} - \text{Current liabilities}$$

Net working capital for Oakmont Marketing Company in Table 11.1 is calculated as follows:

$$\text{Net working capital} = \$830,000 - \$300,000$$

$$= \$530,000$$

A large amount of net working capital indicates that current assets easily cover current liabilities.[2] When net working capital is positive, the current ratio is greater than 1.0.

Figure 11.2 graphically depicts net working capital and suggests an alternative definition for it: dollar amount of current assets financed with long-term debt and equity. Thinking of net working capital in this way reminds you that it is affected by the long-term items on the balance sheet—the long-term *sources* of financing (long-term debt and equity) and the long-term *uses* of financing (fixed assets):

$$\text{Net working capital} = (\text{LTD} + \text{Equity}) - \text{Fixed assets}$$

---

[1] A small number of financial ratios are presented in this chapter and the following three chapters. Seeing selected financial ratios in the context of working-capital management makes it easier to understand them. Be sure to learn the definition, calculation, and interpretation of these ratios, because you will use them in Chapter 15 to analyze financial statements. Becoming familiar now with a few financial ratios will lessen the task in Chapter 15, which presents several more ratios.

[2] Some financial managers use the terms *working capital* and *net working capital* interchangeably. To lessen confusion in this book, we clarify the use of each term as follows: *Working capital* is current assets. *Net working capital* is current assets minus current liabilities.

FIGURE 11.2   **Graphic Portrayal of Net Working Capital**

Net working capital is current assets minus current liabilities. Alternatively, net working capital can be viewed as the portion of current assets financed with long-term debt and equity.

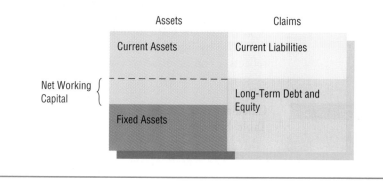

where LTD is long-term debt. Applying the equation to Oakmont Marketing Company yields $530,000 (as previously calculated):

$$\text{Net working capital} = (\$432,\!000 + \$488,\!000) - \$390,\!000$$
$$= \$530,\!000$$

Oakmont has used $920,000 ($432,000 + $488,000) of long-term financing to invest $530,000 in net working capital and $390,000 in fixed assets.

The liquidity measures for Oakmont Marketing Company reflect a conservative working-capital policy. Figure 11.3 graphically portrays a conservative working-capital policy wherein current assets amply cover current liabilities, indicating a high degree of liquidity. Net working capital is positive, suggesting that the company can comfortably meet its current liabilities with its current assets. Potential profitability declines, however, because the large investment in current assets is partially financed with long-term sources of capital. In other words, expensive long-term financing is supporting current assets when it could be employed more profitably in long-term investments.

aggressive working-capital policy
Policy that emphasizes profitability over liquidity.

In contrast to the conservative policy, an **aggressive working-capital policy** emphasizes profitability at the expense of liquidity. Figure 11.3 shows that an aggressive policy results in a small current ratio and a small net working capital. Although liquidity is low under an aggressive policy, the potential for superior profitability is high.

Figure 11.4 draws another distinction between aggressive and conservative working-capital policies: At each sales level the aggressive policy calls for a smaller investment in current assets than does the conservative policy.[3] Thus the company with an aggressive policy works its current assets harder than the company with a conservative policy. The extent to which a company works its cur-

---

[3] Figure 11.4 shows current assets rising at a decreasing rate with increases in sales revenues. Although current assets must be increased to support higher sales levels, they need not be increased proportionately to sales levels. Most companies experience economies in current assets as company sales grow. For example, a doubling of sales normally does not require a doubling of inventory; customer service will continue unabated with less than a doubling of inventory.

FIGURE 11.3

Conservative and Aggressive Working-Capital Policies: Effect on the Current Ratio and Net Working Capital

A conservative working-capital policy produces a large amount of current assets relative to current liabilities and results in a large current ratio and a large net working capital. An aggressive policy produces a small amount of current assets relative to current liabilities and results in a small current ratio and a small net working capital.

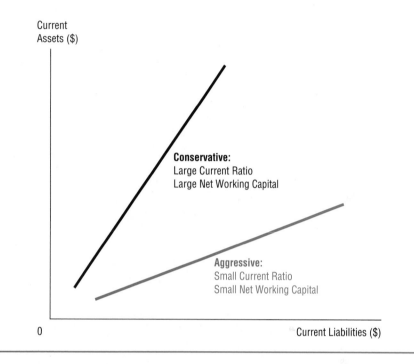

current asset turnover
Sales per dollar of current assets.

rent assets is measured by the **current asset turnover,** the ratio of its sales to current assets:[4]

$$\text{Current asset turnover} = \frac{\text{Sales}}{\text{Current assets}}$$

EXAMPLE

If Oakmont Marketing Company's sales are $6,100,000, what is the company's current asset turnover?

$$\text{Current asset turnover} = \frac{\$6,100,000}{\$830,000}$$

$$= 7.35$$

Oakmont Marketing generates $7.35 in sales for each $1 of current assets.

---

[4]In finance, *turnover* commonly refers to a ratio with sales revenue in the numerator and a balance sheet item in the denominator. Chapter 15 presents additional asset turnovers: fixed asset turnover and total asset turnover, among others.

FIGURE 11.4

Conservative and Aggressive Working-Capital Policies:
Effect on Current Asset Turnover (Sales/Current Assets)

A conservative working-capital policy produces a large amount of current assets relative to sales, resulting in a small current asset turnover. An aggressive policy produces a small amount of current assets relative to sales, resulting in a large current asset turnover.

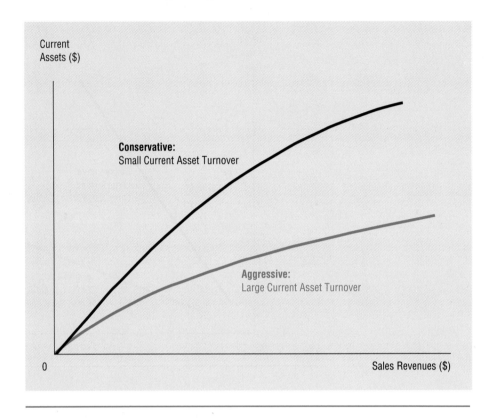

The current asset turnover shows sales revenue over a period of time per dollar of current assets. A company employing the aggressive policy seeks to obtain "more bang for the buck"—that is, more sales revenue generated for each dollar invested in current assets and thus a higher current asset turnover. An aggressive policy carries with it a lower liquidity level and a higher risk.

Table 11.2 shows the financial implications of conservative and aggressive working-capital policies for Oakmont Marketing Company. Balance sheet information for Oakmont's conservative policy comes from Table 11.1, and we add expected sales revenues and earnings after taxes. The table shows that Oakmont's aggressive working-capital policy takes the following form: (1) Reduce current assets from $830,000 to $530,000, using the $300,000 of released funds to retire $300,000 of the long-term debt, and (2) increase current liabilities from $300,000 to $432,000 through bank borrowings, using the additional $132,000 to retire the rest of the long-term debt.

Expected sales revenues decline from $6,100,000 to $5,900,000 because of the reduction in current assets, especially the following: (1) A reduction in inventory causes Oakmont to miss some sales because of stockouts, and (2) management's increased stringency in granting trade credit to customers not only reduces

TABLE 11.2	**Oakmont Marketing Company: Effects of Conservative and Aggressive Working-Capital Policies**		
		Conservative Policy (Table 11.1)	**Aggressive Policy**
	Assets		
	Current assets	$ 830,000	$ 530,000
	Net fixed assets	390,000	390,000
	Total assets	$1,220,000	$ 920,000
	Liabilities and Equity		
	Current liabilities	$ 300,000	$ 432,000
	Long-term debt	432,000	0
	Shareholder equity	488,000	488,000
	Total liabilities and equity	$1,220,000	$ 920,000
	Income Statement		
	Expected sales revenues	$6,100,000	$5,900,000
	Expected earnings after taxes	$ 122,000	$ 144,200
	Expected Performance Measures[a]		
	Current ratio	2.8	1.2
	Net working capital	$530,000	$98,000
	Current asset turnover	7.3	11.1
	Return on total assets	10.0%	15.7%

[a]Performance measures: Current ratio = Current assets/Current liabilities
Net working capital = Current assets − Current liabilities
Current asset turnover = Sales/Current assets
Return on total assets = Earnings after taxes/Total assets

accounts receivable but also causes lost sales to competitors. Despite the lost sales, expected earnings after taxes increase from $122,000 to $144,200, because of the interest savings on long-term debt, the reduced bad-debt expense from granting credit, and the reduced storage costs for inventory.

The balance sheet accounts in Table 11.2 show what happens to liquidity under the aggressive alternative. If Oakmont's management decides to institute the aggressive policy, then the company's liquidity level declines. The current ratio falls from 2.8 to 1.2, indicating that the company will no longer have $2.80 in current assets for each $1.00 of current liabilities; it will now have only $1.20. Net working capital with the aggressive policy falls to $98,000, about one-fifth of its former level ($530,000) with the conservative policy. Although greatly lowered, the new liquidity level of the company permits it to continue operations.

The aggressive policy causes decreases in both current assets and expected sales. Current asset turnover increases, however, from 7.3 to 11.1. Under the aggressive policy, management is able to generate $11.10 in sales for each $1.00 invested in current assets. In addition, the aggressive policy increases the company's expected return on assets from 10 percent to 15.7 percent, a sizable increase in profitability. **Return on assets** is earnings after taxes per dollar of total assets:

return on assets (ROA)
Earnings after taxes per dollar of total assets; measure of a company's profitability.

$$\frac{\text{Return on}}{\text{assets (ROA)}} = \frac{\text{Earnings after taxes}}{\text{Total assets}}$$

Conservative   *Aggressive*

$$\text{ROA} = \frac{\$122,000}{\$1,220,000} \qquad \text{ROA} = \frac{\$144,200}{\$920,000}$$

$$= 0.10, \text{ or } 10\% \qquad = 0.157, \text{ or } 15.7\%$$

Oakmont is expected to generate $0.157 in earnings per $1 of assets if it implements the aggressive working-capital policy.

Observe from the Oakmont Marketing Company example that a reduction in liquidity can lead to increased expected profitability. Whether or not management should implement the aggressive policy, however, depends on whether doing so would increase the price of Oakmont's common stock. The financial manager's task is to balance the company's liquidity needs against the pursuit of higher profitability. Industry averages for the performance measures shown in Table 11.2 would provide useful guidelines for the decision. The financial manager should also consider the timing of company cash inflows and outflows, sales variability, financial leverage, and other operating factors when setting working-capital policy. One of those factors is the matching principle, described in the following section.

THE MATCHING PRINCIPLE OF WORKING-CAPITAL MANAGEMENT

matching principle
Matching the maturity of
capital sources with the
maturity of their uses.

The **matching principle** advises management to match the maturity of capital sources with the maturity of their uses. In other words, use short-term sources of capital for short-term uses and long-term sources of capital for long-term uses. The following example shows what happens when management violates the matching principle.

EXAMPLE

Erika Holbert plans to acquire for $1,000,000 an apartment complex consisting of 50 units. By converting and selling the units as condominiums, Ms. Holbert estimates the project will produce $350,000 each year for 5 years. Consider what happens if Ms. Holbert's down payment is $100,000 and she borrows $900,000 for *one year* at 12 percent. At year-end she must repay $1,008,000 (1.12 × $900,000), but the project produces only $350,000 for the year. The project generates sufficient cash flow to repay the $900,000 loan over 5 years but not over 1 year. It would be imprudent of Ms. Holbert to use a 1-year loan to finance the 5-year project because she would need to refinance the project in the face of uncertain future interest rates. Moreover, she might be unable to obtain financing at the end of the year.

Now consider her position if she follows the matching principle and borrows the $900,000 for 5 years, the life of the project. If she pays 13 percent annually, her annual payment is $255,883 for 5 years. The project's annual cash inflow of $350,000 would easily cover the annual payment. Following the matching principle, Ms. Holbert has sufficient annual cash flow to maintain liquidity and to make a profit.

permanent current assets
Base level of current assets over an operating cycle.

temporary current assets
Part of current assets that changes with seasonal demand.

To apply the matching principle requires an understanding of the distinction between permanent and temporary current assets. **Permanent current assets** form a base level of total current assets that does not change from season to season. **Temporary current assets,** by contrast, are the part of total current assets that change with seasonal demand. A seasonal increase in the level of inventory, cash, or receivables is a temporary current asset because the company soon eliminates the increase. For example, a florist's increase in roses preceding Valentine's Day is a seasonal component of inventory because the increase will soon be eliminated as the florist sells roses to people in love. The minimum investment in current assets across seasons is the shop's permanent current assets. The minimum number of roses the florist maintains throughout the year is the permanent level of its inventory of roses.

Although current assets are short-lived and liquid, their level never falls to zero. The florist in the example above keeps some roses on hand to satisfy the occasional customer. Even at the lowest point of the sales year or operating cycle, a company needs some minimum level of inventory and receivables. Moreover, no company can afford to run completely out of cash. Thus at the lowest point of any company's activity an irreducible minimum of current assets remains in the business. And because it remains, management should finance it with long-term debt and equity sources just as management should finance the company's fixed assets, following the matching principle.

On the other hand, a substantial part of a company's current assets is temporary. Inventories and receivables have large bulges at seasonal peaks and during business booms. A toy retailer's inventory around Christmas surges upward but then shrinks back at seasonal low points. Following the matching principle, this changing component of current assets should be financed with short-term sources because the need for financing is temporary.

Using short-term sources to finance short-term needs has two advantages:

- Short-term sources of funds are generally less costly than long-term sources.
- Short-term sources of funds allow management to tailor loan sizes to changing needs. Loans increase during periods of peak needs and contract during the low points as the company repays. Management thus avoids investing in excess working capital.

Figure 11.5 illustrates the matching principle operating over time. It shows a company's fixed assets growing in stair-step fashion, and its permanent current assets increasing steadily as sales grow. The matching principle advises the financial manager to finance both fixed and permanent current assets with long-term debt and equity. The wavy line above permanent current assets shows the company's changing temporary needs for current assets. Because these needs occasionally fall to zero, the matching principle advises that they should be financed with temporary sources, current liabilities.

Some financial managers choose to violate the matching principle. Aggressively seeking to increase profitability, they may use more short-term debt than called for by the matching principle. The upper panel of Figure 11.6 illustrates the aggressive policy of using current liabilities to support not only temporary current assets but also part of the permanent current assets as well. Accompanying this policy is a **refinancing risk,** the possibility of not being able to refinance (roll over) the short-term debt when it matures. Even though the company may be able to roll over the short-term debt, the financial manager may be disapppointed to discover an increase in interest rates.

refinancing risk
Possibility of not being able to refinance short-term debt when it matures; or the possibility of higher interest rates upon refinancing.

FIGURE 11.5

The Matching Principle Operating over Time

The matching principle states that a company should finance its fixed assets and permanent current assets with long-term debt and equity. It should finance its temporary current assets with current liabilities.

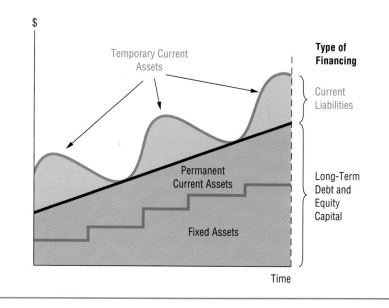

Conservative managers choose to use more long-term debt and equity and less short-term financing. Despite the generally higher cost of long-term sources, they do not have the refinancing risk of short-term sources. The lower panel of Figure 11.6 illustrates the conservative financing policy. As shown there, the conservative policy results in excess working capital during the low points of temporary current assets. Because of the excess working capital and the higher cost of long-term capital, the conservative policy lessens the company's expected profitability.

Managers choosing to violate the matching principle should be aware of the advantages and disadvantages of doing so. Selecting the aggressive policy requires special care because of the added risk incurred from short-term debt. The statement of cash flows, described in the following section, helps managers assess the risk by monitoring the company's cash flows.

STATEMENT OF CASH FLOWS

statement of cash flows
Statement detailing changes in cash during a past operating period.

A **statement of cash flows** details the historical changes in cash during an operating period. It appears along with the balance sheet and income statement in a company's annual report. The statement of cash flows presents an *overview* of activities that cause changes in a company's cash balance between two points in time. Instead of changes in cash only, the statement usually shows changes in cash and *cash equivalents*—money market securities with maturities of 90 days or less.

The statement classifies company activities into three categories:

- *Operating activities:* Producing and delivering goods and services. Includes earnings after taxes plus depreciation and cash flows from changes in current assets and current liabilities.

FIGURE 11.6

Aggressive and Conservative Financing Policies

The upper panel illustrates an aggressive working-capital policy wherein the financial manager uses current liabilities to finance not only temporary current assets but also a part of permanent current assets. The lower panel illustrates a conservative policy wherein the financial manager uses long-term debt and equity to finance not only fixed assets and permanent current assets but also a part of temporary current assets. The financial manager of the company illustrated in the upper panel expects to eat well; the financial manager in the lower panel expects to sleep well.

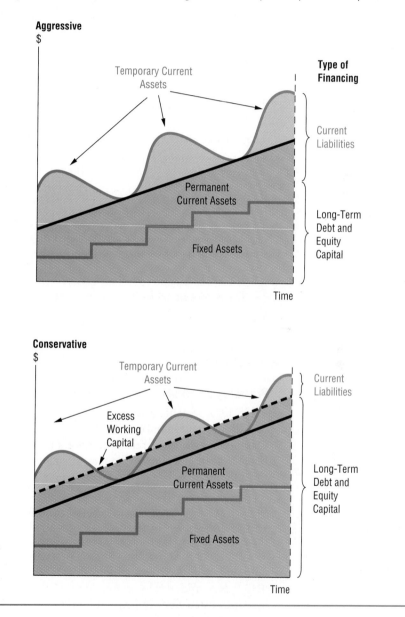

- *Investing activities:* Acquiring and selling fixed assets, lending money, receiving loan repayments, and acquiring and selling marketable securities other than cash equivalents.
- *Financing activities:* Obtaining cash from owners and creditors, paying dividends, repurchasing stock, and retiring debt.

In displaying the impact of these activities on cash, the statement of cash flows shows the financial manager whether cash is increasing or decreasing and the reasons for these changes.

Classifying Changes in Cash

Preparing a statement of cash flows over a year requires information from the beginning and ending balance sheets and the annual income statement. The following listings classify transactions as increases or decreases in cash:

Increases in Cash	Decreases in Cash
1. Earnings after taxes for the year	**1.** Net loss for year
2. Depreciation or other capital consumption allowance	**2.** Dividend payments
3. Sale of fixed assets	**3.** Purchase of fixed assets
4. New equity or long-term debt financing	**4.** Retirement or repurchase of stock or long-term debt
5. Collecting accounts receivable or charging purchases	**5.** Granting trade credit or paying off trade credit

The above lists can be summarized in an easy-to-use framework that emphasizes the impact of changes in balance sheet items on cash:

- *Increases in cash:* Increases in liabilities and decreases in assets.
- *Decreases in cash:* Increases in assets and decreases in liabilities.

This framework tells you to prepare a statement of cash flows by calculating the dollar change in each of the balance sheet items *other than cash.* Since the change in cash is what the statement explains, cash is the balancing item in the statement.

Preparing a Statement of Cash Flows

Table 11.3 presents a work sheet to help with the preparation of a statement of cash flows for Oakmont Marketing Company. It shows two columns added to Oakmont's two most recent balance sheets for recording the changes in selected balance sheet accounts. Changes in each account other than cash are entered in the columns according to the rule above for identifying increases and decreases. Consider, for example, the change in inventories. Inventories are an asset, and they increased $50,000. This change decreases cash. Now consider the change in taxes payable. Taxes payable are a liability, and they increased $30,000. This increase saved Oakmont $30,000 in cash.

Table 11.4 shows the final statement resulting from rearranging the cash amounts in the last two columns of Table 11.3. It includes Oakmont's earnings after taxes and depreciation, a noncash expense. The table shows operating activities listed first, followed by investing and financing activities. Consider the entries under the heading Operating Activities. Notice that there is no entry for the change in retained earnings ($192,000). It is customary to show earnings after taxes and dividends separately, rather than to show the net amount (change in retained earnings on the balance sheet is earnings after taxes less dividends). Table 11.4 follows the customary method: Oakmont had $202,000 in earnings after taxes and paid a $10,000 dividend—the dividend is a part of the company's

TABLE 11.3

Oakmont Marketing Company: Work Sheet for Preparing a Statement of Cash Flows (in Thousands of Dollars)

	19X1	19X2	Increases in Cash	Decreases in Cash
Assets				
Current assets				
Cash	$ 280	$ 230	Ignore cash for now	
Accounts receivable	340	380		$ 40
Inventories	210	260		50
Total current assets	$ 830	$ 870		
Plant and equipment	500	525		25
Less: Accumulated depreciation	(110)	(125)	$15	
Net fixed assets	$ 390	$ 400		
Total assets	$1,220	$1,270		
Liabilities and Shareholder Equity				
Current liabilities				
Accounts payable	$ 220	$ 220		
Taxes payable	80	110	30	
Total current liabilities	$ 300	$ 330		
Long-term liabilities—Bonds, 12 percent, due 19X3	432	240		192
Total liabilities	$ 732	$ 570		
Shareholder equity				
Common stock	280	290	10	
Paid-in capital in excess of par	40	50	10	
Retained earnings	168	360	192	
Total shareholder equity	$ 488	$ 700		
Total liabilities and equity	$1,220	$1,270		

financing activities. Changes in net working-capital items other than cash are included in operating activities.

Oakmont has only one entry under the heading Investing Activities: the increase in plant and equipment. Rather than using the figure for net fixed assets from Table 11.3, we use the changes in gross fixed assets and in accumulated depreciation as two separate items. The $25,000 increase in gross fixed assets decreases cash, and the $15,000 increase in accumulated depreciation (included in operating activities) increases cash. The net change is $10,000 ($25,000 − $15,000), which is the change in net fixed assets on the balance sheet.[5]

Financing activities, in addition to the $10,000 dividend payment, include the issuance of common stock and the retirement of bonds ($192,000). The

---

[5] Disposal of fixed assets sometimes complicates the picture because both fixed assets and accumulated depreciation are written off of the balance sheet. The remaining figures show the net results of fixed assets purchased and sold. To provide such details, we would need specific information about the fixed assets.

TABLE 11.4   **Oakmont Marketing Company: Statement of Cash Flows for 19X2**

Operating Activities

Earnings after taxes	$ 202,000	
Add depreciation	15,000	
Increase in accounts receivable	(40,000)	
Increase in inventories	(50,000)	
Increase in taxes payable	30,000	
Net cash flow from operating activities		$ 157,000

Investing Activities

Increase in plant and equipment	($25,000)	
Other	0	
Net cash used by investing activities		(25,000)

Financing Activities

Payment of dividends	($10,000)	
Issue of common stock	20,000	
Retirement of bonds	(192,000)	
Net cash used by financing activities		(182,000)
Net Increase (Decrease) in Cash		($50,000)

$20,000 stock issue increases the two balance sheet accounts titled Common stock and Paid-in capital in excess of par (Table 11.3). The statement of cash flows records the stock issue as a $20,000 increase in cash. Net cash used by financing activities is $182,000, primarily because of the cash used to retire bonds.

Combining the cash flows produced by operating, investing, and financing activities yields a $50,000 decrease in Oakmont's cash during 19X2:

Net cash flows from:	
Operating activities	$157,000
Investing activities	(25,000)
Financing activities	(182,000)
Decrease in cash	($50,000)

Both the work sheet in Table 11.3 and the statement of cash flows in Table 11.4 show Oakmont's $50,000 decrease in cash.[6]

Different companies use different formats for their statements of cash flows for public reporting. Many are more detailed and complicated than Oakmont Marketing Company's. The basic framework, however, is the same for both simple and complex cases: Change in the cash balance results from changes in other balance sheet items. Table 11.5 presents the statements of cash flows of AT&T for 1991, 1990, and 1989. The format and complexity are representative of audited statements of large U.S. industrial corporations. AT&T developed the statements in much the same way that we developed Oakmont's statement. Table

---

[6] The Financial Accounting Standards Board (FASB) accepts two methods for calculating and reporting net cash flow from operating activities. Most companies use the *indirect method,* illustrated in Table 11.4, which ties earnings after taxes plus depreciation to changes in current assets and current liabilities. Under the alternative *direct* method, operating cash outflows are subtracted from operating cash inflows to calculate the net cash flow from operating activities.

TABLE 11.5			**AT&T: Statements of Cash Flows (Millions of Dollars)**

	Year Ended December 31		
	1991	**1990**	**1989**
Operating Activities			
Net income	$ 522	$ 3,104	$ 3,109
Adjustments to reconcile net income to net cash provided by operating activities:			
Depreciation	3,568	3,721	3,663
Provision for uncollectibles	1,233	1,048	862
Provision for business restructuring	3,572	95	—
(Increase) in accounts receivable	(2,108)	(1,422)	(1,080)
(Increase) decrease in inventories	(59)	230	431
Increase (decrease) in accounts payable	109	(197)	(223)
Net (increase) in other operating assets and liabilities	(1,019)	(108)	(753)
Other adjustments for non-cash items—net	197	(36)	(57)
Net cash provided by operating activities	6,015	6,435	5,952
Investing Activities			
Capital expenditures net of proceeds from sale or disposal of property, plant and equipment of $119, $97 and $124	(3,860)	(4,018)	(3,951)
Increase in finance receivables, net of lease-related repayments of $3,535, $2,952 and $1,956	(3,052)	(2,376)	(631)
Net decrease (increase) in investments	473	(342)	(514)
Acquisitions, net of cash acquired	(29)	(776)	(383)
Other investing activities—net	69	(221)	(51)
Net cash used in investing activities	(6,399)	(7,733)	(5,530)
Financing Activities			
Proceeds from long-term debt issuance	1,300	1,572	917
Retirements of long-term debt	(1,196)	(1,159)	(712)
Issuance of common shares	1,164	726	117
Treasury shares acquired	(3)	(467)	(607)
Dividends paid	(1,563)	(1,496)	(1,390)
Increase in short-term borrowings—net	969	2,197	635
Other financing activities—net	5	(38)	(129)
Net cash provided by (used in) financing activities	676	1,335	(1,169)
Effect of exchange rate changes on cash	(19)	61	(32)
Net increase (decrease) in cash and temporary cash investments	273	98	(779)
Cash and temporary cash investments at beginning of year	1,875	1,777	2,556
Cash and temporary cash investments at end of year	$ 2,148	$ 1,875	$ 1,777

Source: AT&T, *Annual Report,* 1991.

11.5 tells you that the company's cash and cash equivalents increased by $273,000,000 during 1991 because of the following activities:

	Millions of Dollars
Operating activities	$ 6,015
Investment activities	(6,399)
Financing activities	676
Effect of exchange rate changes	(19)
Change in cash and cash equivalents	$ 273

Similar to many other companies, AT&T combines cash and cash equivalents, making no distinction between them in the statement of cash flows. Following the rules of accounting, AT&T shows separately a $19 million loss due to exchange rate changes. Being a multinational company, AT&T owns a substantial amount of foreign currency (for example, French francs and German marks). During 1991 the value of the U.S. dollar increased relative to many foreign currencies, meaning that these currencies became worth fewer U.S. dollars. As a result of the stronger U.S. dollar, AT&T's holdings of foreign currency lost value—19 million U.S. dollars of value.

Using a Statement of Cash Flows

A financial manager uses a statement of cash flows for three purposes:

1. To assess the impact of operations on the company's cash balance.
2. To evaluate the flow of cash from activities other than operations.
3. To determine how the company used cash during the period.

Comparing statements for several periods enables the manager to discern important developing trends.

For Oakmont Marketing Company the $50,000 decrease in cash suggests some decline in liquidity. Oakmont still has $230,000 in cash (Table 11.3), however, which along with other current assets provides it with a reasonable level of liquidity. Table 11.4 shows that operating activities produced a cash flow of $157,000, which was totally consumed by investing ($25,000) and financing ($182,000) activities. Oakmont's management made a major decision to retire $192,000 of the company's outstanding bonds, reducing financial leverage and financial risk, but doing so at the expense of its cash balance.

Oakmont raised $20,000 during the year by issuing new common stock. Combining this total with cash flows from operations and a reduction in the cash balance, Oakmont purchased plant and equipment, retired bonds outstanding, and paid a dividend. Financially speaking, the company appears to have completed a successful year: Earnings after taxes were a hefty $202,000, financial risk declined, and the company was still liquid.

In the appraisal of Oakmont Marketing Company and the preceding overview of working-capital management, we have assumed the constant purchasing power of money, or the absence of inflation. This assumption does not hold during many economic periods. Thus in the following sections we address the special problems inflation creates for working-capital management.

WORKING-CAPITAL MANAGEMENT DURING INFLATION

Inflation decreases the purchasing power of money because of the increase in the average price of goods and services. As a result of inflation, more dollars are needed to purchase the same quantity of goods and services. Components of current assets and current liabilities react differently to changes in purchasing power depending on whether the component is monetary or nonmonetary.

Monetary and Nonmonetary Components

monetary assets
Claims to a fixed number of future dollars.

monetary liabilities
Debts payable in the future with a fixed number of dollars.

Monetary assets are claims to a fixed number of future dollars. **Monetary liabilities** are debts to be paid in the future with a fixed number of dollars. Listed below are typical monetary assets and liabilities on a company's balance sheet:

•

Quoth the Banker, "Watch Cash Flow"

Once upon a midnight dreary as
  I pondered weak and weary
Over many a quaint and curious
  volume of accounting lore,
Seeking gimmicks (without scru-
  ple) to squeeze through some
  new tax loophole,
Suddenly I heard a knock upon
  my door.
  Only this, and nothing more.

Then I felt a queasy tingling and I
  heard the cash a-jingling
As a fearsome banker entered
  whom I'd often seen before.
His face was money-green and in
  his eyes there could be seen
Dollar-signs that seemed to glitter
  as he reckoned up the score.
"Cash flow," the banker said,
  and nothing more.

I had always thought it fine to
  show a jet black bottom line,
But the banker sounded a
  resounding "No,

Your receivables are high, mount-
  ing upward toward the sky:
Write-offs loom. What matters is
  cash flow."
  He repeated, "Watch cash flow."

Then I tried to tell the story of our
  lovely inventory
Which, though large, is full of
  most delightful stuff.
But the banker saw its growth,
  and with a mighty oath
He waved his arms and shouted,
  "Stop! Enough!
  Pay the interest, and don't give
  me any guff!"

Next I looked for non-cash items
  which could add ad infini-
  tum
To replace the ever-outward flow
  of cash,
But to keep my statement black I'd
  held depreciation back,
And my banker said that I'd done
  something rash.

He quivered, and his teeth
  began to gnash.

When I asked him for a loan, he
  responded, with a groan,
That the interest rate would be
  just prime plus eight,
And to guarantee my purity he'd
  insist on some security—
All my assets plus the scalp upon
  my pate.
  Only this, a standard rate.

Though my bottom line is black, I
  am flat upon my back.
  My cash flows out and
  customers pay slow.
The growth of my receivables is
  almost unbelievable;
The result is certain—unremitting
  woe!
And I hear the banker utter an
  ominous low mutter,
  "Watch cash flow."

Source: Herbert S. Bailey, Jr., "Quoth the Banker, 'Watch Cash Flow': A Lament," *Publishers Weekly,* 207, Jan. 13, 1975, 34. Copyright © 1975 by Xerox Corporation. Reprinted from *Publishers Weekly,* published by R. R. Bowker Company, a Xerox Company, by permission.

Monetary Assets	Monetary Liabilities
Cash and bank deposits	Accounts and notes payable
Marketable securities	Accrued expenses
Accounts and notes receivable	Bank loans
Cash surrender value of life insurance	Long-term debt
	Preferred stock

nonmonetary assets
Claims to items whose value changes with the general price level.

nonmonetary liabilities
Obligations to deliver a specified quantity of goods or services whose value changes with the general price level.

Note that monetary assets are primarily current assets less inventory, and monetary liabilities are primarily current liabilities plus long-term liabilities.

In addition to monetary assets and liabilities, a company has nonmonetary assets and liabilities. **Nonmonetary assets,** often called *real assets,* are claims to items whose dollar value changes with the general price level. Inventory, plant, and equipment are examples. **Nonmonetary liabilities** are obligations to deliver a specified quantity of goods or services whose value changes with the general price level. There are very few nonmonetary liabilities. An example is a contract to deliver a specified number of hours of labor or a specified quantity of equipment at a prearranged price.

Net Monetary Position. A company's net monetary position is the difference between its monetary assets and its monetary liabilities. If its monetary assets are greater than its monetary liabilities, the company is a **net monetary creditor.** If, on the other hand, its monetary assets are less than its monetary liabilities, then the company is a **net monetary debtor.** In summary, the following rule can be used to determine whether a company is a net monetary debtor or creditor:

net monetary creditor
Company whose monetary assets are greater than its monetary liabilities.

net monetary debtor
Company whose monetary assets are less than its monetary liabilities.

- Monetary assets > Monetary liabilities: Net monetary creditor
- Monetary assets < Monetary liabilities: Net monetary debtor

As an exercise, review the balance sheet for Oakmont Marketing Company in Table 11.1. Identify the company's monetary assets and monetary liabilities. Verify that the company is a $112,000 net monetary debtor.

Purchasing-Power Gains and Losses. Because the money value of monetary items is fixed in dollar terms, inflation leads to a **purchasing-power loss** (monetary loss) in monetary assets and to a **purchasing-power gain** (monetary gain) in monetary liabilities. If losses in assets exceed gains in liabilities, then a net purchasing-power loss occurs and shareholder wealth measured in real terms declines. If gains in liabilities exceed losses in assets, then a net purchasing-power gain occurs and shareholder wealth measured in real terms increases. The general impact of inflation relates directly to a company's net monetary position in the following way:

purchasing-power loss
Decline in the real value of a company's monetary assets during inflation; causes a decline in shareholder wealth.

purchasing-power gain
Decline in the real value of a company's monetary liabilities during inflation; causes an increase in shareholder wealth.

Position	Impact of Inflation
Net monetary creditor	Net purchasing-power loss
Net monetary debtor	Net purchasing-power gain

EXAMPLE

Suppose that Oakmont Marketing Company's balance sheet on December 31, 19X2, is the same as that shown in Table 11.1 for December 31, 19X1; in other words, the balance sheet stays the same over the year. Suppose also that the consumer price index (used to measure inflation) rises from 264 to 295.7 during the year, reflecting an inflation rate of 12 percent:

$$\text{Inflation rate} = \frac{295.7 - 264}{264} = 0.12, \text{ or } 12\%$$

Oakmont's purchasing-power loss on its $620,000 of monetary assets (cash and accounts receivable) is $74,400 (0.12 × $620,000). Oakmont's purchasing-power gain on its $732,000 of monetary liabilities (accounts payable, taxes payable, and bonds) is $87,840 (0.12 × $732,000). Combining the loss and the gain produces a net purchasing-power gain of $13,440 ($87,840 − $74,400).

Because Oakmont Marketing Company in the preceding example is a $112,000 ($732,000 − $620,000) net monetary debtor during a year of 12 percent inflation, it gains $13,440 (0.12 × $112,000).[7] During the same year net monetary creditors lose purchasing power.

Managing Working Capital during Inflation

What are the implications of inflation's impact on monetary items for working-capital management? They should be clear as long as you remember that inflation causes net monetary debtors to gain and net monetary creditors to lose purchasing power. A company's shareholders are best served if prior to *unexpected inflation* a company is a net monetary debtor—using current and long-term debt to finance nonmonetary assets.

Financial managers find it difficult, however, to capitalize on the wealth transfers inflation causes. First, creditors add an inflation premium to their real, or constant-dollar, interest rate, so that the cost of a monetary liability rises with *expected inflation* rates. This inflation premium shows up as an increase in interest expense on the income statement. Second, inflation is hard to forecast, and if the actual inflation rate differs from the expected rate, then purchasing-power gains and losses differ from what was expected. For example, suppose you expect inflation to be 6 percent next year and agree to pay 10 percent interest on a loan to finance a nonmonetary asset. Also suppose that actual inflation turns out to be only 4 percent. How does this affect your purchasing-power gain? The gain on the monetary liability is less than the real (price-level-adjusted) interest expense you pay. In other words, you lose more in interest than you gain in balance sheet purchasing power. Finally, the decision to expand monetary liabilities may violate other company policies: It may lead to an excessive debt-equity ratio and to a decline in liquidity, both of which affect shareholder wealth.

Despite the difficulty in capitalizing on inflation, a financial manager should understand its role because it results in additional benefits and costs in working-capital management. Other things being equal, financial managers would expand monetary liabilities prior to inflation unexpected by creditors. But in the absence of an accurate inflation forecast, financial managers might be better off to **hedge** against unexpected inflation by holding equal amounts of monetary assets and monetary liabilities. In this way a gain or loss on a monetary asset would exactly offset a loss or gain on a liability.

In summary, this chapter overview of working-capital management points out three trade-offs faced by financial managers: (1) liquidity versus expected profitability, (2) aggressive versus conservative financing of current assets, and (3) a hedged versus an unhedged monetary position. Taking an extreme position in any of these trade-offs presents its own special set of advantages and disadvantages, or expected return and risk. Balancing expected return against risk suggests that financial managers should adopt a position between the extremes. The

hedge

Take equal but opposite financial positions so that gains on one position offset losses on the other.

---

[7]Keeping Oakmont Marketing Company's balance sheet constant over the year simplifies the calculation, because if its monetary position changes, then the gain or loss on the *change* needs to be calculated. For example, suppose that Oakmont's net monetary debtor position gradually (and evenly) increases over the year from $112,000 to $122,000, a $10,000 change. On average during the year, only one-half of the $10,000 change, or $5,000, is outstanding. Multiplying the average change of $5,000 times the 12 percent inflation rate yields a $600 gain. Adding the $600 gain to the $13,440 gain in the example yields a total gain of $14,040.

Managing the Multinational's Working Capital

The assistant treasurer of National Semiconductor Corporation saved the company several thousand dollars by transferring $500,000 from the company's Japanese account to its Philippine operations. This transfer eliminated the need for the Philippine affiliate to borrow the money. For multinational companies, global transfers of cash are an integral part of working-capital management.

Centralization of international cash management generates efficiencies of size and information. These efficiencies enable a company to hold one centralized cash balance that is smaller than the sum of individual local cash balances. Centralized payment systems eliminate unnecessary movements of cash among company business units. Payments due to and from the units are recorded and netted out to company-wide totals. The results are large savings in fees and a reduced exposure to foreign-exchange risk, the uncertainty in the value of foreign currency.

Effective international cash management ensures adequate but not excessive liquidity both locally and company-wide. Multinational companies often face obstacles, however, in their attempts to transfer cash from one business unit to another. A government, especially that of a developing country, may impose limitations on the international movement of the country's currency. In addition to such currency blockages, the differential income tax rates among countries also impede the natural flow of intracorporate cash.

Currency blockages most often affect dividend payments from a foreign subsidiary to its parent company. To overcome the blockage, a company might try to disguise dividend payments as royalties on patents, fees for parent services, or charges for overhead allocations. To be politically acceptable, however, such fees and charges must reflect objective, arm's-length prices.

Transfer pricing (intracompany billing) of goods and services can also be used to minimize a multinational's worldwide income taxes. By inflating the invoice price of goods supplied to a subsidiary in a high-tax-rate country, the parent reduces the subsidiary's tax payments. The tax savings of the subsidiary exceed the increase in tax payments of the parent, which operates in the lower-tax-rate country. Governments, of course, are aware of these tax-minimization ploys and have regulations to prevent or slow down abuse.

In managing international accounts receivable, companies distinguish between accounts with affiliates and those with outside customers. Although intracompany account balances do not affect the company's consolidated balance, they are exposed to foreign-exchange risk. For example, say that a French subsidiary owes its U.S. parent FF1,000,000 (French francs) and that before payment the French franc declines in value. The company as a whole loses money because of the depreciation in the currency. To avoid such risk, companies may speed up collections in weak currencies and convert the receipts to strong currencies. Alternatively, companies can sell weak currencies in the currency market, with delivery delayed until the date of their receipt. Such forward contracts to sell currencies lock in the price to be received in the future.

International accounts receivable from customers outside the company present other problems in addition to foreign-exchange risk. Differing legal systems may lessen the value of the company's claim represented by the receivable, which explains why companies often require a bank letter of credit or other guarantee before selling to a customer abroad. Also, evaluating the creditworthiness of foreign customers is often hampered by scarcity of information.

Finally, centralization of international inventory management creates efficiencies of size and information, just as it does in cash management. Efficiencies in international inventory management are particularly helpful in offsetting inventory buildups due to long transportation times. In some countries the carrying costs of inventory are offset by high inflation rates and depreciating currency, which cause the value of inventory in terms of local currency to increase.

following three chapters present ideas and procedures that help financial managers make the trade-offs in working-capital management:

- Chapter 12, "Cash Management," describes the motivations for holding cash and the techniques for managing cash.
- Chapter 13, "Managing Receivables and Inventory," describes the credit policies that give rise to accounts receivable and the opposing costs that create optimal inventory levels.
- Chapter 14, "Managing Current Liabilities," describes the three dominant sources of short-term financing and their associated costs and benefits.

Cash management, credit management, inventory management, and the management of short-term financing are the key components of the next three chapters.

SUMMARY

- The liquidity of an asset is the ease with which it can be converted into cash at the prevailing market value without large transaction costs. The liquidity of a company is its ability to pay short-term financial obligations. Liquidity shields a company against unexpected problems and thus lessens default risk, but it comes with costs: the cost of managing liquid assets and the cost of financing them.

- The benefits and costs of liquidity create a trade-off between it and expected profitability. A company's balance sheet reflects the trade-off: Higher levels of liquidity generally lessen expected profitability and vice versa.

- Aggressive and conservative working-capital policies are characterized in the following way:

Aggressive:	*Conservative:*
Low current ratio	High current ratio
Small amount of net working capital	Large amount of net working capital
High current asset turnover	Low current asset turnover

where each term is defined as follows:

$$\text{Current ratio} = \text{Current assets/Current liabilities}$$
$$\text{Net working capital} = \text{Current assets} - \text{Current liabilities}$$
$$\text{Current asset turnover} = \text{Sales/Current assets}$$

Aggressive managers seek higher expected profitability at the expense of lower liquidity. Conservative managers give up higher expected profitability for the accompanying higher liquidity.

- The matching principle of working-capital management advises managers to match the maturity of capital sources with the maturity of their uses. Permanent current assets and fixed assets should be financed with long-term sources of capital. Temporary current assets (seasonal increases in current assets) should be financed with short-term (temporary) debt sources. Aggressive managers use more short-term debt than is called for by the matching principle and conservative managers use less.

- The statement of cash flows shows the financial manager the details of past activities that caused a change in the company's cash balance. The statement classifies activities as operating, investing, and financing. Changes over time in balance sheet accounts (other than cash) have the following impact on the cash balance:

Cash increase: Increase in liabilities and decrease in assets.
Cash decrease: Increase in assets and decrease in liabilities.

The change in cash is the balancing item of the statement of cash flows. Financial managers use the statement to evaluate a company's ability to generate cash from operations and to determine sources and uses of cash during the operating period.

• Inflation forces management to consider the purchasing-power losses and gains associated with monetary assets and liabilities. A net monetary debtor gains purchasing power during inflation, and a net monetary creditor loses purchasing power. Although it seems that management would serve shareholders best by maximizing monetary liabilities, creditors add an inflation premium to their loans, charging the company a higher interest rate. The uncertainty in forecasting the rate of inflation makes it difficult for a financial manager to determine the precise level of debt to use. In addition, a company's policy on liquidity level may conflict with the decision to increase monetary liabilities and decrease monetary assets.

Key Terms

working-capital policy	matching principle	nonmonetary assets
conservative working-capital policy	permanent current assets	nonmonetary liabilities
current ratio	temporary current assets	net monetary creditor
net working capital	refinancing risk	net monetary debtor
aggressive working-capital policy	statement of cash flows	purchasing-power loss
current asset turnover	monetary assets	purchasing-power gain
return on assets (ROA)	monetary liabilities	hedge

Questions

11.1. Briefly explain how you would go about assessing the difference in liquidity between General Motors Corporation and Chrysler Corporation.

11.2. *(Library assignment)* Use financial information from Standard & Poor's *Industry Survey* or from *Value Line Investment Survey* to calculate three liquidity measures for General Motors and Chrysler. Interpret the measures and identify the company that is more liquid. Defend your choice.

11.3. Explain the trade-off between a company's liquidity and its expected profitability.

11.4. *(CMA examination, modified)* Working-capital policy raises issues relating to a company's profitability and liquidity. Which one of the following statements would most accurately describe a company's financial relationships if it were aggressively pursuing high profits?
a. The company would probably have a high ratio of current assets to total assets and a high ratio of long-term debt to total debt.
b. The company would probably have a low ratio of current assets to total assets and a low ratio of current liabilities to total debt.
c. The company would probably have a high ratio of fixed assets to total assets and a high ratio of current liabilities to total debt.
d. The company would probably have a low ratio of fixed assets to total assets and a low ratio of current liabilities to total debt.

11.5. Working-capital management may be aggressive or conservative. How must the financial manager adjust the company's reliance on the matching principle in pursuing either working-capital policy?

11.6. Four companies are alike in every way except for the following financing arrangements:

Company A: Uses short-term debt to finance seasonal buildups in current assets.

Company B: Uses long-term debt to finance seasonal buildups in current assets.

Company C: Uses short-term debt to finance fixed assets.

Company D: Uses long-term debt to finance fixed assets.

What is the impact of each of these financing arrangements on the company's risk and on its expected profitability? Explain.

11.7. The first equation below describes a company's balance sheet. Each succeeding equation is a modification of the one preceding it:

$$\text{Assets} = \text{Liabilities} + \text{Shareholder equity}$$

$$\begin{array}{l}\text{Changes} \\ \text{in assets}\end{array} = \begin{array}{l}\text{Changes in} \\ \text{liabilities}\end{array} + \begin{array}{l}\text{Changes in} \\ \text{shareholder} \\ \text{equity}\end{array}$$

$$\begin{array}{l}\text{Changes} \\ \text{in cash}\end{array} + \begin{array}{l}\text{Changes in} \\ \text{assets other} \\ \text{than cash}\end{array} = \begin{array}{l}\text{Changes in} \\ \text{liabilities}\end{array} + \begin{array}{l}\text{Changes in} \\ \text{shareholder} \\ \text{equity}\end{array}$$

$$\begin{array}{l}\text{Changes} \\ \text{in cash}\end{array} = \begin{array}{l}\text{Changes in} \\ \text{liabilities}\end{array} + \begin{array}{l}\text{Changes in} \\ \text{shareholder} \\ \text{equity}\end{array} - \begin{array}{l}\text{Changes in} \\ \text{assets other} \\ \text{than cash}\end{array}$$

$$\begin{array}{l}\text{Increases} \\ \text{in cash}\end{array} = \begin{array}{l}\text{Increases in} \\ \text{liabilities}\end{array} + \begin{array}{l}\text{Increases in} \\ \text{shareholder} \\ \text{equity}\end{array} + \begin{array}{l}\text{Decreases in} \\ \text{assets other} \\ \text{than cash}\end{array}$$

a. Write the equation for *Decreases in cash*.

b. Why is an understanding of the preceding equations important in the construction of a statement of cash flows?

c. Suppose that over the past year a company's assets other than cash decreased $1,000, shareholder equity increased $2,000, and liabilities decreased $3,000. What is the net effect of these changes on the company's cash balance? Explain.

11.8. Examine the statement of cash flows for Oakmont Marketing Company. Explain how net working capital can increase and cash decrease over the same period. Which measure—cash or net working capital—more accurately reflects the company's liquidity? Explain your choice.

11.9. Adco Company has the following balance sheet at the beginning of 19X9:

Assets		Liabilities and Equity	
Cash	$ 1,000	Accounts payable	$ 1,500
Receivables	2,000	Wages payable	500
Inventory	5,000	Mortgage bonds	5,000
Fixed assets	4,000	Common equity	5,000
	$12,000		$12,000

a. Define the terms *monetary assets, monetary liabilities, nonmonetary assets,* and *nonmonetary liabilities.*

b. Identify Adco's monetary assets and monetary liabilities.

c. Identify Adco's nonmonetary assets.

d. What, if any, nonmonetary liabilities does Adco's balance sheet show?

11.10. Why do monetary liabilities incur a purchasing-power gain and monetary assets a purchasing-power loss during inflation?

11.11. Do you think that a company should hedge itself against inflation? Explain your answer.

11.12. Larko Industries has the following balance sheet (in thousands of dollars) at the beginning of 19X3:

Assets		Liabilities and Net Worth	
Cash	$ 200	Accounts payable	$ 700
Receivables	500	Taxes payable	300
Inventory	1,000	Bonds payable	600
Fixed assets	500	Net worth	600
	$2,200		$2,200

a. *True or false:* Larko Industries is a net monetary creditor.

b. *True or false:* During inflation Larko Industries will receive a purchasing-power gain on its monetary assets and a purchasing-power loss on its monetary liabilities.

Strategy Problem

New Jersey Manufacturing and Distributing Company has the following balance sheet as of December 31, 19X8:

Assets		Liabilities and Equity	
Cash	$ 2,000	Accounts payable	$ 30,000
Receivables	18,000	Notes payable	10,000
Inventory	20,000	Long-term debt	20,000
Fixed assets	80,000	Shareholder equity	60,000
Total	$120,000	Total	$120,000

The company's sales in 19X8 were $240,000.

a. Define the terms *net working capital, current ratio,* and *current asset turnover.*

b. Calculate the following liquidity measures for New Jersey Manufacturing and Distributing Company: net working capital (NWC), current ratio (CR), and current asset turnover (CATO).

c. Suppose that companies in the same industry as New Jersey Manufacturing and Distributing have current ratios averaging 1.5 and current asset turnovers averaging 5. Assess the company's liquidity level relative to the industry average.

d. If the consumer price index increased from 256 to 276.5 during 19X8, then what was the net purchasing-power gain (loss) for New Jersey Manufacturing and Distributing during the year? (Assume that the balance sheet remains unchanged during the year.)

Strategy

Solution

a. *Net working capital* is current assets less current liabilities, although it can be measured as long-term debt and equity less fixed (noncurrent) assets. *Current ratio* is the dollar amount of current assets per dollar of current liabilities. *Current asset turnover* is sales per dollar of current assets.

Subtract current liabilities from current assets or subtract fixed assets from long-term debt and equity.

b.

$$NWC = \$40,000 - \$40,000 = 0, \text{ or}$$

$$NWC = (\$20,000 + \$60,000) - \$80,000 = 0$$

Divide current assets by current liabilities.

$$CR = \frac{\$40,000}{\$40,000} = 1.0$$

Divide sales by current assets.

$$CATO = \frac{\$240,000}{\$40,000} = 6.0$$

c. This company's liquidity is substantially less than the industry average, suggesting that it may have problems meeting its short-term cash obligations. The low degree of liquidity increases the company's default risk, which lessens the value of the company's common stock.

d. Calculate the inflation rate during 19X8:

Inflation rate equals change in CPI divided by beginning CPI.

$$\text{Inflation rate} = \frac{276.5 - 256}{256} = 0.08, \text{ or } 8\%$$

Sum up the monetary assets:

Monetary assets are fixed financial claims.

Cash	$ 2,000
Receivables	18,000
Total	$20,000

Multiply the inflation rate times the total to obtain the purchasing-power loss:

$$\$1,600 = 0.08 \times \$20,000$$

Sum up the monetary liabilities:

Monetary liabilities are fixed payables.

Accounts payable	$30,000
Notes payable	10,000
Long-term debt	20,000
Total	$60,000

Multiply the inflation rate times the total to obtain the purchasing-power gain:

$$\$4,800 = 0.08 \times \$60,000$$

Purchasing-power gain minus purchasing-power loss.

Net purchasing-power gain is $3,200 ($4,800 − $1,600).

◆ **Demonstration Problem**

Nalco Chemical Company (NCC) is the world's largest producer of chemicals and services for water and waste treatment. NCC's balance sheets ending December 31 for two recent years are as follows (in millions of dollars):

Assets	19X1	19X0	Liabilities and Equity	19X1	19X0
Cash and equivalents	$ 120.1	$ 35.2	Accounts payable	$ 98.0	$ 93.5
Receivables	208.3	190.9	Other current liabilities	163.6	82.3
Inventories	87.3	82.4	Total current liabilities	$ 261.6	$ 175.8
Other current assets	102.2	97.0	Long-term liabilities	534.1	405.5
Total current assets	$ 517.9	$ 405.5	Preferred stock	9.5	7.8
Noncurrent assets	806.5	631.5	Common equity	519.2	447.9
Total assets	$1,324.4	$1,037.0	Total claims	$1,324.4	$1,037.0

During the fiscal year ending 19X1, NCC earned $137.8 million after taxes and paid $66.5 million in cash dividends. NCC's net sales were $1,237.3 million and $1,068.1 million for 19X1 and 19X0, respectively.

a. A U.S. Treasury bill is highly liquid. Also, some companies are highly liquid and some are not. Define the term *liquidity* as it applies to a U.S. Treasury bill and to a company.

b. "The balance sheet lists *cash and cash equivalents, receivables,* and *inventories* according to decreasing liquidity." Define each italicized term and explain why inventories are less liquid than receivables.

c. Calculate NCC's current ratio, net working capital, and current asset turnover for 19X1 and 19X0. Based on these measures and the change in NCC's cash and cash equivalents, has NCC's liquidity increased or decreased over the year? Explain.

d. Define the *matching principle* of working-capital management. Despite the absence of information on NCC's permanent current assets, do you believe that the company is aggressive or conservative in financing its current assets? Explain.

e. Prepare NCC's statement of cash flows for 19X1. What are the principal activities that caused NCC's cash and cash equivalents to rise by $84.9 million? (*Note:* Ordinarily, depreciation is included in operating activities, and change in gross fixed assets [noncurrent assets] is included in investing activities. These two entries combine to show the change in net fixed assets. NCC's noncurrent assets are net of depreciation, so the change in noncurrent assets accounts for both the change in gross fixed assets and for depreciation, neither of which appears on the company's statement of cash flows.)

f. (1) Define the terms *monetary assets* and *monetary liabilities.* (2) Is NCC a net monetary debtor or a net monetary creditor at the end of 19X1? Explain. (3) During inflation would NCC realize a net purchasing-power gain or loss? Explain. (*Note: Other current assets* consist of 1-year marketable securities, and *other current liabilities* consist of bank loans.)

g. Companies face three trade-offs in the management of working capital: (1) liquidity versus expected profitability, (2) aggressive versus conservative financing of current assets, and (3) a hedged versus an unhedged monetary position. Evaluate NCC's profitability and describe the trade-offs it has made in working-capital management.

Problems

Financial ratios and the balance sheet

11.1. Luca Pacioli (pronounced pat-CHEE-oh-lee) is considered the father of accounting because of his seminal work in 1494 on double-entry bookkeeping. The basic accounting equation, assets equal liabilities plus shareholder equity, reflects Pacioli's work, as does the following balance sheet (in thousands of dollars):

Assets		Liabilities and Equity	
Cash and cash equivalents	$ 890	Accounts payable	$ 620
Accounts receivable	1,050	Notes payable	910
Inventory	1,170	Long-term debt	1,230
Fixed assets	3,260	Common equity	3,610
Total assets	$6,370	Total claims	$6,370

a. Define each current asset and each current liability shown.
b. Use the balance sheet to demonstrate the basic accounting equation: Total assets equal total debt plus shareholder equity.
c. Calculate the following items: (1) net working capital, (2) current ratio, and (3) debt-equity ratio.
d. Does the company appear to be financially sound? Explain.

Comparison of financial ratios

11.2. Luciano Company has the following balance sheet ending December 31, 19X6:

Assets		Liabilities and Equity	
Current assets	$360,000	Current liabilities	$180,000
Fixed assets	280,000	Long-term debt	140,000
		Common equity	320,000
Total assets	$640,000		
		Total claims	$640,000

Luciano's sales during 19X6 were $960,000, and its total expenses were $880,000.
a. Calculate the company's current ratio, current asset turnover, return on assets, and net working capital.
b. The average current ratio of other companies in Luciano's industry is 1.5, and the average current asset turnover is 4.1. Is Luciano's working-capital policy conservative or aggressive? Explain.

Alternative working-capital policies

11.3. Dana O'Doule, vice president of Spur Enterprises, is assessing the risk and return of her company's working-capital policy. She is considering the following two policies (in thousands of dollars):

Policy	Current Assets	Current Liabilities	Long-Term Debt	Projected Earnings after Taxes
Conservative	$700	$350	$500	$ 88
Aggressive	500	500	150	121

Fixed assets would be $700,000 under both policies, but total assets would be $1,400,000 under the conservative policy and $1,200,000 under the aggressive policy.
a. Construct Spur's *pro forma* balance sheet for each policy.
b. Calculate Spur's current ratio, net working capital, and return on assets for each policy.
c. Describe the trade-off between liquidity and expected profitability for each policy.
d. Which policy do you think Ms. O'Doule should adopt? Explain.

Alternative working-capital policies

11.4. American Home Products (AHP) is a leading manufacturer and marketer of health-care products—prescription drugs, medical devices, and nutritional supplements. AHP's abbreviated income statement and balance sheet for 19X1 are:

Income Statement, Year Ending 19X1 (Thousands of Dollars)

Net sales	$7,079,443
Total expenses	5,704,170
Net income	$1,375,273

Balance Sheet, December 31, 19X1 (Thousands of Dollars)

Current assets	$4,119,057	Current liabilities	$1,270,135
Plant and equipment	1,476,841	Long-term liabilities	1,368,115
Other assets	342,899	Shareholder equity	3,300,547
Total assets	$5,938,797	Total claims	$5,938,797

AHP's current assets include $2.1 billion of cash and cash equivalents. Daniel Schneid, a security analyst in the pharmaceutical industry, believes that AHP should use part of its cash to retire all of its long-term liabilities. Such action, in Mr. Schneid's opinion, would save interest expenses, raise net income to $1.48 billion, and leave the company financially sound.

a. Calculate the following items based on AHP's 19X1 financial statements: (1) net working capital, (2) current ratio, (3) debt-equity ratio, (4) current asset turnover, and (5) return on assets.

b. Assume that Mr. Schneid's idea is implemented and AHP's net income rises to $1.48 billion, its long-term liabilities are eliminated, and its current assets decline by the amount of the long-term liabilities. (For simplicity, ignore the increase in shareholder equity due to the increase in net income.) Now calculate the following items: (1) net working capital, (2) current ratio, (3) debt-equity ratio, (4) current asset turnover, and (5) return on assets.

c. Do you think Mr. Schneid's idea is a good one? Explain.

Conservative policy versus aggressive policy

11.5. Apex Company and Apogee Company operate in the same industry but follow different financial policies. The differences in their financial policies are reflected in the comparison of their financial statements below.

a. Which company follows the more aggressive working-capital policy? Support your answer with appropriate calculations.

b. Does the comparison of Apex with Apogee illustrate the trade-off between liquidity and expected profitability? Support your answer with appropriate calculations.

Balance Sheets

	Apex	Apogee
Cash and cash equivalents	$ 120,000	$ 30,000
Accounts receivable	220,000	60,000
Inventory	360,000	70,000
Total current assets	$ 700,000	$160,000
Fixed assets, net	900,000	120,000
Total assets	$1,600,000	$280,000
Accounts payable	$ 510,000	$ 75,000
Accrued liabilities	140,000	15,000
Total current liabilities	$ 650,000	$ 90,000
Long-term debt	250,000	50,000
Common equity	700,000	140,000
Total claims	$1,600,000	$280,000

Income Statements

	Apex	Apogee
Net sales	$2,700,000	$330,000
Cost of goods sold	1,700,000	200,000
Gross profit	$1,000,000	$130,000
Operating expenses	685,000	101,000
Earnings before interest and taxes	$ 315,000	$ 29,000
Interest expense	25,000	5,000
Earnings before taxes	$ 290,000	$ 24,000
Income taxes	115,000	4,000
Earnings after taxes	$ 175,000	$ 20,000

Matching principle and working-capital management

11.6. The financial manager of Oakmont Marketing Company considers herself aggressive in working-capital management. The company's current assets and seasonal components of current assets are:

	Total	Seasonal
Cash	$280,000	$ 40,000
Net accounts receivable	340,000	80,000
Inventory	210,000	80,000
Total	$830,000	$200,000

Oakmont has $300,000 in current liabilities and $1,830,000 in total assets, and sales equal $5,000,000.

a. Calculate the company's net working capital, current ratio, and current asset turnover.

b. Is the company violating the matching principle? Support your answer with calculations.

c. Is the financial manager aggressive in working-capital management? Explain your answer.

Assembling a statement of cash flows

11.7. Adolph Rupp, CEO of Rupp Corporation, is perplexed. His accounting service sent him the following listing of year-to-year dollar changes in Rupp Corporation's balance sheet (parentheses indicate decreases):

Cash and cash equivalents	($45,933)
Accounts receivable	35,823
Other current assets	15,783
Fixed assets	191,877
Other noncurrent assets	(4,063)
Accounts payable	43,840
Other current liabilities	(12,642)
Long-term debt	20,575
Dividends paid	16,593

Appended to the listing, a note says: "Dear A. R.: FYI. Also, net income is $46,875 and depreciation is $111,432. Glad to be of service." Mr. Rupp summons you, his new assistant, and gives you these instructions: "Look over these numbers and get back to me after lunch with an interpretation of their meaning." In preparation for your meeting with Mr. Rupp, assemble the data provided by the accounting service into a statement of cash flows.

CMA examination, modified: Preparing and interpreting a statement of cash flows

11.8. Campbell Company has not yet prepared a formal statement of cash flows for the 19X8 fiscal year. Presented on page 433 are comparative balance sheets as of December 31, 19X7 and 19X8, and a statement of income and retained earnings for the period ended December 31, 19X8.

a. Prepare a statement of cash flows for Campbell.

b. Discuss and interpret Campbell's change in liquidity.

Preparing and interpreting a statement of cash flows

11.9. Wallace Jones, an assistant controller for Feldspar Supplies, is asked by the controller to prepare the statement of cash flows for 19X2. He is given the comparative balance sheets shown on page 434.

a. Prepare Feldspar's statement of cash flows for 19X2 and discuss its financial implications. (Feldspar paid no dividend.)

b. Does the change in net working capital and the change in cash provide the same message? Support your answer by referring to each change.

Purchasing-power gain and loss

11.10. Sandy Sinclair is chief financial officer of Mote Enterprises. She wishes to estimate the impact of inflation on her company's monetary assets and monetary liabilities during the year 19X1. During 19X1 the company was a $41,000 net monetary creditor:

Campbell Company: Balance Sheets as of December 31 (Thousands of Dollars)

	19X7	19X8
Assets		
Current assets		
Cash	$ 100	$ 60
U.S. Treasury bills (60 days)	50	0
Accounts receivable	500	610
Inventory	600	720
Total current assets	$1,250	$1,390
Long-term assets		
Land	$ 70	$ 80
Buildings and equipment	730	840
Accumulated depreciation	(120)	(205)
Total long-term assets	$ 680	$ 715
Total assets	$1,930	$2,105
Liabilities and Ownership		
Current liabilities		
Accounts payable	$ 300	$ 360
Taxes payable	20	25
Notes payable	400	400
Total current liabilities	$ 720	$ 785
Term notes payable—due 2002	200	200
Total liabilities	$ 920	$ 985
Owner equity		
Common stock outstanding	$ 700	$ 830
Retained earnings	310	290
Total owner equity	$1,010	$1,120
Total liabilities and equity	$1,930	$2,105

Campbell Company: Statement of Income and Retained Earnings, Year Ending December 31, 19X8 (Thousands of Dollars)

Sales		$2,408
Less expenses and interest		
Cost of goods sold	$1,100	
Salaries and benefits	850	
Heat, light, and power	75	
Depreciation	85	
Property taxes	18	
Miscellaneous expense	10	
Interest	55	2,193
Earnings before taxes		$ 215
Less income taxes		105
Earnings after taxes		$ 110
Retained earnings—Dec. 31, 19X7		310
Total		$ 420
Less dividend paid		130
Retained earnings—Dec. 31, 19X8		$ 290

Feldspar Supplies: Balance Sheets as of December 31

	19X1	19X2
Assets		
Current assets		
Cash	$ 50,000	$ 40,000
Marketable securities	40,000	30,000
Accounts receivable (net)	100,000	120,000
Inventory	150,000	180,000
Prepaid expenses	10,000	0
Total current assets	$350,000	$370,000
Investments	20,000	40,000
Plant and equipment	400,000	450,000
Less accumulated depreciation	(80,000)	(100,000)
Net plant and equipment	$320,000	$350,000
Total assets	$690,000	$760,000
Liabilities and Shareholder Equity		
Current liabilities		
Accounts payable	$ 80,000	$100,000
Notes payable	10,000	0
Accrued expenses	20,000	10,000
Total current liabilities	$110,000	$110,000
Long-term liabilities		
Bonds payable, 19X3	200,000	170,000
Total liabilities	$310,000	$280,000
Shareholder equity		
Preferred stock, $100 par value	90,000	90,000
Common stock, $1 par value	50,000	60,000
Capital paid in excess of par	160,000	230,000
Retained earnings	80,000	100,000
Total shareholder equity	$380,000	$480,000
Total liabilities and shareholder equity	$690,000	$760,000

Monetary assets	$1,726,000
Less monetary liabilities	1,685,000
Net monetary creditor position	$ 41,000

During 19X1 inflation was 16 percent.

a. Calculate the purchasing-power gain or loss on the monetary position during 19X1.

b. Write a brief memo to Ms. Sinclair explaining the advantage of being a net monetary debtor during inflation.

c. What advice would you give to Ms. Sinclair if you believe the economy is entering a deflationary period? (*Deflation* is a decline in the average price level.)

Rate of inflation and purchasing-power gain and loss

11.11. Pat Campbell is completing a class assignment for his business finance course. The assignment is to calculate the purchasing-power gain or loss for a company for the year 19X8. He decides to use his mom and dad's company, the Campbell Company. Problem 11.8 presents the company's financial statements. He goes to the *Survey of Current Business* (published by the U.S. Department of Commerce) to find price level information. On December 31, 19X7, the consumer price index is 146.80, and on December 31, 19X8, it is 171.12.

a. Is Campbell Company a net monetary debtor on December 31, 19X7? Show calculations to support your answer.

b. Calculate the rate of inflation during calendar 19X8.

c. Calculate the net purchasing-power gain or loss for Campbell Company during calendar 19X8 and interpret your answer.

Rate of inflation and purchasing-power gain and loss

11.12. Examine the 19X1 balance sheet for Feldspar Supplies in Problem 11.9.

a. Calculate the net monetary position of the company.

b. Calculate the changes in Feldspar's net working capital and net monetary position from Year-end 19X1 to Year-end 19X2. What do the differences tell the financial manager?

c. The consumer price index at Year-end 19X1 was 274.8 and at Year-end 19X2 it was 305.03. Calculate the net purchasing-power gain (loss) for Feldspar and interpret your answer.

Selected References

Gentry, James A. "State of the Art of Short-Run Financial Management." *Financial Management,* Summer 1988: 41–57.

Gilmer, R H, Jr. "The Optimal Level of Liquid Assets." *Financial Management,* Winter 1985: 39–43.

Hawawini, Gabriel, Claude Viallet, and Ashok Vora. "Industry Influence on Corporate Working Capital Decisions." *Sloan Management Review,* Summer 1986: 15–24.

Kamath, Ravindra. "How Useful Are Common Liquidity Measures?" *Journal of Cash Management,* January/February 1989: 24–28.

Kroll, Yoram. "On the Differences Between Accrual Accounting Figures and Cash Flows: The Case of Working Capital." *Financial Management,* Spring 1985: 75–82.

Mehta, Dileep. *Working Capital Management.* Englewood Cliffs, N.J.: Prentice-Hall, 1974.

Richards, Verlyn D., and Eugene J. Laughlin. "A Cash Conversion Cycle Approach to Liquidity Analysis." *Financial Management,* Spring 1980: 32–38.

Sartoris, William L., and Ned C. Hill. "A Generalized Cash Flow Approach to Short-Term Financial Decisions." *Journal of Finance,* May 1983: 349–360.

Stancill, James McNeill. "Where Is There Cash in Cash Flow?" *Harvard Business Review,* March-April 1987: 38–49.

Viscione, Jerry A. "How Long Should You Borrow Short Term?" *Harvard Business Review,* March-April 1986: 20–24.

Chapter 12

CASH MANAGEMENT

Nutrition Company Speeds Up Cash Flow

General Nutrition Corporation (GNC), headquartered in Pittsburgh, Pennsylvania, owns and operates more than 1,100 stores in 49 states. Located principally in shopping malls and highway shopping centers, the stores sell vitamins, sports nutrition, and other health-related products. Like other retailers with far-flung operations, GNC faces the daunting task of collecting its cash efficiently and inexpensively.

Total cash flow collected by GNC headquarters comes from three different sources: 85 percent from deposits by stores in their local banks; 10 percent from credit-card sales—American Express, MasterCard, Visa, and Discover; and 5 percent from commercial sales. Prior to implementing a new cash-collection system, the average time for headquarters to collect cash from outlying banks was four days; even worse, the collection of cash from credit-card sales took ten days. Linda Zang, a new assistant treasurer for GNC, says: "The inadequacy of GNC's systems for collecting 95 percent of its cash was obvious."

To solve the problem, GNC solicited the help of (1) National Bankcard Corporation (Nabanco), a credit-card processor, and (2) Verifone, a manufacturer of computer terminals. Together with GNC, these companies designed computer hardware and software to link the more than 1,100 stores with headquarters. The system incorporates two cash management techniques: (1) ACH (automated clearing house) electronic transfers of cash from outlying banks to the headquarters bank and (2) electronic data processing of credit-card receipts. Processing time for store receipts dropped from four days to three days, and processing time for credit cards dropped from ten days to three days. During the first four months of operation, the customized electronic system produced a net savings of $312,510. Ms. Zang notes: ". . . GNC's cash flow has been significantly improved and expenses related to cash collection [have been] reduced by the new system."

Source: Linda A. Zang, "Cash Management at a Mid-Sized Retailer," *Journal of Cash Management,* January/February 1990: 12–15.

Cash management is the planning and controlling of cash flows to increase a company's profitability and to maintain its liquidity. Carefully managing cash flows helps a company to pay operating expenses and debt service and to make capital investments and dividend payments. This chapter describes the techniques a financial manager uses to manage the most liquid part of a company's working capital, its cash. Beginning with a discussion of the reasons companies hold cash balances, the chapter describes the way cash circulates within a company. Managers use a cash budget to anticipate cash shortages and surpluses. After learning how to construct a cash budget, you will learn about the impact on profitability of speeding up cash inflows and controlling cash outflows. The chapter concludes with an examination of the criteria for investing temporarily excess cash and the reduction of risk by hedging.

WHY HOLD CASH?

Holding cash is a necessary evil for a company. Companies hold cash because the timing and amount of cash inflows do not match the timing and amount of cash outflows. For example, a company may make sales daily but pay salaries monthly. The timing and amount of cash from sales may differ greatly from the company's monthly cash outflow for salaries. Holding cash, as with any monetary asset, is an evil in the sense that it subjects the company to purchasing-power risk and to an opportunity cost.

purchasing-power risk
Uncertainty about how much future purchasing power today's money will have.

Purchasing-power risk (sometimes called *inflation risk*) is the uncertainty about how much purchasing power today's money will have at some future point in time. You will recall from Chapter 11 that holding a monetary asset during inflation subjects the company to a purchasing-power loss.

Even in the absence of inflation, a company holding cash incurs an opportunity cost. Cash invested elsewhere earns a return, but an idle cash balance, say, in a non-interest-bearing checking account, does not. The financial manager's objective is to balance the benefit of holding cash against the cost in order to arrive at the optimal cash level.

Although a company may have only one account in which it keeps cash, the cash balance can be viewed as consisting of several parts. For example, the company needs a pool of cash because its receipts and expenditures are not perfectly synchronized. This pool of cash is a **transactions balance,** which acts as a buffer between unmatched cash inflows and outflows.

transactions balance
Cash held to meet payments because of timing differences between cash inflows and outflows.

The financial manager cannot infallibly forecast the company's future cash flows. Unexpected losses or emergencies may occur that cause greater cash outflows than anticipated. To guard against such events, a company needs a rainy-day fund of cash, a **precautionary balance.** With this balance the company avoids the short-term financial embarrassment of failing to meet its financial obligations in a timely fashion. For example, severe weather around Christmas may close the airports in New York City, making it impossible for mail to get through. A New York City company expecting to receive checks in payment for merchandise it has shipped may find itself without cash receipts until the airports reopen. If the company does not have a precautionary balance of cash, then the unexpected interruption may prevent the company from paying its own bills in a timely fashion. As a result, its suppliers may place the company on a cash-only basis or stop selling to it.

precautionary balance
Cash held to protect against emergencies.

A company may also keep cash on hand to take advantage of unexpected opportunities. Whereas a precautionary balance relates to downside protection,

speculative balance
Cash held to take advantage of unexpected opportunities.

a **speculative balance** relates to the upside potential for discovering investment opportunities. How large a speculative cash balance should be depends on a company's lines of credit at commercial banks and the potential for squeezing cash out of operations by delaying payables, running down inventories, and so on. The financial manager normally invests speculative balances in marketable securities such as U.S. Treasury bills, negotiable certificates of deposit (CDs), commercial paper, and other money market securities.

Another reason a company maintains cash balances or their equivalent is to make planned future capital investments. Instead of issuing securities to raise cash for an investment, the company may retain earnings over time, building up cash for the expected outlay. Moreover, not all cash proceeds from a security issue are likely to be paid out immediately. Thus the company has a temporary **planning balance.**

planning balance
Cash held for expected capital expenditures.

compensating balance
Cash in a bank account as a condition for obtaining a bank loan or service.

A company often maintains a **compensating balance** with a commercial bank, which may further increase its cash requirements. Such a balance may be required as a condition for a loan, or it may be necessary to compensate the bank for services such as free checking, credit information, and investment advice. Compensating balances increase the bank's profitability and generally increase the cost of a loan. If the company would not normally keep these cash balances for regular operations, then compensating balances add to the company's overall cash balance.[1]

CIRCULATION OF CASH

As cash flows into and out of a company, its cash balance rises and falls. The reasons for changes in the cash balance will become clear as we explore the cash circulation system of a company.

One distinction we should make before examining the circulation of cash is the difference between cash flows and earnings. Cash management focuses only on transactions that change the level of cash within a company. Earnings after taxes depend on noncash transactions such as credit sales, credit purchases, and depreciation expense. Furthermore, earnings after taxes do not reflect the cash flows from issuing new common stock and selling depreciable assets. Consider a profitable company whose revenues exceed its expenses during an operating period. According to accounting principles, earnings after taxes are positive; retained earnings (on the balance sheet) will increase if dividends are less than the earnings after taxes. If the company invested a large amount of cash in equipment during the period, however, then cash flow could be negative and the company's cash balance would decline. Even profitable companies can experience cash shortages. Managers of rapidly growing companies frequently discover the difficulty of managing cash flows during periods of high sales growth.

---

[1] As the text indicates, a company must have cash balances for various reasons. The company's overall cash balance, however, is not merely a sum of all the cash balances described. Some cash balances may serve more than one purpose. Cash budgeting, examined later in this chapter, provides some insight into the overall cash balance needed. For models that estimate optimal cash balances, see William J. Baumol, "The Transactions Demand for Cash: An Inventory Theoretic Approach," *Quarterly Journal of Economics,* November 1952, 545–556; and Merton H. Miller and Daniel Orr, "The Demand for Money by Firms: Extensions of Analytic Results," *Journal of Finance,* December 1968, 735–759.

FIGURE 12.1

Cash Flows to and from a Company

A company's cash balance increases and decreases as it makes and receives cash payments. Government (taxes), suppliers (purchases), customers (sales), and employees (wages) normally have a one-way flow of cash. Financial markets and institutions have a two-way flow of cash. Cash inflows are indicated by arrows toward Cash Balance; cash outflows are indicated by arrows from Cash Balance.

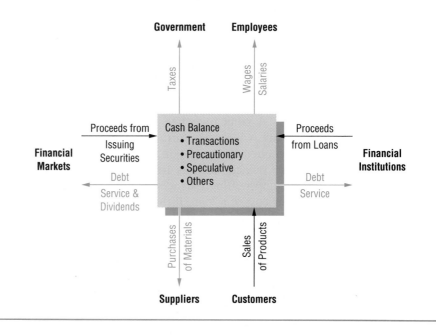

To illustrate the difference between cash flows and earnings, consider several transactions and their effects on cash balances and earnings after taxes during an accounting period:

Transaction	Cash Impact	Earnings Impact
Sell a product on credit	0	+
Buy office supplies on credit	0	−
Collect a receivable	+	0
Pay for depreciable equipment	−	0
Pay dividends	−	0
Purchase a U.S. Treasury bill	−	0
Issue new common stock	+	0
Retire a bond issue	−	0

Figure 12.1 further illustrates the cash flows to and from a company. At the center of the figure is the company's cash balance, maintained for transactions, precautionary, speculative, and other reasons. Leaving the company's cash balance are outflows for taxes, wages and salaries, debt service, purchases, and dividends. Entering the cash balance are inflows from product sales to customers, loan proceeds from financial institutions, and proceeds from issuing securities in the financial markets.

For simplicity, Figure 12.1 excludes some transactions. For example, a company may buy or sell fixed assets, which usually occurs intermittently over time. In addition, the company may purchase money market securities when the cash balance becomes temporarily large, then sell them when the need for cash again

FIGURE 12.2

The Cash Operating Cycle (Purchases and Sales on Credit)

A company uses its cash balance to pay accounts payable, which occur as a result of buying materials on credit. A company increases its cash balance by collecting receivables, which occur as a result of selling products on credit.

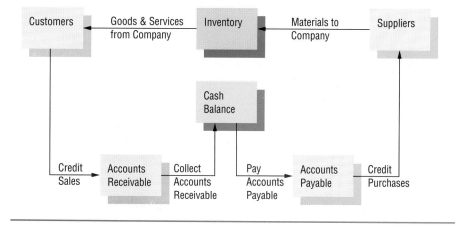

arises. On a somewhat continual basis, most companies buy and sell inventory. Moreover, large parts of the purchases and subsequent sales are made on credit.

Figure 12.2 depicts the **cash operating cycle** for a company that buys and sells on credit. The company purchases materials from suppliers, which increases inventory and accounts payable (for credit purchases). Products are sold to customers, which reduces inventory and increases accounts receivable (for credit sales). The company's cash balance increases when it collects accounts receivable and declines when it pays accounts payable. Will the dollar reduction in inventory equal the dollar increase in accounts receivable? Only if the company sells the products at cost. If the company sells the products at a markup over cost, then accounts receivable increase by a greater amount than inventory declines. The difference is earnings, which registers as an increase, or credit, in shareholder equity via the income statement.

In practice, a company can do little to control the timing of payments to the government for taxes, to employees for wages and salaries, to creditors for debt service, and to shareholders for dividends (after declaring the dividends). Substantial control can be exercised, however, in the management of the cash operating cycle depicted in Figure 12.2. Thus financial managers pay a great deal of attention to the cash operating cycle and the payments to suppliers and the collection of receivables. Before studying these issues, consider the development of a cash budget to forecast a company's cash needs.

cash operating cycle
Flow of cash to inventory, then to receivables, and back to cash.

CASH BUDGETING

cash budgeting
Process of forecasting cash inflows and outflows.

Cash budgeting is the process of forecasting cash inflows and cash outflows; it is the centerpiece of cash management. Prudent financial managers forecast monthly, weekly, and sometimes even daily cash flows. A financial manager might, for example, forecast cash flows for the following periods:

• Monthly for the next twelve months, updated each month.

- Weekly for the next four weeks, updated each week.
- Daily for the next two weeks, updated each week.

By periodically updating the cash budget, the financial manager provides current information for projecting the cash balances the company must have on hand to meet its financial obligations.

The Cash Budget

cash budget
Schedule of expected cash inflows and outflows.

The **cash budget** is a time-based schedule of expected cash receipts (inflows) and disbursements (outflows). The following calculations summarize the cash budget:

Cash inflows	XXXXXX
Less cash outflows	XXXX
Net cash gain (loss)	XXX
Add beginning cash balance	XX
Ending cash balance	XXXX

By anticipating the ending cash balance, management is in a position to make plans well in advance of need, to arrange for loans, and to invest excess cash balances in marketable securities. Management uses the cash budget to anticipate influences on the cash balance resulting from operations and other transactions, as portrayed in Figures 12.1 and 12.2. A well-organized cash budget summarizes in a single document the events that management expects will affect the company's cash balance.

Cash budgeting begins with a work sheet that shows the planning period (often a year) broken into days, weeks, or months—the increments depending on the desired detail. Next, the periodic cash receipts from sales are estimated followed by the cash outlays for operations—purchases of labor, materials, office and factory overhead, and so on. Combining the operating cash flows from the work sheet with other cash flows and the desired cash balance produces the cash budget.

EXAMPLE

Shermant Company's marketing manager has estimated monthly sales for next year. The financial manager uses these figures, the most important estimates in cash budgeting, to prepare the cash budget. Shermant's financial manager believes that an annual budget broken down by month will adequately serve the company's planning purposes. Furthermore, Shermant's management likes to maintain a minimum $3,000 cash balance to meet its precautionary and trans-actions needs. Management anticipates the following operating and financing events during the budget period:

- The beginning cash balance is $7,000.
- Most sales occur in late winter and early spring.
- The company extends trade credit to customers. As a result, 30 percent of Shermant's sales are cash and 70 percent are credit sales collected during the month following the sale.
- Purchased materials and parts amount to 80 percent of sales. The purchasing manager buys materials and parts during the month preceding sales to allow for assembly and distribution, but the company makes payment in the month following purchases.

- The personnel manager expects wages and salaries to change over the year.
- The company will make income tax payments in March, June, September, and December, and it will make a debt repayment in June.

Developing a cash budget for Shermant Company begins with a work sheet detailing the cash operating cycle—the expected cash receipts and disbursements from operations. The following discussion shows how to prepare and combine the work sheet with other information to derive the final cash budget.

Cash Budget Work Sheet. Table 12.1 presents the work sheet for calculating expected monthly operating cash flows for Shermant Company over the year. It shows when the company expects to collect cash from its sales and to pay for its purchases and operating expenses. Because cash receipts flow into the company during the month the company makes a sale and during the following month too, the work sheet has two entries for receipts. Look at the first three lines in Table 12.1. For example, March sales of $22,000 generate cash receipts in March of $6,600 (30 percent of sales are cash) and in April of $15,400 (70 percent of sales are credit-collected in the next month).

Shermant pays for purchases during the month following a purchase, which accounts for the timing of cash payments. Consider, for example, the cash outlay in April associated with purchases. The company orders materials and parts for April's sales in March. It then writes a check in April for the $19,200 March purchases (80 percent of anticipated April sales). Now look at the entry for September. Shermant pays in September for the $9,600 August purchases.

Table 12.1 shows wages and salaries rising and falling in a pattern supplied to the financial manager by the company's personnel manager. The sum of the payments for purchases and for wages and salaries equals total operating outflows.

Final Cash Budget. Combining the forecast of operating cash flows with other cash outflows and inflows and then entering the desired cash balance completes the budget. Table 12.2 shows Shermant Company's cash budget in final form.

The top part of the cash budget includes the cash inflows and outflows from the work sheet in Table 12.1. Each month's anticipated tax payment and the $15,000 debt retirement scheduled for June are also included in the cash budget. Net cash gain (or loss) from each month's transactions equals total operating inflows less total cash disbursements. Adding the net cash gain to (or subtracting the net cash loss from) the beginning cash balance yields the ending cash balance for each month.

To complete the budget, we compare each month's ending cash balance with the desired balance to see if the company is falling short of or exceeding the desired balance. The bottom line of Table 12.2 highlights the company's cash invested and borrowed. Each month's entry in this line is a cumulative total measuring cash excesses (and thus investments in marketable securities) or shortages (and thus borrowings). Each month's dollar amount is the total borrowings (if shortage) or investments (if excess) outstanding at that time. *Changes* in the bottom line of Table 12.2 equal the amount entered in Line 3, net cash gain (loss) during a month. The rationale is that management uses any net cash gain to

TABLE 12.1

Shermant Company: Cash Budget Work Sheet for 19X9

	January[a]	February	March	April	May
Sales revenues	$10,000	$ 8,000	$22,000	$24,000	$ 9,000
Cash receipts					
1st month 30%	$ 3,000	$ 2,400	$ 6,600	$ 7,200	$ 2,700
2nd month 70%		7,000	5,600	15,400	16,800
Total Operating Inflows	$ 3,000	$ 9,400	$12,200	$22,600	$19,500
Purchases (80% of next month's sales)	$ 6,400	$17,600	$19,200	$ 7,200	$ 4,000
Cash payments (purchases from preceding month)		6,400	17,600	19,200	7,200
Add wages and salaries		800	1,500	1,500	850
Total Operating Outflows		$ 7,200	$19,100	$20,700	$ 8,050

[a]In order to simplify the example, we show no entries for cash receipts from December 19X8 sales and no cash payments for December 19X8 purchases. In practice, the cash budget would include these amounts.

TABLE 12.2

Shermant Company: Cash Budget for 19X9

	January	February	March	April	May
(1) Total operating inflows	$3,000	$9,400	$12,200	$22,600	$19,500
Operating outflows					
Payments for purchases		$6,400	$17,600	$19,200	$ 7,200
Wages and salaries		800	1,500	1,500	850
Other cash payments					
Taxes			2,000		
Debt repayment					
(2) Total cash disbursements		$7,200	$21,100	$20,700	$ 8,050
(3) Net cash gain (loss) (Line 1 − Line 2)		$2,200	($ 8,900)	$ 1,900	$11,450
(4) Add beginning cash balance		7,000	9,200	300	2,200
(5) Ending cash balance (Line 3 + Line 4)		$9,200	$ 300	$ 2,200	$13,650
(6) Less cash balance desired		3,000	3,000	3,000	3,000
(7) Cumulative cash invested (borrowed) (Line 5 − Line 6)		$6,200	($ 2,700)	($ 800)	$10,650

TABLE 12.1 *continued*

	June	July	August	September	October	November	December
	$5,000	$5,000	$10,000	$12,000	$12,000	$30,000	$33,000
	$1,500	$1,500	$ 3,000	$ 3,600	$ 3,600	$ 9,000	$ 9,900
	6,300	3,500	3,500	7,000	8,400	8,400	21,000
	$7,800	$5,000	$ 6,500	$10,600	$12,000	$17,400	$30,900
	$4,000	$8,000	$ 9,600	$ 9,600	$24,000	$26,400	$ 6,400
	4,000	4,000	8,000	9,600	9,600	24,000	26,400
	800	800	900	1,000	1,000	2,000	2,500
	$4,800	$4,800	$ 8,900	$10,600	$10,600	$26,000	$28,900

TABLE 12.2 *continued*

	June	July	August	September	October	November	December
	$ 7,800	$5,000	$6,500	$10,600	$12,000	$17,400	$30,900
	$ 4,000	$4,000	$8,000	$ 9,600	$ 9,600	$24,000	$26,400
	800	800	900	1,000	1,000	2,000	2,500
	2,200			2,000			3,000
	15,000						
	$22,000	$4,800	$8,900	$12,600	$10,600	$26,000	$31,900
	($14,200)	$ 200	($2,400)	($ 2,000)	$ 1,400	($ 8,600)	($ 1,000)
	13,650	(550)	(350)	(2,750)	(4,750)	(3,350)	(11,950)
	($ 550)	($ 350)	($2,750)	($ 4,750)	($ 3,350)	($11,950)	($12,950)
	3,000	3,000	3,000	3,000	3,000	3,000	3,000
	($ 3,550)	($3,350)	($5,750)	($ 7,750)	($ 6,350)	($14,950)	($15,950)

discharge debt or for investing in marketable securities and borrows cash or sells marketable securities to cover any loss.[2]

Usefulness of the Cash Budget

The cash budget is a useful financial management tool because it helps to focus management's attention on future cash surpluses and deficits. In this way it helps management to avoid surprises and aids in planning, communication, and control. It also serves to buttress a loan application by increasing the lender's confidence in the borrower.

Consider the situation confronting Shermant Company's management. During February it expects a $6,200 excess of cash (see the bottom line of Table 12.2) that it can temporarily invest, but in March cash outflows will be $8,900 greater than cash inflows. This net outflow will pull the cash level down to $300 ($9,200 − $8,900), which is $2,700 below the desired $3,000 cash balance. The company's financial manager will borrow $2,700 to meet the company's target cash level. In April cash inflows exceed outflows by $1,900. Adding this amount to March's $300 ending balance, the manager sees that Shermant will end April with a balance of $2,200. Comparing this amount with the balance desired shows that the company must borrow $800 in April. May generates an $11,450 net cash gain, which leaves the company with excess cash equaling $10,650. Each month after May, however, finds Shermant with a cash shortage. Because the cash shortage does not turn around during the planning period, the financial manager should determine whether Shermant needs long-term financing or has problems in marketing or production. A cash budget is a short-term planning tool, but here it provides information that could be used in making long-term decisions.

A cash budget disciplines management's cash planning because management must forecast events that influence cash flows during the planning period. With the cash budget as a guide, the financial manager plans necessary actions to cope with cash gains and losses—investing or repaying loans with gains, and borrowing or liquidating assets to cover shortages. Thus the financial manager preserves company liquidity and increases profitability. The cash budget improves the company's ability to borrow by communicating to bankers in advance the planned loans and their repayment.

SPEEDING UP INFLOWS AND CONTROLLING OUTFLOWS

By maintaining no more than the minimum necessary cash balance, the financial manager can keep company cash working in more profitable assets such as marketable securities and operating assets. Speeding up cash inflows to the company also increases company profitability, as does controlling cash outflows. The manager can invest the cash gained in profitable assets.

An example of a corporation that follows these principles is CARE Inc., the American arm of the international aid organization. In the 1980s CARE hired a professional receiving service to process donations on the same day they arrived.

---

[2] Table 12.2 does not include interest expense for short-term borrowing to cover cash shortages, nor does it show interest earned from short-term investments. In some cases these omissions roughly balance each other. If not, then net interest for each period should be included. We omit this consideration in order to focus on more important features of cash budgeting.

The Problem of Too Much Cash

Some companies have an enviable problem: too much cash. At the beginning of 1992, American Home Products held more than $2 billion in cash and cash equivalents. Other cash-rich companies in the early 1990s included Merrill Lynch and Schering-Plough. Unfortunately for these companies, a decline in interest rates sharply reduced their earnings on short-term investments.

According to a survey of corporate practice, more companies invest excess cash in repurchase agreements than in any other type of money market security. Second in popularity are negotiable certificates of deposit. Commercial paper ranks third, followed by foreign short-term securities and U.S. Treasury securities.

When yields on money market securities drop (as they did in the early 1990s), financial managers start looking at alternatives. After all, a percentage point drop in annual return on $2 billion is $20 million! "We used to

do an awful lot of certificates of deposit and government paper," says one financial manager. "Now we're looking at variable-rate preferred stocks."

Variable-rate (or adjustable-rate) preferred stocks, pioneered by Chase Manhattan and Manufacturers Hanover, have floating dividends tied to U.S. Treasury securities. The dividend rate rises and falls with changes in rates on Treasury securities, thereby keeping the value of the preferred stock relatively constant.

Besides a relatively stable value, adjustable-rate preferred stock (ARPS) conveys another benefit to *corporate* investors. The Tax Reform Act of 1986 exempts from federal income taxes 70 percent of dividends received by a corporation. If the corporation owns 20 percent or more (by vote and value) of the dividend-paying corporation's common stock, then it may exempt 80 percent of the dividends. These exemptions greatly increase the attractiveness

of ARPS to corporate investors.

Consider, for example, a corporation with a 34 percent marginal tax rate that receives $100,000 in dividends on a $1,000,000 investment in ARPS. Assuming that the corporate investor owns less than 20 percent of the paying corporation, the corporate investor pays $10,200 in taxes: 0.34(0.30)($100,000). The effective tax rate is 10.2 percent ($10,200/$100,000), and the after-tax rate of return is 8.98 percent ($89,800/$1,000,000). If the $100,000 were received in interest instead of dividends, then the corporate investor would pay $34,000 in taxes—an effective tax rate of 34 percent—and the after-tax rate of return would be only 6.6 percent.

Clearly, U.S. tax rules favor corporate investment in dividend-paying securities. You should remember, however, that such securities are usually riskier than money market securities.

Source: Ravindra R. Kamath, Shahriar Khaksari, Heidi Hylton Meier, and John Winklepeck, "Management of Excess Cash: Practices and Developments," *Financial Management*, Autumn 1985, 70–77; Bernard J. Winger, Carl R. Chen, John D. Martin, J. William Petty, and Steven C. Hayden, "Adjustable Rate Preferred Stock," *Financial Management*, Spring 1986, 48–57; and a report in *The Wall Street Journal*, Mar. 21, 1990, C1.

Before the service was engaged, donations sent at Christmas were not completely processed until the following April. In addition, CARE moved about $1,700,000 from a checking account into interest-earning accounts and exchanged some short-term investments for long-term ones. These changes increased interest income by more than $500,000 annually.

collection float time
Time required to collect cash after a customer issues a check.

disbursement float time
Time required for a payer's bank to reduce the checking balance after the payer issues a check.

Float Time

Speeding up inflows and controlling outflows become tactics in cash management because of float time. **Collection float time** is the time required for a company to collect cash after a customer issues a check for payment to the company. In contrast, **disbursement float time** is the time required for cash to be subtracted

FIGURE 12.3

Illustration of Six-Day Float Time for Receiving and Sending Cash Payments

Collection float time is the number of days that elapse from the time a customer writes a check to a company until the company counts it as cash in the bank. Disbursement float time is the number of days that elapse from the time a company writes a check until the check clears the company's bank account.

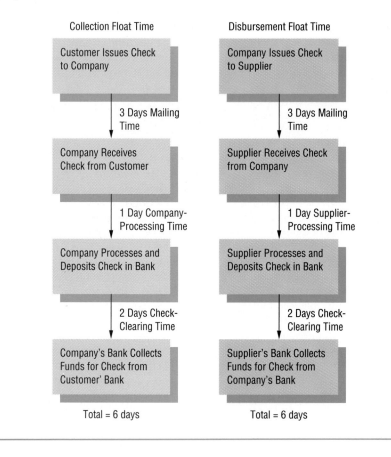

Collection Float Time

Customer Issues Check to Company

↓ 3 Days Mailing Time

Company Receives Check from Customer

↓ 1 Day Company-Processing Time

Company Processes and Deposits Check in Bank

↓ 2 Days Check-Clearing Time

Company's Bank Collects Funds for Check from Customer' Bank

Total = 6 days

Disbursement Float Time

Company Issues Check to Supplier

↓ 3 Days Mailing Time

Supplier Receives Check from Company

↓ 1 Day Supplier-Processing Time

Supplier Processes and Deposits Check in Bank

↓ 2 Days Check-Clearing Time

Supplier's Bank Collects Funds for Check from Company's Bank

Total = 6 days

---

direct send

Mechanism to reduce check-clearing time; bypasses the Federal Reserve and sends checks directly to a correspondent bank for clearing.

from the company's checking account after it issues a check for payment to a supplier.

Figure 12.3 illustrates the factors causing collection and disbursement float time. Depending on the origin and destination of the check, mailing time often constitutes a large part of both float times. After receiving a check, a company experiences *processing time*—the time required to log the check, credit the appropriate account, and take the check to the bank. On depositing the check, the company incurs *check-clearing time*—the time required for the depositor's bank to collect funds from the payer's bank.[3] Banks usually make available to their commercial depositors the check-clearing time schedules for various geographic locations. **Direct sends** connect major money centers like New York City and Los Angeles so that check-clearing time is greatly reduced. The maximum

[3] Bankers use their own discretion, subject to pressure from the customer, to decide how long a customer must wait for check clearance. For new or infrequent customers, bankers may put a hold on a check for up to two weeks, depending on the check's point of origin. Check clearances are much faster for a customer with an ongoing relationship with the bank.

time necessary to clear checks through the Federal Reserve System is two working days.

Speeding Up Cash Inflows

lockbox

Post office box rented by a company and serviced by a local bank.

Lockboxes.   One method for speeding up inflows is the use of a **lockbox,** a post office box rented by a company and serviced by a local bank with which the company keeps its account. The purpose of a lockbox is to reduce collection float time. For instance, if a company based in New York City has many West Coast customers, then it can trim its float time by directing those customers to send their checks to a lockbox in, say, Los Angeles instead of to the company's New York City headquarters. The bank picks up the checks, credits the company's account, and keeps the company informed of all transactions. Company officers never see the checks, although the bank may send copies of the checks to the company's credit department. The financial manager could have the company's funds wired to another bank, perhaps a local one. Wire transfers mean that credit for funds is sent electronically through the Federal Reserve System (or private wire system). Wire transfers eliminate mailing time and check-clearing time.

collection float

Dollar amount of cash inflows in transit to a company.

A reduction in collection float time reduces a company's **collection float,** the dollar amount of cash inflows in transit. By freeing up collection float, the company captures cash that it can invest to earn a return. Alternatively, the company might use the cash to reduce short-term borrowing, thereby reducing interest expense.

EXAMPLE

Kocur Affiliates has annual credit sales of $30,000,000; 95 percent of the company's sales, or $28,500,000, are paid for by checks delivered through the mail. An analysis of its collection system discloses that total float time in the collection system is 6 days. Kocur establishes a lockbox system in several parts of the country and directs the lockbox banks to wire collections to the company's local bank. The lockbox and wire transfer system will reduce float by 2 days. Kocur makes its sales over 5 working days each week, and the company closes for 2 weeks over the Christmas holidays. Thus it makes its sales over 5 days × 50 weeks = 250 working days each year. What is the annual dollar return associated with implementing the lockbox system?

For the above example, begin by calculating sales per working day paid by mail. Multiply daily sales paid by mail times the number-of-days reduction in float time:

$$\begin{aligned}
\text{Reduction in collection float} &= \frac{\text{Daily sales}}{\text{paid by mail}} \times \frac{\text{Days reduction}}{\text{in float time}} \\
&= \left(\frac{\$28,500,000}{250}\right) \times 2 \\
&= \$114,000 \times 2 \\
&= \$228,000
\end{aligned}$$

The lockbox system frees $228,000 from Kocur's pipeline of incoming cash. As long as Kocur can maintain this 2-day reduction in float time, the company has an extra $228,000 annually to use elsewhere.[4]

If Kocur's management can invest the cash in money market securities yielding 8 percent annual interest, then the before-tax benefit of the lockbox system is $18,240, calculated as follows:

Reduction in collection float	$228,000
Multiplied by annual rate available	× 0.08
Annual dollar return	$ 18,240

This $18,240 benefit is not without a cost because most banks charge a handling fee per transaction and a fixed fee per year for lockbox service. In addition, the banks might require the company to maintain compensating balances in non-interest-bearing accounts. Only when the cash benefit exceeds the cost should management implement the lockbox system.

Other Methods.   A financial manager can develop other ways to speed up cash inflows. The financial manager's ingenuity and the company's economic muscle are the major limits to the number of ways. Some of the methods are presented in Chapter 13, which discusses the management of accounts receivable, but here are a few methods in brief:

- Deliver deposits to the bank in person. It is faster than mail service.
- Deposit receipts on the day they are received.
- Make deposits before the bank's cutoff time for the day.
- Consider factoring accounts receivable. *Factoring* is the process of selling receivables to a factor, a company that buys accounts receivable. (Factoring is examined in Chapter 14.)
- Modify terms on credit sales to promote faster payments by customers.
- Mail invoices promptly.
- Keep the bank informed of management's desire to learn methods for minimizing its deposit balance. The banker will then be more likely to pass on suggestions to the company.
- Guard against the tendency for nonroutine receipts (for example, tax refunds and proceeds from the sale of fixed assets) to slow down processing.

Controlling Cash Outflows

The financial manager controls cash outflows, like cash inflows, to improve profitability. By keeping cash in the possession of the company for as long as possible, the financial manager maximizes company earnings. A rule of cash management is: "Pay on time, but never pay early."

---

[4] Another way to look at the cash freed from the pipeline is to consider what happens to the accounts receivable on the company's balance sheet. The 2-day float time saved reduces the company's average collection period (days' sales in accounts receivable) by 2 days. The reduction in receivables makes cash available for use elsewhere. The average collection period is discussed in Chapter 13.

EXAMPLE

Andrews Gunite Company purchases, on average, $200,000 of material daily. Vendors give Andrews 30 days from the date of purchase to make payment. Instead of paying on the 30th day after purchase, Andrews always pays on the 29th day. If Andrews would pay on the 30th day, not the 29th, its accounts payable would be $200,000 (1 day × $200,000 daily) larger and its reliance on other sources of financing $200,000 smaller. Suppose that Andrews has a bank loan outstanding on which it pays 10 percent interest annually. Andrews pays $20,000 (0.10 × $200,000) a year more in interest expenses than is necessary because its bank loan is $200,000 larger than it would be with Andrews paying on the 30th day.

Financial managers use several methods to control cash outflows. Even though legal, some of the methods suggest questionable ethics. In part, ethical issues arise because financially powerful companies can more easily use the methods against the financially weak than the reverse. Consider the practice of **remote disbursement:** drawing a check on a remotely located bank and mailing it from a remote location in order to maximize mailing and clearing times. Suppliers with little influence might put up with the practice, whereas strong suppliers might protest and thus be able to stop it.

Controlling cash outflows involves, in part, the lengthening of disbursement float time in order to increase **disbursement float,** the dollar amount of cash outflows in transit. A larger disbursement float increases the disbursing company's cash balances and the earnings on them. Some of the methods described below increase disbursement float while others simply improve the efficiency of handling cash:

remote disbursement
Drawing a check on a remotely located bank and mailing it from a remote location to maximize disbursement float time.

disbursement float
Dollar amount of cash outflows in transit from a company.

payable through draft (PTD)
Written order to pay cash to the payee only after the payer agrees to the order.

overdraft
Withdrawal of money in excess of the company's deposit balance.

zero balance accounts
Bank accounts into which cash is transferred when needed but which otherwise have zero balances.

depository transfer check (DTC)
Check used to transfer cash from a company's account at one bank to its account at another bank.

- Mail checks at the end of the day.
- Use a **payable through draft (PTD)** instead of a check to make payments. A check is drawn against a bank, but a PTD is drawn against a payer. The bank notifies the payer that it has received a PTD drawn on the payer's account, who then has 24 hours during which either to accept the PTD or reject it. The payer has time to make sure the payment is in order and has use of the cash for an additional 24 hours.
- Establish an overdrafting agreement with a bank. An **overdraft** is a withdrawal of money in excess of the company's deposit balance. The bank automatically extends a loan to cover the overdraft.
- Establish **zero balance accounts,** enabling the company to reduce its cash deposits at banks. Zero balance accounts have zero balances except when checks are cleared against them, at which time the bank transfers cash from the company's master account at the bank. Only the master account carries a cash balance, thereby reducing excess balances in several accounts.
- Use a **depository transfer check (DTC)** to move cash from one of the company's banks to another of its banks. A company uses DTCs to move cash from its lockbox banks to its *concentration bank(s).* Having its cash concentrated in one or only a few banks reduces excess balances and simplifies a company's decisions on short-term investing and borrowing.

TEMPORARILY EXCESS CASH

A company has temporarily excess cash whenever its cash balance exceeds what it needs for transactions and precautionary purposes and for the compensating balances required by banks.[5] The purpose of the excess may be to support forthcoming seasonal increases in receivables and inventory, make long-term investments, retire debt, or take advantage of opportunities. Whatever the purpose, management needs to control temporarily excess cash. The financial manager seeks to maximize return on excess cash subject to constraints imposed by its purpose.

Investing Temporarily Excess Cash

Constraints on investing temporarily excess cash are normally severe, ruling out many types of investments. The overriding purpose of the cash is to achieve a specific goal. Because the cash is earmarked for a specific purpose, financial managers do not take many chances with its investment. For example, a company may declare $430,000 in dividends payable to shareholders in 60 days. The company's financial manager may invest the cash during the interim in a safe security so that the company will have it available on the payment date. Failure to have the $430,000 would be financially embarrassing and lead to a decline in the price of the company's common stock.

In determining where to invest temporarily excess cash, financial managers usually consider the following criteria in addition to *expected return:*

- *Low default risk.* The investment must have little or no chance of default on the return of principal and interest. This criterion generally rules out, for example, low-rated bonds.
- *Low interest rate risk.* Volatility of investment price due to changes in interest rates must be low. This criterion rules out long-term bonds, even those issued by the U.S. Treasury.
- *Low purchasing-power risk.* Changes in the expected inflation rate lead to changes in interest rates and changes in security prices. Similar in effect to interest rate risk, this criterion rules out long-term bonds. Because the excess cash is temporary, long-term inflation hedges such as real estate are also inappropriate investments.
- *Low liquidity risk.* The investment must be easily salable at its market price. Second best is an investment with no secondary market but with a maturity matching the time period of the available excess cash. The presence of a secondary market is especially important when there is uncertainty about the time that the excess cash will be available.
- *Low foreign-exchange risk.* Volatility of the foreign-exchange rate (price of foreign currency) must be low for investment in foreign securities. This criterion rules out securities denominated in the currency of a financially weak country.

---

[5] Some analysts define *temporarily excess cash* as the amount exceeding the transactions and compensating balances, thus omitting the precautionary balance. In many cases, however, a company needs precautionary balances in the form of cash, not marketable securities. Precautionary *cash* balances need to be available because of the uncertainty surrounding the nonsynchronous cash inflows and outflows.

A convenient investment outlet for temporarily excess cash is *repurchase agreements* (called *repos*) with commercial banks or securities dealers. Repos represent an indirect way of investing in the money market. A company agrees to purchase a U.S. Treasury bill from a commercial bank with the stipulation that the bank will repurchase it on a specified date at the then-prevailing price. Maturities of repos can be as short as one day and may extend to several months. Flexibility in maturity enables the financial manager to select a maturity matching the company's need. With rare exceptions, repos have proven to be very safe short-term investments.

Alternatively, a financial manager may participate directly in the money market by investing temporarily excess cash in money market securities. As Chapter 2 indicates, the money market is any place where securities trade with maturities of one year or less. Money market securities generally are high-quality instruments. Still, safety and liquidity do vary, and the financial manager must balance these attributes against the promised yields.

Money market securities commonly used for investing temporarily excess cash include:[6]

- *U.S. Treasury bills:* Short-term debt securities issued by the U.S. Treasury.
- *U.S. agency paper:* Short-term debt securities issued by government agencies—for example, Federal Land Banks and the Bank for Cooperatives.
- *Commercial paper:* Short-term promissory notes issued by corporations.
- *Negotiable certificates of deposit:* Large-denomination deposits at commercial banks, traded by securities dealers.
- *Bankers' acceptances:* Irrevocable obligations of the accepting bank, which promises to pay the bearer a face amount at maturity. These usually arise out of international transactions.
- *Eurodollar deposits:* Dollar-denominated deposits in banks outside the United States. The term *Eurodollar deposit* applies to dollar-denominated deposits in all countries, not just European countries. Two types of deposits are available: interest-bearing time deposits and certificates of deposit (Eurodollar CDs), which trade in a secondary market. Interest rates on the deposits are often based on the London interbank offered rate (LIBOR)—the rate offered by large banks in London to obtain dollar deposits from other banks (hence *interbank*).
- *Foreign short-term securities:* Debt securities issued by foreign companies and countries—for example, the Canadian Treasury bill.

Hedging Temporarily Excess Cash

interest rate futures
Contracts to buy or sell at a later date securities whose prices change with changes in interest rates; agreement specifies price and quantity of the security and the future settlement (delivery) date.

Investing temporarily excess cash in money market securities instead of long-term securities greatly lessens exposure to interest rate risk, but some degree of risk still remains. If interest rates rise, then the market value of the securities will fall. To reduce risk further, the financial manager can use **interest rate futures** to hedge against future changes in interest rates. Interest rate futures are contracts made today to buy or sell a financial security (for example, T-bills, negotiable CDs, and Eurodollar deposits) in the future. The contract specifies (1) the dollar amount of the security to be delivered, (2) the exact day of delivery, and (3) the

---

[6]Money market mutual funds also serve as investments for temporarily excess cash, especially for small companies with small amounts of cash. The large denominations of many money market securities may prevent the direct participation in the money market by small companies.

price that will be paid for the security. By selling futures contracts, the financial manager protects the company from loss on its short-term portfolio.

To *hedge* means to take equal but opposite financial positions so that gains on one position offset losses on the other. Financial managers hedge not to make a profit but to protect a profit on an investment by assuring the company of the future price of the investment. Through hedging, a loss in the **spot market** (sometimes called the *cash market*) is offset by a gain in the futures market or vice versa. The spot market is the market for immediate delivery—say, the market for buying and selling T-bills with immediate delivery. The **futures market** is the market for contracts specifying delivery of a security sometime in the future. Examples of commodity exchanges where financial futures trade are the Chicago Board of Trade; the Chicago Mercantile Exchange; the New York Cotton Exchange; and the New York Futures Exchange.[7]

spot market

Market for immediate delivery.

futures market

Market for contracts to deliver a security in the future on a specified date.

Interest Rate Futures.   The trading unit of some interest rate futures is $1,000,000, with delivery dates spaced at 90-day intervals into the future—more than one year for some contracts. Since traders buy and sell contracts in the futures market on margin, a company does not need $1,000,000 to buy or sell a futures contract. The minimum amount of initial margin (cash) for 90-day T-bill futures is $2,000 to $2,500 for a $1,000,000 contract.

marked to market

Daily adjustment to cash in a margin account to reflect changes in price of the underlying security in a futures contract.

A trader's margin account is **marked to market** each day—a daily adjustment reflecting the change in market value of the security described in the futures contract. For the futures contract buyer, cash is added to the margin account when interest rates decline and the value of the security increases. In contrast, cash is subtracted from the margin account when interest rates increase and the value of the security decreases. If the cash value of the margin account falls below a specified *maintenance margin*, then the futures contract buyer receives a *margin call* requesting sufficient cash to bring the account up to the initial margin requirement. To protect the buyer, futures exchanges establish a *daily limit* on price changes. When the daily limit is reached, trading in the futures contract ceases until the next business day. This gives the buyer a chance to sell the contract when trading resumes and thus limit losses. Daily limits typically are about equal to the initial margin requirement.

Buyers of interest rate futures rarely take delivery of the underlying financial security. Instead, they close out their positions by selling the futures contract before the expiration date. (In like manner, sellers rarely make delivery.) The amount of money in the buyer's margin account upon closing depends on the relationship between the prevailing security price and the price agreed to at the time the futures contract was purchased. If the prevailing security price exceeds the contract's price, then the buyer wins and the seller loses; otherwise, the buyer loses and the seller wins.

Figure 12.4 presents quotations for 90-day Treasury bill futures from *The Wall Street Journal* (February 5, 1993). The first column shows the delivery months for the 90-day T-bills extending from March 1993 to December 1993. The next four columns contain quotations for the opening trade of the day, the day's high, the day's low, and the settlement value (which approximates a closing value). *Chg* is the change in settlement value from the preceding trading day. Because financial managers tend to focus on interest rates rather than on T-bill

---

[7]These exchanges deal in many different commodity futures: corn, oats, soybeans, wheat, cattle, hogs, lumber, cocoa, coffee, sugar, orange juice, gold, silver, platinum, propane gas, gasoline, heating oil, and others. Indeed, agricultural futures were the earliest ones traded, beginning in the mid-1800s. The Chicago Board of Trade first introduced financial futures in 1975.

FIGURE 12.4

**Treasury Bill Quotations of the CME
(Chicago Mercantile Exchange) Futures Contract[a]**

						Discount		Open
	Open	High	Low	Settle	Chg	Settle	Chg	Interest
Mar	97.03	97.06	97.02	97.05	+ .05	2.95	− .05	20,344
June	96.83	96.86	96.82	96.85	+ .05	3.15	− .05	10,828
Sept	96.53	96.57	96.53	96.56	+ .08	3.44	− .08	1,240
Dec	96.19	96.20	96.18	96.19	+ .07	3.81	− .07	253

TREASURY BILLS (CME)—$1 mil.; pts. of 100%

Est vol 5,529; vol Wed 3,351; open int 32,665, +133.

[a] Trades on Thursday, February 4, 1993.
Source: The Wall Street Journal, February 5, 1993, C12.

prices, *The Wall Street Journal* provides annualized discount yields based on settlement prices. Changes in yields from the previous trading session are also provided. Thus the columns under *Discount* say that the T-bill in the March contract offers a 2.95 percent discount yield, down 0.05 percentage point, or 5 basis points (100 basis points = 1 percentage point). The final column shows the open interest in the contracts—that is, the number of contracts outstanding. Open interest reflects the attractiveness of a contract to investors: 20,344 March contracts represent $20.344 billion of U.S. T-bills at face value. The bottom of the table shows the estimated number of contracts traded during the day, the actual number traded the preceding day, the total open interest in all contracts, and the change in total open interest from the preceding day.

The quotations in Figure 12.4 are *not* prices of T-bill futures but are index values, calculated as follows:

$$\text{Index value} = 100 - \text{Annual discount yield}$$

Applied to the settlement value of the March contract, the index is:

$$\text{Index value} = 100 - 2.95$$
$$= 97.05$$

Because the index values depend on *annualized* discount yields, the quotations for the 90-day T-bills to be delivered during different months can be compared with each other. Unfortunately, however, this quotation method masks the contract's actual price of the T-bill to be delivered.

To illustrate the relationship between quotations and prices, consider the settlement price of the March contract, which requires delivery of a 90-day, $1,000,000 T-bill. Securities dealers calculate the annual discount yield on T-bills as follows (presented in Chapter 2):

$$\frac{\text{Annual}}{\text{discount yield}} = \frac{\text{Face value} - \text{Purchase price}}{\text{Face value}} \times \frac{360}{\text{Days to maturity}}$$

Insert the known values of the March contract into the equation and solve for the purchase price:

$$0.0295 = \frac{\$1,000,000 - \text{Purchase price}}{\$1,000,000} \times \frac{360 \text{ days}}{90 \text{ days}}$$

$$0.007375 = \frac{\$1,000,000 - \text{Purchase price}}{\$1,000,000}$$

$$\$7,375 = \$1,000,000 - \text{Purchase price}$$

$$\text{Purchase price} = \$992,625$$

Although the quotation is 97.05, the price of the T-bill is $992,625. The purchaser of the futures contract agrees to pay $992,625 in March (3-day settlement period begins the third Thursday) for a 90-day, $1,000,000 T-bill. To illustrate gains and losses on the contract, suppose the annual discount yield declines from 2.95 percent to 1.95 percent immediately after the purchaser buys the contract: The price of the T-bill would increase from $992,625 to $995,125, a $2,500 gain for the purchaser and a $2,500 loss for the seller.[8] A change of one basis point in the annual discount yield results in a $25 change in price of the T-bill, so 100 basis points (one percentage point) results in a price change of $2,500.

Short and Long Positions.   When financial managers hedge an investment, they take either a short or a long position in the financial futures market. A **short position** means an agreement to deliver the underlying security at the specified price on the settlement date. It is equivalent to *selling* the security at a future date and is opposite to a long position. A **long position** means an agreement to accept delivery of the underlying security at the specified price on the settlement date. It is equivalent to *buying* the security at a future date.

A financial manager can use interest rate futures to hedge interest rate risk associated with riding the yield curve. To **ride the yield curve** means to invest in a security with a maturity different from the investment horizon. For example, a financial manager may invest cash that the company will need in 2 months (the investment horizon) in a 9-month Treasury bill to receive the higher interest rate on the 9-month bill (generally the longer the maturity, the higher the interest rate). In the absence of hedging, the financial manager in this example would be exposing the company to undue interest rate risk.

To illustrate the benefit of hedging interest rate risk when riding the yield curve, consider first an investment horizon *shorter* than the maturity of the security. Chandy Company has excess cash that it will need in 60 days to repay a maturing bank loan. Because of its higher yield, Mr. Chandy wants to invest in a 150-day T-bill instead of the 60-day T-bill. Mr. Chandy hedges by buying the 150-day T-bill in the spot market and at the same time taking a short position in a contract for a 90-day T-bill to be delivered in 60 days. When the 60 days

short position
Agreement to deliver a security in the future at a specified price on a specified date.

long position
Agreement to accept delivery of a security in the future at a specified price on a specified date.

ride the yield curve
Invest in a security with a maturity different from the investment horizon.

---

[8] An equation for calculating purchase price directly can be derived from the preceding equation. For convenience, let Y represent the annual discount yield and D the days to maturity:

$$Y = \frac{\text{Face value} - \text{Purchase price}}{\text{Face value}} \times \frac{360}{D}$$

$$\frac{DY}{360} = \frac{\text{Face value} - \text{Purchase price}}{\text{Face value}}$$

$$\text{Purchase price} = \text{Face value} - \frac{DY(\text{Face value})}{360}$$

$$\text{Purchase price} = \text{Face value}\left(1 - \frac{DY}{360}\right)$$

Application to the 90-day T-bill futures contract with a 1.95 percent annual discount yield produces the following:

$$\text{Purchase price} = \$1,000,000\left[1 - \frac{90(0.0195)}{360}\right]$$

$$= \$1,000,000(1 - 0.004875)$$

$$= \$995,125$$

FOCUS ON PRACTICE

•

Little-Known Cash Facts

- The word *cash* comes from the French *casse*, meaning money box. In other words, what used to *be* the box is now *in* the box!

- The one-dollar silver certificate of 1886 was the first U.S. bill with a portrait of a woman. Martha Washington graced its face.

- The largest denomination of a U.S. bill is the $10,000 bill. It portrays Salmon Portland Chase, who was Secretary of the Treasury during the war between the states. The last $10,000 bill was printed in 1944.

- The first FDIC (Federal Deposit Insurance Corpora-

tion) payment was made to depositors of the Fond du Lac State Bank in East Peoria, Illinois, in July 1934.

- Flipping a coin to make decisions can be traced to Rome in the first century B.C. Caesar's image was on the head side, so if the coin landed heads up it meant he agreed in absentia with the decision.

- The first U.S. coin to use the phrase "E Pluribus Unum" was the 1792 half eagle.

- The largest government-issued gold coin is the Indian 1,000-mohur struck in 1613 at Agra. It is $7\frac{7}{8}$ inches in diame-

ter and weighs over 350 troy ounces.

- The bank with the most branches is the State Bank of India. It had 11,171 branches as of January 1, 1987.

- The earliest recorded banks were the national temples in Greece. Private bankers first appeared in Babylon in 600 B.C.

- In 1938 Frances Estelle Mason became the first woman president of a bank in the United States. She was elected president to replace her father after his untimely death.

Source: Adapted from the 1989–1990 Catalogue of Sheshunoff Information Services Inc.

are up, he sells what was a 150-day T-bill but is now a 90-day T-bill and buys a 90-day, T-bill futures contract to close out his short position. A rise or fall in interest rates does not affect his hedged position. Any change in the T-bill spot price is offset by an opposite change in the T-bill futures price. Mr. Chandy locked in his yield 60 days ago.

Now consider an investment horizon *longer* than the maturity of the security. Damsel Corporation will need cash in 4 months to purchase a mainframe computer for its headquarters. The company's cash for buying the computer is invested in a 1-month T-bill. Damsel's financial manager hedges by taking a long position in a 1-month futures contract for a 3-month T-bill (the money will not be needed for an additional 3 months). Damsel Corporation has guaranteed not only the purchase price of the T-bill one month from now, but also the yield that this bill will provide.

We close our discussion of the techniques associated with cash management by emphasizing the close link between cash and the other components of net working capital. Cash increases and decreases with changes in collections, payments, inventory levels, bank loans, and so on. The study of each component of net working capital is in some respects a study of cash management. With this thought in mind, we concentrate on receivables and inventory in Chapter 13 and current liabilities in Chapter 14.

SUMMARY

• Holding cash subjects a company to purchasing-power risk and to opportunity cost. A company holds cash as a buffer against nonsynchronous cash inflows and outflows. There are other reasons for maintaining cash balances, including precaution, speculation, planned investments, and compensating balances.

• Cash travels between a company and several different parties: owners, creditors, suppliers, customers, employees, and the government. One of the important cash cycles within the company is the cash operating cycle: (1) purchase of materials on credit and, later, payment of the accounts payable, (2) sale of inventory on credit and, later, collection of the accounts receivable.

• A cash budget is a forecast of cash inflows and outflows. It enables the financial manager to anticipate borrowing needs and to plan for the short-term investment of cash. A cash budget shows the following information for each future time period:

Cash inflows	XXXXXX
Less cash outflows	XXXX
Net cash gain (loss)	XXXX
Add beginning cash balance	XX
Ending cash balance	XXX

• Collection float time is the time required for a company to collect cash after a customer issues a check to the company. Reducing this float time speeds up cash inflows to the company. Methods used to reduce collection float include using lockboxes, delivering bank deposits in person, depositing receipts daily, and making bank deposits before the bank's cutoff time for the day. Other methods for speeding up cash inflows include mailing invoices promptly, offering prompt-payment (cash) discounts, and factoring receivables.

• Disbursement float time is the time required for the bank to subtract cash from the company's checking account after it issues a check. Increasing this float time slows down cash outflows. Methods for increasing disbursement float include using remote disbursement locations, delaying payments for purchases, mailing checks at day's end, and using drafts instead of checks.

• Rather than holding cash in a non-interest-bearing account, the financial manager can improve company profitability by investing in money market securities: Treasury bills, short-term securities issued by U.S. government agencies, commercial paper, negotiable certificates of deposit, bankers' acceptances, and Eurodollar deposits. Criteria for investing temporarily excess cash include expected return and risk: default risk, interest rate risk, purchasing-power risk, liquidity risk, and foreign-exchange risk.

• Hedging an investment of temporarily excess cash with interest rate futures permits a financial manager to reduce interest rate risk. Futures contracts reduce the interest rate risk associated with riding the yield curve. If the investment horizon is shorter than the maturity of the security owned, then the financial manager hedges by taking a short position in the futures market. If the investment horizon is longer than the maturity of the security owned, then the financial manager hedges by taking a long position in the futures market.

Key Terms

purchasing-power risk

transactions balance

precautionary balance

speculative balance

planning balance

compensating balance

cash operating cycle

cash budgeting

cash budget

collection float time

disbursement float time

direct send

lockbox

collection float

remote disbursement

disbursement float

payable through draft (PTD)

overdraft

zero balance accounts

depository transfer check (DTC)

interest rate futures

spot market

futures market

marked to market

short position

long position

ride the yield curve

Questions

12.1. Holding cash subjects a company to purchasing-power risk and opportunity cost. Do you agree with this statement? Explain your answer.

12.2. Companies may have at least five motives for holding cash. List and explain these motives.

12.3. Which one of the following types of risk typically arises from holding cash? Define each type of risk.
   a. Interest rate risk.
   b. Business risk.
   c. Purchasing-power risk.
   d. Default risk.

12.4. Describe the cash operating cycle of a company.

12.5. What is the managerial purpose of a cash budget?

12.6. Orr Company is in the 40 percent marginal tax bracket. If Orr's depreciation expense for tax purposes increases by $10,000, what will be the impact on the company's cash budget? Explain your answer.

12.7. List and discuss three methods each for speeding up cash inflows and for slowing down cash outflows. Does each method for slowing outflows seem ethical to you? Explain your answer.

12.8. Circle T or F to show whether each of the following is true or false, then explain the italicized word. One method for slowing down cash outflows would be to:
   T F Install a *lockbox* system.
   T F Pay bills with *payable through drafts*.
   T F Use a *remote disbursement* system.
   T F Use *overdrafts*.
   T F Use *zero balance accounts*.
   T F Use *depository transfer checks*.

12.9. Which one of the following investment alternatives is commonly used to hold cash earmarked to meet a company's short-term, periodic variation in cash needs? Explain why the other choices are unacceptable.
   a. U.S. Treasury bills.
   b. Real estate.
   c. High-grade corporate bonds.
   d. Deep-discount, long-maturity bonds.
   e. Zero-coupon bonds.

12.10. A recent survey of corporate cash management practices revealed that *preservation of capital* is the most important consideration in the investment of temporarily excess cash. Second in importance is *expected rate of return*, followed by *liquidity*, and then *convenience*. Explain the rationale for these rankings.

12.11. List and describe four money market securities. How much are these securities presently yielding? (Refer to the money market section of *The Wall Street Journal*.)

12.12. The director of treasury operations at Campbell Soup Company states: "We use this [ACH] system to issue one-day payments through an automated clearing house for third-party and intercompany transfers. We also use it to pay certain tax bills that require electronic payments. The ACH system is efficient and less expensive than issuing checks or wire transfers. For Campbell Soup, a wire transfer costs $7; an ACH transaction costs 8 cents." Does Campbell Soup actually send cash via electronic networks? Explain.

12.13. (1) What is the primary difference between a *spot market* and a *futures market*? (2) What are interest rate futures?

12.14. Trilling Company owns a $1,000,000 U.S. Treasury bill maturing in 9 months. Trilling's financial manager was told that the T-bill must be sold in 6 months so that the company can invest in new equipment. How can the financial manager use the futures market to lessen interest rate risk?

12.15. A Baxter Travenol Corporation quarterly report to shareholders contained the following passage:

> *Interest rates have moved very favorably since the beginning of this year. Due to the large amount of floating-rate debt incurred to finance the merger [with American Hospital Supply], the company used various hedging techniques to*

minimize the risk of unfavorable movements in interest rates in the future. Although this lowers the risk to the company, it also reduces the benefit from recent favorable movements in interest rates.

a. Describe the hedging action that Baxter Travenol might have taken.
b. Why does management sound apologetic about hedging? Explain your answer.
c. Should management continue to hedge? Explain your answer.

Strategy Problem

Albert Seberg, controller for Carload Toys Inc., is asked to prepare a 5-month cash budget. He calls on you to help him do so. The company is faced with the following situation:

1. The marketing department expects sales in each of the next 5 months to be, respectively, $10,000, $15,000, $30,000, $30,000, and $10,000.
2. The company wishes to have a $4,000 minimum cash balance.
3. On the last day of the month preceding the forecast period, the company's cash balance is $6,000.
4. Sixty percent of sales revenue is collected in the month of the sale and 40 percent is collected in the succeeding month. Purchases for a given month amount to 90 percent of sales expected in that month. Payments are made in the month after the company purchases materials.

5. Carload Toys had $9,000 of sales in the month preceding the budgetary period.
6. Miscellaneous cash outlays will be $2,000 monthly. In the second month the company must repay a $5,000 loan to State Bank of California.

a. Prepare a monthly cash budget covering the next 5 months.
b. Using the cash budget, explain what the financial manager does with the $8,500 net cash gain in Month 3.
c. What is Carload Toy's purchasing-power loss on its $4,000 minimum cash balance over the period if the consumer price index rises from 227 to 247.43?

Strategy	Solution

a.

		Month				
		1	**2**	**3**	**4**	**5**
	Sales	$10,000	$15,000	$30,000	$30,000	$10,000
	Cash inflows					
Recognize the delay in collections.	First month 60%	$ 6,000	$ 9,000	$18,000	$18,000	$ 6,000
	Second month 40%	3,600	4,000	6,000	12,000	12,000
	Less cash outflows					
Recognize the delay in payments.	Payments (90% S_{t-1})	$ 8,100	$ 9,000	$13,500	$27,000	$27,000
	Miscellaneous	2,000	2,000	2,000	2,000	2,000
	Loan repayment		5,000			
	Net cash gain (loss)	($ 500)	($ 3,000)	$ 8,500	$ 1,000	($11,000)
Recognize the beginning balance as the previous ending balance.	Add beginning cash balance	6,000	5,500	2,500	11,000	12,000
	Ending cash balance	$ 5,500	$ 2,500	$11,000	$12,000	$ 1,000
	Less desired cash balance	4,000	4,000	4,000	4,000	4,000
	Cumulative cash excess (shortage)	$ 1,500	($ 1,500)	$ 7,000	$ 8,000	($ 3,000)

b. The financial manager uses the $8,500 net cash gain to repay the $1,500 outstanding loan from Month 2 and invests the remainder in money market securities. Because the company will have a $3,000 cash shortage 2 months later (in Month 5), the financial manager will either invest the $7,000 cash surplus in a security with a 2-month maturity or ride the yield curve (invest longer term) and hedge by taking a short position in the financial futures market.

c. Carload Toy's purchasing-power loss on the $4,000 cash balance is:

Inflation rate is change in CPI divided by initial CPI.

$$\text{Inflation rate} = \frac{247.43 - 227}{227}$$

$$= 0.09, \text{ or } 9\%$$

Multiply the inflation rate times the cash balance.

$$\text{Purchasing-power loss} = 0.09 \times \$4,000$$

$$= \$360$$

Demonstration Problem

Human Resources Management (HRM), a temporary-employment company, needs to retire its $150,000 bank loan at the end of November. The treasurer asks you, the cash manager, to develop a cash budget and to prepare answers for several questions, which you will present at the upcoming executive meeting in October. HRM's September sales totaled $780,000, and its forecast sales for each of the next three months are as follows: October, $840,000; November, $850,000; December, $920,000. HRM collects 40 percent of sales in the month of sale and 58 percent in the following month. The remaining 2 percent is bad debt and is never collected. Other expected cash outflows are as follows:

1. Salaries of temporary employees: 50 percent of sales.

2. Salaries of permanent staff: $160,000 per month.

3. Office lease payment: $8,000 per month.

4. Other expenses: 5 percent of sales.

5. Purchase of a new computer system in December: $210,000.

HRM's cash balance on September 30 is $125,000, but management's desired cash balance is $160,000.

a. What are the disadvantages of holding cash? In view of these disadvantages, what are management's possible motivations for a desired cash balance of $160,000?

b. According to a recent survey of corporate cash management practices, 85 percent of the sample companies prepare a cash budget. What is the managerial purpose of a cash budget?

c. Prepare a cash budget for HRM covering October, November, and December. Will HRM be able to retire its $150,000 bank loan in November?

d. (1) Define *collection float time* and *disbursement float time.* (2) What is a *lockbox system* for speeding up cash inflows? (3) Suppose that HRM instituted a lockbox system, causing collections to change to 60 percent of sales in the month of sale and 38 percent in the following month. In what way is this lockbox system beneficial to HRM? (No calculations are necessary.)

e. List and describe several suitable investment outlets for HRM's temporarily excess cash. Why are the investment outlets on your list suitable for investing temporarily excess cash?

f. What are interest rate futures? If you expect interest rates to *rise,* should you buy or sell interest rate futures? If you expect interest rates to *decline,* should you buy or sell interest rate futures? Explain.

g. Suppose that you plan to purchase a 90-day, $1,000,000 T-bill in 4 months. Furthermore, you are considering two alternatives: (1) Wait 4 months and purchase the T-bill, which you believe will have an annual discount yield of 2.15 percent; or (2) purchase a 90-day T-bill futures contract with a 4-month delivery date, which is presently quoted at 96.85. Calculate the T-bill purchase price associated with each alternative. Which appears better? What risk do you face with each alternative?

Problems

Two-month cash budget

12.1. Diana Ellis is the cash manager for Suntex, a producer of roofing products. Ms. Ellis has been asked by the corporate treasurer to prepare a 2-month cash budget covering June and July. Based on her preliminary investigation, Ms. Ellis has developed the following forecasts:

Forecasts	June	July
Sales	$100,000	$200,000
Purchases of materials	25,000	50,000
Labor costs	25,000	50,000
Other costs	30,000	60,000

Ms. Ellis has also discovered the following facts: (1) May's sales were $140,000. (2) On average, 60 percent of sales is cash, and 40 percent is paid in the month following the sale. (3) May's purchases of materials were $37,500. (4) Suntex pays for purchases 30 days after the purchase date. (5) All other costs are paid during the month incurred. (6) Although its target cash balance is $6,000, Suntex held $9,000 in cash at the end of May.

a. Assist Ms. Ellis by preparing the 2-month cash budget for her.

b. What is the implication of the cash budget for Suntex's short-term borrowing and investing? Explain.

Cash budgeting and purchasing-power loss

12.2. Refer to the information regarding the cash budget for Carload Toys Inc. in the Strategy Problem above. The same conditions prevail in this problem except that sales in the month preceding the budget period were $8,000 rather than $9,000.

a. Prepare a monthly cash budget for the 5-month period.

b. What is Carload Toy's purchasing-power loss on its $4,000 minimum cash balance over the period if the consumer price index rises from 227 to 254.24?

Cash budgeting and earnings after taxes

12.3. Suppose you have been retained as a consultant by Stewart Steel, a manufacturer of rolled steel products. Your task is to prepare a 5-month cash budget covering the period January through May. Having spent the first week collecting data, you have developed the following forecasts (in thousands of dollars):

Month	Sales	Purchases of Materials	Labor Costs	Other Cash Costs	Earnings after Taxes[a]
January	$ 9,500	$ 4,550	$ 3,600	$1,000	$350
February	9,200	4,600	3,650	1,000	(50)
March	9,600	4,650	3,700	1,100	150
April	9,600	4,700	3,800	1,100	0
May	9,700	4,750	3,800	1,100	50
Totals	$47,600	$23,250	$18,550	$5,300	$500

[a] Earnings after taxes but before depreciation.

Your employer tells you that he is most pleased by the forecast total earnings after taxes ($500,000). He notes that the company's current cash balance is $200,000, although he would prefer to maintain a balance of twice that amount.

Further into the conversation, you discover the following: (1) December sales were $9,200,000. (2) Stewart Steel sells products on credit only and collects receivables in the month following sales. (3) All purchases of materials and costs are paid in the month they occur.

a. Prepare the 5-month cash budget for Stewart Steel.

b. How much cash do you expect Stewart Steel to generate over the 5-month period?

c. Explain to your employer why Stewart Steel must borrow money to maintain the desired cash balance of $400,000, despite the $500,000 earnings after taxes.

Cash budgeting and investing

12.4. Eastern Technologies (ET) is a highly successful manufacturer of audiometers and other precision measuring instruments. ET is a profitable "cash cow"; that is, it generates a substantial cash flow each month. Prepare a cash budget to measure these cash flows using the following forecasts:

- Expected sales: Month 1, $9,000,000; Month 2, $10,200,000; Month 3, $12,000,000. Sales last month were $8,500,000 and the month before they were $8,000,000.

- ET collects 60 percent of sales in the month of sale, 30 percent the month after sale, and 10 percent the second month after sale.

- Monthly purchases are 70 percent of sales expected for the following month. Payments for purchases are made 30 days after the purchase date.

- All cash costs other than payments for purchases are $1,400,000 monthly.

- ET's cash balance at the beginning of Month 1 is $4,500,000, but management prefers to maintain a $2,500,000 balance.

After you have prepared the cash budget, prepare a recommendation for investing ET's temporarily excess cash. Because of plans to expand operations, ET will invest all excess cash in fixed assets at the end of Month 3. The following money rates from Section C of *The Wall Street Journal* should be considered in the formulation of your recommendation:

MONEY RATES

Tuesday, February 9, 1993

The key U.S. and foreign annual interest rates below are a guide to general levels but don't always represent actual transactions.

PRIME RATE: 6%. The base rate on corporate loans posted by at least 75% of the nation's 30 largest banks.

FEDERAL FUNDS: 2 15/16% high, 2 13/16% low, 2¾% near closing bid, 2 13/16% offered. Reserves traded among commercial banks for overnight use in amounts of $1 million or more. Source: Prebon Yamane (U.S.A.) Inc.

DISCOUNT RATE: 3%. The charge on loans to depository institutions by the Federal Reserve Banks.

CALL MONEY: 5%. The charge on loans to brokers on stock exchange collateral. Source: Telerate Systems Inc.

COMMERCIAL PAPER placed directly by General Electric Capital Corp.: 3.06% 30 to 59 days; 3.08% 60 to 89 days; 3.10% 90 to 149 days; 3.12% 150 to 179 days; 3.17% 180 to 239 days; 3.20% 240 to 270 days.

COMMERCIAL PAPER: High-grade unsecured notes sold through dealers by major corporations in multiples of $1,000: 3.13% 30 days; 3.16% 60 days; 3.18% 90 days.

CERTIFICATES OF DEPOSIT: 2.63% one month; 2.68% two months; 2.73% three months; 2.82% six months; 2.99% one year. Average of top rates paid by major New York banks on primary new issues of negotiable C.D.s, usually on amounts of $1 million and more. The minimum unit is $100,000. Typical rates in the secondary market: 3.05% one month; 3.10% three months; 3.23% six months.

BANKERS ACCEPTANCES: 3.01% 30 days; 3.02% 60 days; 3.03% 90 days; 3.06% 120 days; 3.11% 150 days; 3.15% 180 days. Negotiable, bank-backed business credit instruments typically financing an import order.

LONDON LATE EURODOLLARS: 3⅛% - 3% one month; 3 3/16% - 3 1/16% two months; 3¼% - 3⅛% three months; 3¼% - 3⅛% four months; 3 5/16% - 3 3/16% five months; 3⅜% - 3¼% six months.

LONDON INTERBANK OFFERED RATES (LIBOR): 3⅛% one month; 3¼% three months; 3⅜% six months; 3 11/16% one year. The average of interbank offered rates for dollar deposits in the London market based on quotations at five major banks. Effective rate for contracts entered into two days from date appearing at top of this column.

FOREIGN PRIME RATES: Canada 6.75%; Germany 9%; Japan 4.50%; Switzerland 7.50%; Britain 6%. These rate indications aren't directly comparable; lending practices vary widely by location.

TREASURY BILLS: Results of the Monday, February 8, 1993, auction of short-term U.S. government bills, sold at a discount from face value in units of $10,000 to $1 million: 2.94% 13 weeks; 3.09% 26 weeks.

FEDERAL HOME LOAN MORTGAGE CORP. (Freddie Mac): Posted yields on 30-year mortgage commitments. Delivery within 30 days 7.56%, 60 days 7.64%, standard conventional fixed-rate mortgages; 4.375%, 2% rate capped one-year adjustable rate mortgages. Source: Telerate Systems Inc.

FEDERAL NATIONAL MORTGAGE ASSOCIATION (Fannie Mae): Posted yields on 30 year mortgage commitments (priced at par) for delivery within 30 days 7.54%, 60 days 7.63%, standard conventional fixed-rate mortgages; 5.45%, 6/2 rate capped one-year adjustable rate mortgages. Source: Telerate Systems Inc.

MERRILL LYNCH READY ASSETS TRUST: 2.85%. Annualized average rate of return after expenses for the past 30 days; not a forecast of future returns.

Cash from accounts receivable

12.5. The Fresh Company is preparing its cash budget for the month of May. The following information is available concerning its accounts receivable:

Estimated credit sales for May	$200,000
Actual credit sales for April	$150,000
Estimated collections in May for credit sales in May	20%
Estimated collections in May for credit sales in April	70%
Estimated collections in May for credit sales prior to April	$12,000
Estimated write-offs in May for uncollectible credit sales	$8,000

What is the estimated cash inflow from accounts receivable collections in May?

Benefit from using drafts

12.6. Arkadia Finance Company makes cash payments averaging $800,000 daily. The company is considering changing from using checks to using drafts, which will permit the company to hold onto its cash for one extra day. If the company can use the increased cash to earn 5 percent annually, what annual dollar return will Arkadia Finance earn? Show your calculations.

Benefit from using a lockbox

12.7. Hari Seldon wants to implement a lockbox system to accelerate his company's cash collections. Presently the company has $36,000,000 of credit sales annually (250 working days), and the float time is 7 days. A lockbox system coupled with wire transfers will reduce float time by 3 days.
a. Define the terms *lockbox* and *wire transfer.*
b. Calculate the collection float made available by the lockbox and wire transfer system.
c. Mr. Seldon's company can invest in a money market fund yielding 5 percent annually. Calculate the annual before-tax cash benefit associated with the lockbox and wire transfers.
d. Does a bank offer such services without charge? Explain your answer.

Benefit from using a lockbox

12.8. Sherman's Soups Company is considering whether or not it should implement a lockbox system with Greenwich State Bank to service its collections in the northeast United States. Greenwich State Bank will charge $750 annually for the service. Sherman's Soups has collected the following information regarding the decision:

Daily credit sales in the Northeast	$4,000
Present average collection period	40 days
Days saved with lockbox system	5 days
Annual interest rate	6%

Calculate Sherman's Soups' annual before-tax profit from the lockbox system.

Benefit from using a lockbox

12.9. Farm Implement Company is considering whether or not it should implement a lockbox system with Farmingdale National Bank to service its collections in the western United States. Farmingdale National Bank will charge $1,200 annually for the service. Farm Implement's management has collected the following information regarding the decision:

Daily credit sales in the West	$2,500
Present average collection period	46 days
Days saved with lockbox system	4 days
Annual interest rate	7%

Calculate Farm Implement's annual before-tax profit from the lockbox system.

T-bill price in a futures contract

12.10. Joe Malesky purchases a 90-day, $1,000,000 T-bill futures contract with a 6-month delivery date. The T-bill quotation of the futures contract is 96.70.
a. Calculate the annual discount yield of the T-bill.
b. What purchase price has Mr. Malesky agreed to pay in 6 months for the T-bill?

Hedging with a T-bill futures contract

12.11. Kathy Kosnik has temporarily excess cash that she will need in 60 days to repay a bank loan. She is considering the following two strategies for investing the cash:

1. Purchase a 60-day, $1,000,000 T-bill with an annual discount yield of 3.0 percent.
2. Purchase a 150-day, $1,000,000 T-bill with an annual discount yield of 3.5 percent and sell a 90-day, $1,000,000 T-bill futures contract with a 60-day delivery date. The T-bill quotation of the futures contract is 96.7. After 60 days have passed, Ms. Kosnik will deliver the 150-day T-bill (now a 90-day T-bill) at the agreed-upon delivery price.
   a. Calculate the purchase price of the 60-day T-bill in Strategy 1 and Ms. Kosnik's potential dollar gain.
   b. Calculate the purchase price of the 150-day T-bill in Strategy 2. Now calculate the delivery price of the T-bill in the futures contract. What is Ms. Kosnik's potential dollar gain from Strategy 2?
   c. Which investment strategy should Ms. Kosnik choose?

Hedging with a T-bill futures contract

12.12. Jane Nelson, treasurer of Itco Company, is concerned about the company's plans to issue $10,000,000 of 90-day commercial paper in 3 months. She fears that the rate then might be higher than the current discount rate of 9 percent, which would raise borrowing costs. She therefore decides to hedge by selling ten 90-day T-bill futures contracts, each with a 3-month delivery date. Futures contracts on commercial paper would create a better hedge than T-bill futures, but no exchange deals in such contracts. The present T-bill quotation of the futures contract is 92.20.
   a. Suppose Ms. Nelson's fears are realized and the discount rate on the commercial paper rises to 10 percent. Calculate the company's *additional* interest cost because of the one percentage point increase. (*Hint:* The 10 percent is an annualized rate, and Itco's commercial paper has a 90-day maturity.)
   b. Calculate the price of the $1,000,000 T-bill implied by the 92.20 quotation. (*Hint:* The quotation equals 100 minus the discount yield.)
   c. Calculate the price of the $1,000,000 T-bill assuming the discount yield increases one basis point (100 basis points = 1 percentage point). (Note that the one-basis-point increase causes the quotation to drop to 92.19.)
   d. For each change of one basis point, what is the dollar change in the T-bill price? (Refer to answers in Parts *b* and *c*.)
   e. Suppose the 3 months have elapsed, the quotation for the T-bill futures contract is 91.20, and Itco issues commercial paper for 10 percent. To close out the hedged position, Ms. Nelson purchases ten 90-day T-bill futures contracts, which offset those sold 3 months ago. Calculate the net gain or loss on the company's hedged position. (Net gain or loss equals the difference between the additional interest expense on commercial paper and gains on the 10 futures contracts. Ignore commission costs and the opportunity cost of funds kept in the margin account.)
   f. What would be your answer to Part *e* if the quotation for the T-bill futures contract were 91.50?
   g. A comparison of your answers to Parts *e* and *f* reveals one reason why hedges may be imperfect. What is this reason? Other reasons include: (1) The delivery date of the futures contract may not be exactly the same as the date for issuing the commercial paper; in the problem both are 3 months. (2) The maturity of the contract security may differ from the maturity of the commercial paper; in the problem both are 90 days. (3) The dollar amount to be hedged may not be an even multiple of $1,000,000; in the problem $10,000,000 is an even multiple of $1,000,000.

Computer Problems 🖫

Cash budget: template CASHBUD

12.13. Jackson Refrigeration's sales in January and February 19X7 and forecast sales for March through August are $110,000, $120,000, $130,000, $160,000,

$175,000, $200,000, $180,000, and $160,000. Twenty percent of the sales revenue is collected in the month of sale and 40 percent in each of the following two months. Purchases each month amount to 60 percent of the sales of the previous month. The company pays for 10 percent of its purchases in the month of purchase and the balance one month later. Other expected cash outflows during March through August are:

- Rent—$5,000 per month.
- Salaries and wages—$12,000 per month.
- Sales promotion expenses—5 percent of monthly sales.
- Interest payments—$10,000 due in April and in July.
- Repayment of principal—$40,000 in June.
- Cash dividends—$15,000 payable in May and in August.
- Purchase of equipment—$50,000 in July.
- Taxes—$60,000 in April.
- Other expenses—10 percent of the preceding month's sales.

Company management desires to have a minimum $20,000 cash balance; the balance on March 1 is $26,000.
a. Prepare the cash budget for March through August 19X7.
b. If management wants to cover additional financing requirements with a line of credit from the bank, then how large must this line of credit be? Explain your answer.
c. What would be your answer to Part *b* if the March through August sales:
(1) Were 20 percent greater than those given above?
(2) Were 20 percent less than those given above?
d. If the probability of 20 percent lower sales is 30 percent, of originally projected sales is 50 percent, and of 20 percent higher sales is 20 percent, then what line of credit would be required? Explain your answer.

Cash budget: template
BUDGET2

12.14. Pedersen Oil Company is required by its bank to reduce its short-term loan balance to zero for the month of July each year. As of March 31, the balance is $675,000. Pedersen's management wants a cash budget for the months of April, May, June, and July to see whether or not it will have any problem meeting the bank's condition and, if so, what can be done about it.
Actual and forecast sales for the period in question are given below:

	March	April	May	June	July	August
Sales (thousands)	$1,600	$1,200	$1,100	$800	$800	$400

Pedersen normally collects 70 percent of sales in the month of sale and 28 percent in the following month. The remaining 2 percent represents bad debts and is never collected. Inventory purchases are 85 percent of sales, ordered and paid for in the month before they are sold. Other cash outflows are:

1. Fixed salaries, $30,000 per month.
2. Rent and leases, $10,000 per month.
3. Interest on long-term debt, $20,000 in June.
4. Miscellaneous, 5 percent of sales.
5. Purchase of new equipment, $100,000 in May.

Pedersen's cash balance on March 31 is $100,000, which is the desired minimum cash balance.
a. Given the assumptions above, will Pedersen Oil be able to eliminate its short-term loan balance by the end of June and avoid additional borrowing in July?

b. Recompute Part *a* assuming that Pedersen runs a summer "top your tank" promotion that will increase sales for June, July, and August by 20 percent, but reduce gross profit to 10 percent, i.e., purchases will rise to 90 percent of sales.

c. Recompute Part *a* assuming Pedersen defers the equipment purchase planned for May until July.

d. Recompute Part *a* assuming that Pedersen offers its regular customers the opportunity to prepurchase oil during the month of June at the lower summer price. This offer is expected to increase June sales by $400,000, but will not change May inventory purchases because the oil will be delivered during the winter months as needed. (The sale will be recorded on Pedersen's books as a current liability called Unearned Income.) All advance sales will be for cash only.

VIDEO CASE PROBLEM

Dos Amigos Petro Stores

Nguyen Tran, CFO of Dos Amigos Petro Stores, completed his review of the previous month's bank deposits. He confirmed that the collection float time on checks from credit-card customers averages 7 days. Mr. Tran knew from his studies of finance that one of the objectives of cash management is to move funds as rapidly as possible from customer bank accounts to the company's bank account. Each day that funds are delayed in the mail or in the bank-clearing system is a day's loss of return on those funds.

Dos Amigos Petro Stores owns and manages self-service convenience stores. In 1980 Juan Reyes and Nguyen Tran formed a new corporation and purchased the operating assets of a bankrupt convenience store company. They retained existing profitable locations and focused expansion in the southwestern region of the United States. New stores are located at highway intersections outside larger cities and inside smaller towns.

The two partners built Dos Amigos into a successful regional company with 97 store locations from Texas to southern California. One reason for the success of Dos Amigos was the introduction of a company credit-card program for retail customers. As a result of the increase in store locations and the credit-card program, credit-card sales grew to $35 million in 1993.

Having concluded that he should examine the possibility of reducing collection float, Mr. Tran contacted the business services department at Interstate Bank. Amy Scholz, Interstate's vice president for business services, analyzed Dos Amigos' receipts and deposits and agreed that Interstate Bank could assist in accelerating the availability of the company's cash receipts. Ms. Scholz reported that the company currently deposits 500,000 checks annually with an average amount of $70 per check deposited. She indicated that management could expect a reduction in collection float time from the current 7 days to approximately 4 days through the use of a lockbox system. The bank offers a number of plans, however, ranging from a single-city system in Houston to interstate systems. The actual reduction in float time would depend on the plan adopted by management.

Ms. Scholz explained that at management's request she would conduct additional analyses of the customer base and provide detailed descriptions of lockbox plans suitable for the company. Her report would also include the bank's fee schedule for managing each plan. At that time management could determine which plan was best for the company.

Mr. Tran was impressed by Ms. Scholz's knowledge of lockbox systems and was ready to proceed with the development of specific plans. Mr. Reyes, who is the Chief Executive Officer of Dos Amigos, was not impressed by the prospects of paying large bank fees for depositing checks. Despite his reservations, he agreed that Ms. Scholz should submit a complete report on the company's current cash collection procedures and the workings of a lockbox system.

After reading Ms. Scholz's report, which appears on the following page, Messrs. Tran and Reyes began to analyze the costs and benefits of the three alternative lockbox plans. Their analysis assumes credit-card collections of $35 million annually over a 250-day work year. Their analysis also assumes investment of accelerated funds at 8 percent per year.

Ms. Scholz's Report

Dos Amigos receives checks in pre-addressed envelopes and deposits them the next day. The current 7-day collection float consists of three components: mail float (4 days), processing float (2 days), and check-clearing float (1 day).

Retail Lockbox System

A retail lockbox system is designed to process a large volume of checks and invoices where each check has a relatively low value. In contrast a wholesale lockbox system is designed to process a few large checks received each month that may accompany different kinds of invoices. Dos Amigos would benefit from a retail system to process the large number of small checks accompanying standard invoice forms.

A lockbox system consists of post office boxes strategically located in cities where return envelopes from those areas are routed. Employees of the bank or of a correspondent bank retrieve the envelopes from the post office boxes several times each day. At each regional lockbox bank, referred to as a processing center, the envelopes are opened by machine, amounts of the checks and the amounts indicated on the invoices are verified, the checks are deposited in that bank for local or regional clearing, and the remitted invoices are forwarded to you for posting. Each day the available deposit balances in the regional lockbox processing centers are transferred instantaneously to your deposit bank in Houston through the Federal Reserve's wire transfer system.

Benefits of a Lockbox System

The objective of a lockbox system is to reduce collection float. This is accomplished by reducing mailing and processing times. Check-clearing time is reduced by clearing checks locally rather than at your bank in Houston. By wire transferring deposit balances collected in regional banks, your funds are available more quickly.

Accelerated funds may be invested in marketable securities or used to reduce notes payable. In either case Dos Amigos would realize a cash benefit. Also, your company would save the approximately 4,000 clerical hours per year used to process checks received in the mail. At $7.50 per hour for clerical work, you would save $30,000 annually in labor costs.

Costs of a Lockbox System

As do other banks, Interstate Bank charges a fee for operating a lockbox system. The typical fee arrangement is a fixed charge per month plus a variable charge for each item processed. For example, if the bank's fee were $1,000 per month plus $0.05 per item processed and the bank processed 10,000 checks each month, the total annual fee would be $18,000:

$$\text{Lockbox fee} = \$12,000 + (\$0.05 \times 10,000 \times 12)$$
$$= \$18,000$$

Clearly, the decision to adopt a lockbox system depends on a comparison of benefits and costs. I propose that you evaluate the following three plans developed to meet Dos Amigos' cash collection needs.

Lockbox Plan 1

1. *Lockbox processing centers: Dallas, San Antonio, El Paso, San Diego, Denver, Albuquerque, and Phoenix.*
2. *Deposit balance wire transferred to Houston daily.*
3. *Total checks processed annually: 500,000.*
4. *Average float time: 3.5 days.*
5. *Interstate Bank's fee: $12,000 per year plus $0.05 per check processed.*

Lockbox Plan 2

1. *Lockbox processing centers: Dallas, San Diego, Albuquerque, and Phoenix.*
2. *Deposit balance wire transferred to Houston daily.*
3. *Total checks processed annually: 500,000.*
4. *Average float time: 4 days.*
5. *Interstate Bank's fee: $8,000 per year plus $0.04 per check processed.*

Lockbox Plan 3

1. *Lockbox processing centers: Dallas, El Paso, and Phoenix.*
2. *Deposit balance wire transferred to Houston daily.*
3. *Total checks processed annually: 500,000.*
4. *Average float time: 5 days.*
5. *Interstate Bank's fee: $6,000 per year plus $0.04 per check processed.*

a. Why should Mr. Tran be concerned about accelerating the company's cash collection?

b. What are the three components of collection float time? Describe how a lockbox system reduces collection float time.

c. Suppose that Dos Amigos (1) receives $140,000 worth of checks in the mail each day and (2) reduces collection float time from 7 days to 5 days. What is the dollar reduction in accounts receivable? What is the dollar increase in the company's cash balance?

d. The three lockbox plans list different processing locations. Why are the locations of the processing centers important to the success of a lockbox system?

e. Calculate the annual dollar return from investing the accelerated funds produced by each of the three lockbox plans.

f. Calculate the total annual fee charged by Interstate Bank for each of the three lockbox plans.

g. Calculate the annual before-tax cash benefit of each lockbox plan, including the reduction in clerical labor costs.

h. Which lockbox plan, if any, should Messrs. Tran and Reyes select? Explain.

Reference: Terry S. Maness and John T. Zietlow, *Short-Term Financial Management,* New York: West Publishing Company, 1993.

The author thanks Professor Carl M. Hubbard of Trinity University for contributing this case problem.

Selected References

Batlin, C. A., and Susan Hinko. "Lockbox Management and Value Maximization." *Financial Management,* Winter 1981: 39–44.

Budin, Morris, and Robert J. Van Handel. "A Rule-of-Thumb Theory of Cash Holdings by Firms." *Journal of Financial and Quantitative Analysis,* March 1975: 85–108.

Clements, Joel, and Robert L. Woodall, "Controlled Disbursements: A Cash Management Tool for Growing Concerns." *Management Accounting,* May 1983: 53–55.

French, Kenneth R. "Pricing Financial Futures Contracts: An Introduction." *Journal of Applied Corporate Finance,* Winter 1989: 59–66.

Huggins, Kenneth M., and Donald R. Hakala. "Treasury Bill Futures as a Cash Management Tool." *Financial Executive,* July 1982: 34–40.

Kawaller, Ira G. "How and Why to Hedge a Short-Term Portfolio." *Journal of Cash Management,* January–February 1985: 26–30.

Kish, Richard J. "Discrepancy in Treasury Bill Yield Calculations." *Financial Practice and Education,* Spring/Summer 1992: 41–45.

Little, Patricia Knain. "Financial Futures and Immunization." *Journal of Financial Research,* Spring 1986: 1–11.

Pettijohn, James B. "Hedging: A Forgotten Topic in the Introductory Financial Management Text." *Journal of Financial Education,* Fall 1982: 17–20.

Stone, Bernell K., and Tom W. Miller. "Daily Cash Forecasting with Multiplicative Models of Cash Flow Patterns." *Financial Management,* Winter 1987: 45–53.

Chapter 13

MANAGING RECEIVABLES AND INVENTORY

Captive Financiers

Westinghouse Credit is a captive finance company, wholly owned by the electrical-products manufacturer Westinghouse Electric Corporation. The financial-services subsidiary provides credit to the parent company's customers. In an attempt to diversify out of its cyclical manufacturing business, Westinghouse directed its subsidiary to loan money for highly leveraged real-estate and corporate take-over deals. Ironically, this bit of diversification cost the giant industrial company hundreds of millions of dollars. Many of the loans turned sour, and the company took massive write-offs from bad debt.

Fortunately, not all captive finance companies in the early 1990s suffered Westinghouse's fate. Many adhered to their original goals—granting credit for the purchase of their parent company's products and limiting other lending to businesses in which they had substantial experience. John Deere Capital, subsidiary of the Midwest

manufacturer Deere & Co., out-performed its parent company. Caterpillar's Caterpillar Financial Services reported an increase in earnings even though the parent company's earnings declined. Both companies enjoyed success from conservative lending within their areas of expertise.

While the Big Three of the U.S. automobile industry were losing money in the early 1990s, each of their finance subsidiaries was profitable: General Motors Acceptance Corporation, Ford Motor Credit Corporation, and Chrysler Financial Corporation. Despite having diversified outside of the automobile industry, the bulk of their lending was to car buyers and car dealers. Even car companies, however, are not immune from loan losses. GMAC, with $105 billion in assets, charged off $931.7 million for bad debt during 1990. Any company with accounts receivable on its balance sheet is likely to discover that some are uncollectible.

Source: "In-House Lenders," *The Wall Street Journal,* October 8, 1991, A1 and A14.

Accounts receivable are a company's claims on its customers for inventory sold to them on credit. Inventory is the stock in trade available for sale. A company uses cash to buy or produce items for inventory and then makes sales from inventory on credit to its customers. After a period of time, the length of which is determined in part by the company's credit policy, the company collects its receivables. The interaction of granting credit and maintaining inventory creates the cash operating cycle. The total investment in receivables and inventory constitutes a majority of current assets for many companies, and the financial managers must carefully manage receivables and inventory to keep their companies profitable and liquid.

This chapter describes the management of the cash operating cycle by dividing it into two parts. The first, on receivables management, describes the way a financial manager formulates and administers credit policy. It explains how credit terms influence customer payment behavior, and shows how a company's credit policy affects its profitability. The second part covers inventory management. The objective of inventory management is to minimize a company's investment in the asset while maximizing the return from holding it. You will learn about the opposing forces of carrying costs and ordering costs, and you will see how this conflict enables us to develop the EOQ (economic order quantity) model. The chapter concludes with practical ideas for monitoring a company's inventory level.

ACCOUNTS RECEIVABLE AND CREDIT POLICY

A company grants credit to increase sales and profits. The company might do this to gain an edge on its competitors. Conversely, it may be the competition that forces the company to grant credit. Indeed, credit is so widespread in some industries that selling goods without it would probably be impossible. It is hard to imagine a department store not granting consumer credit to its customers, or a compact disk distributor not granting trade credit to its retailers. Most customers consider credit part and parcel of the product purchased.

Granting credit results in accounts receivable, a current asset of the selling company. The company's investment in accounts receivable is the cash tied up in receivables. The relative size of the company's investment in accounts receivable depends on its credit policy and sales volume. Large companies generally have large investments in receivables. Exceptions to this rule exist, however, particularly for cash-and-carry businesses, which have no receivables and no credit department.

A company must make three principal decisions before it grants credit to customers:

1. What credit standards should be used to evaluate customers? That is, who should receive credit and how much credit should customers receive?

2. What credit terms should the company use for products sold on account? How much time should customers have before being required to pay? Should the company offer cash discounts for prompt payment? If so, how long should the prompt-payment period be?

3. How should the company collect overdue accounts receivable? What steps should it take with laggards and deadbeats? When does a receivable become a bad debt?

The following sections examine the issues surrounding the answers to these questions.

Credit Standards

credit standards
Criteria for determining a customer's creditworthiness.

Credit standards are the criteria a company uses to determine whether or not a potential customer is creditworthy and whether present customers should continue to receive credit. After analyzing a credit application, a financial manager may reach one of the following conclusions:

- Grant credit in the amount requested.
- Grant credit for an amount less than requested.
- Convert the customer to cash on delivery (C.O.D.); reconsider credit application after a few months of sales experience.

Tasks of the Financial Manager. Financial managers normally have little trouble identifying customers with substantial credit strength. Nor do they have difficulty identifying obvious deadbeats. The dilemma occurs in the vast gray area between these two extremes. This dilemma stems from the trade-off between expected benefits and costs associated with extending credit. Expected benefits are the increased profits from incremental sales caused by extending credit. Costs are the increase in expenses necessary to collect slow-paying accounts, bad-debt expense, and the opportunity cost of tying up cash in accounts receivable.

A conservative financial manager might easily minimize bad-debt expense by refusing credit to most of the gray-area customers. In this case, however, the company forgoes potential sales and profit. An aggressive credit manager might grant credit to too many deadbeats in the gray area, causing bad-debt expense and slow payments to negate profit. Successful financial managers strike a balance between being too conservative and being overly aggressive. Moreover, they tend to understand human behavior, and they carefully research the backgrounds of credit applicants.

Five Cs of Credit. Financial managers often use the *five Cs of credit* to determine whether or not an applicant meets the company's credit standards. The five Cs is a mnemonic device for the features of an applicant's creditworthiness:

- Character
- Capacity
- Capital
- Collateral
- Conditions

Character is the moral fabric of a borrower. If the financial manager does not believe that the customer will honor the credit terms, then the company may sell to the applicant on a cash basis. An applicant with a history of meeting financial obligations demonstrates good character, a willingness and a desire to be honest. Without good character an applicant may not pay even though the capacity to do so is present. The financial manager collects payment histories on new applicants from other suppliers, commercial banks, and other organizations that have dealt with the applicants. Credit information can also be obtained from local credit bureaus and national credit agencies such as Dun & Bradstreet,

Equifax Inc., Trans Union Corp., and TRW Inc. These national agencies have computerized data bases on millions of companies and individuals.

Capacity refers to the credit applicant's ability to pay. Financial managers use financial-statement analysis to judge an applicant's credit capacity. Examining the applicant's income statement, balance sheet, and statement of cash flows for several periods tells the financial manager a great deal about the applicant's capacity to pay. Applicants with sound character but poor cash flow may still end up in the bad-debt file if they do not have cash to pay their bills. Financial managers generally gauge capacity to pay financial obligations by looking at projected cash flows. Ideally, the company would have available the applicant's cash budget. In most cases, however, the financial manager must settle for past financial statements from which to judge future cash flows. One measure of the capacity to pay is the company's liquidity. A highly liquid company may be able to discharge its debts even though its cash flows appear weak.

Capital refers to the applicant's equity. A large amount of debt relative to equity tells the financial manager that the applicant is exposed to substantial financial risk. A high debt-equity ratio may suggest that the applicant has used up its debt capacity, indicating poor prospects for survival. A high debt-equity ratio reflects a low net worth (equity), which could disappear through erosion caused by losses. At that point the creditors are no longer afforded protection by an equity cushion. When debts exceed assets, net worth is negative, and declaration of bankruptcy may soon follow.

trade credit

Credit extended by one company to another in the normal course of business.

Collateral is the customer's assets pledged as a promise of repayment. **Trade credit,** credit extended by one company to another in the normal course of business, is seldom associated with collateral (though, as we shall see in Chapter 14, collateral is often a part of bank loans). Highly liquid assets provide good collateral. Financial managers have little interest, however, in actually confiscating assets; the process of obtaining and liquidating them is too troublesome. Still, collateralized assets provide a creditor with some protection against default, and they put continued pressure on customers already behind in making timely payments. The creditor can threaten to seize the debtor's collateralized assets.

Conditions are the special circumstances of the credit-granting company as well as the general economic climate. If the selling company's strategy is to increase market penetration or to broaden its market, then management may be willing to take on more default risk. Furthermore, companies selling products having large markups can tolerate greater default risk than companies with products having small markups. The large gross profit earned from selling to high-quality customers covers more defaults. Also, economically prosperous periods generally decrease default rates among customer groups. If customers are doing well financially, then they are more likely to service their debt in a timely way. Conversely, even normally good customers may be unable to service their debt during recessions.

credit scoring

Quantifying an applicant's creditworthiness.

Financial managers apply each of the five Cs of credit to rate prospective credit customers. Some financial managers use credit scoring to quantify the five Cs. **Credit scoring** is a procedure that usually employs discriminant analysis. *Discriminant analysis* develops an equation that distinguishes, for example, between high-quality and low-quality credit applicants.[1] By inserting information on the credit applicant into the equation, the financial manager calculates a credit score. If the score exceeds some minimum value, then the probability is high that the

[1] You may be interested to know that the Internal Revenue Service uses discriminant analysis to select individuals and companies for audits. The IRS keeps secret the exact form of the equation.

applicant will pay. Otherwise, there is a likelihood that the applicant will default. Credit scoring is useful in sorting credit applications. For those in the middle range, however, the experience and judgment of the financial manager must take over.

Credit Terms

credit terms

Terms of sale; conditions to which a customer must agree in order to receive credit.

Besides setting the standards for granting credit, the financial manager must also determine the credit terms the company offers customers. **Credit terms,** or terms of sale, tell the customer when to pay for the goods purchased on credit. A company uses credit terms to stimulate sales by offering customers a package consisting of a product or service plus credit.

Some credit terms encourage a customer to pay early by offering a cash, or prompt-payment, discount. Other terms simply specify the number of days after purchase within which the debtor-purchaser must make cash payment. Still other terms specify payment by the end of the next month after purchase (net, E.O.M.) or by the middle of the next month after purchase (net, M.O.M.). For example, net, M.O.M. means pay by the middle of next month (the 15th) and do not take any cash discounts.

seasonal datings

Credit terms specifying payment in a subsequent season.

Some companies use **seasonal datings** in which payment is called for during a subsequent season to encourage customer purchases during slack seasons. In other words, buy now, pay much later—in the next season! Many retailers use seasonal datings by selling goods before Christmas and letting customers delay payment until February. The fuel oil industry provides a good example of seasonal datings. Because many of their customers use little fuel oil in the summer, fuel oil dealers offer to fill customer tanks with payment delayed until the fall. In turn, major oil companies offer to summer-fill dealer tanks, permitting dealers to pay in the fall. The advantages to companies offering seasonal datings are that they (1) create demand when there would be none, though at the expense of demand later, (2) push inventory downstream in the distribution channel in order to avoid the cost of carrying inventory, and (3) level production throughout the year to avoid start-up costs, layoffs, and rehiring of personnel. Before instituting seasonal datings, management needs to weigh the costs of carrying additional accounts receivable against the expected benefits from increased sales and lower inventory costs.

Opportunity Costs and Cash Discounts.   Companies create an opportunity (and opportunity cost) for their customers when they offer them cash discounts for early payment. For example, the lumber industry commonly uses the credit terms 2/10, net 30. These credit terms tell the customer to pay either on the tenth day after purchase or on the thirtieth day. In addition, the terms say:

1. If you pay by the tenth day, then take a 2 percent discount from the purchase price.

2. If you do not pay by the tenth day, then you must pay the entire amount by the thirtieth day.

Companies in other industries give similar incentives to their customers for prompt payment:

- Jewelry: 5/30, net 120
- Gasoline: 1/10, net 30
- Drugs: 2/10, net 60

To calculate a customer's opportunity cost of forgoing cash discounts, you should first carefully interpret the opportunity. For convenience, assume that the customer makes a $100 purchase and the credit terms are 2/10, net 30. Figure 13.1 shows that the customer paying on or before the tenth day after purchase pays only $98; otherwise, the customer pays $100 on the thirtieth day after the purchase, or 20 days later. *A customer rejecting the discount pays $2 for the use of $98 for 20 days.* The customer's opportunity cost for the 20 days is calculated in the following way:

$$\text{Opportunity cost for 20 days} = \frac{\$2}{\$98}$$

$$= 0.0204, \text{ or } 2.04\%$$

Most financial managers prefer to think of interest rates and opportunity costs as annual rates. Thus we change the 2.04 percent for 20 days to an annual rate by multiplying 2.04 percent by the number of 20-day periods in a year:

$$\text{Number of 20-day periods in a year} = \frac{365}{20}$$

$$= 18.25$$

The annual opportunity cost of failing to take advantage of the cash discount for prompt payment is 37.2 percent, calculated as follows:

$$\text{Annual opportunity cost} = 0.0204 \times 18.25$$

$$= 0.372, \text{ or } 37.2\%$$

The equation financial managers often use to calculate the opportunity cost of missing cash discounts summarizes in one step the above analysis:[2]

$$\text{Annual opportunity cost} = \frac{D}{1 - D} \times \frac{365}{n}$$

where D = cash discount expressed as a decimal

n = number of days during the period between the deadlines for cash discount and final payment

EXAMPLE Calculate the annual opportunity cost to a customer who forgoes the cash discount with the following credit terms: 1/10, net 40.

---

[2] Because the equation yields an approximate answer anyway, some managers use 360 instead of 365 for the number of days in a year. With 360 the number of 20-day periods in a year is 18, and the annual opportunity cost becomes 2.04% × 18 = 36.7%. Although typically not done in practice, we might wish to calculate the *effective* annual opportunity cost using the equation from Chapter 4:

$$\text{Effective annual rate} = (1 + 0.0204)^{18.25} - 1.0$$

$$= 1.446 - 1.0$$

$$= 0.446, \text{ or } 44.6\%$$

Advocates of this procedure argue that 2.04 percent forgone for 20 days, 18.25 times in a row, effectively costs 44.6 percent per year compounded annually. Regardless of how we evaluate it, the opportunity cost of cash discounts with 2/10, net 30 is large, and customers should pay early to get the discount.

FIGURE 13.1

Interpretation of the Credit Terms 2/10, Net 30

Terms of 2/10, net 30 mean that the customer can take a 2 percent cash discount if payment is made within 10 days of the sale. Otherwise, the entire invoice amount must be paid within 30 days. A customer paying 30 days after the day of purchase pays $2 for the use of $98 for 20 days (30 − 10 days).

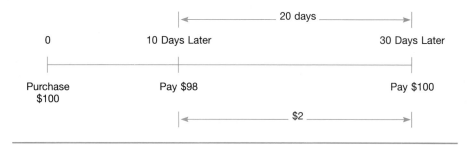

$$\begin{aligned}
\text{Annual opportunity cost} &= \frac{0.01}{1 - 0.01} \times \frac{365}{40 - 10} \\
&= 0.0101 \times 12.167 \\
&= 0.123, \text{ or } 12.3\%
\end{aligned}$$

The answer in the above example implicitly assumes that the customer pays either 10 days or 40 days after purchase. What happens to the opportunity cost if the customer does not pay until 50 days after purchase? The equation tells us the answer:

$$\begin{aligned}
\text{Annual opportunity cost} &= \frac{0.01}{1 - 0.01} \times \frac{365}{50 - 10} \\
&= 0.0101 \times 9.125 \\
&= 0.092, \text{ or } 9.2\%
\end{aligned}$$

The opportunity cost declines, along with the customer's reputation for being creditworthy.

Table 13.1 presents the annual opportunity costs for four different credit terms. Each calculation consists of three steps: (1) Calculate the cost per period, (2) calculate the number of periods in a year, and (3) multiply the cost per period by the number of periods in a year.

Adjusting Credit Terms for Changes in Interest Rates.   The opportunity cost to customers of missing cash discounts affects their payment behavior. The following rules predict their behavior:

• If the opportunity cost of missing cash discounts exceeds customer borrowing rates, then customers will pay early to take the discounts, even if it means borrowing from the bank to do so.

• If the opportunity cost of missing cash discounts is less than customer borrowing rates, then customers will pay later and not take cash discounts.

TABLE 13.1   **Annual Opportunity Cost for Various Credit Terms[a]**

	Credit Terms			
	5/10, Net 120	**1/10, Net 30**	**6/10, Net 60**	**3/20, Net 60**
1. Cost per period	$\dfrac{0.05}{0.95} = 0.0526$	$\dfrac{0.01}{0.99} = 0.0101$	$\dfrac{0.06}{0.94} = 0.0638$	$\dfrac{0.03}{0.97} = 0.0309$
2. Number of periods in a year	$\dfrac{365}{110} = 3.318$	$\dfrac{365}{20} = 18.25$	$\dfrac{365}{50} = 7.300$	$\dfrac{365}{40} = 9.125$
3. Annual opportunity cost (Line 1 × Line 2)	0.0526×3.318 $= 0.175$, or 17.5%	0.0101×18.25 $= 0.184$, or 18.4%	0.0638×7.3 $= 0.466$, or 46.6%	0.0309×9.125 $= 0.282$, or 28.2%

[a] Calculations assume that customers pay either on the discount day or on the final payment day.

Customers in this case will allow their accounts payable (the credit-granting company's accounts receivable) to increase and will reduce their bank loans.

To minimize the investment in accounts receivable, the financial manager must be sure that the opportunity cost of credit terms granted to customers is higher than the general level of interest rates. If interest rates increase dramatically, for example, then credit terms may need changing to increase the opportunity costs of customers and ensure timely payment.

Recall from the earlier calculations that the annual opportunity cost of the terms 1/10, net 40 is 12.3 percent. If bank interest rates increase to 15 percent, then financial managers of the credit-granting company might want to change the credit terms to, say, 1.5/10, net 40 to increase the annual opportunity cost and encourage prompt payment:

$$\frac{\text{Annual}}{\text{opportunity cost}} = \frac{0.015}{1 - 0.015} \times \frac{365}{40 - 10}$$

$$= 0.0152 \times 12.167$$

$$= 0.185, \text{ or } 18.5\%$$

They might also consider changing the credit terms to, say, 1/10, net 30 in order to encourage prompt payment:

$$\frac{\text{Annual}}{\text{opportunity cost}} = \frac{0.01}{1 - 0.01} \times \frac{365}{30 - 10}$$

$$= 0.0101 \times 18.25$$

$$= 0.184, \text{ or } 18.4\%$$

Which course of action a financial manager chooses depends on the projected change in sales and profitability.

In either of the cases in the above example, the goal of the financial manager is to increase the customer's opportunity cost and thereby encourage the prompt payment of bills. If the opportunity cost remains at 12.3 percent when bank-borrowing costs are 15 percent, then the customer will reject prompt payment and use trade credit to the end of the payment period and perhaps even beyond.

The dollar amount of credit sales per dollar of receivables helps the financial manager to monitor the balance between the opportunity cost of credit terms and the borrowing rates of customers. This ratio is the **accounts receivable turnover:**

$$\text{Accounts receivable turnover} = \frac{\text{Credit sales}}{\text{Accounts receivable}}$$

accounts receivable turnover
Dollar amount of credit sales per dollar of receivables.

If customers stop taking cash discounts because of relatively higher borrowing rates, then the accounts receivable of the credit-granting company increase, causing its receivables turnover to decrease.[3]

EXAMPLE

Lormar Products, a manufacturer of beauty aids, generates $780,000 in annual credit sales. Its accounts receivable are $78,000. Lormar's accounts receivable turnover equals 10.0; that is, its annual credit sales are $10 for each $1 of accounts receivable.

If, in the above example, the borrowing rates of Lormar's customers become higher than the opportunity cost of Lormar's credit terms, then Lormar's accounts receivable turnover declines. Table 13.2 illustrates this situation, showing receivables going from $78,000 to $130,000. Lormar's receivables turnover drops from 10.0 to 6.0, indicating that the financial manager needs to consider changing Lormar's credit terms to encourage customers to take advantage of the prompt-payment discount.

Table 13.2 includes a second financial measure for monitoring accounts receivable, the **average collection period,** or days' sales in accounts receivable:

average collection period
Average time required to collect receivables; days' sales in accounts receivable.

$$\text{Average collection period} = \frac{\text{Accounts receivable}}{\text{Average daily credit sales}}$$

Although the accounts receivable turnover is a number with no units attached, the average collection period is measured in days.[4] It represents the average number of days for a company to collect credit sales. Stated differently, the average collection period is the number of average daily credit sales represented in the accounts receivable. If a company's credit terms are 2/10, net 30 and all of its

---

[3] Recall from Chapter 11 the use of the term *turnover:* sales divided by some item from the balance sheet. In this case credit sales divided by accounts receivable is the accounts receivable turnover. Because accounts receivable come from *credit* sales, analysts prefer to use credit sales, not total sales, in the numerator of the ratio. They often settle for total sales, however, because of data limitations. See Chapter 15 for further discussion.

[4] You can verify the units (days) of the average collection period (ACP) by looking at the units of its inputs:

$$\text{ACP} = \frac{\text{Dollar amount}}{\text{Dollar amount/Days}}$$

$$= \text{Days}$$

As stated earlier, some analysts use 360 days, not 365 days, as their measure of a year. The difference is small and does not affect interpretation or action.

TABLE 13.2	**Effect of Borrowing Rates on Lormar Products' Accounts Receivable**	
	Low Borrowing Rates	**High Borrowing Rates**
1. Credit sales (annual)	$780,000	$780,000
2. Accounts receivable	$78,000	$130,000
3. Receivables turnover: Credit sales/Accounts receivable	10.0	6.0
4. Average daily credit sales: (Line 1)/365 days	$2,137	$2,137
5. Average collection period: Accounts receivable/(Line 4)	36.5 days	60.8 days

customers wait until the thirtieth day to pay, then the average collection period will equal 30 days.

| EXAMPLE | Calculate the average collection period (ACP) for Lormar Products in the case of low borrowing rates (see Table 13.2):

$$\text{Average collection period} = \frac{\$78,000}{\$780,000/365}$$

$$= \frac{\$78,000}{\$2,137}$$

$$= 36.5 \text{ days}$$

Using a shortcut method, you can calculate ACP by dividing 365 by the receivables turnover:

$$\text{Average collection period} = \frac{365}{10.0}$$

$$= 36.5 \text{ days}$$

The average collection period is simply a mathematical rearrangement of the receivables turnover. Thus the financial manager can use either or both of the ratios to assess the way credit terms alter the company's accounts receivable.[5] This analysis may uncover a buildup of receivables—low receivables turnover and long average collection period compared with credit terms—suggesting the need to increase collection efforts.

Collection Practices

A sound credit policy includes effective *collection practices*—the methods a company uses to collect receivables. Companies granting credit must earn their money twice: first by making sales, then by collecting the money they are owed.

---

[5] We examine credit terms once again in Chapter 14. There, however, we take the view of the debtor, that is, the customer.

FIGURE 13.2

The Declining Value of an Aging Account Receivable

The expected present value of an account receivable declines for two reasons as it remains out-standing (ages): (1) The probability of collecting the receivable declines and (2) the present value of any amount collected declines with futurity.

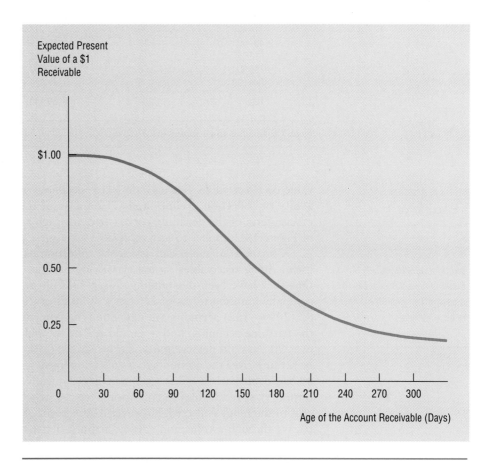

A company should collect receivables approximately within the allowed credit period. Effective treatment of overdue accounts is always an exercise in diplomacy as well as in firmness. Many customers with reputations for slow payments may be sound. Moreover, their business may be much too valuable to lose by abrupt or insulting efforts to collect money a few days sooner than they genuinely intend to pay.

Most companies base collection procedures on a series of periodic and gradually stronger reminders to customers that payment is due. Mailed reminders are called **dunning notices,** and the usual sequence is notices followed by telephone calls. Collection attempts generally begin sooner and become more insistent for customers in lower credit classes than for those in higher ones.

Delay and inattention in the collection process can be costly and ultimately lead to increased bad-debt expense. Bad debts are the scourge of extending credit because they reflect sales made but uncollected. The selling company loses the cost of the goods and the expected profit. Bad debts in some industries can be quite large. For example, a well-run casino oriented toward high rollers normally fails to collect 5 percent of credit extended. Figure 13.2 illustrates the decline in

dunning notice
Letter to a credit customer urging immediate payment.

TABLE 13.3			

Aging Schedule of Accounts Receivable

Age of Account in Days	Number of Accounts	Dollar Value of Accounts	Proportion of Total Dollar Value
0–30	122	$397,598	0.603
31–45	38	104,918	0.159
46–60	19	79,819	0.121
61–75	11	21,802	0.033
76–90	6	13,400	0.020
Over 90	8	41,613	0.064
Total	204	$659,150	1.000

Note: Credit terms to customers are 2/10, net 30.

aging receivables

Classifying accounts based on length of time they have been uncollected.

value of a receivable as it ages. Its value declines with age (1) because the probability of collection declines and (2) because of the time value of money. The precise form of the declining curve varies for each account, but the general form of Figure 13.2 applies to any receivable as it ages.

A financial manager can assess the collection pattern of receivables by aging them. **Aging receivables** means classifying accounts according to the length of time they have been outstanding. Table 13.3 illustrates an aging schedule for a company granting terms of 2/10, net 30: 122 of 204 accounts are current, and 82 (204 − 122) accounts are past due. The company should mail reminders to the past-due accounts, and it should phone the older accounts. The 8 accounts over 90 days old deserve particular attention: (1) Continue the collection effort, or (2) turn over the accounts to a collection agency, or (3) write off the accounts as bad-debt expense. Financial managers typically dislike admitting defeat by turning over receivables to collection agencies, who often charge fees of 50 percent of the funds collected. However, 100 percent of 50 percent, which they may receive through a collection agency, is much better than 100 percent of nothing.

Preparing an aging schedule at regular intervals enables the financial manager to detect trends toward either a slowing or an improving collection process. An aging schedule provides an early warning signal regarding deterioration in receivables collection and the possibility of large and unusual bad-debt expense.

Even without altering credit terms, the financial manager can take steps to accelerate payments and perhaps reduce bad-debt expense. For example, by invoicing customers immediately after purchase, the company receives cash sooner. Including a preaddressed and stamped envelope encourages customers to pay promptly.

captive finance company

Subsidiary that provides credit to the parent company's customers.

Managers of some companies place such great emphasis on the collection process that they form captive finance companies, as discussed in the chapter opening vignette. A **captive finance company** is a subsidiary that provides credit to the parent company's customers. In addition to the examples of captive finance companies already cited—including General Motors Acceptance Corporation and Ford Motor Credit Company—Clark Equipment, General Electric, IBM, Xerox, and Philip Morris also have captive finance companies.[6] The captive

---

[6]Two other methods to accelerate cash flow from receivables are: (1) pledging receivables for loans and (2) factoring (selling) receivables. Chapter 14 discusses these topics.

finance company specializes in credit and collections, and it employs people trained in each area. Presumably the captive finance company will have a better collection experience than the parent company would have.

Evaluating a Change in Credit Policy

Changes in economic conditions make it necessary to evaluate periodically a company's credit policy. A financial manager should occasionally review credit policy to see if change will increase company profitability.

To illustrate the evaluation of a change in credit policy, consider the lowering of credit standards. Relaxing credit standards increases sales because more customers qualify for credit under the less rigorous criteria. This change, however, is not without costs. To determine whether a relaxation of credit standards will improve profitability, the financial manager matches expected benefits against expected costs. One way to do this is to compare the expected after-tax cash inflows from lowering standards with the expected increase in investment in accounts receivable:

$$\frac{\text{Expected after-tax}}{\text{rate of return}} = \frac{\text{Expected after-tax cash inflows}}{\text{Expected increase in investment}}$$

If the expected after-tax rate of return exceeds the company's required rate of return, then the financial manager should implement the policy change because stock price and shareholder wealth will rise. The cash flows associated with a change in credit policy are as follows: (1) increase in contribution margin, a cash inflow; (2) increase in collection expense, a cash outflow; and (3) increase in bad-debt expense, a cash outflow. We explore each of these cash flows by breaking the analysis into several steps.

Step 1. Begin by calculating the expected cash inflows, or the contribution margin, associated with an increase in sales. **Contribution margin** is the amount of sales revenue remaining after paying variable operating costs. The contribution margin contributes toward paying *fixed operating costs,* which do not vary with sales or output levels; they are independent of a company's volume of business. Fixed costs accumulate with the passage of time whether or not the company makes any sales. Panel A of Figure 13.3 illustrates the independence of fixed costs. Economics teaches that all costs are variable in the long run, but for typical planning horizons, we can treat several costs as fixed:

* Depreciation of plant and equipment.
* Rental payments on long-term leases.
* Insurance premiums on assets.
* Salaries of top management and key employees.
* Property taxes on real estate and inventory.
* Cost of minimal maintenance of plant and equipment.
* Some office expenses and energy costs.

Variable operating costs vary directly with sales and output levels. In contrast to fixed costs, which accumulate with the passage of time, variable costs relate to levels of production and sales. If a company produces and sells zero units, then its variable costs equal zero. Higher unit levels lead to higher variable costs.

contribution margin
Revenue remaining after paying variable costs; contribution toward paying fixed costs.

FIGURE 13.3

Behavior Patterns of Fixed, Variable, and Semivariable Costs

Fixed costs (in Panel A) do not change as a company's output and sales change. Variable costs (in Panel B) change as output and sales change, rising with an increase and falling with a decrease. Some costs have a fixed and a variable portion. We call these costs semivariable (in Panel C), and they move in stair-step fashion with changes in output and sales.

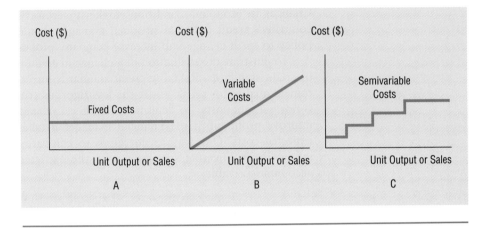

Panel B of Figure 13.3 illustrates the dependence of variable costs on output and sales. Variable costs consist primarily of:

- Direct labor cost of producing products.
- Direct cost of materials in products produced.
- Commissions on sales awarded to the sales force.

Some operating costs have both fixed and variable components. For example, part of energy costs is fixed and part is variable. A company incurs a base level of energy costs even with its doors closed for business, and energy costs increase as production increases. In like manner, management salaries and office expenses may contain both fixed and variable components. Such hybrid costs are *semivariable costs*. Panel C of Figure 13.3 illustrates how semivariable costs are fixed for some range of output before they increase. The resulting relationship is a stair-step function. We assume in the following analysis that the company's cost accountant has classified all costs as either fixed or variable. Thus contribution margin is calculated as follows:

$$\text{Contribution margin} = \text{Sales} - \text{Variable costs}$$

EXAMPLE

Nador Company has sales of $600,000 and variable costs of $330,000. What is Nador's contribution margin?

$$\text{Contribution margin} = \$600,000 - \$330,000$$
$$= \$270,000$$

Nador has $270,000 to contribute toward paying its fixed operating costs.

Step 2. Estimate the expected increase in bad-debt and collection expense. The financial manager can use the five Cs of credit to estimate the likelihood of bad debts associated with relaxed credit standards. Collection expense is the cost to collect receivables. It consists of incremental cash expenses such as telephone, postage, and personnel costs, and fees paid to collection agencies.

Step 3. Estimate the incremental cash invested in accounts receivable. Accounts receivable reflect both a product cost and a markup for profit. Thus the cash invested in accounts receivable is not the total of accounts receivable. Invested cash consists of the variable costs incurred to produce the product. Since management could have used the cash taken by variable costs to invest elsewhere, it should consider this amount as the investment in receivables required to generate the net cash inflow.[7]

variable cost ratio (VCR)

Variable costs per dollar of sales.

To calculate variable costs, the financial manager uses the **variable cost ratio**—variable costs per dollar of sales. The variable cost ratio (VCR) is calculated by dividing variable costs by sales revenue:

$$\text{Variable cost ratio} = \frac{\text{Variable costs}}{\text{Sales revenue}}$$

contribution margin ratio (CMR)

Contribution margin per dollar of sales; sales minus variable costs all divided by sales.

The variable cost ratio is the complement to the **contribution margin ratio (CMR)**, which is the contribution margin per dollar of sales:

$$\text{Contribution margin ratio} = \frac{\text{Contribution margin}}{\text{Sales revenue}}$$

EXAMPLE

Nador Company has $600,000 in annual credit sales and $58,000 in accounts receivable. What is the company's investment in accounts receivable if its contribution margin ratio is 45 percent? Begin by calculating the variable cost ratio:

$$1.00 = \text{VCR} + \text{CMR}$$
$$\text{VCR} = 1.00 - \text{CMR}$$
$$= 1.00 - 0.45$$
$$= 0.55, \text{ or } 55\%$$

Nador Company incurs 55 cents in variable operating costs per dollar of sales:

	Amount	Percent of Sales
Sales	$600,000	100%
Less variable costs	330,000	55
Contribution margin	$270,000	45%

Now multiply the variable cost ratio times the accounts receivable to find the investment in accounts receivable:

---

[7]Most theorists agree that if you consider a change in credit policy as resulting in new sales calling for new production, then the investment in receivables is the variable cost incurred. They reason that if the sales were not made, then the company would not incur the incremental, variable cash costs. On the other hand, if a change in credit policy causes an increase in receivables due to delayed receipt of old credit sales, then the increase in receivables represents the increase in investment.

$$\text{Investment in accounts receivable} = \text{VCR} \times \text{Accounts receivable}$$
$$= 0.55 \times \$58,000$$
$$= \$31,900$$

Step 4. Calculate the expected before-tax rate of return. Subtracting bad-debt and collection expense from the contribution margin yields the expected before-tax cash flow; divide this cash flow by the expected investment in additional accounts receivable to obtain the expected before-tax rate of return.

Step 5. Adjust the expected before-tax rate of return for tax consequences. Multiply the before-tax rate of return from Step 4 by 1 minus the company's marginal tax rate:

$$\frac{\text{Expected after-tax}}{\text{rate of return}} = \frac{\text{Expected before-tax}}{\text{rate of return}} \times (1 - \text{T})$$

Step 6. Make the decision. Compare the expected after-tax rate of return with the company's required rate of return. If the after-tax return is greater than the required return, then the financial manager should recommend that the company implement the proposed relaxation of credit standards. If the after-tax return is less than the required return, then the proposal should be rejected.[8] The decision can also be made using the before-tax analysis, as long as the expected return and the required return are both expressed before taxes.

EXAMPLE

The management of Demos Supplies is considering a proposal from the marketing manager to relax credit standards. From the extension of credit to customers with lower credit ratings, the marketing manager expects the following results:

1. Credit sales will increase from $120,000 annually to $150,000.

2. The average collection period (days' credit sales in accounts receivable) will increase from 30 days to 60 days.

3. Bad-debt expense will increase from 1 percent to 2 percent of credit sales, but collection expense will not rise. The cost accountant calculates the contribution margin ratio to be 18 percent, and the financial manager judges the required rate of return to be 12 percent and the tax rate to be 40 percent.

- *Step 1.* Calculate the expected change in the company's contribution margin:

Contribution margin at new sales level (0.18 × $150,000)	$27,000
Less contribution margin at previous level (0.18 × $120,000)	21,600
Increase in contribution margin	$ 5,400

---

[8] In theory, the required rate of return for investments in accounts receivable can be determined with the capital asset pricing model discussed in Chapter 5. Implementation in practice, however, is difficult. If we view the investment in accounts receivable as a typical investment, then its required rate of return would be the company's marginal cost of capital. Accounts receivable may be less risky than typical investments, however, because the product is already sold and demand risk is therefore absent. This line of argument suggests a required rate of return less than the company's marginal cost of capital.

- *Step 2.* Calculate the change in bad-debt expense associated with the change in credit policy:

Bad debts at new sales level	
(0.02 × $150,000)	$3,000
Less bad debts at previous level	
(0.01 × $120,000)	1,200
Increase in bad-debt expense	$1,800

- *Step 3.* Calculate the change in investment in accounts receivable by using the variable cost ratio and the change in accounts receivable:

New level of accounts receivable:		
Daily sales ($150,000/365 days)	$410.96	
Multiplied by average collection period	× 60	
New accounts receivable		$24,658
Less previous level of accounts receivable:		
Daily sales ($120,000/365 days)	$328.77	
Multiplied by average collection period	× 30	
Previous accounts receivable		9,863
Increase in accounts receivable		$14,795
Multiplied by variable cost ratio		× 0.82
Increased investment in accounts receivable		$12,132

- *Step 4.* Calculate the expected before-tax rate of return:

$$\begin{array}{l} \text{Expected} \\ \text{before-tax} \\ \text{rate of return} \end{array} = \frac{\text{Increase in contribution margin} - \text{Increase in bad debts}}{\text{Increased investment in accounts receivable}}$$

$$= \frac{\$5,400 - \$1,800}{\$12,132} = 0.297, \text{ or } 29.7\%$$

- *Step 5.* Adjust for tax consequences:

$$\begin{array}{l} \text{Expected after-tax} \\ \text{rate of return} \end{array} = 0.297(1 - 0.40)$$

$$= 0.178, \text{ or } 17.8\%$$

- *Step 6. Decision:* Compare the expected after-tax rate of return, 17.8 percent, with the after-tax required rate of return, 12 percent. Because the expected return exceeds the required return, management should relax the company's credit standards.

The preceding analysis assumes that no increases are required in inventory and fixed assets. If increases are required in a particular case, you would add them to the investment in receivables. Also, if accounts payable were to increase as a result of increased sales, the dollar increase would be subtracted from the investment in receivables.

Before turning to the topic of inventory management, we should remember the acronym GIGO: *garbage in, garbage out.* Inputs to the analysis, especially the change in sales, are difficult to estimate. If the estimate is in error, the decision may be in error. Scenario and sensitivity analyses akin to the procedures described in Chapter 10 provide additional refinements to the analysis.

INVENTORY MANAGEMENT

Inventory is a current asset that companies use to support sales and production. For many companies inventory is a large investment. To illustrate, inventories in the automobile industry often average about 60 days of sales. This means that if car assembly plants were to shut down, the industry could make sales for 60 days before running out of cars. The value of the automobile industry's inventory amounts to billions of dollars.

The functions of inventory management are to maintain levels of inventory adequate to meet demand, to order or produce more inventory when stocks run low, and to order or produce sufficient quantities to avoid shortages. Carrying out these functions efficiently maximizes shareholder wealth.

Inventory acts as a buffer between different activities within a company. It removes some of the pressure that might be placed on the production department or suppliers to produce goods in a hurry (possibly with shoddy results). For example, many microcomputer manufacturers and software developers have rushed to fill orders after initial demand exceeded their expectations. The results were flawed products that cost the companies goodwill and future sales. To clarify further the role of inventory, consider the three major types of inventory.

raw materials inventory
Basic inputs of materials to a company's production process.

Raw materials inventory is the basic input to a company's production process. It may consist of commodities such as copper, lumber, and steel, or it may contain processed goods such as woven fabrics, computer circuit boards, and automobile engines. A company's purchasing department buys raw materials for the production department to use. Holding raw materials inventory creates an independence between the purchasing and production departments and prevents delays in production. Raw materials are usually financially liquid because a company in financial distress can sell them quickly to other companies to use in their production.

work-in-process inventory
Partially finished products being produced by a company.

Work-in-process inventory consists of partially finished products being produced by a company. Consider, for example, a production process consisting of two work stations, A and B:

$$\text{Raw material} \rightarrow \boxed{A} \rightarrow \begin{array}{c} \text{A's output is} \\ \text{work in process} \end{array} \rightarrow \boxed{B} \rightarrow \begin{array}{c} \text{B's output is} \\ \text{finished goods} \end{array}$$

Work Station A takes raw material, modifies it, and sends it to Work Station B, where the finishing touches produce finished goods for sale. A's output is a partially finished product—work in process. To make Work Station B independent of A, management may store an inventory of A's output. Longer assembly lines require more work-in-process inventory than do shorter ones to maintain a constant flow of output. Work in process is the least liquid part of inventory because it cannot be easily sold to other companies for use in their production.

finished goods inventory
Products ready to sell; stock in trade available for sale.

Finished goods inventory consists of products that are available for sale. Holding finished goods inventory reduces the dependency of sales on production. The marketing staff will have a supply of finished goods to sell, and the company can meet delivery schedules from its goods on hand. With finished goods inventory, the company can also meet unexpected demand. Were it not for this inventory, the demand might go unmet and sales would be lost.

Inventory Costs

Inventory costs fall into four major categories: (1) cost of designing and implementing the inventory control system; (2) stockout costs, the cost of lost sales because of insufficient inventory; (3) cost of ordering (or setting up to produce) inventory; and (4) cost of carrying inventory.

The *cost of designing and implementing* an inventory control system includes the costs of (1) system design and acquisition of computer capacity to keep track of products stored in inventory, and (2) incremental salaries and compensation needed to staff the system. The company's top management decides on the merit of a system using the capital-budgeting methods examined in Part III of this book.

stockout costs
Lost profit on lost sales attributable to inadequate inventory.

Stockout costs, or shortage costs, occur when a company loses sales because of an insufficient inventory of finished goods. Customers like to have their orders filled promptly—the sooner the better. When disappointed, they may well take their business elsewhere. Stockout costs equal the contribution margin a company loses when its customers fill their orders elsewhere. Stockouts can also cause problems in production. Insufficient raw materials and work-in-process inventories may shut down a production line.

ordering costs
Costs of ordering inventory; include cost of preparing purchase orders and follow-up work, receiving, and processing orders.

Ordering costs (or setup costs) include the costs of such tasks as preparing purchase orders and follow-up work, receiving and processing orders, and making changes in machine setups for production runs. Frequently, the cost per order is independent of the order size. Thus total ordering costs for a year equal the cost per order times the number of orders.

carrying costs
Costs of holding inventory; include cost of capital, storage costs, obsolescence, taxes, and insurance.

Carrying costs are the outlays required to hold or store inventory. Examples of carrying costs are:

- Cost of capital tied up in inventory.
- Storage or space costs (such as rental expense).
- Obsolescence, deterioration, and theft of inventory.
- Taxes on inventory.
- Insurance on inventory.

Carrying costs rise as the dollar size of inventory increases. Moreover, *average inventory levels rise as the frequency of placing orders declines.* Inventory levels rise because infrequent orders mean that the company must acquire more inventory with each order. *Ordering costs over a period vary inversely with carrying costs*—as a company holds larger amounts of inventory, its carrying costs rise and its ordering costs decline because management places fewer orders for materials.

Minimizing Inventory Costs

For most companies the costs of carrying and ordering inventory are unavoidable. The task therefore is to minimize the total of the two costs:

$$\text{Total costs} = \text{Carrying costs} + \text{Ordering costs}$$

For this analysis we assume that management has already decided to implement an inventory control system and that the company has already incurred those costs, meaning that they are sunk costs. Stockout costs are taken care of with safety stock, as discussed below. Safety stock is additional inventory to cover uncertain demand.

Carrying costs and ordering costs can be broken down into their components to express the total costs in greater detail:

$$\text{Carrying costs} = A \times C$$

where A = average size of inventory in units

C = annual cost to carry one unit of inventory

$$\text{Ordering costs} = N \times O$$

where N = number of orders placed per year[9]

O = cost to place one order

Putting these costs together yields the following equation for total costs:

$$\text{Total costs} = (A \times C) + (N \times O)$$

The dilemma facing a manager becomes apparent when you examine how the number of orders placed per year (N) affects the components of total costs:

- Placing a *small* number of large orders per year causes carrying costs to be large because *A* (average inventory size) is large. It causes ordering costs to be small because *N* (number of orders) is small.
- Placing a *large* number of small orders per year causes carrying costs to be small because *A* is small. It causes ordering costs to be large because *N* is large.

economic order quantity (EOQ)

Quantity of inventory units ordered that minimizes the sum of carrying costs and ordering costs.

The trade-off between carrying costs and ordering costs calls for a strategy between the extremes in order to minimize total costs. The strategy is the **economic order quantity (EOQ)**: the quantity of units ordered that minimizes total costs. The following equation is the *EOQ model:*[10]

$$EOQ = \sqrt{\frac{2 \times S \times O}{C}}$$

where EOQ = economic order quantity that minimizes total costs

S = sales per year in units of inventory

[9]The same equation can be used for a period other than for one year by adjusting each value for the time period considered—month, quarter, and so on.

[10]By letting Q be the number of units ordered, average inventory $A = Q/2$; also, by letting S be the number of units sold over the period, the number of orders becomes $N = S/Q$. Express total costs as follows:

$$\text{Total costs} = (Q/2)(C) + (S/Q)(O)$$

To find the minimum total costs, take the derivative of total costs with respect to Q and set the result equal to zero:

$$(C/2) - (SO/Q^2) = 0$$

Solving for Q yields:

$$SO/Q^2 = C/2$$
$$Q^2 = 2SO/C$$
$$Q = \sqrt{(2 \times S \times O)/C}$$

This expression for Q is the economic order quantity.

The EOQ model can also be expressed as follows:

$$EOQ = \sqrt{\frac{2 \times S \times O}{p \times c}}$$

where p = annual carrying cost per unit expressed as a percentage of inventory purchase cost, c

c = purchase cost per unit of inventory or cost per unit to manufacture inventory

If ordering costs (which affect the numerator in the EOQ model) rise relative to carrying costs (which affect the denominator), then the economic order quantity rises. The company increases the order size, places fewer orders each year, and pays more carrying costs. In so doing, it saves more costs through less frequent ordering than it incurs through additional carrying costs. Conversely, as carrying costs increase relative to ordering costs, the company reduces the order quantity, places more orders each year, and pays less in carrying costs. In so doing, the company saves more in carrying costs than it incurs with more frequent ordering.

EXAMPLE

Alton Brothers Hardware sells 2,000 screwdrivers per year (S). Cash ordering costs are $4 per order (O), and each item costs the company $2 (c), with carrying costs 20 percent (p) of the purchase cost. The economic order quantity (EOQ) under these conditions is 200 screwdrivers, calculated as follows:

$$EOQ = \sqrt{\frac{2 \times 2,000 \times \$4}{0.20 \times \$2}} = 200 \text{ screwdrivers}$$

Figure 13.4 illustrates ordering and selling the 200 screwdrivers (EOQ) over time. At time t_0 the company receives 200 screwdrivers and sells them uniformly over the period t_0 to t_1. At t_1 the company orders another 200 screwdrivers and receives them without delay. The company exhausts the order received at t_1 during the period t_1 to t_2. Another order is placed and filled at t_2, and the cycle repeats again. It is assumed in this case that Alton Brothers Hardware receives the orders without delay and that it sells screwdrivers uniformly over the year.

Order Size and Inventory Costs

The economic order quantity (EOQ) minimizes total costs and is therefore the optimal quantity to order. To order either more or less than the EOQ increases total costs, as the following discussion demonstrates.

If a company uses the EOQ model and sells inventory evenly over time, then average inventory in units is the EOQ divided by 2:

$$\text{Average inventory (A)} = \frac{\text{Beginning inventory} + \text{Ending inventory}}{2}$$

$$= EOQ/2$$

FIGURE 13.4

Inventory Levels over Time: Economic Order Quantity (EOQ) Equals 200 Units

The financial manager places an order of size EOQ when the company runs out of inventory. The ordered merchandise is received without delay, and the company starts each period with an inventory of size EOQ (200 screwdrivers). The average size of inventory (100) is the beginning inventory level plus the ending level, all divided by 2. The EOQ is the inventory order size that minimizes the total costs.

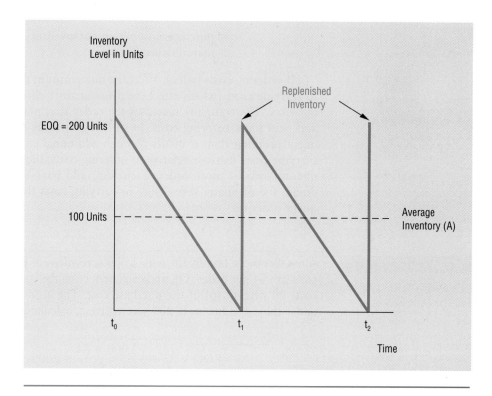

For the Alton Brothers Hardware example illustrated in Figure 13.4, average inventory is:

$$A = 200/2$$
$$= 100 \text{ screwdrivers}$$

Total carrying costs equal the carrying cost per unit times the average number of inventory units:

$$\text{Total carrying costs} = (p \times c)A$$
$$= (p \times c)(EOQ/2)$$

Applying this equation to Alton Brothers Hardware yields the following total carrying costs for the year:

$$\text{Total carrying costs} = (0.20 \times \$2)(200/2)$$
$$= 0.40 \times 100$$
$$= \$40$$

Total ordering costs equal the cost per order times the number of orders placed during the period:

$$\text{Total ordering costs} = \text{Cost per order} \times \text{Number of orders}$$
$$= O(S/EOQ)$$

S/EOQ is the number of orders placed because S is the number of units sold during the period and EOQ is the size of each order. Once again, using the figures of the previous example, we calculate the total ordering costs for Alton Brothers during the year:

$$\text{Total ordering costs} = \$4(2,000/200)$$
$$= \$40$$

Combining these equations yields the equation for total costs based on optimal ordering (EOQ):

$$\text{Total costs} = (p \times c)(EOQ/2) + (O)(S/EOQ)$$

Inserting the figures for Alton Brothers yields:

$$\text{Total costs} = (0.20 \times \$2)(200/2) + (\$4)(2,000/200)$$
$$= \$40 + \$40$$
$$= \$80$$

which is the minimum total costs using the EOQ model.

You can see that the EOQ yields the minimum total costs by looking at the way total costs change with changes in the number of units the company orders. If Alton Brothers increases the quantity ordered by one unit or decreases it by one unit, then total costs increase:

EOQ + 1 unit (carrying costs increase and ordering costs decrease):

$$\text{Total costs} = (0.20 \times \$2)(201/2) + (\$4)(2,000/201)$$
$$= \$40.20 + \$39.801$$
$$= \$80.001$$

EOQ − 1 unit (carrying costs decrease and ordering costs increase):

$$\text{Total costs} = (0.20 \times \$2)(199/2) + (\$4)(2,000/199)$$
$$= \$39.80 + \$40.201$$
$$= \$80.001$$

Clearly, the difference in total costs caused by a one-unit variation from the EOQ is very small. Larger variations, however, cause more significant differences; and larger inventory levels increase the dollar costs.

Figure 13.5 shows the way carrying and ordering costs change with changes in the number of units ordered. Here total carrying costs increase as order size increases and total ordering costs decrease as order size increases. Summing the two curves yields the total costs of inventory. The minimum point on the total cost curve is the EOQ.[11]

[11] Figure 13.5 shows the minimum total costs occurring where carrying costs intersect ordering costs. This location of the minimum occurs because of the assumed linear carrying costs as order size increases. If carrying costs increase at an increasing rate (curve is concave upward), then the minimum occurs to the left of the intersection. If carrying costs increase at a decreasing rate (curve is concave downward), then the minimum occurs to the right of the intersection. For proof, see Robert M. Brown, "On Carrying Costs and the EOQ Model: A Pedagogical Note," *Financial Review,* November 1985, 357–360.

FIGURE 13.5

Minimizing Total Costs of Inventory with the EOQ Model

The total cost curve is derived by taking the sum of carrying costs and ordering costs. The EOQ (economic order quantity) is the order size that minimizes the total costs.

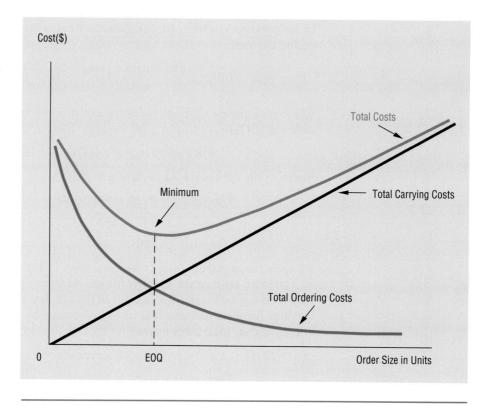

order point

Quantity of remaining inventory units at which management orders the EOQ.

To avoid stockouts, an inventory control system relies on the order point and safety stock. The **order point** is the level of remaining inventory at which management places an order (EOQ size) for additional units. The order point depends on how rapidly the company uses inventory and the delivery time. If delivery time and unit sales were certain, then management could place an order at an inventory level dictated by the rate of use and the time lapse between ordering and delivery. Under these conditions the order point (OP) is a combination of the sales rate (S) over the period and lead time (L) required for delivery:

$$OP = S \times L$$

The equation requires that *S* and *L* be expressed in the same time measure—days, weeks, and so on.

EXAMPLE

Recall that Alton Brothers Hardware sells 2,000 screwdrivers annually. Because the store closes on weekends and holidays, Alton Brothers is open 260 days during a year. As a result, the store sells 2,000/260 days = 7.69 screwdrivers daily. Suppose that there is a 3-day delivery time. The order point is 7.69 × 3 = 23.07 screwdrivers. Because the store cannot order a fraction of a screwdriver, the order point must be rounded upward. The order point in this example becomes 24 screwdrivers; that is, the store places an order of size EOQ when inventory falls to 24 units.

The **safety stock (SS)** is a cushion against the uncertainty surrounding changes in inventory use and in delivery time. Safety stock would be unnecessary if the use rate and delivery time were absolutely certain because an order for new units (of EOQ size) would be placed so that new units arrive at the precise moment that inventory is zero. In the real world of uncertainty, however, a company needs safety stock.

A company holds safety stock to avoid stockouts. This benefit is not without costs, however. Holding safety stock increases inventory carrying costs and therefore total costs. Safety stock needs to be monitored over time to make sure it is neither too large (never completely used) nor too small (frequent stockouts).

Holding safety stock does not influence the EOQ. It does, however, raise the order point. The result is an increase in the average size of inventory and therefore an increase in the total costs of inventory.

EXAMPLE

To illustrate the influence of safety stock on total costs and order point, consider the impact of a 12-screwdriver safety stock for Alton Brothers Hardware. Recall that total inventory costs equal $80 before the store acquires a safety stock. A 12-screwdriver safety stock (SS) increases the average size of inventory to 112 screwdrivers:

$$A = (EOQ/2) + SS$$
$$= (200/2) + 12$$
$$= 112 \text{ screwdrivers}$$

Figure 13.6 illustrates the impact of safety stock on Alton Brothers' inventory levels over time. Average inventory rises from 100 to 112 screwdrivers, and total inventory costs rise to $84.80, calculated as follows:

$$\text{Total costs} = \text{Carrying costs} + \text{Ordering costs}$$
$$= (p \times c)[(EOQ/2) + SS] + [O(S/EOQ)]$$
$$= (0.20 \times \$2)[(200/2) + 12] + [\$4(2,000/200)]$$
$$= \$44.80 + \$40$$
$$= \$84.80$$

Inventory costs rise by $4.80 ($84.80 − $80.00) because of the safety stock. These 12 units increase carrying costs by $0.40 × 12 = $4.80.

The order point increases by the number of units in safety stock. In the example the order point for screwdrivers rises to 36 units:

$$OP = (S \times L) + SS$$
$$= (7.69 \times 3) + 12$$
$$= 36 \text{ screwdrivers (rounded)}$$

FIGURE 13.6

Inventory Levels over Time with Safety Stock

Safety stock increases the beginning and ending levels of inventory and therefore increases the average size of inventory. Inventory levels shift upward by the amount of the safety stock. Alton Brothers Hardware sells 8 screwdrivers daily, and 3 days are required to receive delivery. The store orders 200 screwdrivers when the level of inventory is 36 screwdrivers.

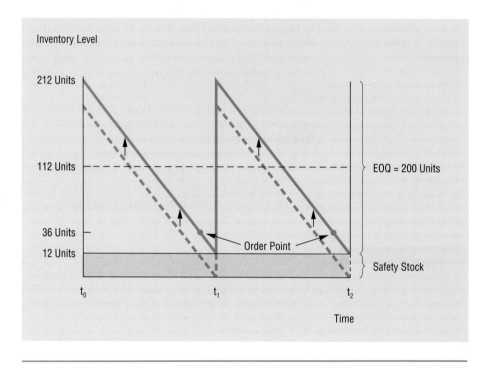

Alton Brothers needs to order more inventory (of size EOQ = 200 screwdrivers) when the number of screwdrivers on the shelf reaches 36.

Monitoring Inventory Levels

The EOQ model serves as a useful first approximation in establishing inventory levels and order sizes. But because of the model's assumptions (for example, perfectly forecast, uniform sales over the year), the financial manager needs to use additional methods to be sure there are sufficient goods on hand to meet production and sales demands.

ABC system
System for monitoring inventory levels based on prioritized groups of items.

One method for monitoring inventory levels is called the **ABC system.** Under this system the inventory manager classifies inventory items into one of three groups: A, B, or C. Group A contains the inventory items requiring the closest scrutiny: high-cost and high-volume items for which the company wants to assure availability for customers. Groups B and C contain second- and third-priority items.

80–20 rule
Rule of thumb that a company makes 80 percent of sales from 20 percent of inventory items.

It is common for 80 percent of a company's sales to come from 20 percent of the items inventoried (the **80–20 rule**). These items would be in Group A. The other 80 percent of all items representing 20 percent of sales would be placed in Groups B and C. After classifying all inventory items, the financial manager pays most attention to Group A, carefully controlling these items by checking their levels, sales, and delivery times. Items in Groups B and C receive less surveillance.

A company's success or failure at controlling its inventory shows up in its financial statements. Poor inventory control results in an imbalance between the inventory on the balance sheet and the cost of goods sold on the income statement. These two figures are combined into a financial measure called the inventory turnover ratio. **Inventory turnover** is the amount of sales (measured at cost) per dollar of inventory:

$$\text{Inventory turnover} = \frac{\text{Cost of goods sold}}{\text{Inventory}}$$

inventory turnover
Dollar amount of sales (at cost) per dollar of inventory; cost of goods sold divided by inventory.

EXAMPLE

Cooler Company's cost of goods sold for the year is $900,000, and its ending inventory is $100,000, which is typical of the past monthly balances. The company's inventory turnover ratio is 9.0:

$$\text{Inventory turnover} = \frac{\$900,000}{\$100,000}$$

$$= 9.0$$

Cooler Company has $9 of sales (measured at cost) for each $1 in inventory.

Inventory turnover in the above example shows the relationship between the cost of goods sold over a period of time and the end-of-period inventory. Some managers use average inventory (beginning + ending)/2, instead of ending inventory; also, some use sales instead of cost of goods sold. These variations are discussed in Chapter 15.

A company's financial manager examines the inventory turnover ratio for several time periods to see if it is rising or falling. A rising ratio implies that inventory is getting too low, and a falling ratio implies that it is getting too high. The financial manager may compare the ratio with the ratios of other companies in the same industry. A ratio substantially different from the industry average is a red flag telling the financial manager that the company should evaluate its inventory control. For example, suppose that Cooler Company's ratio has been decreasing over the past three years and the average inventory turnover in its industry is 15. This information indicates that Cooler Company is letting its inventory levels increase too far, which suggests that it may be incurring excessive carrying costs.

In the example above, the turnover ratio for Cooler Company applies to all inventory. To examine individual inventory items, financial managers divide the total cost of the item sold by its dollar value in inventory. Repeating this calculation for each item reveals the slow movers and the hot items. Trends over time in individual-item turnovers are particularly meaningful to managers. Items with high and increasing ratios are candidates for additional investment, and those with low and falling ratios are candidates for liquidation.

Another refinement of inventory turnover exists in manufacturing companies. Looking at raw materials, work-in-process, and finished goods inventory, manufacturing managers may want to know values for the following turnovers to determine which inventories are too large or too small:

$$\frac{\text{Raw materials}}{\text{turnover}} = \frac{\$\text{Raw materials transferred to work in process}}{\$\text{Raw materials inventory}}$$

Managers Take Steps to Reduce Inventory

"If you manage inventory properly," says Thomas J. Bass, manager of production control at Ford Motor Co., "your supplier carries all of your cost."

"Inventory is evil, and we sought to eradicate it," says Norman Garrity, who oversees several factories owned by Corning Inc. "If you understand what causes inventory, you get to the root causes of a lot of manufacturing problems."

The comments of both Mr. Bass and Mr. Garrity indicate a distaste for incurring the carrying costs of inventory. Carrying $1,000,000 of inventory for a year typically costs a manufacturer $250,000 to $300,000. To reduce such costs, Corning Inc. installed just-in-time inventory manage-

ment. Now Corning supplies its customers just a few days after receiving an order, and Corning's suppliers do the same. The net result is a reduction in carrying costs for all participants in the channel of distribution.

Since the 1981–1982 U.S. recession, companies have done a remarkable job of managing inventories. For example, Corky Johnson, the manager of fuel-distribution supply for Sun Company's refining and marketing unit, has the job of keeping inventories down, which reduces carrying costs. "Long is wrong," he likes to say.

As the chart below shows, decisions by inventory managers such as Mr. Johnson can make a difference. Inventories of U.S.

manufacturers (in 1982 dollars) declined during the 1980s, reaching 1.48 months of sales late in 1990. In other words, companies would need just under a month and a half to sell off all of their inventory. The inventory turnover of these manufacturers equaled 8.1 (12 months/1.48 months).

The increased skill in controlling inventory owes something to the computerized techniques that have been adopted by many companies in recent years. Computers quickly tell managers exactly how much inventory they have and where it is. Managerial judgment, however, still plays a strong role in determining how much inventory is enough.

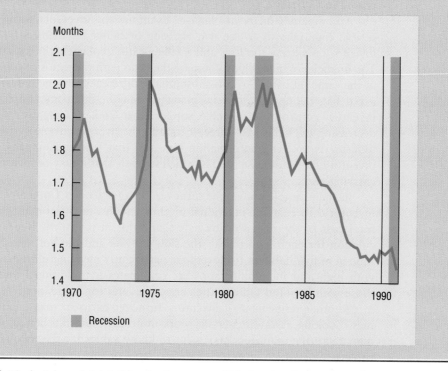

Source: Bill Paul, "Corky Johnson's Job is Trimming Inventory to Help Sun Co. Shine," *The Wall Street Journal,* Apr. 20, 1987, 1, 7; Lindley H. Clark, Jr., "Will Low Inventories Soften a Slump?," *The Wall Street Journal,* Apr. 10, 1989, A1; Thomas F. O'Boyle, "Last In, Right Out," *The Wall Street Journal,* Nov. 19, 1990, A1 and A4.

$$\text{Work-in-process} \atop \text{turnover} = \frac{\text{\$Work in process transferred to finished goods}}{\text{\$Work-in-process inventory}}$$

$$\text{Finished goods} \atop \text{turnover} = \frac{\text{\$Cost of goods sold}}{\text{\$Finished goods inventory}}$$

Monitoring these turnovers enables the financial manager to uncover problems in the three types of inventory. Excessively high turnovers suggest high ordering costs and potential problems with stockouts. Excessively low turnovers suggest inventory buildups and high carrying costs. Managerial judgment is needed to interpret these signals. For example, frequent production stoppages coupled with a historically high raw materials turnover indicate an inadequate stockpile of raw materials. In most cases, other signals are available to corroborate the message of an inventory turnover.

Finally, a recent innovation in inventory management comes to us from Japan, the **just-in-time (JIT) system.** A JIT system attempts to reduce the investment in inventory by coordinating purchasing and manufacturing activities. The goal is to have raw materials arrive just in time for manufacturing processes and to have work-in-process inventory arrive just in time at the next work station. JIT systems tend to push inventories back to suppliers and to increase efficiency in production. Successfully implemented JIT systems reduce inventory levels and carrying costs.

just-in-time (JIT) system
System that tries to move inventory to the production line as close as possible to the time it is needed.

SUMMARY

• A company's credit policy consists of credit standards, credit terms, and collection practices. Financial managers decide whether or not to grant credit to buyers by applying the five Cs: character, capacity, capital, collateral, and conditions. A company manages its accounts receivable by requiring customers to meet its credit standards and terms and by monitoring collections.

• Managers often design credit terms to encourage customers to pay early by giving them a cash discount if they do so. For example, 2/10, net 30 means take a 2 percent discount if you pay by the tenth day after purchase; otherwise, pay the total amount by the thirtieth day. The annual opportunity cost of forgoing this discount is 37.2 percent, calculated with the following equation:

$$\text{Annual} \atop \text{opportunity cost} = \frac{D}{1 - D} \times \frac{365}{n}$$

• When the opportunity cost of forgoing a cash discount is high relative to the general level of interest rates, most customers will take the discount and pay early; otherwise, they will not. Financial managers assess the effects of credit terms using two financial ratios:

$$\text{Accounts receivable} \atop \text{turnover} = \frac{\text{Credit sales}}{\text{Accounts receivable}}$$

$$\text{Average collection} \atop \text{period} = \frac{\text{Accounts receivable}}{\text{Average daily credit sales}}$$

Liberal credit policies lead to low accounts receivable turnovers and long average collection periods. Conservative policies lead to high accounts receivable turnovers and short average collection periods. Aging receivables, classifying receivables according to time outstanding, helps the financial manager evaluate credit policy.

- Evaluating the merit of a change in credit policy requires the financial manager to measure the benefits and costs associated with the change. For example, lowering credit standards leads to an expected increase in sales, profits, bad-debt expense, collection expense, and investment in accounts receivable. If the expected rate of return on the increased investment in accounts receivable exceeds the company's required rate of return, then the financial manager should implement the change; otherwise, the proposed change should be rejected.

- Inventory acts as a buffer between different activities within a company. The inventory of a manufacturer consists of raw materials, work in process, and finished goods. Because carrying inventory involves substantial costs—cost of capital, storage, obsolescence, taxes, insurance, and so on—managers hold only enough inventory to maintain an orderly flow of business.

- Carrying costs and ordering costs are inversely related. A small number of large orders each year leads to a large average inventory and large carrying costs, but small ordering costs. A large number of small orders each year has the opposite effect—a small average inventory and low carrying costs, but large ordering costs. To minimize the sum of carrying and ordering costs, a manager can use the EOQ (economic order quantity) model:

$$EOQ = \sqrt{\frac{2 \times S \times O}{C}}$$

where S is sales per year in units of inventory, O is the cost of placing one order, and C is the annual carrying cost of one unit. EOQ increases with increases in S and O; it decreases with increases in C.

- The order point (OP) is the number of units remaining in inventory at which a company places an order for more inventory:

$$OP = S \times L$$

where L is the lead time required for delivery. If the company holds a safety stock—an inventory cushion against uncertainty—then the order point increases by the number of units in the safety stock.

- Some financial managers control the level of investment in inventory using the ABC system. This system often operates on the 80–20 rule: 80 percent of company sales comes from 20 percent of its products. The financial manager classifies this 20 percent as Group A inventory and monitors it carefully for stockouts and delivery times. Lower-priority items are classified as Group B and Group C inventories.

- Inventory turnover ratios help the financial manager to evaluate the success of a company's inventory control system:

$$Inventory\ turnover = \frac{Costs\ of\ goods\ sold}{Inventory}$$

Financial managers calculate turnovers for total inventory, individual products, and classes of inventory—raw materials, work in process, and finished goods. Low turnovers signal inventory buildups; high turnovers signal small inventory quantities and the possibility of stockouts.

- A recent innovation in inventory management is the just-in-time system, in which a company tries to reduce inventory by coordinating purchasing and manufacturing activities. The supplier delivers inventory items just in time to meet the user's needs.

Key Terms

credit standards

trade credit

credit scoring

credit terms

seasonal datings

accounts receivable turnover

average collection period

dunning notice

aging receivables

captive finance company

contribution margin

variable cost ratio (VCR)

contribution margin ratio (CMR)

raw materials inventory

work-in-process inventory

finished goods inventory

stockout costs

ordering costs

carrying costs

economic order quantity (EOQ)

order point

safety stock (SS)

ABC system

80–20 rule

inventory turnover

just-in-time (JIT) system

Questions

13.1. The level of accounts receivable reflects both the volume of a company's sales on account and its credit policy. Explain why this statement is true.

13.2. List the five Cs of credit. Which one is the most important? Second most important? Explain your choices.

13.3. A wholesaler of petroleum products made the following statement: "During oil gluts, credit terms offered by major oil companies are 1/10, net 30. Along comes a shortage and they change the terms to net 10." Explain the rationale for this change in credit terms to wholesalers from the viewpoint of a major oil company.

13.4. The opportunity cost of forgoing cash discounts with 1/10, net 40 is 12.3 percent; for 1/10, net 30 the opportunity cost is 18.4 percent. As a customer, which terms would you prefer? Explain your answer.

13.5. A deterioration of customer quality leads to a change in the accounts receivable turnover. Do you agree? Why or why not?

13.6. Define *average collection period*. How do you calculate it? What does its value tell you?

13.7. The average collection period (ACP) is a mathematical rearrangement of the accounts receivable turnover ratio. Selected values of the turnover ratio and corresponding values of ACP are:

Accounts Receivable Turnover	ACP
1	365.0
2	182.5
5	73.0
10	36.5
20	18.3
30	12.2

Graph ACP as a function of accounts receivable turnover. Put ACP on the vertical axis and accounts receivable turnover on the horizontal axis. Is the relationship linear (that is, a straight line)?

13.8. Why is a 35-day-old account receivable worth more, in many cases, than a 120-day-old account receivable?

13.9. If a company lowers credit standards, accounts receivable probably will rise. Say, for a particular case, that receivables rise $10,000. Does $10,000 represent the increase in the company's investment in accounts receivable? Explain your answer.

13.10. Take a look at a chair in your room. Identify the raw materials used to make it. Visualize how the chair might be manufactured and describe the work in process at various points. What is the purpose of storing work-in-process inventory?

13.11. Ivan Tory, financial manager for Plastics Unlimited, claims that it costs his company 30 percent of the cost of an item each year to hold inventory. He includes both opportunity cost and cash costs in his calculation. Is it possible that Mr. Tory is correct in using such a large percentage? Explain your answer. What does the 30 percent mean in dollars if Plastics Unlimited carries $1,000,000 of inventory for one year?

13.12. Explain why inventory carrying costs and inventory ordering costs are inversely related.

13.13. Four of the following events reduce the size of inventory that a company will hold. Identify the one that does *not* and explain your choice.
   a. Increased computer control.
   b. Increased rate of sales growth.
   c. Standardization of products.
   d. Limited variety of products.
   e. Faster transportation methods.

13.14. Anne Flaxon, controller of Flaxon Industries and oldest daughter of chief executive officer Jonas Flaxon, comments that she is reluctant to raise the company's inventory order point. Her reason is that raising the order point "increases the total inventory costs." Do you agree with her reasoning? Explain your answer.

13.15. Explain the impact of safety stock on (a) the order point and (b) total costs of inventory.

13.16. Describe the ABC system for monitoring inventory levels. What is the 80–20 rule? Does this rule work in every case? Explain. Identify some area other than inventory control where the 80–20 rule might apply.

13.17. *True or false:* High inventory turnovers indicate high inventory levels. Explain your choice.

13.18. Which of the following companies would likely have the larger inventory turnover ratio: Piggly Wiggly Supermarkets or Inland Steel? Explain your choice.

Strategy Problems

I. Managing Accounts Receivable

Chico Cabinet Makers is trying to determine whether or not to grant credit to its marginal customers. The credit terms the financial manager is considering are 2/10, net 45 days. If the company grants the credit, then accounts receivable will rise by an estimated $26,000 and the company's annual sales will rise by $140,000. The contribution margin will be $14,000. The company will have a $3,500 bad-debt expense and a $4,200 collection expense from the increased sales. The before-tax required rate of return on investment in accounts receivable is 18 percent.

a. Calculate the annual opportunity cost to Chico Cabinet Makers' marginal credit customers of forgoing the prompt-payment discount.

b. Calculate the contribution margin and variable cost ratios.

c. Should Mr. Chico extend trade credit to the marginal customers? Support your answer with calculations.

Strategy	Solution

Apply the opportunity-cost equation using the appropriate number of days.

a.
$$\text{Annual opportunity cost} = \frac{0.02}{1 - 0.02} \times \frac{365}{45 - 10}$$
$$= 0.213, \text{ or } 21.3\%$$

b. The contribution margin ratio is the contribution margin per dollar of sales revenue:

Divide the contribution margin by sales.

$$\text{Contribution margin ratio} = \frac{\text{Contribution margin}}{\text{Sales}}$$
$$= \frac{\$14,000}{\$140,000} = 0.10, \text{ or } 10\%$$

The variable cost ratio is the variable cost per dollar of sales. It is the complement of the contribution margin ratio:

Recognize VCR as the complement of CMR.

$$\text{Variable cost ratio} = 1 - \text{Contribution margin ratio}$$
$$= 1 - 0.10 = 0.90, \text{ or } 90\%$$

c. Because the expected rate of return, 26.9 percent, is greater than the required rate of return, 18 percent, Chico Cabinet Makers should extend credit to the marginal customers:

Divide contribution margin less bad-debt and collection expense by the investment in receivables.

$$\text{Expected rate of return} = \frac{\$14,000 - (\$3,500 + \$4,200)}{\$26,000 \times 0.90}$$
$$= 0.269, \text{ or } 26.9\%$$

II. Managing Inventory

Smithson Company is a sporting-goods supplier that sells a number of products to several sporting-goods stores in the area. One of its products is baseballs. It sells the baseballs in packages of 12 for $20 per package. The market-ing manager has determined that the demand for the baseballs is a constant rate of 2,000 packages per month.

The packages cost the Smithson Company $10 each from the Haitian manufacturer and require a 3-day lead time from date of order to date of delivery. The ordering cost is $1.20 per order, and the carrying cost is 10 percent of the cost of inventory annually. Smithson Company buys economic order quantities. Calculate the economic order quantity and the annual total costs of ordering and carrying baseballs for the year.

Strategy	Solution
	Calculating the economic order quantity requires these inputs: unit sales for the year, 24,000 packages; cost per order, $1.20; percentage carrying cost per year, 10 percent; and purchase cost per package, $10:

Apply the EOQ model, clearly differentiating ordering and carrying costs.

$$\text{EOQ} = \sqrt{\frac{2 \times (12 \times 2,000) \times \$1.20}{0.10 \times \$10.00}}$$

$$= 240 \text{ packages}$$

The annual total costs of inventory equal the annual costs of carrying and ordering baseballs:

$$\text{Total costs} = \text{Carrying costs} + \text{Ordering costs}$$

The company's annual carrying costs equal the average size of inventory times the cost of carrying one package of baseballs:

Calculate the average size of inventory.

$$\text{Average inventory} = \frac{\text{Beginning inventory} + \text{Ending inventory}}{2}$$

$$= \frac{240 \text{ packages} + 0}{2} = 120 \text{ packages}$$

The annual cost to carry a package in inventory is 10 percent of the purchase price ($10) of a package of baseballs, or $1. Use this information to calculate the annual carrying costs:

Multiply average inventory by annual carrying cost.

$$\text{Annual carrying costs} = 120 \text{ packages} \times \$1 = \$120$$

Smithson Company places 100 orders annually (24,000/240) at a cost of $1.20 per order. Its annual ordering costs are:

Multiply number of orders by cost per order.

$$\text{Annual ordering costs} = 100 \text{ orders} \times \$1.20 \text{ per order} = \$120$$

Now sum the individual costs to find the annual total costs:

Sum the carrying and ordering costs.

$$\text{Annual total costs} = \$120 + \$120 = \$240$$

◆ **Demonstration Problem**

Browning-Ferris Industries (BFI) provides high quality waste collection, transportation, processing, and disposal services to public and private customers worldwide. BFI's balance sheets on September 30 for two recent years are as follows (in millions of dollars):

Assets	19X2	19X1	Liabilities and Equity	19X2	19X1
Cash and equivalents	$ 389.0	$ 141.0	Accounts payable	$ 208.5	$ 202.7
Receivables	545.2	500.7	Taxes payable	22.6	4.7
Inventories	26.0	24.6	Other current liabilities	548.5	507.7
Other current assets	53.3	52.8	Total current liabilities	$ 779.6	$ 715.1
Total current assets	$1,013.5	$ 719.1	Long-term liabilities	1,827.5	1,826.5
Noncurrent assets	3,054.0	2,936.8	Common equity	1,460.4	1,114.3
Total assets	$4,067.5	$3,655.9	Total claims	$4,067.5	$3,655.9

BFI's partial income statements for the same two years ending September 30 are as follows (in millions of dollars):

	19X2	19X1
Sales revenue	$3,287.5	$3,183.2
Cost of sales	2,353.5	2,195.7
Gross profit	$ 934.0	$ 987.5
Operating expenses	583.9	801.3
Operating income	$ 350.1	$ 186.2

a. Calculate BFI's accounts receivable turnover and average collection period for 19X2 and 19X1. (*Note:* Since the mix of credit sales and cash sales is unknown, use total sales revenue in your calculations.) Do BFI's customers pay on time, assuming credit terms of net 45? Explain.

b. If BFI changed its credit term from net 45 to 1/20, net 45, what would be the annual opportunity cost of its customers who forgo the cash discount and pay on the 45th day? Would these customers likely forgo the cash discount if their bank borrowing rate were 10 percent per year? Explain.

c. BFI's credit manager uses the five Cs of credit to judge whether or not a potential customer meets the company's credit standards. Describe each of the five Cs of credit.

d. Define the terms *variable cost ratio* and *contribution margin ratio*. Calculate each of these ratios for BFI in 19X2, assuming that *cost of sales* equals variable cost.

e. Suppose that BFI's credit manager is analyzing the impact of lower credit standards on profitability and has developed the following estimates: (1) increase in annual credit sales, $40 million; (2) increase in annual bad-debt expense, $4 million; (3) increase in annual collection expense, $6 million; (4) increase in accounts receivable, $25 million. Assume that the ratios you calculated in Part *d* apply here and calculate the expected before-tax rate of return from the change in standards. If the before-tax required rate of return on investment in accounts receivable is 15 percent, should BFI lower its credit standards? Explain.

f. Calculate BFI's inventory turnover for 19X2 and 19X1. For a company of its size, does BFI carry much inventory? Explain.

g. (1) What are the three types of inventory carried by a manufacturer? (2) What is the purpose of each type of inventory? (3) Identify several examples of carrying costs and of ordering costs. (4) Why do carrying costs vary inversely with ordering costs?

h. Suppose that BFI sells 420-cubic-feet trash bins, which it purchases from a manufacturer for $2,500 per bin. The manufacturer puts the BFI logo on the sides of the bins and constructs them according to BFI specifications. Costs to BFI per order total $500, which includes $400 compensation to the manufacturer for setup costs. BFI sells 3,200 bins per year and incurs an annual 20 percent cost to carry the bins—or $500 (0.20 × $2,500) per bin. Calculate BFI's economic order quantity (EOQ) and the total cost of carrying and ordering bins for the year.

i. Define the term *safety stock*. Assume that BFI carries 20 trash bins as safety stock and recalculate the total cost of carrying and ordering bins for the year. (See Part *h* for other information.)

Problems

Opportunity cost of forgoing cash discounts

13.1. Calculate the annual opportunity cost of failing to take a prompt-payment discount for the following credit terms:
   a. 3/10, net 60 days.
   b. 3/10, net 70 days.
   c. 4/20, net 60 days.
   d. 4/20, net 70 days.

Opportunity cost vs. borrowing rate

13.2. The high cost of short-term financing has caused Freemont Corporation to re-evaluate the credit terms it extends to its customers. The current policy is 1/10, net 45. If Freemont customers can borrow at the prime rate, at what prime rate must Freemont change its credit terms to avoid an undesirable extension in its average collection period?

Accounts receivable turnover and average collection period

13.3. Green Chemicals' annual total sales are $2,500,000: 20 percent cash and 80 percent credit. The company's accounts receivable are $125,000.
   a. Calculate the company's accounts receivable turnover.
   b. Calculate the company's average collection period using two methods.
   c. What biases occur in the preceding calculations if you use total sales instead of credit sales?

Interpreting average collection period

13.4. Orion Computer Company sells on terms of net 30. Orion's annual credit sales are $10,000,000, and Orion's accounts receivable are $1,000,000. Do Orion customers pay on time? Explain and support your answer with appropriate calculations.

Cash discounts and customer behavior

13.5. The Carson Container Corporation (CCC) supplies packaging and paper goods to regional companies. It grants credit terms of 1.5/10, net 60, and its customers can borrow from the bank at an annual rate of 12 percent. CCC's annual credit sales are $2,400,000, and its accounts receivable are $434,000.
   a. If CCC's customers typically pay on the sixtieth day after purchase, what is their annual opportunity cost of not taking the cash discount for early payment?
   b. Calculate CCC's average collection period.
   c. Calculate the annual opportunity cost of not taking cash discounts for CCC's typical customer, one who pays at the end of the average collection period.
   d. In view of the bank rate, is CCC's typical customer acting rationally? Explain.

Variations in calculating inventory turnover

13.6. Calculate the inventory turnover under each of the following conditions:
   a. Annual cost of goods sold = $600,000; inventory = $100,000.
   b. The company's inventory represents 10 days of sales.

Interpreting inventory turnover

13.7. Warden Company's cost of goods sold for 19X8 is $560,000. Its inventory level generally stays around $80,000. The average inventory turnover in Warden's industry is 10.
   a. Calculate Warden's inventory turnover.
   b. Does Warden's inventory level appear too high or too low? Explain your answer.
   c. What are the possible negative financial consequences indicated by Warden's inventory turnover?

Accounts receivable and inventory

13.8. Baxter International (BI) is the world's leading manufacturer and marketer of health-care products for use in hospitals and clinics. BI's current assets on December 31 for two recent years are as follows (in millions of dollars):

Current Assets	19X1	19X0
Cash and cash equivalents	$ 328	$ 40
Accounts receivable	1,701	1,518
Inventories	1,596	1,532
Prepaid expenses	141	128
Other current assets	238	225
Total current assets	$4,004	$3,443

BI's partial income statements for the same two years ending December 31 are as follows (in millions of dollars):

	19X1	19X0
Net sales	$8,921	$8,100
Cost of goods sold	5,651	5,197
Gross profit	$3,270	$2,903

a. Use net sales to calculate BI's accounts receivable turnover and average collection period for 19X1 and 19X0. Do BI's customers pay on time, assuming credit terms of net 60? Explain.

b. If BI changed its credit terms from net 60 to 1.5/30, net 60, what would be the annual opportunity cost of its customers who forgo the cash discount? Would these customers likely forgo the cash discount if their bank borrowing rate were 11 percent per year?

c. Use cost of goods sold to calculate BI's inventory turnover for 19X1 and 19X0. Does BI's investment in inventory appear excessive or deficient? Explain. (*Note:* The average inventory turnover in BI's industry is 6.0.)

Relaxing credit standards   13.9.   The marketing vice president of Zeta Marketing Services wants the company's credit standards relaxed. The company's chief financial officer is concerned that such a change may not be in the best interest of shareholders. After a heated argument between the two executives, the chief financial officer retires to her office and examines data to help make the decision. Presently, collection expense is 1 percent of credit sales and bad-debt expense is 2 percent. These rates will rise to 2 percent and 3 percent, respectively, with the credit change. Additional information is given below:

	Present	Policy Change
Annual credit sales	$300,000	$380,000
Contribution margin ratio	8%	8%
Tax rate	40%	40%
Average collection period	26 days	34 days
Accounts receivable	$ _____	$ _____

An 11 percent after-tax rate of return is available on investments with risk comparable to an investment in accounts receivable.

a. Calculate accounts receivable for each policy. Calculate the variable cost ratio and use it to estimate the change in Zeta's investment in receivables.

b. Calculate the return on investment in new receivables. Should management change the credit policy? Explain your answer.

Changing a credit policy   13.10.   Consider the following information for March Company. With a change in credit policy the average collection period will be 76 days. Accounts receivable are $20,000 and credit sales are $100,000 with no change in policy. Credit sales will expand by 30 percent with the policy change, and the contribution margin ratio will remain 16 percent. Management requires a 12 percent after-tax rate of return on investments in receivables. The marginal tax rate is 40 percent. Bad debts will continue to be 5 percent of sales. Collection expense will rise from 2 percent to 3 percent of sales.

a. Should management change the credit policy? Support your answer with the necessary calculations.

b. Suppose that the average size of inventory rises from $8,000 to $17,000 as a result of the increased sales. Calculate the expected rate of return under this condition and state whether or not management should change the credit policy.

Relaxing credit standards   13.11.   Sundale Corporation manufactures and sells an industrial product. All sales are on credit. The corporation has a 30-day average collection period for its accounts receivable, and bad debts are 1 percent of sales. Sundale's production facilities are underutilized at the present time.

The credit manager has proposed that Sundale relax its credit standards. This action should attract new customers, increase sales, and lead to better utilization of its manufacturing facilities. If the credit standards are relaxed, the annual sales will increase from $120,000,000 to $150,000,000. The current manufacturing facilities would support this larger sales level. As a consequence of the relaxed credit standards, the average collection period would increase to 60 days, and bad debts would total 2 percent of sales.

Sundale's product sells for $15 per unit, and the variable costs to manufacture and sell the product amount to $12.30 per unit. The after-tax rate of return required on investments in receivables is 10 percent, and Sundale's marginal tax rate is 34 percent.

a. Should Sundale relax its credit standards? Support your answer with calculations.

b. Suppose that the average inventory rises from $36,000,000 to $45,000,000 with the increased sales. Under this condition should management accept the proposal to relax the credit standards? Support your answer with calculations.

EOQ and inventory costs in retailing

13.12. Trider Groceries is a retailer of fresh fruits and vegetables. Lettuce, its biggest seller, is purchased separately from a wholesaler. Due to the highly perishable nature of lettuce and the refrigeration required for storage, Trider experiences extremely high carrying costs, estimated to be 50 percent annually of cost. Trider's manager forecasts that the demand for lettuce will average 80 cases per month over the next year, at an expected cost of $12 per case. An assistant manager writes and receives the orders. It takes him 10 minutes per order for these tasks, and he is paid $7.80 per hour. Other ordering costs are $0.08 per order.

a. Calculate Trider Groceries' EOQ for lettuce.

b. Assuming a constant sales rate, how often will Trider Groceries place orders for lettuce?

c. Calculate the retailer's total cost of ordering and carrying lettuce for the year.

EOQ and inventory costs in wholesaling

13.13. The Rodale Company is a restaurant supplier that sells a number of products to various restaurants in the area. One of its products is a special meat cutter with disposable blades. It sells the blades in packages of 12 for $20 per package. After a number of years management has determined that the demand for the replacement blades is at a constant rate of 2,000 packages per month. The packages cost Rodale $10 each from the manufacturer and require a 3-day lead time from date of order to date of delivery. The ordering cost is $1.20 per order, and the carrying cost is 10 percent annually. Rodale is going to use the economic order quantity.

a. Calculate (1) the economic order quantity, (2) the number of orders needed per year, and (3) the total cost of ordering and carrying blades for the year.

b. Assuming there is no safety stock and that the present inventory level is 200 packages, when should the next order be placed? (Use 365 days equals one year.)

EOQ and inventory costs in manufacturing

13.14. Hermit Company manufactures a line of walnut office furniture accessories. Hermit executives estimate the annual demand for the double letter tray, one of the company's products, at 6,000 units. The letter tray sells for $80 per unit. The company's cost accountant estimates costs of the letter tray in 19X7 to be as follows:

• Standard manufacturing cost per letter tray unit: $50.

• Costs to initiate a production run: $300.

• Annual cost of carrying the letter tray in inventory: 20 percent of manufacturing cost.

In prior years Hermit's management scheduled the production of the letter tray in two equal production runs. Management is aware that it can employ the economic order quantity (EOQ) model to determine optimal size for production runs.

a. Calculate the EOQ for the Hermit Company.

b. Calculate the total inventory costs (1) before the EOQ model is implemented and (2) after the EOQ model is implemented.

c. What are the dollar savings that are associated with implementing the EOQ model?

EOQ and inventory costs in manufacturing

13.15. Morgan Company is a small manufacturer of lawn mowers. The company has one assembly line on which to produce four different mowers. These four models differ in size, power, and special features. For example, the most expensive model has a 4-horsepower engine and an electric starter, and it is self-propelled. Unit sales of each model are equal, so Morgan has always divided production time equally among them, making two runs per mower per year. Recently, a management consultant recommended that Morgan use the economic order quantity model to determine the size of each production run for each model. Morgan's total annual sales in units are 7,400 mowers. The cost of setting up the production line for each model is $500. The production cost of each model is: Model 1, $80; Model 2, $105; Model 3, $135; and Model 4, $175. Carrying costs for each model are 20 percent of production cost.

a. Calculate the EOQ for each of the four models.

b. Complete the following table for Model 1:

Order Quantity	Average Inventory (Units)	Carrying Costs	Orders per Year	Ordering Costs	Total Costs
320	160	___	___	___	___
340	___	$2,720	5.44	___	___
360	___	___	___	$2,570	$5,450

c. Answer the following questions based on the table in Part *b*: What is the relationship between carrying costs and ordering costs? What is the EOQ for Model 1?

d. Calculate the total carrying and ordering costs incurred by Morgan *prior* to instituting the EOQ model.

e. Calculate the total carrying and ordering costs incurred by Morgan Company *after* instituting the EOQ model.

f. Suppose the management consultant charged Morgan $10,000 for the advice on using the EOQ model. Was the advice worth $10,000 to Morgan? Will the consultant's advice pay for itself during the first year? Explain.

Computer Problems

Economic order quantity: template EOQ

13.16. Swanson Electrical manufactures ceiling fans. An important component of the fans is the motor. The company purchases motors at a constant rate of 10,000 per month at an average cost of $16 each. The usual lead time required by suppliers is 7 days, but in practice, lead time varies from 3 to 14 days. Ordering costs are $20 per order. The annual carrying cost is 20 percent of the inventory value.

a. Calculate the economic order quantity.

b. Determine the effect on EOQ of the following changes taken one at a time:

   (1) The monthly requirement for motors is 8,000 units, 9,000 units, 11,000 units, and 12,000 units.

   (2) Ordering costs are $16, $18, $22, and $24 per order.

   (3) The carrying cost of inventory as a percentage of average inventory value is 16 percent, 18 percent, 22 percent, and 24 percent.

c. How much safety stock should Swanson carry to avoid stockouts?

d. Calculate the order point, the average inventory, and the annual total costs of inventory.

e. How does the annual total cost of inventory change if the order quantity is 800, 1,000, 1,400, 1,600? How sensitive is the annual total cost of inventory to change in order quantity?

Credit policy: template
CREPOL

13.17. Prasad Microprocessors currently sells 500,000 chips annually at $10 each and has variable costs of $4,000,000 and fixed costs of $500,000. Bad-debt expense is 1 percent of sales. Prasad currently extends 30 days credit and has an average collection period of 36 days. To increase sales and profit, management is considering a change in credit policy. Two alternatives are under consideration, and their implications are given below:

Credit period	45 days	60 days
Sales in units	550,000	700,000
Average collection period	55 days	80 days
Bad-debt expense	1.5% of sales	2% of sales

The company's before-tax required return is 20 percent, and its marginal tax rate is 34 percent. Should the company change the existing credit policy? If so, which policy should it adopt? Explain your answer.

Case Problem

CompuFix

CompuFix is a personal-computer repair shop that began in 1980 as a partnership formed by three former computer technicians from National Cash Register. The personal computer (PC) was a recent innovation at that time, and qualified repair technicians were scarce. The three partners believed that the PC market would grow rapidly and that a shop providing competent repair and parts replacement services would be a success. With a loan from a local bank and with assistance from the Small Business Administration, a building was leased, equipment and parts were purchased, and CompuFix was in business.

In its formative years the company had difficulty breaking even. Retail stores provided much of the service on the PCs they sold, and businesses were slow to replace larger mainframe computers with the smaller PCs. Furthermore, each partner needed $55,000 per year in personal income to support his family. After 5 years of operation and slow but steady growth, company profit for 1985 was only $50,000—far short of that needed by the partners.

In 1986 the founding partners received a buyout offer for the company. They were weary of the business and had expressed a willingness to sell. The buyer was Allen Oaks, a former business student who had worked as a consultant to CompuFix in his senior year at State University. A purchase price for the company was negotiated, and Mr. Oaks' parents provided the capital for the purchase of CompuFix.

Mr. Oaks had worked at CompuFix to fulfill the requirements of a small-business management course funded in part by the Small Business Administration. Very early in his work Mr. Oaks appreciated the potential of the computer repair industry and identified some changes in management policy that would increase CompuFix's profits. One of the changes Mr. Oaks had recommended to the previous owners was to sell services to business customers on a 30-day credit basis. All sales and service charges had been on a cash basis only. Consequently, almost all CompuFix sales were to retail customers. Mr. Oaks was convinced that if the credit policy were in place, revenue from sales and service would increase by $250,000. All of the $250,000 in new sales would be credit sales to business customers. From Dun & Bradstreet reports on potential business clients, Mr. Oaks estimated that the average collection period would be 60 days, and he expected that 5 percent of the credit sales would be uncollectible.

Although Mr. Oaks felt certain that the new credit policy would be profitable, the loan committee at the bank where he applied for a line of credit was less sanguine. The committee requested an estimate of the return on investment in the new accounts receivable.

Mr. Oaks began immediately to accumulate the necessary information. An examination of current prices charged and costs of labor and merchandise revealed a variable cost ratio of 80 percent of sales. For $2,000 per month, a local firm offering credit services would provide administrative services and collect past due accounts for CompuFix. Mr. Oaks estimated the after-tax required rate of return associated with accounts receivable to be 14 percent.

a. Calculate the increase in CompuFix's contribution margin assuming the credit policy is adopted.
b. Calculate the expected annual bad-debt and collection expenses.
c. Calculate CompuFix's investment in accounts receivable. (Assume 365 days in a year.)
d. If CompuFix's marginal income tax rate is 25 percent, what is its expected after-tax return on the investment in accounts receivable?
e. Suppose the increase in sales requires an additional investment of $20,000 in inventory. Recalculate Part *d* with the increase in average inventory included.
f. Based on your answer in Part *e,* do you recommend that Mr. Oaks adopt the new credit policy? Explain.
g. Describe the risk Mr. Oaks faces if he implements the new credit policy.

The author thanks Professor Carl M. Hubbard of Trinity University for contributing this case problem.

Selected References

Beranek, William, and Frederick C. Scherr. "On the Significance of Trade Credit Limits." *Financial Practice and Education,* Fall/Winter 1991: 39–44.

Besley, Scott, and Jerome S. Osteryoung. "Survey of Current Practices in Establishing Trade-Credit Limits." *Financial Review,* February 1985: 70–82.

Carpenter, Michael D., and Jack E. Miller. "A Reliable Framework for Monitoring Accounts Receivable." *Financial Management,* Winter 1979: 37–40.

Gentry, James A., and Jesus M. De La Garza. "A Generalized Model for Monitoring Accounts Receivable." *Financial Management,* Winter 1985: 28–38.

Hubbard, Carl M. "A General Working Capital Analysis of Accounts Receivable Policy." *Journal of Cash Management,* July/August 1991: 46–49.

Lewellen, Wilbur G., and Robert W. Johnson. "Better Way to Monitor Accounts Receivable." *Harvard Business Review,* May–June 1972: 101–109.

Oh, John S. "Opportunity Cost in the Evaluation of Investment in Accounts Receivable." *Financial Management,* Summer 1976: 32–36.

Roberts, Gordon S., and Jerry A. Viscione. "Captive Finance Subsidiaries: The Manager's View." *Financial Management,* Spring 1981: 36–42.

Tiernan, Frank M., and Dennis A. Tanner. "How Economic Order Quantity Controls Inventory Expense." *Financial Executive,* July 1983: 46–47, 49–52.

Weston, J. Fred, and Pham D. Tuan. "Comment on Analysis of Credit Policy Changes." *Financial Management,* Winter 1980: 59–63.

Chapter 14

MANAGING CURRENT LIABILITIES

Sears Stretches Payables

The management of Sears, Roebuck & Co. in the early 1990s asked suppliers to wait an extra 30 days for payment, causing suppliers to have to wait 60 days instead of 30 days before Sears paid them for purchases. Management's letter to suppliers said: "As the retailing industry continues to utilize vendor-financed inventory methods to improve its return on investment, we believe Sears must pursue these opportunities more aggressively so that we are not left at a competitive disadvantage."

When retailers delay paying suppliers, it often signals cash flow problems. Carter Hawley Hale Stores Inc. and Best Products Co., for example, postponed payments to suppliers to preserve cash. Both companies later filed for Chapter 11 (of the Bankruptcy Act of 1938) bankruptcy in attempts to reorganize into financially viable entities. Carefully distancing the Giant Retailer from these companies, a

Sears spokesperson said that cash flow was "absolutely not" a problem.

Security analysts and other observers agreed that Sears was not in a cash-short position. Sidney Doolittle, a retail consultant in Chicago, said: "The issue is that they can make money employing that cash somewhere else." Some analysts noted that Sears was stretching accounts payable in order to reduce the company's short-term loans from banks: Delay the payments to suppliers, and accounts payable rise, which, in turn, lessens the need to borrow and reduces interest expense. In essence, Sears switched from one current liability to another—and thus transformed costly notes payable to banks into cost-free accounts payable to suppliers.

Source: Teri Agins, "Sears to Delay Paying Vendors by 30 Days," *The Wall Street Journal,* August 15, 1991, A3.

This chapter focuses on the management of current liabilities: accounts payable to suppliers, notes payable to banks, and commercial paper. These three current liabilities are the major sources of short-term financing for most companies. Current liabilities, or short-term debt, provide temporary funds to keep a company productive. They support current assets and enable a company to tailor debt levels to short-term needs. The term *liability* has a negative connotation, but liabilities are essential to the successful operation of companies.

TRADE CREDIT

A company receives trade credit when it buys goods from a supplier without paying cash on or before delivery. A wholesaler of golf balls may receive 100 dozen golf balls from a manufacturer but not pay for them until 30 days later. Over the 30 days the manufacturer is financing the wholesaler—not lending cash to the wholesaler but providing goods that the wholesaler can use for 30 days prior to making payment.

The manufacturer of golf balls and the wholesaler have an open-book relationship. The wholesaler sends a purchase order to the manufacturer, who in turn sends the goods along with an invoice to the wholesaler. Companies establish open-book relationships with their customers after completing credit checks, arranging credit lines, and settling credit terms. Once established, mutual trust becomes the basis of an open-book account. Where trust is lacking, suppliers may require the customer to sign a promissory note. A **promissory note** is a legal document specifying the amount owed, its due date, any interest charges, and specific restrictions. For example, a note may require the debtor to maintain a minimum level of net working capital during the life of the note. The debtor-purchaser records an open-book purchase as an account payable and a promissory note for goods received as a note payable. The creditor-seller records the transaction as an account or note receivable.

Table 14.1 shows variations in the presentation of current liabilities on the balance sheets of two companies. Browning-Ferris Industries' current liabilities include the current portion of long-term debt, accounts payable, and **accrued liabilities**. Syntex Corporation presents similar accounts but combines some accrued expenses with accounts payable and shows taxes payable and accrued compensation separately. Both companies must repay or roll over a large amount of debt in the coming year.

Using Trade Credit

The convenience of trade credit explains its widespread use. Just as consumers use credit for purchases because writing a check once a month is easier than writing checks for separate purchases, so companies also enjoy the convenience of writing fewer checks. In fact, the convenience for a company is multiplied because it may make hundreds of small and large purchases each month.

In addition to its convenience, trade credit enables purchasers to use elsewhere the cash they would have used to pay for goods on delivery. For example, a company may buy $70,000 of raw material from a supplier with payment due in 30 days. The company can use the $70,000 to invest in a U.S. Treasury bill or commercial paper for 30 days, thereby earning interest that it would have lost by paying cash on delivery (C.O.D.). Also, unlike bank loans, trade credit rarely

promissory note
Legal document for an IOU.

accrued liabilities
Expenses incurred but not yet paid; a current liability.

TABLE 14.1

Current Liabilities of Two Companies (in Millions of Dollars)

Browning-Ferris Industries: September 30, 1992

Current Liabilities

Current portion of long-term debt	$ 29.9
Accounts payable	208.5
Accrued liabilities	398.1
Other	143.1
Total current liabilities	$779.6

Syntex Corporation: April 30, 1992

Current Liabilities

Short-term debt	$ 516.3
Accounts payable and accrued expenses	204.8
Income and other taxes	220.0
Accrued compensation	102.3
Other	89.5
Total current liabilities	$1,132.9

Source: Company annual and quarterly reports.

entails an explicit interest expense. Interest on a bank loan appears on a company's income statement as an expense for all to see. Trade credit looks a great deal like the proverbial free lunch because its cost does not appear on the income statement. However, prices of the goods purchased may be higher because of trade credit. If this is the case, then the purchaser pays for the free lunch. In most instances that is probably what happens because to stay in business over the long run, a seller must recoup all costs, including the cost of financing receivables (the customers' payables). But because the increased price is often slight, the convenience of trade credit usually outweighs its cost.

Competition among sellers largely controls the credit terms a customer receives. Industry standards and customs, which vary according to the product, also play an important role. For example, sellers of fresh fruits and vegetables typically grant credit for no longer than 7 days. Perishability of the goods sold dictates a fast payoff to reduce the risk of customers defaulting. High-turnover products such as dry groceries also often sell net 7 days. In contrast, durable, slow-turnover building materials often sell net 30 days. Larger markups on building materials than on groceries provide yet another reason for the difference in credit terms.

Even within the same industry, credit limits vary among customers. A customer with a good payment record and a sound financial position receives more trade credit than weaker counterparts. Sellers ordinarily grant a larger credit limit to customers having higher current ratios, better profitability, and lower debt-equity ratios because of these customers' lower default risk.

The dollar size of accounts payable depends in large measure on a company's volume of purchases. If management anticipates a sales increase, the company makes larger purchases of raw materials and other inventory. Larger accounts payable, in turn, follow these larger purchases.

Koger Company management expects average daily sales to increase from $10,000 to $15,000. Koger's average daily purchases have been $8,000 and management expects them to increase to $12,000. The company pays for purchases 30 days after the purchase date. Management expects accounts payable to rise from $240,000 (30 days × $8,000 per day) to $360,000 (30 days × $12,000 per day).

The dollar size of accounts payable depends not only on the size of daily purchases, but also on the number of days before the purchaser makes payment. The number of days before payment depends on the credit terms and the purchaser's payment behavior, which is the topic of the next section.

Stretching Accounts Payable

The length of the payment period affects the attractiveness of accounts payable as a financing source. The longer the payment period, the greater will be the advantage of accounts payable as a source of short-term funds.

In the previous example Koger's supplier grants net 30 credit terms, and Koger pays on time. Koger's 50 percent increase in daily sales and purchases causes its accounts payable to rise by 50 percent. If Koger's management decides to stretch payables to 45 days, then a 125 percent rise in payables accompanies the 50 percent increase in sales and purchases:

$$\begin{aligned} \text{Percentage increase in payables} &= \frac{(\$12,000 \text{ purchases daily}) \times 45 \text{ days}}{(\$8,000 \text{ purchases daily}) \times 30 \text{ days}} - 1.0 \\ &= \frac{\$540,000}{\$240,000} - 1.0 \\ &= 1.25, \text{ or } 125\% \end{aligned}$$

stretching accounts payable

Delaying payment beyond the due date of the credit terms.

In the above example, when Koger extends its payment period beyond the due date, it is **stretching accounts payable.** If Koger did not stretch its accounts payable, then it might have to take out a bank loan. This loan would require interest payments, whereas the accounts payable are interest-free to Koger. Without stretching payables, Koger's expected payables rise from $240,000 to $360,000 because of the sales increase. With stretching, management adds $180,000 ($540,000 − $360,000) to accounts payable. This $180,000 reduces, dollar for dollar, the need for a bank loan, which in turn reduces interest expense. If Koger's borrowing rate were 10 percent, then it would save $18,000 (0.10 × $180,000) per year in interest payments.

Stretching accounts payable produces not only benefits but also a cost. Habitually slow-payment behavior increases the risk of ruining the company's credit rating. Suppliers react quickly to slow payment, and word travels quickly among suppliers and bankers. Additionally, Dun & Bradstreet and other credit-rating agencies note payment behavior in their reports. Thus a slow payer's reputation spreads rapidly, which may lead to more restrictive credit terms—in the extreme, C.O.D.

Despite the risk to the company's reputation, a financial manager may want to stretch accounts payable in some cases. Suppliers may go along with such behavior to retain the business. Many suppliers tolerate periodic stretching of payables but not habitual stretching. If informed of the need to pay late but assured of the intent to pay, then suppliers are less likely to place a customer in a higher risk class.

In addition to the potential damage to a company's reputation, stretching accounts payable may involve another cost, the loss of a cash discount. If a supplier offers a customer a cash discount for prompt payment, then stretching payables causes the customer to lose the discount. Chapter 13 shows that the annual opportunity cost of missing cash discounts can be calculated with the following equation:

$$\frac{\text{Annual}}{\text{opportunity cost}} = \frac{D}{1 - D} \times \frac{365}{n}$$

For terms of 2/10, net 30, the annual opportunity cost of forgoing the cash discount and paying on the thirtieth day is:

$$\frac{\text{Annual}}{\text{opportunity cost}} = \frac{0.02}{1 - 0.02} \times \frac{365}{30 - 10}$$

$$= 0.0204 \times 18.25$$

$$= 0.372, \text{ or } 37.2\%$$

This calculation assumes that the customer pays on either the tenth or the thirtieth day after purchase. If instead, the customer stretches payables to 40 days, then the annual opportunity cost declines to 24.8 percent:

$$\frac{\text{Annual}}{\text{opportunity cost}} = \frac{0.02}{1 - 0.02} \times \frac{365}{40 - 10}$$

$$= 0.0204 \times 12.167$$

$$= 0.248, \text{ or } 24.8\%$$

In this case the customer forgoes the 2 percent discount for 30 days (by stretching) rather than the 20 days in the previous calculation.

In general, missing cash discounts results in an opportunity cost that declines as buyers stretch payables. Figure 14.1 shows the declining opportunity cost for 2/10, net 30 as a company stretches payables: pay on the thirtieth day, 37.2 percent; the fortieth day, 24.8 percent; the fiftieth day, 18.6 percent; and so on. Opportunity cost declines at a decreasing rate as buyers continue to stretch payables.

Figure 14.1 implies that the buying company should never pay before the due date because it would lose the value of the declining opportunity cost. The figure, however, does not imply that the buyer *should* stretch accounts payable. That decision requires weighing the benefits against the potential damage to the buyer's reputation. J. P. Morgan was aware of the importance of character in credit relationships:

> *Mr. Untermyer:* Is not commercial credit based primarily upon money or property?
> *Mr. Morgan:* No, sir; the first thing is character.

FIGURE 14.1

The Effect of Stretching Accounts Payable on the Annual Opportunity Cost of Forgoing Cash Discounts: 2/10, net 30

The annual opportunity cost of forgoing cash discounts declines as the company stretches its payables. With terms of 2/10, net 30, a company paying the invoice amount on the thirtieth day incurs an opportunity cost of 37.2 percent; paying on the fiftieth day reduces the cost to 18.6 percent. A company should never pay in advance of the due date (here, Day 10) because the opportunity cost of cash is not offset by the benefit of a discount.

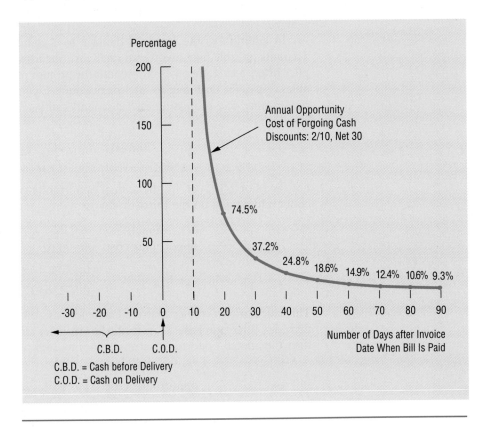

Mr. Untermyer: Before money or property?

Mr. Morgan: Before money or anything else. Money cannot buy it. . . .[1]

COMMERCIAL BANK BORROWING

When a company needs to finance current assets, it often turns to a commercial bank. Commercial bank credit is the second largest total-dollar volume of short-term credit used by businesses.[2] For small and medium-sized companies, banks

---

[1] Quoted in Frederick Lewis Allen, *The Great Pierpont Morgan,* New York: Harper & Row Publishers, 1949, 226; and in Vincent P. Carosso, *Investment Banking in America: A History,* Cambridge, MA: Harvard University Press, 1970, 150. J. P. Morgan was founder of the investment banking firm that is today Morgan Stanley and Company. Samuel Untermyer was chief counsel to the congressional committee investigating competition in the investment banking industry.

[2] Actually, bank credit is the largest *nonbusiness* source for the business sector. Because trade credit is an intrabusiness source, the total of trade receivables must equal the total of trade payables. In this way receivables and payables cancel out between creditor-sellers and debtor-purchasers.

play an especially important role in financing business growth. Unlike large companies, small companies do not have easy access to the money and capital markets.

Whereas collateral usually secures loans from finance companies, banks offer companies both unsecured and secured loans. Historically, bankers preferred to make secured loans called **short-term, self-liquidating loans,** which are repaid out of the cash flows from a specific investment. A typical short-term, self-liquidating loan is characterized by a company borrowing to buy inventory, then selling the inventory to generate enough cash to pay off the loan. Bankers view such loans as having low default risk. Today, as a result of the deregulation of the banking system and increased competition, bankers make several different types of loans and are more aggressive lenders than in the past.

Types of Short-Term Loans

Companies use short-term bank loans to finance temporary or seasonal increases in current assets.[3] Unlike accounts payable from trade credit, notes payable from bank loans do not rise spontaneously with increases in sales volume and purchases. The financial manager negotiates a bank loan, applying for one of the following types.

Direct Loan.   The financial manager applies for a **direct loan** (or *one-time loan*) for a specific purpose. Common among these loans are notes to finance seasonal bulges in current assets. The manager negotiates each loan, tailoring it to company needs. Bank loan officers analyze the application and decide whether or not to extend the loan. If the decision is to extend the loan, then the financial manager signs a promissory note, and the bank credits (increases) the company's checking account with the loan proceeds.

Line of Credit.   A **line of credit** is an *informal* agreement between a company and a bank that defines the maximum loan the company may have during a year. The line is based on the availability of funds at the bank, which means that the line may not be available if the bank itself runs short of funds. After the line is established, the company may, at any time during the year, draw (borrow) on the line up to the maximum amount. Lines of credit are particularly useful for companies with uncertain and periodic needs for short-term financing during the year. Credit investigation and negotiation of terms take place when the bank and the company establish the line of credit, and the company can draw against the line throughout the year without any delays. Banks impose two limitations on lines of credit:

- *Annual renewal.* The borrower must reapply each year for the line of credit. This provision requires the borrower to renegotiate the line and gives the bank another opportunity to run a credit check and to adjust terms.
- *Annual cleanup.* The borrower cannot use the line of credit for 30 consecutive days (or some stated period) during the year. This **annual cleanup** provision assures the banker that the company is not using short-term loans for long-term purposes.

short-term, self-liquidating loan
Short-term loan for a specific purpose that generates sufficient cash flows to repay the loan.

direct loan
Negotiated bank loan intended for a specific purpose; one-time loan.

line of credit
Informal agreement establishing the maximum amount a company may borrow during a year.

annual cleanup
Loan provision requiring the borrower to be out of debt to the bank for at least 30 consecutive days during a 12-month period.

[3] Commercial banks also make term loans to companies. Term loans, described in Chapter 20, have maturities longer than one year.

TABLE 14.2	**Distinctions between a Line of Credit and a Revolving Credit Agreement**	
	Line of Credit	**Revolving Credit Agreement**
Degree of Formality	Informal agreement on the credit ceiling; bank may cancel at any time.	Legal commitment on the credit ceiling; bank cannot legally cancel.
Commitment Fee	Bank does not charge a commitment fee.	Bank charges a commitment fee.
Length of Time	A one-year agreement subject to renewal each year.	Agreement may extend beyond one year, with 18 and 24 months being common; normally less than 3 years.
Annual Cleanup	Company must not have loans against the line for 30 (or more) consecutive days.	Cleanup restriction usually does not apply, hence a revolving loan.

revolving credit agreement
Formal agreement establishing the maximum amount a company may borrow during a period of time.

commitment fee
Dollar amount charged by a bank to maintain a revolving credit agreement.

Revolving Credit Agreement.   A **revolving credit agreement** is a *formal* agreement between a company and a bank that establishes the maximum loan balance permissible during a period of time. The company receives a credit line for a specified amount against which it can borrow at a rate negotiated at the time the agreement is signed. The rate is usually stated as "prime plus," which means the borrower will pay interest at the prime rate (discussed below) plus a premium of one or more percentage points. A bank may terminate a line of credit, but the legal commitment of a revolving credit agreement prohibits termination.

For giving up the option to terminate a revolving credit agreement, banks charge a **commitment fee** (or *standby fee*)—an amount paid a bank to maintain a revolving credit agreement. For example, a banker may charge 0.5 percent (50 basis points) on the unused portion of the credit ceiling specified in the agreement. If the agreement specifies a ceiling of $10,000,000, and the company averages $6,000,000 borrowed, then the commitment fee equals $20,000 (0.005 × $4,000,000). The financial manager views the $20,000 as an insurance premium—insurance on the availability of funds when needed. Of course, the borrower must pay interest on the $6,000,000 *takedown,* the amount borrowed. Some banks charge the commitment fee against the entire credit line, but like other loan terms, the commitment fee is negotiable.

Table 14.2 summarizes the four major distinctions between a line of credit and a revolving credit agreement. In contrast to lines of credit, revolving credit agreements may extend beyond one year. Companies and banks often make revolving credit agreements for 12 to 24 months. In some cases agreements are made for as long as 3 years. The following footnote from the annual report of Browning-Ferris Industries gives a description of a revolving credit agreement:

> The $1 billion Revolving Credit Agreement with Texas Commerce Bank National Association as administrative agent and Credit Suisse First Boston Limited as co-agent for a group of U.S. and international banks, requires a facility fee of .2% per annum on the total commitment, whether used or unused. The bank credit agreement is used primarily to support the company's commercial paper program which was established in 1990. The agreement contains a net worth requirement of $1 billion for the year ended September 30, 1992. This requirement increases annually by 25% of the consolidated net income of the preceding year and excludes the effect of any foreign currency translation adjustments to net worth. The agreement also restricts the incurrence or assumption of additional debt if the

debt to capitalization ratio after considering such additional debt exceeds .65 to 1. At September 30, 1992 and 1991, the Company had no outstanding borrowings under its bank credit agreements.

Secured vs. Unsecured Loan.   The preceding three types of loans are *unsecured loans*. The borrower does not pledge assets to secure them. For unproven and financially weak companies, bankers may require that loans be *secured*—interest and principal guaranteed with assets. The assets most commonly pledged are inventory and accounts receivable, discussed later in the chapter.

Prime Rate and Compensating Balances

Historically, banks offered the prime rate to their better and lower-risk customers. To be a prime-rate bank customer was a matter of some distinction. Today, however, the highly visible prime rate has lost some of its luster, and has become merely a benchmark banks use for setting interest rates on other loans. Some companies actually borrow at rates below prime, but most companies borrow at prime or prime plus. Another benchmark rate is the London interbank offered rate (LIBOR), a European money market rate. Bank loan rates based on LIBOR are especially appealing to multinational companies with access to markets abroad.

The prime rate is less volatile than money market rates because it is administered by bankers. The timing and magnitude of changes in the prime rate occur at their discretion. In contrast, market rates change in direct response to the forces of supply and demand. Large banks in New York City (Citibank, Chase Manhattan, and others) normally set the pace for prime rates, which other banks follow. Because the cost of many sources of bank funds reflects interest rates generally, the prime rate changes (with leads and lags) with money market rates. Figure 14.2 shows the recent history of changes in the prime rate and the rate on 3-month Treasury bills. The stair-step movement in the prime rate indicates the times when bankers decided to change it to reflect money market rates.

In addition to charging short-term borrowers interest on loans, many banks require the borrower to maintain a compensating balance as a condition for the loan. A *compensating balance* is a cash deposit kept at the bank. Banks require compensating balances primarily for unsecured loans. The requirement is usually stated as a percentage of the amount borrowed or of the size of the loan commitment.

Banks often require a compensating balance of 15 or 20 percent of the amount of a direct loan. On lines of credit (and revolving credit agreements) the requirement may be 10 percent on the unused portion and 20 percent on the used portion (the takedown), which causes the compensating balance to slide between 10 and 20 percent of the credit line:

Amount of Credit Line Used	Compensating Balance ÷ Credit Line
0%	10%
50	15
100	20

EXAMPLE

Alpena Products has a $1,000,000 line of credit. Alpena National Bank requires a 10 percent compensating balance on the unused portion of the line and 20

FIGURE 14.2

Changes in Short-Term Interest Rates

Bankers change the prime rate to reflect changes in money market rates. In contrast to the T-bill rate, which is a market rate, the prime rate is an administered rate. Its changes reflect bankers' decisions about what the appropriate level should be.

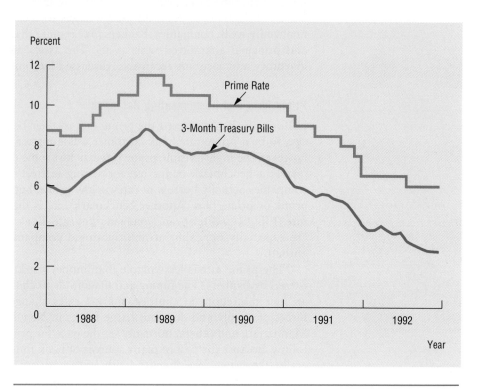

Source: Standard & Poor's Statistical Service, Current Statistics, January 1992, 1993.

percent on the takedown. Alpena Products has taken down $600,000 of its credit line. What is the size of its compensating balance?

$$\text{Compensating balance} = (0.10 \times \$400{,}000) + (0.20 \times \$600{,}000)$$
$$= \$40{,}000 + \$120{,}000$$
$$= \$160{,}000$$

The compensating balance is 16 percent ($160,000/$1,000,000) of the company's credit line.

Banks may require compensating balances to be met either by (1) average deposit balances over time or (2) minimum deposit balances over time. They also may allow the balances to be held in either (1) demand deposits—non-interest-bearing checking accounts—or (2) interest-bearing time deposits (CDs). The most disadvantageous arrangement for the borrower is a minimum deposit balance in a demand deposit. Having to meet a minimum requirement means less flexibility, and a demand deposit does not earn interest. The borrower can usually negotiate these features.

Banks require compensating balances for the following reasons: (1) to increase bank deposits, (2) to increase bank earnings, (3) to increase lending capacity, and (4) to allow more borrowing at prime. As you will see in the following section, a compensating balance increases the effective interest cost of a loan.

CALCULATING THE COST OF BANK LOANS

The true cost of a bank loan depends on the amount of cash received by the borrower and the timing and amount of cash paid by the borrower. Measuring the true cost enables the financial manager to compare the costs of bank loans with the costs of other sources of short-term financing. In this way the financial manager can choose the least expensive means to finance seasonal assets. The true cost of a bank loan is rarely the stated interest rate that the bank quotes, called the *nominal rate*. In most cases the true, or effective, rate exceeds the nominal rate because of compensating balance requirements and the timing of interest payments. The following sections present the techniques that financial managers use to calculate effective rates of interest.

Simple Interest

There is one type of loan where the effective rate equals the nominal rate. It is a loan for which there is no compensating balance and the bank charges simple interest.

EXAMPLE

The First National Bank will grant Pinconing Cheese Company a loan of $200,000 for one year at 12 percent annual interest. The bank does not require a compensating balance, and Pinconing will pay interest at maturity. What is Pinconing's effective annual rate?

For the above example, begin the solution by calculating the dollar interest on the loan:

$$\text{Interest} = \text{Principal} \times \text{Rate} \times \text{Time}$$
$$= \$200,000 \times 0.12 \times 1$$
$$= \$24,000$$

The following time line shows the cash flows associated with the loan:

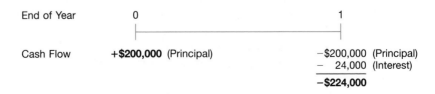

End of Year	0	1
Cash Flow	+$200,000 (Principal)	−$200,000 (Principal)
		− 24,000 (Interest)
		−$224,000

In this example the effective annual rate equals the nominal rate. The effective annual rate for *one-year loans* can be calculated as follows:

$$\text{Effective annual rate} = \frac{\text{Interest}}{\text{Usable loan proceeds}}$$

usable loan proceeds
Cash available from a loan for the borrower's use.

Usable loan proceeds are cash available from a loan for the borrower's use. For the bank loan to Pinconing, the equation yields the following:

$$\text{Effective annual rate} = \frac{\$24,000}{\$200,000}$$

$$= 0.12, \text{ or } 12\% \text{ per year compounded annually}$$

Note that the effective annual rate is compounded annually.[4]

Many loans are made for periods of less than one year. In these cases the effective annual rate depends on a nominal rate with a compounding frequency of more than once a year. Consider the situation above but now assume that Pinconing borrows the $200,000 for only 6 months, and refinances (rolls over) the loan for the second 6 months. In this case the dollar interest for 6 months is $12,000 ($200,000 × 0.12 × 6/12). The combined cash flows for the series of two loans net out as follows:

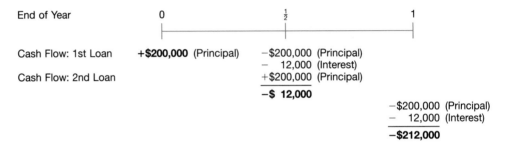

End of Year	0	$\frac{1}{2}$	1
Cash Flow: 1st Loan	+$200,000 (Principal)	−$200,000 (Principal) − 12,000 (Interest)	
Cash Flow: 2nd Loan		+$200,000 (Principal)	
		−$ 12,000	−$200,000 (Principal) − 12,000 (Interest)
			−$212,000

The nominal rate of these two loans is 12 percent per year compounded semi-annually. The effective annual rate of this nominal rate is calculated using the following equation from Chapter 4 (i is the nominal rate and m is the frequency of compounding):

$$\text{Effective annual rate} = \left(1 + \frac{i}{m}\right)^m - 1$$

$$= \left(1 + \frac{0.12}{2}\right)^2 - 1$$

$$= (1.06)^2 - 1$$

$$= 1.1236 - 1$$

$$= 0.1236, \text{ or } 12.36\% \text{ per year compounded annually}$$

In summary, making two 6-month loans with simple interest is more costly (12.36 percent) than making one 1-year loan (12.0 percent). With two 6-month loans the company pays interest sooner than with one 1-year loan, which

[4] For an alternative procedure, recall the equation from Chapter 4 for converting a future value (FV) to a present value (PV):

$$PV = FV/(1 + i)^n$$
$$\$200,000 = \$224,000/(1 + i)^1$$
$$1 + i = \$224,000/\$200,000$$
$$i = 1.12 - 1$$
$$= 0.12, \text{ or } 12\% \text{ per year compounded annually}$$

increases the effective annual rate. The effective annual rate (12.36 percent per year compounded annually) exceeds the nominal rate (12.0 percent per year compounded semiannually).

Discount Interest

discount-interest loan

Borrower pays interest in advance; contrasts with a simple-interest loan in which the borrower pays interest at maturity.

Instead of making simple-interest loans, banks often make **discount-interest loans** to companies. A discount-interest loan means that the borrower pays interest in advance rather than at the end of the loan period. The bank deducts interest from the loan principal, and the borrower repays the principal at maturity. With discount interest the usable loan proceeds are less than the loan principal by the amount of the interest.

Pinconing's one-year loan on a discount basis produces the following cash flows:

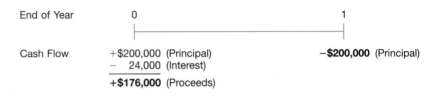

End of Year	0	1
Cash Flow	+$200,000 (Principal) − 24,000 (Interest) **+$176,000** (Proceeds)	**−$200,000** (Principal)

The bank deducts interest of $24,000 (0.12 × $200,000) from the $200,000 principal, causing usable loan proceeds to equal $176,000. The effective annual rate is calculated as follows:

$$\text{Effective annual rate} = \frac{\text{Interest}}{\text{Usable loan proceeds}}$$

$$= \frac{\$24,000}{\$176,000}$$

$$= 0.1364, \text{ or } 13.64\% \text{ per year compounded annually}$$

Discounting increases the effective cost of the loan, moving it from 12 percent with simple interest to 13.64 percent.

If Pinconing needs $200,000, not just $176,000, the company must borrow what it needs plus an additional amount to pay the discount interest. The principal of the loan required is calculated in the following way, letting usable loan proceeds be the amount the company needs:

$$\text{Usable loan proceeds} = \text{Principal} - \text{Discount interest}$$
$$= \text{Principal} - (\text{Nominal rate} \times \text{Principal})$$
$$\$200,000 = \text{Principal} - (0.12 \times \text{Principal})$$
$$= 0.88 \times \text{Principal}$$
$$\text{Principal} = \$200,000/0.88$$
$$= \$227,272.73$$

The cash flows and effective annual rate in this case are:

End of Year	0	1
Cash Flow	+$227,272.73 (Principal) − 27,272.73 (Interest) **+$200,000.00** (Proceeds)	**−$227,272.73** (Principal)

$$\text{Effective annual rate} = \frac{\$27,272.73}{\$200,000.00}$$

$$= 0.1364, \text{ or } 13.64\% \text{ per year compounded annually}$$

The size of the loan does not influence the effective annual rate because the dollar interest and the proceeds increase proportionally. Whether Pinconing borrows $200,000 or $227,272.73, its effective borrowing rate is 13.64 percent with 12 percent discount interest.

If Pinconing borrows the $200,000 with discount interest for only 6 months and refinances the loan for the second 6 months, then the relevant cash flows for each loan are:

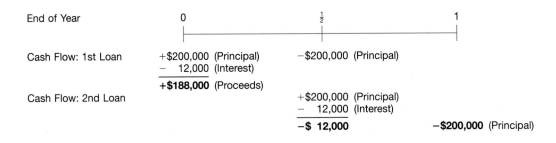

Discount interest for 6 months is $12,000 ($200,000 × 0.12 × 6/12); thus loan proceeds from each loan are $188,000 ($200,000 − $12,000). Each loan requires Pinconing to pay $12,000 at the beginning of the period and to repay the principal ($200,000) at maturity.

To calculate the effective interest rate for the first 6-month loan, simply divide interest paid by usable loan proceeds:

$$\text{6-Month rate} = \frac{\text{Interest}}{\text{Usable loan proceeds}}$$

$$= \frac{\$12,000}{\$188,000}$$

$$= 0.0638, \text{ or } 6.38\% \text{ per 6 months compounded semiannually}$$
$$\text{or } 6.38\% \times 2 = 12.76\% \text{ per year compounded semiannually}$$

The effective *annual* rate is calculated as follows (i = 0.1276 and m = 2):

$$\text{Effective annual rate} = \left(1 + \frac{0.1276}{2}\right)^2 - 1$$

$$= 1.1317 - 1$$

$$= 0.1317, \text{ or } 13.17\% \text{ per year compounded annually}$$

In summary, the effective annual rate (13.17 percent) for the two 6-month discount loans is *less than* the effective annual rate (13.64 percent) for one 1-year discount loan because the borrower pays interest only 6 months in advance with the 6-month loan. With a 1-year discount loan, the borrower pays interest 12 months in advance. Contrast this result with the simple-interest case: The effective annual rate (12.36 percent) of two 6-month loans is *more than* that of the one 1-year loan (12.0 percent) because the borrower pays interest at the end of each period. The four effective annual rates are:

	Two 6-Month Loans	One 12-Month Loan
Simple interest	12.36%	12.00%
Discount interest	13.17	13.64

These relationships show that the financial manager minimizes interest costs with the following strategies: (1) Choose a 1-year loan over fractional-year loans for simple interest but not for discount interest. (2) Choose simple-interest loans over discount loans for all loan maturities.

Simple Interest with a Compensating Balance

If Pinconing pays 12 percent simple interest on its $200,000 loan, and if the bank requires a *compensating balance* equal to 20 percent of the $200,000, then Pinconing's effective interest rate increases. The company pays interest on the total borrowed, but it cannot use the total borrowed because of the compensating-balance (CB) requirement. From Pinconing's perspective the cash flows appear as follows:

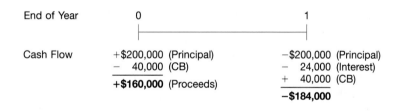

End of Year	0	1
Cash Flow	+$200,000 (Principal)	−$200,000 (Principal)
	− 40,000 (CB)	− 24,000 (Interest)
	+$160,000 (Proceeds)	+ 40,000 (CB)
		−$184,000

Pinconing borrows $200,000 but may use only $160,000 because it must keep $40,000 (0.20 × $200,000) in a compensating balance in the bank. We assume the required compensating balance is kept in a demand deposit that Pinconing would not maintain in its ordinary course of business. At maturity Pinconing pays the bank $224,000, using the $40,000 compensating balance to repay part of the principal.

The effective annual rate calculated with the following equation yields 15 percent:

$$\text{Effective annual rate} = \frac{\text{Interest}}{\text{Usable loan proceeds}}$$

$$= \frac{\$24,000}{\$160,000}$$

$$= 0.15, \text{ or } 15\% \text{ per year compounded annually}$$

The usable loan proceeds are $160,000 because Pinconing must use $40,000 of the principal for a compensating balance. Despite this restriction, Pinconing still pays $24,000 interest on the entire $200,000. Hence the effective annual rate with simple interest is 15 percent if the borrower must maintain a compensating balance.[5]

Discount Interest with a Compensating Balance

If Pinconing pays 12 percent *discount interest* on its $200,000 loan, and if the bank requires a compensating balance equal to 20 percent of the $200,000, then the effective annual rate increases once again. The borrower pays interest on the principal, but the bank deducts interest in advance. From Pinconing's perspective the cash flows appear as follows:

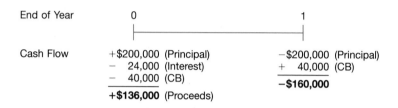

Despite borrowing $200,000, Pinconing's usable loan proceeds are only $136,000. Pinconing cannot use the $40,000 compensating balance during the year, and at year-end it reverts to the bank.

The effective annual rate calculated with the following equation yields 17.65 percent:

$$\text{Effective annual rate} = \frac{\text{Interest}}{\text{Usable loan proceeds}}$$

$$= \frac{\$24,000}{\$136,000}$$

$$= 0.1765, \text{ or } 17.65\% \text{ per year compounded annually}$$

Combining discount interest with the compensating-balance requirement increases the effective annual rate from 15.0 percent to 17.65 percent compounded annually.

Suppose that Pinconing actually needs $200,000 cash. The company must then borrow enough (1) to pay the discount interest of 12 percent and (2) to

---

[5] Another way to calculate the effective annual rate is to divide the nominal rate by $(1 - CB)$, where CB is the compensating-balance rate expressed as a decimal. For Pinconing we get:

$$\text{Effective annual rate} = \frac{0.12}{1 - 0.20}$$

$$= 0.15, \text{ or } 15.0\% \text{ per year compounded annually}$$

Recall that the effective annual rate is independent of the amount borrowed. For example, if Pinconing actually needs usable loan proceeds of $200,000, it would have to borrow $250,000:

$$\text{Principal} = \frac{\text{Usable loan proceeds}}{1 - CB}$$

$$= \frac{\$200,000}{1 - 0.20}$$

$$= \$250,000$$

The compensating balance on $250,000 is $50,000 (0.20 × $250,000). Pinconing gets to use $200,000 and pays $30,000 interest (0.12 × $250,000). The effective annual rate is:

$$\frac{\$30,000}{\$200,000} = 0.15, \text{ or } 15.0\% \text{ per year compounded annually}$$

TABLE 14.3 **Impact of Loan Conditions on Effective Annual Rate: 1-Year $200,000 Loan at a 12-Percent Nominal Rate**

(1) Loan Conditions	(2) Loan Amount	(3) Compensating Balance	0.12 × (2) = (4) Dollar Interest	(5) Usable Loan Proceeds	(4)/(5) = (6) Effective Annual Rate
Simple interest	$200,000	None	$24,000	$200,000	12.00%
Discount interest	200,000	None	24,000	176,000	13.64
Simple interest with a compensating balance (20%)	200,000	$40,000	24,000	160,000	15.00
Discount interest with a compensating balance (20%)	200,000	40,000	24,000	136,000	17.65

meet the 20 percent compensating-balance requirement. Usable loan proceeds to the company after borrowing sufficient cash to cover these needs are calculated as follows:

$$\text{Usable loan proceeds} = \text{Principal} - \left(\frac{\text{Discount}}{\text{interest}} + \frac{\text{Compensating}}{\text{balance}} \right)$$

Inserting Pinconing's data into this equation shows that the company must borrow $294,117.65 (principal) to get usable loan proceeds of $200,000:

$$\$200,000 = \text{Principal} - [(0.12 \times \text{Principal}) + (0.20 \times \text{Principal})]$$
$$= \text{Principal} - (0.32 \times \text{Principal})$$
$$= 0.68 \times \text{Principal}$$
$$\text{Principal} = \frac{\$200,000}{0.68}$$
$$= \$294,117.65$$

In this case the effective annual rate (17.65 percent) is calculated as follows:

$$\text{Effective annual rate} = \frac{\text{Interest}}{\text{Usable loan proceeds}}$$
$$= \frac{0.12 \times \$294,117.65}{\$294,117.65 - (\$35,294.12 + \$58,823.53)}$$
$$= \frac{\$35,294.12}{\$200,000}$$
$$= 0.1765, \text{ or } 17.65\% \text{ per year compounded annually}$$

Whether Pinconing borrows $294,117.65 or $200,000, the effective annual rate is 17.65 percent for a discount interest of 12 percent and a compensating balance of 20 percent.

Table 14.3 summarizes the impact of loan conditions on the effective annual rate for a 1-year $200,000 loan at a 12 percent nominal rate. The lowest-cost condition is simple interest, with an effective annual rate equaling 12.0 percent. Most costly is discount interest with a 20 percent compensating balance, 17.65 percent. The last two rates in Table 14.3 are based on the assumption that (1) the company holds the compensating balance in a non-interest-bearing account, and (2) the company does not have excess cash to satisfy the compensating-balance requirement. When a company places the compensating balance in an interest-bearing account such as a CD or uses cash that it would keep in the bank anyway, the effective annual rates for the last two conditions in Table 14.3 are lower.

SECURED LOANS AND FACTORING

Some companies are unable to obtain unsecured short-term loans. A company may be too new to have established a strong credit history. Or perhaps the credit history suggests poor character or a lack of capacity. In other cases, the company may have used up its unsecured borrowing capacity.

Because of these conditions, a company may be able to obtain only a loan secured with collateral. For these loans the borrower signs a promissory note and a security agreement describing the assets that will serve as collateral. Whether or not collateral persuades the lender to make the loan depends partly on the lender's assessment of the four remaining Cs of credit: character, capacity, capital, and conditions.

Collateral value well in excess of the loan amount provides incentive to the lender to make the loan. The excess provides a margin of safety in case the borrower defaults. Highly liquid collateral adds to the margin of safety. Companies can borrow a higher percentage of collateral value if their pledged property can be sold quickly and reasonably close to market prices. Because of their liquidity, the likely candidates for collateral of secured loans are accounts receivable and inventory.

Pledging and Factoring Receivables

A company generates cash from receivables by either pledging them as collateral for a secured loan or by selling (factoring) them outright. Both procedures accelerate the cash flow from a company's receivables.

Pledging Receivables. Commercial banks and finance companies lend money against receivables pledged as collateral. How much they lend depends on their assessment of the quality of receivables—the perceived default risk of the receivables. The average size of the receivables also plays a role. Numerous small receivables are costly to administer and process. From the lender's viewpoint, a few large high-quality receivables are better than many small low-quality receivables. Lenders typically limit loans to between 50 and 80 percent of the pledged receivables because of the variations in quality and size.

The borrower promises to repay the loan by signing a promissory note and gives the lender a lien (legal claim) on the receivables by signing a security agreement. In the event the borrower's customers default and the receivables become worthless, the lender has legal recourse against the borrower. Signing the promissory note makes the borrower responsible for repaying the loan.

nonnotification loan
Receivables loan in which the borrower's customers are not told that their accounts secure a loan.

notification loan
Receivables loan in which the borrower's customers are told that their accounts secure a loan.

Borrowers generally prefer a **nonnotification loan.** In this type of loan the lender does not notify the borrower's customers that their accounts are collateral for a loan. Upon receipt of payments from customers, the borrower simply forwards a portion of the money to the lender. The lender then credits the borrower by reducing the loan amount. In a **notification loan** the lender notifies the borrower's customers of the loan transaction and asks them to make payments directly to the lender. This arrangement gives the lender more control by cutting out the handling of payments by the borrower.

Lenders typically require an interest rate of prime plus two to four percentage points on a receivables loan. They also charge a processing fee of 1 to 2 percent of the pledged receivables to cover expenses of administering the loan. Effective rates on receivables loans often exceed the rates on unsecured loans because of the greater risk and increased administrative costs associated with receivables loans.[6]

factor receivables

Sell receivables to a financial institution for cash.

Factoring Receivables.   To **factor receivables** means to sell them. Unlike pledging receivables for a loan, factoring is the outright sale of receivables. When a company pledges receivables, it retains title to them; with factoring, the company transfers title to the factor, the financial institution buying the receivables. Factors include subsidiaries of bank holding companies, finance companies, and institutions specializing in buying receivables. Industries in which factoring is commonly used include finished apparel, textile products, and furniture manufacturing.

Factoring often is a long-term relationship in which the factor takes care of three functions: (1) credit analysis, (2) risk bearing, and (3) lending.

- *Credit analysis.* Factors determine the creditworthiness of the seller's customers. If a customer falls short of the factor's standards, then the factor refuses to accept the receivable. In this case the seller may refuse to extend credit to the customer to avoid the exposure to default risk. A seller who trusts the factor's judgment does not need a credit department.

- *Risk bearing.* Factors bear the default risk of the seller's receivables; that is, they usually purchase receivables without recourse to the seller-borrower in the event of default. Factoring receivables therefore relieves the seller of collection and bad-debt expenses.

- *Lending.* Factors advance cash to the seller prior to collecting on the receivables. Factors essentially turn credit sales into C.O.D. sales and reduce the seller's average collection period to zero days.

Factors charge a fee for credit checking and risk bearing, normally in the range of 1 to 3 percent of the receivables. For the lending function they typically charge prime plus two to four percentage points. Combining these costs makes factoring appear far more expensive than unsecured bank borrowing. Bank loans, however, fulfill only the lending function. Factors check credit and bear risk in addition to lending money. Factoring eliminates bad-debt expense and the need for a credit department.

Inventory Loans

inventory loan

Loan secured by a company's inventory.

Inventory loans are secured by a company's inventory. Many types of inventory have reasonable degrees of liquidity, making them suitable for collateral. For example, an automobile dealer uses cars as collateral, a cannery uses canned foods, a lumber wholesaler uses lumber products.

Lenders do not accept all inventory as collateral. Work-in-process inventory, for example, generally makes poor collateral because it is difficult to liquidate. Most raw materials and finished goods are acceptable collateral because they

---

[6]Care should be taken when comparing the interest rates of different loan arrangements. For example, compensating balances increase the effective rates of unsecured loans. Lenders often do not require compensating balances on secured loans.

may be easily liquidated. Concern for liquidity also makes lenders dislike highly specialized goods for collateral. For example, a banker might be reluctant to make a loan to a computer software developer who offers an inventory of software as collateral. Software becomes obsolete quickly and requires a highly specialized sales force that can advise and service buyers. Consequently, if the borrower were to default on the loan, the bank might find itself holding an asset worth, say, 30 cents on each dollar of loan principal.

Commercial banks and finance companies make inventory loans. How much they lend depends on the salability of the inventory. Because of low liquidity and high liquidation costs, some inventory, such as metal-fabricating equipment, commands as little as 50 percent of its book value. At the other extreme, a lender might advance 90 percent against standardized, highly liquid inventory such as lumber, rolled steel, and copper wire.

The procedures lenders use to secure a lien against inventory depend on the physical characteristics of the inventory. Two procedures, *floating liens* and *trust receipts,* leave inventory in the possession of the borrower. Lack of lender control in these procedures occasionally leads to fraud. For example, a borrower might sell the pledged inventory without repaying the lender. Two other procedures, *public warehousing* and *field warehousing,* place inventory under control of a third party. The lender exerts substantial control in these arrangements.

floating lien
Legal claim against all of a company's inventory.

Floating Liens.   A **floating lien** grants to the lender a lien against all of the borrower's inventory. The borrower continues to buy (or manufacture) and sell inventory in the normal course of business and pays the interest on the loan. At any point during the period covered by the loan agreement, all of the borrower's inventory is considered collateral for the loan. The lender has no control over the inventory, which increases the lender's possibility of loss if the borrower defaults. Because of this risk, the lender will evaluate the borrower's creditworthiness on other grounds in addition to the value of the inventory.

trust receipt
Legal claim against specific inventory items with identification numbers.

floor planning
Another name for a trust receipt loan; for example, car dealers floor-plan cars in inventory.

Trust Receipts.   Under a **trust receipt** arrangement, the borrower gives the lender signed trust receipts acknowledging that designated inventory is held in trust for the lender. The borrower must use proceeds from the sale of specific inventory items to repay the lender, who then returns the trust receipts.

Trust receipt loans, also called **floor planning,** are used for inventory items that the lender can easily identify. For example, automobile dealers floor-plan their inventoried vehicles by identification numbers. Appliance dealers use serial numbers from televisions, stoves, and refrigerators. In each case the lender can identify exactly the inventory pledged as collateral.

Trust receipts give more control to the lender than does a floating lien. Trust receipts specifically identify the inventory held as collateral, whereas the floating lien does not. Still, in practice, a lender sometimes loses control. To maintain control, the lender must frequently inspect inventory at the site of the borrower. Inspections can be expensive and inconvenient, especially if borrowers have numerous, geographically dispersed locations.

warehouse receipt
Legal claim against specific inventory in a warehouse.

public warehousing
Pledged inventory maintained in an off-premise warehouse.

Warehouse Receipts.   To lessen the inconvenience of trust receipts in some situations, lenders use a **warehouse receipt** arrangement, in which the lender has a lien against specific inventory in a warehouse. With **public warehousing,** the lender requests the borrower to place the inventory in a public warehouse. Upon delivery, warehouse personnel issue receipts for the inventory to the lender, who in turn makes the loan to the borrower. The warehouse authority releases inventory to the borrower only on instructions from the lender. The borrower reclaims the inventory as the loan is paid.

Some inventory—for example, coal, wheat, and liquid fertilizer—cannot be taken conveniently to a public warehouse. In these cases, field warehousing may be the best alternative. In **field warehousing**, the lender stores pledged inventory on the borrowing company's premises. The lender employs a custodian to control the flow of inventory into and out of a roped-off or walled area. The custodian issues receipts describing the inventory to the lender and releases inventory to the borrower only with the lender's authorization. Except for the location of the inventory, field warehousing works the same as public warehousing.

Warehouse-receipt financing has two costs: (1) the interest on the money borrowed and (2) the inventory-handling costs and storage fees. Lenders typically charge two to four percentage points over prime for the loan. Inventory-handling and storage costs depend on the space taken and the requirements for handling inventory. Storage costs are often calculated as a percentage of the value of inventory stored, and handling charges are a monthly fee. Offsetting these costs to some extent is a reduction in the borrower's inventory carrying costs. The financial manager considers each of these benefits and costs in calculating the effective interest rate of a warehouse-receipt loan. The rate can then be compared with the effective interest rates of other short-term sources.

field warehousing
Pledged inventory maintained on the borrower's premises.

Banking Relations

The bank loan market is a personal market in which borrower and lender meet face to face. Consequently, there is room for personal persuasion on the borrower's part—a financial manager may be able to influence a banker and so obtain loans on better terms. For this reason a financial manager is well advised to cultivate a strong professional relationship with a banker. The manager may do this in several ways: by referring other people to the bank, by opening personal and family accounts at the bank, by using the services of its trust department, and so on. Most important of all, the manager can alert the banker to the company's potential needs, a procedure facilitated by preparing a cash budget. This attention to budgeting and advance notification increases the banker's confidence in the borrower's capabilities.

In addition to being a source of financing, a commercial bank can supply a business borrower with valuable help that may be unavailable from other sources. For example, it may supply credit information on customers. A knowledgeable banker will be familiar with developments in an industry or region and know about business conditions in general. Often a banker can make a cool, rational assessment of the profit potential in a new venture, an ability sometimes lacking in operating and financial managers too close to the trees to see the forest. Clear, objective advice from a good banker-adviser can be a major advantage to a company.

COMMERCIAL PAPER

Unlike the personalized banking market, the commercial paper market is impersonal. On the other hand, the cost of commercial paper is often one to two percentage points below the benchmark prime rate. Commercial paper is a security with a long history, and this longevity partly explains its widespread acceptance today. Figure 14.3 shows the interest rate on high-quality commercial paper from 1935 to 1991. The commercial paper rate in early 1993 was slightly higher than

Goodbye Prime, Hello Cost-Based Lending and Securitization

Many bankers have reduced their emphasis on the prime rate as a basis for determining interest charges on business loans and have moved to a new system to price loans. Bankers call the new loan-pricing system *direct cost-based lending*. "The new direction, I think, is clear," observed a vice president at Bank of America. "We're moving toward direct cost-based lending, tying rates to the cost of funds."

Cost-based lending isn't an entirely new lending concept. Citibank tried in 1971 to transform the prime rate into a rate that automatically responded to changes in its cost of funds as measured by the yield on 90-day CDs. But the rest of the banking community didn't follow Citibank's lead, so the attempt failed. Many bankers are now pricing loans at rates explicitly tied to what they expect will be the cost of funding the loans—a policy that leads to a fragmentation of loan rates.

To some bankers, the decline in the role of the prime is a welcome development given the fact that, as a Morgan Guaranty banker points out, "there is always a political element to it; the cosmetics are always a consideration in setting the prime."

Cost-based lending is developing, in part, because of the securitization of loans, which helps bankers relate a loan to a specific cost of capital. *Securitization* is the pooling and repackaging of loans into securities, which are then sold to investors. For example, a financial manager can use inventory as collateral for a bank loan, and the bank can, in turn, securitize the loan by issuing securities with the trust receipts as collateral. The bank collects debt service from the borrower, subtracts an administrative fee, then distributes the remainder to the security holders.

Auto loans (called CARs— certificates of automobile receivables), computer leases, credit card loans (called CARDS—certificates of amortizing revolving debts), and other receivables have been securitized. Salomon Brothers, a large investment banking firm headquartered in New York,

developed and issued the first CARs in 1985. Salomon privately placed $10,000,000 of CARs for a firm specializing in floor planning for auto dealers. Now several large money center banks (banks in New York City, Chicago, and a few other large metropolitan areas in the United States) securitize loans.

Securitizing loans benefits business borrowers because it leads to greater liquidity and diversification of the loan portfolios of banks. The ability to package and sell these assets in an established secondary market increases their liquidity. The lending bank can achieve greater diversification because it can hold the same dollar amount of a particular type of loan in the form of a security backed by the loans of numerous borrowers, as opposed to holding whole loans of relatively few borrowers. Increased liquidity and marketability mean that the lending bank can ᴄ lower rates of interest to business borrowers.

Sources: Harvey D. Shapiro, "Is the Prime a Second-Rate Rate?" *Institutional Investor,* March 1981, 245; Christine Pavel, "Securitization," Federal Reserve Bank of Chicago, *Economic Perspectives,* July-August 1986, 16–31; and *Journal of Applied Corporate Finance,* Fall 1988.

3 percent. This nearly 60-year history reflects the changing levels of interest rates generally.

Market for Commercial Paper

The traditional definition of commercial paper describes it as a short-term, unsecured promissory note issued by a large, financially strong company. Although this description still holds for many issues of commercial paper, it no longer holds for all issues. Increasingly, for example, small companies are able to issue commercial paper by paying insurance companies and commercial banks to guarantee repayment. Another innovation is the use of collateral, thus transforming

FIGURE 14.3

Commercial Paper Rates: Annual Averages, 1935–1991[a]

Interest rates on commercial paper reflect changes in the supply of and demand for commercial paper. Beginning in 1966, commercial paper rates became more volatile and higher than in most of their previous history. The changes in commercial paper rates reflect the changes in all short-term rates.

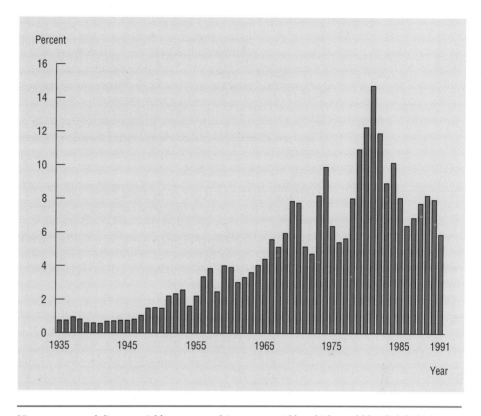

[a] Rates are annual discount yields, not annual investment yields, which would be slightly higher.
Source: Federal Reserve Bulletin.

the issue into a secured promissory note. Each of these enhancements reduces risk and enables otherwise nonqualifying companies to issue commercial paper.

Rating agencies such as Moody's Investors Service and Standard & Poor's Corporation rate commercial paper. The ratings, described in Table 14.4, reflect the likelihood that the issuing company will be timely in its repayments to investors. Major investors in commercial paper are other companies, money market mutual funds, insurance companies, pension funds, and banks.

Companies raise money by issuing commercial paper in large denominations. The basic trading unit is $100,000, and million-dollar denominations are commonplace. Smaller units occur less frequently. Commercial paper, usually issued to the bearer, trades at a discount from face value. The issuer redeems the paper at face value on the maturity date. Maturities at time of issuance usually range from 60 to 180 days; 270 days is the maximum if management wants to avoid registering the issue with the Securities and Exchange Commission. This 270-day rule effectively caps maximum maturity at 270 days.

Companies issue commercial paper in two ways. Large sales-finance companies such as General Motors Acceptance Corporation and Aetna Finance make

TABLE 14.4

Commercial Paper Ratings

Rating Agency	Rating Designations (High to Low)[a]
Moody's Investors Service	P-1, P-2, P-3
Standard & Poor's	A-1, A-2, A-3, B, C, D
Fitch Investor Services	F-1, F-2, F-3, F-4
Duff and Phelps	Duff 1+, Duff 1, Duff 1−, Duff 2, Duff 3
McCarthy, Cristani, Maffei	MCM-1 to MCM-6

[a] Commercial paper ratings reflect the likelihood of timely repayment to investors. For example, Standard & Poor's A-1, A-2, and A-3 represent extremely likely, very likely, and likely timeliness of repayment. A rating of B represents adequate capacity for timely repayment, but a rating of C represents doubtful capacity. A rating of D represents default or expected default. Pluses and minuses indicate shades of difference in quality within a rating designation, making A-1+ Standard & Poor's highest rating.

direct placement
Commercial paper sold without a dealer directly to investors.

dealer-placed paper
Commercial paper sold through a dealer network.

direct placements: They issue their paper directly to investors through a permanent sales force. Many industrial and utility companies issue **dealer-placed paper:** They sell their paper to dealers who resell it to investors at a markup. Major dealers include Merrill Lynch, Goldman Sachs, First Boston, and Salomon Brothers. To use direct placements, a company must ordinarily be a frequent issuer of large dollar amounts of commercial paper; otherwise, supporting a direct sales force is uneconomical.

Using Commercial Paper

bridge loan
Interim financing for investments in fixed assets.

funding
Replacing short-term debt with long-term debt.

Commercial paper is an alternative to bank loans for companies. Typically, companies use it to finance temporary needs and seasonal increases in current assets. Companies also use commercial paper as **bridge loans**—interim financing for investments in fixed assets. Later the company issues bonds to pay off the commercial paper. Replacing short-term debt with long-term debt is known as **funding.**

In order to facilitate the sale of commercial paper, companies frequently choose to back it dollar for dollar with a revolving credit agreement at a large bank or with a consortium (group) of banks. The agreement increases the cost of commercial paper by the amount of the standby commitment, but it also improves its rating and lowers the market's required rate of return. The financial manager must decide whether or not the savings on interest resulting from the higher credit rating outweigh the cost of the standby commitment. During buoyant economic times, 100 percent backing by banks may not be necessary because the general risk of default is low; backing sometimes drops as low as 20 cents on the dollar.

The effective cost of issuing commercial paper includes: (1) the discount from face value offered to investors, (2) the placement costs, typically $\frac{1}{8}$ percent of face value (12.5 basis points) if placed through dealers, and (3) the commitment fee to banks for the revolving credit agreement (when used), typically $\frac{1}{4}$ percent of the credit line (25 basis points). The effective percentage cost reflects the proceeds to the company and the amount paid by the company at maturity.

EXAMPLE

Willamette Corporation issues commercial paper with a $5,000,000 face value maturing in 90 days. The discount from face value offered to investors is

$56,250. In addition, the dealer fee (12.5 basis points) and the bank commitment fee (25 basis points) are based on face value. What is the effective annual percentage cost of the issue?

For the above example begin the solution by calculating the costs of the dealer fee and bank commitment fee:

$$\text{Dealer fee:} \quad 0.00125 \times \$5,000,000 = \$6,250$$

$$\text{Commitment fee:} \quad 0.0025 \times \$5,000,000 = \$12,500$$

The following time line illustrates the cash flows associated with the issue:

Time	0	90 days
Cash Flow	+$4,925,000	−$5,000,000

Cash inflow at time zero is:

Face value		$5,000,000
Less costs		
Discount	$56,250	
Dealer fee	6,250	
Commitment fee	12,500	
		75,000
Proceeds to company		$4,925,000

Willamette's effective annual percentage cost is calculated by first determining its percentage cost for 90 days:

$$\text{90-day rate} = \frac{\text{Discount and fees paid}}{\text{Proceeds to company}}$$

$$= \frac{\$75,000}{\$4,925,000}$$

$$= 0.01523, \text{ or } 1.523\% \text{ per 90 days}$$

or 1.523% × (365/90) = 6.18% per year compounded every 90 days

The effective annual rate is calculated as follows (frequency of compounding is 365/90):

$$\text{Effective annual rate} = (1 + 0.01523)^{365/90} - 1$$

$$= 1.0632 - 1$$

$$= 0.0632, \text{ or } 6.32\% \text{ per year compounded annually}$$

This calculation assumes that Willamette will roll over its commercial paper at the same rate (1.523 percent per 90 days) throughout the year. If so, Willamette pays 6.32 percent per year compounded annually.

Knowing the effective annual rate on commercial paper enables Willamette's financial manager to make comparisons with other sources of short-term financing. For example, if the effective annual rate on commercial paper is less than the effective annual rate on a bank loan, then the financial manager may choose commercial paper. Using the cheaper source makes sense in the short run, but rejecting the bank alternative may jeopardize Willamette's future banking relationship. Moreover, the bank may be providing advisory services not available in the commercial paper market. As in many areas of business financial management, the final choice involves more than a comparison of costs, but such a comparison is a good starting point.

SUMMARY

• Trade credit arises from an open-book relationship between companies transacting business with each other. Credit among companies is so widely used that trade credit ranks first in dollar volume among all short-term sources of funds.

• Stretching accounts payable means delaying payment beyond the due date of the credit terms. By stretching payables, a customer lessens the need for bank loans and reduces interest expense. The customer may also incur two costs: (1) loss of cash (prompt-payment) discounts and (2) a lower credit rating. Stretching accounts payable lessens the annual opportunity cost of forgoing cash discounts.

• Commercial banks provide the second largest total dollar volume of short-term funds. Unsecured bank loans include direct loans, lines of credit, and revolving credit agreements. Borrowing rates on these loans are often linked to the prime rate—a nominal, benchmark lending rate.

• Effective (true) borrowing rates often exceed the stated, or nominal, rate. Only with simple interest does the effective annual rate equal the nominal rate. The effective annual rate is a percentage per year compounded annually. If the banker discounts the interest payment—makes the borrower pay the interest in advance—then the effective annual rate rises. If, in addition to discount interest, the banker also requires the borrower to maintain a compensating balance, then the effective annual rate rises again. A compensating balance is a cash deposit required by the bank as a condition for a loan.

• Newly developing and financially weak companies may be unable to obtain unsecured bank loans. However, they may be able to obtain a secured bank loan. Companies frequently pledge receivables and inventory as collateral for their loans. Inventory loan arrangements include floating liens, trust receipts, and warehouse receipts.

• Factoring is an alternative to secured bank loans. Factoring is selling accounts receivable to a factor. A factor performs three functions: (1) credit checking, (2) risk bearing, and (3) lending money. Factoring offers several benefits but involves substantial costs as well.

• Companies have another option for raising short-term funds: issuing commercial paper—short-term promissory notes. The yield requirement on commercial paper is normally less than the prime rate. The effective cost of commercial paper, however, includes not only the discount provided to investors but also placement costs and any commitment fees to banks. In many cases, a revolving credit agreement between the issuing company and a bank, or consortium of banks, secures commercial paper.

Key Terms

promissory note	stretching accounts payable	direct loan
accrued liabilities	short-term, self-liquidating loan	line of credit

annual cleanup

revolving credit agreement

commitment fee

usable loan proceeds

discount-interest loan

nonnotification loan

notification loan

factor receivables

inventory loan

floating lien

trust receipt

floor planning

warehouse receipt

public warehousing

field warehousing

direct placement

dealer-placed paper

bridge loan

funding

Questions

14.1. Identify and describe the three major sources of short-term funds used by U.S. companies.

14.2. General Motors purchases rolled steel products from Inland Steel. Safeway Supermarkets purchases fresh produce from the Farmer's Market Company. Which company, General Motors or Safeway, probably receives more liberal credit terms? Explain your answer.

14.3. If a company grants a customer credit terms of 2/10, net 30, the customer's annual opportunity cost of missing cash discounts is 37.2 percent. Explain the implicit assumptions of this statement.

14.4. "The bank has turned down our loan request," mutters Greg, the financial manager. "No problem, we just stretch our payables," responds his ebullient assistant, Brent. "By stretching payables, we can reduce the cost below the bank rate." Fumbling some papers, Greg says, "I dunno. I dunno. Won't we get into trouble?" "What trouble? Don't worry. Let's do it," urges Brent.
   a. Explain Brent's proposal.
   b. Explain why Greg *should* worry about the proposal.

14.5. "Frankly," intones the controller for Marwicke and McNeil, "we always take advantage of our cash discounts. We pay with a check upon delivery, so the discount translates into pure profit for us." Critically analyze the controller's policy. Is it a good policy? Explain your answer.

14.6. Historically, factoring accounts receivable in some industries has carried with it a stigma. Why might some people look askance at a company that factors its receivables?

14.7. What impact does factoring have on a company's current ratio? What steps can management take to offset the potential liquidity effects of factoring?

14.8. Which arrangement for inventory loans gives the lender more control of the inventory: (a) floating liens or trust receipts? (b) floating liens or warehouse receipts?

14.9. Identify specific inventoried products suitable (a) for trust receipt loans and (b) for warehouse receipt loans.

14.10. Honest Charlie is a used-car dealer specializing in cars 7 to 10 years old. Mr. Charlie actually changed his name from Anthony to Honest because he likes to emphasize his honest deals. "Honest car deals" is Mr. Charlie's slogan. He floor-plans cars for his east-side lot and his west-side lot.

   Honest Charlie's banker is Wally Peeps, vice president of Valley National Bank. Mr. Peeps visits Mr. Charlie at his east-side lot to check the inventory of cars against the trust receipts the bank holds. The bank has 30 trust receipts and Mr. Peeps counts 30 cars. After Mr. Peeps finishes the count, Mr. Charlie coaxes him to go to Edna's Diner for lunch. Mr. Charlie says, "Wally, you can check the west-side lot after lunch." Mr. Peeps agrees, and they go to lunch. Mr. Peeps later counts 23 cars at the west-side lot as indicated by trust receipts.

   Comment critically on the diligence of Mr. Peep's field inspection. If Mr. Charlie were crooked, what sleight of hand might he have used on Mr. Peeps?

14.11. Commenting on his preference for bank loans instead of commercial paper, Maynard Wayne, treasurer of Okenite Inc., said, "Commercial paper don't take you to lunch." What do you make of this cryptic remark? Explain your answer.

14.12. List several attributes of commercial paper and describe the way it is marketed.

Strategy Problem

MicroMark is a microcomputer and software retailer with several stores in the Pacific Northwest. The Seattle head-quarters needs to finance a seasonal increase in the inventory at its 9 stores for the 60 days preceding Christmas. The company plans to purchase microcomputers and software having a total invoice price of $3,000,000 from various suppliers. These suppliers grant a 2 percent cash discount if payment is made within 10 days of delivery of the merchandise. The full payment is due in 40 days (2/10, net 40). There is a finance charge of 4 percent for each 30-day period beyond the initial 40 days.

MicroMark has an investment in a money market fund, but using these funds to pay for the merchandise would exhaust its near-liquid assets. Therefore Micro-

Mark's financial manager is considering the following two alternatives:

1. Miss the cash discount from the suppliers and pay for the merchandise at the end of the 70-day period.
2. Borrow the necessary funds from MicroMark's commercial bank on a 12 percent per year (2 percent for 60 days) discounted, unsecured, 60-day note. The bank will require a 15 percent compensating balance. The note must cover the compensating balance and interest charges.

Calculate the effective annual rate for each of the financing alternatives available to MicroMark. Which alternative should the financial manager select?

Strategy

Draw a time line.

Solution

For the *first alternative*, if MicroMark pays on the 10th day, then it will pay its suppliers $2,940,000 [(1 − 0.02) × $3,000,000]. Alternatively, the company must pay the full amount plus a 4 percent penalty, or $3,120,000 (1.04 × $3,000,000), on the 70th day. The time line and calculations for the effective annual rate of this alternative are as follows:

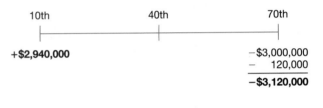

Calculate the 60-day rate.

$$60\text{-day rate} = \frac{\$3,120,000 - \$2,940,000}{\$2,940,000}$$

$$= 0.0612, \text{ or } 6.12\% \text{ per 60 days}$$

The effective *annual* rate is calculated as follows:

Transform the 60-day rate into an annual rate. Frequency of compounding is 365/60.

$$\text{Effective annual rate} = (1 + 0.0612)^{365/60} - 1$$

$$= 1.435 - 1$$

$$= 0.435, \text{ or } 43.5\% \text{ per year compounded annually}$$

Forgoing the cash discount for prompt payment is a costly alternative—43.5 percent.

For the *second alternative*, MicroMark must borrow enough to cover the compensating balance and pay the discount interest. The actual principal borrowed is:

Calculate the principal of the loan.

$$\text{Proceeds} = \text{Principal} - [(0.15 \times \text{Principal}) + (0.02 \times \text{Principal})]$$

$$\$2,940,000 = \text{Principal} - (0.17 \times \text{Principal})$$

$$\$2,940,000 = 0.83 \times \text{Principal}$$

$$\text{Principal} = \frac{\$2,940,000}{0.83} = \$3,542,169$$

The time line and calculations are as follows:

Draw a time line.

10th	70th

+$3,542,169 (Principal)
−   531,325 (CB)
−   70,844 (Interest)
+$2,940,000 (Proceeds)

−$3,542,169 (Principal)
+   531,325 (CB)
−$3,010,844

Calculate the 60-day rate.

$$60\text{-day rate} = \frac{\$3{,}010{,}844 - \$2{,}940{,}000}{\$2{,}940{,}000}$$

$$= 0.0241, \text{ or } 2.41\% \text{ per 60 days}$$

The effective *annual* rate is calculated as follows:

Transform the 60-day rate into an annual rate. Frequency of compounding is 365/60.

$$\text{Effective annual rate} = (1 + 0.0241)^{365/60} - 1$$

$$= 1.156 - 1$$

$$= 0.156, \text{ or } 15.6\% \text{ per year compounded annually}$$

The effective annual rate on the bank loan is 15.6 percent per year. The financial manager should select the bank loan because it is less costly than forgoing the cash discount.

◆ ### Demonstration Problem

Englehard Crafts (EC) manufactures and markets speedboats, ranging from small models to ocean-going vessels. The company's sales are highly seasonal, with the bulk of its sales occurring during the summer months. To support the buildup in inventory prior to the peak sales season, EC uses several sources of short-term funds. The following list contains examples of EC's past financing arrangements:

1. Lycoming Engines Inc. sold boat engines to EC for $2,500,000, with credit terms of 2/10, net 30.

2. Frost National Bank loaned $5,000,000 to EC for one year under the following terms: stated annual interest rate, 9 percent on a discount basis; compensating balance, 15 percent of loan value.

3. Broadway Bank granted EC a $10,000,000 line of credit with the following terms: stated annual interest rate, 8 percent simple interest; compensating balance requirement, 20 percent of the amount borrowed; annual renewal required; annual cleanup period of 30 days required.

4. A group of banks provided EC with a $20,000,000 revolving credit agreement, which included the following terms: stated annual interest rate, 10 percent simple interest; agreement period, 2 years; commitment fee, 30 basis points annually on the credit limit.

5. EC issued 90-day commercial paper with a $20,000,000 face value and incurred the following costs: $250,000 discount from face value offered to investors; dealer fee of 15 basis points and bank commitment fee of 20 basis points, each based on face value.

In addition to these five examples of short-term financing, EC in its early years of operation used factoring, receivables loans, and inventory loans to finance seasonal buildups in current assets. Assume that EC faces the preceding financial arrangements once again and answer the following questions:

a. If EC pays on the 10th day after purchase, how much money does EC pay to Lycoming Engines Inc.? How much money does EC save by paying on the 10th day instead of the 30th?

b. What is EC's annual opportunity cost of forgoing the cash discount and paying on the 30th day? 60th day? What are the benefits and costs to EC of stretching its accounts payable?

c. What is the effective annual rate of EC's loan from Frost National Bank?

d. How much money does EC have to borrow from Frost National Bank to have usable loan proceeds of $5,000,000? (Assume that the loan must cover the discount interest and compensating balance.) What is the effective annual rate of the loan?

e. Compare and contrast, in general, a *line of credit* and a *revolving credit agreement.* Why do companies make these financial arrangements?

f. Suppose that EC uses the line of credit with Broadway Bank to borrow $10,000,000 for 180 days. What is the effective annual rate of the loan?

g. How much money does EC pay per year if it does not borrow against the revolving credit agreement? What is the effective annual rate if EC borrows the entire $20,000,000 for one year?

h. Describe the attributes of commercial paper and note the ways that companies issue it.

i. What is EC's effective annual percentage cost of issuing commercial paper?

j. (1) What is the primary difference between pledging receivables for a loan and factoring receivables? (2) What three services does a factor provide to a company? (3) Describe the following arrangements for inventory loans: floating liens, trust receipts, and warehouse receipts.

Problems

Annual opportunity cost of trade credit

14.1. A company purchases material from its supplier on credit terms of 2/10, net 45.
  a. What is the annual opportunity cost of forgoing cash discounts and paying on the 45th day?
  b. What is the annual opportunity cost if the company pays on the 90th day? 120th day?

Graphing the annual opportunity cost of trade credit

14.2. For credit terms of 2/10, net 60, graph the annual opportunity cost of forgoing cash discounts as a function of the payment date. Put the annual opportunity cost on the vertical axis. On the horizontal axis put the number of days after the invoice date when the bill is paid. What principle does the graph illustrate?

Approximate and effective rates

14.3. Carrie Porterfield has a dilemma. She can borrow from the bank at an effective annual rate of 14 percent. She can also forgo cash discounts on purchases with terms of 1/10, net 30. Either action solves Ms. Porterfield's cash flow problem.
  a. Calculate Ms. Porterfield's annual opportunity cost of forgoing cash discounts using each of the following equations:

$$\frac{\text{Annual}}{\text{opportunity cost}} = \frac{D}{1-D} \times \frac{365}{n}$$

$$\text{Effective annual rate} = \left(1 + \frac{i}{m}\right)^m - 1$$

  b. Why do the two equations in Part *a* give you slightly different answers?
  c. To solve her problem, should Ms. Porterfield borrow from the bank or forgo the cash discounts? Explain.

Amount of financing from stretching accounts payable

14.4. Lee Puchala, controller for Intrafirst Company, expects average daily credit sales to increase from $80,000 to $120,000. Suppliers give Intrafirst credit terms of net 30. Intrafirst's credit purchases equal 70 percent of credit sales. Ms. Puchala pays for credit purchases 30 days after the invoice date.
  a. What is the dollar volume of Intrafirst's accounts payable before the sales increase? After the sales increase?
  b. Assume that Ms. Puchala begins paying suppliers 40 days after invoice dates.

What is the percentage increase in Intrafirst's payables after the sales increase?

c. Discuss the financial advantage of Ms. Puchala's decision to stretch accounts payable. What disadvantage might there be?

Line of credit with compensating balance

14.5. Sunnyvale State Bank grants lines of credit only if the borrower maintains compensating balances in demand deposits at the bank. Sunnyvale's policy calls for balances of 10 percent of the unused portion of the line and 20 percent of the used portion. Gunderman Hardware has a $100,000 credit line at Sunnyvale.

a. If Gunderman takes down $30,000 of the line, then how large must the compensating balance be?

b. Draw a graph of Gunderman's compensating balance as a function of how much Gunderman has borrowed. Put the dollar amount of compensating balances on the vertical axis and the amount borrowed on the horizontal axis.

Revolving credit agreement with commitment fee

14.6. Carol Beggs has a revolving credit agreement with her local bank for her Stanton, Michigan, auto supply stores. The agreement states that Ms. Beggs can borrow up to $200,000 any time during the next 12 months. For this commitment the bank charges a fee of 50 basis points on the unused portion of the credit limit. The bank charges her 12 percent annually for loans.

a. If Ms. Beggs does not borrow any money against the agreement, how much must she pay the bank?

b. If she borrows the entire $200,000 for the year, how much must she pay the bank in fees and interest?

c. Draw a graph of Ms. Beggs's payments of fees and interest to the bank as a function of the amount borrowed. Put fees and interest on the vertical axis and the amount borrowed on the horizontal axis.

Simple vs. discount interest

14.7. Basic Greeting Cards Company borrows $500,000 from U.S. National Bank for one year. The bank charges a stated 10 percent interest per year.

a. How much interest will Basic pay on the loan if the bank charges simple interest? When will Basic actually pay the interest? What is the effective annual rate on the loan?

b. Answer the three questions in Part *a* assuming that the bank discounts the interest.

Effective rates at alternative banks

14.8. Hoffman Industries can borrow from either of two local banks, Founders Trust or Security Bank. The stated loan rate at Founders Trust is 9 percent, and at Security Bank it is 10 percent. Another difference is that Founders Trust discounts the interest, and Security Bank uses simple interest. Hoffman Industries needs loan proceeds of $850,000 for one year.

a. How much money would Hoffman have to borrow from Founders Trust to have proceeds of $850,000? Answer the same question for Security Bank.

b. Should Hoffman borrow from Founders Trust or Security Bank? Support your answer with calculations.

CMA examination, modified: Discount interest and a compensating balance

14.9. A company recently negotiated a $9,000,000 loan with a bank. The stated interest rate is 8 percent. What is the effective annual rate if the bank discounts the loan, the loan is repaid at the end of the year in a single payment, and the bank requires a 10 percent compensating balance?

Discount interest and a compensating balance

14.10. First State Bank loans $700,000 to Mayfield Stores on January 1, 19X6. The loan carries an annual 9 percent rate, and interest is discounted. The bank requires a compensating balance equal to 10 percent of the principal, and the loan matures in one year.

a. Calculate the dollar proceeds available to Mayfield.

b. What is the effective annual rate on this loan?

Principal and effective interest rate

14.11. Jemco Manufacturing needs $330,000 to meet a maturing note repayment. The only source of cash available to Jemco is a local bank. The bank offers to loan Jemco the money for one year. The interest rate is 16 percent annually, a compensating balance equal to 20 percent of the principal is required, and interest is discounted.

a. How much must Jemco actually borrow?

b. What is the effective annual rate on the loan? Show your calculations.

Effective interest rate for a 6-month loan

14.12. Major Productions needs $480,000 to acquire an automated editing system for its print shop. American National Bank agrees to loan the money for 6 months at 10 percent annual interest. The bank discounts all loans.

a. How much money must Major Productions actually borrow?

b. What is the effective annual rate on this loan?

Effective interest rate for a 9-month loan

14.13. Battle Creek Cereals has negotiated a bank loan with the following terms: loan amount, $500,000; nominal rate of interest, 11 percent; compensating balance, 15 percent of the principal; and term of loan, 9 months. The bank discounts all loans, including this one. Calculate the effective annual rate that Battle Creek will pay.

Effective rate on commercial paper with a standby commitment

14.14. Arkansas Cartage Inc. will issue $200,000,000 of commercial paper for 6 months. Current conditions in the money market necessitate a 70 percent backing for any commercial paper issue. The company's commercial bank arranges a revolving credit agreement for a $\frac{1}{4}$ percent standby fee for the 6-month period. Dealer fees are $\frac{1}{8}$ percent of the face value of the commercial paper.

a. How large a credit line with the bank is needed?

b. What is the effective annual rate on the commercial paper if the paper carries a 10 percent annual discount rate?

Cost of an inventory loan

14.15. Larsen Furniture needs $350,000 cash for the next 6 months to finance a sales project. Having a good but brief credit history, Larsen has to use collateral for bank loans. The company will use inventory to secure as much of the $350,000 as the bank will lend. Larsen's bank limits loans to 85 percent of raw-materials inventory and 65 percent finished goods inventory. Under these conditions the bank charges a 12 percent stated annual interest rate. Furthermore, the interest will be discounted. Larsen's raw-materials inventory is $150,000, and its finished goods inventory is $175,000.

a. How much cash can Larsen borrow against its inventory?

b. If Larsen borrows the maximum against its inventory, what will be the net proceeds from the loan? How much cash will Larsen have to obtain from other sources?

c. Calculate the effective annual rate of the bank loan.

Cost of inventory financing vs. a bank loan

14.16. Harriston Refrigeration needs $600,000 cash to finance inventory that the company expects to have on hand for 6 months. The inventory will be completely sold at the end of that time, and the loan can be repaid from the sales proceeds. Jay Harriston, the company's financial manager, is considering warehouse receipt financing. American Financial agrees to loan Harriston Refrigeration the money under the following conditions: Loan amount is 90 percent of Harriston's $666,667 invested in inventory; nominal interest rate is 15 percent per annum; monthly handling charge is $280; storage charge, based on value of inventory stored for each month, is 0.4 percent. All interest and fees are payable at the end of 6 months. Mr. Harriston also contacts Western State Bank about borrowing the money. The effective annual rate on the bank loan is 18 percent.

a. Calculate the effective annual percentage cost of financing with warehouse receipts for Harriston Refrigeration.

b. Should the company borrow from the bank or use warehouse receipts? Explain your choice.

Effective rates on alternative financing sources

14.17. Maxiscribe is a large, fast-growing manufacturer of computer hard drives. Its rapid growth has put a strain on its cash balance, and the company now needs to raise $11,750,000. Maxiscribe needs the financing for 6 months and has identified three alternative sources:

1. Borrow the necessary funds from a local bank on a 9 percent (per year) discounted, unsecured, 6-month note. The bank requires a 20 percent compensating balance, and the note will cover the compensating balance and interest charge.

2. Issue commercial paper with a $12,000,000 face value and a maturity of 6 months. Without bank backing, the paper must offer a 6-month discount rate of 5 percent to investors. Dealer fees are $\frac{1}{8}$ percent of face value. The remaining funds needed can be borrowed at an effective annual rate of 16 percent.

3. Issue 6-month commercial paper with a $12,000,000 face value, with bank backing. Because of the bank backing, investors will require a 6-month discount rate of only 4.5 percent. Dealer fees are $\frac{1}{8}$ percent of face value, and the bank's commitment fee is $\frac{1}{4}$ percent. The remaining funds needed can be borrowed at an effective annual rate of 16 percent.

Based on the effective annual rate, which financing alternative should Maxiscribe choose? Support your answer with appropriate calculations.

14.18. *CMA examination, modified: Opportunity cost of trade credit; bank loan with discount interest and compensating balance; and inventory loan*

Paiport Company is a wholesale distributor that needs to finance a seasonal increase in its inventory for 90 days. The company plans to purchase merchandise having an invoice price of $8,000,000 from various suppliers at the beginning of this 90-day period. These suppliers grant a 5 percent cash discount if payment is made upon delivery of the merchandise. The full payment is due in 60 days. There is a finance charge of $1\frac{1}{2}$ percent for each 30-day period beyond the initial 60 days.

Paiport has an investment in a money market fund, but using these funds to pay for the merchandise would exhaust its near-liquid assets. Therefore Paiport is considering the following three alternatives:

1. Miss the cash discount from the suppliers and pay for the merchandise at the end of the 90-day period.

2. Borrow the necessary funds from a commercial bank on a 16 percent (per year) discounted, 90-day note. The bank will require a 10 percent compensating balance. The note must cover the compensating balance and interest charges.

3. Borrow the necessary funds from a commercial finance company with a note secured by the merchandise inventory. The finance company would provide funds equal to 80 percent of the merchandise's total invoice price ($8,000,000) at an 18 percent annual interest rate. The note principal and interest would be paid at the end of the 90-day period, at which time the floating lien on Paiport's inventory would be removed. The balance of the funds needed to buy the merchandise would be obtained by liquidating part of Paiport's investment in the money market fund. There would be no charge for withdrawing from the fund. The money market fund has been earning $12\frac{1}{2}$ percent per year, but Paiport's financial manager expects it to earn 12 percent per year over the foreseeable future.

   a. Calculate the effective annual rate for each of the three financing alternatives available to Paiport. Which alternative should Paiport's financial manager select?
   b. Some banks and finance companies prefer collateral other than inventory for secured loans. Explain why inventory may not be the preferred collateral.
   c. What problems, if any, is Paiport likely to have with its suppliers by delaying payment 30 days beyond the normal credit period? Explain your answer.

Computer Problems

Trade credit: template
TRCREDIT

14.19. Kim Young Inc. manufactures television sets. The company purchases picture tubes from four suppliers: Miyagi Tubes, Kono Electronics, Ogimura Trading Co., and Tanaka Enterprises. The tubes from the four suppliers are of equivalent quality and are priced identically. The credit terms are:

Miyagi Tubes	2/10, net 30
Kono Electronics	2/15, net 60
Ogimura Trading Co.	3/10, net 45
Tanaka Enterprises	1/15, net 70

a. Calculate the annual opportunity cost of forgoing the cash discount from each supplier.
b. If Kim Young Inc. can borrow at a cost of 15 percent against a line of credit from Sun Kook Bank, from which suppliers should it take the cash discount?
c. If the company decides to take cash discounts, then which supplier should be selected?
d. If the company is short of funds and is not able to take cash discounts, then which supplier should be selected?
e. How would the annual opportunity cost of forgoing cash discounts change if suppliers are paid 10 days past net date, 20 days past net date, and 30 days past net date?

Inventory loan: template
INVLOAN

14.20. Barret Sportswear needs to build up additional inventory of approximately $200,000 worth of swimsuits for the summer season. The suppliers have offered credit terms of 3/20, net 80. The additional inventory needs to be carried for a period of 60 days. The company could either pay after 80 days or borrow the necessary funds and take advantage of the cash discount. The company can tap any of the following sources of financing:

1. It could obtain a warehouse receipt loan of $200,000 from Interstate Bank & Trust Co. The interest rate would be 16 percent per year on the outstanding balance. Inventory handling and storage fees would be 0.5 percent of the average amount borrowed. The average loan balance is expected to be $160,000.

2. First National Bank is willing to loan money to the company in exchange for a floating lien against inventory at an annual interest rate of 15 percent.

3. Peoples Bank will loan money to the company on a 13 percent per year, discounted, unsecured, 60-day note. The bank requires a 20 percent compensating balance.

a. As Barret's financial manager, would you take the cash discount? If so, what source of financing would you select?
b. Consider a changed scenario in which, due to inflation, the warehousing loan interest rate is 19 percent per year, the floating lien interest rate is 19 percent per year, and the unsecured-note interest rate is 16 percent per year. All other factors remain unchanged. What should the company do under such circumstances?

(|VHS|)

VIDEO CASE PROBLEM

Northwest Lumber Inc.

Anita Munsinger, president and CEO of Northwest Lumber Inc., walked by her secretary's desk saying: "Would you please ask Bryan to join me in my office?" Ms. Munsinger had recently recruited Bryan Bilbrey from Anderson Consulting to become Northwest's chief financial officer. Sitting at her desk, she reviewed the Money Rates report in *The Wall Street Journal* and noted with interest the difference between the bank prime rate and commercial paper rates.

Northwest Lumber purchases lumber products from mills in the northwest United States and resells the products to wholesalers and large home center stores. In addition, Northwest ships large quantities of lumber to Japan. Known as a drop-shipper, Northwest sells lumber products to customers without taking physical possession of the inventory. Qualified customers purchase lumber from Northwest on trade credit terms of net 30 days after delivery date.

The mills that supply Northwest with lumber offer 2/10, net 30 trade credit terms. To take advantage of the 2 percent discount, the company uses short-term bank loans to finance payments to the mills. The bank loans, which often total $25 million, are provided by several banks where Northwest maintains lines of credit. To date, the company has never used any other form of short-term financing other than trade credit and bank loans.

After exchanging greetings in her office, Ms. Munsinger and Mr. Bilbrey enter into the following conversation:

Munsinger: Northwest Lumber's interest expense is becoming excessive. If possible, we need to lower our costs by using financing sources other than banks.

Bilbrey: I agree, but we need to maintain our banking relationships. In my opinion we should examine the possibility of issuing $15 million of commercial paper to replace about 60 percent of our bank loans.

Munsinger: Tell me more about commercial paper.

Bilbrey: Commercial paper is an issue of short-term notes, usually unsecured and sold at a discount from face value. Investors earn the difference between the discounted price and face value received at maturity. Term to maturity for newly issued paper usually ranges from 60 to 180 days, with a maximum of 270 days in order to avoid registration with the Securities and Exchange Commission. Money market mutual funds are major

buyers, especially of highly rated paper. The top two ratings provided by Standard & Poor's and Moody's are A-1 and P-1, respectively. We would need either the top rating or next to the top to lower our costs.

Munsinger: How can Northwest qualify for one of the top two ratings?

Bilbrey: We can enhance the rating by arranging a back-up line of credit with our banks. The line of credit would guarantee our ability to retire the commercial paper at maturity. Although this arrangement would reduce the risk and discount cost of the paper, the banks would charge us a commitment fee.

Munsinger: How do we get the paper into the hands of investors?

Bilbrey: The best approach for Northwest is to sell the paper to commercial paper dealers, who in turn resell it to investors. We're not equipped to sell directly to investors.

Munsinger: Give me the bottom-line cost to Northwest.

Bilbrey: I can't give you a bottom-line cost just yet, but I did obtain some information. The annual discount yield on prime commercial paper is approximately 3.5 percent, or 58 basis points for 60 days. Therefore the discount from face value ($15 million) offered to investors is $87,000. Dealers would charge us 0.15 percent of face value for placement; and the banks would charge us 0.20 percent of face value for a back-up line of credit.

Munsinger: Northwest currently pays an effective annual rate of 7.5 percent on 60-day bank loans. I wonder how that compares to the commercial paper rate. Let me see your recommendation before the board meeting next week.

a. If Northwest pays its suppliers on the 30th day after purchase instead of the 10th day, what is its annual opportunity cost? Should Northwest use bank loans, if necessary, to pay suppliers on the 10th day? Explain.

b. Describe commercial paper and the way it is marketed.

c. Explain why Northwest should maintain its banking relationships and not rely solely on commercial paper for short-term financing.

d. In what way does a back-up line of credit lower the risk of a commercial paper issue?

e. Calculate Northwest's proceeds from the sale of $15 million of commercial paper.

f. Calculate Northwest's effective annual percentage cost of issuing commercial paper.

g. Should Northwest issue commercial paper to replace some of its bank loans? Explain.

_____

The author thanks Professor Carl M. Hubbard of Trinity University for contributing this case problem.

Selected References

Boldin, Robert J., and Patti D. Feeny. "The Increased Importance of Factoring." *Financial Executive,* April 1981: 19–21.

Cooley, Philip L., and Richard J. Pullen. "Small-Business Use of Commercial Bank Services." *Banker's Magazine,* January–February 1979: 72–75.

Goldberg, Michael A. "The Sensitivity of the Prime Rate to Money Market Conditions." *Journal of Financial Research,* Winter 1984: 269–280.

Hawkins, Gregory D. "An Analysis of Revolving Credit Agreements." *Journal of Financial Economics,* March 1982: 59–81.

Herskowitz, Barry, and David A. Kaplowitz. "Asset-Based Revolvers: Financing Growth with a Loan That Minimizes the Balance." *Journal of Accounting,* July 1986: 97–104.

Loeys, Jan G. "Interest Rate Swaps: A New Tool for Managing Risk." *Business Review,* May–June 1985: 17–25.

Merris, Randall C. "Business Loans at Large Commercial Banks: Policies and Practices." *Economic Perspectives,* November–December 1979: 15–23.

Stancill, James McNeil. "Getting the Most from Your Banking Relationship." *Harvard Business Review,* March–April 1980: 20–28.

Stone, Bernell K. "Allocating Credit Lines, Planned Borrowing, and Tangible Services over a Company's Banking System." *Financial Management,* Summer 1975: 65–78.

Titman, Sheridan. "Interest Rate Swaps and Corporate Financing Choices." *Journal of Finance,* September 1992: 1503–1516.

ANALYZING AND PLANNING FINANCIAL PERFORMANCE

SMALL-BUSINESS PERSPECTIVE

Financial Planning in a Small Company

Kathy Griffin had considered borrowing money to ease the cash flow problems of In Shape, the retail outlet for exercise equipment that she and Jim Sutherland had opened several years ago. However, after reviewing the company's accounts receivable and inventory, she thought that better control of those assets would help ease the cash shortage. An analysis of the inventory indicated that it had been increasing steadily and that many items were not selling as fast as Kathy and Jim had anticipated. Similarly, the accounts receivable were increasing in part because many accounts were not being collected on time. Kathy decided to develop stricter controls for these items before borrowing any funds.

Because of the rapid growth of the company, Kathy and Jim worked long hours but still found it difficult to complete all of the tasks that should be performed. The daily operations consumed so much time that there was never any time for long-range planning. During the first few years, when the company was relatively small, that had not been a problem. The company had grown so rapidly, however, that Kathy and Jim now felt that the company was running them rather than vice versa.

They hoped that as the years went by the profits and

550

and profitability of the company would increase. This hope seemed reasonable because as sales increased, many overhead expenses would not increase proportionately. For several years profits increased steadily, as shown below:

Year	Earnings after Taxes
19X6	$ 7,480
19X7	8,200
19X8	13,260
19X9	17,510

Kathy expected sales of $600,000 by 19X0 and earnings after taxes of $22,500. However, she was shocked to find at the end of the year that earnings after taxes were only $10,030.

In addition, it became clear by year-end that the cash shortage had not been resolved completely by tighter controls on receivables and inventory. Kathy and Jim believed that additional financing was still necessary, but they were not sure how much they should borrow. Kathy decided that financial planning was essential.

This part of the text illustrates how to analyze the financial position and performance of a company using financial ratios, company trends, and industry comparisons. Methods of forecasting and financial planning are explained and illustrated.

Chapter 15

ANALYZING FINANCIAL PERFORMANCE

Great Expectations

Harley-Davidson's management announced proudly that quarterly earnings were $0.49 per share of the company's common stock. After all, the announced earnings represented a 36 percent increase over the corresponding quarterly earnings of the preceding year. Despite the apparent good news, however, the company's common-stock price declined 31 percent. What's going on? Why did the price decline? Security analysts were surprised because they had been expecting $0.70 per share.

Security analysts examine companies, analyze their financial statements, and make buy-sell recommendations to investors. When a company's earnings fall short of expectations, analysts often reduce their earnings forecast for the future and may even recommend selling the company's stock instead of buying it. Acting on the information provided by analysts and the disappointing

earnings announcement, more investors want to sell than want to buy the stock, driving its price downward.

A company disappoints the stock market at the peril of its shareholders. For example, Hewlett-Packard, the giant electronics manufacturer, announced a quarterly sales increase of 15 percent, but earnings were flat and fell short of expectations. The company's shareholders lost $3 billion as the stock price plummeted 18 percent. The new information on earnings caused investors to revise downward their expectations of future earnings and dividends—and the stock price followed.

Source: Baruch Lev, "The Curse of Great Expectations," *The Wall Street Journal,* November 30, 1992, A12. *Photo Source:* © B. Leng/West Light.

The financial manager must step back from time to time to assess the operations of the entire company. In doing this, the financial manager compares the company's profits and activities with its past performance and with the performance of other companies in the industry. The company's suppliers, creditors, and shareholders also have an interest in analyzing performance because they need assurances that their stakes in the company are secure. Suppliers assess a company's liquidity and solvency because of their concern about the company's ability to meet short-term debts. In addition to liquidity and solvency, long-term creditors are concerned with projected profitability because they seek assurances that the company will be able to service its debt over several years. Company managers need to assess all aspects of financial performance to determine whether or not their investment and financing decisions are maximizing shareholder wealth. Like company managers, shareholders need to assess potential cash flows and the attendant risk in order to estimate the future performance of the price of the common stock. This chapter describes how stakeholders assess the financial strengths and weaknesses of a company through analysis of its financial statements.

FINANCIAL-STATEMENT ANALYSIS

Analyzing financial performance begins with the company's income statement and balance sheet. Analysts use past financial statements to evaluate the company's current condition and financial future. By analyzing the statements, analysts can assess the company's financial strengths and weaknesses. Financial-statement analysis helps answer such questions as:

- Why is the company more profitable or less profitable than other companies in the industry?
- Has management been efficient in using company assets to generate sales?
- Is company liquidity sufficient to satisfy the claims of suppliers and lenders?
- Is the company's debt position overextended, or does the company have additional borrowing power?
- Does management follow aggressive or conservative credit policies?
- Does the company carry excessive or inadequate inventories?

The first step in developing answers to these questions is the calculation of financial ratios that relate one item with another on the company's financial statements. Financial ratios are tools that help analysts interpret the company's financial health. Trends in the ratios and comparisons of them with industry average ratios reveal the financial strengths and weaknesses within the company.

Taken by themselves, the dollar amounts on a balance sheet and an income statement have only limited usefulness. For example, what interpretation can be applied to a company with earnings of $150,000 (revenues less operating and financial expenses)? For a small company these earnings might represent a banner year. For a large company, however, these earnings could spell disaster.

EXAMPLE

Two companies each earn a $150,000 profit for a particular year. Without further information an investor would consider the companies equally desirable. But suppose that one company had $500,000 in total assets and the other had $7,500,000. As return on assets indicates, the small company is more profitable than the large one. To measure return on assets, divide earnings after taxes (profit) by total assets:

<table>
<tr><td align="center">*Small Company*</td><td align="center">*Large Company*</td></tr>
<tr><td align="center">$\dfrac{\$150,000}{\$500,000} = 0.30$, or 30.0%</td><td align="center">$\dfrac{\$150,000}{\$7,500,000} = 0.02$, or 2.0%</td></tr>
</table>

Management of the small company appears to be doing a better job of generating earnings per dollar invested in assets.

profitability
Dollar profit as a percentage of some other quantity.

Relating profit to the investment in total assets provides a measure of **profitability**—the ability of total assets to generate profit. Profit is measured in dollars, but profitability is measured in percentages. Other financial ratios are expressed in percentages as well, and some are merely numbers representing how much larger one item is relative to another. Financial ratios are rarely expressed as 2 to 1, 2/1, or 2:1.

Because of the number of items on a balance sheet and an income statement, analysts can calculate hundreds of financial ratios for a company. Fortunately for our memory capacities, some of these ratios are nonsensical and others are unnecessary. Only a few ratios are needed to develop the picture of a company's overall financial condition and performance.

This chapter would be much shorter if we could discover one ratio that revealed the entire picture of a company's financial health. Pursuing such a ratio, however, is futile. Just as during a physical examination a physician takes readings on temperature, pulse, and blood pressure, so the financial analyst must look at several indicators of business health. Without results from a combination of tests and measurements, the physician might diagnose a patient as having chicken pox when, in fact, the patient suffers from a mild allergy. Accordingly, without several financial ratios serving as indicators, the financial analyst might erroneously conclude that a company is performing well when, in fact, mismanagement is causing a decline in shareholder wealth.

COMPANY TRENDS AND INDUSTRY COMPARISONS

Interpreting financial ratios requires a standard for comparison. Suppose, for example, that a company's earnings after taxes equal 15 percent of its common equity (book-value net worth). Should you conclude that the company is highly profitable, mediocre in profitability, or doing poorly? To reach a conclusion, you must know which values represent good performance and which do not. The most commonly used standards in financial-statement analysis are developed from trend analysis and industry averages.

trend analysis
Interpretation of financial ratios displayed in time series.

return on common equity (ROE)
Earnings after taxes per dollar of common equity.

Trend Analysis

Tracking a financial ratio over time is called **trend analysis.** Figure 15.1 illustrates information obtained from using trend analysis. Consider, for example, the company trend in Figure 15.1A. There you see the company's **return on common equity,** a profitability ratio, trending downward. Something ominous seems to be happening. The company earned more than 20 percent on its common equity in 19X5, but in 19X9 the return fell to less than 10 percent.

Trends and Comparisons: Return on Common Equity

Trend analysis and industry comparative analysis are aids for interpreting financial performance. Worked in combination, these two types of analysis reveal whether managerial or environmental factors are the cause of variation in company performance.

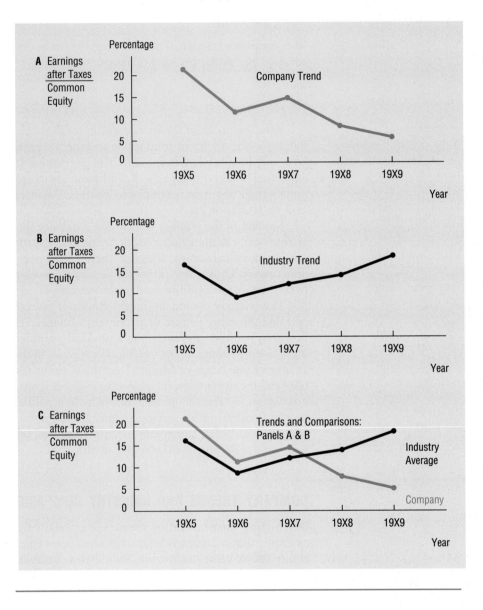

Reflect for a moment about the nature of trend analysis: It compares a financial ratio with itself at an earlier point in time. The ratio at the earlier point in time becomes the standard for comparison. It is entirely possible, of course, for this standard to be inappropriate. Perhaps the company's earlier performance was unusually superior. Comparison with an unusually superior standard will make a ratio appear worse than it actually is. Nonetheless, trends upward and downward provide you with the general pattern of a company's performance.

The key advantage of trend analysis stems from the way that accountants construct financial statements. They follow generally accepted accounting principles and apply them consistently over time, which means that dollar values are calculated in much the same way from year to year. Consistent application of accounting principles produces financial statements that are comparable over time. Financial ratios calculated from such financial statements are also comparable.

Industry Comparative Analysis

Analysts supplement trend analysis with **industry comparative analysis**—the process of comparing a company's ratios with industry average ratios. To illustrate industry comparative analysis, consider the three possible reasons for the decline in company profitability shown in Figure 15.1A. First, poor decisions by the company's management may be responsible. Second, uncontrollable factors in the operating environment may be the cause. Finally, a combination of managerial and environmental influences may be to blame. Without industry averages you cannot easily distinguish between internal and external causes. Industry averages help isolate the managerial effects from the nonmanagerial effects, which is the key advantage of industry comparative analysis.

Figure 15.1B shows the industry trend in profitability measured by return on common equity. Each point on the industry trend line is an average return of all companies within the industry. Note that industry profitability declines from 19X5 to 19X6, then increases each year to 19X9.

Combining the company and industry trends in Figure 15.1C shows company profitability paralleling that of the industry in 19X5, 19X6, and 19X7. In 19X8, for the first time, the company's profitability becomes inferior to the industry average; and in 19X9 company profitability falls far below the industry average. Using this information, the company's management, its suppliers, creditors, and shareholders can see that internal operations are the cause of the below-average performance.

Variation in accounting procedures from company to company lessens comparability across companies. For example, companies may use different depreciation methods for public reporting, allow for different estimates of bad debts, and have different fiscal years.[1] These and other accounting decisions affect a company's balance sheet and income statement. In addition, no two companies have the same product mix, and their costs may differ because of unionized and nonunionized labor forces. Company location and age of company assets will most likely differ as well. With all of these potential intercompany differences, the industry to be used for comparison with a company must be selected with care. As a practical matter in most analyses, the companies in the industry selected for comparison (1) have product lines similar to the company being analyzed and (2) are approximately the same size, as measured by total assets.

A thorough analysis based on financial ratios will uncover the reasons for a decline in profitability. In the sections that follow we examine the ratios analysts use to make such assessments. Before doing that, we review some of the sources of industry data available to the analyst.

---

[1] Companies may use one of several depreciation methods for financial reporting purposes. For tax reporting they use the modified accelerated cost recovery system (MACRS). See the discussion in Chapter 8.

Industry Data Sources

Prior to conducting an industry comparative analysis, the analyst should carefully define the industry encompassing the company. Many companies do not fit exactly into a specific industrial classification. For example, Pfizer Corporation is in pharmaceuticals, health care, and specialty chemicals in the United States, Europe, Asia, and Africa. American Brands is in distilled beverages, tobacco products, golf and leisure products, and financial services in the United States, Europe, and Canada. Classifying such companies in the proper industrial group is a challenging task. For most companies, however, the analyst can find a sufficiently similar industry so that fruit is compared with fruit, if not apples with apples. In the absence of published industry averages, the analyst may need to compile averages from similar companies before undertaking the analysis.

Libraries usually subscribe to several publications of industry-average financial data. Among the popular ones are the following four sources:

- *Annual Statement Studies* is published by Robert Morris Associates (RMA), an association of bank loan officers. This publication provides financial data on over 345 industries of small and medium-sized companies and reports medians and 25 percent deviations (quartiles) from medians for several financial ratios. Table 15.1 presents an abbreviated version of a report from the *Annual Statement Studies* for computer and software retailers. The report presents averaged values from company balance sheets and income statements according to asset size (M = $thousand and MM = $million).

- *Key Business Ratios* is published by Dun & Bradstreet. This publication provides median and quartile values for 14 financial ratios for hundreds of industry groupings.

- *Quarterly Financial Report for Manufacturing Companies* is published by the Federal Trade Commission and the Securities and Exchange Commission. This government report contains quarterly financial ratios by industry groupings and asset sizes.

- *Almanac of Business and Industrial Financial Ratios* is published by Prentice-Hall. It contains averages for 22 financial ratios for almost 200 industries. Eleven company groups by size are included for each industry.

Other useful sources of financial information are Standard & Poor's *Industry Surveys* and Moody's Investors Service's manuals on various industry groupings. Annual reports of competing companies can be used to compile key ratios, as can Forms 10K and 10Q filed with the Securities and Exchange Commission. Finally, a diligent analyst can normally obtain industry averages from trade associations.

CLASSIFICATION OF FINANCIAL RATIOS

Assessing the financial strengths and weaknesses of a company requires four groups of financial ratios: profitability ratios, asset management ratios, debt management ratios, and liquidity ratios. A complete financial analysis includes ratios from each of these groups.

profitability ratios
Ratios measuring profit relative to assets, equity, and sales.

Profitability ratios reflect the effectiveness of all managerial policies and decisions. A company's production, marketing, and financial activities all culminate in a particular level of profitability. Different profitability ratios measure different aspects of profitability. The example in Figure 15.1 uses return on common

TABLE 15.1   **Example of Published Financial Ratios: Computer and Software Retailers**

	Current Data Sorted by Assets						Type of Statement	Comparative Historical Data	
		9	13	9	3	3	Unqualified	46	26
	6	39	9	1			Reviewed	51	49
	30	35	5				Compiled	76	74
	1	2	1				Tax Returns		
	38	31	7	3	1		Other	70	69
		77(4/1–9/30/91)			169(10/1/91–3/31/92)			6/30/87–3/31/88	6/30/88–3/31/89
	0-500M	500M-2MM	2-10MM	10-50MM	50-100MM	100-250MM	**NUMBER OF STATEMENTS**	ALL	ALL
	75	116	35	13	4	3		243	218
	%	%	%	%	%	%	**Income Data**	%	%
	100.0	100.0	100.0	100.0			Net Sales	100.0	100.0
	36.7	29.6	25.7	28.1			Gross Profit	36.1	34.1
	33.9	27.3	25.8	26.5			Operating Expenses	32.5	30.4
	2.8	2.3	−.1	1.7			Operating Profit	3.6	3.7
	.9	.4	.7	−.2			Other Expenses (net)	.9	.9
	1.9	1.9	−.8	1.9			Profit Before Taxes	2.7	2.8
							Ratios		
	2.2	1.8	1.6	2.1			Current	1.9	1.9
	1.6	1.3	1.3	1.8				1.3	1.5
	1.2	1.2	1.1	1.1				1.1	1.2
	1.3	.9	.9	1.5			Quick	1.0	1.0
(74)	.9	.7	.7	.7				.7	.7
	.5	.6	.6	.5				.4	.5
	18 20.6	24 15.2	34 10.7	21 17.5			Sales/Receivables	22 16.8	24 15.5
	30 12.1	36 10.2	41 8.9	49 7.4				34 10.6	37 9.8
	41 9.0	49 7.5	54 6.7	60 6.1				48 7.6	50 7.3
	13 28.0	20 18.3	30 12.2	28 13.0			Cost of Sales/Inventory	33 11.0	35 10.5
	43 8.5	41 8.8	41 8.8	44 8.3				59 6.2	58 6.3
	83 4.4	64 5.7	76 4.8	73 5.0				94 3.9	79 4.6
	11 33.6	17 22.0	27 13.5	31 11.8			Cost of Sales/Payables	14 25.8	16 23.2
	28 13.2	29 12.6	39 9.4	40 9.2				32 11.3	32 11.3
	49 7.5	49 7.5	56 6.5	52 7.0				62 5.9	54 6.8

Source: © Robert Morris Associates 1992, *Annual Statement Studies*, p. 526. Reprinted with permission. RMA cautions that the Studies be regarded only as a general guideline and not as an absolute industry norm. This is due to limited samples within categories, the categorization of companies by their primary Standard Industrial Classification (SIC) number only, and different methods of operations by companies within the same industry. For these reasons, RMA recommends that the figures be used only as general guidelines in addition to other methods of financial analysis.

equity to measure profitability, showing it in decline. To discover the reasons for this decline would require the use of several other financial ratios.

asset management ratios
Ratios measuring sales per dollar invested in a specific type of asset.

Asset management ratios measure the effectiveness with which management employs assets to generate sales revenue. Companies use assets to generate sales from which they earn profit. Assets not needed for making sales reduce a company's return on assets and return on common equity. Chapter 13 presented two asset management ratios: accounts receivable turnover (credit sales/accounts receivable) and inventory turnover (cost of goods sold/inventory). Chapter 11 introduced the current asset turnover (sales/current assets).

debt management ratios
Ratios measuring the use of debt capital to finance assets.

Whereas asset management ratios measure efficiency in the use of assets, **debt management ratios** measure (1) the way the company's assets are financed and

TABLE 15.2   **Cert Company: Balance Sheets as of December 31**

	19X8	19X9
Assets		
Cash	$ 60,000	$ 79,820
Marketable securities	40,000	50,000
Accounts receivable	200,000	142,380
Inventory	210,000	250,000
Total current assets	$510,000	$522,200
Fixed assets (net of depreciation)	450,000	380,000
Total assets	$960,000	$902,200
Liabilities and Shareholder Equity		
Accounts payable	$ 75,000	$ 65,000
Notes payable, banks	74,000	12,000
Current portion of long-term debt	30,000	30,000
Accrued expenses	11,000	9,000
Total current liabilities	$190,000	$116,000
Long-term debt	330,000	310,000
Total liabilities	$520,000	$426,000
Common stock (30,000 shares)	270,000	270,000
Paid-in capital in excess of par	100,000	100,000
Retained earnings	70,000	106,200
Total shareholder equity	$440,000	$476,200
Total liabilities and equity	$960,000	$902,200

(2) the company's ability to service debt. Chapter 7 introduced the debt-equity ratio (debt/common equity), one of several debt management ratios.

liquidity ratios

Ratios measuring a company's potential for paying its bills.

Liquidity ratios show a company's potential for paying its short-term and maturing long-term debt. Without adequate liquidity even the most profitable companies find themselves in financial trouble. Chapter 11 discussed a commonly used measure of liquidity, the current ratio (current assets/current liabilities).

To illustrate the calculation and interpretation of these ratios, we use the financial statements of Cert Company in Tables 15.2 and 15.3. The balance sheets in Table 15.2 show snapshots of Cert's financial position at two points in time—the fiscal years ending December 31, 19X8 and 19X9. Each balance sheet reflects the basic accounting equation: Total assets equal total liabilities plus shareholder equity.[2] For Cert in 19X9 the equation is:

$$\text{Total assets} = \text{Total debt} + \text{Equity}$$
$$\$902,200 = \$426,000 + \$476,200$$

If Cert's balance sheet is similar to a snapshot, then its income statement (Table 15.3) is akin to a motion picture: The balance sheet shows financial accounts at a point in time, but the income statement shows flows over a period of time. For example, Cert generated $840,000 in sales revenue over the 12

---

[2] The following terms are used interchangeably: shareholder equity, stockholder equity, owner equity, net worth, and common equity. These five terms admittedly overkill one concept, but analysts use each frequently. If a company has preferred stock outstanding, then common equity, which excludes preferred stock, would differ from stockholder equity, which usually includes preferred stock.

TABLE 15.3   **Cert Company: Income Statement for Year Ending December 31, 19X9**

	Dollars	Percent of Net Sales	
1. Net sales (90% on credit)	$840,000	100.0%	
2. Cost of goods sold	440,000	52.4	
3. Gross profit (Line 1 − Line 2)	$400,000	**47.6%**	**Gross Profit Margin**
Operating expenses			
General and administrative	138,000	16.4	
Selling and promotion	90,000	10.7	
Lease payments	12,000	1.4	
Depreciation	70,000	8.3	
4. Total operating expenses	$310,000	36.9%	
5. Earnings before interest and taxes (Line 3 − Line 4)	$ 90,000	**10.7**	**EBIT Margin**
6. Interest expense	18,000	2.1	
7. Earnings before taxes (Line 5 − Line 6)	$ 72,000	**8.6%**	**Before-Tax Margin**
8. Income taxes	10,800	1.3	
9. Earnings after taxes (Line 7 − Line 8)	$ 61,200	**7.3%**	**After-Tax Margin**

Change in retained earnings:

Retained earnings, Dec. 31, 19X8	$ 70,000
Add earnings after taxes, 19X9	61,200
Less common-stock dividends	(25,000)
Retained earnings, Dec. 31, 19X9	$106,200

months ending December 31, 19X9. Its cost of goods sold, expenses, and taxes are also for the 12-month period, and they occurred throughout the year. Sales minus cost of goods sold, operating expenses, interest expense, and income taxes equals $61,200 earnings after taxes, the bottom line.

The lower part of Table 15.3 shows the link between Cert's income statement and its balance sheet. Retained earnings for 19X8 ($70,000, see Table 15.2) are increased by Cert's earnings after taxes in 19X9 ($61,200). Cert's board of directors declared a dividend totaling $25,000. Subtracting this amount from the previous sum ($70,000 + $61,200) yields the ending retained earnings, $106,200.[3] Note the retained earnings of $106,200 in Table 15.2.

PROFITABILITY RATIOS

profit margin
Profit per dollar of sales.

return on investment
Profit per dollar of investment.

Two kinds of financial data produce profitability ratios: (1) Data from the income statement only. A profit figure divided by net sales is a **profit margin**.[4] (2) Data from both the income statement and the balance sheet. A profit figure divided by a balance sheet number is a **return on investment.**

[3] When a company has preferred stock outstanding, subtract preferred-stock dividends from earnings after taxes to find earnings available to common shareholders.

[4] Net sales equal gross sales less any returned merchandise or allowances given to customers. Net sales represent the revenue generated from selling products during the period.

Margins on Net Sales

The percentages of net sales shown in Table 15.3 conveniently summarize the margins used in financial analysis. An income statement with all items expressed as percentages of net sales is a **common-size income statement.** Common-size income statements over several years are useful for analyzing trends in both profit margins and expense percentages. Because comparative industry data on individual expenses are often unavailable, the analyst usually must turn to the trends in expense percentages for information on company expense control.

Table 15.3 contains four commonly used profit margins. The first one is the **gross profit margin,** where gross profit is net sales less cost of goods sold. This ratio shows gross profit per dollar of net sales:

$$\text{Gross profit margin} = \frac{\text{Gross profit}}{\text{Net sales}}$$

$$= \frac{\$400,000}{\$840,000}$$

$$= 0.476, \text{ or } 47.6\%$$

Cert Company has $0.476 gross profit per dollar of sales. Cert's gross profit margin reflects its product pricing and efficiency in keeping down its cost of goods sold. If Cert could raise its product prices without reducing the demand for its products, then its sales revenues, gross profit, and gross profit margin would all rise. Cert could also increase its gross profit margin by finding ways to improve production efficiencies, thereby lowering cost of goods sold per dollar of sales.

The next profit margin uses earnings before interest and taxes (EBIT), also known as net operating profit (income). EBIT equals net sales less both cost of goods sold and all operating expenses. Although not shown in Table 15.3, details accompanying an income statement often separate operating expenses into dozens of individual expenses (wages and salaries, utilities, legal expense, advertising expense, and so on). Dividing EBIT by net sales yields the **EBIT margin:**

$$\text{EBIT margin} = \frac{\text{Earnings before interest and taxes}}{\text{Net sales}}$$

$$= \frac{\$90,000}{\$840,000}$$

$$= 0.107, \text{ or } 10.7\%$$

Cert's earnings before interest and taxes are $0.107 per dollar of sales. This ratio reflects not only the factors affecting gross profit margin (product prices and cost of goods sold), but also operating expenses. If the gross profit margin stays relatively constant over time while the EBIT margin falls, then you know that operating expenses are rising disproportionately. Trend analysis of individual expenses would isolate the excessive expenses, allowing management to remedy the problem.

Two final profit margins in Table 15.3 are the **before-tax** and **after-tax profit margins.**[5] Each reflects the amount of earnings (before or after taxes) per dollar of sales:

---

[5] Companies occasionally experience extraordinary gains and losses: income or loss from a lawsuit, income or loss on the sale of plant and equipment, uninsured losses from storms, floods, and fire, and so on. Accountants add these extraordinary items to (or subtract from, as necessary) earnings after taxes. For simplification, we ignore these adjustments in this chapter.

$$\text{Before-tax profit margin} = \frac{\text{Earnings before taxes}}{\text{Net sales}}$$

$$= \frac{\$72,000}{\$840,000}$$

$$= 0.086, \text{ or } 8.6\%$$

$$\text{After-tax profit margin} = \frac{\text{Earnings after taxes}}{\text{Net sales}}$$

$$= \frac{\$61,200}{\$840,000}$$

$$= 0.073, \text{ or } 7.3\%$$

Cert Company earned $0.086 and $0.073, respectively, before and after taxes per dollar of sales. The before-tax margin is particularly useful for proprietorships, partnerships, and S corporations because these organizations pay no income taxes; earnings before taxes are allocated to the owners, and they pay personal income taxes. Even for some regular corporations, the before-tax margin is more useful than the after-tax margin. Consider a corporation that pays no income taxes in a particular year because of a tax-loss carryforward. On an after-tax basis, comparing such a company with the industry average makes the company appear more profitable than is actually the case. The potential benefits from using both the before- and after-tax margins should remind you that one ratio does not make an analysis.

Two ratios related to profit margins are **earnings per share (EPS)** and **dividends per share (DPS)**. Cert Company's EPS and DPS are calculated as follows:

earnings per share (EPS)
Earnings after taxes per share of common stock outstanding.

dividends per share (DPS)
Dividends paid to common shareholders on a per-share basis.

$$\text{Earnings per share} = \frac{\text{Earnings after taxes}}{\text{Number of shares outstanding}}$$

$$= \frac{\$61,200}{30,000}$$

$$= \$2.04$$

$$\text{Dividends per share} = \frac{\text{Common dividends paid}}{\text{Number of shares outstanding}}$$

$$= \frac{\$25,000}{30,000}$$

$$= \$0.83$$

Table 15.3 shows both earnings after taxes and total dividends paid. Table 15.2 shows the number of shares outstanding. Cert did not issue new shares nor buy back outstanding shares during the year; thus the number of outstanding shares is a constant 30,000 for the year. Had the number varied, you would calculate EPS and DPS with the weighted-average number of shares outstanding—each number weighted by its respective proportion of the year.[6]

[6] For companies with preferred stock, earnings per share of common stock equal earnings after taxes less preferred-stock dividends, all divided by the number of common-stock shares outstanding. For companies with preferred stock or bonds convertible into common stock, accountants report two additional figures for EPS: *primary EPS* and *fully diluted EPS*. Primary EPS is based on the number of shares outstanding plus the number of shares created if equity-equivalent securities were converted. (See an accounting textbook for the definition of *equity-equivalent security*.) Fully diluted EPS is based on the number of shares outstanding plus the number of shares created if equity-equivalent securities were converted plus the number of shares created if all other dilutive securities were converted. Fully diluted EPS are always less than or equal to primary EPS.

Return on Investment

Return on investment, or simply ROI, is a widely used term in financial analysis. When using the term, however, you need to specify the investment being addressed. Two variations of ROI are return on total assets and return on common equity. Each measure combines data from the income statement with data from the balance sheet.

The ratio of earnings after taxes to total assets measures return on total assets (ROA):

$$\frac{\text{Return on}}{\text{total assets}} = \frac{\text{Earnings after taxes}}{\text{Total assets}}$$

$$= \frac{\$61,200}{\$902,200}$$

$$= 0.068, \text{ or } 6.8\%$$

Cert Company earned $0.068 per dollar invested in total assets. Return on assets relates the shareholders' portion of sales revenues (earnings after taxes) to the resources both they and creditors contributed to the company (total assets equal total debt plus equity). Put differently, ROA indicates the owners' profitability from *all* of the resources used in the business.

earning power ratio

Earnings before interest and taxes per dollar of total assets.

A variation of ROA, called the **earning power ratio,** divides earnings before interest and taxes (EBIT) by total assets:

$$\text{Earning power ratio} = \frac{\text{Earnings before interest and taxes}}{\text{Total assets}}$$

$$= \frac{\$90,000}{\$902,200}$$

$$= 0.100, \text{ or } 10.0\%$$

This ratio shows the earning power of company assets irrespective of the way the company finances them. Cert's assets earn $0.10 on the dollar before financing costs (interest) and taxes. The earning power ratio measures overall return on both shareholder and creditor capital.

The preceding two ratios divide an earnings figure that develops throughout the year by an asset figure at year-end. To increase accuracy, you could divide earnings by an *average* of the total assets the company uses throughout the year, say, a monthly average. Two factors work against this more accurate calculation, however: (1) Users of ratios, except company management, normally do not have access to monthly balance sheets. (2) Industry averages usually are ratios based on year-end amounts; for comparisons, company ratios should be calculated the same way as the industry ratios. If industry comparisons are not part of the analysis, then you might want the increased accuracy from the following adjustment:

$$\frac{\text{Average}}{\text{total assets}} = \frac{\begin{array}{c}\text{Beginning} \quad \text{Ending}\\ \text{total assets} + \text{total assets}\end{array}}{2}$$

Using this adjustment causes the earning power ratio of Cert Company to decline from 10 percent to 9.7 percent:

$$\text{Earning power ratio} = \frac{\$90,000}{(\$960,000 + \$902,200)/2}$$

$$= 0.097, \text{ or } 9.7\%$$

Similar adjustments can be made for any ratio relating a value from the income statement to a value from the balance sheet. Whether or not the adjustment is made depends on data availability and the need for greater accuracy.

The ratio of earnings after taxes to common equity (total shareholder equity) measures return on common equity (ROE):

$$\text{Return on common equity} = \frac{\text{Earnings after taxes}}{\text{Common equity}}$$

$$= \frac{\$61,200}{\$476,200}$$

$$= 0.129, \text{ or } 12.9\%$$

Cert Company earned $0.129 after taxes for each dollar of shareholder equity. Return on equity expresses the relationship between the shareholders' share of revenues and their previously contributed capital, including retained earnings. A large ROE attracts additional external equity capital, enables the retention of earnings, and makes possible large dividends. From the shareholders' point of view, ROE is the most important profitability ratio.

Return on common equity (ROE) is often called *return on book value* because equity is measured as a book value (based on historical costs) rather than a market value. The market counterpart to ROE is **earnings yield**—earnings per share divided by stock price per share:

earnings yield

Earnings per share divided by price per share; reciprocal of the P-E ratio.

$$\text{Earnings yield} = \frac{\text{Earnings per share}}{\text{Stock price per share}}$$

Note that the reciprocal of earnings yield is the familiar price-earnings (P-E) ratio from Chapter 3. By bidding up stock prices, investors assign high P-E ratios to companies with high expected profitability, which causes low earnings yields. Investors accept a low earnings yield when they expect a high future growth rate in the stock price.[7]

ASSET MANAGEMENT RATIOS

Asset management ratios measure the efficiency of using assets to generate sales revenue. Asset management ratios are called *turnover ratios,* net sales divided by a balance sheet item. A turnover ratio shows the sales revenue generated per dollar invested in assets. The following sections present the total asset turnover and various individual asset turnovers.

Total Asset Turnover

total asset turnover

Net sales per dollar of total assets.

The most comprehensive measure of efficiency in using assets is the **total asset turnover,** which shows a company's sales revenue per dollar of total assets:

---

[7]Companies with high P-E ratios tend to have high market-book ratios—stock price per share divided by book value per share. Book value per share equals a company's total shareholder equity divided by the number of shares outstanding. For example, book value per share for Cert Company in Table 15.2 is $15.87 ($476,200/30,000 shares). If the company's stock price were $22 per share, then its market-book ratio would be 1.4 ($22/$15.87).

$$\text{Total asset turnover} = \frac{\text{Net sales}}{\text{Total assets}}$$

$$= \frac{\$840,000}{\$902,200}$$

$$= 0.93$$

Cert Company's turnover ratio is 0.93 for fiscal year 19X9; that is, Cert generated $0.93 in sales per dollar of total assets.

Larger turnovers indicate that more sales dollars are being squeezed from each dollar invested in total assets. Excess assets in the form of idle plant and equipment decrease total asset turnover. The same result occurs with a liberal credit policy leading to a buildup of accounts receivable; or slack inventory control may cause slow-moving inventory to accumulate excessively. The impact of such events is to increase total assets proportionally more than net sales, thus reducing total asset turnover. Because holding assets costs money—cost of financing the assets, storage costs, depreciation, bad-debt expense, and so on—excessive assets reduce profitability ratios. A reduction in both the total asset turnover and profit margins leads to smaller returns on total assets and common equity.

If management finds that the company's total asset turnover is low, then the seemingly obvious course of action is to reduce assets. Attempting to reduce assets may not, however, increase the turnover. Stringent credit policies, inadequate inventory, or insufficient equipment could lead to reduced net sales and thus to a reduced turnover. For successful asset management, managers must strike a balance in company policies between too large and too small an investment in assets.

Individual Asset Turnovers

Turnovers of individual assets or asset groupings determine the total asset turnover. To verify this statement, take a closer look at the calculation of total asset turnover:

$$\frac{\text{Total asset}}{\text{turnover}} = \frac{\text{Net sales}}{\text{Total assets}}$$

$$= \frac{\text{Number of units sold} \times \text{Price per unit}}{\text{Cash} + \text{Accounts receivable} + \text{Inventory} + \text{All other assets}}$$

Net sales equals the number of units of various products sold times their respective prices. If competition or poor pricing policy causes a low price per unit, net sales and total asset turnover decline. In addition, poor marketing practices can cause the number of units sold to be low, thereby lowering net sales and total asset turnover. The combination of poor pricing policies and poor marketing practices has a double effect: (1) It reduces total asset turnover and (2) it reduces profit margin.

As the preceding equation shows, the other set of potential causes of low total asset turnover stems from buildups in assets. Buildups may occur in current assets as evidenced by a small current asset turnover, or in fixed assets as evidenced by a low fixed asset turnover. Furthermore, individual current assets may be responsible for lowering the total asset turnover.

Current Asset Turnover. The *current asset turnover* shows company sales revenue per dollar of current assets:

$$\text{Current asset turnover} = \frac{\text{Net sales}}{\text{Current assets}}$$

$$= \frac{\$840,000}{\$522,200}$$

$$= 1.61$$

Cert Company's current asset turnover is 1.61 for fiscal year 19X9, indicating that it had $1.61 in net sales for each dollar of current assets. If Cert's current asset turnover differs markedly from the industry average, then you would proceed to investigate the turnovers for receivables and inventory. If receivables and inventory are not responsible for the difference, then you know to look at other current assets for an explanation.

Accounts receivable turnover is credit sales per dollar of accounts receivable:

$$\text{Accounts receivable turnover} = \frac{\text{Credit sales}}{\text{Accounts receivable}}$$

Lower values for the turnover indicate larger amounts of receivables relative to sales volume. Cert Company's accounts receivable turnover based on credit sales in 19X9 is as follows:

$$\text{Accounts receivable turnover} = \frac{0.90 \times \$840,000}{\$142,380}$$

$$= 5.31$$

Cert generated $5.31 in credit sales per dollar of accounts receivable.

Accounts receivable turnover compares credit sales with the asset resulting from credit sales—accounts receivable. In many cases, however, the use of total sales in place of credit sales is necessary. For example, the split between cash and credit sales may not be known. *Moreover, many publications of industry averages use total sales, which for comparability requires the use of the company's total sales.*

Average collection period (ACP) is another ratio for evaluating the level of accounts receivable. ACP shows the number of days of average daily credit sales represented by the accounts receivable. Equivalently, it measures the average number of days for the company to collect accounts receivable:

$$\text{Average collection period} = \frac{\text{Accounts receivable}}{\text{Annual credit sales}/365}$$

Cert Company's ACP for 19X9 is 68.7 days:

$$\text{Average collection period} = \frac{\$142,380}{\$756,000/365}$$

$$= \frac{\$142,380}{\$2,071}$$

$$= 68.7 \text{ days}$$

If Cert's ACP is materially longer than the industry average, the reasons for it should be explored. In addition, if Cert's credit terms to customers are net 30 days, then it clearly has several overdue accounts receivable. The company is either granting credit to customers who should not receive credit, or its collection policy is deficient.

Excessive investment in accounts receivable leads to a reduction in the current asset and total asset turnovers (and in profitability). In contrast, stringent credit policies leading to a high accounts receivable turnover and to a shorter average collection period may cause the loss of profitable sales. Prudent credit policies would fall between these extremes.

In seasonal industries, accounts receivable may change from month to month. Thus the values of accounts receivable turnover and average collection period may depend greatly on the month the company uses to end the fiscal year. Using the monthly average of accounts receivable lessens this seasonality effect.

Accounts receivable turnover and average collection period (ACP) provide essentially the same information. Simply dividing 365 days (a year) by the accounts receivable turnover yields the ACP. Cert Company's data illustrate the relationship:

$$\text{Average collection period} = \frac{365 \text{ days}}{5.31}$$

$$= 68.7 \text{ days}$$

For Cert Company we use annual credit sales to calculate turnover and ACP. When the mix of cash and credit sales is unknown, we use total sales in place of credit sales.

Effective control of inventory is as important to a company's profitability as the effective control of accounts receivable. In either case an excessive buildup reduces asset turnover and profitability. Because the cost of holding inventory normally exceeds the cost of holding receivables, inventory requires a watchful eye. Inventory carrying costs may exceed \$0.30 annually per dollar of inventory; these costs include capital costs, storage, insurance, taxes, handling, and spoilage. Thus excessive inventory not only reduces the asset turnover; it also reduces the profit margin.

Inventory turnover equals cost of goods sold divided by inventory:[8]

$$\text{Inventory turnover} = \frac{\text{Cost of goods sold}}{\text{Inventory}}$$

$$= \frac{\$440,000}{\$250,000}$$

$$= 1.76$$

Based on year-end inventory, Cert Company turns over its inventory 1.76 times per year; the company has \$1.76 in sales, measured at cost, per dollar of inventory. If Cert's inventory were low compared with the industry average, then we might suspect an accumulation of: (1) slow-moving inventory items, (2) obsolete inventory items, (3) spoiled inventory items, or (4) simply too much inventory.

---

[8] Dun & Bradstreet defines inventory turnover as *sales* divided by inventory. Because inventory is recorded on the balance sheet at cost, many analysts prefer *cost of goods sold* divided by inventory. In this way they divide a cost figure by a cost figure. When comparing one company with another, they also avoid interpretation problems caused by the differential markups reflected in the sales figures. Of course, when comparing inventory turnovers with D&B averages, analysts use sales in the calculation for comparability.

days' sales in inventory
Average number of days required to sell inventory items.

Dividing Cert Company's inventory turnover into 365 days yields **days' sales in inventory**—or the average number of days required to sell inventory items:

$$\text{Days' sales in inventory} = \frac{365 \text{ days}}{\text{Inventory turnover}}$$

$$= \frac{365 \text{ days}}{1.76}$$

$$= 207.4 \text{ days}$$

If the usual and customary stockpile of inventory were 60 days, then Cert would appear to have excessive inventory at the end of 19X9. Whether or not Cert's year-end inventory level is typical could be determined with monthly balance sheets. Table 15.2 presents two year-end balance sheets from which an average inventory can be calculated: beginning plus ending inventory divided by 2. Based on this average, Cert's inventory turnover is calculated as follows:

$$\text{Average inventory turnover} = \frac{\$440,000}{(\$210,000 + \$250,000)/2}$$

$$= 1.91$$

Cert's average inventory turnover, 1.91 times, still appears quite low.[9]

fixed asset turnover
Net sales per dollar of fixed assets.

Fixed Asset Turnover. The **fixed asset turnover** is the company's sales per dollar of fixed assets. In addition to buildups in current assets, excessive fixed assets relative to sales volume also reduce total asset turnover. For example, a wholesaler who has trucks not used year-round has an investment not generating sales each day. In comparison, a wholesaler who discovers a way to keep the trucks rolling generates more sales and increases its fixed asset turnover.

For Cert Company, fixed asset turnover is 2.21:

$$\text{Fixed asset turnover} = \frac{\text{Net sales}}{\text{Net fixed assets}}$$

$$= \frac{\$840,000}{\$380,000}$$

$$= 2.21$$

Cert generates $2.21 in sales for each dollar invested in fixed assets. Higher fixed asset turnovers within an industry generally indicate greater efficiencies in using fixed assets.

Several factors other than differences in efficiency may cause fixed asset turnover to differ among companies. Two important ones are the age of the company (and its assets) and the extent of leasing:

1. Older companies may be using fully depreciated assets not shown on the balance sheet, which increases turnover. In contrast, newer companies may have a substantial part of fixed assets recorded at recent market values, which reduces turnover.

---

[9] Another problem in interpreting inventory turnover stems from the methods used to value inventory—for example, last-in first-out (LIFO) and first-in first-out (FIFO). During inflationary periods LIFO companies tend to have high inventory turnovers (cost of goods is high, inventory low). Under identical circumstances FIFO companies have smaller inventory turnovers. When LIFO distortions become significant, analysts often adjust the balance sheet inventory toward the market value.

2. Companies that lease assets tend to have high turnovers if they do not capitalize them by putting the present value of the future lease payments on the balance sheet.

Because of these factors, fixed asset turnover should be interpreted with caution. Whether fixed assets are excessive or deficient should be interpreted with informed judgment assisted by the turnover ratio.

DEBT MANAGEMENT RATIOS

Debt management ratios measure the impact of using debt capital to finance assets. Management employs debt in an attempt to leverage return on common equity—that is, to increase it. Too much debt, however, increases financial risk excessively, and fear of default limits use of debt for financing. Debt management ratios can be divided into two groups: (1) *debt ratios,* measured with balance sheet data, and (2) *coverage ratios,* measured with income statement data. Debt ratios help you to analyze total debt, short-term debt, and long-term debt. By definition, current debt (liabilities) matures within one year, and long-term debt matures over periods extending beyond one year.

Total Debt Ratio

total debt ratio
Total debt per dollar of total assets.

One of the most widely employed measures of total debt usage is the **total debt ratio.** It measures the amount of total debt per dollar of total assets:

$$\text{Total debt ratio} = \frac{\text{Total debt}}{\text{Total assets}}$$

$$= \frac{\$426,000}{\$902,200}$$

$$= 0.472, \text{ or } 47.2\%$$

Cert Company's total debt ratio for fiscal year ending 19X9 is 47.2 percent, meaning that it has $0.472 total debt per dollar of total assets. Expressed as a percentage, the total debt ratio shows the extent to which debt finances total assets. The lower the total debt, the lower the financial leverage, and the greater the protection afforded creditors by common equity.[10]

An alternative to the total debt ratio is the *debt-equity ratio:*

$$\text{Debt-equity ratio} = \frac{\text{Total debt}}{\text{Common equity}}$$

$$= \frac{\$426,000}{\$476,200}$$

$$= 0.89$$

Cert Company's total debt is 0.89 times the size of its common equity, meaning that the company has $0.89 total debt per dollar of common equity. Whether an

---

[10] Like debt, preferred stock creates financial leverage and magnifies return on equity. Preferred stock as a percentage of total assets is analogous to the total debt ratio.

analyst uses the debt-equity ratio or the total debt ratio is a matter of personal preference. They tell the same story, as the following equation indicates:

$$\text{Debt-equity ratio} = \frac{\text{Total debt ratio}}{1 - \text{Total debt ratio}}$$

$$= \frac{0.472}{1 - 0.472}$$

$$= 0.89$$

Cert's debt-equity ratio (0.89) is simply a mathematical transformation of its total debt ratio (0.472).[11]

Another alternative to the total debt ratio is the **equity multiplier**—the dollar value of total assets per dollar of equity:

equity multiplier

Total assets per dollar invested (equity) by owners.

$$\text{Equity multiplier} = \frac{\text{Total assets}}{\text{Common equity}}$$

$$= \frac{\$902,200}{\$476,200}$$

$$= 1.89$$

Cert Company's total assets are 1.89 times larger than its common equity, meaning that the company has $1.89 in assets per dollar of shareholder equity. A financial model presented later in the chapter uses this ratio.

Figure 15.2 illustrates the relationships among the three measures of total debt usage. As Balance Sheet A shows, when a company borrows $1 for each $1 that owners supply, the total debt ratio equals 50 percent, the debt-equity ratio equals 1.0, and the equity multiplier equals 2.0. Borrowing $2 for each $1 of owners' money increases the total debt ratio to 67 percent; once again, the equity multiplier (3.0) exceeds the debt-equity ratio (2.0) by 1.0. In general, the following relationship prevails:

$$\text{Equity multiplier} = \text{Debt-equity ratio} + 1.0$$

The balance sheet for Cert Company bears out this relationship (1.89 = 0.89 + 1.0). *Note that the equity multiplier less 1.0 equals the debt-equity ratio, the debt owed for each $1 of common equity.*

Current and Long-Term Debt Ratios

Current debt normally costs less than long-term debt, but it creates more risk. The additional risk springs from two sources. With most long-term debt (except when it has a **floating interest rate**), a company locks in the interest rate for a

floating interest rate

Interest rate on debt changes (floats) with a specified market rate.

[11] Note that (1 − Total debt ratio) equals common equity divided by total assets. Thus the debt-equity ratio can be expressed as:

$$\text{Debt-equity ratio} = \frac{\text{Total debt ratio}}{\text{Common equity/Total assets}}$$

$$= \frac{\text{Total debt/Total assets}}{\text{Common equity/Total assets}}$$

Total assets divide out, leaving total debt divided by common equity, which is the debt-equity ratio. The following equation converts the debt-equity ratio to the total debt ratio:

$$\text{Total debt ratio} = \frac{\text{Debt-equity ratio}}{1 + \text{Debt-equity ratio}}$$

FIGURE 15.2

Relationships among the Total Debt Ratio, Debt-Equity Ratio, and Equity Multiplier

The total debt ratio, debt-equity ratio, and equity multiplier are equivalent measures of total debt usage. Each ratio is mathematically linked to the other two.

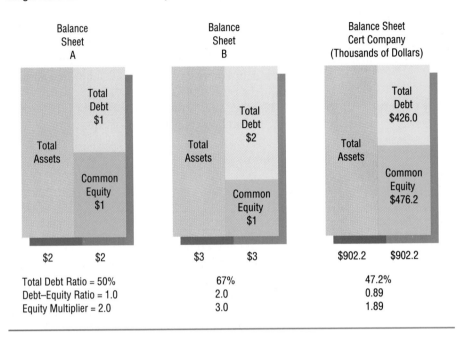

		Balance Sheet Cert Company (Thousands of Dollars)
Total Debt Ratio = 50%	67%	47.2%
Debt–Equity Ratio = 1.0	2.0	0.89
Equity Multiplier = 2.0	3.0	1.89

long period of time. With current debt, future interest costs are uncertain. In the case of accounts payable from trade credit, future credit terms are uncertain. Current debt carries with it a *refinancing risk* (roll-over risk). Bankers may reevaluate the company as having become too risky to receive another loan, or they may increase interest rates. Major suppliers may put the company on a C.O.D. payment basis.

Because of the added risks of current debt, it should be analyzed separately from long-term debt. The relevant ratios for Cert Company in 19X9 are as follows:

$$\text{Current debt ratio} = \frac{\text{Current liabilities}}{\text{Total assets}}$$

$$= \frac{\$116,000}{\$902,200}$$

$$= 0.129, \text{ or } 12.9\%$$

$$\text{Long-term debt ratio} = \frac{\text{Long-term debt}}{\text{Total assets}}$$

$$= \frac{\$310,000}{\$902,200}$$

$$= 0.343, \text{ or } 34.3\%$$

The sum of the percentages (12.9% + 34.3%) for current and long-term debt ratios equals the percentage for the total debt ratio (47.2%). By breaking total debt into its parts, you can analyze the trends of the parts and their comparisons with industry averages.[12]

Coverage Ratios

coverage ratio
Earnings per dollar of financing payments.

Coverage ratios contain only income statement items and refer to the number of times a company's earnings exceed its financing payments. Large ratio values mean that a company's earnings easily cover its payments. Low ratio values mean that small decreases in earnings will cause earnings to become smaller than the payments.

times-interest-earned ratio
Earnings before interest and taxes per dollar of interest expense.

The coverage of interest expense is measured by the **times-interest-earned ratio,** which equals earnings before interest and taxes (EBIT) divided by interest expense:

$$\text{Times interest earned} = \frac{\text{EBIT}}{\text{Interest expense}}$$

$$= \frac{\$90,000}{\$18,000}$$

$$= 5.00$$

Cert Company covered its interest expense 5.00 times in fiscal year 19X9; the company had $5.00 in EBIT per dollar of interest expense. EBIT could have shrunk 80 percent (from $90,000 to $18,000) before leaving interest expense uncovered. Interest coverage is part of the debt management ratios because it is evidence of a company's ability to meet the fixed cost of its debt. Generally, companies with large debt ratios have small times-interest-earned ratios.

fixed charge coverage ratio
Earnings available to pay fixed financing charges per dollar of fixed charges.

The **fixed charge coverage ratio** is a more comprehensive coverage measure in that it includes lease payments as a fixed financing charge. Companies may lease (rent) some assets long term instead of borrowing to buy them. Therefore the fixed charge coverage treats lease payments like interest expense:

$$\text{Fixed charge coverage} = \frac{\text{EBIT} + \text{Lease payments}}{\text{Interest expense} + \text{Lease payments}}$$

$$= \frac{\$90,000 + \$12,000}{\$18,000 + \$12,000}$$

$$= \frac{\$102,000}{\$30,000}$$

$$= 3.40$$

Cert Company covered its fixed charges 3.40 times in fiscal year 19X9; the company had $3.40 available to pay $1 of fixed charges. Adding lease payments to EBIT produces an earnings figure before both interest and lease payments have been paid. This figure is the one covering a company's interest and lease payments.

---

[12] Additional insight into current debt is provided by the *average payment period,* which focuses on accounts payable. Average payment period is the number of days, on average, for a company to pay its accounts payable:

$$\frac{\text{Average payment}}{\text{period}} = \frac{\text{Accounts payable}}{\text{Average daily credit purchases}}$$

When information on average daily credit purchases is not available, analysts use the following proxy for it: annual cost of goods sold divided by 365 days. Annual cost of goods sold is assumed to equal annual credit purchases, which is a good assumption if beginning inventory equals ending inventory.

The preceding coverage ratios have two shortcomings: (1) They use earnings in the numerator instead of cash flow, and (2) they ignore other fixed financing charges in the denominator. To remedy the first shortcoming, some analysts use operating cash flow, as calculated in Chapter 8, instead of earnings before interest and taxes. To remedy the second shortcoming, some analysts include not only interest expense and lease payments but also principal repayments and preferred-stock dividends. Because principal repayments (and preferred-stock dividends) come from after-tax earnings, analysts divide them by 1 minus the company's tax rate to find their equivalent before-tax amounts. For example, to repay a $100,000 loan principal requires $166,667 [$100,000/(1 − 0.40)] in before-tax earnings for a company in the 40 percent tax bracket. Although not usually available to outsiders, a company's cash budget provides an even broader assessment than the preceding ratios of how well a company can meet its fixed financing charges.

Coverage ratios coupled with debt ratios enable the analyst to assess a company's debt management. The debt ratios (from the balance sheet) illustrate the way in which the company finances its assets. The coverage ratios (from the income statement) show how readily the company can meet its fixed financing charges.

LIQUIDITY RATIOS

A company holds liquid assets to meet its approaching obligations. Liquid assets represent the company's potential to discharge current liabilities. Highly liquid companies have a large proportion of liquid assets compared with their current liabilities. Two widely used measures of liquidity are the current ratio and the quick ratio.

The *current ratio* measures current assets per dollar of current liabilities. It indicates the extent to which current assets can meet the claims of short-term creditors—a company's most pressing claims. The current ratio is calculated as follows:

$$\text{Current ratio} = \frac{\text{Current assets}}{\text{Current liabilities}}$$
$$= \frac{\$522,200}{\$116,000}$$
$$= 4.50$$

At year-end 19X9 Cert Company had $4.50 in current assets per dollar of current liabilities. Cert is a highly liquid company; if it becomes necessary, Cert could readily satisfy all of its short-term debt from current assets. As with any going concern, however, it is not likely that Cert will be put to the test of paying its current liabilities all at once. Still, the current ratio indicates the ability to do so.

A trade-off exists between liquidity and expected profitability (see Chapter 11). Financial managers view excessive liquidity as an investment in unproductive assets. Excessive liquidity depresses the total asset turnover (Net sales/Total assets) and, in turn, the return on total assets (and on common equity). Extremely low liquidity, however, is a signal that the company may have trouble paying its

Average Ratio Values for Ten U.S. Industries

Does the public have an accurate idea of the average after-tax profit margin in corporate America? Evidently not, judging by responses to recent surveys by Opinion Research Corporation, which indicate that the public's estimate of the typical manufacturers' after-tax profit margin is in the

30 percent to 40 percent range. The actual margin is more like 5 percent.

Seasoned bankers and other analysts learn—by experience— reasonable ballpark values for financial ratios. Having such values in mind is helpful when perusing financial statements in

the absence of industry averages. The accompanying table of financial ratios will help you to get a feel for reasonable ratio values, and studying the table will help you to avoid gross misconceptions about financial ratios.

Industry	ROE	ATM	TATO	EM	ACP	ITO	CR	QR
Coal mining services	47.0%	8.9%	2.4 x	2.2 x	32.6 days	67.2 x	1.8 x	1.3 x
Cotton agriculture	20.4	8.5	1.5	1.6	13.7	5.7	1.7	0.9
Crude oil production	12.6	10.6	0.7	1.7	70.5	20.9	4.0	1.2
Department stores	3.5	1.6	1.3	1.7	44.5	1.8	3.1	1.0
Frozen dessert manufacturers	24.8	5.1	2.7	1.8	23.6	8.9	2.0	1.0
Hardware stores	10.4	2.9	2.0	1.8	21.6	2.5	2.8	0.8
Meat packing plants	13.2	1.1	6.3	1.9	14.7	28.9	2.0	1.3
Optical goods stores	40.0	6.5	2.8	2.2	14.7	4.0	1.8	0.8
Taxicab companies	13.1	2.5	2.5	2.1	30.9	224.4	1.4	1.1
Travel agencies	44.1	2.7	8.6	1.9	11.9	782.2	1.9	1.7

Note: ROE: Return on Equity; ATM: After-Tax Margin; TATO: Total Asset Turnover; EM: Equity Multiplier; ACP: Average Collection Period; ITO: Inventory Turnover; CR: Current Ratio; QR: Quick Ratio.

Source: Industry Norms and Key Business Ratios 1991–1992, Dun & Bradstreet, various pages.

bills. Prudent financial management calls for moderate liquidity, trending upward for highly levered companies and downward for conservatively financed companies.

The second measure of liquidity recognizes that not all current assets have the same liquidity. Cash, marketable securities, and accounts receivable are more liquid than inventory. Cash is completely liquid, the conversion of marketable securities to cash takes little time, and accounts receivable are one step away— collection—from cash. Inventory, on the other hand, is two steps away from cash—sales and collection. Thus the **quick ratio** (also called the *acid test ratio*) excludes inventory from its calculation and shows the cash and near-cash assets per dollar of current liabilities:

quick ratio

Cash and near-cash assets per dollar of current liabilities.

$$\text{Quick ratio} = \frac{\text{Current assets} - \text{Inventory}}{\text{Current liabilities}}$$

$$= \frac{\$522,200 - \$250,000}{\$116,000}$$

$$= 2.35$$

Cert Company's quick assets (near to cash) are 2.35 times its current liabilities; the company has $2.35 in quick assets for each dollar of current liabilities.[13] Despite the penalty placed on its inventory by the quick ratio, Cert still looks highly liquid.[14] A quick ratio of 1.0 indicates that a company's most liquid assets exactly equal its current liabilities. Many analysts use 1.0 as their rule of thumb for a satisfactory quick ratio.

Despite the emphasis on the current and quick ratios, you should remember that companies pay bills with cash. Liquidity exists only when a company has cash available to pay a bill at the moment payment is due. Thus the analyst should check a company's cash balance and marketable securities in addition to its current and quick ratios when assessing liquidity.

ASSESSING OVERALL FINANCIAL PERFORMANCE

Ralph Waldo Emerson said, "The value of a principle is the number of things it will explain." We could benefit from a guiding principle to interpret the mosaic created by the diverse groups of financial ratios: profitability, asset management, debt management, and liquidity. Fortunately, there are two related models that bring order to financial ratios: (1) The Du Pont model ties together profitability and asset management. (2) The extended Du Pont model ties together profitability, asset management, and debt management. Liquidity is handled outside of the models.

Du Pont Model (ROA)

Du Pont model

Equation showing ROA as the profit margin times total asset turnover.

Du Pont Corporation management developed a method for monitoring the profitability of the company's various divisions. The **Du Pont model** is an equation that relates profit margin and total asset turnover to return on assets:

$$\frac{\text{Return on}}{\text{total assets}} = \frac{\text{After-tax}}{\text{profit margin}} \times \frac{\text{Total asset}}{\text{turnover}}$$

The after-tax profit margin and total asset turnover demonstrate that this equation holds true:

$$\frac{\text{Return on}}{\text{total assets}} = \frac{\text{Earnings after taxes}}{\text{Net sales}} \times \frac{\text{Net sales}}{\text{Total assets}}$$

Net sales cancel out, leaving earnings after taxes divided by total assets, or the return on total assets (ROA). The equation applied to Cert Company for 19X9 is:

---

[13] The quick ratio may also be calculated by totaling its components:

$$\text{Quick ratio} = \frac{\text{Cash} + \text{Marketable securities} + \text{Accounts receivable}}{\text{Current liabilities}}$$

This calculation excludes not only inventory but also miscellaneous current assets such as prepaid expenses (for example, prepaid rent and insurance), which have low liquidity.

[14] Occasionally a company is encountered whose inventory is financially liquid and which therefore should not be penalized by use of the quick-ratio measure. Consider, for example, gasoline distributors and fuel oil dealers. Both types of companies can easily sell their inventories near market prices. Because of the uncertainties in collecting accounts receivable, some participants in these industries argue that their inventories are more liquid than their receivables. In cases of this type, the analyst should focus more on the current ratio and less on the quick ratio for assessing company liquidity.

$$\text{Return on total assets} = \frac{\$61,200}{\$840,000} \times \frac{\$840,000}{\$902,200}$$

$$= 0.073 \times 0.93$$

$$= 0.068, \text{ or } 6.8\%$$

Cert earns $0.068 after taxes for each dollar invested in total assets, the same figure calculated earlier in the chapter ($61,200/$902,200 = 6.8 percent).

Why should we take the indirect route of multiplying two ratios together to calculate return on assets when we can simply divide after-tax earnings by total assets? The reason is that the Du Pont equation breaks the profitability measure ROA into two determinant parts. Multiplying profit margin times total asset turnover enables us to find the reason for a company's low or high ROA.

EXAMPLE

Comparing Cert Company with its industry averages reveals that its profit margin is healthy but its turnover is not:

Cert Company: $0.073 \times 0.93 = 0.068$, or 6.8%

Industry average: $0.061 \times 1.67 = 0.102$, or 10.2%

Cert's problem, and the reason for its failure to achieve the industry average ROA, lies in asset management. Pursuing the problem would require investigation of the turnovers of accounts receivable, inventory, and fixed assets to assess whether or not Cert has an excessive investment in one of these assets.

Combinations of profit margins and total asset turnovers vary widely among industries. For example, retail grocery chains have low profit margins and high turnovers, but telephone companies have high profit margins and low turnovers.

Although in many cases the analyst is interested in after-tax return on assets, the before-tax figure is obtained easily by inserting the before-tax margin into the equation. In either case the ROA figure reflects company profitability on all resources used in the business. Because total assets equals liabilities plus shareholder equity, some analysts prefer to use earnings available to all capital contributors. In this case the EBIT margin (EBIT/Net sales) is inserted into the equation to calculate the earning power ratio. Each of these variations has merit. For illustrative purposes in the following paragraphs, however, we use after-tax ROA, a figure of considerable interest to both shareholders and company managers because it discloses the company's ability to pay dividends.

Extended Du Pont Model (ROE)

extended Du Pont model Equation showing ROE as the profit margin times total asset turnover times the equity multiplier.

The Du Pont model above combines a profitability measure with an asset management measure to calculate return on assets. The **extended Du Pont model** adds the debt management dimension to calculate return on common equity (ROE):

$$\begin{array}{c}\text{Return on} \\ \text{common equity}\end{array} = \begin{array}{c}\text{After-tax} \\ \text{profit margin}\end{array} \times \begin{array}{c}\text{Total asset} \\ \text{turnover}\end{array} \times \begin{array}{c}\text{Equity} \\ \text{multiplier}\end{array}$$

$$\frac{\text{Earnings after taxes}}{\text{Common equity}} = \frac{\text{Earnings after taxes}}{\text{Net sales}} \times \frac{\text{Net sales}}{\text{Total assets}} \times \frac{\text{Total assets}}{\text{Common equity}}$$

Note that net sales and total assets cancel out, leaving earnings after taxes divided by common equity (ROE). ROE relates to ROA in the following way:

$$ROE = ROA \times Equity\ multiplier$$

ROA equals after-tax profit margin times total asset turnover, and substituting these two ratios for ROA yields ROE.[15]

Applying the extended Du Pont model to Cert Company for 19X9 yields the following results:

$$\frac{Return\ on}{common\ equity} = \frac{\$61,200}{\$840,000} \times \frac{\$840,000}{\$902,200} \times \frac{\$902,200}{\$476,200}$$

$$= 0.073 \quad \times \quad 0.93 \quad \times \quad 1.89$$

$$= 0.129,\ or\ 12.9\%$$

Cert earns $0.129 after taxes for each dollar of common equity. Note that return on assets (0.068) times the equity multiplier (1.89) also equals ROE (0.129).

To illustrate the usefulness of the extended Du Pont model, compare the component ratios for Cert Company with industry averages:

Cert Company: $0.073 \times 0.93 \times 1.89 = 0.129$, or 12.9%

Industry average: $0.061 \times 1.67 \times 2.31 = 0.235$, or 23.5%

Cert earns substantially less for its shareholders (12.9 percent) than does the industry generally (23.5 percent). Cert's relatively low return on equity occurs despite its higher-than-average after-tax profit margin. The reason for Cert's lower ROE is that its total asset turnover and equity multiplier are smaller than those of the industry. The smaller turnover is a signal that Cert has excessive and unprofitable investments in some assets. The smaller equity multiplier suggests that Cert is more conservatively financed than the industry average, resulting in two consequences: (1) lower financial risk and (2) lower potential returns on common equity. Even if Cert's equity multiplier equaled the industry's (2.31), however, its ROE would still be only 15.7 percent.

Figure 15.3 depicts the extended Du Pont model as a flowchart. The flowchart performs the same function as the preceding equations but does so pictorially: It shows the financial ratios that determine ROE (and ROA). The upper part of the flowchart is based on data from the income statement; the middle part is based on both the income statement and the balance sheet; and the lower part is based only on the balance sheet. To illustrate, net sales less all costs including income taxes equals earnings after taxes, which divided by net sales equals after-tax profit margin; after-tax profit margin times total asset turnover equals ROA, which times the equity multiplier equals ROE.

Although Figure 15.3 contains only one year's data for Cert Company, typical use of the flowchart would proceed as follows:

1. Place in each box the latest three years of data for the company being analyzed.

2. Place in each box the industry averages.

3. Compare the company to the industry benchmarks over time.

---

[15] An alternative way to view the extended Du Pont model is as follows:

$$ROE = ROA\ (Debt\text{-}equity\ ratio + 1)$$

FIGURE 15.3

Extended Du Pont Model: Cert Company

The flowchart for Cert Company shows the ratios that determine return on assets (ROA) and return on equity (ROE):

$$ROA = 0.073 \times 0.93 = 0.068, \text{ or } 6.8\%$$

$$ROE = 0.073 \times 0.93 \times 1.89 = 0.129, \text{ or } 12.9\%$$

Expressing ROA and ROE in terms of other financial ratios shows the reasons for inferior or superior profitability performance.

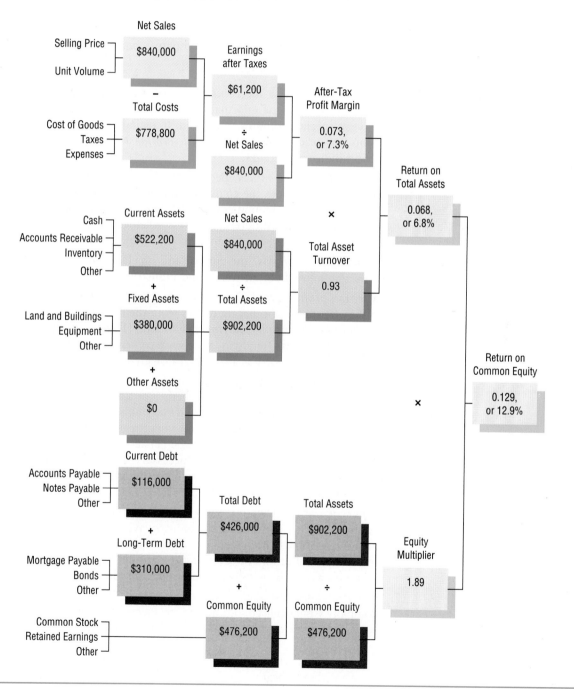

Using the flowchart in this way, the analyst conducts both a trend analysis and an industry comparative analysis.

A PROCEDURE FOR FINANCIAL-STATEMENT ANALYSIS

Experienced analysts normally settle into routines for analyzing a company's financial performance, and there are probably as many routines as there are analysts. Moreover, one procedure for analysis is as good as another if each unlocks the story embedded in the financial statements.

A useful procedure for analyzing a company's financial statements consists of the following steps:

1. *Familiarization with the company.* Look over the company's financial statements for general information. Note company size, product mix, fiscal year, special footnotes, and so on. If available, obtain financial statements for prior years. *Carefully determine the relevant industry* and obtain industry averages.

2. *Extended Du Pont model.* Begin with this model, and apply it to each year of data for both the company and the industry. Compare the company's return on common equity with that of the industry, and identify the reasons for the differences. Assess whether the company has problems in profitability, asset management, or debt management.

3. *Liquidity position.* Use the current and quick ratios to assess the company's liquidity. Look at trends and industry comparisons.

4. *After-tax profit margin.* Determine whether or not the company's trend in the after-tax profit margin differs from the industry average. *Develop a common-size income statement.* Examine (1) gross profit margin, (2) EBIT margin, and (3) individual expense percentages, if available. Trends in expenses expressed as percentages of gross profit may also point to areas needing expense control.

5. *Total asset turnover.* Determine whether or not the company's trend in the total asset turnover differs from the industry average. Examine the current asset turnover and the fixed asset (or noncurrent asset) turnover, followed by the subsidiary turnovers: (1) accounts receivable, (2) inventory, and (3) other asset items, if necessary. Low turnovers may reflect excessive investment in assets, which creates added expense and reduces profit margins.

6. *Equity multiplier.* Determine whether or not the company's trend in the equity multiplier differs from the industry average. Examine current debt and long-term debt as percentages of total assets. Also analyze the times-interest-earned ratio. For safety, an exceptionally high debt ratio should be accompanied by a solid liquidity position (Step 3).

7. *Interpretation.* List several key observations. Write a narrative of the company's financial condition and performance, covering *profitability, asset management, debt management, and liquidity.*

This procedure suggests that, after gaining general familiarity with the company, the analyst should begin with the extended Du Pont model to get an overview of profitability, asset management, and debt management. Step 3 adds the fourth financial dimension, liquidity. Steps 4, 5, and 6 probe each of the three basic determinants of return on common equity. *Essentially, asking the right questions until the cause of a problem is discovered captures the underlying spirit of the analysis.* The seventh and last step requires interpretation of the findings developed in the first six steps.

To illustrate the dissection of the after-tax profit margin, consider the case of a wholesaler or retailer. The company's profit margin is defined as follows:

$$\text{After-tax profit margin} = \frac{\text{Earnings after taxes}}{\text{Net sales}}$$

$$= \frac{\text{Net sales} - \text{Cost of goods sold} - \text{Expenses}}{\text{Net sales}}$$

Net sales equal the number of units sold times the selling price per unit, and cost of goods sold equals the number of units purchased (and sold) times the buying price per unit. Thus the profit margin can be expanded as follows:[16]

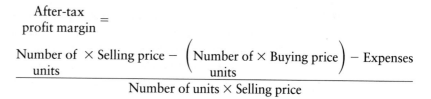

The equation simplifies to:

$$\underset{\text{profit margin}}{\text{After-tax}} = 1.0 - \frac{\text{Buying price}}{\text{Selling price}} - \frac{\text{Expenses}}{\text{Number of units} \times \text{Selling price}}$$

The properties of this last equation reveal the following possible reasons for a low after-tax profit margin:

1. Buying price per unit sold is too high. Cost of goods sold is excessive because of high unit prices paid to suppliers.
2. Selling price per unit is too low. Stiff competition or poor pricing policies lead to a low price per unit sold and low sales revenue.
3. Expenses are out of control and take too large a portion of sales revenues.
4. The company is operating below capacity, selling too few units for its size. Management of companies operating below capacity needs to consider trimming fixed costs.

The gross profit margin provides information on the first two reasons for a low after-tax profit margin:

---

[16]The general principles developed here apply to manufacturers as well. Simply replace *buying price* with *unit cost*. Strictly speaking, the equation represents a one-product company. The equation can be transformed to represent a multiproduct company by using summation signs.

$$\text{Gross profit margin} = \frac{\text{Gross profit}}{\text{Net sales}}$$

$$= \frac{\text{Net sales} - \text{Cost of goods sold}}{\text{Net sales}}$$

$$= 1.0 - \frac{\text{Cost of goods sold}}{\text{Net sales}}$$

$$= 1.0 - \frac{\text{Number of units} \times \text{Buying price}}{\text{Number of units} \times \text{Selling price}}$$

$$= 1.0 - \frac{\text{Buying price}}{\text{Selling price}}$$

A low gross profit margin indicates that an imbalance exists between buying prices and selling prices. It does not say whether one, the other, or both are out of line. Data beyond the financial statements are needed to resolve the question further.

In the pursuit of what makes the after-tax profit margin too low, you discover the importance of expressing expense items as percentages of net sales. Sharp upward trends in expense percentages that exceed industry averages suggest that excessive expenses are the cause of the below-average profit margin. A company operating below capacity typically has both a low fixed asset turnover and excessive expenses.

SCOPE AND LIMITATIONS OF FINANCIAL RATIOS

Francis Bacon observed, "If you give a man a hammer, everything becomes a nail." Whether someone wields a shovel, swings a tennis racket, or uses financial ratios, there always exists the danger of the tool ruling the person rather than the person ruling the tool.

Despite their usefulness in assessing and projecting a company's financial condition and performance, ratios should not be employed mechanically. Common sense must prevail. A general familiarity with the financial statements themselves enables an analyst to get a feel for a company and to use common sense before applying the ratios.

EXAMPLE

Consider the current ratio calculated from the following balance sheet:

Cash	$ 200	Current liabilities	$ 300
Other current assets	400	Long-term debt	200
Fixed assets	400	Common equity	500
Total assets	$1,000	Total claims	$1,000

The company's current ratio equals 2.0 ($600/$300). If the company uses $200 of its cash to pay $200 of its current liabilities, its current ratio increases to 4.0 ($400/$100). Mechanically interpreted, the change in the current ratio indicates that liquidity has improved. If the company has no cash left, however, the company's liquidity has been severely impaired.

INTERNATIONAL DIMENSIONS

Beware of Foreign Financial Statements

Analysts should proceed carefully as they interpret the financial statements of foreign companies. The regulations for financial reporting vary substantially from country to country, and most do not meet the disclosure requirements of the United States.

A West German truck company reported that its profits had declined. The company chairman said, however, that profits actually had risen substantially, allowing it to set aside $40 million. This difference does not appear in the company's annual report, nor could an analyst calculate it from the reported figures. Yet the company's reporting satisfies German requirements.

Most foreign countries do not require consolidated financial statements. Thus when one part of a business suffers a loss, it can be omitted from the parent's financial

statements. For example, tire-maker Pirelli of Italy does not provide information on its foreign subsidiaries, although it operates in 16 countries.

Fortunately, the trend is toward more factual and consistent reporting. Some countries, such as Great Britain, the Netherlands, and Japan, require detailed financial disclosure. The European Community is developing a new body of accounting regulations. More foreign countries are beginning to adopt international accounting standards, which are based on the generally accepted accounting principles (GAAP) in the United States.

Daunting challenges remain, however, in the analysis of a multinational company's financial statements—even those based on GAAP. For example, net losses on assets and liabilities denominated in foreign currency are subtracted from shareholder equity but do not affect the company's reported profits. Thus a company might report profits when it is actually losing money because of foreign-exchange losses.

Distortions in a multinational's financial statements often occur because of management's attempts to reduce taxes and to avoid foreign-exchange losses. By charging excessive prices to a subsidiary operating in a country with high tax rates, management reduces company-wide taxes but also causes the subsidiary's profitability to appear unduly low. In an attempt to avoid losses on inventory denominated in a depreciating currency, management reduces the subsidiary's inventory, which increases the inventory turnover ratio. In contrast, management may substantially increase the inventory of a subsidiary operating in a country with appreciating currency, which reduces inventory turnover.

The foregoing factors, and others such as the effects of hyper-inflation, introduce complexities into the analysis of financial statements. Despite the improvements in disclosure of information, substantial challenges still confront the analyst. Modifying the maxim *buyer beware*, we say *analyst beware!*

Judgments concerning differences between company and industry ratios should be made with care. Because after-tax profit margins are often small numbers, they require particular caution. A naive analyst might erroneously conclude that a company with a 3 percent margin performs about the same as the industry with a 4.5 percent margin. Yet the company's margin is only two-thirds (0.03/ 0.045) the industry average. For a company with net sales equaling $20,000,000, an additional 1.5 percentage points means $300,000 in after-tax earnings, which is significant. In general, to judge the significance of differences in ratios, the analyst should look at the implications in dollars for the company being analyzed.

The determination of "good" or "bad" financial ratios should take into consideration alternative managerial policies. For example, a large inventory turnover ratio may demonstrate efficient control over inventory; alternatively, it may point to a company that has reduced its inventory to the point of providing poor service to customers. The analyst needs to seek additional, corroborating evidence to determine how the company's inventory level affects sales. In the absence of conclusive evidence, the tone of the conclusion should be softened by stating, "One possible reason for this result. . . ."

Finally, during periods of inflation the methods companies use to value inventories and to depreciate assets substantially influence profitability as measured with financial statements. Accounting measures of profitability may differ greatly from cash flow measures of profitability. For example, return on total assets may be 10 percent based on financial statements; but after adjusting assets for replacement values (increasing the value of depreciable assets and the accompanying depreciation charges, which reduces earnings), the return on total assets may be much lower. Adjustments for gains and losses on monetary assets and liabilities would affect the return as well (see Chapter 11).

Despite these potential problems, financial-statement analysis is useful to corporate managers, suppliers, creditors, and shareholders. The analysis provides these groups with insight into a company's financial condition and performance. Moreover, it provides the basis for assessing a company's financial future.

SUMMARY

• Financial managers, suppliers, creditors, and shareholders use financial ratios developed from financial statements to analyze a company's financial condition and performance. Table 15.4 lists and defines selected financial ratios used by analysts.

• Trends in financial ratios show where a company has been and suggest where it is heading. Industry averages enable the analyst to compare the company's performance with companies in its industry. Used in combination, trend and comparative analyses enable the analyst to sort out managerial and environmental influences on the company.

• A complete analysis consists of measuring financial condition and performance with four groups of ratios:

> *Profitability ratios* measure the effectiveness of all policies and decisions.
>
> *Asset management ratios* measure the company's efficiency in using assets to generate sales.
>
> *Debt management ratios* measure how the company finances assets and its ability to service debt.
>
> *Liquidity ratios* measure the company's ability to pay short-term debts.

• Profitability ratios include (1) profit margins—earnings figures divided by sales and (2) return on investment—earnings figures divided by total assets or common equity (shareholder equity). Profit margins are included in a common-size income statement, which expresses all items as percentages of sales. Important margins include the gross profit margin, the EBIT margin, and the before-tax and after-tax margins. Return on total assets (ROA) can be calculated before and after taxes or with EBIT, which produces the earning power ratio. Return on common equity (ROE) equals earnings after taxes divided by common equity.

• Asset management ratios are called *turnovers,* measured as sales divided by a specific asset. Financial managers and other analysts calculate turnovers of total assets, current assets, fixed assets, accounts receivable, and inventory. In lieu of sales, cost of goods sold is often used to calculate inventory turnover. Turnovers decrease as the investment in assets increases disproportionately to sales.

TABLE 15.4		**Summary of Selected Financial Ratios**	
Ratio	**Calculation**	**Ratio**	**Calculation**
Profitability		*Asset Management*	
Return on common equity	$\dfrac{\text{EAT}}{\text{Common equity}}$	Total asset turnover	$\dfrac{\text{Net sales}}{\text{Total assets}}$
Return on total assets	$\dfrac{\text{EAT}}{\text{Total assets}}$	Current asset turnover	$\dfrac{\text{Net sales}}{\text{Current assets}}$
Earning power ratio	$\dfrac{\text{EBIT}}{\text{Total assets}}$	Fixed asset turnover	$\dfrac{\text{Net sales}}{\text{Fixed assets}}$
Gross profit margin	$\dfrac{\text{Gross profit}}{\text{Net sales}}$	Accounts receivable turnover	$\dfrac{\text{Credit sales}}{\text{Accounts receivable}}$
EBIT margin	$\dfrac{\text{EBIT}}{\text{Net sales}}$	Average collection period	$\dfrac{\text{Accounts receivable}}{\text{Annual credit sales/365}}$
Before-tax profit margin	$\dfrac{\text{EBT}}{\text{Net sales}}$	Inventory turnover	$\dfrac{\text{Cost of goods sold}}{\text{Inventory}}$
After-tax profit margin	$\dfrac{\text{EAT}}{\text{Net sales}}$	Days' sales in inventory	$\dfrac{365}{\text{Inventory turnover}}$
Debt Management		*Liquidity*	
Equity multiplier	$\dfrac{\text{Total assets}}{\text{Common equity}}$	Current ratio	$\dfrac{\text{Current assets}}{\text{Current liabilities}}$
Total debt ratio	$\dfrac{\text{Total debt}}{\text{Total assets}}$	Quick ratio	$\dfrac{\text{Current assets} - \text{Inventory}}{\text{Current liabilities}}$
Current debt ratio	$\dfrac{\text{Current liabilities}}{\text{Total assets}}$		
Long-term debt ratio	$\dfrac{\text{Long-term debt}}{\text{Total assets}}$		
Times interest earned	$\dfrac{\text{EBIT}}{\text{Interest expense}}$		

• Debt management ratios consist of (1) debt ratios measured with balance sheet items and (2) coverage ratios measured with income statement items. Total debt as a percentage of total assets equals current plus long-term debt as percentages of total assets. Times-interest earned (EBIT/Interest expense) is a coverage ratio. This coverage ratio and others measure a company's ability to pay its financing payments.

• The current and quick ratios measure liquidity. The current ratio relates current assets to current liabilities; the quick ratio relates only the most liquid current assets (excluding inventory) to current liabilities. Both ratios are measures of company potential for meeting short-term financial obligations.

• The Du Pont model expresses return on total assets as the product of two ratios, a margin and a turnover:

$$\text{ROA} = \frac{\text{After-tax}}{\text{profit margin}} \times \frac{\text{Total asset}}{\text{turnover}}$$

The extended Du Pont model expresses return on common equity as the product of three ratios:

$$\text{ROE} = \frac{\text{After-tax}}{\text{profit margin}} \times \frac{\text{Total asset}}{\text{turnover}} \times \frac{\text{Equity}}{\text{multiplier}}$$

This model provides an overview of the company's profitability, asset management, and debt management, and it conveniently presents three determinants of ROE.

• A useful procedure for analyzing financial statements includes these steps: (1) Review the company's financial statements, (2) apply the extended Du Pont model, (3) assess company liquidity, (4) probe each ROE determinant in the extended Du Pont model to discover reasons for trends and differences from industry averages, and (5) list observations and interpret results, linking where possible the corroborating evidence from different financial ratios.

• Using financial ratios requires the understanding of their definition, calculation, and interpretation. Learning definitions and calculations requires diligence and study. The interpretation of ratios, however, takes practice to gain experience in their application.

Key Terms

profitability	gross profit margin	total debt ratio
trend analysis	EBIT margin	equity multiplier
return on common equity (ROE)	before-tax profit margin	floating interest rate
industry comparative analysis	after-tax profit margin	coverage ratio
profitability ratios	earnings per share (EPS)	times-interest-earned ratio
asset management ratios	dividends per share (DPS)	fixed charge coverage ratio
debt management ratios	earning power ratio	quick ratio
liquidity ratios	earnings yield	Du Pont model
profit margin	total asset turnover	extended Du Pont model
return on investment	days' sales in inventory	
common-size income statement	fixed asset turnover	

Questions

15.1. What are the major differences between an income statement and a balance sheet?

15.2. What additional information does industry comparative analysis provide to trend analysis?

15.3. Identify and describe the four basic groups of financial ratios used in the analysis of a company's financial performance and condition.

15.4. *(Library assignment)* Collect financial data on International Business Machines (IBM) for the calculation of the following financial ratios: (a) after-tax profit margin, (b) total asset turnover, and (c) equity multiplier. What fourth ratio can you calculate from the preceding three ratios?

15.5. Suppose you overhear the following exchange:

Student: In my opinion the company should use some of its $3,600,000 retained earnings to increase salaries and dividends.

Professor: I'm not sure that I understand your proposal.

Student: In fairness, the company should use half, or $1,800,000. Just write checks in proportion to each employee's salary and each stockholder's number of shares.

Professor: I think we may have a conceptual problem here.

Does the student confuse cash with retained earnings? Explain your answer.

15.6. One of your friends tells you, "Learn what margins and turnovers are and you have learned about ten ratios." Explain this advice by pointing out the important role of sales in each type of ratio.

15.7. What is the relationship between the Du Pont model and the extended Du Pont model?

15.8. "I don't get it," Steve comments on the performance of his mother's company. "The company had a much higher after-tax profit margin than its competition, but the competition made a much higher return on assets." Steve mutters, "I better check my calculations." Assume that Steve's calculations are correct and explain how these company results could occur.

15.9. Can a company have an inventory turnover that is too large? Too small? Explain your answers.

15.10. *True or false:* The earning power ratio shows the profitability of company assets irrespective of how they are financed. Explain your answer.

15.11. Which of the following measures probably reflects effective management of an asset or group of assets by a company relative to other companies in the same industry? Explain your choice.

a. High number of days' sales uncollected relative to the industry average.
b. High turnover of accounts receivable relative to the industry average.
c. High number of days' sales in inventory relative to the industry average.
d. Low turnover of total assets relative to the industry average.

15.12. How does the extended Du Pont model combine income and balance sheet items to help management ask meaningful questions about a company's performance?

15.13. "There are simply too many distortions in accounting data for meaningful interpretation," laments Jack. "Like what?" inquires Ellen. "Like all kinds of things," says Jack. "Differing depreciation methods, differing inventory valuation methods, differing accounting for cash discounts—the list goes on and on." "Maybe you should become a carpenter," Ellen jabs with a smirk.

Respond to Jack's lament. Persuade him that the world of financial ratios is not so bleak as he thinks.

Strategy Problem

Selected industry average ratios for Clayton Products are as follows:

After-tax margin: 1.9%	Gross margin: 11.0%
Total asset turnover: 7.0	Expenses/Net sales: 7.1%
Equity multiplier: 2.1	Current asset turnover: 12.6
Current ratio: 2.1	Fixed asset turnover: 11.5
Current debt ratio: 25.0%	

Analyze the financial strengths and weaknesses of Clayton Products using the procedure outlined in the chapter. Begin with the extended Du Pont model, then assess the liquidity position. Next, examine the determinants of return on equity. Finally, interpret the results of the analysis. Clayton Products' financial statements are shown below.

Balance Sheet, December 31, 19X1

Current assets	$ 7,500,600	Current liabilities	$ 6,000,000
Fixed assets	6,801,000	Long-term debt	1,300,800
		Total equity	7,000,800
Total assets	$14,301,600	Total claims on assets	$14,301,600

Income Statement for 12 Months Ending December 31, 19X1

		Percentage of Sales
Net sales	$81,000,000	100.0%
Less cost of goods sold	70,000,000	86.4
Gross profit	$11,000,000	13.6
Less expenses	7,800,000	9.6
Earnings before interest and taxes	$ 3,200,000	4.0
Less interest expense	130,000	0.2
Earnings before taxes	$ 3,070,000	3.8
Less taxes	1,043,800	1.3
Earnings after taxes	$ 2,026,200	2.5

Strategy

Analyze the determinants of ROE using the extended Du Pont model.

Solution

1. *Extended Du Pont Model:*

$$\frac{\text{Profit}}{\text{margin}} \times \frac{\text{Total asset}}{\text{turnover}} \times \frac{\text{Equity}}{\text{multiplier}} = \frac{\text{Return on}}{\text{common equity}}$$

Clayton: $\dfrac{\$2,026,200}{\$81,000,000} \times \dfrac{\$81,000,000}{\$14,301,600} \times \dfrac{\$14,301,600}{\$7,000,800} = \dfrac{\$2,026,200}{\$7,000,800}$

$$2.50\% \times 5.66 \times 2.04 = 28.9\%$$

Industry: $1.9\% \ \times 7.0 \ \times 2.1 \ = 27.9\%$

Clayton's return on common equity (28.9 percent) compares favorably with that of the industry (27.9 percent) because it has a higher profit margin. Clayton earns $0.025 per dollar of sales versus only $0.019 for the industry average. Its advantage with profit margin, however, is largely offset by its poor total asset turnover. Clayton generates only $5.66 in sales for each dollar of total assets, while the industry generates $7.00. Clayton earns more on its sales than is typical, but it makes fewer sales from employing its assets. Clayton's total debt usage is similar to the industry average: It owes $1.04 (equity multiplier minus 1.0) for each dollar of owner equity; the industry average is $1.10.

Assess the company's liquidity position.

2. *Liquidity Position:*

$$\text{Current ratio} = \frac{\$7,500,600}{\$6,000,000}$$

$$= 1.25$$

Clayton Products has $1.25 in current assets for each dollar of current liabilities. Compared with the industry average, 2.1, Clayton's current ratio is small. Clayton is much less liquid than is typical in its industry; its current assets cover its current liabilities but by a much smaller margin than normal.

Evaluate the company's profit margins.

3. *After-Tax Profit Margin.* Clayton's common-size income statement (percentage of sales) is presented alongside its regular income statement. The common-size statement shows that Clayton earns $0.136 in gross profit for each dollar of sales; the industry averages only $0.11. Compared with the industry, Clayton has an advantageous balance between buying prices (or production costs per unit) and selling prices. Part of this advantage is dissipated through higher expenses; Clayton's expenses take $0.096 of each sales dollar compared to $0.071 for the industry. Clayton's high gross margin more than offsets its high expense ratio, though, producing a higher-than-average after-tax profit margin, 2.5 percent.

Evaluate the company's asset turnovers.

4. *Total Asset Turnover.* Clayton earns a healthy 28.9 percent on equity because of its large profit margin (2.5 percent) and despite its small total asset turnover (5.66). If Clayton could increase its total asset turnover to the industry average (7.0), then its return on common equity would be 35.7 percent:

$$2.5\% \times 7.0 \times 2.04 = 35.7\%$$

Analysis of the individual asset turnovers identifies Clayton's problem area:

	Clayton	Industry
Current asset turnover	10.8	12.6
Fixed asset turnover	11.9	11.5

In comparison with the industry, Clayton's current asset turnover is too low. Clayton generates only $10.80 in sales per dollar of current assets, $1.80 ($12.60 − $10.80) less than that of the industry. Clayton should investigate individual current assets (for example, accounts receivable and inventory) to see which one(s) is excessive. Any reduction in current assets should be accompanied by a reduction in current liabilities in order to increase Clayton's current ratio.

Evaluate the company's debt position.

5. **Equity Multiplier.** Clayton's equity multiplier (2.04) is similar to the industry's (2.1). Despite the similarity, Clayton's current debt is excessive in comparison with the industry average (25.0%):

$$\frac{\text{Current debt}}{\text{Total assets}} = \frac{\$6,000,000}{\$14,301,600}$$

$$= 0.420, \text{ or } 42.0\%$$

If Clayton were to replace part of its current debt with long-term debt, causing its CD/TA to equal 25.0 percent, then its current debt would equal \$3,575,400 (0.25 × \$14,301,600). With this new debt level, Clayton's current ratio would improve to 2.1:

$$\text{Current ratio} = \frac{\$7,500,600}{\$3,575,400}$$

$$= 2.1$$

Also, if Clayton were to reduce its current assets to \$6,428,571 in order to increase its current asset turnover to 12.6, then its current ratio would equal 1.8 (\$6,428,571/ \$3,575,400).

Interpret the company's financial performance and condition.

6. **Summary Interpretation.** Clayton Products is a highly profitable company in a highly profitable industry. Clayton could increase its profitability even more by taking two steps: (1) Reduce expenses as a percentage of sales to the industry average (7.1 percent) and (2) increase the total asset turnover by reducing current assets. This second step should be accompanied by a reduction in current debt to prevent the company from becoming illiquid. Clayton's total debt is comparable to that of the industry, so current debt could easily be replaced by long-term debt to achieve the desired liquidity level. Currently Clayton is highly profitable, below average in asset management, solvent (assets exceed liabilities), and low in liquidity.

◆ **Demonstration Problem**

Nike Inc., originally established in Oregon, is a leader in its industry. The company designs, develops, and markets athletic footwear and apparel. Selected industry average ratios and financial statements for Nike Inc. are provided below. Your task is to analyze the financial strengths and weaknesses of this industry leader.

Industry Averages

Return on common equity: 22.3%	Noncurrent asset turnover: 7.8
After-tax profit margin: 6.2%	Average collection period: 46.5 days
Total asset turnover: 2.0	Inventory turnover: 3.3
Equity multiplier: 1.8	Current debt ratio: 30.1%
Gross profit margin: 39.2%	Long-term debt ratio: 14.1%
EBIT margin: 10.9%	Times-interest-earned ratio: 15.1
Before-tax profit margin: 10.2%	Current ratio: 2.5
Current asset turnover: 2.7	Quick ratio: 1.1

Balance Sheet, May 31, 19X1
(in Thousands of Dollars)

Cash and equivalents	$ 119,804	Accounts payable	$ 165,912
Accounts receivable	521,588	Notes payable	300,364
Inventory	586,594	Other current liabilities	162,196
Other current assets	52,274	Total current liabilities	$ 628,472
Total current assets	$1,280,260	Long-term liabilities	46,869
Noncurrent assets	428,170	Shareholder equity	1,033,089
Total assets	$1,708,430	Total claims	$1,708,430

Income Statement,
Year Ended May 31, 19X1
(in Thousands of Dollars)

Net sales	$3,003,610
Less cost of goods sold	1,850,530
Gross profit	$1,153,080
Less operating expenses	664,018
EBIT	$ 489,062
Less interest expense	27,316
Earnings before taxes	$ 461,746
Less taxes	174,700
Earnings after taxes	$ 287,046

a. Apply the extended Du Pont model to Nike and to its industry. Explain why Nike's return on equity (ROE) differs from the industry's. What are the implications of the three determinants of Nike's ROE?

b. Use the current ratio and quick ratio to assess Nike's liquidity relative to the industry's. Is Nike a reasonably liquid company? Explain.

c. Probe for the reasons that cause Nike's after-tax profit margin to differ from the industry's: (1) Develop a common-size income statement for Nike and for the industry. (2) Interpret the implications of the differences in margins between the company and the industry.

d. Probe for the reasons that cause Nike's total asset turnover to differ from the industry's: (1) Calculate five asset management ratios for Nike. (2) Interpret the implications of the differences in asset management ratios between the company and the industry.

e. Probe for the reasons that cause Nike's equity multiplier to differ from the industry's: (1) Calculate four debt management ratios for Nike. (2) Interpret the implications of the differences in debt management ratios between the company and the industry.

f. Summarize Nike's financial strengths and weaknesses.

g. *Quiz questions:* (1) What are the four basic groups of financial ratios? (2) What are *margins* and *turnovers*? (3) How does trend analysis differ from industry comparative analysis? (4) How does the Du Pont model differ from the extended Du Pont model?

Problems

Extended Du Pont model

15.1. Selected financial ratios for a company and its industry are as follows:

	Company	Industry
After-tax profit margin	1.3%	2.1%
Total asset turnover	4.2	5.6
Equity multiplier	2.1	2.0
Return on common equity	11.5%	23.5%

a. Define each of the above financial ratios.

b. Apply the extended Du Pont model to the company and to the industry.

c. Interpret the company's financial performance.

Extended Du Pont model and current ratio

15.2. Acme Oil Company's balance sheet at year-end 19X8 is as follows:

Current assets	$240,000	Current liabilities	$253,000
Fixed assets	708,000	Long-term debt	175,000
		Common equity	520,000
Total assets	$948,000		
		Total claims	$948,000

Acme earned $156,000 on $6,600,000 net sales for the year.

a. Apply the extended Du Pont model to Acme Oil.

b. Calculate Acme Oil's current ratio.

c. Despite the absence of industry averages, what financial interpretation can you give to Acme Oil?

Average collection period

15.3. Nickel Publishing has sales of $860,000 in 19X9. Of this amount $60,000 are for cash. Accounts receivable during 19X9 average $35,000. Calculate Nickel's average collection period. Comment on Nickel's position assuming the collection period within the industry averages 26 days.

Average collection period

15.4. McDonald Sheetrocking has $128,000 in total annual sales, $100,000 in credit sales, and $20,000 average accounts receivable. Management expects credit sales to increase by 10 percent during the next annual operating period, and it expects accounts receivable to increase by 20 percent.

a. What is the level of receivables before and after the sales increase?

b. Calculate the accounts receivable turnover and average collection period before and after the sales increase.

c. What are the implications of the increase in sales?

Inventory turnover

15.5. Selected information from the accounting records of Coda Company is as follows:

Cost of goods sold for 19X8	$1,200,000
Inventories at Dec. 31, 19X7	350,000
Inventories at Dec. 31, 19X8	310,000

a. What is the inventory turnover in 19X8 based on cost of goods sold and average inventory?

b. Coda has a 20 percent gross profit margin. Calculate Coda's net sales and inventory turnover in 19X8 based on net sales and average inventory.

Slim margins

15.6. Supermarket chains typically earn between $0.01 and $0.02 after taxes for each dollar of sales.

a. How is it possible for supermarkets to stay in business with such slim margins?

b. If a thief steals a $10 ham from a supermarket with a 1 percent after-tax profit margin, how many future sales dollars must the supermarket generate to cover the loss? Assume that the supermarket paid $9 for the ham and pays income taxes at a 34 percent rate. Also, the cost of the stolen ham is tax deductible.

Ratio relationships

15.7. Dunston Company has a 12 percent earning power ratio. It has $2,000,000 in sales and turns its assets over 3 times a year.

a. Calculate the dollar value of Dunston's total assets.

b. Calculate Dunston's EBIT margin.

Du Pont model

15.8. Hampton Company is a small company operating in the competitive golf equipment industry. Some of its financial ratios are:

Fixed asset turnover	5.0	Quick ratio	0.9
Total asset turnover	2.5	After-tax margin	6.5%
Total debt to total assets	40.0%	Average collection period	28 days
Current ratio	1.6		

Hampton has $400,000 in fixed assets (plant and equipment) and $200,000 in its common-stock account. Hampton's sales are $2,000,000. Using the Du Pont model, calculate the company's after-tax return on assets (ROA).

Dividends and EPS

15.9.   Roxby Company has earnings after federal and state income taxes of $252,000. It has preferred and common stock outstanding:

Number of Shares	Type	Annual Dividend per Share
40,000	Preferred stock	$4
40,000	Common stock	1

a. Calculate total dividends paid to preferred stockholders.
b. Calculate earnings available to common shareholders and earnings per share of common stock.

Weighted-average shares outstanding

15.10. For the first 8 months of 19X5 the Phina Company had 600,000 shares of common stock outstanding. On September 1 the company issued 50,000 new shares. The company's balance sheet shows that the company had the following amounts in its shareholder equity at the close of 19X5:

Common stock (650,000 shares, $1 par value)	$ 650,000
Paid-in capital in excess of par	1,250,000
Retained earnings	3,000,000
	$4,900,000

Phina's earnings available to common shareholders for 19X5 were $900,000, and the price-earnings ratio of the company's common stock at the end of 19X5 was 6.

a. Calculate the weighted-average number of shares that were outstanding in 19X5.
b. Calculate the earnings and price per share of common stock.

ROE, EPS, yield, P-E, and retained earnings

15.11. Dethero Drilling Corporation (DDC) has the following balance sheet on September 30, 19X8 (in thousands of dollars):

Cash	$ 500	Current liabilities	$ 100
Receivables	1,000	Preferred stock (20,000 shares, $15 par value)	300
Inventory	1,500	Common stock (90,000 shares, $1 par value)	90
Total current assets	$3,000	Paid-in surplus	810
Fixed assets	2,000	Retained earnings	3,700
Total assets	$5,000	Total claims	$5,000

DDC's earnings after taxes were $1,053,500 for the year ending September 30, 19X8, and it paid $30,000 in dividends to its preferred stockholders. The corporation paid 35 percent of earnings available to common shareholders as common-stock dividends. The market price of DDC's common stock is $160 per share.

a. Calculate DDC's return on common equity.
b. Calculate DDC's earnings per share of common stock.
c. Calculate DDC's earnings yield and P-E ratio.
d. Calculate DDC's retained-earnings balance on September 30, 19X7.

Trend analysis and the extended Du Pont model

15.12. McPhail Company has been in business for 25 years. As the assistant to Mr. McPhail, your task is to interpret the company's performance over the past 5 years. The only data available to you are the following:

End-of-Year Data
(in Thousands of Dollars)

Item	19X4	19X5	19X6	19X7	19X8
Net income	$ 157	$ 158	$ 180	$ 185	$ 188
Net sales	2,616	2,725	3,500	4,300	5,000
Total assets	1,308	1,520	1,933	2,621	3,995
Common equity	783	958	1,138	1,541	2,350

a. Calculate McPhail's return on equity (ROE) for each year using the extended Du Pont model.

b. Based on your answers in Part *a*, describe the trend in McPhail's ROE and the reasons for it.

Calculating financial ratios

15.13. Bunne Bakery has the following balance sheet on June 30, 19X7 (in thousands of dollars):

Current assets	$1,308	Current liabilities	$ 710
Fixed assets	607	Long-term debt	51
		Net worth	1,154
Total assets	$1,915	Total claims	$1,915

Bunne's net sales equal $21,100,000, and its earnings after taxes equal $48,760. Given this limited information, calculate as many relevant financial ratios as you can. Sort the ratios calculated into the four basic categories.

Interpreting financial statements

15.14. Federal Express Corporation provides overnight, door-to-door delivery of packages and documents through its own air-ground transportation system. The company has offices in more than 300 U.S. cities and provides international service to more than 100 countries. Selected industry averages and financial statements for Federal Express are provided below.

Industry Averages

Return on common equity: 8.4%   Average collection period: 59.8 days
After-tax profit margin: 2.4%   Inventory turnover (sales): 20.6
Total asset turnover: 1.3   Current debt ratio: 34.7%
Equity multiplier: 2.7   Long-term debt ratio: 28.5%
EBIT margin: 7.3%   Times interest earned ratio: 5.1
Current asset turnover: 2.8   Current ratio: 1.3
Noncurrent asset turnover: 2.3   Quick ratio: 1.0

Balance Sheet, May 31, 19X1
(in Thousands of Dollars)

Cash and equivalents	$ 117,692	Accounts payable	$ 466,621
Accounts receivable	924,773	Notes payable	0
Inventory	154,941	Other current liabilities	1,027,151
Other current assets	85,441	Total current liabilities	$1,493,772
Total current assets	$1,282,847	Long-term liabilities	2,510,069
Noncurrent assets	4,389,614	Shareholder equity	1,668,620
Total assets	$5,672,461	Total claims	$5,672,461

Income Statement, Year Ended May 31, 19X1
(in Thousands of Dollars)

Revenues	$7,688,296
Less operating expenses	7,465,474
EBIT	$ 222,822
Less interest expense	181,880
Earnings before taxes	$ 40,942
Less taxes	35,044
Earnings after taxes	$ 5,898

a. Apply the extended Du Pont model to Federal Express (Fed Ex) and to its industry. Interpret your findings.

b. Use the current ratio and quick ratio to assess Fed Ex's liquidity relative to the industry's.

c. Probe the reasons that cause Fed Ex's after-tax profit margin to differ from the industry's.

d. Probe the reasons that cause Fed Ex's total asset turnover to differ from the industry's.

e. Probe the reasons that cause Fed Ex's equity multiplier to differ from the industry's.

f. Summarize Fed Ex's financial strengths and weaknesses.

Interpreting financial
statements

15.15. Selected industry average ratios and financial statements for Shill Wholesale Company are given below. Analyze Shill's financial position and performance by applying the seven-step procedure outlined in the chapter.

Industry Averages

After-tax margin: 1.2%	Long-term debt/Total assets: 30%
Total asset turnover: 6.7	Gross margin: 9.0%
Equity multiplier: 2.0	Expenses/Net sales: 7.1%
Current ratio: 1.4	Current asset turnover: 12.8
Current debt/Total assets: 20%	Fixed asset turnover: 16.8

Balance Sheet, December 31, 19X8

Current assets	$ 5,321,600	Current liabilities	$ 6,218,400
Fixed assets	8,382,600	Long-term debt	382,000
		Total equity	7,103,800
Total assets	$13,704,200	Total claims on assets	$13,704,200

Income Statement for 12 Months Ending December 31, 19X8

Net sales	$74,318,270
Less cost of goods sold	65,845,990
Gross profit	$ 8,472,280
Less expenses	7,709,770
Net operating profit	$ 762,510
Less interest expense	42,000
Earnings before taxes	$ 720,510
Less taxes	311,680
Earnings after taxes	$ 408,830

Interpreting financial
statements

15.16. Industry averages and financial statements for J. R. Retailing Inc. are given below. Analyze and interpret the financial position and performance of the company by applying the seven-step procedure outlined in the chapter.

Industry Averages

After-tax profit margin: 2.4%	Gross margin: 12.0%
Total asset turnover: 5.0	EBIT margin: 4.0%
Equity multiplier: 2.2	Debt-equity ratio: 1.2
Current ratio: 1.5	Total debt ratio: 54.5%
Accounts receivable turnover: 15.0	Current debt ratio: 30.0%
Inventory turnover: 21.0	Average collection period: 24.3 days

Balance Sheet, December 31, 19X2

Assets		Liabilities and Net Worth	
Cash	$ 14,400	Accounts payable	$ 66,000
Accounts receivable	129,300	Notes payable	34,000
Inventory	147,000	Total current liabilities	$100,000
Total current assets	$290,700	Long-term debt	155,000
Fixed assets	135,000	Total debt	$255,000
		Common stock	120,000
		Retained earnings	50,700
Total assets	$425,700	Total liabilities and net worth	$425,700

Income Statement for 12 Months Ending December 31, 19X2

Net sales	$1,038,000
Cost of goods sold	931,000
Gross profit	$ 107,000
Less operating expenses	78,000
EBIT	$ 29,000
Less interest expense	11,000
EBT	18,000
Less taxes	3,060
Earnings after taxes	$ 14,940

Computer Problems

Ratio analysis—shareholder's view: template RASV

15.17. As a member of the investment club of the business school, Jane Rose has been assigned the task of analyzing Global Motors and International Motors, two giant automobile companies, and recommending which company's stock to buy. She has collected the balance sheets and income statements of the two companies for the past 3 years. Shares of each company are priced at $80. The club members are interested in a brief on the financial strengths and weaknesses of the two companies. Ms. Rose's current task is to provide an analysis of the profitability of each company using the extended Du Pont model. Additional analyses will be conducted by other club members. Based solely on Ms. Rose's analysis, which stock should she recommend to the club? Explain your answer.

Income Statements (in Millions of Dollars)

	Global Motors			International Motors		
	19X5	19X4	19X3	19X5	19X4	19X3
Sales	$98,852	$86,476	$76,447	$54,121	$53,763	$45,385
Cost of sales	81,655	70,218	60,719	44,435	43,425	37,316
Gross profit	$17,197	$16,258	$15,728	$ 9,686	$10,338	$ 8,069
Selling and adm. expenses	4,294	4,006	3,235	3,216	3,211	3,043
Depreciation	6,208	4,966	5,120	2,393	2,308	2,292
Operating income	$ 6,695	$ 7,286	$ 7,373	$ 4,077	$ 4,819	$ 2,734
Interest expense	1,065	965	1,418	447	536	568
Pre-tax profit	$ 5,630	$ 6,321	$ 5,955	$ 3,630	$ 4,283	$ 2,166
Taxes	1,630	1,805	2,223	1,115	1,376	299
Profit after taxes	$ 4,000	$ 4,516	$ 3,732	$ 2,515	$ 2,907	$ 1,867

Balance Sheets (in Millions of Dollars)

	Global Motors			International Motors		
	19X5	19X4	19X3	19X5	19X4	19X3
Cash and cash items	$ 5,114	$ 8,567	$ 6,217	$ 5,903	$ 5,944	$ 3,152
Accounts receivable	7,282	7,358	6,964	2,852	2,526	2,767
Inventories	11,860	7,788	7,619	4,859	4,861	4,900
Total current assets	$24,256	$23,713	$20,800	$13,614	$13,331	$10,819
Fixed assets	39,577	28,432	24,894	17,990	14,155	13,050
Total assets	$63,833	$52,145	$45,694	$31,604	$27,486	$23,869
Accounts payable	$ 8,567	$ 6,623	$ 4,782	$ 6,577	$ 6,190	$ 5,247
Notes payable	1,410	1,212	1,116	1,277	1,348	1,042
Accruals	12,321	9,602	9,011	4,923	4,430	4,027
Total current liabilities	$22,298	$17,437	$14,909	$12,777	$11,968	$10,316
Long-term debt	12,011	10,493	10,019	6,556	5,681	6,007
Total liabilities	$34,309	$27,930	$24,928	$19,333	$17,649	$16,323
Common equity	29,524	24,215	20,766	12,271	9,837	7,546
Total liabilities and equity	$63,833	$52,145	$45,694	$31,604	$27,486	$23,869

Ratio analysis—management's view: template RAMV

15.18. Federal Tools is a manufacturer of machine tools. Over the years the company had been losing ground to competition and was on the verge of closing. In January 19X2 a new management team took over to try to revamp the company. You have been commissioned by the board of directors to review the performance of the new management team. Income statements for 19X2, 19X3, and 19X4 and balance sheets for the years ending December 31, 19X2, 19X3, and 19X4 are available to you, as are common-size income statements and balance sheets of the industry for the same years. In 19X4 two important events took place:

1. The dollar fell sharply compared with the Japanese yen and the German mark, making imports, which had a substantial market share, much costlier. Most U.S. manufacturers raised prices significantly.
2. The market reacted sharply to the price increases and manufacturers were able to maintain sales only by offering costly low-interest loans and other promotional activities that virtually eliminated the benefit of the price increases.

Despite these events, Federal Tools neither increased its prices significantly nor embarked on costly sales promotion programs. From the common-size financial statements and ratios that the computer template calculates, provide an interpretation of the company's profitability, asset management, debt management, and liquidity. Provide a summary for the board of directors.

Income Statements

	Federal Tools			Industry (Common Size)		
	19X2	19X3	19X4	19X2	19X3	19X4
Sales	$3,232,561	$3,557,822	$4,387,230	100.0	100.0	100.0
Cost of sales	2,641,002	2,878,278	3,470,299	79.5	79.2	73.7
Gross profit	$ 591,559	$ 679,544	$ 916,931	20.5	20.8	26.3
Selling and adm. expenses	200,419	202,796	214,974	8.5	8.5	13.8
Depreciation	265,070	295,299	315,881	7.0	7.0	6.9
Operating income	$ 126,070	$ 181,449	$ 386,076	5.0	5.3	5.6
Interest expense	103,442	117,408	122,842	0.9	1.4	1.7
Pre-tax profit	$ 22,628	$ 64,041	$ 263,234	4.1	3.9	3.9
Taxes (34%)	7,694	21,774	89,500	1.4	1.3	1.3
Profit after taxes	$ 14,934	$ 42,267	$ 173,734	2.7	2.6	2.6

Balance Sheets

	Federal Tools			Industry (Common Size)		
	19X2	19X3	19X4	19X2	19X3	19X4
Cash and cash items	$ 97,135	$ 44,984	$ 100,879	7.4	8.5	7.2
Accounts receivable	1,267,380	1,355,456	1,354,947	18.2	17.7	19.0
Inventories	1,873,318	2,078,034	2,177,224	45.1	46.5	48.0
Total current assets	$3,237,833	$3,478,474	$3,633,050	70.7	72.7	74.2
Fixed assets	1,387,643	1,544,822	1,639,383	29.3	27.3	25.8
Total assets	$4,625,476	$5,023,296	$5,272,433	100.0	100.0	100.0
Accounts payable	$1,411,519	$1,522,901	$1,473,456	15.2	15.2	16.5
Notes payable	499,551	506,329	513,487	13.7	13.9	17.9
Accruals	716,949	723,459	766,894	14.6	14.5	11.6
Total current liabilities	$2,628,019	$2,752,689	$2,753,837	43.5	43.6	46.0
Long-term debt	623,455	832,564	817,319	13.8	15.0	14.6
Common equity	1,374,002	1,438,043	1,701,277	42.7	41.4	39.4
Total liabilities and equity	$4,625,476	$5,023,296	$5,272,433	100.0	100.0	100.0

Ratio analysis—creditor's view: template RACV

15.19. Ricardo Refrigeration is a manufacturer of refrigerators. From its inception 7 years ago in 19X1 until 2 years ago, the company had a steady record of growth in sales, assets, and profits. During the second half of 19X6 the company experienced a drop in demand for refrigerators. The following year, 19X7, continued to be poor and, despite intense marketing efforts that included high discounts and extended credit, sales barely increased. Inventories ballooned and the company's payments to suppliers slowed considerably.

In January 19X8 Ricardo Modigliani and his finance manager Alice Thompson were reviewing the prospects for 19X8. Mr. Modigliani anticipated a surge in demand in the coming years. He felt that production facilities needed to be expanded in order to meet future demand. He anticipated that if steps were initiated immediately, the expansion program could be completed by the middle of 19X8. By then, the company's bulging inventories could be brought down. In order to finance the expansion, he proposed to obtain a $1,000,000 loan from the company's bank. He instructed Ms. Thompson to prepare a forecast for 19X8 excluding the expansion plan and based on the following assumptions:

Increase in sales and cost of goods sold	10%
Selling and administrative expenses	11% of sales
Average collection period	45 days
Inventory (days' sales)	72
Accounts payable	75% of the 19X7 figure

Analyze the financial statements for 19X6 and 19X7 and the projected statements for 19X8. If you were the loan officer of the company's bank, would you sanction the loan? If yes, what conditions would you attach? Explain your answer.

Income Statements (in Thousands of Dollars)

	Ricardo Refrigeration			Industry (Common Size)
	19X6	19X7	19X8	
Net sales	$74,251.00	$76,140.00	$83,754.00	100.00
Cost of goods sold	60,368.00	64,444.00	70,888.00	81.00
Gross profit	$13,883.00	$11,696.00	$12,866.00	19.00
Selling and adm. expenses	7,600.00	9,089.00	9,212.00	10.00
Depreciation	666.00	820.00	950.00	1.00
Operating profit	$ 5,617.00	$ 1,787.00	$ 2,704.00	9.00
Interest expense	705.00	1,202.00	1,023.00	1.00
Pre-tax profit	$ 4,912.00	$ 585.00	$ 1,681.00	7.00
Tax at 34 percent	1,670.08	198.90	571.54	2.38
After-tax profit	$ 3,241.92	$ 386.10	$ 1,109.46	4.62
Dividends	1,252.00	150.00	600.00	
Retained earnings	$ 1,989.92	$ 236.10	$ 509.46	
Number of shares (000)	1,450	1,450	1,450	
Stock price per share	$13	$9		

Balance Sheets (in Thousands of Dollars)

	Ricardo Refrigeration			Industry (Common Size)
	19X6	19X7	19X8	
Cash	$ 1,610.00	$ 1,579.00	$ 1,600.00	3.50
Accounts receivable	7,424,00	11,804.00	10,325.00	28.00
Inventory	13,281.00	18,762.00	13,983.00	47.00
Total current assets	$22,315.00	$32,145.00	$25,908.00	78.50
Net fixed assets	6,211.00	6,506.00	7,964.00	21.50
Total assets	$28,526.00	$38,651.00	$33,872.00	100.00
Accounts payable	$ 4,224.00	$ 8,041.00	$ 6,031.00	15.00
Notes payable	2,051.00	7,331.00	3,862.00	9.00
Accruals	2,050.00	2,948.00	3,242.80	7.50
Total current liabilities	$ 8,325.00	$18,320.00	$13,135.80	31.50
Long-term debt	4,891.00	4,784.90	4,680.64	19.00
Total liabilities	$13,216.00	$23,104.90	$17,816.44	50.50
Common equity	15,310.00	15,546.10	16,055.56	49.50
Total liabilities and equity	$28,526.00	$38,651.00	$33,872.00	100.00
Quick ratio				1.00
Current ratio				2.49
Inventory turnover				6.60
Average collection period				35.00
Return on equity				17%
Debt ratio				50.5%
Times interest earned				8

Selected References

Backer, Morton, and Martin L. Gosman. "The Use of Financial Ratios in Credit Downgrade Decisions." *Financial Management,* Spring 1980: 53–56.

Bedingfield, James P., Philip M. J. Reckers, and A. J. Stagliano. "Distributions of Financial Ratios in the Commercial Banking Industry." *Journal of Financial Research,* Spring 1985: 77–81.

Chen, Kung H., and Thomas A. Shimerada. "An Empirical Analysis of Useful Financial Ratios." *Financial Management,* Spring 1981: 51–60.

Cooley, Philip L., and Le Roy D. Brooks. "Financial Analysis and Inflation." *Business and Economic Review,* October 1977: 11–16.

Findlay, M. Chapman, III, and Edward E. Williams. "Toward More Adequate Debt Service Coverage Ratios." *Financial Analysts Journal,* November–December 1975: 58–61.

Fleming, Mary M. K. "The Current Ratio Revisited." *Business Horizons,* May–June 1986: 74–77.

Gombola, Michael J., and J. Edward Ketz. "Financial Ratio Patterns in Retail and Manufacturing Organizations." *Financial Management,* Summer 1983: 45–56.

Grove, Hugh, and Ron Rizzuto. "How to Lie with Accounting: A Unique Extension of Security Analysis." *Journal of Financial Education,* Fall 1981: 33–37.

Townsend, Henry. "Stockholder Earnings." *Financial Analysts Journal,* January–February 1990: 47–57.

Walker, Ernest W., and J. William Petty II. "Financial Differences between Large and Small Firms." *Financial Management,* Winter 1978: 61–68.

Appendix 15A   AN EXERCISE IN ANALYZING FINANCIAL STATEMENTS

EXCERPTS FROM THE 1991 ANNUAL REPORT OF THE COCA-COLA COMPANY

Excerpts from The Coca-Cola Company's 1991 Annual Report illustrate representative components of a company's annual report and provide the opportunity to analyze the financial statements of a large, well-known company. The excerpts include (1) letter to shareholders, (2) balance sheets, (3) income statements, (4) statements of cash flow, (5) report of independent auditors, and (6) shareholder information. The material in this Appendix enables you to compare Coca-Cola with its nearest competitor, PepsiCo.

In 1991 The Coca-Cola Company's sales were $11.6 billion, and its total assets were $10.2 billion. The company's two major lines of business are soft drinks and juice-based beverages, including Coca-Cola Classic, Diet Coke, Sprite, Fanta Orange, and Minute Maid products. So dominant are the company's soft drinks that it has captured about 40 percent of the U.S. market. PepsiCo is hot on its trail, however, with approximately one-third of the U.S. market. PepsiCo's brands include Pepsi Cola, Diet Pepsi, Mountain Dew, and 7UP, along with snacks such as Doritos, Ruffles, and Fritos. PepsiCo also owns Kentucky Fried Chicken, Pizza Hut, and Taco Bell. Coca-Cola's market share in the 185 foreign countries in which it operates is about 45 percent. PepsiCo's foreign-market share is roughly 15 percent.

These two giants of the soft-drink industry supply approximately two out of every three soft drinks consumed in the United States. Both companies have financial strength, massive bottling networks, and aggressive marketing skills. They compete with each other not only for bottled and canned drinks, but also for fountain drinks. Coca-Cola has exclusive franchise in McDonald's, Burger King, and Hardee's; PepsiCo has exclusive franchise in its own restaurants, as well as in Shakey's Pizza, Subway Sandwiches, and Ground Round.

PepsiCo's financial performance in 1990 and 1991 is shown by the financial ratios in the table below. The ratios represent four basic financial dimensions of PepsiCo: profitability, asset management, debt management, and liquidity. Using these ratios and the following procedure, compare and contrast Coca-Cola's financial performance with that of PepsiCo:

a. Read the excerpts from Coca-Cola's 1991 annual report to become familiar with the company.

b. Apply the extended Du Pont model to each company for 1990 and 1991: Describe and interpret (1) the differences between the two companies and (2) the changes from 1990 to 1991.

c. Compare and contrast the liquidity positions of the two companies.

d. Which company has the larger after-tax profit margin? What are the reasons for the difference?

e. Which company has the larger total asset turnover? What are the reasons for the difference?

f. Compare and contrast the debt positions of the two companies.

g. Write a summary comparing and contrasting the financial performance and condition of Coca-Cola and PepsiCo.

PepsiCo Inc. and Subsidiaries: Selected Financial Ratios

Financial Ratio	1991	1990
After-tax profit margin	5.51%	6.05%
Gross profit margin	52.1%	52.0%
EBIT margin	11.7%	13.2%
Return on total assets[a]	5.8%	6.3%
Return on common equity[a]	19.4%	22.0%
Total asset turnover	1.04	1.04
Current asset turnover	4.3	4.4
PP&E turnover[b]	3.0	3.1
Average collection period[c]	27.6 days	29.0 days
Inventory turnover[d]	14.2	14.6
Equity multiplier[e]	3.39	3.50
Total debt ratio[f]	70.5%	71.4%
Current debt ratio	19.8%	27.8%
Times interest earned[g]	3.8	3.3
Current ratio	1.2	0.9
Quick ratio[h]	0.9	0.7

[a] After-tax returns based on end-of-year assets and equity.

[b] Net sales divided by net property, plant, and equipment.

[c] Based on total sales and end-of-year net receivables.

[d] Based on cost of goods sold and end-of-year inventories.

[e] 1991 total assets = $18.8 billion, including $5.9 billion of intangibles; for 1990 the figures are $17.1 billion and $5.8 billion, respectively.

[f] Includes current and long-term debt, deferred income taxes, and other long-term obligations; deferred income taxes at year-end 1991 and 1990 are $1.07 billion and $0.94 billion, respectively.

[g] Excludes nonoperating income such as interest income and gain on sales of assets.

[h] Excludes prepaid expenses and miscellaneous other assets.

Technical Note on Deferred Income Taxes

Deferred income taxes arise from timing differences in the reporting of revenue and expenses for financial reporting (as in annual reports) versus tax reporting. Consider the case where an expense is reported earlier for tax purposes than it is for financial reporting purposes: A company uses accelerated depreciation for tax purposes and straight-line depreciation for financial reporting to the public. In this case the company's actual taxes owed are less than those implied in the annual report, which reflects straight-line depreciation. The difference is deferred income taxes, a noncash charge to the company's publicly reported income.

To illustrate, consider a company with sales revenue of $100,000 and cash expenses of $60,000. Straight-line depreciation for financial reporting is $20,000 for the year, and accelerated depreciation for tax reporting is $40,000. The company's two income statements are as follows:

	Financial Reporting	Tax Reporting
Sales	$100,000	$100,000
Less cash expenses	60,000	60,000
Less depreciation	20,000	40,000
Earnings before taxes	$ 20,000	0
Income taxes (15%)	3,000	0
Earnings after taxes	$ 17,000	0

The company actually pays no income taxes but reports to the public income taxes equaling $3,000, called deferred income taxes. Since deferred income taxes are a noncash expense, the company's cash flow for the year is $40,000: earnings after taxes ($17,000) plus depreciation ($20,000) plus deferred income taxes ($3,000). Deferring income taxes in financial reporting creates a long-term liability (Deferred Income Taxes) on the balance sheet, not to be confused with the current liability Income Taxes Payable. In the example above, income taxes payable for the year are zero, but deferred income taxes are $3,000. For companies that purchase a sufficient amount of depreciable assets each year, deferred income taxes are effectively postponed in perpetuity. Insufficient purchases, however, lead to a reduction in deferred income taxes as reported on the balance sheet and income statement.

The Coca-Cola Company's 1991 balance sheet shows $200,027,000 deferred income taxes accumulated over the past years. A footnote in the company's annual report states: "Deferred taxes are provided principally for depreciation, certain employee compensation-related expenses and certain capital transactions that are recognized in different years for financial statement and income tax purposes." When analyzing a company's balance sheet, some analysts view deferred income taxes as "a zero-interest, long-term loan from the government," because the government grants the company the right to use accelerated depreciation. Pushing this view further, an analyst might view deferred income taxes for some companies as having characteristics similar to common equity.

The Coca-Cola Company's 1991 income statement shows income taxes equaling $765,277,000. A footnote discloses that current income taxes equal $831,424,000 and deferred income taxes equal −$66,147,000; combining the two figures yields $765,277,000. Because of this and for other reasons, the company's actual tax payments on operations in 1991 are approximately $672,000,000.

Share Owners

Message to

For our Company, the year 1991 could be characterized by the words **challenging** and **rewarding**. It was **challenging** because of the harsh economic conditions which prevailed in several of our most important markets, *e.g.*, Australia, Canada, the United States and the United Kingdom. Balancing those economic negatives, however, were the strong free market economies emerging in Latin America with their resulting positive impact on our business; the new markets evolving in eastern Europe; and the continued strong showing of our soft drink business in the Pacific Rim countries. In addition, we achieved share gains relative to the competition in most countries where soft drink industry growth was affected by the local economies.

1991 was especially **rewarding** because our Company, together with the global Coca-Cola system, demonstrated an extraordinary capability to adapt to local market conditions so as to derive the greatest benefits for our soft drink business. This pragmatic adaptability is largely responsible for our Company's ability to continue to produce consistent and reliable profitable growth.

Last year our share price gained nearly 73 percent, almost three times the increase of the S&P 500. Adding the annual dividend of 96 cents per share to the stock price appreciation gave the owners of this Company a total return of 75 percent on their investment. The annualized total return over the past five and 10 years, assuming reinvestment of dividends, has been 37 percent and 34 percent, respectively.

In 1991 the market value of The Coca-Cola Company **increased** by more than $22 billion, an amount $6 billion greater than our Company's **total** market value at January 1, 1989. **In other words, last year, in terms of market capitalization, we created the equivalent of another company larger than The Coca-Cola Company was less than three years ago.**

At year-end 1991, our Company was the sixth-largest public company in the U.S. in terms of market value, worth over $53 billion. This market value is more than three times what it was three years ago, and more than 12 times what it was 10 years ago, back on January 1, 1982, when it stood at $4.3 billion. Stated differently, **$49 billion of additional wealth**

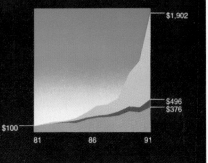

Total Return

Appreciation plus reinvested dividends on $100 investment on 12/31/81. From 1982 to 1991, the Company's common stock outperformed the S&P 500 by approximately 4-to-1 and the Dow Jones Industrial Average by approximately 5-to-1.

■ The Coca-Cola Company
■ Standard & Poor's 500
■ Dow Jones Industrial Average

$1,902

$496
$376

$100

81   86   91

Roberto C. Goizueta,   *Chairman, Board of Directors, and Chief Executive Officer (left), and*
Donald R. Keough, *President and Chief Operating Officer, at the Dunkirk, France, megaplant.*

has been created for the owners of our Company over the last 10 years, $37 billion over the last three years alone.

Our net earnings available to common share owners of $1.62 billion for the year and earnings per share of $2.43 increased 18.6 percent and 19.1 percent respectively over 1990. Our return on share-owners' equity reached 39.5 percent, and we ended the year with a net-debt-to-net-capital ratio of 21 percent. For 1992 our Directors voted to raise our quarterly dividend 17 percent to 28 cents per share, equivalent to an annual dividend of $1.12 per share.

In 1991 the global Coca-Cola system sold 9.9 billion unit cases of our soft drinks, an increase of 474 million unit cases, or 5 percent, over 1990. To put this growth into perspective, if our incremental 1991 volume were considered as a single country, it would rank as our fifth-largest international market, between Germany and Spain.

Coca-Cola Foods continued to maintain its leadership in the U.S. orange juice business in 1991 and to be totally focused on juice and juice-drink products. We won't allow any distractions to take our attention away from our efforts to enhance our leadership position in the citrus business in this country. We view this as a growth business, and we have the plans in place to fully benefit from it and consistently grow profits.

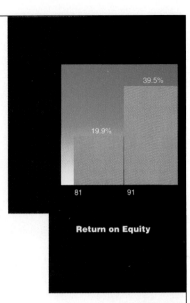

Return on Equity

As an organization, we are not wasting our energy forecasting what the future of the soft drink industry will be like in the many countries around the world in which we operate. And neither are we spending our time forecasting what the future holds for this Company. We will use our resources to construct today the foundation on which **our** future**... the future we are creating for ourselves...** will be built.

We don't view the future as preordained, but as an infinite series of openings, of possibilities. What is required to succeed in the middle of this uncertainty is what the Greeks called "practical intelligence." Above all else, this "practical intelligence" forces adaptability and teaches constant preparedness. It acknowledges that nothing succeeds quite as planned, and that the model is not the reality. But it also teaches that choice and preparation can influence the future. This Annual Report details many of the choices we are making today which will profoundly influence the exciting future we are shaping for our global system.

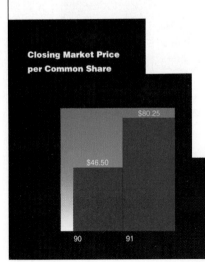

Closing Market Price per Common Share

We do not want to leave our share owners with the false impression that this wonderful soft drink business of The Coca-Cola Company is totally impervious to any and all setbacks. However, we are running this business today at a high efficiency, and we have the attitude and the financial resources, as well as the management team, needed to take care of any negative eventuality which may come our way. So... when it does, if we don't completely neutralize it, at the very least, we will minimize its impact.

On the other hand, and as with everything in life, there will also surely be unexpected positive events in the future of this Company. When they happen, we will quickly put them to work to our advantage. In the past we have demonstrated that our system has such capabilities, and we will continue to take advantage of every opportunity in the future.

We do not foresee 1992 as being any less challenging than 1991 or any less rewarding. We are confident that we have the building blocks in place to continue into 1992 and beyond the profitable growth pattern we have established over the last few years.

We are proud of our associates throughout the world who form a loyal, dedicated and talented global team. We are appreciative of the support, advice and counsel we receive from our most distinguished group of Directors, who continuously challenge us to ever higher levels of achievement. We are fortunate to have as key members of the Coca-Cola system, bottling partners who share our same vision for profitable growth. We thank our suppliers for joining us in committing to product quality and customer service. We express our gratitude to our customers and consumers, without whom The Coca-Cola Company and the enterprise we call the Coca-Cola system would cease to exist. Finally, we take this opportunity to once again thank you, the owners of this business, for the confidence you continue to demonstrate by having chosen our Company as the object of your investment.

Ten Years 1982-1991	Five Years 1987-1991
15%*	22%*

Compound Growth Rates
Income per Common Share
from Continuing Operations
*Excludes unusual items

Roberto C. Goizueta
Chairman, Board of Directors,
and Chief Executive Officer

Donald R. Keough
President and
Chief Operating Officer

February 20, 1992

Consolidated Balance Sheets *The Coca-Cola Company and Subsidiaries*

December 31, *(In thousands except share data)*	**1991**	1990
Assets		
Current		
Cash and cash equivalents	**$ 1,058,250**	$1,429,555
Marketable securities, at cost (approximates market)	**58,946**	62,569
	1,117,196	1,492,124
Trade accounts receivable, less allowances of $34,567		
in 1991 and $29,510 in 1990	**933,448**	913,541
Finance subsidiary—receivables	**36,172**	38,199
Inventories	**987,764**	982,313
Prepaid expenses and other assets	**1,069,664**	716,601
Total Current Assets	**4,144,244**	4,142,778
Investments and Other Assets		
Investments		
Coca-Cola Enterprises Inc. (CCE)	**602,776**	666,847
Coca-Cola Amatil Limited	**570,774**	569,057
Other, principally bottling companies	**980,465**	788,718
Finance subsidiary—receivables	**288,471**	128,119
Long-term receivables and other assets	**442,135**	321,977
	2,884,621	2,474,718
Property, Plant and Equipment		
Land	**172,781**	147,057
Buildings and improvements	**1,200,672**	1,059,969
Machinery and equipment	**2,680,446**	2,204,188
Containers	**390,737**	374,526
	4,444,636	3,785,740
Less allowances for depreciation	**1,554,754**	1,400,175
	2,889,882	2,385,565
Goodwill and Other Intangible Assets	**303,681**	275,126
	$10,222,428	$9,278,187

December 31,	1991	1990
Liabilities and Share-Owners' Equity		
Current		
Accounts payable and accrued expenses	$ 1,914,379	$1,576,426
Loans and notes payable	845,823	1,742,179
Finance subsidiary—notes payable	346,767	161,432
Current maturities of long-term debt	109,707	97,272
Accrued taxes	900,884	719,182
Total Current Liabilities	4,117,560	4,296,491
Long-Term Debt	985,258	535,861
Other Liabilities	493,765	332,060
Deferred Income Taxes	200,027	264,611
Share-Owners' Equity		
Preferred stock, $1 par value—		
Authorized: 100,000,000 shares; Issued: 3,000 shares of Cumulative Money		
Market Preferred Stock in 1991 and 1990; Outstanding: No shares in 1991;		
750 shares in 1990, stated at aggregate liquidation preference	—	75,000
Common stock, $.50 par value—		
Authorized: 1,400,000,000 shares; Issued: 843,675,547 shares in 1991;		
840,487,486 shares in 1990	421,838	420,244
Capital surplus	639,990	512,703
Reinvested earnings	7,425,514	6,447,576
Unearned compensation related to outstanding restricted stock	(114,909)	(67,760)
Foreign currency translation adjustment	(4,909)	4,031
	8,367,524	7,391,794
Less treasury stock, at cost (179,195,464 common shares in 1991;		
172,248,315 common shares in 1990)	3,941,706	3,542,630
	4,425,818	3,849,164
	$10,222,428	$9,278,187

See Notes to Consolidated Financial Statements.

Consolidated Statements of Income *The Coca-Cola Company and Subsidiaries*

Year Ended December 31, *(In thousands except per share data)*	**1991**	1990	1989
Net Operating Revenues	**$11,571,614**	$10,236,350	$8,622,287
Cost of goods sold	**4,648,385**	4,208,850	3,548,570
Gross Profit	**6,923,229**	6,027,500	5,073,717
Selling, administrative and general expenses	**4,604,184**	4,075,936	3,347,932
Operating Income	**2,319,045**	1,951,564	1,725,785
Interest income	**175,406**	169,985	205,035
Interest expense	**192,515**	230,979	308,034
Equity income (1991 reduced by $44 million related to restructuring charges recorded by CCE)	**39,975**	110,139	75,490
Other income—net	**41,368**	13,727	66,034
Income from Continuing Operations before Income Taxes	**2,383,279**	2,014,436	1,764,310
Income taxes	**765,277**	632,532	571,471
Income from Continuing Operations	**1,618,002**	1,381,904	1,192,839
Equity income from discontinued operation	**—**	—	21,537
Gain on sale of discontinued operation (net of income taxes of $421,021)	**—**	—	509,449
Net Income	**1,618,002**	1,381,904	1,723,825
Preferred stock dividends	**521**	18,158	21,392
Net Income Available to Common Share Owners	**$ 1,617,481**	$ 1,363,746	$1,702,433
Income per Common Share			
Continuing operations	**$ 2.43**	$ 2.04	$ 1.69
Discontinued operation	**—**	—	.77
Net Income per Common Share	**$ 2.43**	$ 2.04	$ 2.46
Average Common Shares Outstanding	**666,472**	668,570	691,962

See Notes to Consolidated Financial Statements.

Consolidated Statements of Cash Flows *The Coca-Cola Company and Subsidiaries*

Year Ended December 31, (In thousands)	1991	1990	1989
Operating Activities			
Net income	$1,618,002	$1,381,904	$1,723,825
Depreciation and amortization	261,427	243,888	183,765
Deferred income taxes	(66,147)	(30,254)	37,036
Equity income, net of dividends	(16,013)	(93,816)	(76,088)
Foreign currency adjustments	65,534	(77,068)	(31,043)
Gain on sale of businesses and investments before income taxes	(34,577)	(60,277)	(1,006,664)
Other noncash items	33,338	97,752	24,360
Net change in operating assets and liabilities	222,837	(178,202)	279,382
Net cash provided by operating activities	2,084,401	1,283,927	1,134,573
Investing Activities			
Additions to finance subsidiary receivables	(210,267)	(31,551)	(57,006)
Collections of finance subsidiary receivables	51,942	58,243	188,810
Purchases of investments and other assets	(399,183)	(186,631)	(858,510)
Proceeds from disposals of investments and other assets	180,058	149,807	126,850
Proceeds from sale of businesses	—	—	1,680,073
Decrease (increase) in marketable securities	2,735	16,733	(3,889)
Purchases of property, plant and equipment	(791,677)	(592,971)	(462,466)
Proceeds from disposals of property, plant and equipment	43,958	19,208	60,665
Purchases of temporary investments and other	(2,246)	(113,875)	(145,009)
Proceeds from disposals of temporary investments	—	241,373	—
Net cash provided by (used in) investing activities	(1,124,680)	(439,664)	529,518
Net cash provided by operations after reinvestment	959,721	844,263	1,664,091
Financing Activities			
Issuances of debt	989,926	592,417	336,370
Payments of debt	(1,246,664)	(81,594)	(410,690)
Preferred stock redeemed	(75,000)	(225,000)	—
Common stock issued	39,394	29,904	41,395
Purchases of common stock for treasury	(399,076)	(306,667)	(1,166,941)
Dividends (common and preferred)	(640,064)	(552,640)	(490,655)
Net cash used in financing activities	(1,331,484)	(543,580)	(1,690,521)
Effect of Exchange Rate Changes on Cash and Cash Equivalents	458	32,852	(22,896)
Cash and Cash Equivalents			
Net increase (decrease) during the year	(371,305)	333,535	(49,326)
Balance at beginning of year	1,429,555	1,096,020	1,145,346
Balance at end of year	$1,058,250	$1,429,555	$1,096,020

See Notes to Consolidated Financial Statements.

Report of Independent Auditors

Board of Directors and Share Owners
The Coca-Cola Company

We have audited the accompanying consolidated balance sheets of The Coca-Cola Company and subsidiaries as of December 31, 1991 and 1990, and the related consolidated statements of income, share-owners' equity and cash flows for each of the three years in the period ended December 31, 1991. These financial statements are the responsibility of the Company's management. Our responsibility is to express an opinion on these financial statements based on our audits.

We conducted our audits in accordance with generally accepted auditing standards. Those standards require that we plan and perform the audit to obtain reasonable assurance about whether the financial statements are free of material misstatement. An audit includes examining, on a test basis, evidence supporting the amounts and disclosures in the financial statements. An audit also includes assessing the accounting principles used and significant estimates made by management, as well as evaluating the overall financial statement presentation. We believe that our audits provide a reasonable basis for our opinion.

In our opinion, the financial statements referred to above present fairly, in all material respects, the consolidated financial position of The Coca-Cola Company and subsidiaries at December 31, 1991 and 1990, and the consolidated results of their operations and their cash flows for each of the three years in the period ended December 31, 1991, in conformity with generally accepted accounting principles.

Ernst & Young

Atlanta, Georgia
January 24, 1992

Share-Owner Information

Common Stock

Ticker symbol: KO

The Coca-Cola Company is one of 30 companies in the Dow Jones Industrial Average.

Common stock of The Coca-Cola Company is listed and traded on the New York Stock Exchange, which is the principal market for the common stock, and also is traded on the Boston, Cincinnati, Midwest, Pacific and Philadelphia stock exchanges. Outside the United States, the Company's common stock is listed and traded on the German exchange in Frankfurt and on Swiss exchanges in Zurich, Geneva, Bern, Basel and Lausanne.

Share owners of record at year-end: 117,874

Shares outstanding at year-end: 664 million

Dividends

At its February 1992 meeting, the Company's Board of Directors increased the quarterly dividend to 28 cents per share, equivalent to an annual dividend of $1.12 per share. The Company has increased dividends each of the last 30 years.

The Coca-Cola Company normally pays dividends four times a year, usually on April 1, July 1, October 1 and December 15. The Company has paid 283 consecutive quarterly dividends, beginning in 1920.

Dividend and Cash Investment Plan

All share owners of record are invited to participate in the Dividend and Cash Investment Plan. The Plan provides a convenient, economical and systematic method of acquiring additional shares of the Company's common stock. The Plan permits share owners of record to reinvest dividends from Company stock in shares of The Coca-Cola Company. Share owners also may purchase Company stock through voluntary cash investments of up to $60,000 per year.

All costs and commissions associated with joining and participating in the Plan are paid by the Company.

The Plan's administrator, First Chicago Trust Company of New York, purchases stock for voluntary cash investments on or about the first of each month, and for dividend reinvestment on April 1, July 1, October 1 and December 15.

At year-end, 37 percent of share owners of record were participants in the Plan. In 1991, share owners invested $12.78 million in dividends and $16.35 million in cash in the Plan.

Stock Prices

Below are the New York Stock Exchange high, low and closing prices of The Coca-Cola Company stock for each quarter of 1991 and 1990, adjusted for a 2-for-1 stock split in May 1990.

Quarter	1991 High	Low	Close
Fourth	81.75	62.38	80.25
Third	66.50	54.50	64.50
Second	58.00	51.38	54.50
First	55.50	42.63	54.25

Quarter	1990 High	Low	Close
Fourth	49.00	39.75	46.50
Third	48.38	37.25	39.50
Second	46.88	37.13	44.38
First	39.00	32.63	37.38

Annual Meeting of Share Owners

April 15, 1992, at 9:00 a.m. local time
The Georgia World Congress Center Ballroom
285 International Boulevard, N.W.
Atlanta, Georgia

Publications

The Company's annual report on Form 10-K and quarterly report on Form 10-Q are available free of charge from the Office of the Secretary, The Coca-Cola Company, P.O. Drawer 1734, Atlanta, Georgia 30301.

A *Notice of Annual Meeting of Share Owners* and *Proxy Statement* are furnished to share owners in advance of the annual meeting. *Progress Reports*, containing financial results and other information, are distributed quarterly to share owners.

Also available from the Office of the Secretary are *Coca-Cola, A Business System Toward 2000: Our Mission in the 1990s, The Chronicle of Coca-Cola Since 1886* and other booklets about the Company and its products.

Equal Opportunity Policy

The Coca-Cola Company employs 28,900 people worldwide and maintains a long-standing commitment to equal opportunity and affirmative action. The Company strives to create a working environment free of discrimination and harassment with respect to race, sex, color, national origin, religion, age, disability or being a veteran of the Vietnam era as well as to make reasonable accommodations in the employment of qualified individuals with disabilities. The Company continued to increase minority and female representation in 1991. In addition, the Company provides fair marketing opportunities to all suppliers and maintains programs to increase transactions with firms that are owned and operated by minorities and women.

Chapter 16

FINANCIAL FORECASTING AND PLANNING

Fearsome Forecasting

Forecasting economic and financial events is not an activity for the mild and meek among us. Forecasters are almost always wrong, and feelings of inadequacy are daily companions. A forecaster's main hope is just to be near the mark. Paul Volker, former chairman of the Federal Reserve Board, once noted that economic forecasters and arthritis doctors have two things in common: Both are better at diagnosis than at cures, and both are better at explaining the past than at predicting the future.

Economic forecasters do a particularly poor job at predicting interest rates. Stephen McNees, an economist at the Federal Reserve Bank of Boston, studied the consensus forecasts of a group of well-known economists and concluded: "As an investor, you clearly would have done much better flipping a coin or assuming that rates would remain unchanged." Guru Peter Lynch, former portfolio manager at Fidelity Investments, says: "If an economist at General Motors tells you steel prices are going up after being weak for four

years, that's useful. If an economist at Sears tells you about a new trend in the appliance business, that's useful. But if an economist tells you where interest rates and the economy will be 12 months from now, that's weather forecasting."

In general, economic forecasters have a poor record of forecasting interest rates, stock prices, and turning points in the gross national (domestic) product (GNP and GDP). Surprisingly, though, economists forecast inflation rates reasonably well. At least they beat the prediction of no change in the inflation rate from the preceding six-month period.

Despite problems in developing accurate forecasts, the attempt to do so continues. The stakes for investors, creditors, and corporate managers are too high not to try. For corporate managers macroeconomic forecasts are a key ingredient in planning for production, marketing, and financing.

Source: Tom Herman, "How to Profit from Economists' Forecasts," *The Wall Street Journal,* January 22, 1993, C1 and C6. *Photo Credit:* J. Zuckerman/ West Light.

Financial managers cannot forecast the future with certainty, but they can plan for the most likely scenarios and make provisions for dealing with contingencies. By so doing, they are prepared to arrange financing for planned investments, to pay for advertising programs, to make purchases of materials, and to provide funds for other company activities. Much of a company's success in increasing shareholder wealth depends on how well the financial manager plans for company needs. Because of its central role, the idea of planning pervades much of this book. Whether financial managers are using the capital-budgeting methods of Chapter 9 or developing cash budgets as described in Chapter 12, they are engaged in some aspect of planning. This chapter adds two new techniques to the arsenal of financial-planning methods—*percent-of-sales forecasting* and *break-even analysis*. The chapter begins with methods for forecasting sales. It then describes how sales forecasts are used for planning a company's requirements for external financing—debt and equity. This planning procedure, called percent-of-sales forecasting, forms the basis for developing *pro forma* financial statements. The second procedure, break-even analysis, shows how sales revenue, variable costs, and fixed costs interact to determine a company's break-even point. Break-even analysis is used for planning profit levels of company investments.

SALES FORECASTING

Forecasting future sales is the starting point for financial-planning models because sales affect the size of all other financial variables. Sales increases and decreases affect both sides of the balance sheet—assets on the left side and claims against assets (liabilities and shareholder equity) on the right side. Changes in sales also affect each element of the income statement: cost of goods sold, operating expenses, financial expenses (if there is additional borrowing), and income taxes. An accurate sales forecast enables the financial manager to develop accurate projected financial statements known as the *pro forma* balance sheet and the *pro forma* income statement.

A company's marketing department may use a variety of methods to prepare a sales forecast. Marketing managers use statistics on past total sales, sales by product, sales by territory, and so on to produce sales forecasts based on subjective judgment, trend analysis, and correlation analysis. The following sections discuss each of these methods.

Subjective Forecasts

subjective forecast
Forecast of expected values using personal experience and intuition.

A **subjective forecast** develops expected values based on personal experience and intuition. It relies exclusively on the judgment of the person making the forecast. A marketing manager may state: "Based on a survey of my sales force, I believe we will sell 125,000 units next year in my territory." In this case the forecast of 125,000 units rests on the judgments of several sales representatives. Summing the forecasts for each territory leads to the total number of units forecast for the company. Multiplying the expected price per unit by the expected number of units produces the sales revenue forecast, on which many financial variables depend.

Although it is unsophisticated, this method of sales forecasting has three advantages: (1) It is simple and inexpensive to implement, (2) it draws upon the knowledge of persons in the field who have specific information on customer needs and plans, and (3) the individuals responsible for making the sales prepare the forecast. Offsetting these advantages are the following disadvantages: (1) Sales representatives may make overly optimistic or overly pessimistic forecasts, (2) they may place too much emphasis on recent sales experience, and (3) they may be unable to distinguish trends from seasonal variations and to spot temporary accumulations in customer inventories.

The relative accuracy of subjective forecasts in practice implies that the method has merit. To increase accuracy, upper-level management may temper the forecasts from sales representatives with its own judgment. To refine the forecasts, management can use the **Delphi technique**—utilization of a panel of experts and several iterations to modify forecasts. With this technique management identifies several people knowledgeable about company sales and solicits a forecast from each of them. Each forecaster is then provided with the group consensus (the median forecast) and requested to make another forecast. Those who deviate substantially from the consensus submit a detailed explanation of their difference of opinion. The process continues until the forecasters stop making adjustments in their estimates. Management uses the results of the final round as the basis for its sales forecast.

Delphi technique

Process of modifying the subjective forecast of each person on a panel to derive a consensus forecast.

Trend Forecasts

Trend forecasts of sales are estimates based on past sales data. Sales for future years are extrapolated from (inferred from) the known sales for preceding years. Trend forecasting is a time-series analysis that expresses sales as a function solely of time.

The simplest application of trend analysis is the no-change scenario. In this case the most recent annual sales volume is used as the forecast; sales in previous years are ignored. More common applications of trend analysis base the sales forecast on trends over a number of years. Figure 16.1 illustrates a trend forecast of company sales for 19X9 based on the previous nine years of sales data. Extending the nine-year line to 19X9 produces a forecast of $670,000 in sales revenue.

The easiest way to fit the line to the nine data points is by drawing it freehand, trying to split the difference between the points above and below the line. A more scientific way to draw the line is through the use of mathematical techniques developed to improve the fit of the line to the points.[1] Many of the techniques assign greater weight to more recent sales levels than to earlier ones. This type of weighting makes sense when management believes the recent sales levels are more important and relevant than the earlier ones.

Trend forecasts are usually more accurate when used for short-term sales forecasts of, say, one year. For longer periods, extrapolating from past sales is more likely to miss significant turning points, either upward or downward. Even for the short-term, trend forecasts do not take into consideration potential labor strikes, increased foreign competition, oil embargoes, and the like. Management can improve trend forecasts by making adjustments based on personal knowledge of the company and the industry. For example, management may know that

trend forecast

Forecast based on historical data arrayed in order of time.

---

[1] For a sophisticated treatment of trend forecasting, see George E. P. Box and Gwilym M. Jenkins, *Time Series Analysis: Forecasting and Control* (San Francisco: Holden-Day, 1970).

FIGURE 16.1

Trend Forecast of Sales for 19X9

The forecast sales revenue for 19X9 is $670,000. This forecast is an extrapolation from the sales levels of the past nine years.

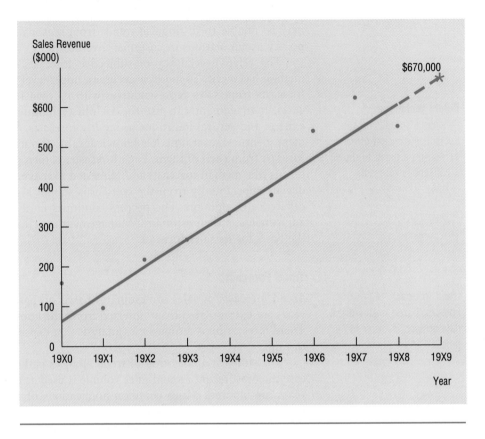

a labor contract must be renewed and that a strike is likely. This information will probably cause the forecast to differ from simple extrapolation.

Correlation Forecasts

correlation forecast
Statistical forecast based on the systematic link between the forecast variable and one or more other variables.

Trend forecasts do not account for what is expected to happen in the economy and in the company's industry. To overcome this shortcoming, **correlation forecasts** can be used to relate company sales to economic variables. The trend forecast in Figure 16.1 ignores changes in the business cycle. If an economic downturn were expected for 19X9, then the sales forecast of $670,000 would likely turn out to be overly optimistic because demand for products tends to decline during economic recessions.

Figure 16.2 shows the relationship between the company's sales revenue and the economic climate as measured by gross national product (GNP). In general, as gross national product increases, so do company sales. Each point in the figure represents a past value for company sales and gross national product for a specific year. The equation of the line best fitting the points is generated by a computer program for regression analysis. In this case the equation is:

$$\text{Sales} = \$95,000 + 150(\text{GNP})$$

FIGURE 16.2

Correlation Forecast of Sales for 19X9 Based on the Forecast of Gross National Product

The forecast sales revenue for 19X9 is $650,000 [$95,000 + (150 × $3,700)]. This sales forecast is based on (1) an equation estimated from the past relationship between sales and GNP and (2) the forecast GNP for 19X9.

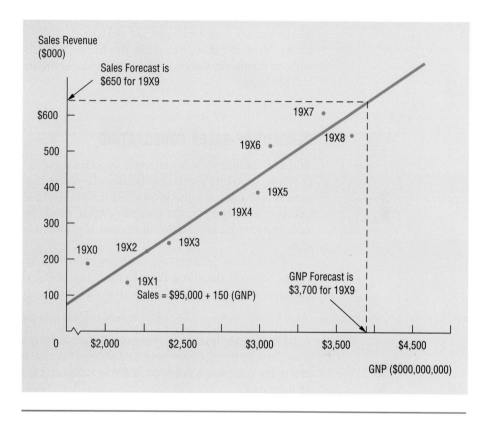

where GNP is measured in billions of current dollars. Thus if management's best forecast of GNP is $3,700 billion, the sales forecast is:

$$\text{Sales} = \$95,000 + 150(\$3,700)$$
$$= \$95,000 + \$555,000$$
$$= \$650,000$$

Forecasts of smaller GNP lead to forecasts of smaller sales and vice versa.

Accuracy of the preceding correlation forecast depends in part on the accuracy of the forecast of gross national product. If that forecast is in error, then the sales forecast will be too. Variables such as GNP, which receive the scrutiny of numerous economists and are readily available in *Business Week, Barron's,* and several other publications, are often (though not always) forecast with a reasonable degree of accuracy.

A second determinant of the accuracy of a correlation forecast is the selection of the predictor (the independent or right-side) variable—gross national product in this case. In place of such a broad measure of business activity, a narrower measure may have more predictive value for a specific company's sales. For example, a manufacturer of slacks might use expected expenditures on clothing;

a manufacturer of cardboard boxes might use an index of packaging activity, and so on. Even more predictive power might be generated by using more than one predictor variable. The manufacturer of slacks might use the forecast of population over 16 years of age in addition to expected expenditures on clothing. Forecasts of these and numerous other predictor variables are available in government and industry publications.

Both trend and correlation forecasts help in the projection of future sales by narrowing the range of expected outcomes. If the sales forecast is grossly inaccurate, then decisions based on the financial methods discussed below will be wide of the mark. Careful sales forecasting is the foundation of successful financial planning.

PERCENT-OF-SALES FORECASTING

When a company's sales change, its investment in assets changes as well. For example, accounts receivable become larger as the company sells to more customers and sales volume grows. To maintain product availability for the larger number of customers, the company must invest in additional inventory. If the sales increase is large, then additional investment in fixed assets will be needed also.

An increase in assets necessitates increased financing from either debt or equity sources. Recalling the equation describing the balance sheet shows that increases in assets must be accompanied by increases in debt or equity:

$$\text{Total assets} = \text{Debt} + \text{Equity}$$

A sales decrease leads to a decrease in the need for assets, which in turn leads to a decrease in the need for debt and equity. Because sales increases, not decreases, create the company's need for additional financing, we concentrate on the effects of increases.

Armed with the forecast of increased sales, the financial manager's task is to estimate the increase in total assets and to plan the financing for the increase. Because arrangements for borrowing from financial institutions and for issuing securities (new stocks and bonds) in the financial markets take time, the financial manager must anticipate the company's need for financing. The following sections describe **percent-of-sales forecasting,** a procedure that the financial manager can use to anticipate a company's financing needs.

percent-of-sales forecasting
Forecasting a company's external financing required because of growth in sales.

Pro Forma **Method of Percent-of-Sales Forecasting**

Forecasting financing needs begins with the company's current balance sheet and the sales forecast for the planning period, usually a year. The first step is to forecast the increase in total assets, which equals the total financing required. The second step is to forecast the funds that the company will generate internally from profit and other sources. *Total financing required less funds generated internally equals the external financing required for the planning period.* By forecasting the external financing required, the financial manager has time to develop the optimal financing strategy.

EXAMPLE   Dalton Company's net sales were $200,000 for the year ending December 31, 19X1. Its after-tax profit margin was 2 percent. Dalton pays 30 percent of its after-tax earnings in dividends to shareholders; it retains 70 percent for reinvestment in the company. Dalton's marketing manager forecasts 19X2 sales at $220,000, a 10 percent increase. Dalton's expected sales increase means that its assets will increase as well. The financial manager's task is to analyze and plan how to finance these assets.

Forecasting Total Financing Required. Estimating Dalton Company's total financing required begins with the expression of total assets as a percentage of sales—the reciprocal of the total asset turnover ratio. Dalton's current balance sheet (see Table 16.1) shows total assets (A) to be $75,000, 37.5 percent of its sales:

$$\frac{A}{S} = \frac{\$75,000}{\$200,000}$$

$$= 0.375, \text{ or } 37.5\%$$

capital intensity ratio
Assets per dollar of sales; reciprocal of the total asset turnover ratio.

where S is Dalton's sales for the year ending 19X1. A/S measures the company's assets per dollar of sales and is called the **capital intensity ratio.** Capital-intensive industries such as electric utility companies and oil refineries tend to have high capital intensity ratios; labor-intensive service industries tend to have low capital intensity ratios.

If the capital intensity ratio stays constant from 19X1 to 19X2, then the percentage change in assets will be exactly the same as the percentage change in sales. In this case Dalton's 10 percent increase in sales—from $200,000 to the forecast sales (FS) of $220,000—will be matched by a 10 percent increase in assets. Only with matching percentage changes will the capital intensity ratio remain unchanged:

$$\text{19X2 total assets} = \text{19X1 total assets} \times (1 + 0.10)$$

$$= \$75,000 \times 1.10$$

$$= \$82,500$$

$$Check: \quad \frac{\text{19X2 total assets}}{\text{FS}} = \frac{\$75,000 \times 1.10}{\$200,000 \times 1.10}$$

$$= 0.375$$

total financing required
Required increase in total debt and equity associated with increases in assets and sales.

The $7,500 ($82,500 − $75,000) change in total assets is Dalton's **total financing required;** that is, if Dalton's sales increase 10 percent ($200,000 to $220,000), then its total assets (assuming a constant capital intensity ratio) increase by 10 percent as well ($75,000 to $82,500). The $7,500 of new assets must be financed with $7,500 of new debt and equity.

Column 3 in Table 16.1 shows each of Dalton's assets as a percentage of sales, total assets being 37.5 percent of sales. Assuming that these percentages hold for 19X2, we multiply them in decimal form times Dalton's forecast sales ($220,000) to obtain, in Column 4, the forecast assets for year-end 19X2.

EXAMPLE

Suppose that Dalton Company's financial manager believes that some assets will not increase with Dalton's sales increase. Consider, for example, the following conditions, each of which changes the capital intensity ratio:

TABLE 16.1

Dalton Company: 19X1 Balance Sheet Accounts as Percentages of 19X1 Sales, and the 19X2 *Pro Forma* Balance Sheet

	(1)	(2) Balance Sheet Values on 12/31/X1	(3) [(2)/$200,000] Selected Accounts as % of 19X1 Sales ($200,000)	(4) [(3) × $220,000] *Pro Forma* 12/31/X2 Balance Sheet (19X2 Sales Forecast = $220,000)
Assets				
Cash		$ 4,000	2.0%	$ 4,400
Marketable securities		2,000	1.0	2,200
Accounts receivable		8,000	4.0	8,800
Inventory		11,000	5.5	12,100
Total current assets		$25,000	12.5%	$27,500
Net fixed assets		50,000	25.0	55,000
Total assets		$75,000	37.5%	$82,500[b]
Liabilities and Equity				
Accounts payable		$10,000	5.0%	$11,000[c]
Taxes payable		4,000	2.0	4,400[c]
Bank notes payable		6,000	NA[a]	9,020[d]
Total current liabilities		$20,000	NA	$24,420
Long-term debt		22,000	NA	22,000[e]
Total liabilities		$42,000	NA	$46,420
Common stock		14,000	NA	14,000[f]
Retained earnings		19,000	NA	22,080[g]
Total common equity		$33,000	NA	$36,080
Total liabilities and equity		$75,000	NA	$82,500

[a]NA (not applicable) means that the account does not vary proportionally with changes in sales.

[b]$82,500 = 0.375 × $220,000; for each asset and asset total, multiply the percentage for 19X1 times the forecast sales for 19X2.

[c]$11,000 = 0.05 × $220,000; $4,400 = 0.02 × $220,000; spontaneous liabilities vary automatically with changes in sales.

[d]Plug factor, the amount needed to balance the *pro forma* balance sheet. External financing required equals $3,020 ($9,020 − $6,000); assumed to be provided by bank loans.

[e]Assumed to remain constant; no new long-term debt, no retirement of principal.

[f]No new issue of common stock.

[g]$22,080 = $19,000 + $4,400 − $1,320; 19X2 ending retained earnings equal 19X1 retained earnings plus projected earnings after taxes less dividends paid.

1. Because of slack in operations, Dalton operated below capacity in 19X1. A 10 percent sales increase in 19X2 will not require additional plant and equipment. If net fixed assets stay at $50,000 and *pro forma* current assets equal $27,500 (0.125 × $220,000), then *pro forma* total assets equal $77,500 ($27,500 + $50,000). In this case Dalton's total financing required in 19X2 is $2,500 ($77,500 − $75,000), and its capital intensity ratio declines.

2. The financial manager plans to relax credit standards. Dalton's average collection period (ACP) for year-end 19X1 is 14.6 days, and the relaxed standards will lead to a 20-day ACP. The increased ACP means that the

increase in accounts receivable will be greater than the percentage suggested by the percent-of-sales forecast:

$$\text{ACP before change} = \frac{\$8,000}{\$200,000/365}$$

$$= 14.6 \text{ days}$$

Relaxing credit standards will cause the ACP to increase to 20 days. Under this scenario year-end 19X2 accounts receivable equal $12,055:

$$\text{ACP after change} = 20 \text{ days} = \frac{\text{Accounts receivable}}{\$220,000/365}$$

$$\text{Accounts receivable} = 20 \text{ days} \times \frac{\$220,000}{365 \text{ days}}$$

$$= 20 \text{ days} \times \$602.74 \text{ per day}$$

$$= \$12,055$$

Comparing $12,055 with the $8,800 for receivables in Table 16.1 (Column 4), we conclude that Dalton's total financing requirements increase $3,255 ($12,055 − $8,800), from $7,500 to $10,755, and the capital intensity ratio rises.

The financial manager should be alert to the possible need to make similar adjustments for cash, marketable securities, inventory, and other assets. Although the assumption that all assets increase proportionally with sales is a useful guide in estimating changes in future periods, any estimated variation should be included in the analysis. For convenience, however, we assume proportional increases here, which means that Dalton Company must raise $7,500 to support asset growth.

Forecasting External Financing Required.　Like all companies, Dalton Company obtains financing from both internal and external sources, classified as follows:

- *Internal sources:* (1) spontaneous liabilities and (2) earnings retained during the year.
- *External sources:* (1) short-term and long-term debt and (2) new common stock.

spontaneous liabilities
Costless short-term debt that arises in the normal course of company operations.

Spontaneous liabilities are costless sources of financing that arise from the normal operations of the company. Accounts payable, taxes payable, and accrued wages are primary examples.

Spontaneous liabilities tend to rise proportionally with sales. For example, accounts payable rise with sales because credit purchases are closely associated with sales. As Dalton Company makes more sales to its customers, it purchases more goods on credit from its suppliers, thereby increasing its accounts payable. Taxes payable rise proportionally with sales if the before-tax profit margin and tax rate are constant. Accrued wages rise proportionally with sales as long as labor costs remain a constant percentage of sales revenue and the company maintains the frequency (say, twice a month) with which it pays its employees. Notes payable, bank loans, and long-term debt are *not* spontaneous liabilities. They do not rise automatically with sales increases but must be negotiated by management.

Table 16.1 shows that Dalton Company's spontaneous liabilities (L) equal $14,000 ($10,000 + $4,000) at year-end 19X1. Expressing L as a percentage of 19X1 sales (S) yields 7 percent:

$$\frac{L}{S} = \frac{\$14,000}{\$200,000}$$
$$= 0.07, \text{ or } 7.0\%$$

If L/S stays constant from 19X1 to 19X2, then Dalton's spontaneous liabilities will increase by the same percentage as its sales. Only with matching percentage changes will the ratio of spontaneous liabilities to sales remain unchanged:

$$\begin{array}{c} \text{19X2 spontaneous} \\ \text{liabilities} \end{array} = \begin{array}{c} \text{19X1 spontaneous} \\ \text{liabilities} \end{array} \times (1 + 0.10)$$
$$= \$14,000 \times 1.10$$
$$= \$15,400$$

$$\textit{Check: } \frac{\text{19X2 spontaneous liabilities}}{FS} = \frac{\$14,000 \times 1.10}{\$200,000 \times 1.10}$$
$$= 0.07, \text{ or } 7\%$$

The $1,400 ($15,400 − $14,000) change in spontaneous liabilities defrays part of Dalton's $7,500 total financing required: Dalton still needs $6,100 more ($7,500 − $1,400) financing.

Retained earnings from 19X2 operations are Dalton's second source of internal financing. Dalton earned 2 percent after taxes on sales during 19X1. If Dalton earns 2 percent after taxes on its *expected* sales, then its earnings after taxes in 19X2 will be $4,400 (0.02 × $220,000). Recall, however, Dalton's policy of paying 30 percent of its earnings in dividends: 0.30 × $4,400 = $1,320. Dalton's financial manager expects the company to retain $3,080 during 19X2, calculated in the following way:

$$\begin{array}{c} \text{Earnings retained} \\ \text{during 19X2} \end{array} = \begin{array}{c} \text{Earnings} \\ \text{after taxes} \end{array} - \text{Dividends}$$
$$= \$4,400 - \$1,320$$
$$= \$3,080$$

As Table 16.1 shows, the $3,080 is added to Dalton's accumulated retained earnings for year-end 19X1 ($19,000) to get $22,080 for year-end 19X2.

External financing required to support Dalton's expected increase in sales equals the total financing required less additional spontaneous liabilities and earnings retained during 19X2:

external financing required
Funds raised outside of a company to support growth; total financing required less internal sources of funds.

Total financing required	$7,500
Less:	
Additional spontaneous liabilities	1,400
Earnings retained during 19X2	3,080
External financing required	$3,020

The financial manager weighs the choices of external financing using the risk-return analysis covered in Chapter 7 (debt versus equity) and in Chapter 11 (short-term versus long-term sources). Forecasting the external financing that will

TABLE 16.2	**Dalton Company: *Pro Forma* Income Statement and Statement of Retained Earnings for Year Ending 19X2**

	Forecast Amount	Forecast Method or Source
***Pro Forma* Income Statement**		
Sales revenue	$220,000	Subjective, trend, and correlation analyses
Less cost of goods sold	143,000	Historical percentage of sales
Gross profit	$ 77,000	
Less total operating expenses	68,200	Trend analysis of individual expense accounts
Earnings before interest and taxes[a]	$ 8,800	
Less interest expense	3,624	Interest rates $\times$ Debt amounts
Earnings before taxes	$ 5,176	
Less income taxes	776	Statutory rate (15%)
Earnings after taxes	$ 4,400	
Statement of Retained Earnings		
Retained earnings, 12/31/X1	$ 19,000	19X1 balance sheet
Earnings after taxes, 19X2	4,400	*Pro forma* income statement
Total retained earnings and EAT	$ 23,400	
Less common-stock dividends	1,320	30% payout policy
Retained earnings, 12/31/X2	$ 22,080	19X2 balance sheet

[a] EBIT is often called net operating income.

be required to sustain growth gives the financial manager time to (1) analyze the alternative sources of financing and (2) arrange for advantageous financial terms. Table 16.1 shows that Dalton Company plans to raise the $3,020 through bank borrowing, which increases its bank notes payable from $6,000 to $9,020. If the company planned to raise the $3,020 through long-term borrowing or a stock issue, then one of these accounts would have increased from 19X1 to 19X2.

To this point the *pro forma* method of percent-of-sales forecasting has been used to (1) estimate the amount of external financing Dalton needs and (2) develop Dalton's year-end *pro forma* balance sheet.[2] Development of Dalton's *pro forma* income statement requires additional information. Suppose, for example, that Dalton's cost of goods sold is normally 65 percent of sales; trend analysis of individual expenses shows that total operating expenses are likely to be 31 percent of sales; and expected interest expense is $3,624. Table 16.2 combines this information with the sales forecast to produce Dalton's *pro forma* income statement. Once again, the sales forecast influences the change from current activity levels. Historical relationships between sales, cost of goods sold, and expenses provide the basis for the forecasts. Interest expense depends on outstanding debt

[2] *Pro forma* balance sheets can also be developed from a cash budget (Chapter 12). The cash budget conveniently indicates the ending cash balance and the amount of short-term borrowing. Levels of accounts receivable and inventory are calculated from the work sheet. The expected sales, profit margin, and dividend payout ratio enable you to calculate retained earnings on the balance sheet. Planned expenditures for fixed assets plus the initial balance sheet and depreciation rates lead to expected fixed assets, and so on.

and interest rates.[3] Taxes are calculated with statutory rates. Combined with the *pro forma* balance sheet, the *pro forma* income statement provides a picture of Dalton's planned financial performance. In addition to their use in financial planning, Dalton's *pro forma* statements strengthen the company's applications for loans from financial institutions.

Economies of Scale.   The percent-of-sales forecasting method is particularly useful if the percentage sales increase is not very large. For large increases, say 30 percent and more, greater accuracy may be obtained by adjusting the relationship between assets and sales. The reason for the adjustment is **economies of scale** in the use of assets.

economies of scale
Benefits from large-scale production; an increase in sales does not require a proportional increase in assets.

Economies of scale occur when an increase in sales does not require a proportional increase in assets. Such economies are most significant for large sales increases. For example, a doubling of sales is not likely to require a doubling of inventory. A company maintains a base amount of inventory and an increase in sales generally requires an increase in that inventory, but the percentage increase in inventory may be less than the percentage increase in sales.

Figure 16.3 illustrates two ways of relating inventory to sales. Figure 16.3A shows the relationship between Dalton Company's inventory and sales as assumed in percent-of-sales forecasting: Inventory equals a constant 5.5 percent of sales. Thus a 10 percent increase in sales ($200,000 to $220,000) is matched with a 10 percent increase in inventory ($11,000 to $12,100). One-to-one matching holds for other percentage changes as well.

Analysis of the historical levels of inventory and sales might imply the alternative relationship noted in Figure 16.3B. Here a minimum inventory level exists for low levels of sales. Furthermore, in contrast to the preceding method, inventory increases more gradually as sales increase. Specifically, inventory equals $5,000 plus 3 percent (0.03) of sales. When Dalton Company's sales equal $200,000, both methods yield $11,000 in inventory, or 5.5 percent of sales. For economies of scale, however, inventory as a percentage of sales *declines* as sales *increase*:

		Inventory/Sales (%)			
	Sales	**Constant Proportions**		**Economies of Scale**	
	$200,000	5.5%		5.5%	
If sales double	220,000	5.5	Inventory doubles	5.3	Inventory fails
	400,000	5.5		4.3	to double

In this scenario, the assumption of constant proportions in the face of economies of scale may lead to forecasting errors: For a doubling of sales the error is 1.2 percentage points (5.5% − 4.3%).

---

[3]Calculation of the interest expense on new debt ($3,020 for Dalton) is complicated. The amount of debt cannot be determined until the *pro forma* income statement is developed, from which retained earnings on the balance sheet is calculated. However, the *pro forma* income statement cannot be developed until the amount of debt on the *pro forma* balance sheet is known. Fortunately, this endless circle of logic need not deter us, because the amount of interest involved is frequently relatively small. If it is significant, then we make revisions to the estimates of interest expense after we have made the preliminary estimates of new debt. Such iterations reduce error.

FIGURE 16.3

Alternative Relationships between the Inventory and Sales of Dalton Company: Constant Proportions and Economies of Scale

Panel A shows inventory as a constant percentage of sales. This assumption of percent-of-sales forecasting may be a poor one if economies of scale exist. The relationship in Panel B depicts one way to accommodate the existence of economies of scale. Inventory starts at a minimum level and then increases with increases in sales.

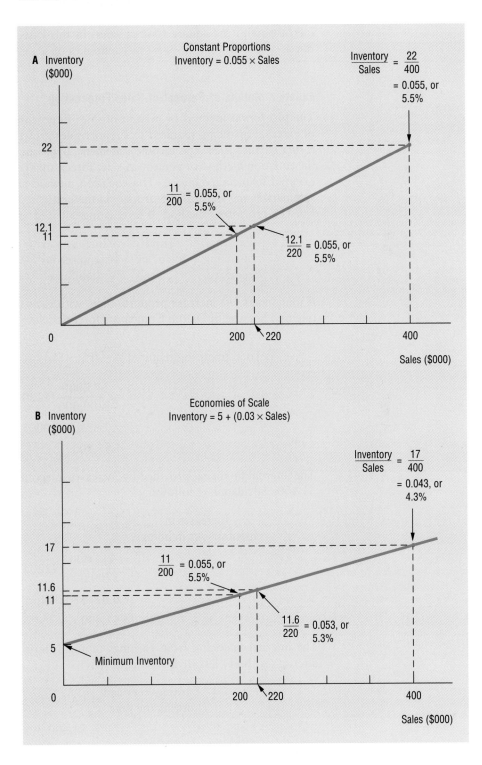

Graphs similar to Figure 16.3B can be used to improve the forecasts of accounts receivable and other assets. In some cases the historical data may imply a curvilinear relationship instead of the linear relationships in Figure 16.3. A curvilinear relationship is one in which the line of best fit is a curve. For companies using the economic order quantity (EOQ) model (Chapter 13), inventory increases with the square root of sales. In this case, inventory rises with sales, but at a decreasing rate—just as economies of scale would suggest.

Equation Method of Percent-of-Sales Forecasting

The *pro forma* method of percent-of-sales forecasting develops (1) an estimate of external financing required to support sales growth and (2) the resulting *pro forma* balance sheet and income statement. Bypassing the *pro forma* statements, the equation method of percent-of-sales forecasting goes directly to the estimated external financing required. The equation method conveniently and compactly summarizes the steps of the *pro forma* method.

The *pro forma* method of forecasting is based on the following equation:

$$\begin{array}{c} \text{External} \\ \text{financing} \\ \text{required} \end{array} = \begin{array}{c} \text{Total} \\ \text{financing} \\ \text{required} \end{array} - \left(\begin{array}{c} \text{Increases in} \\ \text{spontaneous} \\ \text{liabilities} \end{array} + \begin{array}{c} \text{Earnings} \\ \text{retained} \\ \text{during the year} \end{array} \right)$$

If total assets (A) increase proportionally with sales (S), then the total financing required because of Dalton Company's forecast sales (FS) is calculated as follows:

$$\begin{aligned} \text{Total financing required} &= \frac{A}{S}(FS - S) \\ &= \frac{\$75,000}{\$200,000}(\$220,000 - \$200,000) \\ &= 0.375(\$20,000) \\ &= \$7,500 \end{aligned}$$

The internal financing provided by increases in spontaneous liabilities (L) equals $1,400, calculated as follows:

$$\begin{aligned} \begin{array}{c} \text{Increases in} \\ \text{spontaneous liabilities} \end{array} &= \frac{L}{S}(FS - S) \\ &= \frac{\$14,000}{\$200,000}(\$220,000 - \$200,000) \\ &= 0.07(\$20,000) \\ &= \$1,400 \end{aligned}$$

The internal financing from earnings retained during the year equals earnings after taxes (EAT) less dividends paid (Div):

$$\begin{aligned} \begin{array}{c} \text{Earnings retained} \\ \text{during the year} \end{array} &= EAT - Div \\ &= \$4,400 - \$1,320 \\ &= \$3,080 \end{aligned}$$

Combining the preceding three terms yields the equation for percent-of-sales forecasting:

$$\begin{array}{l}\text{External} \\ \text{financing} \\ \text{required}\end{array} = \frac{A}{S}(FS - S) - \left[\frac{L}{S}(FS - S) + (EAT - Div)\right]$$

$$= 0.375(\$20,000) - [0.07(\$20,000) + (\$4,400 - \$1,320)]$$

$$= \$7,500 - (\$1,400 + \$3,080)$$

$$= \$3,020$$

Dalton Company needs to raise $3,020 externally to support a sales increase of $20,000, the same amount found by using the *pro forma* method.

The equation method of percent-of-sales forecasting is particularly useful for examining the external financing required under different scenarios. Programming the equation on a computer provides quick answers to "what if" questions: What if sales increase more than expected? What if the profit margin declines? Even without being programmed, the equation method provides answers more quickly than does the *pro forma* method.

EXAMPLE

David Dalton, financial manager of Dalton Company, wonders what impact a 15 percent inflation rate would have on the company's capital needs. In this case company sales revenue increases from $200,000 to $230,000 (1.15 × $200,000) even though the number of units sold remains constant. Mr. Dalton assumes that inflationary sales growth will affect only current assets (12.5 percent of sales in Table 16.1); fixed assets will remain the same. He also assumes that (1) spontaneous liabilities increase with inflationary growth (0.07 × $30,000 = $2,100); (2) the after-tax profit margin stays at 2 percent (EAT = 0.02 × $230,000 = $4,600); and (3) the dividend payout ratio stays at 30 percent of earnings after taxes (0.30 × $4,600 = $1,380). Mr. Dalton's analysis follows:

$$\begin{array}{l}\text{External} \\ \text{financing} = 0.125(\$30,000) - [0.07(\$30,000) + (\$4,600 - \$1,380)] \\ \text{required}\end{array}$$

$$= \$3,750 - (\$2,100 + \$3,220)$$

$$= -\$1,570$$

The negative $1,570 indicates that Dalton Company has more than enough internal financing to handle the inflationary growth in sales; therefore, external financing is not required. Dalton would likely need to raise external funds if (1) its current assets were a larger percentage of total assets, (2) its spontaneous liabilities were smaller, or (3) its profitability were lower.

Whether the financial manager should use the *pro forma* or the equation method of forecasting depends on the purpose at hand. The *pro forma* method results in *pro forma* financial statements that are useful for financial planning and for presentations to creditors. The equation method is quicker and lends itself to modeling. Using the equation method, the financial manager can easily analyze the impact of changes in input values on external financing needs.

Forecasting and Inflation

Forecasting a company's external financing takes audacity. Forecasts rarely coincide with what actually happens. The forecaster's fond hope is simply that the error will not be excessively large. Dante's *Inferno* describes what happens to forecasters in error:

> *Here are the souls of all those who attempted by forbidden arts to look into the future. . . . Characteristically the sin of these wretches is reversed upon them: Their punishment is to have their heads turned backwards on their bodies and to be compelled to walk backwards through all eternity, their eyes blinded by tears.*

Now you know why it takes audacity to be a forecaster.

Among the many things that can go wrong in a forecast are unexpected changes in the inflation rate. Forecasters build in expected rates in their forecasts of sales. Unexpected changes in the inflation rate can easily topple these forecasts, causing company financing needs to change as well.

With so much riding on the inflation rate, forecasters need an accurate way to measure it. Many forecasters use the consumer price index (CPI) designed by the Bureau of Labor Statistics (BLS) to measure inflation. Whether the CPI is relevant in these applications is debatable, considering how the BLS constructs the CPI. The BLS puts together a market basket of goods and services purchased by "typical" consumers. It then applies weights to the prices

of the items in proportion to their relative importance in household budgets. The BLS collects about 1,000,000 prices from some 25,000 establishments, feeds the prices into a computer programmed with the market basket, and then compares the result with a base period (1982–1984) when the CPI was 100.

If the prices of the items in the CPI market basket increase, does it follow that a given company's product prices will also rise and cause sales revenue to rise? Answering this question is critical in deciding whether to use the CPI to measure the impact of inflation on company sales. The CPI may be appropriate in many cases, but for some companies a different index may be more applicable.

BREAK-EVEN ANALYSIS

break-even analysis
Analysis of the relationships among sales revenue, operating costs, and profits; at the break-even point, sales revenue equals total operating costs, and EBIT = 0.

Break-even analysis is the process of forecasting the level of sales at which a company breaks even on its operations—that is, before considering the impact of interest expenses and taxes. The break-even point is where the company has zero earnings before interest and taxes (EBIT), so that it makes neither a profit nor a loss on its operations. For EBIT to be greater than zero, the company must have sales exceeding the break-even point. If sales are below the break-even point, then the company operates at a loss.

Forecasting the break-even sales level enables the financial manager to assess a company's prospective profitability. High break-even points create substantial downside risk—the possibility of sales falling below the break-even level. On the other hand, high break-even points are often accompanied by large profits for high sales levels. Low break-even points greatly reduce the downside risk, but they generally limit the upside profit potential. By comparing a company's forecast sales with its forecast break-even sales, the financial manager can assess the company's prospects for making a profit.

Calculating the Break-Even Point

A company's break-even point is determined by the relationship between its sales revenue and its operating costs:

$$EBIT = \text{Total sales revenue} - \text{Total operating costs}$$

The break-even point occurs when sales revenue exactly equals total operating costs and EBIT is zero. At break-even, then, total sales revenue equals total operating costs:

$$\text{Total sales revenue} = \text{Total operating costs}$$

The separation of total operating costs into the variable and fixed components creates the following equation:

$$\text{Total sales revenue} = \text{Total variable costs} + \text{Total fixed costs}$$

Variable costs are directly proportional to sales volume, but fixed costs are independent and remain the same regardless of sales volume. Sales revenue equals the price per unit sold (P) times the quantity of units sold (Q). Total variable costs equal the variable cost per unit sold (V) times Q. Combining these symbols with total fixed costs (F) yields an expression that includes all of the elements determining the break-even point:

$$P \times Q = (V \times Q) + F$$

Solving this equation for Q yields the number of units causing the company to break even on its operations:

$$(P \times Q) - (V \times Q) = F$$
$$Q(P - V) = F$$
$$Q_B = \frac{F}{P - V}$$

Q_B is the break-even quantity in units produced and sold. In words, Q_B equals total fixed operating costs divided by the unit contribution margin—the contribution toward covering fixed costs from each unit sold.

EXAMPLE

To illustrate the unit contribution margin, consider the following example:

Price per unit (P)	$26
Less variable cost per unit (V)	21
Unit contribution margin ($P - V$)	$ 5

In this example $5 of each unit sold contributes toward paying fixed costs.

To forecast break-even sales revenue (S_B), the financial manager multiplies price per unit sold (P) times Q_B, the number of units required to break even. The accuracy of the forecast of break-even sales depends on the accuracy of the following estimates: (1) total fixed costs, (2) variable cost per unit, and (3) price per unit sold. Uncertainty in these estimates creates uncertainty in the forecast.

EXAMPLE

The financial manager of Maxel Corporation has estimated the company's fixed operating costs at $450,000. The marketing manager expects to sell compact disks to regional distributors for $7 each. Variable cost (labor and materials) per unit sold is estimated to be $4. The financial manager's remaining task is to calculate the break-even point in units (Q_B) and in sales revenue (S_B):

- *Step 1.* Calculate the break-even point in units:

$$Q_B = \frac{\$450,000}{\$7 - \$4}$$

$$= 150,000 \text{ units}$$

- *Step 2.* Calculate the break-even point in sales revenue:

$$S_B = \$7 \text{ per unit} \times 150,000 \text{ units}$$

$$= \$1,050,000$$

Maxel's financial manager expects to break even with 150,000 compact disks and sales revenue of $1,050,000.

Instead of calculating the break-even point in units and multiplying by price per unit, Maxel's financial manager can use the contribution margin ratio to arrive at the break-even sales revenue directly. The contribution margin ratio is the percentage of price per unit (P) or sales revenue (S) that contributes toward paying fixed costs. The contribution margin ratio can be calculated using either per-unit or total dollar amounts:

$$\text{Contribution margin ratio} = \frac{P - V}{P}$$

$$= 1 - \frac{V}{P} \qquad \text{(per unit)}$$

$$\text{Contribution margin ratio} = \frac{S - TVC}{S}$$

$$= 1 - \frac{TVC}{S} \quad \text{(total dollars)}$$

where TVC = total variable costs

V = variable cost per unit

The break-even sales revenue equals fixed costs divided by the contribution margin ratio calculated with either of the above methods. Thus both of the following equations yield the same break-even sales revenue:[4]

[4]To derive these equations, begin with the following definition:

$$EBIT = S - (TVC + F)$$

Multiply *TVC*, the total variable costs, by *S/S* in order to incorporate the variable cost ratio, *TVC/S*:

$$EBIT = S - [(TVC/S)S + F]$$

Factor out *S*:

$$EBIT = S(1 - TVC/S) - F$$

EBIT = zero at the break-even sales revenue S_B:

$$0 = S_B(1 - TVC/S) - F$$

$$S_B(1 - TVC/S) = F$$

$$S_B = \frac{F}{1 - (TVC/S)}$$

Divide *TVC* and *S* by number of units to get $1 - (V/P)$, which we use in the other equation:

$$S_B = \frac{F}{1 - (V/P)}$$

$$S_B = \frac{F}{(P - V)/P}$$

$$= \frac{F}{1 - (V/P)} \quad \text{(per unit)}$$

$$S_B = \frac{F}{(S - TVC)/S}$$

$$= \frac{F}{1 - (TVC/S)} \quad \text{(total dollars)}$$

EXAMPLE   Calculate directly the break-even sales revenue for Maxel Corporation in the preceding example:

$$S_B = \frac{F}{(P - V)/P}$$

$$= \frac{\$450,000}{(\$7 - \$4)/\$7}$$

$$= \$1,050,000$$

When Maxel's sales revenues are $1,050,000 (150,000 units × $7), its total variable costs are $600,000 (150,000 units × $4). Calculate the company's break-even sales revenue using *S* and *TVC*:

$$S_B = \frac{F}{(S - TVC)/S}$$

$$= \frac{\$450,000}{(\$1,050,000 - \$600,000)/\$1,050,000}$$

$$= \$1,050,000$$

Graphing Break-Even Analysis

The relationships among sales revenue, costs, and profit can be plotted on a graph illustrating the break-even point. The graph makes it easier to understand the break-even point and to see the way costs affect it.

Figure 16.4 shows Maxel Corporation's sales revenue and operating costs as functions of the number of units produced and sold. The following three steps are used to draw the graph:

1. Draw a horizontal line at $450,000 for total fixed costs.

2. Draw the sales revenue line. Sales revenue equals price per unit times the number of units sold (S = P × Q). *The sales revenue line radiates from the origin with a slope (rise over run) equaling price per unit sold ($7).* The sales revenue line intersects the following two points: the origin and the break-even point.

3. Draw the line for total operating costs, and note that it intersects the vertical axis at $450,000 (total fixed costs), not at the origin. The total cost line begins at $450,000 because Maxel incurs this cost when sales are zero. The total cost line reflects total variable costs plus total fixed

FIGURE 16.4   **Break-Even Graph for Maxel Corporation**

A break-even graph illustrates the sales revenue, costs, and profit from operations. If Maxel Corporation produces and sells 150,000 units, then its EBIT will be zero. Producing and selling more than 150,000 units generates profit; producing and selling less generates loss.

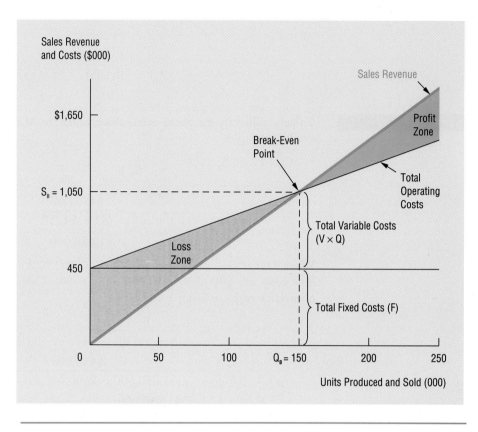

costs (TC = TVC + F). *The slope equals variable cost per unit ($4), and the line passes through the following two points: fixed costs at zero sales and the break-even point.*

Maxel Corporation's break-even point occurs where the lines for sales revenue and total operating costs intersect. At this point the company's earnings before interest and taxes are zero, and the company breaks even on its operations:

Sales revenue ($7/unit × 150,000 units)	$1,050,000
Less variable costs ($4/unit × 150,000 units)	600,000
Contribution margin	$ 450,000
Less fixed costs	450,000
Earnings before interest and taxes	0

Note that Figure 16.4 shows the break-even point and the profit and loss zones for Maxel Corporation. If Maxel produces and sells one less compact disk, then it has a loss; if it produces and sells one more compact disk, then it earns a profit.

Produce and sell 149,999 units:

Sales revenue ($7/unit × 149,999 units)	$1,049,993
Less variable costs ($4/unit × 149,999 units)	599,996
Contribution margin	$ 449,997
Less fixed costs	450,000
Earnings before interest and taxes	−$3

Produce and sell 150,001 units:

Sales revenue ($7/unit × 150,001 units)	$1,050,007
Less variable costs ($4/unit × 150,001 units)	600,004
Contribution margin	$ 450,003
Less fixed costs	450,000
Earnings before interest and taxes	$3

Using Break-Even Analysis

Financial managers use break-even analysis to analyze past performance as well as to forecast future performance. By changing the inputs to the analysis, they are able to calculate the effects on the break-even point. To illustrate, consider the effects of increased fixed costs, variable cost per unit, and price per unit:

1. *Increased fixed costs:* The horizontal line in Figure 16.4 moves parallel upward, and the break-even point increases.

2. *Increased variable cost per unit:* The slope of the line for total operating costs in Figure 16.4 becomes steeper, and the break-even point increases.

3. *Increased price per unit:* The slope of the sales revenue line in Figure 16.4 becomes steeper, and the break-even point decreases. The price increase may cause a decrease in the quantity of the product demanded.

As a planning tool, break-even analysis aids company managers in several areas of planning and control. Financial managers use it in capital budgeting and financing decisions, marketing managers use it in product-pricing decisions, and production managers use it in operational decisions:

- *Capital budgeting:* To supplement net present value analysis. Compare expected sales with the level of sales a project must generate to break even.

- *Financing decisions:* To assess the company's ability to pay interest. Compare expected sales with break-even sales and compare interest coverage at the sales levels.

- *Product pricing:* To assess the impact of various product prices on the break-even point. Analyze the impact of competitive prices on the break-even point.

- *Operational decisions:* To evaluate the break-even consequences of using automation with high fixed costs in place of manual operations with low fixed costs.

Nonlinear Break-Even Analysis

The break-even graph in Figure 16.4 shows sales revenue and total operating costs increasing linearly with increases in units produced and sold. The depiction of sales revenue and total operating costs as straight lines is based on the following two assumptions: (1) Selling price per unit remains constant at all levels of output, and (2) variable cost per unit remains constant for all levels of output.

FIGURE 16.5

Nonlinear Break-Even Graph

Reducing the price per unit sold leads to increases in output and causes sales revenue to increase at a decreasing rate. Total operating costs level out with increases in output because of economies of scale. Approaching full capacity at high levels of output causes total operating costs to increase rapidly because of strain on equipment and overtime wages paid to workers.

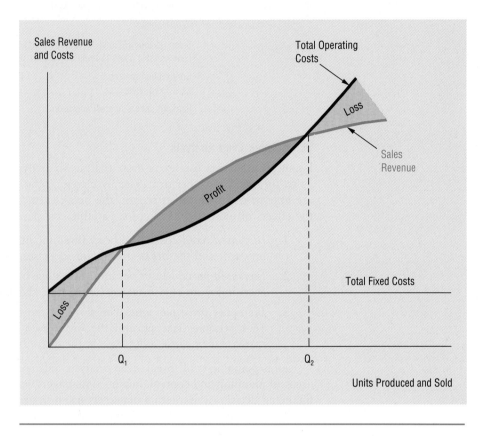

For a limited range of output, these assumptions probably serve as reasonable approximations.

Because of its simplicity, financial managers generally use linear analysis in practice. In some applications, however, nonlinear analysis more accurately describes the behavior of sales revenue and total operating costs. Figure 16.5 illustrates a nonlinear break-even graph in which sales revenue and total operating costs are drawn as curves. The curves reflect the following assumptions:

1. To sell more units, management reduces prices; sales revenue increases, but at a decreasing rate with output.

2. Variable cost per unit declines at low levels of output as the company reaches a critical size (economies of scale from more efficient production methods and quantity discounts on purchases); variable cost per unit begins to increase as the company approaches its full capacity (overtime labor costs and increasing wear on equipment).

Nonlinear break-even analysis may result in more than one break-even point. Figure 16.5 illustrates two of them, one at Q_1 and one at Q_2. If the company operates below Q_1 or above Q_2, then it experiences operating losses. Operating between Q_1 and Q_2 produces positive earnings before interest and taxes.

When nonlinear analysis is called for, the challenging task is to estimate the shapes of the curves for sales and total costs. Linear analysis is easier to use than nonlinear analysis, and it serves as a useful approximation in many cases.

PROFIT AND FIXED COSTS

An increase in fixed costs increases the break-even point if the selling price and variable cost per unit stay the same. Usually, however, companies incur fixed costs in order to reduce the variable cost per unit. For example, when General Motors automates an assembly plant with robotics, fixed costs (depreciation, maintenance, and a portion of energy costs) increase, but variable cost (direct labor) per automobile produced decreases. By increasing fixed costs in place of variable costs, a company earns large profits at high sales levels. Offsetting this advantage, fixed costs in place of variable costs also cause large losses at low sales levels. In other words, fixed costs increase both GM's risk and potential profitability.

leverage
Power of a change in sales to change profit at a greater rate.

Fixed costs result in **leverage,** the power of a change in sales to change profit at a greater rate. For example, if sales increase by 7 percent, then a company with leverage will have an increase in profit greater than 7 percent. A company without leverage will have a change in profit equal to the percentage change in sales. Leverage stems from two aspects of a company's financial management—its investments (operating leverage) and its financing (financial leverage):

- *Operating leverage* arises from the use of fixed *operating* costs. Replacing labor with machines increases fixed operating costs (depreciation and maintenance) and operating leverage.

- *Financial leverage* arises from the use of fixed *financing* costs. As Chapter 7 discusses, replacing common equity with debt (or preferred stock) increases fixed financing costs—interest (or preferred-stock dividends)—and financial leverage.

Degree of Operating Leverage

degree of operating leverage (DOL)
Measure of the change in EBIT resulting from a change in sales.

The **degree of operating leverage (DOL)** measures the magnification of earnings before interest and taxes for a given change in sales revenue. Degree of operating leverage is calculated as follows:

$$\text{Degree of operating leverage (DOL)} = \frac{\text{Percentage change in EBIT}}{\text{Percentage change in sales}}$$

A large number for DOL indicates that a large percentage change occurs in earnings before interest and taxes for a percentage change in sales.

EXAMPLE

Table 16.3 presents the operating results for Orion Corporation during 19X1. The marketing manager forecasts a 10 percent increase in unit sales for 19X2, going from 180,000 to 198,000 units. Sales price per unit is a constant $4. Thus the manager forecasts an increase in sales revenue from $720,000 to $792,000,

TABLE 16.3		**Orion Corporation: Degrees of Operating and Financial Leverage Illustrated by the Effects of a 10 Percent Increase in Sales and Unit Output**		
		Results for 19X1	**Forecast Output for 19X2**	**Percentage Increase**
Output (Units)		180,000	198,000	10%
Sales ($4 per unit)		$720,000	$792,000	10
Less variable costs ($2 per unit)		360,000	396,000	10
Contribution margin		$360,000	$396,000	10
Less fixed operating costs		**300,000**	**300,000**	**0**
Earnings before interest and taxes		$ 60,000	$ 96,000	60
Less interest expense		**20,000**	**20,000**	**0**
Earnings before taxes		$ 40,000	$ 76,000	90
Less income taxes (20%)		8,000	15,200	90
Earnings after taxes		$ 32,000	$ 60,800	90

a 10 percent increase. Orion Corporation has fixed operating costs of $300,000. Its degree of operating leverage is 6.0:

$$\text{Degree of operating leverage (DOL)} = \frac{(\text{Change in EBIT})/\text{EBIT}}{(\text{Change in sales})/\text{Sales}}$$

$$= \frac{(\$96,000 - \$60,000)/\$60,000}{(\$792,000 - \$720,000)/\$720,000}$$

$$= \frac{60\%}{10\%}$$

$$= 6.0$$

The company's expected sales increase of 10 percent causes a 60 percent (6 × 10 percent) increase in earnings before interest and taxes, a magnification of 6.0.

A substantial portion of Orion Corporation's operating costs are fixed. Thus a large part of its expected increase in sales revenue flows through to earnings before interest and taxes. If management could discover a way to increase sales by one more percentage point, then EBIT would increase another six percentage points. A large degree of operating leverage provides a great incentive for management to try to increase sales. Besides added marketing effort, management might consider cutting selling prices to increase total sales revenue. Break-even analysis and the DOL equation show the expected effects on profit from such decisions.

Expressing the degree of operating leverage as the percentage change in earnings before interest and taxes for a given percentage change in sales follows from the definition of DOL. Although less intuitive, the following equation is easier to use:[5]

$$\text{Degree of operating leverage (DOL)} = \frac{\text{Contribution margin}}{\text{EBIT}}$$

$$= \frac{\$360,000}{\$60,000}$$

$$= 6.0$$

EXAMPLE

Suppose that Orion Corporation achieves its 10 percent sales forecast, and the marketing manager forecasts another 10 percent sales increase for 19X3: from $792,000 to $871,200. Total variable costs increase 10 percent, from $396,000 to $435,600. Fixed costs stay at $300,000:

	(1) 19X2	(2) 19X3	(3) [(2)/(1)] − 1 Increase
Sales	$792,000	$871,200	10.00%
Less variable costs	396,000	435,600	10.00
Contribution margin	$396,000	$435,600	10.00
Less fixed costs	300,000	300,000	0
EBIT	$ 96,000	$135,600	41.25

Orion's degree of operating leverage for 19X2 can be calculated with either of the following equations:

$$\text{DOL} = \frac{\text{Percentage change in EBIT}}{\text{Percentage change in sales}}$$

$$= \frac{41.25\%}{10\%}$$

$$= 4.125$$

$$\text{DOL} = \frac{\text{Contribution margin}}{\text{EBIT}}$$

$$= \frac{\$396,000}{\$96,000}$$

$$= 4.125$$

[5] To derive this equation for DOL, rearrange the definitional equation for DOL as follows:

$$\text{DOL} = \frac{\text{Change in EBIT}}{\text{EBIT}} \times \frac{\text{Sales}}{\text{Change in sales}}$$

The change in EBIT equals the contribution margin ratio [CMR = (S − TVC)/S] times the change in sales:

$$\text{DOL} = \frac{\text{CMR} \times \text{Change in sales}}{\text{EBIT}} \times \frac{\text{Sales}}{\text{Change in sales}}$$

$$= \frac{\text{CMR} \times \text{Sales}}{\text{EBIT}}$$

Because CMR × Sales equals the contribution margin, we have:

$$\text{DOL} = \frac{\text{Contribution margin}}{\text{EBIT}}$$

FIGURE 16.6

Degree of Operating Leverage at Various Sales Levels of Orion Corporation

The degree of operating leverage declines as Orion's sales level moves away from the break-even point (S_B). Orion's break-even sales level is $600,000 = $300,000/[1 − ($360,000/$720,000)].

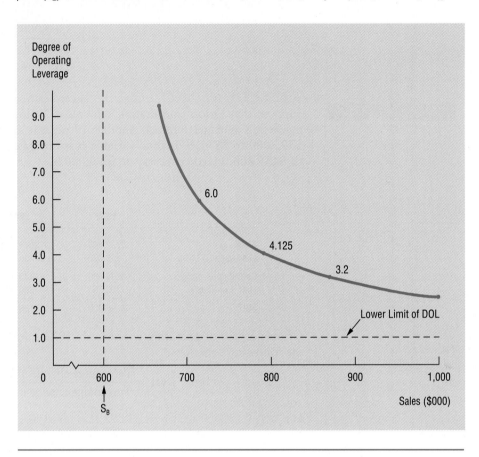

Orion's degree of operating leverage drops from 6.0 in 19X1 to 4.125 in 19X2. Furthermore, if Orion achieves its forecast for 19X3, then its DOL drops even more, to 3.2 ($435,600/$135,600).

Figure 16.6 shows the relationship between Orion Corporation's degree of operating leverage and its sales level. At the break-even sales level ($600,000), DOL is undefined because the contribution margin is divided by a zero earnings before interest and taxes. Moving above the break-even sales causes DOL to decrease, as the decline in Orion's DOL from 19X1 to 19X2 and from 19X2 to 19X3 illustrates. For extremely high sales levels, DOL asymptotically approaches (gets closer and closer to) 1.0. Because Orion has $300,000 in fixed costs, its DOL will never equal 1.0; the percentage change in EBIT will always exceed the percentage change in sales. If Orion had no fixed operating costs, then its DOL would be 1.0 at each level of output.

The use of fixed-cost operations to replace variable-cost operations—and the accompanying operating leverage—affects a company's business risk. *Business risk is the uncertainty of the company's future earnings before interest and taxes.* By definition, fixed costs must be paid whether or not the company prospers. If Orion sells only 125,000 units, then its sales are $500,000 and total variable costs are $250,000. Subtracting both variable and fixed costs ($300,000) from sales leaves Orion with a $50,000 loss, and a degree of operating leverage of −5.0 ($250,000/−$50,000). DOL = −5.0 means that a 1.0 percent increase in sales reduces losses by 5.0 percent (from −$50,000 to −$47,500).

Business risk reflects the uncertainty inherent in a company's operations. Uncertain future product prices and demand for products together with uncertain operating costs combine to create business risk. Adding operating leverage through fixed costs to these risk factors usually increases business risk still more. Yet the potential for large profits in the presence of fixed costs is attractive. To maximize shareholder wealth, the financial manager must carefully weigh the potential for profits against the added risks.

Degree of Financial Leverage

The use of debt for which a company pays a fixed interest cost creates financial leverage. Chapter 7 shows the effect of financial leverage on earnings per share and stock prices; Chapter 15 presents several financial ratios for measuring debt levels. Here we examine the **degree of financial leverage (DFL)**—a measure of the magnification of earnings after taxes for a given change in EBIT:

degree of financial leverage (DFL)

Measure of the change in earnings after taxes resulting from a change in EBIT.

$$\frac{\text{Degree of financial}}{\text{leverage (DFL)}} = \frac{\text{Percentage change in EAT}}{\text{Percentage change in EBIT}}$$

where EAT represents earnings after taxes. A large number for DFL indicates that a large percentage change occurs in EAT for a given percentage change in EBIT.[6]

The degree of financial leverage for Orion Corporation (see Table 16.3) is calculated as follows:

$$
\begin{aligned}
\frac{\text{Degree of financial}}{\text{leverage (DFL)}} &= \frac{(\text{Change in EAT})/\text{EAT}}{(\text{Change in EBIT})/\text{EBIT}} \\
&= \frac{(\$60,800 - \$32,000)/\$32,000}{(\$96,000 - \$60,000)/\$60,000} \\
&= \frac{90\%}{60\%} \\
&= 1.5
\end{aligned}
$$

The 60 percent increase in earnings before interest and taxes causes a 90 percent increase in earnings after taxes. Stated differently, a 1 percent increase in EBIT translates into a 1.5 percent increase in earnings after taxes. This magnification takes place because of the fixed interest expense.

---

[6]If a company has preferred stock in its capital structure, then *earnings available to common shareholders* should be substituted for earnings after taxes in the calculation of DFL. Earnings per share of common stock can be used in place of EAT.

Alternatively, the degree of financial leverage for Orion Corporation can be calculated with the following equation:[7]

$$\text{Degree of financial leverage (DFL)} = \frac{\text{EBIT}}{\text{Earnings before taxes}}$$

$$= \frac{\$60,000}{\$40,000}$$

$$= 1.5$$

This equation yields the same DFL (1.5) for Orion as did the preceding one.

Using fixed-cost debt instead of common stock to raise capital increases a company's financial risk. *Financial risk refers to the uncertainty of a company's future earnings after taxes.* Fixed interest cost is only one cause of this uncertainty. All of the factors that cause business risk—operating leverage and uncertainty in product prices, demand, and operating costs—also add to the uncertainty of earnings after taxes. For this reason, managers of companies with large business risk typically prefer to use small amounts of debt. To add a large financial risk from using debt onto an already existing large business risk greatly increases earnings volatility and the risk to the company's common shareholders.

Degree of Combined Leverage

degree of combined leverage (DCL)

Measure of the change in earnings after taxes resulting from a change in sales.

The combined influence of fixed operating costs and fixed financial costs is measured by the **degree of combined leverage (DCL)**. DCL relates the percentage change in earnings after taxes to the percentage change in sales:

$$\text{Degree of combined leverage (DCL)} = \frac{\text{Percentage change in EAT}}{\text{Percentage change in sales}}$$

DCL combines the effects of both operating and financial leverage.

The degree of combined leverage for Orion Corporation (see Table 16.3) is calculated as follows:

$$\text{Degree of combined leverage (DCL)} = \frac{(\text{Change in EAT})/\text{EAT}}{(\text{Change in sales})/\text{Sales}}$$

$$= \frac{(\$60,800 - \$32,000)/\$32,000}{(\$792,000 - \$720,000)/\$720,000}$$

$$= \frac{90\%}{10\%}$$

$$= 9.0$$

---

[7]Derivation of this equation is too involved to show here. Note, however, that the degree of financial leverage (DFL) can also be expressed as follows:

$$\text{Degree of financial leverage (DFL)} = \frac{\text{EBIT}}{\text{EBIT} - \text{I}}$$

where *I* is dollar interest and (EBIT − I) is earnings before taxes. If a company has preferred stock outstanding, then we modify the equation as follows:

$$\text{Degree of financial leverage (DFL)} = \frac{\text{EBIT}}{\text{EBIT} - \text{I} - [D_p/(1 - T)]}$$

where $D_p/(1 - T)$ represents the before-tax earnings required to pay preferred-stock dividends (D_p).

Because of its operating and financial leverage, a 10 percent increase in Orion's sales leads to a 90 percent (9 × 10 percent) increase in its earnings after taxes. Combined leverage for Orion is large: A 1 percent sales increase produces a 9 percent increase in earnings after taxes! DCL also magnifies declines in sales by 9 times. Overall, small percentage changes in sales produce large changes in Orion's earnings.

The degree of combined leverage (DCL) is the product of the degree of operating leverage (DOL) and the degree of financial leverage (DFL). DCL is calculated directly as follows:

$$DCL = DOL \times DFL$$
$$= 6.0 \times 1.5$$
$$= 9.0$$

This method yields the same degree of combined leverage calculated previously, and it shows the direct effects of operating and financial leverage.

In summary, operating and financial leverage combine to widen the swings in earnings after taxes resulting from any change in sales. Consequently, other things being equal, the more operating leverage a company has, the less financial leverage it can afford. But other things are not necessarily equal. An important third consideration is the stability of product demand. The more stable the demand, the higher the degree of financial leverage a company can undertake for any degree of operating leverage.

The nature of a company's products and the production methods in the industry largely determine the mix of variable and fixed operating costs. Thus, to a large extent, management must accept operating leverage as a given factor. An electric utility, for example, has a large degree of operating leverage because a huge proportion of its costs are fixed. Its annual product demand is quite stable and predictable, however, so it can afford to finance about two-thirds of its assets with bonds. By contrast, a microcomputer producer (in a highly competitive industry) may have such unstable product demand and large operating leverage that it should use little debt. Sales stability becomes the critical link between how much operating and financial leverage is advisable.

SUMMARY

• Any analysis designed to assist management in understanding and controlling a company's financial future is part of financial planning. This chapter discusses two planning techniques: percent-of-sales forecasting and break-even analysis. A company's sales forecast is the starting point for financial planning. Three methods of forecasting sales are: (1) subjective forecasts, which use sales estimates based on projections from the sales staff; (2) trend forecasts (time series), which extrapolate from past sales data using various statistical methods; and (3) correlation forecasts, which relate past company sales to macroeconomic variables.

• A forecast of increased sales leads to an expected increase in total assets to support the sales growth. Increased assets require increased liabilities and shareholder equity to finance them. Financial managers need to forecast future financing requirements to provide for an orderly entry into the financial market. The percent-of-sales forecasting method is a technique for forecasting the external financing required. Both the *pro forma* and equation methods of percent-of-sales forecasting are based on the following relationship:

$$\begin{array}{c} \text{External} \\ \text{financing} \\ \text{required} \end{array} = \begin{array}{c} \text{Total} \\ \text{financing} \\ \text{required} \end{array} - \left(\begin{array}{c} \text{Increases in} \\ \text{spontaneous} \\ \text{liabilities} \end{array} + \begin{array}{c} \text{Retained} \\ \text{earnings} \\ \text{for the year} \end{array} \right)$$

The *pro forma* method develops a detailed projected balance sheet and income statement. The equation method is a useful shortcut to forecasting external financing required because it does not require the development of *pro forma* financial statements:

$$\begin{array}{c} \text{External} \\ \text{financing} \\ \text{required} \end{array} = \frac{A}{S}(FS - S) - \left[\frac{L}{S}(FS - S) + (EAT - Div) \right]$$

- Break-even analysis shows the relationships among forecast sales, operating costs, and profit. Operating costs consist of fixed costs (depreciation, rent, insurance, and so on) and variable costs (direct labor and material). Break-even analysis is used in investment and financing decisions, product-pricing decisions, and the evaluation of production processes.

- The break-even point occurs where sales revenue equals total operating costs, causing earnings before interest and taxes to be zero. Dividing fixed operating costs (F) by the unit contribution margin (price per unit, P, less variable cost per unit, V) yields the operating break-even point in units (Q_B):

$$Q_B = \frac{F}{P - V}$$

To calculate break-even sales revenue (S_B), either multiply *P* times Q_B or use the following equation:

$$S_B = \frac{F}{(P - V)/P}$$

where $(P - V)/P$ is the contribution margin ratio. Alternatively:

$$S_B = \frac{F}{(S - TVC)/S}$$

where *TVC* represents total variable costs and *S* is total sales revenue.

- Traditional break-even analysis assumes that sales revenue and operating costs are linear functions of output. Nonlinear break-even analysis allows for price reductions at high output levels and economies of scale in operating costs.

- Companies that have fixed costs have leverage, the power of a change in sales to change earnings at a greater rate. There are two types of leverage: (1) operating leverage, which arises from fixed operating costs, and (2) financial leverage, which arises from fixed financing costs. Increases in operating leverage increase business risk—the uncertainty of future earnings before interest and taxes. Increases in financial leverage increase financial risk—the uncertainty of future earnings after taxes.

- The degree of operating leverage (DOL) and the degree of financial leverage (DFL) are calculated as follows:

$$\text{DOL} = \frac{\text{Percentage change in EBIT}}{\text{Percentage change in sales}} \quad \text{or} \quad \text{DOL} = \frac{\text{Contribution margin}}{\text{EBIT}}$$

$$DFL = \frac{\text{Percentage change in EAT}}{\text{Percentage change in EBIT}} \quad \text{or} \quad DFL = \frac{EBIT}{EBT}$$

where EBT and EAT are earnings before and after taxes, and contribution margin is sales less total variable costs.

• Operating and financial leverage combine to relate changes in sales to changes in earnings after taxes. The degree of combined leverage (DCL) measures the percentage change in EAT per percentage change in sales. DCL can be expressed in terms of degree of operating leverage and degree of financial leverage:

$$DCL = DOL \times DFL$$

A manager of a company with a large DOL typically chooses a small DFL by using less debt and more equity.

Key Terms

subjective forecast

Delphi technique

trend forecast

correlation forecast

percent-of-sales forecasting

capital intensity ratio

total financing required

spontaneous liabilities

external financing required

economies of scale

break-even analysis

leverage

degree of operating leverage (DOL)

degree of financial leverage (DFL)

degree of combined leverage (DCL)

Questions

16.1. Identify and describe three methods for forecasting company sales. Why is forecasting company sales so important?

16.2. The percent-of-sales forecasting method helps a financial manager to estimate external financing required. Explain what the term *external financing required* means, and state why it is important to forecast this dollar figure.

16.3. Analyze the following statement: "The percent-of-sales forecasting method assumes that total assets and spontaneous sources of financing change by the same dollar amount." Do you agree with this statement? Explain your answer.

16.4. Suppose that a marketing manager forecasts a 12 percent increase in sales but the actual increase is 18 percent. How would this difference likely affect the *total financing required* by the company? Explain.

16.5. An important source of financing for a company is its spontaneous liabilities. Explain what spontaneous liabilities are and why financial managers call them automatic sources of financing.

16.6. In November 1984 PepsiCo Inc. decided to use aspartame alone to sweeten its diet drinks rather than a combination of aspartame and saccharin, even though aspartame was more expensive and PepsiCo's competitors were using the combined sweeteners. The article in *The Wall Street Journal* (November 2, 1984) reporting the decision stated, "Although the change will boost Pepsi's costs, the company expects greater volume to compensate for the expense."

a. In your opinion, would the decision to use aspartame have increased PepsiCo's fixed or variable operating costs? Explain your answer.

b. Use a break-even graph to explain how greater volume could compensate for the additional expense and thus increase PepsiCo's earnings before interest and taxes.

16.7. Draw a break-even graph.

a. Illustrate what happens to the break-even point when fixed costs increase.

b. Illustrate what happens to the break-even point when variable cost per unit decreases.

16.8. Linear break-even analysis requires that sales revenue and variable costs be plotted as straight lines. What factors in practice might cause a nonlinear relationship between sales revenue and output? Between costs and output?

16.9. One way to calculate break-even sales revenue (S_B) is with the following equation:

$$S_B = \frac{F}{(S - TVC)/S}$$

Obtain the income statement of a company and calculate S_B making these substitutions: (1) Use operating expenses for fixed costs, F, and (2) use gross profit for $(S - TVC)$, where S is net sales. If possible, based on what you know about the company, assess the accuracy of your estimate. What factors might cause your estimate to be in error?

16.10. Compare and contrast *operating* leverage with *financial* leverage.

16.11. A company's degree of operating leverage declines as its sales level moves up from the break-even point.

    a. What is the smallest DOL that a company can have at an output level where earnings before interest and taxes exceed zero?

    b. What is the largest DOL that a company can have?

    c. What is the meaning of a negative sign attached to a DOL?

16.12. A company's degree of financial leverage (DFL) is a useful measure to a financial manager. Explain how to calculate DFL, show the equation, and discuss how DFL is useful.

16.13. Compare and contrast *business* risk with *financial* risk.

16.14. A company's degree of operating leverage and degree of financial leverage combine to cause proportionally larger changes in earnings after taxes as sales revenue changes. Show the equation for degree of combined leverage. Comment on why a company with a high DCL is *probably* risky.

16.15. Prove that degree of combined leverage (DCL) equals contribution margin divided by earnings before taxes. Use this relationship to calculate Orion Corporation's (see Table 16.3) degree of combined leverage and check your answer with that provided in the text.

Strategy Problem

Audrey Herrera, CFO of LawnCare Company, is planning the company's acquisition of external financing for the 19X5 fiscal year. As part of the planning process, Ms. Herrera wants to forecast the company's need for external financing under two scenarios. She also wants to calculate the company's break-even point for the past year and determine how changes in variable costs would have affected the company's profitability. Ms. Herrera believes such analyses will give her a better understanding of the company's cost structure and potential profitability. To assist bankers with an evaluation of the company's risk, she will supply each potential lender with information regarding the company's degree of combined leverage.

The company's cost accountant supplied Ms. Herrera with the operating statement on the next page for the year ending December 31, 19X4. LawnCare's total assets at year-end 19X4 totaled $2,105,000, and its spontaneous liabilities (accounts payable and taxes payable) totaled $385,000.

a. Calculate the external financing LawnCare Company will need during 19X5 based on the equation method of percent-of-sales forecasting under two conditions: (1) sales increase by 12 percent and (2) sales increase by 24 percent. Assume that LawnCare's after-tax profit margin stays the same from 19X4 through 19X5.

b. What is the company's break-even point in units and in dollars? If total variable costs in 19X4 had been 10 percent greater than they actually were, then how many units would the company have needed to sell in order to earn the same operating profit?

c. What is the company's degree of combined leverage?

LawnCare Company: Operating Statement for the Year Ending December 31, 19X4 (Thousands of Dollars)

Sales (10,203 units × $236 average price)		$2,408
Less variable costs		
Materials and supplies	$380	
Wages	420	
Utilities	67	
		867
Contribution margin		$1,541
Less fixed operating costs		
Salaries and benefits	$416	
Advertising	30	
Utilities	85	
Depreciation	70	
Property taxes	18	
Patent amortization	28	
Miscellaneous	60	
		707
Operating profit (EBIT)		$ 834
Less interest		82
Earnings before taxes		$ 752
Less taxes (34%)		256
Earnings after taxes[a]		$ 496

[a]The company's board of directors typically declares a common-stock dividend equal to 40 percent of the company's earnings after taxes.

Strategy

Solution

a. The amount of external financing the company will need varies with the growth rate of sales:

Calculate forecast sales.

1. Growth rate of 12 percent ($2,697 = 1.12 × $2,408):

Use forecast sales in the equation for external financing required.

$$\text{External financing required} = \frac{\$2,105}{\$2,408}(\$2,697 - \$2,408)$$

EAT ($555.6) equals last year's profit margin (0.206) times forecast sales ($2,697).

$$- \left[\frac{\$385}{\$2,408}(\$2,697 - \$2,408) + (\$555.6 - \$222.2)\right]$$

$$= \$252.6 - (\$46.2 + \$333.4) = -\$127$$

LawnCare Company will have more than enough internal financing to support its 12 percent growth rate in sales. Based on this forecast, it can plan to pay an extra dividend, retire debt, or build liquidity.

Calculate forecast sales.

2. Growth rate of 24 percent ($2,986 = 1.24 × $2,408):

Use forecast sales in the equation for external financing required.

$$\text{External financing required} = \frac{\$2,105}{\$2,408}(\$2,986 - \$2,408)$$

EAT ($615.1) equals last year's profit margin (0.206) times forecast sales ($2,986).

$$- \left[\frac{\$385}{\$2,408}(\$2,986 - \$2,408) + (\$615.1 - \$246)\right]$$

$$= \$505.3 - (\$92.4 + \$369.1) = \$43.8$$

Based on this forecast, the company should prepare to raise $43,800 during 19X5.

Calculate variable cost per unit.

b.   Variable cost per unit $= \dfrac{\$867,000}{10,203} = \$85$

Divide fixed operating costs by the unit contribution margin.

$$Q_B = \dfrac{\$707,000}{\$236 - \$85}$$

$$= 4,682.12 \text{ or } 4,683 \text{ units (rounded to next whole unit)}$$

Multiply unit break-even by sales price per unit.

$$S_B = 4,683 \text{ units} \times \$236 \text{ per unit}$$

$$= \$1,105,188$$

The company breaks even with 4,683 units and sales revenue of $1,105,188. If total variable costs had been 10 percent greater, then the company would have needed to generate more sales revenue to have EBIT = $834,000.

Use the break-even equation and multiply variable costs by 1.10.

$$\text{EBIT} = \text{Sales revenue} - \text{Total costs}$$

$$= S - (\text{TVC} + F)$$

$$\$834,000 = S - [(\$867,000 \times 1.10) + \$707,000]$$

$$\$834,000 = S - \$1,660,700$$

$$S = \$2,494,700$$

The number of units needed to produce this much sales revenue is:

Divide sales revenue by sales price per unit.

$$\text{Number of units} = \dfrac{\$2,494,700}{\$236 \text{ per unit}}$$

$$= 10,570.8 \text{ or } 10,571 \text{ units}$$

c. To calculate the degree of combined leverage, first calculate the degree of operating and financial leverage:

Use the shortcut equation to calculate DOL.

$$\text{DOL} = \dfrac{\text{Contribution margin}}{\text{EBIT}}$$

$$= \dfrac{\$1,541,000}{\$834,000} = 1.85$$

For each 1 percent change in sales revenue, LawnCare's EBIT changes 1.85 percent.

Use the shortcut equation to calculate DFL.

$$\text{DFL} = \dfrac{\text{EBIT}}{\text{EBT}}$$

$$= \dfrac{\$834,000}{\$752,000} = 1.11$$

For each 1 percent change in EBIT, the company's earnings after taxes change 1.11 percent.

Now combine the degrees of operating and financial leverage to calculate the degree of combined leverage:

Multiply DOL times DFL to obtain DCL.

$$\text{DCL} = \text{DOL} \times \text{DFL}$$

$$= 1.85 \times 1.11 = 2.05$$

For each 1 percent change in sales revenue, LawnCare's earnings after taxes change 2.05 percent.

Demonstration Problem

Chock Full O'Nuts (CFON) processes and sells coffees, teas, peanuts, and other food products. The company's net sales for 19X1 were $270,169,000, and its after-tax profit margin was 3.2543 percent. Other key figures from the company's 19X1 income statement are as follows: Cost of sales, $193,329,000; Operating expenses, $54,851,000; Earnings before taxes, $15,523,000; Earnings after taxes, $8,792,000. CFON's balance sheet as of July 31, 19X1 is provided below (in thousands of dollars):

Assets		Liabilities and Equity	
Cash and equivalents	$ 1,861	Accounts payable	$ 9,570
Accounts receivable	26,672	Accrued expenses	9,904
Inventories	34,098	Short-term debt	2,143
Other current assets	3,934	Total current liabilities	$ 21,617
Total current assets	$ 66,565	Long-term liabilities	109,762
		Common stock	38,662
Net fixed assets	49,181	Retained earnings	21,430
Other noncurrent assets	75,725	Total claims	$191,471
Total assets	$191,471		

a. Construct CFON's income statement for 19X1 (in thousands of dollars).
b. Describe three methods for forecasting CFON's 19X2 net sales.
c. Use the equation method of percent-of-sales forecasting to estimate CFON's external financing requirements in 19X2. Assume the following conditions: (1) Net sales will increase 10 percent. (2) The 19X1 after-tax profit margin will prevail in 19X2. (3) The dividend payout ratio will be 40 percent. (4) The company is operating at full capacity.
d. Repeat the calculation in Part *c* but assume a 20 percent growth rate in net sales. What principle is illustrated by your answer here and your answer in Part *c*?
e. Construct CFON's *pro forma* balance sheet for 19X2. Assume that the conditions in Part *c* prevail and external financing is raised via long-term debt.
f. Calculate CFON's 19X1 break-even sales level in thousands of dollars assuming that (1) cost of sales equals total variable costs and (2) operating expenses equal fixed costs. Check your answer by constructing CFON's income statement at the break-even level.
g. Draw a break-even graph based on Part *f*. (*Note:* Instead of Units Produced and Sold, put Sales Revenue on the horizontal axis.)
h. Calculate CFON's degree of operating, financial, and combined leverage using the assumptions in Part *f*. Interpret the meaning of each of your three answers.
i. What is the difference between *business risk* and *financial risk*? Considering both business risk and financial risk, do you think CFON is highly risky, moderately risky, or marginally risky? Explain.

Problems

Percent-of-sales forecasting and the *pro forma* balance sheet

16.1. In 19X4 Kieso Petroleum's sales were $1,250,000. Its abbreviated balance sheet at the end of 19X4 was as follows:

Assets	Liabilities and Shareholder Equity	
	Accounts payable	$ 200,000
	Taxes payable	100,000
	Long-term debt	300,000
	Shareholder equity	400,000
$1,000,000		$1,000,000

The company's profit margin after taxes is 6 percent and management expects this rate to prevail in 19X5. Management also expects sales to expand in 19X5 by 15 percent, and Kieso has a 40 percent dividend payout rate (it pays out 40 percent of its after-tax earnings in dividends). How much external financing will Kieso need during 19X5? Develop Kieso's *pro forma* balance sheet for 19X5 assuming that external financing is raised via long-term debt.

Percent-of-sales forecasting and financing

16.2. Consider the original position of Kieso Petroleum in the preceding problem. Now assume that management expects sales to expand by 30 percent. The company's profit margin after taxes remains at 6 percent and the dividend payout rate remains at 40 percent.

a. How much external financing will be needed in 19X5?

b. Develop Kieso's *pro forma* balance sheet for 19X5 assuming that external financing is raised via long-term debt.

c. What factors should Kieso's management consider in deciding which sources of financing to use?

Percent-of-sales forecasting and financing

16.3. Saxon-Muckett Company's latest financial statements appear below and on the next page. The company's management expects its after-tax profit margin to persist over the near future. Heather Prewitt, the company's marketing manager, anticipates a 30 percent sales increase for next year. Saxon-Muckett subscribes to a 30 percent dividend payout rate to common shareholders.

a. How much external financing does the company need in 19X9?

b. Develop Saxon-Muckett's *pro forma* balance sheet for 19X9 assuming that external financing is raised via long-term debt.

c. Should the external financing be debt or equity? Explain.

Saxon-Muckett Company: Balance Sheet as of December 31, 19X8 (Thousands of Dollars)

Assets		Liabilities and Shareholder Equity	
Cash	$ 10,000	Accounts payable	$ 20,000
Marketable securities	20,000	Taxes payable	10,000
Accounts receivable (net)	30,000	Accrued pension contributions	
Inventories	40,000	payable	5,000
Plant and equipment (net)	100,000	Bonds payable	50,000
Trademarks, patents, and goodwill	10,000		
		Equity	
		Preferred stock (100,000	
		shares; $8 dividend)	10,000
		Common stock (1,000,000	
		shares)	100,000
		Retained earnings	15,000
Total assets	$210,000	Total liabilities and equity	$210,000

Saxon-Muckett Company: Income Statement for Year Ending December 31, 19X8 (Thousands of Dollars)

Sales	$320,000
Less cost of goods sold	275,000
Gross profit	$ 45,000
Less operating expenses	9,500
Net operating income	$ 35,500
Less interest expense	4,700
Earnings before taxes	$ 30,800
Less taxes (40%)	12,320
Earnings after taxes	$ 18,480
Preferred-stock dividends	800
Earnings available to common shareholders	$ 17,680

Percent-of-sales forecasting and growth rates

16.4. Maytag Corporation designs, manufactures, and distributes home appliances, including the brand names Maytag, Magic Chef, Hoover, Jenn-Air, Admiral, and Norge. The company's net sales for 19X1 were $2,977,695,000, and its after-tax profit margin was 2.6536 percent. Other key figures from the company's 19X1 income statement are as follows: Cost of sales, $2,254,221,000; Operating expenses, $524,898,000; Earnings before taxes, $123,417,000; Earnings after taxes, $79,017,000. Maytag's balance sheet as of December 31, 19X1 is provided below (in thousands of dollars):

Assets		Liabilities and Equity	
Cash and equivalents	$ 48,752	Accounts payable	$ 273,731
Accounts receivable	457,773	Accrued expenses	246,803
Inventories	489,082	Short-term debt	47,074
Other current assets	81,026	Total current liabilities	$ 567,608
Total current assets	$1,076,633	Long-term liabilities	956,875
		Common stock	313,840
Net fixed assets	835,493	Retained earnings	696,745
Other noncurrent assets	622,942		
		Total claims	$2,535,068
Total assets	$2,535,068		

a. Construct Maytag's income statement for 19X1.
b. Use the equation method of percent-of-sales forecasting to estimate Maytag's external financing requirements in 19X2. Assume the following conditions: (1) Net sales will increase 5 percent. (2) The 19X1 after-tax profit margin will prevail in 19X2. (3) The dividend payout ratio will be 20 percent. (4) Maytag is operating at full capacity.
c. Construct Maytag's *pro forma* balance sheet for 19X2. Assume that the conditions in Part *b* prevail and external financing is raised via long-term debt.
d. Suppose that Maytag's 19X2 net sales increase 10 percent, not 5 percent, and the other conditions in Part *b* remain the same. How would this difference affect the *external financing requirements?* Explain.

Contribution margin and
pro forma income statement

16.5. Gujarti Corporation is preparing its operating budget for the third quarter of 19X3. The operating budget will be a *pro forma* income statement that does not include interest expense. Management has determined the following relationships:

- Raw materials expense is 12 percent of sales.
- Labor is 16 percent of sales.
- Utilities are $4,600 plus 6 percent of sales.
- Factory overhead is 5 percent of sales.
- Selling and administrative expenses are $6,800 plus 5 percent of sales.
- Fixed overhead and salaries are $40,000 in each quarter.
- Depreciation expense will be $50,000.

The company's marketing department has forecast that third-quarter sales will be $218,000.
a. Calculate the contribution margin and contribution margin ratio for the third quarter.
b. Construct the *pro forma* income statement for Gujarti Corporation's third quarter.

Contribution margin ratio
and EBIT

16.6. U.S. Paper Company has a 20 percent contribution margin ratio. Sales revenues are currently $360,000, and earnings before interest and taxes are $40,000.
a. After meeting variable costs, what amount of sales revenue is left to contribute toward the payment of fixed costs?
b. If sales decline to $300,000, what will be the level of earnings before interest and taxes?

Break-even point in units
and sales revenue

16.7. A company has $980,000 in fixed costs, an $11 price on its product, and a $7 variable cost per unit. Calculate the following:
a. Unit contribution margin.
b. Break-even point in units of output.
c. Break-even point in sales revenue.
d. Draw a break-even graph based on units of output.

Contribution margin ratio
and break-even analysis

16.8. Pamela Tudsbury, financial officer of Central Broadcasting, wants to calculate the company's break-even point in sales dollars (revenue from advertisers). Total operating costs for the company are expected to be $1,760,000 during the upcoming period. Total fixed costs are $1,200,000. Anticipated advertising revenues are $2,600,000.
a. Calculate Central Broadcasting's contribution margin ratio.
b. Calculate the company's break-even point in sales dollars. Interpret your answer.
c. Write a brief memo to Ms. Tudsbury explaining the implications of the company's break-even point.

Break-even analysis and
target EBIT

16.9. Sexton Company manufactures and sells one product. Price and cost data relating to Sexton's product and operations are as follows:

Selling price per unit	$29.80
Variable costs per unit:	
Raw materials	$11.00
Direct labor	5.00
Manufacturing overhead	2.50
Selling expenses	1.30
Total variable costs per unit	$19.80

	Annual fixed costs:	
	Manufacturing overhead	$ 292,000
	Selling and administrative	276,000
	Total fixed costs	$ 568,000
	Forecast annual sales	$3,000,000

a. What is Sexton Company's break-even point in units?
b. How many units must Sexton sell in order to have $260,000 earnings before interest and taxes for the year?
c. Sexton's management estimates that direct labor costs will increase 8 percent next year. How many units must the company sell next year to reach break-even?

CMA examination, modified: contribution margin and break-even analysis

16.10. Enzio Perronne started a pizza restaurant in 19X0. For this purpose he rented a building for $400 per month. He hired one employee to work full time at the restaurant and six college students to work part time delivering pizza. An outside accountant was hired for tax and bookkeeping purposes, whom Mr. Perronne pays $300 per month. The necessary restaurant equipment and delivery cars were purchased with equity financing. Mr. Perronne has noticed that expenses for utilities and supplies have been rather constant. The accountant has suggested that the restaurant's only variable cost is the cost of food. The average pizza price is $2.50.

Mr. Perronne increased his volume of business between 19X0 and 19X3, with profits more than doubling since 19X0. He does not understand why his profits have increased faster than his volume.

The accountant has prepared the accompanying *pro forma* income statement for 19X4.
a. Calculate the unit contribution margin for the restaurant.
b. What is the break-even point in number of pizzas sold?
c. Draw a break-even graph for the restaurant.
d. Briefly explain to Mr. Perronne why profit has increased at a faster rate than sales.

Perronne Company: *Pro Forma* Income Statement for the Year Ending December 31, 19X4

Sales		$95,000
Cost of food sold	$28,500	
Wages and fringe benefits of restaurant help	8,150	
Wages and fringe benefits of delivery help	17,300	
Rent	4,800	
Accounting services	3,600	
Depreciation of delivery equipment	5,000	
Depreciation of restaurant equipment	3,000	
Utilities	2,325	
Supplies (soap, floor wax, etc.)	1,200	
		$73,875
Net income before taxes		$21,125
Income taxes		6,338
Net income		$14,787

Degrees of operating, financial, and combined leverage

16.11.   The following statements are for Avery Firearms Company:

Avery Firearms: Operating Statements Ending December 31 (Thousands of Dollars)

		19X3		19X4
Sales revenues		$28,000		$35,000
Less total costs				
Variable	$7,000		$8,750	
Fixed	9,000	16,000	9,000	17,750
EBIT		$12,000		$17,250
Less interest		600		600
EBT		$11,400		$16,650
Less taxes (40%)		4,560		6,660
EAT		$ 6,840		$ 9,990

a. Using percentage changes, calculate the following: (1) degree of operating leverage, (2) degree of financial leverage, and (3) degree of combined leverage.
b. Repeat Part *a* using alternative methods.

Degrees of leverage at different levels of output

16.12.   The following information applies to Griffith Telechronics:

	19X1	19X2
Output (units)	90,000	100,000
Sales revenue	$450,000	$500,000
Less:		
Variable selling and production costs ($4.50 each)	$405,000	$450,000
Fixed costs: selling and administrative	30,000	30,000
Net operating profit (EBIT)	$ 15,000	$ 20,000
Less interest	4,000	4,000
Profit before taxes	$ 11,000	$ 16,000
Less taxes (40%)	4,400	6,400
Profit after taxes	$ 6,600	$ 9,600

a. Calculate the degree of operating, financial, and combined leverage for Griffith Telechronics at its sales level in 19X1 and in 19X2.
b. Interpret your calculations in Part *a*.
c. Explain why each level of output has a different degree of operating leverage.

Break-even graph, EBIT, and
DOL.

16.13.   Spreads Inc. and Sheets Company manufacture bedspreads in Greenville, South
Carolina. Spreads is highly automated, whereas Sheets does a lot of manual
work. Because of their different manufacturing processes, Spreads has high fixed
costs and a low variable cost per bedspread, and Sheets has low fixed costs and
a high variable cost per bedspread. Summary data for 19X9 are as follows:

	Spreads Inc.	Sheets Company
Fixed costs	$600,000	$300,000
Variable cost per unit	$15	$24
Selling price per unit	$40	$40

a. Calculate break-even points in units and sales revenue for each company.
b. Draw break-even graphs for Spreads and Sheets, placing them side by side on

graph paper so that you can easily see the differences between the two companies.

c. Calculate earnings before interest and taxes for each company assuming $1,000,000 in sales revenue.

d. Calculate the degree of operating leverage for each company assuming $1,000,000 in sales revenue.

e. Check your answers in Part *d* by assuming a 10 percent increase in sales revenue and noting the percentage increase in earnings before interest and taxes.

f. If the general economy were headed into a boom period, which company— Spreads or Sheets—would you prefer to own? Explain.

Computer Problems

Percent-of-sales forecasting: template FORECAST

16.14. Robin Marlow, vice president of finance for Willard Batteries, is assessing the financing required to meet planned investments in 19X2. The company's income statement and balance sheet for 19X1 are given below.

Willard Batteries: Income Statement for the Year Ending December 19X1 (Thousands of Dollars)

Sales	$53,465
Cost of goods sold	39,874
Gross profit	$13,591
Operating expenses	9,785
EBIT	$ 3,806
Interest expense	1,287
Earnings before taxes	$ 2,519
Taxes	856
Earnings after taxes	$ 1,663

Willard Batteries: Balance Sheet as of December 31, 19X1 (Thousands of Dollars)

Assets	
Cash	$ 1,057
Marketable securities	867
Accounts receivable	2,573
Inventory	9,345
Total current assets	$13,842
Net fixed assets	18,623
Total assets	$32,465

Liabilities and Equity	
Accounts payable	$ 2,761
Accruals	1,329
Notes payable	2,543
Total current liabilities	$ 6,633
Long-term debt	9,621
Total liabilities	$16,254
Common stock	10,000
Retained earnings	6,211
Total liabilities and equity	$32,465

The company has 1,000,000 shares of common stock outstanding. Additional shares can be issued to net $20 per share. The company's dividend payout ratio is 50 percent. Interest is 9 percent per year on short-term loans and 11 percent per year on long-term debt. The contract on the outstanding long-term debt stipulates a minimum current ratio of 2.0 and maximum total debt ratio of 0.5. The company is in the 34 percent tax bracket. Mr. Marlow anticipates a 10 percent sales increase in 19X2. In 19X1 fixed assets were operated at full capacity and current assets were at desirable levels.

Prepare the *pro forma* income statement and balance sheet for 19X2 and calculate the amount of external financing required. Considering the constraints on the current ratio and total debt ratio, how much of the external financing should be short-term debt, long-term debt, and equity? Support your answer with calculations.

Break-even analysis: template BRKEVEN

16.15. Super Sales Corporation is assessing the viability of wholesaling computer diskettes, a new product line it plans to add to its present business. The marketing manager, Barbara Williamson, expects the company to sell 250,000 diskettes annually at a price of 80 cents each. They will be purchased from the manufacturer at a cost of 60 cents each. Two new sales representatives must be hired; they will be compensated at the rate of 5 cents per diskette. Fixed costs associated with the new product line are: rental expenses at $500 per month, personnel costs at $1,000 per month, and other expenses at $10,000 per year.

a. Calculate the break-even sales volume in units and in dollars.

b. Nancy Patty, the financial manager, is a bit skeptical about the figures. In a market as competitive as computer diskettes, the selling price could be anywhere between 70 and 80 cents each, and the sales figure between 200,000 and 250,000 diskettes. Recalculate Part *a* assuming selling prices of 70 cents and 75 cents.

c. The personnel manager, Cyril Walsh, thinks that the estimated rental expense is reasonable but believes personnel costs could rise as high as $1,200 per month and other expenses could go to $15,000 per year. Recalculate Part *a* using Mr. Walsh's estimates.

d. Do you think that Super Sales should add computer diskettes to its line of products? Explain your answer.

DOL, DFL, and DCL: template LEVERAGE

16.16. Malliaris Corporation is considering three alternative technologies for manufacturing ballpoint pens. It could choose a labor-intensive technology, intermediate technology, or automated technology. The investment outlay, fixed costs, and variable cost per unit for each alternative are given below:

Technology	Investment Outlay	Fixed Costs	Variable Cost per Unit
Labor-intensive	$2,000,000	$ 500,000	$1.90
Intermediate	2,500,000	1,000,000	1.50
Automated	3,000,000	2,000,000	0.80

The selling price of the pen will be $2.50. The company proposes to finance the project with 50 percent debt and 50 percent equity. The debt capital will be raised by issuing 10 percent coupon bonds at par value with a 15-year maturity, and the equity capital will be raised by issuing common stock to net the company $10 per share. Management expects to sell 2,000,000 ballpoint pens each year. Malliaris Corporation is in the 34 percent tax bracket.

a. Calculate the degree of operating leverage, degree of financial leverage, degree of combined leverage, earnings after taxes, and earnings per share for each of the technologies being considered.

b. Recalculate Part *a* for projected sales of (1) 1,500,000 pens and (2) 2,500,000 pens.

c. As sales increase, how will business risk, financial risk, and total risk change? Explain your answer.
d. Which technology has the greatest risk? Explain your answer.
e. Which technology would you prefer (1) in a recession and (2) in a boom economy? Explain your answers.

((VHS))

VIDEO CASE PROBLEM

Rolled Oats Company

Rolled Oats Company (ROC) is a diversified food company established more than 100 years ago by two entrepreneurs. Now a publicly held company, ROC is a major competitor in the grocery products business, with sales of $5,421 million in 19X3. Besides its famous Rolled Oats Cereal, the company also manufactures and distributes other hot and cold breakfast cereals, granola snacks, cake mixes, syrups and frozen foods, sports drinks, and pet foods.

ROC's long-range strategic plan includes the following mission statement: *Maximize shareholder value by developing and defending franchise brand names*. Paul W. Burgheim, CEO of ROC, has challenged company employees to carry out the mission by maintaining: (1) a 15 percent annual growth rate in sales, (2) a 5 percent after-tax profit margin, and (3) a constant or increasing total asset turnover. Mr. Burgheim emphasizes that the company must become more efficient, operate at lower cost, and be more profitable.

The company's sales growth rate from 19X2 to 19X3 fell short of Mr. Burgheim's goal, as the following table shows:

	19X3	**19X2**	**% Change**
Sales ($ millions)	$5,421	$4,888	10.9
Earnings after taxes ($ millions)	$173	$202	(14.4)
Total assets ($ millions)	$3,012	$3,070	(1.9)
After-tax profit margin	3.19%	4.13%	—
Total asset turnover	1.80X	1.59X	—

Sales grew only 10.9 percent, not the 15 percent desired by Mr. Burgheim. Moreover, earnings after taxes declined 14.4 percent from $202 million to $173 million. As a consequence, the after-tax profit margin declined from 4.13 percent to 3.19 percent. If sales had grown 15 percent and if the profit margin had been 5 percent, then company earnings would have been $281 million, not $173 million. Although pleased with the total asset turnover, Mr. Burg-

heim believes that ROC can achieve higher levels of profit and profitability.

To achieve a 15 percent annual growth rate in sales, ROC's new-product pipeline must constantly be filled with innovations. To be consistent with corporate philosophy, the new food products must be nutritious and low in fat content; ready to consume or easy to prepare; and respond to needs and wants of customers. Mr. Burgheim demands that new products not be faddish; he wants them "to stand the test of time." In addition, ROC must be able to achieve economies of scale in production and be able to create brand loyalty for each new product.

During the past five years, while ROC increased its market share of oatmeal cereals, fierce competition caused a decline in the company's market share of cereals overall. Sales of granola bars declined because of a scientific study questioning their health benefits. To compensate for these declining product markets, ROC's strategic plan calls for the development of several new products. One new product nearing completion of market testing is a snack food called Cinnamon Oat Circles. Market researchers forecast annual demand at 45 million boxes, with a wholesale price of $1.95 per box. Variable operating cost per box is $0.45, and total fixed operating costs are $49.5 million. A substantial part of the fixed costs is allocated for advertisement and promotion to differentiate the product from competing snack foods.

Variable operating costs for the company as a whole approximately equal the company's cost of goods sold; fixed operating costs approximately equal the company's operating expenses. Based on these approximations and the income statement provided below, ROC's variable operating costs were $2,790 million and its fixed operating costs were $2,233 million in 19X3. Financing costs in 19X3 included $110 million of interest expense and $51.9 million of common-stock dividends.

Any additional financing in the near future will come from long-term borrowing. Mr. Burgheim believes that ROC's financial position is strong, as reflected by the company's balance sheet provided on the next page.

Balance Sheet, December 31, 19X3
(in millions of dollars)

Cash and equivalents	$ 110	Accounts payable	$ 370
Accounts receivable	625	Accrued expenses	437
Inventories	432	Short-term debt	284
Other current assets	121	Total current liabilities	$1,091
Total current assets	$1,288		
		Long-term liabilities	638
Net fixed assets	1,416	Common stock	165
Other noncurrent assets	308	Retained earnings	1,118
Total assets	$3,012	Total claims	$3,012

Income Statement,
Year Ended December 31, 19X3
(in millions of dollars)

Net sales	$5,421
Cost of goods sold	2,790
Gross profit	$2,631
Operating expenses	2,233
EBIT	$ 398
Interest expense	110
Earnings before taxes	$ 288
Income taxes	115
Earnings after taxes	$ 173

a. Use the equation method of percent-of-sales forecasting to estimate ROC's external financing requirements in 19X4. Assume that ROC reaches Mr. Burgheim's goals: Net sales increase 15 percent, and the after-tax profit margin is 5 percent. Also assume that the dividend payout ratio is 30 percent, and ROC is operating at full capacity.

b. Suppose ROC's 19X4 performance is similar to its 19X3 performance: Net sales increase 10.9 percent, and the after-tax profit margin is 3.19 percent. Assume once again that the dividend payout ratio is 30 percent, and ROC is operating at full capacity. Estimate the external financing requirements under the preceding conditions.

c. Why are external financing requirements under the conditions in Part *b* smaller than those under the conditions in Part *a*?

d. Construct ROC's *pro forma* balance sheet in millions of dollars for 19X4 assuming Mr. Burgheim's goals are achieved—i.e., under the conditions in Part *a*.

e. Calculate the following measures for ROC in 19X3: (1) break-even sales level in millions of dollars, (2) degree of operating leverage, (3) degree of financial leverage, and (4) degree of combined leverage.

f. Which of the following costs creates more risk for ROC: (1) fixed operating costs or (2) fixed financing costs? Explain.

g. (1) Calculate the break-even point for Cinnamon Oat Circles in number of boxes produced and sold. (2) Draw a break-even graph for Cinnamon Oat Circles. (3) Show the profit (EBIT) level on the graph from producing and selling 45 million boxes, the forecast demand level.

h. Describe the competitive advantage sought by Mr. Burgheim in introducing new products that enable ROC to "achieve economies of scale in production" and "create brand loyalty."

Selected References

Chambers, John C., Mullick K. Satinder, and Donald D. Smith. *An Executive's Guide to Forecasting.* New York: Wiley, 1974.

Cooley, Philip L., and John W. Cunningham. "Managing Discretionary Fixed Costs." *Managerial Planning,* July–August 1977: 13–16.

De Bondt, Werner F. M., and Mary M. Bange. "Inflation Forecast Errors and Time Variation in Term Premia." *Journal of Financial and Quantitative Analysis,* December 1992: 479–496.

Edwards, Charles E., and Philip L. Cooley. "Leverage Financing Choices for Real Estate Investments." *Real Estate Appraiser and Analyst,* Summer 1984: 73–78.

Georgoff, D. M., and R. G. Murdick. "Manager's Guide to Forecasting." *Harvard Business Review,* January–February 1986: 110–120.

Johnson, James M., David R. Campbell, and James L. Wittenbach. "Identifying and Resolving Problems in Corporate Liquidity." *Financial Executive,* May 1982: 41–46.

Lev, Baruch. "On the Association Between Operating Leverage and Risk." *Journal of Financial and Quantitative Analysis,* September 1974: 542–550.

Strischek, Dev. "Break-even Analysis and Operating Leverage." *Journal of Commercial Bank Lending,* October 1983: 32–41.

Wheelwright, Steven C., and Spyros Makridakis. *Forecasting Methods for Management,* 2nd ed. Somerset, NJ: Wiley/Interscience, 1977.

Wood, Edwin A., and Robert G. Murdick. "A Practical Solution to Forecasting Problems." *Management Accounting,* May 1980: 45–48.

INSTITUTIONAL
FEATURES OF
LONG-TERM FINANCING

Part VI

SMALL-BUSINESS PERSPECTIVE

*Financing Expansion
of the Company*

A financial analysis of In Shape Inc., the exercise equipment outlet operated by Kathy Griffin and Jim Sutherland, identified several areas in which expenses were unnecessarily high. If these expenses were controlled, profitability would increase substantially. The analysis of the company also highlighted the poor cash flow resulting from the large investment in receivables and inventory.

Kathy and Jim wondered if there might be a complementary product or service they could offer that would increase the return on their investment. A possible solution came unexpectedly.

As part of its promotional efforts, In Shape often sponsored biking and jogging marathons. This sponsorship resulted in excellent publicity for the company through radio and television announcements and also provided Kathy and Jim with opportunities to meet potential customers.

At one of the biking marathons, they met John Heatherly, a resident of London, England. John was vacationing in the United States and had entered the marathon to meet others who enjoyed biking. John found that he shared many interests with Jim. John was employed at a health club, just as Jim had been prior to opening In Shape. John also dreamed of opening his own business someday but at present did not have enough capital to do so.

John, Jim, and Kathy met several times after the marathon. They discussed the possibility of opening a health club outfitted with In Shape's exercise equipment. John would be part owner and manager, but In Shape would also own stock in the club in return for furnishing the equipment.

Establishing a health club seemed to be a good idea because, if it were successful, its excellent cash flow would offset some of the cash flow problems of In Shape. Members would always pay in advance for their memberships—either semiannually or annually—and there would be very little inventory and no accounts receivable.

John, Jim, and Kathy discussed ownership and liability issues. Although Kathy and Jim wanted to be owners, they were hesitant to assume any financial or legal liabilities. If the club were not located near In Shape's outlet, it would be difficult for Kathy and Jim to monitor its operations. Also, because of the long hours Kathy and Jim worked at In Shape, they did not have much time to devote to a new health club.

It was also necessary to determine the proportional ownership that In Shape would receive for its investment in equipment. Kathy and Jim believed that this issue could not be settled until the total start-up costs were determined. A plan could then be developed to establish the ownership structure. They decided not to make any final decisions until the exact location of the club was chosen and the total start-up costs were known.

Companies of all sizes face financing decisions through all of their growth stages. This part of the text provides information on the various types of long-term financing. Bonds, stock, and retained earnings are discussed, and the legal restrictions of each are explained.

Chapter 17

BONDS, OPTIONS, CONVERTIBLES, AND WARRANTS

Strange Corporate Securities

Corporate managers and investment bankers have active imaginations when it comes to designing securities. "Plain vanilla" stocks and bonds seem too mundane for some companies. General Cinema Corporation, theater operator and owner of the publisher of this book, illustrates the point. In the 1980s General Cinema issued exchangeable bonds—a type of convertible bond. The strange part is this: Instead of being convertible into the common stock of the issuer, the bonds were convertible into the common stock of RJR Nabisco. At the time, General

Cinema owned a large number of shares of RJR Nabisco. Although an unusual security, exchangeable bonds have been issued by other companies: Corning Glass bonds exchangeable for Owens-Corning stock; Cigna bonds exchangeable for PaineWebber stock; Petrie Stores bonds exchangeable for Toys "R" Us stock.

Another entry into the world of strange securities are bonds backed (collateralized) by hospital bills. Lehman Brothers, an investment banking firm, called them HeARTS—an acronym for Healthcare Accounts-Receivable-backed

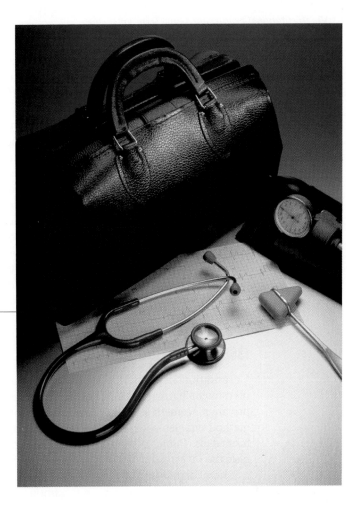

Tranche Securities. As you might guess, this unwieldy acronym did not become popular on Wall Street. The bond itself, however, may well become popular in the 1990s.

Transforming hospital bills into securities is called *securitization,* which works as follows: An investment banking firm (1) buys a large number of accounts receivable from hospitals, (2) pools the receivables into a group of several millions of dollars, (3) repackages the pool into bonds, notes, or commercial paper, (4) sells the asset-backed securities to investors, and (5) pays interest and repays principal from collections on the receivables. Investment bankers have had great success in securitizing student loans, home mortgages, car loans, and other consumer debt. Now they hope to add hospital bills, which represent a large portion of consumer debt, to the list. Tom Capasse, co-head of Merrill Lynch's asset-backed securities group, says: "It's an area of focus for us . . ."

Source: Robert L. Rose, "A Little-Known Type of Convertible Bond Can Be a Profitable Investment for Some," *The Wall Street Journal,* June 9, 1986, 21; George Anders, "Wall Street Hopes for Some Good in an Ill Wind," *The Wall Street Journal,* December 4, 1992, C1 and C9. *Photo Credit:* R. Price/West Light.

The preceding chapters treat bonds as generic securities issued to raise funds for financing long-term assets. This chapter covers descriptive features that differentiate one bond from another and that affect the interest rate a company must pay. Financial managers need to be aware of these features in order to design bonds that minimize the cost of capital. The chapter begins with a review of the way companies issue bonds and the pricing of bonds in the capital market. Following this review, the chapter describes variations in the bonds companies issue. Some of these variations may drastically alter your present perception of corporate bonds. For example, some bonds do not pay interest at all! Still other bonds pay interest that changes from payment to payment. Convertible bonds may be exchanged for common stock; bondholders have the option to make the exchange when they want to, but some companies force them to do so. Some companies give investors an *option* to buy common stock with each bond purchased, but others do not. All of these bond features, and the reasons they exist, are discussed in this chapter. The concluding section arrays several of these types of bonds on the security market line to illustrate their risk-return trade-off.

ISSUING CORPORATE BONDS

Corporations issue bonds to investors in a public offering with the help of an investment banking syndicate, or they issue them to financial institutions in a private placement (often with an investment banker serving as an adviser). Either method enables companies to raise large amounts of money by incurring long-term debt. Public offerings require the establishment of marketing channels, a task the investment banking syndicate performs, as described in Chapter 3.

Immediately prior to a public offering, investment bankers normally place advertisements in newspapers to announce the availability of the bond. Figure 17.1 presents an example of one of these advertisements, called a *tombstone* because of its appearance. This offering is for $625,000,000 of **debentures,** unsecured corporate bonds, maturing in the year 2026. Pacific Bell is issuing the debentures with the help of three investment banking firms. The top part notes that anyone interested can obtain a prospectus. Each bond is priced at 98.106 percent of par value ($1,000) and buying it entitles the bondholder to $71.25 interest annually (in two semiannual payments of $35.625).

After underwriters sell corporate bonds in the primary market to the public, the bonds may trade in the secondary market. Most bonds trade in the over-the-counter market, although several thousand are listed on organized exchanges. The secondary market is thin for many bonds because the initial buyers hold them until maturity. Tracking the prices of bonds that do trade enables the financial manager to calculate bond yields that can be used in setting rates on new bond issues.

THE BOND INDENTURE

Unlike the bank loan market, lenders and borrowers in the bond market rarely meet one another. Investors in St. Paul, Spokane, Miami, or Portland may buy the bonds of a New York company without ever contacting the company management. To protect the rights of widely dispersed bondholders, the company issuing bonds writes a contract called an **indenture** specifying the features and legal requirements surrounding the bond. In addition, the company appoints a

debenture
Unsecured corporate bond.

indenture
Bond contract describing the issuer's obligations to its bondholders.

FIGURE 17.1

A Tombstone Announcing a New Bond Issue

A tombstone announces to the public that a corporation is offering a new bond issue. The tombstone gives only basic information about the issue and tells interested investors that they may obtain a prospectus from any member of the syndicate.

This announcement is not an offer to sell or a solicitation of an offer to buy any of these securities. The offering is made only by the Prospectus, copies of which may be obtained in any State in which this announcement is circulated only from such of the several underwriters as may lawfully offer these securities in such State.

March 11, 1993

$625,000,000

PACIFIC✖BELL.
A Pacific Telesis Company

7⅛% Debentures due March 15, 2026

Price 98.106%

Lehman Brothers

Merrill Lynch & Co.

Salomon Brothers Inc

Source: The Wall Street Journal, Mar. 11, 1993, C21.

trustee
Legal representative of bondholders who ensures that the issuer does not violate the terms of the indenture.

protective covenant
Clause in an indenture guaranteeing specific rights to bondholders.

acceleration of maturity
Principal of a bond becomes immediately payable if the issuer violates terms of the indenture.

trustee, as required by the Trust Indenture Act of 1939, to supervise the indenture. The trustee, which is usually a trust company or a trust department of a commercial bank, has the following three primary duties:

- Certify that the bond is in its specified form and that it entitles the holder to the benefits described in the indenture, the legal document detailing the agreement between lender and borrower (property pledged, restrictions, dates, and so on).
- Enforce the terms and **protective covenants** of the indenture.
- Take action on behalf of the bondholders if the issuing corporation fails to conform with the requirements of the indenture. This action may lead to an **acceleration of maturity,** which causes the principal to become immediately payable. Bondholders need the acceleration clause to give them the right of immediate foreclosure.

Protective Covenants

Protective covenants are legal restrictions that prevent an issuer from taking action that would increase the bond's default risk. Without such restrictions, a safe company might issue bonds at a low interest rate, then take action causing higher risk. The higher risk would, in turn, cause bond prices in the secondary market to drop as investors seek to obtain a higher rate of return. In the meantime the original buyers of the bonds suffer a capital loss because of the higher risk. To lessen the problem and to lessen interest costs, the issuing company includes protective covenants in the indenture.

Protective covenants vary widely. An examination of some typical covenants demonstrates the kinds of restrictions placed on issuers and the protection afforded bondholders. An indenture may specify that the company's debt ratio (total debt/total assets) must not exceed a specific percentage. If the company violates the covenant, then the acceleration of maturity empowers the trustee to force immediate repayment of bond principal. The inclusion of this covenant assures bondholders that the company's financial risk will not be unduly increased.

Protective covenants attractive to bondholders are generally unattractive to the company. Still, carefully designed covenants need not be onerous and they alleviate bondholder fears—and reduce company interest costs. A covenant might restrict common-stock dividends by specifying that dividends become limited if the current ratio drops below a specified level. The bond indenture might restrict the sale of fixed assets by specifying that fixed assets can be sold during the life of the bond only with permission from the trustee. A bond indenture might also restrict liquidity by requiring that the company maintain a specified net working capital during the bond's life. In designing covenants, financial managers try to strike a balance between being overly restrictive and insufficiently restrictive and thus meaningless to bondholders.

Bond Retirement Methods

The indenture spells out the steps that the company can take to retire a bond at or before the maturity date. For some bonds the issuer establishes a systematic retirement plan at the time of issuance. The issuer retires some percentage of **serial bonds** each year beginning at a specified time in the future. Bondholders select at the time of purchase the part of the series they wish to buy. By retiring a portion of the bonds each year, the company pays its debt in a manner similar to paying an installment loan. Without some means of retiring bonds over time, the company has a sizable **balloon payment** at the time of maturity.

Call Provision. Many indentures include a **call provision**, which enables companies to *call* (buy back) their bonds after issuance. The **call price**, or the price specified in the indenture, exceeds bond par value by the **call premium**. Typically, the initial call premium is set equal to one year's coupon interest.

---

serial bonds
Bond issue that matures in installments on successive dates.

balloon payment
Large repayment of principal at maturity.

call provision
Clause in the indenture allowing the issuer to buy back its outstanding bonds at a specified price.

call price
Price at which an issuer may buy back a bond.

call premium
Excess of call price over par value.

EXAMPLE

A 20-year debenture has a coupon rate of 10 percent. The indenture stipulates call protection for 5 years, which prohibits a call during the first 5 years. Any time during Year 6 the company may call the bond for $1,100. During Year 7 the call price is $1,090, during Year 8 it is $1,080, and so on until Year 15, when the call price is $1,010. From Year 16 to Year 20 the call price is par, $1,000.

The example above illustrates four common features of call provisions:

1. The bond offers call protection for several years. Call protection keeps the bondholder from losing the interest the bond provides in the event that interest rates decline and the issuer wants to retire the bond.
2. The call premium is one year's interest in the first year of call.
3. The call price (and call premium) declines as the bond grows older.
4. There is no call premium in the years near the bond's maturity date.

refunding
Retirement of outstanding bonds with the proceeds of a new bond issue.

Management may call a bond to lower the company's debt ratio or to obtain relief from overly restrictive covenants. Typically, however, a call is made in order to refund an outstanding bond. **Refunding** is the replacement of an outstanding bond with a new bond issue. Bond refunding before maturity presents a company with benefits if the outstanding issue can be replaced with one carrying a lower coupon rate. A lower coupon rate may become available because the general level of interest rates declines or the credit rating of the company improves. In either case, calling a bond works to the detriment of bondholders because the cash they receive can be reinvested only in bonds offering a lower interest rate. *Thus bondholders require a higher rate of return on callable bonds than on equivalent noncallable bonds.*

Management does not necessarily call a bond for refunding the moment that interest rates drop below the coupon rate. For one reason, bondholders may have call protection. In addition, management may expect interest rates to fall further. Finally, the present value of the interest savings may not exceed the present value of the costs of refunding—call premium, flotation costs, and payment of temporarily overlapping interest on two bond issues. (See Appendix 17A for a refunding analysis.)

Sinking-Fund Provision.   A sinking-fund provision in an indenture provides the issuing company with another means of retiring its outstanding bonds. For example, a company might have to retire 5 percent of the outstanding bonds each year during the life of a 20-year issue. If the issue consists of serial bonds, then bondholders know in advance when the bonds will be retired; they do not know in advance when bonds will be retired with a sinking fund. Most sinking-fund provisions allow companies either to call the necessary number of bonds for retirement or to buy them in the secondary market. Under the call procedure, companies randomly select the bonds for retirement. If interest rates are high relative to the coupon rate (causing bond prices to be depressed), then companies choose to retire bonds with purchases in the secondary market. In other words, the financial manager compares the market price with the call price (par value for sinking funds) and retires the bonds in the least costly way.

Note the differences between calling bonds for refunding and for sinking funds: (1) Calls for refunding are optional for management; for sinking funds they are not. (2) Calls for refunding include all bonds outstanding; for sinking funds, only a small portion is retired. (3) Calls for refunding include a call premium; sinking-fund calls are at par value. (4) Most importantly, calls for refunding invariably work to the detriment of bondholders; sinking-fund calls do so only when interest rates have fallen and bond prices have risen. In general, bondholders view sinking funds as risk-reducing mechanisms because of the orderly retirement of debt over time.

TYPES OF BONDS

Corporate bonds come in varieties too numerous to catalog completely here. The imaginations of management and of the advising investment bankers are the chief limitations on bond types. Nonetheless, by examining several ordinary and some not-so-ordinary bonds, you get a feel for the features that management should consider when issuing bonds.

Secured and Unsecured Bonds

Secured bonds have assets pledged to protect the bondholders in the event of bankruptcy. Proceeds from the sale of pledged assets reimburse secured bondholders for any losses. Unsecured bonds are backed only with the faith and credit of the issuing company. Figure 17.2 identifies three types of secured bonds and two types of unsecured bonds, which the following paragraphs briefly discuss.

Mortgage Bonds.   Company assets identified in the bond indenture secure a **mortgage bond**. A mortgage pledges real property—plant, land, and buildings—to the mortgagee. **Closed-end** first mortgages prohibit a company from issuing additional bonds with the same claim on pledged assets as a previous bond issue. The company may, however, issue bonds with a second mortgage (secondary claim), called a junior mortgage. In the event of bankruptcy, holders of second-mortgage bonds have a claim on the pledged assets inferior to the claim of the first-mortgage bondholders—the senior claimants. Holders of a second mortgage receive cash from pledged assets only after the holders of the first mortgage receive all cash due them. **Open-end** mortgages allow a company to issue additional first-mortgage bonds under the existing indenture. These mortgages give companies flexibility but potentially reduce the protection afforded bondholders. To appease bondholders, companies can include the **after-acquired clause:** Any future assets acquired of the kind specified in the indenture will also serve as collateral for the bond.

Collateral Trust Bonds.   **Collateral trust bonds** are similar to mortgage bonds, but they are secured by securities (stocks or bonds) deposited with the trustee. As long as the issuing company does not default on its bonds, the trustee remits to the company any dividends or interest earned on the pledged securities. Holding companies are the major issuers of collateral trust bonds. A *holding company,* or parent company, owns controlling interests in other companies, called *subsidiaries.* In many cases the primary assets of the holding company are the securities of its subsidiaries. Using these securities as collateral, the holding company borrows in the bond market and lends money, in turn, to its subsidiaries. The holding company can often borrow on more favorable terms than its subsidiaries.

Equipment Trust Certificates.   **Equipment trust certificates** are issued primarily by railroads and by some airlines and trucking companies. The equipment owned by these companies serves as collateral. Because the rolling stock of railroads—locomotives, boxcars, tanker cars, flatcars—is standardized and easily sold, investors view it as high-quality collateral. Historical experience justifies this view, for equipment trust certificates have an excellent record of timely payments of interest and principal. Even when Penn Central Railroad defaulted in 1970 on its other debts, it met the financial obligations of its equipment trust certificates. The Penn Central episode attests to the strong security this financing arrangement provides.

---

mortgage bond
Bond secured with real property—plant, land, and buildings.

closed end
Property already pledged may not be used as collateral for another bond issue with the same claim as the first bond issue.

open end
Property already pledged may be used as collateral for another bond issue with the same claim as the first bond issue.

after-acquired clause
Issuer pledges future acquired property as collateral for an outstanding bond issue.

collateral trust bond
Bond secured with securities of other companies.

equipment trust certificate
Bond secured with mobile equipment—railroad cars, trucks, or planes.

FIGURE 17.2

Types of Secured and Unsecured Bonds

Corporate bonds may be either secured or unsecured. Secured bonds provide bondholders with cash from pledged assets in the event of default. Unsecured bonds provide no assurance of repayment other than the good faith and credit of the issuer.

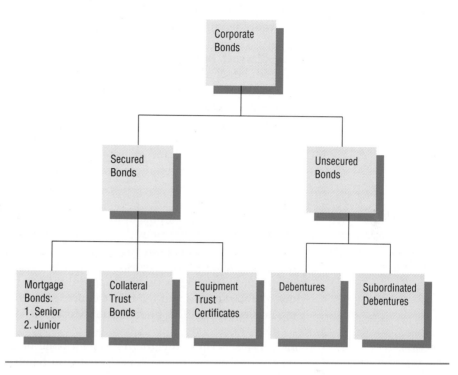

Debentures. Debentures are unsecured bonds. The issuing company does not pledge any specific assets as collateral for debentures. Only the company's credit standing provides protection for debenture owners. In the event of bankruptcy, debenture owners share with other creditors claims on any unpledged assets. Because of the absence of collateral, prudent investors are willing to purchase debentures from companies only with strong financial records. Companies such as Exxon, Sears, and Citicorp have little trouble issuing debentures. In fact, debentures of financially strong companies often have less risk than the first-mortgage bonds of weaker companies.

subordinated debenture
Unsecured bond with a claim secondary to those of specified other creditors.

Subordinated Debentures. To *subordinate* means to place below another in rank. Hence **subordinated debentures** are not only unsecured bonds, but they also place the holder's claims in bankruptcy below those of specified other creditors. For example, the bond indenture may make the subordinated debenture holder's claim inferior to all creditors, whether short or long term. In many cases companies subordinate debentures to bank loans because bankers insist on it as a condition for a loan. (Chapter 21 presents a detailed analysis of the way subordination affects the distribution of cash in a bankruptcy proceeding.) Because of their greater default risk, subordinated debentures carry higher interest costs than most other types of bonds. To reduce costs, the financial manager can make a subordinated debenture convertible into the company's common stock. By issuing subordinated debentures instead of mortgage bonds, a company preserves its ability to pledge assets later, should that become necessary.

Special-Feature Bonds

In addition to the traditional bonds above, companies issue numerous other types of bonds with special features. Financial managers add the features in an attempt to appeal to various segments of the market, thus increasing demand and price and reducing the company's cost of borrowing. Many of the bonds described below are recent creations.

deep-discount bond
Bond with a market price far below par value because of its low coupon rate.

Deep-Discount Bonds. In 1981 Martin Marietta Corporation issued a **deep-discount bond,** a bond that pays low interest and trades at a deep discount from face value. What investors lose in interest, they make up in capital appreciation on the bond price. At maturity investors receive the bond face value ($1,000). An extreme form of a deep-discount bond is the *zero-coupon bond,* which pays no interest at all. Investors are especially attracted to zero-coupon bonds when interest rates are high and expected to fall. Buying a zero-coupon bond means that they need not worry about investing future interest receipts at a lower interest rate.

floating-rate bond
Bond with a coupon rate that changes with a market interest rate.

Floating-Rate Bonds. Unlike traditional bonds with fixed interest rates, **floating-rate bonds** pay interest rates that vary with prevailing market rates. Companies typically tie the floating rate to U.S. Treasury securities rates (either long or short term, depending on the terms of the indenture), adding a specified percentage premium. Floating rates on bonds appeal to both issuers and buyers during periods of uncertainty about the future course of interest rates. Citicorp issued floating-rate bonds in 1974, and General Motors in 1980.

junk bond
Bond with high default risk and high expected yield to maturity.

Junk Bonds. The derogatory term **junk bond** describes high-risk, high-yielding bonds. Any bonds of companies verging on bankruptcy might appropriately be called junk. The junk-bond label, however, came into wide use in the 1980s with the wave of leveraged buy-outs. In a *leveraged buy-out* a group of investors buys control of a company with money raised by issuing bonds. The company's assets are collateral for the bond issue. Typically, the investors place little equity into the deal, using primarily the proceeds from the bond issue to buy the target company. The resulting high debt ratios create substantial financial risk, and the bonds trade at high yields.

income bond
Bond that pays interest contingent on the company's level of earnings.

Income Bonds. Interest payments on most bonds are legal obligations of the issuer. Not so with **income bonds,** which pay interest only to the extent that the company has sufficient earnings before interest and taxes. If the company has an operating loss, then it pays no interest on its income bonds. Like preferred stock, some income bonds have a cumulative feature—missed interest payments accumulate and must be paid in the future. Historically, income bonds have been used by trustees to reorganize the capital structure of failing companies. In these circumstances income bonds might be given to creditors in lieu of cash payments. Today, companies rarely issue income bonds, perhaps because of the failing-company stigma. The Missouri Pacific Railroad has an income bond outstanding that matures in the year 2030. Because the company issued the bond several years ago when interest rates were much lower, the bond pays only $4\frac{3}{4}$ percent per year on face value ($1,000).

put bond
Bond that gives the holder the option to sell (put) the bond back to the issuer at face value before maturity.

Put Bonds. Put bonds allow the bondholder to sell (put) the bond back to the company at face value prior to maturity. The put option becomes especially valuable to the bondholder if interest rates rise causing the bond price to decline

Creative Financing

Financial managers in recent years have been tinkering with the features of corporate securities. As a result, ordinary stocks and bonds are beginning to look like "plain vanilla." Financial managers are intensely interested in designing securities that will appeal to investors, thereby reducing the cost of each source of capital. Here is a list of some recent twists:

- *CMOs:* Collateralized mortgage obligations. Debt obligations backed by a pool of mortgages or mortgage-backed securities such as Ginnie Mae (Government National Mortgage Association) bonds.

- *Securitized receivables:* Debt securities collateralized by a pool of accounts receivable. They include CARDs (certificates of amortizing revolving debts) backed by credit-card debt; CARs (certificates of automobile receivables) backed by automobile loans; and CLEOs (collateralized lease equipment obligations) backed by lease receivables.

- *LYONs:* Liquid yield option notes. Zero-coupon convertible bonds with an option to sell the bonds after a fixed period at a specified yield that rises over time.

- *Rising-coupon (or step-up coupon) bonds:* Bonds whose coupon rate rises over time according to a published schedule. Typically, these notes are issued at a discount based on the expected yield over the life of the note.

- *Stripped government securities:* A type of zero-coupon bond. A brokerage house "strips" the interest payments from a government bond and sells a claim to the payments separate from the claim on the bond principal. Stripped securities are known as CATs (certificates of accrual on Treasury bonds) and TIGRs (Treasury investment growth certificates).

- *Drop-lock bonds:* Floating-rate debt that converts into fixed-rate debt automatically when interest rates fall below a specified benchmark level.

- *Flip-flop notes:* Notes that allow investors to convert to and from two types of securities. The investor could, say, flip from a floating-rate bond to a three-month note bearing a lower rate of interest and then flop back to the bond at maturity.

Source: David Fairlamb and Leah Nathans, "New Boom in Creative Financing," *Dun's Business Month,* August 1986, 44–46; John E. Stewart, "The Challenge of Hedge Accounting," *Journal of Accountancy,* November 1989, 48–60.

below face value. Put bonds appeal to investors worried about an unexpected increase in interest rates. In 1976, for example, Beneficial Corporation issued a put bond to appeal to such investors and to save on interest costs.

Put bonds are just one example of a corporate security that provides investors with an option (a put). Two other prominent corporate securities with option features are *convertibles* and *warrants*. The following discussion of options (*puts* and *calls*) lays the groundwork for understanding convertibles and warrants.

OPTIONS

option

Contract giving the holder the right to buy or sell an asset at a stated price during a specified period of time.

An **option** is a contract that gives the holder the right, but not the obligation, to buy or sell an asset *at a stated price during a specified period of time.* Companies issue options when they issue convertible bonds, convertible preferred stock, or warrants. For example, a convertible security gives the holder the option to exchange (convert) the security for a specified number of shares of common stock. A warrant is an option to buy a specified number of shares of common stock at a stated price during a specified period of time. The put bond described above gives the holder the right (option) to sell the bond back to the company. In contrast, when a company makes a bond callable, it reserves to itself the right (option) to buy back the bond from the holder.

Puts and Calls

Unlike the options originated by companies, puts and calls are originated by investors through stockbrokers. One investor sells (writes) a put or call and another investor buys it. A **put option** is a contract to *sell* common stock, usually 100 shares. A **call option** is a contract to *buy* common stock, again usually 100 shares. Just like common stock, puts and calls trade on organized exchanges and over-the-counter. In terms of number of option contracts traded, the largest exchanges are the Chicago Board Options Exchange (CBOE) and the American Stock Exchange. Other options exchanges include the Philadelphia Stock Exchange, Pacific Stock Exchange, and New York Stock Exchange. Because of the tendency of investors to buy long (bullish) rather than sell short (bearish), the trading volume of call options greatly exceeds that of put options.

put option
Contract to *sell* shares of stock at a stated price during a specified period of time.

call option
Contract to *buy* shares of stock at a stated price during a specified period of time.

Listed Options Quotations.   To illustrate the mechanics of options, consider the listed option quotations shown in Figure 17.3. The names of companies that have options traded on their common stock are listed in the first column. Look at the first entry for Chrysler Corporation and interpret the information as follows:

exercise (strike) price
Price paid by the holder of a call option to acquire a share of common stock; price received by the holder of a put option when selling a share of common stock.

Option/Strike Chryslr Apr $22\frac{1}{2}$	Chryslr is an abbreviation of the company's name. Apr, or April, is the month when the option expires. Actual expiration dates occur the Saturday following the third Friday of the month. The figure $22\frac{1}{2}$ is the strike price (**exercise price**) of the option—the dollar price the holder of the call option pays to acquire one share of the company's common stock. *Note:* The absence of the small letter *p*, for put option, means that the quotation represents a call option.
Vol 100	The number of call options (each for 100 shares) traded between investors is 100; i.e., volume (Vol) is 100 contracts.
Exch CB	The call options on Chrysler's common stock trade on the Chicago Board Options Exchange.
Last 17	Last (or latest) price per call option traded is $17. Total price of a contract for 100 shares is $1,700 (100 shares $\times$ $17).
Net Chg $-\frac{1}{2}$	Net change in the last price per call option from the preceding trading day is $-\frac{1}{2}$, or $-$0.50. The last price the preceding day must have been $17.50 ($17 + $0.50).
a-Close 39	The closing (or latest) price per share of the **underlying common stock,** Chrysler's in this quotation, is $39.
Open Int 302	Open interest is the number of 100-share call options currently outstanding, or open. Larger numbers indicate greater investor interest in the option.

underlying common stock
Common stock that the holder of a call option may buy at the exercise price; common stock that the holder of a put option may sell at the exercise price.

Figure 17.3 shows a total of 11 different options on Chrysler's common stock: 3 put options and 8 call options. Differing expiration dates and differing strike prices distinguish one option from another. The exchange (Chicago Board of Options Exchange in this case) introduces new options as old ones expire and as the price of the underlying stock changes. Because put and call options derive their existence from the underlying stock, investors call them *derivative securities*.

Option Pricing.   Investors call the price paid for an option the *option premium*. Brokers charge a commission in addition to the option premium to buy options

FIGURE 17.3

Listed Options Quotations from *The Wall Street Journal*

A listed option—a put or call—is one that trades on an organized exchange such as the CBOE (Chicago Board Options Exchange). Price quotations are for the last trades of the day. Trading units are usually 100 shares, even though the price quotations are for options on one share of common stock.

Thursday, March 11, 1993

Volume, close, net change and open interest of the 1,400 most active equity and 100 most active long-term contracts. Volume figures are unofficial. Open interest is total outstanding for all exchanges and reflects previous trading day. **CB**-Chicago Board Options Exchange. **AM**-American Stock Exchange. **PB**-Philadelphia Stock Exchange. **PC**-Pacific Stock Exchange. **NY**-New York Stock Exchange. **a**-Underlying stock on primary market. **c**-Call. **p**-Put.

MOST ACTIVE CONTRACTS

Option/Strike			Vol Exch	Last	Net Chg	a-Close	Open Int
I B M	Mar 55		4,171 CB	15/16 −	1/2	54 7/8	16,505
I B M	Mar 55	p	3,565 CB	11/16 +	7/16	54 7/8	8,074
Pfizer	Mar 60	p	2,765 AM	3/8 +	3/16	62 3/8	3,969
Ph Mor	Apr 60	p	2,696 AM	13/16 −	3/16	65 3/4	3,333
Merck	Apr 40		2,429 CB	3/8 −	3/8	39 1/4	11,746
Citlcp	Apr 25		2,293 CB	3 7/8	...	28 5/8	10,527
Citlcp	Apr 30		2,286 CB	3/4 −	1/8	28 5/8	3,487
Compaq	Mar 50		2,142 PC	1 5/8 +	1/4	50 5/8	6,255
I B M	Mar 55		2,080 CB	2 −	9/16	54 7/8	25,301
Blkbst	Mar 12 1/2		2,034 CB	6 7/8 +	5/8	19 1/2	2,958
Novell	Mar 30		1,950 AM	3 1/8 + 1	9/16	33 1/4	4,715
Micsft	Mar 85		1,944 PC	2 11/16 +	1 1/8	86 1/2	4,023
Ph Mor	Apr 60	p	1,922 AM	1/16 −	3/16	65 3/4	7,396
I B M	Apr 55		1,879 CB	2 +	3/8	54 7/8	7,494
SunMic	Jul 35	p	1,731 PC	4 5/8 +	1	32 1/4	178
Boeing	May 35		1,613 CB	1 3/8	...	34 5/8	6,068
Pfizer	Apr 65		1,562 AM	1 1/8 −	1/4	62 3/8	7,639
G M	Mar 40		1,530 CB	1/4 −	1/2	38 1/2	19,158
I B M	Apr 60		1,515 CB	9/16 −	1/8	54 7/8	23,330
I B M	Apr 50		1,499 CB	1/2 +	1/16	54 7/8	11,362
Chase	Mar 35		1,411 AM	5/8 +	1/8	35	1,292
Gen El	Mar 85		1,378 CB	2 7/8 −	1/8	87 1/2	5,406
Citlcp	Jul 30		1,334 CB	2	...	28 5/8	4,895
Compaq	Apr 50		1,319 PC	3 1/8 +	1/4	50 5/8	5,395
Pfizer	Mar 60		1,301 AM	2 5/8 −	5/8	62 3/8	9,917

-A-B-C-

Option/Strike			Vol Exch	Last	Net Chg	a-Close	Open Int
A M D	Mar 20		142 PC	4 1/8 +	1/4	23 3/4	2,921
A M D	Apr 20		300 PC	4 1/8 +	1/8	23 3/4	3,761
A M D	Apr 20	p	605 PC	1/4	...	23 3/4	2,347
A M D	Mar 22 1/2		377 PC	1 1/2 +	1/4	23 3/4	6,273
A M D	Mar 22 1/2	p	207 PC	1/4	...	23 3/4	1,364
A M D	Apr 22 1/2		187 PC	2	...	23 3/4	3,603
A M D	Apr 22 1/2	p	607 PC	3/4 −	1/16	23 3/4	708
A M D	Jul 22 1/2	p	98 PC	1 3/4 −	3/8	23 3/4	1,049
A M D	Mar 25		211 PC	1/4 +	1/16	23 3/4	512
A M D	Apr 25		160 PC	7/8 −		23 3/4	3,066
A M D	Apr 25	p	273 PC	2 1/8 −	3/8	23 3/4	218
A M D	Jul 25		66 PC	2 1/8 +	1/8	23 3/4	934
A M P	Mar 60		78 CB	1/2 −	1/8	58 3/4	134
A M R	Mar 55	p	129 AM	1/16 −	1/16	60 1/2	776
A M R	Mar 60	p	145 AM	5/8 −	3/4	60 1/2	786
A M R	Apr 65		70 AM	3/4 −		60 1/2	298
A M R	May 65		139 AM	1 1/2 +	3/8	60 1/2	1,915
A M R	May 70		200 AM	1/2 −	1/8	60 1/2	1,503

Option/Strike			Vol Exch	Last	Net Chg	a-Close	Open Int
Cadenc	May 17 1/2	p	70 AM	3/4 −	1/8	19 1/4	50
Cadenc	Mar 20		255 CB	9/16 −	1/16	19 1/4	122
Cadenc	Mar 20		200 AM	5/16 −	1/4	19 1/4	122
Cadenc	Apr 20		60 AM	13/16 +	1/4	19 1/4	223
Cadenc	Apr 20		110 CB	1	...	19 1/4	223
CaesrW	Mar 45		260 AM	1 +	1/4	44 3/8	746
CaesrW	Apr 45		139 AM	2 1/8 +	1/16	44 3/8	235
CaesrW	May 45		111 AM	3 +	1/4	44 3/8	394
CaesrW	May 45	p	78 AM	3 1/8 −	1 3/8	44 3/8	113
Catels	Mar 7 1/2		80 CB	5/16 +	1/16	7 1/2	224
Chase	Jun 25		120 AM	10 +	1 1/8	35	969
Chase	Mar 30		148 AM	5 +	1/4	35	8,586
Chase	Mar 30	p	75 AM	1/16	...	35	4,849
Chase	Jun 30		227 AM	5 1/2 +	1/4	35	2,304
Chase	Jun 30	p	200 AM	1 −	1/16	35	3,703
Chase	Mar 35		1,411 AM	5/8 +	1/8	35	1,292
Chase	Mar 35	p	220 AM	1/16 −	13/16	35	202
Chase	Apr 35		1,147 AM	1 1/4 +	3/16	35	2,015
Chase	Apr 35	p	84 AM	1 1/8 −	1/4	35	27
Chase	Jun 35		233 AM	1 15/16 +	3/16	35	2,384
Chase	Sep 35		65 AM	2 11/16 +	3/16	35	1,228
Chase	Sep 35	p	90 AM	3 −	3/8	35	638
ChemBk	Jun 40		124 AM	4 1/2 −	1/8	43 3/8	3,106
ChemBk	Jun 40	p	110 AM	1 3/16 +	3/16	43 3/8	1,279
ChemBk	Mar 45		130 AM	5/16 −	1/8	43 3/8	1,102
ChemBk	Apr 45		93 AM	3/4 −	1/4	43 3/8	236
ChemBk	Jun 45		168 AM	1 13/16 −	1/16	43 3/8	1,874
Chevrn	Mar 75		313 AM	2 3/4 −	5/8	77 1/2	3,864
Chevrn	Apr 75		253 AM	3 1/2 −	1/2	77 1/2	30
Chevrn	Apr 80		125 AM	7/8 −	1/4	77 1/2	1,009
Chevrn	Jun 80		77 AM	1 3/4 −	3/16	77 1/2	2,061
CheySf	Mar 30		146 CB	1 1/4 −	1/4	31	1,353
Chiron	Apr 45	p	205 CB	2 5/16 +	3/16	51 1/2	1,100
Chiron	Apr 45		93 AM	2 3/8 +	3/8	51 1/2	1,100
Chiron	Mar 50		101 AM	3 1/8 −	5/8	51 1/2	991
Chiron	Apr 50	p	134 CB	2 −	3/8	51 1/2	582
Chiron	Apr 55		61 AM	1 −	1/8	51 1/2	906
Chiron	Apr 55		75 AM	1 −		51 1/2	1,024
Chryslr	Apr 22 1/2		100 CB	17 −	1/2	39	302
Chryslr	Jul 30		97 CB	10 1/4 −	3/8	39	2,177
Chryslr	Apr 35		87 CB	4 1/2 −	7/8	39	9,054
Chryslr	Apr 35	p	281 CB	3/8 +	3/8	39	3,767
Chryslr	Jul 35		72 CB	5 5/8 −	1	39	3,987
Chryslr	Mar 40		452 CB	1/2 −	1/2	39	7,081
Chryslr	Apr 40		935 CB	1 7/16 +	1/2	39	1,566
Chryslr	Apr 40	p	640 CB	1 1/2 −	7/16	39	10,178
Chryslr	Apr 40	p	89 CB	2 5/16 +	7/16	39	1,261
Chryslr	Jul 40		429 CB	3 3/8 −	5/8	39	7,596
Chryslr	Jul 45		75 CB	1 9/16 −	3/16	39	6,140
CirCty	Mar 50		76 PC	3 7/8 +	1/4	53 5/8	357
CirCty	Apr 55		106 PC	2 3/8 −	1/4	53 5/8	359
Circus	Mar 40		68 AM	6 3/8 +	1 3/4	46 1/4	202
Circus	Mar 40	p	165 AM	1/16 −	1/16	46 1/4	659
Circus	Mar 45		229 AM	1 3/4 +	7/16	46 1/4	704
Circus	Apr 50		67 AM	1 +	3/8	46 1/4	54
Cirrus	Jun 30	p	60 PC	4 −	7/8	29 3/4	37
Cirrus	Sep 30		60 PC	5 1/2 +	2 1/8	29 3/4	63
Cirrus	Jun 35		100 CB	2 +	1/2	29 3/4	398
Cisco	Mar 85		73 CB	8 7/8 +	1 5/8	94	1,266
Cisco	Mar 90		205 CB	4 1/8 +	3/4	94	1,138
Cisco	Mar 90	p	622 CB	5/8 −	3/4	94	1,025
Cisco	Apr 90		138 CB	7 3/8 +	1	94	2,601
Cisco	Apr 90	p	90 CB	3 1/4 −	1	94	1,926

Source: The Wall Street Journal, Mar. 12, 1993, C11.

on behalf of investors. Brokers retain the buyer's commission and pass the premium (less the seller's commission) to the investor who sold the option. Like prices of all securities trading in the market, option prices are established through the buying and selling behavior of investors.

Suppose you were considering buying the Chrysler call option having an exercise price of $22.50 and expiring in April. According to Figure 17.3, your purchase would cost 17, or $17.00. For the usual contract on 100 shares, your total cost would be $1,700.00 plus a brokerage commission. Buying the call option entitles you to pay $22.50 per share of Chrysler stock worth 39, or

exercise value

Value of an option when it is exchanged for the underlying common stock.

$39.00. The **exercise value,** or *intrinsic value,* of the call option on each share equals the stock price minus the exercise price (strike price):

$$\text{Exercise value (call)} = \text{Stock price} - \text{Exercise price}$$
$$= \$39.00 - \$22.50$$
$$= \$16.50$$

speculative value

Portion of the option price in excess of the exercise value.

The excess of the option price over the exercise value represents **speculative value** (or *time value*):

$$\text{Speculative value} = \text{Option price} - \text{Exercise value}$$
$$= \$17.00 - \$16.50$$
$$= \$0.50$$

For a contract on 100 shares, the speculative value is $50 ($1,700 − $1,650). Note that option price equals exercise value plus speculative value.

The speculative appeal of options entices investors to pay a price in excess of exercise value. To illustrate, consider what happens to the exercise value of the "Chrysler April $22\frac{1}{2}$ call" in Figure 17.3 if Chrysler's stock price rises from $39 to $59, a rise of 51.3 percent. The exercise value rises from $16.50 to $36.50 ($59.00 − $22.50), a rise of 121.2 percent! At the same time, the most the investor can lose is 100 percent, the price of the option. Total loss on the option occurs at expiration if Chrysler's stock price is $22.50 or less per share. The high degree of leverage created by options (because of the fixed exercise price) gives them enormous upside potential and speculative appeal.

Instead of considering buying a call option, suppose you were bearish and were considering buying the "Chrysler April 40 put." According to Figure 17.3, your purchase would cost $2\frac{5}{16}$, or $2.3125. For a contract on 100 shares, your total cost would be $231.25 plus a brokerage commission. Buying the put option entitles you to *sell* Chrysler stock for $40.00 per share when it is worth only $39.00 per share. The exercise value of the put option on each share equals the exercise price (strike price) minus the stock price:

$$\text{Exercise value (put)} = \text{Exercise price} - \text{Stock price}$$
$$= \$40.00 - \$39.00$$
$$= \$1.00$$

The speculative value of the put is $1.3125 ($2.3125 − $1.00), the price of the put minus its exercise value. If the price of Chrysler stock declines, the value of the put increases. For example, a $5 decline in stock price to $34 would cause the exercise value of the put to become $6.00 ($40.00 − $34.00), a 500 percent increase. If the price of Chrysler stock rises to $40 or more, however, the exercise value of the put becomes zero. Option holders do not exercise options with negative exercise values, so all negative values are treated as zero.

In practice, owners of puts and calls rarely exercise them to buy common stock. Instead, they usually sell their options in the market prior to the expiration date. Owners neither exercise nor sell worthless options but simply let them expire. Options are highly risky securities, and many do expire without value.

Buying options has obvious appeal to speculators willing to face a large probability of loss for a small probability of large gains. Perhaps less obvious is the usefulness of options to conservative investors. Consider the nervous investor who has a large unrealized capital gain on a stock. Buying a put option on the stock protects the investor from a decline in stock price. Any loss on the stock is offset by gain on the put option. Alternatively, the investor might choose to sell a call option on the stock—known as *writing covered options*. The investor receives the call price (premium) less commissions but gives up any subsequent large gains on the stock to the buyer of the call. Writing options is conservative only if the investor already owns the underlying stock. Otherwise, the action is speculative and is known as *writing naked options*.

Valuation Concepts

Three factors that affect the market value (price) of call options are apparent from the preceding discussion: (1) price of the underlying stock, (2) exercise price of the option, and (3) time to expiration of the option. Two additional factors, though less apparent, have been identified by Black and Scholes (developers of a widely used option pricing model): (4) market interest rates, and (5) price volatility of the underlying stock.[1]

Price of the Underlying Stock. *The market value of a call option is positively related to the price of the underlying stock.* An increase in stock price causes the exercise and market value of the call option to increase. When stock price exceeds exercise price, the option is said to be *in-the-money;* otherwise, it is *out-of-the-money* (stock price is less than exercise price) or *at-the-money* (stock price equals exercise price). The maximum market value of a call option equals the price of the underlying stock. Imagine, for example, a 3-month option to buy a $50 stock for $0.01, the exercise price. In this unusual case, the market value of the option almost equals the stock price.

Exercise Price of the Option. *The market value of a call option is inversely related to its exercise price.* For a given stock, increasing the exercise price lowers the market value of the option. To illustrate, consider the "Chrysler April calls" described in Figure 17.3. Market value of the option is 17 for an exercise price of $22.50, $4\frac{1}{2}$ for an exercise price of $35.00, and $1\frac{1}{2}$ for an exercise price of $40.00. As exercise price increases, exercise value decreases and investors perceive a smaller and smaller probability of the stock price exceeding the exercise price prior to expiration. The minimum value of a call option is zero.

Time to Expiration of the Option. *The market value of a call option is positively related to its time to expiration.* Longer periods of time to expiration increase the likelihood that stock price will rise during the life of the option, adding value to the option. The value added is speculative value, or *time value*. To illustrate, consider the "Chrysler 40 calls" described in Figure 17.3. Market value of the option is $\frac{7}{16}$ for the March expiration, $1\frac{1}{2}$ for the April expiration, and $3\frac{3}{8}$ for the July expiration. At the end of the last trading day (third Friday of the month) prior to expiration, the market value of a call option equals stock price minus exercise price, or the exercise value. When time remains until expiration and investors perceive a possibility that the stock price will exceed the exercise price, then the market value of the option exceeds its exercise value.

---

[1] The Black-Scholes option pricing model (OPM) is developed in Fisher Black and Myron Scholes, "The Pricing of Options and Corporate Liabilities," *Journal of Political Economy,* May–June 1973, 637–654. Many investment textbooks provide a description of the Black-Scholes OPM; for example, see Frank K. Reilly, *Investment Analysis and Portfolio Management,* 3rd ed. (Hinsdale, IL: Dryden Press, 1989).

Market Interest Rates. *The market value of a call option is positively related to market interest rates.* To understand the reason, consider the purchase of a call option as being akin to buying stock with two installment payments. The first payment is the price of the option, and the second payment is its exercise price paid sometime later when the stock is acquired. Deferring this second payment becomes increasingly valuable as market interest rates rise, because the present value of the payment declines. The reduction in present value of the second payment makes the call option more valuable. Hence increases in market interest rates lead to higher market values for call options.

Price Volatility of the Underlying Stock. *The market value of a call option is positively related to the price volatility of the underlying stock.* Greater volatility in stock price increases the potential for gain on the option. A call option on a stock with zero volatility is worth only its exercise value. In contrast, a call option on a stock whose price might halve or double has speculative value in addition to exercise value. To illustrate, consider a 3-month call option with a $50 exercise price. If the price of the underlying stock is also $50 and there is no chance for it to change, then the value of the option is zero. In contrast, if there is 50 percent probability of the stock trading for either $25 or $100 before the option expires, then the option has value. A $25 stock price causes the option to be worth zero, but a $100 stock price causes it to be worth $50. Based on the probabilities, the expected value of the option is $25 [0.5(0) + 0.5($50)]. Unlike the stockholder, the owner of the call option benefits from a volatile stock price.

CONVERTIBLE BONDS

convertible bond

Bond that an investor may exchange for common stock.

A **convertible bond** permits the investor to exchange (convert) the bond for a specified number of shares of common stock.[2] The investor in a convertible bond essentially owns a straight bond plus a call option on the company's common stock. To exercise the call option, the investor must give the convertible bond to the company. The investor has the choice of when to exercise the call option, or equivalently, when to convert the bond. When conversion occurs, the company's number of shares outstanding increases, and its debt level decreases along with its interest expense.

Convertibility is a sweetener that lowers the interest rate demanded by investors. During periods of high interest rates, companies encourage investors to buy bonds with relatively low coupon rates by adding a conversion option. Convertibility also makes it easier for companies to issue junk bonds and subordinated debentures at reasonable interest costs.

Besides being a sweetener, convertibility offers a company an indirect way of issuing common stock. If the financial manager believes the company's stock price is depressed, then a stock offering should be delayed until the future. Issuing convertible bonds accomplishes this delaying tactic: When investors convert the bonds to common stock, it will be at a higher effective stock price. To understand this financing tactic better, you need to understand the terminology of convertible bonds.

---

[2] Preferred stock may also be convertible into common stock. Chapter 18 discusses convertible preferred stock.

Valuing Convertible Bonds

The market price of a convertible bond, like all securities, depends on investor perceptions of its intrinsic value. The market price reflects the value of a straight bond combined with a conversion option.

conversion ratio

Number of shares of common stock into which a bond may be converted.

Conversion ratio is the number of shares into which investors can convert each convertible bond. The indenture designates the conversion ratio. To illustrate, a convertible debenture with a $1,000 par value has a conversion ratio of 20: The bondholder may convert one debenture into 20 shares of common stock.

conversion price

Effective price per share paid for common stock in a conversion; equals par value divided by the conversion ratio.

Conversion price is the effective price per share paid by the bondholder (received by the company) when conversion occurs. The conversion price in the preceding example is related to the conversion ratio as follows:

$$\text{Conversion price} = \frac{\text{Par value of the convertible bond}}{\text{Conversion ratio}}$$

$$= \frac{\$1,000}{20}$$

$$= \$50 \text{ per share}$$

The conversion price is a mathematical transformation of the conversion ratio.

conversion value

Value of a convertible bond in terms of the underlying common stock; equals the conversion ratio times the price per share of stock.

Conversion value is the total value of the common stock for which the bondholder exchanges the convertible bond. If the price per share of stock equals $60, then the conversion value of the preceding convertible debenture is $1,200:

$$\begin{array}{l} \text{Conversion} \\ \text{value} \end{array} = \begin{array}{l} \text{Conversion} \\ \text{ratio} \end{array} \times \begin{array}{l} \text{Price per} \\ \text{share of stock} \end{array}$$

$$= 20 \times \$60$$

$$= \$1,200$$

When traded in the market, the convertible debenture is worth at least $1,200, its conversion value.

straight-bond value

Value of a convertible bond without its conversion option.

Straight-bond value is the value of the convertible bond *without* its conversion option. If the convertibility feature were stripped away, then the remaining value would be the straight-bond value. Without its convertibility, the security in the preceding example becomes a regular, or straight, debenture. A convertible bond's straight-bond value is estimated using a discount rate equal to the yield to maturity on a nonconvertible bond with the same default risk and maturity.

EXAMPLE

To illustrate the calculation of straight-bond value, assume that the convertible debenture above has a 10-year life and a coupon rate of 8 percent annually, payable semiannually. Further assume that the annual yield to maturity is 12 percent on bonds similar in all respects to the convertible debenture, excepting the convertibility feature. The convertible pays $80 (0.08 × $1,000) per year in interest, payable in $40 installments each 6 months. The discount rate is 12 percent per year, or 6 percent per 6-month period:

$$\text{Straight-bond value} = \$40(\text{PVIFA}_{6\%,20}) + \$1,000(\text{PVIF}_{6\%,20})$$

$$= (\$40)(11.4699) + (\$1,000)(0.3118)$$

$$= \$458.80 + \$311.80$$

$$= \$770.60$$

This straight-bond value is interpreted as follows: (1) The convertible is worth $770.60 as an interest-paying bond. Even if the convertibility feature becomes worthless because of a decline in stock price, the convertible is still worth $770.60 as a straight bond. (2) The straight-bond value, $770.60, is the convertible's *floor value* below which its price will not fall—assuming that interest rates and the company's default risk do not change.

Graphing the Value of a Convertible Bond

Figure 17.4 plots the conversion value and straight-bond value of the sample convertible as functions of price per share of common stock. Conversion value equals the conversion ratio (20) times the stock price. Thus the conversion-value line starts where the stock price is zero, at the origin, and slopes upward to the right (its slope is the conversion ratio). As noted earlier, when the stock price is $60 per share, conversion value is $1,200 (20 × $60).

The straight-bond value is depicted in Figure 17.4 by the horizontal line at $770.60. Straight-bond value does not depend on the stock price, and so Figure 17.4 shows it positioned horizontally. The straight-bond line moves parallel to the horizontal axis, moving up and down, respectively, as interest rates move down and up.[3]

Straight-bond value ($770.60) equals the conversion value (conversion ratio times stock price) when the stock price is $38.53 ($770.60/20 shares).[4] Figure 17.4 shows this point to be the intersection of the lines representing conversion value and straight-bond value. Below a stock price of $38.53 the convertible is worth at least its straight-bond value; above $38.53 it is worth at least its conversion value. The blue line in Figure 17.4 shows which value dominates the other.

The market price of a convertible bond usually exceeds the greater of its straight-bond value and its conversion value. Figure 17.5 illustrates the **conversion premium** at which the sample convertible trades in the marketplace when the stock price is $60 per share and the convertible bond price is $1,230:

conversion premium
Excess of the price of a convertible bond over its conversion value.

$$\frac{\text{Conversion}}{\text{premium}} = \frac{\text{Price of}}{\text{convertible}} - \frac{\text{Conversion}}{\text{value}}$$

$$= \$1,230 - \$1,200$$

$$= \$30$$

Stated as a percentage, the conversion premium is 2.5 percent ($30/$1,200) of conversion value.

Essentially, the convertible bond in Figure 17.5 trades in the market as a portfolio of 20 shares of $60 common stock. Laying claim to those 20 shares with the convertible bond costs investors $1,230, $30 more than if they were to buy the shares directly. *What do investors get for their $30?* First, they earn inter-

---

[3] Strictly speaking, for low stock prices the straight-bond line would probably curve toward the origin. Low stock prices would likely reflect increased risk and required rates of return, causing a decline in straight-bond value.

[4] Stock prices are quoted in increments of one-eighth of a dollar. Thus the nearest quote to $38.53 would be $38\frac{1}{2}$.

FIGURE 17.4

A Convertible Bond's Conversion Value and Straight-Bond Value as Functions of Common-Stock Price

A convertible bond will trade for at least its conversion value or straight-bond value, whichever is greater. Here a common-stock price above $38.53 per share causes the bond to trade for at least its conversion value. A common-stock price below $38.53 causes the bond to trade for at least its straight-bond value.

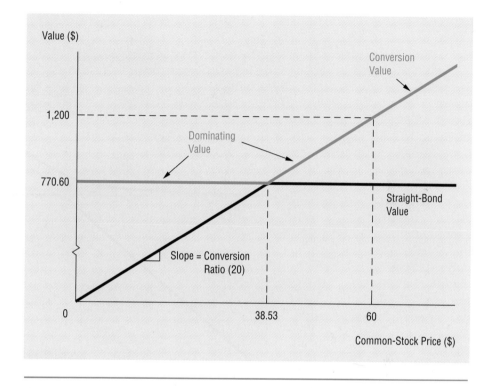

est ($80 per year) on the convertible bond, which may or may not be more than the dividends they would earn on 20 shares of stock. Second, the convertible bond offers investors downside protection. The straight-bond value puts a $770.60 floor under the convertible's price. In this example the floor ($770.60) is a long way from $1,230. Still, the convertible's expected rate of return is less risky than that on the 20 shares of stock; and if the stock price increases, then the conversion feature causes the price of the convertible to increase as well.

EXAMPLE

If the price per share of the underlying stock of the convertible shown in Figure 17.5 were to drop to $35, what would be the approximate price of the convertible? At $35 the conversion value is $700 (20 × $35). Assuming no change in interest rates and default risk, the conversion value ($700) is less than the straight-bond value ($770.60). Thus the price of the convertible would exceed $770.60 by an amount called the **straight-bond premium**. For illustrative purposes, Figure 17.5 shows this premium to be $59.40 ($830 − $770.60).

FIGURE 17.5

Market Price of a Convertible Bond as a Function of Common-Stock Price

The market price of a convertible bond exceeds conversion value by an amount called the conversion premium. In this figure the conversion premium is $30 ($1,230 − $1,200) when the common stock trades at $60 per share. The market price of the convertible exceeds the straight-bond value by an amount called the straight-bond premium: $59.40 = $830 − $770.60, when the common stock trades at $35 per share.

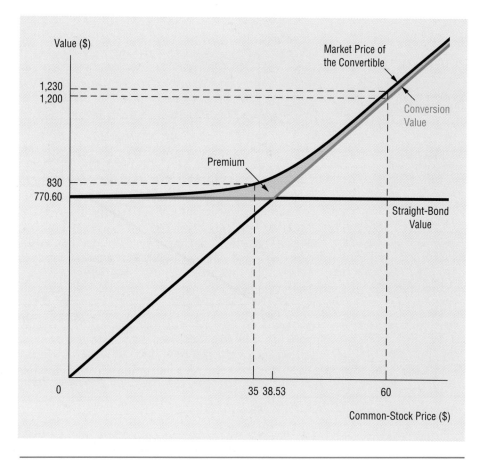

Features of Convertible Bonds

A convertible bond has three special features that relate to its underlying common stock. These features are dilution protection, conversion pricing, and forced conversion.

Dilution Protection.   To be attractive to investors, the value of the conversion option must be protected from dilution. Thus the indenture for a convertible bond usually includes an **antidilution clause.** The clause provides for an increase in the conversion ratio if the company issues new shares of common stock at below-market prices. For example, to reduce its current $60 stock price to $30 a share, a company could simply double the number of shares outstanding by matching each shareholder's present holdings.[5] Keeping other factors constant

antidilution clause
Covenant requiring the conversion ratio to be increased if the company issues new shares of common stock at below-market prices.

[5] The example describes a stock split, which Chapter 19 discusses.

and doubling the shares outstanding causes the stock price to split in half to $30. For the example case the antidilution clause would require the conversion ratio to be doubled from 20 to 40. Forty shares of $30 stock is equivalent to 20 shares of $60 stock, and the convertible bondholders own $1,200 in conversion value per bond in either case.

Setting Conversion Price.   Recall that conversion price equals the par value ($1,000) of a convertible divided by the conversion ratio; it is the effective stock price per share received by the company from the conversion of the bond. Financial managers typically set the conversion price 15 to 30 percent above the market price of the common stock at the time of issuing the convertible bond. In this way, they take advantage of both the bond and stock characteristics of the convertible. The convertible should initially trade primarily on the basis of its straight-bond value, although the possibility of conversion should seem attainable to investors. Setting the conversion price too high causes the convertible to sell as a straight bond, and investors will require a high coupon rate; the company might as well issue a straight bond in this case. Setting the conversion price too close to the prevailing stock price causes the convertible to sell as though it were a portfolio of shares of stock; the company might as well sell common stock in this case. In setting the conversion price, financial managers consider the effects of conversion price on the bond's coupon rate and on the estimated time until conversion: High conversion prices (low conversion ratios) lead to high coupon rates and lengthen the time to conversion.

Encouraging and Forcing Conversion.   Conversion rids the company of debt and reduces interest costs. The issuer can either encourage or force convertible bondholders to convert their bonds to common stock. The company encourages conversion by raising the dividends paid on common stock. If total dividends on the shares received upon conversion greatly exceed the interest paid on the convertible, then investors may be willing to give up the bond protection afforded by the convertible for the stock. Convertible bondholders in this way make a voluntary risk-return decision encouraged by dividend policy.

Most indentures of convertible bonds contain a call provision, which gives the company some control over the timing of conversion. *Calling the convertible when the conversion value is higher than the call price forces investors to convert their bonds into the higher-valued shares rather than accept the lower call price.* Stated differently, when stock price per share exceeds call price per share (call price divided by the conversion ratio), the company can force conversion. Another strong incentive for conversion is provided by scheduling step-downs in the conversion ratio. If the indenture states that the conversion ratio declines according to a schedule, then investors feel pressure to convert before the date of the step-down. Like any feature disadvantageous to investors, step-down clauses increase the company's interest cost.

EXAMPLE

Asto Industries' convertible bond has a 10 percent coupon rate, a conversion ratio of 40, and a call price of $1,100. The call price per share is $27.50 ($1,100/40). If Asto calls the convertible when the stock price equals $35 per share, then the bondholders will present each bond for 40 shares of common stock valued at $1,400 (40 × $35) rather than for $1,100 cash (the call price).

Conversion of convertible bonds reduces a company's financial leverage by erasing debt from the balance sheet and increasing common equity. It also reduces interest expense on the income statement and increases the number of shares outstanding. In practice, it is difficult to predict the impact of conversion on stock price. What happens depends on the price-earnings ratio, which depends on the optimal capital structure. The interest expense saved and the number of new shares issued also play roles in determining the new stock price.

WARRANTS

warrant

Long-term, company-issued option to buy a specified number of shares of common stock at a stated price.

A **warrant** is an option to buy a specified number of shares of common stock at a stated price during a specified period of time. *Companies issue warrants primarily for the purpose of selling bonds.*[6] Purchasers of the bonds receive as a bonus a warrant that allows them to buy the company's stock at a fixed price over time. For this reason a warrant is sometimes called an *equity kicker*. Similar to making the bond convertible, adding a warrant to a bond sweetens the deal and lessens the coupon interest that issuers must pay on bonds.

Valuing Warrants

Most warrants are detachable from the bond with which they are issued. After issuance the warrants take on lives of their own and trade in secondary markets similarly to other securities. Historically, warrants traded primarily in the over-the-counter market. Since 1970, when AT&T issued a large volume of bonds with warrants, several warrants have traded on the New York Stock Exchange. About 100 different warrants currently trade on the NYSE.

A warrant has value to an investor because it allows the holder to buy a company's common stock for a fixed price, the *exercise price* (or *strike price*). Moreover, depending on the warrant, the holder may have this right for a large number of years, forever in some cases.

EXAMPLE

Warren Company issues bonds with five warrants accompanying each bond. Each warrant entitles the holder to purchase one share of Warren's common stock for $20 any time during the next 10 years. Warren's common stock currently trades for $15 a share. Do Warren's warrants have any value? As you may suspect, Warren's warrants have speculative value.

Financial managers typically set the exercise price of a warrant 15 to 30 percent above the prevailing stock price at the time of issuance. In the above example, one of Warren's warrants allows the holder to pay $20 for a stock trading for $15. The exercise value is currently zero, but it may exceed zero sometime in the future. If Warren's stock price exceeds the warrant's exercise price ($20)

---

[6] In recent years warrants have been used on occasion to sell common and preferred stock. Buyers of the common or preferred stock receive a warrant to buy more shares of common stock in the future. In comparison to the CBOE call options discussed earlier, a warrant is (1) issued by a company, not an investor, and (2) issued with a long-term life, not a short-term life.

at any time during the next 10 years, then the *exercise value* will be positive. The probability of a positive exercise value over the decade may be quite high.

The exercise value of a warrant is calculated with the following equation:

$$\begin{matrix} \text{Exercise} \\ \text{value} \end{matrix} = \left(\begin{matrix} \text{Stock} \\ \text{price} \end{matrix} - \begin{matrix} \text{Exercise} \\ \text{price} \end{matrix} \right) \times \begin{matrix} \text{Number of shares} \\ \text{acquired per warrant} \end{matrix}$$

Because warrant holders do not exercise warrants when they have negative exercise values, we consider all negatives to be zero. The exercise value of Warren's warrants takes on a positive value for all stock prices greater than $20, the exercise price.

Despite its zero exercise value, Warren Company's warrants in the preceding example will trade at a price above zero because of *speculative value*. To illustrate, assume that the warrants trade in the secondary market for $2 per warrant. In this case, speculative value equals the market price of the warrant:

$$\text{Speculative value} = \text{Warrant price} - \text{Exercise value}$$
$$= \$2 - 0$$
$$= \$2$$

A term often used interchangeably with speculative value is *premium value* or simply *premium*. Investors pay a $2 premium for Warren's warrants because they believe some chance exists for Warren's stock price to go above $20 (exercise price) during the next 10 years. Note that the market price of a warrant consists of two parts: exercise value and speculative value.

Warrant Premium

Warrants carry premiums because of the potential to earn high rates of return on them when the underlying stock price increases. Investors can buy more warrants than shares of the underlying stock for the same dollar investment. For example, with $1,500 an investor can buy 750 of Warren Company's warrants but only 100 shares of its common stock. If the stock price subsequently increases, then investors earn higher returns on the warrants than on the underlying stock. Contrast a $1,500 investment in 100 shares of Warren's stock to a $1,500 investment in 750 of Warren's warrants. A 50 percent increase in stock price ($15 to $22.50) produces the following results:

	Stock Investment	Warrant Investment
From:	100 shares × $15 = $1,500	750 warrants × $2 = $1,500
To:	100 shares × $22.50 = $2,250	750 warrants × $4.50 = $3,375
Produces:	50% gain	125% gain

The new exercise value is calculated as follows:

$$\text{Exercise value} = (\$22.50 - \$20) \times 1$$
$$= \$2.50$$

If the premium stays at $2, then the warrant price (exercise value plus premium) is $4.50:

$$\text{Warrant price} = \$2.50 + \$2$$
$$= \$4.50$$

FIGURE 17.6   **Exercise Value and Warrant Price as Functions of Common-Stock Price**

The exercise value of a warrant is zero until the stock price exceeds the exercise price, then it rises with increases in the stock price. The warrant price is larger than the exercise value by a premium that investors pay because of the speculative appeal of warrants.

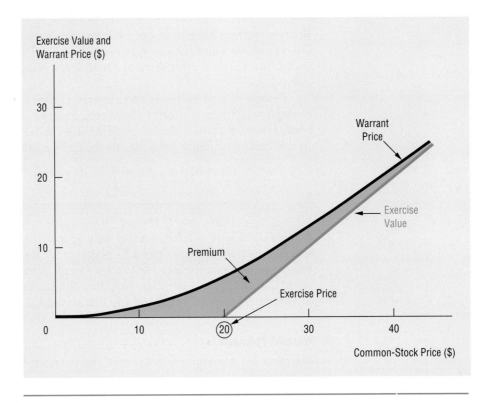

Thus a 50 percent gain in the stock price produces a 125 percent gain in the warrant price. It is this leverage associated with warrants (and call options generally) that provides their speculative appeal.

Figure 17.6 depicts the exercise value and the price of Warren Company's warrant as functions of Warren's stock price. The exercise value is zero for stock prices ranging from zero to the exercise price of $20. Above $20 the exercise value increases dollar for dollar with increases in stock price. The warrant price exceeds the exercise value for all levels of stock price.

At low stock prices the premium is small because the chances are remote that the stock price will increase enough to give the warrant a positive exercise value. At high stock prices the premium once again is small—this time because warrants lose much of their leverage at high stock prices. For example, when the price of Warren Company's stock is $50, the exercise value of its warrant is $30 = ($50 − $20) × 1; a 20 percent increase in the stock price to $60 causes the exercise value to increase to $40 = ($60 − $20) × 1, a 33.3 percent increase from $30. Thus a 20 percent increase in the stock price is associated with a 33.3 percent increase in the exercise value. At higher stock prices the percentage increases in the exercise value become closer to the percentage increases in the stock price.

At very high stock prices investors might as well buy the stock instead of the warrant. Besides, investors receive dividends with stock, and with warrants they do not. For example, when the price of Warren Company's stock is $100, the exercise value of its warrants is $80 = ($100 − $20) × 1. A 10 percent increase in the stock price leads to an exercise value of $90 = ($110 − $20) × 1, which is a 12.5 percent increase from $80. *At very high stock prices relative to exercise prices, the percentage changes in warrant prices approximate the percentage changes in stock prices.*

Warrants vs. Convertible Bonds

The financial manager can use either the conversion option or warrants to help the company issue bonds at a low coupon rate. In both cases the company pays less interest, but it may have to issue common stock in future years at prices below then-current market values. From the investor's point of view, convertibles and bonds with warrants yield less in interest, but they provide the opportunity to participate in gains on the company's common stock. Convertibles and warrants represent attempts by financial managers to lower a company's average cost of capital by appealing to the preferences of various segments of the financial market.

Because of differences in their features, convertibles and warrants present financial managers with a choice for sweetening a bond issue. Financial managers need to weigh each of the following three differences:

- *Exercise effect on future cash:* Conversion of bonds does not provide the company with additional cash, although it does reduce interest expense. In contrast, when holders of warrants exercise them, they pay the exercise price per warrant to the company, thereby providing the company with additional cash.

- *Exercise effect on outstanding debt:* Conversion of bonds reduces a company's outstanding debt and the accompanying interest expense. Exercising warrants does not reduce company debt or interest expense; it does increase the company's equity, however, because warrant holders pay the exercise price for the new shares of common stock.

- *Management control:* The call feature of convertibles gives management some control over when conversion takes place. Warrants are often not callable.[7] Similar to the scheduled step-down in the conversion ratio of convertibles, the exercise price of warrants is sometimes scheduled for a step-up. In both cases the holders are encouraged to take action (convert or exercise) before the scheduled change.[8]

SECURITY MARKET LINE

Chapters 5 and 6 discuss the relationship between required rate of return and the risk investors perceive in securities. Because investors are risk averse, they require higher returns on securities with higher risks. If a company issues a secu-

[7] Rapid American Corporation issued the first callable warrant in the early 1970s. Managers often ignore the call provision for warrants, although callability does add a measure of control.

[8] Companies provide dilution protection for warrants similar to that provided for convertible bonds. If the company issues new common stock at below-market prices, then the exercise price is lowered accordingly. The lower exercise price nullifies the effect of the lower stock price on exercise value.

FIGURE 17.7

The Risk-Return Relationships for a Company's Securities and U.S. Treasury Securities

Illustrated on the security market line (SML) are securities issued by a company and the U.S. Treasury. Although approximate, the position of each security on the SML illustrates the higher rate of return required on securities with higher risk.

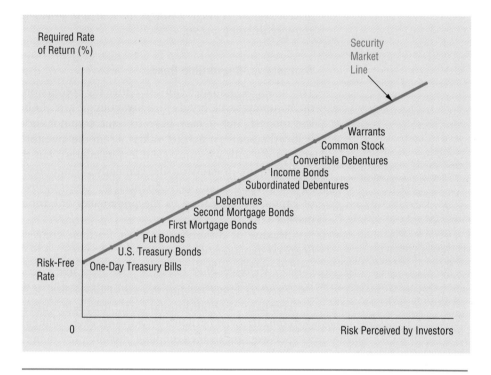

rity with high risk to the investor (and low risk to the company), then the company must pay a high explicit cost for the issue.

Figure 17.7 arrays along the security market line (SML) several of the securities described in this chapter. The security market line shows that investors require higher returns on securities with higher risks. To hold constant differing risk between companies, the line in Figure 17.7 locates corporate securities for an individual company. Security risk to the investor ranges from that of a one-day Treasury bill to a company's warrants. Between these extremes fall the several bonds that a company might issue. Well-secured mortgage bonds have less risk than debentures. Income bonds and convertible debentures have characteristics making them similar in risk to common stock. Each innovation in bond design represents an attempt by financial managers to fill in a gap on the security market line continuum.

Financial managers get feedback from rating agencies on the risk perceived in the bonds issued by their companies. Table 17.1 lists the corporate bond ratings assigned by the two major agencies, Standard & Poor's Corporation and Moody's Investors Service Inc. Although the symbols used by these agencies are slightly different, they mean essentially the same thing. Triple A bonds have high quality (low default risk), and bonds rated with Cs have low quality (high default risk). In general, the agencies base their ratings on: (1) probability of default, (2) protective covenants in the indenture, and (3) the bondholders' claims in the

TABLE 17.1	**Corporate Bond Ratings**

Standard & Poor's[a]		Moody's[a]	
AAA	Highest grade	Aaa	Best quality
AA	High grade	Aa	High quality
A	Upper-medium grade	A	Upper-medium grade
BBB	Medium grade	Baa	Medium grade
BB	Lower-medium grade	Ba	Speculative elements
B	Speculative elements	B	Generally lack characteristics of a desirable investment
CCC	Outrightly speculative		
CC	Speculative to a high degree	Caa	Poor; may be in default
C	Bankruptcy petition may have been filed	Ca	Speculative to a high degree; often in default
D	In default	C	Lowest grade

[a]Standard & Poor's applies modifiers (plus and minus) to ratings AA through CCC to indicate variations in quality. Moody's applies numerical modifiers (1, 2, and 3) to ratings Aa through B to indicate variations in quality: 1 indicates that the bond ranks at the high end of a category; 2, in the middle; and 3, at the low end.

event of bankruptcy. Company factors that cause low ratings include subordination clauses, high debt ratios, low earnings stability, low current ratios, and so on. If company factors change after a company issues a bond, Standard & Poor's places the bond on its *CreditWatch* list for changes in rating. Financial managers observe this process closely because a change in bond rating alters the company's cost of capital.

SUMMARY

• Companies issue bonds through investment bankers to the public or directly to institutional investors. A trust company or trust department of a bank enforces the bond indenture (contract) in a public offering.

• A bond indenture fully describes the nature of a bond: principal, coupon rate, maturity date, and assets pledged as collateral, if any. It also includes protective covenants, which are restrictions on company behavior that would expose bondholders to more risk after the company issues the bond. If the company retains the right to buy back (call) the bond before it matures, then the indenture describes the conditions for the procedure. The indenture may have a sinking-fund provision that requires the company to retire a percentage of the outstanding bonds each year.

• Companies issue different types of bonds. Secured types include mortgage bonds, collateral trust bonds, and equipment trust certificates. Unsecured bonds are debentures. Subordinated debentures place the holders' claims below those of specified senior creditors. Bonds with special features include deep-discount bonds, floating-rate bonds, income bonds, and put bonds. Financial managers issue different types of bonds in an attempt to appeal to various investor preferences, thereby reducing the company's cost of capital.

• A put option is a contract to sell common stock, and a call option is a contract to buy common stock. Puts and calls trade in the securities market, including several organized exchanges. Options trading attracts speculators seeking the potential for large gains and investors seeking to hedge existing investments. The concepts associated with options crop up in business financial management in various ways: (1) Convertible securities and warrants convey call options from the company to investors. (2) Callable securities convey a call option from investors to the issuing company. (3) Put bonds convey a put option from the company to investors. (4) Standby underwritings convey a put option from investment bankers to the company issuing securities (see Chapters 3 and 18).

- The exercise value of a call option equals the stock price minus the exercise price (strike price):

$$\text{Exercise value (call)} = \text{Stock price} - \text{Exercise price}$$

In contrast, the exercise value of a put option equals the exercise price (strike price) minus the stock price:

$$\text{Exercise value (put)} = \text{Exercise price} - \text{Stock price}$$

Speculative value (time value) of a call option and a put option equals the option price minus exercise value:

$$\text{Speculative value} = \text{Option price} - \text{Exercise value}$$

The high degree of leverage created by options gives them enormous upside potential and speculative appeal.

- A convertible bond permits the investor to exchange the bond for a specified number of shares of the company's common stock. Companies add convertibility to sweeten bonds so that investors will require less interest. A convertible bond has two important values: (1) Conversion value is the total value of the common stock for which the convertible may be exchanged; conversion value equals the conversion ratio times the price per share of the stock. (2) Straight-bond value is the value of the convertible as an interest-paying security; strip away convertibility and what remains is straight-bond value. The market price of a convertible bond exceeds the greater of its conversion value and its straight-bond value.

- Bondholders may voluntarily exchange a convertible bond for stock when it is to their advantage—for example, when total stock dividends greatly exceed bond interest. Financial managers may force conversion by calling the convertible when its conversion value exceeds the call price. In either case conversion rids the company of its bond debt, lowers its interest expense, and increases its number of shares of common stock outstanding.

- A warrant is an option to buy a specified number of shares of common stock at a stated price during a specified period of time. Companies issue warrants primarily for the purpose of selling bonds at lower interest costs. Instead of making a bond convertible, the financial manager may choose to add a warrant.

- The exercise value of a warrant, which can trade separately from the bond, is expressed as follows:

$$\begin{array}{l}\text{Exercise} \\ \text{value}\end{array} = \left(\begin{array}{l}\text{Stock} \\ \text{price}\end{array} - \begin{array}{l}\text{Exercise} \\ \text{price}\end{array}\right) \times \begin{array}{l}\text{Number of shares} \\ \text{acquired per warrant}\end{array}$$

The fixed exercise price causes proportionally greater changes in exercise value for a given change in stock price. These changes in turn cause warrants to be highly speculative investments. The speculative value (premium) of a warrant is given as follows:

Speculative value = Warrant price − Exercise value

Stated differently, the market price of a warrant consists of two parts: exercise value and speculative value.

- Convertibility and warrants enable a company to issue bonds with low coupon rates. To determine which one to use, the financial manager evaluates their differences: (1) exercise effect on future cash, (2) exercise effect on outstanding debt, and (3) managerial control over timing of exercise or conversion.

- Standard & Poor's Corporation and Moody's Investors Service are major suppliers of financial information, including ratings of corporate bonds. High ratings (AAA and Aaa) reflect a low probability of default, good protective covenants, and high claims priority in the event of bankruptcy. Low ratings (say, CC and Ca) indicate the opposite.

Key Terms

debenture	open end	exercise (strike) price
indenture	after-acquired clause	underlying common stock
trustee	collateral trust bond	exercise value
protective covenant	equipment trust certificate	speculative value
acceleration of maturity	subordinated debenture	convertible bond
serial bonds	deep-discount bond	conversion ratio
balloon payment	floating-rate bond	conversion price
call provision	junk bond	conversion value
call price	income bond	straight-bond value
call premium	put bond	conversion premium
refunding	option	straight-bond premium
mortgage bond	put option	antidilution clause
closed end	call option	warrant

Questions

17.1. Obtain a recent tombstone advertisement for a corporate bond from *The Wall Street Journal* or other newspaper. Describe the information provided in the advertisement.

17.2. Explain why financial managers put protective covenants in a bond indenture. Why should managers protect bondholders? Are not managers supposed to take care of shareholders?

17.3. Why does the call provision increase the required rate of return on bonds and the sinking-fund provision reduce it? Note that both provisions are designed to retire a bond issue.

17.4. List six different types of corporate bonds in descending order of risk to investors (start with the most risky bond). Briefly comment on the rank-determining feature(s) of each bond.

17.5. Fill in the blanks of the following statements: A

_____ option enables you to buy shares of common stock at the _____ price. A _____ option enables you to sell shares of common stock at the _____ price. Bullish investors normally buy _____ options but not _____ options. The market value of an option equals its _____ value plus its _____ value.

17.6. Explain each of the following statements: (1) The maximum market value of a call option equals the price of the underlying stock. (2) The minimum market value of a call option is zero. (3) At the end of the last trading day prior to expiration, the market value of a call option equals its exercise value. (4) The market value of a call option prior to its expiration date is greater than its exercise value.

17.7. Suppose that after you buy a call option several changes occur. What effect does each of the fol-

lowing changes, considered separately, have on the market value of your call option?
a. Price of the underlying stock increases.
b. Exercise price increases.
c. Time to expiration decreases.
d. Market interest rates increase.
e. Price volatility of the underlying stock decreases.

17.8. Explain whether each of the following circumstances involves a put option or a call option.
a. A company issues convertible debentures.
b. A company issues debentures with warrants attached.
c. A company issues bonds that the investors can sell back to the company at par value.
d. A company issues a first mortgage bond, redeemable by the company at par value.
e. A company issues common stock through an investment banker that underwrites (guarantees the success of) the issue.
f. A company gives stock options to executives as a reward for superior performance.
g. A company pays $10,000 for a 3-month option to purchase a plot of land.

17.9. Why do companies issue convertible bonds?

17.10. Explain the relationship between the terms in each of the following pairs of terms associated with convertible bonds:
a. Conversion ratio and conversion price.
b. Conversion ratio and conversion value.
c. Conversion value and price of the underlying stock.
d. Conversion value and market price of the convertible bond.
e. Straight-bond value and market price of the convertible bond.

17.11. a. How can a company encourage conversion of a convertible bond?
b. How can a company force conversion of a convertible bond?

17.12. Explain the downside protection afforded by convertible bonds. What is meant by the *bond floor* of a convertible?

17.13. The following statements refer to a company's reasons for using warrants in a debenture offering. Identify the statements as true or false and explain the reasons for your choices.
T F A warrant lowers the interest cost of a bond issue.
T F A warrant decreases the company's future debt-equity ratio.
T F A warrant makes a debenture more attractive to investors.

T F A warrant permits management to retire a debenture before maturity.
T F A warrant increases the future cash available to the company.

17.14. How does a warrant differ from a call option that is listed on the Chicago Board Options Exchange?

17.15. Explain the relationship between the terms in each of the following pairs of terms associated with warrants:
a. Warrant price and exercise value.
b. Exercise value and exercise price.
c. Warrant price and price of the underlying stock.
d. Warrant premium and price of the underlying stock.

17.16. Evaluate the differences between convertible bonds and bonds with warrants from the company's viewpoint along the following dimensions: (1) exercise effect on future cash, (2) exercise effect on outstanding debt, and (3) management control.

17.17. Compare and contrast the following two bond ratings: AAA and CCC. What variables do the analysts at Standard & Poor's Corporation consider when they rate a bond issue?

17.18. (*CMA examination, modified*) Chrysler Corporation obtained loan guarantees from the U.S. government in 1980 as part of a federal bailout package. In exchange for the loan guarantees, the U.S. government received 14,400,000 of Chrysler warrants exercisable until 1990. In addition, the Chrysler Loan Guarantee Board was established by Congress in conjunction with the loan guarantees for the purpose of overseeing Chrysler's operations.

In August 1983, the Chrysler Loan Guarantee Board announced its decision to sell the 14,400,000 warrants. The exercise of the warrants at that time would have yielded the government a profit of approximately $180,000,000.

Lee Iacocca, then chairman of Chrysler, asked the government to delay the sale of the warrants. On September 12, 1983, Chrysler outbid three groups of securities firms and agreed to purchase the 14,400,000 warrants from the U.S. government for $311,000,000. Chrysler's bid was $14,000,000 higher than the next closest bidder.

The purchase of the warrants eliminated the last obligation Chrysler had with respect to the government's bailout of the company. Chrysler's management indicated that the warrants would be retired.

a. Explain what a warrant is, and describe the circumstances under which companies issue them.

b. Identify and discuss the advantages and disadvantages of warrants to (1) the issuing company and (2) the investor.

c. Explain the advantages and disadvantages to Chrysler of its purchasing the warrants from the government.

Strategy Problem

David Uhrick, financial vice president of Aramco Manufacturing and Distributing Company, has completed the analysis of the company's capital investment program for the upcoming year. The planned investments will require $40,000,000 of new capital, and the company will raise $20,000,000 from equity and $20,000,000 from debt financing. To raise the debt capital, Mr. Uhrick is considering issuing callable bonds either convertible into common stock or with warrants attached.

The company's investment banker tells Mr. Uhrick that Aramco can issue convertible bonds with a coupon rate of $5\frac{3}{4}$ percent. At that coupon rate the conversion ratio will have to be 40. Were it not for the conversion option, the bonds would have to yield 10 percent annually. Each convertible bond would pay interest semiannually, mature in 15 years, and have a $1,000 par value.

If Aramco issues 15-year bonds with warrants, then the coupon rate would be 6 percent. Each of the 20,000

bonds would have 15 detachable warrants, and each warrant would enable the holder to buy one share of Aramco common stock for $30. The warrants would expire at the end of 15 years.

Aramco's common stock currently trades for $22\frac{1}{8}$ per share on a regional stock exchange. Mr. Uhrick expects that price to prevail during the bond-offering period.

a. Calculate the conversion value and straight-bond value of the convertible bond. Which value is dominant?

b. Calculate the exercise value of each warrant. Will the warrant trade in the market at its exercise value? Explain.

c. Aramco's investment banker advises Mr. Uhrick that the company can safely call the bond and force conversion when conversion value is 20 percent above the call price—par value plus one year's interest. Calculate the stock price necessary for forcing conversion.

d. Describe the key differences between the financing alternatives confronting Aramco.

Strategy	Solution

Multiply the conversion ratio times the stock price.

a.

$$\text{Conversion value} = 40 \times \$22.125$$
$$= \$885$$

Discount the interest payments and principal at 5% for 30 six-month periods.

$$\text{Straight-bond value} = \$28.75(15.3725_{5\%,30}) + \$1,000\,(0.2314_{5\%,30})$$
$$= \$441.96 + \$231.40$$
$$= \$673.36$$

Conversion value dominates straight-bond value; at minimum the convertible bond is worth $885.

Stock price minus exercise price, all times 1.0 equals exercise value.

b.

$$\text{Exercise value} = (\$22.125 - \$30) \times 1.0$$
$$= -\$7.875 \text{ or } \$0.00$$

Negative exercise values are considered to be zero because investors do not exercise warrants with negative exercise values. Despite the zero exercise value, the warrant would trade at a positive market price, reflecting its speculative value.

First calculate the call price; then add 20%; divide this result by the conversion ratio.

c. The call price is par value ($1,000) plus one year's interest ($57.50): $1,057.50. The conversion value 20 percent above the call price is $1,269 (1.2 × $1,057.50). To attain this conversion value, the stock price must be $31.73 ($1,269/40). Following the investment banker's advice, Aramco will call the convertible bonds when its stock price reaches $31.73.

d. Key differences between the financing alternatives:

- *Exercise effect on future cash:* Conversion of convertible bonds provides no additional cash, but Aramco receives $9,000,000 when investors exercise all the warrants:

Investors pay Aramco the $30 exercise price of each warrant.

$$\text{Cash inflow} = (20,000 \text{ bonds})(15 \text{ warrants/bond})(\$30)$$

$$= \$9,000,000$$

Interest expense of the convertibles differs from that of the bonds with warrants.

- *Exercise effect on outstanding debt:* Conversion of convertible bonds reduces Aramco's debt by $20,000,000 and its interest expense by $1,150,000 ($57.50 × 20,000 bonds). Exercising warrants does not reduce Aramco's $20,000,000 debt nor its $1,200,000 (0.06 × $20,000,000) interest expense.

- *Management control:* Aramco's management has more control of when conversion occurs than when exercising the warrants occurs. Management can force conversion by calling the convertible bonds when the conversion value exceeds the call price. Investors probably will not exercise the warrants until the day before they expire in 15 years. To exercise the warrants any earlier would mean giving away their speculative value.

◆ ## Demonstration Problem

General Appliance Products (GAP) manufactures and distributes small kitchen appliances. Because of dramatic changes in its 19X6 models, GAP needs to invest $50,000,000 in new equipment and the redesign of its factory layout. Ayen Wen, GAP's CFO, has the primary responsibility for raising the needed funds. In her opinion, GAP should issue neither common stock nor straight bonds because: (1) The P-E (price-earnings) ratio of the stock is too low and does not reflect the exceptional profitability she expects on the new appliance models. (2) Interest rates are currently too high, which would necessitate a high coupon rate on straight bonds. Ms. Wen is therefore considering the following two financing alternatives:

1. Ten-year, 6 percent coupon convertible bonds with a conversion ratio of 35, callable at par value ($1,000 per bond) plus one year's interest after 5 years; interest is payable semiannually.

2. Ten-year, 7 percent coupon bonds with 20 detachable warrants per bond, callable at par value ($1,000 per bond) plus one year's interest after 5 years; interest is payable semiannually. Each warrant entitles the holder to purchase one share of GAP common stock for $25.

GAP's common stock currently trades for $20 per share.

a. Identify several different types of corporate bonds that GAP might have issued had interest rates been lower.
b. What is an indenture? Identify several significant provisions contained in an indenture.
c. On March 16, 19X6, the Chicago Board Options Exchange listed the following call options and put options on GAP common stock:

Option/Strike	Vol	Exch	Last	Net Chg	a-Close	Open Int
GAP Apr 20	87	CB	$1\frac{1}{2}$	$+\frac{1}{4}$	20	306
GAP May 20	95	CB	$2\frac{1}{2}$	$+\frac{3}{8}$	20	418
GAP Apr 25 p	67	CB	$6\frac{1}{4}$	$-\frac{1}{8}$	20	195
GAP May 25 p	60	CB	$7\frac{3}{8}$	$-\frac{1}{4}$	20	236

(1) Calculate the exercise value and speculative value for each GAP option. (2) Why do the speculative values differ for the two call options? Put options? (3) If the strike prices were lowered, what would happen to the market prices of the call options and

the put options? (4) Assume that GAP's stock price rises 20 percent and speculative value of the options remains unchanged; then calculate the percentage change in market price of the May call and the May put. (5) Assuming that GAP's stock price is $25 per share on the day before expiration of each option, what is the market price of each option?

d. Calculate the following values per bond based on the proposed convertible bonds: (1) conversion price, (2) conversion value, and (3) straight-bond value assuming the annual yield to maturity on GAP's 10-year nonconvertible bonds is 8 percent compounded semiannually. Now estimate the market value of each convertible bond. No calculations are necessary, but explain your answer.

e. At what minimum price per share of stock can GAP force conversion of the convertible bonds?

f. In what ways are warrants and call options similar, and in what ways do they differ?

g. Calculate the following values based on the proposed bonds with 20 detachable warrants: (1) exercise value of each warrant and (2) market value of each bond assuming an annual required rate of return equal to 8 percent compounded semiannually.

h. If you expect market interest rates to remain unchanged and the price of GAP's stock to be $35 per share at year's end, which bond—the convertible or the bond with warrants—would you prefer to purchase at a cost of $1,000 per bond? Assume each warrant has a speculative value of $2, and support your answer with calculations.

i. Suppose your expectations in Part *h* come true. Which financing alternative is more costly to GAP? Explain.

Problems

Annual rate on a zero-coupon bond

17.1. Claremont Beverages issued zero-coupon bonds with a 6-year maturity. The bonds will mature with an $80,000,000 face value. If the offering price is $50,413,570, what is the compound annual interest rate on the issue?

CMA examination, modified: Financing with coupon bonds vs. zero-coupon bonds

17.2. Darty Corporation needs to raise $2,600,000 to finance plant expansion and renovation. Management is considering issuing zero-coupon bonds. This bond issue would be sold with an original-issue discount and would not bear interest. The financing alternative is to issue 14 percent coupon bonds. The pertinent facts about each bond issue are as follows:

	Coupon Bond Issue	Zero-Coupon Bond Issue
Face value	$1,000	$1,000
Annual interest (coupon) rate	14%	—
Selling price	$1,000	$270
Maturity	10 years	10 years

a. What annual rate of return do investors earn on the coupon bond? On the zero-coupon bond?

b. How many bonds will Darty issue under each alternative?

c. Describe Darty's before-tax cash flows with each type of bond issue.

d. Discuss the advantages and disadvantages of the zero-coupon bond from Darty's viewpoint.

Exercise value of call and put options

17.3. Omega Phi Company's (OPC) common stock currently trades in the market for $35 per share. Investors also buy and sell call options and put options on the company's common stock.

a. For an exercise price of $30, calculate the exercise value of the OPC call option and the OPC put option.

b. For an exercise price of $40, calculate the exercise value of the OPC call option and of the OPC put option.

Interpreting listed options
quotations

17.4. The following two quotations on Chevron call options are from *The Wall Street Journal,* dated March 12, 1993:

Chevrn Apr 80	125	AM	$\frac{7}{8}$	$-\frac{1}{16}$	$77\frac{1}{2}$	1,009
Chevrn Jun 80	77	AM	$1\frac{3}{4}$	$-\frac{3}{16}$	$77\frac{1}{2}$	2,061

a. On which exchange do these call options trade?
b. Calculate the exercise value and speculative value of each call option.
c. Why is the price of the "Chevrn Jun 80" greater than the price of the "Chevrn Apr 80"?
d. Why are options called *derivative securities*?
e. Identify an alternative term for each of the following terms: (1) exercise price, (2) exercise value, and (3) speculative value.

Interpreting listed options
quotations

17.5. *The Wall Street Journal* quoted an IBM call option and an IBM put option as follows:

IBM Mar 55	4,171	CB	$\frac{15}{16}$	$-\frac{1}{2}$	$54\frac{7}{8}$	16,505
IBM Mar 55 p	3,565	CB	$1\frac{1}{16}$	$+\frac{7}{16}$	$54\frac{7}{8}$	8,074

a. Identify each part of the two quotations.
b. Is the call option *in-the-money* or *out-of-the-money*? Explain.
c. Is the put option *in-the-money* or *out-of-the-money*? Explain.
d. Calculate the exercise value and speculative value of the call option and of the put option.
e. Are these two options issued by IBM? Explain.

Percentage gain on a call
option and the underlying
stock

17.6. Suppose you buy 100 shares of common stock for $10 per share, and a friend of yours buys a 3-month call option on 100 shares of the same common stock. Her call option has an exercise price of $12 per share and thus trades out-of-the-money, but she paid $100 for it.
a. On the last trading day of the option, the stock trades for $15 per share. Ignoring commission costs, calculate your percentage gain and the percentage gain of your friend.
b. Recalculate Part *a* assuming the stock trades for $12 per share.
c. What principle do your answers to Parts *a* and *b* illustrate?

Stock price volatility and the
value of a call option

17.7. The following probability distributions describe the possible prices per share of two different common stocks 3 months from now:

Probability	**Stock A**	**Stock B**
0.10	$34	$30
0.20	42	40
0.40	50	50
0.20	58	60
0.10	66	70

Three-month call options on Stock A and B each have an exercise price of $55.
a. Calculate the expected price per share of Stock A and of Stock B.
b. Calculate the expected value of the call option on Stock A and on Stock B during the last trading day.
c. Why is the call option on Stock B more valuable than the call option on Stock A?
d. The expected price per share of Stock A is less than the exercise price of the call option. How, then, is it possible for the call option on Stock A to have value?

Call date of a convertible bond	**17.8.** Okay Productions has issued callable convertible bonds. Each bond has a $1,000 face value, and the coupon rate is 9 percent. The conversion ratio is 20, and the bonds are callable at par value plus one year's interest. The common stock is presently trading at $24\frac{5}{8}$. How long can you reasonably expect the bond to be outstanding if the growth rate of the stock price is expected to be 17 percent per year? State your assumptions.

Analysis of a convertible bond

17.9. Askew Company issues a convertible bond on January 1, 19X3, with a call provision. The conversion ratio is 20; the coupon rate, 8 percent; the face value, $1,000. The bond is callable at par plus one year's interest, and it matures in 8 years. Market price of the common stock is $40 per share.

a. Calculate the conversion price.

b. Calculate the bond's conversion value on January 1, 19X3.

c. If interest rates rise, why wouldn't the bond's market price fall below $800, assuming the stock price remains at $40?

d. What is the straight-bond value of the convertible? The annual required rate is 12 percent (compounded semiannually) on Askew's nonconvertible bonds. The convertible pays interest semiannually.

e. Calculate the conversion premium and the straight-bond premium of the convertible bond, assuming its market price is $950.

Analysis of a convertible debenture

17.10. Bauer Corporation has debentures outstanding (face value of $1,000 per bond) that are convertible into the company's common stock at a price of $25 per share. The convertibles have a coupon interest rate of 11 percent per year and mature 10 years from now. Interest is payable semiannually. In addition, each convertible debenture is callable with a call premium of one year's interest.

a. Calculate the conversion value assuming the stock price is $30 per share.

b. Calculate the straight-bond value assuming that bonds of equivalent risk and maturity are yielding 10 percent per year compounded semiannually.

c. Based on your answers to Parts *a* and *b,* estimate the market price of the convertible. No calculations are required, but explain your answer.

Interpreting information on a convertible bond

17.11. In January 1993 NovaCare Inc. issued $175,000,000 of $5\frac{1}{2}$ percent convertible subordinated debentures due January 15, 2000. *Moody's Bond Survey* describes the convertibles as follows:

> *Rating:* Ba3
> *Offering price:* 100
> *Underwriter:* Smith Barney, Harris Upham & Co. Incorporated; Alex, Brown & Sons Incorporated
> *Yield:*
>   Current: 5.50%
>   Maturity: 5.50%
> *Interest payment dates:* Semiannually on each January 15 and July 15, beginning July 15, 1993.
> *Call features:* Nonredeemable, at the company's option, prior to January 15, 1996.
> *Put option:* Redeemable at par plus accrued interest, at the option of the holder, upon a change of control.
> *Conversion feature:* Convertible at any time prior to maturity, at a conversion price of $26.65 per share.
> *Sinking fund:* None
> *Purpose:* Proceeds will be used for general corporate purposes and to acquire contract services and orthotic and prosthetic services companies, rehabilitation hospitals, and potentially other rehabilitation businesses.
> *Price to company:* 97.85

a. Interpret the meaning of Moody's Ba3 bond rating.

b. How many dollars must an investor pay to acquire one bond?

c. How many dollars does the company receive for each bond issued? Why does the company receive fewer dollars per bond than the investor pays?

d. Show calculations for the current yield (5.50 percent) and the yield to maturity (5.50 percent).

e. Which provision—the call feature or the put option—is more attractive from the investor's viewpoint? Explain.

f. Calculate the conversion value of the convertible, assuming that NovaCare's stock trades at $16.75 per share.

Interpreting information on a convertible bond

17.12. In October 1989 Drug Emporium Inc. issued $50,000,000 of convertible subordinated debentures. *Moody's Bond Survey* describes the convertibles as follows:

Rating: B2.

Offering price: 100.

Underwriter: Goldman, Sachs & Co.

Yield:

    Current: 7.75%

    Maturity: 7.75%

Interest payment dates: Payable April 1 and October 1, commencing April 1, 1990, to holders of record on the preceding March 15 and September 15.

Call features: In the twelve-month period beginning October 1, 1992, the debentures are redeemable, in whole or in part, at 104.9; thereafter, the price declines 0.7, annually, to par on or after October 1, 1999.

Put features: If a risk event, as defined, occurs prior to October 1, 1999, the holder can put the debenture back to the company at par. The company, however, has the option to pay the repurchase price in common stock, valued at 95% of the average closing balance for the five days ending the third day preceding the repurchase date.

Conversion feature: Convertible into the company's common stock at any time prior to maturity at $15.35 per share, subject to certain adjustments.

Sinking fund: Beginning October 1, 2000, and continuing through October 1, 2013, the company must make sinking fund payments sufficient to redeem $2.5 million aggregate principal amount; scheduled to retire $35 million principal amount prior to maturity.

Purpose: To finance new store openings, repay outstanding debt, provide working capital to certain subsidiaries, and for other general corporate purposes.

Form: Registered, without coupons.

Denomination: $1,000 and multiples thereof.

Indenture date: October 5, 1989, with The Huntington National Bank as trustee.

Security: The debentures will be unsecured, convertible, subordinated debt of the company.

Sr. debt outstanding: As of August 31, 1989, approximately $11.1 million of senior debt was outstanding.

Restrictions: The indenture prohibits the company from consolidating with or merging into another person unless that person is (1) a U.S. corporation, partnership, or trust which expressly assumes the debentures and the indenture, and (2) no default occurs as a result of the merger.

Price to company: 97.625.

Effective interest cost: 8.03%.

a. How much were the dollar proceeds to the company?

b. Calculate the conversion ratio of the convertible.

c. Calculate the conversion value of the convertible assuming the underlying stock trades for $7.50 per share.

d. Calculate the minimum price per share of stock necessary for the company to be able to force conversion on November 15, 1992.

e. Explain the impact that each of the following features has on the return required by investors in the convertible: (1) call feature, (2) put feature, and (3) sinking-fund feature. (No calculations are necessary.)

f. According to *Moody's Bond Survey*, how risky is the convertible? Explain.

Warrant pricing and values   17.13. Homer Drug Corporation's warrants entitle holders to buy one share of common stock at $2 per share through March 6, 1999. The corporation's stock trades for $4.75 per share, and the market price per warrant is $3.125.

a. Calculate the exercise value and premium (speculative value) of the warrant.

b. Holding other factors constant, what do you expect will happen to the warrant price if the stock price becomes more volatile? Explain.

c. Holding other factors constant, what do you expect will happen to the warrant price as time goes on? Explain.

Behavior of speculative value of a warrant   17.14. ELA Microsystems' common stock currently trades for $11 per share. The warrants on its common stock currently trade for $3 per warrant. Each warrant entitles the holder to purchase one share of ELA common stock for $10. The recent 52-week highs and lows for the securities are as follows:

Security	High	Low
Common stock	$15	$8
Warrant	6	1

a. Calculate the current exercise value and speculative value per warrant.

b. Calculate the speculative value per warrant when the stock price is $8 and the warrant price is $1.

c. Calculate the speculative value per warrant when the stock price is $15 and the warrant price is $6.

d. Why does the speculative value of a warrant decline as the price of the underlying stock becomes increasingly small?

e. Why does the speculative value of a warrant decline as the price of the underlying stock becomes increasingly large?

Pan Am Corporation's warrants   17.15. *Moody's Transportation Manual* describes Pan Am Corporation's warrants as follows: "Each warrant entitles its holder to purchase one common share of Pan Am Corp. for $8.00 (subject to adjustment) by tendering cash or debenture $13\frac{1}{2}$s, 2003, which will be valued at 100% of principal amount, or a combination thereof. Warrants may be exercised until May 1, 1997...." On May 9, 1990, the company's stock price closed at $2\frac{3}{4}$, and its warrant price closed at $\frac{9}{16}$. The recent 52-week highs and lows for the securities are as follows:

Security	High	Low
Common stock	$5\frac{1}{8}$	$2\frac{1}{2}$
Warrant	$1\frac{1}{4}$	$\frac{11}{32}$

a. Calculate the exercise value and premium (speculative value) of the warrant on May 9, 1990.

b. If you had bought the stock at its low price and sold at its high price, what would your percentage gain have been?

c. If you had bought the warrant at its low price and sold at its high price, what would your percentage gain have been?

d. Recalculate your answers to Parts *b* and *c* assuming you bought the securities at their highs and sold at their lows.

e. Which security is riskier? Explain.

f. Assuming Pan Am Corporation's stock price remains at $2\frac{3}{4}$ until January 31, 1997, explain what will happen to its warrant price. (No calculations are needed.)

Comparison of gains on a warrant and the underlying stock

17.16. Sitting next to Jan at a business luncheon, Nancy exclaimed, "I feel positively brilliant. I bought American Desk at $20 a share and it's gone to $40." "Poor dear," said Jan. "You should have bought American's warrants. I did." Looking less brilliant, Nancy asked, "What are you trying to say, Jan?" "I'm saying that you bought a 4-door sedan, and I bought a Ferrari!"

a. What *is* Jan trying to say?

b. The exercise price of American Desk's warrants is $18. Jan purchased the warrants for $4 each when American Desk's stock price was $20 a share. Each warrant entitles Jan to purchase one share of American stock. Assuming the $2 warrant premium drops to $1 when the stock price is $40, what is the current price of the warrant?

c. Calculate Jan's percentage gain when the stock price is $40 and the warrant premium is $1. Calculate Nancy's percentage gain.

Comparison of losses on a warrant and the underlying stock

17.17. Jan and Nancy of the preceding problem met 6 months later at another business luncheon. Nancy looked sad. Jan looked sadder. "I feel terrible," intoned Nancy. "What's wrong?" Jan solicitously inquired. "Remember that stock I told you about? Well, it plummeted. Fell out of bed. Dropped like a stone. It now sells for $5 a share, and I bought it at $20." "You think you have problems. I bought 1,000 of American Desk's warrants at $4 each. They now sell for 25 cents," replied Jan. "One-upmanship," mumbled Nancy. "Your Ferrari investment strategy is making you manic-depressive, Jan."

a. Calculate the percentage losses of both Nancy and Jan.

b. What attribute of warrants causes their price to be more volatile than the underlying stock price?

c. "*Debt* is to interest expense and earnings volatility as *warrant* is to _____ and warrant price volatility." Fill in the blank and explain the analogy.

Computer Problem

Convertible bonds and warrants: template CONWAR

17.18. Leslie DeRego, financial manager for Go Go Sales, is reviewing the long-term financing needs of the company. The *pro forma* financial statements suggest that the entire external financing needs can be met by issuing $25,000,000 in new debt securities.

In view of the currently high interest rates and the possibility that interest rates may fall, Ms. DeRego is considering the issuance of callable bonds. The company's investment bankers suggested the following alternatives:

1. 15-year, 8 percent coupon bonds callable after 5 years.

2. 15-year, 6.5 percent coupon convertible bonds with a conversion ratio of 25, callable after 5 years.

3. 15-year, 7 percent coupon bonds with 10 detachable warrants, callable after 5 years. Each warrant would enable the buyer to buy one share of common stock for $48 any time before maturity, but only on January 1 of each year.

The call premium in each alternative is 1 year's interest. The company is expected to force conversion when the conversion value exceeds the call price by 20 percent.

The company currently has a $50,000,000 noncallable straight-bond issue outstanding. Coupon interest is 7.5 percent and the bond issue will mature in 12 years. The new bonds will be issued in January 19X1.

The *pro forma* statements indicate that the expected earnings before interest and taxes in the coming years are as follows:

19X1	$16,834,000
19X2	$17,296,000
19X3	$18,764,000
19X4	$20,236,000
19X5	$22,109,000
19X6	$24,002,000
19X7	$25,236,000

The company's common stock currently trades for $30 per share, with 1,500,000 shares outstanding. The current dividend is $2 per share and is expected to grow at 10 percent per year. The stock price is expected to grow at the same rate as the dividend. Go Go Sales is in the 34 percent tax bracket.

a. Calculate the conversion value of the convertible bond.

b. Calculate the exercise value of each warrant.

c. Recalculate Parts *a* and *b* for stock prices of $40, $50, $60, and $70.

d. Suppose the company can force conversion only on January 1 of any year. In what year can conversion be forced?

e. What is the first year in which holders of the warrants might exercise them?

f. For each of the alternative bond issues, calculate the company's earnings per share in 19X1 and 19X7.

Selected References

Alexander, Gordon J., and Roger D. Stover. "The Effect of Forced Conversion on Common Stock Prices." *Financial Management,* Spring 1980: 39–45.

Chang, S. J., and Son-Nan Chen. "A Study of Call Price Behavior Under a Stationary Return Generating Process." *Financial Review,* August 1989: 335–354.

Chatfield, Robert E., and R. Charles Moyer. "Putting Away Bond Risk: An Empirical Examination of the Value of the Put Option on Bonds." *Financial Management,* Summer 1986: 26–33.

Ederington, Louis H. "Why Split Ratings Occur." *Financial Management,* Spring 1986: 37–47.

King, Raymond, "Convertible Bond Valuation: An Empirical Test." *Journal of Financial Research,* Spring 1986: 53–69.

Laber, Gene. "Bond Covenants and Forgone Opportunities: The

Case of Burlington Northern Railroad Company." *Financial Management,* Summer 1992: 71–77.

Lin, Ji-Chai, and K. C. Chen. "Partially Anticipated Convertible Calls." *Financial Review,* November 1991: 501–515.

Malitz, Ileen. "On Financial Contracting: The Determinants of Bond Convenants." *Financial Management,* Summer 1986: 18–25.

Perry, Larry G. "The Effect of Bond Rating Agencies on Bond Rating Models." *Journal of Financial Research,* Winter 1985: 307–315.

Wansley, James R., and Terrence M. Clauretie. "The Impact of *CreditWatch* Placement on Equity Returns and Bond Prices." *Journal of Financial Research,* Spring 1985: 31–42.

Appendix 17A ANALYSIS OF REFUNDING A BOND

Refunding occurs when a corporation calls an outstanding bond issue and replaces it with a new bond issue. Corporations refund an issue to reduce interest expense. When interest rates fall over time, management has the opportunity to retire old bonds carrying high coupon rates with new bonds carrying low coupon rates. To capture the future annual savings in interest, a company must incur expenses: call premium on old bonds, flotation cost of new bonds, interest expense during the overlapping period, and tax adjustments. Thus refunding is a capital-budgeting problem: a cash outlay followed by a series of cash inflows. To illustrate, consider the refunding decision of Bell Company.

Bell Company has outstanding a $10,000,000, 8 percent bond, originally issued 10 years ago with a 15-year maturity. The principal has not been amortized, so the entire $10,000,000 still remains to be paid. Original placement costs were amortized on a straight-line basis, and $50,000 remains to be amortized. Management believes that refunding may be worthwhile.

The financial manager's task is to determine the feasibility of refunding the issue with a new 5-year, $10,000,000 bond issue having a 5 percent coupon rate. An investment banking company will charge $200,000 to sell the issue at face value. Bell Company can call the outstanding issue at an 8 percent call premium. The investment banker advising the Bell Company suggests that 2 months will be required to call the outstanding issue. Thus the new bond will have to be sold 2 months before the outstanding issue is retired.

The company is in the 40 percent marginal tax bracket and uses the straight-line method to calculate annual amortization charges for tax purposes. Table 17A.1 shows details of the 7-step analysis.

Step 1.   The after-tax yield to maturity on the new issue is 5 percent multiplied by $(1 - T)$, where T is Bell's marginal tax rate:

$$\frac{\text{After-tax yield}}{\text{to maturity}} = 0.05\,(1 - 0.40)$$
$$= 0.03, \text{ or } 3\%$$

This rate is used to discount all future cash flows in the refunding analysis because it reflects the risks involved.

Step 2.   Unamortized flotation costs on the outstanding issue are immediately expensed, and the tax savings are $(0.40)($50,000) = $20,000$. Table 17A.1 shows the $20,000 as a benefit.

Bell Company forgoes the future tax savings resulting from amortizing the unamortized flotation costs of the outstanding issue. The annual rate of amortization is $50,000/5 = $10,000$, and the annual forgone tax savings are $(0.40)($10,000) = $4,000$ at the end of each of the next 5 years. In present value the loss of tax savings is $($4,000)(4.5797) = $18,319$. (See Column 4 of Table 17A.1.)

Step 3.   Flotation costs on the new issue affect cash at two different times: The *immediate* impact is a cash outflow that is not tax deductible. The *subsequent* impact is a tax savings as Bell Company amortizes the flotation costs on its corporate tax return. Total flotation costs ($200,000) on the new issue are incurred immediately. The amortization is $200,000/5 = $40,000$ per year, and the tax savings are $(0.40)($40,000) = $16,000$. The discount factor at 3 percent annually is 4.5797, and the present value of the future annual tax savings is $73,275.

Step 4.   The $800,000 call premium is an immediate reduction in cash, but its tax deductibility makes the after-tax cost $480,000 = $800,000(1 - 0.40)$. This amount is entered in Column 4 of Table 17A.1, and Column 5 shows that it is a cost, or cash outlay.

Step 5.   Bell Company pays additional or overlapping interest for 2 months. Two months of interest payments on the old issue total $133,333, calculated by using 2 months as a fraction of the year multiplied by the annual dollar interest:

$$\$133,333 = (\tfrac{2}{12}) \times \$800,000$$

TABLE 17A.1

Benefits and Costs from Refunding an 8 Percent, $10,000,000 Bond with a 5 Percent, $10,000,000 Bond[a]

(1) Financial Impact	(2) After-Tax Amount	(3) Present- Value Factor (3%)[b]	(4) Present Value	(5) Benefit (B) or Cost (C)
Flotation costs				
Outstanding issue				

Tax savings from immediate
    write-off of unamortized
    amount
	$ 20,000	1	$ 20,000	B

Annual tax savings forgone (straight-line amortization)	$ 4,000	4.5797	$ 18,319	C
New issue				
Total flotation costs	$200,000	1	$200,000	C
Annual tax savings from amortization (straight-line)	$ 16,000	4.5797	$ 73,275	B
Call premium	$480,000	1	$480,000	C
Two months additional interest	$ 80,000	1	$ 80,000	C
Annual interest savings	$180,000	4.5797	$824,346	B

Net Present Value

Total benefits	$917,621
Less total costs	778,319
Net present value	$139,302

Decision: Proceed with refunding

[a]All amounts are rounded to the nearest dollar.

[b]The present-value factor is determined by the after-tax yield on the new issue.

This amount is tax deductible, so the after-tax cash outflow of the overlapping interest is:

$$\$80,000 = \$133,333(1 - 0.40)$$

Column 5 shows that the $80,000 is a cost, or cash outlay. (For simplicity, we ignore any interest earned on the refunding proceeds.)

Step 6.   The annual interest savings over the remaining years is the difference in the annual dollar interest on the two bond issues:

Annual dollar interest, outstanding issue	$800,000
Less annual dollar interest, new issue	500,000
Annual savings	$300,000

The annual savings on an after-tax basis is $180,000 = $300,000(1 − 0.40). The present value of the after-tax savings of interest is $824,346. This capitalized amount is a benefit, so a B is entered in Column 5 of Table 17A.1.

Step 7. Subtract the present value of the costs, or cash outlays (the Cs in Table 17A.1), from the present value of the benefits, or cash inflows (the Bs in Table 17A.1):

Total benefits	$917,621
Less costs	778,319
Net present value	$139,302

Refunding increases shareholder wealth by $139,302, so Bell Company should refund the outstanding bond issue.

Questions

Consider the entries in Table 17A.1 in answering the following questions:

17A.1. Which items are tax shelters? Explain your answer.

17A.2. At what interest rate are benefits and costs discounted? Why are some items associated with a tax factor of T and others with a tax factor of $(1 - T)$?

Problem

17A.1. Knudson Book Publishing Company issued a $20,000,000 bond 15 years ago. The coupon rate is 14 percent and it originally had a 20-year maturity. Unamortized flotation costs are $70,000, and the company is amortizing them for tax purposes at a rate of $14,000 annually. Management can call the issue at face value plus 1 year's interest.

The company can place a new 5-year $20,000,000 issue with a coupon rate of 10.6 percent. The investment banking firm serving as adviser will charge $250,000 to complete the deal for Knudson. This placement cost will be amortized on a straight-line basis for tax purposes. The company must place the new issue 3 months before retiring the outstanding issue. Knudson is in the 34 percent marginal tax bracket.

Should Knudson refund the bond? Support your answer by calculating the net present value of refunding.

Computer Problem 🖫

Bond refunding: template
BNDREF

17A.2. Sanjit Bhattacharya, financial director of Diagnostics Inc., believes that it may be profitable to refund the company's outstanding bond issue. Fifteen years ago the company issued $2,000,000 of $1,000 par value bonds with a 10 percent coupon rate and having 30 years to maturity. Flotation costs were $150,000 and are being amortized on a straight-line basis at $5,000 per year. The bonds became callable 5 years after the issue date at a premium of 10 percent of par value, declining by 0.5 percent per year thereafter. For example, if the bonds were called at the end of the tenth year, then the call premium would be 7.5 percent. No portion of the issue has been called or purchased from investors.

The company's investment banker believes that a new $2,000,000 bond issue carrying an 8 percent coupon and a 15-year maturity can be sold at par. Flotation costs of $75,000 would be amortized straight line over 15 years. New bonds would have to be sold 1 month before the outstanding issue is retired. The company is in the 34 percent tax bracket.

a. Should the company refund the bond issue? Explain your answer.

b. Mr. Bhattacharya estimates that when the bonds are actually issued, the coupon rate required for issuing the bonds at par could be between 7 percent and 9 percent. The following probability distribution describes his beliefs:

Probability	Coupon Rate
0.10	7.0%
0.10	7.5
0.50	8.0
0.17	8.5
0.13	9.0

At what maximum coupon rate would the bond refunding be profitable? Based on the above probability distribution, should Diagnostics Inc. refund the outstanding bond?

Chapter 18

COMMON STOCK AND PREFERRED STOCK

The Importance of Pictures

The number of investors taking possession of stock certificates is declining. Many investors, nowadays, leave their stock in "street name," the name of their broker. The investor owns the stock but receives declared dividends, the annual report, and other company publications through the broker.

Although many investors never see their stock certificates, companies still try to project a good corporate image through the vignettes on their certificates. Traditional vignettes are dominated by figures of Greek gods, pictures of factories, and other symbols of industrial might. Companies pay substantial sums for original engraving of the vignettes and subsequent printing of the certificates. Engraving alone often runs to $10,000, and printing the certificates costs much more.

Reflecting changes in cultural tastes, many companies are changing the face of their certificates: (1) Ryder System Inc. replaced two scantily clad Adonises with a picture of two well-dressed business people. (2) K mart Corp. now shows three young executives, instead of a

mother and a daughter happily shopping at a K mart store. (3) Reliance Electric Co. still has a Greek god sitting among factories, but the chimneys no longer belch smoke. (4) Playboy Enterprises Inc. switched from Miss February 1971, to a woman holding a globe aloft in a cityscape of famous buildings from around the world. Playboy's certificate was redesigned to better reflect Playboy Enterprises' expanding global presence and to show that Playboy had become more than just a publishing company.

The motivation for changing the picture on stock certificates varies from company to company. Many want to convey an up-to-date image, a reflection of modern-day thinking. Others want to impart the glory and majesty of the company, its aspirations and dreams of becoming a world leader. Some companies, such as Ford Motor Co., are happy with their old and enduring pictures of the past: The car company's stock certificate shows Henry Ford with his 1896 Quadricycle.

Source: Steven E. Levingston, "Stock Certificates Get a Makeover for the '90s," *The Wall Street Journal,* January 19, 1993, C1 and C11. *Photo Credit:* Courtesy of Playboy Enterprises, Inc.

Companies issue common and preferred stock in exchange for funds to finance long-term assets. Investors purchase the stock for the rights of ownership and in anticipation of receiving dividends. The difference between the rights of common and preferred shareholders is substantial. This chapter examines the differing rights common and preferred stock convey, distinctions that give these securities their individual character. What does a company give up and what does it get from issuing common and preferred stock? Why do companies issue different kinds of stock? What are the variations in types of common and preferred stock? These are some of the questions addressed in the two major sections of the chapter, the first dealing with common stock and the second with preferred stock.

COMMON STOCK

stock certificate
Document evidencing corporate ownership.

Common stock is a security that conveys ownership in a company, and the **stock certificate** is evidence of this ownership. Figure 18.1 presents an example of a typical common-stock certificate. The upper right-hand corner of the certificate shows the number of shares owned by the shareholder. The name of the company and its state of incorporation are located near the center of the certificate. Beneath the spelled-out number of shares in the middle of the certificate is a statement noting that the shares are fully paid (the original purchaser paid at least par value) and nonassessable (creditors cannot force the shareholder to contribute cash in the event of bankruptcy). The corporate secretary and chairman of the board sign the certificate. Corporations must by law designate a transfer agent (to change names of the shareholders on certificates) and a registrar (to maintain an official list of shareholders), and these parties countersign the certificate. Irving Trust Company serves both functions for The Gilbert Companies Inc. The CUSIP number is a unique and permanent identifier, much like a person's Social Security number, that is assigned to the stock of a company. CUSIP stands for Committee on Uniform Securities Identification Procedures—a group associated with the American Bankers Association.

closely held company
Company with few shareholders.

publicly held company
Company with many shareholders.

A company's shareholders as a group own the company, and the ownership of individual shareholders is proportional to the number of shares they own of the total. **Closely held companies** are owned by only a few shareholders. In contrast, **publicly held companies** are owned by a large and diverse group of shareholders.[1] Publicly held stock trades frequently in the market, but closely held stock trades infrequently.

Common shareholders are residual claimants, meaning that they are the last to be paid when earnings are distributed or upon liquidation of the company. A company pays all expenses—wages, salaries, cost of goods, interest, and taxes—before paying a dividend to owners. In the event of bankruptcy and liquidation, the claims of all others must be satisfied before the common shareholders receive anything, and liquidation often leaves shareholders with nothing.

To attract investors, the residual claim that common stock offers must be balanced by the expectation of sizable rewards. Without the offsetting rewards, a company would be unable to sell common stock to raise capital. It is the rights given to common shareholders that create the offsetting rewards.

---

[1] Use of these terms is rather loose because no specific number of shareholders separates a closely held company from a publicly held company.

FIGURE 18.1

Example of a Common-Stock Certificate

A stock certificate shows the number of shares the shareholder owns, name of the issuing company, state of incorporation, and name of the shareholder. Company officers, the transfer agent, and the registrar sign the certificate. Companies by law must provide certificates for all shares of stock they issue.

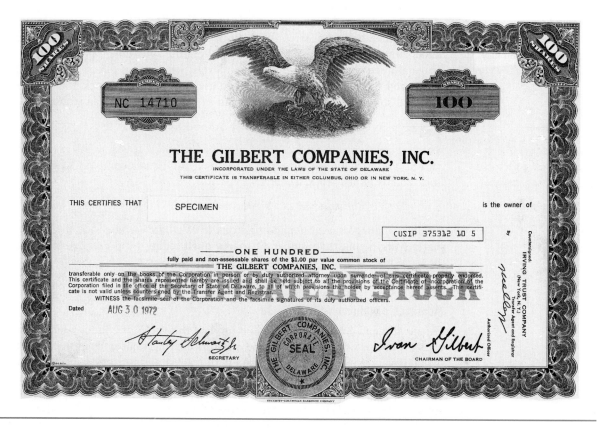

The modern-day corporation is a descendent of the joint-stock company that developed in England in the seventeenth century. Owners of joint-stock companies had limited liability and were residual claimants, but they did not receive a certificate that could be used to transfer all or part of their ownership. Widely issued common stock accompanied the development of modern-day corporations and enabled companies to tap a large source of financing. Soon after the signing of the Articles of Confederation in 1781, states granted corporate charters on a case-by-case basis. In the early 1800s states developed laws of incorporation enabling the creation of corporations without legislative acts. From these early days to the present, corporations have been creatures of individual states, not of the federal government.[2]

To incorporate, individuals file articles of incorporation with a state. The filing becomes the company's **charter,** or contract with the state, if the state grants

charter
Contract with a state establishing a corporation's existence.

---

[2]Exceptions include federal charters granted to some commercial banks and savings and loan associations.

it. Potential investors in shares of a corporation may be interested in examining the charter because it lists the name of the company, the location of its headquarters, its purpose, numerous bylaws and special provisions, and the authorized number of shares of common stock. States charge an incorporation fee and may charge an annual franchise tax based on the number of authorized shares or on the book value of stock.

Authorized stock is the maximum number of shares the corporation can issue without amending its charter. Amending a charter takes time because the shareholders must vote on such a proposal. To avoid the amendment process, the charter usually sets authorized stock at high levels, which gives the corporation some authorized but unissued stock for later use. **Issued stock,** stock that has been issued to shareholders, must be less than or equal to authorized stock:

$$\text{Issued stock} \leq \text{Authorized stock}$$

issued stock
Authorized shares distributed to investors.

When a company repurchases some of its issued stock, it becomes **treasury stock,** with no voting right and no claim to a dividend. Thus a company's **outstanding stock** equals issued stock less treasury stock:

treasury stock
Issued shares repurchased by the issuing corporation.

$$\text{Outstanding stock} = \text{Issued stock} - \text{Treasury stock}$$

outstanding stock
Issued shares in the hands of shareholders.

Financial managers use outstanding stock to calculate earnings and dividends per share. Multiplying the number of shares outstanding by price per share equals the total market value of a company's common equity.

Measures of Common-Stock Value

Financial managers and investors often view the value of common stock differently from the way accountants do when preparing financial reports. Financial managers and investors are concerned with market and intrinsic values. The market value of a share of stock, or its price per share, reflects the expectations of buyers and sellers. Buyers and sellers ordinarily hold different perceptions of the stock's *intrinsic value*—the present value of its expected future dividends—when a trade occurs.[3] When estimated intrinsic value exceeds market value, the investor should buy the stock. Conversely, when intrinsic value falls short of market value, the investor should not buy the stock (or should sell it).

Accountants are concerned with several other measures of value, in addition to market and intrinsic value. One of these is **par value,** an arbitrary dollar amount selected by the company founders. Many states permit companies to issue stock with no par value at all or with some arbitrarily stated value that does not even appear on the stock certificate. A company's charter indicates the par or stated value of its common stock.

par value
Arbitrary value appearing on a stock certificate; used on the balance sheet in the common-stock account.

Par value serves two functions. First, it measures the extent of the liability of the shareholder. Legally, investors who purchase common stock from a company for less than par value can be held liable to creditors for the difference between par value and the purchase price. Because of this potential liability, the company founders usually set a low par value, typically $1 and rarely above $5. Second, par value determines the amount of external equity allocated to the common-stock account on the balance sheet. Accountants record the aggregate par value of a stock issue under the label *Common stock* in the equity section of the

---

[3] Investors also may sell common stock to increase their liquidity or simply to rebalance their portfolios to change risk levels.

balance sheet. They record the amount of capital exceeding the aggregate par value as *Capital in excess of par.*

EXAMPLE

Perkison Enterprises issues 10,000 shares of common stock for $50 a share. Perkison's corporate charter sets par value at $1 a share. The accountant sets up the equity section of the balance sheet as follows:

Common stock (10,000 shares, par $1)	$ 10,000
Capital in excess of par	490,000
Total common equity	$500,000

Accountants record stock with a stated value in a manner similar to the way they record par-value stock. If Perkison had issued a no-par stock, then the entire $500,000 would be carried to the common-stock account.

At the time of issuing stock, Perkison's *book value* is $50 a share: $500,000 divided by the number of shares outstanding (10,000). As Perkison generates and retains earnings, its book value increases. Conversely, if Perkison incurs losses, then its book value decreases.

EXAMPLE

By year-end Perkison Enterprises earns and retains $50,000 after taxes. Its updated equity section looks as follows:

Common stock (10,000 shares, par $1)	$ 10,000
Capital in excess of par	490,000
Retained earnings	50,000
Total common equity	$550,000

Book value per share is $55 ($550,000/10,000 shares). If Perkison loses $50,000 instead of earning $50,000, then its equity section would be:

Common stock (10,000 shares, par $1)	$ 10,000
Capital in excess of par	490,000
Retained earnings	(50,000)
Total common equity	$450,000

Book value per share is $45 ($450,000/10,000 shares).

Perkison's book value may bear little resemblance to its market value because book value is based on historical-cost accounting procedures, and market value reflects investors' assessment of future cash flows (expected dividends and selling price). Perkison's future cash flows depend on how management invests the capital it raises. Some stocks trade above book value and others below.

liquidation value

Piecemeal disposal value of assets less total liabilities.

Perkison's **liquidation value** is the value of equity upon dissolution of the company. The current piecemeal value of assets less liabilities equals liquidation value. Because the value of nonmonetary assets increases with inflation, the proceeds from selling a company's individual assets may exceed their historical (book) values; in this case liquidation value per share exceeds book value per share. When a company's liquidation value exceeds its *market value,* it is "worth

Measures of Value Associated with Common Stock

The book value of common stock equals the historical cost of assets less liabilities; replacing historical cost of assets with their replacement value yields liquidation value. Adding organizational value to liquidation value produces market value, or going-concern value. Market value exceeds book and liquidation value if management is successful in maximizing the price per share of common stock.

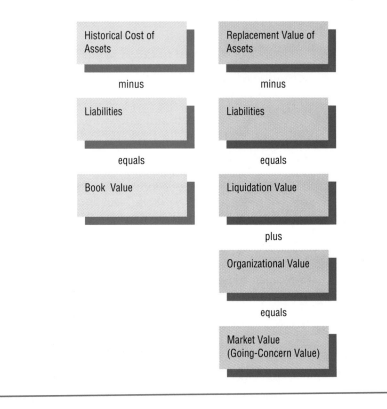

more dead than alive." *Forbes* calls such companies *loaded laggards.*[4] The amount by which a company's market value exceeds its liquidation value is its **organizational value**. Organizational value results from the skill that management employs in making investment and financing decisions. Positive organizational value occurs because of **synergy**. The total value of the company is greater than the sum of the values of its individual assets.

Figure 18.2 summarizes the relationships among several of the measures of value. Book value provides no information beyond the historical cost of assets and the book value of liabilities. Liquidation value equals the *replacement value* of assets less liabilities. Adding organizational value to liquidation value yields market value, the most important value to shareholders.

organizational value
Market value less liquidation value.

synergy
Condition in which the total exceeds the sum of its parts.

---

[4] *Forbes* publishes annually a list of publicly held companies whose book values (not liquidation values) per share are greater than their market price per share. For some companies even working capital per share exceeds market price per share. These companies are loaded and lagging because their assets are not being used productively, making them tempting targets for takeover specialists. Wresting control from entrenched shareholders or management, however, is often difficult, a point emphasized in Chapter 21.

Ⅹ Legal Rights of Shareholders

The corporate charter spells out the rights of shareholders. A shareholder who owns 100 percent of a company's common stock has little trouble with the legal rights of ownership. Most large corporations, however, are owned by numerous, geographically dispersed shareholders and are operated by professional managers. This separation of ownership from management makes it necessary to spell out the legal rights of shareholders because management may choose to operate the company in its own best interest rather than in the best interest of the shareholders.

Shareholders of common stock have the fundamental right to elect the directors of the company. In other words, shareholders have power over corporate affairs through their representatives. The directors are agents of shareholders (the principals) and establish broad policies for managers to follow.

The company's charter describes specific shareholder rights, while general rights have evolved as a result of court decisions over time. For example, shareholders have the right to:

- Own a stock certificate and to sell it to others whenever they wish to transfer their ownership.
- Receive information on company operations through annual and, perhaps, quarterly reports.
- Attend the annual shareholders' meeting.
- Limited liability from company creditors; the most shareholders can lose is what they paid for the stock they own.
- Inspect company books and records, although they may have to prove in court the need to do so.

In addition to these rights, shareholders have rights pertaining to earnings, voting, and buying new shares of company stock.

Right to Earnings.   Most investors own common stock because of the right to earnings. Shareholders receive company earnings directly only when the board of directors declares a dividend. Declared dividends become a current liability of the company and must be paid. Shareholders benefit indirectly from retained earnings through gains in stock price. When retained earnings are invested in profitable projects, they increase the value of the company and therefore cause the price of the stock to rise.

Right to Vote.   Each share of stock usually entitles a shareholder to one vote in elections to select directors, amend the company charter, adopt or modify bylaws, and make other changes in company policies. Legally, the ultimate control of a company resides with its shareholders. They elect the board of directors, which in turn selects the management to operate the company. Selected members of management often serve on the board.

Shareholders may vote in person on company matters at the annual shareholders' meeting, or they may vote by signing a **proxy,** a document empowering others to vote on their behalf. Because a majority of shareholders do not or cannot attend annual meetings, most cast their votes via proxy.

In a **proxy fight,** competing groups solicit proxies, usually seeking control of the company. By soliciting proxies, the groups attempt to install their own board of directors, replace selected members of management, and thus take control.

proxy
Document empowering someone else to vote on behalf of a shareholder.

proxy fight
Competition among groups for the proxies of shareholders.

Most outside challenges fail, however, partly because management and the board have the resources of the company—people and money—at their disposal. Probability of a successful outside challenge increases when (1) the board controls only a small percentage of outstanding shares and (2) company performance has been poor.

To maintain voting control, the board can authorize two types of common stock, Class A and Class B. For example, holders of Class A stock might have the right to receive dividends but not the right to vote. Holders of Class B stock might or might not have the right to receive dividends, but they do have the right to vote. If both classes have identical rights to dividends, then Class B stock will trade at a higher price because of the value of voting power. Keeping the voting stock in friendly hands assures control. In recent years, beginning when General Motors issued Class E common stock to purchase Electronic Data Systems and Class H common stock to purchase Hughes Aircraft, the New York Stock Exchange has allowed companies to list more than one class of common stock. Most companies, however, still have only one class of common stock.

A second way the board maintains corporate control is through majority voting. With **majority voting**, a shareholder with 100 shares casts 100 votes for each director position—say, five positions. With **cumulative voting**, that same shareholder can cast votes in any combination—all 500 votes for one director or allocated in any other way. The majority-voting system ensures that majority shareholders elect each director. The cumulative-voting system provides the possibility that a minority shareholder (one who owns less than 50 percent of the shares) can elect at least one director.

majority voting
Shareholder must allocate votes equally among elective positions on a board of directors.

cumulative voting
Shareholder may allocate votes among elective positions in any combination.

EXAMPLE

Suppose that a company has 1,000 shares outstanding, and that 5 directors are to be elected. Under majority voting, 501 votes (shares) cast for each position elect the entire slate of 5. A shareholder with fewer shares would not be able to elect even one director if the other 501 shares were in opposition. The majority shareholders with 501 shares would win each directorship.

With cumulative voting the minimum number of shares needed to elect a specified number of directors is given as follows:

$$\text{Minimum number of shares needed} = \frac{\text{Number of shares outstanding} \times \text{Number of directors sought}}{\text{Number of directors up for election} + 1} + 1$$

Applying the equation to the example above shows that at least 167 shares are needed to elect 1 director:

$$\text{Minimum number of shares needed} = \frac{1{,}000 \times 1}{5 + 1} + 1$$

$$= 167.7, \text{ or } 167 \text{ (rounded downward)}$$

A minority shareholder with 167 shares is able to elect 1 director even with the other 833 shares in opposition.

Accumulating votes (5 directors × 167 shares = 835 votes), the minority shareholder casts 835 votes for one director, ignoring the other four. The best that the 833 opposing shares can do is shown here:

| | Number of Votes | |
Directorship	Majority	Minority
1	833	0
2	833	0
3	833	0
4	833	0
5	833	835

The majority shareholders get four directors but lose on the fifth because only 833 votes combat the minority shareholder's 835 votes. Thus in this case 16.7 percent (167/1,000) of the outstanding shares entitles the minority shareholder to representation on the company's board of directors. Roughly half of the states (including California, Michigan, and South Carolina) require cumulative voting for directors. Some observers consider cumulative voting to be more democratic than majority voting because it gives minority shareholders a better chance for representation on the board of directors.

preemptive right

Shareholder's right of first refusal on the purchase of additional shares of common stock issued by the company.

Preemptive Right.   The **preemptive right** of shareholders grants them the right of first refusal on the purchase of additional shares of common stock issued by the company. The right of first refusal means that the company must first offer a new issue of common stock to its shareholders before trying to sell it to other investors. Preemptive rights protect shareholders from dilution of control and of value. When a company issues common stock to outsiders, it reduces the voting control of existing shareholders. Moreover, if the company prices the stock below the current market value, then shareholders experience a dilution of value. To see the effects of exercising the preemptive right by shareholders, consider the following example.

EXAMPLE

Triniton Corporation has 10,000 shares of common stock outstanding, trading at $100 a share. Triniton issues 10,000 new shares for $50 each. Before the stock offering, the market value of Triniton's equity is $1,000,000 (10,000 shares × $100); after the offering, its value is $1,500,000—(10,000 × $100) + (10,000 × $50). The $500,000 increase in value reflects the capital raised from issuing new stock. The price per share of Triniton's stock falls to $75 ($1,500,000/ 20,000).

rights offering

Issuance of new common stock to shareholders of a company.

The preemptive right enables shareholders to purchase new shares in a **rights offering**—the issuance of new common stock to company shareholders—on a *pro rata* basis; that is, they buy a number of shares in proportion to their ownership. Thus a shareholder owning 10 percent of a company may purchase 10 percent of the new issue of common stock.

EXAMPLE

The shareholder who owns 10 percent of Triniton and does not purchase new shares suffers dilution of control: (1) Before the offering the shareholder has 10 percent (1,000/10,000) of all votes; (2) after the offering the same shareholder has 5 percent (1,000/20,000) of all votes. Moreover, the shareholder suffers dilution of value: (1) Before the offering the shareholder's stock is worth $100,000 (1,000 shares × $100); (2) after the offering the stock is worth $75,000 (1,000 shares × $75).

To prevent dilution of control and of value, the shareholder must purchase 10 percent of the new stock issue (1,000 shares $\times$ \$50 = \$50,000). The shareholder would then own 2,000 of 20,000 shares (10 percent control) outstanding with an average share price of \$75. The shareholder's \$150,000 investment equals 10 percent (\$150,000 ÷ \$1,500,000) of the company's equity value. By exercising the preemptive right, the shareholder with 10 percent of the ownership before the new offering maintains 10 percent voting control in the company and 10 percent of the value of the company.

In most states the preemptive right exists unless specifically denied in the company charter; in other states the preemptive right does not exist if the company charter is silent on the matter. Under either of these conditions the shareholders may vote to eliminate the preemptive right.

Issuing Common Stock through Subscription Rights

subscription right
Option to buy a new share of common stock at a specified subscription price.

A company satisfies the preemptive right by permitting shareholders to subscribe *pro rata* to any new issue of stock or by letting them sell their **subscription rights** to others. The board of directors approves the new issue, and an officer of the company formally announces the new stock issue in a letter to shareholders. The letter describes the subscription rights and specifies the record date for determining who is entitled to the rights. It also explains how long the offer will remain open and when subscription warrants to evidence the subscription rights will be mailed.

subscription price
Price at which a shareholder exercises a right.

After the record date the corporate officer mails subscription warrants to shareholders of record. The warrant describes the terms of the issue, the **subscription price** (or *exercise price*) per share, the final date for exercising the rights, and the date the new stock will be issued. A subscription agreement to be signed by the subscriber is on the back of the warrant. By paying the subscription price and remitting the warrant, the subscriber buys a share of the new issue.

Dates of a Rights Offering.   Rights have a fleeting life. They exist in most cases for only a few weeks before expiring. To understand the events that take place during a rights offering, examine the time line in Figure 18.3. The board of directors announces on October 3 its intention to raise equity capital through a rights offering and specifies October 25 as the date of record, the date when the names of shareholders entitled to subscribe will be compiled. An officer of the company mails the subscription warrants on November 17 to shareholders holding the stock on the date of record. The final date for exercising rights is November 28. New stock is issued on December 16, with shares being sent to subscribers or (in the event of unsubscribed shares) being sold to investors.

ex-rights date
Day beginning the period when the purchase of a share of stock does not include a right.

To receive a right, an investor must purchase the stock five days before the date of record. Under the rules of most stock exchanges (for example, the New York and American Stock Exchanges), shares trade *ex* rights four trading days before the date of record. *Ex* rights means without or beyond rights. The four-day lead time allows four business days to inform the transfer agent and registrar that share ownership has changed. Figure 18.3 shows that on the *ex*-**rights date,** October 21, the stock trades without rights. In fact, the period from October 21 through November 28 is the *ex*-rights period. The period prior to the *ex*-rights date (October 21) is the **rights-on period**—denoting that *stock purchasers will receive one right per share purchased.*

rights-on period
Period during which purchase of stock conveys one right for each share.

FIGURE 18.3

Dates Associated with a Rights Offering

Common stock trades *ex* rights when buying shares no longer entitles the shareholder to subscribe to new shares at the subscription price. For listed stocks the *ex*-rights date is four trading days preceding the date of record.

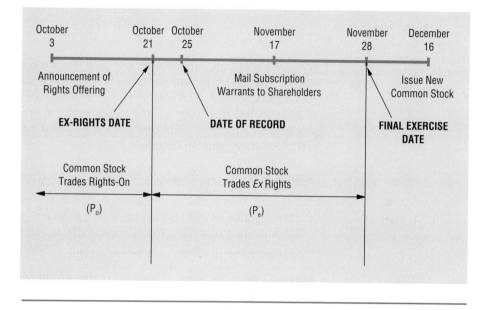

Setting the Subscription Price.   At the time of announcing a rights offering, the board also announces the subscription price per share. By setting the subscription price below the prevailing market price per share, the board ensures that the rights have value, which encourages holders to exercise them and allows the company to raise the capital needed. Typically, directors set the subscription price 15 to 30 percent below the current market price.

EXAMPLE

Klaxton Company plans to raise $10,000,000 through a rights offering. Klaxton has 1,000,000 shares outstanding, trading at $50 a share, although the price has ranged from $44 to $53 over the past three months. Klaxton's management believes that a $40 subscription price per share will assure a successful offering. How many shares must the company issue?

In the above example, the number of new shares issued is calculated by dividing the capital needed by the subscription price:

$$\text{Number of new shares} = \frac{\text{Capital needed}}{\text{Subscription price}}$$

$$= \frac{\$10,000,000}{\$40}$$

$$= 250,000$$

Klaxton needs to issue 250,000 shares to raise the $10,000,000. Each of Klaxton's 1,000,000 outstanding shares entitles the holder to one right to maintain a *pro rata* share of ownership in the company. Thus the number of shares (N), or number of rights, needed to subscribe to a new share is calculated as follows:

$$N = \frac{\text{Number of shares outstanding}}{\text{Number of new shares}}$$

$$= \frac{1,000,000}{250,000}$$

$$= 4$$

A shareholder can subscribe to one new share of stock for every four shares already owned by paying the $40 subscription price per share and submitting four rights. Should shareholders choose not to exercise their rights to subscribe to new shares, they may sell the rights to other investors. Rights to buy listed stocks trade on the stock exchanges; the prices of rights are quoted in the financial press along with stock prices.

Valuing a Right.   In the above example, the total market value of the common stock is $60,000,000:

Market value of old shares (1,000,000 shares × $50)	$50,000,000
Market value of new shares (250,000 shares × $40)	10,000,000
Market value of all shares after new issue	$60,000,000

Klaxton's price per share of stock after the offering equals the total market value of all shares divided by the number of shares outstanding. Thus the *ex*-rights price per share of common stock (P_e) equals $48:

$$P_e = \frac{\text{Total market value of all shares}}{\text{Number of shares outstanding}}$$

$$= \frac{\$60,000,000}{1,250,000}$$

$$= \$48 \text{ per share}$$

If Klaxton issues all 250,000 new shares at $40 each, then its stock price drops from $50 to $48 on the *ex*-rights date. Shareholders are compensated for the $2 drop in price by receiving one subscription right worth exactly $2. Four rights plus $40 enable shareholders to buy a stock worth $48. The value of each right (R) is therefore $2:

$$R = \frac{P_e - S}{N}$$

$$= \frac{\$48 - \$40}{4}$$

$$= \$2$$

where P_e = *ex*-rights price per share of stock

S = subscription price per share of stock

N = number of old shares (or rights) needed to buy one new share of stock

During the *ex*-rights period, when the stock trades without rights, the price per share of stock is P_e. Buyers and sellers of rights must use P_e, the only available stock price, to estimate the value of a right.

During the rights-on period, when the stock trades with rights, the price per share of stock is P_o. Buyers and sellers of rights must use P_o, the only available stock price, to estimate the value of a right. Rights trade in the market on a *when-issued* basis before the subscription warrants are mailed; delivery of the subscription warrants between buyers and sellers takes place when they become available. Using the *rights-on price,* we calculate the value of a right (R) as follows:

$$R = \frac{P_o - S}{N + 1}$$

$$= \frac{\$50 - \$40}{4 + 1}$$

$$= \$2$$

The value of the right is the same $2; its value does not change, although a different equation is used for its computation.[5] Figure 18.4 shows why a different equation is used for the rights-on and *ex*-rights periods. During the rights-on period, investors receive one subscription right with each share they purchase; thus they are buying the share of stock in the secondary market plus the right to subscribe to the new issue at $40 per share. Dividing *(P_o − S)* by N *plus 1* during the rights-on period gives recognition to the right included in the stock price *P_o*. *On the ex-rights date the price per share of stock drops by the value of one right,* and *(P_e − S)* divided by N equals the value of a right. Either equation is a shorthand method to calculate the decline in market value per share that shareholders experience as a result of the new issue.

Effect on Shareholder Wealth.   Despite the value of a right being merely compensation for the decline in price per share of stock, shareholders may be inclined to look upon the receipt of rights as a bonus. A rights offering mistakenly implies that shareholders receive something for nothing—a number of valuable rights. In fact, their wealth remains unchanged as long as they (1) exercise the rights to purchase the new stock or (2) sell the rights to other investors.

EXAMPLE

Consider the courses of action open to a shareholder who owns 100 shares of Klaxton's common stock. Letting rights expire unexercised or unsold causes the shareholder to lose $200 (100 rights × $2):

Rights-on market value of stock (100 shares × $50)	$5,000
Less *ex*-rights market value of stock (100 shares × $48)	4,800
Loss on unexercised and unsold rights	$ 200

---

[5] The rights-on equation is derived as follows: The *ex*-rights price *(P_e)* equals the rights-on price *(P_o)* less the value of one right *(R)*:

$$P_e = P_o - R$$

Substitute *(P_o − R)* for *P_e* in the *ex*-rights equation:

$$R = \frac{(P_o - R) - S}{N}$$

Now use algebra to solve for the value of a right *(R)* in terms of *P_o*:

$$RN = P_o - R - S$$

$$RN + R = P_o - S$$

$$R(N + 1) = P_o - S$$

$$R = \frac{P_o - S}{N + 1}$$

FIGURE 18.4

Behavior of Stock Price per Share on the *Ex*-Rights Date

The value of a right is merely compensation to shareholders for the decline in value of their shares. The price per share of common stock drops as a result of the new issue of stock at a below-market price, and the amount of the drop is the market value of the right.

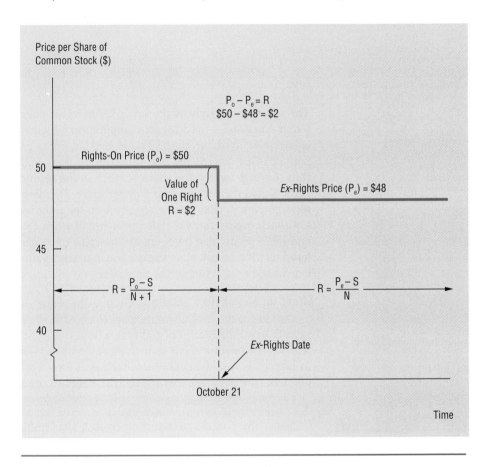

Clearly, as the above example shows, a shareholder who ignores rights suffers a loss in wealth. What happens to wealth if the shareholder exercises or sells the rights? It remains unchanged because the market value of a right exactly equals the loss in value of a share of stock.

Assume that the shareholder in the above example exercises rights to purchase new shares. Before the rights offering, the shareholder's stock is worth $5,000 (100 shares × $50). The shareholder may purchase 25 new shares for $40 each and 100 rights; it takes 4 shares (4 rights) and $40 to buy a new share. To exercise the rights requires an additional investment of $1,000 (25 shares × $40). After exercising the rights, the shareholder has a $6,000 ($5,000 + $1,000) investment and 125 shares, for an average cost of $48 a share ($6,000/125 shares). Because Klaxton's *ex*-rights price per share also equals $48, the shareholder's wealth is unchanged: The shareholder has invested a total of $6,000, which equals the market value of the stock.

Alternatively, the shareholder may sell the 100 rights in the market for $200 (100 rights × $2). Recall from earlier calculations that the new issue causes the stock price to drop from $50 to $48 a share. Adding the cash from selling the rights ($200) to the $4,800 (100 shares × $48) stock value reveals that the shareholder's investment remains at $5,000. Selling rights causes a change in the composition of the shareholder's portfolio: What was once 100 shares of $50 stock is now $200 in cash and 100 shares of $48 stock. The shareholder's wealth remains unchanged.

A rights offering forces shareholders to decide either to invest more money or to divest part of their holdings if they are to avoid losing wealth. Shareholders divest holdings by selling their rights to other investors. Investors may buy rights to reduce brokerage commissions on the purchase of shares. For example, an investor can buy 20 shares of Klaxton's stock from a broker for $48 per share or buy 80 rights for $2 each and then 20 shares for $40 each from the company. Although each course of action results in a $960 investment, exercising rights reduces transaction costs.

Typically, only a small portion of all rights expire unexercised when the subscription price remains below the stock price. To ensure the complete sale of the new stock, the company can use an **oversubscription privilege** permitting shareholders to buy on a *pro rata* basis all of the unsubscribed shares in the initial offering. The company might also make a standby agreement with an investment banker to purchase the stock at the subscription price in the event that the market price of the stock falls below the subscription price.[6] Because of the substantial fees involved in such an agreement, shareholders might be better served if management were to set the subscription price so low that a successful offering is guaranteed without the standby agreement.

oversubscription privilege
Subscribers may buy, at the subscription price on a pro-portional basis, all new shares not purchased in a rights offering.

Rights vs. Warrants. The time line in Figure 18.3 indicates that on November 17 the company mails subscription warrants to the shareholders of record. Although subscription warrants might appear to be much like the warrants associated with bonds (Chapter 17), substantial differences exist between the rights evidenced by subscription warrants and the warrants associated with bonds:

- *Purpose:* Companies use rights in order to issue new common stock, but they usually use warrants to *help* issue bonds. Warrants sweeten a bond issue and allow the company to pay a lower interest rate.

- *Time period:* Rights are short-lived, existing only a few weeks before they expire. Warrants are long-term securities with lives measured in years and some in perpetuity.

- *Exercise price at time of issuance:* The subscription price of a right is less than the underlying stock price at the time a company issues rights. In contrast, the exercise price of a warrant is *above* the prevailing stock price at the time of issuance. The warrant has speculative value, whereas the right is too short-lived to have much speculative value.

When issuing common stock to raise funds, a company must necessarily grant participation in company ownership. To limit that participation, the company may issue preferred stock in place of common stock.

---

[6]The company essentially buys a put (sell) option with an exercise price equal to the subscription price; that is, for a period of time the company can sell the new stock at a specified price.

FOCUS ON PRACTICE

A Tale of Two Issues

When closely held companies have an initial public offering (IPO) of common stock, they try to sell shares to a wide circle of investors. *Going public* is attractive to closely held companies because it (1) establishes a market value for the company, (2) creates liquidity for shareholders, and (3) establishes a market for future financing.

On the other hand, going public involves substantial costs: legal fees, accounting fees, and investment banking fees. In addition, company owners lose their privacy and may lose control of their company.

Here then is a tale of two issues—a happy IPO and a not-so-happy IPO.

Before he was 30 years old, William Gates III cofounded Microsoft, a manufacturer of software for personal computers. A few years after its founding, Microsoft held its initial public offering of common stock. In March 1986 Microsoft stock was offered to the public for $21 per share. It soon zoomed to $35.50

per share in OTC trading before settling at $31.25.

Microsoft's IPO consisted of new shares from the company and shares owned by the founders. In total, Microsoft and its founders raised $61,000,000. Mr. Gates received $1,600,000 for the shares he sold. The shares he kept had a market value of $350,000,000!

In early 1990 the technocratic Mr. Gates was putting the finishing touches on software called Windows 3.0. Since its IPO, Microsoft, and therefore Mr. Gates, have been financially very successful. The company's new and previous inventions have made Mr. Gates a multibillionaire.

The intrusion of outsiders into a previously private domain does not seem to bother Mr. Gates as much as it does Ronald Massa, founder of Dynatrend Inc. About going public Mr. Massa says, "It has basically changed my whole world." "I have a new boss," he observes. "I don't work for myself anymore."

A general malaise developed at Dynatrend after its IPO. Mr.

Massa says, "We've all become circumspect and a little jittery. What used to be no one's business must be disclosed now. My wife thinks it's terrible that everyone knows my salary."

Being public costs Dynatrend more than $100,000 per year. There are fees for the transfer agent, lawyers, and accountants plus the costs for printing and mailing. "It's very bad to be a small company and a public company. You just don't have the wherewithal the big companies have," says Mr. Massa.

Going public produced $2,450,000 for Dynatrend, but the underwriters took 10 percent, and the other costs consumed $350,000. Dynatrend was left with $1,885,000 for development of its product lines. Meanwhile, Mr. Massa is in the grip of outside forces that he believes are not entirely good for the company. One of Dynatrend's underwriters serves on the board, and he reminds Mr. Massa of Wall Street's views and demands.

Source: *The Wall Street Journal*, Nov. 15, 1982, 31; Bro Uttal, "Inside the Deal That Made Bill Gates $350,000,000," *Fortune*, July 21, 1986, 23–33; G. Pascal Zachary, "Opening of Windows Shows How Bill Gates Succeeds in Software," *The Wall Street Journal*, May 21, 1990, A1.

PREFERRED STOCK

Preferred stock grants a preference over common stock in the payment of dividends. Like common stock, preferred stock represents legal ownership in a company. Preferred shareholders, like all shareholders, are entitled to the rights of ownership except where limited by contract and custom. These limitations combine to make preferred stock a hybrid of common stock and corporate bonds. Despite the substantial limitations imposed on the rights of preferred stockholders, they have a senior position over common shareholders—hence the adjective *preferred* instead of *common*.

Claims on Earnings and Assets

Preferred stockholders have junior (lower) claims relative to bondholders. Corporate bonds create default risk because a company contractually agrees to pay interest on bonds, and failure to do so can result in bankruptcy. In contrast, a company pays dividends on preferred stock only when such dividends are declared by the board of directors. Neither common nor preferred stockholders have the legal power to force bankruptcy because of omitted dividends. The trustee acting on behalf of bondholders, however, can force bankruptcy if a company omits interest payments.

Bondholders and other company creditors view preferred stock in much the same way that they view common stock. Bonds confer senior claims over preferred and common stock, both of which represent a company's net worth. In fact, accountants usually include preferred stock along with common equity in the Net Worth or Shareholder Equity accounts of a company's balance sheet, as illustrated in the following excerpt from an annual report:

Shareholder Equity	**1993**	**1992**
Capital shares:		
Cumulative preferred stock—		
$25 par value per share; authorized 50,000 shares, issuable in series—Series of 1956—5% cumulative preferred stock, redeemable at $25.25 per share; authorized 42,758 shares, outstanding 447 shares in 1993 and 472 shares in 1992	$ 11,175	$ 11,800
Common stock—		
$.15 par value per share; authorized 6,010,000 shares in 1993 and 1992; issued 4,826,364 shares in 1993 and 4,626,028 shares in 1992	723,954	693,904
	$ 735,129	$ 705,704
Capital surplus	29,371,195	26,116,890
Retained earnings	14,116,744	14,995,972
	$44,223,068	$41,818,566

Preferred stock adds to the protection afforded creditors by common equity and increases a company's borrowing capacity. Creditors realize that they will receive interest before the company pays preferred dividends and that in liquidation they may lay claim to the assets purchased with the proceeds of the preferred-stock issue.

Common shareholders view preferred stock in much the same way they do a bond. Its dividend, like bond interest, is usually a fixed amount that the company must pay before common shareholders receive their dividend. Both the fixed dividend of preferred stock and the fixed interest of bonds create financial leverage, which increases financial risk and the potential for a high rate of return on common equity.

Table 18.1 illustrates the differing impact on earnings caused by preferred stock and corporate bonds. The company in the illustration has $1,000,000 of earnings before interest and taxes. By order of appearance, interest is deducted first, then preferred-stock dividends, then common-stock dividends. Unlike interest, preferred- and common-stock dividends are not tax deductible. Because of the tax deductibility of interest, bond financing carries with it a distinct advantage over preferred-stock financing.

The example in Table 18.1 shows the consequences of financing with $2,000,000 of bonds and $2,000,000 of preferred stock, each paying a rate of

| TABLE 18.1 | **Differing Impact on Earnings Caused by Corporate Bonds and Preferred Stock (Thousands of Dollars)** |

	Corporate Bonds[a]	Preferred Stock[b]
Earnings before interest and taxes	$1,000	$1,000
Less interest expense	**200**	0
Earnings before taxes	$ 800	$1,000
Less income taxes (40%)	320	400
Earnings after taxes	$ 480	$ 600
Less preferred-stock dividends	0	**200**
Earnings available to common shareholders	$ 480	$ 400
Less common-stock dividends	100	100
Retained earnings	$ 380	$ 300

[a] $2,000,000 of bonds outstanding at 10 percent coupon interest.
[b] $2,000,000 of preferred stock outstanding at a 10 percent dividend rate.

10 percent. Earnings available to common shareholders are $480,000 with bond financing and $400,000 with preferred-stock financing. The additional earnings of $80,000 accompanying bonds arise because of the tax savings associated with interest: The tax rate (0.40) times interest expense ($200,000) equals $80,000. Accompanying this advantage of bonds is the increase in default risk caused by the company's legal obligation to pay interest. In contrast, preferred-stock dividends need be paid only when the board of directors declares them, although the dividends may be *cumulative*.

Dividend Payments

A financial manager usually designs a preferred stock with either (1) a fixed dollar dividend or (2) a dividend stated as a fixed percentage of par value. For example, a preferred stock with a $100 par value may pay an annual dividend of $10 per share, perhaps in quarterly installments of $2.50. Equivalently, a 10 percent preferred stock with a par value of $100 also pays a $10 annual dividend.

In addition to serving as the basis for the dividend calculation, the par value (or other stated value) of a preferred stock represents the maximum dollar amount collectible by preferred stockholders in the event of bankruptcy and liquidation. These two functions make par value a more important concept for preferred stock than for common stock.

Cumulative Dividends. Most preferred stocks have cumulative dividends—unpaid dividends accumulate from year to year until paid by the company. The

dividends in arrears
Prior-period dividends presently payable by a company.

company must pay **dividends in arrears** to preferred stockholders before it pays any dividends to common shareholders. The cumulative feature puts substantial pressure on directors and management to keep current on preferred-stock dividends. Without the cumulative feature, preferred stock offers little assurance or protection to investors, thus greatly reducing its marketability.

| EXAMPLE | Marquette Mills has not paid dividends for 5 years on its $4 cumulative preferred stock. Marquette's 100,000 outstanding shares of preferred stock trade in the |

FIGURE 18.5

Footnote Reference to an Adjustable-Rate, Callable Preferred Stock

An adjustable-rate preferred stock pays a dividend that changes with some specified market rate. A callable preferred stock, like a callable bond, gives the company an opportunity to retire the preferred issue at a specific call (redemption) price.

At December 31, 1985, United Jersey Banks had 4,000,000 shares of preferred stock authorized and 600,000 shares outstanding. Each outstanding share of $50 stated value preferred stock is non-convertible and has no voting rights. Dividends are cumulative and are payable quarterly on February 1, May 1, August 1, and November 1 of each year. The dividend rate on the preferred stock is determined in advance of each quarterly period, and is .30% above the highest of the Three Month Treasury Bill Rate, the Ten Year Constant Maturity Rate and the Twenty Year Constant Maturity Rate. The dividend rate for any dividend period may not be less than 7.5% per annum or greater than 13% per annum.

The preferred stock is redeemable at the option of United Jersey Banks, in whole or in part, on or after May 1, 1988, and prior to May 1, 1993, at a redemption price of $51.50 per share and thereafter at $50 per share, plus accrued and unpaid dividends. In the event of any voluntary or involuntary liquidation or dissolution of United Jersey Banks, the holders of shares of preferred stock are entitled to receive out of assets of the Company, liquidating distributions in the amount of $50 per share plus accrued and unpaid dividends.

Source: United Jersey Banks, *Annual Report to Shareholders, 1985.*

market on speculation of whether the company will ever be able to pay the $20 per-share arrearage (5 years × $4) and future dividends. Marquette's preferred and common shareholders have been clamoring for a resolution to the problem because they have not received dividends for 5 years.

Adjustable Rates.   Traditionally, companies have paid a constant, fixed dividend on preferred stock. Like the special features of other corporate securities designed to attract investors, some companies have modified the dividend feature on their preferred stock to accommodate changing interest rates. **Adjustable-rate preferred stock (ARPS)** first appeared in 1982, issued by Chase Manhattan, Aetna Insurance, and Ensearch, among other companies. Figure 18.5 presents details of an adjustable-rate preferred stock issued by United Jersey Banks.

Dividends on this type of preferred stock change with changes in interest rates. For example, the preferred stock might pay 30 basis points (0.30 percentage point) above the highest of the (1) 3-month Treasury bill rate, (2) 10-year Treasury bond rate, or (3) 20-year Treasury bond rate. Furthermore, the preferred-stock rate is normally confined by a maximum and minimum rate, called the interest rate *window,* set in advance. Some corporate treasurers invest temporarily idle cash in adjustable-rate preferred stock for two reasons: (1) 70 percent of the dividends earned are exempt from corporate federal taxation and (2) the floating rate reduces price volatility compared with fixed-income securities.

Participation Feature.   Some preferred stocks have a **participation feature** entitling the preferred stockholders to dividends in excess of the stipulated rate under specified conditions. Like adjustable rates, the participation feature causes the dividend on a preferred stock to vary over time. Although participation details vary, a common one allows preferred stockholders to share equally with common shareholders after each receives a dividend equal to the stated rate on the preferred. For example, one company has outstanding a 4 percent, participating preferred stock with a $50 par value. Preferred stockholders must be paid $2 a share

adjustable-rate preferred stock (ARPS)
Preferred stock with a floating dividend based on some U.S. Treasury security.

participation feature
Provision permitting preferred stockholders to participate in earnings beyond the stated dividend level.

before common shareholders receive dividends. The preferred stockholders share equally with common shareholders after the common-stock dividend reaches $2 a share. Thus if common shareholders receive $3 per share, then preferred stockholders must receive an extra $1, bringing their dividends to $3 per share.

Preferred-Stockholder Protection

Besides the protection afforded by its claims priority on earnings and assets, preferred stock offers investors additional protection through voting rights and protective covenants.

Voting Rights. Preferred stock may convey limited voting rights to preferred stockholders. Unlike common shareholders, preferred stockholders often do *not* have full voting rights on directors or other matters presented at the company's annual meeting. Preferred stock typically has voting rights on specified company matters only when the company is in arrears on its preferred-dividend payments. For example, if a company fails to pay dividends for six months, then preferred stockholders might have the right to elect at least two members of the board of directors. Furthermore, they might be empowered to vote on mergers, sales of fixed assets, and the issuance of additional preferred stock and bonds.

Because of the limited voting rights, preferred stock often figures in the succession of ownership of small, closely held companies. For example, an owner-manager of a company might give the common stock to a son or a daughter but retain the preferred stock. In this way the owner-manager transfers ownership of the company through a gift of common stock and provides for retirement income from the dividends on preferred stock.

Protective Covenants. Voting rights, though often limited, provide a measure of protection to preferred stockholders. Protective covenants in the registration statement filed with the Securities and Exchange Commission at the time the company issues the preferred stock provide additional protection. These covenants take on many shapes and forms, but the following examples illustrate their nature:

- The company cannot pay dividends to common shareholders if the debt ratio exceeds a specified percentage.
- Consent of a majority of preferred stockholders is needed to issue additional preferred stock if such issuance would cause the coverage ratio (Earnings after taxes/Preferred-stock dividends) of the preceding year to fall below a specified level.
- The board of directors may not declare a dividend on common stock if the company's current ratio and net working capital fall below specified levels.

Retirement Methods

Like common stock and unlike corporate bonds, preferred stock is issued in perpetuity—that is, it has an infinite maturity. Issuing a perpetuity with claims senior to those of common shareholders potentially reduces future maneuverability in financing. Thus management usually establishes a method to retire preferred stock. The three most widely used retirement methods are callability, sinking funds, and convertibility.

Callable Preferred Stock.   Most issues of preferred stock are callable at the company's discretion for a price exceeding or equaling the original offering price. Figure 18.5 describes a preferred stock callable at $51.50 per share for a limited time and at its $50 stated value thereafter. Similar to the callability of bonds, the callability of preferred stock is usually deferred for the first several years after issuance. Also, the call price usually declines over the life of the preferred stock.

Calling preferred stock is more convenient and less expensive than many alternatives for retiring preferred stock. To retire a noncallable preferred stock, a company may need to undergo major reorganization, merge with another company, or repurchase the stock in the market.

The rationale for issuing new preferred stock to replace an old issue (refunding) is equivalent to that of bond refunding. If interest rates decline, then the company may have the opportunity to (1) issue new preferred stock with a lower dividend rate and (2) use the proceeds to call the outstanding issue. Whether or not a company ought to refund depends on the present value of dividends saved versus the present value of refunding costs. If the net present value of refunding is positive, then the company should go forward with the refunding operation because it will increase shareholder wealth.

Sinking Fund.   Since the late 1970s many new issues of preferred stock have contained a provision for a sinking fund. This provision requires the company to redeem annually a percentage of the outstanding issue. In this way the company systematically retires the preferred stock.

Typically, a company redeems preferred stock from investors at par or stated value. Investors do not receive a premium, because the sinking fund is merely a preprogrammed way of retiring preferred stock; it is not a discretionary managerial decision like that in refunding when interest rates decline. In recent years issues of preferred stock with sinking funds have sold to yield 80 basis points less than issues without sinking funds, suggesting an investor preference for the provision.[7]

Convertible Preferred Stock.   Many issues of preferred stock are convertible into the company's common stock at the discretion of the investor. Upon conversion, the company replaces the preferred stock with common stock. The conversion ratio dictates how many shares of common stock the preferred stockholders receive upon conversion. For example, CBS Inc. has outstanding a preferred stock convertible into 0.6886 of a share of its common stock. CBS can call the preferred for $43.50 per share plus any accrued or unpaid dividends. The company holds several thousand authorized but unissued shares of common stock to provide for conversion of the preferred stock. Preferred stockholders of CBS might convert their holdings voluntarily if the dividends on 0.6886 of a share of common stock exceed the dividends on a share of preferred. Like most other convertible issues, CBS's convertible preferred stock is callable, which means that the company can force conversion. By calling the convertible when its conversion value (conversion ratio times price per share of common stock) exceeds the call

---

[7] For an analysis of the changing role of sinking funds for preferred stock, see Eric H. Sorensen and Clark A. Hawkins, "On the Pricing of Preferred Stock," *Journal of Financial and Quantitative Analysis,* November 1981, 515–528. As the authors indicate, insurance companies carry sinking-fund preferreds at book value and other preferreds at market value. Because managers of insurance companies prefer, for regulatory reasons, to carry preferreds at book value, they tend to bid up the prices of sinking-fund preferreds, causing their yields to decline.

FIGURE 18.6

Earnings, Risk, and Control Conveyed by Corporate Securities

Common stock conveys the largest expected return, the most risk, and the greatest voting control to investors. Bonds convey the smallest expected return, least risk, and least voting control to investors. Preferred stock falls between common stock and bonds.

	Expected Distribution of Earnings	Risk to Investors	Voting Control Granted
Common Stock	Most	Most	Most
Preferred Stock	Intermediate	Intermediate	Intermediate
Bonds	Least	Least	Least

price by a comfortable margin, CBS management can be assured that preferred stockholders will convert into common stock. Thus, by making a convertible preferred stock callable, management preserves some control over the retirement of the preferred stock.

FINANCING WITH CORPORATE SECURITIES

Companies issue bonds, preferred stock, and common stock to finance their investments. These securities enable companies to raise the necessary funds to invest in new projects and thereby maximize shareholder wealth. The mix of securities should be selected to balance the risk and cost to company shareholders. By issuing bonds, preferred stock, and common stock in optimal proportions, the company's financial manager helps minimize the average cost of capital and maximize shareholder wealth.

In an attempt to lower the cost of each source of capital, the company accepts restrictions on corporate activity and grants rights to investors. Securities serve to distribute these benefits among company investors. Each security with its individual features and attributes holds different implications for the distribution of the company earnings, risk, and control to investors. Figure 18.6 illustrates the distribution flowing from three basic securities: common stock, preferred stock, and bonds.

Management and investors expect common shareholders in the long run to receive the largest portion of a company's earnings, with bondholders receiving the least and preferred stockholders receiving a middling portion. To compensate bondholders for the expectation of low earnings, the company arranges through priorities and protective covenants for bondholders to share the least risk. As residual claimants, common shareholders share the most risk, with preferred stockholders once again falling in the middle. As the owners of the company, common shareholders have the most voting control. Bondholders normally vote only if a company is undergoing bankruptcy proceedings, and then they vote as members of the creditor committee. Short of bankruptcy proceedings, preferred stockholders often have a voice in corporate governance only when dividends are in arrears.

SUMMARY

• States grant charters to corporations. Among other things, the charter specifies the maximum number of common shares that a company can issue. The number of shares the company issues must be less than or equal to the number of shares authorized in the charter:

$$\text{Issued stock} \leq \text{Authorized stock}$$

When a company repurchases outstanding shares, these shares become treasury stock. Thus outstanding stock equals issued stock less treasury stock:

$$\text{Outstanding stock} = \text{Issued stock} - \text{Treasury stock}$$

• In addition to market and intrinsic values, which investors and financial managers use to evaluate assets, several other values are associated with a company's common equity. For example, par value is an arbitrary dollar amount assigned to common stock by a company's founders. Equally arbitrary, stated value serves as an alternative to par value in accounting for common equity. Book value per share equals a company's net worth (from the balance sheet) divided by the number of shares outstanding. In contrast to the historical-cost basis of book value, liquidation value is based on what the assets would bring if they were sold piecemeal in the market less all liabilities. When market value is less than liquidation value, a company is worth more if its assets are sold with the proceeds distributed to creditors and shareholders than if it continues to operate. Market value of a company's common equity equals price per share of common stock times the number of shares outstanding.

• Among other legal rights, common shareholders have the right to vote on important company matters such as the election of members to the board of directors. With majority voting, the shareholders holding a majority of the votes can elect the entire board. With cumulative voting, a minority shareholder with less than 50 percent of the votes might be able to elect at least one member to the board. In practice, most shareholders vote by the proxy method.

• The preemptive right requires a company to offer any new issue of common stock to current shareholders on a *pro rata* basis. Preemptive rights protect shareholders from dilution of value and control.

• A rights offering is the issuance of new common stock to the company's shareholders. All shareholders prior to the *ex*-rights date have the right to subscribe to new shares in proportion to the number of shares owned, at a subscription price (S) below market value. Because new stock is offered to shareholders at a below-market price, the subscription rights have a market value:

$$R = \frac{P_o - S}{N + 1}$$

where P_o is price per share of stock during the rights-on period. During the *ex*-rights period the following equation is used to value a right:

$$R = \frac{P_e - S}{N}$$

where P_e is the *ex*-rights price per share of stock. Despite the value of a right being merely compensation to shareholders for the decline in price per share of common stock, some shareholders mistakenly look upon the receipt of rights as a bonus.

• Common shareholders can either exercise rights to buy more of the company's stock or sell the rights through brokers to other investors. Exercising rights requires shareholders to invest more money in the company. Selling them requires shareholders to reduce their proportional ownership in the company. Shareholders neither gain nor lose wealth from a rights offering as long as they either exercise or sell their rights. Taking no action causes shareholders to lose the value of their rights.

• Like common stock, preferred stock conveys legal ownership in a company. The ownership rights accompanying preferred stock are normally severely limited, however. In return for these limitations, preferred stockholders receive preferential treatment over common shareholders on earnings and on assets in the event of bankruptcy and liquidation.

• A disadvantage of preferred stock to the issuing company is that dividend payments are not tax deductible. Offsetting this disadvantage are three advantages: (1) Because dividends are not legal obligations, preferred stock does not contribute to the issuing company's default risk. (2) The common shareholders usually do not give up voting power unless the company falls behind in paying preferred-stock dividends. (3) Corporate borrowing capacity is enhanced.

• Most preferred stocks have cumulative dividends, meaning that dividends accumulate from one year to the next until they are finally paid in full by the company. Although preferred-stock dividends are usually fixed by contract, dividends on some issues vary with interest rates or company profitability.

• Companies retire preferred stock by (1) calling the issue and paying the call price, (2) using a sinking fund, or (3) making the stock convertible, then later forcing conversion by calling the stock when the conversion value exceeds the call price.

Key Terms

stock certificate	liquidation value	subscription right
closely held company	organizational value	subscription price
publicly held company	synergy	*ex*-rights date
charter	proxy	rights-on period
authorized stock	proxy fight	oversubscription privilege
issued stock	majority voting	dividends in arrears
treasury stock	cumulative voting	adjustable-rate preferred stock
outstanding stock	preemptive right	participation feature
par value	rights offering	

Questions

18.1.   Suppose that in thumbing through your school's newspaper you come across the following letter to the editor:

> *In 19X0, 66 percent of the total U.S. GNP was controlled by fewer than 3,500 mem-*

bers of corporate boards of directors. Imagine, two-thirds of the nation's total economy controlled and directed by only 3,500 people! The major counterpoint brought against this figure is that it overlooks all the men and women who own stock in those corporations (a favorite argument of any chamber of commerce). But that argument is nearsighted, for it does not clarify the distinction between common stock (what you or I might own) and preferred stock (what a Ford or a Rockefeller might own).

Write a critique of this letter.

18.2. Define the following terms and identify their key relationships with one another: (a) authorized stock, (b) issued stock, (c) outstanding stock, and (d) treasury stock.

18.3. Explain how it is possible for book value per share of common stock to be less than market value per share.

18.4. Explain the difference between book value and liquidation value.

18.5. List several rights of common shareholders. Which two, in your opinion, rank highest in importance? Explain your selection.

18.6. Evaluate the relative fairness to common shareholders of majority and cumulative voting for boards of directors. In your opinion, which is the fairer procedure? Defend your answer.

18.7. Which security listed below presents the *greatest* risk for the issuing company?
a. Convertible preferred stock.
b. First mortgage bonds.
c. Common stock.
d. Preferred stock.

Explain your choice and state why each of the other alternatives is unacceptable.

18.8. Which security listed below presents the *least* risk for the issuing company?
a. Subordinated debentures.
b. Convertible preferred stock.
c. First mortgage bonds.
d. Common stock.
e. Preferred stock.

Describe each security listed above.

18.9. For a small company whose shareholders are concerned about maintaining control over the company, the *least* desirable form of financing is:
a. A rights offering.
b. Preferred stock.
c. Convertible bonds.
d. Subordinated debentures.
e. Income bonds.

Explain your choice and state why each of the other alternatives is unacceptable.

18.10. Some companies issue new common stock by

using a rights offering. Explain why a company would use this method, and describe what happens to the price of a share of common stock when it begins to trade *ex* rights.

18.11. "We're rich, we're rich," exclaims Harry Hudson to his wife. "What are you talking about?" inquires his wife, Harriet. "In the mail. Angus Company sent us 1,000 rights in the mail." "What are rights? Are they worth anything?" asks Ms. Hudson. "I don't know what they are, but our broker says they're worth $8 each. We have an extra $8,000 to blow!"
a. Describe a right.
b. Is Mr. Hudson correct? Does the Hudson family have an extra $8,000 to blow? Explain your answer.

18.12. Cousins Corporation is planning a large capital expenditure program to add plant capacity and to modernize manufacturing equipment. Management's projections of cash flows reveal that internal equity will not be adequate to finance the capital investment program. Lynch Capital Markets, the company's investment banker, has suggested a preferred-stock issue. The board of directors has asked the financial manager to investigate thoroughly the general attributes of preferred stock. Major points that came immediately to the financial manager's mind included cost, financial risk, and capital structure flexibility. The financial manager plans to address these points as well as other issues in her analysis.
a. Identify and explain the principal provisions and features of preferred stock.
b. From the viewpoint of a prospective issuer, explain the advantages and disadvantages of preferred stock with respect to the financing alternatives of common stock and long-term debt.

18.13. Preferred stock has features that may make it a more desirable form of financing than long-term debt. Indicate whether each of the following statements is true or false:
T F Preferred-stock dividends are a weaker legal obligation than bond interest for the issuing company.
T F Preferred stock has default risk but long-term debt does not.
T F Preferred stock adds to the company's equity base, which strengthens its borrowing capacity.
T F Preferred stockholders cannot force a company into bankruptcy due to unpaid dividends.

Explain your choices.

18.14. Would you prefer to invest in a traditional preferred stock with a fixed annual dividend or in an adjustable-rate preferred stock? Explain your answer.

18.15.   Compare and contrast the callability feature with the sinking-fund provision of preferred stock.

Strategy Problem

Roger Kelly, financial manager of Dialysis International, a manufacturer and distributor of artificial kidney (dialysis) machines, has been asked by the company's board of directors to analyze the impact of issuing $4,250,021 of new common stock on the company's financial position and stock price. At present the company's shareholder equity appears as follows on the balance sheet:

Common stock (1,000,000 shares, par $1)	$ 1,000,000
Capital in excess of par	7,500,000
Retained earnings	12,500,000
Total common equity	$21,000,000

The company's common stock trades on a major stock exchange at 2.6 times its book value, and the board has decided to issue new shares through a rights offering. The new shares will be issued at a 20 percent discount from the current market price. The date of record will be Friday, March 27, 19X9.

a. How many new shares must Dialysis International issue?

b. On what day will the shares begin to trade *ex* rights? By what dollar amount will the stock price decline on that day?

c. Calculate the value of a right.

Strategy	**Solution**

Use the market/book-value ratio to calculate market price.

a.   Market price per share = Book value × Market-to-book ratio

$$= \frac{\$21,000,000}{1,000,000} \times 2.6$$

$$= \$54.60$$

Subscription price is 80% (1 − 0.20) of the market price.

Subscription price = Market price per share × (1 − Discount)

$$= \$54.60(1 - 0.20)$$

$$= \$43.68$$

Issue size divided by subscription price equals number of shares to be issued.

Number of shares = Issue size/Subscription price

$$= \frac{\$4,250,021}{\$43.68}$$

$$= 97,299 \text{ shares}$$

b. The shares will trade *ex* rights 4 trading days before the date of record (March 27)—on Monday, March 23. The price of the stock will decline as a result of the new shares issued:

	(1) Shares	(2) Number	(3) Price per Share	(2) × (3) = (4) Total Market Value
Price of the stock after the new issue is total market value divided by total shares outstanding.	Outstanding shares New issue	1,000,000 97,299	$54.60 43.68	$54,600,000 4,250,021
		1,097,299		$58,850,021
		└─── $53.63 ───┘		

$$\frac{\text{Decline in price}}{\text{per share}} = \text{Price before issue} - \text{Price after issue}$$

$$= \$54.60 - \$53.63$$

$$= \$0.97 \text{ per share}$$

Begin by calculating N.   c.

$$N = \frac{1,000,000 \text{ old shares}}{97,299 \text{ new shares}}$$

$$= 10.28$$

One right is issued for each share, so it takes as many rights (10.28) as it does shares to buy one new share. Calculate the value of the right as follows:

Use the rights-on equation with the calculated N.

$$R = \frac{\$54.60 - \$43.68}{10.28 + 1}$$

$$= \$0.97$$

Compare the value of a right with the decline in price calculated above.

Note that the value of the right equals the decline in price per share of stock.

◆   **Demonstration Problem**

Gates Furniture Company (GFC) manufactures and markets office furniture. To increase market penetration and to expand geographically, GFC's management plans to raise $10,000,000 for additional facilities. GFC's current capital structure appears on its balance sheet as follows:

Debentures (10%, 2012)	$ 9,500,000
Preferred stock (7%, $50 par)	5,500,000
Common stock (800,000 shares, $1 par)	800,000
Capital in excess of par	12,000,000
Retained earnings	8,200,000
Total	$36,000,000

Management expects company earnings before interest and taxes (EBIT) to be $6,500,000 during the first year after expansion. Based on consultations with an investment banker, management is considering the following three sources to finance the expansion:

1. Issue $10,000,000 of mortgage bonds at par value with an annual coupon rate of 9 percent.

2. Issue $10,000,000 of preferred stock yielding 10 percent annually.

3. Issue $10,000,000 of common stock through a rights offering, with a subscription price of $25 per share.

GFC pays income taxes at a 40 percent rate, and its common stock trades in the secondary market for $34 per share.

a. GFC has 800,000 shares of common stock outstanding. What are the relationships among outstanding stock, authorized stock, issued stock, and treasury stock?

b. Calculate the book value per share of GFC's common stock. What possible reasons explain the market value of GFC's common stock exceeding its book value?

c. Calculate the projected earnings available to common shareholders (EACS) assuming (1) the company issues mortgage bonds and (2) the company issues preferred stock. Explain the two causes of the difference in EACS for the two financing alternatives.

d. Answer the following questions related to the rights offering: (1) How many subscription rights must GFC issue in total? (2) How many new shares of common stock must GFC issue? (3) How many rights are required to purchase one new share for $25? (4) What is the value of one right? (5) What is the market price per share of stock *ex rights*? (6) Suppose an investor who owns 100 shares of GFC stock sells the 100 rights received from GFC. Compare and contrast the investor's portfolio before and after the rights offering. (7) Suppose an investor who owns 100 shares of GFC stock exercises the 100 rights received from GFC. Compare and contrast the investor's portfolio before and after the rights offering.

e. Suppose GFC goes ahead with the rights offering, and EBIT is $6,500,000 during the first year after expansion: (1) Calculate EACS for the year and (2) show GFC's capital structure as it would appear on the company's year-end balance sheet. (*Note:* GFC does not pay common-stock dividends.)

f. Rights and warrants are options to buy common stock. In what three major ways do rights differ from warrants?

g. Many issues of preferred stock are *callable, cumulative,* and *convertible.* Define each of the italicized terms.

h. Suppose GFC has a board of directors consisting of only three members, who must stand for election after the rights offering: (1) With majority voting, what minimum number of shares must you control to assure yourself of a board position? (2) With cumulative voting, what minimum number of shares must you control to assure yourself of a board position? Using your answer, prove that you cannot be defeated. Which method of voting, majority or cumulative, do you think is fairer?

Problems

Book value and par value

18.1. Riverdale Corporation has the following abbreviated balance sheet:

Assets	Claims	
	Current liabilities	$121,300
	Long-term debt	58,000
	Shareholder equity	
	Common stock (10,000 shares, $5 par)	50,000
	Paid-in capital in excess of par	64,200
	Retained earnings	50,000
$343,500		$343,500

a. Calculate Riverdale's book value per share.

b. What does the $5 par value tell an investor?

c. Does the above information give you much insight into Riverdale's market value per share? Explain.

Interpretation of common-equity accounts

18.2. IBM Corporation's common-equity accounts on December 31, 19X2, are as follows (in million of dollars):

Capital stock (par value $1.25 per share; shares authorized, 750,000,000; shares issued, 571,791,950)	$ 6,563
Retained earnings	19,124
Translation adjustments	1,962
Treasury stock, at cost (356,222 shares)	(25)
Total stockholder equity	$27,624

Note: Translation adjustments are gains on the translation of foreign-currency-denominated operations into U.S. dollars. *Capital stock* includes capital in excess of par value.

a. Calculate IBM's book value per share.

b. Why is *Treasury stock* shown as a negative $25,000,000?

c. How many more shares of common stock can IBM issue without amending its corporate charter?

Transaction effects on common-equity accounts

18.3. USTA Company's common-equity accounts on January 1, 19X8, are as follows:

Common stock (210,000 shares, $1 par)	$ 210,000
Capital in excess of par	2,100,000
Retained earnings	8,465,194
Total common equity	$10,775,194

During the year USTA (1) earns $2,000,000 after taxes, (2) pays dividends totaling $1,000,000, and (3) issues 100,000 shares of stock at $75 a share.
a. Calculate USTA's book value per share on January 1, 19X8.
b. Show USTA's common-equity accounts on December 31, 19X8, and calculate the new book value per share.
c. Explain why USTA's common stock might trade in the market at a price above its book value per share.

Cumulative voting and a proxy fight

18.4. Millar Corporation has four members on its board of directors, and each member must stand for election this year. Michael Isberg owns 4 percent of the 10,000 shares of outstanding common stock. He wants to be a board member and is engaged in a proxy fight with Millar's management, who do not want him on the board. Millar's corporate charter requires the use of cumulative voting to elect board members.
a. What is a proxy fight?
b. How many shares must Mr. Isberg control to assure himself a position on the board of directors?
c. Show that it is impossible for Mr. Isberg to lose if he has the number of shares you calculated in Part *b*.

Majority vs. cumulative voting

18.5. Teltronics has 750,000 shares of common stock outstanding, of which Paul Piper owns 10 percent. Mr. Piper wants to be a member of Teltronics' 20-person board of directors, and he doubts that he will receive votes from anyone other than himself.
a. With majority voting, is Mr. Piper likely to become a board member? Explain.
b. With cumulative voting, is Mr. Piper likely to become a board member if all directors are up for election? Explain.

CMA examination, modified: *Ex*-rights price per share of stock

18.6. Sumner Company plans to issue 500,000 new shares of common stock through a rights offering. Each common shareholder will be entitled to subscribe to one additional share of common stock at $55 per share for each four shares held. The 2,000,000 shares of stock currently outstanding trade for $75 a share. What is the value of one share of stock when it goes *ex* rights?

Rights offering and related values

18.7. Oblesk Corporation's common stock trades for $18 per share during the rights-on period. The company has 1,200,000 shares outstanding. In its rights offering, the company plans to issue new stock for $12 per share. One new share will be issued for each three shares currently existing.
a. How much money does the company plan to raise?
b. In total, how many subscription rights will the company issue?
c. Calculate the value of one right.
d. Calculate the *ex*-rights price per share.
e. Assume that bad news about the company arrives in the stock market one week after the announced rights offering. As a consequence of the news, the price per share of the stock drops to $11. What impact will the price decline have on the rights offering? Explain.

Rights offering and related values

18.8. The value of a right is $4.20. The company has 8,000 shares outstanding before the new flotation, and 4 rights are required to buy one new share. Shares (rights on) currently trade at $51.25 each.
a. How many new shares are being offered?
b. What is the subscription price?
c. What is the market price of a share *ex* rights?
d. Explain why the market price declines by the value of one right on the *ex*-rights date.

Rights offering and the investor's portfolio

18.9. WYSIWYG Inc.'s common stock trades for $50 per share. In its rights offering, the company will offer new stock for $38 per share. One new share will be issued for each two shares currently existing.
a. Calculate the value of one right.
b. Calculate the *ex*-rights price per share.

c. Suppose you own 100 shares and you sell your rights. Compare and contrast your portfolio before and after the rights offering.

d. Suppose you own 100 shares and you exercise your rights. Compare and contrast your portfolio before and after the rights offering.

Rights offering, book value, EPS, and ROE

18.10. Clark Enterprises needs new equity and can sell new shares through a rights offering. The price of its stock is $65 per share and the subscription price will be $58. Book value per share is $20. Clark will sell 400,000 new shares, and it has 1,000,000 shares outstanding. The company now earns an after-tax 18 percent return on equity measured in book value.

a. Calculate the current earnings per share.

b. Determine the value of a right and the market price of a share *ex* rights.

c. Assume that the company sells the entire issue to shareholders and that the rate of return is 15 percent on the new equity. What are the earnings per share after the issue, assuming the return on original equity stays at 18 percent?

d. Explain what happens to the wealth of a shareholder who (1) exercises rights, (2) sells rights, or (3) lets rights expire. (*Note:* No calculations are required.)

Rights offering vs. public offering

18.11. Ellis Electronics Corporation needs $5,000,000 to acquire new distribution facilities that will provide an estimated after-tax return of 12 percent. A review of the company's financial position and current capital markets has led corporate officials to decide on equity financing rather than debt financing. E. G. Morris, vice president of finance, has obtained information to be used in comparing a rights offering of common stock with a public offering of common stock through an investment banker.

Present after-tax earnings are $11,250,000 annually. The 4,500,000 outstanding shares now trade for $50 each in the market. The price-earnings ratio is 20 and is expected to continue at this level. The proposed rights offering would permit Ellis shareholders to subscribe at $40 for one new common share for each 36 shares of common stock they hold.

The investment banking firm advising Ellis believes that a public offering of stock at the current market price would succeed. The firm will charge $2 per share to underwrite the issue. (Consider the underwriting fee a tax-deductible expense.)

a. Compute the earnings and price per share of the common stock assuming that the company is in the 30 percent marginal tax bracket and that management carries out (1) the rights-offering proposal and (2) the public offering of stock.

b. Assuming the company selects the rights proposal, (1) calculate the value of a right and (2) calculate the price per share of the stock when it trades *ex* rights.

Financing with bonds vs. preferred stock

18.12. The management of Moon Chemical expects the company to earn $3,400,000 before interest and taxes during the coming year. Moon Chemical's capital structure is as follows:

Debentures (12%, 2010)	$ 4,500,000
Preferred stock (8%, $100 par)	3,000,000
Common stock (100,000 shares, $2 par)	200,000
Capital in excess of par	4,800,000
Retained earnings	6,500,000
	$19,000,000

Moon Chemical pays $100,000 interest on short-term debt in a typical year. Management plans to raise $2,500,000 either through an issue of preferred stock or through a bond issue. Preferred stock would be sold to yield 11 percent, and bonds would be sold at par with a coupon rate of 10 percent. The $2,500,000 will produce an additional $500,000 earnings before interest and taxes. The company pays taxes at the 34 percent rate.

a. Calculate the projected earnings available to common shareholders assuming (1) the company issues bonds and (2) the company issues preferred stock.

b. Calculate earnings per share of common stock assuming (1) the company issues bonds and (2) the company issues preferred stock.

c. Explain the reason for the difference in earnings per share for the two financing alternatives.

Cumulative preferred stock and dividends in arrears

18.13. South Pacific Paper issued $100,000,000 of cumulative preferred stock 10 years ago and has not paid any dividends for the past 2 years. The stock has a par value of $25 a share, and it is supposed to pay a per-share preferred dividend of $2.50 each year. Management believes the company will be able to pay the dividends in arrears and the current dividend for the approaching year. Management expects the company's earnings after taxes to be $50,000,000 this year. What is the maximum dividend per share of common stock that South Pacific can pay based on earnings if conditions work out as management expects and if 10,000,000 shares of common stock are outstanding?

Convertible preferred stock and conversion value

18.14. TEC Limited has 500,000 shares of convertible preferred stock outstanding. Each share of the preferred stock is convertible into 2.6 shares of common stock. TEC's charter from the state of Delaware authorizes the issuance of 30,000,000 shares of common stock, but only 20,000,000 shares have been issued. TEC's outstanding common stock trades in the market for $20 a share, and its indicated dividend is $1 per share annually. The preferred stock has a par value of $40, and it pays a dividend of $1.50 per share annually. The call price per share of preferred stock is $45.

a. Calculate the conversion value of the preferred stock.

b. If you owned the preferred stock, would you voluntarily convert at this time? Explain your answer.

c. Is TEC able to force conversion at this time? Explain your answer.

d. What is the impact of the call price on the market price of the preferred stock?

Computer Problems

Preferred stock vs. bond financing: template PFSTBND

18.15. Special Steels Inc. has begun to recover from an unprecedented slump in the steel industry. After 5 years of losses the company made a small profit last year. Management expects sales and profits to grow substantially during the next 5 years. In order to support the higher expected sales, the company needs additional long-term financing of $15,000,000. It is not appropriate to issue additional common stock at this time because of its low market price. Management is considering three financing alternatives:

1. Issue 15,000 bonds: par value of $1,000, 12 percent coupon, and 5-year maturity.

2. Issue 150,000 shares of preferred stock: par value of $100, 10 percent dividend, and callable after 5 years.

3. Issue 150,000 shares of cumulative preferred stock: par value of $100, 9 percent dividend, and callable after 5 years.

The company's accumulated losses equal $4,375,231 at the beginning of 19X0. Dividends on preferred stock will be paid only after accumulated losses have been recovered and adequate earnings are available to pay a full year's dividend. Dividends are paid in multiples of a full year's dividend. The company's forecast of earnings before interest and taxes for the next 5 years is:

19X0	$2,560,000
19X1	$3,235,000
19X2	$4,197,000
19X3	$5,217,000
19X4	$5,673,000

a. Calculate the present value of earnings available to common shareholders using a discount rate of 13 percent and marginal tax rates of 15 percent, 25 percent, and 34 percent. What form of financing should the company choose? Explain your answer.

b. Recalculate Part *a* assuming the company has no accumulated losses. Does this assumption change your decision? Explain your answer.

Rights offering: template
RIGHTS

18.16. Kimberly James, president of James Sportswear Co., called a board meeting to finalize the issue of $10,000,000 of new common stock. The company has 1,000,000 shares outstanding, and the prevailing market price of its common stock is $50 per share. The company has a marginal tax rate of 34 percent.

There were two proposals before the board:

- *Proposal 1:* Issue shares to the shareholders via a rights offering without using the services of an investment banker.

- *Proposal 2:* Employ an investment banker to manage the issue. The investment banker will charge $300,000 for services rendered and guarantee the purchase of the unsubscribed portion of the issue at the subscription price.

Paul Ben-Gurion, an investment banker, strongly supported Proposal 2. He argued that since equity financing is required to meet the debt ratio stipulated in the company's bond indenture, it is vitally important to ensure that the targeted amount be raised. Using an investment banker would guarantee a successful offering. Mr. Ben-Gurion suggested a subscription price of $42 per share. In Mr. Ben-Gurion's opinion a lower subscription price, which would be necessary if an investment banker is not used, would lower the stock price too much.

Ronald Pickwick, a major shareholder in the company, strongly disagreed with Mr. Ben-Gurion's position. He argued that a subscription price of $35 would ensure that the issue would be fully subscribed. At this price, he noted, the rights would be far too valuable to expire unexercised.

a. If Proposal 2 is accepted, how many shares will have to be issued? What would be the value of each right and the market value of the company?

b. Recalculate Part *a* assuming Proposal 1 is accepted and the subscription price is $37.50, $35.00, and $32.50.

c. Which alternative should Ms. James select? Explain your answer.

Selected References

Ang, James S., and William L. Megginson. "Restricted Voting Shares, Ownership Structure, and the Market Value of Dual-Class Firms." *Journal of Financial Research,* Winter 1989: 301–318.

Bhagat, Sanjai. "The Effect of Preemptive Right Amendments on Shareholder Wealth." *Journal of Financial Economics,* November 1983: 287–310.

Borstadt, Lisa F., and Thomas J. Zwirlein. "The Efficient Monitoring Role of Proxy Contests: An Empirical Analysis of Post-Contest Control Changes and Firm Performance." *Financial Management,* Autumn 1992: 22–34.

Dodd, Peter, and Jerold B. Warner. "On Corporate Governance: A Study of Proxy Contests," *Journal of Financial Economics,* April 1983: 401–438.

Emannuel, David. "A Theoretical Model for Valuing Preferred Stock." *Journal of Finance,* September 1983: 1133–1156.

Ferreira, Eurico J., Michael F. Spivey, and Charles E. Edwards. "Pricing New-Issue and Seasoned Preferred Stocks: A Compari-

son of Valuation Models." *Financial Management,* Summer 1992: 52–62.

Finnerty, John D. "Preferred Stock Refunding Analysis: Synthesis and Extension." *Financial Management,* Autumn 1984: 22–28.

Heinkel, Robert, and Eduardo S. Schwartz. "Rights Versus Underwritten Offerings: An Asymmetric Information Approach." *Journal of Finance,* March 1986: 1–18.

Lease, Ronald C., John J. McConnell, and Wayne H. Mikkelson. "The Market Value of Control in Publicly Traded Corporations." *Journal of Financial Economics,* April 1983: 439–471.

Moyer, R. Charles, M. Wayne Marr, and Robert E. Chatfield. "Nonconvertible Preferred Stock Financing and Financial Distress: A Note." *Journal of Economics and Business,* February 1987: 81–89.

Chapter 19

INTERNAL FINANCING AND DIVIDEND POLICY

A Tale of Two Dividends

Maytag Corporation had been paying steady or rising cash dividends since 1946. Maytag even developed a tradition of paying an "extra dividend" at the end of the year. Investors viewed the Newton, Iowa, manufacturer of Maytag, Admiral, Norge, and Magic Chef as a dependable source of dividends. Individual investors (as opposed to institutional investors) held more than 60 percent of the company's outstanding common stock.

Then it happened. Maytag cut its dividend by more than 40 percent. A company spokesperson said management was confident about the future but needed to conserve cash. Because of the economic recession, sales of appliances were flat, and earnings per share declined. In addition, Maytag had incurred substantial debt in order to acquire two companies and now faced major capital expenditures for improvements. Management found it necessary also to freeze wages and lay off workers.

At about the same time that

Maytag was experiencing difficulties, Entergy Corporation was reporting good news. The chairman of the midsouth electric utility company made the following statements in his quarterly letter to stockholders:

I have good news to report. The Entergy board of directors has increased the quarterly dividend on common stock from 25 cents to 30 cents per share, a 20 percent increase. . . . As evidenced by this dividend increase, we feel we have now placed our company on a firm financial foundation. . . . You should also be encouraged by news that the board authorized an expenditure of up to $150 million to repurchase more Entergy common stock. . . .

In contrast to Maytag's announcements, Entergy's announcements were hailed in the stock market, and its stock price rose.

Source: Robert L. Rose, "Maytag Reduces Payouts in Effort to Conserve Cash," *The Wall Street Journal,* February 8, 1991, B2; *Entergy Quarterly Report,* December 1990, 2. *Photo Credit:* Charles Waller.

In addition to raising funds externally through issuing stocks and bonds, companies generate funds internally by retaining earnings. A company faces a dilemma, however, in the decision to retain earnings for financing investments: The earnings available to common shareholders may be either retained for company purposes or paid to common shareholders as dividends. Retention of earnings for profitable investments increases the expected growth rates in dividends and stock price. In contrast, the payment of dividends provides an immediate cash reward to shareholders for their investment in company stock. Which should a company do: retain earnings or pay dividends?

This chapter focuses on the issues surrounding the retention of earnings and the payment of dividends. The chapter reviews the advantages of retained earnings as a source of financing and explains how these advantages balance against the desires of shareholders to receive dividends. Shareholder preferences, constraints imposed by creditors, the financial position of the company, and the business environment combine to determine dividend policy. The dividend vs. retention decision is a compromise among a number of conflicting forces. Following a discussion of these conflicts, the chapter concludes with an examination of noncash disbursements to shareholders, a company's repurchase of its own common stock, and the signals that dividend policy sends to investors.

INTERNAL FINANCING

As indicated above, a company can raise the equity capital it needs to finance investment projects either externally by issuing new common stock or internally by retaining its earnings. Both sources provide the company with equity capital to invest in assets or perhaps to retire debt.

Issuing common stock forces a company to incur flotation costs for underwriting and distributing shares. Conversely, when the company uses retained earnings for financing, it does not incur flotation costs. Because of the absence of flotation costs, the cost of retaining earnings is lower than the cost of issuing new common stock. This cost advantage encourages companies to raise more equity capital internally than externally. The total dollar volume of annual earnings retained by U.S. corporations often exceeds three times the dollar volume of new issues of common stock.

Another incentive for using internal instead of external equity financing stems from *asymmetric information,* where corporate managers (insiders) have better information about a company's financial prospects than do investors (outsiders). Ask yourself this question: "Are corporate managers more likely to issue new common stock (1) when they believe the stock is overpriced or (2) when they believe the stock is underpriced?" If you and all other investors answer, "When they believe the stock is overpriced," then the announcement of a new stock issue conveys negative information to the stock market. The announcement becomes an admission by corporate insiders that in their view (a very good one) the stock is overpriced. According to **signaling theory,** the announcement of a new stock issue will cause investors to revise downward their estimates of the company's stock value. The resulting drop in price per share of stock is another cost of using external equity financing.[1]

signaling theory

Theory based on information asymmetry stating that investors interpret equity cash flows as a managerial forecast of a company's financial prospects.

[1] Empirical studies reveal a small decline in stock price, on average, when companies announce a new issue of common stock. Many of these study results are summarized in: Clifford W. Smith, Jr., "Investment Banking and the Capital Acquisition Process," *Journal of Financial Economics,* January–February 1986, 3–29.

For companies that choose internal equity financing, their choice necessarily involves the decision to pay dividends, as the following equation shows:

$$\text{Earnings available to common shareholders} = \text{Dividends} + \text{Earnings retained}$$

The percentage of earnings paid in dividends is the *dividend payout ratio,* and the percentage retained is the *retention ratio.* Summing the two ratios yields 100 percent. Financial managers and investors use these ratios for comparing dividend policies among companies.

The analysis of internal financing is closely linked to a company's dividend policy. To analyze one requires consideration of the other. The following discussion treats the payment of dividends as the decision variable and draws from it the implications for internal financing. The analysis begins with the procedure for paying cash dividends.

MANAGING DIVIDEND PAYMENTS

After the board of directors decides on the size of a dividend payment, the procedure for paying it is routine. Most companies that pay cash dividends on common stock pay them once each quarter. Only a few companies deviate from this practice, and they typically pay monthly, semiannually, or yearly. A company's board of directors declares the dividend, specifies its size, and determines when it will be paid. Once declared, the dividend is recorded as a dividend payable, a current liability of the company. Declaration of a dividend increases the company's current liabilities and reduces its liquidity as measured by the current ratio (current assets/current liabilities) and net working capital (current assets less current liabilities).

Figure 19.1 presents a time line containing the key dates in managing dividend disbursements. On the **declaration date** the board of directors publicly announces the amount of the dividend, the date of record, and the payment date. Formal announcement of the dividend constitutes an enforceable contract between the company and its shareholders. The **date of record** is the day on which the corporate secretary obtains the list of shareholders from the registrar, the bank trust department maintaining the list. The **payment date** is the day on which the company mails the dividend checks to shareholders on the registrar's list. To receive the dividend, an investor must purchase the stock prior to the *ex*-**dividend date,** which usually occurs four trading days prior to the date of record. Purchasers of stock on the *ex*-dividend day will not receive the dividend. These four trading days allow time for the transfer agent (a bank trust department) to inform the registrar of ownership changes and for the registrar to update the list of company shareholders.

To illustrate the disbursement of dividends, consider the procedures of W. R. Grace & Company. Grace mails dividend checks so that shareholders receive them around the tenth day of March, June, September, and December. The company publishes the quarterly record and *ex*-dividend dates for the convenience of investors.

On the *ex*-dividend date a company's stock price drops by the amount of the dividend. For example, if W. R. Grace's common stock trades for $40 per share, and the board of directors announces a $0.70 dividend per share, then Grace's stock price drops to $39.30 on the *ex*-dividend date. The explanation for this behavior is simple: When investors buy the stock on the *ex*-dividend day, they

declaration date

Day on which the board of directors declares a dividend.

date of record

Day on which the registrar provides the list of shareholders eligible to receive the declared dividend.

payment date

Day on which the company distributes dividend checks to shareholders of record.

***ex*-dividend date**

First trading day on which purchase of stock does not entitle the purchaser to the declared dividend; four trading days preceding the date of record.

FIGURE 19.1

Key Dates in Managing Dividend Disbursements

The board of directors declares a dividend and specifies the date of record and the dividend payment date. To receive the dividend, investors must have purchased the stock prior to the *ex-dividend* day, which occurs four trading days prior to the date of record.

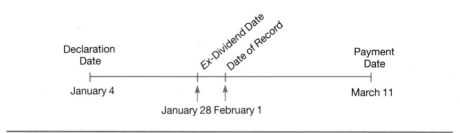

do not receive the $0.70 dividend per share; the sellers do. As a result, the buyers will offer, and sellers will accept, $0.70 less per share.

In practice, the decline in price per share might not exactly equal the dividend per share for the following reasons: (1) Other news events may cause changes in the stock price. (2) Shares of common stock trade in increments of eighths of a dollar—$39.30 for W. R. Grace is not a one-eighth increment. (3) Tax laws and transaction costs may prevent the stock price from dropping by exactly the amount of the dividend.[2]

INFLUENCES ON THE DIVIDEND DECISION

A recent *Annual Report* states that the future dividends W. R. Grace pays "will depend upon Grace's earnings, capital requirements, and other factors." Larger earnings and smaller capital requirements presumably will lead to larger dividends. Moreover, the directors will consider other factors before declaring future dividends. Grace's directors are not unique in their deliberations on the declaration of dividends.

The group interested in the payment of dividends can be quite large, particularly for publicly held companies. For example, W. R. Grace has about 48,000,000 shares of common stock outstanding and 30,000 shareholders. To satisfy this diverse group is difficult because the proper means for maximizing shareholder wealth can be interpreted differently by each shareholder, director, and manager. Perceptions and preferences will likely differ from person to person. Table 19.1 lists three influences on dividend policy operating through shareholder perceptions and preferences. The table also lists five company influences based on operations and business environment. The following sections discuss each of these influences.

Shareholder Perceptions and Preferences

Differing circumstances and prospects may cause individual shareholders to desire different dividend policies. In particular, shareholders may differ in their needs for dividend income, their perception of risk reduction through dividend payments, and their personal tax brackets.

---

[2] A great deal of research suggests that, on average, stock price does not drop as much as the dividend paid. For a sophisticated analysis, see A. Kalay, "The *Ex*-Dividend Day Behavior of Stock Prices: A Re-examination of the Clientele Effect," *Journal of Finance*, September 1982, 1059–1070.

TABLE 19.1   **Influences on the Dividend Decision**

Shareholder Perceptions and Preferences

Preference for dividend income
Risk reduction through dividends
Taxes on income and capital gains

Company Operations and Business Environment

Capital investment needs
Cash position
Stability of earnings
Legal restrictions
Inflation outlook

---

widows and orphans clientele

Facetious term for shareholders preferring dividends to earnings retention and capital gains.

Preference for Dividend Income.   Some shareholders, such as retired people and full-time investors, use dividend income for living expenses. Stockbrokers refer to this group as the **widows and orphans clientele.** Any omission or reduction of dividends would work a hardship on these shareholders. Some theorists argue that to make up for an omission or reduction, the proceeds from selling the stock can substitute for dividends. A company's stock price increases when, instead of paying dividends, the company retains earnings. Shareholders therefore can sell shares of stock to create *homemade dividends.* Some shareholders, however, have an aversion to liquidating their share of ownership in a company and are opposed to creating homemade dividends. In addition, selling stock requires them to pay brokerage fees and perhaps a tax on the increase in price above their original investment. Receiving dividends does not involve these costs, and homemade dividends are therefore not a perfect substitute for dividends.

Risk Reduction through Dividends.   Most shareholders are averse to risk and require higher rates of return for higher risk levels. Hence if the directors of a company could reduce the risk perceived by shareholders through dividend payments, then the shareholders would require a smaller return and bid up the price of the company's stock. Supporters of this view claim that dividends provide a partial payback to shareholders, thus reducing their total capital at risk. To adapt a common adage, "A dividend in the hand is worth more than a capital gain in the bush." The expected rate of return on common stock can be viewed as the expected dividend yield plus the expected capital gain yield:

$$K_c = \frac{D_1}{P_0} + g$$

where D_1/P_0 = expected dividend yield

g = expected capital gain yield

If shareholders view D_1/P_0 as less risky than g, then they would place a higher value on the dividend than on the capital gain. By declaring dividends, a company's directors lessen shareholder risk and the accompanying required rate of return, which increases price per share of the common stock. Opponents of this reasoning assert that risk of future dividends and risk of capital gains are equivalent. They argue that the risk to shareholders lies solely in the risk of a company's operating cash flows.[3] How the company splits these operating cash flows between retention and payment, they say, does not affect risk to shareholders.

Taxes on Income and Capital Gains.   The Internal Revenue Service (IRS) taxes both dividends and capital gains received by shareholders. Beginning in 1987, the IRS taxed each at the same ordinary-income tax rate. Although shareholders pay taxes either way—on dividends as they are received or on the capital gains at the time of sale—capital gains lead to a deferment of taxes. By retaining earnings, a company increases its stock price and postpones the taxes its shareholders pay. The tax-deferment advantage of capital gains is especially helpful to shareholders in high tax brackets. For all tax-paying shareholders, postponing the payment of taxes reduces the present value of future tax payments.

Prior to the Tax Reform Act of 1986, the Internal Revenue Service taxed capital gains at a rate equal to approximately one-half of the taxpayer's ordinary tax rate. Hence shareholders in high tax brackets tended to prefer capital gains to dividends. While all shareholders benefit from earnings retention and a rising stock price, this benefit was especially important to well-to-do shareholders whose cash dividends would be largely taxed away. Consequently, the differential tax rates on dividends and capital gains provided a strong incentive for directors to retain earnings. Although the differential-tax incentive disappeared in 1987, a new version of it reappeared in 1993. In any case, postponing shareholder taxes is an incentive for directors to retain earnings instead of paying dividends.

A company's board of directors tries to satisfy the bulk of the shareholders by establishing a consistent dividend policy that meets shareholder needs. Consistency in the dividend policy leads to a **clientele effect:** Investors gravitate toward companies with dividend policies they prefer. If company directors change the established dividend pattern, then the clientele may become dissatisfied and sell its stock. Selling pressure may in turn cause a decline in the price per share of stock. Therefore, to establish the optimal dividend policy, the directors should consider (1) preferences for dividend income, (2) perceptions of risk reduction through dividends, and (3) deferment of taxes on capital gains. The problem facing company directors consists of weighing the value its shareholders place on each of these factors.

clientele effect

Dividend policy attracts a specific type of investor group, one that prefers the company's pattern of dividends to that of other companies.

Company Operations and Business Environment

In addition to setting dividend policy to serve shareholder interests, directors weigh company needs for investment funds, the company's ability to pay dividends, and the general business climate. The following sections describe five company factors that influence the dividend decision.

Capital Investment Needs.   Directors of a company with many investment opportunities may want to retain a large portion of the company earnings or possibly all of the earnings. A company with many profitable opportunities, such as a high-growth company, will benefit its shareholders by reinvesting earnings and driving up the price of the common stock. A company without these opportunities should pay out its earnings in dividends because the shareholders can probably earn a higher return by investing dividends elsewhere. The size of a company's earnings is the basis for dividend payments over the long run.

---

[3] Merton H. Miller and Franco Modigliani make this point in "Dividend Policy, Growth, and the Valuation of Shares," *Journal of Business,* October 1961, 411–433. Given their assumptions, the authors demonstrate the irrelevance of dividend payout—one payout is as good as another.

Cash Position.   Paying cash dividends requires a company to have cash balances. In addition to earnings, directors make the dividend decision based on the company's short-term cash needs. Although earnings may be substantial, as in the case of a rapidly growing company, they may be tied up in inventory or other assets and unavailable for dividends. Large cash dividends normally come with company maturity. As growth in sales slows (causing growth in assets to slow), a company typically begins to pay a cash dividend. Payment may start at a modest 10 percent or 20 percent payout rate, then increase as the sales growth declines further. A mature company whose capital investment needs are limited primarily to replacement projects and whose sales are reasonably stable may have a payout rate of 80 percent.

Stability of Earnings.   Companies with reasonably stable earnings over business cycles are better able to pay higher dividend rates than are companies with volatile earnings. With stable earnings, directors feel assured that future earnings will cover the established dividend level. In contrast, highly volatile earnings provide little assurance that the company can maintain dividends at any level.

dividend-signaling hypothesis

Hypothesis that changes in dividend payments furnish information to investors and cause the stock price to change.

Company directors are reluctant to set dividend payments at levels unsustainable in the future. According to the **dividend-signaling hypothesis,** announcing a dividend reduction sends a strong negative signal to investors, who interpret dividend changes as statements by managers and directors about the company's future profitability. Thus decreases in dividends suggest a managerial forecast of poor profitability; increases imply a forecast of superior profitability.

Investors view announcements of changes in dividends as having *information content* that is much more objective than, say, public statements by company managers or directors. A managerial statement describing a bright future for the company would be viewed with skepticism if company directors simultaneously cut the dividend. As one disgruntled shareholder told a company executive, "Put your dividend where your mouth is." Because of the information content, a decrease in stock price usually follows an announced dividend cut. Conversely, an increase in stock price usually follows an announced dividend increase.

Legal Restrictions.   Legal restrictions on the payment of dividends arise from federal tax laws, state requirements, and contractual agreements. As the following examples illustrate, some restrictions mandate the payment of dividends and others prohibit them:

1. *Improper accumulation of earnings.* A closely held corporation that has unusually large cash balances or large investments in marketable securities may be charged by the Internal Revenue Service with improperly accumulating earnings. The IRS interprets an excessive accumulation of earnings as a means of avoiding dividend payments and—more importantly—as a means for shareholders to defer paying taxes. Managers of closely held corporations usually argue in tax court that the balances are needed for liquidity and for planned expansions—as noted in the minutes of company board meetings.

2. *Impairment of capital.* The statutory laws of many states prohibit dividend distributions if the distributions reduce shareholder capital— defined as the par value of common stock and, in some states, including the capital in excess of par. Stated differently, in many states a company must have retained earnings in order to pay dividends. These laws

   protect the security interest of creditors by limiting wealth transfers from
   creditors to shareholders through dividend payments.

3. *Protective covenants.* Indentures with bondholders and other restraints
   placed on the company by creditors and preferred stockholders limit the
   company's freedom to pay dividends on its common stock. For example,
   a bond indenture may prohibit dividend payments in the event that the
   current ratio, interest coverage ratio, and other financial ratios fall below
   specified levels. Cumulative preferred stock disallows common-stock dividends when preferred-stock dividends are in arrears.

Inflation Outlook.   Earnings during a period of rising product prices may not jus-
tify dividend payments otherwise acceptable during a period of stable prices.
Current costs (replacement values) of assets usually increase with the general
price level, forcing a company to retain a greater portion of its earnings to replace
deteriorating equipment. Depreciation calculated on historical costs may be
insufficient to provide for replacement, requiring the company to retain a higher
percentage of earnings or to raise capital externally.

EXAMPLE

Suppose that the current cost of Startec Corporation's depreciable assets rises by
20 percent. This increase means that the company needs 20 percent more financing—debt and equity—to replace the deteriorating assets. Because of the cost
increases, the company's directors feel pressure to reduce the dividend on common stock and to provide for replacement of assets.

---

distributable earnings
Current-cost earnings that
can be paid as dividends
without impairing the
income-producing potential
of the company.

Table 19.2 illustrates the effect of a 20 percent increase in the replacement
value of Startec Corporation's $2,600,000 depreciable assets. Based on historical
costs, depreciation equals $200,000 per year; based on current costs of depre-
ciable assets, depreciation must be 20 percent larger to reflect the 20 percent
increase in current costs. The $40,000 increase in depreciation gives recognition
to the increased cost of the depreciable assets. If sales, cost of goods sold, and
taxes are held constant, then earnings after taxes decline by $40,000, from
$204,000 to $164,000.[4] The new earnings after taxes, $164,000, represent **dis-
tributable earnings**, the amount of earnings available for paying dividends. Inflation may cause net working capital to increase as well, which further reduces the
distributable portion of earnings after taxes.

Based on historical costs, Startec Corporation pays 60 percent ($122,400/
$204,000) of its earnings in dividends. Adjusting for inflation, however, causes
the percentage to rise to 74.6 percent ($122,400/$164,000). If management plans
capital expenditures for expansion based on the 60 percent rate, then the company cannot sustain the 74.6 percent rate. For many companies an inflationary
economy pressures company directors to reduce the dividend payout ratio.

---

[4] Companies cannot use current-cost accounting to calculate income taxes. Thus income taxes are the
same for the historical and current-cost cases in Table 19.2. We assume that sales and cost of goods
sold remain constant under inflation at $800,000 and $260,000, respectively. If both sales and cost
of goods sold increase by the same inflation rate, say 20 percent, then gross profit remains the same
$540,000. Only if sales increase more than cost of goods sold does gross profit increase. To nullify
the negative inflationary effects on depreciable assets and net working capital, gross profit must rise
substantially.

TABLE 19.2

Startec Corporation: Historical and Current-Cost Income Statements

Depreciable Assets

Historical Basis		Current-Cost Basis		
Historical cost	$2,600,000	Replacement value:		
Annual depreciation	200,000	1.20 × $2,600,000 = $3,120,000		
		Annual depreciation:		
		1.20 × $200,000 = $240,000		

Income Statements

	(1) Historical Cost	(2) Current Cost	(2) − (1) = (3) Difference
Sales	$800,000	$800,000	0
Less cost of goods sold	260,000	260,000	0
Gross profit	$540,000	$540,000	0
Less depreciation expense	200,000	240,000	$40,000
Earnings before taxes	$340,000	$300,000	($40,000)
Less taxes (40%)	136,000	136,000	0
Earnings after taxes	$204,000	$164,000	($40,000)
Less dividends	122,400	122,400	0
Earnings available for expansion	$ 81,600	$ 41,600	($40,000)

DIVIDEND POLICIES

Boards of directors have several alternatives when attempting to balance the conflicting forces that affect the payment of dividends. A single dividend policy is unlikely to meet each shareholder's personal goals and to satisfy the cash requirements of the company. The optimal policy makes the best compromise among these factors and maximizes shareholder wealth. The following sections describe the advantages of four general types of dividend policy.

Residual Dividend Policy

residual dividend policy
Company pays dividends only when earnings exceed the equity needed for financing investment projects.

According to the **residual dividend policy,** a company pays dividends only when earnings exceed the equity needed for financing investment projects. Allowing the dollar amount of a company's planned projects to determine its dividends means that dividends are residual, or left over, from investment decisions. Managerial decision making in this scenario would follow these steps: (1) Estimate the dollar requirements of the planned projects, (2) determine the amount of common equity needed to finance the projects and to maintain the optimal debt-equity ratio, and (3) pay a cash dividend equal to the residual earnings (if any).

EXAMPLE

The management of B&G Manufacturing estimates that the company's optimal capital structure consists of 40 percent debt and 60 percent common equity. Management expects that earnings available to common shareholders will equal $6,000,000 for the year. What dividend should B&G pay if the company follows the residual dividend policy? The solution depends on the dollar requirements of the planned projects; consider the impact of three different capital budget levels: $7,000,000, $10,000,000, and $12,500,000.

The $10,000,000 budget in the preceding example means that B&G needs to raise $10,000,000 to finance the projects. For this budget, management must use $6,000,000 (0.60 × $10,000,000) equity financing in order to keep the capital structure unchanged and at its optimal level. Thus the company pays no dividend because management invests all earnings in capital projects totaling $10,000,000:

Earnings retained	$ 6,000,000
New debt financing	4,000,000
Capital budget	$10,000,000

Consider next the $12,500,000 capital budget. To maintain the optimal capital structure (40/60), B&G needs to raise $7,500,000 (0.60 × $12,500,000) from equity. Because B&G's earnings are only $6,000,000, the company cannot pay a dividend. As a matter of fact, the company must issue new common stock in order to maintain its optimal capital structure. Its sources of financing are:

Earnings retained	$ 6,000,000
New common stock ($7,500,000 − $6,000,000)	1,500,000
New debt financing	5,000,000
Capital budget	$12,500,000

Finally, consider the residual dividend dictated by the $7,000,000 capital budget. To maintain the optimal capital structure (40/60), B&G needs $4,200,000 (0.60 × $7,000,000) from equity and $2,800,000 from debt to finance the planned projects. B&G's $6,000,000 earnings easily cover its equity need of $4,200,000. In fact, B&G has earnings remaining for a dividend payment to common shareholders:

Earnings available to common shareholders	$6,000,000
Less earnings retained (0.60 × $7,000,000)	4,200,000
Residual dividend	$1,800,000

By paying dividends only when the company does not need the earnings for internal financing, B&G's directors accomplish two financial objectives: (1) They maximize capital gains on stock and postpone taxes paid by shareholders, and (2) they minimize the flotation costs of issuing new common stock. On the other hand, B&G's dividend payment and payout ratio will vary, depending on both its capital investment needs and its earnings level. In the example B&G's payout ratio ranges from a high of 0.30 ($1,800,000/$6,000,000), or 30 percent, to a low of zero. Shareholders who prefer dividend income may frequently be disappointed, and the volatile dividends may increase the risk they perceive.

Figure 19.2 illustrates the residual dividend policy over time for B&G Manufacturing. The company pays dividends each year from 19X0 to 19X2 and 19X6 to 19X9 because its earnings exceed the common equity needed for capital investments. From 19X3 to 19X5, however, the company pays no dividends

FIGURE 19.2

Residual Dividend Policy for B&G Manufacturing: Pay Dividends Only When Earnings Exceed the Need for Equity Capital

Following the residual dividend policy, B&G Manufacturing pays a dividend only when earnings exceed the common equity needed for capital investments. When earnings are less than the common equity needed, B&G does not pay dividends and issues new common stock. Following this policy causes B&G's dividend payments to be erratic over time.

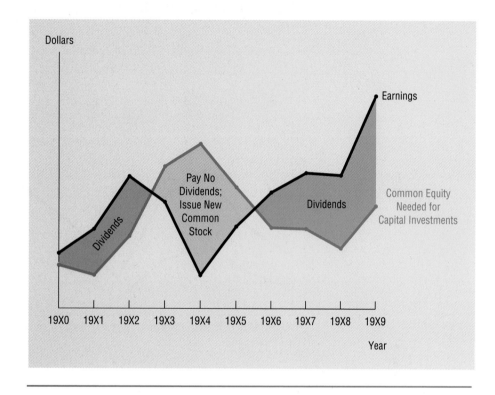

because it needs all earnings for investments. Also during the 19X3–19X5 period, the company issues new common stock to make up for the deficiency in earnings. Following the residual dividend policy causes B&G to pay an erratic stream of dividends over time to its common shareholders.

Because announcements of decreases in dividends send negative signals to investors, company directors usually adopt a dividend policy that smooths the changes in dividends over time. Companies rarely follow the residual dividend policy blindly. Nevertheless, the policy does reduce the amount of new stock issued and the accompanying flotation costs; it also postpones the taxes shareholders pay. To obtain these advantages, yet keep dividends reasonably stable over the years, requires directors to follow a compromise residual dividend policy. For example, the compromise might be as follows:

- Attempt to maintain stable dividends over time.

- Set the dividend payout ratio so that in the long run total dividends equal total earnings less the equity needed for capital projects. In the short run, dividends may be more or less than the difference between earnings and equity needs.

FIGURE 19.3

Constant Payout Ratio: Dividends Divided by Earnings Equal a Constant Percentage

Following a constant payout policy requires that dividends be a constant percentage of earnings. Changes in earnings cause similar changes in dividends, making it difficult for shareholders to depend on dividend income.

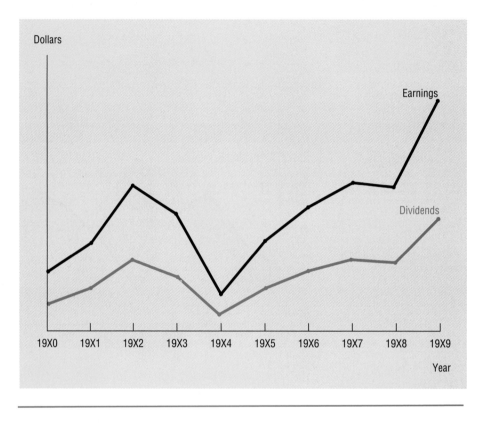

Constant Payout Policy

constant payout policy

Company pays a constant percentage of its earnings as dividends.

Under the **constant payout policy**, directors declare dividends based on a constant percentage of earnings. Using a 70 percent payout ratio, for example, a company pays $0.70 to shareholders for each $1.00 of earnings available to common shareholders.

Figure 19.3 illustrates the pattern of a constant payout policy for dividend payments. Keeping the payout ratio constant causes dividends to change pace with earnings: Soaring earnings cause dividends to soar, crashing earnings cause dividends to crash. Only to the extent that shareholders can predict earnings can they predict future dividend payments. Statistical studies show that shareholders cannot predict future earnings with much accuracy; it follows, therefore, that shareholders are poor forecasters of dividends under the constant payout policy.

Few companies adhere to the constant payout policy because of the uncertainty the future dividend stream creates and the negative signals sent to shareholders. Rigidly applying the policy causes short-run volatility in dividends. Companies may follow a constant payout policy in the long run, however, and smooth the short-run volatility. They smooth dividends by accumulating earnings in the form of cash and marketable securities during prosperous years for dividend payments in later, less prosperous years.

In recent years U.S. companies have paid out, on average, 40 to 60 percent of their earnings in dividends. The payout percentage varies from year to year in large part because companies pay relatively stable dividends in the face of fluctuating earnings.

Stable Dividends with Growth

Many directors emphasize the need for dividend stability and growth when setting dividend policy. To avoid stock price swings because of variable dividends, company directors may employ the following policy of maintaining stable dividends with growth:

- Pay conservatively low, sustainable dividends.
- Increase dividends only with the assurance that the company can maintain the new level for several years into the future. Allow the payout ratio to fall with temporary increases in earnings.
- Reduce dividends only when it becomes apparent that future earnings cannot support the present level of dividends. Allow the payout ratio to rise with temporary decreases in earnings.

Figure 19.4 illustrates a policy of stable dividends with growth. As shown, the company directors increase dividends per share in 19X1 and 19X2, consistent with the increases in earnings per share. Undeterred by the drop in earnings during 19X3 and 19X4, the directors maintain the dividend level set in 19X2. This action causes the dividend payout ratio to increase in 19X3 and to exceed 100 percent in 19X4. Despite the increase in earnings during 19X5, 19X6, and 19X7, the directors refrain from increasing dividends until 19X7. This action causes the payout ratio to fall over the period. Correctly signaling an increase in future earnings, the directors increase the dividend level once again in 19X8 and maintain it in 19X9. Only when the directors conclude that future earnings cannot sustain the 19X9 dividend level will they reduce the dividend level in subsequent years.[5]

Stable Dividends with an Extra Dividend

Directors of some companies modify the policy of stable dividends with growth by including an extra year-end dividend in prosperous years. Declaring the extra dividend toward year-end allows the directors to match the dividend with an accurate estimate of earnings. By identifying the dividend as extra, directors hope to signal investors that a recurrence of the dividend may not be forthcoming.

Distinguishing between the regular, stable dividend and the extra dividend provides directors with a measure of flexibility, which is especially useful for companies with volatile earnings. If a company pays an extra dividend repeatedly, however, then investors might begin to expect it. At that point, omitting the extra dividend conveys the same negative information to the market as omitting the regular dividend. This turn of events defeats the purpose of extra dividends and causes directors to lose the flexibility they seek.

---

[5] Reflecting investor interest in dividends, *Barron's Financial Weekly* publishes a list of changes in dividends and the payment dates. The list contains companies that have national followings of investors.

FIGURE 19.4

Stable Dividends per Share with Growth

Following a policy of stable dividends with growth requires directors to declare conservatively low dividends, increasing them only when the company can sustain the higher level. When earnings fall temporarily, the directors do not cut dividends, making it easier for shareholders to depend on dividend income.

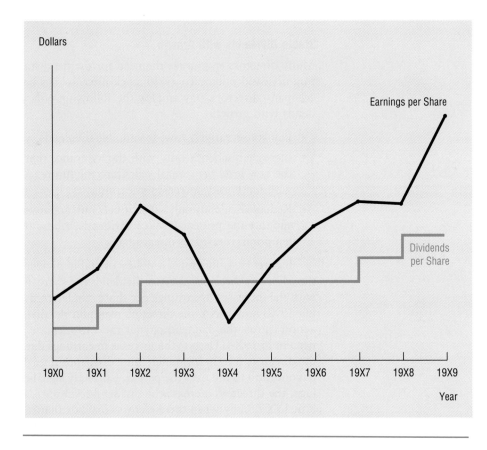

The dividend policy a company follows depends on the attitudes of shareholders and the needs of the company. Young, newly organized companies are attracted to the residual policy because of the need for funds and the expectation of large returns from investments in projects. More mature companies are attracted to stable dividends with growth. At maturity, successful companies are able to generate cash flows exceeding their needs.

STOCK DIVIDENDS AND STOCK SPLITS

Most dividend policies include rules for distributing company earnings in the form of cash to company owners. Broadly defined, however, a dividend policy may include the distribution of any asset to shareholders. For example, a cosmetics company with excess inventory might pay a dividend with inventory items. Upon liquidation, a company might pay a combination of cash and other assets as a dividend, known as a **liquidating dividend.**

liquidating dividend
Final dividend that dissolves the company or part of the company.

In contrast to paying dividends with assets, a company may distribute new shares of stock to shareholders. Such a distribution is called a **stock dividend** or a **stock split,** depending on the accounting treatment of the transaction. Neither a stock dividend nor a stock split is equivalent to a cash dividend, or to any asset dividend for that matter. With both stock dividends and splits shareholders receive additional shares of stock in proportion to their current holdings. For example, Shoreline Financial announced a 5 percent stock dividend to all share-holders of record on March 16, 1993, payable on April 1, 1993. For each 100 shares held, shareholders received another 5 shares. Cheyenne Software announced a 3-for-2 stock split; for each 100 shares held, shareholders received another 50 shares. A 3-for-2 stock split is equivalent to a 50 percent stock div-idend in terms of the extra shares a shareholder receives.

Accounting for Stock Dividends and Stock Splits

An easy way to understand stock dividends and splits is to examine the account-ing treatment of each. For stock dividends the paying company transfers from retained earnings to its permanent capital accounts an amount equal to the mar-ket value of the stock dividend. Assets and *total* shareholder equity are unaf-fected. Only accounts *within* shareholder equity change.

EXAMPLE

The directors of Hartford Company declare a 10 percent stock dividend. Prior to the stock dividend, Hartford's equity accounts appear as follows:

Common stock (100,000 shares, $10 par)	$1,000,000
Capital in excess of par	500,000
Retained earnings	3,500,000
Total shareholder equity	$5,000,000

A 10 percent stock dividend means that Hartford will distribute 10,000 (0.10 × 100,000) additional shares to its common shareholders: one additional share for each 10 shares held. Hartford's common stock trades in the market for $25 per share. What is the effect of the stock dividend on the company's balance sheet?

Because Hartford's stock price in the above example is $25 per share and the stock dividend requires issuing 10,000 new shares, the company's accountant transfers $250,000 (10,000 shares × $25) from retained earnings to the other two equity accounts:

1. $100,000 (10,000 shares × $10 par) goes in the common-stock account.
2. The residual, $150,000, goes into the account labeled Capital in Excess of Par.

After the stock dividend Hartford's equity accounts appear as follows:

Common stock (110,000 shares, $10 par)	$1,100,000
Capital in excess of par	650,000
Retained earnings	3,250,000
Total shareholder equity	$5,000,000

Total shareholder equity remains $5,000,000, although the accountant shifts amounts among the individual accounts.[6]

Prior to the stock dividend Hartford's book value per share equals $50 ($5,000,000/100,000); afterwards it equals $45.45 ($5,000,000/110,000). A shareholder with 10 shares before the stock dividend owned stock with a total book value of $500 (10 shares × $50). Moreover, the shareholder's total book value stays the same after the stock dividend: 11 shares × $45.45 = $500.

In contrast to a stock dividend, a stock split does not require a transfer from retained earnings to the other equity accounts. A stock split changes two figures within the common-stock account: the number of shares outstanding and the par value per share. None of the aggregate amounts within shareholder equity changes.

EXAMPLE

To illustrate the accounting impact of a stock split, consider again the original equity section of Hartford Company's balance sheet. If instead of a 10 percent stock dividend, Hartford's directors declare a 2-for-1 stock split, what is the effect on the company's balance sheet?

In the above example the split leaves unchanged the total assets and the total of each component within shareholder equity, but it causes a shift within the common-stock account:

Common stock (200,000 shares, $5 par)	$1,000,000
Capital in excess of par	500,000
Retained earnings	3,500,000
Total shareholder equity	$5,000,000

The 2-for-1 stock split means that each shareholder receives another share of stock for each one held. Thus Hartford's total number of shares outstanding increases from 100,000 to 200,000. Par value drops from $10 to $5 a share, and the common-stock account stays at $1,000,000 (200,000 × $5).

As with a stock dividend, total shareholder equity stays the same after a stock split—$5,000,000 for Hartford Company. Book value per share of Hartford stock, however, declines from $50 ($5,000,000/100,000 shares) to $25 ($5,000,000/200,000 shares) because of the 2-for-1 stock split. A shareholder with 10 shares before the stock split owned stock with a total book value of $500 (10 shares × $50). After the stock split the shareholder still owns stock with a total book value of $500 (20 shares × $25).

To summarize, stock dividends and splits do not change the total shareholder equity of a company. The total book value of each shareholder's stock remains unchanged as well.

Effect on Shareholder Wealth

Essentially, stock dividends and stock splits cut the company pie into more pieces but do not create new wealth. A 100 percent stock dividend (or its equivalent,

---

[6] Accountants refer to the transfer from retained earnings to the other equity accounts as recapitalizing (or permanently capitalizing) earnings. If a stock has no par value, then the accountant transfers the entire amount from retained earnings to the common-stock account.

•

Anatomy of a Stock Split

Are stock splits worth the paper they're printed on? Perhaps not, if we can judge by the experience of Exxon Corporation's 2-for-1 split in 1981.

Exxon's nearly 700,000 shareholders received their bright new stock certificates in June 1981. Planning for the stock split began in December of the previous year with employees of the treasurer's office gathering information requested by the board of directors. Based on the information gathered, the board resolved that the split would "be in the best interest of the corporation and its shareholders" because it would attract a wider base of ownership.

After the board's resolution, the company notified the New York Stock Exchange (NYSE), and the company's shareholder-relations office prepared proxies for the shareholders' vote on the split. Lawyers prepared documents to amend the corporate charter, and company officers met with officials from both the NYSE and Morgan Guaranty Trust Company. Morgan Guaranty would mail the new certificates because it kept the records on Exxon's 700,000 shareholders. More than 50 people at Morgan Guaranty would later spend two weeks signing, registering, checking, and counting the new certificates.

American Bank Note Company printed the certificates following the exacting standards of the NYSE: (1) include at least 20 square inches of intricate patterns of lines and circles, (2) include a human face in the vignette on the certificate, and (3) print with the same engraving process used to print U.S. currency. These steps, and others, make it tough on counterfeiters. Certificates cannot be used as money, but they can be used as collateral for bank loans.

Printing the certificates took American Bank Note Company approximately 32 days, 13 hours per day. Piled in a stack, the certificates would be as high as a 40-story building. Placed end to end, they would reach 125 miles. It took several trucks just to transfer the certificates from the printer's to Morgan Guaranty. After Morgan Guaranty employees processed, addressed, and sorted the certificates by zip code, the certificates were taken to the post office.

How many tons of paper does it take to produce the stock certificates for a stock split? The answer for Exxon's 2-for-1 split in 1981 is 10 tons—and 3,000 pounds of ink.

Source: Basia Hellwig, "Anatomy of a Stock Split."

a 2-for-1 stock split) gives shareholders two half-sized pieces for each piece they formerly owned.[7] If other variables are held constant, then a 2-for-1 stock split will cause a $60 per-share stock to fall to $30; a 3-for-1 split will cause it to fall to $20 per share, and so on. A shareholder with 100 shares of $60 stock is no better off with 200 shares of $30 stock.

In view of the foregoing logic, why do directors declare stock dividends and splits? Many financial managers believe that stock dividends and splits have a favorable psychological impact on investors, thereby increasing demand for the stock. They point out that the road taken by a successful company is paved with a series of stock dividends and splits. Although supporting evidence is scarce for the psychological impact, there is evidence supporting the second point. Stock market data show that the price of a company's stock rises, on average, around the day of an announced split in the stock. In part, the stock price increases because directors often increase the cash dividend simultaneously with the announced split. The information content of the increased cash dividend and the

[7]The New York Stock Exchange classifies all stock dividends exceeding 25 percent as stock splits. But the NYSE's rule is arbitrary, and the large majority of stock dividends actually are less than 25 percent. How the distribution of shares is classified matters little to shareholders.

split itself signal the market that management and directors believe company earnings will increase. Being company insiders, managers and directors usually have better estimates of company prospects than do outsiders. If subsequent earnings fail to meet investor expectations, however, then the stock price will decline. Increases in stock price around the time of announced splits depend on perceived growth in earnings, not on the split itself.[8]

Paying stock dividends and declaring stock splits involves numerous people: corporate officers, engravers, printers, lawyers, accountants, computer analysts, and investment bankers. Total administrative costs can therefore be substantial for large companies. Why do directors cause companies to incur these costs if the effect of the dividends and splits is to leave shareholder wealth unchanged? Proponents and opponents of stock dividends and splits offer the following arguments:

Proponents	Opponents
Splits and stock dividends provide signals to investors that management expects financial prosperity for the company.	Splits and stock dividends are costly signals of what will soon become clear when company earnings rise.
Splits and stock dividends reduce high stock prices to a more popular trading range. Shareholders prefer to purchase round lots but cannot afford to do so when the price per share is high.	Fees for odd lots (1 to 99 shares) are small. Also, institutional investors, with millions of dollars to invest, purchase far more stock than do individuals. Institutional investors are indifferent to price levels as long as they perceive expected returns commensurate with risk.
Recapitalization of retained earnings through stock dividends provides creditors with assurance (because of state laws) that this part of equity cannot be reduced by the payment of cash dividends.	Recapitalization of retained earnings provides for a remote eventuality that can be taken care of at less cost with protective covenants.
Management can use stock dividends in place of cash dividends to conserve company cash.	Stock dividends and cash dividends are not substitutes for one another. Giving shareholders more stock certificates from the same company will not fool them into thinking that they have received something of value. Cash dividends represent a real transfer of wealth and provide more potent signals to the market than do stock dividends.

Where do these arguments leave us? For purposes other than signaling the market, there is little theoretical support for the value of stock dividends and splits. Perhaps signaling alone justifies the administrative costs of stock dividends and splits, but more research is needed to provide a definitive answer. Behavioral research might be able to explain why many shareholders enjoy receiving additional stock certificates even though they do not increase wealth.

---

[8] Company directors can reduce the number of shares outstanding by declaring a *reverse stock split*—for example, a 1-for-2 split. A 1-for-2 reverse stock split would cause a stock trading for $5 a share to go to $10 a share. Stock market data show that investors generally view announcements of reverse splits as bad news. They seem to believe that directors of companies in financial difficulty are more likely to announce reverse splits than the directors of healthy companies. On average, the market value of a company's common equity declines on the day that its directors announce a reverse split.

REPURCHASE OF COMMON STOCK

Rather than pay a cash dividend, some company managers choose to repurchase shares of the company's outstanding stock. By using cash for repurchases instead of dividends, they drive up the stock price, producing a capital gain for their shareholders. Using cash for repurchases instead of dividends effectively defers taxes on dividends for the remaining shareholders. Companies must obtain approval for repurchases from the Securities and Exchange Commission, which means that repurchases are not perfect substitutes for the routine payment of dividends.

Companies often repurchase their common stock for reasons other than its being an alternative to paying dividends. For example, management may want to change the company's financial leverage. Issuing bonds and using the proceeds to repurchase outstanding stock increases financial leverage, presumably toward the optimal level. To illustrate, a company may issue $5,000,000 of bonds, then use the cash to repurchase $5,000,000 of common stock. The common stock becomes *treasury stock*—stock issued as fully paid and returned to the company, where it is kept in the treasury (meaning it can be reissued). The company's total assets remain unchanged (except for the transaction costs involved), but the capital structure will show a $5,000,000 increase in bonds payable and a $5,000,000 decrease in shareholder equity.

Management may view the company's stock as being underpriced, making it a better investment than, say, additional plant and equipment. IBM, for example, began a share repurchase program in 1990 when its stock dropped below $100 per share. Management announced that the reason for the repurchase program was to take advantage of an "artificially" depressed stock price. Subsequent events proved management wrong as IBM's stock price fell below $50 per share in early 1993.

Another reason to repurchase stock is to thwart a takeover attempt by a hostile raider. A raider is a person or organization that takes control of a company in a manner unfriendly to the management and directors. For example, T. Boone Pickens attempted raids on Phillips Petroleum and Unocal in 1985. Both were unsuccessful because of tactics the target companies undertook, including competing with Mr. Pickens for shares trading in the market and buying shares from him at a premium above market.

Whatever the reason, companies usually choose one or more of the following methods for repurchasing stock: (1) buy the stock in the secondary market through a broker, (2) negotiate a purchase with the holder of a large block of stock (normally defined to be 10,000 shares or more), or (3) issue a tender offer to all shareholders for a specified number of shares. When a company announces a **tender offer,** it offers to pay a specific price for a specified number of shares currently held by shareholders.

tender offer

Announcement of willingness to purchase outstanding shares of stock under specified conditions.

Whether shareholders view the repurchase of common stock as a financially suitable substitute for cash dividends remains an unsettled issue. The new tax law of 1993 reinstated one attraction of the method, the lower tax rate on capital gains than on cash dividends for high-income investors. Shareholders can create homemade dividends by selling shares of stock, but to do so causes them to incur transaction costs. Also, companies usually pay dividends quarterly, whereas they only sporadically repurchase shares of stock. In practice, therefore, companies normally use share repurchases to complement cash dividend payments.

FIGURE 19.5

Signaling Effects of Equity Cash Flows

Company managers and directors have more and better information than do investors about the company's future performance. Because of this asymmetry in information, investors interpret equity cash outflows as signals that the company is performing well and prospects are bright. If this were not the case, so the argument goes, then the managers and directors would retain cash to survive the uncertain future. For opposite reasons, investors interpret equity cash inflows as bad news.

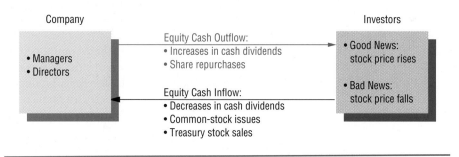

DIVIDEND POLICY AND SIGNALING

A well-designed dividend policy maximizes shareholder wealth. To achieve this goal, the policy needs to coordinate cash dividends, stock dividends and splits, share repurchases, and the company's need for equity funds to invest in capital projects. Unfortunately, the company's need for funds may have a short-run negative effect on its stock price.

Research shows that investors read equity cash flows to and from a company as signals of its current and future performance. **Equity cash flows** include cash dividends, share repurchases, treasury stock sales, and new issues of common stock. According to *signaling theory*, equity cash flows are objective expressions of management's perceptions of the company's financial prospects. Cash flows are much more objective and believable signals than, say, news releases and publicity announcements. Moreover, managers and directors are company insiders who have better access than investors to inside information. Based on this premise, investors interpret equity cash flows as illustrated in Figure 19.5.

Equity cash outflows (increases in cash dividends and share repurchases) generally signal good news to investors, resulting in a rising stock price. Outflows demonstrate management's confidence in the ability of the company to generate more cash in the future to replace the outflows. Increases in dividends give management an incentive to continue performing well to avoid the adverse effect of a dividend cut. In addition, share repurchases signal investors that management interprets the present stock price to be depressed, and that future earnings and dividends will increase. Exceptions to this interpretation include: (1) small repurchases for administrative purposes, such as funding pension plans and (2) massive repurchases to combat a takeover attempt.

The bottom part of Figure 19.5 shows that equity cash inflows (decreases in cash dividends, new common-stock issues, and treasury stock sales) generally signal bad news to investors, resulting in a falling stock price. Decreases in dividends signal management's loss of confidence in the ability of the company to generate cash flows. Investors interpret new issues of common stock as an attempt by management to take advantage of a high stock price. No company, the argument goes, would issue new shares or sell treasury stock when its stock

equity cash flows

Cash flows between a company and its shareholders; cash dividends, share repurchases, treasury stock sales, and new issues of common stock.

price is depressed (unless management is desperate, itself a negative signal). Therefore the issuance of new shares and the sale of treasury stock signal management's belief that the stock is overpriced. Investors react by bidding down the stock price.

Signaling theory provides strong support for the policy of stable dividends with growth and for that policy's corollaries: (1) Set dividends at a low, sustainable level and (2) avoid cutting dividends. Because stock dividends and splits do not produce equity cash flows, the theory classifies these events as weak signals of management's beliefs. In contrast, share repurchases demonstrate management's strong belief in the company's financial future. Finally, signaling theory suggests that companies should issue new shares of common stock only under one or more of the following conditions: (1) The stock is overpriced, (2) earnings retention is insufficient to finance the company's profitable projects, or (3) the company has insufficient debt capacity to finance profitable projects through borrowing. Some combination of these conditions may cause the benefits of issuing new stock (or selling treasury stock) to outweigh the negative impact on the stock price.

THEORETICAL PERSPECTIVES ON DIVIDEND POLICY

The impact of a company's dividend policy on its market value has been the focus of theoretical study for many years. Hundreds of financial theorists have sought to answer the question: Does dividend policy matter? Depending on their assumptions, some theorists say that dividend policy is irrelevant; others say that it *does* affect the company's market value; and still others say that dividend policy is a puzzle yet to be solved.

dividend irrelevance proposition

Proposition, developed by Miller and Modigliani, that a company's dividend policy does not affect its market value.

The debate on dividend policy began in 1961 with the theoretical modeling of Merton Miller and Franco Modigliani (hereafter MM).[9] They developed the **dividend irrelevance proposition** and described the conditions necessary for it to hold true. MM view dividend policy as the following trade-off: retaining earnings versus paying cash dividends and issuing new shares of stock. According to MM, a company can offset any dividends it pays (reduction in retained earnings) by issuing new shares of stock. Furthermore, if a company does not pay dividends, then shareholders can sell shares, thus creating homemade dividends. Since any dividend policy can easily be offset, MM argue that dividend policy is irrelevant and does not affect the value of a company.

To arrive at their startling conclusion, MM assume the existence of a *perfect capital market,* one characterized by: (1) *no taxes*—which rules out investor tax-based preferences for capital gains over dividends; (2) *no flotation costs*—which means that the issuance of new shares of stock is costless just like the retention of earnings; (3) *no transaction costs*—which means that buying and selling stock is costless, and that therefore investors can costlessly create homemade dividends; and (4) *no information costs*—which means that corporate managers (insiders) and investors (outsiders) share the same information about the company's financial prospects, and that therefore dividend payments have no information content and do not provide valuable signals to the market.

In addition to assuming the simplified world of perfect capital markets, MM carefully separate dividend policy from *investment policy* and *financing policy.* They note that dividend payments need not affect a company's investment in

[9]See Note 3 for the bibliographic reference to Miller and Modigliani's seminal article.

INTERNATIONAL DIMENSIONS

Dividend Policy and the Multinational Company

The flow of dividends in a multinational company includes two major steps: (1) cash dividends from foreign subsidiaries or affiliates to the parent company and (2) cash dividends from the parent company to its shareholders. The second step involves issues similar to those that confront a domestic company, but the first step involves issues unique to the multinational company.

Among the issues surrounding a foreign subsidiary's payment of dividends to its parent company are taxes, currency controls, liquidity and opportunity costs, and the cash needs of joint-venture partners.

Dividend payments from subsidiaries can affect company-wide tax liabilities and after-tax profitability. Some countries (e.g., Germany and Japan) levy higher taxes on earnings retained than on earn-

ings paid out as dividends, which encourages the payment of dividends. In addition to this two-tier income tax, a 3 percent to 5 percent *withholding tax* on dividends is levied by some countries, which discourages the payment of dividends. To reduce double taxation, however, most countries give companies a foreign tax credit for taxes already paid by subsidiaries.

When a country experiences persistent deficits in its balance of payments with other countries, currency controls, which impede dividend payments, often result. Managers of companies with a history of regular dividend payments are well positioned to argue that the payments are a normal cost of doing business. A consistent dividend policy may create a favorable mindset among government officials toward the company, especially if the policy is followed by company subsidiaries in other countries. Accordingly, many multinational companies attempt to elude currency controls by maintaining consistent dividend policies over time and across countries.

Dividend payments reduce a subsidiary's liquidity and may force it to borrow funds from local institutions. Whether or not dividend payments in these cases are sensible depends in part on the subsidiary's local borrowing rate. Shareholder wealth maximization suggests that large dividend payments and some borrowing would be advisable where rates are low. Small (or no) dividend payments and no borrowing would be preferable, however, where rates are high. In politically risky countries, borrowing at high rates may be necessary in order to hedge against expropriation. If the foreign government seizes the subsidiary, the parent company could then default with impunity on the local loans.

Finally, when a company enters into a joint venture with a foreign partner, an additional issue surrounds dividend payments. Dividend policy becomes a shared managerial decision, and the viewpoints of the partners may differ. To avert conflict, the partners often agree to conservatively low, sustainable dividend payments.

assets nor its mix of debt and equity. A company can maintain its capital structure and follow the residual dividend policy: Pay dividends only when earnings exceed the equity needed for financing investment projects. According to MM, the market value of a company arises primarily (if not solely) from its investment decisions, not from its dividend and financing decisions.

By identifying the assumptions accompanying their dividend irrelevance proposition, MM simultaneously identify the real-world factors that might cause dividend policy to matter. Indeed, the controversy over dividend policy often centers on the importance placed on these factors. Despite differences of opinion, many financial theorists believe: (1) Tax laws favor the stocks of companies that pay low (or no) dividends. (2) Paying conservatively low dividends minimizes flotation costs and avoids the costs of negative signals associated with issuing stock. (3) A company's repurchase of stock in lieu of dividends is probably a better way to distribute cash to shareholders. (4) Because of the signals they send to the stock market, sudden changes in dividend payments lead to sudden changes in stock price.

Although the foregoing statements seem to represent consensus beliefs among financial theorists, even that is debatable. The controversy over dividend policy continues to boil and will likely do so for some time to come.

SUMMARY

- Companies either retain earnings for internal financing or pay out earnings as cash dividends to common shareholders. Dividend policies are guidelines for balancing the conflicting forces affecting the proportion of earnings that a company should pay to shareholders as dividends.

- Company directors publicly declare dividends on common stock, which then become a current liability of the company. At the time of declaration, the directors also set the date of record and the payment date. The *ex*-dividend date usually occurs four business days prior to the date of record. To receive the declared dividend, shareholders must own the stock prior to the *ex*-dividend date.

- Three shareholder attributes potentially affect the dividend decision: (1) Some shareholders need dividend income for meeting personal expenses. (2) Some shareholders perceive dividends as a risk-reducing mechanism. (3) Shareholders in high tax brackets often prefer companies to retain earnings and postpone dividends. Shareholder characteristics such as these combine to form dividend clienteles.

- Company characteristics potentially affect the cash dividend decision in the following ways:

Company Characteristic	Dividend Effect
Capital investment needs increase	Reduction
Company cash balances decline	Reduction
Company earnings stabilize	Increase
Legal restrictions on company	Conflicting effects
Current costs of assets increase	Reduction

- The dividend policy that a board of directors adopts is a compromise influenced by shareholder perceptions and preferences and company characteristics. Types of dividend policies are:

    Residual dividend policy: The company pays dividends from earnings not needed for internal financing—dividends are a residual amount left over after investing in profitable projects.

    Constant payout policy: The company pays a constant percentage of earnings as dividends. Under this policy the company maintains a constant dividend payout ratio (dividends per share divided by earnings per share) and allows dividends to change with earnings.

    Stable dividends with growth: The company pays a conservatively low dividend and increases it only when it is sustainable. The company does not reduce dividends unless absolutely necessary.

    Stable dividends with an extra dividend: The company pays low sustainable dividends and pays an extra dividend at year-end during highly profitable years.

- When company directors declare stock dividends or stock splits, the company distributes additional shares of stock to its shareholders. For example, a

100 percent stock dividend and a 2-for-1 stock split mean that shareholders receive a new share for each share of stock currently held. The number of pieces in the company pie increases, but the size of the pie does not increase. A stock dividend and a stock split cause stock price per share to drop. Shareholders own more shares of a lower-priced stock, and the aggregate market value of the shares remains unchanged. Although the price effects of stock dividends and splits are the same, their accounting treatments differ.

• As an alternative to paying cash dividends, a company may use cash to repurchase the company's outstanding common stock in the secondary market; the stock also may be purchased from large-block holders or through tender offers. Stock repurchases in place of cash dividends have the effect of deferring taxes on dividends for shareholders not selling stock.

• According to signaling theory, equity cash flows are objective expressions of management's perceptions of the company's financial prospects. Share repurchases and increases in cash dividends send positive signals and increase stock price. Selling treasury stock, issuing new common stock, and decreasing cash dividends send negative signals and reduce stock price.

• The impact of dividend policy on a company's market value has been the focus of debate for many years. In a well-crafted article published in 1961, Miller and Modigliani (MM) develop the dividend irrelevance proposition. Since 1961, many theorists have attacked MM's theoretical assumptions and have argued that dividend policy does indeed affect a company's market value. Some theorists think that dividend policy is still an intellectual puzzle.

Key Terms

signaling theory	clientele effect	stock dividend and stock split
declaration date	dividend-signaling hypothesis	tender offer
date of record	distributable earnings	equity cash flows
payment date	residual dividend policy	dividend irrelevance proposition
ex-dividend date	constant payout policy	
widows and orphans clientele	liquidating dividend	

Questions

19.1. What factors make the retention of earnings preferable to issuing stock for long-term financing?

19.2. Explain the following dates associated with dividends. Which date is most important to common shareholders? Why?
   a. Declaration date.
   b. *Ex*-dividend date.
   c. Date of record.
   d. Payment date.

19.3. List the influences that tend to discourage paying dividends on common stock. In view of your list, why do companies pay dividends on common stock?

19.4. What is the difference between the dividend payout ratio and the dividend yield? Which one does *The Wall Street Journal* report?

19.5. Give the arguments for and against the residual dividend policy employed in its pure form.

19.6. A financial economist commented: "Paying stable dividends per share with growth is an attempt to veil changes in earnings per share. Such attempts are futile because investors easily see through the veil. Dividend policy cannot reduce the risk inherent in the cash flows produced by a company's assets." Discuss this statement, explaining your position on the issue.

19.7. In 1986 Congress modified the tax law so that capital gains and dividends became taxable in 1987 at the ordinary-income rate. Before then, capital gains were taxed at roughly one-half of the ordinary-income rate applicable to dividends.

Explain the impact of this tax change on the decision to retain earnings or to pay dividends.

19.8. Satel Company is a producer of electronic components for computers. Satel is only 3 years old and has never paid a dividend. Chris Perkins, CEO of Satel, recently announced that Satel's return on capital investments averages 35 percent annually. He went on to say that Satel would not pay a dividend in the foreseeable future. In your opinion, will investors view Mr. Perkins's comments as good news or bad news? Explain your choice.

19.9. On November 11 of last year the Yatsabishi Cycle Company declared its fourth-quarter dividend. Rather than its usual $2 per share, the company declared $1. On the declaration day Yatsabishi's stock price declined from $28 to $23 per share. Provide a rationale based on *asymmetric information* for this price decline.

19.10. Suppose that you overhear the following dialogue between Marla and Corine at an office meeting:

> *Marla:* In my opinion, it's foolish for U.S. companies to pay dividends.
> *Corine:* Why's that?
> *Marla:* Because a typical company pays a dividend and at the same time issues common stock. They'd be better off to retain earnings instead of paying dividends. Retained earnings are an inexpensive source of capital, but issuing new shares reduces shareholder wealth.
> *Corine:* You do realize, Marla, that you've just challenged the thinking of thousands of business people. Marla versus thousands of experienced practitioners—what a headline!
> *Marla:* Right is right. It's foolish. I rest my case.

Do you agree with Marla? Explain your answer, and note which dividend policy she implicitly endorses.

19.11. Explain the differences and similarities between stock dividends and stock splits.

19.12. Would you be pleased to learn that a company in which you own 100 shares of common stock is planning an 8-for-5 stock split? Explain your answer.

19.13. When a company repurchases its common stock, the stock becomes classified as treasury stock. A company's treasury stock has no claim to assets, receives no dividend, and conveys no vote in corporate elections. Why does a company repurchase its stock?

19.14. Equity cash flows signal either good news or bad news to investors. Identify each type of equity cash flow and explain its impact on share price.

19.15. Miller and Modigliani identify a special world in which the payment of dividends becomes an irrelevant detail.
   a. What is the nature of this world?
   b. Explain the argument for dividend irrelevance. In what way and to whom are dividends irrelevant?

19.16. There are no taxes, flotation costs, transaction costs, nor information costs in the land of Phantasia. Managers of Phantasian companies have a different view of the dividend decision than do their counterparts in the United States. Explain the difference in viewpoints.

Strategy Problem

Ersatz Fashions owns a chain of stores that specialize in selling clothing accessories. In 19X5 company sales were $4,150,000, earnings after taxes were $555,000, and dividend payments were $222,000. Management expects sales to be $6,000,000 in 19X6, based in part on planned capital expenditures totaling $800,000. In addition, management expects the after-tax profit margin to be 10 percent. Ersatz Fashions' target debt ratio (total debt/total assets) is 45 percent, and its stock price is $25 per share. The company's balance sheet on December 31, 19X5, is as follows:

Assets		Liabilities and Equity	
Current assets	$ 600,000	Current liabilities	$ 200,000
Fixed assets	1,400,000	Long-term debt	700,000
		Common stock	
		(100,000 shares, $1 par)	100,000
		Capital in excess of par	250,000
		Retained earnings	750,000
Total assets	$2,000,000	Total claims	$2,000,000

a. Calculate the company's 19X5 earnings per share, dividends per share, dividend payout ratio, and dividend yield.
b. If the company maintains its 19X5 dividend payout ratio and its target debt ratio, how much external equity will it need to raise during 19X6?
c. If the company follows the residual dividend policy, how much external equity will it need to raise during 19X6?

d. Calculate the dividends per share resulting from the policies described in Parts *b* and *c*. (Ignore the issuance of any new shares of stock.)
e. Do the implications of signaling theory favor the dividend policy in Part *b* or the one in Part *c*? Explain.
f. Show the changes in the balance sheet that would occur if Ersatz Fashions declares and pays a 10 percent stock dividend.

Strategy

The balance sheet shows 100,000 shares outstanding.

Dividend payout is DPS divided by EPS.

Dividend yield is DPS divided by price per share.

Forecast earnings equal profit margin times forecast sales.

Target debt ratio is 45%; target equity ratio is 55%.

You need to understand the residual dividend policy.

Total equity needed equals the equity ratio times $800,000.

Solution

a.
$$\text{Earnings per share} = \frac{\$555,000}{100,000}$$

$$= \$5.55$$

$$\text{Dividends per share} = \frac{\$222,000}{100,000}$$

$$= \$2.22$$

$$\text{Dividend payout ratio} = \frac{\$2.22}{\$5.55}$$

$$= 0.40, \text{ or } 40\%$$

$$\text{Dividend yield} = \frac{\$2.22}{\$25}$$

$$= 0.089, \text{ or } 8.9\%$$

b. The forecast earnings after taxes equal $600,000 (0.10 × $6,000,000), of which $360,000 (60 percent) will be retained and $240,000 (40 percent) will be paid in dividends.

To maintain the target capital structure, the company will finance the $800,000 capital expenditures as follows: 45 percent debt, or $360,000; and 55 percent equity, or $440,000.

The company needs $440,000 equity but will generate only $360,000 from internal equity. Therefore the company needs $80,000 external equity.

c. The residual dividend policy states that a company will pay dividends only when earnings exceed the equity needed for financing investment projects. Ersatz Fashions needs equity totaling $440,000 (0.55 × $800,000). Since forecast earnings are $600,000, the company will retain the $440,000 and pay $160,000 in dividends. No external equity is needed to support the $800,000 capital expenditures.

d. For Part *b*:

$$\text{Dividends per share} = \frac{\$240,000}{100,000}$$

$$= \$2.40$$

For part *c*:

$$\text{Dividends per share} = \frac{\$160,000}{100,000}$$

$$= \$1.60$$

e. The implications of signaling theory favor the dividend policy in Part *b* because it causes dividends per share to increase from $2.22 to $2.40, a positive signal to the stock market. The dividend policy in Part *c* causes dividends per share to fall from $2.22 to $1.60, a negative signal to the stock market. Unlike negative signals, positive signals lead to increases in stock price.

f. A 10 percent stock dividend means that 10,000 more shares will be outstanding:

Recapitalize retained earnings: $250,000 = 10,000 × $25 per share. Transfer $10,000 to common stock and $240,000 to capital in excess of par.

Common stock (110,000 shares, $1 par)	$ 110,000
Capital in excess of par	490,000
Retained earnings	500,000
Total equity	$1,100,000

Note that total equity stays the same, $1,100,000.

◆ Demonstration Problem

Solarius Products Company (SPC) manufactures and distributes alternative-energy devices, including solar screens, photovoltaic cells, and windmills. SPC plans to invest $30,000,000 in 19X7 to expand its operations. The following table provides selected information from the company's 19X6 financial statements:

Net sales	$96,575,000
Earnings after taxes	11,589,000
Common-stock dividends	3,476,700
Total assets	$94,782,000
Total liabilities	$52,130,100
Common stock (par value $1; authorized shares 8,500,000; issued shares 2,100,000)	$ 2,100,000
Capital in excess of par value	20,300,000
Retained earnings	23,751,900
Treasury stock at cost (100,000 shares)	(3,500,000)
Total shareholder equity	$42,651,900
Total liabilities and shareholder equity	$94,782,000

SPC's target debt ratio (total debt/total assets) is 55 percent, and its common stock currently trades for $60 per share. Management expects sales to increase to $125,000,000 in 19X7 but expects the after-tax profit margin to decline to 11 percent.

a. Why is treasury stock a negative number on SPC's balance sheet? How many shares of common stock are outstanding?
b. Based on signaling theory, what was the stock market's likely reaction to SPC's repurchase of common stock? Explain.
c. Calculate SPC's 19X6 earnings per share, dividends per share, dividend payout ratio, dividend yield, and price-earnings ratio.
d. The date of record for SPC's most recent quarterly dividend was Friday, November 18, 19X6: (1) When was the *ex*-dividend date? (2) What is the latest date that you could have purchased SPC stock and still have received the dividend?
e. (1) How much equity does SPC need to finance the planned expansion? (2) What is the dollar forecast for 19X7 earnings after taxes? (3) Calculate 19X7 dividends per share assuming that SPC follows the residual dividend policy. (4) Compare the dividends per share calculated in Part *(3)* with those paid in 19X6, and explain the implications of signaling theory.
f. Many companies follow the dividend policy of *stable dividends with growth*: (1) Describe this policy. (2) What are the advantages and disadvantages of this policy?
g. What is a 2-for-1 stock split? Show the changes in SPC's balance sheet caused by a 2-for-1 stock split.

h. What is a 10 percent stock dividend? Show the changes in SPC's balance sheet caused by a 10 percent stock dividend.
i. Merton Miller and Franco Modigliani (MM) developed the *dividend irrelevance proposition*: (1) What is MM's proposition? (2) Describe MM's perfect capital market and its implications for dividend payments. (3) Since the real-world capital market is not perfect, what is the value of MM's proposition?

Problems

Ratios related to dividends

19.1. Maxwell Company's annual report contains the following data:

Number of shares of common stock outstanding	500,000
Number of shares of preferred stock outstanding	150,000
Earnings after taxes	$2,500,000
Latest price-earnings ratio	9
Dividends per share of common stock	$1.00
Dividends per share of preferred stock	$0.80

a. Calculate earnings available to common shareholders and earnings per share of common stock.
b. Calculate the dividend payout ratio and the retention ratio.
c. Calculate the dividend yield.

Repurchase of common stock

19.2. Microtech Industries (MI) has 100,000 shares of common stock outstanding, annual earnings of $2 per share, and a price-earnings ratio of 12. Holding other things constant, suppose MI repurchases 20,000 shares of its common stock.
a. Calculate MI's annual earnings per share after the repurchase of common shares.
b. Calculate MI's stock price per share after the repurchase of common shares.
c. By how many dollars does MI's total market value of equity change as a result of the repurchase of common shares?
d. Do MI's remaining shareholders benefit from the repurchase of common shares? Explain.

Stock split and *ex*-dividend day

19.3. Suppose that you own 400 shares of common stock of Columbus Lighting, which later splits 9-for-5. Later still, Columbus Lighting declares a $1 dividend per share to all shareholders of record on Friday, June 23, with payments to be made on July 25.
a. What will be the total amount of your dividend check?
b. What will be the amount of your dividend check if you sell your stock on Thursday, June 22?
c. What will be the amount of your dividend check if you sell your stock on June 15?

Size of capital budget and dividend payout ratio

19.4. Indiana Granite limits its capital expenditures to the amount that internal equity can support. Determine the size of Indiana Granite's capital budget if its optimal debt-equity ratio is 0.40, its earnings after taxes are $620,000, and its dividend payout ratio is 45 percent.

Paying dividends while issuing common stock

19.5. Doral and Associates has $15,000,000 in earnings available to common shareholders and pays all of it as a cash dividend in 19X7. The company's debt-equity ratio is 0.60, and its capital budget is $80,000,000. Doral and Associates issues new common stock to finance the portion of its capital budget that will maintain its 0.60 debt-equity ratio.
a. Calculate the company's ratio of total debt to total assets.
b. How much new equity must the company issue to finance the capital budget?
c. Discuss the decision of the directors to pay a dividend and issue common stock in the same period. Do you believe that it is in the shareholders' best interest?

Residual dividend policy

19.6. The management of Smite Products has developed the company's capital budget for the next planning period. According to plans, the amount needed for investing is $800,000. Jan Smite, the company's financial manager, is advising the directors on the amount of dividends that the company should pay. The company's forecast calls for $320,000 in after-tax earnings, and Ms. Smite estimates that the company's optimal capital structure has 30 percent debt and 70 percent equity.

a. If Smite Products subscribes to the residual dividend policy, how large will the company's dividend be? What dollar amount of new common stock must it issue?

b. Henry Pirenne, the company's phlegmatic and aging board member, rouses himself from a daydream and suggests to Ms. Smite that the policy followed by the company "puts the cart before the horse." He continues, "I suggest that we declare and pay a $100,000 dividend and issue common stock to help finance the equity part of our capital budget." How much common stock must be issued if the company follows Mr. Pirenne's advice? What arguments can you make to support his suggestion? What arguments can you make against his suggestion?

Distributable earnings, tax rate, and payout ratio

19.7. Wascomb Enterprise's income statement for 19X8 is presented below. A search of corporate records indicates that the average age of depreciable assets is 8 years and that replacement values of depreciable assets during 19X8 increased an average of 16 percent.

Wascomb Enterprises: Income Statement for the Year Ended December 31, 19X8

Sales	$260,000
Less costs	120,000
Gross income	$140,000
Less depreciation	80,000
Net operating income	$ 60,000
Less interest expense	36,000
Earnings before taxes	$ 24,000
Less taxes	3,960
After-tax earnings	$ 20,040
Less dividend (40%)	8,016
Earnings retained	$ 12,024

a. Calculate distributable earnings.

b. Calculate the following on both historical and current-cost bases: (1) effective tax rate, (2) dividend payout ratio, and (3) amount of internal financing available for expansion.

Identifying and justifying dividend policy

19.8. Fenton Affiliates of North America has experienced rapid growth in the past 5 years. In order to finance the growth, the board of directors has followed a policy of controlled borrowing, a low dividend payout rate, and regular stock dividends.

The percentage of debt in the capital structure has remained constant since 19X4, and the funds generated from operations have been reinvested in productive assets. Each January for the past 4 years Fenton's board of directors has declared and paid a 10 percent stock dividend. Each November for the past 5 years the company has paid a $0.20 cash dividend per share.

The board anticipates a challenge to its intention to continue its dividend policy from two corporate raiders who have recently bought large blocks of the common stock. Management fears that they intend to take over the company.

Selected data relating to the company's earnings and dividends are as follows:

Year	Earnings	Shares Outstanding 12/31	Dividend per Share	Total Payout	Price per Share 12/31
19X2	$100,000	100,000	$0.20	$20,000	$10.00
19X3	120,000	110,000	0.20	22,000	12.00
19X4	144,000	121,000	0.20	24,200	14.30
19X5	172,800	133,100	0.20	26,620	17.00
19X6	207,360	146,410	0.20	29,282	22.00

a. Calculate the dividend payout ratio for each year. Is Fenton following a constant payout policy?

b. Assume that you own 1,000 shares of Fenton stock at the end of 19X2 and do not buy more shares in subsequent years. How many shares of Fenton stock would you own at the end of 19X6? How many dollars in dividends would you have received each year? What is the market value of your original investment at the end of 19X6?

c. Prepare a response from the perspective of Fenton's board of directors that (1) justifies the low dividend payout ratio and (2) explains the benefits of the dividend policy for Fenton's shareholders.

Effect of dividend transactions on the balance sheet

19.9. York Company's abbreviated balance sheet (in thousands of dollars) is as follows:

Assets		Liabilities and Shareholder Equity	
Cash	$ 200	Current liabilities	$ 80
Other	1,800	Long-term liabilities	600
		Shareholder equity	
		Common stock (50,000 shares outstanding, $1 par)	50
		Paid-in capital in excess of par	70
		Retained earnings	1,200
Total	$2,000	Total	$2,000

York's common stock trades for $60 per share on the day of each of the transactions below. Treat each transaction independently of the others, and show the balance sheet following each transaction.

a. A $1 per share cash dividend is declared and paid.

b. A 10 percent stock dividend is declared and paid.

c. A 4-for-1 stock split occurs.

d. A 1-for-4 reverse stock split occurs.

Stock split, ratios, and value

19.10. Alabama Metal (AM), a manufacturer of metal fasteners, has been highly profitable for the past 5 years. Its profitability has caused its stock price to soar, and management is considering a 2-for-1 stock split. AM's recent financial data are as follows:

Dividend payout ratio	60%
Earnings after taxes	$75,000,000
Number of common shares outstanding	9,375,000
Price per share of common stock	$100

a. Based on AM's recent financial data, calculate earnings per share, dividends per share, price-earnings ratio, and total market value of common stock.

b. Recalculate your answers in Part *a* assuming that AM carries out its 2-for-1 stock split.

c. Explain the meaning of the following quote: "A stock split unaccompanied by an increase in the cash dividend is like giving someone 5 singles for a $5 bill."

Effect of a stock split on price per share, dividend yield, and shareholder wealth

19.11. Ted Born owns 1,000 shares of Crystal Frames, which recently split its stock 7-for-5. Crystal's stock price per share was $48 preceding the day of the split. Also, Crystal paid a $2 dividend per share before the split.

    a. What do you expect will happen to the price per share on the day of the split? Support your answer with calculations.

    b. Assume that Crystal maintains its $2 dividend per share after the split. What is the dividend yield based on your solution to Part *a*? What has happened to Mr. Born's wealth?

    c. Assume that Crystal pays the same aggregate dividends after the split that it paid before the split. What dividend yield will a shareholder receive based on the stock price calculated in Part *a*? What has happened to Mr. Born's wealth?

Computer Problem

Effect of dividend policy on growth and earnings: template DIVIDEND

19.12. The treasurer of Colorful Plastic Devices Inc. expects after-tax earnings this year (19X0) of $1 million on $20 million of sales. Because of strong demand for its products, Colorful's sales growth will be limited only by production capacity. For each of the next four years, sales will increase by 40 percent of the amount invested in capital assets during the preceding year.

    Colorful will maintain a 5 percent profit margin. The company's policy is to finance growth only with internal equity and debt. Its target debt ratio is 45 percent, and 750,000 shares of common stock are outstanding.

    The company has never paid a dividend, but to satisfy the demands of disgruntled investors, will do so for the first time this year. The treasurer believes that the percentage of income paid out in dividends in 19X0 will determine policy for the next four years.

    a. Compute earnings per share, dividends per share, and the capital budget for 19X0. Fifty percent of earnings will be paid out as dividends.

    b. Compute sales, net income, earnings per share, dividends, dividends per share, and the capital budget for each year during 19X1 to 19X4.

    c. Compute the annual growth rate of sales, net income, and dividends for the period 19X0 through 19X4.

    d. Recompute Parts *a, b,* and *c* assuming dividend payout ratios of 40 percent, 30 percent, 20 percent, and 10 percent.

Case Problem

Barfield Materials Inc.

The mood in the boardroom grows tense as the directors of Barfield Materials Inc. (BMI) take their chairs to begin the last meeting of fiscal year 19X9. Three of the seven directors represent minority stockholders, several of whom have communicated their strong preference for regular cash dividends. The remaining four directors are members of the Barfield family, which holds a 55 percent interest in the corporation. BMI's long-standing policy of reinvesting after-tax earnings and not paying dividends is going to be challenged. The first item on the agenda for the board meeting is the company's dividend policy.

    BMI was founded in 1950 as a proprietorship by Rudolph Barfield. The company leases gravel rights on several hundred acres in southern Pennsylvania. The rock is mined from quarries and crushed into aggregate for use in concrete. Most of the gravel is sold to paving companies and to municipalities. Sales grew and Mr. Barfield added new crushing equipment and dump trucks in response to the increased demand.

    It soon became obvious to Mr. Barfield that more capital was required than he alone could provide. In 1970 he incorporated and sold 45 percent of the shares to several local investors. The additional equity investment allowed BMI to expand and take advantage of growth opportunities. Over the next few years the minority shares traded in the local over-the-counter market. BMI stock split 2-for-1 in 1975 and again in 1980. Currently, 100,000 shares of common stock are outstanding.

Abbreviated financial statements for the most recent 2 years and estimated figures (in thousands of dollars) for 19X9 are given below:

	19X7	**19X8**	**19X9e**
Net sales	$7,112	$9,014	$10,107
Earnings after taxes	436	475	492
Current assets	$2,409	$3,054	$ 3,424
Net fixed assets	2,562	4,588	5,512
Total assets	$4,971	$7,642	$ 8,936
Current liabilities	$1,180	$1,495	$ 1,677
Long-term debt	633	2,514	3,134
Common equity	3,158	3,633	4,125
Total claims	$4,971	$7,642	$ 8,936
Average price per share	$42.00	$49.00	$59.00
Earnings per share	4.36	4.75	4.92

After approval of the minutes and agenda, the directors took time to review the 19X9 financial estimates. During the discussion of dividend policy, Delbert Thomas, a minority director, spoke up: "BMI has earned a profit every year since incorporation in 1970, and minority stockholders have yet to see any return on their investment. How can we expect to benefit from our shares in BMI if the company never pays a dividend?"

To diffuse tension, James Barfield, president and chairman of the board, asked Mr. Thomas what kind of dividend policy he would propose. "I propose a policy of paying 50 percent of the after-tax earnings in cash dividends to shareholders on a quarterly basis beginning next year. With such a policy our stockholders would always be assured of dividend income. As an act of good faith, we should declare a $0.60 per share dividend for the fourth quarter of 19X9." "Hear! Hear!" shouted another minority director.

Jill Barfield, BMI's chief financial officer and treasurer, was anxious to join the discussion. "Dividend policy in the long run should be determined by the investment and growth opportunities we may have. If paying dividends becomes the overriding goal, we shall have to curtail growth and in doing so, forgo profitable opportunities.

"I have just completed my forecast of external funds requirements for 19X0," Jill continued. "Assuming a 10 percent increase in net sales and a 5 percent net profit margin, we shall need to raise $170,000 next year. And that's with no dividend!"

"We can easily increase our borrowing to cover a dividend," Thomas rebutted.

"Yes, the bank will lend us the additional funds," Jill replied. "However, we are well above our target debt-to-assets ratio as a result of financing the EPA-mandated equipment and the land acquisition. Now we need the retention of earnings to reduce our indebtedness. Furthermore, other problems are just over the horizon that will require equity capital; our trucks and loading equipment are aging and are scheduled for replacement. I am generally in favor of cash dividends when the company can afford it. Right now we can't afford it."

Noon approached and Mr. Barfield suggested that Jill complete a thorough study of the feasibility of a cash dividend and report to the executive committee next week.

a. Evaluate Mr. Thomas's statement that minority shareholders have realized no return on their investment in BMI stock.

b. Combine Ms. Barfield's sales growth and earnings assumptions with a 50 percent dividend payout policy, and calculate next year's annual dividend per share.

c. List and briefly discuss Ms. Barfield's arguments against declaring a dividend.

d. Assume that Ms. Barfield used the percent-of-sales method to forecast external funds required. If the company is operating at capacity and all current liabilities are spontaneous, is her $170,000 estimate correct? Assume no dividends and support your answer with calculations.

e. Ms. Barfield is opposed to additional indebtedness to pay a cash dividend. Does BMI's debt level seem excessive? Explain.

f. Should the board consider issuing new common stock to provide funds for growth as well as for dividends? Explain your answer.

g. Summarize a recommendation for the board of BMI regarding dividend policy. What is another way shareholders can realize returns in cash? What disadvantages does that alternative have?

The author thanks Professor Carl M. Hubbard of Trinity University for contributing this case problem.

Selected References

Asquith, Paul, and David W. Mullins. "Signalling with Dividends, Stock Repurchases, and Equity Issues." *Financial Management,* Autumn 1986: 27–44.

Baker, H. Kent, Gail E. Farrelly, and Richard B. Edelman. "A Survey of Management Views on Dividend Policy." *Financial Management,* Autumn 1985: 78–84.

Baker, H. Kent, and Patricia Gallagher. "Management's View of Stock Splits." *Financial Management,* Summer 1980: 73–77.

Baker, H. Kent, Patricia L. Gallagher, and Karen E. Morgan. "Management's View of Stock Repurchase Programs." *Journal of Financial Research,* Fall 1981: 233–247.

Brealey, Richard A. "Does Dividend Policy Matter?" *Midland Corporate Finance Journal,* Spring 1983: 17–25.

Hanson, Robert C. "Tender Offers and Free Cash Flow: An Empirical Analysis." *Financial Review,* May 1992: 185–209.

Maloney, Michael T., and J. Harold Mulherin. "The Effects of Splitting on the Ex: A Microstructure Analysis." *Financial Management,* Winter 1992: 44–59.

Miller, Merton H., and Kevin Rock. "Dividend Policy Under Asymmetric Information." *Journal of Finance,* September 1985: 1031–1051.

Murray, Dennis. "Further Evidence on the Liquidity Effects of Stock Splits and Stock Dividends." *Journal of Financial Research,* Spring 1985: 59–67.

Netter, Jeffry M., and Mark L. Mitchell. "Stock-Repurchase Announcements and Insider Transactions after the October 1987 Stock Market Crash." *Financial Management,* Autumn 1989: 84–96.

Spudeck, Raymond E., and R. Charles Moyer. "Reverse Splits and Shareholder Wealth: The Impact of Commissions." *Financial Management,* Winter 1985: 52–56.

Wansley, James W., and Elayan Fayez. "Stock Repurchases and Securityholder Returns: A Case Study of Teledyne." *Journal of Financial Research,* Summer 1986: 179–191.

SPECIAL TOPICS

Part VII

SMALL-BUSINESS PERSPECTIVE

Leasing and International Expansion

After several weeks of an unsuccessful search for a suitable location for the health club that he planned to operate with Kathy Griffin and Jim Sutherland, John Heatherly considered the possibility of opening the club in England. Health clubs there were not so numerous as in the United States, and John thought it might be an excellent opportunity to capitalize on the market potential. If he opened the club in England, he could also serve as a distributor for some of In Shape's equipment. If he bought equipment from In Shape instead of from the manufacturers, he could buy in small quantities at an excellent price. These purchases would also help ease the cash flow problems of In Shape. John decided to return to England to see if a good location could be found.

The possibility of the club-distributorship in England and the rapid growth of their outlet in the United States caused Kathy and Jim to consider the purchase of a computer system to help manage information. Kathy and Jim spent some time evaluating computer systems that would provide them with the functions they would need. The one they decided to purchase had the capacity to handle a varied inventory, to print invoices, and to complete financial statements. Also, it was capable of interfacing with the cash register so that sales records would be automated.

The bank agreed to finance the computer for 3 years at an interest rate of 12 percent, but the bank also required a 20 percent down payment. This presented a problem for two reasons. First, because the company was extremely short of cash, a large down payment would create an additional strain. Second, if the balance were financed over 3 years, the monthly payments would be much higher than what Kathy and Jim wanted.

The computer sales company had offered a lease arrangement, but Kathy and Jim were reluctant to use this method of financing because of their inexperience with leasing. However, there were several attractive features to the lease. These included a down payment of only $500, an option to buy the system at the end of the lease for $100, and a 5-year payment schedule. Kathy and Jim wondered which alternative would be less costly.

They now had two business decisions to make. They had to decide whether to proceed with the investment in a company in England. Managing a company there would be very different from managing their outlet in the United States, particularly since they were not familiar with international business procedures. Then they had to decide whether to lease or buy the computer system.

The decisions that Kathy and Jim have to make confront many small-business managers. At each stage of growth, new opportunities and challenges arise and new decisions must be made. Successful financial decisions are continually demanded to ensure the success of the company.

This part of the text provides information on several special topics, including leasing and international financial management. Leasing, often used as an alternative method of financing by small companies, is especially important to those companies that do not wish to employ debt financing. International financial management is becoming a common concern for many small companies that see expansion opportunities abroad.

Chapter 20

TERM LOANS AND LEASES

Something Borrowed, Something New

What do the following companies have in common: (1) GATX Corp., (2) Ryder System Inc., (3) Polaris Aircraft Leasing Corp., and (4) Comdisco Inc.? *Answer:* Each is an equipment lessor; that is, each company purchases equipment and leases it to other companies. GATX is one of the largest lessors of railroad tank and freight cars. Ryder is by far the largest full-service truck lessor. Polaris specializes in short-term aircraft leases. And Comdisco concentrates on high-tech equipment, ranging from mainframe computers to medical equipment.

In recent years leasing has accounted for about one-third of the investment in equipment by U.S. companies. In some leases the lessor's only role is that of a financial institution providing asset financing and collecting lease payments. To increase their business, however, many lessors are adding asset management services. For example, GATX

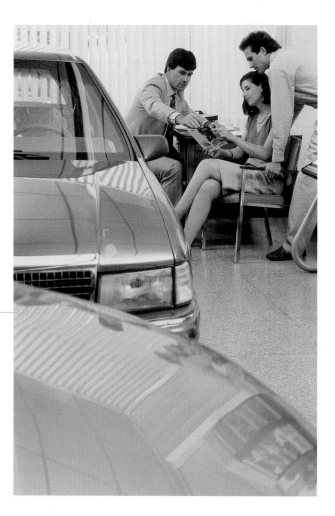

designs and maintains specialized tank cars for its customers. A recent GATX annual report states: "Tank cars . . . come in a variety of sizes with virtually infinite combinations of valving, coils, linings, and other features. Maintenance of tank cars is substantially different from the maintenance of box, gondola, or hopper cars. For these reasons, railroads have stayed out of this business, leaving it to leasing companies or owner/shippers."

Despite the proliferation of services available with leases, many companies choose to own their equipment. They finance the equipment through commercial banks or other financial institutions and provide their own maintenance and other services. Only careful analysis can resolve the question companies face: Will leasing or owning an asset maximize shareholder wealth?

Source: Jim Mele, "Leasing: Preparing for the 1990s," *Business Week,* March 19, 1990, 24ff; *GATX Annual Report,* 1991, 7.

Some types of financing do not fit into the classifications of short- and long-term financing. Between these extremes lies a middle ground called the intermediate term. Although rather arbitrary, the intermediate term is usually thought to include the period between one and ten years—short term being one year or less and long term being ten years or more. The two primary types of intermediate-term financing are term loans and leases. Each of these alternatives is a method for financing company assets. To assess the merits of these financing methods, the financial manager must evaluate their individual terms as well as their costs. The goal of this chapter is to describe this evaluative process.

TERM LOANS

term loan

Multiyear business loan that a borrower repays with periodic payments.

A **term loan** is a multiyear business loan that the borrower agrees to repay with periodic payments. A wide variety of financial institutions make these loans available, including commercial banks, life insurance companies, finance companies, pension funds, and small-business investment companies. Commercial banks are the major source of term loans, and this part of their business has been growing rapidly in the past decade.

Because companies negotiate term loans privately with lending institutions, the provisions of the agreements vary widely. The origination costs of term loans usually exceed those of short-term loans because of the increased documentation of provisions and the need for the lender to monitor the loan for a longer period of time. In contrast, the origination costs of term loans are usually less than those associated with bond issues. For many types of bond issues, companies pay registration fees to the Securities and Exchange Commission, investment banking fees, and printing costs for the prospectus. Thus the cost of taking out a term loan is usually less than the cost of issuing bonds.

Financing with Term Loans

Companies use term loans to finance permanent increases in assets, for interim financing, and for repaying other borrowings. The permanently added assets often take the form of an increase in working capital or additional equipment. As interim financing, a term loan might be used to finance the early stages of development of a new product; then, when the product is developed, the company may shift from the term loan to a long-term source of capital.

Because their maturities fall in the middle range, term loans share characteristics with both short-term loans and bonds. Like short-term loans, term loans involve negotiation between the company and the lender. In contrast, companies issue bonds through investment bankers, and the lenders (bond purchasers) rarely make contact with the company. The borrower repays a term loan in periodic installments beginning no more than one year after the loan is made. Similarly, bonds often require repayments of principal through a sinking-fund provision. Term loans command higher interest rates than do short-term loans because banks require compensation for their loss of liquidity from loans with longer maturities. In addition, banks often require collateral for term loans to reduce exposure to default risk.

The borrower provides additional assurances to the lender by agreeing to protective covenants as a condition for a term loan. These restrictions originate

The author thanks Michael Gombola, Professor of Finance at Drexel University, for his contributions to this chapter.

in the negotiation process. Covenants are usually more restrictive for term loans to companies perceived as high risks. Restrictiveness generally increases also with the maturity of term loans. Examples of protective covenants are as follows:

- The borrower's current ratio must not fall below a specified level, and the borrower's debt ratio must not rise above a specified level.
- Limits may be placed on the amount of dividends paid to shareholders.
- Acquisition of new plant and equipment may be limited in amount during the period the loan is outstanding.

Failure to meet such covenants triggers default and empowers the lender to demand repayment of the entire loan. In most cases, however, the lender stops short of "pulling the trigger." Instead, the lender uses the legal leverage to make the borrower take corrective action.

Repaying Term Loans

Borrowers usually repay term loans in equal monthly, quarterly, or semiannual installments, which differs from their repayment of most short-term loans with one payment at maturity. A term loan is fully *amortized*, meaning that some of its principal is repaid in each period and the last payment repays the loan balance. Term loans seldom require balloon payments. Lenders view balloon payments as risky because they delay repayment of the loan, and the borrower may have trouble making the final large payment.

Calculation of Payments. Debt-service payments include both interest expense and principal. On the basis of these payments, the financial manager develops an amortization schedule, which shows the amount of each payment going to interest and principal.

EXAMPLE

William & Company borrows $50,000 for 3 years at 8 percent annual interest compounded quarterly. The company must repay the term loan in quarterly payments beginning at the end of the first quarter. How much are the quarterly debt-service payments?

The series of 12 (3 years × 4 quarters) equal quarterly payments in the above example constitutes an ordinary annuity. Use either a financial calculator or Appendix B.4 and the following procedure to calculate the quarterly payments:

$$PVA = PMT(PVIFA_{i,n})$$
$$\$50,000 = PMT(PVIFA_{8\%/4, 3 \times 4})$$
$$\$50,000 = PMT(10.5753)$$
$$PMT = \$4,728$$

The company pays $4,728 at the end of each of the next 12 quarters to fully amortize (pay off) the $50,000 loan. Table 20.1 shows the amortization schedule detailing each interest payment (Column 4) and repayment of principal (Column 5). At the beginning of Quarter 1, the loan balance is $50,000, and the company pays $1,000 interest, or 2 percent of the loan balance for the quarter. Subtracting $1,000 from the $4,728 debt-service payment yields the $3,728 repayment of

TABLE 20.1   **Amortization Schedule of a $50,000 Term Loan at 8 Percent Annual Interest Compounded Quarterly for 3 Years (Quarterly Payments)**

(1) Quarter	(2) Beginning Balance	(3) Payment	(0.08/4) × (2) = (4) Interest	(3) − (4) = (5) Repayment of Principal	(2) − (5) = (6) Ending Balance
1	$50,000	$4,728	$1,000	$3,728	$46,272
2	46,272	4,728	925	3,803	42,469
3	42,469	4,728	849	3,879	38,590
4	38,590	4,728	772	3,956	34,634
5	34,634	4,728	693	4,035	30,599
6	30,599	4,728	612	4,116	26,483
7	26,483	4,728	530	4,198	22,285
8	22,285	4,728	446	4,282	18,003
9	18,003	4,728	360	4,368	13,635
10	13,635	4,728	273	4,455	9,180
11	9,180	4,728	184	4,544	4,636
12	4,636	4,728	92	4,636	0

principal. Subtracting $3,728 from the $50,000 beginning loan balance yields the $46,272 ending loan balance. Similar calculations for the remaining quarters complete the amortization schedule. As loan maturity approaches, the quarterly interest payments decrease and the quarterly repayments of principal increase. The final repayment of principal equals the quarterly beginning loan balance, causing the ending loan balance to be zero—and the loan is repaid.

After-Tax Payments.   A loan amortization schedule is needed for calculating after-tax payments, the actual cash outflows experienced by the company. Interest payments are tax deductible, but the repayments of principal are not. Financial managers calculate after-tax payments to measure the actual cash flows required to service company debt.

After-tax payments can be calculated in either of two ways: (1) repayment of principal *plus* the after-tax cost of interest or (2) the debt payment *less* the tax savings of interest.

Suppose that William & Company in the preceding example has a 34 percent income tax rate. Calculate the after-tax loan payment for the first quarter using two different methods:

Method 1		*Method 2*	
Repayment of principal	$3,728	Debt payment	$4,728
Plus after-tax interest		Less tax savings	
$1,000 − (0.34 × $1,000)	660	(0.34 × $1,000)	340
After-tax payment	$4,388	After-tax payment	$4,388

Each subsequent after-tax payment is calculated similarly.

TABLE 20.2

After-Tax Payments on a $50,000 Loan at 8 Percent Annual Interest Compounded Quarterly for 3 Years (Quarterly Payments)

(1) Quarter	(2)[a] Repayment of Principal	(3)[b] After-Tax Interest	(2) + (3) = (4) After-Tax Payment
1	$3,728	$660	$4,388
2	3,803	611	4,414
3	3,879	560	4,439
4	3,956	510	4,466
5	4,035	457	4,492
6	4,116	404	4,520
7	4,198	350	4,548
8	4,282	294	4,576
9	4,368	238	4,606
10	4,455	180	4,635
11	4,544	121	4,665
12	4,636	61	4,697

[a]From Column 5 of Table 20.1.
[b]Dollar interest from Column 4 of Table 20.1 multiplied by (1 − 0.34).

For the above example, Table 20.2 shows that the quarterly after-tax payments (Column 4) increase over time. The increase occurs as maturity approaches because the quarterly interest payments (tax deductible) fall and the quarterly repayments of principal rise. Figure 20.1 shows the time line for the after-tax payments. Discounting the payments at the after-tax interest rate—0.02(1 − 0.34) = 0.0132, or 1.32 percent per quarter—yields a present value of $50,000, the original loan principal.

Discounting the before-tax payments ($4,728) at the before-tax interest rate (2 percent per quarter) yields the same present value ($50,000) as discounting the after-tax payments at the after-tax interest rate. Moreover, both discounting procedures yield the original loan principal. Note that after-tax payments should never be discounted at the before-tax interest rate; nor should before-tax payments be discounted at the after-tax rate. After-tax discounting is used in the analysis of the cost of leasing assets.

LEASES

lessee
User of the asset in a lease agreement.

lessor
Owner of the asset in a lease agreement.

A lease is a rental agreement under which a company (the **lessee**) acquiring use of an asset obligates itself to the owner (the **lessor**) for periodic rental payments. Any asset can be the subject of a lease. As lessors, IBM leases computers, Xerox leases copiers, and GATX leases railroad cars. Automobile dealers lease cars, heavy-equipment manufacturers lease bulldozers, real estate developers lease buildings, and airplane manufacturers lease airplanes.

Leasing is neither a new type of financing nor an uncommon one. Around 1400 B.C. the Phoenicians were leasing ships to the merchants of other nations to carry goods to and from trading ports. These merchants were more interested

FIGURE 20.1   **After-Tax Payments on a $50,000, 8 Percent Term Loan with Quarterly Payments**

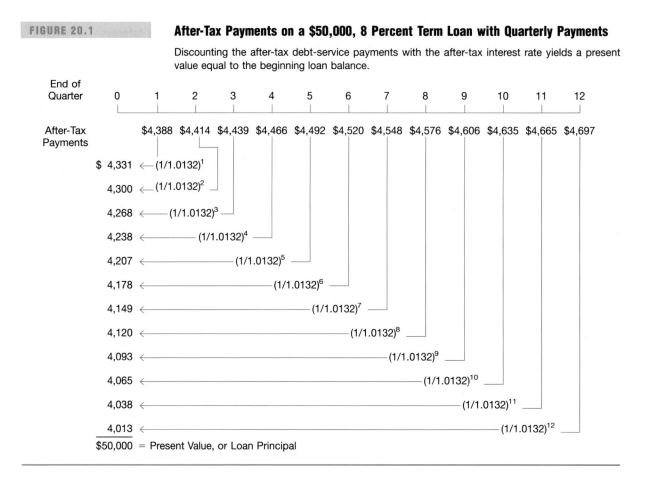

Discounting the after-tax debt-service payments with the after-tax interest rate yields a present value equal to the beginning loan balance.

in trade than in owning ships, so the lease agreement was an expedient way to have the use of a ship. Although leasing has its roots in ancient history, only since World War II has it become widely used as a financing tool. The principal reason is the entry of commercial banks into the leasing market. In the mid-1950s the Comptroller (pronounced *controller*) of the Currency permitted national banks to be lessors.

A lessor, as legal owner of the asset, depreciates it and reports lease payments as taxable rental income. A lessee deducts from taxable income the full amount of lease payments. For lease payments to be deductible, however, the lease must conform to technical guidelines provided by the Internal Revenue Service. The IRS seeks assurance that the lease is not a disguised installment sale. Lessees (and lessors) have incentives to disguise installment sales as leases because lease payments are fully tax deductible and payments (interest plus repayment of principal) on installment sales are not. With an installment sale, the buyer deducts depreciation and interest payments but not repayments of principal. To assure itself of a "true" lease, the IRS requires that (1) the term of the lease be less than the useful life of the asset, (2) the lessor receive a reasonable rate of return, and (3) the lessee pay the fair market value of the asset if purchased upon expiration of the lease. Leases that satisfy the IRS requirements fall into two categories: capital leases and operating leases.

Capital Leases

capital lease

Rental agreement that provides effective ownership of an asset; financial effects of the lease are shown on the lessee's balance sheet.

A **capital lease** (also called a *financial lease*) is a rental agreement in which the lessee acquires a substantial portion of the rights to an asset and incurs a liability, both of which are recorded on the lessee's balance sheet. The lessee includes the value of the leased property in assets and the present value of future lease payments (financial portion) in liabilities. The financial portion of a lease payment is the part that pays for financing (net of any **executory costs**—maintenance, service, and insurance). To calculate the liability created by the lease, the lessee discounts the financial portion of lease payments at the lower of (1) its incremental borrowing rate or (2) the lessor's implicit interest rate (if that rate can be determined). The lessee records the corresponding asset value as equaling the liability created by the lease or the fair market value of the asset, whichever is lower.

executory costs

Nonfinancial expenses necessary to maintain and operate a leased asset.

A capital lease conveys, in substance, the benefits and risks associated with owning the asset. A lease meeting one of the following conditions is a capital lease. Meeting *one* of the conditions is sufficient for a capital lease, although some leases may not meet the IRS requirements for a "true" lease.[1]

- Lease contract transfers to the lessee the asset title at the end of the lease term.

- Lease contract contains an option that permits the lessee to purchase the asset upon expiration of the lease at a price lower than fair market value.

- Lease term equals 75 percent or more of the economic life of the asset.

- Present value of the lease payments (net of any executory costs—maintenance, service, and insurance) equals 90 percent or more of the fair market value of the asset.

Two types of capital leases are net leases and service leases.

net lease

Lease in which lessor provides only financing; lessee provides maintenance and insurance.

Net Leases.   With a **net lease** the lessee is responsible for all service and maintenance of the asset, which means that the lessor supplies only the financing. A net lease is similar to borrowing money to buy the asset.

A special type of net lease is the **sale and leaseback.** Here, a company owning land, buildings, or equipment sells the asset and simultaneously executes an agreement to lease it back for a specific period of time. The lessor could be an insurance company, a bank, a specialized leasing firm, the finance division of an industrial company, or an individual.

sale and leaseback

Lease in which the seller of an asset immediately leases it back from the buyer.

The lessee participates in a sale and leaseback (1) to obtain cash from the asset while continuing to use it and (2) to decrease future tax payments. The lessee's future tax payments decline when the arrangement involves either equipment that has been completely depreciated or land. Neither fully depreciated assets nor land provides any tax shelter. Leasing these assets, however, provides tax-deductible lease payments. The lessor receives title to the asset and earns a rate of return on the investment.

EXAMPLE

Casey Appliances owns a building constructed in 19X4 for $10,000,000. The building has a $60,000,000 replacement value but is depreciated on its low historical cost. Casey wants to take advantage of the building's increased value and

---

[1]Financial Accounting Standards Board *Statement No. 13* deals with the accounting procedures required to capitalize leases. This *Statement* applies to the financial reporting and not to the tax deductibility of lease payments.

also continue to occupy it. Casey accomplishes its objectives by entering into a sale-and-leaseback arrangement with the State University Endowment Fund. The lessee receives $60,000,000 for the building but must pay the fund $5,620,714 per year for 25 years.

In the above example the Fund buys the building for $60,000,000, then leases it back to Casey at an annual rental of $5,620,714 for 25 years; Casey pays all upkeep and taxes. The annuity formed by these payments provides a yield of 8 percent per year and returns the Fund's entire investment with profit over the 25-year period.[2] Casey gets $60,000,000 in cash (before considering taxes on the gain), continued use of its building, and a $5,620,714 tax deduction annually because of its rental payments.

Sale-and-leaseback arrangements are often leveraged leases. A **leveraged lease** is a lease in which a third party loans money to the lessor. For example, Leasco Inc. may agree to lease a jumbo jet to Delta Air Lines. If Leasco puts up 25 percent of the cost and borrows 75 percent from Chase Manhattan Bank, then the financing arrangement is a leveraged lease. From the lessee's viewpoint, there is no apparent difference between a leveraged and a nonleveraged lease. A leveraged lease, however, may result in lower lease payments. Competition among lessors may force the lessor to pass to the lessee a portion of the tax savings from the interest payments on the money borrowed to buy the asset.

leveraged lease

Lease in which the lessor acquires the asset partly with borrowed money.

Service Leases.   The second major type of capital lease is the **service lease**, which includes both financing and executory services provided by the lessor. In a service lease the lessor is assured that taxes are paid and the asset is adequately insured and maintained. Although some capital leases include executory services, most service leases are properly classified as operating leases.

service lease

Lease in which the lessor provides financing and other services to the lessee.

Operating Leases

An **operating lease** is a rental agreement in which effective ownership and use of the asset are separate. Typically, the lessee uses the asset for a short period of time relative to its useful life. Because the lease period is relatively short, an operating lease does not convey, in substance, the rights of ownership.

An operating lease is called *off-balance-sheet financing* because the lessee does not report it as a liability. This practice causes the lessee's balance sheet to understate liabilities and assets. As a consequence, the lessee's total asset turnover (sales/total assets) will be overstated. Profitability and debt ratios will also be affected. Careful analysis of financial statements requires consideration of the effects of operating leases.

Figure 20.2 shows lease information disclosed in the *Annual Report* of AT&T. It presents information regarding both capital and operating leases in a footnote appended to its financial statements. The footnote shows the total rental commitments and their distribution between capital and operating leases. The

operating lease

Rental agreement that does *not* provide effective ownership of an asset; financial effects of the lease are *not* shown on the lessee's balance sheet (off-balance-sheet financing).

[2]Use a calculator or Appendix B.4 to find the 8 percent annual rate of return:

$$\$60,000,000 = \$5,620,714(\text{PVIFA}_{i,25})$$

$$10.6748 = \text{PVIFA}_{i,25}$$

Appendix B.4 shows that the annual rate of return associated with an n of 25 and PVIFA of 10.6748 is 8 percent.

FIGURE 20.2

Footnote Disclosure of AT&T's Capital and Operating Leases

AT&T leases land, buildings, and equipment through contracts that expire in various years through 2008. Future minimum lease payments due under noncancelable leases at December 31, 1992, are as follows:

	Capital Leases	Operating Leases
		(Millions)
1993	$126	$ 780
1994	111	564
1995	66	447
1996	32	328
1997	22	277
Later years	4	1,280
Total minimum lease payments	**$361**	**$3,676**
Less: Estimated executory cost	1	
Imputed interest	58	
Present value of net minimum lease payments	**$302**	

Source: AT&T 1992 Annual Report, Note I.

present value of the capital lease commitments is $302 million, which AT&T shows as a long-term asset and a long-term liability (less the portion due within one year, a current liability). The larger operating-lease commitments ($3,676 million vs. $361 million, undiscounted) are not capitalized on AT&T's balance sheet.

ADVANTAGES OF LEASING

Leasing assets instead of owning them can potentially reduce a company's costs and increase shareholder wealth. The lessor may be economically powerful and therefore able to purchase or manufacture an asset at a low price. If the lessee lacks the equivalent economic power, then the lessor may be able to acquire the asset and pass part of the savings to the lessee through reduced rental payments.

Allied Transport Company is considering buying a truck for $84,000. U.S. Leasing Inc. purchases 100 trucks each year, which it then leases to other companies and individuals. Because it buys trucks in large quantities, U.S. Leasing pays $75,000 per truck. If U.S. Leasing will pass on part of the $9,000 ($84,000 − $75,000) savings to Allied through reduced rental charges, then leasing a truck may be less costly than owning it.

Leasing reduces the uncertainty surrounding a lessee's expected cash flows by transferring to the lessor the task of estimating the disposal value of the leased asset. A lessor who repeatedly handles specific types of assets may be in a better position than the lessee to estimate an accurate disposal value. Moreover, the lessor may be able to lease used, outmoded assets. Thus the lessor is able to avoid the costs of obsolescence that a lessee would face.

The flexibility of leasing enables the lessee (1) to acquire use of an asset for exactly the time period it is needed and (2) to upgrade the asset if necessary. Many leases contain a cancellation clause permitting the lessee to enter into a new contract with the lessor or to return the equipment and cancel the contract. Such a clause is negotiable and usually comes at a cost in capital leases (cancellation costs often are zero in operating leases). For example, the clause permitting Allied Transport Company to cancel its lease with U.S. Leasing in the example above may call for a $15,000 payment if cancellation occurs during the first three years of the contract. Although cancellation comes at a cost to Allied Transport, this cost may be small compared with being stuck with an unneeded or inefficient truck.

Depreciation rules also provide an advantage to lessees. A company cannot depreciate land for tax purposes. It can, however, deduct lease payments for the use of land. Thus by leasing land the lessee gets a tax deduction that would not accompany ownership. Offsetting this advantage, however, the lessee loses any future appreciation in land values and improvements to the property.

Lease agreements do not include protective covenants, which can be an advantage to some companies. Unlike banks providing term loans, lessors maintain ownership of leased assets and can take possession quickly in the event that lessees default on payments. Whether or not the absence of protective covenants produces a net benefit to the lessee depends on the cost of the lease. If lease payments are high, then the advantage may be totally offset. A financial manager must weigh the lease cost against all of the purported advantages of a lease to determine whether leasing an asset is more beneficial to shareholders than owning.

FINANCIAL ANALYSIS OF LEASING

Capital and operating leases use up a lessee's debt capacity, as do term loans from banks. Agreeing to a lease obligates a lessee to a series of payments similar to the debt-service payments on a loan. The present value of the financial portion of lease payments represents the loan equivalent to the lease.[3] Leasing an asset is therefore a substitute for buying it with borrowed money.

Leasing offers the advantage of tax deductibility of lease payments, but borrowing to buy offers the advantage of tax deductibility of interest and depreciation expenses. Often the greatest attraction of buying an asset lies in the expectation of a large residual cash flow. For example, land and buildings may cost $1,000,000 today and, thanks to inflation, have a $3,000,000 value after a generation of use. A company buying these assets would have enjoyed both their full use and a large capital gain. Best of all, it would be assured of continued possession at no added cost. By contrast, a company leasing the land and buildings for 25 years would end up with nothing but a file of rent receipts. If at the end of 25 years the company wished to renew the lease, it would likely find rental payments tripled.

---

[3] Each year the lessee reduces the capitalized lease liability and leasehold improvement (asset) by the amount of *principal* included in each payment. For example, a 3-year lease of a $50,000 asset with payments of $4,728 at the end of each quarter would have an amortization schedule like the one in Table 20.1. At the end of Year 2 (Quarter 8) the lessee will have an asset and a liability of $18,003.

Analysis of Leasing vs. Borrowing to Buy

The financial analysis of a lease is the same irrespective of the type of lease. It makes no difference whether you analyze a capital lease or an operating lease, one with or without maintenance, or one with or without a cancellation clause. The analysis consists of measuring the impact of the lease on the company's cash flows and comparing that impact with the cash flows from borrowing to buy the asset.

Before working through an example, consider the four major steps in the analysis of leasing vs. borrowing to buy:[4]

1. Calculate the after-tax interest rate on an equivalent bank loan having the same maturity as the lease. Use this rate to discount all future cash flows.

2. Calculate the cost of leasing. Determine the present value of the after-tax lease payments. Include the effects of executory costs and purchase option, if present.

3. Calculate the cost of borrowing to buy. Determine the purchase price of the asset plus the present value of after-tax costs for maintenance, insurance, and other nonfinancial costs. Subtract from this amount the present value of the tax savings from depreciation and the present value of the after-tax disposal cash flow.

4. Compare the present value from Step 2 (leasing) with the present value from Step 3 (borrowing to buy) and choose the alternative with the lower cost.

Using these steps, we analyze in the following section whether leasing or borrowing to buy is a better choice for Calvert Company.

Application of Leasing Analysis

Calvert Company is considering leasing equipment for three years as an alternative to borrowing to buy it. The lease calls for three annual payments of $9,967 to be made at the beginning of each year. U.S. Leasing, the lessor, will maintain and insure the equipment to protect its investment. In response to Calvert's query, the lessor says that maintenance and insurance average $600 annually. The lessor offers a purchase option: Calvert may purchase the equipment for $700 at the end of Year 3. Calvert's management expects the equipment's disposal value at that time to be $15,000.

Calvert Company's purchasing manager finds equipment that the company can purchase for $24,000. A call to Chase Chemical Bank establishes that a 3-year loan for the equipment is available at 12.86 percent effective annual interest. Calvert has its own maintenance department with enough excess capacity to service the equipment, so the marginal maintenance expense is zero. A local insurance company will insure the equipment for $1,500 annually, with payments to be made at the beginning of each year.

Calvert Company will depreciate the equipment for tax purposes using the straight-line method with the half-year convention. The company's marginal tax rate, including state income taxes, is 30 percent.

---

[4]There are several methods for evaluating leases. For a discussion of alternatives, see Richard S. Bower, "Issues in Lease Financing," *Financial Management*, Winter 1973, 25–34.

Step 1. *Discount Rate.* Determine the after-tax interest rate on a loan equivalent to the lease:

$$\text{After-tax borrowing rate} = 0.1286 \times (1 - 0.30)$$
$$= 0.09, \text{ or } 9\%$$

Step 2. *Lease Analysis.*

a. Calvert's financial manager discounts at 9 percent the after-tax cost of the financial portion of the lease payments. The after-tax financial portion of each lease payment is $6,557, calculated as follows:

$$\text{After-tax payment} = (\$9,967 - \$600) \times (1 - 0.30)$$
$$= \$6,557$$

The present value of the annuity due formed by these payments is:[5]

$$\text{PVA(Due)} = \$6,557(\text{PVIFA}_{9\%,3})(1 + 0.09)$$
$$= \$6,557(2.5313)(1.09)$$
$$= \$18,092$$

b. The present value of after-tax maintenance and insurance, $420 [$600 (1 − 0.30)], payable at the beginning of each year as part of the lease, is:[6]

$$\text{PVA(Due)} = \$420(2.5313)(1.09)$$
$$= \$1,159$$

c. Calvert has a purchase option in the leasing agreement. The expected net gain from the option is:

Expected disposal value	$15,000
Less purchase option price	700
Expected net gain	$14,300

Assuming that Calvert will liquidate the equipment for $15,000, the company pays taxes of $4,290 on the gain:

Expected net gain	$14,300
Multiplied by tax rate (30%)	× 0.30
Taxes	$ 4,290

Net cash flow from the purchase option is the disposal value less the cash required to exercise the option and the tax payment:

Cash inflow		$15,000
Less cash outflows		
Option price	$ 700	
Taxes	4,290	4,990
Net cash flow		$10,010

The present value of the net cash flow expected at the end of Year 3 discounted at 9 percent is $7,730 = $10,010(0.7722).

---

[5] See Chapter 4 for a discussion of an annuity due.

[6] If the lessor allowed the lessee to take care of maintenance, then maintenance cost would be zero because of the lessee's excess capacity.

d. The net cash flows of the leasing arrangement appear on a time line as follows:

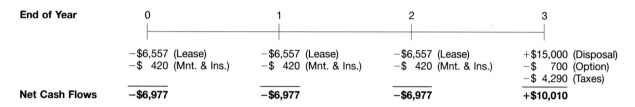

End of Year	0	1	2	3
	−$6,557 (Lease)	−$6,557 (Lease)	−$6,557 (Lease)	+$15,000 (Disposal)
	−$ 420 (Mnt. & Ins.)	−$ 420 (Mnt. & Ins.)	−$ 420 (Mnt. & Ins.)	−$ 700 (Option)
				−$ 4,290 (Taxes)
Net Cash Flows	−$6,977	−$6,977	−$6,977	+$10,010

The cost of the leasing alternative to Calvert is the present value of the net cash flows shown on the time line:

$$\text{Cost of leasing} = \frac{-\$6,977}{(1 + 0.09)^0} + \frac{-\$6,977}{(1 + 0.09)^1} + \frac{-\$6,977}{(1 + 0.09)^2} + \frac{+\$10,010}{(1 + 0.09)^3}$$

$$= -\$11,521$$

Equivalently, the cost of leasing is the sum of the individual present values:

Present value of after-tax lease payments	($18,092)
Add present value of after-tax maintenance and insurance	(1,159)
Less present value of purchase option	7,730
Cost of leasing	($11,521)

Step 3. *Borrowing to Buy.*

a. First, consider the after-tax debt-service payments on the loan discounted at the after-tax borrowing rate. Discounting the debt-service payments leads to the purchase price, as Figure 20.1 illustrates earlier in the chapter. Thus no calculation is necessary, and this part of the cost of borrowing to buy is the purchase price, $24,000.

b. Add to the purchase price the present value of the after-tax costs of maintenance and insurance. Calvert Company's only marginal cost is the after-tax cost of insurance, $1,050 [$1,500 × (1 − 0.30)], because the company has excess capacity in its maintenance department. The present value of the insurance cost discounted at 9 percent is $2,897:

$$\text{PVA(Due)} = \$1,050(\text{PVIFA}_{9\%,3})(1 + 0.09)$$

$$= \$1,050(2.5313)(1.09)$$

$$= \$2,897$$

c. Calculate next the present value of the tax savings from depreciation expense (depreciation tax savings, or DTS). Table 20.3 shows the annual depreciation expense using straight line with the half-year convention and a 3-year life. Column 5 contains the tax savings for each year, which we discount at the 9 percent rate and assume to occur at the end of each year. The present value of DTS is calculated for only 3 years to make buying and leasing cover the same 3-year period:

$$\text{Present value of DTS} = \frac{\$1,200}{(1 + 0.09)^1} + \frac{\$2,400}{(1 + 0.09)^2} + \frac{\$2,400}{(1 + 0.09)^3}$$

$$= \$1,101 + \$2,020 + \$1,853$$

$$= \$4,974$$

TABLE 20.3   **Tax Savings from Depreciation (Straight Line with Half-Year Convention)**

(1) Year	(2) Depreciable Basis	(3) Rate	(2) × (3) = (4) Depreciation	(4) × 0.30 = (5) Tax Savings (End of Year)
1	$24,000	$(\frac{1}{3})/2$	$ 4,000	$1,200
2	24,000	$\frac{1}{3}$	8,000	2,400
3	24,000	$\frac{1}{3}$	8,000	2,400
4	24,000	$(\frac{1}{3})/2$	4,000	1,200
		1.00	$24,000	

The present value of the depreciation tax savings ($4,974) reduces the cost of buying, and Calvert Company receives it only with the purchase of the equipment.

d. The final cash flow comes from the $15,000 disposal value of the equipment. If Calvert Company sells the equipment at the end of Year 3, it will pay taxes on the gain at the ordinary-income rate:

Expected disposal value		$15,000
Less book value at end of Year 3		
Purchase price	$24,000	
Less accumulated depreciation	20,000	
		4,000
Gain on sale		$11,000
Multiplied by tax rate (30%)		× 0.30
Taxes		$ 3,300

The disposal cash flow is calculated as follows:

Cash inflow	$15,000
Less cash outflow (taxes)	3,300
Disposal cash flow	$11,700

The present value of the disposal cash flow expected at the end of Year 3 and discounted at 9 percent is $9,035 = $11,700(0.7722).

e. The net cash flows from borrowing to buy the equipment appear on a time line as follows:

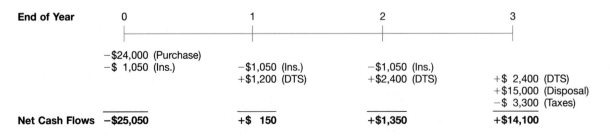

The cost of borrowing to buy the equipment is the present value of the net cash flows shown on the time line:

$$\text{Cost of borrowing} \atop \text{to buy} = \frac{-\$25,050}{(1 + 0.09)^0} + \frac{+\$150}{(1 + 0.09)^1}$$

$$+ \frac{+\$1,350}{(1 + 0.09)^2} + \frac{+\$14,100}{(1 + 0.09)^3}$$

$$= -\$12,888$$

Equivalently, the cost of borrowing and buying is the sum of the individual present values:

Purchase price	($24,000)
Add present value of maintenance and insurance	(2,897)
Less present value of depreciation tax savings	4,974
Less present value of disposal cash flow	9,035
Cost of borrowing to buy	($12,888)

Step 4.   Should Calvert Company lease or borrow to buy the equipment? The answer is clear: Calvert should lease because its cost is less than the alternative— $11,521 vs. $12,888. If Calvert leases the equipment rather than borrowing to buy it, then shareholder wealth will be greater by the difference between the two costs, $1,367:

Cost of borrowing to buy	$12,888
Less cost of leasing	11,521
Advantage to leasing	$ 1,367

Notice that the purchase option strongly influences the decision. First, it determines the time period used in the analysis. Even though the useful life of the equipment may extend beyond the time at which the lessee may exercise the purchase option, the option period (3 years) is used in the analysis. Second, the option value influences the final decision. Without the option, the cost of leasing becomes $19,251 ($18,092 + $1,159). Under this condition, Calvert Company should borrow to buy the equipment because its cost would be less than the cost of leasing ($12,888 vs. $19,251).

Finally, Calvert's financial manager should realize that the Internal Revenue Service may disallow the lease because the $700 option price is far lower than the $15,000 expected disposal value. The IRS may claim that the bargain option price enables the lessor to charge excessive lease payments, which in turn gives the lessee excessive tax deductions in the early years. Only if the IRS requirements for a "true lease" are met will the analysis of cash flows likely lead to the correct decision and the maximization of shareholder wealth.

SUMMARY

• A term loan is a multiyear business loan that the borrower repays in periodic installments to the lender: a commercial bank, life insurance company, or finance company. Companies use term loans to finance permanent additions to working capital and fixed assets.

• The effective interest rate on a term loan is the discount rate that equates the present value of debt-service payments to the loan proceeds. The after-tax cost of a term loan is less than its before-tax cost because interest is tax deductible.

A Tax Boost to Leasing

The Tax Reform Act of 1986 gave a big boost to the leasing industry by making it more attractive for individuals and corporations to lease assets.

When Congress enacted the new tax law, it eliminated the tax deductibility of interest paid by individuals on car loans. (Lease payments made by individuals have never been tax deductible unless the car is used for business purposes.) The elimination of interest deductions increases the relative cost of individual borrowing to buy in comparison with leasing.

The Tax Reform Act of 1986 also introduced an alternative minimum tax on corporations, which had the side effect of boosting lease activity. The tax law provides for an alternative minimum tax (AMT) equal to 20 percent of half the difference between the income reported in a company's

tax return and that reported in its financial statements (book income). The company must pay the AMT if it is more than the tax on taxable income.

When companies buy equipment, they often use straight-line depreciation (without the half-year convention) for financial reporting and the modified accelerated cost recovery system (MACRS) for tax reporting (see Chapter 8). MACRS procedures make for higher depreciation and lower taxable income during the early years of an asset's life, which widens the gap between taxable and book income. This gap may lead to higher taxes when the Internal Revenue Service applies the AMT rule.

Leasing equipment reduces the gap and lessens the alternative minimum tax because lease payments are the same on a company's tax return and financial statements. For example, a com-

pany may buy airplanes worth $100,000,000 and deduct $20,000,000 in depreciation using MACRS and $8,000,000 using straight line. A $12,000,000 gap occurs between taxable and book income, which subjects the company to an AMT of $1,200,000, calculated as shown in the table.

By leasing the airplanes, the company applies the same dollar deduction for rent on both sets of books. There is no gap and no AMT.

As you might expect, lessors were quick to promote the leasing implications of the Tax Reform Act. An executive of BankAmerilease, a unit of BankAmerica Corporation in San Francisco, chortled, "Buying equipment is a sure-fire way to trigger the AMT trap." BankAmerilease expected its leasings to increase substantially as a result of the change in tax law.

MACRS depreciation	$20,000,000
Less straight-line depreciation	8,000,000
Excess of book income over taxable income	$12,000,000
Multiplied by 0.50	× 0.50
Half the difference between the incomes	$ 6,000,000
Multiplied by AMT 20% rate	× 0.20
Alternative minimum tax	$ 1,200,000

Source: Based on a report in *The Wall Street Journal*, May 29, 1986, 1; and Lee Barton, "Surprise Loophole: Firms Expect Leasing to Save Them Millions under the New Tax Law," *The Wall Street Journal*, Mar. 11, 1987, 1.

After-tax debt-service payments discounted at the after-tax interest rate equal the principal of the loan. Before-tax debt-service payments discounted at the before-tax interest rate also equal the principal of the loan.

• Capital (financial) leases and operating leases are the two major types of leasing arrangements. A capital lease is a rental agreement in which the lessee acquires a substantial portion of the benefits and risks associated with owning the asset. The lessee records capital leases on the balance sheet. Net and service leases are two types of capital leases. An operating lease is a rental agreement that does not provide effective ownership of an asset. An operating lease is called off-balance-sheet financing because the lessee discloses its effects only in a footnote to the balance sheet.

• Leasing potentially offers the lessee several financial advantages relative to ownership. If lessors provide services at costs lower than the lessee can provide itself, then leasing is advantageous. In many cases lessors have more economic power than do lessees, and lessors, by sharing the benefits of this power reduce a lessee's costs. Lessors specializing in particular assets may have better information about the disposal value of the asset, thereby reducing risk. Lessors may be able to lease outmoded assets, thereby reducing the costs of obsolescence below the costs that lessees would face. Many leases contain cancellation clauses, which permit the lessee to respond to changes in production technology by canceling the lease and acquiring new assets.

• A complete analysis of the decision to lease or borrow to buy an asset is complicated. All cash flows in the analysis are discounted at the after-tax interest rate on a loan equivalent to the lease. The cost of leasing is the present value of the after-tax financial portion of the lease payments and the costs of executory services less the present value of the cash flow from exercising the purchase option. The cost of borrowing to buy is the asset purchase price plus the present value of costs of services equivalent to those provided in the lease; from this sum are subtracted the present value of the tax savings of depreciation and the disposal cash flow. The financial manager selects the alternative with the lower cost.

Key Terms

term loan	executory costs	service lease
lessee	net lease	operating lease
lessor	sale and leaseback	
capital lease	leveraged lease	

Questions

20.1. Describe the major characteristics of a term loan.

20.2. The costs of term loans differ from the costs of short-term loans. Briefly discuss why term loans typically have higher interest costs than do short-term loans.

20.3. Commercial banks have been aggressively making term loans and leasing arrangements, which have increased the maturity of their assets. Checkable deposits and other short-term deposits are the major sources of financing for banks. Some corporate treasurers see this move by banks as a threat to banking liquidity. Explain how such a policy might be a threat. (*Hint:* Recall the matching principle from Chapter 11.)

20.4. The following examples illustrate affirmative covenants and negative covenants in a typical term-loan contract:

Affirmative Covenants

• Borrower will submit monthly financial statements.

• Borrower will maintain adequate insurance.

Negative Covenants

• Borrower will not allow the debt-equity ratio to exceed 1.50.

• Borrower will not allow the current ratio to be less than 1.70.

a. What is the basic difference between an affirmative covenant and a negative covenant?

b. Which type of covenant—affirmative or negative—is more likely to cause trouble for the borrower?

20.5. Assume that you are the CFO of a company planning to apply for a 5-year term loan of $1,000,000. Describe the information that you will supply to the bank's corporate loan officer.

20.6. There are two major types of leases, capital and operating. List the distinctive characteristics of each type of lease, and comment on the off-balance-sheet financing provided by one of them.

20.7. Which of the following statements concerning leases is false?
   a. Restrictive covenants included in loan agreements are usually not found in lease agreements.
   b. Lessees may deduct lease payments for tax purposes.
   c. Lease financing has no effect on a company's ability to borrow money.

   Explain your choice.

20.8. "Leasing real estate effectively allows a company to depreciate land." In what sense is this statement true? Illustrate your answer by discussing a sale and leaseback.

20.9. "Leasing assets increases the instability of a company's earnings." Do you agree with this statement? Explain why or why not.

20.10. When financial managers analyze leasing vs. borrowing to buy an asset, what factors should they consider in the analysis?

Strategy Problem

The financial manager of Areff Distributing has been asked by the chief executive officer to determine whether the company should lease or buy two Peterbilt trucks for the company to use in hauling electronic equipment between its manufacturing facilities in Atlanta and its stores in New Orleans, Dallas, and Phoenix. If Areff buys the trucks, it must pay $167,271. The trucks will be depreciated for tax purposes using the straight-line method with the half-year convention and a 5-year life. The company has located a source that will maintain and insure both trucks for $12,000 annually, with payments at the beginning of each year.

Leasco Industry of Des Moines, Iowa, will lease the trucks to Areff for $70,000 annually for 3 years, with lease payments at the beginning of each year. Leasco will also maintain and insure the trucks. In response to a query from Areff's financial manager, Leasco agrees to reduce the lease payments by $6,800 if Areff will maintain and

insure the trucks. As added inducement, Leasco offers Areff an option to buy the trucks for $22,000 at the end of the contract (end of Year 3). Areff's financial manager expects the trucks to have a market value of $87,000 at that time.

Instead of leasing, Areff can take out a term loan from the Atlanta State Bank and Trust to purchase the trucks. The bank will make the loan for prime plus $3\frac{1}{8}$ percentage points. The prime rate is presently 9 percent, and the financial manager expects that it will stay at 9 percent for the life of the loan. The company is in the 34 percent marginal tax bracket.

Calculate the costs of leasing the trucks and of borrowing to buy them. Based on your analysis, which of the financing methods is better for Areff shareholders?

Strategy	Solution

Solution

1. Calculate Areff's after-tax borrowing rate and use it to discount cash flows:

Adjust the borrowing rate for percentage premium and tax deductibility.

$$\text{After-tax borrowing rate} = (0.09 + 0.03125)(1 - 0.34)$$

$$= 0.08, \text{ or } 8\%$$

2. Calculate the cost of leasing by discounting the after-tax cash flows: (a) financial portion of the lease payment, (b) cost of executory services (maintenance and insurance), and (c) gain on the purchase option.
   a. Financial portion of the lease payment: $63,200 = $70,000 − $6,800.

Adjust for tax deductibility and use annuity-due equation.

$$\text{PVA(Due)} = \$63,200(1 - 0.34)(\text{PVIFA}_{8\%, \, 3})(1 + 0.08)$$

$$= \$41,712(2.5771)(1.08)$$

$$= \$116,096$$

   b. Cost of executory services: $6,800.

Adjust for tax deductibility and use annuity-due equation.

$$\text{PVA(Due)} = \$6,800(1 - 0.34)(\text{PVIFA}_{8\%, \, 3})(1 + 0.08)$$

$$= \$4,488(2.5771)(1.08)$$

$$= \$12,491$$

   c. Gain on purchase option: Option price = $22,000; value of trucks = $87,000.

Calculate expected net gain.	Expected disposal value	$87,000
	Less purchase option price	22,000
	Expected net gain	$65,000
	Multiplied by tax rate (34%)	× 0.34
Calculate dollar taxes.	Taxes	$22,100
Calculate net cash flow.	Cash inflow	$87,000
	Less cash outflows	

Option price	$22,000	
Taxes	22,100	44,100
Net cash flow		$42,900

Calculate the present value.

$$\text{Present value of net cash flow} = \$42,900/(1 + 0.08)^3 = \$34,055$$

d. Leasing cash flows on a time line:

End of
Year

	0	1	2	3
	$-$41,712 (Lease)$ $-$ 4,488 (Mnt. & Ins.)$	$-$41,712 (Lease)$ $-$ 4,488 (Mnt. & Ins.)$	$-$41,712 (Lease)$ $-$ 4,488 (Mnt. & Ins.)$	$+$42,900 (Disposal)$
Net Cash Flows	**$-$46,200$**	**$-$46,200$**	**$-$46,200$**	**$+$42,900$**

The cost of leasing is the present value of the net cash flows.

$$\text{Cost of leasing} = \frac{-\$46,200}{(1 + 0.08)^0} + \frac{-\$46,200}{(1 + 0.08)^1} + \frac{-\$46,200}{(1 + 0.08)^2} + \frac{+\$42,900}{(1 + 0.08)^3}$$

$$= -\$46,200 - \$42,778 - \$39,609 + \$34,055$$

$$= -\$94,532$$

Alternatively, calculate the cost of leasing as follows:

Present value of financial portion of payments	($116,096)
Add present value of maintenance and insurance	(12,491)
Less present value of purchase option	34,055
Cost of leasing	($ 94,532)

3. Calculate the cost of borrowing to buy the trucks by discounting the after-tax cash flows: (a) purchase price, (b) cost of maintenance and insurance, (c) depreciation tax savings, and (4) disposal cash flow.

Begin with purchase price.

a. Purchase price: After-tax debt-service payments discounted at the after-tax interest rate is $167,271, the purchase price.

Adjust for tax deductibility and use annuity-due equation.

b. After-tax cost of maintenance and insurance: $7,920 = $12,000(1 − 0.34).

$$\text{PVA(Due)} = \$7,920(\text{PVIFA}_{8\%, 3})(1 + 0.08)$$

$$= \$7,920(2.5771)(1.08)$$

$$= \$22,043$$

c. Depreciation tax savings:

Construct a depreciation schedule; adjust for half-year convention.

(1) Year	(2) Depreciable Basis	(3) Rate	(2) × (3) = (4) Depreciation	(4) × 0.34 = (5) Tax Savings (End of Year)
1	$167,271	$(\tfrac{1}{5})/2$	$16,727	$ 5,687
2	167,271	$\tfrac{1}{5}$	33,454	11,374
3	167,271	$\tfrac{1}{5}$	33,454	11,374
4	167,271	$\tfrac{1}{5}$	33,454	11,374
5	167,271	$\tfrac{1}{5}$	33,454	11,374
6	167,271	$(\tfrac{1}{5})/2$	16,727	5,687

Calculate the present value of depreciation tax savings (DTS) for the first 3 years, the planning horizon of the analysis:

Use only the years prior to the purchase option.

$$\text{Present value of DTS} = \frac{\$5,687}{(1 + 0.08)^1} + \frac{\$11,374}{(1 + 0.08)^2} + \frac{\$11,374}{(1 + 0.08)^3}$$

$$= \$5,266 + \$9,751 + \$9,029$$

$$= \$24,046$$

d. Disposal cash flow:

Expected disposal value		$87,000
Less book value		
Purchase price	$167,271	
Less accumulated depreciation	83,635	
		83,636
Gain on sale		$ 3,364
Multiplied by tax rate (34%)		× 0.34
Taxes		$ 1,144

Use the book value at time of exercising the option.

Calculate dollar taxes.

Calculate disposal cash flow.

Cash inflow	$87,000
Less cash outflow (taxes)	1,144
Disposal cash flow	$85,856

Calculate the present value.

Present value of disposal cash flow = $85,856/(1 + 0.08)^3

$$= \$68,155$$

e. Borrowing-to-buy cash flows on a time line:

End of Year	0	1	2	3
	−$167,271 (Purchase)	+$5,687 (DTS)	+$11,374 (DTS)	+$11,374 (DTS)
	−$ 7,920 (Mnt. & Ins.)	−$7,920 (Mnt. & Ins.)	−$ 7,920 (Mnt. & Ins.)	+$85,856 (Disposal)
Net Cash Flows	−$175,191	−$2,233	+$ 3,454	+$97,230

The cost of borrowing to buy is the present value of net cash flows.

$$\text{Cost of borrowing to buy} = \frac{-\$175,191}{(1 + 0.08)^0} + \frac{-\$2,233}{(1 + 0.08)^1} + \frac{+\$3,454}{(1 + 0.08)^2} + \frac{+\$97,230}{(1 + 0.08)^3}$$

$$= -\$175,191 - \$2,068 + \$2,961 + \$77,185$$

$$= -\$97,113$$

Alternatively, calculate the cost of borrowing to buy as follows:

Purchase price	($167,271)
Add present value of maintenance and insurance	(22,043)
Less present value of depreciation tax savings	24,046
Less present value of disposal cash flow	68,155
Cost of borrowing to buy	($ 97,113)

4. Should Areff lease or borrow to buy the trucks? Although it is a close call, Areff should lease the trucks. Leasing provides an additional $2,581 to shareholder wealth in comparison with borrowing to buy:

Subtract the lower cost from the higher cost.

Cost of borrowing to buy	$97,113
Less cost of leasing	94,532
Advantage to leasing	$ 2,581

◆ **Demonstration Problem**

Booker Washington Inc. (BWI) manufactures and distributes sports apparel. To reduce the variable costs associated with its line of knit shirts, BWI plans to acquire a technologically advanced assembly machine. The machine is available for lease or purchase from the manufacturer based on the following terms:

> *Lease terms.* Leasing period, 3 years; beginning-of-year lease payments, $98,000—includes service contract for insurance and maintenance valued at $10,000 per year; purchase option at the end of Year 3, $40,000.
> *Purchase price.* $223,000.

If BWI purchases the machine, the company will depreciate it for tax purposes using the straight-line method with the half-year convention and a 3-year life. The machine can be sold for $50,000 at the end of 3 years. BWI has located a company that will insure and maintain the machine for $11,000 annually, payable at the beginning of each year. To purchase the machine, BWI will take out a term loan from a local bank at an effective annual rate of 10 percent. BWI's income tax rate is 40 percent.

a. What is a term loan? Describe the information provided in a term-loan contract.
b. State the primary differences between the following types of leases: (1) a capital lease and an operating lease; (2) a net lease and a service lease.
c. Calculate the present value of BWI's cost of leasing the machine.
d. Calculate the present value of BWI's cost of borrowing to buy the machine.
e. Should BWI lease or buy the machine? Explain.
f. What are the potential advantages of leasing an asset instead of owning it?

Problems

Present value of an ordinary annuity and annuity due

20.1. Calculate the present value of $85,000 per year for 9 years under the following conditions (the discount rate is 15 percent per year):
a. Payments occur at the *end* of each year.
b. Payments occur at the *beginning* of each year.

Effective interest rate on a term loan

20.2. A company needs $340,000 to acquire an asset. Union Finance Company will loan the company the money for 5 years at 10 percent compound annual interest. As part of the loan agreement, the company must pay $11,438 in origination and legal fees, payable on the day the company receives the loan proceeds. Calculate the effective interest rate on the loan.

Interest and principal of debt-service payments

20.3. Security National Bank loans $530,000 to Bentham Broadcasting Group. The loan is for 6 years at 12 percent compound annual interest. Calculate the annual debt-service payments assuming that Bentham Broadcasting must make equal annual payments. How much of the first payment goes for interest and how much for principal? How much of the second payment goes for interest and how much for principal?

Amortization schedule of a term loan

20.4. Bell Financial Services negotiates a 3-year, $720,000 term loan from the Sanford State Bank. The bank quotes an annual rate of 12 percent compounded semiannually and requires semiannual debt-service payments. Construct an amortization schedule for the loan.

Before- and after-tax payments

20.5. Bladen Inc. borrows $82,000 from the United National Bank. The loan is for 4 years at 10 percent compound annual interest. Equal payments are made at the end of each year, and Bladen is in the 40 percent marginal tax bracket.
a. Calculate the annual before-tax payments.
b. Calculate the after-tax payments in Years 1 through 4.
c. Calculate the after-tax interest rate on the loan.
d. Calculate the present value of (1) the after-tax payments discounted at the after-tax interest rate and (2) the before-tax payments discounted at the before-tax interest rate.

<table>
<tr><td>Interest rate implicit in a contract</td><td>20.6.</td><td>Malley Enterprises is considering whether or not it should enter into a contractual agreement to finance equipment. The manufacturer offers the equipment to Malley with 8-year financing and payments of $23,500 annually. The contract calls for payments at the end of each year. Malley's purchasing manager finds that the company can buy the equipment for $105,452 from an alternative source.</td></tr>
</table>

Interest rate implicit in a contract

20.6. Malley Enterprises is considering whether or not it should enter into a contractual agreement to finance equipment. The manufacturer offers the equipment to Malley with 8-year financing and payments of $23,500 annually. The contract calls for payments at the end of each year. Malley's purchasing manager finds that the company can buy the equipment for $105,452 from an alternative source.

   a. Calculate the interest rate implicit in the contract.

   b. Assuming the contract calls for payments at the beginning of each year, what is the implicit interest rate?

Interest rate implicit in a lease

20.7. Jackson Inc. leases several hydraulic jacks from Disden Suppliers. Lease payments are $24,000 annually for 4 years. Jackson must make lease payments at the beginning of each year. The hydraulic jacks wear out after 4 years, and Jackson can purchase them today for $79,719 from an alternative source.

   a. What is the before-tax interest rate implicit in this lease?

   b. Jackson is in the 34 percent marginal tax bracket. Show its after-tax cost of leasing as a percentage rate.

Implicit interest rates

20.8. Marinay Company has found a machine that will produce substantial cost savings over the next 5 years. The company can acquire the machine by outright purchase for $240,000. Marinay could obtain a 5-year loan from a local bank to pay for the purchase. The bank would charge interest at an annual rate of 12 percent compounded quarterly on the outstanding balance of the loan. The loan would be repaid in quarterly installments due at the end of each quarter.

   A local financier heard of Marinay's need and offered the company an unusual proposition: She would advance the company $240,000 to purchase the machine. The company must sign a promissory note to pay her a lump sum of $504,082 at the end of 5 years.

   The manufacturer will finance the machine under a sales contract. Marinay would pay $70,000 at the beginning of each year for the 5-year period.

   a. Calculate the effective annual interest rate in each alternative.

   b. Which source of financing should Marinay use? Explain your choice.

Lease vs. borrow-to-buy analysis

20.9. Highlights Illuminating has decided to acquire a lighting display to use at automobile exhibitions during the next 2 years. The display can be purchased or it can be leased for a 2-year period. If purchased, the lighting display will require a $10,000 outlay, and Highlights Illuminating anticipates that maintenance will be $800 at the end of each year. The display has an expected $1,000 market value at the end of the 2-year period. The company will use straight-line depreciation with the half-year convention and a 3-year life for tax purposes. Highlights Illuminating is in the 34 percent marginal tax bracket, and no investment tax credit is available.

   Lumenescence Leasing offers to lease the lighting display to Highlights for $5,934 annually, with payments at the beginning of each of the 2 years. Lease payments include maintenance, and Lumenescence agrees to reduce each lease payment by $600 if Highlights Illuminating wants to provide its own maintenance. The lease has a $400 purchase option exercisable at the end of 2 years.

   Highlights Illuminating's financial manager calls the company's commercial bank and is told by a loan officer that the company can borrow up to $10,000 for 2 years at an effective interest rate of 8 percent annually.

   a. Should the display be leased or should it be purchased with borrowed money? Support your answer with analysis.

   b. Suppose that during negotiations Lumenescence Leasing cancels the purchase option. How does this cancellation affect the decision? Show all calculations necessary to support your answer.

CMA examination, modified: lease vs. borrow-to-buy analysis

20.10. LeToy Company produces a wide variety of children's toys, most of which are manufactured from stamped parts. One of the company's employees recommended that the company acquire a new stamping machine. The capital-budgeting committee concurred with the recommendation and assigned Ann Mitchum of the budget and planning department to supervise the acquisition and to analyze the alternative financing available.

After careful analysis and review, Ms. Mitchum has narrowed the financing of the project to two alternatives. The first alternative is a lease provided by American Midland Bank. The bank will lease the machine to LeToy for 5 years even though it has a useful economic life of 10 years. The lease agreement calls for LeToy to make annual payments of $62,000 at the beginning of each year. Included in the lease agreement is an $8,000 purchase option at the end of 5 years. The second alternative would be for LeToy to purchase the machine outright from the manufacturer for $240,000. Preliminary discussions with Bruton Bank & Trust, LeToy's local bank, indicate that LeToy would be able to finance the purchase with a 15 percent term loan. The company would depreciate the equipment for tax purposes using straight-line depreciation with the half-year convention and a 5-year life. Ms. Mitchum expects the market value of the machine to be $45,000 at the end of 5 years.

All maintenance, taxes, and insurance would be paid by LeToy under each alternative. LeToy is subject to a 34 percent marginal corporate income tax rate.
a. Which alternative should LeToy accept? Support your answer with analysis.
b. Suppose that during the negotiations the manufacturer increases the purchase option to $35,000. How does this change affect your choice of alternatives? Support your answer with analysis.

Computer Problem

Leasing: template LEASING

20.11. William Tilden started Tilden Trucking Co. 2 years ago with one truck. He believes that the time is ripe to buy another truck. Sheila Tilden, his wife and the company's accountant, suggested that he lease a truck instead of buying one. Mr. Tilden contacted 20th Century Leasing and was informed of the following terms and conditions:
(1) Annual lease payments payable at the beginning of each year: $32,000, including $4,000 for executory costs—insurance and maintenance.
(2) Purchase option at the end of Year 3: $20,000.
According to Mr. Tilden's estimate, the market value of the truck will be $50,000 at the end of Year 3.

If the company borrows money from the bank to purchase the truck, the bank will charge interest at 14 percent per year. The truck would cost $90,000. Insurance payments would be $3,000 per year payable at the beginning of the year. Maintenance expenses would be $1,500 per year payable at the end of the year to a truck repair company. The truck would be depreciated for tax purposes on a 3-year straight-line basis with the half-year convention. Tilden Trucking is in the 15 percent tax bracket.
a. Calculate the difference between the cost of leasing and borrowing to buy the truck. Interpret your solution.
b. Recalculate Part *a* using a marginal tax rate of 25 percent and 34 percent.
c. At what annual lease payment would Mr. Tilden be indifferent to buying or leasing? (Calculate to the nearest $100.)

Selected References

Ang, James, and Pamela Peterson. "The Leasing Puzzle." *Journal of Finance*, September 1984: 1055–1065.

Bierman, Harold, Jr. "Buy versus Lease with an Alternative Minimum Tax." *Financial Management*, Winter 1988: 87–91.

Copeland, Thomas E., and J. Fred Weston. "A Note on the Evaluation of Cancellable Operating Leases." *Financial Management*, Summer 1982: 60–67.

Hodges, Stewart D. "The Valuation of Variable Rate Leases." *Financial Management*, Spring 1985: 68–74.

Hull, John C. "The Bargaining Positions of the Parties to a Lease Agreement." *Financial Management*, Autumn 1982: 71–79.

Lewis, Craig M., and James S. Schallheim. "Are Debt and Leases Substitutes?" *Journal of Financial and Quantitative Analysis*, December 1992: 497–511.

McConnell, John J., and James S. Schallheim. "Valuation of Asset Leasing Contracts." *Journal of Financial Economics,* August 1983: 237–261.

Mukherjee, Tarun K. "A Survey of Corporate Leasing Analysis." *Financial Management,* Autumn 1991: 96–107.

Smith, Clifford W., Jr., and L. MacDonald Wakeman. "Determinants of Corporate Leasing Policy." *Journal of Finance,* July 1985: 895–908.

Sorensen, Ivar W., and Ramon E. Johnson. "Equipment Financial Leasing Practices and Costs: An Empirical Study." *Financial Management,* Spring 1977: 33–40.

Chapter 21

MERGER, REORGANIZATION, AND LIQUIDATION

Expansion and Contraction

- AT&T launched a hostile takeover of NCR Corp. and eventually gained control for $7.89 billion. NCR's management acquiesced after resisting the takeover for six months.
- Union Carbide created a new company through a $1.99 billion spinoff of its Praxair Inc. industrial-gas division. Union Carbide "set the business free" by distributing shares in the newly created company to Union Carbide shareholders.
- Lockheed Corp. paid $1.53 billion for General Dynamics' fighter-jet business. Reflecting ongoing consolidation in the defense industry, Martin Marietta Corp. announced its intention to buy General Electric Co.'s aerospace business for $3.05 billion.

Buying and selling companies often entails massive amounts of money, but not always. Consider the case of John Henning, president of Austin Electronics. National Gypsum owned the small manufacturer of fire-training equipment and offered to sell it to Mr. Henning for $6 million. Mr. Henning had only $100,000 to invest, which he got by mort-

gaging his house. Impressed by the potential buyer's managerial expertise and the manufacturer's business, Chase Manhattan Bank financed $4 million of the acquisition. National Gypsum financed most of the rest, and Mr. Henning became owner of the company, now called Symtron Systems Inc.

The Austin Electronics deal is called a leveraged buyout (LBO), in which a large part of the purchase price is financed with debt using the target company's assets as collateral. The most famous LBO is Kohlberg Kravis Robert's $25 billion purchase of RJR Nabisco. To service the large debt levels in LBOs, the new owners often find it necessary to divest (sell) corporate assets: subsidiaries, divisions, or product lines. In some cases divestitures are inadequate to the task, and the companies enter bankruptcy to reorganize or liquidate. Examples of LBOs gone wrong are Resorts International, Revco D.S. Inc., and Hillsborough Holdings.

Source: Randall Smith, "Merger Activity Falls for Fourth Straight Year But Some Say the Worst Is Finally Over," *The Wall Street Journal,* January 4, 1993, R8; Terri Thompson, "Engineering Your Own LBO," *U.S. News & World Report,* January 30, 1989, 74–76.

Merge. Reorganize. Liquidate. Divest. Acquire. These and other terms reflect the varied business activity always at work in the economy: some companies robust and growing, some fighting off takeover attempts by other companies, some making modest profits, some losing money, and others in bankruptcy. Such activity partly reflects the life cycle of a company, the concept that provides background for the two principal topics of this chapter: merger and bankruptcy. Mature companies often find mergers and acquisitions attractive solutions to declining markets and eroding market shares. In contrast, companies experiencing financial difficulties may find it necessary to file bankruptcy petitions, seeking court protection from creditors. In combination, merger and bankruptcy describe expansion and contraction in the life cycle of a company.

LIFE CYCLE OF A COMPANY

life cycle of a company
Stages of a company's existence from formation through decline.

Depicting the stages of business growth, the **life cycle of a company** suggests general trends during the company's existence. A typical life cycle consists of start-up, growth, maturity, and decline:

- In the start-up stage, management organizes production and begins to develop markets for the company's products. Cash and equity are scarce and earnings are low or negative.

- Sales and earnings grow rapidly during the growth stage, and short-term debt is high. To alleviate continued cash shortages, growth companies issue stocks and bonds to investors.

- The maturity stage is characterized by stable, high earnings and rising dividend payments. Cash is plentiful, the debt level is moderate, and mergers and acquisitions are attractive.

- In the decline stage the company's sales fall, and excess capacity develops. Earnings decline and growth rates become negative. Management may try to postpone decline through product innovation or mergers and acquisitions. Declaration of bankruptcy—reorganization or liquidation—becomes imminent.

This division of the economic history of a company into a life cycle was first described by Alfred Marshall, an early-twentieth-century economist. Unlike a person, who has no fountain of youth, a company can use techniques that prolong the growth stage. For example, Arm & Hammer increased the annual sales of its baking soda from $15,600,000 to $57,900,000 in five years as a result of advertising it for use as a refrigerator freshener. Johnson & Johnson increased the market for its shampoo by advertising it for use by adults as well as babies. Each of these companies prolonged the growth stage. In addition to internal growth from product innovation, many companies grow externally from mergers and acquisitions, the topic of the following section.

MERGERS AND ACQUISITIONS

When one company buys another company, it can proceed in various ways. For example, it may offer in payment cash or securities such as bonds, preferred stock, and common stock. Also, how companies join together may vary. A com-

The author thanks Professor James W. Wansley of the University of Tennessee for his contributions to this chapter.

merger
Combination of two or more companies into one company; corporate identity of only one company survives and the other companies cease to exist as legal entities.

consolidation
Combination of two or more companies to form a new company.

holding company
Parent company owns all of or a controlling interest in another company, the subsidiary.

hostile takeover
Acquisition fought and resisted by the management of the target company; usually involves a tender offer.

horizontal merger
Merger between companies in the same line of business.

Sherman Antitrust Act
Federal law, passed in 1890, making restraint of trade both a criminal and a civil violation.

conglomerate merger
Merger between companies in totally unrelated lines of business.

monplace way is the **merger**—a combination in which the acquiring company survives and the acquired company ceases to exist as a legal entity. To illustrate, the 1988 merger of Philip Morris and Kraft caused the legal disappearance of Kraft, with Philip Morris the surviving company. This merger may alternatively be called an acquisition because Philip Morris acquired Kraft. The terms *merger* and *acquisition* are often used interchangeably.

Unlike a merger, a **consolidation** causes both corporations to disappear and a new company to form. The 1986 combination of Burroughs and Sperry is an example of a consolidation. The newly created company is Unisys Corporation; Burroughs and Sperry no longer exist as independent corporations.

Another type of business combination is the **holding company**—the acquiring company buys all of or a controlling interest in another company's common stock. If the parent company owns at least 80 percent of the subsidiary's stock, then the dividends the parent receives are exempt from federal income taxes. For example, Associates Corporation of North America (with 1988 revenues of $1.6 billion) is a wholly owned subsidiary of Gulf & Western, the parent company. Gulf & Western does not pay income tax on dividends from Associates Corporation of North America.

Mergers and acquisitions can be friendly or hostile. Hostile ones occur despite the wishes of the target company's management and directors, and thus are called **hostile takeovers**. The target company, said to be "in play," is the one being acquired. Management of the acquiring company usually takes its bid directly to the shareholders of the target company. Takeover bids are *tender offers*, meaning that the acquiring company asks shareholders of the target company to tender (submit) their shares directly to the acquiring company. In a tender offer the acquirer offers to pay an above-market price directly to shareholders to circumvent opposition from management and directors of the target. To fend off advances, management of the target may seek a friendly partner (called a *white knight*) to take over the company. For example, Borg-Warner Corporation thwarted GAF's attempt in 1987 to acquire it by promoting and approving a tender offer by a group led by Merrill Lynch (acting as both investor and adviser). Borg-Warner shareholders ended up receiving more money from the Merrill Lynch group than they would have received had the acquisition attempt by GAF been successful.

Types of Mergers and Acquisitions

Mergers and acquisitions are often classified according to the relationship between the companies involved. For example, a merger between companies in the same line of business is called a **horizontal merger**. A wave of horizontal mergers took place from 1893 to 1904, resulting in the formation of giant monopolies such as Standard Oil and U.S. Steel (now USX Inc.). This merger wave ended when the U.S. Supreme Court ruled that the **Sherman Antitrust Act** prohibited not only collusion but also mergers that lead to monopoly power. A second wave of horizontal mergers took place from 1926 to 1930, resulting in oligopolies, where a few large companies dominated the product markets. This wave ended with the collapse of the securities markets and the depression of the 1930s. A different type of merger wave occurred from the mid-1950s to 1970. The combinations during this period were **conglomerate mergers**—companies merged with other companies in totally unrelated lines of business. For example, Ling-Temco-Vought Inc. was a conglomerate consisting of aerospace products, steel, airlines, and meat packing.

TABLE 21.1

Ten Large Corporate Mergers

Merging Companies[a]	Value (Billions)	Year
Kohlberg Kravis Roberts and RJR Nabisco	$25.0	1989
Philip Morris and Kraft	13.4	1988
Chevron and Gulf	13.3	1984
Texaco and Getty	10.1	1984
Reed International and Elsevier	9.3	1992
DuPont and Conoco	8.0	1981
British Petroleum and Standard Oil	7.8	1987
U.S. Steel and Marathon Oil	6.6	1982
Campeau and Federated	6.5	1988
General Electric and RCA	6.0	1986

[a] Acquiring company followed by the acquired company.

Source: The Wall Street Journal, Jan. 8, 1989, 1R; and Jan. 4, 1993, R8.

vertical merger
Merger between companies that have a supplier-customer relationship.

In the early 1980s a new wave began. This wave consisted, in large part, of **vertical mergers**—business combinations between suppliers and customers. For example, a steel company merged with a coal company, and a construction company merged with a forest products company. This wave was a result of two events: (1) the U.S. Justice Department's removal of antitrust rules against vertical mergers in 1982 and (2) the deregulation of specific industries (especially the airline and financial industries) beginning in 1978.

Recent mergers have involved extraordinary dollar amounts, dwarfing predecessors in this respect. Table 21.1 shows ten large mergers (acquisitions) since 1981.

Government Regulation

As in many other areas of business activity, federal and state laws impose regulations on mergers. Some observers believe that restrictions now in place are not strict enough, given the rash of takeovers in the 1980s, and some members of Congress feel inclined to impose further restrictions on takeover activity. A financial manager should be familiar with the legal environment surrounding mergers because of its financial implications.

Congress designed the U.S. antitrust laws to preserve competition in the American economic system. The Sherman Act was the first *antitrust law*—a law to curtail monopolistic power—and it made collusion to restrain trade both a criminal and a civil violation. The law provided that anyone injured by another's violation of the act could sue the offending party and, if the injury was established judicially, recover treble damages—three times the amount of the ascertained damage.

Clayton Act
Antitrust law prohibiting mergers that lessen competition or create monopoly.

Congress in 1914 supplemented the Sherman Act with the Clayton Act. The **Clayton Act** attacks antitrust activity through a preventive approach rather than the corrective approach of the Sherman Act. Part of the Clayton Act directly prohibits mergers that would "substantially lessen competition" or "tend to create" a monopoly. The Federal Trade Commission (FTC) enforces the Clayton Act, and if the FTC believes that an interstate business practice is collusive or monopolistic, then it may issue a cease and desist order to halt the activity. The

Justice Department will, at the FTC's direction, prosecute parties believed to be in violation of the Sherman and Clayton Acts.

Presently, neither the FTC nor the federal courts interpret literally the Sherman and Clayton Acts. Instead, they apply a *rule of reason*. This rule prohibits only actions that impose *unreasonable* restraints on trade, and the court determines what is unreasonable. In addition to the rule-of-reason doctrine, there are **per se violations** of the acts. Per se violations are actions in and of themselves proving the existence of a restraint of trade without regard to reasonableness. Examples of per se violations are: (1) *horizontal price fixing*—conspiring to set prices with companies in the same industry, and (2) *predatory pricing*—lowering prices with the intent of driving competition out of the market.

In contrast to the Sherman and Clayton Acts, which impose restrictions in product markets, the following laws impose restrictions in securities markets: (1) The *Williams Act* (1968) requires issuers of tender offers to disclose their plans for the target company. (2) The Securities and Exchange Commission requires investors who purchase 5 percent of a company's common stock to file Form 13d stating their intentions. (3) Beginning with Indiana in 1987, some states prohibit investors who acquire 20 percent of a company from voting their shares unless approval is given by the "disinterested" shareholders—everyone except company managers, directors, and the takeover investor. Together, these regulations effectively increase the barriers to hostile takeovers. The barriers increase the job security of incumbent management and lessen the competition for corporate control by different management teams.

per se violation

Action in and of itself proving an unreasonable restraint of trade.

Reasons for Mergers and Acquisitions

The primary financial rationale in favor of mergers and acquisitions is the creation of value. If the value of the combined shares is greater than the sum of the values before merging, then *synergy* exists between the two companies—the whole is greater than the sum of its parts when synergy exists. Think of a basketball team with individual players who are mediocre but who excel as a team. Synergy exists on that team, and synergies exist in some corporate mergers.

Synergy arises from two sources in a merger: *operating synergies* and *financial synergies*. Operating synergies include economies of scale, market power (and the possibility of monopolistic pricing), and increased efficiency. An example of an operating synergy is the elimination of duplicate support facilities by combining marketing, purchasing, and accounting functions. In addition to these direct benefits, the merger may reduce competition so that earnings before interest and taxes increase or become more stable.

Financial synergies result from three sources: tax benefits, reduced flotation costs, and the reduced probability of incurring bankruptcy costs. First, tax benefits occur because the U.S. tax code permits companies to apply operating losses in any one year against operating income in other years, thereby reducing taxes in profitable years; a company can carry a loss back three years and forward fifteen years, and the acquiring company may use the loss of the acquired company. Thus a highly profitable company may acquire a company with large accumulated tax losses and immediately turn those losses into tax savings. Second, the increased size of the combined companies may give them better access to capital markets and reduce flotation costs. Third, as long as the cash flows of the two merging companies are not perfectly correlated, the uncertainty of the cash flows after the merger will be less than the uncertainties of the pre-merger cash flows of the two independent companies. Merging the two companies produces a less volatile stream of cash flows, thereby reducing default risk and the probability of incurring bankruptcy costs.[1]

Diversification itself, in the absence of operating and financial synergies, is *not* a justifiable rationale for a merger. Shareholders can diversify their own portfolios by purchasing shares of different companies. Besides being superfluous, corporate diversification is more costly than shareholder diversification. It also decreases the ability of shareholders to diversify by reducing the number of companies outstanding. In general, if a merger offers investors nothing that they cannot get for themselves in the market by purchasing shares, then investors are better off without the merger.

EXAMPLE

Gypsum and Raybestos are considering merging. Before management announces the merger, the companies have the following values:

	Gypsum	**Raybestos**
Market value	$1,000,000	$2,000,000
Beta	1.0	0.90

The value of the combined companies in the absence of operating and financial synergies is the total of the individual market values: $1,000,000 + $2,000,000 = $3,000,000. Weights for the combination are each company's proportion of the combined market value: Gypsum, $\frac{1}{3}$, and Raybestos, $\frac{2}{3}$. The beta (nondiversifiable risk) of the combined companies is 0.93:

$$\beta_p = (1/3)(1.0) + (2/3)(0.90) = 0.93$$

Investors can combine stocks in their own portfolios and do not need a merger to do it for them. In the absence of operating and financial synergies, a company cannot improve its market value by combining with another company.

The foregoing reasons for merging suggest rational, economically sound decisions. In some instances, however, managers and directors simply have the urge to merge. Other mergers occur because managers want to manage a larger company and receive more recognition or income. Some mergers may *not* occur, even though it would be in the shareholders' best interests; managers may fear losing their jobs in the new corporation. An investor may hold a well-diversified portfolio, but a manager has nondiversifiable *employment risk*. Part of the efficiencies of merging may include termination of the manager's position.

EVALUATING TARGET COMPANIES

After the acquiring company finds a potential acquisition candidate that appears to offer operating and financial synergies, the financial manager employs the valuation techniques described in Part III of this book, along with an assessment of

[1] For a more complete discussion of the benefits from mergers, see Joseph T. Marren, *Mergers and Acquisitions: Will You Overpay?* Homewood, IL.: Dow Jones-Irwin, 1985.

the price necessary to obtain the target company. Evaluating an acquisition requires two basic steps: (1) estimating the value of the target company and (2) determining the means of paying for the acquisition.

Capital-Budgeting Analysis

Using capital-budgeting analysis, the financial manager of the acquiring company estimates the value of the target company and subtracts the necessary investment, which yields net present value (NPV). Similar to the evaluation of any proposed capital project, a positive NPV indicates a good investment and a negative NPV indicates a bad one.

The value of the target company to the acquiring company is the value of assets less the value of liabilities assumed by the acquirer. These values are *not* those reported on the target's balance sheet, which provides the *book value* of owners' equity. The financial manager seeks the *going-concern value* of the target as part of the acquiring company. Going-concern value in this context will likely differ not only from book value but also from liquidation value and market value.

The first step in the analysis is the valuation of target-company assets based on discounted cash flows. Because of operating and financial synergies, these cash flows may be larger than those of the target company operating independently. The incremental cash flows included in the analysis are as follows: (1) operating cash flows, (2) cash outflows for increases in net working capital (or cash inflows for decreases), and (3) cash outflows for increases in fixed assets (or cash inflows for decreases). Operating cash flow (OCF) is calculated as follows:

$$OCF = EBIT(1 - T) + Depreciation$$

where EBIT = earnings before interest and taxes generated by the target company, including the effects of synergy

T = marginal corporate tax rate applicable to the target company's earnings

Discounting all incremental cash flows (including OCF, operating cash flow) at a rate of return commensurate with the risk level—the target company's weighted-average cost of capital, K_a—yields the intrinsic value of the target's assets.

If the acquiring company assumes the target's liabilities, then estimated acquisition value equals intrinsic value of assets less market value of the liabilities:

$$\text{Acquisition value of target company} = \text{Intrinsic value of assets} - \text{Market value of liabilities assumed}$$

Acquisition value is the value of the target's common equity, or the value of owning the target company. The acquiring company should pay no more than acquisition value to buy the target:

$$\text{Maximum price for target's equity} = \text{Acquisition value of target company}$$

If the acquirer negotiates and buys the target for less than acquisition value, then the acquisition will have a positive net present value and will increase the wealth of the acquirer's shareholders.

The mechanics of valuation are fairly easy to apply, but in practice accurately estimating cash flows is difficult. Based on differing assumptions, the following procedures sometimes are used to value acquisitions:

1. Assume an infinite life for the target company and use the perpetuity model:

$$\frac{\text{Acquisition value}}{\text{of target company}} = \frac{\text{OCF}}{K_a} - \frac{\text{Market value of}}{\text{liabilities assumed}}$$

OCF is operating cash flow, and K_a is the target's weighted-average cost of capital.

2. Assume an infinite life for the target company and use the constant-growth model:

$$\frac{\text{Acquisition value}}{\text{of target company}} = \frac{\text{OCF}_1}{K_a - g} - \frac{\text{Market value of}}{\text{liabilities assumed}}$$

OCF_1 is the expected operating cash flow one year from now, and g is the expected growth rate of OCF.

3. Estimate the target's annual cash flows (CF) for a finite planning horizon, say, 5 to 15 years:

$$\text{CF} = \text{OCF} - \text{Increase in NWC} - \text{Capital expenditures}$$

NWC is net working capital, and capital expenditures are investments in fixed assets necessary to generate the operating cash flow. Next, estimate and discount the terminal (end of planning horizon) value of the target company's common equity using one of the following methods: (a) Multiply a price-earnings ratio (based on similar publicly held companies) by after-tax earnings in the final year of the planning horizon and discount the result to the present. (b) Apply the perpetuity model to the cash flow in the final year of the planning horizon (CF_n/K_a) and discount it to the present $[(\text{CF}_n/K_a)/(1 + K_a)^n]$. (c) Apply the constant-growth model to the cash flow in the final year of the planning horizon $[\text{CF}_{n + 1}/(K_a - g)]$ and discount it to the present. Based on the foregoing cash flows, the acquisition value of the target company is:

$$\frac{\text{Acquisition value}}{\text{of target company}} = \sum_{t = 1}^{n} \frac{\text{CF}_t}{(1 + K_a)^t} - \frac{\text{Market value of}}{\text{liabilities assumed}} + \frac{\text{Present value of}}{\text{terminal value}}$$

The planning horizon is n years (usually 5 to 15) in duration.

EXAMPLE

Wingo Industries is considering the acquisition of Amatech Corporation. Amatech's most recent (abbreviated) balance sheet is as follows:

Assets		Liabilities and Equity	
Current assets	$350,000	Current liabilities	$200,000
Fixed assets	500,000	Bonds	150,000
		Shareholder equity	500,000
Total	$850,000	Total	$850,000

Wingo's financial manager estimates Amatech's annual operating cash flows (OCF) to be $176,000, calculated in the following way:

$$OCF = EBIT(1 - T) + Depreciation$$
$$= \$190,000(1 - 0.34) + \$50,600$$
$$= \$176,000$$

Based on Amatech's weighted-average cost of capital, the financial manager judges the required rate of return to be 18 percent per year. Amatech will repay its current liabilities before the acquisition, but Wingo will assume the long-term liabilities, which have a market value of $120,000. Assuming the operating cash flows form a perpetuity, the financial manager estimates that Amatech is worth $857,778:

$$\text{Acquisition value of target company} = \frac{\$176,000}{0.18} - \$120,000$$
$$= \$857,778$$

After tough negotiations, Wingo agrees to pay $630,000 for ownership of Amatech. Because the price paid is less than acquisition value, the financial manager expects the wealth of Wingo's shareholders to increase by the difference, $227,778 (NPV = $857,778 − $630,000).

Financing an Acquisition

The acquiring company may use cash or issue securities as payment to the target company. If it pays cash or issues debt securities, then the selling company or its shareholders are taxed immediately on any capital gains. In contrast, if common stock or voting preferred stock is used, then capital gains are postponed until the sale of the securities. The selling company is responsible for taxes on capital gains when its assets are purchased, but the shareholders are responsible when its common stock is purchased. The selling company may continue to exist (perhaps as a corporate shell) after the sale of assets, but it ceases to exist and is merged with the acquiring company after the sale of common stock. Target-company managers and their shareholders usually prefer payment in common stock or voting preferred stock in order to postpone paying taxes until they decide to sell the securities.

When an acquiring company offers common stock as payment for the target company, the companies must agree on an **exchange ratio**—the number of shares of the combined companies' stock per share of the target company's stock. For example, an exchange ratio of 1 to 3 means that the acquiring company exchanges one share of stock for three shares of the target company's stock. The exchange ratio is negotiable, but its value is determined in large part by the relative stock prices of the acquiring and target companies and by operating and financial synergies.

Table 21.2 presents an illustration of the exchange ratio necessary for the target company to break even. In the absence of synergy, the operating cash flow ($4,500,000) of the combined companies equals the sum of the individual cash flows ($3,000,000 + $1,500,000). Furthermore, the market value ($12,500,000) of the combined companies equals the sum of the individual market values ($10,000,000 + $2,500,000). For the target company (or its shareholders) to break even, the market value of its portion of the combined companies must equal its market value before merger:

$$\text{Market value of target before merger} = \text{Target's percentage of combined companies} \times \text{Market value of combined companies}$$

exchange ratio
Number of shares of the combined companies offered by the acquirer for one share of the target company.

TABLE 21.2

**Exchange Ratio Necessary for the Target Company to Break Even:
An Illustration without and with Synergy**

	Before Merger: Individual Companies		After Merger: Combined Companies	
	Acquiring Company	Target Company	Without Synergy	With Synergy
Operating cash flow	$3,000,000	$1,500,000	$4,500,000	$5,000,000[a]
Market value	$10,000,000	$2,500,000	$12,500,000	$15,000,000
Shares outstanding	500,000	250,000	625,000[b]	600,000[c]
Price per share	$20.00	$10.00	$20.00	$25.00
Exchange ratio	—	—	0.50	0.40

[a] Greater than the sum of individual cash flows because of operating synergies.

[b] Acquiring company offers 125,000 shares for the 250,000 shares of the target company, an exchange ratio of 0.50. After merger and *without* synergy, price per share is $20.00, or $12,500,000 divided by 625,000 shares. Target company breaks even because its after-merger market value, 125,000 shares times $20 per share, equals its before-merger market value, $2,500,000.

[c] Acquiring company offers 100,000 shares for the 250,000 shares of the target company, an exchange ratio of 0.40. After merger and *with* synergy, price per share is $25.00, or $15,000,000 divided by 600,000 shares. Target company breaks even because its after-merger market value, 100,000 shares times $25 per share, equals its before-merger market value, $2,500,000.

Let N be the target's number of shares of the combined companies and apply the equation to the without-synergy case in Table 21.2:

$$\$2,500,000 = \frac{N}{500,000 + N} \times \$12,500,000$$

$$N = 125,000 \text{ shares}$$

The target company breaks even with 125,000 shares of the combined companies because its after-merger market value, 125,000 shares times $20 ($12,500,000/625,000) per share, equals its before-merger market value, $2,500,000. At break-even, the exchange ratio is 0.50, or 125,000 shares of the combined companies for 250,000 shares of the target company (a 1-to-2 ratio). The *acquiring* company's break-even exchange ratio in this case is the same as the target company's. In a 1-for-2 exchange of stock, the acquiring company has $10,000,000 of value before and after the merger.

In the absence of synergy, the break-even exchange ratio can be calculated more directly and simply with the following equation:

$$\frac{\text{Break-even exchange}}{\text{ratio (without synergy)}} = \frac{\text{Target company's stock price}}{\text{Acquiring company's stock price}}$$

$$= \frac{\$10}{\$20}$$

$$= 0.50$$

This shortcut yields the same answer (0.50) for the without-synergy case as that provided by the alternative procedure. When synergy exists, however, the shortcut equation yields a different answer and should not be used.

In the presence of synergy, the combined companies described in Table 21.2 produce an operating cash flow of $5,000,000 (not $4,500,000). Synergy brings forth additional operating cash flow ($500,000) and additional market value ($2,500,000). Once again, for the target company (or its shareholders) to break even, the market value of its portion of the combined companies must equal its market value before merger:

$$\$2,500,000 = \frac{N}{500,000 + N} \times \$15,000,000$$

$$N = 100,000 \text{ shares}$$

The target company breaks even with 100,000 shares because its after-merger value, 100,000 shares times $25 ($15,000,000/600,000) per share, equals its before-merger value, $2,500,000. The target company's break-even ratio is 0.40, or 100,000 shares of the combined companies for 250,000 shares of the target company (a 2-for-5 ratio).

Because of the $2,500,000 ($15,000,000 − $12,500,000) market value brought forth by synergy, the *acquiring* company's break-even exchange ratio differs from the target's 0.40. For the acquiring company (or its shareholders) to break even, the market value of its portion of the combined companies must equal its market value before merger:

$$\frac{\text{Market value of}}{\text{acquirer before merger}} = \frac{\text{Acquirer's percentage}}{\text{of combined companies}} \times \frac{\text{Market value of}}{\text{combined companies}}$$

$$\$10,000,000 = \frac{500,000}{500,000 + N} \times \$15,000,000$$

$$N = 250,000 \text{ shares}$$

The acquiring company breaks even if it gives 250,000 shares of the combined companies to the target company, an exchange ratio of 1.00. Total shares outstanding equal 750,000 and price per share becomes $20 ($15,000,000/750,000). The acquiring company's portion of the combined companies is $10,000,000 (500,000 × $20), which equals its market value before merger.

To summarize, in the absence of synergy, both companies have the same break-even exchange ratio, 0.50, and neither company gains value in the exchange. In the presence of synergy, however, the companies have differing break-even exchange ratios, and they do have the opportunity for gains in the exchange:

1. The target company's break-even exchange ratio is 0.40, representing 100,000 shares valued at $25 per share. Its gain is zero, and the acquirer's gain is $2,500,000. In other words, the acquirer gets all of the value created by synergy.

2. The acquirer's break-even exchange ratio is 1.00, representing 250,000 shares valued at $20 per share. Its gain is zero, and the target's gain is $2,500,000. In other words, the target gets all of the value created by synergy.

Because the companies will negotiate the actual exchange ratio, it will likely fall between the break-even points 0.40 and 1.00. The corresponding number of shares issued to the target company will fall between 100,000 and 250,000, with a market value between $2,500,000 and $5,000,000. The resulting **acquisition premium** equals the actual value paid less the market value of the target company's stock. In practice, acquisition premiums are often 20 to 35 percent above market value, and they sometimes soar much higher. An acquisition premium

acquisition premium
Acquisition payment in excess of the target company's market value.

TABLE 21.3

Abnormal Stock Price Increases from Successful Acquisitions

	Increase in Stock Price[a]	
Type of Acquisition	Target Companies	Acquiring Companies
Hostile	30%	4%
Friendly	20	0

[a] Stock price changes are statistically adjusted to eliminate the effects of marketwide price changes.
Source: Michael C. Jensen, "Takeovers: Folklore and Science," *Harvard Business Review,* November–December 1984, 109–121.

helps the acquiring company (1) to induce shareholders of the target company to tender shares in a hostile takeover, or (2) to gain approval of the acquisition from the target company's board of directors in a friendly merger.

PROFITABILITY OF MERGERS AND ACQUISITIONS

A company that plans and completes an acquisition devotes a large amount of time and resources to the effort, so it is logical to ask: Are mergers and acquisitions profitable? If so, who profits? These questions have been the subject of debate by financial theorists, investors, legislators, and financial managers. One way to answer these questions is to examine the impact of mergers and acquisitions on the prices of the common stock of the acquiring and target companies.

Table 21.3 summarizes the results of several studies on the stock prices of companies involved in acquisitions. The data suggest that both hostile and friendly acquisitions are profitable, on average, for shareholders of target companies. Shareholders in hostile acquisitions receive abnormal returns on the order of 30 percent during the interval immediately surrounding the original announcement of the tender offer.[2] Shareholders of target companies in friendly acquisitions receive a 20 percent abnormal return. Shareholders of acquiring companies receive small abnormal returns in hostile takeovers, but in friendly ones they earn no abnormal return attributable to the acquisition.

When shareholders of the acquiring company receive a zero abnormal return, the acquisition has a zero net present value. In other words, the acquisition earns exactly (no more than) the risk-adjusted required rate of return. One way to interpret the numbers in Table 21.3 is as follows: Markets for whole companies are efficient so that acquiring companies must pay acquisition premiums that equal the values of synergy in acquisitions.

Besides depending on whether the acquisition is hostile or friendly, abnormal returns to target-company shareholders also depend on the means of payment. Figure 21.1 shows the way that stock prices of a group of target companies performed around the day of their announced acquisition by other companies. The figure illustrates the results of two types of payment for the acquisitions, cash

---

[2] Abnormal return is the difference between an actual and expected return. The researcher estimates the expected return using the stock's beta and the return on a market index such as Standard & Poor's 500 Index. In other words, the researcher controls the effect of marketwide movements in stock prices. Any return not explained by the market is the abnormal return.

FIGURE 21.1

Abnormal Stock Price Movement around Announcement of Acquisitions Paid by Cash and Securities

Acquisitions paid by cash lead to a greater return to target-company shareholders than acquisitions paid by securities. In each case the abnormal returns attributable to the merger are received by the announcement day (Time 0).

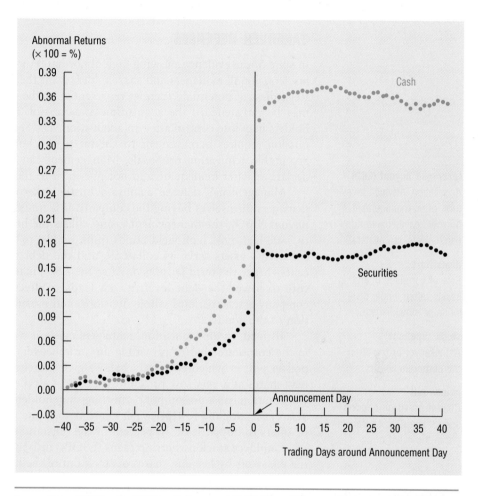

Source: James W. Wansley, William R. Lane, and Ho C. Yang, "Abnormal Returns to Acquired Firms by Type of Acquisition and Method of Payment," *Financial Management,* Autumn 1983, 16–22.

and securities. The abnormal returns measured on the vertical axis (cumulated from 40 days before the announcement) are attributable to the announced acquisition. Because hostile takeovers are usually cash offers, and friendly acquisitions are usually exchanges of securities, the numbers in Figure 21.1 relate closely (though not exactly) to those in Table 21.3. Differences in tax treatment also contribute to the different levels of abnormal returns. When target-company shareholders receive cash for shares, they pay any capital-gains taxes in the year of the acquisition. The difference between the returns illustrated in Figure 21.1 results in part from the timing difference between taxes paid for a securities exchange (deferred taxes) and for a cash acquisition (immediate taxes). Because shareholders must immediately pay taxes in cash deals, they demand a high price for their shares of stock.

Figure 21.1 shows that abnormal returns attributable to the acquisition have been received by the announcement day.[3] Only normal returns are earned after the announcement day. To take advantage of an impending merger, therefore, investors must make their stock purchases before news of the merger becomes public information.

TAKEOVER DEFENSES

In spite of the evidence showing high abnormal returns to target-company shareholders, not all managers and shareholders want their companies to be acquired. Regardless of potential synergies represented by the acquisition, a manager's job may be threatened if the acquisition is successful. In addition, majority shareholders may lose control after an acquisition. The Securities and Exchange Commission requires management to submit to the board of directors potentially acceptable acquisition proposals. Management can simply choose, however, to declare an offer inadequate and not present it to the board.

Management's defense against a hostile takeover sometimes leads to the managers themselves buying the company. In a transaction known as a **leveraged buyout (LBO),** the management group enlists the help of an investment banker to issue high-risk, high-yield bonds (junk bonds) to finance the acquisition. The company's assets serve as collateral, and the debt ratio often exceeds 90 percent—hence the term *leveraged.* After the LBO, management usually feels pressure to lower the debt level, which leads to **divestitures.** Management sells company assets, perhaps whole divisions, and uses the proceeds to repay a portion of the bonds.

To fend off an acquisition, managers may use a **shark repellent,** a provision in the corporate charter providing an antitakeover maneuver. An example is a **poison pill,** in which corporate bylaws give shareholders the right to purchase new shares at a very low price in the event of a takeover. For example, Questar Corporation has a poison pill permitting shareholders to buy new common stock at an exceptionally low price per share if someone acquires at least 20 percent or offers to buy at least 30 percent of the outstanding shares.

Employee stock ownership plans (ESOPs) help management to ward off hostile takeovers by keeping shares of stock out of the hands of hostile investors. In an ESOP a trust is created that borrows funds for purchasing an employer's stock for employees, who also contribute funds to the trust. Because of federal tax breaks to ESOP lenders, ESOPs can borrow at below-market rates. Another advantage stems from the antitakeover laws in some states that provide ESOPs with disproportionate control over the approval of takeovers.

When these and other defenses fail, the target company may resort to **greenmail,** in which it repurchases shares from the raider at a substantial premium above market value. Greenmail now has limited attractiveness as a defense because the target company must expense the dollar amount of greenmail in its financial statements. This requirement has encouraged managers and directors to turn to **golden parachutes,** severance pay to those losing their positions as a result of the takeover.

---

[3]The trend in stock prices prior to merger announcements could indicate that investors are trading on insider information about forthcoming mergers (which is illegal), or it might simply reflect trading on rumors of mergers (which is legal).

---

leveraged buyout (LBO)
Acquisition in which investors, often management, borrow heavily using company assets as collateral.

divestiture
Sale of company operating assets, often whole divisions or subsidiaries.

shark repellent
Antitakeover provision in the corporate charter.

poison pill
Charter provision offering special favors to shareholders in the event of an attempted hostile acquisition.

employee stock ownership plan (ESOP)
Tax-advantaged trust that purchases the employer's common stock on behalf of employees.

greenmail
Repurchase of shares from a raider at a price above market value.

golden parachute
Large severance payment to a manager discharged following a hostile acquisition.

INTERNATIONAL DIMENSIONS

Global Mergers and Acquisitions

Acquisitions of foreign companies are often the easiest way for businesses to enter foreign markets, and the number of international mergers has increased dramatically in recent years.

During the 1980s, several events fueled an international merger mania. European and Japanese companies were particularly active in the acquisition of U.S. companies. The sharp decline in the value of the dollar caused U.S. companies to become bargains for those with foreign currency.

In addition to favorable foreign-exchange rates, companies overseas were attracted to the relative political and economic stability of the United States. Japanese companies, which came under increasing pressure to limit exports, found that they could maintain their U.S. market share by merging with or acquiring U.S. businesses.

Many economists, politicians, financial analysts, and workers feel that the infusion of foreign capital benefits the U.S. economy, improves the prospects of the acquired firms, and creates new job opportunities. Others worry that foreign interests are becoming a threat to U.S. enterprise and ownership of capital. This concern was evident when the U.S. government blocked a proposed merger between the Japanese company Fujitsu and Fairchild Semiconductor on grounds that U.S. national security would have been compromised.

Caution is not unique to the United States. When the British securities markets were deregulated, many foreign firms (notably U.S. mortgage bankers and financiers) attempted to take control of the top British merchant banks. The British government responded by limiting the stake that any foreign investor could have in such institutions unless approved by the Bank of England.

Despite the problems, mergers and acquisitions are tactics that global companies use to expand markets, improve product lines, and increase the wealth of shareholders. Illustrative of these tactics are the top ten U.S. acquisitions of European companies listed in *Acquisitions Monthly:*

Top 10 U.S. Acquisitions of European Companies, 1984–1992

Bidder	Target	Value (Billions of Dollars)
SmithKline	Beecham Group	$7.65
Philip Morris	Jacobs Suchard	3.80
Ford	Jaguar	2.46
Philip Morris	Freia Marabou	1.49
PepsiCo	Smiths/Walkers	1.35
Pembridge Associates	DRG PLC	1.03
General Electric	Avis Lease	0.87
St. Paul Cos.	Minet Holdings	0.72
Whirlpool	Whirlpool Inter. (43%)	0.70
Reebok	Pentland Holdings	0.66

EXAMPLE

Pantry Pride's hostile takeover of Revlon in 1985 illustrates the cost of waging a defense. The $1.83 billion takeover generated more than $100,000,000 in fees. The Pantry Pride–Revlon fees went to investment banking firms and advisers involved in the hostile takeover:

Drexel Burnham Lambert	$60,000,000
Morgan Stanley	30,000,000
Lazard Frères	11,000,000

Goldman, Sachs	3,000,000
Chemical Bank	4,300,000
Legal fees	10,000,000

That was not the only tab. Revlon established $42,200,000 in golden parachutes to pay managers for severance if they lost their jobs when Pantry Pride took over. Michel C. Bergerac, Revlon's chairman and chief executive officer, pulled his rip-cord quickly. The value of his parachute: $21,400,000.

The propriety of greenmail and golden parachutes is questionable. Many argue that company resources should not be used for such purposes. Some might even question the value of mergers and acquisitions, based on the small average percentage gain to the acquiring-company shareholders. In many cases, however, mergers and acquisitions provide a useful way for a company to stave off the stage of decline in its life cycle.

BANKRUPTCY

bankruptcy
Legal declaration of a company's inability to meet claims against it.

Mergers and acquisitions and internal investments in capital projects are ways for a going concern to prolong its growth. Unfortunately, financial plans some-times fail to meet the expectations of managers and shareholders. In extreme cases of such failure, companies may be forced to seek protection from creditors in the bankruptcy courts. **Bankruptcy** is a legal declaration of financial distress that places the company under court supervision. During bankruptcy the court makes sure that all creditors and claimants are treated fairly and that no indi-vidual group gains advantage over other groups.

Companies at one time vital and profitable may become financially distressed for one of several reasons. Incompetent management, however, often lies at the foundation of business failures: For example, selling fountain pens in a ballpoint-pen world is difficult. In some cases the reason for failure seems to stem more from the business climate. Foreign competition has driven some companies to failure, particularly in the apparel industry. The lower cost of foreign labor puts U.S. apparel manufacturers at a competitive disadvantage. Whatever the reason for failure—managerial or environmental—its frequency suggests the need to understand how to cope with it.

recapitalization
Retiring outstanding securi-ties with new ones to sat-isfy claims of creditors and to lessen financial pressure on the debtor.

Companies suffering temporary setbacks can often make arrangements with creditors to continue operations. Creditors will sometimes agree to a **recapitali-zation,** an exchange of new securities with less restrictive conditions for the ones currently held. If creditors do not agree to a recapitalization, then the company must sell assets to satisfy the claims of creditors. When these actions fail, the company can turn to the bankruptcy courts.

The Bankruptcy Act

The Bankruptcy Act of 1938 (amended in 1978 and 1984) is the principal law governing bankruptcy. The act has several sections, called chapters, but we deal with only two of them because of their applicability to business financial man-agement: *Chapter 7* deals with liquidation, selling the debtor's assets and dis-tributing the cash proceeds among the creditors. *Chapter 11* addresses reorganization, the means for a debtor to restructure debts so that creditors will be treated fairly. A company may voluntarily file a court petition for bankruptcy under either chapter. Also, creditors may, under specified circumstances, file a petition to have the debtor company declared bankrupt by the court; this is called an *involuntary bankruptcy*. It is not uncommon for companies to petition initially under Chapter 11 to try to reorganize, then, if reorganization attempts are unsuccessful, to convert to Chapter 7 for liquidation.

A company petitioning the court need not be insolvent (have negative net worth). The Bankruptcy Act makes it possible for companies to file petitions if they *anticipate* being insolvent. Consider the following examples of companies using the Bankruptcy Act for protection against claimants:

- *Manville Corporation.* Manville's bankruptcy petition in 1982 was intended to let it grapple with $2.5 billion of asbestos-related lawsuits. At the time of filing, the company had a net worth of $1.1 billion.

- *Continental Airlines.* Continental filed a bankruptcy petition in 1983. At the time of filing, the airline had $500,000,000 cash, and its chairman commented that the problem was not cash, but labor. Operating under the protection of the court, the company used the bankruptcy law to break union contracts and establish lower wage rates.

- *A. H. Robins.* Robins filed a bankruptcy petition in 1985 to freeze the 6,000 claims pending against the company arising from its Dalcon Shield, an intra-uterine contraceptive device. The company was solvent at the time of its filing, with its common stock trading around $11 per share.

- *Texaco.* Texaco filed a bankruptcy petition in 1987 to protect itself from a judgment of more than $10 billion awarded to Pennzoil as a result of Texaco's $10.1 billion acquisition of Getty Oil in 1984. Texaco was found guilty of tampering with a merger agreement between Getty and Pennzoil. At the time of filing, Texaco had $34 billion of total assets and $13.7 billion of net worth. In April 1988, Texaco paid $3 billion to Pennzoil and emerged from bankruptcy.

- *Pan Am.* Pan Am Corp., the parent of Pan American World Airlines, filed a Chapter 11 bankruptcy petition in 1991. In its filing, Pan Am listed assets of $438 million and liabilities of $89 million. Pan Am was in a cash bind in a highly competitive industry. Bankers Trust of New York required the bankruptcy filing as a condition for a $150 million loan called debtor-in-possession financing. Lending to a bankrupt company gave Bankers Trust priority liens on all of Pan Am's unencumbered assets.

Chapter 11 Proceedings

Chapter 11
Bankruptcy provision allowing the bankrupt company to operate while attempting to reorganize.

trustee
Court-appointed person who oversees a company's reorganization proceedings.

Reorganization under **Chapter 11** begins with a petition to the court by a company or its creditors. The court protects the company from any actions by creditors while it attempts to reorganize. The court also protects creditors by appointing (1) creditor committees to investigate the debtor's financial position and potential profitability and (2) a trustee to oversee the operations of the company. The **trustee** is a disinterested party, someone not having a vested interest in the company's reorganization, who supervises the proceedings. After investigating for possible malfeasance, the trustee submits the findings to the court and notifies creditors and shareholders that they may submit proposed reorganization plans.

feasible plan
Reorganization plan that allows the debtor to function financially and to pay its bills.

The company has 120 days to present a plan acceptable to its creditors. After the company has submitted its plan, the creditors may submit their own plan. The court holds a hearing on the proposed plans to determine whether they are feasible and whether they are fair and equitable. A **feasible plan** permits the company to operate and to pay its bills. A **fair and equitable plan** treats each class of securities and creditors according to legal priority.

EXAMPLE

Jenrette Company petitions the court for protection from its creditors. The company is unable to pay its creditors in a timely fashion, and its net worth has become negative. Jenrette's financial problems began two years ago when a U.S. district court ordered the company to cease selling its line of monoclonal antibodies. A competitor had sought the injunction because of an alleged patent infringement. Jenrette Company petitions for Chapter 11 reorganization and develops a feasible and a fair and equitable plan.

---

fair and equitable plan
Reorganization plan that treats each class of securities and creditors according to legal priority.

Table 21.4 shows an example of a feasible and a fair and equitable reorganization plan for the Jenrette Company. The plan is fair and equitable because it fully covers the principal amounts of the senior securities (first mortgage bond and secured bank loan) and allocates remaining values to the junior creditors. The reorganization is also feasible because it reduces the interest on each issue and makes renewed financial difficulties unlikely: The annual interest payments decline from $750,000 ($250,000 + $180,000 + $320,000) to $340,000 ($200,000 + $140,000). To make the burden of debt less onerous, the new bonds are income bonds, which pay interest only when operating income covers it. The subordinated debenture holders and trade creditors of Jenrette Company come out with what may be a bucket of air. They obtain an equity interest (preferred and common) in the reorganization, which may turn out to be of little value. Jenrette's original shareholders lose their entire investment.[4]

The federal judge tentatively approves a proposed plan and asks the creditors to approve it. The court accepts the plan if creditors holding two-thirds of the dollar claims vote approval. If the debtor company is solvent (has positive net worth), then a majority of the common shareholders must also accept the plan. When the affected parties have accepted the plan, the federal judge confirms it and the plan becomes binding upon the bankrupt company and all creditors. When the affected parties cannot agree to a plan, the bankruptcy petition converts to a Chapter 7 liquidation.

Chapter 7 Proceedings

Chapter 7
Bankruptcy provision under which the court liquidates assets of the bankrupt company.

Chapter 7 liquidation is a procedure in which the court takes over the assets of a bankrupt company and sells them for cash. The cash is distributed among the company's creditors. Secured creditors receive the cash from the assets securing their claims, and if any portion of their debt is unsatisfied, then that portion is included along with other unsecured claims. Some claims receive a higher priority

---

[4]Under the absolute priority rule, common shareholders receive nothing until senior claimants are completely satisfied. However, the rule may be broken in practice. Senior claimants often agree to payments to common shareholders even when not required by law. The payments speed up the legal proceedings and reduce bankruptcy costs, which offset the payments to common shareholders.

TABLE 21.4

Jenrette Company: Reorganization Plan

Debt	Before Reorganization		After Reorganization	
	Principal	Annual Interest	Principal	Annual Interest
First mortgage bond, 5% coupon, due 19X3	$5,000,000	$250,000	$5,000,000	$200,000
Secured bank loan	3,000,000	180,000	3,000,000	140,000
Subordinated debenture, 8% coupon, due 19X7	4,000,000	320,000	Received *pro rata* $4,000,000 of 3 percent noncumulative preferred stock and all of the company's common stock	
Trade creditors	3,800,000			

than others. Claims are paid in order of their priority, with each class of claims being paid in full before the court makes any payment to claims of a lower priority. If there is not enough cash to pay fully all claims within a class, then the cash available is prorated among the creditors in that class. All claims that exceed the amount allowed as a priority become general claims. The claims in order of *decreasing* priority are:

1. *Administrative expenses.* These include the trustee's actual and necessary expenses and the filing fees (paid by creditors in involuntary filings).

2. *Additional administrative expenses.* Expenses occurring in the ordinary course of the debtor's business after filing of the case but prior to the appointment of the trustee.

3. *Wages, salaries, and commissions.* The court next pays wages and salaries due employees and commissions due sales personnel payable within 90 days before the petition date. Maximum settlement to each person is limited.

4. *Claims for contributions to employee benefit plans.* The court pays claims arising from services rendered within 180 days of filing of the petition. Maximum settlement to each person is limited.

5. *Deposits on consumer goods.* The court pays a limited amount per claim for deposits made on consumer goods and services that were not received.

6. *Taxes to federal and state authorities.*

After all classes of priority claims have been paid, any remaining cash is distributed on a *pro rata* (proportional) basis to unsecured creditors. Preferred stockholders receive nothing until unsecured creditors are completely paid, and common shareholders receive nothing until preferred stockholders receive the par (or stated) value of their shares.

EXAMPLE

Table 21.5 presents Dataline Corporation's liabilities. The debenture is subordinated specifically to the bank loan. In addition to the financial claims in Table 21.5, administrative costs are $40,000, taxes are $30,000, and wages for the period preceding the petition total $70,000. Real estate secures the first mortgage

TABLE 21.5	**Dataline Corporation: Liabilities on the Bankruptcy Date**

Liability	Amount
Accounts payable	$ 60,000
Bank loan	150,000
Current portion of mortgage bond	20,000
First mortgage bond	340,000
Subordinated debenture (subordinated to bank loan)	400,000
	$970,000[a]

[a] Note that preferred stockholders and common shareholders do not share in the allocation.

bond. How are the claims against the company settled in a Chapter 7 distribution?

The first allocation in the above example is the distribution of secured property. The trustee sells the real estate for, say, $200,000 and applies this amount against the first mortgage bond (current and noncurrent portions due). That leaves unpaid $160,000 ($360,000 − $200,000) of the mortgage bondholders' claim. What happens to the unpaid claim? The court combines the $160,000 claim with unsecured claims.

According to the list of priorities, the liquidated assets are distributed for administrative expenses, then for wages, and finally for taxes. If the court liquidates the petitioner's remaining assets for $400,000, then the cash remaining for unsecured creditors is calculated as follows:

Liquidated assets (after disposing of secured property)		$400,000
Less priority claims		
Administrative expenses (Priority 1)	$40,000	
Wages (Priority 3)	70,000	
Taxes (Priority 6)	30,000	
		140,000
Cash remaining for unsecured creditors		$260,000

The court distributes the remaining cash to unsecured creditors and unsatisfied secured creditors on a *pro rata* basis. However, it must recognize subordination. In this example the $400,000 debenture is subordinated to the bank loan. The relationship between a subordinated debt and its senior security in liquidation is clear: Subordinated claims receive nothing until the senior claim is completely repaid. For Dataline Corporation this relationship means that the bank (senior claim) must receive $150,000 before any cash is distributed to the subordinated debenture holders.

The following steps are taken to determine the distribution of cash among unsecured creditors when subordination exists: (1) List the unsecured liabilities (including the unsatisfied claims of mortgagees) and calculate the proportion that each claim represents. Table 21.6 shows the procedure for Dataline Corporation. The cash from liquidating secured property (Column 3) reduces the claim of the mortgage bondholders, and the remaining claim is included in Column 4. Each remaining claim is then expressed as a proportion of the total claims (Column 5).

TABLE 21.6

Dataline Corporation: Distribution of Liquidation Cash Flows

(1) Liability	(2) Balance Sheet Amount	(3) Less Secured Property	(4) Remaining Claim	(4)/$770,000 = (5) Proportion
Accounts payable	$ 60,000		$ 60,000	0.0779
Bank loan (senior issue)	150,000		150,000	0.1948
First mortgage bond	360,000	− $200,000 =	160,000	0.2078
Subordinated debenture (junior issue)	400,000		400,000	0.5195
Total	$970,000		$770,000	1.0000

(1) Liability	$260,000 × (5) = (6) Initial Distribution		(7) Final Distribution
Accounts payable	$ 20,254		$ 20,254
Bank loan (senior issue)	50,648	+ $99,352 =	150,000
First mortgage bond	54,028		54,028
Subordinated debenture (junior issue)	135,070	− $99,352 =	35,718
Total	$260,000		$260,000

(2) Determine the initial distribution as shown in Column 6 based on the proportions in Column 5. The amounts in Column 6 would be the final distribution if it were not for subordination. (3) Include the effect of subordination by reducing cash to the subordinated claim and increasing cash to the senior claim to provide full compensation to the senior claim. Column 7 shows the result of applying this step to Dataline Corporation. The bank loan requires an additional $99,352 ($150,000 − $50,648) to be completely repaid. This amount comes out of the subordinated claim, leaving the subordinated debenture holders with $35,718 ($135,070 − $99,352). Because the liquidation cash flow does not completely cover the claims of unsecured creditors, there is no cash left to distribute to preferred stockholders and common shareholders.

Three disinterested appraisers appointed by the court appraise the assets of the bankrupt company to determine that the trustee liquidated the assets at a fair value. The trustee then files final accounts with the court within 15 days of the distribution of the liquidated assets. If the accounts show proper administration of the activities, the court approves them and closes the proceedings.

SUMMARY

• A company, like a person, has a life cycle consisting of start-up, growth, maturity, and decline. Mergers and acquisitions help to stave off corporate decline. A merger is a combination of companies in which only one company survives and the others cease to exist as legal entities. Mergers may be horizontal, vertical, or conglomerate. A consolidation is a combination of companies for the purpose of forming a completely new company. A holding company is a parent organization that owns all or controlling interests in other companies called subsidiaries. Mergers and acquisitions may be hostile or friendly toward the management and directors of the acquired company.

• Federal and state laws impose regulations on mergers and acquisitions. The Sherman and Clayton Acts deal directly with mergers and acquisitions that may restrict competition. Except in instances of per se violations, federal government agencies and courts follow the rule of reason in interpreting the acts: Only those actions that impose unreasonable restraints on trade are condemned. States may enact their own laws to limit mergers and acquisitions.

• Mergers and acquisitions have two economic justifications: operating synergy and financial synergy. Operating synergies include economies of scale, market power, and increased efficiency. Financial synergies include tax benefits, reduced flotation costs, and the reduced probability of incurring bankruptcy costs. Because investors can diversify their own portfolios, corporate diversification to reduce risk on their behalf is not economically justifiable.

• The value of a prospective acquisition is estimated with capital-budgeting analysis. Discounting the incremental cash flows attributable to the target company produces the estimated intrinsic value of its assets. Subtracting from this estimate the market value of liabilities that the acquiring company will assume yields the acquisition value of the target company:

$$\text{Acquisition value of target company} = \text{Intrinsic value of assets} - \text{Market value of liabilities assumed}$$

The maximum price an acquirer should pay for the target company is its acquisition value. Paying less than the acquisition value results in a positive net present value and an increase in wealth of the acquiring company's shareholders.

• Paying cash or issuing debt securities in payment for an acquisition causes the target company or its shareholders to pay applicable capital-gains taxes. If common stock or voting preferred stock is the means of payment, then the taxes are deferred until sale of the stock. The value of the common-stock shares paid by the acquiring company depends on the value of the combined companies. In the absence of synergy, the break-even exchange ratio is the same for the target and acquirer, and it equals the target's stock price divided by the acquirer's stock price. In the presence of synergy, however, a different calculation is required, and the break-even exchange ratio of the target company differs from the acquirer's. The difference provides a range for negotiation of the acquisition price.

• Shareholders of acquired companies receive, on average, abnormally large returns in both hostile and friendly acquisitions. Shareholders of acquiring companies receive, on average, small abnormal returns in hostile takeovers and zero abnormal returns in friendly ones. Cash payments generally result in larger abnormal returns to acquired-company shareholders than do payments with securities.

• Managers and directors of target companies defend themselves against hostile takeovers by using LBOs, ESOPs, poison pills, and greenmail. If these tactics fail, then they often provide themselves with golden parachutes.

• Bankruptcy is a legal declaration of a company's inability to meet claims against it. Companies may voluntarily petition for bankruptcy or creditors may force bankruptcy. Chapter 11 of the Bankruptcy Act deals with reorganization in which the debtor company continues to operate under the direction of a trustee. Chapter 7 of the Bankruptcy Act deals with liquidation of the debtor company's assets and distribution of the cash among the claimants. Owners of mortgage bonds have a high priority in comparison with owners of subordinated debentures, and common shareholders have the lowest priority of all.

Key Terms

life cycle of a company

merger

consolidation

holding company

hostile takeover

horizontal merger

Sherman Antitrust Act

conglomerate merger

vertical merger

Clayton Act

per se violation

exchange ratio

acquisition premium

leveraged buyout (LBO)

divestiture

shark repellent

poison pill

employee stock ownership plan (ESOP)

greenmail

golden parachute

bankruptcy

recapitalization

Chapter 11

trustee

feasible plan

fair and equitable plan

Chapter 7

Questions

21.1. Describe the stages of a company's life cycle.

21.2. Suppose that General Motors Corporation is considering a merger with either Chrysler Corporation or General Mills. Which merger would likely be in violation of federal antitrust laws? Which merger promises operating synergies? Explain your choices.

21.3. Operating synergy and financial synergy are two financial justifications for mergers and acquisitions. Which of these synergies is more likely to exist in a horizontal merger? In a vertical merger? Explain your answers.

21.4. Theorists contend that, in the absence of synergy, corporate diversification is irrelevant and does not affect the price of common stock. Explain this assertion.

21.5. In 1981 Mobil Oil Corporation offered $85 per share for Marathon Oil Company. Marathon's stock was trading for around $60 per share, and Mobil offered to pay cash for the shares.
   a. Is this an example of a conglomerate, vertical, or horizontal merger? Explain your answer.
   b. What are the tax consequences for a Marathon shareholder who tenders stock? Would the shareholder prefer to receive Mobil shares instead of cash? Why or why not?
   c. Calculate the cash outlay that Mobil makes, assuming that 40 million shares are tendered.
   d. List two reasons for an acquiring company to offer an acquisition premium for target-company shares.

21.6. Evaluating a target company to determine its benefit to the acquiring company involves capital-budgeting analysis. Explain the influence of each of the following items on the net present value of the acquisition.

   a. Expected operating and financial synergies increase.
   b. The acquiring company agrees to assume an increased amount of the target company's liabilities.
   c. The expected terminal value of the target company decreases.
   d. The target company's weighted-average cost of capital rises.
   e. Intense negotiation results in the acquiring company paying more for the target company than originally planned.

21.7. Determine whether each of the following statements is true or false. In an acquisition, shareholders of the target company often prefer a stock payment to a cash payment because:
   T F Capital gains realized on the sale of the firm need not be recognized for tax purposes until the stock is subsequently sold.
   T F The profit resulting from a cash payment is taxed immediately.

21.8. Pipkin United is acquiring Clint Corporation in a stock-for-stock transaction. At present Pipkin United common stock is $26 per share. After acquiring Clint Corporation, Pipkin United's earnings per share will be $4.00 and the price-earnings ratio will be 7.0. On the basis of this information, should Pipkin United complete the acquisition? Explain your answer.

21.9. One of your classmates in marketing looks at your finance textbook and comes across Figure 21.1, which portrays abnormal stock-price movements around the time of merger announcements. She comments: "It looks as though you can make a lot of money in a merger if you buy the target company's stock."
   a. Explain the term *abnormal return*.

b. Comment on the returns to target-company shareholders in an acquisition and explain to your friend when a person would need to buy the stock in order to earn an abnormal return.

21.10. Are common shareholders of the target company harmed in hostile takeovers? What evidence supports your answer?

21.11. Luby's Cafeterias amended its corporate charter to include a *poison pill*, which makes it more difficult for a corporate raider to take over the company.
a. What is a poison pill?
b. Why may it be in the target shareholders' best interest for management to offer some resistance to takeover attempts?

21.12. Explain the difference between Chapter 7 and Chapter 11 of the Bankruptcy Act.

21.13. Rank the following claims in order of priority in a bankruptcy (1 = highest priority, 9 = lowest priority):
____Taxes
____Wages
____Common stock
____Unsecured debt
____Additional administrative expenses
____Administrative expenses
____Deposits on consumer goods
____Preferred-stockholder claims
____Contribution to employee benefit plans

21.14. Examine the claims arrayed against Dataline Corporation's assets in Table 21.5.
a. Why is shareholder equity absent from the list of claims?
b. Explain what *subordination* entails for the subordinated debenture holders. No calculation is necessary.

Strategy Problem

Warner American Corporation is considering acquiring Linden Industries, one of Warner's major competitors in the Midwest. The financial manager of Warner has estimated that the annual operating cash flow generated by Linden will be $128,358 for the foreseeable future if it continues to operate as an independent company. Merged with Warner, however, Linden could probably generate $186,200 annually because of operating synergies. Furthermore, no annual outlays for net working capital and fixed assets would be necessary to generate the cash flow. Warner's capital-budgeting guidelines call for the financial manager to evaluate a horizontal merger using a 16 percent discount rate. Linden's most recent balance sheet is shown below.
a. Calculate the intrinsic value of Linden Industries' assets to the shareholders of Warner American. What is the maximum price that Warner should pay for Linden if Warner must pay Linden's debts? (Assume that market value of the debts equals book value.)
b. Preliminary discussions with the directors of Linden industries have collapsed. As a result, Warner American plans to make a tender offer to the shareholders of Linden. If Linden's stock is presently trading at 1.2 times book value, then what is the maximum acquisition premium (expressed as a percentage) that Warner can offer without causing the price of its own stock to decline?
c. The CEO of Linden Industries tells the CEO of Warner American about a shark-repellent provision in Linden's corporate charter. He says the provision permits the company to petition for Chapter 7 bankruptcy if any one shareholder acquires more than 20 percent of the outstanding shares of common stock. Moreover, he asserts that Linden will take this poison pill if Warner persists with its tender offer. Thinking to himself, the Warner CEO notes that this could be a bluff. He asks Warner's financial manager to estimate the liquidation value of Linden's assets and to determine the distribution of the resulting cash. Perhaps Linden is a worthy takeover target even in Chapter 7 bankruptcy! The financial manager estimates that Linden's mortgaged assets can be sold for $120,000 and its other assets for $450,000. Determine the distribution of Linden's cash under a Chapter 7 bankruptcy. Does the poison pill pose a threat to Warner?

Linden Industries: Balance Sheet as of April 15, 19X7

Assets		Liabilities and Shareholder Equity	
Cash	$ 60,000	Accounts payable	$ 75,000
Marketable securities	40,000	Notes payable, banks	74,000
Accounts receivable	200,000	Current portion of mortgage bond	30,000
Inventory	210,000	Accrued expenses	11,000
Total current assets	$510,000	Total current liabilities	$190,000
Fixed assets (net of depreciation)	450,000	Mortgage bond	180,000
		Convertible subordinated debenture	150,000
Total assets	$960,000	Total liabilities	$520,000
		Common stock (30,000 shares)	$270,000
		Paid-in capital in excess of par	100,000
		Retained earnings	70,000
		Total shareholder equity	$440,000
		Total liabilities and equity	$960,000

Strategy

Use the perpetuity model to calculate present value of operating cash flows; the discount rate is 16 percent.

Subtract liabilities from intrinsic value to calculate the maximum price for Linden's equity.

Divide maximum price by total market value and subtract 1 to calculate acquisition premium.

Reduce mortgage bond by liquidated value of property.

Solution

a. The intrinsic value of Linden Industries' assets is the present value of operating cash flows (OCF), which form a perpetuity:

$$\text{Intrinsic value} \atop \text{of assets} = \frac{\text{OCF}}{K_a}$$

$$= \frac{\$186,200}{0.16} = \$1,163,750$$

The maximum price that Warner American should pay for Linden is the acquisition value—the intrinsic value of Linden's assets less the liabilities that Warner assumes:

$$\text{Acquisition value} \atop \text{of target company} = \text{Intrinsic value} \atop \text{of assets} - \text{Market value of} \atop \text{liabilities assumed}$$

$$= \$1,163,750 - \$520,000 = \$643,750$$

b. Linden Industries' market value is 1.2 times its book value of $440,000, or $528,000. The maximum price that Warner American should pay for Linden is $643,750, which represents a 21.9 percent acquisition premium:

$$\text{Acquisition premium} = \frac{\$643,750}{\$528,000} - 1$$

$$= 0.219, \text{ or } 21.9\%$$

c. The liquidation must recognize the claims of all creditors according to the priority rules of the Bankruptcy Act:

(1) Liability	(2) Balance Sheet Amount	(3) Less Secured Property	(4) Remaining Claim	(4)/$400,000 = (5) Proportion
Accounts payable	$ 75,000		$ 75,000	0.1875
Notes payable	74,000		74,000	0.1850
Accrued expenses	11,000		11,000	0.0275
Mortgage bond	210,000	− $120,000 =	90,000	0.2250
Conv. subordinated debenture	150,000		150,000	0.3750
Total	$520,000		$400,000	1.0000

	$450,000 \times (5) = (6)$	(7)
Liability	**Initial Distribution**	**Final Distribution**
Accounts payable	$ 84,375	$ 75,000
Notes payable	83,250	74,000
Accrued expenses	12,375	11,000
Mortgage bond	101,250	90,000
Conv. subordinated debenture	168,750	150,000
Total	$450,000	$400,000 + $50,000 left over for common shareholders

Calculate initial distribution; reduce each amount to equal actual claims.

Linden's liquidation value covers all claims with $50,000 left over for common shareholders. In contrast, the market value of Linden's stock is $528,000. Linden should not be liquidated because it would cause a loss of $478,000 ($528,000 − $50,000). If the CEO and directors of Linden act with economic rationality, then the poison pill does not pose a threat to Warner. If the CEO and directors were to act irrationally and petition for Chapter 7, then liquidation of Linden would cause Warner to lose money on any stock position it might take.

◆ Demonstration Problem

If agreeable terms can be worked out, Markle Industries (MI) will acquire Sabine Enterprises (SE) in a stock-for-stock exchange. John Markle, MI's CEO, has developed the following information on the two companies:

	Markle Industries	**Sabine Enterprises**	**Combined Companies**
Market value of equity	$20,000,000	$5,000,000	$30,000,000
Number of shares outstanding	500,000	250,000	—
Price per share	$40	$20	

Separately, Mr. Markle is evaluating the potential cash purchase of Redwood Products (RP). RP's most recent balance sheet and Mr. Markle's forecast of RP's cash flows if acquired by MI are shown below. Mr. Markle also estimates the following values for RP: (1) average cost of capital (K_a), 12 percent; (2) market value of shareholder equity at the end of Year 19X6, $11,000,000.

Redwood Products: Balance Sheet

Current assets	$3,340,000	Total debt	$3,120,000
Fixed assets	5,610,000	Shareholder equity	5,830,000
Total assets	$8,950,000	Total claims	$8,950,000

Mr. Markle's Forecast	**19X3**	**19X4**	**19X5**	**19X6**
Operating cash flow	$1,400,000	$1,500,000	$1,600,000	$1,600,000
Increase in net working capital	100,000	100,000	100,000	100,000
Capital expenditures	200,000	200,000	200,000	200,000

a. If MI and SE cannot agree on merger terms, Mr. Markle will attempt a hostile take-over. How can Mr. Markle gain control of SE against the wishes of the company's management?

b. Describe the defensive tactics that SE's management might use against Mr. Markle's advances.

c. Because of synergy, the market value of equity in the combined companies (MI + SE) exceeds the total market value of the independent companies. What are the possible sources of this synergy?

d. (1) How many shares of stock in the combined companies must SE receive to break even? (2) Show that SE's pre-merger market value equals its share of the post-merger market value at the break-even point. (3) Calculate SE's break-even exchange ratio.

e. (1) How many shares of stock in the combined companies can MI give to SE and still break even? (2) Show that MI's pre-merger market value equals its share of the post-merger market value at the break-even point. (3) Calculate MI's break-even exchange ratio.

f. (1) How many shares of stock in the combined companies must MI give to SE to provide a 30 percent acquisition premium? (2) Show that SE's share of the post-merger market value exceeds its pre-merger market value by 30 percent. (3) Calculate the exchange ratio necessary for MI to pay a 30 percent acquisition premium to SE.

g. What is the tax advantage to SE shareholders of a stock-for-stock exchange instead of a cash-for-stock exchange?

h. Calculate the acquisition value of RP to MI under the following condition: MI assumes responsibility for RP's total debt, which has a market value (and book value) of $3,120,000.

i. The following questions relate to your calculations in Part *h*: (1) What is the theoretical justification for using RP's K_a instead of MI's K_a as the discount rate? (2) What is the intrinsic value (in dollars) of RP's assets to MI? (3) What is the maximum price that MI should pay for RP? (4) What is the theoretical justification for MI to pay more than book value, $5,830,000, for RP's shareholder equity? (5) What is the net present value of the acquisition, assuming that MI pays $6,000,000 for RP?

j. Suppose that MI operates RP as an independent subsidiary for four years, at which time RP declares Chapter 7 bankruptcy. The bankruptcy court liquidates RP's assets for $6,200,000, administrative expenses of the bankruptcy are $200,000, and RP's liabilities are as follows:

Accounts payable	$ 1,500,000
Bank loan	3,400,000
Debenture (subordinated to bank loan)	5,600,000
Total	$10,500,000

(1) How much cash does each creditor class receive from the liquidation? (2) What percentage of its total claims does each creditor class receive? (3) How much cash does MI receive?

k. What is the difference between a Chapter 11 bankruptcy and a Chapter 7 bankruptcy?

Problems

Valuing an acquisition: perpetuity

21.1. Wolverine Shoes Inc. plans to purchase Care Shoe Company. Lea Mitchell, financial manager, has collected the following data on Care:

Earnings before interest and taxes	$550,000
Annual depreciation expense	$ 75,000
Weighted-average cost of capital	10%
Total liabilities	$200,000

Incremental earnings from the acquisition will be taxed at a 34 percent rate. As a first approximation, Ms. Mitchell assumes that Care's EBIT and depreciation expenses will persist at their current levels into the foreseeable future, with no additional investments in net working capital and fixed assets. She also assumes that Wolverine will become responsible for Care's liabilities.

a. Estimate the intrinsic value of Care Shoe Company's assets based on Ms. Mitchell's assumptions.

b. What is the maximum price Wolverine Shoes should pay for Care Shoe Company? Calculate the net present value of the acquisition at that price.

Valuing an acquisition: finite planning horizon

21.2. As a consultant to a group of investors, your task is to estimate the value of a target company called Contempo Fabrics. To date, you have gathered the following information:

Earnings before interest and taxes	$2,500,000
Weighted-average cost of capital	15%
Total liabilities	$500,000

Your planning horizon is five years, at the end of which you expect the acquisition to be sold for 10 times earnings after taxes. You expect Contempo to generate an annual EBIT of $2,500,000 during the first five years. You assume that annual depreciation charges will average $150,000 and that earnings after taxes will be $1,500,000 during the fifth year. Your client will pay the liabilities of Contempo. Assuming a tax rate of 40 percent, what is the estimated value of Contempo?

Net present value of an acquisition

21.3. Striker Corporation is considering the acquisition of Ekutrim Company, a manufacturer of cuticle scissors. The market values of Ekutrim's debt and preferred stock equal the book values shown below on the balance sheet. Striker's financial manager expects that synergy will contribute an additional $70,000 to the net operating income shown below on Ekutrim's income statement. Tax-reported depreciation, included in the cost of goods sold, is $56,000. The financial manager estimates the weighted-average cost of capital of Ekutrim to be 12 percent. Although Ekutrim's tax rate (state and federal) is 17 percent, in combination with Striker the effective tax rate will be 34 percent.

a. Calculate expected annual operating cash flow based on Ekutrim's income statement, the effect of synergy, and Striker's effective tax rate.

Ekutrim Company: Balance Sheet as of September 13, 19X9

Assets		Liabilities and Net Worth	
Cash	$ 14,400	Accounts payable	$ 66,000
Accounts receivable	129,300	Notes payable	34,000
Inventory	147,000	Total current liabilities	$100,000
Total current assets	$290,700	Long-term debt	155,000
Fixed assets	135,000	Total liabilities	$255,000
		Preferred stock	70,000
		Common stock	60,000
		Retained earnings	40,700
Total assets	$425,700	Total liabilities and net worth	$425,700

Ekutrim Company: Income Statement for Year Ending September 13, 19X9

Net sales	$1,038,000
Less cost of goods sold	931,000
Gross profit	$ 107,000
Less operating expenses	78,000
Net operating income	$ 29,000
Less interest expense	11,000
Earnings before taxes	$ 18,000
Less taxes (17%)	3,060
Earnings after taxes	$ 14,940

b. Use the perpetuity model to calculate the intrinsic value of Ekutrim's assets. (Assume that no additional investments will be made in net working capital and fixed assets.)

c. Calculate the acquisition value of Ekutrim, assuming that Striker becomes liable for Ekutrim's debt and preferred stock.

d. Ekutrim's CEO says that the company is worth three times its book value. Based on net present value, should Striker be willing to pay that price if necessary? Explain.

Exchange ratio and value with no synergy

21.4. Murphy and Johnson Incorporated is considering merging with Wilmo Construction Company in a stock-for-stock exchange based on the relative market values of their common stock:

	Murphy and Johnson	Wilmo Construction
Common-stock price	$52	$13
Number of shares		
Authorized	140,000	126,000
Outstanding	70,000	100,000

a. In the absence of synergy, how many shares of Murphy and Johnson common stock must management offer at a minimum for each share of Wilmo Construction?

b. Calculate the market value of the combined companies assuming the absence of synergy.

c. Given the exchange ratio in Part *a*, what percentage of the combined companies will Murphy and Johnson and Wilmo Construction each own?

Exchange ratio, earnings per share, and acquisition premium

21.5. The Jenner Company plans to acquire Zates Mining Company. The financial data are as follows:

	Jenner	Zates
Earnings after taxes	$600,000	$400,000
Number of shares	200,000	100,000
Sales	$12,000,000	$9,000,000
Book value (total)	$800,000	$600,000
Price (per share)	$24	$15

Management negotiates a stock-for-stock acquisition on the basis of price per share. No synergy will result from the acquisition.

a. How many shares of Jenner Company common stock are outstanding after the acquisition if Jenner pays the minimum price to Zates?

b. Calculate the earnings per share for Jenner after the acquisition.

c. What is the net present value of the acquisition if Jenner pays a 25 percent premium? Should Jenner pay an acquisition premium to Zates? Explain.

Exchange ratios with synergy

21.6. Deder Company's common stock trades for $60 per share, and Ober Company's common stock trades for $40 per share. Deder has 200,000 shares outstanding, and Ober has 100,000 shares outstanding. If Deder and Ober merge, their total market value will be $18,000,000.

a. How many shares can Deder Company offer Ober Company and break even in the acquisition?

b. Calculate the percentage acquisition premium implied in Part *a*.

c. How many shares can Ober offer Deder and break even in the acquisition?

d. Calculate the percentage acquisition premium implied in Part *c*.

Exchange ratios and values with synergy

21.7. Wyngard Inc. is considering whether or not to acquire Sonrise Inc. Jerri Wyngard, financial manager of Wyngard (and oldest daughter of phlegmatic Edsel Wyngard), collects the following data:

	Wyngard	Sonrise	Combined Companies
Operating cash flow	$900,000	$400,000	$1,600,000
Market value	$6,000,000	$2,400,000	$10,000,000
Shares outstanding	200,000	100,000	—
Price per share	$30	$24	—

Ms. Wyngard plans to negotiate a stock-for-stock exchange but is unsure about the appropriate exchange ratio. Your task is to help her.

a. How many shares of the combined companies must Sonrise receive to break even? Calculate Sonrise's break-even exchange ratio. At this break-even point, what is the market value of each company's portion of the combined companies?

b. How many shares of the combined companies can Wyngard give to Sonrise and still break even? Calculate Wyngard's break-even exchange ratio. At this break-even point, what is the market value of each company's portion of the combined companies?

c. Assume that after negotiation the companies settle on an exchange ratio equaling 1.0. Calculate the percentage acquisition premium.

Distribution of liquidation cash flows

21.8. Genco Inc. files for bankruptcy under the Bankruptcy Act of 1938 as amended. Its balance sheet is as follows:

Assets		Liabilities and Net Worth	
Real estate	$12,000,000	Trade creditors	$ 2,000,000
Other assets	8,000,000	Mortgage loan	6,000,000
		Subordinated debentures	4,000,000
		Shareholder equity	8,000,000
Total	$20,000,000	Total	$20,000,000

All of the company's real estate secures the $6,000,000 mortgage loan. The debenture is subordinated specifically to the mortgage loan. Administrative expenses are $150,000. Accumulated rent, not shown in the balance sheet, is $80,000, and wages payable, also not shown in the balance sheet, are $9,000. The court liquidates the real estate for $5,000,000 and all other assets for $7,000,000.

a. How much cash do the mortgage holders receive in liquidation?

b. How much cash do the subordinated debenture holders receive in liquidation?

c. How much cash do the common shareholders receive in liquidation?

Distribution of liquidation cash flows

21.9. The accompanying balance sheet for Helms Corporation overstates its true worth, and because of declining sales, the corporation files for bankruptcy. Additional information on Helms follows: (1) $150,000,000 of net plant and equipment secures long-term bonds, (2) debentures are subordinated to the long-term bonds, and (3) the $150,000,000 of mortgaged plant and equipment is sold for $80,000,000 so that $70,000,000 of the long-term bonds remain unsatisfied. The court sells assets of the bankrupt Helms Corporation, excluding the pledged net plant and equipment, for $320,000,000. Consequently, the amounts for which the court sells all assets are as follows:

	Book	Cash Realized
Pledged	$150,000,000	$ 80,000,000
All other assets	739,350,000	320,000,000
Total	$889,350,000	$400,000,000

Administrative fees in the proceedings are $380,000.

**Helms Corporation: Balance Sheet as of Date of Bankruptcy
(Thousands of Dollars)**

Assets

Cash	$ 1,800
Accounts receivable	81,900
Inventories	134,700
U.S. Treasury bills	33,450
Total current assets	$251,850
Land	117,500
Plant and equipment (net of accumulated depreciation)	391,500
Patents (less accumulated amortization)	128,500
Total assets	$889,350

Liabilities and Equity

Accounts payable	$136,500
Taxes payable	3,000
Notes payable	30,000
Current portion of debentures	6,000
Total current liabilities	$175,500
Bank loan	11,400
Long-term bonds	150,000
Subordinated debentures	111,000
Total liabilities	$447,900
Common stock	360,000
Retained earnings	81,450
Total liabilities and equity	$889,350

a. After secured claims and administrative fees and taxes are paid, how much cash remains to distribute among the creditors?
b. Show the distribution of cash to the creditors.
c. What proportion of the debenture holders' claim is satisfied?

Computer Problem

Value of an acquisition: template ACQUIS

21.10. Jules Letombeau had reached the age of 65 and was contemplating retirement from the funeral parlor business he had acquired in 1956. His only child, Marie, had majored in finance and mathematics at a large state university. She was now an actuary with a local insurance company and had no interest in taking over the business. Through a broker, Mr. Letombeau contacted R.I.P. Inc., a large corporation that had bought out several local funeral parlors and was running them at the original locations, usually under the original name.

An appraiser estimated that the physical assets of the business (which consisted of the funeral parlor, formerly a large Victorian home on 1.6 acres of land with a parking lot, a two-story garage that doubled as a showroom for caskets, a hearse, a limousine, and various fixtures and inventory) had a market value of $620,000. The company's only liabilities were $5,000 in accounts payable and a $20,000, 5-year loan used toward purchase of the limousine.

R.I.P. initially offered Mr. Letombeau $695,000, broken down as follows:

Physical assets	$620,000
Goodwill, use of name	100,000
Subtotal	$720,000
Less liabilities	25,000
Total	$695,000

Marie suggested that R.I.P. was less interested in the physical assets than in the cash flows the business could generate. R.I.P. would be able to take advantage of economies of scale and depreciation on the newly purchased assets to generate considerably higher cash flows from the same sales revenue.

The 1989 income statements below show the actual figures for the company and Marie's estimates of income and cash flow had R.I.P. owned the funeral parlor during the past year:

	Letombeau	R.I.P.
Sales revenue	$310,000	$310,000
Cost of goods (caskets, etc.)	103,000	93,000
Other operating expenses	40,000	76,000
Depreciation	10,000	27,000
Director's salary	75,000	—
Net income before taxes	$ 82,000	$114,000
Taxes	15,500	38,760
Net income after taxes	$ 66,500	$ 75,240
Add back depreciation	10,000	27,000
Cash flow	$ 76,500	$102,240

Marie believed that sales revenue would increase at the rate of 10 percent per year for the next eight years and thereafter at the rate of 4 percent. She believed that R.I.P.'s after-tax profit margin would be approximately 25 percent of sales revenue. To simplify computations, she assumed that depreciation expense would be $27,000 per year and that vehicle replacement and other capital expenses would be $10,000 in 1990 and grow at the same rate as sales for the next eight years. Over the same period, she estimated that net working capital would increase by 10 percent of the *increase* in sales. She estimated that R.I.P.'s required rate of return was between 12 and 16 percent.

a. Construct a table showing revenue, net income, depreciation, increase in net working capital, capital expenses, and cash flows for each of the next eight years. Assume that R.I.P. is operating the business.
b. Compute the present value of the Letombeau Funeral Parlor's cash flows for 1990 through 1997, the value of the business at the end of 1997, and the present value of the business assuming R.I.P.'s required rate of return is 12 percent.
c. Recompute Part *b* assuming R.I.P.'s required rate of return is 16 percent.
d. What is the highest price Mr. Letombeau can expect to be offered for his business? What is the lowest price he should accept?

Case Problem

Adams Drugstore Inc.

Julie Adams reread the letter from John Klein, the president of J-K Stores, with mixed emotions. In his letter Mr. Klein offered $500,000 cash to purchase her majority interest in the family drugstore. Mrs. Adams looked forward to selling the company, but she was unsure how to evaluate the offer.

The author thanks Professor Carl M. Hubbard of Trinity University for contributing this case problem.

The offer from Mr. Klein was the culmination of a series of events that had begun with the lengthy illness of Bill Adams, Mrs. Adams's late husband. Mr. Adams had grown up working for his father in the family drugstore. His father had established the business as a family-owned corporation in 1932 and had carefully built up a large pharmacy clientele in the community. The store also had an excellent reputation among local physicians.

As her husband's illness worsened, Mrs. Adams assumed responsibility for the management of the store. After her husband's death she inherited his 80 percent interest in Adams Drugstore Inc. When, after some reflection, Mrs. Adams decided to sell her interest in the drugstore, her attorney made some discreet inquiries and ultimately contacted Mr. Klein. Then, in order to obtain a professional opinion on Mr. Klein's offer, Mrs. Adams made an appointment with a financial analyst to discuss the value of her shares.

The analyst first explained that because the company was small and closely held, no stock market information was available to provide an objective market value. Therefore a value had to be estimated. He then discussed three approaches to the valuation of a company: book value, liquidation value, and going-concern value. The book value is shown on the company's balance sheet. The liquidation value is the sum of the piecemeal market values of the company's assets less all liabilities. The going-concern value is the present value of future cash flows less all liabilities. After reviewing the company's financial statements for 19X6 and 19X9, which are shown below, the analyst recommended the going-concern approach. At the close of the meeting with Mrs. Adams, he agreed to advise her in the matter of Mr. Klein's offer.

	12/31/X6	12/31/X9
Cash	$ 21,000	$ 35,000
Accounts receivable	125,000	205,000
Inventories	325,000	420,000
Net fixed assets	125,000	50,000
Total assets	$596,000	$710,000
Accounts payable	$225,000	$200,000
Accrued wages and taxes	30,000	50,000
Mortgage payable	30,000	25,000
Common stock	1,000	1,000
Retained earnings	310,000	434,000
Total claims	$596,000	$710,000
Sales revenue	$1,290,000	$1,650,000
Cost of sales	900,000	1,160,000
Cash operating expenses	200,000	250,000
Depreciation	20,000	5,000
EBIT	$ 170,000	$ 235,000
Interest paid	6,000	2,500
Earnings before taxes	$ 164,000	$ 232,500
Income taxes	65,000	70,000
Earnings after taxes	$ 99,000	$ 162,500
Dividends paid	$ 64,000	$ 82,000
Common shares	1,000	1,000

Notes: Accounting policies are conservative. Receivables are primarily due from insurance companies and Medicare and are net of an allowance for doubtful accounts. Inventories are valued at the lower of cost or market value. Net fixed assets are the residual book value of the land and building occupied by the store, fixtures, and a delivery van. The land and building were purchased in 1950, and the building, although in good condition, has a depreciated book value of $1.

A few days later, having assembled the necessary data, the analyst estimated the average cost of capital (K_a) for small drugstore corporations like Adams Drugstore to be 15 percent. Following the going-concern approach, he chose a discounted-cash-flow model to estimate the value of the company's equity. The first part of the model is the following equation:

$$PV = \frac{CF_1}{(1 + K_a)} + \frac{CF_2}{(1 + K_a)^2} + \cdots + \frac{CF_n}{(1 + K_a)^n} + \frac{CF_n/K_a}{(1 + K_a)^n}$$

where PV is the value of the company's total assets, CF is the annual cash flow, and n is the forecast horizon—five years in this case. Beyond the five years the cash flows are assumed to be constant, thus forming a perpetuity. The last term in the equation is the present value of the perpetuity. The value of the company's equity is:

$$\text{Value of equity} = PV - \text{Total liabilities}$$

Each annual cash flow (CF) consists of an operating cash flow (OCF) defined as:

$$OCF = EBIT(1 - T) + \text{Depreciation}$$

where EBIT is earnings before interest and taxes and T is the marginal income tax rate. Subtracting the annual increase in net working capital (NWC) and capital expenditures from OCF yields the annual cash flow:

$$CF = OCF - \text{Increase in NWC} - \text{Capital expenditures}$$

Following an assessment of the local market, the analyst forecasts annual sales as follows:

Year	Sales Forecast
19X0	$1,765,500
19X1	1,871,430
19X2	1,965,002
19X3	2,063,252
19X4	2,166,414

Historically, EBIT has been approximately 14 percent of sales, and the analyst expects that margin to continue. Depreciation is expected to be $15,000 per year, and capital expenditures for replacement of fixed assets are expected to be $12,000 per year. The company's marginal income tax rate is 34 percent. Increases in net working capital are expected to be 40 percent of annual *increases* in sales.

a. Construct a table containing the annual sales revenue, EBIT, depreciation, increases in net working capital, and capital expenditures for each of the next five years.
b. Based on your answer to Part *a*, calculate (1) the expected annual cash flows and (2) the expected value of the company's assets at the end of Year 5.
c. Calculate the value (PV) of the company.
d. Calculate the value of the company's common equity. Assume that market value of the liabilities equals book value.
e. What is the value of Mrs. Adams's 80 percent interest in Adams Drugstore? Should she receive a premium for her controlling interest?
f. Should Mrs. Adams accept Mr. Klein's offer? Why or why not?

Selected References

Ang, James S., and Jess H. Chua. "Corporate Bankruptcy and Job Losses among Top Level Managers." *Financial Management,* Winter 1981: 70–74.

Banerjee, Ajeyo, and James E. Owers. "Wealth Reduction in White Knight Bids." *Financial Management,* Autumn 1992: 48–57.

Bruner, Robert F., and Kenneth M. Eades. "The Crash of the Revco Leveraged Buyout: The Hypothesis of Inadequate Capital." *Financial Management,* Spring 1992: 35–49.

Davidson, Wallace N., III, Sharon Hatten Garrison, and Glenn V. Henderson, Jr. "Examining Merger Strategy with the Capital Asset Pricing Model." *Financial Review,* May 1987: 233–247.

Mohan, Nancy, M. Fall Ainina, Daniel Kaufman, and Bernard J. Winger. "Acquisition/Divestiture Valuation Practices in Major U.S. Firms." *Financial Practice and Education,* Spring 1991: 73–81.

Ott, Mack, and G. J. Santoni. "Mergers and Takeovers—The Value of Predators' Information." Federal Reserve Bank of St. Louis, *Review,* December 1985: 16–28.

Roy, Asim. "Partial Acquisition Strategies for Business Combinations." *Financial Management,* Summer 1985, 16–23.

Scholes, Myron S. "Employee Stock Ownership Plans and Corporate Restructuring: Myths and Realities." *Financial Management,* Spring 1990: 12–28.

Wansley, James W., Rodney L. Roenfeldt, and Philip L. Cooley. "Abnormal Returns from Merger Profiles." *Journal of Financial and Quantitative Analysis,* June 1983: 149–162.

Weston, J. Fred. "Divestitures: Mistakes or Learning?" *Journal of Applied Corporate Finance,* Summer 1989: 68–76.

Chapter 22

INTERNATIONAL FINANCIAL MANAGEMENT

World Business

Improvements and technological changes in transportation and communication have made it easy for U.S. companies to transact business in foreign countries and for foreign companies to transact business in the United States. As a consequence, international business dealings now take many forms. U.S. companies export goods and services to expand their markets and import foreign-made products to take advantage of low costs. Some companies engage in joint ventures to manufacture U.S. products in foreign countries. Large companies like IBM, General Motors, and General Electric have built factories in foreign countries and operate them as subsidiaries. In some cases, establishing a foreign subsidiary enables the U.S. company to take advantage of cheap labor to make parts for products sold in the United States. For example, Mexico permits U.S. companies to establish manufacturing facilities there, as well as to ship equipment and materials to Mexico duty free, manufacture or assemble products using Mexican labor, then export the products to the United States.

How risky is Mexico as a country for foreign corporate investments? The *International Country Risk Guide (ICRG)* judges Mexico relatively low in risk, placing the country 32nd of the 129 countries ranked. *ICRG* publishes an overall risk rating for each country based on: (1) political risk—possible seizure of assets and stability of government, (2) financial risk—strength of currency and level of country debt, and (3) economic risk—inflation rate and balance of payments. The ten lowest-risk and the ten highest-risk countries according to *ICRG* are:

Lowest Risk	Highest Risk
Switzerland	Liberia
Luxembourg	Somalia
Norway	Sudan
Austria	Iraq
Germany	Burma
Netherlands	Uganda
Brunei	Ethiopia
Japan	Haiti
Singapore	Zaire
United States	Guinea-Bissau

Country risk is a critical variable in the decision of a company to invest abroad.

The study of international financial management adds some new wrinkles to financial theory and practice. Regardless of the type of foreign transaction that U.S. companies engage in, the differences in the value of the dollar in foreign currencies add complexity to the transaction. The financial manager must adjust cash flows for currency and risk differences. Foreign transactions offer advantages to companies, notably the expansion of product markets, opportunities for production at lower costs, and alternative sources of financing. If companies decide to invest abroad and to obtain financing from foreign sources, then they must be prepared for the risks unique in foreign business. These are the aspects of international financial management that we explore in this chapter.

FOREIGN-EXCHANGE MARKETS

Any company buying or selling goods and services abroad deals with foreign currency. Individuals deal with foreign currency as well when they travel abroad. If you vacation in Italy, then you will need lira, not dollars, to buy food, get a hotel room, and buy souvenirs. If you subscribe to a British magazine, then you will pay for it in pounds sterling. Lira and pounds sterling are two examples of foreign currencies to U.S. citizens. The U.S. dollar is foreign currency to Italian and British citizens.

How can individuals and companies obtain foreign currency? Like other goods and services, it is sold in a market—the foreign-exchange market. There are three types of foreign-exchange markets, as discussed in the following section.

Types of Markets

Different foreign-exchange markets accommodate different needs of financial managers and investors. For example, a company importing South Korean computer parts might need to pay for them immediately. In this case the financial manager would use the spot market to buy won (pronounced *wan*), the South Korean currency. The **spot market** is the market in foreign currencies for immediate delivery, and it is often called the *cash market*. Financial managers use the spot market whenever they need to buy foreign currency to make immediate payments. An importer of Hyundai automobiles would buy won in the spot market to pay the exporter, if the cars were shipped C.O.D. payable in won.

When a transaction calls for future payment in foreign currency, the financial manager might want to use either the forward or the futures market. The **forward market** is a telecommunications market dealing in tailor-made contracts to buy and sell foreign currencies for future delivery. The forward market is similar in organization to the over-the-counter market for stocks in that neither has a centralized trading facility. Commercial banks will write a contract to sell or buy a negotiated amount of foreign currency for delivery in the future at a price set today. The forward market offers flexibility to companies needing foreign currency in the future by allowing the contract size and settlement date to be tailored to the company's needs.

The **futures market** is a centralized trading facility that specializes in standardized contracts to buy and sell foreign currencies for future delivery. The futures market is similar to organized exchanges for stocks in that it has centralized trading facilities. A financial manager can call a securities broker and arrange a contract to deliver (sell) or to accept delivery of (buy) foreign currency

spot market
Market in which foreign currencies trade for immediate delivery; cash market.

forward market
Network of banks that write tailor-made contracts for future delivery of foreign currencies.

futures market
Centralized trading facility in which standardized contracts trade for future delivery of foreign currency.

The author thanks Professor David A. Ricks of the American Graduate School of International Management for his assistance in preparing this chapter.

TABLE 22.1

Comparison of the Forward Market and Futures Market

Feature	Forward Market	Futures Market
Contract size	Tailored to meet individual needs	Standardized
Delivery date	Tailored to meet individual needs	Standardized
Commissions	Set by spread between bank's buy and sell prices	Standardized
Marketplace	Telephone	Central exchange floor
Regulation	Self-regulating	Commodity Futures Trading Commission
Frequency of delivery	Greater than 90% settled by actual delivery	Less than 1% settled by delivery
Speculation	Not widespread	Widespread
Price change	No daily limit	Daily limit imposed by the exchange

Source: Based on *Understanding Futures in Foreign Exchange,* Chicago: International Monetary Market, 10–11.

in the future at a price set today. Contracts have standardized maturity dates and are written for standardized monetary amounts.

Table 22.1 shows the principal differences between the forward and futures markets. Which market the financial manager uses depends on the relative benefits and costs for the task at hand. Financial managers normally use the forward market when they expect actual delivery of the currency to occur. They normally use the futures market for hedging risk. The forward market provides the additional advantage of working with a banker who may be able to give advice on political and economic developments in a foreign country.

Foreign-Exchange Rates

foreign-exchange rate
Number of currency units of one country needed to buy the currency unit of another country; the price of foreign currency.

A **foreign-exchange rate** is the number of currency units of one country needed to buy the currency unit of another country. In other words, it is the price of foreign currency. Foreign-exchange rates result from competitive forces in foreign-exchange markets as individuals, companies, commercial banks, and central banks such as the Federal Reserve System buy and sell foreign currency. Figure 22.1 illustrates the adjustment of a foreign-exchange rate to an increase in demand for foreign currency. Suppose the foreign currency Figure 22.1 illustrates is the South Korean won, although any foreign currency would serve equally well. An increase in demand for won occurs when U.S. imports of South Korean products increase, U.S. citizens travel to South Korea, U.S. **multinational companies**—companies with facilities abroad—expand facilities there, and foreign aid and military assistance to South Korea increase. Increased demand for won from D_1 to D_2 increases its price from P_1 to P_2. The higher price causes an increase in the quantity of won that holders of the currency willingly supply.

multinational company
Company with operations in more than one country.

appreciation
Increase in the price (often measured in U.S. dollars) of foreign currency.

An increase in the price of foreign currency means that it **appreciates,** and a decrease in the price of foreign currency means that it **depreciates.**[1] When one

depreciation
Decrease in the price (often measured in U.S. dollars) of foreign currency.

[1] These terms differ from devaluation and revaluation. *Devaluation* is the formal act of a government that reduces the value of its currency and the price at which it will buy and sell its currency. For example, in May 1987 Brazil devalued the cruzado by 8.49 percent to 27.5 per dollar in an effort to revive the country's slumping trade performance. *Revaluation* is the formal act of raising the value at which the government will buy and sell its currency.

FIGURE 22.1

Supply of and Demand for Foreign Currency

The foreign-exchange rate, or price of foreign currency in U.S. dollars, depends on the market forces of supply and demand. As demand for a foreign currency shifts upward, price rises and quantity supplied increases.

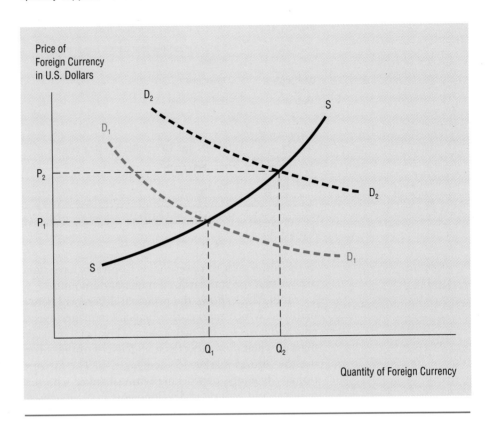

currency appreciates, the other necessarily depreciates, and vice versa. In Figure 22.1 the won appreciates from P_1 to P_2 and the U.S. dollar depreciates.

If South Korea later imports an increasing quantity of U.S. equipment and other goods, then demand for the U.S. dollar increases. Increased demand for the U.S. dollar by South Koreans causes it to appreciate. At the same time the South Korean won depreciates.

Reading Foreign-Exchange Rates. Foreign-exchange rates may change rapidly when investors are busily buying one currency and selling another. For example, a U.S. company may be buying won to invest in the working capital of its South Korean affiliate, and speculators may be buying won based on their expectations that it will continue to appreciate. Financial managers and investors watch exchange rates closely because of their volatility. Figure 22.2 presents foreign-exchange rates quoted in *The Wall Street Journal*. The text at the top indicates that the quotations apply to wholesale transactions of $1,000,000 or more; Bankers Trust Company, Telerate, and other sources provide the quotations as of 3 P.M. in New York City. At the lower right of the figure are shown quotations for two collections of different currencies. An SDR is a special drawing right originally developed by the International Monetary Fund, an agency organized

FIGURE 22.2   **Foreign-Exchange Rate Quotations**

EXCHANGE RATES

Wednesday, April 7, 1993

The New York foreign exchange selling rates below apply to trading among banks in amounts of $1 million and more, as quoted at 3 p.m. Eastern time by Bankers Trust Co., Telerate and other sources. Retail transactions provide fewer units of foreign currency per dollar.

Country	U.S. $ equiv. Wed.	U.S. $ equiv. Tues.	Currency per U.S. $ Wed.	Currency per U.S. $ Tues.
Argentina (Peso)	1.01	1.01	.99	.99
Australia (Dollar)	.7063	.7076	1.4158	1.4132
Austria (Schilling)	.08780	.08816	11.39	11.34
Bahrain (Dinar)	2.6522	2.6522	.3771	.3771
Belgium (Franc)	.03008	.03015	33.25	33.16
Brazil (Cruzeiro)	.0000390	.0000395	25656.02	25325.00
Britain (Pound)	1.5135	1.5145	.6607	.6603
30-Day Forward	1.5102	1.5109	.6622	.6619
90-Day Forward	1.5035	1.5044	.6651	.6647
180-Day Forward	1.4950	1.4958	.6689	.6685
Canada (Dollar)	.7930	.7947	1.2610	1.2583
30-Day Forward	.7917	.7935	1.2631	1.2603
90-Day Forward	.7888	.7906	1.2677	1.2649
180-Day Forward	.7837	.7854	1.2760	1.2733
Czechoslovakia (Koruna)				
Commercial rate	.0357654	.0357654	27.9600	27.9600
Chile (Peso)	.002568	.002565	389.37	389.87
China (Renminbi)	.174856	.174856	5.7190	5.7190
Colombia (Peso)	.001536	.001536	651.10	651.10
Denmark (Krone)	.1609	.1614	6.2155	6.1941
Ecuador (Sucre)				
Floating rate	.000549	.000549	1822.02	1822.02
Finland (Markka)	.17087	.17082	5.8523	5.8540
France (Franc)	.18260	.18315	5.4765	5.4600
30-Day Forward	.18160	.18203	5.5065	4.4935
90-Day Forward	.17987	.18023	5.5595	5.5485
180-Day Forward	.17778	.17809	5.6250	5.6150
Germany (Mark)	.6180	.6203	1.6180	1.6120
30-Day Forward	.6155	.6176	1.6247	1.6192
90-Day Forward	.6110	.6132	1.6367	1.6309
180-Day Forward	.6055	.6076	1.6516	1.6458
Greece (Drachma)	.004521	.004544	221.20	220.05
Hong Kong (Dollar)	.12935	.12936	7.7310	7.7305
Hungary (Forint)	.0115660	.0115848	86.4600	86.3200
India (Rupee)	.03226	.03226	31.00	31.00
Indonesia (Rupiah)	.0004831	.0004831	2070.01	2070.01
Ireland (Punt)	1.5102	1.5133	.6622	.6608
Israel (Shekel)	.3704	.3704	2.6995	2.6996
Italy (Lira)	.0006287	.0006285	1590.51	1591.06
Japan (Yen)	.008805	.008777	113.57	113.93
30-Day Forward	.008805	.008777	113.57	113.93
90-Day Forward	.008805	.008778	113.57	113.93
180-Day Forward	.008808	.008781	113.54	113.89

Country	U.S. $ equiv. Wed.	U.S. $ equiv. Tues.	Currency per U.S. $ Wed.	Currency per U.S. $ Tues.
Jordan (Dinar)	1.4896	1.4896	.6713	.6713
Kuwait (Dinar)	3.3167	3.3167	.3015	.3015
Lebanon (Pound)	.000574	.000574	1742.00	1742.00
Malaysia (Ringgit)	.3875	.3874	2.5808	2.5813
Malta (Lira)	2.6350	2.6350	.3795	.3795
Mexico (Peso)				
Floating rate	.3233107	.3233107	3.0930	3.0930
Netherland (Guilder)	.5498	.5519	1.8187	1.8120
New Zealand (Dollar)	.5351	.5335	1.8688	1.8744
Norway (Krone)	.1451	.1455	6.8903	6.8728
Pakistan (Rupee)	.0377	.0377	26.53	26.53
Peru (New Sol)	.5514	.5514	1.81	1.81
Philippines (Peso)	.03960	.03960	25.25	25.25
Poland (Zloty)	.00006307	.00006329	15856.15	15800.01
Portugal (Escudo)	.006642	.006686	150.55	149.56
Saudi Arabia (Riyal)	.26702	.26702	3.7450	3.7450
Singapore (Dollar)	.6158	.6146	1.6240	1.6270
South Africa (Rand)				
Commercial rate	.3133	z	3.1923	z
Financial rate	.2197	z	4.5525	z
South Korea (Won)	.0012555	.0012569	796.50	795.60
Spain (Peseta)	.008626	.008662	115.93	115.45
Sweden (Krona)	.1304	.1309	7.6693	7.6369
Switzerland (Franc)	.6714	.6718	1.4895	1.4885
30-Day Forward	.6691	.6705	1.4945	1.4914
90-Day Forward	.6683	.6687	1.4964	1.4955
180-Day Forward	.6664	.6668	1.5005	1.4998
Taiwan (Dollar)	.038745	.038790	25.81	25.78
Thailand (Baht)	.03954	.03954	25.29	25.29
Turkey (Lira)	.0001059	.0001061	9441.01	9423.00
United Arab (Dirham)	.2723	.2723	3.6725	3.6725
Uruguay (New Peso)				
Financial	.000261	.000261	3835.00	3835.00
Venezuela (Bolivar)				
Floating rate	.01196	.01197	83.63	83.53
		– – –		
SDR	1.40208	1.40275	.71323	.71289
ECU	1.20190	1.20530	....	....

Special Drawing Rights (SDR) are based on exchange rates for the U.S., German, British, French and Japanese currencies. Source: International Monetary Fund.

European Currency Unit (ECU) is based on a basket of community currencies.

z-Not quoted.

Source: *The Wall Street Journal*, April 8, 1993, C15.

to stabilize international exchange and to expand trade. An ECU is a European currency unit, an average value of the currencies of countries in the European Community. *The Wall Street Journal* quotes these rates because some international transactions are stated in SDRs and ECUs rather than in an individual currency.

Foreign-exchange quotations are expressed in *American terms* as the U.S. dollar cost of foreign currency (numerical Columns 1 and 2 in Figure 22.2). The quotations are expressed in *European terms* as the amount of foreign currency per U.S. dollar (numerical Columns 3 and 4). In other words, Column 3 is the reciprocal of Column 1, and Column 4 is the reciprocal of Column 2. For example, on Wednesday, April 7, 1993, the Canadian dollar in the spot market cost $0.7930 (Column 1), and 1.2610 (Column 3, 1/0.7930) Canadian dollars could buy one U.S. dollar.

Some countries have more than one foreign-exchange rate. For example, Venezuela has an official (not shown) and a floating rate, and South Africa has a commercial (trade) and a financial rate. These countries have implemented foreign-exchange controls to influence specific types of transactions.

Spot and Forward Rates.

Figure 22.2 shows spot rates for each currency and forward rates for several actively traded currencies. A financial manager buys foreign currency in the spot market at the spot rate. The price of foreign currency for future delivery is the forward rate. For example, the British pound (pounds sterling) costs $1.5135 in the spot market (Wednesday quotation), $1.5102 for delivery in 30 days, $1.5035 for delivery in 90 days, and $1.4950 for delivery in 180 days. The forward rate does not equal the spot rate but is an unbiased forecast of the future spot rate. Where a forward rate stands in relation to its spot rate helps the financial manager to forecast a currency's eventual spot price.

forward discount

Forward exchange rate below the spot rate, indicating a weak currency.

A currency is weak if the forward rate is below the spot rate (a **forward discount**). The British pound trades at a forward discount, as shown in Figure 22.2:

- Merchants receiving the weak currency in the next few weeks are selling it in the forward market to avoid potentially larger losses than the forward discount if the exchange rate topples. For example, if a U.S. exporter expects to receive £100,000 (100,000 pounds sterling) in 90 days, the financial manager may enter a contract to deliver them in 90 days for $150,350 ($1.5035 × £100,000) rather than risking a large decline in the spot rate.

- Speculators are selling the weak currency in the forward market, hoping that it will collapse before their sales contracts mature. If the eventual spot rate is below the contract rate, they buy the currency at the new spot price and profit from the difference.

forward premium

Forward exchange rate above the spot rate, indicating a strong currency.

By similar reasoning, a currency is strong if the forward rate is above the spot rate (a **forward premium**).[2] Merchants are buying the currency in the forward market to lock in the price, and speculators are buying it to profit if the future spot price is above the contract price. For example, comparing the spot rate and the 180-day forward rate for the Canadian dollar and for the Japanese yen in Figure 22.2 reveals that the Canadian dollar is weak and the Japanese yen is strong.

FINANCING MULTINATIONAL BUSINESS

U.S. companies buy goods and services from and sell goods and services to foreign companies for cash and on credit, typically consisting of various types of drafts. Multinational companies requiring long-term financing have the option of issuing common stock and bonds in foreign capital markets.

Short-Term Financing

Foreign transactions sometimes take longer to complete than domestic transactions and present additional risks to U.S. companies. Because of these factors, U.S. companies use alternatives to the domestic methods of short-term financing. To assist U.S. companies, banks provide the service of guaranteeing payment from the time merchandise is shipped or ordered to the time payment is received.

---

[2] The forward discount or premium reflects in part the principle of *interest rate parity*, which holds that, in an efficient market with no transaction costs, the forward differential depends on the interest rate differential between countries. Thus countries with low interest rates (such as Japan) compared with those in the United States will have a currency trading at a forward premium.

I N T E R N A T I O N A L   D I M E N S I O N S

Roller Coaster Currency Markets

Above the Barclays Bank's sprawling currency-trading floor in London, the air is filled with cigarette smoke and shouts. The foreign-exchange dealers, row after row of them, . . . are umbilically linked to the market with three video screens and two telephones each. It is an arena of split-second decision making.

This is the rawest nerve of the international financial system, the foreign-exchange market, where only seconds after some news announcement—trade figures, housing starts, election results, whatever—an impact is felt in the value of the affected country's most visible asset, its currency. For the major players—banks, securities houses, multinational corporations, and investing institutions— the risks in this huge market can be staggering unless properly hedged and managed.

With its staff of 140 people trading more than $9 billion a day, the Barclays dealing room is one of the biggest in London, the world's currency-trading capital. . . .

. . . there is an inherent conflict between the government officials and the currency traders. The governments may want stability, but foreign-exchange dealers desire the opposite. . . . An axiom of the business is that any trader complaining of exchange-rate volatility is a trader who lost money in the market [that day]. . . . "Foreign-exchange speculators make convenient scapegoats for the central bankers and finance ministers," said Claude Tygier, a New York foreign-exchange consultant, who was formerly a bank currency dealer. ". . . And those market conditions are created not by the speculators but usually by failed government policies and poor economic performance."

Still there is no denying that exchange rates have become increasingly volatile in recent years, and much of the difference is explained by changes within the market itself. Because of new technology, financial deregulation, and huge trade imbalances among major nations, the foreign-currency market is mushrooming in size and increasing in importance. . . .

Today, 90 percent of all turnover in the currency markets is trading among dealers, mostly banks, while only 10 percent is

generated by outside investors or corporations buying currencies to finance trade or for investment purposes. Trades are typically done in blocks of several million dollars. . . .

Banks make money on razor-thin arbitrage profits—for example, selling a currency on slightly more favorable terms to one bank than the terms it acquired it on from another. Most profits, however, come from positioning—correctly anticipating short-term movements in currencies.

Bank traders typically focus on where rates are headed over the course of a few hours. Carrying large inventories of a given currency overnight is a risk the banks usually avoid. Because dealers tend not to carry large positions for long, most currency economists agree that the traders have far less impact on exchange-rate trends than do major investors such as corporations. . . . The traders, of course, are speculators. But their speculation would mostly affect currency prices for a few hours, while it is longer-term investors whose decisions can influence rates over the course of weeks or months.

Source: Adapted from Steve Lohr, "Currency Nerve Center: A Penchant for Volatility," *New York Times*, Mar. 23, 1987. Reprinted with permission. Copyright © 1987 by The New York Times Company. Reprinted by permission.

A short-term financing source often used to finance international trade is the draft, an order written by an exporter, or seller, requesting the importer, or buyer, to pay a specified amount of money on a specified date. If the importer agrees to pay the draft (that is, accepts it), then the draft is a *trade draft*. If the importer's bank agrees to pay the draft, then it is a *bank draft*. Drafts conforming to specific terms become negotiable by signature, which means they can be transferred by endorsement. Trade and bank drafts may be one of two types. A **sight draft** is payable upon presentation. When the importing company receives the draft, it must make payment immediately. Sight drafts are similar to buying on terms of

sight draft
Draft payable upon presentation by the exporter to the importer.

time draft
Draft payable on a future date.

C.O.D. in a domestic transaction. A **time draft** permits the importer to pay after some delay, thereby allowing time to raise cash for payment. When an importer accepts a time draft, it becomes a *trade acceptance*. When the importer's bank accepts the time draft, it becomes a *banker's acceptance*. The acceptance is returned to the exporter, who may either hold it until maturity or sell it at a discount from face value. The discount is usually less than the bank prime rate, and the acceptance is negotiable by signature. Financial publications such as *The Wall Street Journal* quote rates on bankers' acceptances each day.

Eurocurrency
Currency held outside its country of origin.

Some banks make loans denominated in foreign currency. They obtain foreign currency to lend from a deposit of foreign currency, called a **Eurocurrency**. The addition of the prefix *Euro* to *currency* denotes U.S. dollars or any other currency outside the currency's country of origin. For example, a deposit in England denominated in U.S. dollars is a Eurodollar deposit.

Eurocurrency loans are often made on a floating-rate basis. Interest rates are set at LIBOR plus, which means that lenders set the rate at the London interbank offered rate plus a percentage point premium. LIBOR is the interest rate at which London banks loan Eurodollars to each other. Lenders usually adjust rates on outstanding loans every six months. For example, if the interest rate is stated as LIBOR plus 75 basis points, then the borrower will pay 9.75 percent annual interest when LIBOR is 9 percent. If LIBOR is different at the end of six months, then the borrower will pay the new rate plus 75 basis points for the next six months. *The Wall Street Journal* publishes LIBOR daily in its column on money rates. Because large companies can borrow in either the U.S. money market or the Eurocurrency market, the interest rates in these two markets tend to move together.

Common-Stock Financing

U.S. companies may issue stock in a foreign country as long as they conform to the regulations of the country. There are a few countries, however, that prohibit foreign companies from issuing securities, and some that simply do not have large enough capital markets to meet corporate financing needs. The number of such countries, though, is declining, and many countries now encourage U.S. companies to enter their capital markets. *The Wall Street Journal* reports selected stock prices daily on exchanges in London, Frankfurt, Milan, Sydney, Toronto, and Tokyo.

Each stock exchange establishes its own set of requirements and fees for listing. Charges can be substantial, so most multinational companies list shares only in the countries in which they are the most active. Because foreign companies typically pay out a high percentage of earnings in dividends, U.S. companies issuing shares in these markets are pressured to do the same to attract investors. Overseas equity markets are not as liquid as their U.S. counterpart. It is therefore more difficult to raise large sums without paying higher costs. For this and other reasons, U.S. companies typically shun foreign markets for issuing common stock.

Long-Term Debt Financing

Eurobond
Bond issued outside the country in whose currency the interest and principal are paid.

Although U.S. companies generally shun foreign equity markets, they often use foreign markets to issue **Eurobonds**. The prefix *Euro* means that the bonds are issued outside the country in whose currency they are denominated. An example of a Eurobond is as follows: Exxon sells bonds denominated in U.S. dollars (interest and principal paid in U.S. dollars) in Japan.

Multinational companies consider the Eurobond market an important source of financing. U.S. companies issue about 40 percent of their bonds in the Eurobond market. About half of the Eurobond issues have floating rates based on LIBOR. Eurobonds may be denominated in almost any currency or stated in terms of the European currency unit (ECU). Most Eurobonds, however, are denominated in U.S. dollars.

In addition to Eurobonds, companies also issue foreign bonds. A **foreign bond** is issued by a foreign company and is denominated in the domestic currency. For example, a bond marketed by Sony Corporation in the United States with interest and principal denominated in dollars is a foreign bond. A bond issued by General Electric in Germany and denominated in marks is also a foreign bond.

Eurobonds offer benefits in comparison with foreign bonds. First, the Eurobond market permits a company to issue a bond with interest and principal payable in its own country's currency. For example, in 1984 Texaco issued $1.5 billion in Eurobonds to finance its acquisition of Getty Oil. Although the bonds were sold in France, Italy, Great Britain, and West Germany, interest and principal were payable in U.S. dollars. This feature eliminated Texaco's uncertainty surrounding future exchange rates; any unexpected appreciation or depreciation of the U.S. dollar would not affect Texaco's debt-service payments. Second, the Eurobond market is much larger and can accommodate larger issues than the foreign-bond market. Third, flotation costs and the time required to issue a Eurobond are less than those associated with foreign bonds because the Eurobond market is largely unregulated. The issuer does not need to file a registration statement, furnish the buyer with a prospectus, pay filing fees, or conform with security regulations. As a result, big borrowers such as Texaco can often raise money more cheaply and quickly in the Eurobond market than they can in the U.S. bond market. Fourth, Eurobonds are usually in bearer form without the owner's name on the bond or elsewhere listed. Some investors prefer the anonymity of bearer bonds.

RISKS IN FOREIGN BUSINESS

A company transacting business across national boundaries faces risks beyond those present in domestic operations. Domestic companies must contend with business and financial risks. In addition to these, multinational companies face social, political, and foreign-exchange risks.

Laws, languages, and business customs differ widely from one country to another, and it is these differences that create **social risk**. Unfamiliarity with the laws, language, and customs of a country increases the risk of foreign transactions in comparison with domestic transactions. Failure to consider the belief systems and traditions of people in foreign countries can cause foreign projects to fail. For example, written contracts are more readily repudiated in some countries than in the United States, and some English words have totally different meanings when translated into other languages.

Each nation is a sovereign power with the right under international law to repudiate contracts with citizens of other countries, confiscate their property, or subject them to punitive or discriminatory regulations. The possibility that assets may be seized *(expropriated)* by a foreign sovereign power creates **political risk**. For example, the 1987 decision by Brazil to suspend interest payments on $67 billion of its debt and to force its creditors to accept lower interest rates and

foreign bond
Bond issued in a country foreign to the issuer and denominated in the foreign country's currency.

social risk
Uncertainty of future cash flows as a result of different laws, languages, and customs.

political risk
Uncertainty of future cash flows as a result of a country's sovereign power.

longer maturities on loans cost Brazil's creditors billions of dollars. Its two largest creditors, Citicorp and Chase Manhattan, lost about $2.5 billion.

In addition to social and political risks, a company transacting business abroad faces **foreign-exchange risk** from the uncertainty of exchange rates. Since the price of foreign currency changes each day, forecasting the value of foreign currency is a challenging task. The following sections discuss how companies cope with the risks arising from the volatility in exchange rates.

foreign-exchange risk
Uncertainty of future cash flows arising from unexpected changes in foreign-exchange rates.

Foreign-Exchange Risk

Foreign-exchange risk creates the possibility that an actual return will differ from its expected value. A multinational company faces three types of foreign-exchange risk: translation (or accounting) risk, economic risk, and transaction risk.

translation risk
Foreign-exchange risk arising from the translation of foreign-currency-denominated values into the company's home currency.

Translation risk arises from the translation of foreign-currency-denominated operations into the company's home currency for reporting operating results. To *translate* means to calculate amounts denominated in one currency in terms of another currency. When U.S. companies translate and present in their financial statements the results of foreign operations denominated in foreign currency, they recognize foreign currency gains or losses depending on whether the foreign currency has appreciated or depreciated. The change in foreign-exchange rates during a reporting period affects assets and liabilities, perhaps causing net worth to change. Although translation recognizes an economic event that has already taken place—change in foreign-exchange rates—the translation may cause net worth to differ from what management and investors expect.[3]

EXAMPLE

Boulder Associates Inc. (BAI) has an affiliate in Lucerne, Switzerland, with $F_{Sw}760,000$ (Swiss francs) in assets and $F_{Sw}426,000$ in liabilities that it must report at the current exchange rate. During the accounting period, the Swiss franc depreciated by 12 percent from $0.58 to $0.51. BAI will therefore show a *translation loss* on assets and a *translation gain* on liabilities. Had the Swiss franc appreciated, BAI would show a translation gain on assets and a translation loss on liabilities. Because the dollar value of the Swiss franc declined, BAI reports a net translation loss calculated as follows:

Change in value of assets:

Value before depreciation ($F_{Sw}760,000 \times \$0.58$)	$440,800	
Less value after depreciation ($F_{Sw}760,000 \times \$0.51$)	387,600	
Translation loss on assets		$53,200
Change in value of liabilities:		
Value before depreciation ($F_{Sw}426,000 \times \$0.58$)	$247,080	
Less value after depreciation ($F_{Sw}426,000 \times \$0.51$)	217,260	
Translation gain on liabilities		$29,820
Net translation loss		$23,380

BAI's book-value net worth declines by $23,380.

---

[3] FASB *Statement No. 52: Foreign Currency Translation* describes the accounting rules for translation. Accountants carry translation gains and losses to shareholder equity on the company's balance sheet, which means that earnings per share are unaffected. (FASB stands for Financial Accounting Standards Board.)

economic risk

Foreign-exchange risk arising from changes in operating cash flows from foreign operations.

transaction risk

Foreign-exchange risk arising from settling a transaction in foreign currency.

Economic risk is the uncertainty in operating cash flows of foreign operations resulting from unexpected changes in exchange rates. *Unexpected* changes are emphasized because financial managers and investors include expected exchange rates in their evaluation and projection of operating results. Only unexpected changes in exchange rates cause changes in the price of the company's common stock. Economic risk has significance for the long-run performance of a company because it arises from future, long-run cash flows over several periods.

Transaction risk results from an unexpected change in foreign-exchange rates during the period between the agreement to pay foreign currency and the actual payment date. It has a short-term impact on cash receipts and payments because buyers and sellers usually write such contracts for a few months or less. For example, if you pay 50 Swiss francs (F_{Sw}) for a Swiss magazine subscription and the franc is worth $0.68, then your dollar cost is $34 ($0.68 $\times$ 50). But if you wait to pay until the publisher bills you for the subscription and the franc appreciates to $0.80, then the subscription costs you $40. Your dollar cost differs from what you expected because the Swiss franc appreciated after you agreed to pay but before you actually paid—transaction risk.

Economic and Transaction Risks

Economic and transaction risks differ in the time period of their impact on cash flows. Transaction risk has a short-term impact and economic risk has a long-term impact. Each risk means that when a financial manager converts dollars into foreign currency or foreign currency into dollars, the company's cash account will likely differ from what was originally expected. To *convert* foreign currency means physically exchanging one currency for another.

Transaction risk results from conversion in the immediate future, but economic risk results from conversion in the distant future. An unexpected change in exchange rates creates economic risk for the following reason: It may cause a foreign affiliate to lose sales and to experience an increase in its cost of operations, each unexpectedly changing the parent company's operating cash flows. For example, unexpected appreciation of the Italian lira may cause the Italian affiliate to lose customers as Italian customers and other customers begin to purchase from companies in other countries (remember, other currencies have depreciated relative to the lira). When the U.S. parent subsequently *repatriates* (transfers) lira from the Italian affiliate to the parent, there will be fewer dollars received because of the decline in sales. Unexpected depreciation of the British pound may cause the British affiliate to experience a reduction in its operating cash flows because the cost of raw materials it purchases from Spain has increased (remember, other currencies have appreciated relative to the pound). When the U.S. parent subsequently repatriates pounds from its British affiliate, there will be fewer dollars received.

Managing Economic Risk.   Economic risk is a long-term problem that a company addresses by making adjustments in its foreign production and marketing strategies. The company might take one of the following steps:

- Locate a new plant in the foreign country.
- Increase advertising for its products to increase sales.
- Market products targeted toward high-income, less price-sensitive customers.
- Reduce costs by altering production processes.

Each one of these steps is strategic (long run) and requires a commitment of large expenditures by the company. For example, following the substantial dollar devaluation of 1971, Volkswagen revised its product line for the U.S. market to keep mark-denominated operating cash flow high: It introduced and emphasized Rabbits and Audis rather than the previously successful low-priced Bug. When the Japanese yen appreciated in the middle 1980s, Honda did the same with its introduction of the upscale Acura. In this way the dollar could depreciate by, say, 20 percent, but the dollar price of the product could increase by about 20 percent, and the yen-denominated operating cash flow would remain roughly unchanged. Toyota adjusted to the dollar depreciation by constructing production facilities in the United States, launching a joint venture with General Motors to produce the Chevrolet Nova, and introducing the upscale Lexus. Economic risk was counteracted because U.S. sales were maintained and yen-denominated operating cash flow was preserved.

Managing Transaction Risk.   Transaction risk is a short-term problem that only one participant in a foreign transaction incurs—the participant with settlement stated in foreign currency. For example, trade between an Italian company and a German company presents the German company with transaction risk if payment is in Italian lira, and presents the Italian company with transaction risk if payment is in German marks. It makes no difference which one is to receive or pay—only the currency denomination is important.

A U.S. company dealing in international transactions can reduce transaction risk in several ways. First, the company might require payment in U.S. dollars. Then whenever foreign currency appreciates or depreciates, the U.S. dollar cash flow does not change. A requirement such as this may not be financially wise, however, because the U.S. company may be unable to force foreigners to pay or accept dollars.

Another way to lessen transaction risk is to pay or receive cash at the time of ordering or selling merchandise. By including (or requiring) payment with an order, the U.S. company's cash flow is unaffected by subsequent changes in the foreign-exchange rate. The U.S. company may not want to make payment when ordering, however, because it would incur an opportunity cost; delaying payment would permit the company to earn a return on the invested cash. Also, the U.S. company may not be in an economic position strong enough to require its foreign customers to pay when ordering.

In general, companies cope with transaction risk by adjusting credit terms, collection policy, and payment policy. They delay payments and accelerate collections in weak currencies and accelerate payments and delay collections in strong currencies. Exporting companies use credit and collection strategies to minimize transaction risk, and importing companies use payment strategies:

- *Credit terms:* Grant liberal credit terms to customers whose currencies are likely to appreciate (strong currencies). Insist on strict credit terms—or on cash payment—with customers whose currencies are likely to depreciate (weak currencies).

- *Collection policy:* Accelerate collections from customers whose currencies are weak. Relax pressure on collections from customers whose currencies are strong.

- *Payment policy:* Accelerate payment to suppliers whose currencies are strong; consider paying cash. Delay payment to suppliers whose currencies are weak.

EXAMPLE

Intec Gypsum Inc. borrows $F_{Sw}400,000$ from a Swiss bank with repayment in Swiss francs. Because the Swiss franc may appreciate between now and maturity, Intec Gypsum's financial manager requests a clause permitting early repayment. When the spot price of Swiss francs is $0.6793, Intec Gypsum pays $271,720 to retire the loan:

$$\$0.6793 \times F_{Sw}400,000 = \$271,720$$

Suppose after two months that Intec Gypsum's financial manager expects the Swiss franc to appreciate to $0.722. If the company were to delay paying until after the appreciation, then the U.S. dollar cost of the loan would be $288,800:

$$\$0.722 \times F_{Sw}400,000 = \$288,800$$

Accelerating payment eliminates the foreign-exchange loss because appreciation of the franc will not affect principal previously paid.

In addition to adjusting credit and payment policies, companies also adjust prices to nullify the effect of varying foreign-exchange rates. For example, companies often increase the resale price of imported products to compensate for appreciation of foreign currency. Competition allowing, such price increases enable companies to maintain their contribution margin ratios. The rise in price of foreign currency increases the variable costs of importing, which are recouped through a higher resale price.[4] If sales revenues increase by the same percentage as variable costs, then the contribution margin ratio remains constant.

Hedging Transaction Risk

Conducting business in dollars, adjusting credit and payment policies, and adjusting prices help U.S. companies to reduce risk from uncertain exchange rates. To reduce risk further, many companies add hedging techniques. To *hedge* means to establish a currency position in the forward (or futures) market opposite to the currency position in the spot market. Companies hedge to preserve cash flows, not to make a profit.

A company expecting to receive payment in foreign currency (an asset indicated by an account receivable) hedges in the forward market by contracting with a bank to deliver foreign currency (a liability). A company expecting to make a payment in foreign currency (a liability indicated by an account payable) hedges by contracting with a bank to accept delivery of foreign currency (an asset). In each case the company takes a position in the forward market equal and opposite to an actual or developing position in the spot market. In this way receivables and payables denominated in foreign currency equal each other, and appreciation or depreciation of the foreign currency does not affect the dollar cash flow from the transaction.

EXAMPLE

U.S. Grain and Wheat sells wheat to a British company with payment stipulated to be £250,000 payable in 90 days. The U.S. company is exposed to transaction risk because payment is specified in pounds (£) and the pound may depreciate

---

[4]Elasticity of demand enters the picture here. The analysis assumes an inelastic demand, suggesting that increased costs can be passed on to the customers. Such a condition is unlikely to hold in all cases.

I N T E R N A T I O N A L   D I M E N S I O N S

Misinterpretation and a Financial Blunder

Sometimes errors in translating foreign-exchange rates lead to capital-budgeting mistakes and large financial losses. Consider the investment decision of a U.S. multinational corporation that invested $2,000,000 to double the size of its Brazilian facilities. Management based the decision on the affiliate's past performance, which appeared to be mind-boggling. You see, the U.S. managers thought that sales and earnings had more than doubled during the previous 5 years, but

they were deceived because of the company's method of translating foreign operations into dollars. The company's policy was to translate the current month's operations at the new rate and to compare it with historical results based on previous rates. The result is what you would expect when comparing apples and oranges: meaningless information.

The translation method made the foreign affiliate's sales appear to increase more in dollars than they really had because the Brazilian cruzado (now called cruzeiro) appreciated over the period. Thus cruzado-denominated sales did not increase at anything like the dollar-denominated sales. When the U.S. headquarters calculated the

annual growth rate in U.S. dollars without considering the impact of the cruzado appreciation, it was completely fooled. Consider in the table, for example, how meaningless the dollar increase in sales is.

The dollar values suggest that sales increased by 260 percent, ($23,780,000/$6,600,000) − 1. But sales in cruzados increased by 93.3 percent, (Cr580,000,000/Cr300,000,000) − 1. Most of the increase in dollars is attributable to the appreciation in the cruzado. If the company's financial manager had correctly interpreted the Brazilian affiliate's reports, then the company might have avoided a $2,000,000 blunder.

Year	Cruzado Sales	Exchange Rate	Dollar Sales
19X0	Cr300,000,000	$0.022	$ 6,600,000
19X5	580,000,000	0.041	23,780,000

Source: Based on David A. Ricks, Marilyn Fu, and Jeffrey S. Arpan, *International Business Blunders,* Columbus, OH: Grid Publishing, 1974, 52–53.

during the 90-day period, causing the U.S. company's dollar cash flow to be less than expected. To minimize risk, the financial manager of U.S. Grain and Wheat hedges by calling the company's commercial bank and negotiating a forward contract to sell (deliver) pounds 90 days forward against the dollar. Thus the receivable is matched with a payable to the buyer of the forward contract.

Suppose that the pound is trading spot at $1.5135 and 90-days forward at $1.5035. U.S. Grain and Wheat's financial manager can lock in a cash flow (excluding transaction costs) of $375,875 ($1.5035 × £250,000). In 90 days U.S. Grain and Wheat collects the receivable and discharges the liability by delivering pounds to the bank. The value of the contract is $375,875 regardless of where the pound stands in 90 days. If the pound depreciates, then U.S. Grain and Wheat avoids a loss. Of course, it gives up any gains from appreciation of the pound because it must deliver the pounds as promised.

A forward exchange rate like those in Figure 22.2 is an unbiased estimate of the future spot exchange rate. In other words, the odds are equal that the eventual spot rate will be above or below the forward rate. Although unbiased, the estimate is still likely to be in error. Therefore companies that hedge in the forward market face equal probabilities of gaining (avoiding loss) or losing (forgoing gain) on the transaction relative to not hedging. A company might forgo a gain because of hedging, but managers and shareholders presumably prefer to profit from producing and selling products (wheat in the example above) rather than from speculating in foreign currency by not hedging.

CAPITAL BUDGETING

Capital budgeting for a foreign project of a company is similar to that for a domestic project: Calculate the present value of future cash inflows using a risk-adjusted discount rate and subtract the net investment cash outflow. For foreign projects, however, the procedure is a two-stage process: (1) Calculate the present value of the project's cash flows from the perspective of the foreign affiliate at the affiliate's required rate of return, and (2) calculate the present value of cash distributed from the affiliate to the parent company at the parent's required rate of return.

In more detail, the process for a U.S. multinational company consists of the following steps:

1. The foreign affiliate estimates incremental cash flows from the foreign project. It then discounts these cash flows at the affiliate's required rate of return. The affiliate's capital-budgeting committee accepts projects with positive net present value and rejects those with negative net present value.

2. For projects surviving Step 1, the U.S. parent company calculates net present value based on the cash flows that are distributed to the parent company:
   a. Management estimates the timing and amounts of cash flows that the foreign affiliate will distribute to the U.S. parent. These may differ from the timing and amounts of the project's own cash flows because the affiliate may retain cash and because tax rates may differ between the two countries.
   b. Management translates foreign-denominated incremental cash flows into dollars at exchange rates expected to prevail at the time the parent repatriates cash to the United States.
   c. Management discounts the incremental cash flows at the parent's required rate of return to find the project's net present value. Only with a positive net present value from the parent's viewpoint is a project finally accepted.

Although the principles of capital budgeting are similar for foreign and domestic investments, differences exist as a result of the risks in foreign business: (1) Foreign-exchange risk—uncertain future exchange rates add uncertainty to the cash flows the parent company expects to receive; (2) political risk—using their sovereign authority, foreign governments may expropriate foreign investments; (3) social risk—language and cultural inexperience may cause the company to incur a loss. In practice, substantial effort is directed toward understanding the potential impact of each of these risks.

SUMMARY

- Uncertain foreign-exchange rates present a problem to companies engaged in foreign transactions. Values of foreign currencies change daily, adding risk to company cash flows. Managing exchange-rate risk is a central part of international financial management.

- Foreign-exchange markets include: a spot market for buying and selling foreign currency with immediate delivery; a forward market comprising commercial banks where contracts can be bought and sold for delivery of foreign currency at future points in time; and a futures market with centralized trading facilities in which standardized contracts trade for future delivery of foreign currency. Supply and demand conditions in these markets determine foreign-exchange rates.

- The financial press presents daily quotations of foreign-exchange rates for many free-world currencies. The quotations include spot rates and forward rates, which reflect expectations of market participants. A forward rate above its spot counterpart (a forward premium) suggests that participants expect strengthening in the currency. A forward discount suggests an expected weakening.

- Foreign sources of financing consist of short-term debt, common stock, and long-term debt. Common sources of short-term debt are sight and time drafts. A time draft honored by a bank is a banker's acceptance. Companies also borrow money in the Eurocurrency market, in which principal and interest are denominated in a currency other than that of the country in which the loan originates. The rate on a Eurocurrency loan is usually stated as LIBOR plus basis points. U.S. multinational companies issue common stock less frequently than bonds in foreign countries. Two important types of long-term debt are foreign bonds and Eurobonds.

- Transacting international business subjects a company and its shareholders to three types of risk—social, political, and foreign exchange. There are three types of foreign-exchange risk:

    Translation risk for a U.S. company results from translating foreign-currency-denominated income statements and balance sheets into U.S. dollars.

    Economic risk is the uncertainty of operating cash flows caused by unexpected changes in foreign-exchange rates. It is a long-term phenomenon.

    Transaction risk results from unexpected changes in foreign-exchange rates between the time that a transaction occurs and the time that payment is made. Transaction risk is a short-term phenomenon.

- Management reduces the company's economic risk by taking steps to preserve long-term operating cash flows. These steps include locating plants in foreign countries, increasing advertising in foreign countries, marketing upscale products, and reducing operating costs of foreign facilities by altering production processes.

- Management reduces transaction risk by adjusting policies on granting credit, on paying for purchases, and on pricing products. Other strategies include forward hedging: establishing a currency position in the forward (or futures) market opposite to the currency position in the spot market.

- Adjustments for social risk, political risk, and foreign-exchange risk complicate capital budgeting by a multinational company. The financial manager first calculates net present value of a project from the perspective of the foreign affiliate. Then the financial manager estimates the timing and amounts of cash flows from the affiliate to the parent company. After translating the foreign currency at the expected exchange rate, the financial manager discounts the cash flows at the parent company's required rate of return. The resulting net present value tells management whether or not to accept the project.

Key Terms

spot market	forward discount	social risk
forward market	forward premium	political risk
futures market	sight draft	foreign-exchange risk
foreign-exchange rate	time draft	translation risk
multinational company	Eurocurrency	economic risk
appreciation	Eurobond	transaction risk
depreciation	foreign bond	

Questions

22.1. Match the item in Column A with its closest counterpart in Column B. Use each item only once.

	A	B
a.	Spot market	____Fixed commission
b.	Conversion	____Increase in price
c.	Translation	____Restate foreign values
d.	Futures market	____Cash market
e.	Forward market	____Physically exchange
f.	Appreciate	____Negotiated contract
g.	Depreciate	____Decrease in price

22.2. Use Wednesday's quotations in Figure 22.2 to answer the following questions:
  a. How many Indian rupees can you buy for one U.S. dollar?
  b. How many U.S. dollars can you buy for 1,000 pesetas?
  c. What is the currency unit of each of the following countries: Saudi Arabia, Kuwait, Greece, Israel, Ireland, and Ecuador?
  d. What is the currency unit of each of the following countries: Taiwan, Singapore, New Zealand, Hong Kong, Canada, Australia, and the United States?
  e. In European terms, what is the spot rate of French francs? What is the spot rate in American terms?

22.3. What does the relationship between a currency's spot and forward rates tell you? Explain your answer.

22.4. Define the following terms: *Eurodollar, Eurocurrency, Eurobond, bank draft, sight draft,* and *time draft.*

22.5. Describe the difference between a *Eurobond* and a *foreign bond* and give an example of each.

22.6. "In a foreign transaction only one participant incurs transaction risk." Do you agree with this statement? Why or why not?

22.7. Explain how management uses pricing policy to offset the increased costs of imports resulting from appreciation in foreign currency.

22.8. Suppose that foreign-currency traders expect the U.S. dollar to appreciate against foreign currencies. A company pays for its imported raw materials with foreign currencies and sells its exported finished goods for foreign currencies. Explain why the company should accelerate collection of receivables and stretch payments to trade creditors.

22.9. There are three types of foreign-exchange risk: (1) translation, (2) economic, and (3) transaction. Preceding each of the following items, place the appropriate number (1, 2, and/or 3) identifying these risks:
  ____a. Exists during the period between transaction and payment.
  ____b. Affects long-run operating cash flows.
  ____c. Hedged in the forward market.
  ____d. Virtually impossible to hedge because it is long run.
  ____e. Faced by individuals buying foreign merchandise.
  ____f. Has an impact on a company's financial statements according to FASB *Statement No. 52.*
  ____g. Associated with unexpected changes in foreign-exchange rates.

22.10. The Amerigo Airframe Company, a U.S. multi-national, has an affiliate in Thailand. The Thai baht appreciates during an operating period. Explain whether the U.S. parent company has a gain or loss under each of the following circumstances:

a. The Thai entity has assets greater than liabilities.
b. The Thai entity has liabilities greater than assets.
c. The Thai entity's assets equal its liabilities.

Strategy Problem

Securities Investing Associates has an affiliate in Canada responsible for advising new companies on sources of venture capital, underwriting security issues, and brokering securities in the Canadian secondary market. The net working capital of the Canadian affiliate at the end of the third quarter of 19X7 appears, in Canadian dollars (C$), as follows:

Assets		Liabilities	
Cash	C$124,000	Accounts payable	C$ 78,000
Securities	286,000	Taxes payable	46,000
Receivables	204,000	Bank loans	254,000
Total	C$614,000	Total	C$378,000

The foreign-exchange rate on the statement date is the Wednesday spot rate in Figure 22.2.

The financial manager of Securities Investing Associates is evaluating the impact of recent volatility of the Canadian dollar on the U.S. parent. In addition, the U.S. parent is selling C$40,000 of securities today through its Canadian affiliate, which expects to collect the cash and remit it to the U.S. parent at the end of 90 days. The financial manager wants to hedge the parent company's expo-sure to transaction risk. Use the foreign-exchange rates of the Canadian dollar in Figure 22.2 to make all calculations.

a. At the beginning of the third quarter of 19X7, the Canadian dollar was $0.75 (C$1.3333 per U.S. dollar). Did Securities Investing Associates incur a translation gain or loss during the quarter? Assume that its net working capital remained constant over the period.

b. Describe how the financial manager could use a forward hedge to minimize the company's exposure to the transaction risk associated with the C$40,000 receivable created by today's sale of securities.

c. Securities Investing Associates prices the C$40,000 of securities to return the company a 16 percent contribution margin ratio. In U.S. dollars the contribution margin is $5,075.20 (C$40,000 × 0.793 × 0.16). The financial manager expects the Canadian dollar to depreciate to its 90-day forward rate in Figure 22.2. Suppose that company policy does not authorize the financial manager to use forward hedges. At what price must the company sell the issue today to preserve its contribution margin when it collects and transfers the cash to the U.S. parent?

Strategy

Calculate gain on assets from the Canadian dollar appreciation.

Calculate loss on liabilities from the Canadian dollar appreciation.

Use the 90-day forward rate to calculate the price of the forward contract.

Solution

a. Appreciation of the Canadian dollar means that the U.S. parent realizes a translation gain on assets and a loss on liabilities denominated in Canadian dollars:

Change in value of assets:

Value after appreciation (C$614,000 × 0.793)	$486,902	
Value before appreciation (C$614,000 × 0.75)	460,500	
Translation gain on assets		$26,402

Change in value of liabilities:

Value after appreciation (C$378,000 × 0.793)	$299,754	
Value before appreciation (C$378,000 × 0.75)	283,500	
Translation loss on liabilities		$16,254
Net translation gain		$10,148

b. A forward hedge requires a forward contract matching the receivable. The financial manager arranges a contract to deliver C$40,000 in 90 days. The price is based on the 90-day forward rate in Figure 22.2:

$$\text{Contract price} = \frac{\text{Forward rate on}}{\text{Canadian dollar}} \times \frac{\text{Number of}}{\text{Canadian dollars}}$$

$$= \$0.7888 \times C\$40,000$$

$$= \$31,552$$

In 90 days the company collects C$40,000, which it delivers for $31,552.

c. To preserve the contribution margin (CM) in U.S. dollars, the company must price the securities to reflect the expected exchange rate upon conversion of Canadian dollars to U.S. dollars:

Determine the Canadian dollar price using the expected spot rate.

$$\text{Forward rate} = \text{Expected spot rate} = 0.7888$$

$$\frac{\text{CM in U.S.}}{\text{dollars}} = \frac{\text{Canadian}}{\text{price}} \times \frac{\text{Expected}}{\text{spot rate}} \times 0.16$$

$$\$5,075.20 = \frac{\text{Canadian}}{\text{price}} \times 0.7888 \times 0.16$$

$$\frac{\text{Canadian}}{\text{price}} = \text{C}\$40,212.98$$

By pricing the securities at C$40,212.98, the firm will preserve its $5,075.20 contribution margin.

◆ **Demonstration Problem**

Exim Commodities Company (ECC) is a U.S. wholesaler of commodities, including lumber, steel, and nonferrous metals. The company has sales offices in Japan, South Korea, England, France, Mexico, Venezuela, and Brazil. Each sales office has approximately ten employees who market company products and provide service to customers. Prior to being assigned to a sales office, an employee must attend a four-week training session on local culture and folkways, marketing procedures, and international financial management. At the end of the training session, the employee must take an exam covering each of the three areas of study. Suppose that you have just completed the training session and must now take the following exam on international financial management.

a. Kenichi Ohmae (author of *Beyond National Borders*) notes that multinational companies evolve as follows: They begin as exporters and importers operating through foreign distributors; next they open their own sales offices overseas; then they establish production facilities overseas to accompany sales and service; finally, they establish autonomous subsidiaries overseas responsible for research and development, engineering, manufacturing, marketing, sales, and service. Why do multinational companies tend to evolve as Mr. Ohmae suggests?

b. Exchange rates for the French franc are as follows:

	U.S. $ equiv.		Currency per U.S. $	
	Wed.	Tues.	Wed.	Tues.
France (Franc)	.18260	.18315	5.4765	5.4600
30-day forward	.18160	.18203	5.5065	5.4935
90-day forward	.17987	.18023	5.5595	5.5485
180-day forward	.17778	.17809	5.6250	5.6150

(1) Which of the preceding quotations are expressed in *American terms* and which are expressed in *European terms*? (2) Show the relationship between Wednesday's spot rate in American terms and European terms. (3) Did the French franc appreciate or depreciate from Tuesday to Wednesday? Explain. (4) What is the difference between the spot market and the forward market? (5) Does the French franc trade at a *forward discount* or at a *forward premium*? Explain.

c. Use the preceding exchange rates and suppose that ECC exports goods to France for 1,000,000 French francs, payable in 90 days: (1) If the French franc depreciates 3 percent, what is the U.S. dollar equivalent of the payment received by ECC? (2) Explain how ECC can use the forward market to hedge this transaction.

d. A *draft* is an order written by an exporter requesting the importer to pay a specified amount of money on a specified date. What is a trade draft? Bank draft? Sight draft? Time draft? Trade acceptance? Banker's acceptance?

e. What is the difference between a Eurodollar and a Euroyen? A Eurobond and a foreign bond?

f. Because of its investments in foreign countries, ECC faces social risk, political risk, and foreign-exchange risk. Define each of these risks. What can ECC do to lessen social risk? Political risk?

g. ECC's foreign-exchange risk includes translation risk. For example, ECC's sales office in Mexico has P2,500,000 (Mexican pesos) in assets and P1,600,000 in liabilities. During a recent accounting period the Mexican peso depreciated 10 percent from $0.3592341 to $0.3233107. Calculate ECC's net translation loss.

h. ECC's foreign-exchange risk also includes economic risk and transaction risk. Define each of these risks. What steps can ECC take to manage economic risk? Transaction risk?

i. How does capital budgeting for a foreign project differ from that for a domestic project?

Problems

Foreign-exchange rates

22.1. Exchange rates for the Japanese yen are as follows:

	U.S. $ equiv.		Currency per U.S. $	
	Wed.	**Tues.**	**Wed.**	**Tues.**
Japan (Yen)	.008805	.008777	113.57	113.93

a. How many yen is $10,000 worth on Wednesday? On Tuesday?
b. How many U.S. dollars is 1,000,000 yen worth on Wednesday? On Tuesday?
c. Did the Japanese yen appreciate or depreciate from Tuesday to Wednesday? Explain.

Foreign-exchange rates

22.2. Exchange rates for the Greek drachma are as follows:

	U.S. $ equiv.		Currency per U.S. $	
	Wed.	**Tues.**	**Wed.**	**Tues.**
Greece (Drachma)	.004521	.004544	221.20	220.05

a. How many drachmas is $10,000 worth on Wednesday? On Tuesday?
b. How many U.S. dollars is 1,000,000 drachmas worth on Wednesday? On Tuesday?
c. Did the Greek drachma appreciate or depreciate from Tuesday to Wednesday? Explain.

Foreign-exchange rates

22.3. Austrian Motor Works sells AMWs in Austria for S330,705 (330,705 schillings). The schilling presently trades at the rate stated for Wednesday in Figure 22.2. Investors expect the schilling to depreciate by 4 percent within six months.
a. Calculate the U.S. dollar price of an AMW in the spot market.
b. What is the U.S. dollar price of an AMW in terms of the future (6-month) schilling?

Foreign-exchange rates and hedging

22.4. Destructo Racket Distributing orders $4,200 worth of Danish graphite tennis rackets at a time when the krone costs $0.16. Shipment will be made in 30 days, with payment due 30 days thereafter. The Danish krone costs $0.17 in the 60-day forward market. The transaction is fixed in krones.

a. Calculate the krone price of the order in the forward market.

b. Describe how Destructo Racket can hedge the transaction in the forward market.

c. The relationship between the krone's cash and forward rate suggests that the krone will depreciate over the ensuing 60 days. Is this statement true or false? Why?

d. Destructo insists on an 8 percent contribution margin ratio on its rackets. As an alternative to hedging, management can price the rackets to reflect a change in the expected cost of the krone. Assuming that management expects the krone to change at the rate the spot-forward relationship indicates, what should the percentage price change be in order for the company to preserve its 8 percent contribution margin ratio?

Foreign-exchange rates and hedging

22.5. Switzerland is one of the leading financial centers of the world. Consequently, many U.S. corporations buy securities sold by the Swiss government. Suppose that Micro Corporation has cash to invest for 180 days, at which time the company will need it to pay a dividend. The company's financial manager wishes to buy a 180-day $F_{Sw}100,000$ security sold by the Swiss government. The security pays 8 percent annual interest at maturity and the company purchases it at face value.

a. What is the amount of interest this security pays in Swiss francs? Use a 365-day year in your calculation.

b. How many U.S. dollars are invested? Use the spot rate on Wednesday in Figure 22.2.

c. How many U.S. dollars does the financial manager of Micro expect to receive when the Swiss francs (including interest) are converted to U.S. dollars? Use the 180-day forward rate in Figure 22.2.

d. Explain how Micro can make use of the forward market to hedge this transaction.

Foreign-exchange rates and hedging

22.6. Lando Marketing orders R173,913 (173,913 renminbi) worth of merchandise from China, payable in 30 days. The renminbi is presently trading at $0.18, and the supplier insists on payment in renminbi. Alf Lando, president and financial manager of Lando Marketing, anticipates a 15 percent appreciation in the renminbi in the next 30 days.

a. What is the dollar cost of the merchandise before and after the expected appreciation?

b. The 30-day forward exchange rate of the renminbi is $0.22.
    1. What is the dollar cost of the merchandise based on the forward exchange rate?
    2. Should Mr. Lando hedge this transaction? Explain your answer.

Foreign-exchange rates and contribution margin

22.7. Staja Inc. imports Moto Guzzi and Kagiva motorcycles from Italy for sale in the United States. The company's financial manager expects the price of the Italian lira to appreciate by 12 percent during the next 12 months. Presently Staja's contribution margin ratio is 15 percent. Anticipated U.S. sales, ignoring the appreciation, are $700,000.

a. What is the expected foreign-exchange rate of the lira after appreciation? The present rate (Wednesday's) is shown in Figure 22.2.

b. What must be the percentage increase in price to preserve Staja's contribution margin ratio? Support your answer with calculations showing the contribution margin ratio (1) before the appreciation and (2) after the appreciation.

c. Does Staja face transaction or translation risk? Explain your answer.

Foreign-exchange loss

22.8. The British pound has depreciated by 12 percent from its previous rate of $1.64. A U.S. company has assets of £80,000 and liabilities of £60,000 during the period. Calculate the company's foreign-exchange loss over the period.

Translation gains and losses

22.9. Barnes Food Processors has an affiliate in Saudi Arabia that packages and distributes food items in that country. At present the Saudi riyal (R) costs $0.29 and the 90-day forward riyal costs $0.33. Barnes Food Processors has a R72,400 net exposed position calculated as follows:

Exposed assets	R393,000
Less exposed liabilities	320,600
Net exposed position	R 72,400

Stacey Barnes, the company's financial manager, is concerned about the stability of the riyal and wants to protect her company against unexpected changes in the foreign-exchange rate.

a. Does the relationship between the spot and 90-day forward riyal suggest that the riyal will appreciate or depreciate? Explain your answer.

b. If the net exposed position remains the same and the riyal becomes $0.33, will Barnes Food Processors show a translation gain or loss on its consolidated statements? Support your answer with calculations.

Translating financial statements denominated in foreign currency

22.10. StyCo Corporation is a manufacturing company with several overseas subsidiaries. Chantille S.A., StyCo's principal French subsidiary, operates entirely within France and submits financial statements translated into U.S. dollars to corporate headquarters on a regular basis. The projected year-end balance sheet as of December 31, 19X6, and the projected income statement for the month of December 19X6 for Chantille S.A. had been submitted to corporate headquarters in November. The financial statements below were prepared when the exchange rate was 6.8 French francs to the dollar (French franc = $0.147).

During December the spot franc depreciated 10 percent against the U.S. dollar, dropping the exchange rate from $0.147 at the beginning of the month to $0.132 (0.90 × $0.147) on December 31. StyCo Corporation instructs the management of its foreign subsidiaries to use current exchange rates when translating the financial statements. Chantille S.A. used the exchange rate current in November—$0.147 per French franc—for the projected December statements. Had Chantille management known that the franc was to depreciate 10 percent, it would have used the $0.132 exchange rate for all accounts on the balance sheet and the average rate of $0.1395 for all accounts in the December income statement. Projected statements assume that inventory would not be acquired during December. All local (French) transactions are measured in French francs.

a. Calculate the translation gain or loss experienced by Chantille S.A. on its projected balance sheet accounts as of December 31, 19X6, due to the depreciation of the French franc.

b. Briefly describe how StyCo's management can hedge an anticipated depreciation of the French franc.

c. What relationship probably prevailed between the spot and forward franc on December 1?

d. *(Optional)* Explain the meaning of *S.A.* in the company name.

Chantille S.A.: Projected Balance Sheet, December 31, 19X6 (F_F = $0.147)

Assets		Liabilities and Shareholder Equity	
Cash	$ 100,000	Accounts payable	$1,200,000
Receivables	500,000	Other current liabilities	600,000
Prepaid expenses	50,000	Long-term debt	1,000,000
Inventory	1,200,000	Deferred income	200,000
Plant and equipment (net)	2,000,000	Shareholder equity	1,000,000
Goodwill	100,000	Total liabilities and shareholder equity	$4,000,000
Deferred charges	50,000		
Total assets	$4,000,000		

Chantille S.A.: Projected Income Statement for the Month of December 19X6 (F$_F$ = $0.147)

Sales	$400,000
Less costs and expenses	
Cost of sales	307,000
Depreciation	9,700
Other operating expenses	35,000
Amortization of goodwill	300
Interest	8,000
Total costs and expenses	$360,000
Net income before income taxes	$ 40,000
Less income taxes	16,000
Net income	$ 24,000

Selected References

Adler, Michael, and Bernard Dumas. "Exposure to Currency Risk: Definition and Measurement." *Financial Management,* Summer 1984: 41–50.

Banker, Pravin. "You're the Best Judge of Foreign Risks." *Harvard Business Review,* March–April 1983: 157–165.

Brewer, Thomas. "Political Risk Assessment for Foreign Direct Investment Decisions: Better Methods for Better Results." *Columbia Journal of World Business,* Spring 1982: 5–12.

Kim, Suk H., Martha Rowland, and Seung H. Kim. "Working Capital Practices by Japanese Manufacturers in the U.S." *Financial Practice and Education,* Spring/Summer 1992: 89–92.

Marr, M. Wayne, John L. Trimble, and Raj Varma. "On the Integration of International Capital Markets: Evidence from Euroequity Offerings." *Financial Management,* Winter 1991: 11–21.

Mathur, Ike, and David Loy. "Foreign Currency Translation: Survey of Corporate Treasurers." *Management Accounting,* September 1981: 33–42.

Oblak, David J., and Roy J. Helm, Jr. "Survey and Analysis of Capital Budgeting Methods Used by Multinationals." *Financial Management,* Winter 1980: 37–41.

Ouyang, Ling-Nan. "Joint Ventures in China: Problems and Solutions." *Financial Review,* May 1988: 175–181.

Stanley, Marjorie T. "Capital Structure and Cost of Capital for the Multinational Firm." *Journal of International Business Studies,* Spring-Summer 1981: 103–120.

Swanson, Peggy E. "Interrelationships among Domestic and Eurocurrency Deposit Yields: A Focus on the U.S. Dollar." *Financial Review,* February 1988: 81–94.

ANSWERS TO
ODD-NUMBERED
PROBLEMS

Appendix A

Note: Your answers may differ slightly from some of the answers provided here, because of rounding errors.

1.1. $106,000.

1.3. Bondholders.

1.5. 13.3%; 1.4 percentage points.

1.7. $300,000.

1.9. (a) $150; (b) $210; 40% increase.

1.11. $0.25.

1.13. Diminishing marginal utility.

1.15. Increase the quantity of goods sold.

1.17. $1,500.

1.19. 12.04%.

2.1. 4.10%.

2.3. No answer provided.

2.5. **a.** U.S. Treasury bills: 4.29%; U.S. agency paper: 5.22%; prime commercial paper: 6.77%; bankers' acceptances: 6.14%.
b. No answer provided.

2.7. **a.** Bid price = $996,396.67; Asked price = $996,447.78.
b. 2.83%.

2.9. 7%.

2.11. **a.** $1,066.67.
b. 8.61%.
c. 6.5%; 8.3%; 8.0%; yield curve not provided.

3.1. **a.** $1,100,000.
b. 6.3%.
c. $2.20.

3.3. **a.** $17,750.
    b. $14,750.
    c. 16.9% loss.

3.5. **a.** No answer provided.
    b. $49\frac{5}{8}$.
    c. 3.9%.

3.7. **a.** Thursday.
    b. Coca-Cola; 2.4%; 1.9%.
    c. $3.03; $3.15.
    d. 45.6%; 32.3%.

3.9. **a.** $10,400.
    b. $862.50.
    c. 8.3%.
    d. No answer provided.

3.11. **a.** 5.7%.
    b. 2001.
    c. $1,000.
    d. $95.

3.13. 18.4%.

4.1. **a.** $1,771.56.
    b. $1,771.60.

4.3. **a.** $4,943.69.
    b. $7,457.65.
    c. $8,000.

4.5. 5.2%.

4.7. 14.5%.

4.9. $23,182.58 (based on Appendix B.1).

4.11. $681,550 (based on Appendix B.3).

4.13. 9.6%.

4.15. $20,000.

4.17. $500 loss.

4.19. **a.** $500.
    b. Price declines to $416.67.
    c. Inverse relationship.
    d. $83.33 loss.

4.21. $6,209.21; $6,139.13; $6,102.71; $6,077.89.

4.23. 20.

4.25. **a.** 16.08%.
    b. $150.

4.27. **a.** $8,137.23 (based on Appendix B.4).
    b. $31,372.30.

4.29. **a.** $127,201.74 (based on Appendix B.4).
    b. $22,282.40.
    c. $62,776.28 (based on Appendix B.4).

4.31. **a.** $32,923.98 (based on Appendix B.4).

b.

(1) Year	(2) Beginning Balance	(3) Annual Payment	0.12 × (2) = (4) Dollar Interest	(3) − (4) = (5) Principal Repayment	(2) − (5) = (6) Ending Balance
1	$100,000	$32,924	$12,000	$20,924	$79,076
2	79,076	32,924	9,489	23,435	55,641
3	55,641	32,924	6,677	26,247	29,394
4	29,394	32,921[a]	3,527	29,394	0

[a]The final payment differs due to rounding in previous calculations.

    c. $31,693.

4.33. $16,567.12.

4.35. Choose Plan 1 with PVA = $13,583.19, not Plan 2 with PVA = $14,010.58.

4.37. a. 9.417% per year compounded annually.
    b. Yes.
    c. 9.53% per year continuously compounded.

4.39. a. 6%.
    b. 3%.
    c. 9 years; 18 years.
    d. 0.72 years; 1 year.

5.1. a. 15%; 13%.
    b. 15.5%; 9.8%.
    c. No answer provided.
    d. No answer provided.

5.3. a. $1,000,000; $1,000,000.
    b. No answer provided.
    c. No answer provided.
    d. No answer provided.
    e. No answer provided.

5.5. 17.5%.

5.7. a. 12%.
    b. 10%.

5.9. $\beta = 1.32$; more risky than average.

5.11. a. $\beta = 0.725$.
    b. $\beta = 0.58$.
    c. Part *a*.

5.13. a. $\beta = 1.30$.
    b. 15.8%.
    c. 13.4%; 15.2%; 18.8%; 15.8%.

6.1. $724.06 (based on Appendixes B.2 and B.4).

6.3. a. Bond A, $982.27; Bond B, $937.70.
    b. Bond A, $948.03; Bond B, $827.95; Bond B has more interest rate risk than Bond A.

6.5. 9.6%.

6.7. a. $2.14.

    b. $71.33.

    c. **(1)** Price increases; **(2)** price decreases; **(3)** price increases.

6.9. $31.89.

6.11. **a.** $1; $1.50; $2.25; $3.38; $5.07; $5.42.

    b. $0.48; $0.62; $0.80; $1.03; $1.33.

    c. $60.22; $15.84.

    d. $20.10.

6.13. No; VC declines from $23.73 to $20.25.

6.15. 14% per year compounded semiannually.

6.17. 10% per year compounded semiannually; $K_i = 6\%$.

6.19. **a.** 10.6%.

    b. 10.6%.

6.21. **a.** 3% per year.

    b. 17.3%.

    c. 21.2%.

6.23. **a.** No.

    b. $2,660,000; $1,040,000.

    c. $2.74.

    d. 14.1% and 15.5%.

7.1. **a.** 14.0%.

    b. No answer provided.

    c. No answer provided.

7.3. **a.** 0.11; 1.0; 4.0.

    b. Optimal capital structure is 50 percent debt and 50 percent equity, which causes K_a to be 11.2 percent.

    c. No answer provided.

    d. No answer provided.

7.5. **a.** $K_c = 15.2\%$ and $K_{nc} = 15.6\%$.

    b. $K_a = 12.1\%$.

    c. Budget = $1,000,000.

    d. $K_a = 12.4\%$.

7.7. Break points are $10,000,000 and $20,000,000; $K_a = 10.85\%$, 11.40%, and 11.85%.

7.9. **a.** $K_{mortgage} = 6\%$; $K_{debenture} = 7.5\%$; $K_p = 13.8\%$; $K_c = 14\%$; $K_{nc} = 14.3\%$.

    b. $K_a = 11.16\%$.

    c. $K_a = 11.31\%$.

    d. Budget = $108,000,000.

    e. No answer provided.

7.11. **a.** 133,333.33 shares.

    b. $2,666,667.

    c. Yes.

    d. Yes.

7.13. **a.** EBIT* = $480,000.

    b. EPS = $2.88 for each alternative when EBIT = $480,000.

    c. True, because expected EBIT exceeds EBIT*.

    d. No answer provided.

8.1. a. 17.9%.
      b. 25.0%.
      c. Marginal tax rate.

8.3. Average tax rate and marginal tax rate are the same, 34%; answer holds for all taxable income equal to or greater than $335,000.

8.5. $207,400.

8.7. a. $978,000.
      b. $978,000.

8.9. $58,400.

8.11. a. (1) $141,648; (2) $67,200; (3) $49,248.
      b. This decision is unwise.

8.13. NICO = $430,000; OCF_1 = $148,662; OCF_2 = $171,464; OCF_3 = $142,319; OCF_4 = $142,599; disposal cash flow = $83,000.

9.1. a. Payback = 3.57 years; IRR = 22.5%; NPV = $18,604; PI = 1.07 (based on Appendix B.4).
      b. Yes.

9.3. a. $2,060,000 and $60,000.
      b. $640,000.
      c. 3.22 years; no.
      d. $168,348 (based on Appendixes B.2 and B.4); yes.

9.5. a. 12%.
      b. 14%.
      c. No answer provided.
      d. No answer provided.

9.7. a. NPV = $507,685 (based on Appendix B.4).
      b. $5,007,685.
      c. No answer provided.
      d. No answer provided.

9.9. $89,633.

9.11. a. 17.3% and 15%; prefer Fast Payoff.
      b. $28,690 and $31,380; prefer Slow Payoff.
      c. Choose Fast Payoff if the reinvestment rate is greater than 11.1%.

9.13. a. 15%.
      b. Project A; you assume that Richmond can invest the $100,000 at a rate greater than 15%.

9.15. a. $530,000.
      b.

	Year 1	Year 2	Year 3	Year 4	Year 5
OCF	$165,333	$198,667	$198,667	$165,333	$132,000
Add disposal					73,200
					$205,200

      c. 2.84 years; reject the project.

d. $22,908; accept the project.

e. 21.9%; accept the project.

9.17. a. No answer provided.

b. (1) 2.69 years, accept the proposal; (2) $635, accept the proposal; (3) 1.038, accept the proposal; (4) 21.8%, accept the proposal.

c. Yes. Each evaluation method indicates acceptability of the proposal.

10.1. a. $\overline{\text{NPV}}_A = \$49,500$; $\overline{\text{NPV}}_B = \$49,500$. Based solely on $\overline{\text{NPV}}$, each project is equally desirable because the $\overline{\text{NPV}}$s are the same amount.

b. Project B.

10.3. a. $38,772.

b. $54,714.

c. 15.87%.

d. 99.997%.

10.5. a. $\overline{\text{CF}}_1 = \$16,000$; $\overline{\text{CF}}_2 = \$14,400$.

b. NPV = $4,801.

c. Yes, stock price and shareholder wealth will rise if the project is accepted.

10.7. a. $130,635; $40,738; and −$38,160 (based on Appendix B.4).

b. No answer provided.

10.9. a. NPV = $13,969.

b. Z-Mart should invest in the project.

c. How valid are the certainty equivalent factors?

10.11. a. K = 15%.

b. OCF = $105,144.

c. NPV = −$14,814; reject the project.

10.13. a. K_a = 11.46%.

b. K = 14.7%.

c. Yes, because 15% > 14.7%.

10.15. a. *Worst case:* NPV = −$299,788; IRR = 8.6%, PI = 0.77, payback = 5.1 years; *most likely case:* NPV = $162,160, IRR = 21.5%, PI = 1.15, payback = 3.7 years; *optimistic case:* NPV = $630,510, IRR = 33.0%, PI = 1.63, payback = 2.9 years.

b. No answer provided.

c. No answer provided.

11.1. a. No answer provided.

b. $6,370 = $2,760 + $3,610.

c. (1) $1,580; (2) 2.03; (3) 0.76.

d. No answer provided.

11.3. a. No answer provided.

b. Conservative policy: 2.0, $350,000, and 6.3%; aggressive policy: 1.0, 0, and 10.1%.

c. No answer provided.

d. No answer provided.

11.5. a. Apex follows the more aggressive working-capital policy as indicated by its lower current ratio (1.08 vs. 1.78) and higher current asset turnover (3.86 vs. 2.06).

b. Yes, Apex's lower liquidity is accompanied by a higher return on assets (10.9% vs. 7.1%).

11.7.

Net cash flow from operating activities	$137,899
Net cash flow from investing activities	(187,814)
Net cash flow from financing activities	3,982
Net decrease in cash	($45,933)

11.9. a.

Net cash flow from operating activities	$20,000
Net cash flow from investing activities	(70,000)
Net cash flow from financing activities	40,000
Net decrease in cash	($10,000)

b. No, Feldspar's net working capital increased $20,000 while cash decreased $10,000.

11.11. a. Yes, Campbell's net monetary debtor position is $270,000.

b. Rate of inflation = 16.6%.

c. Net purchasing-power gain = $44,820. (Plus $3,735 on the increase.)

12.1. a. Cumulative cash excess: June, $26,500; July, $51,500.

b. No answer provided.

12.3. a. Cumulative cash excess (shortage); January, ($150,000); February, $100,000; March, ($150,000); April, ($150,000); May, ($200,000).

b. Cash generated = 0.

c. No answer provided.

12.5. $157,000.

12.7. a. No answer provided.

b. $432,000.

c. $21,600.

d. No answer provided.

12.9. −$500.

12.11. a. $995,000 and $5,000.

b. $985,416.67; $991,750; and $6,333.33.

c. Choose Strategy 2.

13.1. a. 22.6%.

b. 18.8%.

c. 38.0%.

d. 30.4%.

13.3. **a.** 16.
   b. 22.8 days.
   c. Accounts receivable turnover will be overstated, and the average collection period will be understated.

13.5. **a.** 11.1%.
   b. 66 days.
   c. 9.9%.
   d. Yes, because the customer's opportunity cost (9.9%) is less than the borrowing rate (12%).

13.7. **a.** 7.
   b. Too high, because Warden's inventory turnover is low relative to the industry average.
   c. Excessive carrying costs.

13.9. **a.** Accounts receivable: $21,370 and $35,397; variable cost ratio, 0.92; increased investment in accounts receivable, $12,905.
   b. −16.7%; no, because expected after-tax return (−16.7%) is less than the required rate of return (11%).

13.11. **a.** Yes, because the expected after-tax return (19.6%) is greater than the required rate of return (10%).
   b. Yes, because 11.2% > 10%.

13.13. **a.** (1) 240 packages; (2) 100 orders; (3) $240.
   b. Immediately.

13.15. **a.** EOQ: 340.0, 296.8, 261.8, and 229.9.
   b. No answer provided.
   c. Inversely related; EOQ = 340.
   d. $49,787.50.
   e. $26,787.83.
   f. Yes. Yes.

14.1. **a.** 21.3%.
   b. 9.3% and 6.8%.

14.3. **a.** 18.4% and 20.1%.
   b. 18.4% per year compounded every 20 days is a nominal rate; 20.1% per year compounded annually is an effective rate.
   c. She should borrow from the bank.

14.5. **a.** $13,000.
   b. No answer provided.

14.7. **a.** $50,000; end of the year; 10%.
   b. $50,000; beginning of the year; 11.1%.

14.9. 9.8%.

14.11. **a.** $515,625.
   b. 25.0%.

14.13. 14.6%.

14.15. **a.** $241,250.
   b. $226,775; $123,225.
   c. 13.2%.

14.17. Alternative 1, 12.3%; Alternative 2, 11.3%; Alternative 3, 10.7%; choose Alternative 3.

15.1. **a.** No answer provided.
 b. Company: 1.3% × 4.2 × 2.1 = 11.5%; Industry: 2.1% × 5.6 × 2.0 = 23.5%.
 c. No answer provided.

15.3. 15.97 days.

15.5. **a.** 3.6.
 b. $1,500,000 and 4.5.

15.7. **a.** $666,667.
 b. 4.0%.

15.9. **a.** $160,000.
 b. $92,000 and $2.30.

15.11. **a.** 22.25%.
 b. $11.37.
 c. 7.1% and 14.1.
 d. $3,034,725.

15.13. No answer provided.

15.15. No answer provided.

16.1. $53,250.

16.3. **a.** $36,243,200.
 b. No answer provided.
 c. No answer provided.

16.5. **a.** $122,080 and 56.0%.
 b. No answer provided.

16.7. **a.** $4.
 b. 245,000 units.
 c. $2,695,000.
 d. No answer provided.

16.9. **a.** 56,800 units.
 b. 82,800 units.
 c. 59,167 units.

16.11. **a.** DOL = 1.75; DFL = 1.053; DCL = 1.84.
 b. Same as Part *a*.

16.13. **a.** Spreads: 24,000 units and $960,000; Sheets: 18,750 units and $750,000.
 b. No answer provided.
 c. Spreads, $25,000; Sheets, $100,000.
 d. Spreads, 25.0; Sheets, 4.0.
 e. Spreads, 25.0; Sheets, 4.0.
 f. No answer provided.

17.1. 8%.

17.3. **a.** Exercise value of call option = $5; exercise value of put option = 0.
 b. Exercise value of call option = 0; exercise value of put option = $5.

17.5.   **a.** No answer provided.
      b. Out-of-the-money.
      c. In-the-money.
      d. Call option: 0 and $\frac{15}{16}$; put option: $\frac{1}{8}$ and $\frac{15}{16}$.
      e. No.

17.7.   **a.** Stock A, $50; and Stock B, $50.
      b. Call option on Stock A, $1.70; and call option on Stock B, $2.50.
      c. Because the variance in the price of Stock B exceeds that of Stock A.
      d. No answer provided.

17.9.   **a.** $50.
      b. $800.
      c. Bond price will be above or equal to the conversion value of $800.
      d. $797.84.
      e. Conversion premium, $150; straight-bond premium, $152.16.

17.11. **a.** Ba3 indicates relatively high risk.
      b. $1,000.
      c. $978.50; because of underwriting costs.
      d. No answer provided.
      e. Put option.
      f. $628.52.

17.13. **a.** $2.75 and $0.375.
      b. Price increases.
      c. Price decreases.

17.15. **a.** Exercise value = 0; premium = $\frac{9}{16}$.
      b. 105%.
      c. 263.6%.
      d. −51.2% and −72.5%.
      e. Warrant is riskier than the stock.
      f. Price decreases.

17.17. **a.** Jan's loss on the warrants is 93.75%; Nancy's loss on the stock is 75%.
      b. Fixed exercise price.
      c. Exercise price.

18.1.   **a.** $16.42.
      b. No answer provided.
      c. No answer provided.

18.3.   **a.** $51.31.
      b. Book value per share, $62.18.
      c. No answer provided.

18.5.   **a.** No.
      b. Yes.

18.7.   **a.** $4,800,000.
      b. 1,200,000.
      c. $1.50.

d. $16.50.

e. Rights offering will fail.

18.9. **a.** $4.

b. $46.

c. No answer provided.

d. No answer provided.

18.11. **a.** (1) $2.56 and $51.20; (2) $2.54 and $50.80.

b. (1) $0.27; (2) $49.73.

18.13. $2.

19.1. **a.** EACS = $2,380,000; EPS = $4.76.

b. Payout ratio = 21.0%; retention ratio = 79.0%.

c. 2.3%.

19.3. **a.** $720.

b. $720.

c. 0.

19.5. **a.** 0.375.

b. $50,000,000.

c. No answer provided.

19.7. **a.** $7,240.

b. Historical: (1) 16.5%, (2) 40%, and (3) $12,024; current: (1) 35.4%, (2) 110.7%, and (3) −$776.

19.9. No answer provided.

19.11. **a.** Price declines to $34.2857.

b. 5.8%.

c. 4.17%.

20.1. **a.** $405,586 (based on Appendix B.4).

b. $466,424 (based on Appendix B.4).

20.3. Payment = $128,910 (rounded, based on Appendix B.4). *First payment:* interest = $63,600 and principal = $65,310; *second payment:* interest = $55,763 and principal = $73,147.

20.5. **a.** Payment = $25,868.

b. Year 1, $22,588; Year 2, $23,295; Year 3, $24,072; Year 4, $24,930.

c. 6%.

d. (1) PVA_{AT} = $82,000; (2) PVA_{BT} = $82,000.

20.7. **a.** 14%.

b. 9.24%.

20.9. **a.** Cost of leasing = $7,278; cost of borrowing to buy = $7,288. Advantage to leasing.

b. Cost of leasing = $7,635; cost of borrowing to buy = $7,288. Advantage to borrowing to buy.

21.1. **a.** $4,380,000.

b. Maximum price = $4,180,000; NPV = 0.

21.3. **a.** $121,340.

b. $1,011,167.

      c. $686,167.

      d. Yes, because NPV = $384,067.

21.5. **a.** 262,500 shares.

      b. $3.81.

      c. NPV = −$375,000. No.

21.7. **a.** Number of shares = 63,157.9; break-even exchange ratio = 0.631579; Sonrise's portion = $2,400,000; Wyngard's portion = $7,600,000.

      b. Number of shares = 133,333.33; break-even exchange ratio = $1\frac{1}{3}$; Sonrise's portion = $4,000,000; Wyngard's portion = $6,000,000.

      c. 38.9%.

21.9. **a.** $316,620,000.

      b. Accounts payable, $118,441,210; notes payable, $26,029,330; bank loan, $9,891,209; long-term bond, $70,000,000; subordinated debentures, $92,258,252.

      c. 78.9%.

22.1. **a.** 1,135,700 yen; 1,139,300 yen.

      b. $8,805; $8,777.

      c. Appreciate.

22.3. **a.** $29,036.

      b. $27,874.

22.5. **a.** $F_{Sw}3,945$.

      b. $67,140.

      c. $69,269.

      d. No answer provided.

22.7. **a.** $0.0007041.

      b. 12%.

      c. Transaction risk.

22.9. **a.** The riyal will appreciate.

      b. Translation gain = $2,896.

MATHEMATICAL TABLES

Appendix B

Future Value of $1: $FVIF_{i,n} = (1 + i)^n$; $FV = PV(FVIF_{i,n})$

Period, n	1%	2%	3%	4%	5%	6%	7%	8%	9%	10%	11%	12%	13%
1	1.0100	1.0200	1.0300	1.0400	1.0500	1.0600	1.0700	1.0800	1.0900	1.1000	1.1100	1.1200	1.1300
2	1.0201	1.0404	1.0609	1.0816	1.1025	1.1236	1.1449	1.1664	1.1881	1.2100	1.2321	1.2544	1.2769
3	1.0303	1.0612	1.0927	1.1249	1.1576	1.1910	1.2250	1.2597	1.2950	1.3310	1.3676	1.4049	1.4429
4	1.0406	1.0824	1.1255	1.1699	1.2155	1.2625	1.3108	1.3605	1.4116	1.4641	1.5181	1.5735	1.6305
5	1.0510	1.1041	1.1593	1.2167	1.2763	1.3382	1.4026	1.4693	1.5386	1.6105	1.6851	1.7623	1.8424
6	1.0615	1.1262	1.1941	1.2653	1.3401	1.4185	1.5007	1.5869	1.6771	1.7716	1.8704	1.9738	2.0820
7	1.0721	1.1487	1.2299	1.3159	1.4071	1.5036	1.6058	1.7138	1.8280	1.9487	2.0762	2.2107	2.3526
8	1.0829	1.1717	1.2668	1.3686	1.4775	1.5938	1.7182	1.8509	1.9926	2.1436	2.3045	2.4760	2.6584
9	1.0937	1.1951	1.3048	1.4233	1.5513	1.6895	1.8385	1.9990	2.1719	2.3579	2.5580	2.7731	3.0040
10	1.1046	1.2190	1.3439	1.4802	1.6289	1.7908	1.9672	2.1589	2.3674	2.5937	2.8394	3.1058	3.3946
11	1.1157	1.2434	1.3842	1.5395	1.7103	1.8983	2.1049	2.3316	2.5804	2.8531	3.1518	3.4786	3.8359
12	1.1268	1.2682	1.4258	1.6010	1.7959	2.0122	2.2522	2.5182	2.8127	3.1384	3.4985	3.8960	4.3345
13	1.1381	1.2936	1.4685	1.6651	1.8856	2.1329	2.4098	2.7196	3.0658	3.4523	3.8833	4.3635	4.8980
14	1.1495	1.3195	1.5126	1.7317	1.9799	2.2609	2.5785	2.9372	3.3417	3.7975	4.3104	4.8871	5.5348
15	1.1610	1.3459	1.5580	1.8009	2.0789	2.3966	2.7590	3.1722	3.6425	4.1772	4.7846	5.4736	6.2543
16	1.1726	1.3728	1.6047	1.8730	2.1829	2.5404	2.9522	3.4259	3.9703	4.5950	5.3109	6.1304	7.0673
17	1.1843	1.4002	1.6528	1.9479	2.2920	2.6928	3.1588	3.7000	4.3276	5.0545	5.8951	6.8660	7.9861
18	1.1961	1.4282	1.7024	2.0258	2.4066	2.8543	3.3799	3.9960	4.7171	5.5599	6.5436	7.6900	9.0243
19	1.2081	1.4568	1.7535	2.1068	2.5270	3.0256	3.6165	4.3157	5.1417	6.1159	7.2633	8.6128	10.197
20	1.2202	1.4859	1.8061	2.1911	2.6533	3.2071	3.8697	4.6610	5.6044	6.7275	8.0623	9.6463	11.523
21	1.2324	1.5157	1.8603	2.2788	2.7860	3.3996	4.1406	5.0338	6.1088	7.4002	8.9492	10.804	13.021
22	1.2447	1.5460	1.9161	2.3699	2.9253	3.6035	4.4304	5.4365	6.6586	8.1403	9.9336	12.100	14.714
23	1.2572	1.5769	1.9736	2.4647	3.0715	3.8197	4.7405	5.8715	7.2579	8.9543	11.026	13.552	16.627
24	1.2697	1.6084	2.0328	2.5633	3.2251	4.0489	5.0724	6.3412	7.9111	9.8497	12.239	15.179	18.788
25	1.2824	1.6406	2.0938	2.6658	3.3864	4.2919	5.4274	6.8485	8.6231	10.835	13.585	17.000	21.231
26	1.2953	1.6734	2.1566	2.7725	3.5557	4.5494	5.8074	7.3964	9.3992	11.918	15.080	19.040	23.991
27	1.3082	1.7069	2.2213	2.8834	3.7335	4.8223	6.2139	7.9881	10.245	13.110	16.739	21.325	27.109
28	1.3213	1.7410	2.2879	2.9987	3.9201	5.1117	6.6488	8.6271	11.167	14.421	18.580	23.884	30.633
29	1.3345	1.7758	2.3566	3.1187	4.1161	5.4184	7.1143	9.3173	12.172	15.863	20.624	26.750	34.616
30	1.3478	1.8114	2.4273	3.2434	4.3219	5.7435	7.6123	10.063	13.268	17.449	22.892	29.960	39.116
35	1.4166	1.9999	2.8139	3.9461	5.5160	7.6861	10.677	14.785	20.414	28.102	38.575	52.800	72.069
40	1.4889	2.2080	3.2620	4.8010	7.0400	10.286	14.974	21.725	31.409	45.259	65.001	93.051	132.78
45	1.5648	2.4379	3.7816	5.8412	8.9850	13.765	21.002	31.920	48.327	72.890	109.53	163.99	244.64
50	1.6446	2.6916	4.3839	7.1067	11.467	18.420	29.457	46.902	74.358	117.39	184.56	289.00	450.74
60	1.8167	3.2810	5.8916	10.520	18.679	32.988	57.946	101.26	176.03	304.48	524.06	897.60	1530.1

APPENDIX B.1 *continued*

Period, n	14%	15%	16%	17%	18%	19%	20%	21%	22%	23%	24%	25%
1	1.1400	1.1500	1.1600	1.1700	1.1800	1.1900	1.2000	1.2100	1.2200	1.2300	1.2400	1.2500
2	1.2996	1.3225	1.3456	1.3689	1.3924	1.4161	1.4400	1.4641	1.4884	1.5129	1.5376	1.5625
3	1.4815	1.5209	1.5609	1.6016	1.6430	1.6852	1.7280	1.7716	1.8158	1.8609	1.9066	1.9531
4	1.6890	1.7490	1.8106	1.8739	1.9388	2.0053	2.0736	2.1436	2.2153	2.2889	2.3642	2.4414
5	1.9254	2.0114	2.1003	2.1924	2.2878	2.3864	2.4883	2.5937	2.7027	2.8153	2.9316	3.0518
6	2.1950	2.3131	2.4364	2.5652	2.6996	2.8398	2.9860	3.1384	3.2973	3.4628	3.6352	3.8147
7	2.5023	2.6600	2.8262	3.0012	3.1855	3.3793	3.5832	3.7975	4.0227	4.2593	4.5077	4.7684
8	2.8526	3.0590	3.2784	3.5115	3.7589	4.0214	4.2998	4.5950	4.9077	5.2389	5.5895	5.9605
9	3.2519	3.5179	3.8030	4.1084	4.4355	4.7854	5.1598	5.5599	5.9874	6.4439	6.9310	7.4506
10	3.7072	4.0456	4.4114	4.8068	5.2338	5.6947	6.1917	6.7275	7.3046	7.9259	8.5944	9.3132
11	4.2262	4.6524	5.1173	5.6240	6.1759	6.7767	7.4301	8.1403	8.9117	9.7489	10.657	11.642
12	4.8179	5.3503	5.9360	6.5801	7.2876	8.0642	8.9161	9.8497	10.872	11.991	13.215	14.552
13	5.4924	6.1528	6.8858	7.6987	8.5994	9.5964	10.699	11.918	13.264	14.749	16.386	18.190
14	6.2613	7.0757	7.9875	9.0075	10.147	11.420	12.839	14.421	16.182	18.141	20.319	22.737
15	7.1379	8.1371	9.2655	10.539	11.974	13.590	15.407	17.449	19.742	22.314	25.196	28.422
16	8.1372	9.3576	10.748	12.330	14.129	16.172	18.488	21.114	24.086	27.446	31.243	35.527
17	9.2765	10.761	12.468	14.426	16.672	19.244	22.186	25.548	29.384	33.759	38.741	44.409
18	10.575	12.375	14.463	16.879	19.673	22.901	26.623	30.913	35.849	41.523	48.039	55.511
19	12.056	14.232	16.777	19.748	23.214	27.252	31.948	37.404	43.736	51.074	59.568	69.389
20	13.743	16.367	19.461	23.106	27.393	32.429	38.338	45.259	53.358	62.821	73.864	86.736
21	15.668	18.822	22.574	27.034	32.324	38.591	46.005	54.764	65.096	77.269	91.592	108.42
22	17.861	21.645	26.186	31.629	38.142	45.923	55.206	66.264	79.418	95.041	113.57	135.53
23	20.362	24.891	30.376	37.006	45.008	54.649	66.247	80.180	96.889	116.90	140.83	169.41
24	23.212	28.625	35.236	43.297	53.109	65.032	79.497	97.017	118.21	143.79	174.63	211.76
25	26.462	32.919	40.874	50.658	62.669	77.388	95.396	117.39	144.21	176.86	216.54	264.70
26	30.167	37.857	47.414	59.270	73.949	92.092	114.48	142.04	175.94	217.54	268.51	330.87
27	34.390	43.535	55.000	69.345	87.260	109.59	137.37	171.87	214.64	267.57	332.95	413.59
28	39.204	50.066	63.800	81.134	102.97	130.41	164.84	207.97	261.86	329.11	412.86	516.99
29	44.693	57.575	74.009	94.927	121.50	155.19	197.81	251.64	319.47	404.81	511.95	646.23
30	50.950	66.212	85.850	111.06	143.37	184.68	237.38	304.48	389.76	497.91	634.82	807.79
35	98.100	133.18	180.31	243.50	328.00	440.70	590.67	789.75	1053.4	1401.8	1861.1	2465.2
40	188.88	267.86	378.72	533.87	750.38	1051.7	1469.8	2048.4	2847.0	3946.4	5455.9	7523.2
45	363.68	538.77	795.44	1170.5	1716.7	2509.7	3657.3	5313.0	7694.7	11110	15995	22959
50	700.23	1083.7	1670.7	2566.2	3927.4	5988.9	9100.4	13781	20797	31279	46890	70065
60	2595.9	4384.0	7370.2	12335	20555	34105	56348	92709	*	*	*	*

*These interest factors exceed 100,000.

Present Value of $1: $PVIF_{i,n} = 1/(1 + i)^n$; $PV = FV(PVIF_{i,n})$

Period, n	1%	2%	3%	4%	5%	6%	7%	8%	9%	10%	11%	12%	13%
1	.9901	.9804	.9709	.9615	.9524	.9434	.9346	.9259	.9174	.9091	.9009	.8929	.8850
2	.9803	.9612	.9426	.9246	.9070	.8900	.8734	.8573	.8417	.8264	.8116	.7972	.7831
3	.9706	.9423	.9151	.8890	.8638	.8396	.8163	.7938	.7722	.7513	.7312	.7118	.6931
4	.9610	.9238	.8885	.8548	.8227	.7921	.7629	.7350	.7084	.6830	.6587	.6355	.6133
5	.9515	.9057	.8626	.8219	.7835	.7473	.7130	.6806	.6499	.6209	.5935	.5674	.5428
6	.9420	.8880	.8375	.7903	.7462	.7050	.6663	.6302	.5963	.5645	.5346	.5066	.4803
7	.9327	.8706	.8131	.7599	.7107	.6651	.6227	.5835	.5470	.5132	.4817	.4523	.4251
8	.9235	.8535	.7894	.7307	.6768	.6274	.5820	.5403	.5019	.4665	.4339	.4039	.3762
9	.9143	.8368	.7664	.7026	.6446	.5919	.5439	.5002	.4604	.4241	.3909	.3606	.3329
10	.9053	.8203	.7441	.6756	.6139	.5584	.5083	.4632	.4224	.3855	.3522	.3220	.2946
11	.8963	.8043	.7224	.6496	.5847	.5268	.4751	.4289	.3875	.3505	.3173	.2875	.2607
12	.8874	.7885	.7014	.6246	.5568	.4970	.4440	.3971	.3555	.3186	.2858	.2567	.2307
13	.8787	.7730	.6810	.6006	.5303	.4688	.4150	.3677	.3262	.2897	.2575	.2292	.2042
14	.8700	.7579	.6611	.5775	.5051	.4423	.3878	.3405	.2992	.2633	.2320	.2046	.1807
15	.8613	.7430	.6419	.5553	.4810	.4173	.3624	.3152	.2745	.2394	.2090	.1827	.1599
16	.8528	.7284	.6232	.5339	.4581	.3936	.3387	.2919	.2519	.2176	.1883	.1631	.1415
17	.8444	.7142	.6050	.5134	.4363	.3714	.3166	.2703	.2311	.1978	.1696	.1456	.1252
18	.8360	.7002	.5874	.4936	.4155	.3503	.2959	.2502	.2120	.1799	.1528	.1300	.1108
19	.8277	.6864	.5703	.4746	.3957	.3305	.2765	.2317	.1945	.1635	.1377	.1161	.0981
20	.8195	.6730	.5537	.4564	.3769	.3118	.2584	.2145	.1784	.1486	.1240	.1037	.0868
21	.8114	.6598	.5375	.4388	.3589	.2942	.2415	.1987	.1637	.1351	.1117	.0926	.0768
22	.8034	.6468	.5219	.4220	.3418	.2775	.2257	.1839	.1502	.1228	.1007	.0826	.0680
23	.7954	.6342	.5067	.4057	.3256	.2618	.2109	.1703	.1378	.1117	.0907	.0738	.0601
24	.7876	.6217	.4919	.3901	.3101	.2470	.1971	.1577	.1264	.1015	.0817	.0659	.0532
25	.7798	.6095	.4776	.3751	.2953	.2330	.1842	.1460	.1160	.0923	.0736	.0588	.0471
26	.7720	.5976	.4637	.3607	.2812	.2198	.1722	.1352	.1064	.0839	.0663	.0525	.0417
27	.7644	.5859	.4502	.3468	.2678	.2074	.1609	.1252	.0976	.0763	.0597	.0469	.0369
28	.7568	.5744	.4371	.3335	.2551	.1956	.1504	.1159	.0895	.0693	.0538	.0419	.0326
29	.7493	.5631	.4243	.3207	.2429	.1846	.1406	.1073	.0822	.0630	.0485	.0374	.0289
30	.7419	.5521	.4120	.3083	.2314	.1741	.1314	.0994	.0754	.0573	.0437	.0334	.0256
35	.7059	.5000	.3554	.2534	.1813	.1301	.0937	.0676	.0490	.0356	.0259	.0189	.0139
40	.6717	.4529	.3066	.2083	.1420	.0972	.0668	.0460	.0318	.0221	.0154	.0107	.0075
45	.6391	.4102	.2644	.1712	.1113	.0727	.0476	.0313	.0207	.0137	.0091	.0061	.0041
50	.6080	.3715	.2281	.1407	.0872	.0543	.0339	.0213	.0134	.0085	.0054	.0035	.0022
60	.5504	.3048	.1697	.0951	.0535	.0303	.0173	.0099	.0057	.0033	.0019	.0011	.0007

Period, n	14%	15%	16%	17%	18%	19%	20%	21%	22%	23%	24%	25%
1	.8772	.8696	.8621	.8547	.8475	.8403	.8333	.8264	.8197	.8130	.8065	.8000
2	.7695	.7561	.7432	.7305	.7182	.7062	.6944	.6830	.6719	.6610	.6504	.6400
3	.6750	.6575	.6407	.6244	.6086	.5934	.5787	.5645	.5507	.5374	.5245	.5120
4	.5921	.5718	.5523	.5337	.5158	.4987	.4823	.4665	.4514	.4369	.4230	.4096
5	.5194	.4972	.4761	.4561	.4371	.4190	.4019	.3855	.3700	.3552	.3411	.3277
6	.4556	.4323	.4104	.3898	.3704	.3521	.3349	.3186	.3033	.2888	.2751	.2621
7	.3996	.3759	.3538	.3332	.3139	.2959	.2791	.2633	.2486	.2348	.2218	.2097
8	.3506	.3269	.3050	.2848	.2660	.2487	.2326	.2176	.2038	.1909	.1789	.1678
9	.3075	.2843	.2630	.2434	.2255	.2090	.1938	.1799	.1670	.1552	.1443	.1342
10	.2697	.2472	.2267	.2080	.1911	.1756	.1615	.1486	.1369	.1262	.1164	.1074
11	.2366	.2149	.1954	.1778	.1619	.1476	.1346	.1228	.1122	.1026	.0938	.0859
12	.2076	.1869	.1685	.1520	.1372	.1240	.1122	.1015	.0920	.0834	.0757	.0687
13	.1821	.1625	.1452	.1299	.1163	.1042	.0935	.0839	.0754	.0678	.0610	.0550
14	.1597	.1413	.1252	.1110	.0985	.0876	.0779	.0693	.0618	.0551	.0492	.0440
15	.1401	.1229	.1079	.0949	.0835	.0736	.0649	.0573	.0507	.0448	.0397	.0352
16	.1229	.1069	.0930	.0811	.0708	.0618	.0541	.0474	.0415	.0364	.0320	.0281
17	.1078	.0929	.0802	.0693	.0600	.0520	.0451	.0391	.0340	.0296	.0258	.0225
18	.0946	.0808	.0691	.0592	.0508	.0437	.0376	.0323	.0279	.0241	.0208	.0180
19	.0829	.0703	.0596	.0506	.0431	.0367	.0313	.0267	.0229	.0196	.0168	.0144
20	.0728	.0611	.0514	.0433	.0365	.0308	.0261	.0221	.0187	.0159	.0135	.0115
21	.0638	.0531	.0443	.0370	.0309	.0259	.0217	.0183	.0154	.0129	.0109	.0092
22	.0560	.0462	.0382	.0316	.0262	.0218	.0181	.0151	.0126	.0105	.0088	.0074
23	.0491	.0402	.0329	.0270	.0222	.0183	.0151	.0125	.0103	.0086	.0071	.0059
24	.0431	.0349	.0284	.0231	.0188	.0154	.0126	.0103	.0085	.0070	.0057	.0047
25	.0378	.0304	.0245	.0197	.0160	.0129	.0105	.0085	.0069	.0057	.0046	.0038
26	.0331	.0264	.0211	.0169	.0135	.0109	.0087	.0070	.0057	.0046	.0037	.0030
27	.0291	.0230	.0182	.0144	.0115	.0091	.0073	.0058	.0047	.0037	.0030	.0024
28	.0255	.0200	.0157	.0123	.0097	.0077	.0061	.0048	.0038	.0030	.0024	.0019
29	.0224	.0174	.0135	.0105	.0082	.0064	.0051	.0040	.0031	.0025	.0020	.0015
30	.0196	.0151	.0116	.0090	.0070	.0054	.0042	.0033	.0026	.0020	.0016	.0012
35	.0102	.0075	.0055	.0041	.0030	.0023	.0017	.0013	.0009	.0007	.0005	.0004
40	.0053	.0037	.0026	.0019	.0013	.0010	.0007	.0005	.0004	.0003	.0002	.0001
45	.0027	.0019	.0013	.0009	.0006	.0004	.0003	.0002	.0001	.0001	.0001	*
50	.0014	.0009	.0006	.0004	.0003	.0002	.0001	.0001	*	*	*	*
60	.0004	.0002	.0001	.0001	*	*	*	*	*	*	*	*

*These interest factors are less than .0001.

Future Value of an Annuity of $1: $FVIFA_{i,n} = \dfrac{(1 + i)^n - 1}{i}$; $FVA = PMT(FVIFA_{i,n})$

Period, n	1%	2%	3%	4%	5%	6%	7%	8%	9%	10%	11%	12%	13%
1	1.0000	1.0000	1.0000	1.0000	1.0000	1.0000	1.0000	1.0000	1.0000	1.0000	1.0000	1.0000	1.0000
2	2.0100	2.0200	2.0300	2.0400	2.0500	2.0600	2.0700	2.0800	2.0900	2.1000	2.1100	2.1200	2.1300
3	3.0301	3.0604	3.0909	3.1216	3.1525	3.1836	3.2149	3.2464	3.2781	3.3100	3.3421	3.3744	3.4069
4	4.0604	4.1216	4.1836	4.2465	4.3101	4.3746	4.4399	4.5061	4.5731	4.6410	4.7097	4.7793	4.8498
5	5.1010	5.2040	5.3091	5.4163	5.5256	5.6371	5.7507	5.8666	5.9847	6.1051	6.2278	6.3528	6.4803
6	6.1520	6.3081	6.4684	6.6330	6.8019	6.9753	7.1533	7.3359	7.5233	7.7156	7.9129	8.1152	8.3227
7	7.2135	7.4343	7.6625	7.8983	8.1420	8.3938	8.6540	8.9228	9.2004	9.4872	9.7833	10.089	10.405
8	8.2857	8.5830	8.8923	9.2142	9.5491	9.8975	10.260	10.637	11.028	11.436	11.859	12.300	12.757
9	9.3685	9.7546	10.159	10.583	11.027	11.491	11.978	12.488	13.021	13.579	14.164	14.776	15.416
10	10.462	10.950	11.464	12.006	12.578	13.181	13.816	14.487	15.193	15.937	16.722	17.549	18.420
11	11.567	12.169	12.808	13.486	14.207	14.972	15.784	16.645	17.560	18.531	19.561	20.655	21.814
12	12.683	13.412	14.192	15.026	15.917	16.870	17.888	18.977	20.141	21.384	22.713	24.133	25.650
13	13.809	14.680	15.618	16.627	17.713	18.882	20.141	21.495	22.953	24.523	26.212	28.029	29.985
14	14.947	15.974	17.086	18.292	19.599	21.015	22.550	24.215	26.019	27.975	30.095	32.393	34.883
15	16.097	17.293	18.599	20.024	21.579	23.276	25.129	27.152	29.361	31.772	34.405	37.280	40.418
16	17.258	18.639	20.157	21.825	23.657	25.673	27.888	30.324	33.003	35.950	39.190	42.753	46.672
17	18.430	20.012	21.762	23.698	25.840	28.213	30.840	33.750	36.974	40.545	44.501	48.884	53.739
18	19.615	21.412	23.414	25.645	28.132	30.906	33.999	37.450	41.301	45.599	50.396	55.750	61.725
19	20.811	22.841	25.117	27.671	30.539	33.760	37.379	41.446	46.018	51.159	56.939	63.440	70.749
20	22.019	24.297	26.870	29.778	33.066	36.786	40.995	45.762	51.160	57.275	64.203	72.052	80.947
21	23.239	25.783	28.676	31.969	35.719	39.993	44.865	50.423	56.765	64.002	72.265	81.699	92.470
22	24.472	27.299	30.537	34.248	38.505	43.392	49.006	55.457	62.873	71.403	81.214	92.503	105.49
23	25.716	28.845	32.453	36.618	41.430	46.996	53.436	60.893	69.532	79.543	91.148	104.60	120.20
24	26.973	30.422	34.426	39.083	44.502	50.816	58.177	66.765	76.790	88.497	102.17	118.16	136.83
25	28.243	32.030	36.459	41.646	47.727	54.865	63.249	73.106	84.701	98.347	114.41	133.33	155.62
26	29.526	33.671	38.553	44.312	51.113	59.156	68.676	79.954	93.324	109.18	128.00	150.33	176.85
27	30.821	35.344	40.710	47.084	54.669	63.706	74.484	87.351	102.72	121.10	143.08	169.37	200.84
28	32.129	37.051	42.931	49.968	58.403	68.528	80.698	95.339	112.97	134.21	159.82	190.70	227.95
29	33.450	38.792	45.219	52.966	62.323	73.640	87.347	103.97	124.14	148.63	178.40	214.58	258.58
30	34.785	40.568	47.575	56.085	66.439	79.058	94.461	113.28	136.31	164.49	199.02	241.33	293.20
35	41.660	49.994	60.462	73.652	90.320	111.43	138.24	172.32	215.71	271.02	341.59	431.66	546.68
40	48.886	60.402	75.401	95.026	120.80	154.76	199.64	259.06	337.88	442.59	581.83	767.09	1013.7
45	56.481	71.893	92.720	121.03	159.70	212.74	285.75	386.51	525.86	718.90	986.64	1358.2	1874.2
50	64.463	84.579	112.80	152.67	209.35	290.34	406.53	573.77	815.08	1163.9	1668.8	2400.0	3459.5
60	81.670	114.05	163.05	237.99	353.58	533.13	813.52	1253.2	1944.8	3034.8	4755.1	7471.6	11762

Period, n	14%	15%	16%	17%	18%	19%	20%	21%	22%	23%	24%	25%
1	1.0000	1.0000	1.0000	1.0000	1.0000	1.0000	1.0000	1.0000	1.0000	1.0000	1.0000	1.0000
2	2.1400	2.1500	2.1600	2.1700	2.1800	2.1900	2.2000	2.2100	2.2200	2.2300	2.2400	2.2500
3	3.4396	3.4725	3.5056	3.5389	3.5724	3.6061	3.6400	3.6741	3.7084	3.7429	3.7776	3.8125
4	4.9211	4.9934	5.0665	5.1405	5.2154	5.2913	5.3680	5.4457	5.5242	5.6038	5.6842	5.7656
5	6.6101	6.7424	6.8771	7.0144	7.1542	7.2966	7.4416	7.5892	7.7396	7.8926	8.0484	8.2070
6	8.5355	8.7537	8.9775	9.2068	9.4420	9.6830	9.9299	10.183	10.442	10.708	10.980	11.259
7	10.730	11.067	11.414	11.772	12.142	12.523	12.916	13.321	13.740	14.171	14.615	15.073
8	13.233	13.727	14.240	14.773	15.327	15.902	16.499	17.119	17.762	18.430	19.123	19.842
9	16.085	16.786	17.519	18.285	19.086	19.923	20.799	21.714	22.670	23.669	24.712	25.802
10	19.337	20.304	21.321	22.393	23.521	24.709	25.959	27.274	28.657	30.113	31.643	33.253
11	23.045	24.349	25.733	27.200	28.755	30.404	32.150	34.001	35.962	38.039	40.238	42.566
12	27.271	29.002	30.850	32.824	34.931	37.180	39.581	42.142	44.874	47.788	50.895	54.208
13	32.089	34.352	36.786	39.404	42.219	45.244	48.497	51.991	55.746	59.779	64.110	68.760
14	37.581	40.505	43.672	47.103	50.818	54.841	59.196	63.910	69.010	74.528	80.496	86.950
15	43.842	47.580	51.660	56.110	60.965	66.261	72.035	78.330	85.192	92.669	100.82	109.69
16	50.980	55.717	60.925	66.649	72.939	79.850	87.442	95.780	104.93	114.98	126.01	138.11
17	59.118	65.075	71.673	78.979	87.068	96.022	105.93	116.89	129.02	142.43	157.25	173.64
18	68.394	75.836	84.141	93.406	103.74	115.27	128.12	142.44	158.40	176.19	195.99	218.04
19	78.969	88.212	98.603	110.28	123.41	138.17	154.74	173.35	194.25	217.71	244.03	273.56
20	91.025	102.44	115.38	130.03	146.63	165.42	186.69	210.76	237.99	268.79	303.60	342.94
21	104.77	118.81	134.84	153.14	174.02	197.85	225.03	256.02	291.35	331.61	377.46	429.68
22	120.44	137.63	157.41	180.17	206.34	236.44	271.03	310.78	356.44	408.88	469.06	538.10
23	138.30	159.28	183.60	211.80	244.49	282.36	326.24	377.05	435.86	503.92	582.63	673.63
24	158.66	184.17	213.98	248.81	289.49	337.01	392.48	457.22	532.75	620.82	723.46	843.03
25	181.87	212.79	249.21	292.10	342.60	402.04	471.98	554.24	650.96	764.61	898.09	1054.8
26	208.33	245.71	290.09	342.76	405.27	479.43	567.38	671.63	795.17	941.46	1114.6	1319.5
27	238.50	283.57	337.50	402.03	479.22	571.52	681.85	813.68	971.10	1159.0	1383.1	1650.4
28	272.89	327.10	392.50	471.38	566.48	681.11	819.22	985.55	1185.7	1426.6	1716.1	2064.0
29	312.09	377.17	456.30	552.51	669.45	811.52	984.07	1193.5	1447.6	1755.7	2129.0	2580.9
30	356.79	434.75	530.31	647.44	790.95	966.71	1181.9	1445.2	1767.1	2160.5	2640.9	3227.2
35	693.57	881.17	1120.7	1426.5	1816.7	2314.2	2948.3	3755.9	4783.6	6090.3	7750.2	9856.8
40	1342.0	1779.1	2360.8	3134.5	4163.2	5529.8	7343.9	9749.5	12937	17154	22729	30089
45	2590.6	3585.1	4965.3	6879.3	9531.6	13203	18281	25295	34971	48302	66640	91831
50	4994.5	7217.7	10436	15090	21813	31515	45497	65617	94525	*	*	*
60	18535	29220	46058	72555	*	*	*	*	*	*	*	*

*These interest factors exceed 100,000.

Present Value of an Annuity of $1: $PVIFA_{i,n} = \dfrac{1 - [1/(1 + i)^n]}{i}$; $PVA = PMT(PVIFA_{i,n})$

Period, n	1%	2%	3%	4%	5%	6%	7%	8%	9%	10%	11%	12%	13%
1	0.9901	0.9804	0.9709	0.9615	0.9524	0.9434	0.9346	0.9259	0.9174	0.9091	0.9009	0.8929	0.8850
2	1.9704	1.9416	1.9135	1.8861	1.8594	1.8334	1.8080	1.7833	1.7591	1.7355	1.7125	1.6901	1.6681
3	2.9410	2.8839	2.8286	2.7751	2.7232	2.6730	2.6243	2.5771	2.5313	2.4869	2.4437	2.4018	2.3612
4	3.9020	3.8077	3.7171	3.6299	3.5460	3.4651	3.3872	3.3121	3.2397	3.1699	3.1024	3.0373	2.9745
5	4.8534	4.7135	4.5797	4.4518	4.3295	4.2124	4.1002	3.9927	3.8897	3.7908	3.6959	3.6048	3.5172
6	5.7955	5.6014	5.4172	5.2421	5.0757	4.9173	4.7665	4.6229	4.4859	4.3553	4.2305	4.1114	3.9975
7	6.7282	6.4720	6.2303	6.0021	5.7864	5.5824	5.3893	5.2064	5.0330	4.8684	4.7122	4.5638	4.4226
8	7.6517	7.3255	7.0197	6.7327	6.4632	6.2098	5.9713	5.7466	5.5348	5.3349	5.1461	4.9676	4.7988
9	8.5660	8.1622	7.7861	7.4353	7.1078	6.8017	6.5152	6.2469	5.9952	5.7590	5.5370	5.3282	5.1317
10	9.4713	8.9826	8.5302	8.1109	7.7217	7.3601	7.0236	6.7101	6.4177	6.1446	5.8892	5.6502	5.4262
11	10.3676	9.7868	9.2526	8.7605	8.3064	7.8869	7.4987	7.1390	6.8052	6.4951	6.2065	5.9377	5.6869
12	11.2551	10.5753	9.9540	9.3851	8.8633	8.3838	7.9427	7.5361	7.1607	6.8137	6.4924	6.1944	5.9176
13	12.1337	11.3484	10.6350	9.9856	9.3936	8.8527	8.3577	7.9038	7.4869	7.1034	6.7499	6.4235	6.1218
14	13.0037	12.1062	11.2961	10.5631	9.8986	9.2950	8.7455	8.2442	7.7862	7.3667	6.9819	6.6282	6.3025
15	13.8651	12.8493	11.9379	11.1184	10.3797	9.7122	9.1079	8.5595	8.0607	7.6061	7.1909	6.8109	6.4624
16	14.7179	13.5777	12.5611	11.6523	10.8378	10.1059	9.4466	8.8514	8.3126	7.8237	7.3792	6.9740	6.6039
17	15.5623	14.2919	13.1661	12.1657	11.2741	10.4773	9.7632	9.1216	8.5436	8.0216	7.5488	7.1196	6.7291
18	16.3983	14.9920	13.7535	12.6593	11.6896	10.8276	10.0591	9.3719	8.7556	8.2014	7.7016	7.2497	6.8399
19	17.2260	15.6785	14.3238	13.1339	12.0853	11.1581	10.3356	9.6036	8.9501	8.3649	7.8393	7.3658	6.9380
20	18.0456	16.3514	14.8775	13.5903	12.4622	11.4699	10.5940	9.8181	9.1285	8.5136	7.9633	7.4694	7.0248
21	18.8570	17.0112	15.4150	14.0292	12.8212	11.7641	10.8355	10.0168	9.2922	8.6487	8.0751	7.5620	7.1016
22	19.6604	17.6580	15.9369	14.4511	13.1630	12.0416	11.0612	10.2007	9.4424	8.7715	8.1757	7.6446	7.1695
23	20.4558	18.2922	16.4436	14.8568	13.4886	12.3034	11.2722	10.3711	9.5802	8.8832	8.2664	7.7184	7.2297
24	21.2434	18.9139	16.9355	15.2470	13.7986	12.5504	11.4693	10.5288	9.7066	8.9847	8.3481	7.7843	7.2829
25	22.0232	19.5235	17.4131	15.6221	14.0939	12.7834	11.6536	10.6748	9.8226	9.0770	8.4217	7.8431	7.3300
26	22.7952	20.1210	17.8768	15.9828	14.3752	13.0032	11.8258	10.8100	9.9290	9.1609	8.4881	7.8957	7.3717
27	23.5596	20.7069	18.3270	16.3296	14.6430	13.2105	11.9867	10.9352	10.0266	9.2372	8.5478	7.9426	7.4086
28	24.3164	21.2813	18.7641	16.6631	14.8981	13.4062	12.1371	11.0511	10.1161	9.3066	8.6016	7.9844	7.4412
29	25.0658	21.8444	19.1885	16.9837	15.1411	13.5907	12.2777	11.1584	10.1983	9.3696	8.6501	8.0218	7.4701
30	25.8077	22.3965	19.6004	17.2920	15.3725	13.7648	12.4090	11.2578	10.2737	9.4269	8.6938	8.0552	7.4957
35	29.4086	24.9986	21.4872	18.6646	16.3742	14.4982	12.9477	11.6546	10.5668	9.6442	8.8552	8.1755	7.5856
40	32.8347	27.3555	23.1148	19.7928	17.1591	15.0463	13.3317	11.9246	10.7574	9.7791	8.9511	8.2438	7.6344
45	36.0945	29.4902	24.5187	20.7200	17.7741	15.4558	13.6055	12.1084	10.8812	9.8628	9.0079	8.2825	7.6609
50	39.1961	31.4236	25.7298	21.4822	18.2559	15.7619	13.8007	12.2335	10.9617	9.9148	9.0417	8.3045	7.6752
60	44.9550	34.7609	27.6756	22.6235	18.9293	16.1614	14.0392	12.3766	11.0480	9.9672	9.0736	8.3240	7.6873

Period, n	14%	15%	16%	17%	18%	19%	20%	21%	22%	23%	24%	25%
1	0.8772	0.8696	0.8621	0.8547	0.8475	0.8403	0.8333	0.8264	0.8197	0.8130	0.8065	0.8000
2	1.6467	1.6257	1.6052	1.5852	1.5656	1.5465	1.5278	1.5095	1.4915	1.4740	1.4568	1.4400
3	2.3216	2.2832	2.2459	2.2096	2.1743	2.1399	2.1065	2.0739	2.0422	2.0114	1.9813	1.9520
4	2.9137	2.8550	2.7982	2.7432	2.6901	2.6386	2.5887	2.5404	2.4936	2.4483	2.4043	2.3616
5	3.4331	3.3522	3.2743	3.1993	3.1272	3.0576	2.9906	2.9260	2.8636	2.8035	2.7454	2.6893
6	3.8887	3.7845	3.6847	3.5892	3.4976	3.4098	3.3255	3.2446	3.1669	3.0923	3.0205	2.9514
7	4.2883	4.1604	4.0386	3.9224	3.8115	3.7057	3.6046	3.5079	3.4155	3.3270	3.2423	3.1611
8	4.6389	4.4873	4.3436	4.2072	4.0776	3.9544	3.8372	3.7256	3.6193	3.5179	3.4212	3.3289
9	4.9464	4.7716	4.6065	4.4506	4.3030	4.1633	4.0310	3.9054	3.7863	3.6731	3.5655	3.4631
10	5.2161	5.0188	4.8332	4.6586	4.4941	4.3389	4.1925	4.0541	3.9232	3.7993	3.6819	3.5705
11	5.4527	5.2337	5.0286	4.8364	4.6560	4.4865	4.3271	4.1769	4.0354	3.9018	3.7757	3.6564
12	5.6603	5.4206	5.1971	4.9884	4.7932	4.6105	4.4392	4.2784	4.1274	3.9852	3.8514	3.7251
13	5.8424	5.5831	5.3423	5.1183	4.9095	4.7147	4.5327	4.3624	4.2028	4.0530	3.9124	3.7801
14	6.0021	5.7245	5.4675	5.2293	5.0081	4.8023	4.6106	4.4317	4.2646	4.1082	3.9616	3.8241
15	6.1422	5.8474	5.5755	5.3242	5.0916	4.8759	4.6755	4.4890	4.3152	4.1530	4.0013	3.8593
16	6.2651	5.9542	5.6685	5.4053	5.1624	4.9377	4.7296	4.5364	4.3567	4.1894	4.0333	3.8874
17	6.3729	6.0472	5.7487	5.4746	5.2223	4.9897	4.7746	4.5755	4.3908	4.2190	4.0591	3.9099
18	6.4674	6.1280	5.8178	5.5339	5.2732	5.0333	4.8122	4.6079	4.4187	4.2431	4.0799	3.9279
19	6.5504	6.1982	5.8775	5.5845	5.3162	5.0700	4.8435	4.6346	4.4415	4.2627	4.0967	3.9424
20	6.6231	6.2593	5.9288	5.6278	5.3527	5.1009	4.8696	4.6567	4.4603	4.2786	4.1103	3.9539
21	6.6870	6.3125	5.9731	5.6648	5.3837	5.1268	4.8913	4.6750	4.4756	4.2916	4.1212	3.9631
22	6.7429	6.3587	6.0113	5.6964	5.4099	5.1486	4.9094	4.6900	4.4882	4.3021	4.1300	3.9705
23	6.7921	6.3988	6.0442	5.7234	5.4321	5.1668	4.9245	4.7025	4.4985	4.3106	4.1371	3.9764
24	6.8351	6.4338	6.0726	5.7465	5.4509	5.1822	4.9371	4.7128	4.5070	4.3176	4.1428	3.9811
25	6.8729	6.4641	6.0971	5.7662	5.4669	5.1951	4.9476	4.7213	4.5139	4.3232	4.1474	3.9849
26	6.9061	6.4906	6.1182	5.7831	5.4804	5.2060	4.9563	4.7284	4.5196	4.3278	4.1511	3.9879
27	6.9352	6.5135	6.1364	5.7975	5.4919	5.2151	4.9636	4.7342	4.5243	4.3316	4.1542	3.9903
28	6.9607	6.5335	6.1520	5.8099	5.5016	5.2228	4.9697	4.7390	4.5281	4.3346	4.1566	3.9923
29	6.9830	6.5509	6.1656	5.8204	5.5098	5.2292	4.9747	4.7430	4.5312	4.3371	4.1585	3.9938
30	7.0027	6.5660	6.1772	5.8294	5.5168	5.2347	4.9789	4.7463	4.5338	4.3391	4.1601	3.9950
35	7.0700	6.6166	6.2153	5.8582	5.5386	5.2512	4.9915	4.7559	4.5411	4.3447	4.1644	3.9984
40	7.1050	6.6418	6.2335	5.8713	5.5482	5.2582	4.9966	4.7596	4.5439	4.3467	4.1659	3.9995
45	7.1232	6.6543	6.2421	5.8773	5.5523	5.2611	4.9986	4.7610	4.5449	4.3474	4.1664	3.9998
50	7.1327	6.6605	6.2463	5.8801	5.5541	5.2623	4.9995	4.7616	4.5452	4.3477	4.1666	3.9999
60	7.1401	6.6651	6.2492	5.8819	5.5553	5.2630	4.9999	4.7619	4.5454	4.3478	4.1667	4.0000

INDEX